ARGUMENT

Dynamic Argument

Robert Lamm
Arkansas State University

Justin Everett
University of the Sciences in Philadelphia

Houghton Mifflin Company

Boston New York

Publisher: Patricia Coryell
Editor in Chief: Suzanne Phelps-Weir
Senior Development Editor: Meg Botteon
Assistant Editor: John McHugh
Senior Project Editor: Rosemary Winfield
Editorial Assistant: Katherine Leahey
Art and Design Coordinator: Jill Haber
Photo Editor: Jennifer Meyer Dare
Composition Buyer: Chuck Dutton
Manufacturing Coordinator: Karen Fawcett
Marketing Director: Anna Marie Rice

Credits continue on page C-1, which constitutes an extension of the copyright page.

Printed in the U.S.A.

Library of Congress Catalog Card Number 2005936443

Student text ISBN:
0-618-47518-4 or 978-0-618-47518-6

Instructor's exam copy ISBN:
0-618-73202-0 or 978-0-618-73202-9

2 3 4 5 6 7 8 9 - VH - 09 08 07 06

Brief Contents

CONTENTS

CHAPTER 4 The Reader's Response to Arguments 91

CHAPTER 5 Planning Arguments 122

PART 2
READER 395

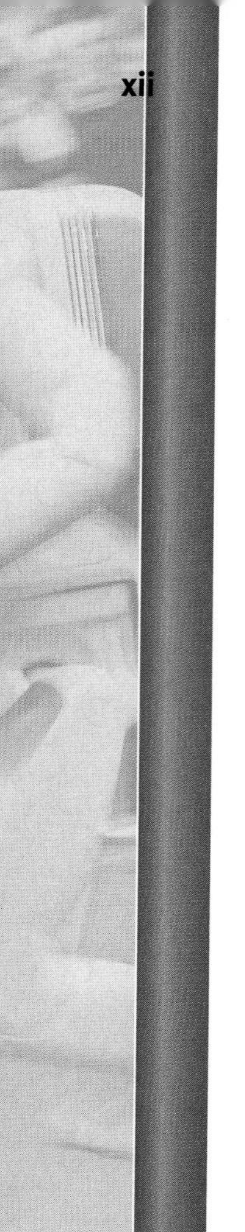

Chapter 19 Popular Culture: Violent Entertainment, Body Modifications, and Consumerism 653

Chapter 20 Classic Arguments 745

Preface

You may have heard the saying, "Life is a banquet, and most people are starving." In the same sense, life is an argument, and most people are speechless. *Dynamic Argument* helps student writers acquire the skills they need to join life's debate. We wrote this book as a practical, down-to-earth guide to understanding the arguments of others and to creating arguments in response.

Dynamic Argument features readings and visuals that engage the lives that students live today as citizens, consumers, and members of families. It avoids prepackaged and antiseptic pro or con, conservative or liberal viewpoints that do not encourage critical or creative thinking. By allowing students to avoid binary thinking and instead explore ambivalence and ambiguity, *Dynamic Argument* challenges students with fresh material that has no preconceived viewpoint. Students in a *Dynamic Argument* classroom engage topics that speak to them. They develop their own points of view, work out logic independently, and determine their own approaches to persuasion.

Features

- ***Really* process oriented:** *Dynamic Argument's* Rhetoric section (Part One) takes the *process* of writing seriously in four chapters that help students plan, draft, revise and edit, and research their writings. Techniques, models, and guided practice make the process clear and as easy as possible. Reflecting the recursive nature of the writing process, these chapters can be revisited productively whenever the student is working on a writing assignment.
- **Visually appealing:** The visual appearance of the text is inviting and dynamic, with creative formatting, abundant illustrations, entertaining yet instructive cartoons, and four-color layouts varying the presentation. Its many photographs provide additional interest and context for the discussion of contemporary issues and challenges. Chapter 12, "Arguing Visually," presents full-color visual arguments on a variety of contemporary and significant issues, encouraging students to read visual arguments critically and to use visuals within their own arguments.

- **Nontechnical:** The terminology and examples used to present argument, rhetoric, and process are nontechnical and user-friendly, with the goal of helping the student become a better writer. The pedagogical approach is not an end in itself. Our approach to logic is not overly prescriptive. *Dynamic Argument* helps students discover persuasion through both the process of logic and the process of writing.
- **More of the useful:** Part One contains the kinds of examples, advice, and materials that teachers often have to provide as supplements to a text. There are chapters on "Quoting, Paraphrasing, and Summarizing" and on "Arguing Visually," revision and editing guides, many models of writing (including student-written essays), and many tips contained in sidebars and textboxes.
- **Dynamic approaches for today's diverse classroom:** Today's students are asked to interact with each other, lead discussions, participate in group activities, and use a wide variety of learning styles from hands-on practice to the creation and interpretation of visual texts. *Dynamic Argument* takes advantage of current research in multiple intelligences, cooperative learning, and other learning styles. By offering strong visuals and group-oriented exercises, it addresses the needs of both traditional and nontraditional learners.
- **Spoken like a mentor:** The style of the book's exposition is cordial. It addresses one reader — the student. Its tone is that of a one-on-one conference between a student and a rather pleasant instructor who is at once challenging and encouraging. We have extensively class-tested this material with our own students, who have been candid and generous in helping us to shape both pedagogy and voice.
- **Thematic and beyond:** The excerpts and articles in Part Two (the Reader) feature clusters on specific topics within a larger subject area. The clusters provide a bigger picture for students to integrate varied materials into an argument.

Organization

Dynamic Argument consists of two major sections—a Rhetoric and a Reader—with a glossary.

Part One, "Rhetoric" Part One, the Rhetoric section of *Dynamic Argument*, comprises fourteen chapters sequenced to lead students through the complete process of writing and two chapters that provide the basics of MLA and APA documentation styles. Conceptually, Part One is based on three pedagogical concepts integrated into every chapter:

- **Elements of argument:** Claims, evidence, and explanations.
- **Rhetoric:** Purpose, audience, structure, and style.
- **The process of writing:** Planning, drafting, revising (with editing), and research are given their own respective chapters. Separate chapters on MLA and APA citation styles provide clear, easy-to-follow examples of key print and electronic sources, as well as student models of MLA and APA research papers.

Part Two, "Reader" Each of the six chapters in Part Two, the Reading section, has a theme (such as Health and Medicine), and within each theme high-interest topics are explored:

- **Health and Medicine:** obesity epidemic, stem-cell research, psychology of success
- **The Individual in Society:** same-sex marriage, poverty, political correctness and freedom of speech
- **Security:** Islam and the West, immigration control, and the culture of fear
- **The Future:** environmental sustainability, artificial intelligence, human longevity
- **Popular Culture:** violent entertainment, body modification, and consumerism
- **Classic Arguments:** Writers use rhetorical strategies—dialogue (Plato), satire (Swift), declaration (the Declaration of Independence), and the letter (King—to illustrate how fundamental issues such as human rights have resonated through the ages.

Resources for Students

Visit <college.hmco.com/pic/lamm1e> to learn more about *Dynamic Argument* and to access the Online Study Center and the Online Teaching Center.

Online Study Center: The Online Study Center icon throughout the text directs students to additional resources on the companion site:

- **Prepare for Class** offers Web links to further information about topics, writers, and themes.

- **Improve Your Grade** hosts suggestions for writing and activities.
- **General Resources** provides writing and research references and student papers.

Plagiarism Prevention Zone: The Plagiarism Prevention Zone has critical instruction on how to take notes, how to cite sources, and how and when to quote, paraphrase, and summarize.

***A Student Guide to Authoring Your Own Work: Understanding Plagiarism* by Rosemarie Menager-Beeley and Lyn Paulos:** This guide helps students avoid the pitfalls of plagiarism and provides sections where students can check their knowledge, including a quiz at the end.

***American Heritage Dictionary*, Fourth Edition:** The *American Heritage Dictionary* is an indispensable tool and desk reference for college and beyond.

Internet Research Guide: The Internet Research Guide has helpful advice and practice for your students on how to conduct research, evaluate sources, build an argument with Internet research, and document papers properly.

SMARTHINKING™ (live, online tutoring): SMARTHINKING links students to experienced writing instructors for one-on-one online tutoring during peak study hours. Please consult your Houghton Mifflin sales representative for more details.

Acknowledgments

We are grateful to our universities and colleagues for their assistance. At Arkansas State University, we thank Charles Carr, Tim Coone, Jeane Harris, Bryan Moore, Lisa Parks, Norman Stafford, and Jennifer Stewart. At the University of the Sciences in Philadelphia, we thank Robert Boughner, Barbara Byrne, Miriam Diaz-Gilbert, Dennis Millan, and C. Reynold Verret.

We thank our students for their contributions to this text. At ASU, we thank Janet Barnett, Kerri Bennett, Melonie Brodbent, Faith Bruns, Ashley Ingram Bowdler, Phillip Campbell, Justin Lynch, Charles Mueller, and Stephen W. Pogue for contributing their writings and models. At USP, we thank Laren Kressaty, Dana Lulias, and Hetal Shah.

We are indebted to our former instructors and colleagues at the University of Oklahoma for the education and experiences they provided us: Michael

Angelotti, Robert Con Davis-Undiano, Frances Dunham, Paul Kline, the late Michael Flanigan, Dorothy Fritz, David Mair, Martha Mills, Ronald Schleifer, Peter Smagorinsky, Alan Velie, and Kathleen Welch.

For their helpful guidance and suggestions through the development of *Dynamic Argument*, we would like to thank the following reviewers:

Susan B. Achziger, Community College of Aurora
Cathryn Amdahl, Harrisburg Area Community College
Martha R. Bachman, Camden County College
Jamie Berthel, Danville Area Community College
Carol Bledsoe, Florida Gulf Coast University
Avon Crismore, Indiana University-Purdue University – Fort Wayne
Anthony Di Renzo, Ithaca College
Larnell Dunkley Jr., Benedictine University
Patricia L. Dunmire, Kent State University
Marie Eckstrom, Rio Hondo College
Ernest J. Enchelmayer, Troy State University
Malvina D. Engelberg, Nova Southeastern University
Anne Erickson, Atlantic Cape Community College
Judith Gardner, University of Texas at San Antonio
Keith Gumery, Temple University
Shelley N. Harper, Rowan-Cabarrus Community College
D. Alexis Hart, University of Georgia
Karen J. Jones, St. Charles Community College
Leanne Maunu, Palomar College
JoAnna Stephens Mink, Minnesota State University
Steven Reynolds, College of the Siskiyous
Peter H. Schreffler, Florida Southern College
Timothy A. Shonk, Eastern Illinois University
David P. Sokolowski, St. Mary's University of Minnesota
Alan Tessaro, University of Missouri – St. Louis
Susan P. Willens, George Washington University
Amy Short Williams, Murray State University

Our course, we owe a lifetime of gratitude to our "textbook widows and orphans": Rob's wife, Martha, and children, John, Alexi, and Mark; and Justin's wife, Diana, and daughter, Hannah.

Finally, we owe gratitude to the wonderful staff of Houghton Mifflin, in particular Suzanne Phelps-Weir, Patricia Coryell, Meg Botteon, Rosemary Winfield, Kathleen Leahey, Anne Leung, John McHugh, Ben Reichman, Cindy Graff Cohen, Susan Holtz, Jill Hobbs, Maria Maimone, and Cia Boynton.

Robert Lamm
Arkansas State University

Justin Everett
University of the Sciences in Philadelphia

Dynamic

ARGUMENT

Writing is an exploration. You start from nothing and learn as you go.

— E. L. Doctorow

Part 1

Argument, Rhetoric, and Process

A blank sheet of paper is the traditional starting place for writers. It symbolizes limitless potential. Like all writers, you will learn to fill the blank page as you go—cautiously at first and eventually with growing confidence and skill. Each of the fourteen chapters in Part 1 of *Dynamic Argument* has tips and examples that will guide you in your exploration of writing and help you master the methods needed to complete your writing assignments. You might even learn to fill the blank page with great thoughts that amaze readers and change the world.

1 Introduction

Most of the change we think we see in life
Is due to truths being in and out of favor.
—Robert Frost

Argument changes the world. It shapes the way people think, offering them alternative ways of seeing what is "true." It motivates people to behave differently, providing them with reasons to take action or to halt. As a result, countries wage war or seek peace. People gain or lose civil rights. Those accused of crimes are convicted and jailed or acquitted and freed. Business deals are made or broken. Personal relationships form, break up, or mend. Politicians are elected or defeated. All these activities are set into motion and resolved through a dynamic process of change known as argument.

Dynamics of Argument

Online Study Center
This icon will direct you to content and resources on the website <college.hmco.com/pic/lamm1e>.

What Is an Argument?

Like many words, *argument* can be applied correctly in different ways. The word can refer to a thing, such as the completed text of a persuasive conversation, speech, or piece of writing. Another meaning is less static and more dynamic: Argument is the process of giving reasons to change the way one thinks or acts. By seeking change in people, argument may affect everything touched by humans.

Chances are that when you first saw the word *argument* in this book, other possible definitions sprang to mind that are not applicable. Let's consider those other meanings before putting them aside.

Argument Is Not . . . One way to define a term is to clarify what it is not. As practiced in this book, argument is not a verbal duel, not quibbling, not a shouting match, not a quarrel, not an altercation. Unfortunately, the word *argument*, as commonly used, carries some negative connotations. When argument based on reasoning fails, the result is often the other kind of argument: a verbal duel. That kind of outcome is loud, emotional, and counterproductive.

Argument Is Not Quite . . . Another way to define a term is to qualify it, which means to tell under which conditions it is or is not true. It is true that argument can be adversarial, meaning that one side can be pitted against the other, as in court trial: The prosecutor offers one interpretation of a crime; the defense offers a different one. In a court of law, both sides claim that their interpretation is true and provide reasons in the form of evidence and explanations to influence the judge or jury to think and act a certain way—that is, to reach a verdict in favor of only one side. Claims and supporting reasons are the basic parts of an argument.

Successful arguments convince an audience to accept a claim.

In writing, effective arguments are seldom one-sided: A reader depends on a writer to present a fair account of all important aspects of the issue being discussed. Because the written product may be the reader's only source of information, the writer acts as both the prosecution and the defense to present a kind of verdict, a claim. A reader who feels misled will usually reject not only the writer's argument but also the writer's credibility in all other matters.

Online Study Center
Prepare for Class
Argument

Argument Is . . . Our definition of argument—"giving reasons to change the way one thinks or acts"—is used throughout this book. The desired "change" is expressed as a claim, which is any statement that needs proof before its acceptance. The "reasons" are the support for the claim; they take the form of evidence and explanations.

ELEMENTS OF AN ARGUMENT

Claim A claim, also known as an argumentative thesis, is an assertion that needs support—specific reasons—to be accepted as true. Claims fill our public and private lives. Politicians make claims about one another and about public policy: "This law is immoral"; "That candidate is uninformed"; "We should (or should not) carry out certain policies." Advertisements claim that you should buy certain products. In your daily life, you deal with claims in many forms, such as friends wanting your help or you wanting theirs, people making excuses, perhaps you explaining why a teacher should accept late homework or change a grade. All of these examples are claims, and all are supportable by reasons. (See Chapter 3, Support, for more information.)

Support Support consists of any reasons you provide to convince an audience to accept your claim. A skeptical audience always wonders, "Why should I accept your claim?" Support lets you answer with "Because. . . ." The "because" of support consists of (1) evidence and (2) explanations of how the evidence applies to the claim.

Evidence: Evidence is information that proves or strongly suggests the claim is true or valid. It includes expert opinions, facts and statistics, history, personal experience, scenarios, and specific examples—almost anything that backs the claim. For example, if you were to make a claim about the legality of downloading music from the Internet, the evidence supporting that claim would be specifically related to downloading—for example, statistics about how just or unjust the punishment is or about how much revenue is lost by music companies, stories about legal prosecutions, or appeals by musicians to stop stealing from them. (See Chapter 3, Support, for more information about evidence.)

Explanation: Evidence often needs to be explained, either because the evidence itself is unclear or because its relevance to the claim needs to be spelled out explicitly. For example, if you cited the Geneva Convention as evidence that al-Qaeda prisoners captured in Afghanistan have certain legal rights, you would have to explain how a document protecting conventional military personnel applies to paramilitary fighters and "nonnative combatants." Explanations take the form of clarification, interpretation, application, analysis, synthesis, and evaluation. (See Chapter 2, Claims, for more information about explanations.)

Cornered by Mike Baldwin

"What's important is that we found some common ground. Let's try not to get bogged down over who found it first."

Successful arguments find common ground.

Carl Rogers and Rhetoric

Carl Rogers (1902–1987) was a humanistic psychologist who focused on conflict resolution, among other things. Rogers believed that the best way to resolve an argument was for the individual making the argument to be required to state his or her opponent's position to the opponent's satisfaction before putting forth the individual's own position. Such Rogerian rhetoric—stating an opposing viewpoint before stating your own—can have the effect of pacifying a potentially hostile audience.

Online Study Center
Prepare for Class
Carl Rogers

Finding Common Ground through Conflict Resolution

Arguments sometimes fail because people tend to leap headlong into the conflict without first identifying those key points on which they already agree. Experienced writers—and counselors and arbitrators—often will first seek common ground to help set a tone of mutual trust and to place a disputed point in the context of agreed-upon points.

Conflict resolution is a method of finding common ground and building consensus. Frequently used by psychologists, counselors, and negotiators, these nonadversarial methods depend on active listening. In other words, your goal is to understand the other person's views. Also known as emphatic or empathetic listening, active listening requires an open mind, trust, and a positive attitude toward a point of view you initially find unacceptable.

CONFLICT-RESOLUTION TECHNIQUES

Conflict resolution often is conducted in small groups consisting of two (or a few more) people, sometimes with an arbitrator or counselor present to guide the session. (Clinical psychologists developed this technique.) In a classroom setting, small groups usually can function without an arbitrator as long as all participants follow the guidelines. Each participant is expected to be positive, honest, and constructive and to expect the same of the other participants.

Following are some guidelines for conducting a conflict-resolution session.

- **Take turns setting the agenda.** Each participant helps decide which parts of the issue should be discussed. For example, if the issue is stem-cell research, one person may be concerned about the use of human embryos, while another may be more concerned about the plight of patients who could be saved by such research. An exception to this rule occurs when the arbitrator sets the agenda.
- **Don't interrupt.** This includes not only maintaining verbal silence but also avoiding body language and facial expressions that convey negative reactions.
- **Respond positively.** As another person speaks, you should indicate when you agree by offering a brief word such as "Yes" or a nod. Avoid reacting emotionally, especially if your reaction is not in sympathy with the speaker. Positive body language—showing interest and openness—is encouraged. Work at creating a supportive atmosphere.
- **Postpone disputing facts or opinions.** Factual disputes may not be resolvable during the session. You may even discover later that some of these disagreements were not worth discussing anyway. Immediately arguing about facts and opinions may sidetrack you from learning the main source of disagreement and discovering possible solutions to the conflict.
- **Restate the other person's position briefly and in your own words.** This approach allows you to check whether you understood not only the idea being expressed but also the feeling behind it. You can begin these statements with phrases such as "You think . . . ," "You seem to feel . . . ," or "What I hear you saying is . . . ."
- **Ask for clarifications.** A nonadversarial way of doing this is to reuse the speaker's own words: "What do you mean when you say that harvesting stem cells from an embryo is murder?"
- **Listen for omissions or evasions.** You can sometimes learn much from what the person has not mentioned. Omissions may indicate what the other person has not considered; evasions may reveal what the other person is reluctant to confront.

In a classroom setting, conflict-resolution techniques can help you find and support a position that can be argued with a greater chance of success: You'll better understand those parties who initially disagree with you. (See Chapter 6, Drafting Arguments, for more on using conflict-resolution techniques in argumentation.)

PRACTICE 1.1 Understanding Conflict

In a brief writing or a group discussion, recall a disagreement (from your personal experiences or a television talk-show debate) that degenerated into a quarrel or even a fight. What was it about? What went wrong? Could you have resolved the conflict in a better way? How? Did the experience have an effect on the way you now deal with disagreements?

PRACTICE 1.2 Conflict Resolution

Working in groups or in a class discussion, practice conflict-resolution techniques to better understand a point of view with which you currently disagree. In your discussion, try to find a middle ground that everyone can agree on. Select an issue that already is on your mind or choose an issue from the options given below. Apply Carl Rogers's method (state your opponent's position to his or her satisfaction before stating your own). How might this approach help make your audience more receptive to your point of view?

1. Should students who are caught cheating on exams at your college or university be expelled?
2. Should illegal immigrants have access to public services such as education and health care?
3. Should a new public housing project be built adjacent to your college or university?
4. Should artists who portray or advocate violence be held responsible when their fans or viewers behave violently?
5. Are restaurants responsible when their customers gain weight?

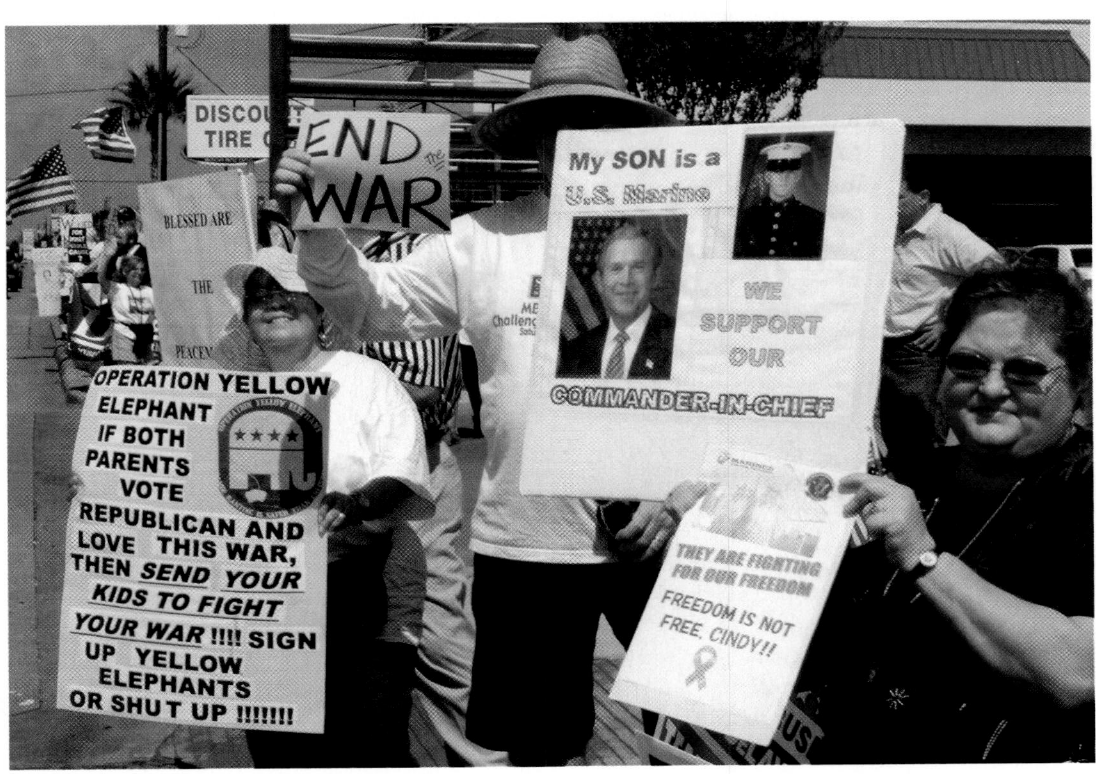

There are at least two sides to every argument.

Online Study Center
Prepare for Class
Classical Greek Rhetoric

Truth and Belief

What is the relationship between argument and truth? The ancient Greeks, who are credited with bringing the arts of argumentation and rhetoric to Western civilization, believed that truth was absolute, pure, and eternal and was out there waiting to be discovered by philosophers. Today we live in an era that is more relativistic and in which truth is often considered tenuous and subjective. It often seems that the only truth today is the idea that there is no absolute truth.

Of course, truth is not relative in the sense that we can violate the laws of nature, but the values we hold true are largely constructed by our cultural beliefs. How an audience responds to a particular issue—gay marriage, medical marijuana, body art, date rape, political correctness, free speech, or stem-cell research—is guided by what they believe to be fundamentally true about what is important in life.

Take marriage, for example. Do you believe it is a holy sacrament created by a divine being? If so, your underlying belief probably is based on religious teachings that a supreme being established rules to guide human behavior. Other people, however, may define marriage primarily as a social contract established by government. Still others may see it as primarily a romantic bond between two people. Is marriage a union of any two (or more) people, or should it be limited to pairs specified by race, religion, gender, age, and so on? Is the union temporary or for life? On top of all these possibilities, do you insist that others should conform to your beliefs—that "there ought to be a law"? However you define marriage, it is your underlying cultural beliefs that guide you in forming that definition.

PRACTICE 1.3 Truth and Claims

For the following issues (or others selected by your instructor), list a claim that particular people make. For each claim, speculate on the belief that underlies it. What do those people believe to be true?

1. Who is responsible for the obesity epidemic among children?
2. If people have large numbers of children because they use fertility drugs, should they be able to receive welfare to support their huge families?
3. What, if anything, should be done about people who hire undocumented workers (illegal immigrants) and pay them at rates below the minimum wage?
4. Should people pay a "congestion tax" for driving their cars in overcrowded cities?
5. Are some poor people being oppressed by society, or are they ultimately responsible for their own station in life because of the choices they make?

Different Audiences Require Different Arguments

"Different strokes for different folks" is a cliché describing how audiences vary not only in their basic beliefs but also in how they may be persuaded in specialized ways. Although some audiences will be homogeneous, many others will be heterogeneous, holding varied and sometimes conflicting beliefs. Environmentalists, for example, would have similar concerns about issues such as clear-cutting of rainforests, while the larger population would have a wider assortment of concerns—the need for more logging jobs, corporate profits, cheap building materials, increased farmland, or fewer government restrictions. As you craft an argument, you must consider the audience, tailoring your claim and support to fit its particular beliefs. (See Chapter 5, Planning Arguments, for more information about understanding audiences.)

PRACTICE 1.4 **Arguing for Different Audiences**

Working individually or in groups, consider the following purposes for writing arguments and their associated audiences. Explain how you would approach each situation and why you would take that approach.

1. You are writing a letter home to your parents to ask them to send you money for living expenses. Would you tell them about any or all of the following: (a) your part-time job, (b) your classes, and (3) your social activities? Explain.
2. You are an attorney who is arguing a case before a jury. Your client has been accused of pedophilia—sexual relations with a minor. Your client is 22 years old, and the minor he had a consensual relationship with was 17 years old. You know the jury includes people who think pedophilia is a horrible crime. How will you convince the jury that your client should not be judged by the standards underlying a law that was intended to prevent the molestation of much younger children? (Could a Rogerian approach be used in this case?)
3. The town you live in wants to build a community center for disadvantaged children; the goal is to encourage these children to continue their education and to keep them away from a life of crime. The center will be located in an affluent neighborhood so that the children can see other ways of living. Some people in the neighborhood where the center will be located do not want nonresidents being bused into their neighborhood. Your job, as a member of the city council, is to convince the people in the well-off neighborhood that the community center will be good for the town as a whole.

Online Study Center
Prepare for Class
Authority, Emotion, and Logic

Formulating Reasonable Arguments: Authority, Emotion, Logic

Reasonable people can be persuaded in several ways—appealing to their trust in authority, their emotions, and their logic. These three appeals, known to debaters and speech makers since at least the fifth century B.C.E., sometimes are referred to by their original Greek names: *ethos* (authority), *pathos* (emotion), and *logos* (logic). Seldom is just one of these approaches adequate to convince an audience to accept a claim. Instead, all of them can be brought into play when arguments are made. (See Chapter 10, Using Logic, for more information.)

AUTHORITY

When you argue, it is necessary to create a sense of your authority. This does not mean that you must necessarily be a leading expert in the field or create an overbearing tone when you write, although some degree of knowledge and self-confidence are part of this perception. The Greek word *ethos* is the same root found in the word *ethical*; it is sometimes translated as *character*. If your readers trust your character, they will be receptive to the claims and support you present.

There are two ways to enhance your authority as a writer: (1) become an "instant authority" through research and (2) use an authoritative yet reasonable tone.

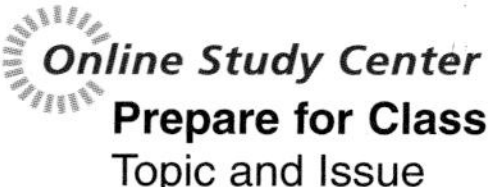

- **Become an "instant authority."** If you know very little about your subject, you can become informed by researching your topic. In this way, you can, in effect, "borrow" the authority of experts in the field. You should also present alternative viewpoints fairly when you write your arguments. If you omit a contrary point of view that is obvious to the readers, they will likely lose faith in you and consequently disregard what you have to say. (When evidence representing only one side is overemphasized while other points of view are diminished or concealed, it is called *card stacking* because it is analogous to cheating at a card game.)
- **Sound authoritative.** Once you have researched your topic and borrowed the authority of your sources, you will be more likely to create an authoritative voice in your writing. Your confidence will make your readers more likely to listen to what you have to say. This approach can be easily overplayed, however, giving the audience the impression that the writer is a pedantic blowhard. Your tone of voice should carry confidence and a sense of authority without seeming arrogant or closed-minded. If you want members of your audience to have open minds, then you, as the author, must lead by example.

Emotion

The persuasive appeal of emotion (Greek: *pathos*) concerns the writer's ability to make an emotional connection with the audience. It can be a powerful tool: Think of how the images of the collapse of the World Trade Center's Twin Towers contributed to support for the "war on terror." Pathos can help you establish common ground by demonstrating your sympathy for your audience's values, beliefs, and worldview. It has the added benefit of increasing your ethos with your audience: Once you have established a sympathetic connection, audience members are more likely to view you as a reliable and authoritative source of information.

Pathos can be overplayed to the point that its emotional element causes the claim to be forgotten. Sometimes the emotional element can be so entertaining that you miss the point of the argument, such as humorous Superbowl commercials that are so humorous that you fail to notice which product is being advertised. At other times it can be disturbing, as illustrated by an ad that tried to warn people of the dangers of abortion by displaying a bloody fetus pinched between a pair of forceps.

Logic

This appeal is equated strongly with logic (Greek: *logos*). Using evidence and specialized kinds of explanations as support, it is considered a very reliable means for reaching decisions. (See Chapter 10, Using Logic, for more information about logic.)

PRACTICE 1.5 Using Authority, Emotion, and Logic

Support each of the following topics using each of the three appeals—emotion, authority, and logic. Because you haven't researched these topics, your support probably will have to be speculative or invented.

1. Violent video games such as *Grand Theft Auto* do not cause young people to become violent.
2. Extreme tattooing, body modification, and scarification are not signs of mental illness but rather are ways of using the body as an artistic canvas.
3. If a fetus has serious mental or physical defects, a parent should be allowed to abort it.
4. Biology teachers should be required to teach intelligent design in public schools because students have a right to be aware of all theories of human origin.
5. To prevent potential threats against the American public, the government should have access to everyone's personal records, including what individuals choose to read in the library or view on the Internet.

Logic is not totally separate from emotion and authority: Trust and feelings are reasons that can matter as much to some people as any logical evidence or explanation. Logic seldom operates with complete detachment from the emotional and authoritative appeals. If readers have no reason to respect the authority of the author and have no emotional investment in what is being said, then their attention will dissipate like smoke.

Why Study Argument?

There are personal reasons for learning how to argue effectively:

Good arguing skills bring many benefits. For example, they can help you make wise decisions in all phases of your life, from life-altering personal issues, such as whether and whom you should marry, to social and civic matters, such as which policy or candidate you should support. Even better, your arguing skills can help resolve both personal and professional disagreements diplomatically, with less chance of a situation degenerating into a quarrel.

"The ability to argue well" is part of most job descriptions, whether it is stated directly or implied. Consider these examples from several different professions:

- Executives make decisions that are essentially claims—developing and marketing a new service or product—guided specifically by whatever evidence is presented about the market for that service and guided generally by the belief that the company must be profitable.
- Doctors make decisions that are essentially claims—treating illnesses based on evidence of symptoms and knowledge of the effectiveness of various treatments—guided primarily by the ethical codes of the Hippocratic Oath.
- Lawyers argue cases, whether for or against a client's particular position. They must sway a judge and sometimes a jury to reach the desired verdict.
- Scientists argue for or against theories. They also must argue for grants and for legal permission. Sometimes they must argue for political action, as in cases such as global warming or stem-cell research.
- Salespeople argue the merits of their products and services, often needing to overcome the skepticism of a customer or client.
- Teachers argue for or against philosophical, aesthetic, and scientific ideas to give their students the tools to develop good critical thinking skills.

Lack of good arguing skills can result in errors of judgment, both small and disastrous, and can cause conflict with others that otherwise could have been avoided. People who cannot evaluate claims, evidence, and explanations are easily misled or cheated. They sometimes must depend more on chance or blind faith because they cannot make well-reasoned decisions.

PRACTICE 1.6 **Arguments in Careers**

Many careers involve some kind of decisions or controversy. Which careers have you considered for yourself?

1. Name a possible career, and list arguments for and against pursuing it.
2. Name some issues that are argued within the career. (For example, physicians argue the pros and cons of "mercy killing.")

Democracy

In addition to the personal benefits afforded by good argumentative skills, the ability to argue effectively has a public benefit: Logical argument is fundamental to the survival of democracy. In a democracy, where all citizens have a right to influence social and political policies, poor decisions can be catastrophic on a national or even global scale. Good citizens understand and practice argument as the best available process for reaching decisions.

PRACTICE 1.7 **Argument and Democracy**

Respond to the following quotation (through a short writing or a group discussion). How does it relate to argumentation?

> Democracy is the recurrent suspicion that more than half the people are right more than half the time.
>
> —E. B. White *(1899–1985)*

Media Arguments

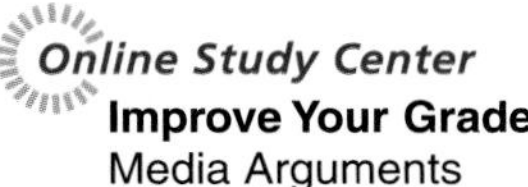

Some arguments are not written on paper but instead are presented through other media. These arguments may take the form of television commercials or pictorial advertisements in magazines; they may be presented on the Internet, in song lyrics, or as the underlying theme of a television show or movie. Whereas written arguments work to persuade an audience primarily through language, media arguments may, in addition to (or in place of) text, use images, color, sound, and motion to emphasize a claim and provide support.

Online Study Center
Prepare for Class
National Youth Anti-Drug Media Campaign

Consider the following examples. The first is from an antidrug campaign sponsored by the National Youth Anti-Drug Media Campaign. It has appeared in magazines and on television (in the form of commercials). The second ad was posted in buses in the Washington, D.C., area by a lobbying organization called Change the Climate. This organization seeks to legalize marijuana.

"The Enforcer" advertisement emphasizes parental authority.

PRACTICE 1.8 **Evaluating Media Arguments: Part 1**

Examine both the text and the images of "The Enforcer" advertisement, and consider the following questions.

1. Which issue is being considered?
2. Who is the target audience for the ad? How do you know? What does your intuition suggest to you about the audience's race, lifestyle, income level, education level, and other demographics? Does the advertisement appear to target parents or children?
3. Why is the woman in the foreground? Does she look concerned, strong, worried? Why is the boy in the background? Why is his image smaller? What does his facial expression suggest? What is his relationship with the woman? Finally, why is there a city in the background?
4. Sum up the ad's argument.
    a. What claim is this ad trying to make?
    b. What evidence is or could be provided to support that claim? How does the woman's image serve as evidence?
    c. Describe how the ad utilizes each of the three appeals (authoritative, emotional, logical) to persuade its audience.

The two advertisements—"The Enforcer" and "Protect Our Children!"—provide claims while leaving it to the viewer to interpret visual evidence and supply the explanation. The fact that they present their arguments mostly with images instead of words does not necessarily make them any less convincing. The important things to remember are that (1) audiences can be targeted and (2) arguments can be made outside of the formal and traditional style of the written or spoken argument. Both advertisements appeal to logic through the text that appears in the ads, authority through the images presented and through the faith the target audience may have in the sponsoring organizations, and emotion through the connections that the images of the mother and the young girl make with their respective audiences. (See Chapter 12, Arguing Visually, for more information about visual arguments.)

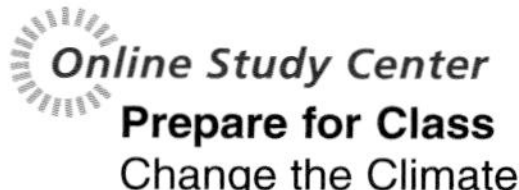

Protect our Children!

Legalize and Tax **Marijuana.**

www.changetheclimate.org

This advertisement emphasizes the importance of individuality.

PRACTICE 1.9 Evaluating Media Arguments: Part 2

Examine both the text and the images of the "Protect Our Children!" advertisement, and consider the following questions.

1. Which issue is being considered?
2. Who is the target audience for the ad? How do you know? What does your intuition tell you about the audience's race, lifestyle, income level, education level, and other demographics? Does the advertisement appear to target parents or children?
3. Why is the girl in the picture shown with a tongue stud and hair braids? Why is she smiling? What does this image suggest about the claim that is being made? What underlying beliefs about individuality and freedom of choice does this ad make? How does that compare to the assumptions about freedom of choice implied by "The Enforcer" ad?
4. Sum up this ad's argument.
   a. What claim is this ad trying to make?
   b. What evidence is or could be provided to support that claim?
   c. Describe its appeal (authoritative, emotional, logical).

PRACTICE 1.10 **Evaluating Media Arguments: Part 3**

Working individually or in groups, compare the two advertisements, "The Enforcer" and "Protect Our Children!"

1. Which do you believe is more effective in conveying its point of view to its target audience?
2. Which has the most explicit claim?
3. Which provides the most compelling support?
4. Which makes the best use of each of the three appeals?
5. How does "Protect Our Children!" differ from the "The Enforcer" in message and method? Which ad do you believe to be more effective, and why?

Note: One ad may not be the most persuasive in all of these areas. You may think that one has better support whereas the other does a better job at appealing to the emotions of the audience, for example.

Writing Arguments

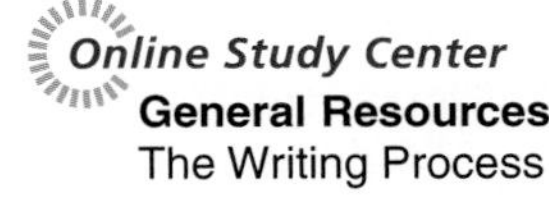

The Writing Process: Planning, Drafting, Revising, Editing, Presenting, Reflecting

Writing includes more than just the physical act of assembling words into visible messages that convey meaning. It also encompasses the mental activities of the writer, including all preparations before and follow-up activities after the physical activity. This comprehensive view of writing is known as the *writing process.* The writing process can be described as consisting of sequential phases—planning, drafting, and revising—although in practice these phases tend to overlap and repeat as the writer discovers what else needs to be done. In other words, the earlier parts of the process are *recursive* (recurring as needed). After the rhetorical and argumentative features are finalized, the writing process terminates with stages that usually occur only once (*nonrecursive*): editing, presenting, and reflecting.

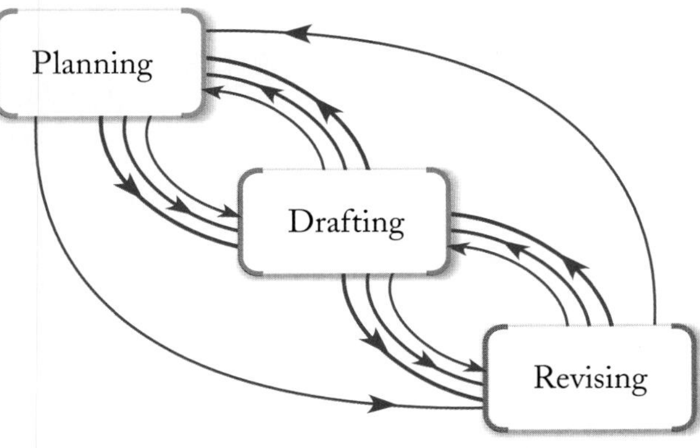

Parts of the writing process are recursive, repeating as needed.

- **Planning:** The planning stage of the writing process helps you create arguments by discovering and organizing your claims, evidence, and explanations. Also known as prewriting, it can make writing remarkably easier. Planning includes understanding the assignment, generating material, and organizing. (These techniques are demonstrated in Chapter 5, Planning Arguments.)

- **Drafting:** Also known as *composing*, the drafting phase involves putting the arguments into particular words, sentences, paragraphs, and overall structure. Drafting is characterized by the many decisions you must make at the verbal level—diction (word choice), syntax (sentence formation), and organization. It seldom is an orderly process because the text will evolve partly according to early planning and partly through trial and error as the drafting occurs. Often you will resume planning when new ideas are needed or engage in revision briefly while drafting. (These techniques are demonstrated in Chapter 6, Drafting Arguments.)
- **Revising:** The word *revision* literally means to "view again." Also known as rewriting, the revising phase is characterized by changing any part of the writ-

Presenting Your Work

Presentation before an audience is the ultimate goal of most arguments. After Terry Schiavo suffered brain damage in 1990, she lived in a semivegetative state that required feeding through a tube. Some argued that her feeding tube should be removed. Here, members of Schiavo's family—who argued that she should continue to be fed through a tube—show her photo to the Pope. The feeding tube was removed on March 18, 2005, and Schiavo died 13 days later.

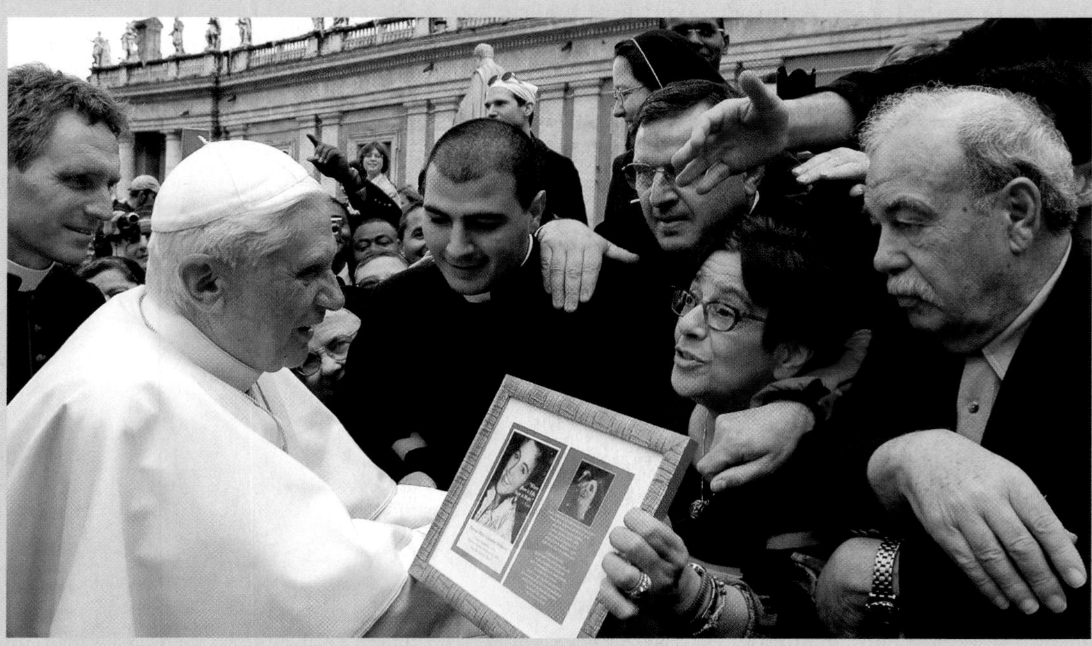

ing that affects the meaning of a text. When revision reveals that more ideas are needed, the writer may return to planning. You might use a rubric (criteria describing qualities of writing) and feedback from peers, teachers, or editors to help "view again" with fresh eyes. If time allows, you might set the text aside for a while so as to gain a new perspective on it. (These techniques are demonstrated in Chapter 7, Revising Arguments.)

- **Editing:** Editing is the "correctness" phase of the writing process. Known also as copy editing, proofing, or proofreading, this phase involves making sure the usage, spelling, punctuation, and other conventions are acceptable. Editing can be aided by various software packages attached to word processors. Experienced writers postpone most editing until after they finish the revision process. Otherwise, time may be wasted editing text that will be changed or deleted later. Even worse, the flow of drafting may halt while the writer deals with technical details.
- **Presenting:** Also known as sharing, publishing, or submitting, this phase is when the writer makes the text public in any way. In most college classes, presenting is accomplished by sharing with classmates and by submitting the work to an instructor. It also may involve reading the text in public or circulating it electronically (via e-mail or Web) or in print. In the workplace, virtually all written works are presented to other employees, administrators, or clients as memos, letters, reports, and proposals.
- **Reflecting:** You learn from your experiences in life, and writing is one of those experiences. You may learn more if your writing process and products become

PRACTICE 1.11 **Your Writing Process**

In a brief writing or in group discussion, reflect on the following questions.

1. Do you like to write? Why or why not?
2. Do you like some kinds of writing better than others? Which do you like best? Which do you like least? Why?
3. How much and what kind of writing do you think your future career might require? Has your ability to write affected your career plans? Why or why not?
4. What percentage of your writing time is spent on the various parts of the writing process: planning, drafting, and revising?
5. In what ways do you want to improve as a writer? How can you make specific improvements?

the subject of reflection, perhaps even the impetus of further writing. Writers sometimes keep a "writer's journal" that is focused on any writing they contemplate, work on, complete, or admire—anything writing-related.

Rhetoric: Purpose, Audience, Structure, and Style

As you write an argument, you must make choices about the best ways to communicate. These choices can be divided into four major considerations:

- **Purpose:** What effect on the audience are you seeking?
- **Audience:** Who will read (or hear or view) your argument?
- **Structure:** What form, genre, or organization will the writing take?
- **Style:** What attitude or "voice" will your writing display?

Online Study Center
Prepare for Class
Purpose, Audience, Structure, and Style

These four considerations—purpose, audience, structure, and style (known by the acronym PASS)—provide the basis for a broad set of rules or guidelines for writing effectively that are known as *rhetoric*. Perhaps without realizing it, you have been learning and practicing rhetoric all your life, communicating in different ways with different kinds of people—friends, teachers, police officers, romantic interests.

The *purpose* is the goal of your communication. In a general sense, your purpose is to argue and to change the audience's thoughts or actions. However, you will always have a specific purpose for arguing—specific opinions or specific actions desired. In writing, that specific purpose forms your thesis, your augmentative claim.

The *audience* consists of the readers, listeners, or viewers of your argument. In everyday communications you may understand your audience well enough to write or converse freely, such as with a friend. More generally, audiences can vary in so many ways (and may even be imaginary scenarios) that it may be overwhelming to comprehend all of the possibilities:

- **Physical characteristics:** Age, race, and gender. For example, an older audience may have different values than a younger audience regarding tastes in music and fashion or ideas about morality.
- **Background:** Ethnic group, level of education, geographic or national origin, heritage, religion, politics.
- **Size, variety, and distance:** Large or small groups, mixed or uniform, near (in your presence) or far (whom you'll never meet).

PURPOSE AND THESIS

We write to attain a purpose—to express our feelings, to entertain, to inform, or to argue. The implied or stated purpose for a particular piece of writing is its central idea—that is, its thesis.

Sample Thesis Statements for Purposes of Writing

- **To express:** "When I turned 21, it was the best year of my life!"
- **To entertain:** "When I was one-and-twenty / I heard a wise man say / Give crowns and pounds and guineas / But not your heart away."—A. E. Housman
- **To inform:** "In most states, 21 years is the minimum age for purchase of liquor."
- **To argue (claim):** "The legal age to vote should be 21, not 18."

An argumentative thesis is called a claim. It differs from other statements of purpose primarily because it is controversial, requiring reasons for an audience to accept it. Keep your primary goal in mind when you write. Arguers sometimes get side-tracked into primarily informing or entertaining an audience or venting their personal feelings.

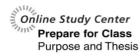

Online Study Center
Prepare for Class
Purpose and Thesis

Structure is the recognizable form that your argument takes. Written arguments are found in the form of essays, certainly, but also as personal letters, ads, print versions of speeches, memoranda, editorials, and blogs (weblogs). Structure also includes the way you organize your ideas within a form, such as comparison/contrast or narration. Your audience, purpose, and style will influence

PRACTICE 1.12 Analyzing Rhetoric

For the following paragraph, analyze the major rhetorical features and explain your analysis by referring to specific parts of the passage. Answer these questions about rhetoric:

1. Purpose: What effect on the audience does the author seek?
2. Audience: To whom is the argument addressed? Who would reject it?
3. Structure: What form, genre, or shape does the writing take?
4. Style: What attitude or voice does the writing display?
5. In what ways could the author use rhetoric differently, perhaps more effectively?

The war on terror is in truth nothing more than an excuse for using aggressive means to open Middle Eastern oil resources to Western corporations—the very corporations that fund the political campaigns of those who engage in the warmaking. All talk of terror here is deception, and the shameful and hypocritical war in Iraq is, in fact, a counterproductive effort that will do nothing except worsen the very predicament whose improvement was its stated objective.

—*Excerpt from a student's essay*

your choice of structure. For example, a letter might influence a friend, whereas a letter to the editor of the local newspaper might influence a community.

Style is how you say something. It is influenced strongly by your purpose, audience, and structure. An informal letter to a friend might begin, "What's up, man?" whereas a letter to a senator might begin, "The Honorable Bill Frist." Style includes voice, which essentially is your personality being expressed through the writing. Your voice is conveyed by your distinctive word choices, sentence formations, and organization as well as by the attitude and tone you convey toward your audience and subject. You vary your writing style to suit the occasion, much the same way that you wear informal clothes to relax with friends but dress up in formal attire to attend a wedding or dinner party.

Online Study Center
General Resources
Student Essay: "Childhood Obesity"

Student Essay

Read the student essay, "Childhood Obesity: Introducing the Fat Card," and complete the associated practices.

PRACTICE 1.13 **Before You Read**

Working individually or in groups, consider your opinion of the problem of childhood obesity in America.

1. Are more of today's young people getting fat than members of previous generations? What makes you think so?
2. If you think childhood obesity is increasing and creating health problems, what might be the cause?
3. Do you think the responsibility for making people healthy rests with society or with the individual? In other words, can you blame McDonald's for making you fat?
4. Examine the essay's title. What does it suggest about the author's thesis?

Janet Barnett

Dr. Robert Lamm

Composition

29 July 2004

Childhood Obesity: Introducing the Fat Card

Nationwide, childhood obesity has increased threefold over the last thirty years, rising to affect a total of nine million obese children ("New Grants Program"). Obesity is creeping up on a majority of children as they eat junk food and rest on their derrieres while watching television and playing video games. It is easy to blame fast-food restaurants and advertisers for enticing children to want supersized portions of junk food. Moreover, it is parents and guardians who provide children with fattening food choices and hours of unlimited television time exposing children to advertisements. Many children will not make wise nutritional choices for themselves; therefore, parents should be setting examples and encouraging children to develop healthy eating habits and active lifestyles.

In an effort to inform parents and guardians about how their children rate according to acceptable standards of height and weight, the government has ordered schools to provide body mass index information in the form of a health report card. Although this information alone cannot change the weight of a child, ideally it will make parents and guardians take the initiative to help their children eat healthier and become more physically fit. Some parents fear that too much emphasis is already put on children to be thin, even without the humiliation of a fat report card. Most students and parents resent schools reporting student body mass information and forcing changes in nutrition and exercise.

Child nutrition and physical activity are the responsibility of adults in the home. Unfortunately, in the United States, approximately 60 percent of adults are overweight. Based on the assumption that children have environmental influences from obese adults, it is not surprising that one-fourth of our high school students are obese or are at risk of becoming obese. Obese children have shorter life expectancies and will cost the government a phenomenal amount of money in health care. According to Claudia Wallis, overweight adolescents have a high risk of becoming overweight adults (68). Many obese students may not be able to work when they are older if they do not change their lifestyles. Only long-term behavior and health improvement will guard against adult obesity, which is the second leading cause of preventable death in the United States ("New Grants Program").

Because so many students are failing the nutrition and exercise practicum, the government has had to take necessary steps to change junk-food habits in American children (Avery). Schools are taking on the tasks of monitoring students' health and adapting fitness goals and junk-food intake while at school.

Some states, such as California, are seeking nutritional standards under which healthier food choices would replace junk food in school vending machines (Sprague). Many schools are afraid if they have to stop selling junk food in vending machines and cafeterias, school programs will suffer because junk food yields high profits. Schools do not want to lose money, and children do not want to give up junk food; but the risks of being overweight are greater.

Obese students are at risk of developing diseases such as heart conditions, hypertension, and diabetes. Type II diabetes is up

Barnett 3

800 percent in the last ten years. Prevention is the best combatant against these diseases caused by obesity.

Promotion of fitness, wellness, active lifestyles, clinical intervention, preventive screenings, and health education are keys to defeating obesity in children and adults nationally ("New Grants Program"). Parents are the most suited to make these changes for children, but it seems the task will be easier if schools help in providing healthier foods and improved physical education plans. In addition, the health report card will hold parents and guardians accountable for information regarding their children's fitness and provide assistance if necessary. The health report card is a good reminder for parents and students as long as too much emphasis is not placed on the report, causing students who are not overweight to go on starvation diets that could lead to serious food disorders.

Barnett 4

Works Cited

Avery, Sarah. "Childhood Obesity Raises Worry, Debate at National Summit." Knight Ridder Tribune Business News 4 Jun. 2004. ABI/INFORM. ProQuest. Arkansas State U Lib., Jonesboro, AR. 22 Jul. 2004 <http://proquest.umi.com>.

"New Grants Program Aims to Prevent Obesity through Promoting Physical Activity." The Daily Record 16 Apr. 2004. ABI/INFORM. ProQuest. Arkansas State U Lib., Jonesboro, AR. 22 Jul. 2004 <http://proquest.umi.com>.

Sprague, Mike. "California State Senator Seeks Junk-Food Ban for Schools." Knight Ridder Tribune Business News 26 Mar. 2004. ABI/INFORM. ProQuest. Arkansas State U Lib., Jonesboro, AR. 22 Jul. 2004 <http://proquest.umi.com>.

Wallis, Claudia. "Guess What F Is for? Fat." Time 15 Sep. 2003. ABI/INFORM. ProQuest. Arkansas State U Lib., Jonesboro, AR. 22 Jul. 2004 <http://proquest.umi.com>.

PRACTICE 1.14 **Understanding the Essay**

1. Identify the writer's central claim (thesis statement). What secondary points does the author make to support the main idea?
2. What sort of evidence does the author provide? Examine the paragraphs one at a time. Are any supporting ideas not really supported?
3. Does the author acknowledge an alternative point of view? Explain.
4. In your own words, summarize the author's (a) argumentative purpose, (b) target audience, (c) method of organization (How does she "break up" the topic into arguable parts?), and (d) style (How does she use language appropriate to the target audience?).
5. How does the author appeal to the audience's logic? How does she attempt to establish an authoritative voice? How does she work to make an emotional connection with the audience?

PRACTICE 1.15 **Responding to the Essay**

1. Do you agree or disagree with the author's claim and supporting ideas? Did the author change your prior opinion in any way? How?
2. Where is the author's support stronger? Where is it weaker? Explain.
3. Does the author's omission of another point of view affect your willingness to believe what she has to say? In what way?
4. What, if anything, would you change about the essay's organization and content? Is there anything missing that you would add?
5. Which of the appeals (logic, authority, emotion) do you think was strongest in this essay? Which was weakest? Why do you think so?
6. Name the essay's greatest strength and most significant weakness. Explain your answer.

Looking Back at Chapter 1

- Argument pervades our lives—in some ways reflecting the way we are but in other ways trying to change thoughts and actions and shape the way we will be.
- The pervasiveness of argument in our culture makes its study significant and weighty in ways that you may find surprising: You can argue back.
- This book aims to provide the experiences, guidance, and tools that will make you an able arguer in your studies and in life.
  1. How to recognize the issues in their various forms
  2. How to analyze, evaluate, and respond to arguments

3. How to effectively present claims, evidence, and explanations
4. How to utilize authority, logic, and emotion when you argue
5. How and why you should argue honestly
6. How to analyze and evaluate the written forms of arguments and write your own arguments using rhetorical principles: audience, purpose, structure, and style

Suggestions for Writing

- Search though magazines and locate advertisements. What claims do they make, and how do they support those claims?
- Write a journal entry describing and reflecting on your best and worst experiences with writing.
- Brainstorm a list of issues that intrigue you and affect your life. Write an essay responding to one of those issues.
- Think of one change that would benefit your hometown. Write a detailed letter to the city council explaining what that change is and why it should be made.

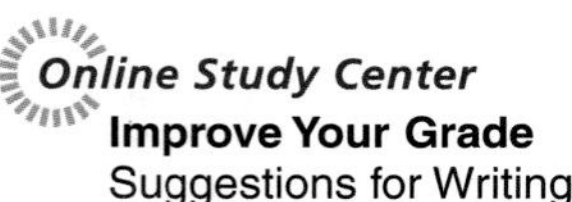

Online Study Center
Improve Your Grade
Suggestions for Writing

2

CLAIMS

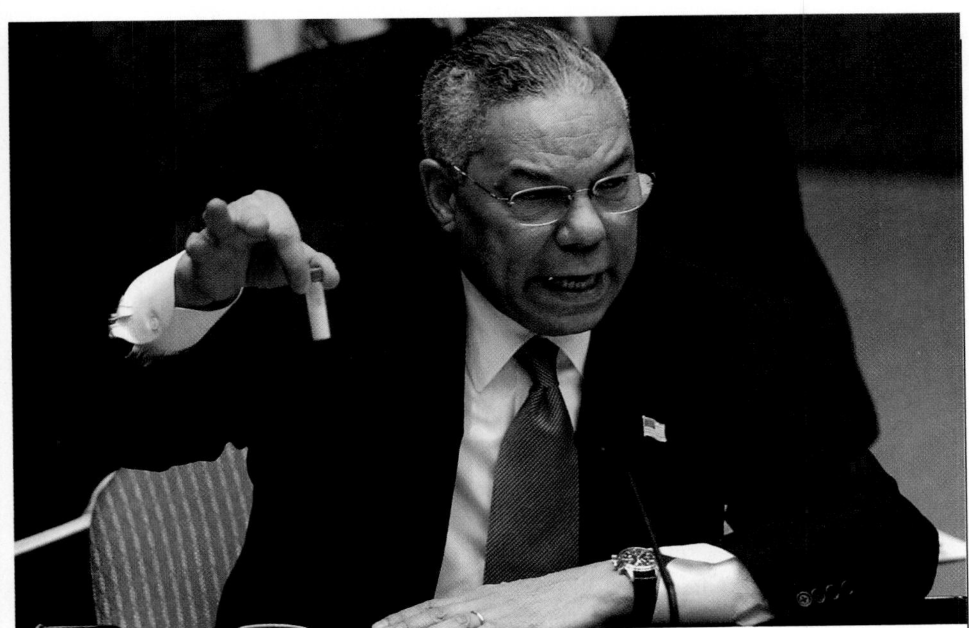

A claim asserts that something is true, but some element of uncertainty or disagreement prevents others from accepting that statement. Arguments always are based on one or more claims, with the goal of convincing reasonable skeptics to believe the claims' validity.

Of course, not all statements are claims, just as not all writings are arguments. Nonargumentative writings have other goals, such as expressing emotions primarily for personal benefits (e.g., a diary, a journal), entertaining readers creatively (e.g., novels, poems), or informing others with noncontroversial facts

A man who makes an assertion puts forward a claim—a claim on our attention and to our belief.
—STEPHEN TOULMIN

REASONABLE SKEPTICISM

Claims are more often presented to a skeptical—that is, nonbelieving—audience. However, their skepticism does not mean that the audience members reject the claim outright. Instead, you should think of a claim as being part of a contract between a writer and an audience. The writer proposes to try to convince the audience that something is true through a series of claims and support, and the audience promises to consider the evidence honestly and with an open mind. If the audience does not approach the argument with a willingness to be convinced, then an argument, in the true sense of the word, cannot really take place (see Chapter 1, Introduction). For instance, the statement "Teenagers should not be allowed to obtain a driver's license until they turn 18" is a claim. This statement is arguable, but it requires proof to be considered valid. Believers would immediately accept the claim as valid. Skeptics would require proof, but—as part of the honest contract between writer and audience—would be willing to be convinced if the writer offered enough proof.

Online Study Center
This icon will direct you to content and resources on the website <college.hmco.com/pic/lamm1e>.

Online Study Center
Prepare for Class
Reasonable Skepticism

(e.g., expository writing). Your understanding of claims will help you avoid drifting into writing for nonargumentative purposes. Also, you will be able to better analyze and critique the way others argue about an issue. Finally, understanding claims will help you reach the decision every writer must make: "What do I want to say?"

To use claims productively, you need to know (1) how they vary in their degree of controversy, (2) how they function within a piece of writing, and (3) what type of statement they make about what is "true."

Degrees of Controversy

A claim is relative, meaning that its degree of controversy depends on the audience to whom it is addressed: One audience may fully agree with your position on an issue, whereas another may disagree completely. Consider, for example, two different claims (theories) about the origins of life on earth: evolution and intelligent design (also known as creationism). A claim based on intelligent design would be controversial at a conference of scientists, whereas some church congregations would accept intelligent design as a reality, not as a claim. Similarly, evolution is regarded as a claim by some religious people but accepted by many scientists as a fact.

Functions in Writing

Claims can vary in how they function within a piece of writing. You could think of claims as ranging from broad to narrow, general to specific, major to minor, or central to supporting—any of these ways will help you see the role a particular claim plays in an overall argument.

Major Claim

An argument usually presents one *major claim*—namely, the arguer's stance on a particular issue. An *issue* differs from a *topic* by being specific and arguable. "Global Warming" is a topic. Whether government should enforce emission standards for automobiles to curb global warming is an issue. The major claim functions as a thesis statement, expressing the main idea. A major claim always needs support in the form of evidence and/or explanations. If, for example, you argue that Ronald Reagan was the greatest American president of the twentieth century, you could support this major claim by citing evidence of his achievements and explanations of how this evidence proves your claim.

Online Study Center
Prepare for Class
Topic and Issue

Supporting Claim

The *supporting claim* is offered as evidence to support the major claim. Whenever evidence contains some element of uncertainty or disagreement, it must be treated as a claim and must be given its own support. If, for example, you said that one reason for Ronald Reagan's greatness was the way that his foreign policies led to the breakup of the Soviet Union, this evidence actually would be a supporting claim and would need its own evidence and explanations. In other words, you would have to argue a cause/effect relationship between Reagan's policies and the collapse of the Soviet Union. Supporting claims sometimes function as topic sentences but may also be used as support for a topic.

Types of Claims

Online Study Center
Prepare for Class
Types of Claims

Claims can also vary in what they assert as being true. This chapter describes five types of claims: fact, identity, cause/effect, value, and proposal. The thesis statement of an argument usually fits into one of these categories. By contrast, the support for the thesis statement often consists of a combination of many types of claims.

- Fact claims make assertions about what is real or not real.
- Identity claims make assertions about what something is.
- Cause-and-effect claims make assertions about how or why things happen.
- Value claims make judgments.
- Proposal claims make assertions about what should be done.

TYPES OF CLAIMS

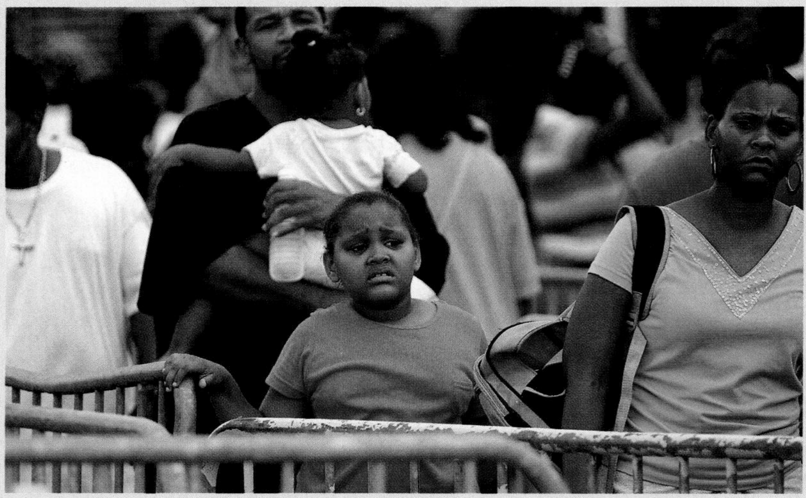

When is someone needy enough to deserve public assistance? In this photo, people wait in line for assistance following hurricane Katrina.

Value claims help citizens make informed decisions in political contests. Here, a woman in Iraq casts a ballot in the referendum to approve the new constitution.

Fact: Is/was it real?

Existence: Does/did it actually exist?

Occurrence: Does/did it actually happen?

Identity: What is it?

Definition: What are its characteristics?

Classification: To which group does it belong?

Comparison/Contrast: How is it alike or different?

Resemblance: What does it resemble?

Cause/Effect: How or why does it work?

Cause: What made, makes, or will make it happen?

Effect: What happened, happens, or will happen?

Value: How is it judged?

Quality: How "good" or "bad" is it?

Ethics/Morality: How "right" or "wrong" is it?

Proposal: Should something be done?

Policy: What should be done?

Procedure: How should it be done?

Fact Claims: Is or Was It Real?

Fact claims make assertions about whether something is or ever was an actuality, answering the question, "Is or was it real?" These claims sometimes deal with whether an event occurs or ever occurred. For example, historians debate whether Viking or Chinese explorers discovered America before Columbus in 1492. Fact claims may also focus on whether a person, place, thing, or phenomenon exists or ever existed. For example, global warming—a theory that human pollution is contributing to a greenhouse effect—has been the subject of much argument.

> **EXAMPLE OF A FACT CLAIM**
>
> Americans know something without a name is undermining the country, turning the mind mushy when it comes to separating truth from falsehood and right from wrong. And they don't like it.
>
> —Charlton Heston, "Winning the Cultural War"

Facts Change Over time, the unearthing of new evidence has shown many earlier claims of fact to be erroneous. For example, from ancient times until the fifteenth century, European astronomers believed that the Earth was the center of the universe; later astronomers such as Copernicus and Galileo discovered new evidence showing that the Earth revolved around the Sun. More recently, the director of the U.S. Central Intelligence Agency, William Tenet, made a factual

Fact claims make assertions about what is real or not real.

claim that Iraqi dictator Saddam Hussein had weapons of mass destruction, saying to President George W. Bush, "It's a slam-dunk case." Not until after Coalition forces invaded Iraq did new evidence reveal the fact claim of Iraqi WMDs to be in error.

PRACTICE 2.1 Fact Claims: Part 1

Online Study Center
Prepare for Class
Fact Claims

Read the following two paragraphs. For each, identify a claim of fact within the paragraph; (2) rephrase the claim in your own words; and (3) write an opposing claim that might be used to refute what each paragraph has to say. *Hint:* This exercise involves being able to identify a generalization in the midst of many facts and specifics. Which sentences in the paragraphs are of a more general nature, and which are more specific?

1. From Lowell Monke, "Charlotte's Webpage: Why Children Shouldn't Have the World at Their Fingertips"

"There have been no advances over the past decade that can be confidently attributed to broader access to computers," said Stanford University professor of education Larry Cuban in 2001, summarizing the existing research on educational computing. "The link between test-score improvements and computer availability and use is even more contested." Part of the problem, Cuban pointed out, is that many computers simply go unused in the classroom. But more recent research, including a University of Munich study of 174,000 students in thirty-one countries, indicates that students who frequently use computers perform worse academically than those who use them rarely or not at all.

2. From Charles Shaw, "A Less Fashionable War"

But as the rare upper-middle-class educated White American in prison, I found myself in a truly alien, self-perpetuating world of crushing poverty and ignorance, violent dehumanization, institutionalized racism, and an entire subculture of recidivists, some of whom had done nine and ten stints, many dating back to the seventies. Most used prison as a form of criminal networking, knowing full well they would be left to fend for themselves when released. We were told on many occasions that an inmate was worth more inside prison than back in society. Considering it costs an average of $37,000 a year to incarcerate offenders, and the average income for black Americans is $24,000, and only $8,000–12,000 for poor blacks, one can easily see their point.

Some Claims Cannot Be Argued Sometimes, a claim that is argued as a fact is based on a personal value rather than on evidence. In such cases, people will hold a position regardless of any evidence presented that shows the opposite to be true. Such arguments are usually irrational, and they do not rely on evidence for their support. For example, if someone argues that you should never shop in a mall because cameras watch you in the dressing rooms, the person is likely stating this position not on the basis of evidence, but on the basis of a personal belief. In such cases, the arguer has short-circuited the contract between the writer and the audience.

PRACTICE 2.2 **Fact Claims: Part 2**

1. What is arguable about the following claims of fact?
   a. Global warming is a myth.
   b. Wearing motorcycle helmets prevents injuries.
   c. Evolution is not believable because it is not mentioned in the Bible.
   d. Stem-cell research will cure Alzheimer's disease.
   e. Playing cops and robbers desensitizes children to killing.
2. State a claim of fact that you have heard or read—a statement that some people accept as valid but others reject. What makes this claim arguable? What evidence and explanations support it? Are there alternative claims of fact?
3. State your own claim of fact. Who would agree or disagree with your claim? How would you defend your position?

Identity Claims: What Is It?

Identification is the ability to assign a name to something by observing its characteristics. The ability to identify things is so basic to our lives that we probably take it for granted. The methods we use for identification include defining, classifying, comparing and contrasting, and observing resemblances.

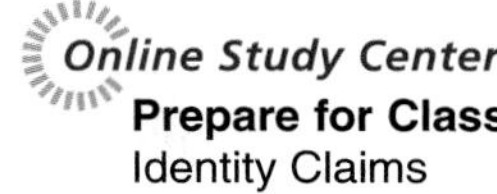

- We define by understanding a thing by the qualities it possesses. Example: "An activist is a person who believes that direct, visible action is necessary to attain a political or social goal."
- We classify by creating groups that help sort out similar things from dissimilar things. Example: "Political demonstrators may be classified either as activists or as rabble."
- We compare and contrast by examining the degree to which one thing is different from or the same as another thing. Example: "Activists tend to be well orga-

Identification claims are based on criteria that are descriptive.

nized and focused on a specific issue, while rabble tend to be disorganized and generally discontented."

- We observe resemblances between two things that are similar yet not identical. Example: "When a rabble stages a demonstration, it is like children throwing a tantrum."

Identity arguments are based on descriptive details known as criteria (also called descriptors, qualities, characteristics, or features). Criteria provide a kind of checklist that helps answer the question, "How do I know what this is?" For example, if you define an activist as "a person who believes that direct, visible action is necessary to attain a political or social goal," then the criteria are expressed in the key words: *person, direct action, visible action, social* or *political goal.*

Identity claims arise from either (1) matching the criteria with a particular thing or (2) establishing particular criteria for the identity:

- **Matching criteria:** If, for example, you define *rabble* as "a crowd of people who are disorganized and generally discontented," then any political demonstrator who matches those criteria can be identified as being part of the rabble. Arguments might arise over whether a demonstrator displays any, some, or all of those criteria. Is the demonstrator actually "disorganized" and "generally discontented"? This kind of identification argument is typical of legal trials, which match the criteria of a law with the actions of the accused: The verdict is based on the match.

- **Establishing criteria:** Sometimes an identity claim is based on reaching an agreement about which criteria actually identify something. For example, you might want to define *rabble* as "unsanitary": You argue for the criterion of "not using soap" to be added. This kind of arguing is a typical of policy makers such as legislators who write laws establishing the difference between legal and illegal actions.

You'll find that definition, classification, comparison and contrast, and resemblance overlap a bit in how they identify things. Each, however, gives a particular perspective on the criteria that answer the question, "What is it?"

Definition Claims: What Are Its Characteristics? Definition claims identify something by detailing its characteristics or features. Most definitions are not controversial, but they become claims when they are not accepted by all or part of an audience.

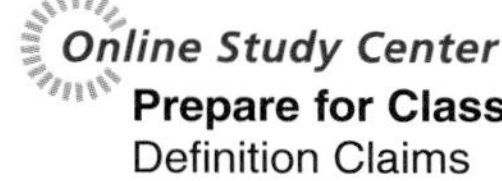

Online Study Center
Prepare for Class
Definition Claims

EXAMPLES OF DEFINITION CLAIMS

If marriage is redefined to include two men in love, on what possible principled grounds can it be denied to three men in love?

—Charles Krauthammer, "When John and Jim Say, 'I Do'"

Defining Kitsch

Kitsch, a German word meaning "ugly," is often applied to a category of collectables that are—or once were, before they became valuable—considered "junk." Kitsch is usually mass-produced and inexpensive when the product is first sold. Pez dispensers, Elvis memorabilia, fuzzy dice, and 1970s black-light posters are all examples of "kitschy" items. Kitsch can be difficult to categorize and define. To do so, it is best to examine several items that seem "kitschy" and work your way backward from there. What makes some junk not junk? In some cases you have to begin with the adage, "I know it when I see it."

PRACTICE 2.3 Definition Claims

1. Use the following statements as the basis of a definition. Is your definition controversial? Who would agree or disagree with it? How would you defend it?
   a. What is the difference between *erotica* and *pornography*?
   b. What does a police officer have to do to be accused of police brutality?
   c. What is the difference between cigarette, alcohol, and drug *abuse* and *use*? Can these substances ever be used without being abused?
   d. What makes someone a *soldier,* a *terrorist,* or a *freedom fighter*?
   e. What makes some expressions objectionable? When can language be said to be *colorful* as opposed to *objectionable*?

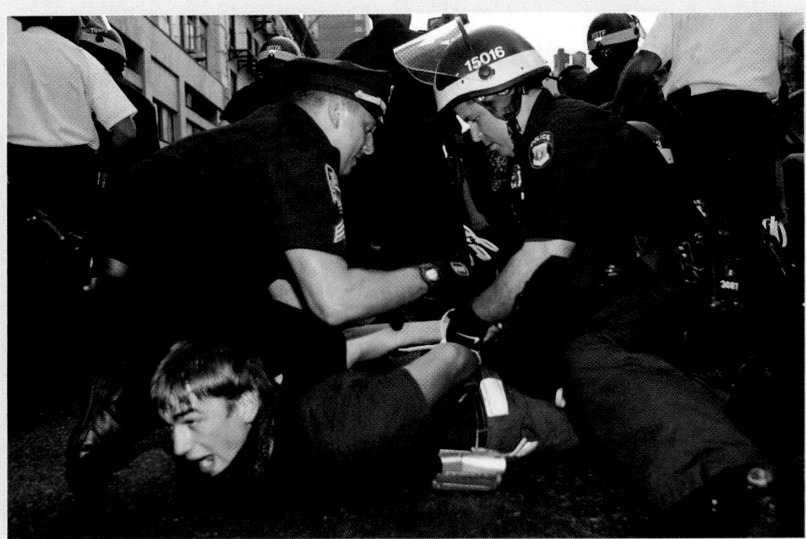

The difference between police brutality and proper procedures is often a matter of definition.

2. State a controversial definition that you have heard or read—a definition that some people accept as valid but that others do not accept. What makes the definition claim arguable?
3. State your own definition claim. Who would agree or disagree with your claim? How would you defend your position?

> We will never get a moral consensus that a single cell, or a clump of 100 cells, is a human being. That definition defies moral sense, rational argument, and several major religious traditions.
>
> —Virginia Postrel, "Should Human Cloning Be Allowed? Yes, Don't Impede Medical Progress"

Definition claims arise either in formulating the definition or in applying it. For example, defining *junk* as "anything that has outlived its usefulness" may be intended to be informative and nonargumentative, but it would become a claim if you applied that label to something (or somebody) that others consider "useful."

Classification Claims: To Which Group Does It Belong? Classification claims offer a system for splitting a large group of people, places, objects, or events into smaller groups. Virtually everything is classified in some way. People are classified by race, gender, age, education, career, nationality, religion, height, weight, blood group, hair color, and many other ways. How people are classified can have many effects on their lives, either opening opportunities or closing doors.

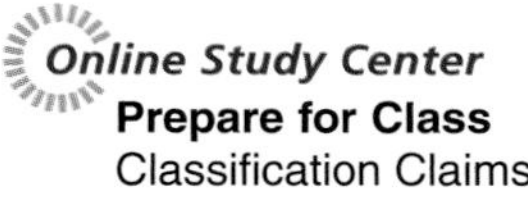

The components of a large group often can be arranged continuously between two extremes, as with human IQ values. This method of sorting is called a range, spectrum, or continuum. A range usually is divided into subgroups, even when none are obvious: We have a need to break large, undifferentiated collections into parts that are easier to understand. For example, the U.S. Department of Homeland Security classifies terrorism threat levels by using a handful of colors to represent degrees of severity, even though the dividing lines between degrees of real-life threats may not be distinct.

Classification claims focus either on creating a system or on applying it.

EXAMPLES OF CLASSIFICATION CLAIMS

The spectrum of body decoration incorporates body painting, body adornment, and body modification.

—Janice Selekman, "A New Era of Body Decoration"

The debate is usually divided into two issues—reproductive cloning (creating cloned human beings) and therapeutic cloning (creating cloned human embryos for research and destruction).

—Eric Cohen and William Kristol, "Should Human Cloning Be Allowed? No, It's a Moral Monstrosity"

Classification becomes important when the groups are treated differently—for example, when one group receives more or fewer benefits or has greater or lesser responsibility. For example, vehicles classified as SUVs (based on the criterion of weighing more than 6,000 pounds) recently have qualified for $100,000 in tax breaks for small businesses. Controversy has erupted because of accusations that this government policy encourages sales of luxury vehicles with low fuel efficiency.

Classification claims are created in three ways: (1) by establishing criteria for a categorical system (e.g., how to classify vehicles); (2) by matching criteria of an existing system with particular subjects (e.g., does a particular vehicle qualify for

PRACTICE 2.4 Classification Claims

1. For the following large groups, describe one existing classification system. Try to create a hierarchy that is at least three levels deep, ending with a specific example (e.g., Automobiles/Trucks/Sports Utility Vehicles/Midsize SUVs/Hyundai Santa Fe). What criteria are used for each system?
   a. Motion pictures
   b. Students
   c. Relationships
   d. Food groups
   e. Music
2. Name a controversial classification system—groupings that some people accept as valid but others reject. What makes the classification system arguable?
3. Devise an original classification system or revise an existing one. Explain the benefits of your system. Who would or would not agree with it?

a tax break); or (3) by establishing the rights, protections, and responsibilities of each group.

If you are proposing a new or revised system of classification, make sure your system is unified, thorough, and exclusive:

- **Unity:** A classification system is usually based on a unifying concept. For example, people can be classified by religion or by political party, but probably not both ways in the same system.
- **Thoroughness:** A classification system usually needs to have a place to put every item being sorted. Of course, some things will resist classification. If too many items don't fit into any of your categories, however, your system probably needs revision.
- **Exclusiveness:** The categories should clearly apply to some items and clearly not apply to others. If many items seem to fit in more than one category, the classification system probably needs revision.

Comparison and Contrast Claims: How Is It Alike or Different?

Comparison and contrast claims identify something in relation to something else: Features of one thing are shown to be essentially the same as or different from the features of the other thing. Claims based on comparisons and contrasts tend to point out the unexpected: how two "different" things are unexpectedly alike, or how two "identical" things are surprisingly different. Shoppers and advertisers frequently make comparisons between products—that is, their product versus an inferior "Brand X." Advocates and opponents of gay marriage sometimes compare the lifestyles of heterosexual and homosexual couples or make a distinction between marriage and civil union.

Online Study Center
Prepare for Class
Comparison/Contrast Claims

EXAMPLES OF COMPARISON AND CONTRAST CLAIMS

> For no matter how true the new feminist analysis might be, there remains a world of difference between a smooth talker on the one hand and a hand holding a knife to your throat on the other. Calling them both rapists may be a fine way of highlighting the malignity of the former, but it is also a way of trivializing the criminality of the latter.
>
> —David Carlin, Jr., "Date Rape Fallacies"

> Compared to marriage, a civil pact is harder to get into (some of its benefits do not arrive until a couple has been together for two or even three years) and much easier to get out of.
>
> —David Frum, "American Conservatism: The Marriage Buffet"

How does a "civil union" between gay partners compare with a heterosexual marriage? What are the features of each? Is one inherently better than the other? By comparing the requirements of each, it is possible to build an argument on the basis of comparison.

PRACTICE 2.5 Comparison and Contrast Claims

1. For the following pairs, list points of comparison and contrast. What kind of claim could you make about how they are alike or different? Which would interest an audience more, the comparison or the contrast?
   a. Healthful dieting and eating disorders
   b. Traditional and nontraditional unions
   c. Animal rights and human rights
   d. Mercy killing and murder
   e. Reasonable fear and paranoia
2. State a controversial comparison or contrast you have heard or read. What makes the comparison/contrast arguable?
3. State your own comparison/contrast claim. Who would agree or disagree with your claim? How would you defend your position?

Resemblance Claims: What Does It Resemble? Sometimes you may identify things by indicating what they resemble. Resemblance claims can help an audience understand something complex or unknown by showing how it mimics something simpler or more familiar. These claims can also raise the prestige of the thing being defined by showing how it resembles other things that are valued and respected.

EXAMPLES OF RESEMBLANCE CLAIMS

> Hip hop is like an interdisciplinary academic community, combining the fields of sociology, psychology, political science, English, ethnomusicology, economics, American studies, African American studies, and offering a choice of electives to its subscribers
>
> —Todd Boyd, *The New H.N.I.C.*

> At first glance, the correlation between piracy and terrorism seems a stretch. Yet much of the basis of this skepticism can be traced to romantic and inaccurate notions about piracy. An examination of the actual history of the crime reveals startling, even astonishing, parallels to contemporary international terrorism.
>
> —Douglas R. Burgess, Jr., "The Dread Pirate bin Laden"

Resemblance claims can take the form of precedents or analogies.

- **Precedent:** As its root word indicates, a precedent "precedes" or comes before something else. In a courtroom, for example, lawyers sometimes cite an earlier

Analogy claims argue for finding similarities between basically dissimilar things.

Body builders and power-lifters are among the athletes who use performance-enhancing drugs such as steroids to win athletic contests. How is this practice similar to or different from cheating on a test?

case as a precedent for the one being tried. Do the same legal rulings that hold bartenders responsible for the inebriation of their customers extend to fast-food restaurants, making the latter responsible for the obesity of their customers?

- **Analogy:** An analogy highlights a similarity between essentially different things. For example, one might argue that the United States' dependence on foreign oil makes the country analogous to a dog on a leash. When you claim two things are analogous, you must usually explain in specific terms which aspects of the analogy are meaningful: Its control over the world's oil supply gives OPEC a degree of leash-like control over the United States, restraining it and coercing it to go where its master leads it.

PRACTICE 2.6 Resemblance Claims

1. For each of the following actions, state something it resembles and briefly explain why. Is the resemblance claim original (your own idea) or is it something you have heard or read before? Do you agree with the resemblance? Why or why not?
   a. Censoring song lyrics is like . . .
   b. Blaming a restaurant for making you obese is like . . .
   c. Using steroids to win an athletic competition is like . . .
   d. Polluting the environment is like . . .
   e. For a democratic society to allow torture is like . . .
2. Name a controversial resemblance claim—a similarity some people accept as valid but others reject. What makes the resemblance claim arguable?
3. State your own resemblance claim. Who would agree or disagree with your claim? How would you defend your position?

PRACTICE 2.7 Identity Claims

The following excerpt from Andrew Sullivan's article, "Why the M Word Matters to Me," contains many claims of identity. As you read it, locate and try to label the kinds of identity claims: definition, classification, comparison/contrast, or analogy. Which claims do you agree or disagree with, and why? Would more evidence and explanation change your mind? Why or why not?

When people talk about gay marriage, they miss the point. This isn't about gay marriage. It's about marriage. It's about family. It's about love. It isn't about religion. It's about civil marriage licenses. Churches can and should have the right to say no to marriage for gays in their congregations, just as Catholics say no to divorce, but divorce is still a civil option. These family values are not options for a happy and stable family life. They are necessities. Putting gay relationships in some other category—civil unions, domestic partnerships, whatever—may alleviate real human needs, but by their very euphemism, by their very separateness, they actually build a wall between gay people and their families. They put back the barrier many of us have spent a lifetime trying to erase.

Cause-and-Effect Claims: How or Why Does It Happen?

Claims of cause and effect argue how or why something takes place. When you argue that an action (or the lack thereof) leads to a particular result, you are making a cause-and-effect claim. Your auto mechanic might warn you that if you don't change the oil in your car regularly, its engine will burn out. Your professor might argue that if you do not do your homework regularly and with care, it will be impossible to make an A.

Cause-and-effect relationships might seem obvious, but in many arguments this kind of link is not immediately clear. An effect might have more than one cause, a cause might have several effects, or the evidence connecting two events might be inconclusive. Because causal relationships are rarely simple, they can be some of the most challenging arguments to make.

When you make a claim about cause and effect, you may want to focus on either a cause or an effect: You'll name a known effect and then claim a cause or causes, or you'll name a known cause and then claim an effect or effects.

Cause Claims: What Made, Makes, or Will Make It Happen?

Cause claims are argued when an effect is known but the cause is uncertain.

Online Study Center
Prepare for Class
Cause Claims

EXAMPLE OF A CAUSE CLAIM

Research conducted . . . at Harvard reveals that even among people who claim to have no bias, the more strongly one supports the ethnic profiling of Arabs at airport-security checkpoints, the more hidden prejudice one has against Muslims.

—Margo Monteith, "Why We Hate"

In this example, the cause—a subconscious prejudice against Arabs and Muslims—leads to the effect of supporting racial profiling at airport security stations.

Cause claims may focus on past, present, or future effects, depending on when the effects are presumed to take place:

- **Past:** Often we know what happened in the past, but we don't know how or why. For example, scientists generally accept that dinosaur species suffered mass extinctions during the Cretaceous Period, but they disagree on the cause or causes of the extinction: Meteor impact, disease, weather changes, and other theories are debated as the source of the dinosaurs' disappearance.
- **Present:** The need to understand a cause can become urgent when detrimental effects are apparent. Problems such as drug abuse, hate crimes, terrorism, illegal immigration, and obesity are known effects, but their causes are the subjects of debate: Finding their solutions will remain "guesswork" until the root causes are understood. When people try to remedy a problem without knowing its true cause, the approach is regarded as "treating the symptoms rather than the disease."
- **Future:** Predictions of future causes are claimed in some arguments. Such predictions already have a desired (or feared) effect in mind and then claim a means to achieve (or to avoid) that effect. For example, if the effect desired was a healthier work force and higher productivity, you might argue that national health insurance would cause that result.

PRACTICE 2.8 Cause Claims

1. In a journal entry or group discussion, consider the effects listed below. What are their causes? How certain are you about these causes? Who might agree or disagree with your position? Why? For each of these five specific situations, try to generalize it into a causal claim.
   a. After a public-transit bombing in a city in another country, a commuter in the United States refuses to take public transportation.
   b. A health club declines to offer membership to a lesbian couple.
   c. A consumer purchases a gas–electric hybrid automobile.
   d. After 20 years of teaching, a professor leaves his university to pursue a career as a business executive.
   e. Although they have always been happy in the city, a couple decides to move to a suburban development that is an hour's drive from work.
2. Name an effect that you have heard or read about. What do some people claim its cause(s) to be? Who would agree or disagree? Why?
3. Name an effect that interests you. What do you claim its cause(s) to be? Who would agree or disagree? How would you defend your claim?

Understanding cause-and-effect relationships can help people avoid undesirable consequences.

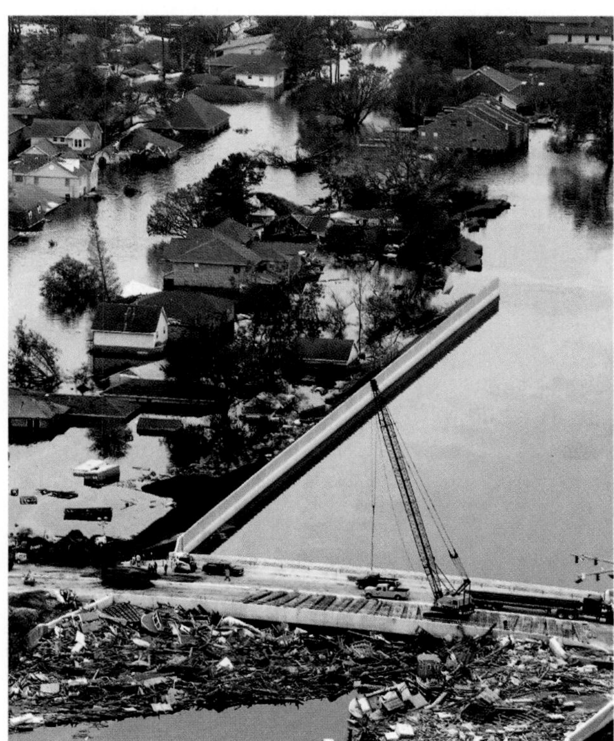

Was the Hurricane Katrina disaster primarily caused by an unusually fierce hurricane or by an inadequate levee system?

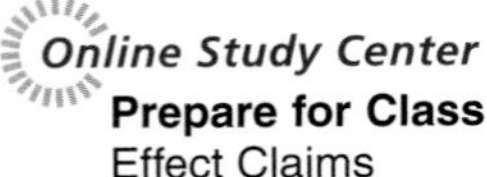

Prepare for Class
Effect Claims

Effect Claims: What Happened, Happens, or Will Happen? Effect claims are argued when a cause is known but its outcome is uncertain.

EXAMPLE OF AN EFFECT CLAIM

More than in the past, children are viewed as a project by perfectionist parents. Today's parents are imposing on their kids a violence of raised expectations. They are using their children for their own needs. We've decreased the threat of physical violence but increased the psychological violence.

—Steven Mintz, *Huck's Raft: A History of American Childhood*

In this example, the focus is on the effect. The cause—parents who drive their children to excel as a sort of status symbol—results in the effect—psychological damage to the children.

Like cause claims, effect claims may focus on past, present, or future effects.

- **Past:** Often, we know what happened in the past, but we don't know what effect it had. For example, scientists know that mass extinctions of dinosaur species took place during the Cretaceous Period, but they debate the effect the extinctions had on the rise of mammals.

PRACTICE 2.9 **Effect Claims**

1. In a journal entry or group discussion, consider the causes listed below. What are their effects? How certain of these effects are you? Who would agree or disagree? Why? Can you rewrite your responses to each of these specific situations as an effect claim of a more general nature?
   a. A mother smokes marijuana while she is pregnant.
   b. In an urban neighborhood with spotty police presence, guns are readily available.
   c. Large numbers of unskilled workers are unable to find employment and are unable to feed their families.
   d. A bright student becomes nervous before tests and performs poorly on standardized tests.
   e. A young woman, although she is thin, is self-conscious about her appearance and refuses to eat.
2. Name a cause that you have heard or read about. What effect claims do some people make regarding this cause? Who would disagree? Why?
3. Name a cause that interests you. What do you claim its effect(s) to be? Who would agree or disagree with your position? Why? How would you defend your claim?

- **Present:** The need to understand an effect can become urgent when the causes are occurring in the present. For example, drug abuse may be an outcome (effect) of psychological or physical problems or even of medical malpractice, but it also may lead to (cause) personal and societal problems such as disease, crime, shortened life span, or death. An effect claim might attempt to show the benefits of drug rehabilitation or the consequences of ignoring or improperly responding to drug addiction.
- **Future:** Predictions of future effects already have a cause or means to an end in mind, but then claim an effect or result. For example, if you oppose the establishment of a national health plan, you might claim the plan's effects would include higher costs to employers, higher taxes, higher-priced and less competitive goods, overseas outsourcing of jobs, and a weaker economy.

Causal Chains Some cause-and-effect claims deal with a sequence of events called a causal chain. In a causal chain, each effect becomes the cause of another effect. A schoolyard rhyme expresses this kind of chain: "First comes love, then comes marriage, then comes Junior in a baby carriage." We know that one thing often leads to another: Lack of education can lead to poverty, poverty can lead to crime, crime can lead to convictions, convictions can lead to a need for more prisons, more prisons can lead to higher taxes, and so on. If your goal is to reduce taxes, you may find yourself arguing for better schools because it could prevent this chain of events from starting. On a lighter note, comedies and comic strips sometimes depict causal chains as a complicated, multistep process that accomplishes very little.

Online Study Center
Prepare for Class
Causal Chains

Vicious Circles Some causal chains are actually causal loops known as vicious circles, such as the historic feud between the Hatfield and McCoy clans: A member of one family shoots a member of the other family, setting off a series

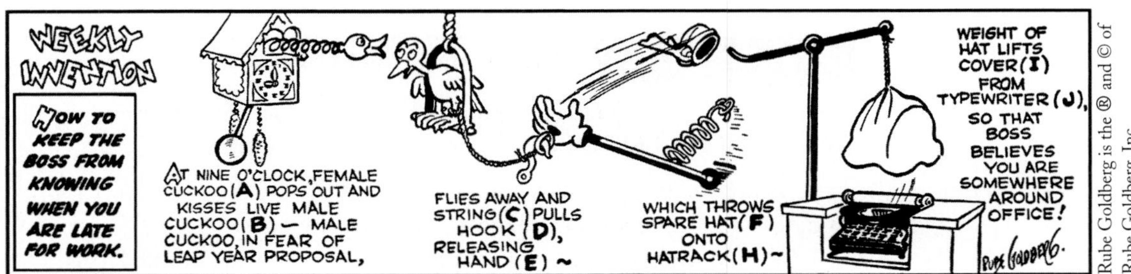

Causal chains clarify how an effect can become a cause of other effects.

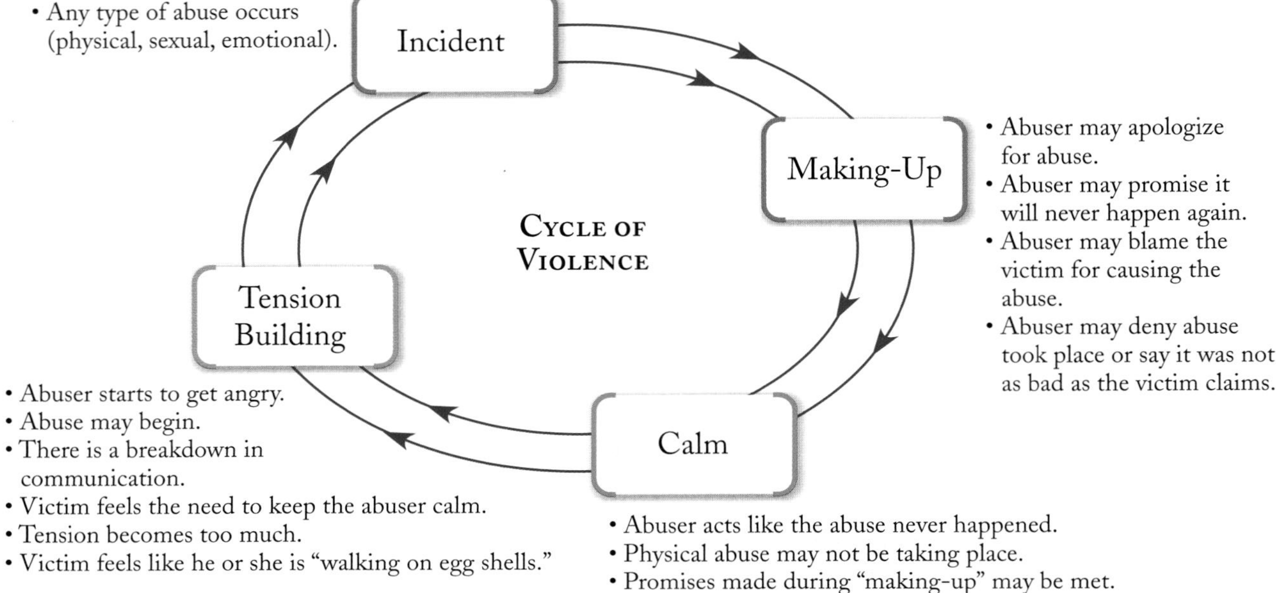
• Any type of abuse occurs (physical, sexual, emotional).
Incident
Making-Up
• Abuser may apologize for abuse.
• Abuser may promise it will never happen again.
• Abuser may blame the victim for causing the abuse.
• Abuser may deny abuse took place or say it was not as bad as the victim claims.
CYCLE OF VIOLENCE
Tension Building
• Abuser starts to get angry.
• Abuse may begin.
• There is a breakdown in communication.
• Victim feels the need to keep the abuser calm.
• Tension becomes too much.
• Victim feels like he or she is "walking on egg shells."
Calm
• Abuser acts like the abuse never happened.
• Physical abuse may not be taking place.
• Promises made during "making-up" may be met.
• Victim may hope that the abuse is over.
• Abuser may give gifts to the victim.

of revenge killings. Sociologists and economists speak of the "cycle of poverty," a self-perpetuating situation in which the deprivations associated with having a low income produce new generations of poor people. It is possible to write an entire essay that focuses on a cycle of causes and effects. For example, domestic-abuse counselors argue that a "cycle of violence" within an abusive relationship (1) begins with an incident of violence, (2) which is followed by making up, (3) which results in a period of calm, (4) which is followed by a period of renewed tension, (5) which eventually explodes into a new incident of violence, and so on.

PRACTICE 2.10 **Cause-and-Effect Claims**

The following excerpt from Frank L. Cioffi's article, "Argumentation in a Culture of Discord," contains claims of cause and effect.

1. As you read, locate any stated cause and the effect.
2. Do you agree with the claims? Why or why not?
3. Would more evidence and explanation change your mind? Explain.

Students typically don't want to attempt "argument" or take a controversial position to defend, probably because they've seen or heard enough of the media's models—Bill O'Reilly, Ann Coulter, or Al Franken, to name a few—and are sick of them. If I were an 18-year-old freshman assigned an argumentative essay, I'd groan in despair, either because I found the food-fight journalism model repulsive or because . . . I didn't feel strongly enough about anything to engage in the furious invective that I had all too often witnessed. Maybe the unanticipated consequence of the culture of contentious argument . . . is the decline in the general dissemination of intellectual, argumentative discourse more broadly construed.

Value: How Is It Judged?

Value claims make judgments about things, answering the question, "How is it judged?" These claims examine specific features or criteria and assess them using standards or a scale. The assessment can be quantitative, which usually means that numbers are involved, or qualitative, which usually means that the assessment is stated in words. Assessments often rank the thing being assessed (e.g., "top of the class") or simply accept or reject the thing (e.g., a "pass/fail exam").

Online Study Center
Prepare for Class
Value Claims

Value claims can be classified as either quality or moral/ethical, based on the kinds of standards applied.

Quality Claims: How Good or Bad Is It? Quality claims assert that a person, place, thing, or event fulfills a function at a particular level of competence. Typically the writer acts as a critic, reviewer, grader, or other kind of evaluator of the quality of performance.

EXAMPLE OF A QUALITY CLAIM

The scenery, effects, and balletic, iconic combats are perfectly wonderful, but there's an emotional black hole where the hero should be.

—Joe Morgenstern, "Lucas Goes to the Dull Side"
(review of *Star Wars Episode III*)

The criteria used to evaluate performances may range along a high-to-low scale, as in the following examples:

- Hotels and restaurants are rated on the quality of service: "four out of five stars."
- Dramas are rated on aesthetic qualities such as the script, costumes, and actors' performances: "two thumbs up."

PRACTICE 2.11 **Quality Claims: Part 1**

Which of the following are quality claims? Which are not? Can you identify what sort of claims they are? Can some of them serve more than one purpose?

1. The houses destroyed in the fire were especially valuable.
2. You should not put modern art in your house because it has a very traditional style.
3. Modern art, being more emotionally expressive than eighteenth-century art, is by far a superior choice for your apartment.
4. *The Parable of the Sower* is a cautionary novel about the economic collapse of the United States.
5. You can't call *The Parable of the Sower* science fiction because there are no space ships, laser battles, or aliens in it.
6. This college campus is especially attractive because it overlooks a pristine river valley.

- Employee performances are rated according to a supervisor's expectations: "excellent," "good," or "bad."

When making quality claims, it is important to use criteria that other people can share. For example, film critics assess the acting, screenplay, musical score, special effects, and other features that an audience values. Critics, judges, and reviewers try to maintain as much objectivity as possible, avoiding claims based

PRACTICE 2.12 **Quality Claims: Part 2**

1. For each of the following (1) give an example, (2) decide on at least one criterion (quality), and (3) evaluate the example based on that criterion. Briefly explain your decisions.
   a. Motion picture or actor
   b. Restaurant or chef
   c. Song or singer
   d. Vacation spot or type of recreation
   e. Food or drink
2. Describe a quality claim that you have heard or read. Who would agree or disagree with it? Why?
3. Select something that interests you and briefly evaluate it. Name and explain the criteria you believe to be important. Who would agree or disagree with your position? Why?

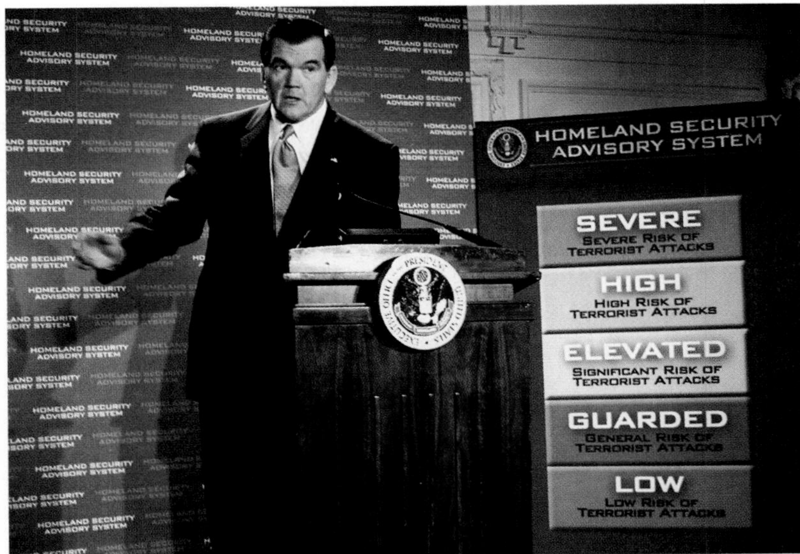

Quality arguments do not always make aesthetic judgments. Many times, when an argument is based on a scale, a claim of quality is being made.

on idiosyncratic, personal tastes. For example, saying "I hate spicy foods" is such a highly personal critique of Cajun cuisine that a mixed audience will find the information in a restaurant review containing this phrase of little use when looking for a place to dine.

Moral and Ethical Claims: How "Right" or "Wrong" Is It? Moral and ethical claims judge human behavior by applying a code of conduct based on a religious or philosophical belief system. These types of claims emerge when

CLAIMS OF QUALITY AND CLAIMS OF FACT

Claims of quality do not always judge the desirability or undesirability of something (as in a movie review or with someone's opinion of the service in a particular restaurant). These types of claims can also make factual statements identifying where something lies on a particular scale. The claim can also be written in a way that accomplishes both purposes.

- **Desirability:** "These mashed potatoes sure are good!"
- **Scale:** "These mashed potatoes are too cold to eat!"
- **Desirability and scale:** "I sure do like warm, buttery potatoes!"

Online Study Center
Prepare for Class
Moral/Ethical Claims

someone (1) matches a standard to a situation or behavior, (2) establishes a moral/ethical standard where none previously existed, and (3) resolves conflicts between competing moral/ethical standards (for example, between mercy killing and allowing someone to suffer). The moral/ethical scale of values typically ranges from right to wrong, from good to evil, or from moral to immoral. Depending on the belief system, this scale may or may not include a middle ground or "gray area."

"Dude, I got the answers for the test in Ethics class from my frat brother ... you want 'em?"

Moral/ethical arguments make judgments about conduct.

EXAMPLES OF MORAL OR ETHICAL CLAIMS

Advocates of the gay and lesbian movement have the responsibility to set forth publicly their alternative proposals.

—*Wall Street Journal* editorial

Contrary to a lot of scary rhetoric, a healthy cloned infant would not be a moral nightmare, merely the not-quite-identical twin of an older person.

—Virginia Postrel, "Should Human Cloning Be Allowed? Yes, Don't Impede Medical Progress"

All normal people make moral/ethical decisions, following their conscience or moral compass—in fact, a lack of conscience is considered a defining trait of a sociopath. Conscience goes beyond an individual's conduct, spilling over into public affairs and taking many forms. Although "separation of church and state" limits religion-based influence on some public issues, it doesn't prevent people from "voting their conscience." Codes of conduct, such as an honor code against cheating, try to make a boundary between ethical and unethical behavior. Your professor may discuss plagiarism in your class. When she tells you that representing someone else's writing as your own is unethical, the professor is making a moral argument. Cheating in academia, like stealing, is viewed as a form of dishonesty, and therefore a violation of moral conscience.

The argument that women and children should be rescued first in a disaster is a moral choice based on conscience and a sense of right and wrong.

PRACTICE 2.13 **Value Claims**

This excerpt is from a speech that was delivered by President George W. Bush on August 9, 2001. It contains value claims.

1. As you read it, locate and try to label any stated value.
2. Do you agree with the claims made in the speech? Why or why not?
3. Would more evidence and explanation change your mind? Explain.

Embryonic stem-cell research is at the leading edge of a series of moral hazards. The initial stem-cell researcher was at first reluctant to begin his research, fearing it might be used for human cloning. . . . I strongly oppose human cloning, as do most Americans. We recoil at the idea of growing human beings for spare body parts, or creating life for our convenience. And while we must devote enormous energy to conquering disease, it is equally important that we pay attention to the moral concerns raised by the new frontier of human embryo stem-cell research. Even the most noble ends do not justify any means.

I also believe human life is a sacred gift from our Creator. I worry about a culture that devalues life, and believe as your President I have an important obligation to foster and encourage respect for life in America and throughout the world.

PRACTICE 2.14 **Moral and Ethical Claims**

1. For each of the following, take a moral or ethical stand. Which criteria are you using? Who might agree or disagree with your values?
   a. Spanking is a good way to discipline children. Spare the rod and spoil the child.
   b. For the advance of science, it is acceptable to use animals in scientific experiments.
   c. If it will save lives, then it is the moral responsibility of government agents to torture suspected terrorists in an attempt to extract useful information from them.
   d. A loving couple has the right to engage in sex before they are married.
   e. If a plane full of people wanders into the airspace surrounding Washington, D.C., it should be shot down on the chance that the president might be harmed.
2. Describe a moral/ethical claim that you have heard or read. Who might agree or disagree with it? Why?
3. Make a claim about something moral or ethical that interests you. Which values influence your claim? Who might agree or disagree your position, and why?

Online Study Center
Prepare for Class
Proposal Claims

PROPOSAL CLAIMS: SHOULD SOMETHING BE DONE?

When you make a proposal, you try to convince an audience that it should take a specific course of action. Familiar examples of proposals are those issued regularly by the American Medical Association and the U.S. Department of Health, which suggest dietary habits that could improve health and longevity. Dietary proposals often are supported by other kinds of claims such as classification (food groups) or value (degree of healthiness of particular foods).

Proposal claims argue what should be done, such as "eat healthy foods."

Proposal claims have two possible aims: prescribing *what* should be done (policy) and indicating *how* it should be done (procedure). Policy and procedure are closely related, and sometimes you may find yourself synthesizing the two into one argument. On other occasions you may be more concerned with one aim than the other. For example, you may want to propose or revise a policy without getting into the details of its implementation, or you may want to propose or revise an implementation plan for an existing policy.

Policy: What Should Be Done? Policies can be rules, guidelines, or laws. They help guide decision makers, enabling them to treat people or situations in a consistent and fair manner. When policies lack consistency or fairness, they are likely to be challenged and eventually revised or repealed.

Online Study Center
Prepare for Class
Policy Claims

EXAMPLE OF A POLICY CLAIM

Equality is not the empirical claim that all groups of humans are interchangeable; it is the moral principle that individuals should not be judged or constrained by the average properties of their group.

—Steven Pinker, *The Blank Slate*

What policies should governments enact to be better prepared to respond to disasters?

Students with cognitive disabilities receive help while enrolled in a special degree program. Should institutions create special bachelor's programs for people who are mentally challenged?

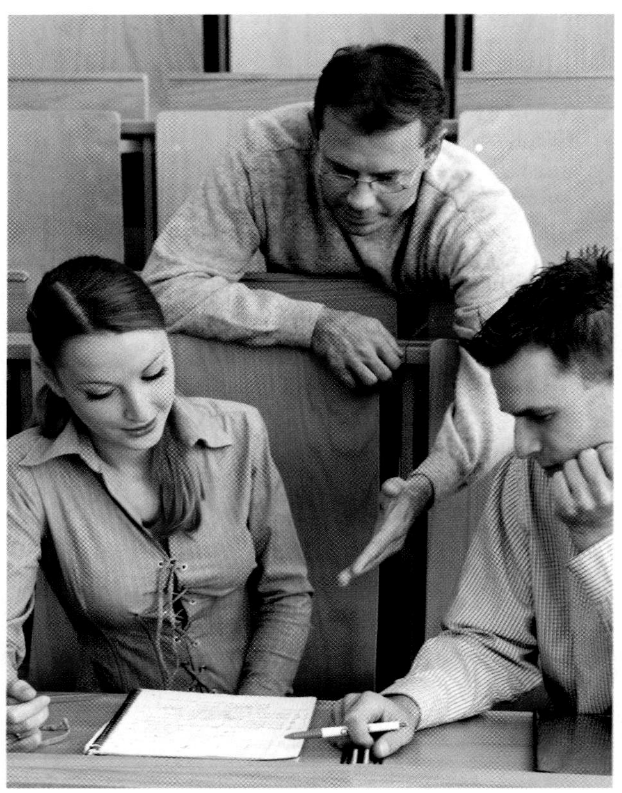

Pinker's claim uses definition as the basis for making a statement about policy. Sometimes, however, claims may be hybrids consisting of two different types of claims. In such cases, it is best to identify the primary argumentative purpose of the claim. In this example, Pinker's primary purpose is not to establish a definition but rather to work from that definition so as to argue in favor of a policy. The definition part of his claim acknowledges that people are different; the policy part of his claim says that in spite of these differences, they should have the same rights.

The following example is a little more straightforward.

> If cities are to survive in Europe or elsewhere, they will need to face this latest threat to urban survival with something more than liberal platitudes, displays of pluck, and willful determination. They will have to face up to the need for sometimes harsh measures, such as tighter immigration laws, preventive detention, and widespread surveillance of suspected terrorists, to protect the urban future.
>
> —Joel Kotkin, "Survival of the City"

PRACTICE 2.15 **Policy Claims**

1. Using the following questions as a guide, write a claim of policy for each issue.
   a. Does the government have the right to limit your privacy in the name of national security? Should it be able to examine your employment history, banking practices, and even keep tabs on what you read or watch on television?
   b. Should people be allowed to commit suicide when they are very sick or have a terminal illness?
   c. Under what conditions should abortion be legal?
   d. Should an employer be allowed to check your credit history as part of the hiring process (and make a decision whether to hire you based on what it says)?
   e. To what extent should fast-food restaurants be held responsible for the health risks associated with their food?
   f. Are affirmative action programs that encourage or require employers to hire a certain number of women and persons of color appropriate and fair? How about if employers were also required to fairly represent minority religions? What if the employer were required to hire people with mental disabilities, such as Down syndrome? Where should the equal-opportunity line be drawn?
2. Describe a policy that you have heard or read. Who would agree or disagree with it? Why?
3. Choose a problem that concerns you. Write a policy claim that will remedy this problem. In what way do you think your policy will be beneficial?

Procedure: How Should It Be Done? A claim of procedure is intended to persuade an audience that a policy should be carried out in a specific way. For example, if your community had a policy of restricting possession of handguns, you might propose a buy-back program through which people could turn in handguns for cash; this procedure would be an alternative to procedures such as having the police execute search warrants in homes and other methods that might be either objectionable or ineffective.

Online Study Center
Prepare for Class
Procedure Claims

EXAMPLES OF PROCEDURE CLAIMS

Given the gravity of the terrorist threat, vigorous questioning [of prisoners] short of torture—prolonged interrogations, mild sleep deprivation, perhaps the use of truth serum—might be justified in some cases.

—*The Economist* editorial

> But what can you do [about political correctness]? How can anyone prevail against such pervasive social subjugation? The answer's been here all along. . . . You simply . . . disobey. Peaceably, yes. Respectfully, of course. Nonviolently, absolutely.
>
> —Charlton Heston, "Winning the Cultural War"

PRACTICE 2.16 **Procedure Brainstorming**

Working individually or in groups, brainstorm (or discuss), outline, and briefly defend a procedure.

1. How do you get a reluctant friend in need of intervention to enroll in a drug or alcohol rehabilitation program?
2. What is the best way to give someone extremely bad news?
3. What is the best way to study for an examination?
4. How should the United States' borders be protected against illegal immigration?
5. How should students be disciplined after cheating on a university exam or submitting a plagiarized paper?
6. What should parents do to encourage their children to eat a healthy diet and exercise regularly?

PRACTICE 2.17 **Procedure Claims**

1. Choose a policy that concerns you. Outline a procedure for implementing it. In what ways do you think your procedure will be effective? In what ways might your procedure be controversial?
2. Describe a procedure that you have heard or read about. Who would agree or disagree with the procedure? Why?
3. Choose a problem that concerns you. Write a procedure claim that will remedy this problem. In what way do you think your procedure will be beneficial?

PRACTICE 2.18 **Proposal Claims**

The following excerpt from Frank L. Cioffi's article, "Argumentation in a Culture of Discord," contains proposal claims. Read the excerpt, and answer the questions that follow it.

I propose that we teach students more about how intellectual discourse works, about how it offers something exciting—yet when it succeeds, it succeeds in only approaching understanding. The philosopher Frank Plumpton Ramsey puts it bluntly but eloquently: “Meaning is mainly potential.” Philosophical and, more generally, argumentative discourse presents no irrefutable proofs, no indelible answers. In fact, the best writing of this kind tends not only to answer but to rain questions, ones that perhaps the audience hadn’t previously considered. Or to put it in terms my college-age nephew uses, when you’re writing argument, don’t go for the slam-dunk.

At the same time, we should make students aware that they’re not alone on the court. We need, that is, to emphasize more the need for counterarguments, which inevitably force writers to place themselves in the audience’s position and attempt to image what the audience values and feels—what objections it might intelligently raise.

1. Locate any proposal claim(s) in the paragraph.
2. How would you state the claim(s) in your own words?
3. What evidence is offered to support the proposal? Do you find it convincing? Why or why not?
4. Do you agree with what is being argued? Why or why not?
5. Would more evidence and explanation change your mind? Why or why not?

Student Essay

In the following essay, a student discusses various ways that American society has reacted to terrorism. Complete Practice 2.19 before reading this essay, and then answer the questions that follow the reading.

PRACTICE 2.19 Before You Read

1. What do you think of when you hear the word *terrorism?* How does it make you feel?
2. Have you ever discussed with friends or family what you thought should be done to stop terrorism? What did you say?
3. What does the essay’s title, “The Horrors of Terrorism” suggest to you? What do you think the author will say?

Justin R. Lynch
Dr. Lamm
Composition
Terrorism Essay
22 July 2004

The Horrors of Terrorism

Terrorism is much like a parasite, relying entirely on the life-sustaining fluids of civilization for sustenance. Like science fiction horrors, terrorism lies in the minds and hearts of evil-minded people, sucking the life fluids of society, leaving fear in the hearts of victims wherever it strikes. It grows, thrives, and spreads, darkening the lives of the innocent and the jaded alike. As a result, society must learn how to deal with this hidden parasite, this ephemeral demon, this horribly real nightmare. We must tread this path with caution. In an attempt to stop terrorism, we do not want to become terrorists ourselves.

The issues of how and when it is necessary for society to deal with terrorism have, fortunately, already begun to be discussed. Hugh Segal, for example, discusses the very problems of when and how to deal with terrorism in his article "Accomodating Evil: Sometimes, Military Action Is Proper and Necessary. Is This Such a Time?" Segal discusses the consequences of dealing with and, conversely, not dealing with U.S.-aimed terrorism based in the Middle East. He specifically discusses military action. On the one hand, military action will result in unfortunate collateral damage—innocents will die and buildings, stores, and other structures that have little or no ties with terrorism will face destruction. Governments that condone and even back terrorism will kill their countries' citizens in the attempt to harm their enemies. On the other hand, he says, those same governments will still harm their citizens: such governments squash freedoms and harass their citizens. Penalties for infractions, however minor, can be harsh. Indeed, the consequences of either option, whether military action or complacency, are bleak indeed, as Segal presents them: harm comes to innocents whether military action is taken or not. Innocents are harmed either way.

Another consequence is offered in Randall Hamud's article, "We're Fighting Terror, but Killing Freedom." This dire outcome that Hamud describes is one that often accompanies terrorism and war. This consequence, born out of fear and hate, manifests itself in harassment of certain peoples based mostly on a common ancestry with those whom are truly at fault. For example, during World War II, Japanese Americans were arrested, interrogated, and put into camps for fear of what they might do. Similarly, Americans of Middle Eastern descent are now being harassed and arrested for fear that they will participate in terrorist activities. Hamud provides examples of what he has faced. He speaks of death threats that he has received through the telephone and other means. Hamud also speaks of some of his clients, arrested primarily for their ancestry. In one case, his clients were arrested because suspects in the September 11, 2001, hijackings met and befriended them. These clients were arrested not because they were believed to have participated in the hijackings but to testify against the suspected hijackers. Essentially, Hamud is talking about a consequence of terrorism that goes beyond physical misfortunes and goes truly and deeply into the realm of the mind and emotions (Hamud).

Related to the harassment and prejudices of innocent Americans is the treatment of prisoners of war and the use of torture. Certain rules, which have been established by the Geneva Convention and other treaties, govern how prisoners of war are to be treated. Ruth Wedgwood and R. James Woolsey discuss in their Wall Street Journal article "Law and Torture" the Convention against Torture (CAT), a treaty ratified by the United States in 1994. Torture, according to CAT, is "the intentional infliction of severe pain or suffering, whether physical or mental . . . on a person for such purposes as obtaining from him or a third person information or a confession" (qtd. in Wedgwood and Woolsey). The treaty goes on to say that torture, under any conditions, is wrong (Wedgwood and Woolsey). In recent years, however, there have been incidents when the rules against the use of torture have been ignored, even tossed aside, as pointed out by Jonathan Gatehouse in his article "Photo Finish?" Gatehouse points out the Abu Ghraib prison scandal, where horrible things happened to prisoners, including rape and physical assault.

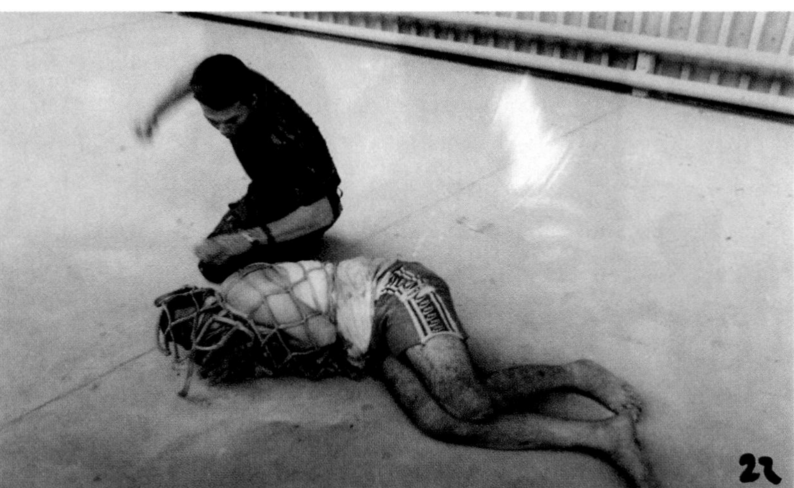

American soldiers abuse prisoners in Iraq.

This and similar events have brought the issue of torture even more to the forefront in terms of the treatment of prisoners of war. When torture is or is not acceptable is the major question, and it is a question that is very hard to answer. After all, terrorists are seemingly willing to use any means to gain their desires: witness the events of September 11, 2001. Torture, in comparison, would almost seem an acceptable means to rid the world of terrorism. However, it is not. It brings the United States and its allies down to the level of the terrorist.

Other problems also arise with the issue of terrorism. Perhaps the largest hurdle, presented capably by Michael Ware in his article "Meet the New Jihad," is that terrorists do not really want to change. Most, as presented by Ware, believe that what they are doing is right and good. As Ware goes on to discuss, they also have plans. Indeed, Ware states, "They [terrorists of Middle Eastern descent] want to transform Iraq into . . . a training ground for young jihadist groups that will form the next wave of recruits for al-Qaeda and like-minded groups." Essentially, those who practice terrorism are seeking to ensure the survival of terrorism (Ware). If this is the case, when the United States and its allies engage in tactics like torture to extract information, they are doing very little to discourage terrorism. From the point of view of the terrorists, these incidents of torture provide justification for their actions. The photos from Abu Ghraib simply provided the terrorists with one more reason to hate the West and gave them yet another wonderful recruitment tool.

Terrorism is a horrifying prospect that must be dealt with soon. While the duty of dealing with terrorism belongs to all society, the duty will prove to be a very difficult, hazardous journey. After all, there is a knife's edge between dealing with terrorism in proper, civilized ways and dealing with terrorism by becoming terrorists ourselves.

Lynch 5

Works Cited

"The Abu Ghraib Prison Photos." Antiwar.com 11 Jun. 2004. Randolph Bourne Institute <http://www.antiwar.com/news/?articleid=2444>.

Gatehouse, Jonathon. "Photo Finish?" Maclean's 17 May 2004: 16. ABI/INFORM. ProQuest. Arkansas State U Lib., Jonesboro, AR. 1 Aug. 2004 <http://www.proquest.umi.com>.

Hamud, Randall. "We're Fighting Terror, but Killing Freedom." Newsweek 1 Sep. 2003: 11. ABI/INFORM. ProQuest. Arkansas State U Lib., Jonesboro, AR. 18 Jul. 2004 <http://www.proquest.umi.com>.

Segal, Hugh. "Accommodating Evil: Sometimes, Military Action Is Proper and Necessary. Is This Such a Time?" Maclean's 24 Mar. 2003: 47. ABI/INFORM. ProQuest. Arkansas State U Lib., Jonesboro, AR. 18 Jul. 2004 <http://www.proquest.umi.com>.

Ware, Michael. "Meet the New Jihad." Time 5 Jul. 2004: 24. ABI/INFORM. ProQuest. Arkansas State U Lib., Jonesboro, AR. 18 Jul. 2004 <http://www.proquest.umi.com>.

Wedgwood, Ruth, and R. James Woolsey. "Law and Torture." Wall Street Journal (Eastern Edition) 28 Jun. 2004: A10. ABI/INFORM. ProQuest. Arkansas State U Lib., Jonesboro, AR. 1 Aug. 2004 <http://www.proquest.umi.com>.

PRACTICE 2.20 Understanding the Essay

1. What is the essay's overall claim? What does it tell you about the author's purpose?
2. Look over the essay, and identify as many supporting claims as you can find. What types of claims are they? (Look carefully; this document includes a number of different types of claims.)
3. What sort of evidence is used to validate the author's supporting ideas?
4. How does the author establish himself as an "authority" on this subject? How does he attempt to connect with the audience on an emotional level?
5. Who do you think might be an appropriate audience for this argument?

PRACTICE 2.21 Responding to the Essay

1. Name one significant strength and one significant weakness of the author's argument. Explain your answer.
2. Study the introductory paragraph. How does the author use analogy to set the tone for his argument?
3. Examine the conclusion. How effectively does the author return to the ideas and images in the introduction to bring his argument full circle? In other words, how effectively does he reemphasize his primary claim?
4. In the second paragraph, the author recognizes a viewpoint contrary to his own. How effective is this tactic in creating a sense that he is taking a fair and balanced approach toward his subject? (And what might this suggest about his intended audience?)
5. Which is the strongest claim in this paper? Which is the weakest? Explain.
6. Sometimes this author uses quotations from one of his sources to support the claim he wants to make. Does this tactic help him establish authority as a writer? If so, how?

Looking Back at Chapter 2

- Arguments always are based on claims, always with the goal of convincing reasonable skeptics of the claims' validity.
- Claims state that something is true, but some element of uncertainty or disagreement prevents others from immediately accepting that statement.
- Claims vary in (1) their degree of controversy, (2) their function within a piece of writing, and (3) the type of statement they make about what is "true."
- The thesis statement of an argument usually will be one of five kinds of claims: fact, identity, cause/effect, value, and proposal.
- Claims always need support in the form of evidence and explanations.

Suggestions for Writing

- Choose an argumentative article and read it carefully, examining its claims and support. Write a short evaluation of the effectiveness of the argument.
- Use the Practice activities in this chapter to guide your planning for writing your own essay on an issue.

Online Study Center
Improve Your Grade
Suggestions for Writing

SUPPORT

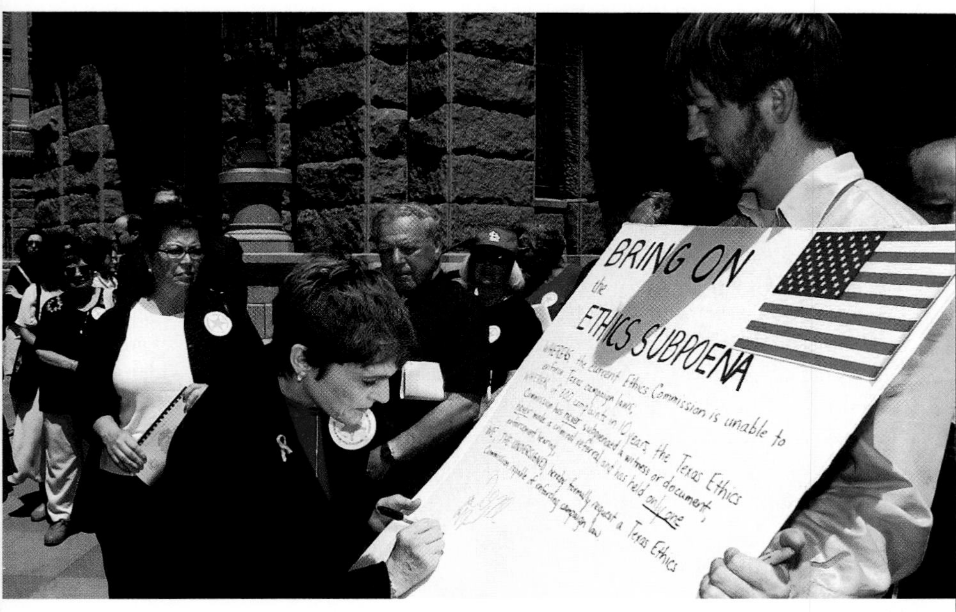

Imagine for a moment that an argument is like a house. A claim resembles a roof, in the sense that it thematically covers all the text and needs support—not by beams, but by reasons in the form of evidence and explanations. Without the right kind of support arranged in rhetorically sensible ways, an argument collapses like a shoddily constructed building. To make your argument sturdy, you need to be as familiar with claims and support as a carpenter is with blueprints and building materials.

> *How can one beam alone support a house?*
>
> —CHINESE PROVERB

All claims have the same general goal: to be accepted by an audience. Thus a defining characteristic of a claim is that an audience will not accept the claim on its own: It needs support. Also known as elaboration, this support comes in the form of evidence and explanations.

Online Study Center
This icon will direct you to content and resources on the website <college.hmco.com/pic/lamm1e>.

Evidence

Evidence gives support to a claim by connecting it to the real world. Also known as data and in logic as a minor premise or grounds, evidence helps answer the question, "What proof is there that the claim is valid?" Your answer could consist of many categories, or kinds, of evidence: anecdotes, expert opinions, facts and statistics, history, scenarios, and specific examples.

ANECDOTES

Anecdotes are real-life accounts of situations or events that have happened to you or to others. They usually are specific and limited, lacking the significant number of cases typical of statistics. However, story-telling techniques (narration and description) can make anecdotes very vivid and appealing to an audience.

> **EXAMPLE OF AN ANECDOTE**
> When my tattoo was finished I floated outside in a state of mild ecstasy and for the next few days did the usual dance of babying it, marveling at it, showing it off. What a high it was to have done a completely superfluous act, to have identified myself in a unique way and at the same time to have become linked through a shared physical experience with other beings.
>
> —Mary Vineyard, "Tattoo Made Its Mark on This Mother"

EXPERT OPINIONS

You could quote, paraphrase, or summarize the opinion of an expert or experts on an issue. The opinion can carry much weight if it is based on research, analysis, and interpretation. Of course, experts disagree on many things, so the opinion of only one may not be enough to convince an audience.

> **EXAMPLE OF AN EXPERT OPINION**
> Some researchers lobbying for funding have unfortunately fed patient's hopes and anger by hyping the potential of embryonic stem cell research far beyond scientific integrity.
>
> —Christian Medical and Dental Associations,
> "Letter to U.S. Congress"

Facts and Statistics

Any evidence that an audience will accept at face value can be considered a "fact"; you may support a claim using facts from science or other sources. A statistic is a fact based on numerous cases. Although statistical evidence may not be as vivid as an anecdote or a scenario, it often can more accurately reveal the "big picture."

> **EXAMPLE OF STATISTICS**
> The vast majority of stored embryos (88.2 percent) are being held for family building, with just 2.8 percent of the total (11,000) designated for research.
>
> —Rand Corporation, "How Many Frozen Human Embryos Are Available for Research?"

History

What happened in the past could resemble the present and thus be used as a precedent or analogy.

> **EXAMPLE OF HISTORY**
> The Tuskegee study is the most notorious episode in the history of American medical research. Begun in 1932, . . . more than 400 of the men were known to have syphilis and were never treated; some of them unknowingly transmitted it to wives and children; many died of the disease.
>
> —Anonymous, "Don't Let It Happen Again"

Scenarios

You can produce hypothetical or fictionalized accounts. Like anecdotes and personal experience, scenarios can be vivid and dramatic. They can also illustrate what *might* happen.

> **EXAMPLE OF A SCENARIO**
> Imagine, for a moment, that a disease like this exists—it affects babies in the womb, is often fatal, but may be treatable using some very fancy new technology. The treatment (which is experimental and not guaranteed to work) involves injecting the unborn fetus with a special extract of human cells. The only drawback is that the cells are derived from living adults. The cells in question must be "harvested" from adults suffering from Alzheimer's disease or Parkinson's disease [who are to be] humanely and quietly killed and their cells used

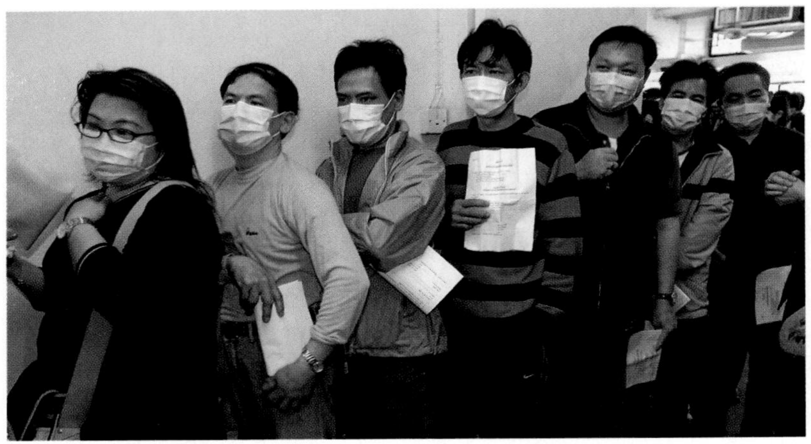

A scenario is a type of evidence that is based on what might happen. Here, birds are slaughtered out of fear that they might spread the avian flu.

> to save the lives of babies. A disturbing scenario—one which would hopefully never be allowed to happen. But the exact reverse of this is, apparently, fine.
>
> —Ed Walker, "We Must Not Kill to Cure"

PRACTICE 3.1 Categories of Evidence

Below you will find information from two media campaigns regarding teens, parents, and marijuana use. Each contains several categories of evidence.

1. Identify as many different types of evidence as you can within the information from these two campaigns.
2. Write a paragraph (or a letter to a parents' group) explaining how parents can talk to their teenaged children about marijuana use. Use at least two different types of evidence in your paragraph.

SPECIFIC EXAMPLES

You sometimes will offer a sampling of evidence to represent a larger body of evidence. Some examples are brief, consisting only of naming the evidence; these brief examples may be illustrative without claiming statistical significance. Other examples may be detailed, perhaps involving description, narration, or other techniques.

EXAMPLE OF A SPECIFIC EXAMPLE

The cartoon carnage that ends each episode of *South Park*, when the character meets different grotesque deaths, has echoes of the comic dismemberment suffered by a stupidly obstinate knight in *Month Python and the Holy Grail* (1975)—not to mention the cretinous head-bashing of the Three Stooges.

—Anonymous, "Moreover: It's Stupidity, Stupid"

THE OFFICE OF NATIONAL DRUG POLICY *Information Sheet*

AN OPEN LETTER TO PARENTS:

HERE'S WHAT THE EXPERTS SAY ABOUT MARIJUANA AND TEENS.

■ "Marijuana is not a benign drug. Use impairs learning and judgment, and may lead to the development of mental health problems."
– *American Medical Association*

■ "Smoking marijuana can injure or destroy lung tissue. In fact, marijuana smoke contains 50 to 70 percent more of some cancer causing chemicals than does tobacco smoke."
– *American Lung Association*

■ "Teens who are high on marijuana are less able to make safe, smart decisions about sex – including saying no. Teens who have used marijuana are four times more likely to have been pregnant or gotten someone pregnant than teens who haven't."
– *National Campaign to Prevent Teen Pregnancy*

■ "Marijuana can impair perception and reaction time, putting young drivers, their passengers and others on the road in danger. Teens, the highest risk driving population, should avoid anything that might impair their ability to operate a vehicle safely."
– *American Automobile Association*

■ "Marijuana use may trigger panic attacks, paranoia, and even psychoses, especially if you are suffering from anxiety, depression or having thinking problems."
– *American Psychiatric Association*

■ "Marijuana can impair concentration and the ability to retain information during a teen's peak learning years."
– *National Education Association*

■ "Recent research has indicated that for some people there is a correlation between frequent marijuana use and aggressive or violent behavior. This should be a concern to parents, community leaders, and to all Americans."
– *The National Crime Prevention Council*

And, according to the National Institute on Drug Abuse, marijuana can be addictive. In fact, more teens are in treatment with a primary diagnosis of marijuana dependence than for all other illicit drugs combined.

Teens say their parents are the single most important influence when it comes to drugs. Know their friends. Ask them where they are going and when they will be home. Take time to listen. Talk to your teens about marijuana. To learn more about marijuana and how to keep your teens drug-free, visit **www.theantidrug.com** or call **800-788-2800.**

PARENTS.
THE ANTI-DRUG.

THE DRUG POLICY ALLIANCE *Information Sheet*

Safety First: Parents, Teens and Drugs

Dear Johnny,

. . . Despite my advice to abstain, you may one day choose to experiment [with drugs.] I will say again that this is not a good idea, but if you do, I urge you to learn as much as you can, and use common sense.

Marsha Rosenbaum,
The San Francisco Chronicle
September 7, 1998

According to a recent government survey, 54 percent of high school seniors have experimented with an illegal drug. Though all parents wish and hope that their children abstain from drug experimentation, the statistic above shows the majority of teenagers will experiment despite 20 years of "Just Say No" messages. Teenagers have become skeptical of the often-exaggerated messages and scare tactics relayed through D.A.R.E. and other prevention programs. While advocating abstinence, our ultimate goal should be safety and the prevention of drug abuse and drug problems.

Drug education should follow the lead of sex education. Though sex education began with abstinence only tenets in the 1970s, the AIDS epidemic of the 1980s focused on efforts to save lives. To help reduce the harm associated with unsafe sexual practices, realistic sex education stressed safety. Today's drug education programs face the same abstinence only versus safety dilemma.

Many parents fear that a reality-based, safety-oriented discussion of drugs may lead to experimentation. Ultimately, teenagers will make the final decision about alcohol and other drug use. Young people need to know which drugs pose the most risks; that mixing certain substances can be deadly; and that driving under the influence or attending school under the influence must be avoided. When talking about drugs, trust and open dialogue is of utmost importance between teens and parents. Though abstinence is preferred, parents need to let their teens know that they care most about their health. Drug education efforts should promote *safety first*.

PRACTICE 3.2 **Finding Evidence**

Make a claim about an issue that concerns you. Using the following list as a guide, speculate upon the kind of evidence you might find:

- Expert opinions
- Facts and statistics
- History
- Personal experience
- Scenarios
- Specific examples

Explanations

Evidence hardly ever "speaks for itself," yet inexperienced writers too often move from one piece of evidence to the next prematurely, leaving their audience to figure things out for themselves. Poorly explained evidence can not only frustrate a reader but also leave the writer struggling to find enough words to fulfill a minimum-length requirement. Explanations can appear before a piece of evidence (as an introduction), after a piece of evidence (as a follow-up), or both. Also, explanations may be combined in various ways—that is, you may explain evidence using more than one approach.

The explanations listed below are based on a system known as Bloom's taxonomy, which identifies six ways we can understand things: knowledge (clarification), comprehension (interpretation), application, analysis, synthesis, and evaluation. (See Chapter 4, The Reader's Response to Arguments, for more on Bloom's taxonomy.)

Knowledge (Clarification): Clarify to Make Sure the Evidence Is Understood

You can explain to ensure that evidence is understood on a basic, literal level. This kind of explanation is known as clarification, or "making clear." Clarification typically entails some kind of repetition. Although repetition and redundancy often are a waste of words, at other times they are necessary to ensure the reader understands your meaning. Paraphrase, summary, and emphasis are types of restatements that help clarify evidence.

Paraphrase: Restate to Translate Some evidence may need to be repeated in more familiar terms. Paraphrasing can make slang, technical jargon, or dialect more intelligible; it can also use synonyms to make important points more clearly relevant to a claim.

> **EXAMPLE OF PARAPHRASING**
> Ann L. Flynn, a psychologist who is associate director of the Counseling Center at College of the Holy Cross, cited the trauma and searingly personal sense of violation that accompanies a sexual assault as another reason such crimes are underreported. "In terms of whether it gets reported, there's a good reason for why not," Flynn said. "It's a medical, psychological, criminal event. When a person is raped, they're responding to the immediacy of their emotional, medical state."
>
> —Ian Donnis, "Campus Rape: A Hidden Problem"

Summarize: Restate to Abbreviate Putting the evidence "in a nutshell" makes it easier to grasp.

> **EXAMPLE OF SUMMARIZING**
> In "The Challenge of Legalizing Drugs" . . . Joseph P. Kane, S.J., presents a compelling description of the devastation wreaked on our society by drug abuse, but draws some troubling conclusions supporting the legalization of drugs. . . .

> The solution, he concludes, is to legalize drugs while at the same time (1) changing attitudes within our society about drugs; (2) changing laws and public policy; and (3) providing drug education and treatment to all those who want it.
>
> —Gerald Lynch and Roberta Blotner, "Legalizing Drugs Is Not the Solution"

Emphasize: Restate to Highlight Sometimes one part of the evidence is more relevant, revealing, or startling than other parts. Emphasis helps your reader see the key points.

EXAMPLE OF EMPHASIZING

> The point is not that consensual sex always involves an explicit "yes, I want to have sex with you," but that nonconsensual sex always involves, at best, a failure to be sure that sex is wanted.
>
> —Richard Orton, "Date Rape: Critiquing the Critics"

Comprehension (Interpretation): Speculate on Its Deeper Meaning and Significance

Sometimes evidence requires an interpreter who can "read between the lines," putting a kind of "spin" on it. If a statistic shows the unemployment rate as 5.4 percent, is that to be regarded with alarm or relief? Your interpretation will put the data into perspective.

EXAMPLE OF COMPREHENSION

> It took 71 eggs to produce a single [cloning] success, and in the best case, the embryo grew to only six cells before dying. That's not a revolution. It's an incremental step in understanding how early-stage cells develop.
>
> —Virginia Postrel, "Should Human Cloning Be Allowing? Yes, Don't Impede Medical Progress"

Application: Explain How the Evidence Applies

Application can be important when the connection between the evidence and the claim isn't immediately clear. An analogy, for example, involves "applying" the principles underlying one thing to another, seemingly different thing.

EXAMPLE OF APPLICATION

> For more than 3 billion years, biological evolution has guided the colonization of our planet by living organisms. Evolution's rules are simple: Creatures that

adapt to threats and master the evolutionary game thrive; those that don't, become extinct. And so it is with the threat posed to the United States by terrorist networks such as al Qaeda. If the genus Americanus wants to overcome this latest challenge to its existence, it must adapt its defense mechanism accordingly.

—Raphael Sagarin, "Adapt or Die"

Analysis: Explain the Parts

Analysis is like a dissection, dividing a whole into its parts and explaining how they work separately and in unison. When an argument is complex, breaking it down into smaller pieces helps the audience understand it more readily.

EXAMPLE OF ANALYSIS

Three horrors come to mind: First, the designing of our descendents, whether through cloning or germ-line engineering, is a form of generational despotism.

—Eric Cohen and William Kristol, "Should Human Cloning Be Allowed? No, It's a Moral Monstrosity"

Synthesis: Relate It to Other Claims or Evidences

One claim or piece of evidence may interact with others, supporting each other piece or disagreeing with it. Synthesis brings two or more arguments together, allowing for comparison/contrast, rebuttal, or accumulation of mutually supporting points.

EXAMPLE OF SYNTHESIS

The ideas of integration and assimilation were key to earlier versions of America's historical narrative, be it the assimilation of European immigrants at the turn of the century, like those in *The Godfather*, or the motive for integration that defined Martin Luther King Jr.'s ideology and that of the civil rights movement.

—Todd Boyd, *The New H.N.I.C*

Evaluation: Explain Its Value

Sometimes evidence needs qualification: an explanation of how reliable and complete it is. Rebuttals often use evaluation to dismiss the other claims or evidence as being weak or erroneous.

EXAMPLE OF EVALUATION

The best discussion I have seen of the role and influence of music in the lives of today's young people occurs in the "Music" chapter of the late Allan Bloom's 1997 book, *The Closing of the American Mind.*

—Lloyd Eby, "The World & I"

In the following exercises, you will practice applying Bloom's taxonomy to a body of evidence. Here is "The Surgeon General's Call to Action to Prevent Overweight and Obesity" from the Office of the Surgeon General's website. Using this set of data as your raw evidence, write paragraphs as described in the Practice activities that follow.

PRACTICE 3.3 Explaining Evidence

In most argumentative paragraphs, you will accomplish three things: (1) You will introduce an idea with a claim; (2) you will present evidence; and (3) you will explain how the evidence validates the claim. Following the claim below you will find a series of facts. Organize the material into a paragraph. (You will have to write the explanation on your own. Be certain it goes into enough depth to convince your reader that the evidence presented validates the claim.)

Claim: Public school science teachers should not be forced to teach creationism and intelligent design theories in their classes because these approaches do not conform to the scientific method.

EVIDENCE

- The intelligent design theory, which presupposes that the universe was intentionally created by God, cannot be tested.
- The theory violates scientific method by assuming its conclusion—that God created the universe—in advance of any supporting evidence.
- There is also no evidence to support the supposition that the universe is too complex to have evolved by accident.
- The theory is also dangerous because it does not emphasize the steps of the scientific method: Form a hypothesis, test the hypothesis, repeat the experiment to be certain you are right, and draw your conclusions based only on the evidence.

OVERWEIGHT AND OBESITY: A VISION FOR THE FUTURE *The Surgeon General*

The Surgeon General identifies the following 15 activities as national priorities for immediate action. Individuals, families, communities, schools, worksites, health care, media, industry, organizations, and government must determine their role and take action to prevent and decrease overweight and obesity.

Communication The nation must take an informed, sensitive approach to communicate with and educate the American people about health issues related to overweight and obesity. Everyone must work together to

- Change the perception of overweight and obesity at all ages. The primary concern should be one of health and not appearance.
- Educate all expectant parents about the many benefits of breastfeeding.
  - Breastfed infants may be less likely to become overweight as they grow older.
  - Mothers who breastfeed may return to pre-pregnancy weight more quickly.
- Educate health care providers and health profession students in the prevention and treatment of overweight and obesity across the lifespan.
- Provide culturally appropriate education in schools and communities about healthy eating habits and regular physical activity, based on the *Dietary Guidelines for Americans*, for people of all ages. Emphasize the consumer's role in making wise food and physical activity choices.

Action The nation must take action to assist Americans in balancing healthful eating with regular physical activity. Individuals and groups across all settings must work in concert to

- Ensure daily, quality physical education in all school grades. Such education can develop the knowledge, attitudes, skills, behaviors, and confidence needed to be physically active for life.
- Reduce time spent watching television and in other similar sedentary behaviors.
- Build physical activity into regular routines and playtime for children and their families. Ensure that adults get at least 30 minutes of moderate physical activity on most days of the week. Children should aim for at least 60 minutes.
- Create more opportunities for physical activity at worksites. Encourage all employers to make facilities and opportunities available for physical activity for all employees.
- Make community facilities available and accessible for physical activity for all people, including the elderly.
- Promote healthier food choices, including at least five servings of fruits and vegetables each day, and reasonable portion sizes at home, in schools, at worksites, and in communities.
- Ensure that schools provide healthful foods and beverages on school campuses and at school events by:
  - Enforcing existing U.S. Department of Agriculture regulations that prohibit serving foods of minimal nutritional value during mealtimes in school food service areas, including in vending machines.
  - Adopting policies specifying that all foods and beverages available at school contribute toward eating patterns that are consistent with the *Dietary Guidelines for Americans.*
  - Providing more food options that are low in fat, calories, and added sugars such as fruits, vegetables, whole grains, and low-fat or nonfat dairy foods.
  - Reducing access to foods high in fat, calories, and added sugars and to excessive portion sizes.
- Create mechanisms for appropriate reimbursement for the prevention and treatment of overweight and obesity.

Research and Evaluation The nation must invest in research that improves our understanding of the causes, prevention, and treatment of overweight and obesity. A concerted effort should be made to

- Increase research on behavioral and environmental causes of overweight and obesity.
- Increase research and evaluation on prevention and treatment interventions for overweight and obesity and develop and disseminate best practice guidelines.
- Increase research on disparities in the prevalence of overweight and obesity among racial and ethnic, gender, socioeconomic, and age groups and use this research to identify effective and culturally appropriate interventions.

OVERWEIGHT AND OBESITY: HEALTH CONSEQUENCES

The Surgeon General

The primary concern of overweight and obesity is one of health and not appearance.

Premature Death

- An estimated 300,000 deaths per year may be attributable to obesity.
- The risk of death rises with increasing weight.
- Even moderate weight excess (10 to 20 pounds for a person of average height) increases the risk of death, particularly among adults aged 30 to 64 years.
- Individuals who are obese (BMI ≥30)* have a 50 to 100 percent increased risk of premature death from all causes, compared to individuals with a healthy weight.

Heart Disease

- The incidence of heart disease (heart attack, congestive heart failure, sudden cardiac death, angina or chest pain, and abnormal heart rhythm) is increased in persons who are overweight or obese (BMI ≥25).*
- High blood pressure is twice as common in adults who are obese than in those who are at a healthy weight.
- Obesity is associated with elevated triglycerides (blood fat) and decreased HDL cholesterol ("good cholesterol").

Diabetes

- A weight gain of 11 to 18 pounds increases a person's risk of developing type 2 diabetes to twice that of individuals who have not gained weight.
- Over 80 percent of people with diabetes are overweight or obese.

Cancer

- Overweight and obesity are associated with an increased risk for some types of cancer, including endometrial (cancer of the lining of the uterus), colon, gallbladder, prostate, kidney, and postmenopausal breast cancer.
- Women gaining more than 20 pounds from age 18 to midlife double their risk of postmenopausal breast cancer, compared to women whose weight remains stable.

Breathing Problems

- Sleep apnea (interrupted breathing while sleeping) is more common in obese persons.
- Obesity is associated with a higher prevalence of asthma.

Arthritis

- For every 2-pound increase in weight, the risk of developing arthritis is increased by 9 to 13 percent.
- Symptoms of arthritis can improve with weight loss.

Reproductive Complications

- Complications of pregnancy:
  - Obesity during pregnancy is associated with increased risk of death in both the baby and the mother and increases the risk of maternal high blood pressure by 10 times.
  - In addition to many other complications, women who are obese during pregnancy are more likely to have gestational diabetes and problems with labor and delivery.
  - Infants born to women who are obese during pregnancy are more likely to be high birthweight and, therefore, may face a higher rate of cesarean section delivery and low blood sugar (which can be associated with brain damage and seizures).
  - Obesity during pregnancy is associated with an increased risk of birth defects, particularly neural tube defects, such as spina bifida.
- Obesity in premenopausal women is associated with irregular menstrual cycles and infertility.

Additional Health Consequences

- Overweight and obesity are associated with increased risks of gallbladder disease, incontinence, increased surgical risk, and depression.
- Obesity can affect the quality of life through limited mobility and decreased physical endurance as well as through social, academic, and job discrimination.

Children and Adolescents

- Risk factors for heart disease, such as high cholesterol and high blood pressure, occur with increased frequency in overweight children and adolescents compared to those with a healthy weight.
- Type 2 diabetes, previously considered an adult disease, has increased dramatically in children and adolescents. Overweight and obesity are closely linked to type 2 diabetes.
- Overweight adolescents have a 70 percent chance of becoming overweight or obese adults. This increases to 80 percent if one or more parent is overweight or obese.

(Continued)

- The most immediate consequence of overweight, as perceived by children themselves, is social discrimination.

Benefits of Weight Loss

- Weight loss, as modest as 5 to 15 percent of total body weight in a person who is overweight or obese, reduces the risk factors for some diseases, particularly heart disease.
- Weight loss can result in lower blood pressure, lower blood sugar, and improved cholesterol levels.
- A person with a body mass index (BMI) above the healthy weight range* may benefit from weight loss, especially if he or she has other health risk factors, such as high blood pressure, high cholesterol, smoking, diabetes, a sedentary lifestyle, and a personal and/or family history of heart disease.

PRACTICE 3.4 **Knowledge (Clarification)**

Write a paragraph rephrasing the section entitled "Communication" in your own words.

PRACTICE 3.5 **Comprehension (Interpretation)**

Working from the section entitled "Action," explain the importance for the nation as a whole to develop good eating habits.

PRACTICE 3.6 **Application**

We often assume that the health dangers presented by obesity are something to worry about in adulthood. Write a paragraph explaining how even children may be in danger from the health risks associated with obesity.

PRACTICE 3.7 **Analysis**

Working from "Overweight and Obesity: Health Consequences," explain how many different elements might contribute to a premature death.

PRACTICE 3.8 **Synthesis**

Write a paragraph comparing the Surgeon General's concern with obesity to ideas that the heath crisis may be blown out of proportion. (See the "Obesity Epidemic" cluster in the Health section at the back of the reader for helpful information.)

PRACTICE 3.9 **Evaluation**

Write a paragraph explaining the positive benefits of weight loss to a skeptical reader. In addition to health benefits like lowered blood pressure and a lower risk of heart disease, such benefits might include more energy and a greater sense of happiness and well-being.

Student Essay

As you read the student essay titled "The Ethical Dilemma of Stem-Cell Research," locate the claims, evidence, and explanations. How effectively do they work together to make an argument?

PRACTICE 3.10 **Before You Read**

1. What do you know about stem-cell research? Why is it considered controversial? If you don't know much about this topic, how could you find out more?
2. What is your opinion of stem-cell research? Should it be banned, funded freely, or closely regulated? Why do you think this?
3. What does the title of the essay suggest about the topic? What do you think the essay will be about?
4. Glance over the essay quickly. Look at the "Works Cited" page. What does it tell you about what the writer will argue?

Brodbent 1

Melonie Brodbent
Composition II
Dr. Lamm
15 August 2004

The Ethical Dilemma of Stem-Cell Research

A human embryo sits in a frozen dish in the back of a freezer at a fertilization clinic. A young boy, once cheerful and vibrant, sits in a wheelchair, paralyzed by a neck injury. Both entities have a potential for a full and healthy life, but who or what determines which life is more important? Should the boy be denied the hope of a cure made possible through harvesting the embryo's stem cells? Or should the embryo be protected from being used for something akin to human experimentation? Certainly stem-cell research poses an ethical dilemma, pitting the sanctity of life against compassion for suffering. Nevertheless, the stakes are too high for a stalemate: the possibility that human lives can be saved is simply too great to be ignored.

Stem cells are like skilled actors waiting to be assigned a part in a drama. They can assume any role in the body, becoming brain cells, blood cells, skin cells, and so on once they receive the necessary signal through physiological mechanisms that are at present a mystery. Medical researchers are hopeful that as they solve the mystery of stem cells, they will be able to cure a host of previously incurable ailments by repairing old cells with new ones. Ron Reagan Jr., son of the late President Ronald Reagan, expresses this optimism, hailing the research as possibly "the greatest medical breakthrough in our or in any lifetime." The elder Reagan died of Alzheimer's disease, one of many ailments that stem-cell research could someday remedy.

Stem-cell research, however, poses two ethical problems that divide well-intentioned people. The first problem deals with how the research begins with the harvesting of stem cells; the second is concerned with where the research may lead—to human cloning and perhaps even to animal-human gene splicing. The debate has led to a legislative stalemate that threatens to slow or even halt the research either by underfunding it or by overregulating it (Reagan).

The first ethical impasse concerns how stem cells are acquired. Although stem cells are attainable from sources such as umbilical cords and adult fat cells, the most pristine and versatile of cells come from embryos. Sacrificing embryos for their cells is objectionable to many people who are concerned with the sanctity of life. They see it as sliding down a slippery slope that validates abortion: "Taking stem cells out of a blastocyst [an embryo of about 100 cells] is, in this view, no different from cutting the heart out of a baby" (Postrel). However, embryos are routinely destroyed in fertility clinics. Proponents of stem-cell research see this as an unethical waste of harvestable stem cells: "Why has the use of discarded embryos for research suddenly become such an issue? Is it more ethical for a woman to donate unused embryos that will never become human beings, or to let them be tossed away in the garbage when they could help save thousands of lives?" (Reeve).

The second ethical issue is about "playing God." Stem-cell research includes experiments with (1) cloning and (2) gene therapy. Stem cells are cloned into "lines" produced in volumes large enough for many researchers to use; in therapeutic uses they are inoculated with a particular patient's DNA to make them compatible with the immune system. Opponents of stem-cell research foresee this kind of research leading to nightmarish misapplications, a kind of evil genie that must be kept in its bottle: "In order to stop the dehumanization of man, and the creation of a post-human world of designer babies, man-animal chimeras, and 'compassionate killing' of the disabled, we may have to forego some research" (Cohen and Kristol). According to Leon Kass, President George W. Bush's bioethics advisor, stem-cell research puts "human nature itself on the operating table, ready for alteration, enhancement, and wholesale redesign" (qtd. in Cohen and Kristol).

Admittedly, no one can guarantee the ethical use of scientific discoveries yet unmade, nor can all future abuses be stopped or even imagined. However, no scientific progress would ever have been made if fear of the unknown prevailed. Proverbial caution says, "If God had meant us to fly, he would have given us wings." The wise proverbial reply is that "God gave humankind the intellect to design wings for itself."

Scientists have already started to attempt to create proper ethical guidelines for the research and use of stem cells. The Chinese National Human Genome Center, for example, proposes that stem cells should be used in a safe, helpful way, with respect for the beliefs and values of the donor, and that stem cells should be gotten only from donors who understand what they are doing and willingly give them (Kennedy Institute of Ethics). With ethical guidelines to guide the hands of stem-cell research, the risk of stem-cell misuse will be lessened considerably.

The ethical dilemma surrounding stem-cell research is undeniable but not beyond resolution. It is right and understandable to be concerned with potential abuses, but those concerned should

Brodbent 4

help provide ethical guidance, not bar the way. The greater good must prevail, and in this case the greater good clearly is the life-saving knowledge that will come from solving the mystery of stem cells.

Brodbent 5

Works Cited

Cohen, Eric, and William Kristol. "Should Human Cloning Be Allowed? No, It's a Moral Monstrosity." Wall Street Journal 5 Dec. 2001: A20. ABI/INFORM. ProQuest. Arkansas State U Lib. 12 Jul. 2004 <http://www.proquest.umi.com>.

Kennedy Institute of Ethics. "Ethical Guidelines for Human Research." Kennedy Institute of Ethics Journal Mar. 2004: 47+. ABI/INFORM. ProQuest. Arkansas State U Lib. 12 Aug. 2004 <http://www.proquest.umi.com>.

Postrel, Virginia. "Should Human Cloning Be Allowed? Yes, Don't Impede Medical Progress." Wall Street Journal 5 Dec. 2001: A20. ABI/INFORM. ProQuest. Arkansas State U Lib. 12 Aug. 2004 <http://www.proquest.umi.com>.

Reagan Jr., Ron. "Remarks by Ron Reagan Jr. to the Democratic National Convention." 27 Jul. 2004. California Stem Cell Research and Cures Initiative 12 Aug. 2004 <http://www.yeson71.com/news_clip_0727_reagan.php>.

Reeve, Christopher. "Using the Body's 'Repair Kit.'" Time 1 May 2000: 60. ABI/INFORM. ProQuest. Arkansas State U Lib. 12 Aug. 2004 <http://www.proquest.umi.com>.

PRACTICE 3.11 **Understanding the Essay**

1. What is the author's primary claim (thesis statement)? What sort of claim is it (what is the author's purpose in this argument)?
2. What supporting claims does the author present to back up her thesis? What categories of claims are they?
3. Look over each paragraph carefully. Which categories of evidence does the author use (anecdotes, expert opinions, facts and statistics, history, scenarios, or specific examples) to support each claim? Explain which kind of evidence is used in each paragraph.
4. Which techniques—that is, which elements of Bloom's taxonomy—does the author use to validate each claim? Explain which techniques are used in each paragraph.

PRACTICE 3.12 **Responding to the Essay**

1. Name one significant strength and one significant weakness of the overall argument.
2. Taking each paragraph one at a time, critique the evidence that was used to support the claim (ignore the explanations for now). In each case, was the evidence the most appropriate choice? Would you have chosen another type of evidence? Explain.
3. Taking each paragraph one at a time, critique the explanation strategies that were used to connect the evidence to the claim. In each case, how well does the evidence validate the claim (how well does it convince you, as a reader, that the evidence establishes this particular claim is true)?
4. Where is the explanation weakest in this paper? If you were the author, would you use different strategies of explanation? Why or why not?
5. Is there anything missing from this argument? (For example, how well does the author address a point of view other than her own? What does this suggest about the intended audience of the essay?)

Looking Back at Chapter 3

- Evidence gives support to a claim by connecting it to the real world. Also known in logic as data, a minor premise, or grounds, evidence helps answer the question, "What proof is there that the claim is valid?"

- Evidence includes anecdotes, expert opinions, facts and statistics, history, scenarios, and specific examples.
- Common methods of explaining are clarifying the knowledge, aiding comprehension by interpreting, analyzing, applying, synthesizing, and evaluating.

Suggestions for Writing

- Choose an argumentative article, and read it carefully, examining its claims and support. Write a short evaluation of the argument's effectiveness.
- Use the Practice activities in this chapter to guide your planning for writing your own essay on an issue.
- Choose an argumentative article, and read it carefully. Examine how explanations are used to support evidence. Write an evaluative essay discussing the effectiveness of the strategies employed.
- Choose an argumentative article, and read it carefully. Using the same evidence employed by the article, write a refutation of the article (or argue an alternative claim that the author did not consider).

Online Study Center
Improve Your Grade
Suggestions for Writing

The Reader's Response to Arguments

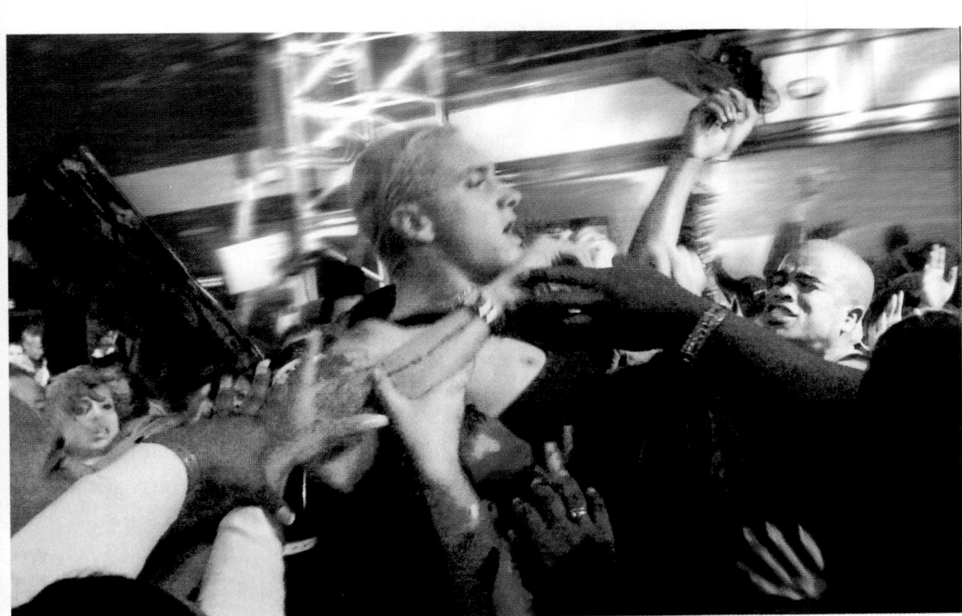

> *On the contrary, Watson, you can see everything. You fail, however, to reason from what you see.*
> —Sherlock Holmes

When Sherlock Holmes would come upon a crime scene, magnifying glass in hand, deerstalker cap upon his head, and Calabash pipe drooping from his mouth, he often solved the case by observing clues that others had overlooked. Holmes had a keenly developed ability to think critically, analyzing and interpreting beyond the surface facts. As you encounter arguments in everyday

Online Study Center
This icon will direct you to content and resources on the website <college.hmco.com/pic/lamm1e>.

Critical thinking resembles detective work.

Topic, Issue, and Claim

A topic is a subject that is under consideration. For example, rap music is a topic. An issue is something related to the topic but more specific and controversial. Rap music issues include violence, disrespect for women, cultural identity, obscenity, freedom of speech, and social/political activism. When you take a side on an issue, you propose a claim, such as the following:

- Even if their lyrics are offensive, rap artists have a constitutional right to freedom of speech.
- Because rap artists are public figures, they should be held to the standards of morality in the communities in which they live.

life (and particularly in this book), you will view, read, and inquire in ways that resemble detective work.

Investigating written arguments requires critical reading. *Critical* does not mean you read solely with the intention of finding fault, but rather that you play the role of a critic, examining the material's strengths and weaknesses. Unlike reading a text solely for the sake of pleasure (such as a Stephen King novel) or to extract information (such as a computer manual), critical reading means you engage a text in multiple ways: to interpret it, to apply it to your own purposes, to analyze its parts, to synthesize it with other information, and to evaluate its qualities.

As you prepare to write an argument, most of your readings will be topically linked, dealing with particular subjects. Obesity, stem-cell research, political correctness, artificial intelligence, longevity, and immigration are among the topics of this book's readings. To model the topical approach to critical reading, this chapter focuses solely on the topic of rap music.

Online Study Center
Prepare for Class
Reader Response Method

Reader Response: How You Read

Your opinion of what you read changes as you work your way through an essay. Although you progress linearly, from left to right and from top to bottom, you also work backward and forward simultaneously—scribbling notes in the margins;

reevaluating your knowledge of the topic, the author, and the argument; reconsidering earlier thoughts; and anticipating what might come in the next sentence or paragraph. Your opinion changes dynamically as you move from word to word, sentence to sentence, paragraph to paragraph. Consider this sentence from the opening paragraph of John McWhorter's "Mean Street Theater," a commentary on rap music:

> Last fall pioneer rapper Jam Master Jay was murdered in his Queens, N.Y., studio at 37, leaving behind a wife and children.

As you read sequentially from the first word to the final period, you apply cognitive thinking skills that build meaning as you go. Let's reconstruct a possible phrase-by-phrase sequence of critical reader-responses prompted by McWhorter's sentence about Jam Master Jay:

> Last fall pioneer rapper Jam Master Jay . . .

The mere mention of this person's name and profession, depending on your cultural mindset and opinion of rap music, may be positive or negative. Now we add a bit more:

> . . . was murdered . . .

Your reaction at this point, unless you are completely hostile to rap and its associated musicians, is probably one of sympathy. A little more:

> . . . in his Queens, N.Y., studio at 37 . . .

While the first part of the phrase might be viewed as mere information, what does the mention of his age imply? With most people, their reaction would be, "That's too young to die!" However, a rap-hater might respond, "Serves him right! How'd it take so long?" Now let's finish the sentence:

> . . . leaving behind a wife and children.

The tragedy is complete. Regardless of your opinion of rap music and rappers, you probably feel sympathy for Jam Master Jay at this point. McWhorter has piqued your interest and earned your ear, if only for a moment.

By reading carefully and tuning in to your responses, you'll gain understanding not only of a text's argumentative and rhetorical strengths and weaknesses, but also its possible uses in your own argument.

PRACTICE 4.1 **How You Read**

In a brief writing or group discussion, reflect on the following questions.

1. Do you like to read? Why or why not?
2. Do you like some kinds of reading better than others? Which do you like best? Which do you like least? Why?
3. How much and what kind of reading do you think your future career might require? Does your ability as a reader affect your career plans? Why?
4. When you read critically, what are some of the things you do to improve your understanding of the text?

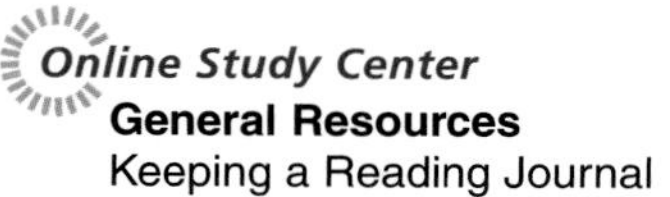

General Resources
Keeping a Reading Journal

KEEPING A READING JOURNAL

When you are investigating any subject for the purpose of writing about it, keeping a journal can be an excellent tool. The journal can help you solidify your reaction to what you have read and make it easier for you to later react to the reading in a formal argument. A double-entry journal can help you separate your understanding of a text (in the form of a summary, for example) from your response to a text (in the form of an analysis or evaluation).

Summary	*Response*
McWhorter argues that the negative image of blacks can be blamed largely on rap music.	*This may be partly true, but the "thug" image is not just a brand. It is also reinforced by news reports, especially in urban areas. Does this mean that news reports should be censored because they present a negative image of some African Americans? McWhorter also ignores the positive images associated with some rappers, as well as their philanthropy and the charitable work they do in their home communities.*

Questioning Critically

There is no single "tried and true" method of critical reading. Instead, most textbooks offer tips, guidelines, or lists of things to do while reading. We suggest that you pursue one major strategy: **Ask questions constantly about what you read.**

Asking Questions

Critical readers know how to ask the right kinds of questions about a reading, questions that go beyond the stated facts. The psychologist Benjamin Bloom classified and described six cognitive skills that often are used as a guide for questioning. Known as Bloom's taxonomy, this system begins with knowledge (understanding the stated meaning of the text) as the most basic type of questioning and then builds by levels: comprehension (interpreting the deeper meaning and significance), application (considering uses for the text), analysis (considering how specific parts of the text function separately and in unison), synthesis (relating the material to other texts and to prior knowledge), and evaluation (judging the qualities of the text). Bloom's taxonomy can lead you to ask questions that you might not otherwise have considered. (For more about Bloom's taxonomy, see Chapters 3 and 5.)

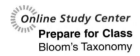

Online Study Center
Prepare for Class
Bloom's Taxonomy

BLOOM'S TAXONOMY *Questions for Critical Reading*

Knowledge/Clarification: Understanding the Stated Meaning or the Knowledge Conveyed Who is the author? What is the title? Where and when was the text published? What issue(s) does the text address? What is the claim? What evidence and explanations are provided? What beliefs are stated? How would I paraphrase or summarize the text?

Comprehension/Interpretation: Inferring Deeper Meaning What is implied but not stated directly? What unstated beliefs lie behind the claims? How does my point of view differ? How does the author use rhetoric (e.g., style) to help make the argument?

Application: Using the Text How does the text apply to real-life situations? How can I use these arguments for my own purposes, such as for support or for rebuttal? How might others use or misuse these arguments? Which argumentative techniques should I adopt or avoid in my own writing? Which rhetorical techniques should I adopt or avoid in my own writing?

Analysis: Understanding Parts in Relation to the Whole Where are the claims, evidence, and explanations expressed in the argument? What are specific instances of rhetorical techniques? How do the parts function separately and in relation to other parts and to the whole?

Synthesis: Relating the Text to Other Texts and Personal Experience Do I have personal experiences that relate to the arguments in the text? To what collective point of view, belief, or "school of thought" does this text belong? How does that school of thought compare to others? What other arguments exist? How do other arguments compare? How do the rhetorical strategies used by this author compare to those employed by other authors?

Evaluation: Judging the Text How well does the text present its major and supporting claims? How valid and convincing are the evidence and explanations? Is the support relevant and sufficient? Do the arguments appeal to the beliefs of the audience? How effective are the rhetorical techniques?

FOCUSING QUESTIONS

As a critical reader, you constantly ask the kinds of questions in Bloom's taxonomy, but not aimlessly. Those questions will be guided by your goals of arguing and writing about a particular issue. You will want to focus your questions in three ways: (1) culturally, about your beliefs and those of others; (2) argumentatively, about the claims, evidence, and explanations; and (3) rhetorically, about the purpose, audience, structure, and style of an article.

1. **Questions about culture**
   a. What is your opinion of the subject matter?
   b. Which beliefs do you hold that influence your opinion?
   c. What is your emotional reaction to the subject matter?
   d. Has your opinion of the subject matter changed any as a result of the reading? Are you firmer in your prior opinion, or have you changed your mind?
2. **Questions about argument**
   a. Where are the claims and support located in the passage?
   b. Which kinds of claims are made and which kinds of support are provided?
   c. Are the claims (thesis statement and supporting claims) arguable?
   d. Is the support—evidence and explanations—adequate? Why or why not?
   e. How could the claims or support be modified to appeal more strongly to you or to a larger audience?
3. **Questions about rhetoric**
   a. **Purpose:** Where does the author state a purpose? What is the purpose? Is it stated or implied?
   b. **Audience:** Is the audience appropriate, considering the topic and purpose? Why or why not? Could you describe the intended audience of the text in any detail? Is the audience too narrow or too broad to be useful in accomplishing the purpose?
   c. **Structure:** Is the form (e.g., essay, letter, speech) appropriate to the purpose and audience? What are its strengths and limitations? What other forms would have been possible? How well is it organized?
   d. **Style:** Does the style (e.g., word choices, sentence structures) accomplish the purpose and reach the audience in question? Why or why not? What is the author's tone? Is the tone appropriate? Do you get a sense of the author as a person? How?

Reading Culturally

To read culturally means to consider your personal place or "niche" in the dominant culture—your beliefs, values, background, prejudices, and the like—in relation to the "niche" represented by the text you are evaluating. It may be helpful to realize that what we broadly call "culture" is actually a conglomeration of subcultures based on religion, race, gender, education, upbringing, national or regional origin, and many other criteria. Clearly, members of these subcultures are highly diverse. Most of the time your cultural mindset is different—sometimes *very* different—from that represented by what you read. If you are a conservative Protestant from the Midwest, for example, you may approach an article advocating gay marriage with a degree of reservation. Because your beliefs and opinions often affect your attitude toward a subject even before you have read the first word of the argument, it is important for you to examine your own cultural point of view prior to reading. In other words, be aware of your opinion as you approach a text. Try to notice the ways that a particular argument affects your opinion as you read—or even after you have read and have thought about or discussed what was proposed.

PRACTICE 4.2 Reading Rap Culturally, Argumentatively, and Rhetorically

Use the culture, argument, and rhetoric "focusing questions" to guide your critical reading of the following passage. Written by Chuck D, founder of the rap group Public Enemy, and excerpted from an article titled "The Sound of Our Young World," it first appeared in *Time* magazine. Record your responses (e.g., as a journal entry) or share in a group discussion.

As we head into the twenty-first century, rap music/hip-hop is in the earth-wide sound stream, the child of soul, R and B and rock 'n' roll, the by-product of the strategic marketing of Big Business, ready to pulse out to the millions on the wild, wild Web. It's difficult to stop a cultural revolution that bridges people together. Discussing differences through artistic communication and sharing interests in a common bond—rap music and hip-hop have achieved that in twenty years. From Lauryn Hill, Wu Tang, Mack 10, to Everlast, all you have to do is look around. Watch, feel, and listen. It's only just begun.

—Chuck D, *"The Sound of Our Young World"*

In addition to making music, Chuck D writes and speaks about rap and its culture.

PRACTICE 4.3 Reading Other Topics Culturally, Argumentatively, and Rhetorically

Use the "focusing questions" to guide your critical reading of an article or passage that is relevant to a topic of interest to you. Record your responses as a journal entry, or share them in a group discussion.

Online Study Center
General Resources
Previewing, Reading, and Responding

Process of Reading: Previewing, Reading, and Responding

Like writing, reading is a dynamic process. Reading occurs in three stages, commonly known as previewing, reading, and responding. It is possible to proceed through these steps one at a time, though in reality most readers move back and fourth between the steps in the process.

PREVIEWING

Previewing is the first step of the reading process. It can help make the reading process easier and more productive by giving you a context—that is, by situating the reading inside a broader picture. Previewing usually considers reflecting on the (1) topic and issues, (2) title, (3) author, and (4) features of the text. You can use questions to guide your previewing activities.

- **Topic and issue:** What do you already know, factually? What do you probably need to know? What is your current opinion? Are you flexible, or are you set in your opinion?
- **Title:** What can you learn from the title?
- **Author:** What do you know or need to know about the author?
- **Text:** What do you learn from the form (e.g., article, letter), formatting, and organization (e.g., headings of sections, tables, and charts)

Online Study Center
Prepare for Class
Online Sources for Contemporary Debates

Previewing Topics and Issues To be a responsive and thoughtful reader, it is important to "tune in" to your own knowledge, opinions, and preconceptions about a particular topic. Your prior experiences with an issue will not only affect your level of interest in the issue, but also influence whether you approach a topic enthusiastically or cautiously. Take inventory of your prior knowledge, beliefs, and information gaps.

PRACTICE 4.4 **Previewing the Topic and Issues of Rap Music**

Use the questions below to guide your preview of the topic and issues of rap music. These questions can be used in brainstorming, journal writing, or group discussion.

- What do you already know (facts, key words, important issues)?
- What else do you probably need to know?
- What is your current opinion?
- Are you flexible, or are you set in your opinion?

PRACTICE 4.5 **Previewing Your Own Topics and Issues**

Use the questions below to guide your preview of a topic and issues that interest you. These questions can be used in brainstorming, journal writing, or group discussion.

- What do you already know (facts, key words, important issues)?
- What else do you probably need to know?
- What is your current opinion?
- Are you flexible, or are you set in your opinion?

Previewing a Title Titles have a dual function: to inform the reader about the content and to attract the reader's interest. Readings intended primarily to inform (such as science articles) tend to have very information-packed titles—for example, "The Effects of Eight-Week Foci of Instruction on the Quality of Argumentative Essays Written by First-Year College Composition Students." Novels, short stories, poems, and similar works have titles meant to attract interest—for example, *The Da Vinci Code.* The titles of argumentative writings usually need to be informative yet still attract interest. To do so, they sometimes combine a title and subtitle, as in "Mean Street Theater: An Awful Image for Black America." Titles can convey information on several levels, ranging from general to specific: topic, issue, claim, and even an author's attitude. For example, "Stop the Madness!" conveys information about the claim, indicating the kind of action being proposed.

Because you will add titles to each of your own essays, you can benefit from learning more about how titles are crafted by other writers.

PRACTICE 4.6 **Previewing a Title**

Consider the following list of titles. Rate your interest in each one on a scale from 1 to 10. Which is the most engaging? Which is the least engaging? Which is the most informative? Which is the least informative? Explain.

1. "Mean Street Theater: An Awful Image for Black America" (article by John McWhorter)
2. "The Sound of Our Young World" (article by Chuck D)
3. "Taking the 'Rap' for Violence in Music" (student essay)
4. "Rap Music" (student essay)
5. *The Language Police* (title of book about censorship)
6. "The Importance of Hip Hop and Rap: A Question of Resistive Vernaculars" (academic source)
7. *Get Rich or Die Tryin'* (movie title)
8. *Bone-a-Fide* (album by T-Bone)

PRACTICE 4.7 **Informative Titles**

Working from the table of contents for Part 2 of this book or from your own knowledge, make a list of ten titles. Then explain in what ways they are interesting and to what degree they are informative.

Your response to an argument often depends on how much authority a writer or speaker has. How is your opinion influenced by obvious signs of authority, such as uniforms?

Previewing the Author Sometimes you may already know something about the author; at other times you may have to conduct some research to learn about him or her. Frequently you can obtain author-related information from the Internet. Books sometimes provide information about the author, and essays occasionally are prefaced with a headnote, a biographical paragraph found at the beginning of an essay. You will find headnotes in many collections of essays as well as in the reading selections found in the latter portion of this book. As you preview the author, consider questions such as these:

- What do you already know about the author (other writings, public statements, reputation, background, personal information)?
- What have you learned from your research directed at learning about the author (such as checking websites or reading *Who's Who?* or a headnote)?
- Do you trust the author's expertise?
- Do you trust the author's integrity?

PRACTICE 4.8 **Previewing the Author**

Read the headnote below, and then answer the following questions. These questions can be answered in brainstorming, journal writing, or group discussion.

1. What do you already know about the author (other writings, public statements, reputation, background, personal information)?
2. What have you learned from the headnote?
3. Do you trust the author's expertise?
4. Do you trust the author's integrity?

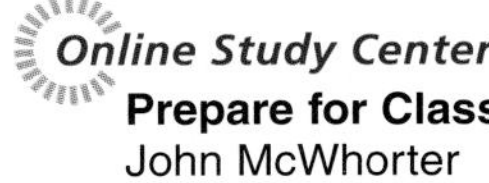

John McWhorter

After receiving his Ph.D. in linguistics from Stanford University in 1993, John McWhorter served as a postdoctoral fellow at the University of California at Berkeley, where he currently serves as associate professor of linguistics. A specialist in Creole languages and typology, he has written extensively about Creole languages, Black English, dialect, and language change. His books include *The Word on the Street: Fact and Fiction about American English* (1998), *The Missing Spanish Creoles: Recovering the Birth of Plantation Creole Languages* (2000), *Losing the Race* (2000), and *The Power of Babel* (2002). McWhorter is also a contributing editor to *The New Republic* and *City Journal*. His writings on race argue that African Americans have held themselves back culturally by emphasizing victimization instead of individual responsibilities. A politically conservative African American, McWhorter argues in his article "Mean Street Theater" about rap's effects on racial identity.

Online Study Center
Prepare for Class
John McWhorter

Good schools!

What do these words mean?

What else has he written? Check out these for more info.

What other articles on rap music has he published?

Previewing the Text A preliminary scan of a text often will reveal features that can help you as you read. Headings of sections, for example, work much like titles, giving you a notion of what the major parts of the reading will discuss. The lengths of paragraphs may suggest something about how thoroughly the topics are discussed. Sentence length hints at how easy or challenging the reading will be. Highlighting (boldface letters, color fonts, italics, underlining) are signs that the author is adding aids; conversely, a lack of highlighting probably means that you will have to work more diligently to uncover key points for yourself. Illustrations (pictures, charts, graphs) may indicate a kind of rest break in the reading; they also offer graphic alternatives to otherwise linguistic information. The presence or absence of bibliographic references (works cited) indicates how scholarly the text will be.

PRACTICE 4.9 Previewing the Text

As you scan the paragraphs of McWhorter's "Mean Street Theater" that follow, analyze the following features: headings, paragraph length, sentence length, highlighting, illustrations, and bibliographic references. What do these features reveal about the reading?

READING

The second stage of the reading process involves the actual reading of the text. As you read, you'll continue to ask questions. In addition, you'll annotate the text by marking it with your questions, observations, and concerns.

On the following pages, you will read McWhorter's essay a few paragraphs at a time. The first three paragraphs have been annotated with commentary to help you understand how cultural, argumentative, and rhetorical factors affect the reading process. Study the paragraphs below, and complete the activities that follow as you proceed through the essay.

ANNOTATING ARGUMENTS

To annotate something means to respond to a text in writing, frequently in the form of marginalia (i.e., annotations in the margins of the paper). You may choose to bracket words, sentences, or paragraphs that seem important to you. Alternatively, you may underline, circle, use asterisks, or even use a highlighter to draw attention to particular parts of the text. You may also write notes, sometimes between the lines of text itself, but usually in the margins. You may pose questions ("What does *sybaritic* mean?"), paraphrase what you think the author is saying ("He is arguing that rappers are getting rich at the expense of their race"), or evaluate the argument ("Weak evidence here").

Annotating what you have read, whether one article or many, will give you the opportunity to think about your own position on the topic at hand, consider the mistakes others have made, and ultimately sharpen your own approach to your subject.

Guidelines for Annotating a Text

Here are some general guidelines that will be useful whenever you read and mark a text:

1. Mark difficult passages, words, and phrases you did not understand. You can develop your own "shorthand," perhaps using symbols for some remarks. Here are some suggestions:
   - **?** A question mark next to a passage can show you don't understand.
   - **!** An exclamation mark can show your surprise about a statement.
   - ***** A star or asterisk can show you think a statement could be valuable.
   - **Q** A Q can mark a statement you think is quotable
   - **_** Underlining can mark an important passage such as a major claim.
2. Highlight points that "stand out" or seem otherwise important to you. Don't over-highlight, however, because it will make the important points indistinguishable from minor points.
3. Indicate (circle) words that are important or need to be defined.
4. Use lines to connect passages, showing relationships between related ideas.
5. Jot down a restatement of the central ideas in the margin

Online Study Center
General Resources
Quotation, Paraphrase, and Summary

Online Study Center
General Resources
Tips for Annotating

Mean Street Theater: An Awful Image for Black America

JOHN MCWHORTER

There goes another one. Last week 21-year-old Savannah-based rapper Camoflauge was shot to death in front of his toddler son. Only two months before, New York rapper Freaky Tah was killed, at age 27, shot while leaving a party. Last fall pioneer rapper Jam Master Jay was murdered in his Queens, N.Y., studio at 37, leaving behind a wife and children.

Engaging hook!

Rappers put their kids in the line of fire?

Look up info on these guys.

Negative tone. Emphasis on rapper's family—not him.

This paragraph involves readers on several levels:

- **Cultural:** Most arguments will affect you on a personal level in one of two ways: They will give you confidence in the author (by showing that he or she is an expert on the subject at hand, for example), or they will tug at your heart-strings. Although some of the information in the paragraph above—like the

Funeral of Jam Master Jay.

second through fourth sentences—shows that the author holds some sympathy for rappers and knows something about rap (which may give you some faith in what he has to say), most of the information is designed to evoke sympathy for the dead men. Note especially the "attention-getting" sentence (the "hook") that both involves your emotions and implies the problem illustrated by the rest of the paragraph—that rappers are dropping like flies.

- **Argumentative:** It is notable that this paragraph lacks argumentative structures—there is no major claim or thesis statement. Is this a problem? If so, can you explain why?
- **Rhetorical:** The paragraph uses carefully selected words to pique your interest. It uses emotional appeals to keep you interested in the topic and encourage you to move on to the next paragraph. Does this paragraph do enough to successfully indicate the problem (rap = violence) that will be treated in the remainder of the essay? What does the word *pioneer* imply? Does it help gain your sympathy or otherwise keep you engaged? Who would you guess the intended audience to be? Does the paragraph "speak" to you? Why or why not?

Negative tone again. Effective, though. Good use of question.

Trivializes serious social problems.

Strong claim but one-sided. Look up words.

Such carnage puts in a certain perspective the mantra that black America is so often taught: "Why can't whites see blacks as equals?" Many claim that a big problem is the depiction of blacks in the media, and there is a point here—but no longer the "whitey did it" point that many suppose. Today the biggest image problem for blacks comes from neither the movies nor television but from the rap industry. The most popular music in black * America presents a grim, violent, misogynist, sybaritic black male archetype as an urgent symbol of authenticity.

The preceding paragraph is more complex than the first one, which engaged your emotions so as to encourage your interest in the topic.

- **Cultural:** While McWhorter does less in this paragraph to engage your emotions, the two quotations are provocative. Each one operates on both emotional and rhetorical levels. What is your emotional response to these quotations?
- **Argumentative:** Does this paragraph include a thesis statement (major claim)? What is it? How do you know it is the thesis of the essay? The first two

sentences make a counterargument—they present a point of view that runs counter to the point McWhorter will make. How do they function argumentatively? (How will they function to help McWhorter prove his point?) How do they function rhetorically? (What is the persuasive advantage of presenting an alternative view first?)

- **Rhetorical:** How do the two quotations affect you rhetorically? Who is the target audience? How might a black person respond to the quotations? How might a white person respond? How does the context of these quotations (the feelings of blacks regarding stereotyping by whites) affect your response to them? What sort of stereotypes of blacks do these quotations imply? Do you know what the words *misogynist, sybaritic,* and *archetype* mean? Look them up. What does their use imply about the intended audience?

Now briefly consider the first two paragraphs together. How do they function together to create an "introduction" for the argument? Is it a good idea to split introductory material into two paragraphs? Why or why not?

Fans object that there is plenty of hip-hop with constructive messages. True, but it's the "thug" brand that sells best. How many hip-hop magazines would there be if the music delivered only positive messages? Camoflauge, despite his searingly profane, violent lyrics, was regularly invited to speak at Savannah high schools. In the hip-hop world, "keeping it real" is everything, and the gutter is considered the "realest."

Acknowledges positive side but does not give enough credit.

Look up bio.

Is this the fault of the rapper or the teachers?

"Gutter" may be the common feeling of many American blacks. Many below poverty line. How did McWhorter grow up? Privileged?

- **Cultural:** Here the words that appeal to the emotions also have rhetorical impact. The use of "hip-hop" words such as *thug, gutter,* and *realest* have negative emotional connotations while invoking notions of "Black English."
- **Argumentative:** English teachers often instruct students to write paragraphs that begin with topic sentences followed by specific examples. Is that what McWhorter does? Which minor claim forms the topic sentence for this paragraph? Now look at the fourth sentence. How does McWhorter use evidence to back up his claims? Is it effective? Why or why not?

- **Rhetorical:** How does the counterargument presented in the first sentence function on a rhetorical level? (How is it used as a persuasive device in conjunction with what follows?) What role does the word *True* play in convincing the audience that rap music creates an image problem for black people in America?

PARAPHRASING AND SUMMARIZING ARGUMENTS

Paraphrasing is putting someone's text into your style—that is, "into your own words." Summarizing is putting someone's text in far fewer words. Both techniques can be used to help you read critically. (See Chapter 9 for more on paraphrasing and summarizing.)

Paraphrasing has two major uses: to add the ideas of others to your own writing and to help you understand what others mean. Researchers use paraphrasing as an alternative to quoting sources: The imported material blends together smoothly with the researcher's own prose. Later in this textbook you will learn paraphrasing techniques that can enhance your writing while allowing you to give proper credit to your sources and thereby avoid plagiarism or "literary theft." In this chapter you will use paraphrasing to help you understand what you read.

A reader often must "translate" or "decode" the written material. This kind of paraphrasing may be as simple as restating a word or phrase, or it may involve more complex, longer portions of text. When you read critically, you essentially paraphrase the material, putting the entire text into your own words, albeit usually without actually rewriting the original text. Occasionally, however, you may find that rewriting the original in your own words helps you not only understand a text but also evaluate both its strengths and its flaws.

Consider this sentence from McWhorter's article about rap music:

> The most popular music in black America represents a grim, violent, misogynistic, sybaritic black male archetype as an urgent symbol of authority.

The sentence contains "elevated" diction—words you might encounter only in an intellectual discussion. You may understand some, most, or all of the words, depending on your previous experiences as a reader. You may need to look up words in a dictionary, including words that you thought you understood but that may have special meanings in the context of the sentence. After conducting such a translation, however, you may discover that the sentence is still difficult to understand.

How would you express McWhorter's sentence in your own words? Here is one student's paraphrase of it:

Rap makes the" ideal" black man look like a dangerous women-hater who cares only about his own pleasure.

Is McWhorter's meaning clearer? Was the paraphrase accurate? Was it complete? For example, did the student clarify what McWhorter meant by "urgent symbol of authority"? What do you think that phrase means?

Paragraphs, too, can be paraphrased. Consider the fourth paragraph in McWhorter's article:

> And most hip-hop, whatever its "message," is delivered in a cocky, confrontational cadence. The "in your face" element is as essential to the genre as vibrato to opera, reinforced as rappers press their faces close to the camera lens in videos, throwing their arms about in poses suggesting imminent battle. The smug tone expresses a sense that hip-hop is sounding a wake-up call, from below, to a white America too benighted to listen. I can count on hearing about a "hip-hip revolution" from at least one questioner at every talk I give these days.

Focus on aggression and anger. Implies it contributes to violence.

Good use of supporting detail form videos. But what good do these guys do?

Language here implies a danger of a real revolution? Over the top!

Here is one student's paraphrase of the preceding paragraph:

According to John McWhorter, the majority of rap, regardless of its meaning, is performed in a self-confident, combative style. The aggressive performance is as basic to the art form as brush strokes are to painting, emphasized as hip-hoppers thrust their visages toward the lens of the camera of a televised video, waving their arms while striking poses like battling warriors. The self-satisfied sound conveys the idea that rap is an alarm bell rung by the underprivileged to awaken American Caucasians too dense to understand. McWhorter wagers that he'll hear a comment about a "rap revolution" from at least one person attending each speech he gives nowadays.

Again, is McWhorter's meaning clearer? Was the paraphrase accurate? Was it complete?

PRACTICE 4.10 **Paraphrasing**

Read the fifth paragraph of McWhorter's essay, and paraphrase it on your own (we will practice annotating next).

But unfocused cynicism is not a promising platform for a revolution. The Hip-Hop Summit Action Network, for instance—founded by rap impresario Russell Simmons—has attempted to "bridge hip-hop and politics" and does deserve credit for its proposed voter registration drive. But then what does the organization want "the hip-hop generation" to vote for? Mostly the bromides that have disempowered blacks for decades.

Consider the sixth and seventh paragraphs of McWhorter's essay, which have been annotated for you:

Diction: "corralled" sounds like they're being forced. Implies animals. Makes them sound stupid. Logic: Just because McWhorter doesn't agree with these initiatives, it doesn't make them wrong.

Implies that the Action Network doesn't care.

What makes him think these will work? How many rappers go to church?

Without "street theater" there would have been no civil rights movement!

Check on his claims about AN. Some rap groups must be doing good. Is "acting up" bad? What about Martin Luther King, Jr.? Rosa Parks?

Stuck in the idea that urban schools fail because of inadequate funding, the group corralled marchers to support the teachers' union opposed to New York Mayor Michael Bloomberg's education budget. It also stuck it to President Bush for invading Iraq and has protested advisory labels on rap CDs.

One has to wonder whether the Action Network will ever sponsor "summits" [supporting the welfare reform now improving countless black women's lives or urging the Bush administration to give more money to faith-based initiatives.] By focusing on the issues that lend themselves to street theater, the organization proposes a "revolution" committed more to the thrills of acting up than to the mundane work of helping people in need.

Clearly, this passage could have been annotated in many other ways. The important thing to consider, however, is that the reader has engaged the writer in a conversation by asking questions, commenting, and paraphrasing what has been said. There are probably as many ways to carry on this conversation as there are ways to write. Ultimately, you must develop your own approach to critical reading.

PRACTICE 4.11 Annotating

Read the last few paragraphs of McWhorter's essay. Annotate them, and then answer the questions that follow the reading.

Of course, "hip-hop intellectuals" would disagree, celebrating hip-hop as an expression of inner-city frustration. But frustration does not require music so willfully alienated and nihilistic: None existed during the centuries when all blacks endured injustice much more concrete. In any case, hip-hop elicits identification across classes, having become a kind of "musica franca" for black identity. One often sees well-heeled young black executives get into their new cars and turn on the same spiky rap that the inner-city black man listens to.

Hip-hop, in short, is not a message from the streets but a histrionic pose. Producers coach aspiring artists to glower for photos. "I'm valid when I'm disrespected," an aspiring black rapper told a reporter for the *New York Times* in 2000, in an article from its "How Race Is Lived in America" series. The piece ended with his recording a CD whose strident vulgarity and sexism chilled the article's writer. The rapper knew the truth—he was indulging in an act that sells, pure and simple.

In the grand view, hip-hop may be seen as a typical American phenomenon—one part the cowboys-and-Indians tradition of heroic conflict and one part the recent "Bobos in Paradise" syndrome of celebrating countercultural gestures as "real." *The Sopranos,* in its violence and vulgarity, shares this mixed cultural parentage. But that TV show is not intended as a guide to living for all Italians. Hip-hop, by contrast, is linked to a particular racial identity. Yes, numerically it has more white listeners. But hip-hop's fans would be up in arms against anyone who claimed that the music was rooted in white culture rather than an African American consciousness.

And what a dismaying symbol of identity for a race just past misery. Rappers slip acrid slams at their rivals into recordings, nurturing "battles" to sell CDs. It was such provocations that likely led to the deaths of Tupac Shakur and "Biggie" Smalls. And that brings us back to "rap and rap sheet," in the artful phrase of the music critic Kelefa Sanneh. Rapper 50 Cent was recently arrested for harboring assault weapons in his car. DJ Funkmaster Flex physically assaulted a female rival DJ in New York last fall. In 2000, a brawl at the Source Hiphop Awards shut the ceremony down—right after a video tribute to slain rappers!

"But white people act up too." Yes, but Garth Brooks does not bring a "piece" to the Grammys, and Martin Scorsese does not get into ugly scuffles on the street. There is a fine line between playing the bad boy and becoming one, and in the "hip-hop community" too often violence jumps out of the quotation marks and becomes a tragic reality.

But calls to combat hip-hop are useless for the moment. As Judith Rich Harris showed us in *The Nurture Assumption,* children identify with their peers more than with their parents. Blacks under a certain age feel this music as their poetry, rattling off extended selections as readily as Russians recite Puskin. It's not going away.

But this is a lowdown, dirty shame. I am just old enough to remember when whites were making the sourest, nastiest pop music while blacks were making the sweetest and truest. White kids listened to hideous screaming, while funk and soul were black America's soundtrack. As a kid in the 1970s I was conscious of that contrast and proud of it. The civil rights protesters a decade before, who made the lives of the "hip-hop generation" possible, would have been appalled to hear the likes of Jay-Z, and we would be hard-pressed to claim that they would have been somehow missing something in that judgment. They accomplished a lot more, too, than any rapper's sideline donations to community efforts ever will.

The staged alienation of the hip-hop scene shows black Americans celebrating attitude over action at best and violence over civility at worst. For 350 years white America told blacks they were beasts. Now a black-generated pop music presents us to whites and ourselves as beasts, while a cadre of black intellectuals celebrate this as "deep" and black impresarios glide by in their limos calling it a "revolution." Revulsion is more like it.

PRACTICE 4.12 Understanding "Mean Street Theater"

1. Identify the primary claim (thesis statement) and the minor claims (supporting statements) in the essay. (It would be valuable to compare your answers to those of your peers to see whether you have identified the same sentences.) Write the sentences word for word, then paraphrase them (put them in your own words without distorting the original meaning).
2. Does McWhorter recognize a point of view other than his own? Are you able to adequately understand the other viewpoint? Explain.
3. Does McWhorter support all of his claims with adequate evidence?
4. Do you consider McWhorter to be a trustworthy, authoritative source? Explain.
5. Who seems to be the target audience? How can you tell? Would McWhorter's view be received with sympathy by that audience? What do you think his target audience is like in terms of race, class, education, politics, and interest in the arts?
6. What is McWhorter's tone? Is it formal or informal? Is it well suited for his audience? Do you think his audience was receptive to his claim? Explain.

Responding

Determining where reading ends and responding begins is difficult, because the acts of reading and responding inevitably occur together. Paraphrasing, annotating, and writing in your reading journal are all aspects of reading as well as elements of responding. At some point, however, you may decide to respond to the text in a more formal way. Perhaps you may write a refutation, a sort of argument in which you explain why you disagree with another argument. Alternatively, you may write a synthesis, in which you discuss how one argument relates to others that consider similar issues. Ultimately, your response will probably involve reacting to the writings of others as you construct your own argument.

PRACTICE 4.13 **Responding to "Mean Street Theater"**

1. Read the first two paragraphs and last two paragraphs of McWhorter's article. How effectively do they introduce and conclude the content of the essay? Are they misleading in any way? How?
2. Do you agree or disagree with McWhorter's analysis of rap and its culture? Explain.
3. Evaluate McWhorter's use of evidence. Where is it strongest? Where is it weakest? Why?
4. If you had written this article, would you have spent more time discussing the rappers' point of view? What advantage would this approach offer?
5. Identify the greatest strength and the greatest weakness of the argument. Explain your answer.

Working with Multiple Arguments

When you investigate written arguments on your own, you will encounter a variety of viewpoints on any given argument. In the news media, political and social issues are often debated in terms of liberal versus conservative, for and against, pro and con. While some issues readily lend themselves to this sort of division (considering whether a law should be passed, for example), most issues have many dimensions. You will encounter people who are strongly in favor of an idea, people who are firmly against the idea, and people who fit somewhere in between the two extremes. To complicate matters further, arguments you read will not always neatly "line up." That is, they will rarely talk about the same aspects of the issue being debated. As a reader, you must consider the overall issue and determine what the various arguments have in common. Some will agree (more

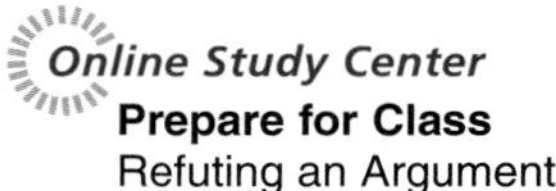

Prepare for Class
Refuting an Argument

or less); others will disagree (more or less). You must decide which features are worth comparing to gain an overall picture of what is at stake.

REFUTATIONS

When one argument directly responds to another argument, it is often called a refutation (see Chapter 6, Drafting Arguments, for more on refutations). When someone refutes another argument, the refutation depends on the original source for its central claims, and often for its organization and support. The argument that follows, "Hip-Hop Activism Buds Beautifully," is a direct response to McWhorter's essay.

READING SELECTION

Hip-Hop Activism Buds Beautifully

OPIO LUMUMBA SOKONI

Opio Lumumba Sokoni is an activist, attorney, and writer who was educated at Howard University. He has worked for the Drug Policy Alliance and Amnesty International, where he worked on issues related to the use of excessive force by police. In addition to his frequent writings on the Internet, his articles have appeared in *Black Commentator*, the *Washington Times*, and the *Boston Globe*. He has written on the drug war, the disproportionate treatment of African Americans in the criminal justice system, and, of course, hip-hop.

BEFORE YOU READ

1. What is your reaction to the name Opio Lumumba Sokoni? How does it compare to the name John McWhorter?
2. What does the title, "Hip-Hop Activism Buds Beautifully," imply?
3. What do you think this author is likely to say in his argument? What does a quick scan of the document tell you?

Hip-Hop Activism Buds Beautifully

Harry Belafonte stated to me in an interview that entertainers have the responsibility to speak out on issues concerning the community. He also said that entertainers are so often used to take people's minds off real issues and that entertainers who do not act are part of the problem. In a recent *Wall Street Journal* article entitled "Mean Street Theater," written by John McWhorter, he called social and political contributions to the community made by rappers' "sideline donations." About the recently slain rap artist

Camoflauge, McWhorter writes, "Despite his searingly profane, violent lyrics, [he] was regularly invited to speak at Savannah high schools." This article could have been more appropriately titled, "Mean Muggin' Hip Hop."

There's more. The article went on to run off other artists (i.e., Tupac, Biggie, and Jam Master Jay) as products of the genre. Never mind the failings of law enforcement, who have yet to find the killers of any of these men. But, they could find any small-time hustlers in the hood and lock them up for years and years for a nonviolent offense (i.e., drug possession).

This brings me to the most appealing part of the piece. While the author gave credit to Russell Simmons's Hip-Hop Action Network for setting a goal to register millions of hip-hop voters for the 2004 elections, he asked a poignant question: "What does the organization want the hip-hop generation to vote for?" If for nothing else, his article should have been printed for this query.

It is true that hip-hop has to have a political issue or issues to mobilize around. And we got issues; no doubt about that. Well, Russell Simmons, P Diddy, Jay Z, and many other hip-hoppers are right on point in their effort to address what should be the number one issue to focus hip-hop activism—fighting against the failed war on drugs. These celebrities are doing exactly what Mr. Belafonte says is expected of them.

This is a perfect issue for hip-hop activism because the lives affected the greatest are in the same communities that hip-hop most represents. In addition, the unchecked drug war is now devastating lives in white communities. But what makes this an even greater issue for the hip-hop generation is the fact that it is The Issue of our time.

No other cause has as many moving parts as the issues associated with the failed drug war. First, the war on drugs has created a prison population that should be an embarrassment to any rational person. I do not know any African American who does not have a personal connection to someone in jail for a drug crime. Most of the over 2 million people in jail are nonviolent, low-level drug offenders who would be better in treatment, therapy, job training, and/or on a job than in jail. But instead, the war on drugs has delivered young bodies to jails that are used to support the heartbreaking reality of the prison industrial complex.

Second, our babies are in foster care in high numbers because their parents have been given long sentences, usually for minor use or possession charges. In Washington, D.C., an estimated 70 percent of the children who are in foster care are there directly or indirectly due to drug addiction. There are no studies that show prison as being better than treatment for a parent.

Finally, aside from the other civil and human rights problems related to the war on drugs (i.e., a person losing the right to vote or a person being denied financial aid for college), there is the matter of racism. The fallout from the drug war has been more devastating than the KKK lynchings of the 1920s. Young people are racially targeted, set up, captured, convicted, sentenced, and jailed at a staggering rate.

A 2000 Human Rights Watch report confirms that in Wisconsin a black man is fifty-three times more likely to go to prison on a drug charge than a white man. This rate is reported to be the second highest in the country and more than four times the national average. Only Illinois ranked higher—there, a black man is fifty-seven times more likely to go to prison on a drug charge.

In New York, 94 percent of the people sentenced under the Rockefeller drug laws are from black and Latino communities. That's right, 94 percent. Debra Small, who works for Drug Policy Alliance, says that the Rockefeller drug laws are the granddaddy of the federal mandatory sentencing laws. A low-level drug offender can be sentenced to fifteen years to life if convicted.

I recently met a victim of the Rockefeller drug laws named Anthony Papa who is the painter of *15 Years to Life: Self-Portrait.* Anthony spent twelve years in a maximum-security prison for passing an envelope containing 4 ounces of cocaine. When asked about this law, he says, "The millions of dollars being spent to house nonviolent persons can be used to feed the hungry, put shoes on children's feet, and spent on education."

Russell Simmons's Hip-Hop Action Network has decided to work with Mothers of the New York Disappeared and other activists, celebrities, and organizations to change these laws. A victory in New York could have a domino effect among other states that have adopted similar drug policies. Further, this may be the catalyst to make drug policy reform front and center in the 2004 elections.

Hip-hop is coming into political maturity and can work to change some of the realities that are reported so vividly in rap lyrics. It is so fascinating how music has always been a part of social action in the black community. During slavery, coded songs were used to take persons to freedom. In the civil rights movement, marchers sang songs like "Ain't Gonna Let Nobody Turn Me Round." Now, there is an entire genre that is budding into full political awareness. How beautiful. And, it does not look like a mere "sideline donation" to me.

Understanding the Reading

1. What is Sokoni's thesis? In what way does it address or respond to McWhorter's primary claim?
2. In what ways is Sokoni's audience different from McWhorter's audience?
3. What are Sokoni's supporting claims? Do they address any of McWhorter's supporting points? Which ones?
4. What points does Sokoni make that are unique to his argument and do not depend on McWhorter's argument?
5. Does Sokoni provide adequate evidence to support his claims? Explain.

Responding to the Reading

1. Do you think Sokoni is an authority on the subject of hip-hop activism? Why or why not? Who is more authoritative for you—Sokoni or McWhorter? Explain.
2. Do you sympathize with Sokoni's view? Explain.
3. How well has Sokoni refuted McWhorter's argument? Be specific.
4. Name one significant strength and one significant weakness of Sokoni's essay. Why do you make this judgment?

Synthesizing Arguments

One of the tasks you may face as you prepare to write about an issue is determining how a particular text relates to other texts, in what has been termed the "universe of discourse." Everything we know relates to something else in this universe of discourse; understanding how an argument relates to other arguments is called synthesis. Synthesis helps a reader tease out details of how different texts relate to one another—how they agree and disagree, where their ideas come together, and where they diverge.

When you write a synthesis, you compare and contrast what different writers have to say about the same subject. In this case, your thesis will generally report on the significant similarities and differences between two or more arguments (or other sources) you have read. A synthesis can be comparative, meaning that it doesn't make critical judgments about one text or the other. A synthesis can also be analytical, meaning that it judges the quality of particular arguments. Finally, a synthesis can be evaluative, meaning that it argues one writer is correct and another writer is wrong.

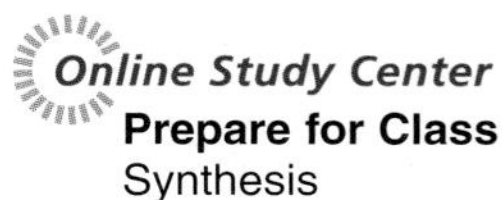

Prepare for Class
Synthesis

Understanding the Universe of Discourse

Perhaps the easiest way to think about the universe of discourse is to consider all mass-distributed discourse (ads on billboards, television shows, articles in newspapers, postings on a website) to be part of the same giant conversation. Think about the last time you went to a party: The room was probably filled with people, not talking in a single large mass, but conversing in various smaller, more intimate groups. Texts function in the same way. They respond to each other. Even if one author does not directly respond to another author (such as when a reader writes to a newspaper complaining about a particular view expressed in an editorial), writers often address common issues so that, in effect, they seem to be talking to one another.

PRACTICE 4.14 **Writing a Synthesis**

Choose one paragraph from McWhorter's argument and one paragraph from Sokoni's response. Make sure that they are linked, such that McWhorter makes a claim and Sokoni then responds to in his argument. Write a synthesis of the paragraphs.

Student Essay

Working individually or in groups, consider this student's response to rap music.

PRACTICE 4.15 **Before You Read**

1. What is your opinion of rap music and hip-hop culture now, after reading and responding to McWhorter's and Sokoni's arguments? Has your opinion changed in any way? Explain.
2. What does the title of the essay suggest to you? What do you think the writer might argue?
3. Scan the essay. What do you think the major divisions of the argument are? Who is the target audience?

Kerri Bennett
Dr. Everett
Composition
22 May 2006

Taking the "Rap" for Violence in Music

Whether or not one appreciates rap music, its prevalence cannot be ignored. In traffic, its aficionados treat other drivers to rap by pumping up the volume of oversized car speakers, booming teeth-rattling rhythms into any automobile within range. Channel surfing the television reveals music videos of rappers snarling their lyrics while striking menacing poses. A trek through a mall or other public places becomes a fashion show featuring youths dressed in droopy pants and draped heavily with gaudy, bling-blingish jewelry in imitation of their favorite rap entertainers. Since its emergence from the break-dancing competitions in the 1970s and 1980s, rap has evolved into one of the most popular and influential genres of music among America's youth.

Of course, the danger of rap music lies in neither its fashion statements nor its driving rhythms. The threat is in its message, a litany of catchy phrases encouraging its audience of young children and teens to commit violence against women and other groups. These young fans of rap are impressionable. Noted child psychologist Judith Rich tells us that instead of looking up to their parents, the young use other youths as role models (McWhorter 3). Shock-rocker Marilyn Manson confirms that musicians lead their young fans: "Music is such a powerful medium now. The kids don't even know who the president is, but they know what's on MTV. I think that if anyone like Hitler or Mussolini were alive now, they would have to be rock stars" (qtd. in Brownback 3).

Bennett 2

Senator Sam Brownback asserts that children who grow up with a stable home life will not be adversely affected by these influences; however, he wonders about the fate of other children: "In some of America's inner cities, where young men grow up without fathers, without good schools, surrounded by violence—how does this affect the way they think about and treat women?" (3). It is these children who are more susceptible to the harmful messages in the songs of their favorite rap artists.

Rapper Eminem (born Marshall Mathers) is a rap music icon, and whether voluntarily or involuntarily, he serves as a role model. Regrettably, his lyrics are rife with violence and with hatred toward women, describing acts of rape and murder in gruesome detail and even aiming some of his most brutal lyrics toward his own mother and the mother of his daughter (Mathers, "Kill"). He is also aware that young children look up to him, as the lyrics to his rap "Stan" indicate: in it, he describes a six-year-old who considers the rapper to be an idol and wants to be like him. Like many other rap singers, Eminem is criminally cavalier as a role model.

The incidents of violence and other crimes committed by the young have increased dramatically in recent years. Rap music may well be the cause:

> Over the last thirty years, violent juvenile crime has jumped more than 500%. Teen suicide has tripled. . . . Crimes against women have increased. Casual teen drug use has jumped by almost 50 percent in the last four years alone. . . . At the same time, there has been a marked increase in violence and misogyny in popular music. (Brownback 4)

In the world of rap, brutality seems to change quickly from an act for the cameras and the words of songs to real guns, knives, or rape (McWhorter 3).

What should we do to stop the violence? Contrary to the suggestions of some extremists, the answer is not to ban rap music: the First Amendment does give rappers the right to "spew their poison" (Hoyt 3). Although freedom of speech may seem to allow the problem, it can also be the solution because the media have the right—indeed, the responsibility—to denounce and expose any person or artistic work that could be harmful. Unfortunately, even though newspapers and magazines are aware that rap songs are violent and misogynistic, they still endorse them as entertaining. For example, Eminem's Slim Shady met with approval from Arizona Republic music critic Victor Barajas: "It's mean-spirited, profane, shocking—and actually quite entertaining if not taken too seriously" (qtd. in Hoyt 2). Ideally, the media can do better.

The news media should act as a spotlight, a kind and informative "Note Nanny" for parents, issuing warnings about particularly obscene or violent music. Magazines, newspapers, and television have the means, opportunity, and mandate to expose the nature of objectionable lyrics in reviews, editorials, and columns so that an informed and concerned public can guide and protect their young. The ironic solution to the problems presented by a constitutionally protected freedom to produce rap music lies not in repression of the arts but in the freedom of the media to expose rap's dark side to the light of reason.

Bennett 4

Works Cited

Brownback, Sam. "Free Speech: Lyrics, Liberty, and License." Vital Speeches of the Day 15 May 1998: 454–56.

Hoyt, Michael. "An Eminem Exposé: Where Are the Critics?" Columbia Journalism Review 1 Sept. 2000: 67.

Mathers, Marshall. "Kill You." Marshall Mathers LP. Interscope Records, 2000.

---. "Stan." Marshall Mathers LP. Interscope Records, 2000.

McWhorter, John. "Taste: Mean Street Theater." Wall Street Journal 30 May 2003: W15. ABI/INFORM Complete. ProQuest. Arkansas State U Lib., Jonesboro, AR. 28 Jun. 2005 <http://www.proquest.umi.com>.

PRACTICE 4.16 Understanding the Reading

1. What is the author's argumentative purpose? Who is her target audience? How can you tell?
2. What claims does the author use to support her thesis?
3. Does she recognize any views other than her own? Explain.
4. How does the author attempt to establish authority and appeal to the emotions of her audience?

PRACTICE 4.17 Responding to the Reading

1. Do you agree with the author's primary claim (thesis statement)? Why or why not?
2. Do her secondary claims serve to support her overall purpose? How? Does the author fail to provide any supporting ideas that have occurred to you? What are they?
3. Is the evidence adequate or weak in places? Explain.
4. How effectively does the author establish authority and appeal to the emotions of her audience?
5. Name one significant strength and one significant weakness of the argument. Explain your answer.

Looking Back at Chapter 4

- Critical reading is a process involving previewing (thinking about the topic), reading (understanding, annotating, and analyzing the argument), and responding (evaluating and writing about what you have read).
- Reading is a dynamic process. Rather than moving neatly from previewing to reading to responding in a linear fashion, you are more likely to switch back and forth between these functions, often performing all of them at once.
- Writing about critical reading involves asking questions about what you have read:
  How the argument is situated culturally—how it relates to you, to its audience, and to the culture in general;
  How it functions logically—how well it presents claims, evidence, and alternative points of view;
  How it functions rhetorically—how it utilizes purpose, audience, structure, and style to establish authority and maintain an emotional link with its audience.

- Responding to what you have read involves learning to paraphrase, properly quote, and summarize what you have read; analyzing arguments for the quality of their logic and rhetoric; synthesizing multiple arguments into a single document; and evaluating an argument to argue whether what it has to say is right or wrong.

Suggestions for Writing

- Select an argument or arguments from the readings in this chapter or other readings in this textbook. Critically read the argument(s). Then write one or more of the following:
  1. An analysis and evaluation of the argument
  2. A response to the argument
  3. A synthesis of one argument with another argument
  4. An analysis and evaluation of the rhetoric within the text(s)
- Choose an article on a subject of interest to you. Apply critical reading strategies, annotating the text thoroughly. Work on developing your own system of annotation.
- Summarize McWhorter's article or another article of your choosing.
- Paraphrase a paragraph from one of the readings in this chapter or from an article of your choosing.
- Synthesize information from two or more readings about a topic or issue that interests you.

Online Study Center
Improve Your Grade
Suggestions for Writing

5 Planning Arguments

> *A journey of a thousand miles begins with a single step.*
>
> —Lao-Tzu (604–531 b.c.e.)

A long journey can be intimidating, especially when it takes you into unknown territory. Completing the quest requires preparation, effort, a commitment of time, and solving problems both expected and unexpected. Ancient wisdom, however, reminds us that even the most arduous journey can be accomplished through a series of manageable steps.

Likewise, writing requires preparation, effort, a commitment of time, and plenty of problem solving. Fortunately, a number of techniques can make this process easier. Known as *planning* or *prewriting*, these techniques help you divide any assignment into a series of smaller, simpler tasks. Just as a journey of a thousand miles begins with a single step, so a book of a thousand pages begins with a single word. Planning can help you to make the first steps, to write the first words.

There are many planning techniques and many situations in which to apply those techniques. As you learn more about writing, you will not only expand your planning repertoire but also identify those methods that work best for you. To plan well, you'll need to (1) understand the assignment, (2) generate material, and (3) organize.

Online Study Center
This icon will direct you to content and resources on the website <college.hmco.com/pic/lamm1e>.

Understanding the Assignment

Online Study Center
Prepare for Class
Rhetorical Context

Whether self-assigned, course-required, or job-related, writing assignments have elements that must be analyzed and understood early and reviewed throughout the writing process. Some of these elements are *task-specific* requirements dictated by an instructor, employer, or publisher: format, length, sources, and deadline. Other elements are based more on the *rhetorical context*: *purpose, audience, structure,* and *style*.

Task Specifications

A writing assignment usually has specifications regarding its format, length, sources, and deadline. Although these specifications are technical in nature, they are the first noticed and most easily assessed features of your finished product. By carefully following the task-specific requirements, you'll make a good initial impression on the reader and use your time efficiently throughout the writing process.

Format Formatting concerns the visual appearance of your text: margins, headings, pagination or headers, font type and size, bullets, indentations, cover sheets, setups and labels for tables and figures, and acknowledgment of sources. Instructors, employers, or publishers sometimes create their own formatting requirements. At other times, they defer to the formatting style prescribed by an authority such as a professional organization—for example, the Modern Language Association (MLA) or the American Psychological Association (APA). Word processors have default (automatic) formats that can be changed by accessing the toolbar. (Chapters 13 and 14 provide more information about formatting issues.)

Length Writing assignments usually have a prescribed length. Although planning can help with assignments of any length, with longer assignments it may be indispensable, helping you conceive of the whole and organize its many parts.

For your convenience, word processors indicate the number of pages automatically and will even count the number of words for you. Plan to stay comfortably within the constraints of any prescribed word or page count: Skimping on length usually looks like you are skimping on effort, while excessive length may indicate an inability to focus your thoughts and be concise. Tweaking the font size, margins, and line spacing to compensate for length problems won't fool anyone!

Sources Some writing assignments require sources; others may exclude their use. If you are using sources, you'll need to know how many, what kind, and how to find, evaluate, use, and acknowledge them. This chapter and most others in this book discuss using sources.

Deadline A deadline is a time limit for the completion and submission of a writing assignment. Also known as a due date, a deadline sometimes is self-imposed and flexible, especially when a project is self-assigned. Deadlines set by an instructor, employer, or publisher, by contrast, are usually beyond your control and firm (or at least regulated by a policy).

Scheduling When facing a firm deadline, you'll want to set up a personal schedule that breaks the assignment into subtasks, each with its own deadline. Scheduling can help you anticipate which parts of the process will take more time than others: ordering books or other research materials through interlibrary loan or from vendors, or working around the schedules of others to conduct interviews. You'll have a much better chance of producing quality material if you pace yourself and budget your time so that you don't have to write frantically at the last minute. A schedule can be mapped out on a daily planner, calendar, or checklist.

SAMPLE SCHEDULE

Task	*Date*
Decide on a topic or subject	________
Begin research	________
Decide on an issue	________
Decide on tentative thesis or major claim	________
Complete rough first draft	________
Complete polished draft for others to review	________
Hold peer review or conference	________
Complete final draft	________
Submit (deadline)	________

Rhetorical Context

Writers select a particular structure or form (for example, an essay or letter) and adjust their style to fit a particular purpose and audience. Together, these considerations define the rhetorical context of a piece of writing.

Purpose You write to achieve a purpose, such as to inform, to entertain, to express yourself, or, of course, to argue. The general goal of argument is to change how an audience thinks and possibly how it acts in response to an issue. More specifically, argument focuses on making a case for particular claims: fact, identity, cause/effect, value, and proposal.

Audience An audience is composed of your readers, listeners, or viewers. In a writing course you know your work is destined for an instructor's scrutiny—an audience of one—and this fact strongly influences how you write. However, instructors often expect you to write for a broader audience. When in doubt, assume your audience to be a reasonable but skeptical stranger who is moderately acquainted with the subject: Don't assume your reader already knows the same things you have read or discussed in class. Your instructor may even create a scenario, giving you a specific "imaginary" audience: expert or uninformed, friendly or hostile. You'll make adjustments in your writing for the audience, adapting your purpose, structure, and style to fit its characteristics. Indeed, some writers create a profile of the audience to help tailor their arguments to fit that particular group.

Structure Structure refers partly to the form, genre, or type of writing produced, and partly to the organization within a form. Formal essays commonly are required in composition courses, but their internal features will vary with the techniques used to argue. Classification, comparison/contrast, description, and narration, for example, have distinctive organizational patterns. Also, arguments need not always be formal essays or even written documents. Editorials and editorial cartoons, letters to the editor, petitions, grant proposals, contract bids, debates, courtroom hearings, advertisements—all are arguments. (Chapter 6, Drafting Arguments, contains more information on structure.)

Style Style refers to *how* something is said rather than *what* is said. It is conveyed by your attitude, tone, voice, sentence structure, and word choice. Think of style as a range of choices between formal and informal, serious and humorous, specialized and general purpose, familiar and distant. You'll want to use a style that fits your rhetorical context—that is, your purpose, audience, and structure.

RANGE OF STYLES

Style in writing is analogous to style in dress, ranging from informal to formal. Research papers tend to be formal, written in an "academic style" that prefers third-person point of view and avoids contractions. In other words, you avoid the use of *I* or *you*, and you write out terms such as *should not* instead of using *shouldn't*.

Informal: I think we should all work together so plagiarism doesn't mess up our school.

Formal: Students, instructors, and administrators should cooperate in promoting a healthy atmosphere of academic honesty.

You have probably noticed that this textbook uses a less formal style, assuming a second-person point of view (POV) to address *you* directly. Second-person POV fits our purpose of acting as your mentor: We want to convey a tone that is friendlier than third-person POV will allow. Also, we would argue that the textbook itself is not a research paper—so cut us some slack, okay? (You wouldn't use slang phrases like "cut us some slack, okay" in a formal research paper.)

While there are no absolute cutoff points distinguishing degrees of formality in writing, you could think of your choices as a continuum, as displayed in this imaginary "formality meter":

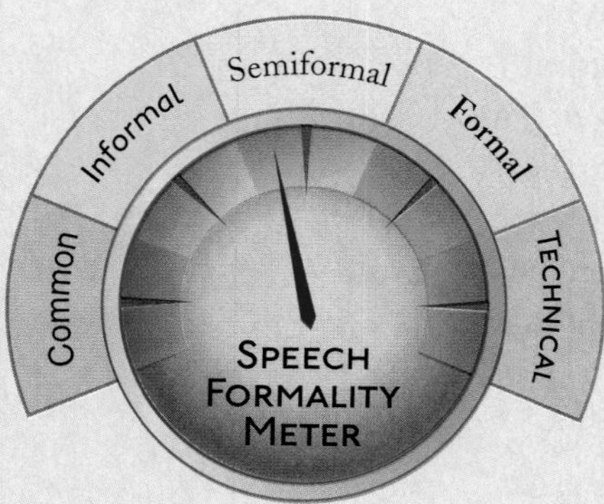

Style can range in degrees of formality.

Common Speech Language is specific to the community where it is used. Incomplete sentences, alternative grammar, and idiomatic expressions are freely employed in some communities. Slang and other "unofficial" words may also be used.

Example of word choice expressing "amount": a bunch.

Informal Language is used broadly outside of one's immediate family, neighborhood, or peer group to communicate with the world at large. Incomplete sentences and contractions are freely used, although alternative grammar, idiomatic speech, slang, and other expressions that might impede communication are avoided.

Example of word choice expressing "amount": a lot.

Semiformal This language is commonly used to communicate, both in writing and speech, at work and in school. Incomplete sentences, alternative grammar, and idiomatic expressions are usually avoided. The writing in newspapers and magazines represents this level of formality.

Example of word choice expressing "amount": many.

Formal This language is carefully written. Rules of punctuation and grammar are strictly followed. Contractions and other signs of informality are avoided. Words are carefully chosen to communicate specific ideas. Generally. a more complex vocabulary is employed.

Example of word choice expressing "amount": an abundance.

Technical Sentences and paragraphs must follow a specific format. Words are often the jargon used by specialists and have very precise meanings. This language is typical of legal documents and technical manuals.

Example of word choice expressing "amount": 6.74 liters.

PRACTICE 5.1 **Rhetorical Context**

Evaluate the rhetorical features of the following excerpts. What are the apparent purpose, audience, structure, and style of each? How would changing one rhetorical feature affect the other features?

One of the oddest job offers I ever received came when a stranger telephoned to ask if I would be interested in researching and writing academic papers for university students. For the uninitiated, so-called "paper mills" sell term papers and essays to desperate students who hand them in as their own work. People picture the mills as a low-rent operation run out of someone's basement. Maybe in the days of bell-bottoms and peace symbols, but not anymore. Thanks to the Internet, email, and fax machines, academic plagiarism is easy—and big business."

—Rhonda Lauret Parkinson, *"Plagiarize at Your Peril"*

Meta-analytic findings have suggested that individual differences are relatively weaker predictors of academic dishonesty than are situation factors. A robust literature on deviance correlates and workplace integrity testing, however, demonstrated that individual difference variables can be relatively strong predictors of a range of counterproductive work behaviors (CWBs).

—Gale Lucas and James Friedrich, *"Individual Differences in Workplace Deviance and Integrity as Predictors of Academic Dishonesty"*

Creating an Audience Profile The audience is a vitally important rhetorical consideration. Identifying the characteristics of your audience through an audience profile can help you understand the readers you wish to persuade and decide how you can adapt your argument to better fit them.

AUDIENCE PROFILE

I. Rhetorical context (preliminary, tentative)
   A. Purpose:
   B. Audience:
   C. Structure:
   D. Style:
II. Profile of primary audience
   A. Audience's relevant demographics (e.g., profession, education, age, gender, race, religion):
   B. Audience's knowledge of the issue (ranging from expert to novice):
   C. Audience's present attitude(s) toward the issue:
      1. Audience's major concerns:
      2. Audience's minor concerns:

AUDIENCE PROFILE *(Continued)*

III. Profile of secondary audience(s)
   A. Secondary audience 1
      Audience:
      Conflicts with primary audience:
   B. [repeat as needed]
IV. Arguments (claims and support) the audience(s) could accept
   A. Argument 1
      Claim:
      Support:
   B. [repeat as needed]
V. Rhetorical considerations (revised after profiling the audience)
   A. Purpose:
   B. Audience:
   C. Structure:
   D. Style:

Below is an audience profile prepared by student Hetal Shah, who plans to write on the topic of plagiarism. (Shah's paper appears in Chapter 6.)

Audience Profile for the Topic of Plagiarism

I. Rhetorical context (preliminary, tentative)
   A. **Purpose:** To persuade instructors to be more understanding of students who plagiarize and to be more lenient on plagiarists
   B. **Audience:** Instructors
   C. **Structure:** Argumentative essay based on research
   D. **Style:** Formal
II. Profile of primary audience: Instructors
   A. **Audience's relevant demographics (e.g., profession, education, age, gender, race, religion):** The most important thing about instructors is their <u>profession</u>: They are obliged to enforce codes of academic honesty. Also, their <u>education</u> level is important: They already know how to write well, so

their standards about writing are high. Their college preparation may have been better than that of the students they now teach, so they may not understand the students' difficulties. Age is an issue because they may have forgotten what it's like to be a student.

B. **Audience's knowledge of the issue (ranging from expert to novice):** Instructors have an expert knowledge of how to use sources in writing. Their knowledge of teaching writing will vary: more with English instructors, less with other disciplines. Their knowledge of their own students' backgrounds and abilities will vary.

C. Audience's present attitude(s) toward the issue:

1. **Audience's major concerns:** Students' learning of subject being taught, students' knowledge of writing, students' understanding of ethics
2. **Audience's minor concerns:** Students' grades, stress, exhaustion, morale, future

III. Profile of secondary audience(s)

A. **Secondary audience 1**

Audience: Administrators who influence policies affecting instruction and disciplinary policies

Conflicts with primary audience: Probably few conflicts. Administrators and instructors probably will agree with one another and can be persuaded with the same arguments. Administrators might be more sympathetic to students, and might be more concerned with public relations and with a policy that is consistent and universal.

B. **Secondary audience 2**

Audience: Students affected by instruction and by disciplinary procedures.

Conflicts with primary audience: Most will already be sympathetic to claims that shift responsibility to instructors and administrators. Their concerns will focus less on ethics and knowledge, and more on grades and fair treatment. However, those who don't plagiarize will likely agree with instructors. They want a level playing field where students don't get high grades without doing the work.

IV. Arguments (claims and support) the audience(s) could accept

A. **Argument 1**

Claim: "When plagiarism is accidental, leniency should be shown."

Support: "It isn't an ethical weakness, only lack of knowledge." "Students are in school to learn, not to be punished."

B. **Argument 2**

Claim: "Instruction about academic honesty could be improved. This would include ethical training and writing training aimed specifically at ways to avoid plagiarism."

Support: "Many educators, philosophers, and religious leaders believe ethics and morality <u>can be learned</u>; therefore, it <u>should be taught</u>." "Students who haven't been taught how to use sources properly may be forced into making unethical choices."

V. Rhetorical context (revised after profiling the audience)

A. **Purpose:** To propose a fairer policy of academic honesty that clarifies the responsibilities of students, instructors, and administrators

B. **Audience:** Students, instructors, and administrators

C. **Structure:** Argumentative essay based on research

D. **Style:** Formal

As the student worked through the profile, she discovered that her preliminary purpose was unlikely to sway her intended audience: Instructors were unlikely to accept responsibility for the academic dishonesty of their students. Her revised purpose was a compromise claiming that students, instructors, and administrators share responsibility for the problem of plagiarism and that the remedy will require them to work together. Her audience was broadened, and her claim became more likely to change the way the audience thought and acted.

PRACTICE 5.2 Creating an Audience Profile

Use Hetal Shah's audience profile as a guide to create a profile of an audience for a topic or an issue you plan to write about.

Generating Material

Much the same way that a carpenter gathers tools and materials before beginning to build a house, the process of generating material helps you gather claims and support before beginning to write a draft. On an intuitive level, you might think anything that keeps you from immediately starting your first draft is a waste of time; in practice, you'll find that generating materials makes drafting proceed more quickly and easily. Generating techniques include brainstorming, critical thinking, discussing, writing, sketching and scrapbooking, discovering, and researching.

TECHNIQUES FOR GENERATING ARGUMENTS

Brainstorming: Rapid listing of ideas, words, or phrases suggested by a topic
Critical thinking: Interpretation, application, analysis, synthesis, and evaluation
Discussing: Vocal or Internet exchanges with others on a topic
Writing: Using prose to generate ideas, not necessarily produce a draft

- Focused freewriting: Full-sentence rapid writing on a topic
- Journaling: Full-sentence reflective writing on a topic
- Blogging: Journal or log entries posted on the Web ("weblogging")

Sketching and scrapbooking: Collecting visual materials on a topic
Discovering: Using lists of points or questions as guidelines
Researching: Gathering information

- Primary research: Generating new information
- Secondary research: Finding information generated by others

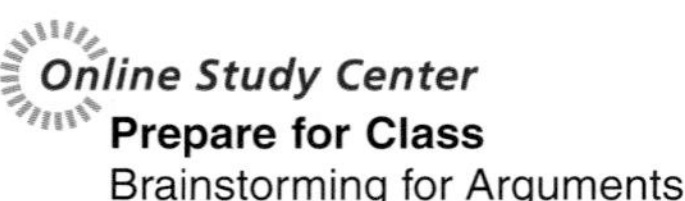

Prepare for Class
Brainstorming for Arguments

BRAINSTORMING

Brainstorming involves the rapid listing of ideas on a given topic. Its goal is quantity: Worries about quality are postponed until after the brainstorming session, when each idea is evaluated. Brainstorming is the most basic and versatile of all planning techniques.

Brainstorming can be performed individually or in any size group. When performed individually, it is a silent writing activity. In contrast, a group working collaboratively is highly vocal, with a designated person recording the ideas as words or phrases (not complete sentences) because speed is of the essence. Discussion of the ideas is suspended until the brainstorming session ends.

A typical brainstorming session lasts five to ten minutes, but it can be expanded or contracted to suit the situation. For a short writing assignment, a minute of brainstorming might suffice, whereas committees or think tanks may brainstorm for hours, days, or longer on major issues. For many writers, brainstorming recurs quite frequently: A writer may first brainstorm possible topics, then select an issue, and finally brainstorm terms, ideas, and claims specific to the selected issue.

Following is a list of terms and ideas that Hetal Shah produced during a two-minute brainstorming session on her topic of plagiarism:

writing is hard	*paraphrasing*	*quoting*	*MLA*
APA	*punishment*	*flunking*	*pressure*
deadlines	*too many papers*	*ethics*	*morality*
tough teachers	*Internet papers*	*Turnitin.com*	*paper mill*
footnotes	*bibliography*	*works cited*	*guilt*
academic dishonesty	*cheating*	*unfair*	*F*

Guidelines for Brainstorming

Brainstorming is the rapid listing of ideas, questions, and information about a topic. It produces a collection of words and phrases that later can be reflected upon, organized, and expanded.

- **Aim for quantity.** Don't stop for any reason. State (orally or in writing) as many ideas as possible in a given period of time.
- **Aim for speed.** Write as quickly as you can. Record your ideas in brief fashion—words, phrases, abbreviations. Don't let recording slow down your generation of ideas.
- **Build from the ideas already recorded.** When the initial stream of ideas starts to slow, expand on things you've already written.
- **Don't worry.** Suspend your inhibitions, never stopping to critique an idea. Write whatever comes to mind. Evaluate later.

PRACTICE 5.3 Brainstorming

Choose a topic, perhaps one you may later argue. With a watch or clock in view, brainstorm and record a list of issues, terms, facts, ideas, and individuals associated with the topic. You are not limited to controversy: At this stage, you simply list anything you know (or want to know) about the topic.

CRITICAL THINKING

Critical thinking involves "reading between the lines," looking beneath the surface meaning of a subject. A productive way to think critically is to ask and answer questions such as those modeled after Bloom's taxonomy. Questions can guide your brainstorming, freewriting, journaling, discussion, or research. (See Chapter 4, The Reader's Response to Arguments, for more on questions and critical thinking.)

Here is a list of terms and ideas produced by one student's ten-minute critical thinking session on the topic of plagiarism. These questions, which are derived from Bloom's taxonomy, also can be used to discover explanations for supporting evidence. (See the "Discovering" section later in this chapter.)

1. **Knowledge and clarification:** Plagiarism is considered cheating or theft. It's easy to plagiarize through websites—old student essays are there for the taking. Internet sources also sell customized essays. It's easy to take a published article and turn it into an essay. Penalties can be severe: failure, suspension, expulsion. Not sure what the school's policy is. Not sure how to completely avoid plagiarizing.

2. **Comprehension and interpretation:** Plagiarism can get you into trouble—a short-term fix that can backfire and end your education and maybe your future. But sometimes it's the last resort for desperate students out of time. Sometimes it's the only resort for students who don't know any other way to use sources.

3. **Application:** Plagiarism can get you out of trouble—a deadline or an overload of work. If you're not caught, it can get you a good grade. If you're caught, it's just the opposite: You're in trouble and you get a bad grade. Knowing how to use sources properly makes it possible to get the benefits and avoid penalties.

4. **Analysis:** The "parts" of plagiarism are materials taken from a source—a book or article—that you pretend you wrote yourself. Or it can be a whole essay someone else wrote, using articles and books legitimately. Or you can pretend you're paraphrasing, when you're really quoting without using quotation marks. Guilt and fear are parts of it—sometimes you're caught years after you plagiarized, so

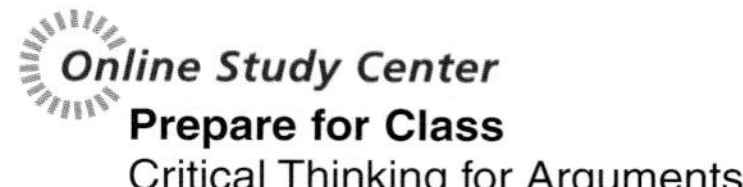

Guidelines for Critical Thinking (from Bloom's Taxonomy)

1. **Knowledge and clarification:** What facts do you know or perhaps need to know?
2. **Comprehension and interpretation:** What is its significance? What does it imply or *really* mean?
3. **Application:** What uses does it have to you or to others?
4. **Analysis:** What are its parts? How do they work together?
5. **Synthesis:** How does it relate to other things?
6. **Evaluation:** What is its importance? How good is it?

From Benjamin S. Bloom et al., *Taxonomy of Educational Objectives*, Book I, *Cognitive Domain* (Boston: Allyn and Bacon).

you're never in the clear. It's a decision made to go over to the dark side.

5. **Synthesis:** It's a form of cheating—"academic dishonesty." It's like stealing from someone (except the person may never miss what you've stolen!). It's also like a lifesaver for a drowning person—someone who might sink academically without it. It's similar to downloading music without paying royalties or copying answers from someone else's test.

6. **Evaluation:** It gets the job done, in a way. It's efficient—you get a grade without much work. It's scary but kind of a rush, like committing a crime and hoping no one knows it was you. Once you realize how bad some people think it is, you start feeling bad about yourself, like you're a fake. The worst thing is you never learn how to write your own stuff in a way that will help you in life.

PRACTICE 5.4 Critical Thinking

Choose an issue, perhaps one that emerged from brainstorming or free writing about a topic. Respond to the following questions and record your answers.

1. **Knowledge and clarification:** What facts do you know or perhaps need to know?
2. **Comprehension and interpretation:** What is its significance? What does it imply or *really* mean?
3. **Application:** What uses does it have to you or to others?
4. **Analysis:** What are its parts? How do they work together?
5. **Synthesis:** How does it relate to other things?
6. **Evaluation:** What is its importance? How good is it?

DISCUSSING

Talking about a subject can be a powerful method for discovering ideas. Interactive, focused discussions often reveal that you know more—or less—about a subject than expected. In either case, it can guide you to the next steps for planning. Discussion adds a social dimension to reading and writing, often making the process more enjoyable because it is interactive and sometimes dramatic. Sometimes discussion is structured around a prepared list of questions, such as those that guide critical thinking or audience profiling, but it can also be freewheeling and spontaneous.

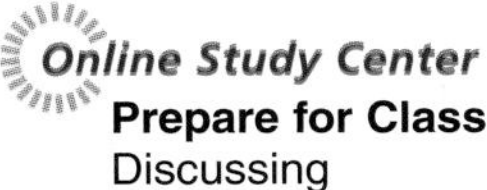

Prepare for Class
Discussing

Discussions can range from cooperative (a team effort to understand issues and solve problems) to adversarial (a debate that reveals points of contention, support, and rebuttals). They can occur in large groups, small groups, or pairs before, during, or after reading or writing—whenever they are useful. Although discussions often occur in classroom settings, they may also take place through e-mail, chat rooms, and instant messaging.

Guidelines for Discussing

The following guidelines are adapted from the conflict resolution techniques introduced in Chapter 1. They can help make discussion more productive and civil.

- Take turns introducing topics or issues.
- Don't interrupt.
- Respond positively.
- Ask for clarifications.
- Listen for omissions or evasions.

PRACTICE 5.5 Discussing

In a small or large group, discuss a controversial issue of your choice. Argue first as adversaries, taking opposite sides in a point-counterpoint fashion. Then change your approach, working collaboratively to solve the issue by finding common ground and making concessions.

Writing

Online Study Center
Prepare for Class
Freewriting, Journaling, and Blogging

Writing can be used as a planning technique. This kind of writing is intended not so much to draft a text but rather to generate ideas before you begin putting the ideas into the form you want. Freewriting, journaling, and blogging are writing techniques used as generative techniques.

Freewriting Freewriting, also known as stream of consciousness writing or rambling, involves nonstop composing on a particular topic. Freewriters usually write in complete sentences, unlike the word-or-phrase listing of brainstorming. Freewriting sessions typically last five to ten minutes but can be expanded or contracted to fit the particular circumstances. Indeed, some essay tests may ask you to perform focused freewriting for an hour or more.

The most important goal while freewriting is to compose nonstop without worrying about anything except volume: The motto here is "The more, the better." To be able to write rapidly, freewriters suspend their "internal editor," ignoring concerns about errors, disorganization, poor word choice, or lack of ideas. Freewriting offers benefits that might not be achieved through other kinds of writing activities:

- Confidence that might otherwise be diminished by self-editing. If you burden yourself with concerns about saying something "just right," you may never get the idea on paper.
- Fluency through writing with a flow resembling conversation. When we speak, we seldom take long pauses and we almost never run to a dictionary to look up words. Freewriting can help a writer capitalize on the ease of oral communication.
- Freedom from "writer's block." You have no choice except to write. If you are stuck, write something like "I'm stuck, I'm stuck . . ." until you find something better to write.

Focused freewriting takes the technique a little further, requiring that you write nonstop on a particular topic or issue. Focused freewriters attempt to make their writing coherent—logically flowing from sentence to sentence—but off-topic drifting is natural and acceptable. The following example is a five-minute focused freewrite on the topic of plagiarism by a student in Hetal Shah's collaborative learning group:

> *I hope nobody reads this because I'm about to confess! I've plagiarized most of my life. In grade school, teachers would assign reports, and most of the time my report was copied straight out of an encyclopedia. It was never questioned, and I always got a good grade when I turned it in. LOL. Book reports were a little harder, except sometimes you could copy a summary straight from the cover of the book! In high school they taught about citing sources and how to make a bibliography, but the English teacher was the only one watching how we used the sources. The biology teacher, the history teacher I think they were more concerned with what we learned about their subjects and not so much about the actual writing. They never questioned how I came up with the wording while I just took the stuff straight from a book but dummied it down into my own style.*

Guidelines for Focused Freewriting

Focused freewriting involves writing nonstop about a topic or issue.

1. **Aim for quantity.** Don't stop for any reason.
2. **Aim for speed.** Write as quickly as you can. It's probably better (faster) if you use cursive rather than printing. If you can't think of something to write, then write something like "I'm stuck" until you're not stuck.
3. **Build from the ideas already recorded.** When the initial stream of ideas starts to slow, expand on things you've already written.
4. **Don't worry.** Suspend your inhibitions, never stopping to solve problems with spelling or word choice—settle for approximate spellings. Write whatever comes to mind about the topic or issue. Evaluate your writing later.

PRACTICE 5.6 Focused Freewriting

Freewrite for a set amount of time on a subject or issue you plan to argue.

Journaling A journal is your record of your experiences and reflections. Also known as a log and resembling a diary, journals can be freewritten. In this textbook, however, we distinguish between journaling and freewriting based on how the passage is produced. Journaling is more meditative, allowing you to pause as needed to think about what to write and even to revise what you have already written. Freewriting is nonstop writing and consequently more spontaneous.

The rhetorical context of a journal is defined by its personal nature: for the purposes of reflection, exploration, and self-expression, for an audience of one (the author), through a freeform structure, in a style that is precisely the voice of the writer. Although *journal* contains a root word from the French *jour* (meaning "day"), writers do not strictly have to write daily. They do need to write regularly, however.

PRACTICE 5.7 Journaling

Keep a journal for an extended period of time—days, weeks, or months. Focus the journal on an issue you plan to argue. You may wish to use freewriting as a means for writing the journal, or you may prefer to employ a slower, more reflective technique.

Blogging A blog (a contraction of *weblog*) is a personal journal made public by posting on a webpage. In the planning phase of writing, a blog may function like a journal while offering some additional benefits: It provides an audience that can respond, creating a community of learners that extends beyond the walls of a classroom to potentially anywhere on the planet. Anything that can be digitalized can be added to the blog—any form of writing, visuals, or music. The public nature of a blog changes the journal's rhetorical context.

Purpose: While the purposes for writing a journal tend to be personal, exploratory, and tentative, a blog may have an effect on other readers, essentially becoming an argument.

Audience: The audience of a journal initially is oneself, whereas the audience of a blog is, potentially, the world.

Structure: Although a blog may retain the relaxed organization of a journal entry, a blogger often will rewrite for the sake of clarifying ideas for an audience.

Style: A blog usually retains the voice of the author. However, because this writing is public, a blogger should observe certain conventions of public discourse, such as avoiding profanity and refraining from the expression of inflammatory ideas such as attacks based on race, culture, gender, or religion. Once a journal becomes public, the writer can be held ethically and legally responsible for its content.

BLOG: CHEATING AND COMMON KNOWLEDGE

I think the problem of cheating in schools is significant and important to address, and we must be aware of the ways that technologies can be used to facilitate cheating. But it would be wrong-headed to see either technologies or the commons as the source of cheating. Instead, we should try to understand the larger social context within which students live (a context that appears to reward cheating on a regular basis) and to develop ways of addressing those issues to encourage more ethical behavior. We should speak out against unethical behavior in all its guises. We should also develop processes within the academic sphere that reward creative behavior rather than promoting obsession with grades and similar phenomenal outputs.

—Frederick Emrich, Info-Commons.org

PRACTICE 5.8 Blogging

Find a blogsite related to an issue you plan to argue. Read through the ongoing discussion and then join in if access is possible—in other words, post a response.

SKETCHING AND SCRAPBOOKING

Writers sometimes keep sketchbooks to help them remember experiences. Sketching often occurs as part of a journal entry, joining images with verbal reflections. Scrapbooks can include photos, clippings, and artifacts (such as a pressed flower or a ticket stub). Nonprint materials sometimes will be the object of your claims or the substance of your evidence. For example, if you were researching sexism in children's toys, you might clip images of Barbie dolls from magazines, photograph the doll or children playing, or download images from Web sources into a file. A scrapbook can be digital, consisting of pictures scanned or copied from Web sources. Digital materials can easily be integrated into a draft of an essay. (For more on visuals, see Chapter 12, Arguing Visually.)

PRACTICE 5.9 Visual Scrapbooking

Begin a scrapbook or sketchbook on an issue you wish to argue. Try to include examples from a variety of sources.

Discovering

Discovery techniques help you find ideas and facts that are accessible but unnoticed; they remind you where to direct your thoughts. Also known as *heuristics* (from the Greek *eureka,* meaning "I found it"), discovery techniques consist of routines or formulas, such as a list of questions.

Some discovery techniques are generic (all-purpose), such as the "reporter's formula," also known as the "five W's and an H": who, what, when, where, why, and how. The leads of most news stories answer these questions. Other discovery techniques are geared toward a specific purpose, such as questions focused on an argument's claims, support, and rhetorical context.

Following are questions designed to help you discover claims, evidence, and rhetorical context. The student responses are focused on the topic of plagiarism.

Discovering Claims: What Are You Trying to Argue?

Fact: Is or was it real? Does or did it actually exist? The theft of ideas has been around for a long time. Copyrights and patents haven't always been part of the law and aren't respected everywhere in the world. Plagiarism may not be as one-sided as instructors think, though—it may be "factual" that instructors contribute to the problem.

Identity: What is it? Cheating. Theft. Borrowing. The sincerest form of flattery. An efficient way to get what you want. A misunderstanding. An epidemic.

Cause and effect: How does it work? Too much pressure on students. Unrealistic expectations. Poor instruction. Lack of ethics or morals.

Value: How is it judged? Harshly by instructors, with stiff penalties when formally investigated and tried. Lightly by students, many of whom don't see it as wrongful conduct.

Proposal: Should something be done? Better teaching not only about how to write but also about the policies that guide and procedures that enforce ethical conduct. Policies and pedagogy should be reviewed and revised.

Guidelines for Discovering Claims

Fact: Is or was it real?
Identity: What is it?
Cause and effect: How does it work?
Value: How is it judged?
Proposal: Should something be done?

Discovering Evidence: How Will You Support Your Argument?

Expert opinions: Research shows lots of experts, mostly instructors and school administrators, comment on the "epidemic" of academic dishonesty. Example: "When Academic Dishonesty Happens on Your

Guidelines for Discovering Evidence

Expert opinions:
Facts and statistics:
History:
Personal experience:
Scenarios:
Specific examples:

Guidelines for Discovering Rhetorical Context

Purpose: What effect on the audience are you seeking?
Audience: Who will be reading (or hearing or viewing)?
Structure: What form or organization will the argument take?
Style: How formally will you present your argument?

Campus" by Karen L. Clos, Dean of Learning and Instructor at Barton County Community College.

Facts and statistics: Number of studies available on why students cheat. Many articles with figures on the increase in cheating, such as "A Culture of Copy-and-Paste" by Jessica Durkin.

History: Apparently Shakespeare borrowed ideas from sources, and imitation has a long intellectual history. In "So, Is It the Real Thing?" Atul Prakash quotes Picasso as saying "a great artist steals."

Personal experience: Careful: I don't want to get into trouble for something I did a long time ago! Better to report what I know others have done or make up a scenario.

Scenarios: I can make up an example about a student under pressure who resorts to plagiarism. I can put a lot of sob-story elements that mitigate things: He wasn't taught properly, she'll lose her scholarship if she fails or if she's punished when caught, etc.

Specific examples: Brief interviews with other students; my observations of cheating by others; my observations of instructors; examples of policies and procedures related to cheating.

PRACTICE 5.10 Discovering Claims

For an issue you wish to argue, try to make each kind of claim: fact, identity, value, cause or effect, value, and proposal.

PRACTICE 5.11 Discovering Evidence

For a claim you wish to make, predict the kinds of evidence you might research or actually do this research.

PRACTICE 5.12 Discovering Rhetorical Context

For a particular assignment, determine the rhetorical context: purpose, audience, structure, and style.

RESEARCHING

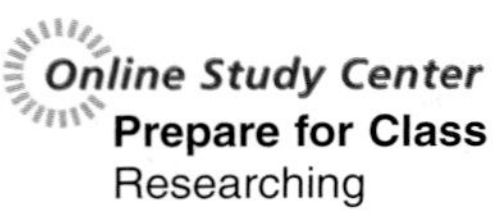

Prepare for Class
Researching

Primary Research Evidence is considered primary when it comes not from other researchers but rather from your own activities: experiences or discoveries made through field work such as in a lab, an archaeological dig, a survey, or an interview. Sometimes the best source of evidence is actual experience, such as eating particular foods over a period of time to understand a popular diet. Field excursions may be useful to get a sense of the real world. Some experiences can be vicarious or simulated, as when you attend a realistic war movie to get a sense of real combat. (For more information on primary research, see Chapter 8, Researching Arguments.)

PRACTICE 5.13 **Experiencing**

List experiences that are relevant to your argument. How practical are they in terms of your ability to attain them? Consider ways of acquiring and using personal experience to support an argument.

Secondary Research Secondary research involves gathering information from the experiences or studies of others. Print materials have long been the mainstay of researchers, but today researchers use a wide variety of sources, including audio recordings, visuals, and electronic texts. (For more information on secondary research see Chapter 8, Researching Arguments.)

PRACTICE 5.14 **Secondary Research: Searching Databases and Libraries**

Find an article, book, and Web source that are relevant to your issue or argument. Copy the bibliographic information, and write a brief summary of each source.

Organizing Materials

Once you have generated materials to use in an argument, you'll want to organize them in some way that makes sense. This exercise can help with the drafting that comes afterward. Organizing also enhances other planning techniques, perhaps revealing the need for more brainstorming, discovery, or research. In fact, some organization techniques do double duty by helping to generate material. Charts, clusters, diagrams, and outlines are all useful guides for organizing.

Online Study Center
Prepare for Class
Charts, Clusters, Diagrams, and Outlines

CHARTING

Writers sometimes create columns and rows to clarify the connections between parts of their argument. Charts typically use columns to show categories of information and rows to show relationships. The intersection of each column and row forms a box called a cell. Here are some possible headings for charts:

CLAIMS AND SUPPORT CHART

Claim ***Evidence*** ***Explanation***

PRO AND CON CHART

Reasons for ***Reasons against***

REBUTTAL CHART

Opposition ***Refutation***

A claims and support chart, for example, would state a claim in one cell. The supporting evidence would appear in an adjacent cell. A third cell could hold an explanation of the evidence. Because a claim may have more than one piece of supporting evidence, charts often need expansion or other modifications. Here is an example of a rebuttal chart:

Opposition	*Refutation*
Students are to blame for giving in to the temptation of an easy way to make a good grade.	*Some students may not know how plagiarism is wrong. They haven't had adequate ethical education.*
The instructor is to blame for not adequately training students in effective use of sources.	*It is less a matter of training by teachers and more a matter of students not applying themselves.*
The institution is to blame for not adequately informing students about policies against cheating.	*Most students already know that they should give credit to their sources. They must take responsibility for knowing the policies.*

DIAGRAMMING

Venn diagrams graphically depict how the elements of an argument are related. They show how much (or how little) two or more things (concepts, groups) have in common by depicting those elements as circles that are overlapping, enclosing each other, or separate. These diagrams often are used to explain logical syllogisms and are useful in conceptualizing a comparison and contrast argument. The following Venn diagram shows similarities and differences between plagiarism and theft.

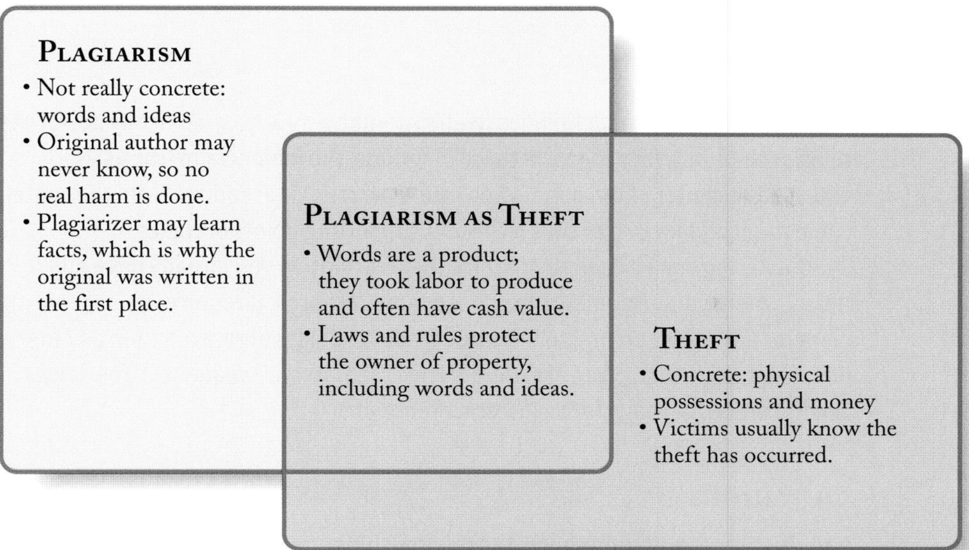

Plagiarism
• Not really concrete: words and ideas
• Original author may never know, so no real harm is done.
• Plagiarizer may learn facts, which is why the original was written in the first place.
Plagiarism as Theft
• Words are a product; they took labor to produce and often have cash value.
• Laws and rules protect the owner of property, including words and ideas.
Theft
• Concrete: physical possessions and money
• Victims usually know the theft has occurred.

A Venn diagram shows the relationships between things.

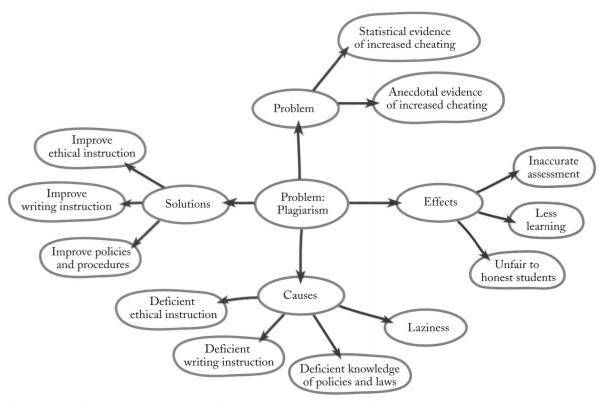

Statistical evidence of increased cheating
Anecdotal evidence of increased cheating
Problem
Improve ethical instruction
Improve writing instruction
Solutions
Problem: Plagiarism
Effects
Inaccurate assessment
Less learning
Unfair to honest students
Improve policies and procedures
Causes
Deficient ethical instruction
Laziness
Deficient writing instruction
Deficient knowledge of policies and laws

Clustering graphically organizes your supporting points.

CLUSTERING

Clustering and similar techniques (webbing, mapping) also graphically depict the relationships between ideas. In these diagrams, the major claim (thesis) is located in the center of the page, often inside a circle. Lines radiate from the center circle to secondary circles that represent supporting points or topics.

Clustering can be used to organize the information you already have and to reveal where your arguments may need more research. It requires no sequencing of major and minor points, so it is more flexible but less organized than an outline. Clusters, in fact, often are pre-outlines that later are sequenced formally. See the preceding page for a clustering template.

Framework for an Outline

I. First item
II. Second item
  A. Subitem
  B. Subitem
    1. Subsubitem
    2. Subsubitem
III. Third item

OUTLINING

Like clustering, outlining shows the relationships among the various parts of an argument. However, outlining sequences the parts, often labeling them with Roman numbers, uppercase and lowercase letters, Arabic numerals, and so on. A combination of letters, numbers, and indentation can distinguish major and supporting evidence and explanations. Following is a template for a possible outline:

Title (tentative): Curing Plagiarism

I. Introduction
  A. Problem: Increased plagiarism
    1. Anecdotal evidence of plagiarism (brief)
    2. Statistical evidence of plagiarism (brief)
  B. Current "solution" is ill informed and unfair.
    1. Places blame solely on students (brief statement)
    2. Present policies ignore some facts (brief statement)
  C. Thesis: A comprehensive and fair solution is needed
II. A problem really does exist (fuller support than introduction).
  A. Statistical evidence of increase in plagiarism
  B. Anecdotal evidence of plagiarism
  C. Expert testimony about plagiarism

III. Current views of the problem are one-sided.
   A. Places blame solely on students (fuller support)
   B. Present policies ignore some facts (fuller support)
IV. A more balanced view of the causes of plagiarism
   A. Students' responsibility for problem
   B. Instructors' responsibility for problem
   C. Administrators' responsibility for problem
V. Conclusion
   A. Students' responsibility to change
   B. Instructors' responsibility to change
   C. Administrators' responsibility to change

PRACTICE 5.15 **Organizing**

Create a chart, cluster, diagram, or outline that organizes your claims, evidence, and explanations.

Looking Back at Chapter 5

- Planning helps you divide a large, complex writing task into a series of smaller, simpler tasks. To plan well, you'll need to (1) understand the assignment, (2) generate material, and (3) organize.
- Some task-specific requirements may be mandated by an instructor, employer, or publisher: length, format, sources, and deadline. Other elements are based on the rhetorical context: purpose, audience, structure, and style.
- Generating techniques that help you gather claims and support before beginning to write include brainstorming, critical thinking, discussing, writing (freewriting, journaling, blogging), sketching, discovering, and researching.
- Organization techniques facilitate writing the first draft and enhance other planning techniques, perhaps revealing the need for more brainstorming, discovery, or research. Charts, clusters, diagrams, and outlines are useful forms of organizing.

Suggestions for Writing

- Create one or more journal entries on your own use of planning. If you already use planning techniques, what works for you and what doesn't? If you don't use these techniques, reflect on why you don't and which ones you might try in the future.
- If you don't already use planning techniques, experiment with them. Then write one or more journal entries reflecting on the results.
- Use planning techniques as you prepare for a writing assignment.

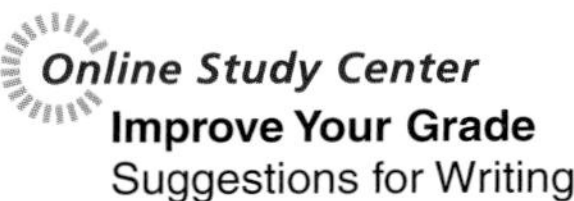

Improve Your Grade
Suggestions for Writing

Drafting Arguments

The word *compose* comes from root words meaning to "place into position" or "put together." Perhaps you are familiar with composing in the musical sense, the process of a musician putting together notes to make a melody. *Composing* also is a synonym for *drafting*, the process of a writer putting together words and the ideas they represent into a unified text—a composition.

Drafting rarely is a straightforward process proceeding sequentially from the first sentence to the conclusion. Experienced writers instead prefer to draft the parts they're clearest about first, in hopes that the other parts will become clearer as the whole takes shape. Sometimes the introduction is written last, because only when the drafting process is complete does the writer fully realize the argument being made.

> *The last thing one discovers in composing a work is what to put first.*
>
> —Blaise Pascal (1623–1662)

Online Study Center
This icon will direct you to content and resources on the website <college.hmco.com/pic/lamm1e>.

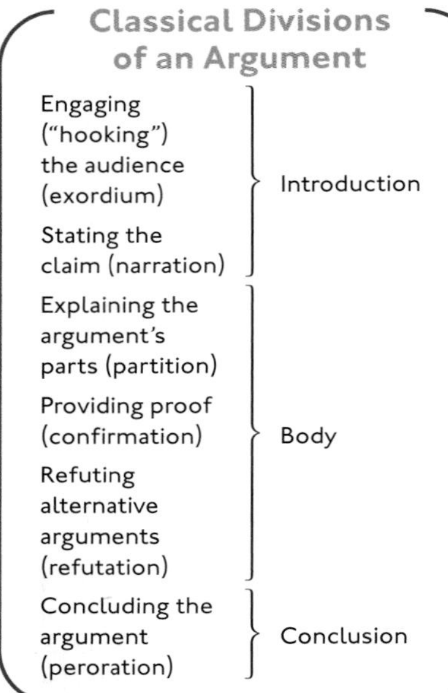

Classical Divisions of an Argument
Engaging ("hooking") the audience (exordium)
Stating the claim (narration)
Introduction
Explaining the argument's parts (partition)
Providing proof (confirmation)
Refuting alternative arguments (refutation)
Body
Concluding the argument (peroration)
Conclusion

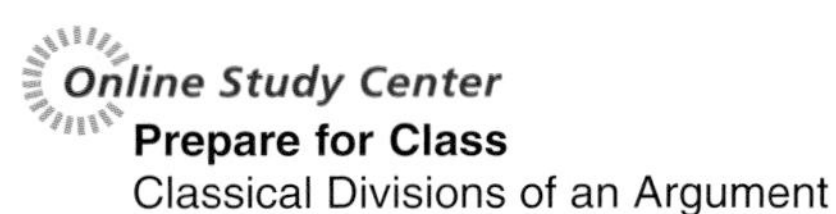

Structure of an Argument

An essay's overall structure consists of three major sections: (1) an introduction that provides a thesis statement or otherwise orients the reader toward a major claim, (2) a body consisting of paragraphs that break down the thesis into specific areas and treat each area in detail, and (3) a conclusion that provides closure. As you draft each section, you'll have to make a number of organizational decisions.

DRAFTING AN INTRODUCTION

When you meet a stranger in a social situation, an introduction is usually needed before any productive conversation can follow. Most people need a little warming up first, such as sharing interesting personal details and general background information, and perhaps finding a purpose for further conversation. When a reader picks up a composition, there is a similar need for warming up—to pique the reader's interest, establish an issue, and make a claim. An introduction to a composition accomplishes these goals by providing a hook, background information, and a thesis or major claim.

- A hook engages the reader's interest and establishes authority.
- Background information lets the reader understand the history, context, and importance of the claim.
- A major claim (an argumentative thesis) states or strongly implies what the author intends to argue. It is sometimes followed by a forecasting statement that partitions the argument into several points.

These three components may vary in the order they are presented and in the emphasis each receives: more, less, or none at all, depending on the relevance to the overall composition.

CLASSICAL DIVISIONS OF AN ARGUMENT

Classical, as we use the term in this book, refers to rhetoric that originated with the public speakers (called *orators*) of ancient Greece and Rome. These arguments, on which modern arguments largely are based, assign specific duties to what we today call the introduction, body, and conclusion. Roman orators such as Cicero (106–43 B.C.E.) argued that good public speaking consisted of five canons: invention, arrangement, style, memory, and delivery. The second of these canons, arrangement, indicates that the parts of a speech should follow a particular order:

1. Exordium (in which the topic is introduced)
2. Narration (in which the central claims and background are given)
3. Partition (in which the parts of the argument are outlined)
4. Confirmation (in which the proof is offered)
5. Refutation (in which contrary arguments are answered)
6. Peroration (in which the matter is concluded, or wrapped up)

It may help to think of the introduction as a "block of text" rather than as a paragraph. Even though it often lasts for only one paragraph, it can also be composed of two and occasionally even more paragraphs, depending on the length of each part. Introductions often are in proportion to the entire text. For example, very short writings might embed the introduction into the first body paragraph, often as the first sentence. Long compositions tend to have long introductions. In fact, books sometimes devote the entire first chapter to the introduction.

Hook

Background information

Major claim

A typical introduction contains a hook, background information, and major claim or thesis.

Drafting a Claim Regardless of which part of the composition you decide to draft, having the major claim written out and visible is essential to keeping yourself on the right track. As you draft your claim, test it by asking these questions:

- Is your claim really a claim? Does it take a position and argue a debatable issue?
- Does your claim fit your audience?
- Is your claim focused?

The Major Claim

An argumentative thesis or major claim can be structured in varying degrees of detail.

- A claim can be stated in a simple form:

  Smoking should be banned in public places.

- It can be associated with a reason explaining the "why" or "because" of it:

  To avoid exposing innocent bystanders to dangerous carcinogens, smoking should be banned in public places.

- Sometimes it may be accompanied by a forecasting statement that briefly announces the divisions of the topic to be covered:

  Smoking should be banned in public places because it endangers the health of nonsmokers, violates individual rights, is a hazard for children, and is a nuisance.

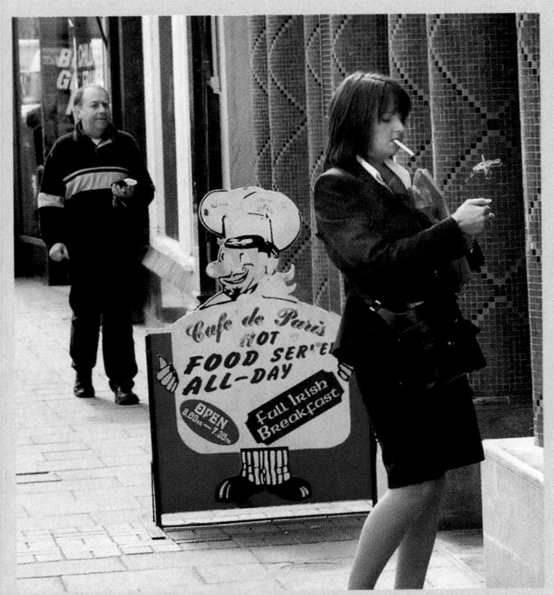

Smokers have been banned from most interior spaces, including most restaurants and bars. Should smoking be banned in all places where people gather? Why or why not?

Online Study Center
General Resources
Expository Writing

Is your claim really a claim? Is it intended to change the audience's opinions and actions on an issue? Or are you unintentionally writing for another purpose: to inform, to entertain, or to express your feelings? Novice writers sometimes drift into other, nonargumentative purposes.

- **Sometimes an argument shifts into expository writing.** An author may think that the audience needs to be led "inductively"—that is, the audience is shown the evidence before being told a conclusion or claim. Unfortunately, this practice often results in a rambling "for your information" download of loosely connected facts, with a brief concluding paragraph stating a claim more as an afterthought. Without the perspective of a claim, readers quickly begin to wonder, "What's the point?"

  > To decide whether to support stem-cell research, we should look at the facts.

  This thesis statement leads to facts that lack the perspective of a claim.

- **Sometimes an argument shifts strongly into self-expression.** When an author has strong emotions about an issue, those feelings may erupt into prose that is strong but rings with the wrong "tone of voice"—a strident ranting or perhaps a fawning tribute. Although this kind of writing can be cathartic for the writer, it can be unintentionally amusing for the reader.

  > It's high time we threw those lying politicians in jail!

  This thesis statement is more suggestive of mob violence than of reasoned action.

Does your claim fit your audience? Are you "preaching to the choir"—readers who already believe as you do—or are you "speaking a foreign language"—addressing readers whose beliefs are hopelessly different from yours? Adjust your claim to fit the audience, finding some practical goal worth arguing.

- **Adjust your claim when you face overwhelming skepticism.** For example, although you might not be able to convince an audience of scientists of the factuality of "creationism" or "intelligent design," you might be able to convince them that because this theory is accepted by some Americans, it should be taught in schools along with other theories of the origin of life.
- **Adjust your claim to address a predisposition of acceptance.** If, for example, you and your audience were already in agreement about the need to conduct stem-cell research, you could argue for a system of safeguards and accountability.

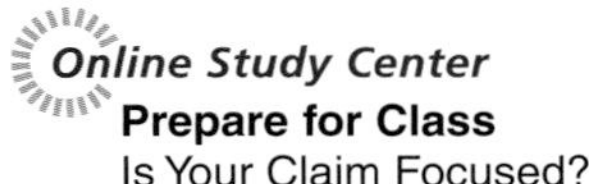
Prepare for Class
Is Your Claim Focused?

Is your claim focused? An overly broad claim weakens an argument. Novice writers understandably would rather deal with an excess of support rather than a shortage, but they often end up with a claim so broad that the composition says very little and consequently is dull to read. Readers often prefer to learn "a lot about a little" than a "little about a lot." This goal can be achieved by (1) focusing on only part of a problem rather than many aspects of it or (2) being more specific about details. Consider the following examples:

> BROAD, WITH SEVERAL PARTS
> Illegal immigration can be controlled by increased vigilance at the border and by strengthened punishment for illegal immigrants and their employers.
>
> FOCUSED, WITH FEWER PARTS
> The most effective way to decrease the number of illegal immigrants is to fine and imprison their employers.
>
> BROAD, WITH LESS-SPECIFIC DETAILS
> The government should ban gay marriage.
>
> FOCUSED, WITH MORE-SPECIFIC DETAILS
> Congress should pass a constitutional amendment defining marriage as a pact between one man and one woman.

Types of Claims

A major claim is an argument's thesis, the author's position on an issue. Below is a list of kinds of claims. (See Chapter 2 for more information about claims.)

- **Fact:** Is or was it real?
- **Identity:** What is it?
- **Cause and effect:** How and why does it work?
- **Value:** How is it judged?
- **Proposal:** Should something be done?

PRACTICE 6.1 Drafting Your Major Claim

Write out your major claim (argumentative thesis). As you draft your claim, test it by asking these questions:

1. Is your claim really a claim?
2. Does your claim fit your audience?
3. Is your claim focused?

Drafting the Background Information Rarely will a reader have all the prior knowledge needed to understand the issues at stake in your argument. In the introduction, your goal is to provide context, thereby helping the reader understand what the issue is, but without going into too much detail too early. The following suggestions and examples may help as you draft the background information for your introduction.

Online Study Center
Prepare for Class
Drafting Background Information

Emphasize the importance of an issue. By establishing the significance of the issue, the reader will be motivated to read on.

> Cheating in college is certainly not a new phenomenon. Underground paper mills, from which students can obtain previously prepared papers to be submitted as their own work, have existed for quite some time. However, with the growth of the Internet has come a concurrent of and explosive growth in the number of online paper mills, drastically increasing the accessibility of previously prepared term papers.
>
> —C. R. Campbell, C. O. Swift, and L. T. Denton, "Cheating Goes Hi-Tech"

Present a quotation relevant to the topic. Quotations can be intriguing, can contribute authority, and can hint at the angle your argument will take.

> Picasso once said, "A good artist borrows, a great artist steals." . . . Ask any writer, music composer, filmmaker, or designer and they'll tell you nothing is created in a vacuum, all ideas are drawn from outside inspiration. But the problem arises when you infringe on someone else's original work.
>
> —Atul Krakash, "So, Is It the Real Thing?"

Present one or more examples. Examples make the issue seem real.

> Last year, our college experienced a rash of cheating incidents that caused us to reevaluate how prepared we were to deal with academic dishonesty. Within two weeks after a seemingly isolated incident in which one of our professors discovered a student cheating on a written assignment, four separate incidents of academic dishonesty were reported in our online program, in outreach and community education, and in on-campus programs as well.
>
> —Karen Clos, "When Academic Dishonesty Happens on Your Campus"

Present interesting facts or statistics. Information your reader does not know can sometimes whet the reader's appetite for more.

> Academic dishonesty, which includes everything from wrongfully getting information by looking at a neighbor's test to plagiarizing information in a term paper, is a growing problem and concern for higher education. Several recent national surveys have found that more than half of all college students in the United States admit to some form of academic dishonesty, at least once during their college years. . . . Research shows a correlation between academic dishonesty and moral development (Barnett and Dalton 1981). That is, individuals with a higher level of moral development are less likely to be engaged in academic dishonesty because they consider that sort of behavior to be morally wrong.
>
> —Mohammed Y. A. Rawwas, Jamal A. Al-Khatib, and Scott J. Vitell, "Academic Dishonesty"

Pose a problem or a mystery. A problem or a mystery gives the issue significance while setting the stage for a solution.

> For years, management educators have learned the tricks of the trade for avoiding academic dishonesty by students by changing assignments from semester to semester and even requiring in-class writing assignments that could be used as samples and compared to writing done outside of class. However, the enhanced opportunities for academic dishonesty presented by online term paper mills raise the bar for management educators in devising assignments that circumvent the offerings of such term paper services.
>
> —Jeffrey Mello, "Commentary on 'Cheating Goes Hi-Tech'"

Briefly explain the issue's history. History can put an issue in context.

> The Internet was still a toddler in the late 1990s. Today, it's a juggernaut. In the last five years, instances of plagiarism from webpages have grown perhaps just as rapidly as the Internet itself. In fact, some sites even boast "original" essays for sale.
>
> —Jennifer Kabbany, "Educators: Digital Plagiarism Rampant"

Dramatize. Make an issue come to life by providing a real-life story or example or by creating a believable scenario or hypothetical situation.

> Imagine a student who had never cheated before, who works hard and sincerely wants to learn and to better herself. This semester, however, she has taken on far too much work. She can't possibly write all the required research papers in the time by the end of the term. Her GPA hangs in the balance, as does her scholarship and her future. Panicking, she turns to what she sees as her last resort: an online paper mill that will provide what she needs—an instant essay.
>
> —Sam Nguyen, "The Temptation of Instant Essays"

Pose one or more questions. Questions that are related to your argument can pique readers' interest and help forecast the answers you will reveal.

> What is the relationship between academic dishonesty and workplace dishonesty? If a student is prone to cheating in college, will that same student be prone to cheating in the workplace?
>
> —Sarath Nonis and Cathy Swift, "An Examination of the Relationship Between Academic Dishonesty and Workplace Dishonesty"

Define a key concept. A definition can provide good background. However, opening with "According to *Webster's Dictionary*" is a very weak hook.

> Indeed, there are many ways to misrepresent the truth. Part of the problem is that not everyone agrees on the definition of lying. Lying by omission, for

example, is a form of passive deceit because a person is withholding information or not volunteering the truth. . . . Plagiarism is another form of lying. Plagiarism is a form of "literary theft," of which I would be guilty, if I didn't tell you that I copied that phrase from the *Merriam-Webster Dictionary*.

—Michael Angelo Caruso, "There Are Many Types of Lies"

Present an analogy. An analogy helps a reader understand a new issue by comparing it to something more familiar.

The 1960s gave us, among other mind-altering ideas, a revolutionary new metaphor for our physical and chemical surroundings: the biosphere. But an even more momentous change is coming. Emerging technologies are causing a shift in our mental ecology, one that will turn our culture into the plagiosphere, a closing frontier of ideas.

—Ed Tenner, "Rise of the Plagiosphere"

Present various sides of the issue. Briefly citing several selected sources can show a range of opinions and the extent of differences.

The ease of use of the Internet technology is the number one factor blamed for the increase in academic cheating (Decamp 2001). Another factor is an increasing number of digital paper mills mushrooming on the Internet such as Buyapapers.com . . . , Term Papers & Term Papers, . . . and Term Papers Amazon.

—Apiwan D. Born, "How to Reduce Plagiarism"

PRACTICE 6.2 Drafting Your Background Information

With your major claim in mind, write an introduction that includes background information. You may wish to experiment with the models presented earlier in this chapter.

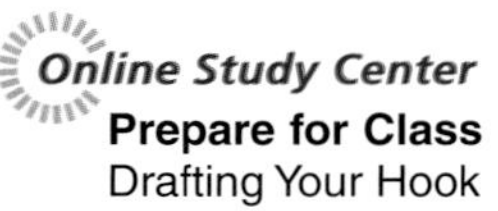

Drafting Your Hook In some ways, the beginning of an essay is the most important part. If the audience members are not engaged immediately, they may never read the rest of the text. A hook is a technique or trick you use to grab your reader's interest. Of course, the title itself is the first chance you have to catch a reader's attention. Once past the title, a reader will decide very soon whether the text is worth pursuing.

In a typical introduction to a college essay, the hook may or may not be distinguishable from the introduction as a whole, especially when the background information is interesting or when the claim is provocative. However, even in a short piece of writing, the first few sentences can be critical. Consider this opening line from David Glenn's article, "Judge or Judge Not?":

> In an ideal world, academe would respond to plagiarism allegations with a sure and swift machinery of justice.

This sentence conveys context—"academe," "plagiarism allegations"—while hinting at frightening, even harsh consequences—"sure and swift machinery of justice." A reader might read on purely for the information, but also might be enticed by the suspense of impending punishment or even by residual guilt from, shall we say, personal plagiaristic indiscretions.

PRACTICE 6.3 Understanding Hooks

Below are the opening lines from the models of background information presented earlier in this chapter. How well do they "hook" you? Why do they work or not work?

1. "Cheating in college is certainly not a new phenomenon."
2. "Picasso once said, 'A good artist borrows, a great artist steals.'"
3. "Last year, our college experienced a rash of cheating incidents that caused us to reevaluate how prepared we were to deal with academic dishonesty."
4. "Academic dishonesty, which includes everything from wrongfully getting information by looking at a neighbor's test to plagiarizing information in a term paper, is a growing problem and concern for higher education."
5. "For years, management educators have learned the tricks of the trade for avoiding academic dishonesty by students by changing assignments from semester to semester and even requiring in-class writing assignments that could be used as samples and compared to writing done outside of class."
6. "The Internet was still a toddler in the late 1990s. Today, it's a juggernaut."
7. "Imagine a student who had never cheated before, who works hard and sincerely wants to learn and to better herself. This semester, however, . . . "
8. "What is the relationship between academic dishonesty and workplace dishonesty?"
9. "Indeed, there are many ways to misrepresent the truth."
10. "The 1960s gave us, among other mind-altering ideas, a revolutionary new metaphor for our physical and chemical surroundings—the biosphere."
11. "The ease of use of the Internet technology is the number one factor blamed for the increase in academic cheating."

PRACTICE 6.4 **Drafting Your Hook**

Examine one of your own introductory paragraphs. Will it catch a reader's interest? Revise your writing, experimenting with alternative hooks.

PRACTICE 6.5 **Analyzing Introductions**

Read the two introductory text blocks below, and locate their parts. Place brackets around the hooks, and underline the claims. Which parts do you find the most compelling? Why? In what way(s) could they compel an audience to read the rest of the argument?

The growth of academic dishonesty is discouraging to faculty, administrators, and ethical students. Faculty, in particular, are often wary of spending time and resources on educating college and university students about academic dishonesty. Administrators, too, are well aware of the costs imposed on the institution by dishonest behavior. And the ethical student knows that rampant cheating can devalue a college degree. But if institutions are to fully educate their students in honesty as well as in particular content areas, they should work to create an ethical campus climate where the rewards of ethical conduct may be as great as mastery of any program of study. Only when institutions treat ethics as an essential element of all conduct—at school, at work, and in personal lives—will students see the importance of infusing ethics in their academic conduct.

—MELANIE STALLINGS WILLIAMS and WILLIAM R. HOSEK, *Strategies for Reducing Academic Dishonesty*

This spring, Jerry Ceppos, vice president for news at Knight Ridder, finished his term as president of the organization that accredits journalism schools. In a speech at the April 30 meeting of the Accrediting Council on Education in Journalism and Mass Communications, Ceppos ticked off a list of plagiarism cases that had cropped up at newspapers over the previous year. They ranged from student papers at the universities of Virginia and Kansas to the *Hartford Courant* and *Milwaukee Journal Sentinel* to *USA Today* and the *New York Times*. "If any outside poked his or her head in this room," Ceppos said, "the first question would obviously be, 'What are you doing about this epidemic of ethical problems in journalism?'"

—JEFF SOUTH, *"Ethics in the Classroom"*

PRACTICE 6.6 **Drafting Introductions**

For an issue that concerns you, draft an introduction that contains a hook, background information, and statement of your major claim.

SHOULD I WRITE MY INTRODUCTION FIRST?

The writing process is both situational and personal: You have your own habits and techniques that must be adapted to different kinds of assignments. You may be comfortable working from beginning to end, or you may prefer to move back and forth through the text as you draft. Here are a few pointers to help you craft your own individual style:

- After planning your argument, write your claim first. Put it on a piece of paper and tape it to the top of your computer screen or in some other visible position. Its presence may serve as a reminder to help you keep your essay focused and on task.
- Don't write your introduction first if you don't feel ready to do so. Jump into the body of the essay after you have figured out your basic organizational strategy.
- Decide how you want to organize your paper—what your main points will be, how you will refute the opposition's arguments, and so on—before you jump into your text. This will save you time reorganizing your text later on.
- If you are composing and the work just isn't moving along, you may need to return to the planning process, generating and organizing material. Do you need to construct a more detailed outline? Would writing out your supporting points help?

DRAFTING THE BODY

The body of a composition consists of paragraphs that support the major claim with reasons in the form of evidence and explanations. Sometimes you can comfortably develop one reason per paragraph; at other times, you can devote several paragraphs to one reason or several reasons to one paragraph. This choice depends entirely upon the volume of evidence and the amount of explanation it needs.

A paragraph has its own unity of purpose that may be either expressed as a topic sentence or implied strongly by the evidence and explanations. As you draft the body, you'll have options about how to arrange the topic sentences and reasons within paragraphs.

Placing Topic Sentences Topic sentences can appear anywhere within a paragraph. For the sake of illustration, we will highlight four paragraph structures:

Online Study Center
Prepare for Class
Placing Topic Sentences

- **Topic at top:** You start with the supporting point (topic sentence) and follow up by supplying the details that will convince the reader that the claim is valid.
- **Topic at bottom:** You work through the details first, which allows the reader to accept the claim that is presented at the end as a sort of concluding sentence.
- **Topic delayed:** You delay the claim by "easing into" a paragraph with a sentence or so of transitional material. Sometimes the topic sentence may not appear until the middle of the paragraph.

TOP TOPIC

Topic or supporting claim

Evidence

Discussion

BOTTOM TOPIC

Evidence

Discussion

Topic or supporting claim

DELAYED TOPIC

Transition

Topic or supporting claim

Evidence

Discussion

IMPLIED TOPIC

Evidence

Discussion

A body paragraph's topic sentence can appear in different locations.

- **Topic implied:** Sometimes you might choose to not state the purpose of a block of text, but leave it for the reader to figure out. This approach can be very effective if the block is well written, but can lead to confusion if it is not.

No method is superior to all of the others. In fact, if you study the readings in Part 2 of this book, you will see that many writers mix all of these approaches to organization.

PRACTICE 6.7 Placing the Topic Sentence

Read the excerpts and then answer the following questions:

1. Which paragraph places the topic at the top? At the bottom? As a delayed topic? As an implied topic?
2. Which paragraph did you find the most engaging to read? The most convincing? Why?
3. Which strategy did you find the most effective? Explain.
4. What point is the final paragraph trying to make?

Excerpt A

Although slenderness is only a look, an image presumably of beauty, it is frankly a narrow stereotype that functions as a badge or token for an accompanying ideology. In America, thinness is a socially recognized sign, for class status, sexuality, grace, discipline, and "being good," whereas fat is now a categorical derogative for those stigmatized as stupid, sick, self-indulgent, neurotic, lazy, sad, bad, and invariably ugly. All such associations, images, and prejudices have coalesced into a modern image of good looks, physical size, and social consequences—a body of culturally specific beliefs that both reflect and reinforce the sexual, racial, and economic politics of the time.

—Jane Caputi and Susan Nance, *"One Size Does Not Fit All: Being Beautiful, Thin, and Female in America"*

Excerpt B

Like the peoples of the nation whose values he defends, Superman is an alien, but not just any alien. He's the consummate and totally uncompromised alien, an immigrant whose visible difference from the norm is underscored by his decision to wear a costume of bold primary colors so tight as to be his very skin. Moreover, Superman the alien is real. He stands out among the host of comic book characters (Batman is a good example) for whom the superhero role is like a mask assumed when needed, a costume worn over their real identities as normal Americans. Superman's powers—strength, mobility, X-ray vision, and the like—are the comic-book equivalents of ethnic characteristics, and they protect and preserve the vitality of the foster community in which he lives in the same way that immigrant ethnicity has sustained American culture linguistically, artistically, economically, politically, and spiritually. The myth of Superman asserts with total confidence and a childlike innocence the value of the immigrant in American culture.

—Gary Engle, *"What Makes Superman So Darned American?"*

(continued)

Excerpt C

What does Michael Jackson's appearance suggest about his attitude toward life? Is it healthy or unhealthy? What makes you think this?

"Proud and insolent youth," said Hook, "prepare to meet thy doom." "Dark and sinister man," Peter answered, "have at thee." And it is this epic battle that so characterized J. M. Barrie's quirky novel and play that Michael Jackson has dramatized as the mortal conflict of celebrity itself: the bright possibility of one's youth fighting against the corruption and compromises of age. It is a sign of our flawed heroism and our majestic immaturity as a public that we accept the battle of our cultural mythmaking in such distorted terms. But Peter Pan is a basic myth of Western life, not the neurotic fantasy of a middle-aged pop singer who didn't want to die before he got old and who didn't want to get old either.

—GERALD EARLY, *"Never-Never Land"*

Excerpt D

Thursday nights my parents went bowling, and we kids stayed home alone. It was the night of Gene Roddenberry's original *Star Trek,* and the program made a big impression on me. I came to accept its notion that humans had a future in space, Western-style, with big heroes and adventures. Roddenberry's vision of the centuries to come was one with strong moral values, embodied in codes like the Prime Directive: to not interfere in the development of less technologically advanced civilizations. This had an incredible appeal to me; ethical humans, not robots, dominated the future, and I took Roddenberry's dream as a part of my own.

—BILL JOY, *Why the Future Doesn't Need Us*

EVIDENCE

Whenever you make a claim, a skeptical audience will require proof that it is true or reasons to accept it—in short, evidence. (For more on evidence, see Chapter 3, Support.) Evidence comes in the following forms:

Anecdotes: Narrate or describe real-life accounts of situations or events that have happened to you or to others.

Expert opinions: Quote, paraphrase, or summarize the opinion of an expert or experts on an issue.

Facts and statistics: Provide evidence that an audience will accept at face value.

History: Tell what happened in the past if it is relevant to the present or the future.

Scenario: Produce hypothetical or fictionalized accounts that dramatize typical or possible situations.

Specific examples: Offer a sampling of evidence to represent a larger body of evidence.

Organizing Evidence When you present evidence in an argument, it cannot stand alone. No bit of data is self-evident. It must be explained to establish its validation of the truth of the claim. The explanation of evidence within a block of text is typically organized in one of two ways:

- The *point-by-point method* discusses the evidence one piece at a time. This approach is useful when each piece of evidence needs its own explanation.
- The *block method* is used either when one piece of evidence is followed by several explanations or when several pieces of evidence can be lumped together and explained once.

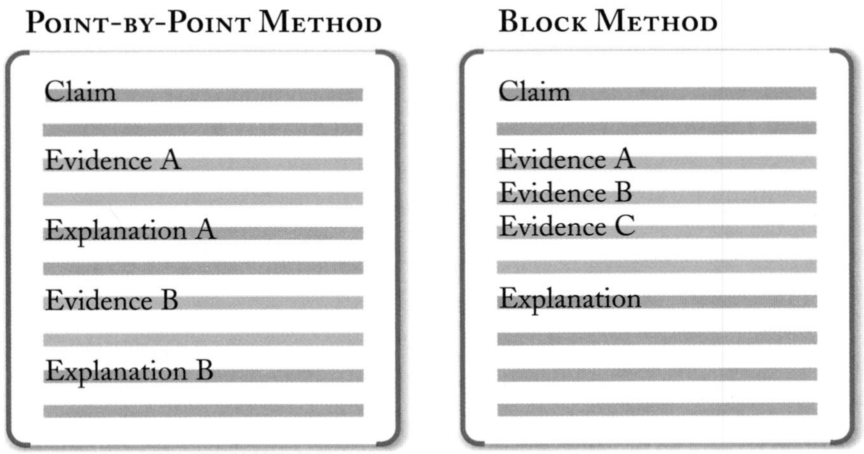

Point-by-Point Method	Block Method
Claim	Claim
Evidence A	Evidence A
Explanation A	Evidence B
Evidence B	Evidence C
Explanation B	Explanation

Evidence and explanations can be presented point by point or separated into blocks.

Online Study Center
Prepare for Class
Bloom's Taxonomy

EXPLAINING EVIDENCE

Evidence almost always needs some kind of explanation or discussion to strengthen its connection to the claim. The kinds of explanations below are based on a list of thought processes known as "Bloom's taxonomy." (For more on explaining evidence, see Chapter 3, Support.)

Clarification (knowledge): Restate to make sure the evidence is understood. Paraphrase, summary, and emphasis help clarify evidence.

Interpretation (comprehension): Speculate on its significance. Evidence often requires an interpreter who can "read between the lines" and put it into perspective.

Application: Explain how the evidence applies. Application can show the connection between evidence and claim when the relationship isn't immediately clear.

Analysis: Explain the parts. Analysis divides a whole into its parts and explains how they work separately and in unison.

Synthesis: Relate it to other claims or other forms of evidence. Synthesis brings two or more arguments together, allowing for comparison/contrast, rebuttal, or an accumulation of mutually supporting points.

Evaluation: Explain its value. Evaluation is a kind of qualification, explaining how applicable the evidence is to the claim or how reliable and accurate it is.

PRACTICE 6.8 Organizing Evidence and Explanations

Read the excerpt from Lawrence Shames's book *The Hunger for More,* and then answer the following questions. The claim has been underlined, and the evidence bracketed.

1. What method does Shames use in organizing and explaining his evidence? Why do you think he used this method? Is it convincing? Why or why not?
2. What kind of evidence (statistics, facts, case study, and so on) does Shames use? Should he have used a different type? Why do you think so?
3. Do you agree with Shames's claim? Are we running out of "more"? Why do you think so?

The country is not running out of wealth, drive, savvy, or opportunities. We are not facing imminent ruin, and neither panic nor gloom is called for. But there have been ample indications over the past two decades that we are running out of more.

(continued)

Consider productivity growth—according to many economists, the single most telling and least distortable gauge of changes in real wealth. [From 1947 to 1965, productivity in the private sector (adjusted, as are all the following figures, for inflation) was advancing, on average, by an annual 3.3 percent.] This means, simply, that each hour of work performed by a specimen American worker contributed 3.3 cents worth or more to every American dollar every year; whether we saved it or spent it, that increment went into a national kitty of ever-enlarging aggregate wealth. [Between 1965 and 1972, however, the "more factor" decreased to 2.4 percent a year, and from 1972 to 1977 it slipped further, to 1.6 percent. By the early 1980s, the number productivity growth was at a virtual standstill, crawling along at 0.2 percent for the five years ending in 1982.] Through the middle years of the 1980s, the numbers rebounded somewhat—but by then the gains were being neutralized by the gargantuan carrying costs on the national debt.

—LAURENCE SHAMES, *"The More Factor"*

PRACTICE 6.9 Organizing Evidence

Using the same evidence, rewrite Shames's paragraph using a different organizational strategy.

PRACTICE 6.10 Drafting Body Paragraphs

For an issue that concerns you, draft a body paragraph that contains a topic sentence, evidence, and explanation.

PROVIDING EVIDENCE

While drafting, you must decide what kind of evidence is needed and how much to use. (See Chapter 3, Support, for more about evidence.) As a rule, provide evidence that is sufficient, relevant, and appealing:

Sufficient: Use only the minimum amount of information you need to establish the truth value of your claim, and no more.

Relevant: Use only evidence that supports your claim; avoid anything that "sort of" or "might" support your claim. If the relationship between evidence and claim is blurry to you, it will be even more blurry to your readers.

Appealing: Use evidence that will be received sympathetically by your readers. Avoid sources or types of evidence they might not respect or might find offensive.

Arguments and Alternative Arguments The body of an argument argues for a major claim not only by supporting it with reasons (evidence and explanations), but also by rebutting significant alternative arguments.

As your readers consider your argument, they may think of positions and claims that contradict the point you are seeking to prove. These positions contrary to your own are sometimes called *opposition arguments* or *alternative arguments*. The process of neutralizing them is called *refutation* or *rebuttal*. It is important for you to recognize these opposing positions and either (1) neutralize them by explaining their weaknesses, (2) show your claim to be better, or (3) propose a compromise.

Refutation can be vital to a successful argument. There are four ways to organize the refutation of alternative arguments:

- *Early refutation* deals with alternative arguments shortly after the introduction or within the introduction.
- *Late refutation* deals with alternative arguments in a separate section near or in the conclusion.
- *Occasional refutation* deals with alternative arguments as they become relevant to topics within the body of the composition.
- *Complete refutation* deals with alternative arguments as the chief purpose of the composition. Typically, this approach entails a point-by-point organization.

Early refutation Early refutation meets the opposition "head on," listing and usually discussing the alternative arguments in the early paragraphs and sometimes even in the introduction. Writers who opt for early refutation do so for several reasons:

- When an audience is clearly aware of opposing claims—perhaps even sympathetic to them—there is a danger that readers will resist your own claims until their doubts are allayed. Early acknowledgment of alternative arguments can remove these doubts or at least put your audience in a more receptive frame of mind.
- Acknowledging the opposition is a way to establish your own credibility, your *ethos*. You let the audience know not only that you have done your homework but also that your argument will not be one-sided. The audience will pick up clues from the tone of your writing style about how fairly you will treat the opposition.

- Introductions and early paragraphs often are used to establish the context of an issue, so identifying alternative arguments may be essential for clarifying the purpose and major claims of your composition.

Late refutation. Sometimes writers postpone dealing with alternative arguments until the conclusion of the composition. This tactic has advantages for some purposes and some audiences:

- When an audience is unaware of the opposing arguments, the composition can become bogged down by introducing topics that have to then be dismissed before proceeding to your major claim.
- When an audience is aware of the opposing arguments but either is unconcerned by them or is sympathetic and receptive toward your claims, the refutation can be delayed.

Sometimes you cannot directly discredit or diminish the opposition. In fact, sometimes the opposition claim is not only valid but also appealing. In such cases, refutation does not occur in the literal sense of the word *refute*, which means "to prove something is false or in error." Instead, the alternative argument is neutralized by presenting your claim as being better than the rival claim. You offer the audience the greater of two goods; it is like concluding, "Now that you've seen my claim, isn't it better than my opposition's claim?"

Occasional refutation Sometimes you may decide that it is more advantageous to refute alternative arguments as the need arises. This method offers several advantages:

- Many arguments incorporate a number of claims, but not all of these claims have opposing claims needing refutation. Opposing arguments can occur anywhere in the body of your composition, whenever the occasion (the topic) calls for dealing with opposing views.
- Some arguments and opposing arguments have symmetry—for every pro, there is con; for every point, there is a counterpoint. A point-by-point organization can pair up each claim with an opposing claim, perhaps in the same paragraph or in juxtaposed paragraphs. For example, suppose that you have decided to argue in favor of the legalization of medical marijuana. Your opposing argument might line up with the opposition's argument something like this:

POINT / COUNTERPOINT

Introduction
Forecast (optional)
(1) Refutation
(1) Argument
(2) Refutation
(2) Argument
(3) Refutation
(3) Argument
Conclusion

Point and counterpoint organization.

	Opposition's Argument	*Your Argument*
MAJOR CLAIM	Medical marijuana should not be legal.	Medical marijuana should be legal.
SUPPORTING POINT	It has no legitimate medical application.	It is used to treat cancer, multiple sclerosis, glaucoma, eating disorders, and chronic pain.
SUPPORTING POINT	It is a gateway drug that leads to harder drugs.	It is nonaddictive and less habit-forming than most prescription drugs.
SUPPORTING POINT	There are other legitimate drugs to treat the illnesses marijuana would treat.	In some cases, when other therapies have failed, marijuana is the only alternative.

Such a research paper would likely have the structure shown in the figure on the left.

Complete refutation. Your argument can be structured completely as a reaction to an opposing argument while not offering an alternative argument of your own. Sometimes it is important enough to expose a misconception or to advise against a course of action. Your argument would be saying, basically, "I don't know what the solution is to Problem X, but I know the opposition's solution is wrong." For example, you might give reasons why a U.S. embargo on Cuban products is an unwise policy without proposing your own plan for discouraging that dictatorship.

DRAFTING THE CONCLUSION

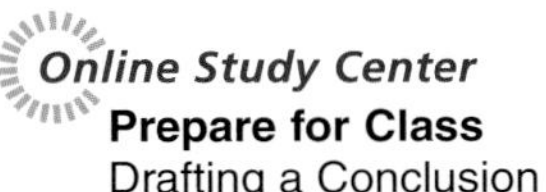

Online Study Center
Prepare for Class
Drafting a Conclusion

Conclusions, like introductions, are specialized paragraphs. They let the readers know that the essay is coming to an end and remind them of the main idea of the essay. A writer will often remind the readers of the thesis and sometimes summarize the main points of the essay. In arguments, the conclusion is usually the place to mention the major claim (thesis statement) again and to summarize some of the topics or supporting points that made up the body of the piece.

If you have difficulty concluding your composition, consider these three techniques: (1) revisit the claim, (2) summarize the supporting points, and/or (3) offer a final parting statement. The first two techniques are relatively easy to understand. Sometimes the third is not. The parting statement may be thought of as the reverse of the hook that you used initially to gain the reader's attention and give some hint of the topic. Like the hook, the parting statement casts a wide net, but is intended to "ease" the reader out of the topic. It is like a train slowing down to let you off at your stop.

Here are some points to remember when writing a conclusion:

- Write the conclusion only after you know the final shape of your essay.
- Restate your claim, but don't quote it verbatim from the introduction.
- The claim can appear anywhere within the conclusion. When it appears at the bottom, it may serve as the parting statement.
- Summarize the most important supporting points, but don't make the conclusion read like a staccato-like laundry list. Some writers will restate their response to an alternative argument before reintroducing their overall claim.
- Use transitional words and phrases.
- End with a general statement related to your topic. In most cases, it will be broader than your claim.

PRACTICE 6.11 Working with Conclusions

Read the concluding paragraphs and then answer the following questions. Major claims have been underlined. Supporting points have been bracketed, and parting statements surrounded with angle brackets.

1. Which conclusion did you like the best? Why?
2. One of the paragraphs is inductive (moving from specific to general); the other is deductive (moving from general to specific). Which is which? What are the strengths and weaknesses of each approach?
3. How does the anecdote about Cleanth Brooks help transition into McCrellis's claim? What does this story imply? (*Hint:* What are the similarities between Brooks's situation and Eminem's situation?)
4. McCrellis does not summarize the supporting points from his article. Is this approach effective or ineffective? Explain.

Excerpt A

Ultimately, the legitimization of pseudoscientific research and paranormal phenomena by trusted news sources cannot occur without the simultaneous devaluation of science and reason. If the trend continues, the American public will be left with two disconcerting options: [(1) They can learn to distrust the information provided by mainstream news sources; or (2) They can learn to readily accept scientifically baseless claims as provided by mainstream news sources.] <The implications are profound.>

—Shari Waxman, *"Mind Over Media: How the News Legitimizes the Paranormal and Why It Matters"*

(continued)

Excerpt B

I once asked the late Cleanth Brooks, professor of English at Yale University and proponent of the New Criticism, why the literary theory that he and Robert Penn Warren had so enthusiastically promoted in the 1950s and '60s had come under such sharp attack in the 1980s and '90s. He said to me, "I don't know. All we ever wanted was to show what made literature good." I suspect that neither Brooks nor Warren, were they alive today, would be fans of Eminem, but they most certainly would be interested in how his poems managed to have such a popular appeal. It could be the case that Eminem is simply the next stage in America's cultural and intellectual decline. However, I don't think so. As an artist, Eminem may be mischievous, but he is no fool. Perhaps one good thing that will result from putting his lyrics under the microscope is that hip-hop will finally be recognized as a culturally diverse and artistically sophisticated musical genre. <Someday, perhaps, even the artists themselves will get the respect they deserve from academics as well.>

—M. P. McCRELLIS, *"Why Eminem Is Important"*

The Five-Paragraph Theme

The three major parts of an essay are the introduction, body, and conclusion, and the number of paragraphs in each part can vary. Sometimes, however, instructors will specify how many paragraphs you should write for a particular essay assignment. The traditional "five-paragraph theme" is an essay that includes the following parts:

- **Introduction:** An introductory paragraph includes a thesis statement.
- **Body:** Each of the three body paragraphs has a topic sentence followed by some minor points.
- **Conclusion:** A conclusion paragraph draws the previous four paragraphs together.

This template or pattern often works well for an essay of approximately 250 words, but one size doesn't fit all. Sometimes the five-paragraph theme forces you to invent or ignore points to fit the three paragraphs that are prescribed for the theme's body. Ideally, a writer should adapt the structure to fit the argument and not the argument to fit the structure.

Tying It All Together

Readers expect precision and unity in any kind of writing. In part, this is accomplished through a thesis and topic sentences. In addition, writers use qualifiers and transitions to smooth out the flow of words.

Using Qualifiers

By their very nature, claims tend to be accompanied by a degree of uncertainty. Arguers often must qualify their claims by (1) explaining under which circumstances the claim is true or (2) estimating the probability that a claim is true.

Circumstantial Qualifiers Some claims apply only under certain circumstances. For example, you might claim that certain Homeland Security measures or parts of the Patriot Act should apply only during times of "high terror alert." In the following excerpt, the qualifier is underlined:

> It remains true that there are legitimate and honorable forms of love other than marriage. . . . In the current climate, it becomes imperative to affirm the reality and beauty of sexually chaste relationships.
>
> —"Morality and Homosexuality," *Wall Street Journal* editorial

Probability Qualifiers So many things in life are unknown, but decisions still must be made based on our "best guess." Sometimes you can find statistical data that will give you a numerical estimate of probability. At other times, you'll have to offer verbal qualifiers ranging from long explanations to simple adjectives such as *possibly, sometimes, potentially,* or *probably*.

Qualifiers

Qualifiers describe the limits of a claim. Below are some examples:

absolutely	occasionally
probably	always
possibly	sometimes
most of the time	as a rule
seldom	typically
regularly	hardly ever
never	potentially
usually	tentatively
generally	often
least	frequently

Using Transitions

Readers appreciate when you help them see how the parts of a composition relate to each other. You do this in part by directly stating the relationships in your thesis and topic sentences and in part by showing the relevance of your evidence. In addition,

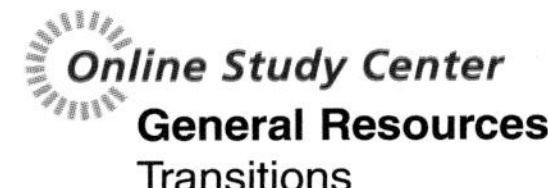

TRANSITIONS

Addition: again, also, and, as well, besides, in addition, furthermore, moreover

Cause and effect: accordingly, because, consequently, since, so, therefore, thus

Clarification: i.e., in other words, that is to say, to put it another way

Concession: granted that, naturally, of course, to be sure

Comparison: by the same token, comparably, in the same way, likewise, similarly

Contrast: but, conversely, however, in spite of, nevertheless, on the other hand

Emphasis: by all means, certainly, indeed, in fact, no doubt, of course, surely

Illustration: e.g., for example, for instance, specifically, to demonstrate

Purpose: in order that, in order to, intending to, so that

Sequence: finally, first (second, and so on), then, next, numbered list (1., 2., and so on)

Space: above, adjacent, adjoining, beyond, far, here, near, there

Summary: briefly, in conclusion, in the final analysis, to summarize, to sum up

Time: after, before, immediately, later, meanwhile, occasionally, soon you can use transitions—that is, words or phrases that state how the parts are related. Without transitions, your reader may have to work harder to understand how sentences or whole paragraphs relate to each other and to the thesis.

Consider, for example, one of the most frequently used transitions in this book: "for example." It signals that something concrete will illustrate a generality. In addition, consider the transitional phrase "in addition." It signals that you are being given an additional example. You get the idea.

PRACTICE 6.12 Using Transitions to Achieve Coherence

Read the following excerpts. Transitional words and phrases have been underlined.

Excerpt A

The origins of the success myth can be traced back to the days of our country's first settlement. The private diaries and journals of some of the New World's first settlers as well as their public accounts for the folks back home can quickly confirm this. For a long time, Europeans had dreamed of a "brave new world" which would offer them freedom from the oppression of a largely feudal system where a few profited from the ownership of land while the many worked the land hard and reaped only minimal fruits for their labor. And because of the unified religious tradition in Europe at the time, these longings began to shape themselves around the Biblical story of the Garden of Eden, that paradise where the first humans had been perfectly in tune because they were uncorrupted by sin and lived harmoniously with nature. Influenced by their economic and political longings as well as their Christian education, many of the first explorers and settlers of the new land sent back to Europe accounts which tended to confirm that the American continent might indeed be a New Eden.

—MADONNA MARSDEN, *"The American Myth of Success"*

Excerpt B

But it's wishful thinking to suppose that we can have good schools without paying teachers good salaries. Comparisons to the good old days ignore the fact that times have changed. Back then, low wages could secure top talent because half the population was restricted to just two or three jobs, one of which was teaching. The best still had to compete to be teachers, and only the best of the best got in. Today, potential teachers—men or women—have so many other options that it's the teaching profession that must compete, against other lines of work, to reel in the top talents. Otherwise, instead of teaching, those top talents might choose to be . . . Well, let's see: police officers, accountants, department store buyers, architects, computer systems analysts, engineers, attorneys, professors, or doctors, for example.

—TAMIM ANSARY, *Are Teachers Overpaid?*

(continued)

Excerpt C

Spurious gender difference is maintained and rewarded in bodybuilding through the discriminatory valorization of certain aesthetic categories. Indeed, bodybuilding tries to limit the achievements of female physique athletes by adding "femininity" to the list of aesthetic categories they are expected to fulfill. The film *Pumping Iron II: The Women* (1985) dramatically documents this sexism by recording a conflict which erupts in a sequestered conference room among those judging the 1983 "Miss Olympia" (now the "Ms. Olympia"), America's most prestigious bodybuilding competition for women. A man apparently serving his first stint as judge is puzzled and angry to find that he is supposed to judge the women on the basis of their "femininity." He points out to the other, more experienced judges that, while the men are ranked on the basis of their muscle density, definition, over-all symmetry, and proportionality, as well as for the style, skill, and fluidity of their posing, the women are in addition judged for a quality called "femininity" which surreptitiously but effectively limits all the others. How, this judge queries, is anyone supposed to determine how muscular a woman's body can be before it ceases to be feminine? Furthermore, in what other sport could a female competitor be expected to limit her achievement for fear of losing her proper gender?

—Marcia Ian, *"From Abject to Object: Women's Body Building"*

Discuss these excerpts in a small group or in a class discussion and respond to the following questions:

1. How are the transitions in the three paragraphs similar and/or different? How often are they used in each case? Are there places where transitions do not appear where you think they are needed? Explain.
2. Do the transitions seem to be all of the same type, or are they of different types? How are they different? Which type seems more sophisticated to you? Which type would you be inclined to use? How does the type of transition used affect the style of the piece?
3. How well is each paragraph tied together? Is one more unified than the others? Explain.
4. Are there places where formal transitions are not needed to move effectively from one sentence to another? How is this effect achieved?

PRACTICE 6.13 Using Transitions

Examine one of your own essays. Circle all of the transitions. Insert (pencil in) additional transitions wherever a transition would help the flow.

Plagiarism is literary theft.

Student Essay

As you read the following student essay, identify and evaluate its structural features: introduction (hook, background, major claim), supporting and rebutting body paragraphs (types of claims, evidence, and explanations; their organization), and conclusion. What does the author do well, and what could she improve?

Hetal Shah

EN 101

Dr. Everett

November 11, 2005

Curing Plagiarism

Academic dishonesty is spreading like an epidemic across colleges and universities. Its symptoms range from copying a friend's homework to looking at another student's answers during a test to turning in a term paper that is plagiarized. Plagiarism, which is taking credit for someone else's words or ideas, in particular has increased at an alarming rate. Schools and colleges seek to understand not only the causes for rampant plagiarism but also ways to treat it more effectively. The remedy lies in cooperation between instructors, administrators, and students: instructors should improve how they teach academic honesty, administrators should revise and publicize policies treating academic misconduct, and students should value ethics over grades.

Statistics show a tremendous increase in academic dishonesty across the nation. According to a study conducted by Plagiarism.org 58.3 percent of high school students in 1969 allowed others to copy their work. In 1989, about 97.3 percent allowed their work to be copied by other students. Even more students today are copying homework answers and cheating on tests to maintain high grades.

There are many causes of plagiarism. One reason is the pressure on students to achieve, varying from maintaining a high GPA in high school to get into a good college to keeping up grades while in college to hold on to scholarships (Durkin). A second reason is the competitive nature of grading: a student must be not just acceptable but better than others (Fanning 8). Plagiarism also occurs because it is socially acceptable: many students do not consider it to be cheating because all their friends are doing it. In addition, cheaters are convinced that they are not going to get caught (Lincoln 47); 95 percent of high school students who cheated were never found out (Gomez 42). Finally, rigorous course loads have led many students, often those who are near the top of their classes, to cheat in an effort to keep up with the workload.

Acting as a kind of safety valve for the pressures on students, modern technology has contributed greatly to the rise of plagiarism. The Internet has broadened the horizons for those who plagiarize because it is easily accessible and its resources are huge. At least 305 "cheat sites" with names such as "schoolsucks.com" and "lazystudents.com" sell recycled and custom-made papers (Clos). A study performed by Education Week found that 54 percent of American students admitted using prewritten Internet essays as a source for completing assignments at least once (Durkin).

According to Apiwan D. Born, an educator who specializes in information systems, instructors tend to react to plagiarism after the fact, when instead they should be proactive, stopping it before it starts: "an instructor should focus on 'how to reduce and discourage cheating activities' rather than 'why students cheat and how they did it.'" Proactive measures include teaching writing as a process rather than as a product, using more group rather than solitary activities, conducting more writing activities in class rather than out of class, and educating students better about what plagiarism is and why it is wrong (Born 223).

Establishing a campuswide program for educating students about plagiarism and instructors about plagiarism prevention is an administrative task. Just as campuses provide seminars for faculty members to help them better serve students with handicaps or to avoid practices that might be taken as sexual harassment, training should take place to help faculty understand the causes of and solutions to academic dishonesty. Administrative policies regarding cheating should be not only judicial and punitive, as they are now, but also proactive and preventive: writing instruction and ethical instruction need to be highlighted, promoted, and practiced universally.

Finally, students should be held responsible. At present there is a culture of complicity, where honest students tolerate the cheating done by their peers: students who would without hesitation report the theft of physical property instead look the other way when intellectual property is stolen. Something like an honor code needs to be established. Without the support of the average student, any program that promotes academic honesty is doomed to failure.

The epidemic of cheating will continue to plague academia until instructors, administrators, and students work together to treat it. This means more than posting a policy statement in a syllabus or handbook. This means more than assigning the "avoid plagiarism" passage for students to read in their composition textbooks. This means more than using antiplagiarism websites and software to catch plagiarists and then punish them after the fact. It means, instead, a cooperative effort to cure plagiarism through improved instruction, improved administration, and improved student ethics.

Shah 4

Works Cited

Born, Apiwan D. "How to Reduce Plagiarism." Journal of Information Systems Education 14.3 (2003): 223–24.

Clos, Karen. "When Academic Dishonesty Happens on Your Campus." Innovation Abstracts 24.26 (2002): 1–2.

Durkin, Jessica. "A Culture of Copy-and-Paste." Spiked Online 28 Apr. 2005. 22 Oct. 2005 <http://www.spiked-online.com/Articles/0000000CAAD2.htm>.

Fanning, Karen. "Is Honesty Still the Best Policy?" Junior Scholastic 107.17 (2005): 8–9.

Gomez, Dina S. "It's Just So Easy to Cheat." NEA Today 19.7 (2001): 42.

Lincoln, Margaret. "Internet Plagiarism." Multimedia Schools 9.1 (2002): 46–49. ABI/INFORM. ProQuest. Lib. of the U of the Sciences, Philadelphia. 3 Nov. 2005 <http://proquest.umi.com>.

Plagiarism.org. 2005. IParadigms, LCC. 3 Nov. 2005 <http://www.plagiarism.org/plagiarism_stats.html>.

Looking Back at Chapter 6

- An essay's basic structure consists of three major sections: (1) an introduction that provides a thesis statement or otherwise orients the reader toward a major claim, (2) a body of paragraphs that break down the thesis into specific areas and treat each area in detail, and (3) a conclusion that provides closure.
- A basic introduction to a composition contains a hook, background information, and a thesis or major claim.
- The body of an argument argues for the major claim (1) by supporting it with reasons (evidence and explanations) and (2) by rebutting significant alternative arguments.
- A topic can be stated at the top of a text block or paragraph, at the bottom of a text block or paragraph, as a delayed topic (after a transition sentence), or as an implied topic (not directly stated).
- There are four ways to organize the refutation of alternative arguments: early, late, occasional, and complete.
- Arguers often must qualify their claims by explaining under which circumstances the claim is true or by estimating the probability that a claim is true.
- Transitions help maintain coherence within a composition.

Suggestions for Writing

- Write a journal entry about your own process of drafting.
- After choosing an issue that interests you, follow the suggestions in the chapter as you draft an argument.

Online Study Center
Improve Your Grade
Suggestions for Writing

7 Revising and Editing Arguments

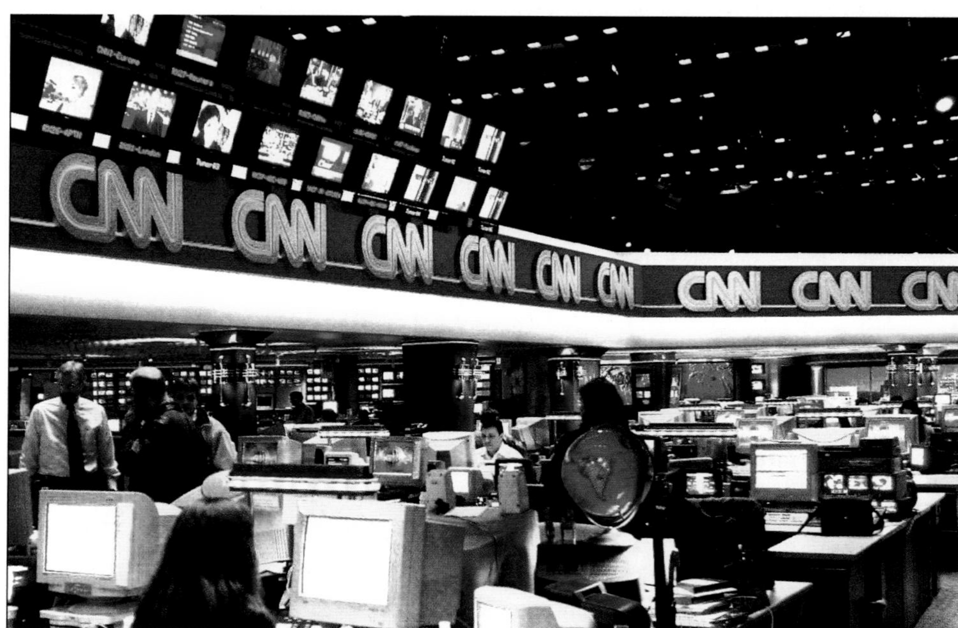

There I am paying big money to you writers, and for what? All you do is change the words.
—Samuel Goldwyn, former CEO of MGM Studios

Writing is a process of change. Through your efforts, a blank sheet of paper changes into a text. As you then evaluate what you've written, the text undergoes improvements in form and content. The latter changes are the result of revision and editing.

Revising an Argument

Online Study Center
This icon will direct you to content and resources on the website <college.hmco.com/pic/lamm1e>.

The word *revision* is derived from root words that mean "see again." Revision is expressed as alterations of your words, phrases, and larger blocks of text. Yet these external, visible changes emerge from invisible thought processes within you. The greater part of "seeing again" is internal, growing with your understanding of the needs of people (an audience), your own needs (your purpose for writing), and the ways in which rhetoric and argument can satisfy those needs.

Looking at your own writing with fresh eyes can be tricky. Some authors find they benefit from putting their texts aside for a while, allowing a kind of "distancing" or perspective. Unfortunately, many writing assignments come with deadlines that rule out a prolonged cooling-off period for works in progress. Fortunately, writers have several methods that they can use to quickly re-see and improve their work. For example, revision guides, checklists, and rubrics can all be used to evaluate your own writing. These three methods can also be used to gather and organize feedback from your peers and from your writing instructor, as well as to guide you in giving feedback to other writers in your class.

Revision Isn't Editing

Although the phrase "revision and editing" often is uttered in the same breath, as though the two are the same activity, they are actually fundamentally different processes. Revision is closely related to planning and drafting, in that these processes are primarily concerned with the content—the meaning or message—of a text. Like planning and drafting, revision is recursive, with the writer repeating this process as often as necessary until he or she is satisfied with what the text has to say. By contrast, editing is nonrecursive, a terminal phase that normally doesn't lead to the production of content. The primary concern of editing is the correctness of technical features—spelling, punctuation, usage, and other features that affect meaning only if they are performed incorrectly.

Efficient writers postpone editing as long as possible because it slows the writing process: You pause to look up a spelling or stop writing a particular thought because you can't figure out the punctuation or think of the right word. Inexperienced writers have difficulty turning off their "internal editor," the part of them that resists writing anything that isn't correct. If your writing has ever come to a screeching halt because of technical matters, your internal editor needs to take a break. To make matters worse, the technical changes that slow down your writing process may end up in the scrap heap later on as you revise.

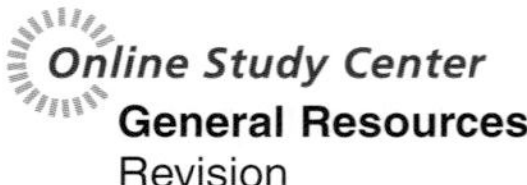

REVISION GUIDES, CHECKLISTS, AND RUBRICS

Revision guides, checklists, and rubrics all direct you to find and evaluate particular features (criteria) of your draft:

- They present the criteria (characteristics, descriptors) of good writing.
- They assume you can detect particular weaknesses and revise them once your attention is directed that way.
- They can be used to guide an evaluation of your own writings or the writings of others.

These three revision tools differ somewhat in how they are structured and used. For instance, revision guides tend to be long and detailed, whereas checklists are brief. A rubric adds a grading scale to the criteria.

Feedback from others also can be directed by a revision guide, checklist, or rubric. Feedback, which will be discussed later in this chapter, can occur in one-on-one discussion sessions (with an instructor or a peer such as another student) and group work or, less personally, through a reviewer's written or recorded comments.

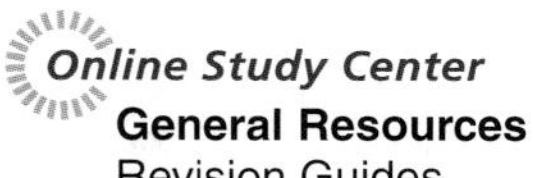

USING A REVISION GUIDE

Here are some suggestions for using a revision guide productively:

- **Consider every question.** Not all questions will be useful, but as a whole the guide should help pinpoint significant strengths and weaknesses or concerns.
- **Mark and annotate.** Show the locations of specific strengths and weaknesses.
- **Evaluate.** Finish by writing a brief statement about the strengths, your concerns, and your recommendations.

USING A REVISION CHECKLIST

A revision checklist contains criteria that are similar to those in a revision guide but presents those criteria in a briefer form. Think of the revision guide on page 181 as a training program: Using the guide is slow at first, but you eventually internalize the criteria. Once you become familiar with the guide, you can switch to the shorter, quicker checklist. The checklist is also useful for peer evaluation, as we will soon see.

The checklist presented in this book includes criteria for argument and rhetoric. In addition, it includes criteria for technique, which encompasses

REVISION GUIDE

ARGUMENT: Claims, Evidence, Explanations, Qualifications, and Refutations

Claims

- What is the major claim? Where is it stated or how is it implied?
- Is the major claim significant (worth arguing), clear, arguable, and relevant to an issue?
- What, if any, are the supporting claims? Where are they stated?
- Are the supporting claims clear, arguable, and relevant to the major claim?
- How could the claim(s) be improved?

Evidence

- What evidence supports the claim(s)? Where is it located?
- Is the evidence adequate, current, credible, and relevant to the claim(s) or supporting points (topic sentences)? Why or why not?
- How could the evidence be improved?

Explanations of Evidence

- What explanations are provided? Where are they located?
- Are the explanations clear, adequate, and relevant to claim(s) and evidence?
- How could the explanations be improved?

Qualifications

- What qualifications are provided? Where are they located?
- Are the qualifications accurate and clearly phrased?
- How could the qualifications be improved?

Refutations

- What are the opposition arguments? Are the opposition arguments refuted? Where are they stated and refuted?
- Are the opposition arguments presented and refuted fairly and adequately?
- How could the presentation and refutation of opposition arguments be improved?

RHETORIC: Purpose, Audience, Structure, and Style

Purpose

- What does the author want to accomplish? (The purpose may be identical to the major claim but more precisely is the change that the author seeks in the reader.)
- In what ways could the intended purpose be reconceptualized (broadened, narrowed, redirected) by the author?

Audience

- Who is the audience? Where is the audience stated or how is it implied?
- Is the audience compatible with the other rhetorical features: purpose, structure, and style?
- In what ways could the intended audience be reconceptualized (broadened, narrowed, redirected) by the author?

Structure

- What form does this argument take (e.g., essay, letter, editorial)?
- Is the type of argument appropriate to the assignment and rhetorical context?
- Are the basic organizational features (introduction, body, conclusion, thesis and topic sentences, transitions, paragraphing) present and effective?
- If needed, are specialized organizational features (e.g., for definition, comparison/contrast, narration) present and effective?
- How could the structure be improved?

Style

- **Diction:** Are the word choices appropriate? Why or why not? What might be improved?
- **Voice:** Is the voice appropriately formal or informal? Do you have a sense of the personality of the author? What are the strongest and weakest examples of voice? What might be improved?
- **Tone:** Is the tone appropriate to the other rhetorical considerations: purpose, audience, and structure? Why or why not? What are the strongest and weakest examples of tone? What might be improved?
- **Point of view:** Is the point of view appropriate to the rhetorical context and task specifications? (For example, research papers tend to be written in the third-person perspective, whereas personal narratives such as anecdotes are typically written in the first-person perspective.) What might be improved?
- **Sentence variety:** Are the sentences appropriately varied in length and form (simple, compound, complex)? What might be improved?

PRACTICE 7.1 **Using a Revision Guide**

Use the revision guide as you evaluate the following passage from Hetal Shah's rough draft of her essay on plagiarism. Mark, annotate, and evaluate the passage. Focus on strengths, concerns, and suggestions.

Academic dishonesty can come into play when students feel that many pressures are being placed on them. Pressures from parents, for example, can lead students to look for the easy way out. Plagiarism also occurs because it is socially acceptable and students do not consider it cheating. Meeting various expectations can cause students to turn to cheating. Pressures can vary from maintaining a high GPA in high school to get into a good college to keeping up grades while in college to hold on to scholarships. American high school students feel pressure from parents as well as teachers to attend good colleges or universities (Durkin). Students in all grade levels competing for grades are causing a great increase in academic dishonesty (Fanning 8). Many high-achieving students are turning to ways of cheating to get their A's in their demanding classes (9). Rigorous course loads and high expectations have led many students, often those who are near the top of their classes, to cheat.

PRACTICE 7.2 **Revising a Paragraph**

Revise the paragraph in Practice 7.1, using your evaluation of it as a guide.

PRACTICE 7.3 **Using a Revision Guide on Another Writer's Paragraph**

Choose a paragraph of your own or one from another student's paper. Using the revision guide, evaluate the paragraph.

Online Study Center
General Resources
Using a Checklist

grammar and usage, mechanics, and task specifications. Technique is a concern of editing. Editing and technique will be discussed more thoroughly later in this chapter.

Use a checklist much as you would a revision guide:

- **Consider every point.** Not all points will be useful, but as a whole the checklist should help pinpoint significant strengths and weaknesses or concerns.
- **Mark and annotate.** Show the locations of specific strengths and weaknesses.
- **Evaluate.** Finish by writing a brief statement about the strengths, your concerns, and your recommendations.

REVISION CHECKLIST

Argument Claims, support (evidence and explanations), qualifications, and refutations are thorough, honest, and convincing.

- ☐ **Claim(s):** Clear, significant, arguable, and relevant to the issue.
- ☐ **Evidence:** Adequate, current, credible, and relevant to the claim(s).
- ☐ **Explanations:** Clear, adequate, and relevant to the claim(s) and evidence.
- ☐ **Qualifications:** Clearly and accurately show to what extent a claim is applicable.
- ☐ **Refutation:** Opposition arguments are presented and refuted fairly and adequately.

Rhetoric Purpose, audience, structure, and style are effective.

- ☐ **Purpose:** Author's goal is clearly stated or strongly implied. (Purpose is the major claim plus the change the author seeks in the reader.)
- ☐ **Audience:** Appropriate for the purpose, structure, and style.
- ☐ **Structure:**
  - Basic organizational features (introduction, body, conclusion, thesis and topic sentences, transitions, paragraphing) are present and effective.
  - If needed, specialized organizational features (e.g., for definition, comparison/contrast, narration) are present and effective.
- ☐ **Style:** Diction, voice, tone, point of view, and syntax are appropriate for the purpose, audience, and structure.

Technique Technical elements are correct.

- ☐ **Grammar and usage:** Sentences and their parts are formed according to accepted standards.
- ☐ **Mechanics:** Spelling, capitalization, punctuation, and formatting are correct.
- ☐ **Task specifications:** Topic, deadline, length, sources, and referencing style are as required.

Using Rubrics

Checklists and revision/editing guides both present criteria that describe good writing. When you take criteria a step further and add a rating scale, the result is an evaluation tool known as a scoring guide or rubric. Letter grades are a traditional kind of rating scale: A, B, C, D, F. In recent years the trend has been to use a numeric scale—such as 0 to 3, 1 to 5, 1 to 6, or 0 to 9—for the convenience of calculating scores mathematically.

Instructors, institutions, and testing programs (such as AP and ACT) have developed their own rubrics. Although rubrics are most often used for assessments ("grading"), they also can be used by writers in much the same way they use checklists and revision/editing guides. In fact, knowing the value of criteria can be formative (instructional), not just summative (evaluative).

Students sometimes use rubrics (rather than revision guides or checklists) to help them evaluate one another's essays or sample essays provided by instructors. Typically, the instructor will later reveal the actual rubric value for the writing sample, helping the students determine how well they do or do not understand the criteria. Professional evaluators call this kind of training *calibration*: the process of tuning one's ability to assess. Sample essays with established values are called *range finders*.

RUBRICS

This rubric is holistic: Each score evaluates all of the qualities as a whole.

Score 5: Essays meriting a score of 5 are of high quality, exhibiting advanced skill with argument, rhetoric, and technique:

- **Argument:** Claims, evidence, explanations, qualifications, and opposition arguments/refutations are presented in a thorough, honest, and convincing manner.
- **Rhetoric:** Purpose, audience, structure, and style consistently work in harmony to advance the argument.
- **Technique:** Grammar, usage, mechanics, and task specifications are nearly flawless.

Score 4: Essays meriting a score of 4 are of good quality, exhibiting proficient skill with argument, rhetoric, and technique. Minor lapses are evident in one category.

Score 3: Essays meriting a score of 3 are of adequate quality, exhibiting passable skill with argument, rhetoric, and technique. Minor lapses are evident in two or more categories.

Score 2: Essays meriting a score of 2 are of inconsistent quality, exhibiting developing skill with argument, rhetoric, and technique. Minor lapses in all categories or a major weakness in one area is evident.

Score 1: Essays meriting a score of 1 are of low quality. Major lapses in all categories are evident.

PRACTICE 7.4 **Using a Rubric: "Curing Plagiarism"**

Using the preceding rubric, assess the complete draft of "Curing Plagiarism" presented later in this chapter (page 189). In group discussion or a brief writing, justify your assessment.

Online Study Center
General Resources
Giving Feedback

Giving and Receiving Feedback

Feedback is the advice you give to or receive from others. Advice can come from face-to-face exchanges, from written or recorded comments, or from a combination of these encounters. In a classroom setting, advice often comes from other students. This kind of feedback goes by many names, often including the word *peer* followed by another term: peer conferencing, peer response, peer review, or peer editing. *Peer evaluation* is the preferred term in this textbook.

When you evaluate the writing of others, additional guidelines should be followed to ensure the advice is constructive: Be positive and be specific.

Be Positive

Even the best examples of writing likely will contain flaws, especially in earlier drafts, and sooner or later those flaws will have to be addressed. Nevertheless, it is vitally important to be constructive and considerate when giving feedback.

GIVING FEEDBACK

When giving advice to other writers, your major goals are to be positive and to be specific. One way to accomplish both these goals is to phrase advice as questions. This method also lets you indicate problems (being descriptive) without offering solutions (being prescriptive). In fact, it is better if the writer is the one who figures out the solution.

Below is a list of problems typically faced by writers and examples of questions that can lead to solutions. The list is not comprehensive; you'll have to react to other problems with questions (feedback) of your own creation.

Problem	*Question*
Thesis isn't a claim.	What kind of change in the reader do you want?
	Where do you state your major claim or thesis?
	Can you turn this thesis into a fact claim? Identity claim? Cause and effect claim? Value claim? Proposal claim?
Claim is too broad.	Which part of the issue is most significant?
	Are you arguing more than one major claim?
Evidence is insufficient.	What are some reasons you could give?
	Where do you give some support?
	Can you restate? Interpret? Apply? Analyze? Synthesize? Evaluate?
Evidence is irrelevant.	How does that evidence fit your claim?
	Could you delete part of that quotation?
Evidence is excessive.	Do you need all that information to support your claim?
Quotations need work.	Who is the source, and why is he or she worth quoting?
	Could you paraphrase some of these quotations?
	Could some of the quotation be deleted?
Evidence needs explaining.	How does the evidence fit your claim?
	What does this statement mean?
Explanation isn't clear.	How could you make this clearer?
	Should you restate? Interpret? Apply? Analyze? Synthesize? Evaluate?
Style is inappropriate.	How will a reader react to your tone?
	Is your word choice appropriate to the reader?
	Is a first-person point of view appropriate for this writing?
Writing is disorganized.	What is the main idea of this paragraph? Does that point fit?
	Would a forecast statement in the introduction help show your organization?
	How does this idea or sentence lead to the next one?
Wording is repetitive.	Could you eliminate some repeated phrases or ideas?
	Could you combine some related sentences?
	Could you vary the way you say this?

Working Effectively with Others

When you work with other students in groups, whether to create an original project (such as a group presentation) or to receive feedback about something you bring to the group (such as a rough draft of a paper you have written), this activity is often termed collaborative learning or cooperative learning. Such activities give students an opportunity to learn from one another in a way that is not possible in a whole-class activity. You should take advantage of this time by doing the following:

- Come prepared to your group meeting. When you come unprepared, you affect the performance of the entire group.
- Be an active participant. Passive group members hinder the learning of everyone involved.
- Avoid dominating the group. When one person dominates the conversation, others do not have as much of a chance to contribute.
- Respect other group members. Treating others with respect contributes to group cohesion and makes the experience more pleasant for everyone involved.

Any writer who has made a serious attempt at producing a piece of writing will be sensitive about its reception. It is unrealistic to expect complete emotional "detachment" of an author from a work.

Unfortunately, evaluators tend to have a keener eye for flaws than for virtues: *Error marking* traditionally is synonymous with *paper grading*. Fortunately, there are several ways to make criticism more constructive:

- **Limit the number of critical "summary" remarks.** Few people are able to assimilate more than three or four new concepts in a feedback session. Also, you don't want to make the person despair.
- **Balance the negative with the positive.** Always find positive traits in the writing: People tend to learn very well from positive feedback.
- **Soften criticism by phrasing an observed weakness as a question.** For example, instead of saying "Your evidence is outdated," you could ask, "Have you looked for more recent data?"

BE SPECIFIC

Broad, generic feedback is quick and easy to give and receive, but it has little constructive value. For example, labeling an entire piece of writing as "good" or "I don't like it" seldom tells the author enough to lead to better writing. A writer needs to know very specifically *what* is effective or ineffective: a particular word, a particular example, or a particular sequence of sentences. It is even more useful if the writer knows *why* something works or fails.

Learning to evaluate writing may be one of the best ways to grow as a writer: *Identifying* quality can take you most of the way toward *producing* quality. At first it may be easier to evaluate others' writing than to evaluate your own work, probably because you are "too close" to your own material. As you learn to spot the best and worst qualities of other people's writings, you begin to "internalize" those criteria and to understand them better in your own work.

Hetal Shah shared an early draft of her essay "Curing Plagiarism" with a peer evaluation group in her writing class. Here is the introduction to her essay, with handwritten annotations Shah made during discussion of her draft. (The complete version of the rough draft is presented later in this chapter; Shah's final draft appears in Chapter 6.)

The cheating epidemic is spreading rapidly. Consequently, many colleges and universities are being caught in the middle of this growing epidemic. Academic dishonesty can vary from copying a friend's answers in a homework assignment to turning in a term paper bought from any of the various "cheat sites" available on the Internet. Plagiarism is a prime example of a type of academic dishonesty that has hit campuses very hard. The use of someone's work without giving appropriate credit is defined as plagiarism. Educators have been pondering over the thought as to why so many of their students today are turning to the easy way out of assignments. In order for academic integrity to be maintained in their schools, educators and administrators need to understand the various reasons that caused students to turn to acts of dishonesty.

Repetitive?

Good trans.

Good examples

Good to define

Possibly combine with previous sentence?

Repetition: Combine some sentences, and eliminate others.

Expository? What is your claim?

Lack of logical flow: Sequence should begin generally and end with a specific thesis.

Lack of argumentative thesis or claim: Make a stronger claim.

Shah's writing teacher reviewed the early draft of her essay and sent her an e-mail with the following suggestions about her introduction:

FROM: Justin Everett
TO: Hetal Shah
DATE: 12/19/2005 09:22 AM
CC:
BCC:
SUBJECT: Your essay draft

Dear Hetal,

I've read the rough draft of your essay, "Curing Plagiarism." It's coming along nicely. Below are some suggestions to help you make it even better.

Strengths

- It displays some elements of a good introduction: It establishes an issue—a problem to be solved.

- The issue or problem has significance and a sense of urgency.
- Overall organization is good. It begins generally (about "dishonesty"), narrows to "plagiarism," and then focuses on a manageable thesis: "[E]ducators and administrators need to understand the various reasons that cause students to turn to acts of dishonesty."

Concerns

- It seems to repeat some ideas and phrases nonproductively. For example, the first and second sentences mention that the epidemic is growing, and later you say it "has hit campuses very hard."
- The major claim doesn't seem like an argument. It seems to be mostly expository—as though it's mainly going to report information rather than argue.

Suggestions

- Could you give the thesis statement an argumentative edge? What kind of claim could you make?
- Could you combine sentences and eliminate some repetition?
- I like the "epidemic" analogy. Could you use it more?

I look forward to reading your revised draft by next Thursday.

Best wishes,
Professor Everett

After reflecting on the feedback from her classmates and instructor, Shah revised the introduction to her essay:

Academic dishonesty is spreading like an epidemic across colleges and universities. Its symptoms range from copying a friend's homework to looking at another student's answers during a test to turning in a term paper that is plagiarized. Plagiarism, which is taking credit for someone else's words or ideas, in particular has increased at an alarming rate. Schools and colleges seek to understand not only the causes of rampant plagiarism but also ways to treat it more effectively. The remedy lies in cooperation between instructors, administrators, and students: Instructors should improve how they teach academic honesty, administrators should revise and publicize policies treating academic misconduct, and students should value ethics over grades.

PRACTICE 7.5 Using a Revision Guide or Checklist to Give Feedback

Using the revision guide or checklist discussed earlier in the chapter, evaluate the following complete rough draft of Hetal Shah's essay. Mark, annotate, and evaluate, focusing on strengths, concerns, and suggestions. Phrase some suggestions in the form of questions. Share your comments and suggestions with your classmates. What are the most useful and constructive ways to deliver feedback? At what points does it become challenging to evaluate someone else's writing?

Shah 1

Hetal Shah
EN 101

Curing Plagiarism

The cheating epidemic is spreading rapidly. Consequently, many colleges and universities are being caught in the middle of this growing epidemic. Academic dishonesty can range from copying a friend's answers in a homework assignment to turning in a term paper bought from any of the various "cheat sites" available on the Internet. Plagiarism is a prime example of a type of academic dishonesty that has hit campuses very hard. The use of someone's work without giving appropriate credit is called plagiarism. Educators have been pondering why so many of their students today are turning to the easy way out of assignments. For academic integrity to be maintained in their schools, educators and administrators need to understand the various reasons that cause students to turn to acts of dishonesty.

Academic dishonesty can come into play when students feel that many pressures are being placed on them. Pressures from parents, for example, can lead students to look for the easy way out. Plagiarism also occurs because it is socially acceptable and students do not consider it cheating. Meeting various expectations can cause students to turn to cheating. Pressures can vary from maintaining a high GPA in high school to get into a good college to keeping up grades while in college to hold on to

(continued)

scholarships. American high school students feel pressure from parents as well as teachers to attend good colleges or universities (Durkin). Students in all grade levels competing for grades are causing a great increase in academic dishonesty (Fanning 8). Many high-achieving students are turning to ways of cheating to get their A's in their demanding classes (9). Rigorous course loads and high expectations have led many students, often those that are near the top of their classes, to cheat.

Statistics support the claim of a tremendous increase in academic dishonesty across the nation. For example, according to a study conducted by Plagiarism.org 58.3 percent of high school students in 1969 allowed others to copy their work. In 1989, this increased to about 97.3 percent. Copying their homework, students seem to care only about high grades. Based on these disturbing statistics, it is relevant that pressures are negatively affecting the maintenance of academic integrity in many schools. Plagiarism and cheating are also on the rise in schools because many students do not think, or rather do not even understand, that such acts are illegal. Students don't feel that copying someone else's work is socially unacceptable because all their friends are doing it. They are convinced that they are not going to get caught (Lincoln 47). Ninety-five percent of high school students who cheat admitted that they do not get caught (Gomez 42).

Modern technology has contributed greatly to the unfortunate rise of plagiarism. The Internet has broadened the horizons for those who plagiarize. Trying to save time on assignments, students look for shortcuts. This is made possible by the Internet. The average student uses the Internet to "steal" papers because it is easily accessible to them. A study performed by Education Week illustrated that 54 percent of American students admitted that they have used the Internet asa viable source for completing consignments at least once (Durkin). The easy method of copying and pasting a sentence that is available on the Internet has enabled students to take the easy, dishonest way.

(continued)

Shah 3

Many "cheat sites" are available on the Internet. These websites consist of various term papers and essays that are similar to many college curriculums (Clos).

Research done by Peggy Bates and Margaret Fain shows that there are at least 305 of these "cheat sites" on the Internet. Some of these websites include names such as "schoolsucks.com" and "lazystudents.com" (Clos).

Students who have been buying papers off the Internet tend to buy many more as classes advance and become more rigorous because they do not have the required writing skills needed to achieve a good grade at that specific level. Finding papers on the Internet is very easy for those who know how to conduct specific online searches. Search engines, such as Google and Yahoo, display hundred of results when prompted to search for "buy term paper" (Durkin).

As a result of this increase in plagiarism due to the Internet, administrators need to adopt methods to decrease the rate of academic dishonesty. Integrity could be maintained on the academia level if students are taught about plagiarism and understand how to avoid it. Antiplagiarism websites are at the discretion of the faculty. These sites assist the teachers in pinpointing exact phrases, paragraphs, and papers that have been taken from the Internet. An example of such a site that is being used by many high schools and colleges across the nation is <www.turnitin.com> (Clos). TurnItIn allows teachers to submit portions of papers that they find suspicious. The website then sends a report back to the teacher indicating whether an act of academic dishonesty has been performed (Clos).

Maintaining integrity in academia is not an easy task due to the advanced technology that is available for students. However, those administrators who hope to find solutions to this increasing problem of academic dishonesty in their schools need to work with the students and both the students as well as the teachers need to understand exactly what needs to be done about the situation.

(continued)

Shah 4

Works Cited

Clos, Karen. "When Academic Dishonesty Happens on Your Campus." Innovation Abstracts 24.26 (2002).

Durkin, Jessica. "A Culture of Copy-and-Paste." Spiked Online 28 Apr. 2005. 22 Oct. 2005 <http://www.spiked-online.com/Articles/0000000CAAD2.htm>.

Fanning, Karen. "Is Honesty Still the Best Policy?" Junior Scholastic 107.17: 8–9.

Gomez, Dina S. "It's Just So Easy to Cheat." NEA Today 19.7: 42.

Lincoln, Margaret. "Internet Plagiarism." Multimedia Schools 9.1. (2002): 46–49. Research Lib. Complete ProQuest. Lib. of the U of the Sciences, Philadelphia. Nov. 2005. <http://proquest.com>.

Plagiarism.org. 2005. IParadigms, LCC. 3 Nov. 2005 <http://www.plagiarism.org/plagiarism_stats.html>.

Should My Rough Draft Be Handwritten?

These days, many students prefer to perform all of the stages of the writing process on a computer. While this may seem like a logical approach—after all, you can cut and paste text and move words around more easily—it has some disadvantages. Writing on a computer may tempt you to take shortcuts. The text, if properly formatted, looks very professional and may look and feel "finished" at first glance. However, even the most neatly presented text may include many drafting errors. Also, writing exclusively on a computer may cause you to make errors as you move between research sources on the Internet and your paper. You may accidentally commit "cut and paste" plagiarism, which could cause you to fail the assignment, or even your class.

One advantage of planning, drafting, and even revising by hand is that it forces you to read your text carefully as you reread it and type it. This exercise will help you catch errors that might otherwise slip by unnoticed.

Editing an Argument

Editing is a process of tidying up the technical and mechanical features of a piece of writing—that is, "dotting the i's and crossing the t's." Known sometimes as proofreading, most editing can be postponed until a draft is completed, although fastidious people may have trouble ignoring errors even temporarily. Whether sooner or later, eventually the editing must be done.

Over the years you probably have been taught many rules about spelling, punctuation, grammar/usage, and formatting. As you edit, your personal storehouse of knowledge is your primary resource. However, so many rules exist that you'll probably supplement your own body of knowledge with reference books—a dictionary, a thesaurus, and a writer's handbook (for usage and mechanics). If you use a word processor, these resources may be part of your software package.

Editing on a Word Processor

Electronic versions of dictionaries, thesauruses, and handbooks often are integrated into word processors. These tools alert you to potential errors as you write, highlighting misspelled words or faulty sentences. Clicking on a highlighted passage summons a menu of suggestions and additional tools. At other times, you may choose to activate proofreading and editing software by clicking on typed words or a toolbar.

Commands and Functions Word processors allow you to issue commands and perform functions important in editing and proofreading: copy, count (words, pages), find and replace, insert, delete, move, search. A person who is skilled in the use of a word processor can apply these functions to great advantage, making changes much more rapidly than is possible with pen and paper.

Spelling Checker A checker can spot possible problems and enable you to choose from a menu of suggested spellings or add new spellings to its list. Autocorrect is an option that will empower your word processor to make some changes automatically. A spelling checker, however, can make mistakes. Its lexicon may be limited, omitting some words that are acceptable: The words *prewrite* and *freewrite*, for example, are accepted in the English profession but are not recognized by many spelling checkers. Also, a checker will accept a properly spelled word even when it is the wrong word. If, for example, you mistyped

CANDIDATE FOR A PULLET SURPRISE

Jerrold H. Zar

This poem was originally published in the January–February 1994 issue of the *Journal of Irreproducible Results*. By the author's count, 127 of the 225 words in the poem are incorrect (although all words are correctly spelled).

I have a spelling checker,
It came with my PC.
It plane lee marks four my revue
Miss steaks aye can knot sea.

Eye ran this poem threw it,
Your sure reel glad two no.
Its vary polished in it's weigh.
My checker tolled me sew.

A checker is a bless sing,
It freeze yew lodes of thyme.
It helps me right awl stiles two reed,
And aides me when eye rime.

Each frays come posed up on my screen
Eye trussed too bee a joule.
The checker pours o'er every word
To cheque sum spelling rule.

Bee fore a veiling checker's
Hour spelling mite decline,
And if we're lacks oar have a laps,
We wood bee maid too wine.

Butt now bee cause my spelling
Is checked with such grate flare,
Their are know fault's with in my cite,
Of nun eye am a wear.

Now spelling does knot phase me,
It does knot bring a tier.
My pay purrs awl due glad den
With wrapped word's fare as hear.

To rite with care is quite a feet
Of witch won should bee proud,
And wee mussed dew the best wee can,
Sew flaw's are knot aloud.

Sow ewe can sea why aye dew prays
Such soft wear four pea seas,
And why eye brake in two averse
Buy righting want too pleas.

"spell" as "spiel," the spelling checker would not catch the error because "spiel" is the correct spelling for another word.

Grammar Checker A word processor can check for lapses in accepted grammar and usage. A grammar checker can also give you short lessons in style, explaining why some things are incorrect and offering alternatives. Like spelling checkers, grammar checkers have limitations and sometimes must be ignored or overruled.

Dictionary This resource can be activated by clicking on a word in your text or by clicking onto an icon displayed on a toolbar. Although useful, these dictionaries may be less complete than hardcover collegiate dictionaries.

Synonyms (Thesaurus) Highlighting a word and clicking will activate this resource. The list of synonyms may be useful yet less complete than a print version of a thesaurus.

Translator Some software provides English-to-foreign language translations. Also, a number of websites provide this service.

Evaluator Some software programs will "grade" your writing. This kind of evaluation is not a substitute for a human editor, but it can give you feedback by evaluating features such as sentence and paragraph length and the quality of diction.

PRACTICE 7.6 **Using Word Processing Tools**

While working with a word processor, practice using its commands and tools: copy, count (words, pages), find and replace, insert, format, delete, move, navigate (scroll), search, spelling checker (use it to automatically correct misspellings), grammar checker (use it to automatically correct grammatical errors), synonyms, translation (to or from a foreign language).

EDITING GUIDES

An editing guide, like a revision guide, directs you to find and evaluate particular features of your draft. It aims specifically at correctness: grammar/usage, mechanics, and task specifications. This kind of guide often is joined with a revision guide, forming a dual-purpose "revision and editing guide."

EDITING GUIDE: TECHNIQUE

Grammar and Usage

Sentences: Are the sentences formed correctly? Are there any "fused sentences" (comma splices or run-ons) or fragments?

Words: Are the forms of words correct? Are there incorrect singular or plural nouns or verbs? Do all of the pronouns have antecedents? Do all verbs agree with their subjects?

Meaning of words: Do the words mean what they are intended to mean? Are there errors in diction, "wrong words"?

Positions of words: Are words arranged in correct order? Are any modifiers placed in a way that could be misread (dangling, squinting, misplaced)? Are instances of "parallelism" correct or faulty?

Mechanics Are spelling, capitalization, punctuation, and formatting correct?

Task Specifications Did you use the required topic, deadline, length, sources, and referencing style?

Editing Marks

Professional editors use a variety of symbols and abbreviations to show where and how a text should be corrected. Known as *editing marks* or *proofreading marks*, they are fairly easy to learn and very handy for shortening the time it takes to mark a paper.

EDITING AND PROOFREADING MARKS

Can you think of a way to correct each of the examples?

Symbol	*Meaning*	*Example*
Abr	Abbreviation problem	(Abr) Doct. Peterson is the best pharmacy professor on campus.
Agr	Agreement problem	(Agr) Salar and Won Ho is going to Law Vegas next month for a seminar.
Ante? or Ref?	Pronoun antecedent missing or unclear	My friends Phil and Dave painted (Ante?) his apartment last weekend.
Awk	Awkward language	The earthquake was a (Awk) really awful bad disaster.
Cap (X̳)	Faulty capitalization	Next year I'm going to study at the u̳niversity of l̳ondon. (Caps)
C/S	Comma splice	I'm going to the store, (C/S) I'm going to buy bread.
Delete (~)	Problem word or phrase	Next month five students are going before ~~the~~ (Del) the academic discipline board for plagiarism incidents.

(continued)

EDITING AND PROOFREADING MARKS *(continued)*

Symbol	*Meaning*	*Example*
Dic	Diction problem (word choice)	I performed really good on the test.
Dgl mod	Dangling or misplaced modifier	Lying beside the street in a drainage ditch, I discovered a wallet walking home.
-ed	Problem with -ed verb ending	If you had jog with Fred every morning like you had planned, you would be in better shape these days.
Frag	Sentence fragment	Dealing with angry people on a daily basis at my job at the police department.
F/S	Fused sentence or run-on	I'm going to the store I'm going to buy bread.
Insert (^)	Missing word or phrase	Next month five students are going before the academic discipline board for plagiarism incidents.
lc	Improper capitalization	One of the most important influences on modern life is Market Capitalism.
//	Problem with parallelism	In college, I'm planning on majoring in English and to play football.
P/A	Pronoun agreement problem	The average student gets their chance at success if he studies hard.
Para. (¶)	Make a new paragraph	My supervisor said, "I'll have to let you go if you don't lose weight. It's bad for the company's image." "Try it," I said. "Try it, and I'll sue."
Rep.	Repeated word or phrase	Technically, I'm having trouble understanding technical technology.
SP	Spelling error	My favorite professer is Dr. Roberts.
-s	Problem with -s ending	Dr. Stephens plan to run for public office.
SVA	Subject and verb agreement problem	The committee, which includes Aditi and Kareem, are voting in favor of the amendment.
Tense	Verb tense problem	In Shakespeare's Hamlet, the title character will lecture his mother on morality after he killed Polonius.
Wdy	Wordy phrase needs to be simplified	One of the really major problems with not only American, but the society of the world in general today is the lack of civility and the tendency to be curt and impolite to others.
WW	Wrong word	One affect of higher gas prices is that some people get more exercise.

The passage below is the third paragraph from the student essay, "Curing Plagiarism." Errors have been added to help illustrate the use of editing marks.

(¶) Statistics support the claim of a tremendous increase in academic dishonesty across the nation. For example, according to a study conducted by The State of Americans: This Generation and the Next, 5.3 percent of high school students in 1969 (Tense) allow others to copy their work. (Frag) In 1989, about 97.3 percent. (Dgl mod) Copyright their homework, high grades are all that students seem to care about. (Sp) Bassed on these disturbing statistics, (Wdy) it is relevant that pressures are (Awk) negatively affecting the maintenance of (lc) Academic (lc) Integrity in the many schools. Plagiarism and cheating are also on the rise in schools because many students do not think, or rather do not even understand, that such acts are illegal. (SVA) A student don't feel that copying someone else's work is socially (Sp) inacceptible, (CS) all their friends are going it. They are convinced that (Ref?) they are not going to get caught (Lincoln 47). Ninety-five percent of high school students who cheat (Tense) admitted that they do not get caught (Gomez 42).

PRACTICE 7.7 **Using an Editing Guide and Editing Marks: "Curing Plagiarism"**

Using the editing guide and editing marks, annotate the errors in the following passage from Hetal Shah's rough draft.

Students face pressures and uncertainty, modern technology has contributed greatly to the unfortunate rise of plagiarism. The internet has broaden the horizons for those who plagerize. Saving time on assignments, looking for shortcuts is what students try to do. This is made possible by the Internet. The average student uses the Internet to "steal" a paper because it is easily accessible to them. A study performed by "Education Week" illustrated that fifty-four percent of American students admitted that they have used the Internet as a viable source for completing consignments at least once (Durkin). The easy method of copying and pasting a sentence that is available on the Internet has enabled students to save time and find the easy way of using it.

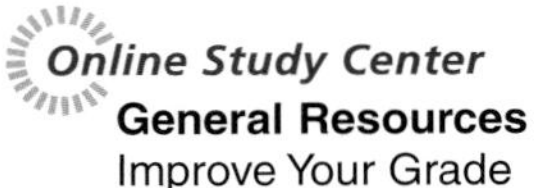

Online Study Center
General Resources
Improve Your Grade

Looking Back at Chapter 7

- Revising is "re-seeing." One way to re-see is to understand the qualities that characterize good writing.
- Checklists, revision guides, and rubrics can not only help you re-see and revise but also help you advise others.
- Postpone editing until you are satisfied with the rhetorical and argumentative features of your draft.
- Use the tools of the trade. A dictionary and thesaurus are basic resources that are typically available as books or as word processing software.
- Word processors offer many tools and commands that facilitate revision.
- Rubrics can help you understand which qualities characterize good writing and how those qualities are evaluated.

Suggestions for Writing

- In both your current and later writing assignments, use a revision/editing guide, checklist, or rubric as you critically read and revise your work.
- In both your current and later writing assignments, use a revision/editing guide, checklist, or rubric as you give feedback to other writers.

Researching Arguments

A claim requires support in the form of evidence. But where does the evidence come from? Sometimes you may be able to draw upon your firsthand observations or you may have gone through enough training to be an expert on some subjects. At other times your personal experience regarding the subject under investigation may be limited. That is when research becomes vitally important. As its root word indicates, research is a search for facts, studies, testimony, and other forms of evidence that can help you develop a claim and persuade your audience.

> *We must cling to the belief that the incomprehensible is comprehensible; otherwise we would not continue to search.*
>
> —Johann Wolfgang von Goethe (1749–1832)

Online Study Center
This icon will direct you to content and resources on the website <college.hmco.com/pic/lamm1e>

The Process of Research

The research process involves three stages: planning, exploring, and evaluating sources.

- In the *planning stage,* you devise a topic, formulate a research question, and develop a plan for finding the answer to that question.
- In the *exploring stage,* you divide your strategy into phases, usually based on the types of sources you plan to use (serial publications, books, the Internet, government documents, and so on) and follow the "trail of evidence" as you move from one source to another. For example, if you notice that certain ideas, people, or other sources are discussed repeatedly as you conduct your research, then you also need to explore these trails of evidence.
- In the *evaluating stage,* you determine whether the evidence is sufficient to answer your question and support the claims you wish to make. If the answer is no (and it usually is no the first time through), then you must return to one of the earlier stages of the research process.

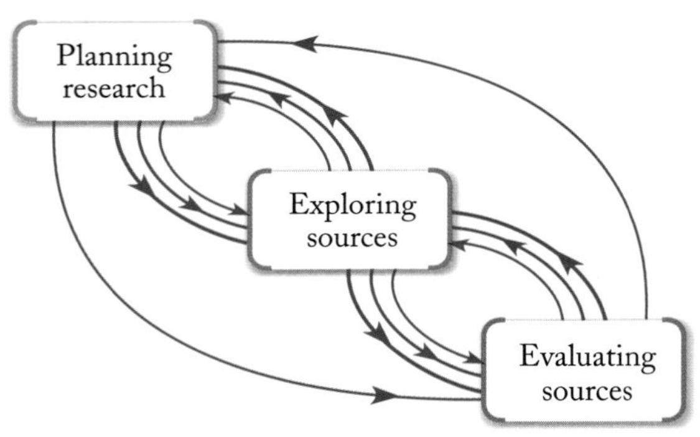

Like the process of writing, the process of researching is recursive: You may need to return to any part of the process at any time. Typically, you will return to the exploration stage to locate more information. Sometimes, though, you will return to the planning stage, perhaps even to rewrite your research question if you discover that it is too narrow (for example, you can't locate enough evidence) or too broad (to adequately argue the case, you might have to write much more than required by the assignment).

Planning Research: From Research Topic to Research Question

Online Study Center
General Resources
Planning Research

Research usually begins with a topic—something you want to investigate. Sometimes your instructor will assign the topic. At other times you will choose your own topic, perhaps selecting from a list or coming up with it on your own. A topic by itself is not very useful, because it doesn't give your research much direction or focus. Instead, you should try to phrase the topic as a *research question*. Then you can seek to discover the answer to the question. Once you have completed your research and believe you have found the answer to your question (or at least have obtained an opinion or some perspective on it), you can rewrite the question in the form of an initial claim or working thesis for your paper. A *working thesis* is an experimental version of your major claim; it is open to changes as new information comes to light. If you already have enough knowledge about your topic (or at least an opinion about it), then you may be able to write a claim instead of a research question. (For more on developing a thesis, see Chapter 5, Planning Arguments, and Chapter 6, Drafting Arguments.)

Let's illustrate this idea with an example. Sarah, a college student, has decided to write about the English author C. S. Lewis for a research assignment in her writing class. From readings in class she knows that Lewis was a writer of fiction and religious literature. At this point Sarah knows she needs to refine her topic, so she checks a biography of Lewis out of her library. In that book, she comes across a reference to "Mrs. Moore," an elderly woman whom Lewis cared for even though she was not a relative. Wanting to know more, Sarah writes her research question:

> What was C. S. Lewis's relationship with Mrs. Moore?

At this point, Sarah can begin planning her research, because she has a specific purpose in mind. What kinds of sources are likely to supply her with information about Mrs. Moore? If she decides to investigate other biographies, articles about Lewis, and follow a "bibliographic trail" from one source to another, Sarah will not be far from the mark. After some research, she is able to turn the question into a working thesis:

> Mrs. Moore, the mother of Lewis's wartime friend Paddy Moore, may have inspired some of the writer's more cantankerous characters.

Now Sarah can begin organizing her research notes and planning the content of her argument.

Following a Bibliographic Trail

Often, you will come across useful information in a source but will not find the "answer" to your research question. However, your efforts may not have been wasted: One of the best ways to find sources is to look at the Works Cited page (bibliography, references) at the end of an article or book on the same subject you are investigating. Even if the article or book itself isn't very useful, its list of references may lead to something better. It is rather like being a detective following a trail of clues.

Types of Sources: Primary and Secondary Research

Research can involve either obtaining information in person—that is, through *primary research*—or reading what others have written about a particular topic—that is, through *secondary research.* If you learned about the college you were attending by visiting the college to take a tour and speak to students and instructors, you were conducting primary research. If you learned about the college through books or the Internet, you were engaging in secondary research.

Primary Research Some types of research projects call for primary research, especially in scientific disciplines. These projects may involve visiting a place (a school or nursing home), interviewing people (teachers, students,

CONDUCTING AN INTERVIEW

An interview is a form of primary research that can yield information that might otherwise be difficult to find or perhaps not even available from any other source. Your interview will be more productive if you plan ahead.

Make an appointment. An interviewee will have to allot time for you; indeed, you may have to wait days or longer to get adequate time for an interview. When you make the appointment, you should inform the interviewee briefly of the nature of your project (subject and possibly your working thesis). This step will ensure that you don't waste your time on someone who can't provide the information you need. Also, give an estimate of how long you think the interview will last.

Prepare a list of questions in advance. As much as possible, target the questions to relevant issues and to specific gaps in your research. In addition, prepare a few broad-spectrum questions that might lead to results you couldn't anticipate. Your interviewee might want to see the list before you arrive, allowing for some reflection or research.

Use a tape recorder, if permissible. A recording can not only provide exact quotations for later use, but also let you reflect on the interviewee's tone of voice and other nuances. Ask in advance for permission to record.

Take copious notes. Write down some statements in brief form—you don't want the pace of the interview to depend completely on your speed as a transcriber. Important points, especially if quotable, should be written verbatim. Ask the interviewee to repeat some key statements, especially if you plan to quote him or her directly. Even if you do use a recorder, don't expect it to completely replace your notes: Recordings sometimes are unintelligible or suffer from technical failures.

Check back with the interviewee before publishing. This courtesy usually is appreciated greatly. No one wants to be misquoted, especially in writing: The misquote could be an embarrassment that is requoted endlessly by others. Your source may want to refine the phrasing a bit, because the impromptu nature of oral interviews sometimes results in awkward sentences or inaccurate wording.

Send a "thank you" note. This courteous gesture need not be elaborate. In many cases, an e-mail message will suffice.

Make a record of the date, time, and location of the interview. You'll need this information as you document your sources. For more information on documenting an interview, see Chapter 13 (for MLA documentation style) and Chapter 14 (for APA documentation style).

patients, nurses) or conducting a study (determining the number of part-time students who attend your school). When you decide to conduct interviews, a university is a goldmine—it employs experts on wide variety of subjects. If you conduct this type of research, you will probably have to carry out secondary research in the library as well to give you the appropriate background with which to pursue the primary research project.

Secondary Research In many academic classes, you will be asked to write research papers that are based on secondary research. To use the library's resources successfully, you should understand how your library organizes this information.

INTEGRATING ELECTRONIC AND CONVENTIONAL RESEARCH

You will probably integrate information gleaned from library research with information obtained from electronic sources. However, if your library has a good collection, begin there. Even if you intend to use primarily electronic resources, your librarians can assist you in locating appropriate resources, Also, your library may have access to specialized databases such as Ebscohost, ProQuest, LexisNexis, Project Muse, and ERIC that you may not be able to use from home. For more on electronic research, see the "Electronic Research" section later in this chapter.

How Your Library Classifies Sources Most libraries divide resources into five general areas: books, periodicals, reference works, government documents, and media. The nature of your topic will help you decide where to focus your search, and your instructor can help you plan the focus of your research. Periodicals generally contain the most up-to-date information, while books hold the most extensive information. You will usually begin with reference materials such as electronic card catalogs and other specialized bibliographies. In addition, you may use encyclopedias or other reference materials that your university holds or can access over the Internet. (Databases and services such as ProQuest, InfoTrac, and Ebscohost have vastly "expanded" the holdings of even the smallest libraries.) Government documents are usually housed in a special area, and may range from land records to extensive research reports. Media resources should not be overlooked. In addition to films and recordings, your library may own CD-ROMs that contain useful information. The best way to begin planning your research—even before you write your research question—is to visit your library and discover what sorts of resources it offers that are related to your topic.

How to Evaluate a Topic Evaluating a topic to plan your research is a part of the prewriting stage of the writing process. As a result, many activities that are useful for brainstorming a topic for an essay that does not require research are useful for those projects that do require it. Writing lists, clustering diagrams, and freewriting can all be used to narrow down a topic (see Chapter 5, Planning Arguments, to learn more about these methods). Initially, you can brainstorm based on your prior knowledge about a particular topic or something you learned in class. As your topic becomes more focused, however, you may need to conduct some preliminary research before you decide on your working thesis or research question.

Using Interlibrary Loan

Although the Internet and electronic databases are valuable for obtaining articles and government documents, at present very few books can be accessed in this way. Part of the difficulty relates to the awkwardness of reading an entire book on a screen; another obstacle is the expense of printing and binding a book in a folder.

Not long ago, if you wanted to obtain a book through interlibrary loan, you had to process your request very early in the semester if you wanted to receive the book in time for it to be useful in your research. Electronic streamlining has since made it very easy to get books though interlibrary loan. Today, they often will arrive within a matter of days. You may be able to request a loan directly from the database where you found the reference just by entering your name or student identification number.

Online Study Center
General Resources
Interlibrary Loan and Google Book/Scholar

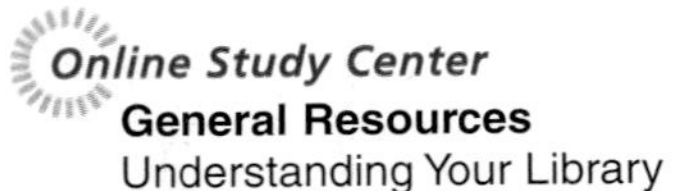

Online Study Center
General Resources
Understanding Your Library

PRACTICE 8.1 Narrowing a Research Topic

Working individually or in groups, evaluate the general topics in the following list. Select one, and use freewriting, listing, or clustering to narrow the topic so that it could become the basis of a research question.

1. Terrorist threats
2. Childhood obesity
3. Gay marriage
4. Violence in video games
5. Plagiarism

Some people argue that excessive television or computer time and diseases related to childhood obesity are connected.

PRACTICE 8.2 Writing a Research Question

Choose the topic you worked on in Practice 8.1 or another topic that interests you, and write a research question for it. Critique your research question in small groups or in class. Is it too narrow? Too broad? Is it researchable? Where might you locate information on this topic?

LEVELS OF SOURCES

Librarians, instructors, and researchers often classify sources by their degree of originality, labeling them as different levels—primary, secondary, or tertiary—depending on the relative distance from firsthand information.

Primary Sources Sources are considered primary when they result from direct experience, such as an article written by scientists to describe the results of their experiments, the diary of soldier during a war, or statistics from surveys. Primary sources are valuable because they are close to the original experience and are not influenced by the analysis, editing, and interpretation added by other people.

Secondary Sources Secondary sources use or build upon primary sources. Examples include a textbook that reports on the history of scientific research, a biography that interprets someone's diary, or a proposal based on statistics from surveys. These second-hand sources may be more comprehensive than primary sources and have the benefit of expert interpretation, analysis, and commentary.

Tertiary Sources Tertiary sources are overviews of fields of information. Dictionaries, encyclopedias, directories, indices, and bibliographies are frequently used as tertiary sources. An index or bibliography is a source of sources, listing many different primary or secondary sources and telling when and in which media they were published. Annotated bibliographies include a brief summary of the content of the source, and many indices include abstracts or longer summaries. Libraries make tertiary sources available as reference books or electronic databases. Writers often begin their research with tertiary sources to gain an overview and to find appropriate primary and secondary sources.

Conducting Research

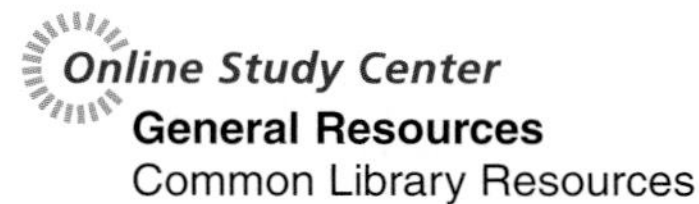

After you have developed a plan of attack, you will have to physically locate the sources that will provide some insight into your working thesis or research question. Inevitably, you will run into difficulties. Books may be checked out. Pages may have been torn out of journals. The sources you find may supply only superficial information. Much-needed websites may deny you access or cannot be found. When this happens, it is a good idea to sit down and review what you have found. Remind yourself that your goal is not just to "fill up" your paper but to provide adequate support for your working thesis or provide insight into your research question.

Your research is complete only when you have enough information to adequately back up the claims you will make in your argument. Sometimes you may have to reevaluate, or even rewrite, your research question or working thesis. Don't hesitate to return to the planning stage and rethink the focus of your project if necessary. If you must refocus, do so early in the process. The worst time to discover that you can't find enough information about your project is the night before it is due.

It's All in the Timing

Don't wait until the night before (or even a few days before) a paper is due to begin your research project. If it is a short research project, begin at least two to three weeks before the paper is due. If it is a major research paper, give it a month or more. This long lead time becomes especially important if you require interlibrary loan articles to write your paper. Remember, you will need time to evaluate what you find and locate other sources as necessary!

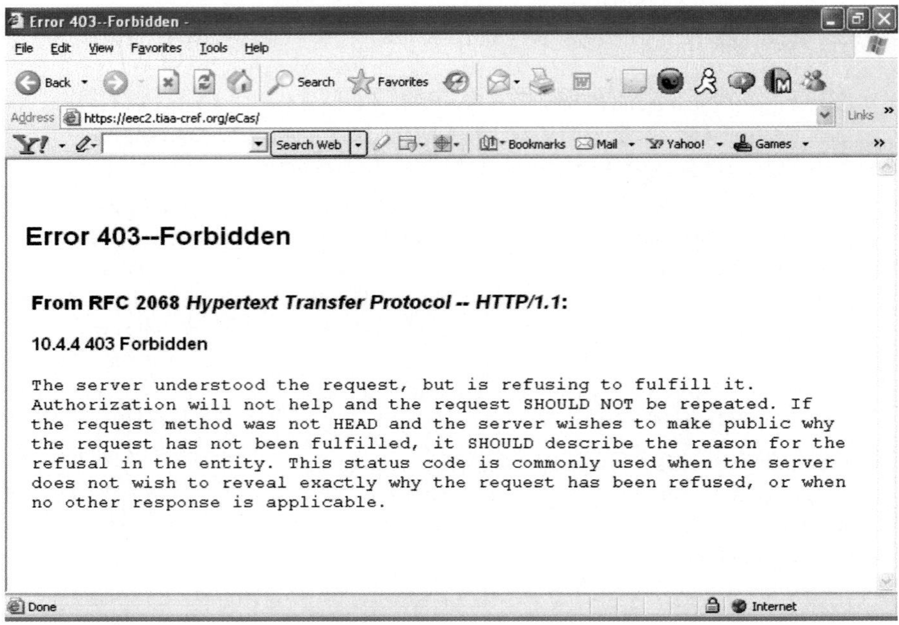

Limited access, especially from home, can make Internet research frustrating.

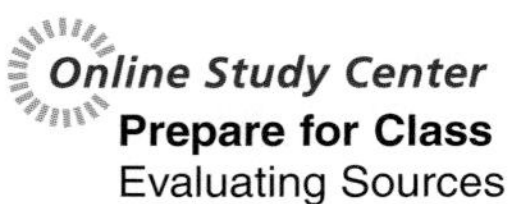

Prepare for Class
Evaluating Sources

Evaluating Sources

The main way you will evaluate your sources is by reading your sources *critically*. This involves several processes:

- Previewing what you will read
- Annotating the text
- Responding to the text
- Organizing with other texts

PREVIEWING WHAT YOU WILL READ

Previewing means that you try to understand the context of something you will read. You can ask questions about the topic, author, title, or publisher. You can also briefly examine the length of a piece, getting an idea about its tone and its level of complexity.

Who Is the Author? Occasionally you will happen across a piece of writing by a famous person, or at least by a person whom you recognize. Ask yourself whether this person will be recognized and respected by the audience. Additionally, as you conduct research, you will start seeing the same names over and over. When a person has written repeatedly about a particular subject, he or she is often (but not always) knowledgeable about the subject area. Sometimes you can obtain information about an author by looking for a headnote, reading a forward to a book, or looking up the author in the library or on the Internet. These days, many active writers have homepages that tell more about them and their writings.

What Does the Title Imply? Sometimes a title will tell you almost nothing about the content of the article or book in question. At other times the title may imply a great deal. For example, *War and Peace* tells you more about the content of Tolstoy's novel than *Hamlet* tells you about Shakespeare's play. Often, the title will tell you something about the point of view presented in the writing. You would naturally expect a different viewpoint from an article entitled "We Need Stem-Cell Research Now" than you would from an article called "The Immorality of Stem-Cell Research." Titles can sometimes help significantly in deciding how you will eventually classify the information you have found.

RELIABILITY OF INTERNET SOURCES

When using sources found on the Internet, you will find that some texts are co-published on the Internet and in print. If you use these sources, you should credit both the print source and the Internet source. When you use Internet-only sources, scrutinize them with care. While many Internet-only sources are very good, always remember that *anyone* can publish on the Web. The website where the information is published can help you gauge the reliability of the source in question. If a website has a long history and is well respected, then you can approach the source with the same level of confidence as you can a reputable print source. Conversely, be wary of information found on personal webpages.

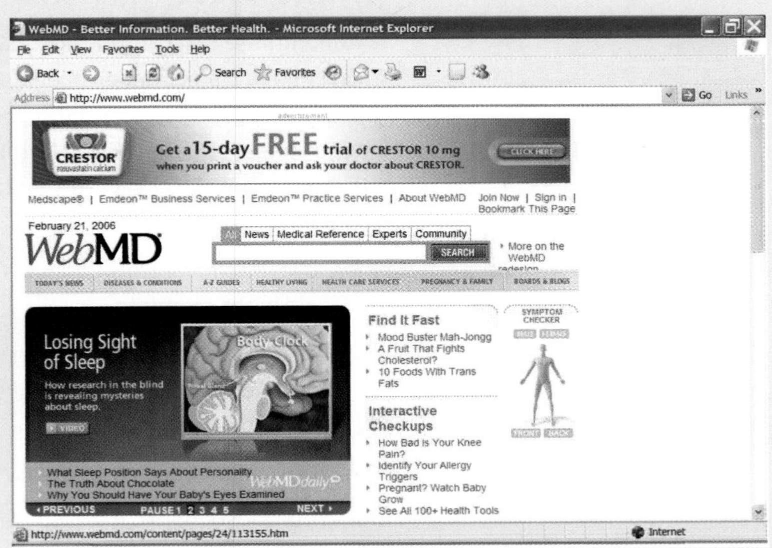

Reliable databases such as WebMD are good sources of Internet-based information.

Who Published the Piece? Publishers can be more important than you may realize. Certain publishers will carry more clout (*Wall Street Journal* and *Time*), while others may be particularly liked or disliked by a given audience. A politically conservative audience, for example, is likely to look positively upon articles from *National Review* and negatively upon articles from *New Republic*. Also, you can expect academic journals to provide more rigorously examined information than popular magazines do. As you become familiar with different publishers, you will also become familiar with the unique viewpoint that each offers.

What Does Skimming Tell Me? If you skim a piece before you read it carefully, you will get an idea about its length and complexity. This information will help you decide how much time it will take you to carefully read and annotate the article. You may also be able to identify the major and minor claims, as well as gain a sense of the article's level of difficulty. A complex academic piece will usually take more time to read and annotate than an article from a popular magazine. The lengths of paragraphs (short ones typically contain less information), illustrations, and the presence of a bibliography can all help you prepare to read.

Annotating the Text

Annotating a text can help you, as a reader, identify structural elements of the text (major claims, minor claims, topical headings, literature reviews, counterarguments, and the like) and document your initial responses to the reading. (See Chapter 4, The Reader's Response to Arguments, for more about annotating.) Here are some ways to annotate the sources you have located (and photocopied or printed via computer):

- Circle unfamiliar words or phrases so that you can look them up and define them in the margins.
- Underline sentences that seem important. Often they contain major and minor claims. Alternatively, put stars or other indicators next to important information.
- Write comments in the margins—especially if you disagree with a point.
- Write questions. If the question is later answered, make a note of it.

- Make a note if the writer addresses a topic you have encountered in another source (this will help you synthesize information from your sources later).
- On a separate sheet of paper, summarize the essay immediately after you have read it.
- Avoid using a highlighter. It just "short-circuits" the annotating process.

Taking Notes There was a time when conducting research meant taking a stack of note cards to the library to write down every quotation and detail you expected to use in your argumentative paper. In more recent years, photocopying machines and the Internet have reduced much of the paperwork involved in taking notes. Even if you are conducting your research exclusively on the Internet or working from a stack of photocopied articles, however, you should take careful notes. In addition to the critical reading practices outlined earlier, you should, at a minimum, create a note card for every source you look at. If you are seriously considering using the material as a source, annotate it and create a note card for it.

Making Note Cards and Bibliography Cards You may use two kinds of cards in your research: note cards and bibliography cards. Bibliography cards contain a complete bibliographic record of the source. Sometimes a bibliography card may include a paragraph summary of the source (its thesis and main supporting points) or notes indicating its usefulness to you under several headings. For example, a bibliography card could contain the following headings, plus a one- or two-sentence comment under each heading:

- Purpose (what the source attempts to accomplish)
- Uses (why you are interested in the source)
- Limitations (how narrow or wide the scope of the work is)
- Weaknesses (where you see a flaw in the source)
- Additional features (what kind of extra elements it includes, such as bibliographies, appendices, or maps)

Buckley, William F. "Other Things about Marriage." Townhall.com. 19 Nov 2004. <http://www.townhall.com/columnists/wfbuckley;printwf020030810>

Purpose: To convince the reader about the value of marriage.

Uses: Good stats on relationship between alternative families and poverty/crime. Reputable author.

Limitations: Very brief. Focuses mostly on the alternative family poverty connection.

Weakness: Card stacking. Considers only the negative elements of alternative families. Bias.

Additional features: None.

When creating bibliography cards using this formula, you must distinguish between sources' limitations and weaknesses. Limitations concern only the depth and focus of the source. Weaknesses consider something that you think is wrong with the argument.

Note cards contain brief reference information at the top (author's name and title of the source), with quotations, paraphrases, and summaries being recorded along with their page number references. If you use note cards instead of working from notes on paper or photocopies, then it is important to put quotation marks around anything you copy directly from the source. Also, you should carefully record all of the features of the original, including spelling, punctuation, and the use of italics. Even if the source misspells a word or is grammatically incorrect, you should reproduce the errors in your quotation. You can acknowledge that the error is not yours by placing the abbreviation *sic* inside of brackets immediately after the error.

Buckley, "Other Things about Marriage" (p. 2 of printout)

"We know that the composite impact of single-parent homes on children is huge. The poverty rate in single-parent homes is 400 percent that for two-parent homes. Among long-term prison inmates, 70 percent grew up without a father in residence. There are comparable figures for illiteracy and drug use."

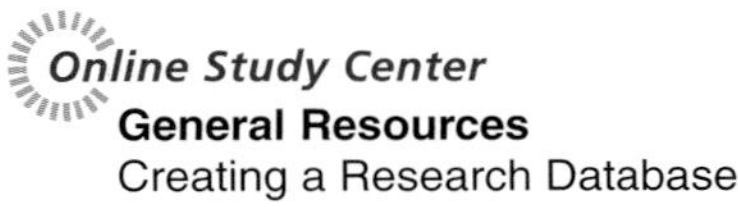

Online Study Center
General Resources
Creating a Research Database

PRACTICE 8.3 **Creating Bibliography and Note Cards**

Gather at least three of the sources that you intend to use for a research project, or use sources as assigned by your instructor. After previewing, reading, and annotating the sources, make bibliography cards for each one. Use the scheme from the earlier example, or another one mandated by your instructor. (Some teachers may prefer summaries to the heading/comment scheme.) Begin by creating a bibliographic heading for the card, in MLA, APA, or whatever style system your instructor has asked you to use. After you have created the bibliography card, set it aside and begin making the note cards. You may choose to use your first note card to write a summary of the work (thesis and main supporting points), and then record quotations and paraphrases on subsequent cards. When you are finished, put the bibliography card back on top of the pile and paperclip each source's cards together or bind them with a rubber band. Binding each source's cards separately will help you stay organized. If you work from notes on sheets of paper or from photocopies directly, paperclip the bibliography to the notes or annotated copy.

SUMMARIZING

Online Study Center
General Resources
Quotation, Paraphrase, and Summary

Some instructors may ask you to write summaries of your sources. For example, you may be asked to write an informal summary, a formal abstract, or a summary recorded on a note card. In some cases, you may wish to summarize a source in your research paper if it provides important background information, even though it does not contain information you plan to paraphrase or directly quote.

A summary may be written in one sentence, one paragraph, or several paragraphs; single-paragraph summaries are probably the most common method. In research writing, summaries are used to establish the context or provide

PRACTICE 8.4 **Writing Summaries**

Select an article from your research, choose one of the readings in Part 2 of this book, or use another source as directed by your instructor. After first carefully previewing and annotating the article, write three summaries: (1) one sentence long, (2) one paragraph long (about 100 words), and (3) one page long (about 250 words). Try this procedure for writing your summaries:

(continued)

1. After you annotate, underline sentences that seem especially important. Try to identify the major and minor claims.
2. Paraphrase the underlined sections in your own words.
3. Compose your summary, introducing transition words to make it flow well.
4. Rewrite the summary, eliminating as many words as possible as long at the information is not compromised and the words flow well. Simplicity is the key to good summarizing.
5. If your summary doesn't seem to "flow," try rearranging, combining, or rewriting sentences.

background information where more specific information (such as that provided with a paraphrase or quotation) is not required. (For more on summaries, see Chapter 9.)

Paraphrasing

Most of the information that eventually ends up in your researched argument will be paraphrased. This means that you do not summarize the material—it is a specific piece of information instead of a general idea—but rather put it in your own words. A summary is usually much shorter than the original source, whereas a paraphrase will be the same length as (if not longer than) the original.

Traditional Notes

Make bibliographic entries on 3-inch by 5-inch cards.
Copy quotations accurately.
Indicate page numbers where information was found.
Clip cards to your note sheets.
Categorize notes, clip them together, label the stacks, and place them in the order you will discuss them before you write.

Electronic Notes

Use a database to record electronic cards, or give each source its own word processing document.
Group documents in folders and subfolders. This will help you categorize your research and make it easier to locate your sources once you are ready to write.
Copy quotations accurately, and indicate the page numbers where the information was found.

Photocopies

As soon as you copy a source, immediately write the complete bibliographic information at the top of the copy. If you wait, you may lose the information in the shuffle.

Read and annotate the source soon after you copy it. Don't wait until later.

Highlight or underline quotations you may wish to use.

Write notes in the margins or on Post-it notes to indicate how and where you plan to use the information.

Stack copies by category, clip stacks together, and label each pile. Arrange stacks in the order you will use them before you write.

Responding to the Text

Responding to the material you have gathered in your research is not something that begins after you have read the article, made note cards, taken notes, and written down summaries, paraphrases, and quotations. Responding actually begins when you preview your reading, and it continues as you annotate your text and take notes. However, after you have absorbed your source, it is a good idea to evaluate its information in depth and make some decisions regarding where it fits into your research project, if at all. (You should never be afraid to toss out a source that "just doesn't fit.") One way you can evaluate a source is to consider once again the particular strengths of the author, the reputation of the publication, the applicability to your research question or claim, and the rhetorical strength of the text.

Author When authors are well known, their "reputations precede them," meaning that the public is aware of their biases and degree of credibility. Other times, you may have to investigate authors to discover whether they are specialists in a field and trustworthy in their judgment and in the presentation of their claims.

How specialized? Whenever the perception of an issue depends on having knowledge beyond common experience, a reasonable audience will pay attention to opinions from experts. For an issue such as censorship, for example, an audience will want to hear from experts on morality to understand certain values, from lawyers to understand legal aspects, from sociologists and psychologists to learn how images and language affect people, and from artists to appreciate free expression. When using an expert as a source, you may want to inform your readers: "Dr. John McWhorter, associate professor of linguistics at

Berkeley, states . . . ." An audience will also weigh the opinions of capable nonspecialists who have taken the time to conduct research into an issue. When using a nonspecialist as a source, you will need to determine that his or her research has been adequate—for example, a list of references at the end of a publication helps indicate the extensiveness of the research. Conversely, you should be wary of an opinion that comes from a nonspecialist who has not conducted adequate research or who might have misunderstood or misrepresented the facts.

How trustworthy? All people have biases—points of view that may influence their opinions. The credibility of authors depends partly on their biases and partly on how reasonably and fairly they deal with those biases. For instance, journalist George Will has a reputation for being moderately conservative and fair-minded, whereas talk show host Rush Limbaugh is known for his unflinching right-wing convictions and extreme positions. A center-of-the-road audience would probably be skeptical about most opinions offered by Limbaugh but would give strong credence to opinions offered by Will. A strong bias may lead authors to overlook or downplay evidence that contradicts their points of view while overestimating the value of other evidence that supports their claims. Even honest people can be blinded by their convictions. Of course, some people are dishonest and will purposely present false claims and evidence to further their goals.

When the reputation of a writer is unknown, you should exercise extra caution before accepting any of his or her conclusions. You can check authors' credentials through reviews of their works, by searching the Internet for entries about them, or by consulting other experts. Some databases are devoted to the backgrounds of authors: Internet authors can be checked through <http://www.writers.net>, for example. A number of *Who's Who* editions, both general and specific to various disciplines, may be useful as well.

Publication Information about a publisher can help you evaluate your source. Publishing houses, periodicals, and sponsors of websites have histories and biases that can be researched. As you check the credentials of publishers, you will want to note how specialized and how trustworthy they are.

How specialized? Some periodicals, such as *Newsweek* and *Time,* have broad interests and appeal to a very diversified readership. Their articles tend to be short, moderately detailed, and aimed at the nonexpert, although some of the feature articles may go into more length and depth. Publications with broad readerships tend to provide information on a "secondary" level that has been summarized, interpreted, and perhaps simplified. Other periodicals, such as the *Journal of the American Medical Association* (*JAMA*), have a readership of specialists; few readers outside the field of medicine would understand the terminology and data presented by *JAMA*, for example. Professional journals often present data that are "primary" in nature, appearing there for the first time.

Articles from specialized journals have high credibility because they are written and reviewed by experts. By contrast, articles from popular journals may require more evaluation because the authors might not be specialists and the articles might not be reviewed by experts before publication. If a book is published by a university press, it has probably been reviewed by experts.

URLs for websites can also provide clues about biases. Those ending with .edu are from educational sources, whereas those ending in .gov are government sites. Both types of websites tend to exist for distributing information. URLs ending in .com are commercial sites and may be motivated by profit.

How trustworthy? Like authors, many publications are well known and are preceded by their reputations. Editors of respected publications accept responsibility for what they publish, often demanding that authors authenticate their texts in various ways. The publishers of *USA Today*, for example, know that its commercial success depends on the readers' faith in its honesty. When some of the newspaper's reporters were discovered to be fabricating and plagiarizing information, not only were reporters dismissed, but the editor also resigned because she felt responsible for maintaining the periodical's journalistic standards.

Of the many thousands of publications available, you may be personally familiar with the reputations of only a few. Yet before you put your faith in a source, you will want to discover something about the publisher. Publications, like authors, have biases. Some biases are political: *New Republic* is considered liberal, and *U.S. News and World Report* is considered conservative—yet both journals are respected for their intellectual content and journalistic standards. Journals published by professional organizations or religious groups may maintain high journalistic standards yet must be read in context: They represent the beliefs of a particular group, and those views will inevitably affect the use of evidence and the statement of claims. Other journals may be biased to the point of being distorted or dishonest, sources of propaganda and lies. When you use some sources, you may want to qualify them to alert your reader of possible bias: "According to *The Watchtower,* the official publication of the Jehovah's Witnesses, ..." The Internet provides some sites that profile periodicals; visit <http://www.world-newspapers.com/news-magazine.html> for more information.

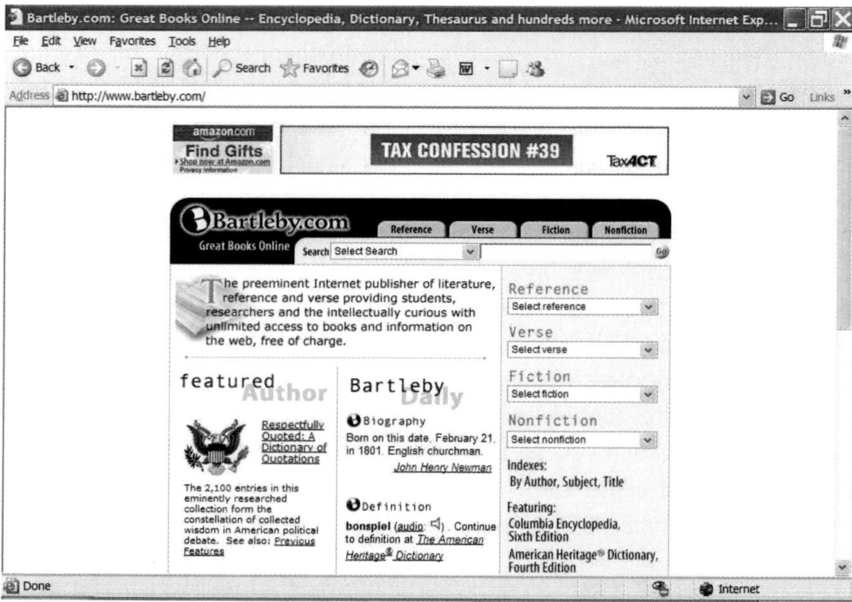

The Bartleby.com site is a reliable resource for electronic texts and reference materials.

Coverage Even when you have found a publication and author who are authoritative and honest, you will still be concerned with the quality of the information. How current and how complete is it?

How current? Some areas of knowledge change rapidly: Scientists make new discoveries, elections and revolutions change governments, laws are passed or repealed, media stars rise and fall. Other areas of knowledge may change very little over long periods of time, such as historical records. Consequently, your sources may have a very long or very short "shelf life," depending on the subject. You will have to assess whether your source is current enough to remain meaningful.

Modes of publication have different speeds of production. For example, the Internet and television and radio media are virtually instantaneous in making updates, followed closely by daily newspapers, and then by periodicals such as weeklies. Books, however, can take years to produce and more years to update. Most publications will provide a date of publication on the title page or somewhere near the beginning. The homepage of a website usually will display the date of its most recent revision; some homepages, such as stock exchange websites, may even display the hour or minute.

How complete? You must determine whether a particular source provides enough information to support your claim. Secondary and tertiary sources can be useful for putting your primary sources in the kind of context you need to evaluate "completeness." Even when you feel you have enough evidence, you should commit to not distorting an issue by omitting relevant facts. A half-truth often is a whole lie. When your research is not complete, you should either continue your research or qualify your results. For example, you can limit your conclusions by scope or by time: "My conclusions on language acquisition apply only to immigrants entering the United States from 1976 to 1988."

How biased? Just as authors and publications can demonstrate bias by selecting what they write and publish, so individual sources can demonstrate bias by deciding which claims they will make, which evidence they will include, and what they will ignore. Is the bias so strong that certain evidence is ignored or misrepresented? Would the slant of the article be distasteful to your audience? What logical fallacies are in play here? If you choose to refute a piece of writing, it is helpful to understand its weaknesses.

Rhetoric Rhetorical features can help you evaluate a text. You will want to consider the source's purpose, audience, structure, and style.

What is the purpose? The author may express a purpose directly in the text, often as part of the introduction, or the purpose may be implied by the text. Is the source intended to inform? To persuade? In some cases the author may have a hidden agenda, an ulterior motive that may not be directly detected by all members of an audience. For example, a scathing denunciation of one politician may actually be an endorsement of a competing politician or an attempt to stop a certain piece of legislation. Knowing the expressed, implied, and ulterior purposes of a source can help you determine how much trust to put in it.

Who is the audience? The intended audience for a source can reveal much about the quality of information contained in a source. Is the audience expert or novice, believer or skeptic, specific or general?

How is it structured? Is the source well or poorly organized? Does its organization affect the quality of the information? Is the structure appropriate to the purpose and audience?

How is the style used? The word choice, tone, and phrasings of a source can reveal an attitude and perhaps an ulterior motive. Is the tone reasonable? Sarcastic? When the author has discretion in choosing a word, is the choice biased or neutral? For example, a "battle" might be described as a "slaughter" or as a "peace-keeping exercise"—all of these word choices reveal something about the author's point of view.

PRACTICE 8.5 Evaluating Print Sources

Working individually or in groups, evaluate an article that you have obtained in your research. Use the following rubric:

Author: How specialized? How trustworthy? To you? To your audience?

Publication: How specialized? How trustworthy? To you? To your audience?

Coverage: How current? How complete? What bias is evident?

Rhetoric: How focused and appropriate is the purpose? Who is the intended audience? What structural weaknesses are evident? What gaps, if any, occur in the text? What, if anything, was confusing? Did the author acknowledge and refute contrary opinions? How effective is the style and tone of the piece? Select a representative paragraph and explain.

Organizing with Other Texts

Online Study Center
Prepare for Class
Evaluating Print Sources

After you have read, annotated, and possibly summarized a number of sources, you will probably have a better idea of what shape your paper will eventually take. At this point, you may find it useful to rewrite your working thesis or research question, or you may decide that you need to obtain more information and refocus your research. Eventually, however, you will decide that you have all the information you need and will begin the process of organizing it. Careful organization at this stage can save a lot of headaches later when you are trying to draft your argument.

Some of your sources will inevitably agree with each other. In fact, some may share the same source material and build upon one another. Other sources will disagree, and when they cite certain people, it will be to refute their views. Also, a few of your sources will likely address your topic directly, as if they were "made" for your paper. Others may scarcely mention your topic at all.

When you begin to organize your material, you will place your sources in categories that you create. Typically, you will place those sources that are in agreement together, and those that represent other viewpoints in other groups.

Ultimately, you will probably want to organize your research material according to how it will be used in your paper.

Suppose you've found ten articles that you want to use in a research paper:

- Literature review: Three in support of your position and two against your position
- Main argument: Three as evidence to support claims
- Counterargument (refutation): Two to represent a counterargument you plan to refute

Of course, this example is an oversimplification. You may reuse sources in your main argument that were introduced in your literature review, for example. Nevertheless, having some kind of plan regarding where you will use your sources can be invaluable. One of the easiest ways to organize your sources is to paperclip the groups together in the order you will use them, and then to place adhesive notes on each of the groups. Some writers will benefit by creating a formal outline; others will work better with informal outlines and organized "stacks" of material.

When determining how to use the sources that you have selected, ask whether source A agrees with B or whether source A has a different, even contrary thesis:

Similarity

- What would you gain from comparing A and B?
- Are A and B related strongly enough that they belong in the same section?
- Do they agree completely, or do they diverge on some points?
- Is one source more "extreme" than the other?

Difference

- Would you gain more from contrasting A and B?
- If two sources disagree, are they "polarized" or do they share some views in common?

Focus

- Do A and B address the same points, or is their "crossover" limited? (Unless one article directly responds to the other, most arguments will have limited crossover and will not "match up" claim to claim.)
- Is there enough crossover for you to discuss the articles together?
- Do A and B provide background information or engage in a current debate?

Sources

- Do A and B share sources in common?
- Does source A elaborate on or draw upon the sources represented in source B (and vice versa)?
- Would sources in their bibliographies be useful?

Electronic Research

These days, many students find it very tempting to conduct all of their secondary research on the World Wide Web. Indeed, many instructors now allow their students to perform part—if not all—of their research on the Internet. So why not do all of your investigation in the privacy of your own home instead of taking an hours-long trip to the library? While electronic research, whether carried out on the Internet or through databases and CD-ROMs that are available at your college library, seems easy at first, it can be as time-consuming as a trip to the library. In fact, research on the Internet, especially from home, can lead to many dead ends and unproductive hours of searching for the right information. Electronic research must be just as well planned as traditional secondary research, and it requires the same evaluative steps as the less high-tech approach.

Just as traditional library research requires knowledge of the ways libraries organize information, some familiarity with the types of electronic resources that are available (and their limitations) can be helpful.

RESEARCH ON THE INTERNET

While no one will deny that the Internet's accessibility from any home computer makes it convenient, its vastness (and its relative lack of organization) can make it difficult to find the kind of information you need. Information in libraries is neatly organized on shelves, where each item has its own special place and number. In contrast, the Internet is rather like a giant pile of books in the middle of the room. When you do a search on the Internet, you are rummaging through that pile (albeit very quickly). If you type the keyword "Shakespeare" into Yahoo!, for example, you will come up with millions of hits (who could ever look at them all?), including community theaters, costume shops, genealogy sites, and several breweries! Also, where these sites are positioned in your "results" has less to do with their quality and more to do with their willingness to pay the search engine company to list the site near the top. Be especially wary of "sponsored links." Usually they are commercial sites that have paid the search engine company

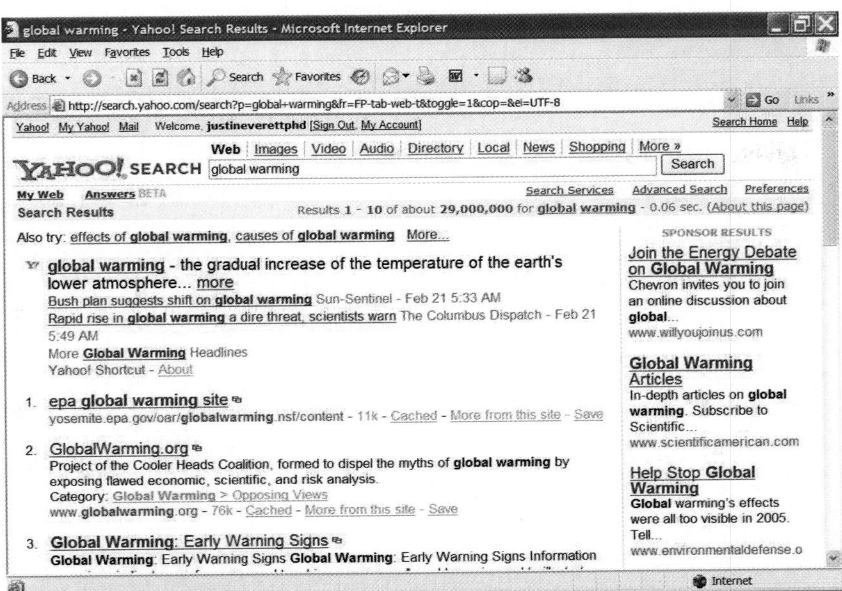

Yahoo! is one of the most popular search engines.

to appear in a very prominent position at the top of the list. While these links may not look like "banner ads," they serve a similar purpose. If your Internet search is not carefully phrased and well planned, it can prove very difficult to find the sort of information you're looking for.

Another consideration when conducting an Internet search is the quality of the material that is published on the World Wide Web. While book and magazine publishers are very careful to select only the best material for publication (largely because of the cash they must invest), anyone with an Internet connection and a little know-how can place information on the Internet. While some of this information is indeed valuable, much of it is amateurish, short-sighted, poorly researched, horribly biased, or just plain wrong. When you obtain information on the Internet, you should evaluate the site carefully for knowledgeable authors, reputable publishers, fair content, and strong, balanced rhetoric.

Research Using Internet Search Engines Although the plethora of material available on the Internet presents a challenge when your goal is to find valuable, authoritative information, you should not ignore this resource. There are two keys to conducting successful Internet research: Use good research techniques, and evaluate Web information carefully for its quality. As with library research, you should formulate a working thesis or research question, create a

Online Study Center
General Resources
Organizing Research: Folders and Piles

How Many Internet Sources Can I Use?

Just a few years ago, many professors would not allow their students to cite documents from the Internet. They deplored the poor quality of the resources their students found and believed using the Internet "short-circuited" the research process. Today, however, most professors encourage their students to cite information obtained on the World Wide Web and even support students who create their own websites. It is becoming increasingly common for professors to require students to create at least one Web-based project. Many students use resources from the Internet exclusively in their papers, whereas others may find some of their sources in the library and other sources on the Internet or in their library's databases. Check with your professor to see what is required. Whenever you rely on Internet sources, they should be of the same quality as information obtained in the library, and they should be properly cited (see Chapters 13 and 14 for more information).

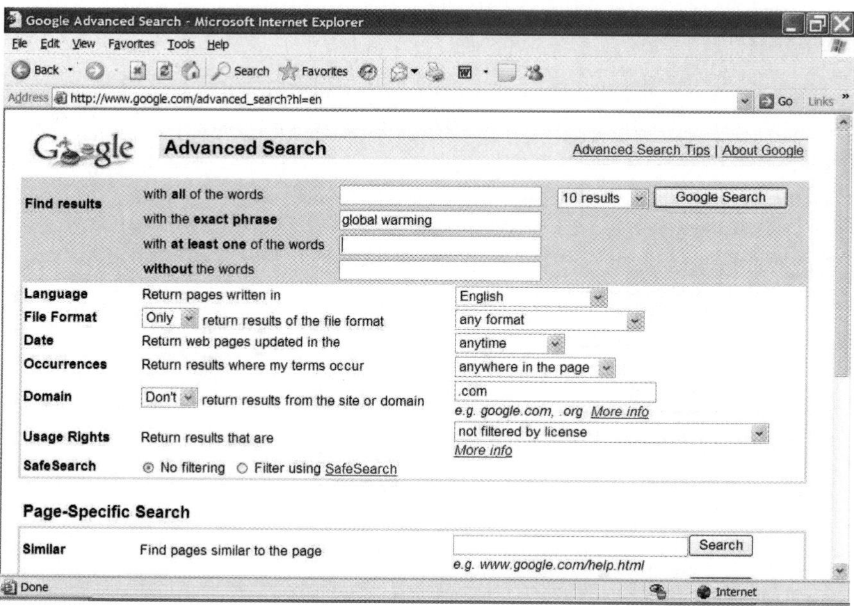

An advanced search lets you limit your results to the specific types of information for which you are searching.

research plan, and carefully read, annotate, and evaluate any information that you find.

Two of the most popular search engines on the Internet are Yahoo! and Google. Whereas Yahoo! is one of the oldest search engines and is famed for its huge collection of categories, Google is known for cataloging an enormous amount of material. These two options are not the only search engines available, however. Many specialized search engines exist, and one may deal specifically with your topic. Some websites even publish catalogs of hundreds of different search engines.

Basically, search engines list things in two ways. First, people submit their URLs to the engine, hoping they will be listed. Second, Internet "robots," sometimes called "spiders," search the Internet for things to list. Thus, even if you don't find success with one engine, you may have better luck using another engine.

How do I conduct an Internet search? If you are looking for something unusual, you may be able to find it using the general search function. More often, however, you will need to use the advanced search function. It allows you to filter your search using a specific sequence of words, determine where those words occur on the page, select sites with a particular type of suffix (such as .edu, .org, or .com), or even limit the search to a particular website (such as the massive Web MD site). Boolean operators—words like *and*, *or*, and *not*—can help you limit your search. Most of the time you can also put phrases in quotation marks if you want to return only pages with words in a particular order (for example, "building concrete dams" in that order, instead of all pages containing the words "building," "concrete," and "dams"). With a little experimentation, you may discover ways to limit your search so that you will have to wade through less irrelevant material. In general, limiting your search to sites that end in .edu (universities and colleges), .org (organizations), and .gov (the U.S. government) is a good idea. Searching on the .com suffix will often yield numerous commercial sites that provide little useful information. Websites in other countries use suffixes with which you may be less familiar. For example, .co.uk designates commercial sites based in the United Kingdom.

Online Study Center
General Resources
Managing Internet Research

How do I evaluate a website? A great deal of information exists on the Internet for evaluating websites. Most university and community college libraries provide some kind of advice for evaluating site content. Here are a few basic things to look for when you evaluate the quality of something you have found on the Web:

Author: Who wrote the piece? What else has he or she published on the Internet or in print (a quick search will help you with this question)? Is the author an authority in this subject area? Will your audience respect him or her? If no author is listed, is the website a reliable source of information?

Publication: Is the home site reputable and reliable? Is it easily recognized? How long has it been up? Does it update its content regularly? How biased is it? Are its writers reputable? Do they also publish in print? Where? If the source is an electronic magazine, how long has it existed? Does it copublish in print?

Coverage: How current, complete, and in-depth is the information? Does it include illustrations? A bibliography? If the information is dated, would it make more sense to use a print source? Does the website offer links to other valuable sources of information?

Rhetoric: How focused and appropriate is the purpose? Who is the intended audience? What structural weaknesses are evident? What gaps, if any, occur in the text? What, if anything, was confusing? Did the author acknowledge and refute contrary opinions? How effective are the style and tone of the piece? Are logical fallacies evident?

Website Reliability

When evaluating a website for reliability, consider the following issues:

- Who sponsors the site?
- How long has it been up?
- How reputable are the authors who appear on the site?
- Has the site won any awards?
- Is it associated with a reputable organization like a university?

Don't let a slick appearance fool you. Some of the best sites look like a train wreck, while many sham sites have a slick, professional appearance.

Online Study Center
Prepare for Class
Evaluating Online Resources

Research on Subscription Databases Most libraries subscribe to specialized databases in a variety of disciplines. Many of these databases allow you to access them from your home computer using a password; others are kept on CD-ROMs that you can search using your library's computers. While some of these services will return only bibliographic references, others provide full-text versions of articles and books. These databases also have the advantage of being up-to-date, unlike the books found on your library's shelves.

LexisNexis and ProQuest are examples of general-purpose databases that are available through many college libraries. Additionally, your college library may subscribe to a number of specialized databases. For example, Project Muse provides access to articles published in a wide range of notable academic journals in the humanities, and ERIC lists conference presentations and articles in the field of education. A visit to your library will allow you to find out which sorts of databases are available in your particular area of research.

Electronic Searches for Articles, Books, and Government Documents Not too many years ago, a trip to the library meant spending hours paging through a cross-referenced "card catalog." In some libraries, these catalogs took up much of the first floor. These days, the space occupied by the paper-based catalogs has been largely usurped by desks and computers. These machines provide access to electronic "card catalogs" that allow you to search not only your own library's holdings, but often the holdings of libraries all over the country. You might even locate a book you need in a library three states away and issue an interlibrary loan request for the source. Usually the book will arrive in just a few days, instead of the two weeks or longer it used to take.

A Final Word on Sources: Currency

So far, we have said only a little about the currency of sources. Most of the time, you want the sources you are relying on to formulate your argument to be as up-to-date as possible. While books usually contain the most detailed information, by the time they are published they are at least two years out of date. Articles contain less detailed information (although they may provide in-depth coverage of a limited topic) and tend to be several months out of date. Newspaper articles are very current, but usually offer only superficial coverage of a particular issue. Likewise, information obtained on the Internet or through your library's other electronic resources may be up-to-date, but may treat your subject in less detail than you need. When you evaluate your resources, you must balance these two issues—currency versus in-depth coverage. As the author of a research-based

Boolean Operators

When you use a search engine to explore the Internet or a database like ProQuest, your results may include books, government documents, and articles from journals and popular magazines. Often, however, these searches will yield too many hits.

Narrowing a search: To narrow your search, you can use Boolean operators:

And will return items listing both words.
Or will return items listing one word or the other.
Not will not return items listing the word that follows it.

For example, if you typed

childhood obesity epidemic

then you would return articles listing any of those words. If you typed

childhood and obesity

or

obesity and epidemic

then you would more likely return the types of articles you were looking for.

Limiting a search: You can focus your search to have more hits and fewer misses by searching a phrase: a group of words together in a set order. Some search engines such as Google require quotation marks around the words to make a phrase: "child obesity epidemic" would omit sources that didn't have those three words together in that order. Other search engines such as EBSCO don't require quotations marks; they assume that any search terms typed together are a phrase.

Note: Different search engines may define Boolean searches in their own particular ways. Be sure to read the instructions for any Boolean or advanced search before typing in your search terms.

argument, you must be the judge about the appropriate balance in your particular case.

Avoiding Plagiarism

Online Study Center
Improve Your Grade
Plagiarism

Plagiarism is the act of representing someone else's words as your own. It is both a form of academic dishonesty and a type of theft. When you commit plagiarism, you steal someone else's ideas and present them as being your own. Universities and colleges enforce strict penalties for plagiarism, including expelling students who commit this offense.

The ready access to the Internet has, unfortunately, increased instances of plagiarism in recent years. The most flagrant examples involve students who purchase papers over the Internet and turn them in as their own work. Some websites have even begun writing custom papers for students—for a hefty fee, of course. Other students have engaged in "cut and paste" plagiarism, in which they may "borrow" information from a website, paste it into their papers, and fail to give credit to the source. This epidemic has forced some professors to take desperate measures, including submitting papers through Internet services such as turnitin.com where they can be electronically checked for stolen material. Turning in work that is not your own cheats you of the education you deserve and is unfair to other students who have worked hard to produce their own papers.

Sometimes plagiarism may be accidental, but it still carries the same severe penalties as deliberate theft. One way students accidentally plagiarize is by improperly paraphrasing a borrowed source. Consider the following passage from page 74 of Richard Fortey's book *Life: A Natural History of the First Four Billion Years of Life on Earth:*

> So what are animals? In the first place, they feed: They feed upon plants, either directly, or by feeding upon some other animal that feeds upon plants. Animals are spongers on the hard work of photosynthesizers: They graze or hunt, or else they absorb nutrients from an organic soup which was ultimately brewed by plants.

If a paraphrase is poorly written, it may consist of groups of the same words used by the original source. This practice is a low-tech form of "cut and paste" plagiarism. In the example that follows, the underlined words were copied directly from the preceding passage:

> <u>Animals feed upon plants.</u> Sometimes they <u>feed upon other animals that feed on plants,</u> or they <u>sponge</u> off the

photosynthesizers. They graze, hunt, and absorb nutrition from the organic soup made by the plants (Fortey 74).

Even though this passage has been rephrased, it contains so much of the original language that it constitutes plagiarism. While it is often not possible to avoid all of the language used in the original ("photosynthesizers" would be hard to replace without a long, awkward phrase because it is a technical term), groups of words and idiomatic language should not be duplicated. The following paraphrase attempts to capture the content of the original without duplicating the original language:

> According to Fortey, animals are organisms that feed upon plants either directly, by eating the plants themselves, or indirectly, by consuming creatures that feed upon plants. In some cases, animals feed upon the chemical by-products that plants produce (74).

In this paraphrase, most of the language is the writer's own. A few of the same words have been used, but not in the same way or in the same order as the original. While the word *directly* was used, it was utilized in a new way, and no other word could replace it without making the paraphrase awkward or changing the meaning of the passage. For example, the writer could have used the words *primarily* and *secondarily*, but they would have changed the meanings that "directly" and "indirectly" imply. In no case did the writer use the same groups of words as in the original, and the idiomatic expressions from the original quotation were left out as well. While it is important for a writer to use his or her own words in the paraphrase, it is equally important for the paraphrase to maintain the same length and emphasis of the original. Chapter 9 includes further guidelines for recognizing and avoiding plagiarism when you quote sources in your work.

PRACTICE 8.6 Paraphrasing a Challenging Passage

Read the following passage from Bill Joy's *Wired* article, "Why the Future Doesn't Need Us." Paraphrase all or part of the passage, being careful not to directly quote the original. If you do use groups of words, place them inside quotation marks.

(continued)

We are being propelled into this new century with no plan, no control, no brakes. Have we already gone too far down the path to alter course? I don't believe so, but we aren't trying yet, and the last chance to assert control—the fail-safe point—is rapidly approaching. We have our first pet robots, as well as commercially available genetic engineering techniques, and our nanoscale techniques are advancing rapidly. While the development of these technologies proceeds through a number of steps, it isn't necessarily the case—as happened in the Manhattan Project and the Trinity test—that the last step in proving a technology is large and hard. The breakthrough to wild self-replication in robotics, genetic engineering, or nanotechnology could come suddenly, reprising the surprise we felt when we learned of the cloning of a mammal.

Looking Back at Chapter 8

- Research is a three-stage process: *planning*, *exploring*, and *evaluating sources*.
- One of the best ways to find sources is to follow a "bibliographic trail."
- Research can involve either obtaining information in person (through *primary research*) or reading what others have written about a particular topic (through *secondary research*).
- Most libraries divide resources into five areas: books, periodicals, reference, government documents, and media.
- Librarians, instructors, and researchers often classify sources by their degree of originality, labeling them as different levels—*primary*, *secondary*, or *tertiary*—depending on the relative distance from "firsthand" information.
- Evaluate your sources by reading them *critically*: previewing, annotating, responding, and organizing.
- In research writing, summaries are used to establish the context or provide background information where more specific information (such as that provided with a paraphrase or quotation) is not required.
- You can evaluate a source by considering the particular strengths of the author, the reputation of the publication, the applicability to what you are researching, and the rhetorical strength of the text.
- Plagiarism—turning in work that is not your own—cheats you of the education you deserve and is unfair to other students who have worked hard to produce their own papers.

Suggestions for Writing

- Select one of the questions in the following list. Using your library and/or the Internet as indicated by your instructor, find the answer to the question. Prepare a presentation (or write a short essay) explaining the research process you followed. Remember to formulate a research plan and record all of your steps in the process.
  1. When was the term *rock and roll* first coined? Where and by whom?
  2. Under what conditions did poet John Milton allow his estranged wife to return to him?
  3. What does *deconstruction* mean? Who coined this term?
  4. What did the Ace Paperback Company do when it discovered that J. R. R. Tolkien did not have a U.S. copyright for *The Lord of the Rings?*
  5. How did the G.I. bill affect writing programs at colleges in the United States in the 1960s and 1970s?
  6. Which fashion model made a thin, rail-like figure popular in the 1960s?
  7. When were American baseball teams desegregated? Who was the first black player to enter an all-white team? How was he treated by other players? By the public?
  8. Who wrote the first "disk operating system" program for personal computers? Which company did he help build? How did he land the deal?
- Use the techniques featured in this chapter to conduct research on a topic of your choice.

Online Study Center
Improve Your Grade
Suggestions for Writing

QUOTING, PARAPHRASING, AND SUMMARIZING

Quote me as saying I was misquoted.
—GROUCHO MARX (1890–1977)

The chapter-opening quotation is known as an *epigraph,* a word of Greek origin meaning "written above or over." Writers sometimes begin a book, chapter, or essay with an epigraph to introduce an issue, set a tone, or grab the reader's interest. When an epigraph serves as a launching point for discussion, it

Quotations often are followed by commentary.

"When you quote a Presidential candidate, Gorman, you do not—I repeat—do not roll your eyes."

Online Study Center
This icon will direct you to content and resources on the website <college.hmco.com/pic/lamm1e>.

becomes the first topic to be addressed—similar to the way this paragraph is taking advantage of the preceding epigraph to introduce a particular use for quotations. Occasionally (and perhaps less effectively), the epigraph simply hovers over the text—not directly discussed, relevant to the argument, yet never enlisted as support for any particular claim.

As you conduct your research into an issue, you will discover sources that provide essential support for particular claims. You then must decide how to add those sources to your text. You can incorporate the words and ideas of others in three distinctive ways: quoting, paraphrasing, and summarizing.

- **Quoting:** You present the ideas and the wording of a source, unchanged from the original.
- **Paraphrasing:** You present the ideas of a source unchanged, but you express them in your own writing style.
- **Summarizing:** You present the important ideas of a source in briefer form and in your own writing style.

Quoting

Online Study Center
General Resources
Quoting

A quotation is an exact repetition of words written or spoken by someone else. Quotations have many uses in writing, but along with their application come responsibilities.

Uses of Quotations

Quotations perform important functions in argumentative writing: They support your views with authoritative sources, add clarifications, provide context for issues, reveal controversies, and add touches of drama and eloquence.

Authority: Using Experts and Documents for Support The original wording from a text can be authoritative. When experts express their thoughts in their own words, it is as if you brought the actual authority to speak personally to your reader. Similarly, quoting from a relevant document can persuade your reader to trust your analysis and interpretation of it. For example, if you were arguing about gun control, you might quote Article II of the Bill of Rights.

> Although the Second Amendment protects the right to bear arms, it also requires regulation: "A well regulated [emphasis mine] Militia, being necessary to the security of a free State, the right of the people to keep and bear Arms, shall not be infringed."

Clarification: Explaining the Original Wording When the original statements are complex, confusing, or subtle, unraveling the meaning may become the focus of your writing.

> When Mae West says, "Marriage is like a book—the whole story takes place between the covers," she humorously uses double entendre to assert the predominance of sex: The second meaning of *covers* refers to a bed.

Context: Revealing a Variety of Views Surrounding an Issue When you wish to reveal the extent, history, or nature of a debate, a series of quotations may be effective.

> Writers disagree on how selfless love should be. Although Emerson exhorts, "Give all to love: Obey thy heart," Yeats cautions, "O never give the heart outright," and Housman writes, "Give not your heart away."

Controversy: Using an Extreme Statement to Focus an Issue A controversial statement may provide an interest-catching "hook" or a thematic focal point for part or all of an essay.

> Vice President Cheney claimed that a vote for John Kerry would be a vote for a terrorist attack: "If we make the wrong choice [for president], then the danger is that we'll get hit [by terrorists] again."

Drama: Using Dialogue to Make an Issue Come Alive Because readers respond more readily to real people rather than to abstractions and concepts, your writing can be enlivened with dialogue or personal statements made by others. Dramatic techniques of description and dialogue can make an issue come alive.

> Her eyes reflecting the flames from the apartment building, she pleaded, "Save my daughter! Won't somebody save my daughter?"

Eloquence: Displaying a Statement That Is Phrased Skillfully Sometimes you may wish to preserve the original wording because its rhetorical style is striking. In the following quotation, John F. Kennedy skillfully used a technique known as inversion or chiasmus, reversing the order of the terms *you* and *your country* in the two parallel clauses.

> Kennedy reminds us of the selflessness of patriotism: "Ask not what your country can do for you; ask what you can do for your country."

Online Study Center
General Resources
How to Quote Effectively

HOW TO QUOTE EFFECTIVELY

Several important responsibilities accompany the use of quotations.

Honesty: Staying True to the Meaning of Your Sources When you quote from a source, one of your most important obligations is to present the original message honestly. Although exact quotations help maintain honesty,

THE QUOTING PROCESS

Plan

- **Read critically and annotate.** Look for passages that can enhance your argument. Such passages can be used to support your argument or to represent opposition arguments.
- **Make choices.** Determine how much of the source you wish to delete, quote, paraphrase, or summarize.

Draft

- **Integrate.** Connect the quotation to your text with an introductory lead-in.
- **Explain.** Restate, interpret, apply, analyze, synthesize, and evaluate the quotation as needed.

Revise

- **Check major features:** honesty, acknowledgment, proportion, integration, and accuracy.

even a precise repetition of a person's words does not convey all of the original meaning. To present another person's ideas honestly, you must (1) provide context when needed and (2) interpret fairly.

Provide context. Surprisingly, quotations don't always "speak for themselves." Consider, for example, this simple, one-word quotation: "Yes." Although we all know the meaning of *yes*, the word itself signifies nothing outside of the context in which it was spoken. Words taken out of context can distort a source's original meaning, sometimes conveying the exact opposite.

> President George W. Bush was quoted as saying, "I don't think we can win the war on terrorism," a statement that sounds like an admission of failed policy. However, the context of the quotation concerned ways in which terrorism was unlike conventional warfare, making a conventional victory involving a peace treaty impossible.

Interpret fairly. When you quote someone, you usually follow up with your own words of explanation and interpretation. A misinterpretation will distort the meaning of a quotation. For example, during the 2004 presidential campaign, Senator John Kerry was quoted as saying he supported authorizing President Bush to declare war on Iraq. Kerry's opponents interpreted this statement as Kerry supporting Bush's decision to go to war; Kerry, however, insisted that his support was only to give Bush discretionary power and not approval to invade Iraq before United Nations weapons inspections were concluded.

Acknowledgment: Giving Credit to Your Sources Whenever you quote a source, you must acknowledge it through an attribution known as a reference or citation. This credit can be in text (within your text but attached externally to the main body of the sentence), integrated (grammatically part of your own sentence), or both (parts of the citation are given in both places).

In-text (formal, nonintegrated, parenthetical) citations. Often you will give credit to your source in a standardized, formal method known as a style. Referencing or documentation styles are distinct from rhetorical style; these guidelines are issued by professional organizations such as the Modern Language Association (MLA) or the American Psychological Association (APA). Styles dictate what kind of reference information must be given and how it must be displayed. MLA and APA, for example, require that references be given inside parentheses that are not grammatically part of a sentence. (MLA and APA styles are fully discussed in later chapters of this book.)

MLA STYLE: AUTHOR'S NAME AND A PAGE NUMBER
"If the microscopic dot is a human being with full human rights, the answer is easy: no stem cell research" (Kinsley 13).

APA STYLE: AUTHOR'S NAME, YEAR OF PUBLICATION, AND A PAGE NUMBER
"If the microscopic dot is a human being with full human rights, the answer is easy: no stem cell research" (Kinsley, 2004, p. 13).

In-sentence (integrated) citations. Sometimes you will decide to place credit for your source within your own sentence as you introduce a quotation; this is especially advisable when the name of the source endows the quotation with more authority. The simplest way to integrate a citation is by including an introductory lead-in that names the source: "According to Jones, . . ." or "Smith states that . . . ." To emphasize the credentials of the authority, you may choose to add brief biographical information.

MLA STYLE
Critical theorist Stanley Fish asserts that "free speech is not an independent value but a political prize" (43).

APA STYLE
Critical theorist Stanley Fish (1993) asserts that "free speech is not an independent value but a political prize" (p. 43).

Proportion: Using Quotations Sparingly Composition students tend to quote excessively—too often and at too great a length. The result seems like a string of oversized pearls of other people's wisdom, with the composition student providing only the string. The chief reason for overquoting probably is a lack of writing experience: Novice writers may not trust their own ability to "turn a phrase" and may be unacquainted with strategies for paraphrasing and summarizing. The temptation to borrow the ready-made words of others is difficult for writers-in-training to resist, especially when they are struggling to meet a deadline and satisfy a word count.

An essay brimming with quotations is seldom a very good essay. The chorus of quoted experts tends to drown out the voice of the author, who then becomes more like an emcee rather than the featured performer. If the quotations are not dead-on relevant to the author's claims, the essay will tend to ramble and consequently will lack focus. Worst of all, the author may inadvertently reveal a very unpersuasive lack of self-confidence by not asserting ownership of the argument. Remember that *you* own the argument. To claim ownership of your writing, use quotations sparingly.

- Quote only those parts of others' writing that relate to your claim. To do so, you may have to delete parts from quoted sentences or remove sentences from quoted paragraphs.

  FULL-LENGTH QUOTATION
  Cohen and Kristol caution against stem-cell research: "And in trying to stamp out disease by any means necessary, we risk beginning the 'compassionate' project of killing off the diseased themselves, something that has already begun with the selective abortion by parents of 'undesirable' embryos."

  SHORTENED QUOTATION
  Cohen and Kristol caution that stem-cell research may lead to euthanasia—"killing off the diseased themselves." [The shortened version focuses specifically on euthanasia.]

- Quote only when necessary for establishing authority, making a clarification, providing context, pinpointing a controversy, creating a dramatic effect, or showcasing eloquence.
- Use paraphrasing and summarizing whenever you need material from sources but quotation is not required by other circumstances. (Paraphrasing and summarizing are demonstrated later in this chapter.)

Integration: Combining Your Words with Those of Others Pretend for a moment that your essay is simply a conversation between you and your reader. If someone known to you but unknown to your reader joins this conversation, etiquette dictates that you should introduce this newcomer. If the newcomer bursts into the conversation without any introduction, your reader may be jolted, puzzled, and perhaps even irritated. The etiquette of writing is similar to the etiquette of conversation: readers benefit not only from knowing when to shift their attention to another speaker but also from knowing something about that new speaker. Through this introductory signaling you integrate ("make whole") the quotation: You join the quotation with your essay not only logically but also grammatically.

Online Study Center
General Resources
Integrating Quotes

Novice writers often integrate quotations weakly or not all. Quoted sources that lack any introduction are known as dropped, floating, free-floating, free-standing, or dumped quotations. Even when dropped quotations follow the logical flow of a paragraph, you are still obliged by convention and common sense to integrate them.

DROPPED QUOTATION
After the tragedy of September 11, 2001, homeland defense will never be the same. "Everything has changed: the nature of threat, the sources of information, the technology use" (Treverton 40).

INTEGRATED QUOTATION

After the tragedy of September 11, 2001, homeland security will never be the same. Gregory Treverton, former vice chairman of the National Security Council, underscores the 9/11 effect: "Everything has changed: the nature of threat, the sources of information, the technology use" (40).

In the first example, the quotation follows the logical flow of the first sentence, but lacks any kind of introduction. In the second example, the quotation is integrated by identifying the source.

The most common method of integrating a quotation is to identify the source. In its briefest form, this identification consists of a personal name or title. This method of integration is known by various names: signal phrase, tag, introductory phrase, or lead-in. Some writers prefer short lead-ins: "in the words of [name]," "according to [name]," "as stated by [name]," or "as [name] has pointed out." However, the "name coupled with a verb" method can become boring to read unless you vary how you write the lead-ins.

Vary where the lead-ins connect to the quotation. Although it makes sense to provide introductory material before beginning a quotation, readers also prefer varied sentence patterns. Minor changes in punctuation will enable you to locate your lead-ins at the beginning, middle, or end of a quotation:

BEGINNING LEAD-IN

As stated by Michael Kinsley, "Embryos that aren't transferred get destroyed or frozen indefinitely—unless, that is, they are used for stem-cell research."

MIDDLE LEAD-IN

"Embryos that aren't transferred get destroyed or frozen indefinitely," states Michael Kinsley, "—unless, that is, they are used for stem-cell research."

ENDING LEAD-IN

"Embryos that aren't transferred get destroyed or frozen indefinitely—unless, that is, they are used for stem-cell research," writes Michael Kinsley.

Vary the wording of the lead-ins. Some verbs and phrases are neutral, including little or no information to influence the reading of a quotation. "Jones writes . . ." or "In the words of Smith . . ." leads a reader into a quotation without revealing how the source is related to the issue or how you feel about the source. As a writer, you would deliberately employ such "neutral" lead-ins when you do not wish to influence the reader.

At the same time, you have the option of including any of hundreds of non-generic lead-in verbs that can add useful information. "Jones agrees that . . ." or

"Smith disputes the fact that . . ." at the very least will provide some variety in your diction. More importantly, informative verbs help your reader anticipate how the quotation relates to the issue under discussion.

Add more information to the lead-ins. Skilled writers go beyond the minimal requirements of a lead-in, expanding it to include many kinds of relevant information:

- **Revealing the credentials of the source:** J. R. R. Tolkein, author of *Lord of the Rings,* defines fantasy as . . . .
- **Clarifying the relevance of a quotation to an issue:** Jones refutes Smith, saying . . . .
- **Sharing an attitude of a source toward an issue:** Smith blusters . . . .
- **Sharing your estimate of the value of the source:** Jones is mistaken when she states . . . .
- **Rather than using a name of a particular source, commenting on the content of the quotation:** Plagiarism can actually be encouraged by policies that seek to discourage it: "We had been operating on an outdated and semi-relevant policy that clearly affected the punishment that could be meted out" (Rouche).

Follow up the lead-ins and quotations with explanations. Experienced writers rarely move past a quotation without discussing it, instead "milking it for all it's worth." Inexperienced writers overlook a quotation's potential for initiating discussion and consequently find themselves in desperate need of quotations to meet a required word count.

Following are some strategies for explaining a quotation, based on Bloom's taxonomy. For more information on explanations, see Chapters 3 and 4.

- **Knowledge (clarification): Clarify to make sure the evidence is understood.** You can restate its key point to ensure that a quotation is understood on a basic, literal level. Paraphrase, summary, and emphasis are types of restatements that help clarify evidence.
- **Comprehension (interpretation): Speculate on the quotation's deeper meaning and significance.** Sometimes a quotation requires an interpreter who can "read between the lines," putting a kind of "spin" on it.
- **Application: Explain how the evidence applies.** Application can be important when the connection between the quotation and your claim isn't immediately clear.

- **Analysis: Explain the parts.** Analysis is like a dissection, dividing a whole into its parts and explaining how they work both separately and in unison. When a quotation is complex, breaking it down into smaller pieces will help your audience understand it.

LEAD-IN VERBS

When introducing a quotation, you have the option of using a verb purposefully—thereby guiding the reader's understanding of the quotation or of the source—or remaining neutral.

- **Neutral influence:** Adds little or no perspective or interpretation in advance of the quotation.

  Patrick Henry states, "Give me liberty, or give me death!"

- **Interpretation:** Suggests the attitude that a source or quotation takes toward an issue. Briefly explains the attitude expressed by each verb.

  Patrick Henry exhorts his fellow legislators, proclaiming, "Give me liberty, or give me death!"

- **Evaluation:** Suggests the attitude that you take toward the source or quoted information. Briefly explains the attitude expressed by each verb.

  Bravely, Patrick Henry placed his life on the line: "Give me liberty, or give me death!"

The verbs listed below are examples of lead-ins. Although this list seems long, it represents only a small fraction of the choices available to a writer.

accentuates
accuses
acknowledges
acquaints
adds
admits
advises
affirms
alleges
announces
answers
applauds
approves
argues
asks
asserts
assumes
attests
avers
avows
believes
bewails
blames
calls attention to
cautions
challenges
charges
claims
clarifies
comments
communicates
compares
complains
conceals
concedes
concurs
condemns
confesses
confirms
confronts
considers
contends
contests
contrasts
counsels
counters
cries
criticizes
declares
declines
decries
defies
deliberates
demonstrates
denies
deprecates
derides
disagrees
disallows
disapproves
discards
discloses
disparages
displays
disproves
disputes
draws attention to
eliminates
emphasizes
endorses
enlightens
establishes
exhibits
explains
exposes
expresses
goes over
grants
grieves
guesses
highlights
illustrates
implies
includes
indicates
informs
inquires
insists
laments
lays bare
maintains
mentions
mourns
muses
notes
notifies
observes
offers
points out
ponders
praises
proclaims
proffers
proposes
protests
proves
proves false
puts forward
reacts
rebuts
recapitulates
recaps
recognizes
recommends
refuses
refutes
rejects
rejoins
remarks
reminds
replies
reports
requests
responds
retorts
reveals
reviews
says
scoffs
shows
specifies
states
stresses
submits
suggests
summarizes
sums up
supports
supposes
tells
thinks
underscores
updates
verifies
views
volunteers
warns
wonders
writes

- **Synthesis: Relate the quotation to other claims or evidences.** One quotation may interact with others, either supporting or refuting those other quotations. Synthesis brings two or more quotations together, allowing for comparison/contrast, rebuttal, or an accumulation of mutually supporting points.
- **Evaluation: Explain the quotation's value.** Sometimes a quotation needs qualification—an explanation of how reliable and complete it is.

PRACTICE 9.1 **Choosing the Right Verb**

For each of the following purposes, list five appropriate lead-in verbs. Briefly explain how each might affect a reader.

1. Neutral influence—adding little or no perspective or interpretation in advance of the quotation
2. Interpretation—suggesting the attitude that a source or quotation takes toward an issue
3. Evaluation—suggesting the attitude that you take toward a source or quoted information

PRACTICE 9.2 **Vary Your Lead-Ins**

Choose one or more quotations from a source you may use in an argumentative essay. Practice writing lead-ins at the beginning, middle, and end.

Accuracy: Being True to the Words of Others When you quote, you are obliged to remain faithful to the original wording. You fulfill this obligation by clearly signaling (1) where your own words make a transition into and out of a quotation and (2) where you make a permissible alteration in the quotation.

To transition into and out of a quotation, you need to clearly signal to the reader where your words end and the source's words begin. A quotation is signaled in one of two ways: (1) by placing quotation marks at the beginning and end of the quotation or (2) by *blocking* (indenting) a long passage to set it off from the rest of your text.

Once you have signaled the beginning of a quotation, you must preserve the original wording. However, under certain circumstances you may change a quotation by (1) adding necessary information, (2) deleting irrelevant parts, or (3) changing grammatical or mechanical elements. Specialized punctuation marks

Online Study Center
Prepare for Class
Changing Quotations While Maintaining Accuracy

are used to signal these changes—a pair of square brackets for each addition and an ellipsis for each deletion.

Add to a quotation. Sometimes quotations need additional material to make them function smoothly in your text. Although technically you are prohibited from changing a quotation, there is a legitimate way to add words—by using brackets. Brackets look like squared-off parentheses [] and, in fact, are often called "square brackets" to distinguish them from "angle brackets" < >. Although parentheses and brackets are both used to enclose words and other additions, they generally are not interchangeable. Brackets have a unique use: They create a zone within a quotation where you momentarily suspend the obligation to quote verbatim. Using brackets, you can include a number of your own additions to a quotation:

- **Changes in the original forms of the words:** To blend or integrate a quotation with your own writing, you may need to change the capitalization of an initial letter, the tense or number of a verb, the person or number of a pronoun, or other features.

  "[A]sk what you can do for your country," directed Kennedy.

- **Clarifications:** Because quotations often are taken out of context, you may need to add words to clarify a name, a pronoun reference, or an event.

  "Lady [Diana] Spencer married Prince Charles on July 29 [1981]."

- **Explanations:** Sometimes you may highlight (underscore, italicize, bold) a portion of the quotation to emphasize something. Brackets allow you to explain that you added the highlighting, using phrases such as "emphasis mine" or "italics added."

  "Ask *not* [emphasis mine] what your country can do for you."

- **Corrections:** A quotation may contain a factual error that you can correct if it doesn't substantially change the meaning of the quotation.

  "Easter is calculated by the 1528 [1582] Gregorian calendar."

- **Disclaimers:** A misspelling or error in typing, grammar, or fact could create confusion about whether you or the source were the origin of the error. Writers traditionally bracket the Latin word *sic* (which means "thus") to indicate that the error immediately before it comes from the original source.

  According to the candidate, "The incumbent is a left-leaning libberal [*sic*]."

PRACTICE 9.3 Adding to a Quotation

Locate a quotation you plan to use in an argument. Add necessary words to it and then integrate the quotation into your own sentence.

Delete from a quotation. Some quotations contain more information than you need to support your claim. If you can remove irrelevant information without distorting the essential meaning of the quotation, the result will be clearer and more concise. To indicate a deletion, you insert an ellipsis where the deletion occurred. Make an ellipsis by typing three spaced periods in a row (. . .).

Although an ellipsis technically is an addition to a quotation, MLA style (2003) does not require it to be enclosed in square brackets. However, MLA does recommend using square brackets around your own inserted ellipsis dots in the rare situation where you're quoting a passage that itself contains an ellipsis.

> Scout seems unaware that she had softened the hearts of the lynch mob: "Well, Atticus, I was just sayin' to Mr. Cunningham that entailments are bad an' all, but [. . .] it takes a long time sometimes . . . that you all'd ride it out together . . ." (Lee 154).

In the preceding quotation from *To Kill a Mockingbird*, the two unbracketed ellipses were written by author Harper Lee to represent speech pauses; the bracketed ellipsis shows where the student writer deleted a part of Scout's speech.

Several other rules guide your use of ellipses. Which rules apply depends on (1) where the deletions occur within a sentence and (2) how the ellipsis interacts with other punctuation marks.

- A deletion at the beginning of a sentence: An ellipsis is not required when the deletion occurs at the beginning of a sentence, as long as the remainder of the quotation preserves the source's meaning. When the sentence deletion causes a sentence to begin with a lowercase letter, use brackets to insert a capital letter.

  ORIGINAL
  "I have a dream that one day this nation will rise up and live out the true meaning of its creed."

  CHANGED
  "[T]his nation will rise up and live out the true meaning of its creed."

- **A deletion within a quoted sentence:** Use the standard ellipsis with a space before and after each ellipsis point.

  "I have a dream that . . . this nation will rise up and live out the true meaning of its creed."

- **A deletion between quoted sentences:** Place the ellipsis in the location of the deletion after the first sentence and before the second sentence. Hold a space before and after each ellipsis point.

Martin Luther King, Jr.'s speeches and writings are frequently quoted.

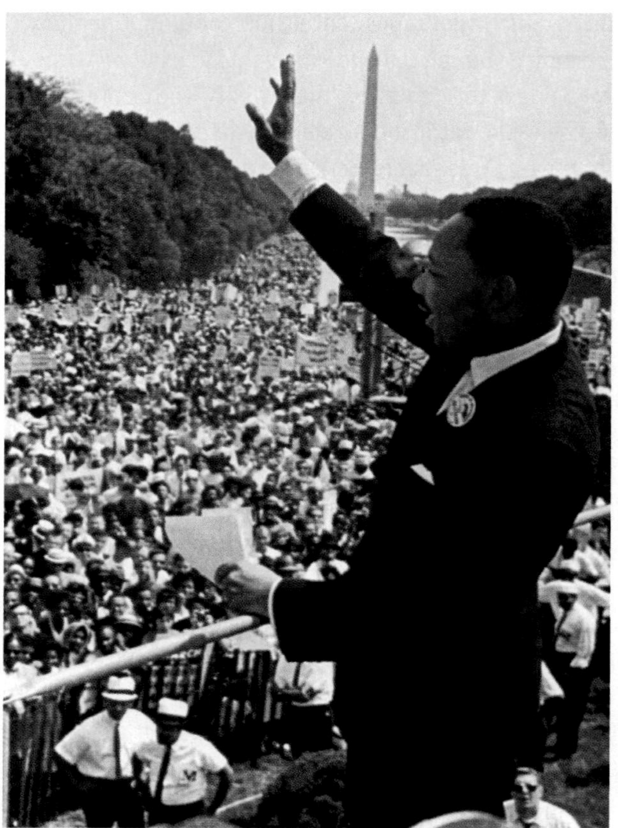

Martin Luther King linked civil rights to American ideals: "And if America is to be a great nation, this must become true. . . . From every mountain side, let freedom ring."

- **A deletion at the end of a quoted sentence ending with a period:** Placement of the final period depends on whether a parenthetical reference concludes your sentence.

  Without a parenthetical reference: When your sentence ends with an ellipsis, the period goes after the last word in the sentence.

  King proclaimed, "I have a dream that one day this nation will rise up. . . ."

  With a parenthetical reference: When your sentence ends with a parenthetical reference, use an ellipsis after the last word of the quotation, and then close the quotation. Place the period after the parenthetical reference.

  "I have a dream that one day this nation will rise up . . ." (King).

PRACTICE 9.4 Deleting from a Quotation

Locate a quotation you plan to use in an argument. Delete unneeded words from it and then integrate it into your own sentence. Use ellipsis marks, as needed.

Change grammatical or mechanical elements in a quotation. When part of a quotation is blended grammatically with part of your sentence, sometimes the forms of some words need be changed. The tense or number of a verb and the number or case of a pronoun are typical changes, but sometimes an adverb or adjective may change forms.

ORIGINAL
"If you are lucky enough to live in Paris as a young man, then wherever you go for the rest of your life it stays with you, for Paris is a moveable feast" (Hemingway).

CHANGED
Hemingway believed that Paris was a "moveable feast" and that "wherever you [went] for the rest of your life, it [would stay] with you."

Under certain circumstances, you can make changes in punctuation without signaling the change to the reader. For example, you may change a period to a comma at the end of a quotation.

ORIGINAL
Sometimes a cigar is only a cigar.

QUOTED
"Sometimes a cigar is only a cigar," admitted Freud.

You may change double quotation marks to single quotation marks for a quotation within a quotation.

ORIGINAL
What does she mean by "glom"?

QUOTED
"What does she mean by 'glom'?"

PRACTICE 9.5 Changing the Grammatical and Mechanical Features

Locate a quotation you plan to use in an argument. Change grammatical and mechanical features as needed to integrate the quotation with your own text.

PUNCTUATING QUOTATIONS

Following are rules for quotation marks, examples of how they interact with other punctuation, and explanations.

1. **A comma follows a partial-sentence introduction to a quotation.**

   Hamlet ponders, "To be, or not to be?" [The introductory lead-in needs the quotation to form a complete sentence.]

2. **A colon follows a complete-sentence introduction to a quotation.**

   Hamlet poses an existential question: "To be, or not to be?" [A colon requires a complete sentence before it. A word, phrase, list, or complete sentence can follow.]

3. **A comma or period goes inside the final quotation mark, unless a parenthetical reference follows it.**

   "Flip flops," said the candidate, "are my opponent's weakness."

   "Flip flops," said the candidate, "are my opponent's weakness" (Bush).

   [This is the preferred style in the United States, but in the British Commonwealth the commas and periods appear outside the quotation marks.]

4. **A period is the only kind of "end punctuation" following a parenthetical reference.**

   The novel *A Tale of Two Cities* begins, "It was the best of times. It was the worst of times" (Dickens 1). [A sentence needs only one period to end it. If a quotation concludes a sentence, its period is postponed until after the parenthetical reference.]

5. **Exclamation marks or question marks remain with the quotation, even if a final period comes after a parenthetical reference.**

   "Families, I hate you!" (Gide 38). [An exclamation mark or question mark conveys information vital to the quotation but not meant to exclaim about or question the parenthetical reference.]

6. **A question mark or exclamation mark is placed according to its relation to the quotation.**

   Nixon proclaimed, "I am not a crook!" [Place the punctuation inside the final quotation mark when the quotation itself is a question or exclamation.]

   Did Nixon proclaim, "I am not a crook!"? [Place the punctuation outside the final quotation mark when the sentence is a question or exclamation about the quotation. A question mark or exclamation mark carries more information than a period and thus has a function beyond that of "end punctuation."]

7. **A semicolon or a colon goes outside the final quotation mark.**

   The W stands for "wrong": This was Kerry's attack on George W. Bush. [Semicolons and colons are never used for end punctuation.]

8. **Two square brackets indicate additions or alterations.**

   - Use brackets to add a comment or correction:

     According to the candidate, "My opponent is a *left-leaning* [emphasis mine] libberal [*sic*]."

   - Use brackets to show changes such as capitalizing a lowercase letter in the original quotation:

     "[C]ome on up and see me sometime," West suggested.

   - Do not use brackets to indicate changing a period to a comma at the end of a quotation:

   ORIGINAL
   "It ain't over 'til it's over."

   CHANGED
   "It ain't over 'til it's over," said Yogi Berra.

Paraphrasing

Through your research you will discover other people's ideas that you wish to use in your writing. Although you sometimes will quote your sources directly, you shouldn't be overly dependent upon other people's words. Paraphrasing is an alternative to quoting. To paraphrase is to express someone else's ideas not merely

PUNCTUATING QUOTATIONS *(continued)*

9. **An ellipsis indicates a deletion.**
   - Type three spaced periods to create an ellipsis:

     "I have a dream that . . . this nation will rise up and live out the true meaning of its creed."
   - To show a deletion at the end of a quoted sentence, place a period at the end of the sentence followed by three spaced-out ellipsis points and the end quotation marks:

     King proclaimed, "I have a dream that one day this nation will rise up. . . ."
10. **An ellipsis is not necessary for a deletion at the beginning of a quotation.**

    Kennedy concluded, "[A]sk what you can do for your country." [The bracketed A of *Ask* provides capitalization for the new beginning of this quotation.]
11. **A pair of single quotation marks is placed inside a pair of double quotation marks to show a quotation within a quotation.**

    "Yogi Berra-isms include 'It ain't over 'til it's over.'"
12. **A block quotation uses indentation to replace a pair of quotation marks.**
    - MLA: Use block quotations when the quotation is more than four lines, Indent the entire blocked quotation ten spaces from the left margin only, not from the right.
    - APA: Use block quotations when the quotation is more than fifty words. Indent five spaces or one return.
    - Include any quotation marks that were part of the original quotation. Place parenthetic references after the blocked quotation's end punctuation.

      The energy, the faith, the devotion which we bring to this endeavor will light our country. . . . And so, my fellow Americans: ask not what your country can do for you; ask what you can do for your country. My fellow citizens of the world: ask not what America will do for you, but what together we can do for the freedom of man. (Kennedy)

President John F. Kennedy delivered his famous "Ask Not" speech at his inauguration in Washington, D.C., on January 20, 1961.

in your own words but in your own style—that is, using your own word choice, sentence structure, and organization of ideas.

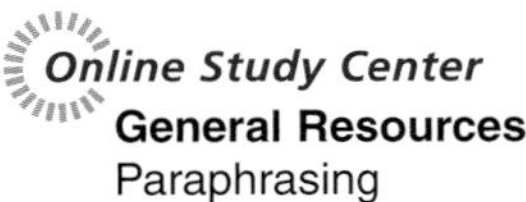

General Resources
Paraphrasing

Uses of Paraphrasing

Use paraphrasing to make yourself the main speaker, to clarify the source, to add zest to the original, or to extract key points without the problem of excessive ellipses.

Make Yourself the Main Speaker Your readers primarily want to read your words—to "hear" what you have to say, even when you are using the ideas of others.

Clarify When the Original Source Is Difficult to Understand Clarification may be necessary to explain difficult concepts or terminology, antiquated language, or unusual phrasing such as one might find in some poetry.

Add Stylistic Zest When the Original Source Is Worded Blandly You probably wouldn't paraphrase famous quotations, such as Kennedy's "Ask not what your country can do for you; ask what you can do for your country." In many other communications, however, it is the meaning—not the means of expression—that is memorable.

Extract Key Points without Excessive Ellipses The original source may contain additional points that are not relevant to your discussion. Irrelevant content in a quotation can mislead or confuse a reader. Of course, you can excise unwanted materials from a direct quotation, but overuse of ellipsis marks can render a passage difficult to read.

YOUR OWN VOICE

Imagine for a moment what it would be like to have a conversation with someone who spoke only in quotations.

You: Our relationship isn't going anywhere.
He/She: Alexander Pope wrote, "Fools rush in where angels fear to tread."
You: But I'm just not happy the way things are.
He/She: Remember what John Stuart Mill says: "Ask yourself whether you are happy, and you cease to be so."
You: Why do you quote all the time instead of speaking for yourself?
He/She: "Words that enlighten are more precious than jewels." Hazrat Inayat said that.

An essay resembles a conversation, with you as the chief speaker. Your reader prefers to hear your "voice" even when the ideas originate from others. Novice writers tend to overuse quotations, perhaps because they feel safer using the original but more likely because quoting is easier than paraphrasing. Fortunately, paraphrasing becomes more natural with practice.

Key Features of Paraphrasing

To paraphrase correctly, you must be true to the source's meaning, state the meaning in your own style, suspend the use of quotation marks, and give credit to the source.

The Essential Ideas of the Original Source Are Complete and Undistorted You have not added any ideas, including your opinion or interpretation. The length of the paraphrase is similar to the original.

The Writing Is in Your Own Style The wording is your own, except for words that cannot be changed without losing the original meaning. The sentence structure is your own. When paraphrasing paragraphs, the sequence of ideas is your own.

No Quotation Marks Are Used Use quotation marks only with direct quotations—when you have not changed the original source at all. Of course, you'll place quotation marks around any unchanged portions of the original that you might include in the paraphrase.

Credit Is Given You must still give credit to your source, either within the text or afterward, following MLA, APA, or other style guidelines.

Misconceptions about Paraphrasing and Plagiarism

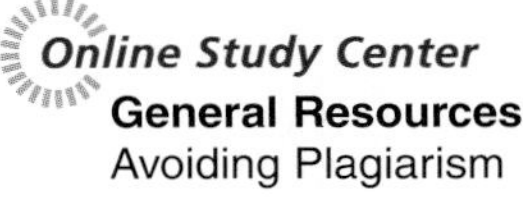

An old rule of thumb dictates you do not have to quote a source as long as you don't use more than four consecutive words from it. This guideline has led some students to believe that you can paraphrase by simply changing every fifth word or so. Wrong! Even if you credit the source of your ideas, formulaic word substitution alone will result in a type of plagiarism (literary theft). When you don't use quotation marks when expressing someone's idea, you are claiming that you are speaking in your own voice. To paraphrase honestly—to avoid plagiarism—you will find it necessary to change the original.

There are three major techniques for paraphrasing. Employing any one of them in isolation may still result in plagiarism, but using them together will help assure that the writing style is your own.

- Substitute key words or phrases. Find synonyms for key words, as long as you can preserve the original meaning.

- Use different sentence patterns than found in the original.
- Rearrange the sequence of points if the sequence is not essential to the original meaning.

Substitute Key Words or Phrases Although simple word substitution alone isn't enough to qualify as honest paraphrasing, you must replace some of the vocabulary of the original material with your own word choices. Choosing which words to change isn't a matter of substituting a percentage of words or satisfying a formula such as "every fifth word," but rather using your voice while not borrowing the voice of the original writer or speaker. For example, if a writer describes someone as "cocky," that word choice also says something about the writer. A cocky person has a brazenly overconfident attitude; when you call someone "cocky," you reveal your attitude toward that person. "Cocky" is a more colloquial way of saying something that can be stated in a less stylized way: "conceited" or "arrogant."

> ORIGINAL
> "**And** most hip-hop...is **delivered** in a **cocky, confrontational cadence.**"
>
> PLAGIARIZED (WORD SUBSTITUTION BUT SAME SENTENCE PATTERN)
> "**Also,** most rap is **performed** in an **overly confident, combative style.**"
>
> PARAPHRASED (WORD SUBSTITUTION AND NEW SENTENCE PATTERN)
> "Rappers' performances tend to display aggression and excessive confidence."

Kinds of words and phrases to substitute. Certain word choices should be treated as the intellectual property of the author of your source materials. Detecting which words and phrases compose the personal voice of your source is one of the first "paraphrasing" skills you must develop. Use your own language in the following situations:

- **Most words or phrases that have accurate synonyms.** For example, *confrontational* can be replaced with other words, such as *combative*.
- **Words or phrases that may be colloquialisms, slang, or figures of speech.** For example, *in your face* is another way of saying *aggressive*.
- **Forms of words.** You can change a word to a different part of speech. For example, *confrontational* could become *confronting* or *confronted*, which leads to a new sentence structure.

Kinds of words and phrases to keep. Keep the original author's language in the following cases:

- **Words without accurate synonyms:** *Stem cells,* for example, would not have many synonyms that nonspecialists would recognize. Some slang terms and dialect also lack synonyms.
- **Function words:** Prepositions (*of, on, in, to*), articles (*the, a, an*), and other style-neutral words can remain as is, unless it is convenient to change them. Such words play a supporting role in a sentence, yet sometimes carry important meaning: A preposition such as *above* indicates direction; a substitution might be misleading.

Use Different Sentence Patterns A number of techniques would compel you to change the structure of a sentence.

- **Change the basic structure.** Vary the sentence structure—simple, compound, or complex.
- **Change parts of speech.** Turn a noun into a verb, or vice versa. This usually forces a significant change in sentence structure.
- **Change the order in which the information emerges in the sentence.** For example, try sentence inversion.
- **Change the modification.** Adjectives, adverbs, and various phrases can be added, subtracted, or moved around.

Rearrange the Sequence of Points Sometimes certain points in a paraphrase are in a fixed order that shouldn't be changed. Preserve the original sequence in the following situations:

- **Standard phrases:** A familiar phrase such as "red, white, and blue" not only describes a flag but is a synonym for it. "Moe, Larry, and Curly" describes the Three Stooges not only as individuals but as a unit. Changing these to "blue, red, and white" or "Larry, Curly, and Moe" is not only unnecessary but also a bit unsettling.
- **Sequences that have a temporal order:** Some events and activities have a natural progression, such as the directions for baking a cake. Changing this progression can create confusion.

- **Patterns that are linked to the meaning of the paraphrased passage:** Sometimes materials are presented in order of importance, in alphabetical order, or in spatial order (such as from left to right or top to bottom). Tampering with a meaning order can result in a disorganized paraphrase of an organized original.

When the sequence of points in the original material does not have an indispensable pattern, however, you should rearrange the sequence. Resequencing helps you distance yourself from the original, showing that your style isn't derivative. For example, the bulleted list and discussion preceding this paragraph are not in a fixed order. A paraphrase might read like this:

> According to Lamm and Everett, a paraphrase should retain the original order of points when the order is essential to the meaning. Chronological order (history, technical procedures), phrases that act as a single entity (such as Old Glory's colors of red, white, and blue), and other meaning-dependent patterns are exempt from being resequenced. On the other hand, when the order is not crucial, the best tactic is to reorganize the materials in an original fashion.

PRACTICE 9.6 Identifying Words to Be Substituted

Read the following passage and list ten words or phrases that you think would be changed if you paraphrased it. Provide synonyms for them.

> And most hip-hop, whatever its "message," is delivered in a cocky, confrontational cadence. The "in your face" element is as essential to the genre as vibrato to opera, reinforced as rappers press their faces close to the camera lens in videos, throwing their arms about in poses suggesting imminent battle. The smug tone expresses a sense that hip-hop is sounding a wake-up call, from below, to a white America too benighted to listen. I can count on hearing about a "hip-hop revolution" from at least one questioner at every talk I gave these days.
>
> —JOHN MCWHORTER, *"Mean Street Theater"*

PRACTICE 9.7 Identifying Words to Remain the Same

In the passage given in Practice 9.6, list five words or phrases that you probably would not change if you paraphrased it. Why would you not want to change them?

PRACTICE 9.8 Evaluating Paraphrased Passages

The following passages are students' paraphrased versions of the McWhorter passage presented in Practice 9.6. What meaning has been retained? What meaning has been lost or changed?

1. According to John McWhorter, the majority of rap, regardless of its meaning, is performed in a self-confident, combative style. The aggressive performance is as basic to the art form as brush strokes are to painting, emphasized as hip-hoppers thrust their visages toward the lens of the camera of a televised video, waving their arms while striking poses like battling warriors. The self-satisfied sound conveys the idea that rap is an alarm rung by the underprivileged to waken American Caucasians too dense to understand. McWhorter wagers that he'll hear a comment about a "rap revolution" from at least one person attending the speeches he gives nowadays.
2. Although delivered in an offensive manner, the style of rap music is defined through the message that is gotten from what is being said. How are the characteristics of body language and slang any different from any other style characteristics in the other various musical categories? The offensive manner has to be somewhat eye-catching to draw the attention of the indifferent stereotyping public. (McWhorter)
3. Rap music, says music critic John McWhorter, is known for its risky, "on the edge," violent tone. The artists acting violently as if they are going to start a brawl is as necessary as coffee is in the morning. Rappers feel this is essential to sell albums. They want the world to notice the music and how they feel. The music has changed the world so much that it's very uncommon to not hear it (or hear about it) on a daily basis.

PRACTICE 9.9 Revise the Paraphrasing

Revise one of the paraphrases of the McWhorter passage from Practice 9.8, but this time put it in your own voice by changing words and phrases, altering sentence structures, and possibly putting some ideas in a different order.

PRACTICE 9.10 Compose Your Own Paraphrase

Choose a passage that you may wish to include in your own essay. Paraphrase it, following the process and other guidelines given in this chapter.

PRACTICE 9.11 Evaluating Paraphrased Sentences

For each of the following quotation–paraphrase pairs, evaluate the quality. Has the original meaning been preserved? Is the style of the paraphrase different enough? Which techniques were used to change the style?

1. ORIGINAL: "Nearly four million Americans are tipping the scales at more than 300 pounds."
   PARAPHRASE: Americans today are more overweight than ever: there are about four million people who weigh more than 300 pounds.
2. ORIGINAL: "A study in *Obesity Research* found that newlyweds gain an average of six to eight pounds in the first two years of marriage" (Koontz).
   PARAPHRASE: According to Koontz, research indicates that typical newlyweds gain six to eight pounds within two years.
3. ORIGINAL: "At the heart of this obesity epidemic is a debate over whether obesity is a biological 'disease' [. . .]."
   PARAPHRASE: The obesity problem has people arguing about whether it should be called a disease.
4. ORIGINAL: "The causes of epilepsy are varied, and one seizure alone doth not an epileptic make."
   PARAPHRASE: Epilepsy has varied causes, and one seizure does not make an epileptic.
5. ORIGINAL: "Both sunlight and tanning beds increase the risk of skin cancer."
   PARAPHRASE: Tanning beds and sunlight pose a threat to skin health by increasing a person's chances of getting skin cancer.

THE PARAPHRASING PROCESS

Plan Read, annotate, and make choices.

- **Read critically and annotate.** Identify the major claim and the important supporting points.
- **Make choices.** Determine how much of the source you wish to delete, to quote, to paraphrase, or to summarize. For a paraphrase, list synonyms for key words and phrases. List major ideas to be expressed in the paraphrase. If sequence is important, organize the ideas by sequence. If not, consider presenting the ideas in an order that differs from the original.

Draft Write in your own style.

- **Avoid looking at the original.** If you work from memory and notes, you'll be less likely to mimic the original.
- **Don't editorialize.** Be as objective as possible. A paraphrase is not a review: Refrain from evaluating the quality of the information or from reacting personally. Don't distort the meaning of the original.
- **Integrate.** Connect the paraphrase to your text with an introductory lead-in.

Revise Cross-reference with the original source.

- Are the wordings, sentence structures, and organization distinctly your own?
- Is the length about the same as the original? (This is a matter of practicality—it will usually take approximately the same length to convey the same meaning.)
- Is the original meaning complete and undistorted?
- Did you give credit to your source?

Summarizing

Online Study Center
General Resources
Summarizing

A summary is a reduction of a longer text into a condensed form. Also know as a précis, brief, or abstract, and figuratively described as "the bottom line" and "talking points," it is shorter than the original text, presenting only the essential information. A summary may be written as a single sentence, as a single paragraph, or in a much longer form, depending on the length of the original and on how much information you wish to convey.

Uses of Summarizing

You will encounter summaries in virtually every field that uses information. Although they lack the elaboration found in full-text documents, they are valued for their conciseness.

- Article databases (such as ABI Inform, Biological Abstracts, and hundreds of others) offer summaries (abstracts) to full-text articles so that researchers can preview longer works, deciding whether the longer readings will be useful before accessing the original versions.
- To cope with information overload, researchers sometimes read summaries almost exclusively, thereby gleaning the main ideas of the original writings.
- Writers present summaries in their writings (1) to be concise and (2) to focus on the relevant points of a source without presenting irrelevant points. If your purpose in a summary is to make a point and not to produce an abstract of a source, you can pick and choose what you will include.

How to Summarize

Sometimes when you summarize, your major goal is to provide a brief yet balanced view of an entire text. An annotated bibliography and an abstract of a journal article, for example, are intended to be read by wide audiences and must be written so that anyone can get an overview. When you summarize to make an argument, however, you can more narrowly target what you present—as long as you don't distort the meaning of the original text.

As you summarize, you will make decisions about what to present fully, what to condense, and what to omit.

- **Present fully.** Major claims sometimes are difficult to present in abbreviated form.
- **Condense.** Some data can be reduced from paragraphs to sentences or from sentences to phrases.

- **Omit.** Much of the explanation or supporting evidence may be disregarded in the summary.

You'll have to decide which points you wish to make and how much depth to give those ideas. Sometimes you can summarize a huge amount of information in a few words. Darwin's *Origin of the Species,* for example, can be reduced to "humans evolved from primate ancestors"; a summary that brief may be adequate to make a point in an argument about intelligent design. At other times, however, you may need to provide more information about the original source.

Following is an excerpt from an argument made by Dr. Gregory Stock on the topic of human longevity. It will help illustrate how to summarize.

> We've developed many ways of trying to accept not only these ravages, but death itself. The first is to ignore descent: We can simply pretend it isn't happening. This works when we're young, but becomes ever less effective as the years march by and our strength seeps from us. The second way is to deny death: We can assert that the soul is eternal, that our memory will live on, that we are young at heart, that we are not older but better. A third way is to battle the process like Ponce de Leon did slogging through Florida, Dorian Gray, or those engaged in anti-aging research because, in the backs of their minds, they hope to extend their own future. Or we can accept this descent as sad but inevitable, and say that it's natural and can't be avoided, or even tell ourselves that it's the best thing and claim, like Leon Kass, the chair of the President's Bioethics Advisory Commission, that death gives meaning.
>
> —Gregory Stock, "Would Doubling the Human Life Span Be a Net Positive or Negative for Us Either as Individuals or as a Society?"

To summarize Dr. Stock's passage, you must decide what to present fully, what to condense, and what to omit.

- **Present fully.** The key point seems to be contained in the first sentence: "We've developed many ways of trying to accept not only these ravages, but death itself." It may be difficult to shorten this statement.
- **Condense.** Dr. Stock has signaled the major supporting points with transitions: *first, second, third, or.* The main point of each sentence could be shortened at all these points and placed in a single sentence.
- **Omit.** Specific examples—references to Ponce de Leon or Leon Kass—probably can be left out of the summary.

Below is a 39-word summary of Stock's 166-word passage:

> According to Dr. Gregory Stock, humankind copes with aging and death in several ways: denial of physical effects, the consolation of eternal afterlife, the development and use of anti-aging treatments, and philosophical resignation to the natural scheme of life.

THE SUMMARIZING PROCESS

Plan

- **Read critically and annotate.** Identify the major claim and the important supporting points. As you read, watch for topic sentences—the author may have already identified important points for you.
- **Make choices.** Decide which information to present fully, which to condense, and which to omit.

Draft Write in your own style.

- **Don't editorialize.** Be as objective as possible. A summary is not a review, so refrain from evaluating the quality of the information or reacting personally. Don't distort the meaning of the original.
- **Integrate.** Connect the quotation to your text with an introductory lead-in.

Revise Check your summary by cross-referencing it with the original source.

- Are the wordings, sentence structures, and organization distinctly your own?
- Is the length shorter than the original?
- Is the original meaning complete and undistorted?
- Did you give credit to your source?

PRACTICE 9.12 Writing Summaries: Part 1

Write a seventy-five-word summary of the following paragraph, an excerpt from Michael Crichton's "Environmentalism as Religion Run Amok."

How about the human condition in the rest of the world? The Maori of New Zealand committed massacres regularly. The Dyaks of Borneo were headhunters. The Polynesians, living in surroundings as close to Eden as one can imagine, fought continually and created a society so hideously restrictive that you could lose your life for stepping in the footprint of a chief. It was the Polynesians who gave us the very concept of taboo, as well as the word itself. The noble savage is a fantasy. That anyone still believes it, 200 years after philosopher Jean-Jacques Rousseau, shows the tenacity of religious myths and their ability to hang on in the face of centuries of factual contradiction. There even was an academic movement, during the latter 20th century, that claimed that cannibalism was a white man's invention to demonize indigenous races. (Only academics could fight such a battle.) It was some 30 years before professors finally agreed that yes, the ritualistic consumption of human flesh indeed does occur. Meanwhile, all during this time, New Guinea highlanders continued to eat the brains of their enemies, until they finally were made to understand that they risked kuru, a fatal neurological disease. Remember, too, that the African Pygmies have one of the highest murder rates on the planet. Conversely, the gentle Tasaday of the Philippines turned out to be a publicity stunt, a nonexistent entity.

PRACTICE 9.13 **Writing Summaries: Part 2**

Select an article from your research, perhaps one of the readings in Part 2 of this book or another source as directed by your instructor. After first carefully previewing and annotating the article, write two summaries: (1) a one-sentence summary and (2) a one-paragraph (about 100 words) summary.

Looking Back at Chapter 9

- A quotation is an exact repetition of words written or spoken by someone else.
- Quotations support your views with authoritative sources, add clarifications, provide context for issues, reveal controversies, and add touches of drama and eloquence.
- To paraphrase is to express someone else's ideas not merely in your own words but in your own style—that is, using your own word choice, sentence structure, and organization of ideas.
- Paraphrasing helps you (1) express another person's ideas in your own voice, (2) clarify points that are unclear in the original, (3) present points in a more interesting way than the original, and (4) smoothly delete unnecessary information from the original.
- A summary is a reduction of a longer text into a condensed form. Also known as a précis, brief, or abstract, and described figuratively as "the bottom line" and "talking points," it is shorter than the original text, presenting only the essential information.
- A summary may be written as a single sentence, as a single paragraph, or in a much longer form, depending on the length of the original and on how much information you wish to convey.

Suggestions for Writing

- Revise the quotations in one of your essays.
  1. Improve your integration and explanations.
  2. Change some quotations into paraphrases or summaries.
- Paraphrase something you have read; include it in an essay you are writing.
- Write a summary for an article you have researched; include it in an essay you are writing.

Online Study Center
Improve Your Grade
Suggestions for Writing

USING LOGIC

In this book we have spent a great deal of time talking about purposes and audiences, structure and style, planning and revision, claims and support. However, we have yet to discuss the thinking that lies beneath the surface of the argument itself: the logic that causes the words to make sense and persuade an audience. If an argument can be thought of as being a ship, a watertight structure of a particular shape with a rudder to steer it and a sail to move it along, then logic might be compared to the water that keeps the ship afloat. When you construct arguments, you may not always pause to think carefully about the logic that guides your writing. Nevertheless, if your argument is to be as logically solid as a watertight ship, then you must devote time to this step.

> *Logic takes care of itself; all we have to do is to look and see how it does it.*
>
> —LUDWIG WITTGENSTEIN (1869–1951)

This chapter begins by considering how the three main aspects of persuasion—authority, logic, and emotion—work together to convince an audience

Online Study Center
This icon will direct you to content and resources on the website <college.hmco.com/pic/lamm1e>.

of the validity of a claim. We then investigate how a logical statement known as a syllogism forms the basis of an argumentative claim. Next, we work through the elements of practical logic as defined by Stephen Toulmin to understand how the various components of argumentation work together to persuade an audience of a claim's validity. Finally, we examine a nonadversarial method of conflict resolution developed by psychologist Carl Rogers (this topic was discussed briefly in Chapter 1).

What Is Logic?

Put in simple terms, logic is the study of establishing a relationship between ideas. In formal logic, this relationship is very abstract and approaches the level of mathematics in its certainty. When we are talking about arguments situated in the real world, however, there are no absolutes. Thus using logic to convince your audience that your claim is valid is not based on a system of absolute proof. Instead, different audiences have different beliefs and assumptions underlying what they will or will not accept as "reasonable" or "true." The importance of logic in this context means that you should try to understand your audience's way of looking at the world and to employ that value system or set of assumptions to your advantage.

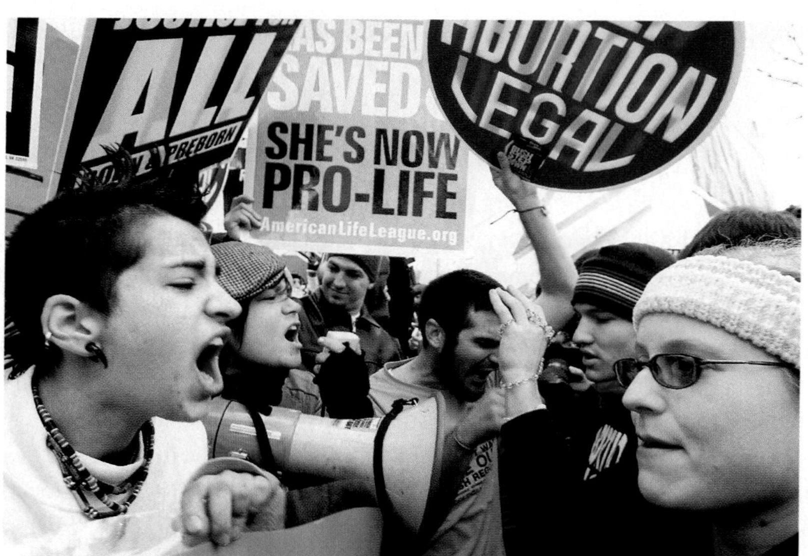

Abortion activists disagree about the definition of human life.

For example, the arguments over stem-cell research and abortion hinge on different definitions of "human life." Some individuals assert that human life begins at birth; others believe that a tiny embryonic-cell cluster counts as a human being. Still others believe that because stem cells can develop into embryos, they are human beings and to use them in the laboratory is murder. All three points of view represent different ways of looking at the world, different assumptions, different beliefs. If you plan to present an argument that deals with a subject such as abortion, therapeutic cloning, or stem-cell research, then you must be aware of which assumptions your audience holds and which sorts of claim/evidence combinations they are willing to entertain.

Authority, Emotion, and Logic

Your ability to persuade your audience relies on more than just your willingness to present clear claims and sound evidence. You must convince your audience that you are an authority on the subject at hand, you must win the audience's sympathy for what you have to say, and you must provide the necessary logical connections to back up your claim. When creating an authoritative voice for your argument, you should always keep your purpose (what you want the audience to think or do) and your audience (whom you wish to convince) firmly in mind. Each time you approach an audience, the impression of authority should be crafted to appeal to those particular individuals.

Online Study Center
Prepare for Class
Authority, Emotion, and Logic

Consider, for instance, the expectations you have when you visit a car dealership to purchase a new automobile. You expect the salesperson to be knowledgeable about the vehicle you are buying. If the salesperson does not seem to know what she is talking about, then you might be less inclined to listen to what she has to say. Even if she is knowledgeable, this authority alone is probably not enough to convince you to purchase the car. The salesperson has to convince you that the particular car is right for you by telling you about its features and backing up these statements with evidence. Finally, the salesperson will probably try to appeal to your emotions. Not only will she make you see the logic of the purchase, but she will also make you desire the car on an emotional level. For example, the salesperson might tell you what a status symbol owning this particular model is, or how good you will look driving it.

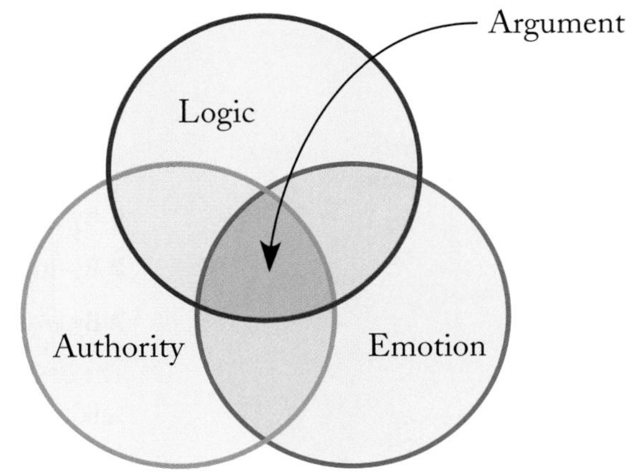

Authority, emotion, and logic are three elements essential to a balanced argument.

All of these elements—appeals to authority, logic, and emotion—come into play in any argument. If the car salesperson does

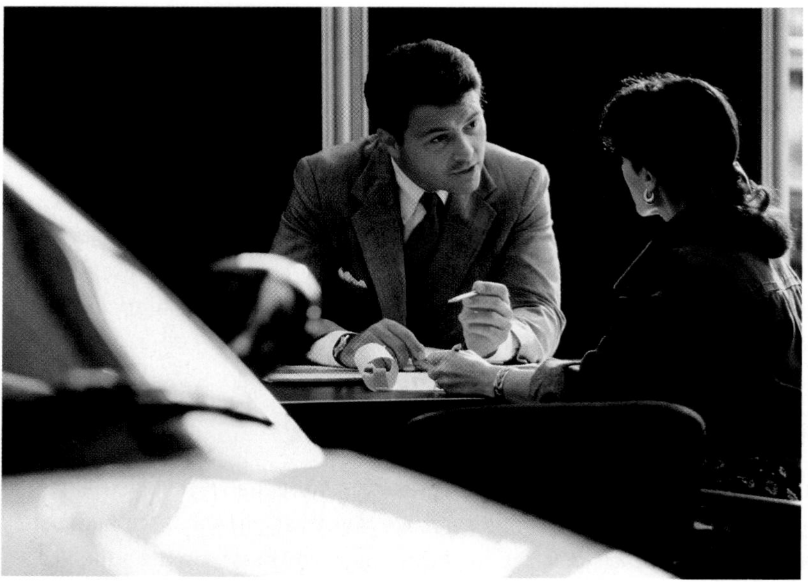

Salespeople use rhetorical skills and logic to try to convince people to purchase cars.

not use them well together, then there will probably be no sale. Moreover, she may vary her "sales pitch" depending on the attitude and interest of the particular person buying the car. She may approach someone who is interested in an economical vehicle by pointing out money-saving features. For someone who is interested in safety, she may talk about the car's air bags, the strength of the frame, and other features.

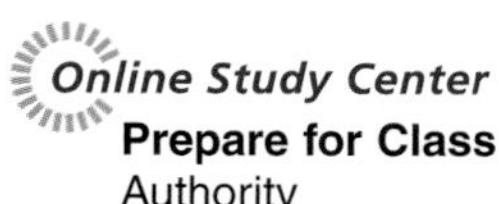

Online Study Center
Prepare for Class
Authority

Establishing Authority

You can establish authority within your argument in several key ways:

- By drawing on your personal experience and knowledge.
- By utilizing research to "borrow" the authority and knowledge of others.
- By writing in an authoritative voice.

The best way to establish credibility with your audience is to know what you are talking about. In some instances, you may already have all of the experience (things that you have done) and knowledge (things that you know) needed to persuade your audience to listen to what you have to say. When an audience is reading what you have written (or is listening to you in some public forum), its members are deferring authority to you. They are thinking, "I'll give this guy a few minutes to convince me that I should listen to what he has to say." If you are able to share experiences and information with your audience that will cause them to consider what you have to say, then they may become "sympathetic listeners" and be more receptive to the claims and evidence you present.

Sometimes, you may choose to write on a topic about which you have little knowledge. In such a case, you must bring yourself up to speed by borrowing the knowledge and authority of others. Research comes in handy in these circumstances. You may research a topic formally by visiting the library to find sources of information, or you may research a topic more informally by interviewing individuals who have knowledge in that particular subject area. For example, although you would probably use traditional academic research for an argument about the dangers of steroid use, you also could obtain information by interviewing athletes who have abused steroids and suffered as a result. No matter how informal your research, however, you should be mindful to avoid plagiarism and give credit where credit is due. (For more on this issue, see Chapter 8, Researching Arguments.) A reader who is aware that you have carefully investigated your subject is more likely to see you as an authoritative source of information.

Speaking with an authoritative voice is important, but by itself it will not persuade an audience to have faith in what you have to say. There must be substance behind your words. What constitutes "authority" may vary from audience to audience, and identifying it requires some intuition on your part. Some audiences will expect a formal level of prose, whereas other audiences can be more easily approached with informality.

MINING YOUR PERSONAL DATABASE

While you may not consider yourself an authority, you might be surprised if you take a moment to inventory your knowledge and personal experiences.

Employment What kinds of jobs have you had? What skills did you obtain? What did you learn about managing your schedule and getting along with co-workers? Have you ever supervised someone? Been fired? Fired someone? What did you learn from those experiences?

Family What kind of family did you grow up in? Do you have siblings? Do you have children of your own? What advice could you give someone else regarding family life?

Tragedy Have you ever dealt with divorce, bankruptcy, the loss of a job, or the death of a loved one? How have these experiences affected you, and how could others learn from them?

Personal interests What hobbies or sports do you engage in? How might these skills be relevant to a particular argument?

Previous research What research projects have you done in the past that have given you a specialized knowledge of a particular subject?

Think for a moment about how this book is written. Is it formal, informal, or somewhere in between? Why do you think so? What assumptions did the authors make about an audience consisting of college students in preparing this text? Likewise, if you were preparing a paper or a talk about binge drinking, you would likely approach an academic audience in a more formal and impersonal way, whereas you would address a group of concerned parents sending their children to college in a more personal fashion. Not only would the formality or informality of your language differ, but the way in which you establish authority, the type of evidence you present, and the degree of emotionality you utilize would also vary depending on the audience.

PRACTICE 10.1 Establishing Authority

Working individually or in a group, consider the following argumentative topics and the two distinct audiences that follow each. Describe each audience in terms of its primary values, likes and dislikes, assumptions, and so forth. Then write a claim designed to appeal to each of the two audiences.

1. Gay couples should be allowed to adopt children.

   Audience A: Evangelical Christians from a small Southern town

   Audience B: Progressive college students from the Midwest

2. Anyone who thinks illegal aliens ("migrant workers") from Mexico should not be given full citizenship in the United States is racist.

   Audience A: Educated professionals from the Southwest

   Audience B: Skilled workers and union members from the Northeast

3. When investigating suspected terrorists, the government should be allowed to arrest people without warrants and hold them indefinitely. The Bill of Rights should not get in the way.

   Audience A: Liberal members of Congress who are interested in reelection

   Audience B: An organization representing Arab Americans

Invoking Emotion Inappropriately

While it is important—even unavoidable—to utilize emotion to convince your audience of your argumentative purpose, this tactic should not be the primary means for moving your audience to action. An argument employs logic—presenting claims and supporting them with evidence—as the primary means of convincing an audience. Other forms of persuasion may use emotion as a primary tool. For example, works of art commonly use emotion as the major way of convincing an audience to hold a particular opinion. When was the last time you went to a particularly memorable movie and said, "That film was certainly persuasive. Its presentation of claims and evidence was flawless!"? More likely you were moved emotionally by the film. You sympathized with the major characters and with their point of view.

Online Study Center
Prepare for Class
Propaganda

Likewise, emotion can be used as the primary means of persuasion in messages such as political propaganda. In such cases, the logic is often overshadowed by the strong emotional element. Look at the following propaganda posters from the 1930s. How do these posters inappropriately use emotion to convince the audience of their claims?

The poster reads, "The Jew: Inciter of war, prolonger of war."

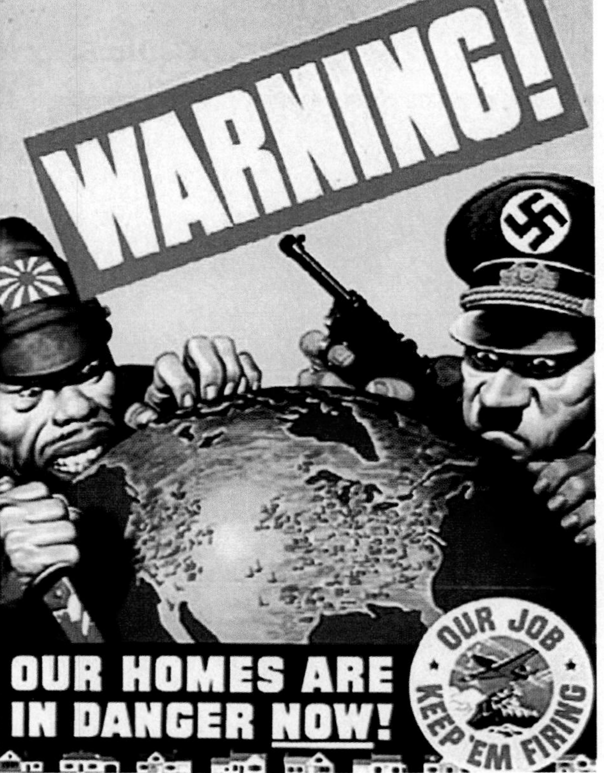

This American propaganda poster from World War II uses fear as its primary means of persuasion.

PRACTICE 10.2 Evaluating Propaganda

Study the posters. Working individually or in groups, answer the following questions.

1. Examine the German poster. What is the purpose of the curtain? What does it imply? Does the face behind the curtain look friendly or threatening? How so? What might the raised fists represent?
2. Now consider the American poster. why does the globe display North America? Explain.
3. In each case, who is the intended audience? How do you know?
4. How do the images in the posters attempt to incite the emotions of the audience?
5. Is logic employed in any way (to validate the claims)? Explain.

Using Emotion Appropriately

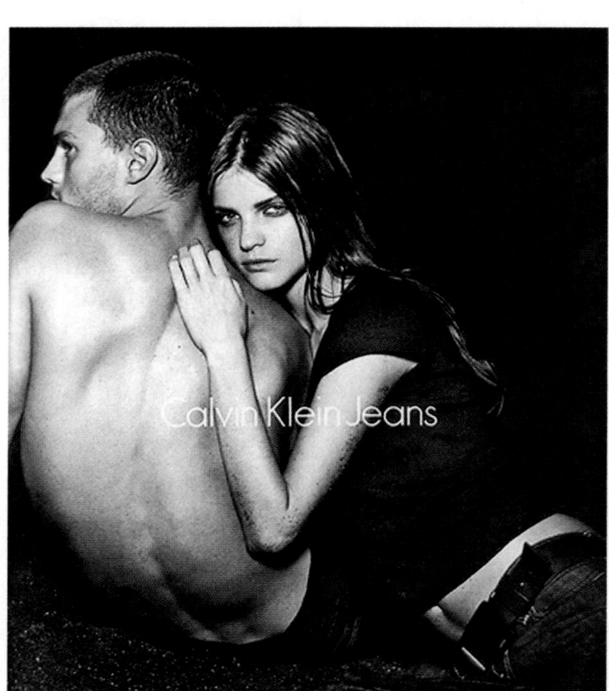

What is argumentative about this image? What is emotionally persuasive? What is the difference?

While emotion is sometimes used inappropriately to motivate an audience (such as using images of attractive women to sell cars), when balanced appropriately with authority and logic, it can cause your audience to view your argument sympathetically. Appealing to emotion is "inappropriate" when it replaces claims and evidence; appealing to emotion is "appropriate" when it reinforces the logic of your argument. Emotion should never be substituted for logic when your goal is to persuade an audience. An advertisement that uses a supermodel to sell beer is persuasive, but it is not argumentative. When using emotion within an argument, it is important to keep this distinction in mind.

Consider the following paragraph from Ann Coulter's article, "Not Crazy Horse, Just Crazy," in which she criticizes the academic practice of professorial tenure:

> Tenure was supposed to create an atmosphere of open debate and inquiry, but instead has created havens for talentless cowards who want to be insulated from life. Rather than fostering a climate of open inquiry, college campuses have become fascist colonies of anti-American hate speech, hypersensitivity, speech codes, banned words, and prohibited scientific inquiry.

Coulter's carefully chosen words—"talentless cowards," "fascist colonies," "anti-American hate speech"—serve to evoke the emotions of her readership. Other audiences may not be equally receptive to her message, however. The paragraph's point may be reasonable, but its presentation is so emotionally charged that Coulter's passion effectively buries the effect that her claim and associated evidence might otherwise have.

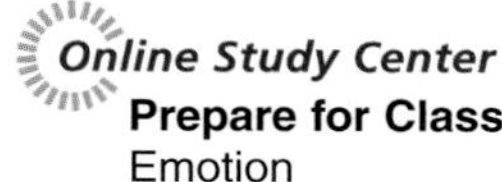

Victor Hanson makes a similar point in his *National Review* article, "Topsy-Turvy," albeit without the same level of emotional intensity:

> There are many explanations for this disturbing picture, both institutional and generational. Lifelong employment through tenure can breed complacency, ensure mediocrity, and foster insularity. Underachieving but tenured academics, despite dismal teaching evaluations and nonexistent scholarship, are virtually immune from meaningful censure—docked pay or dismissal—from their peers. Instead, they are like Brahmins from their seventh year to retirement—essentially three decades and more of institutional unaccountability.

This passage is more successful not only because emotion is not used as the primary means of persuasion, but also because the more balanced tone helps the author create a reasonable, authoritative voice to which the audience may be more likely to respond. The lesson here is clear: An argument that carefully balances authority, emotion, and logic is more likely to be considered sympathetically by a potential audience.

Deductive Logic

Logic provides a set of rules to guide reasoning. There are actually many forms of logic (*deductive*, *epistemic*, *Boolean*, *quantum*, *stoic*, *fuzzy*), each with its own techniques and uses. *Boolean logic*, for example, applies *operators* (such as *and*, *or*, *not*, and *with*) to create the logical flow charts that are essential to software programming and Internet searches. It is a kind of *computer logic* that is compatible with human-to-human communication. *Deductive logic* is based on spoken and written language and also is compatible with human-to-human communication. Deduction begins with a *general* point of agreement (evidence, reason) to convince an audience to accept a point of disagreement.

Aristotle's Formal Logic

The origins of deductive logic can be traced back to ancient Athens, and Aristotle (384–322 BCE) was the first to record its techniques in his book *Rhetorica*. But Greek orators probably used this reasoning to prepare their persuasive speeches for many generations before Aristotle. Literacy was only a few generations old at the time of Aristotle, and little is known of the preliterate, oral practices of rhetoric.

Aristotle presented argument in the form of a word equation called a *syllogism*. In its most basic form, a syllogism presents an argument divided into three parts:

- The *major premise* is a general concept that people can accept as being true.
- The *minor premise* is a specific concept that people can accept as true.
- The *conclusion* is an assertion that emerges from the relationship between the two premises.

The major and minor premises, if accepted by the audience, lead to an *inescapable* conclusion. For example, if you agree with (1) the major premise that all humans eventually die and with (2) the minor premise that a particular being is human, then you *must* agree with (3) the conclusion: the particular being will eventually die.

The following syllogism is a classical example of Aristotle's deductive logic:

Aristotelian Syllogism

Major premise: All men are mortal.
Minor premise: Socrates is a man.
Conclusion: Socrates is mortal.

The order in which the major premise, minor premise, and conclusion are presented is traditional. As a sentence, the syllogism might read like this:

> If all men are mortal, and if Socrates is a man, then Socrates is mortal.

Syllogisms often are phrased as *If . . . , then . . .* or end with *therefore*, *consequently*, or *thus*. However, the parts of the syllogism could easily be inverted, leading to a sentence like this:

> Socrates is mortal because he's a man and all men are mortal.

Toulmin's Practical Logic

In 1958, philosopher Stephen Toulmin published a book entitled *The Uses of Argument*, which ultimately changed the way that modern rhetoricians think about the elements of argumentation. Toulmin challenged the classical view of argument (which was based largely on Aristotle's *Rhetoric* and other works) and sought to create a more practical way of understanding argumentation.

According to Toulmin, arguments are won and lost at the sentence level. For that reason, in this chapter we concern ourselves not with the overall structure of a protracted argument but rather with the very practical business of making claims and convincing an audience that those claims are valid. (For more extensive discussions of organizing an overall argument, see Chapter 5, Planning Arguments, and Chapter 6, Drafting Arguments.)

Toulmin maintained that the certainty required to make Aristotle's logic functional was seldom to be found in real-life situations. In practice, decision makers usually work with incomplete evidence and unsure or contradictory facts. In a courtroom, for example, the prosecution and the defense present very different versions of the truth to the judge and jury. Today, Toulmin's logic is sometimes called "practical" or "informal" in contrast to Aristotle's formal logic.

Toulmin's syllogisms function much like those of Aristotle but conceptually his practical logic is based on probable, not assured, conclusions. His terminology also parallels that of Aristotle:

- **Warrant:** Toulmin's warrant functions like Aristotle's major premise by guaranteeing (like a product's warranty) that the evidence leads to the claim by providing the relevant inference, principle, belief, or law.
- **Reason:** Toulmin's *reason* (*grounds, data,* or *evidence*) functions like Aristotle's *minor premise* by supporting the claim with specific reasons and evidence.
- **Claim:** Toulmin's *claim* functions like Aristotle's *conclusion,* offering an assertion.

Toulmin Syllogism
Warrant (Inference): Personal health is a public issue.
Reason: Smoking is unhealthy.
Claim: Tobacco smoking should be outlawed

Toulmin's approach to logic is used throughout this chapter as a means of analyzing and evaluating the arguments. However, in *Dynamic Argument* we have modified Toulmin's terminology to make it more user-friendly: We replace *warrant* with the term *inference.*

Terminologies of Logics

Function
General principle
Specific principles
Logical outcome

Aristotle's terms
Major premise
Minor premise
Conclusion

Toulmin's terms
Warrant
Reason
Claim

Modified Toulmin terms
Inference
Reason
Claim

The Logical Structure of an Argument

Claim, Reason, and Inference

Frequently, an argument will contain only two parts: a claim and a reason. The third part, the inference, is usually unstated.

Online Study Center
Prepare for Class
Logical Structure of Claims

Claim, Reason, and Inference

- **A claim:** Something that the writer wants the audience to believe
- **A reason:** A statement that explains why the assertion should be believed
- **An inference:** An unstated assumption that is shared by the writer and the audience and that makes it possible to see a valid logical connection between the assertion and the reason

We are using the more familiar term *inference* in the place of the term used by philosopher Stephen Toulmin, *warrant*. We discuss these two terms more a bit later.

Online Study Center
Prepare for Class
Syllogisms and Enthymemes

Sometimes the inference is general enough that the audience can be safely assumed to accept it:

> **Claim:** You should fix this bicycle.
> **Reason:** Because the wheel is about to fall off.
> **Inference:** A broken bicycle can't be ridden and may lead to injury.

The audience does not have to accept the claim as true. If the issue is truly debatable, then readers or listeners may be expected to doubt your claim in some way. In the preceding example, someone might reject the claim because he or she sees the reason as invalid: No, the wheel is not about to fall off. Even if the audience rejects the reason but accepts the inference, the entire logical statement (claim, reason, inference) is still logically valid. In contrast, if someone does not share the inference with the author, then a logical connection between claim and reason is not achieved:

> **Claim:** You should paint this bike pink.
> **Reason:** Because it will be more attractive.
> **Inference:** Pink bikes are attractive.

Although this example is trite, it serves to illustrate the principle: If an individual does not share the inference that pink bikes are attractive, then no logical connection between claim and reason is made. If you have any doubt that your audience will accept your inference as reasonable (if not flatly true), then you should rewrite your argumentative thesis to better "reach" the audience with an inference they will accept.

UNDERSTANDING SYLLOGISMS AND ENTHYMEMES

Aristotelian syllogism In the language of formal Aristotelian logic, a syllogism is a complete logical statement that consists of a major premise, a minor premise, and a conclusion. The argumentative thesis statements discussed in this section are based on this basic logical structure.

> **Major premise:** All fish live underwater.
> **Minor premise:** All trout are fish.
> **Conclusion:** All trout live underwater.

Toulmin syllogism In the language of practical Toulmin logic, a syllogism is a complete logical statement that consists of a warrant (inference), reason, and a claim. A Toulmin syllogism functions like an Aristotelian syllogism. The warrant acts like a major premise, the reason acts like a minor premise, and the claim acts like a conclusion. However, Toulmin logic is considered to be the more practical of the two and is applied to real-life situations where inferences and reasons lack certainty.

> **Warrant (inference):** We should take every opportunity to learn about life.
> **Reason:** The elderly have much to teach us about life.
> **Claim:** We should learn what we can from the elderly.

Enthymemes An *enthymeme* is an incomplete syllogism consisting of a claim (conclusion) but missing one or both of the other parts. Enthymemes typically omit the inference (major premise) when the audience already is aware of the general principle, belief, or law.

> **Enthymeme:** We should learn everything we can from the elderly because of what they can teach us of life.

This enthymeme assumes the audience values knowledge. Sometimes the reason (minor premise) also can be omitted.

> **Enthymeme:** Don't play with fire!

The Basics

A complete syllogistic sentence consists of three elements:

> **Claim + Reason + Inference:** We should not allow racial profiling to be used to search passengers at airports because that is a form of racism, and, as everybody knows, racism is bad.

This sentence is unnecessarily long and complex because it states the obvious. We are making certain assumptions about the audience here: Who are they? If your audience is likely to believe your inference, then you can delete it:

> **Claim + Reason + ~~Inference~~:** We should not allow racial profiling to be used to search passengers at airports because that is a form of racism, ~~and, as everybody knows, racism is bad~~.

Then the thesis can look like this:

> **Thesis:** We should not allow racial profiling to be used to search passengers at airports because that is a form of racism.

Logic Words

Try using some of these words to connect your assertion and your reason:

- As a result . . .
- Because . . .
- Because of this . . .
- For this reason . . .
- If . . . (claim), then . . . (reason)
- It follows . . .
- It is reasonable to assume . . .
- It stands to reason . . .
- So . . .
- The reason is . . .
- Therefore . . .
- Thus . . .

Multiple Reasons

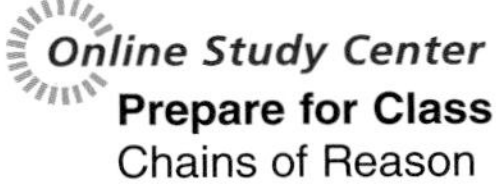

Argumentative thesis statements can have more than one associated reason. Using multiple reasons should be done with care, because the more reasons you give, the more complex the argument becomes:

> **Claim:** Responsible owners will neuter their cats.
> **Reasons:** Neutering prevents pets from wandering, helps control the population of feral cats, and prevents males from spraying.
> **Inferences:** Actions that control cat behavior and overpopulation are desirable.

The advantage of listing several reasons is that they help you structure your paper. If a series of reasons appears in an argumentative thesis, they also provide the reader with a mini-outline of what may appear later in the text of the argument. However, this strategy also limits you somewhat, because you should address everything mentioned in the paper's thesis within the body of the full argument. In addition, the argumentative claim can become very long and unwieldy.

Multiple Inferences

Even if only one reason is stated, certain ideas may be "loaded" with multiple inferences:

Claim: Stem-cell research should be banned.
Reason: Stem-cell research is murder.
Inferences: Stem cells count as human life and to end human life is wrong.

Social and ethical issues rendered as claims tend to have multiple inferences behind them. It may be valuable to list as many of these inferences as you can think of. If the audience finds some of them questionable, you may need to address this skepticism directly as part of your extended argument.

PROBLEM CLAIMS

There are a number of problems you might encounter while formulating a claim. Fortunately, most of them are easy to avoid.

The Audience Doesn't Share Your Assumption Because not all audiences are the same, sometimes your readers may not share your underlying inference.

Claim: Gasoline automobiles should be made illegal.
Reason: Auto emissions promote global warming.
Inference: Things that promote global warming should be avoided.
Problem: The audience might not believe that global warming is a reality.

One solution to this problem is to address the concern by rewriting the claim. By changing either the claim or the reason, the inference will be changed as well:

Claim: Gasoline automobiles should be replaced with hybrids.
Reason: They pollute less and save gas.
Inference: Polluting the air is bad, and saving money is good.

In modifying the claim, the inference—the underlying belief or assumption—was also changed (and ideally will now be accepted by the target audience).

The Language of the Claim Can Be Interpreted in Various Ways If your language is not specific enough, you may leave your claim open to multiple interpretations.

Claim: Dr. Flanagan is an excellent professor.
Reason: Because she knows her subject so well.
Inference: Excellent professors know their subjects.
Problem: The audience may have a different understanding of "excellent." Would an "excellent" professor also have to be an outstanding teacher or an engaging speaker?
Solution (Make the language more specific): Dr. Flanagan is an excellent professor because she is not only a knowledgeable person, but also a dynamic, engaging teacher.

In this case, *excellent* could have been replaced with *informative*, but that would create another problem: a circular claim (see below). By expanding the single reason to two reasons, the writer addresses the reader's assumptions. The inference would now become multiple as well: excellent professors are both knowledgeable and engaging.

The Claim Is Circular The assertion and the reason must make different statements. A claim is thought of as circular if the reason merely rephrases the claim.

Claim: Illegal drugs should be avoided.
Reason: Because they are against the law.
Inference: All illegal things should be avoided.
Problem: The assertion, reason, and inference are almost identical.
Solution (Rewrite the reason to make a different statement): Illegal drugs should be avoided because they are bad for your health.

The inference that things that are bad for your health should be avoided is general enough to be accepted by a wide audience.

One could suggest that this point is not actually arguable because it is a commonly accepted belief and does not address a debatable issue. However, that point turns on the values and beliefs of the target audience. Certain audiences might argue that the right to enjoy the effects of illegal drugs outweighs the health concerns: People should have the right to enjoy illegal drugs regardless of health concerns because individuals, not governments, should bear responsibility for their own health.

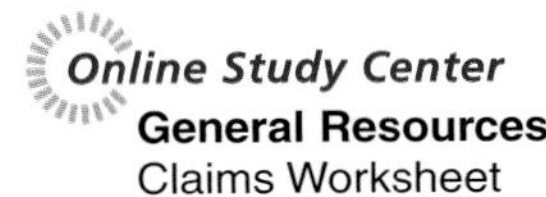

General Resources
Claims Worksheet

CLAIM WORKSHEET

The questions below can help you develop your claim.

1. Which debatable issue is being argued? Example: Should Americans be allowed to buy inexpensive drugs from Canada via Internet pharmacies?
2. What is your opinion regarding this issue? It will become your claim. *Example:* Americans should be able to buy drugs from Canadian Internet pharmacies.
3. Now state a reason that your claim is valid. (Use *because* to get your reason started, although you may rephrase your argumentative claim later.) *Example:* Americans should be allowed to buy drugs from Canadian Internet pharmacies because the prohibition is based on corporate greed.
4. What inference are you making? *Example:* Things that are done purely for profit motives are not legitimate reasons to make something illegal.
5. Who is your audience? *Example:* Pharmacists who work for large pharmaceutical firms and (1) have high standards regarding drug control and quality and (2) stand to profit from higher drug sales in the United States.
6. Is your audience likely to agree with your inference? *Example:* No, because they believe that lax regulations in Canada may result in the availability of drugs that might not meet U.S. standards.
7. If your audience does not accept your claim, how will you attempt to convince them that the inference is valid? *Example:* By arguing that Canadian standards are as good as, and sometimes exceed, U.S. standards.

The Syllogism Is Stated as an Argumentative Claim In the text of an argument, the syllogism will rarely be written in a formal format as presented in this chapter, but rather will typically be rendered in the form of a claim. The claim may consist of one or two sentences (or even more) and usually will not include the inference (unless the arguer believes the audience will not accept it, in which case the inference has to be argued and proven). Sometimes the reason will be stated before the claim. At other times it will follow the claim.

Claim: Pit bulls should not be bred for profit.
Reason: Because they present a danger to society.
Inference: Things that present a danger to society should not be allowed.

- Using a "because" clause:

  Pit bulls should not be bred for profit because they present a danger to society.

- As two separate sentences:

  Pit bulls should not be bred for profit. The reason is that they present a danger to society.

- With the reason and the claim reversed:

  Because they present a danger to society, pit bulls should not be bred for profit.

  Pit bulls present a danger to society. As a result, they should not be bred for profit.

This claim could be written in a variety of ways, employing various transition words, as one or two sentences.

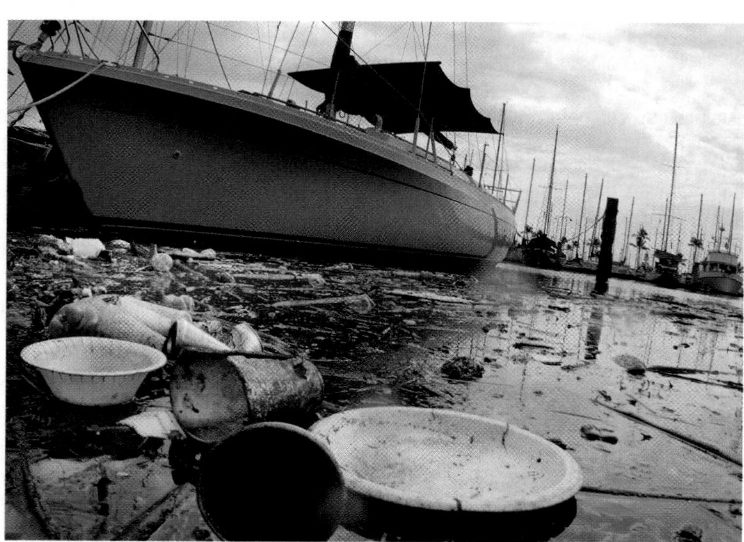

Who is responsible for cleaning up environmental hazards? If the company responsible can't—or won't—deal with the damage, should the taxpayers have to foot the bill?

PRACTICE 10.3 **Transforming a Syllogism into an Argumentative Thesis**

Working individually or in groups, select one of the issues listed below or come up with a topic on your own. Identify a target audience for that issue, and then write a syllogism for it. Decide whether your audience is likely to agree with your inference (and which strategy you must employ to convince them that it is valid). Finally, write an argumentative thesis (Claim + Reason) in at least three different ways. (Use the preceding examples for inspiration and employ the techniques outlined in the sidebar on page 271 as needed.)

1. Should the government pay to clean up pollution caused by corporations? (Assume that the corporations were following all government regulations when the pollution occurred.)
2. Should the president of the United States be allowed to serve more than two terms in office?
3. What should be done (if anything) to deal with illegal immigration from Central America to the United States?
4. Does the use of "politically correct" language foster more equality in the United States (or elsewhere in the world, for that matter)?
5. If delinquent children commit crimes, should their parents be held accountable for their bad parenting?
6. What should your community do to increase employment and/or reduce crime in poverty-stricken areas?

Backing, Grounds, Qualifiers, and Rebuttals

Online Study Center
General Resources
Claims Worksheet

As we have noted, the core of an argument is its claim, reason, and inference. However, other elements of an argument — *backing, grounds, qualifiers*, and *rebuttals* — often are required to make it convincing:

- **Backing:** Inferences sometimes need to be supported with their own evidence and explanations, which are known as *backing*. For example, if you claim that smoking should be banned and your inference/warrant is that personal health is a public issue, your backing might include evidence showing (1) the health expenses of smokers and (2) the effects of those health expenses on overall insurance rates.
- **Grounds:** Reasons, which tend to be stated in generalities or abstractions, often need support in the form of concrete evidence known as *grounds, data,* or *evidence*. For example, if your stated reason for banning smoking is "because it is unhealthy," your grounds might reveal the kinds, frequency, and severity of health problems suffered by smokers.

- **Qualifiers:** Sometimes you must specify under what conditions a claim is true—by using qualifiers such as *always, sometimes, usually,* or *never.*
- **Rebuttals:** Sometimes you must refute or rebut one or more opposition arguments.

The simple syllogism shown in Figure 10.1 maps how these elements work together.

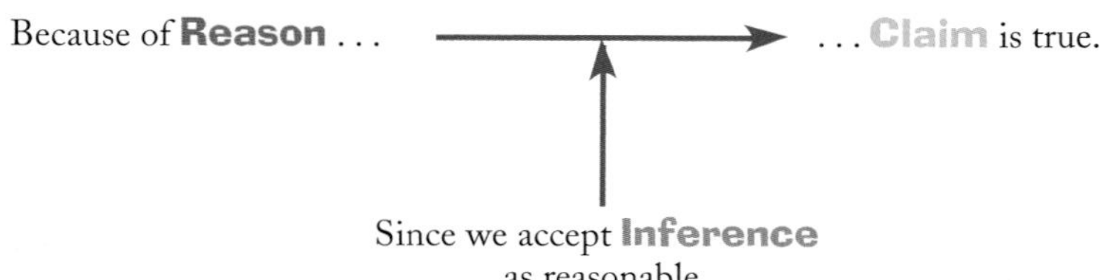

Figure 10.1 A simple three-part Toulmin model

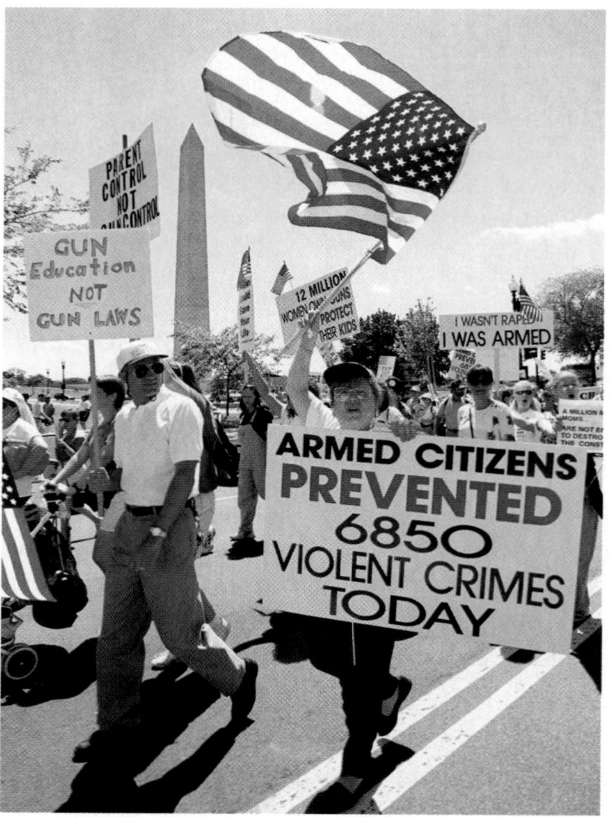

Gun control continues to be hotly debated in the United States.

The essential meaning of this schematic is this:

> Because of the reason and the inference, it is possible for the audience to accept the validity of the claim.

To make this schematic more concrete, let's put it in sentence form:

> Handguns are used more often in the execution of violent crimes than anywhere else. Because of this reason, they should be made illegal.

Although *because* is attached to the claim here, it refers back to the reason stated in the previous sentence. This handgun example is mapped out in Figure 10.2.

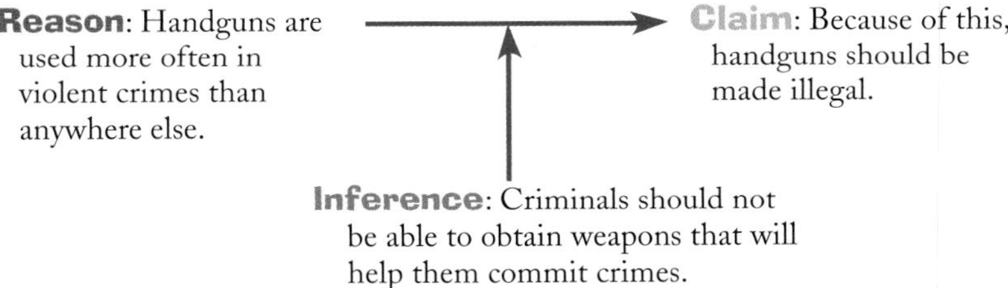
Reason: Handguns are used more often in violent crimes than anywhere else.
Claim: Because of this, handguns should be made illegal.
Inference: Criminals should not be able to obtain weapons that will help them commit crimes.

Figure 10.2 An example using a three-part Toulin model

The example presented here works well if the audience shares the inference. In the real world, of course, logic is rarely a simple matter of writing an argumentative claim that will allow the inference to be shared by the author and the audience. Indeed, in most cases, some measure of disagreement will occur between the assumptions made by the author and the beliefs of the audience. Typically, a number of related inferences may influence the way an audience responds to a claim. This likelihood requires us to consider two ways of looking at evidence.

Approaches to Evidence

When you present an argument, even one as brief as the two sentences outlined above, you can support it in two ways:

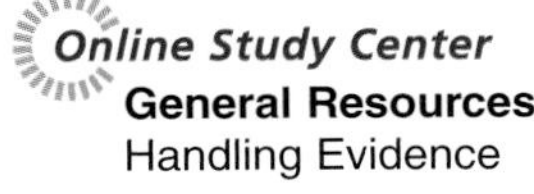
Online Study Center
General Resources
Handling Evidence

- If the audience is likely to see the inference (I) as possibly true, then you should present evidence called grounds (G) to support your reason (R). The assumptions that you are making are that the inference will be accepted by the audience and that you need only to convince them of the truth value of R.
- If the audience is likely to see I as probably false, then—in addition to providing G to support R—you should present evidence called backing (B) to convince the audience that I is valid.

Let's clarify these types of evidence by expanding the schematic a little bit, as is shown in Figure 10.3.

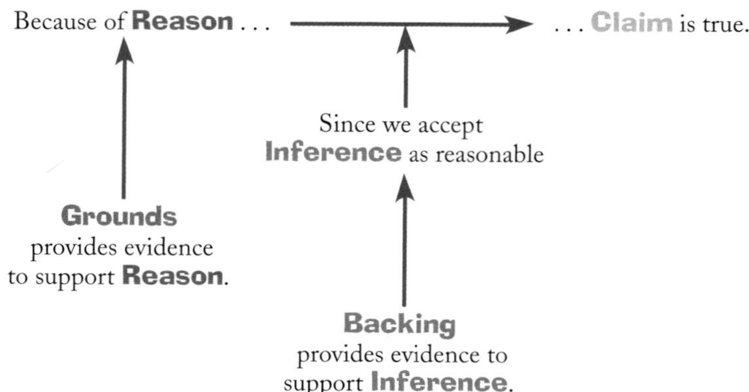
Because of **Reason** . . .
. . . **Claim** is true.
Since we accept
Inference as reasonable
Grounds
provides evidence
to support **Reason**.
Backing
provides evidence to
support **Inference**.

Figure 10.3 A three-part Toulmin model plus grounds and backing

Now let's get specific. If you assume—rightly or wrongly—that your audience shares your inference that "Criminals should not be able to obtain weapons that will help them commit crimes," then your argument may look a bit like the one shown in Figure 10.4.

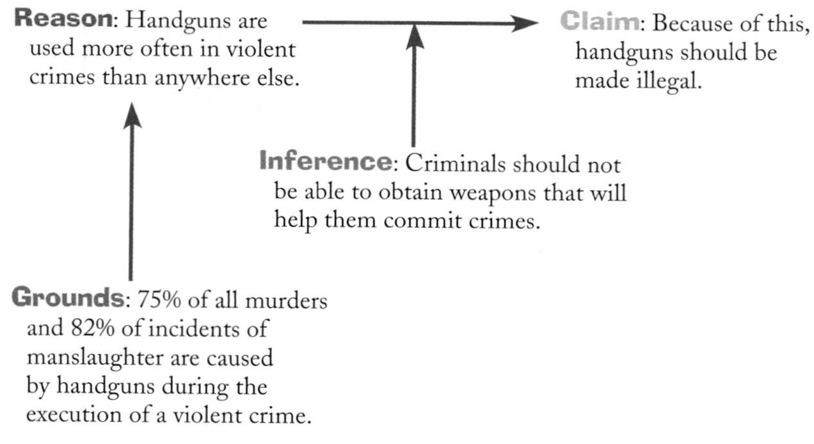
Reason: Handguns are
used more often in violent
crimes than anywhere else.
Claim: Because of this,
handguns should be
made illegal.
Inference: Criminals should not
be able to obtain weapons that will
help them commit crimes.
Grounds: 75% of all murders
and 82% of incidents of
manslaughter are caused
by handguns during the
execution of a violent crime.

Figure 10.4 An example using a three-part Toulin model plus grounds

Conversely, if you are aware that your audience either (1) may not share your inference or (2) may entertain, or otherwise be aware, of multiple inferences, then you must state your inference in the course of the argument. Recall that if

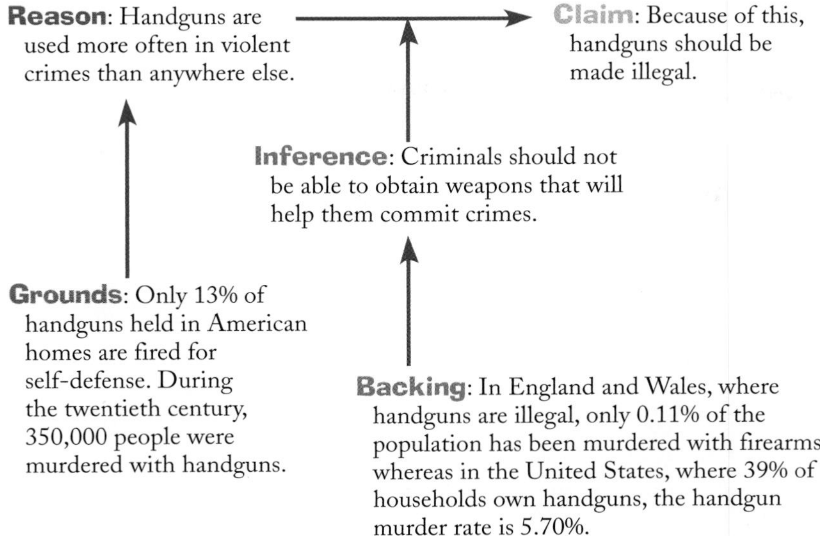

Reason: Handguns are used more often in violent crimes than anywhere else.
Claim: Because of this, handguns should be made illegal.
Inference: Criminals should not be able to obtain weapons that will help them commit crimes.
Grounds: Only 13% of handguns held in American homes are fired for self-defense. During the twentieth century, 350,000 people were murdered with handguns.
Backing: In England and Wales, where handguns are illegal, only 0.11% of the population has been murdered with firearms, whereas in the United States, where 39% of households own handguns, the handgun murder rate is 5.70%.

Figure 10.5 An example using a three-part Toulmin model plus grounds and backing

the inference is shared by author and audience, then it usually remains unstated. However, if it is likely to be the subject of disagreement, then the inference must be stated directly and supported with appropriate evidence—ideally with the result of at least causing the audience to entertain the possibility of the truth value of your claim (see Figure 10.5 above).

In this example, evidence in the form of grounds is not enough to convince the audience, which doubts the validity of the inference. Therefore, further evidence in the form of backing must be provided with the hope that the audience will entertain the possibility that the inference is correct. Only after the audience accepts this inference will they be compelled by grounds in support of the reason. Remember, it is the inference that allows a connection to be made between the claim and its reason.

PRACTICE 10.4 Identifying When Backing Is Needed

Working individually or in groups, determine which inferences connect the claim(s) to the reason(s) in the following brief arguments. Identify an audience that would likely accept the inference as well as an audience that would doubt the inference. Explain how you would present the argument to a skeptical audience.

(continued)

1. Persons convicted of felonies should have to wear tracking devices even after they have served their sentences. It is important for the government to be able to keep track of these criminals so they will be prevented from committing new crimes.

Television celebrity Martha Stewart wore an ankle bracelet while under house arrest for insider trading.

2. Children today have an inability to control their emotions. One reason for this is that many of them do not receive discipline at home, and the law prevents children from being properly disciplined at school. It is my opinion that schools should have the option of punishing children for misbehavior. Such punishment options should include spankings because a little bit of pain and humiliation can be an effective teacher.
3. Various women's groups have argued for equal opportunities for women. In the military, women are allowed to perform most jobs except those involving direct front-line combat. If women are to be truly equal, then all jobs in the military should be open to them. In addition, they should be assigned to such jobs in exactly the same way that men are. If they are going to serve in the military, they should not be able to "opt out" of combat positions.
4. In certain states, Native American tribes are allowed to run "bingo halls" that effectively amount to casinos. Because of treaties that were put in place many years ago, different rules apply to businesses that op

(continued)

erate on Native American–owned land than apply to businesses that are operated by the rest of the population. Because gambling is a dangerous addiction that attracts crime, these casinos should be closed.

Casinos have proliferated on tribal lands, stirring debates about the impact of gambling-based business on traditional Native American cultures and the degree of autonomy guaranteed to tribes.

The Qualifier

A qualifier is a word or phrase that is employed within an argumentative claim or the supporting reason and that serves to limit—to qualify—the claim for specific kinds of cases. Qualifiers can help you avoid making erroneous absolute statements that may cause your audience to reject your claim out of hand. Absolute statements can come off as jarring and dogmatic, and they can put your audience in a defensive state of mind. What would you think if you encountered the following statement on a professor's syllabus?

> NOTICE: ABSENCES ARE NOT ALLOWED. If you miss class FOR ANY REASON, you will receive a FAILING GRADE!

Now how about this:

> NOTICE: Attending class is extremely important. Missing more than three classes will result in a lower grade, although you will be excused for documented illnesses and school-sponsored activities as appropriate.

Most likely you see the second statement as "friendlier" and "more reasonable." The first statement is absolute and lacks qualifiers. The second statement contains qualifiers that limit its application to specific circumstances. Now read the following statement without a qualifier:

> Because the military is required to operate efficiently, civilian employees of military bases should be required to work Monday through Friday without exception.

Now with a qualifier:

> Because the military is required to operate efficiently, with the exception of Muslims who attend prayers on Friday, civilian employees of military bases should be required to work Monday through Friday without exception.

A qualifier limits the application of a claim and thus avoids a potential objection. In the preceding example, a Muslim employee might contend he should be able to trade working on Friday in exchange for working on Sunday. If a qualifier is placed in the claim, then the objection is avoided. Here is another example:

> Video games may desensitize impressionable young people to violence. Therefore, all video games should be banned.

Now here it is with a qualifier:

> Certain video games that reproduce murderous rampages, like *Grand Theft Auto,* may desensitize impressionable young people to violence. While some games are innocent fun, those that realistically simulate murder should be banned.

A qualifier usually makes a claim more acceptable to a potential audience and limits the claim's application to specific cases so it will not be seen as dogmatic or absolute. The qualifier limits the claim so that the inference connecting the claim and the reason may have an exception applied to it. In the first of the two video game examples, the inference might be stated as follows:

> Things that might incite violence should be banned because they will make society safer.

Most people, however, are not likely to accept the idea that all video games (or other forms of popular entertainment, for that matter) are likely to incite violence. By qualifying the claim and limiting it only to games that simulate murder, a more reasonable claim is made that the audience may be more likely to accept.

PRACTICE 10.5 Rewriting with Qualifiers

Working individually or in groups, rewrite the following argumentative thesis statements. Consider whether qualifiers should be used in each case. Be prepared to explain your purpose and target audience to your group, your instructor, or the rest of the class.

1. The first time someone is arrested for a drug offense, that person should be locked up for twenty years with no chance of parole.
2. Gay couples should always be allowed to adopt children.
3. Because automobile emissions contribute to global warming, all gasoline-powered automobiles should be replaced with gas/electric hybrids or with hydrogen fuel-cell cars.
4. Children lose a portion of what they learned in the preceding school year during summer vacation. For this reason, a twelve-month school term should become mandatory.
5. In lieu of prison sentences, convicted felons should be required to perform labor for their victims. The dollar equivalent of their crime should be set by a jury.

Some states have resurrected the concept of "chain gangs" to punish—rather than reform—prisoners. Is this practice "cruel and unusual punishment"? For which crimes might hard labor be warranted?

Objection and Rebuttal

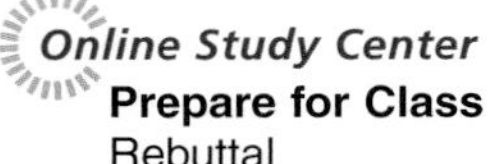
Online Study Center
Prepare for Class
Rebuttal

All audiences (even friendly ones) will inevitably raise questions about your argument. These questions are objections—specific counterclaims that the reader generates or that recur as the reader ponders your argument. The best thing you can do in the course of making your argument is to anticipate potential objections (although you will probably not think of all possibilities) and respond to them. A rebuttal is an argument you make in response to a specific objection. An objection may be stated in the form of a question, or it may be a fully developed argument complete with claim(s), reason(s), inference(s), and supporting evidence in the form of grounds and backing. Likewise, your rebuttal will generally take the form of a fully developed argument. You must (1) summarize the opposing argument, (2) recognize its strengths (this will help you establish authority and build sympathy with your audience), and (3) argue against its weaknesses.

If we return briefly to the gun control example from earlier in this chapter, you can see how this might work:

Your claim: Handguns should be made illegal because they cause thousands of deaths as the result of accidents and their use in violent crimes.

Audience objection: Most handguns are owned by responsible citizens who keep them in their homes for self-defense. Besides, there is a constitutional right to bear arms.

Your rebuttal: Only 13 percent of handguns have ever been used by Americans to protect themselves from criminals. It stands to reason, then, that the majority of these weapons are fired either accidentally or to commit a crime such as murder. Furthermore, 67 percent of all murders in the United States are committed with handguns. In England and Wales, where handguns are illegal, only one-tenth of 1 percent of the population has been killed with firearms, whereas in the United States, almost 6 percent of the population has been murdered with firearms. In the United States, handguns are present in 39 percent of homes. This would seem to suggest that the presence of so many handguns in the United States has led to more murders.

It is even possible for an entire argument to take the form of rebuttal. An argument's purpose can be to summarize and respond to positions that differ from the writer's own position. This technique works rather like an inverted pyramid. The author first outlines a series of objections to a particular point of view, then summarizes each one in turn, and finally refutes each one in turn. By the end of the argument, only one alternative remains; this—generally the author's thesis—is the one the writer endorses.

PRACTICE 10.6 **Identifying the Elements of a Refutation Argument**

A refutation is an argument replete with all of the elements—claim, reason, evidence (grounds and backing), and qualifiers. Working individually or in groups, reread the preceding refutation, and identify or reconstruct the following:

1. The original argument's thesis, complete with claim, reason(s), and inference(s).
2. The claim, reason(s), and inference(s) of the objection.
3. The claim, reason(s), and inference(s) of the rebuttal. Also, identify how the evidence functions as grounds (supporting a reason) and backing (validating an inference).

Does the refutation contain more than one claim?

Carl Rogers: Conflict Resolution

Psychologist Carl Rogers developed an approach to dealing with objections and rebuttals that (at least in theory) has the effect of increasing audience sympathy. When Rogers was working with groups of patients, before he would allow a patient to rebut someone else's point of view about a subject, he required the patient to acknowledge the other person's argument to the second patient's satisfaction. This method, whether used in a live setting such as a therapy session or in writing, forces an individual not only to summarize, but also to recognize the legitimacy of another argument before proceeding. This strategy is very useful for rebutting arguments: If the alternative argument is summarized with care, you will become more aware of its claims, reasons, inferences, and forms of support than you might otherwise.

Rogers's technique is especially valuable if you disagree vehemently with another point of view. If you can see an alternative argument with some degree of clarity and sympathy, you may recognize subtler points within that argument that you might otherwise be inclined to miss. Your acknowledgment of these finer points also may persuade a skeptical audience—especially one that agrees with the opposing argument that you are preparing to summarize and critique—to lend a sympathetic ear to what you have to say.

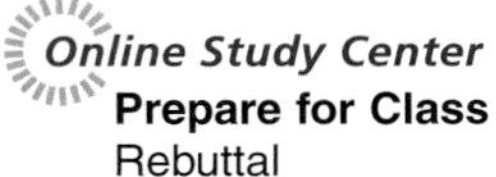

Prepare for Class
Rebuttal

PRACTICE 10.7 Identifying Objections and Preparing a Rebuttal

Working individually or in groups, read the following claims carefully. Identify one or more objections to each, and write a claim/reason statement that rebuts the objection.

1. A private company should have the right to scrutinize the health habits of its employees and to fire those who live unhealthy lifestyles and may cause the company's insurance rate to rise.
2. Because children are especially impressionable, advertising should be banned during children's television shows.
3. If a college athlete is found to have used steroids to enhance his or her performance, then the athlete should have to repay the institution for the cost of his or her education. The athlete has defrauded the institution and has defrauded the public that has paid to see him or her perform.
4. The United States needs a government-subsidized health care program. Health care and drug costs in this country have skyrocketed out of control.
5. Male scientists outnumber female scientists because evolution has given women better social skills and men better spatial acumen. This makes men better mathematicians, and mathematics is the basis of science.
6. If a person dies but some of his or her organs are still functional, the person should be able to put a provision in his or her will allowing the family to sell the functional organs.

Health care is a major issue that results in many kinds of argumentative claims.

Looking Back at Chapter 10

- Logic is a study of establishing a relationship between ideas.
- To be persuasive, you must convince your audience that you are an authority on the subject at hand, you must engage the audience's sympathy for what you have to say, and you must provide the necessary logical connections to back up your claim.
- You can establish authority by drawing on your personal experience and knowledge, by using research to borrow the authority and knowledge of others, and by writing in an authoritative voice.
- Appealing to emotion is inappropriate when it is used in the place of claims and evidence; it is appropriate when it is used to reinforce the logic of your argument.
- Deductive logic, the hallmark of argument, begins with a *general* point of agreement (a law, shared-belief, scientific principle) and applies it to a *specific* point of agreement (evidence, reason) to convince an audience to accept a point of disagreement.
- Aristotle presented argument in the form of a word equation called a *syllogism*, which is composed of the *major premise*, the *minor premise*, and the *conclusion*.
- Stephen Toulmin's logic functions like that of Aristotle, with the conceptual difference that it is practical and based on probable, not assured, conclusions.
- Toulmin's terminology parallels that of Aristotle: *warrant* resembles *major premise*, *reason* resembles *minor premise*, and *claim* resembles *conclusion.*
- Other elements that often are required to make an argument convincing include *backing*, *grounds*, *qualifiers*, and *rebuttals*.
- Psychologist Carl Rogers developed an approach to dealing with objection and rebuttal that (at least in theory) has the effect of increasing audience sympathy.

Suggestions for Writing

Select an argumentative topic for an essay. Before beginning to draft the essay, write the argumentative thesis and the supporting claims of the essay in the form of syllogisms. Anticipate any objections and prepare a rebuttal for each objection. Here are some questions to consider:

- Should uniforms be required in public schools? Why or why not? What are some advantages of uniforms? Some drawbacks?
- Are television commercials partly to blame for increases in childhood obesity? How about the Internet? What responsibility do corporations that advertise unhealthy lifestyles bear for children who end up with diabetes and other diseases?

- Should any form of "shame" punishments become legal? For example, should a judge be able to sentence someone who is convicted of public intoxication to several hours of wearing a sign in public reading, "I was drunk in public"?
- Should people of certain ethnicities be allowed to receive special education in their ethnic group? For instance, should Native Americans receive education in their particular ethnic history? Should this be done in the public schools, and should taxpayers have to foot the bill?
- Should children be allowed to pray in school? When both religious children (who want to pray) and nonreligious children (whose parents do not want them exposed to religion in any form) are present, who has the dominant right? The religious children? The nonreligious children? Why?
- Given that the U.S. divorce rate is close to 50 percent, should state governments be able to require premarriage counseling prior to issuing a marriage certificate? Should state governments be able to require a waiting period (six weeks, for example) before issuing a marriage certificate so that a hasty decision is not made?
- Should persons on welfare be able to undergo plastic surgery? What if the surgery is reconstructive and not cosmetic? Should welfare recipients have access to lifestyle-enhancing drugs such as Viagra, which may not be medically necessary?
- If a university discovers that a tenured professor had been convicted of, and served a sentence for, a serious crime such as murder, should that professor be fired? What if the crime happened thirty years ago and the professor has been a model citizen since then?

Online Study Center
Improve Your Grade
Suggestions for Writing

11 STRATEGIES AND FALLACIES

Earlier chapters of this book focused on the basic strategies of argument: stating a claim, supporting it with evidence and explanations, making qualifications, and rebutting the opposition. This chapter looks more closely at the uses and abuses of specific language strategies—namely, humor, rhetorical questions, figurative language, and fallacies.

> *So on the tip of his subduing tongue,*
> *All kinds of arguments and questions deep. . . .*
>
> —WILLIAM SHAKESPEARE (1564–1616)

Online Study Center
This icon will direct you to content and resources on the website <college.hmco.com/pic/lamm1e>.

Humor

Humor consists of anything that amuses people. In addition to making an audience smile or laugh, it has a number of practical uses:

- It can make or support a claim or discredit the opposition.
- It can make you more aware of strategies used by others.
- It can hook your audience's interest.
- It can make your argument memorable.
- It can form a bond between you and your audience.
- It can be abused as a means of attack or as a distortion of the truth.

PRACTICE 11.1 **Humor**

Your experiences with humor: In a short writing or a group discussion, consider examples of the following topics of humor (perhaps from movies, cartoons, advertisements, jokes, or real-life events). How was the humor presented? Why was it humorous or not humorous?

1. Violence (e.g., "The Three Stooges")
2. Intelligence (blonde or nerd jokes; comedies with foolish characters)
3. Appearance (e.g., clothing, hair, behavior)
4. Political or religious beliefs
5. Culture (e.g., "primitives," other countries, American subcultures)

Humor as argument: In a short writing or a group discussion, reflect on how humor affects people's attitudes about issues and public figures. What argument, if any, does the humor make? For examples you could use any of the cartoons presented in this book or the following quotations from Will Rogers (1879–1935):

- I don't make jokes. I just watch the government and report the facts.
- I belong to no organized party. I am a Democrat.

Online Study Center
Prepare for Class
Using Humor in Arguments

TECHNIQUES OF HUMOR

Classifying humor is not easy—there are hundreds of categories ranging from knock-knock jokes to absurdist drama. Major techniques of humor include exaggeration, irony, ridicule, and literary devices (with a comic twist). These techniques are not discrete but rather can overlap, performing multiple functions.

Overstatement and Understatement Both overstatement and understatement are humorous distortions that function through the same mechanism, as if you looked through one or the other end of a telescope. Caricature, a visual version of overstatement, exaggerates the postures and physical features of the subject.

Overstatement (hyperbole) Sometimes we exaggerate something as though it were larger or more significant than it really is, as in "big as a house." Exaggeration can be used as a form of praise when it emphasizes positive traits, such as the strength of John Henry or Paul Bunyan. Conversely, it can be used for ridicule if it emphasizes flaws, such as the extreme miserliness of Ebenezer Scrooge.

> Badder than a-old King Kong / And meaner than a junkyard dog.
>
> —Jim Croce, "Bad, Bad Leroy Brown"

> This country has come to feel the same when Congress is in session as when the baby gets hold of the hammer.
>
> —Will Rogers

Understatement (litotes) Sometimes we portray something as smaller or less significant than it really is, as in "small as a mouse." Understatement sometimes takes the form of euphemism, replacing an offensive expression with a less offensive alternative.

> Last week I saw a woman flayed, and you will hardly believe how much it altered her appearance for the worse.
>
> —Jonathan Swift

Caricature Artists sometimes exaggerate a person's physical characteristics. Writers also can caricature a person's features through descriptive exaggeration of appearance, behavior, and speech.

> As President Bush so eloquently put it in his address to Congress, "Mathematics are one of the fundamentaries of educationalizing our youths." I could not have said it better with a ten-foot pole.
>
> —Dave Barry

Techniques of Humor

Following are a few techniques of humor that may prove useful as you argue.

Exaggeration
- Overstatement
- Understatement
- Caricature

Irony
- Dramatic irony
- Situational irony
- Verbal irony

Ridicule
- Insult
- Satire
- Parody

Literary Devices
- Word play
- Rhythm and rhyme

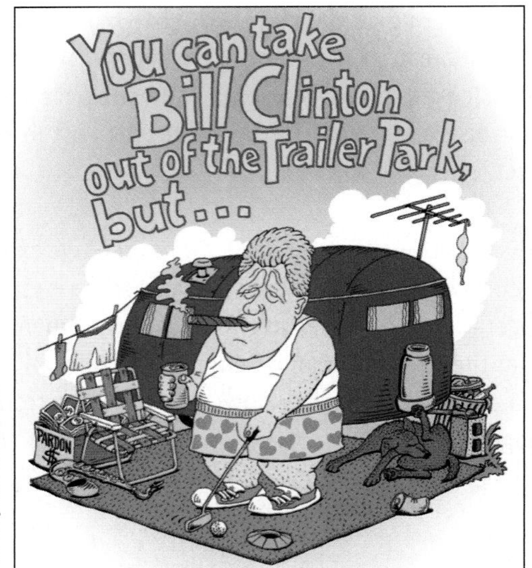

A caricature exaggerates the subject's distinctive characteristics.

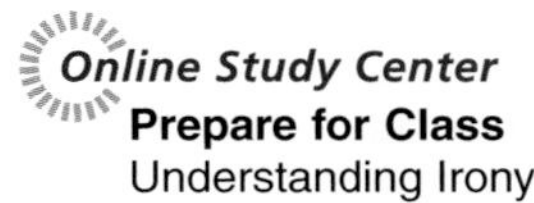

Irony Irony is the contrast between the expected and the actual. Other forms of humor—satire or ridicule, for example—may take inspiration from the gap between the ideal and the real, between expectation and realization, between what is stated and what is meant. Often irony is classified into several categories, such as dramatic, situational, and verbal.

Dramatic irony Dramatic irony is literary and often presented as a tragedy. In such a case, the characters know less about the truth than the audience does. Fate may be important to the plot: the tragic end is inescapable once a choice is made. For example, Sophocles's King Oedipus searches for his father's killer, not knowing that *he* is the killer. The biblical Eve believes the forbidden fruit is the source of happiness but instead discovers that it is the source of misery.

Situational irony Situational irony is a contrast between what is expected to be true and what is actually true. This type of irony often inspires satire, a form of ridicule with an implied claim that the situation should be improved. Examples include medicines that actually make people sick; policies that cause the problems they are meant to prevent; and hypocrites such as police officers who are crooks, religious leaders who are sinners, and experts who are ill informed.

Verbal irony Verbal irony involves a contrast between what is stated and what the speaker or writer really means: the meaning is indirect and sometimes subtle. A more obvious form of verbal irony is known as sarcasm. In his eulogy for Julius Caesar, Mark Anthony refers sarcastically to the assassins as "honorable men":

> For Brutus is an honorable man, so are they all honorable men.
>
> —Shakespeare

> Thus the metric system did not catch on in the United States, unless you count the popularity of the nine-millimeter bullet.
>
> —Dave Barry

> One should always be in love. That is the reason one should never marry.
>
> —Oscar Wilde

> Eternity is very long, especially near the end.
>
> —Woody Allen

PRACTICE 11.2 **Understanding Irony**

In a brief writing or a group discussion, reflect on situations in which there are contrasts between what is expected and what actually occurs. What, if anything, is ridiculous or otherwise humorous about the situation? How might a writer respond to or make use of the irony?

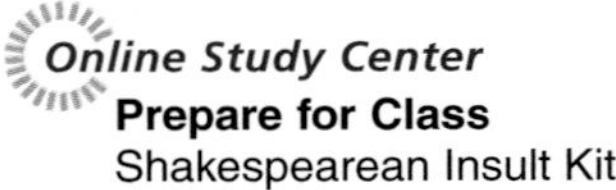

Prepare for Class
Shakespearean Insult Kit

SHAKESPEARE INSULT KIT

To create a Shakespearean insult, begin with "Thou," and follow with one word from each of the three columns below. For example: "Thou beslubbering, toad-spotted, harpy!" The words below were collected from Shakespeare's dialogue.

Column 1	*Column 2*	*Column 3*
beslubbering	beef-witted	codpiece
goatish	beetle-headed	harpy
ruttish	flap-mouthed	lewdster
saucy	ill-breeding	maggot-pie
villainous	toad-spotted	strumpet

Ridicule Much humor takes the form of ridicule, ranging from friendly jibes to scathing attacks. Common forms of ridicule are insults and satire. Parody, which is imitation, mocks a familiar work or genre.

Insult Harsh language (invective) can be intended to offend or show disrespect. It can also be amusing, even though attacking a person rather than an idea is considered an unfair way to argue. (See *ad hominem attacks* in the section on fallacies.)

> She [Katherine Hepburn] ran the whole gamut of emotions from A to B.
>
> —Dorothy Parker

> To those she [Dorothy Parker] did not like, she was a stiletto made of sugar.
>
> —John Mason Brown

PRACTICE 11.3 Insults

Understanding insults: In a brief writing or in a group discussion, reflect on insults.

1. Where have you witnessed insults being hurled? What were they like?
2. Why do people insult each other?
3. Are insults ever justifiable? Explain.
4. In what ways do insults help or hurt an argument?

Writing insults: Using Shakespearean insults as a model (two adjectives followed by a noun), create an insult. Choose the target and wording of your insult carefully so that no one is actually offended and you don't get into trouble.

Thou poisonous bunch-back'd toad!

—Shakespeare, *Richard III* (See the "Shakespeare Insult Kit" on the previous page.)

Ya cheese-eatin' surrender monkeys!

—Groundskeeper Willie of *The Simpsons*, insulting the French

Satire This category of humor is devoted to exposing foolish practices and debunking silly ideas. Satire can range from genial (such as a friend kidding another friend about a bad haircut) or harsh. It often uses other techniques, such as insults, irony, hyperbole, or even taunting rhymes, and can be combined with parody.

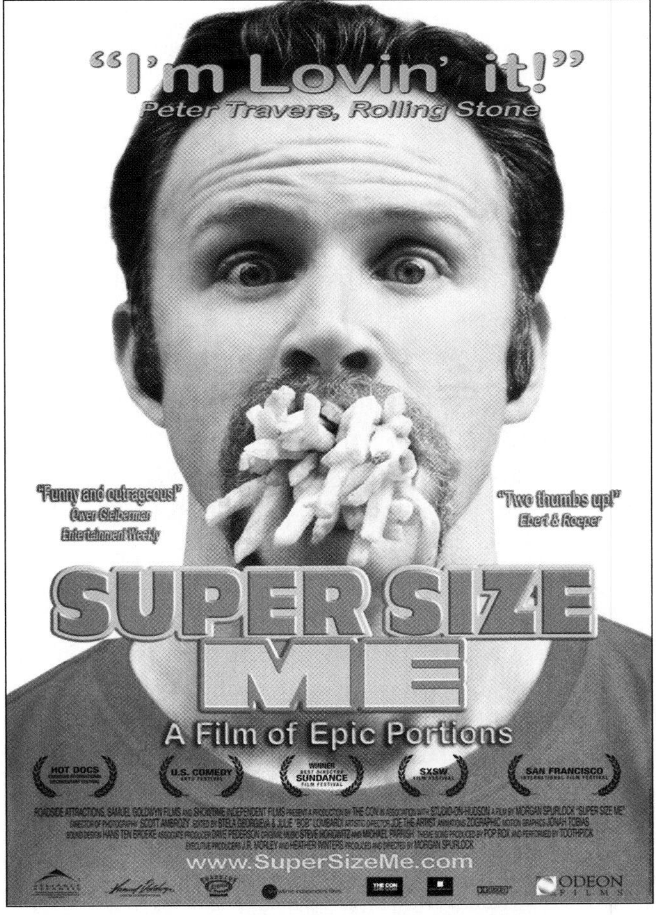

The film *Super Size Me* has biting humor for McDonald's cuisine.

SATIRE: AN EXCERPT FROM "WHY I WANT A WIFE"

The following passage is from a longer essay written by a woman claiming that she wants a wife. Written by Judy Syfers and published in 1971 in *Ms.* magazine, it's not about same-sex marriage but rather about the inequality of traditional gender-based roles. This paragraph focuses on caring for children's needs; subsequent paragraphs deal with satisfying the author's physical, social, and sexual needs.

> Why do I want a wife? I would like to go back to school so that I can become economically independent, support myself, and, if need be, support those dependent upon me. I want a wife who will work and send me to school. And while I am going to school I want a wife to take care of my children. I want a wife to keep track of the children's doctor and dentist appointments. And to keep track of mine, too. I want a wife to make sure my children eat properly and are kept clean. I want a wife who will wash the children's clothes and keep them mended. I want a wife who is a good nurturing attendant to my children, who arranges for their schooling, makes sure that they have an adequate social life with their peers, takes them to the park, the zoo. . . .
>
> —Judy Syfers

"A Modest Proposal," Jonathan Swift's mock-serious essay, proposes cannibalism as a solution to poverty and a food shortage.

The documentary film *Super Size Me* ridicules the fast-food industry generally and McDonald's restaurants in particular.

PRACTICE 11.4 Satire

Understanding satire: In a short writing or a group discussion, respond to the following questions about the preceding passage from Judy Syfers's "Why I Want a Wife."

1. Based on Syfers's definition of *wife*, would you want a wife? Why or why not? How accurate and fair is her definition?
2. What do you think Syfers really wants? To what extent should you take Syfers literally: Does she *really* want a wife?
3. What techniques of humor is she using?
4. How does Syfers's gender affect your understanding of "Why I Want a Wife"? In what ways would your understanding change if the speaker were male?
5. In what ways have laws and customs changed since 1971, the year this article was published? Does the article have the same effect now as it probably did then?

Writing a satire: Syfers's article can be used as a model for writing satire. Think of a similar situation in which roles are predetermined and unequal. Consider the ways a particular role (the boss, a senator, a sports legend, and so on) is desirable yet unfairly rewarded. "Why I Want to Be _____" is one way to start: Syfers could have approached this issue as "Why I Want to Be a Husband."

Parody A parody imitates and sometimes ridicules the style of another literary work. It may derive its humor from the conventions of the form, or it may instead use that form as a vehicle—a convenient mold to organize satire aimed at some other issue. The Austin Powers movies, for example, derive their humor not only from the spy genre but also from the fashions and customs of earlier decades, such as the promiscuity of the 1960s. *The Onion*, an online humor magazine, uses the form of a newspaper and mock-journalistic style as a mold for its satirical pieces.

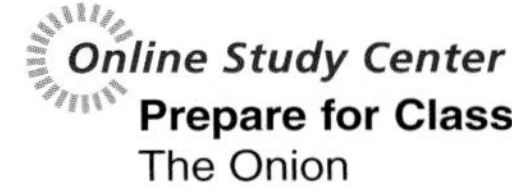

PARODY AND SATIRE

Parody mocks a form or style; satire ridicules foibles and folly. Sometimes these two techniques work together. Below, journalistic style—usually reserved for significant events—is parodied in the March 25, 1998, issue of the online newspaper *The Onion* to satirize an overblown domestic issue.

Area Woman Not Listened to Again

SPENCER, WI—Diane Hamm, 38, a lifelong Spencer resident and part-time clerical assistant at Groelke Home Financing in nearby Plovis, was not listened to yet again Tuesday, when her husband paid no attention to what she was saying as she handed him the morning newspaper.

Officials estimate that the incident marks roughly the 10 billionth time Hamm has not been listened to when attempting to speak.

"I talk and talk and talk and talk and talk and talk," Hamm told reporters at a press conference in the breakfast-nook area of the Hamm household, "and it just goes in one ear and out the other. I might as well be talking to a wall."

Hamm's sister-in-law, Janice Gunderson, who is staying with the Hamms temporarily, was sitting at the family's breakfast table when the non-listening incident occurred.

According to Gunderson, at approximately 7:45 a.m., Hamm's husband Gary, 41, asked his wife to please hand him the newspaper. As Hamm handed it to him, she reportedly said, "Oh, by the way, that reminds me. We need to send off the check for that subscription renewal if you still want to get the paper. Do you?"

According to Gunderson, Gary responded by staring into space, in no way acknowledging that he had heard his wife. Hamm then repeated the question twice, to no avail.

"It was only after Diane waved her hand in front of Gary's face while whistling the *Twilight Zone* theme that she got any reaction out of him at all," Gunderson said. "He just blinked and was like, 'Huh?' I swear, it's like he just tunes her out."

Though Gary, who married Diane in 1983, has denied his wife's allegations, claiming that he "was just zoning out there for a minute," many experts familiar with the Hamm case argue that the incident is merely symptomatic of a severe not-being-listened-to problem that has existed since the beginning of their marriage.

"The specific examples of Gary not listening to Diane are too numerous to list in full. In fact, if laid from end to end,

PARODY AND SATIRE *(continued)*

they'd reach from here to the sun," said Patricia Sloane, renowned feminist author and attorney with the D.C.-based Women's Attention-Payment Project.

Sloane then produced an abridged, 800-page document chronicling some of the prior incidents. Among them: the 1987 episode in which Hamm told her husband not to turn on the kitchen-sink garbage disposal because a fork was lodged in it, but he did anyway, breaking the garbage disposal; the week in early 1991 when she told him five days in a row to pick up their dry cleaning, and he didn't; and the much-discussed May 1993 dinner party thrown by the Engelbreits, at which he ignored 27 attempts by Hamm to contribute to a political discussion.

"It is clear that this is someone who does not hold Diane Hamm's words in the same regard he does those of other people," Sloane said.

According to noted New York–based gender activist Lisa Kopani, Hamm's case is far from uncommon.

"Each day in this country, millions of women go unlistened-to, despite their earnest efforts to make themselves heard," said Kopani, a member of the controversial performance-art group Metric Labia. "Unfortunately, you never hear about them in the media because their cases aren't as glamorous and sensationalized as this one."

"I have just about had it up to here," Hamm told reporters. "Gary can remember the plot of every episode of *Coach*, but my mother's birthday is beyond him? And I don't even want to talk about Jeffy and Craig. Don't even get me started on those kids. Talk about never listening to a word I say!"

The remainder of Hamm's comments are not known, as reporters stopped paying attention to her and just sort of aimlessly wandered off.

PRACTICE 11.5 Parody

Understanding parody: In a short writing or a group discussion, respond to the following questions about "Area Woman Not Listened to Again."

1. Journalistic style reveals the relevant "who, what, when, where, why, and how" as in the lead (the first one or sometimes two sentences). After that, an article will present the details in order of importance. Does this article follow journalistic style? What and where are the "five W's and an H" of this story?
2. News stories usually have some significance. Is this story significant? Explain.
3. In what way, if any, is the story a satire? What is the author satirizing? Explain.
4. Compare the point of view of this satire with Syphers's "Why I Want a Wife." How important is point of view in argument and in humor? To what extent can readers appreciate humor that doesn't reflect their own point of view?

Writing a parody: Think of a situation that isn't really significant but that some people fuss about. Write a news article about the situation. You may even want to submit it to *The Onion* at <http:// www. theonion. com>.

HUMOR IN ACADEMIC WRITING

Academic writing is formal and somewhat emotionally restrained, but humor can be used occasionally, especially when it fits the rhetoric context.

Purpose Humor sometimes can help you accomplish your argumentative goal by acting as a rebuttal or an explanation. It can

- Reveal ironies or inconsistencies in the words or actions of the opposition.
- Create a scenario of what might happen if the opposition gets its way.

Audience Humor can help you win over an audience. Speech makers, for example, often begin with a humorous story or joke. However, humor must be appropriate to the audience:

- *An instructor:* The audience for a student's academic writing usually is an instructor. How will the instructor react to your use of humor? Will the humor be considered effective and appropriate, or will it be considered off-task and a departure from requirements?
- *An unknown audience:* Students may be asked to write for a hypothetical audience or even to present a piece of writing to a real audience (such as the readers of a newspaper). Consider whether the audience might react to your writing according to different cultural backgrounds.

Structure Depending on the form or genre of your assignment, humor may or may not be effective and appropriate:

- If you are asked to write a satire or parody, have fun.
- If you are asked to write in academic style, such as a formal essay, use humor sparingly and with caution. It should not offend your readers or seem irrelevant.

Style Humor *is* a style. However, there are many kinds of humorous styles. Consider how harsh or genial you wish to be. Ridicule, for example, usually is not appropriate to academic writing.

Online Study Center
Prepare for Class
Literary Devices

Literary Devices Literary devices that might otherwise grace fine poetry can be overdone to lend a humorous touch. Jingles, slogans, and titles often use literary devices because they make words noticeable, memorable, and fun.

Word play This type of humor generally consists of puns, identical or similar sounds presented with two meanings. Also know by the Greek name *paronomasia*, it can take the form of double entendre, a pun with a naughty second meaning. GEICO, an insurance company, is sometimes represented by a cartoon lizard called a gecko. Here are some other examples of word play:

> Nothing runs like a Deere.
>
> —Slogan for John Deere tractors

> War decides who's left, not who's right.
>
> —Unknown

> A pun is the lowest form of wit, therefore the foundation of all wit.
>
> —Henry Erskine

Taking the "Rap" for Violence in Music
—Kerri Bennett, title of student essay on rap music

I used to be Snow White, . . . but I drifted.
—Mae West

Alliteration and assonance Alliteration (repeated consonant sounds) and assonance (repeated vowel sounds) can be concentrated in a sentence, creating something like a tongue twister. Here are two advertising slogans that use these techniques:

Picky people pick Peter Pan peanut butter.

Drink Coca-Cola.

Rhythm and rhyme Words that rhyme and sentences that flow may sound "right" even when the logic is flawed. People sometimes say jokingly, "If it rhymes, it must be true!"

If the glove doesn't fit, you must acquit.
—Johnnie Cochran in his successful defense of O. J. Simpson

I Like Ike.
—Political campaign slogan used by Dwight D. Eisenhower

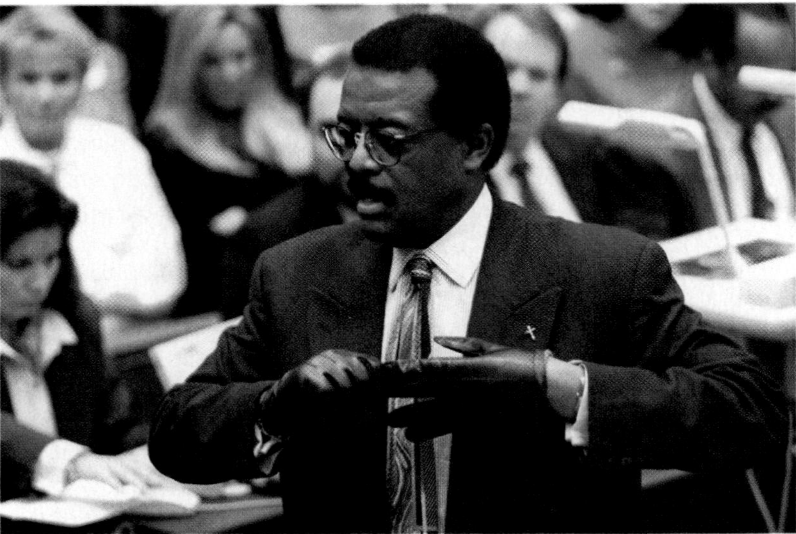

In his summation in defense of O. J. Simpson, Johnnie Cochran's "If the glove doesn't fit, you must acquit" resonated beyond the courtroom into American culture and history.

PRACTICE 11.6 **Literary Devices**

1. **Understanding literary devices:** In a brief writing or in group discussion, consider how literary devices such as the preceding examples can add humor and improve an argument by making it more noticeable, memorable, and fun.
2. **Writing literary devices:** Experiment with writing puns, alliteration and assonance, and rhythm and rhyme as you focus on an issue that has humorous potential. The following examples are based on issues stemming from the war in Iraq.
   - **Puns:** For an issue that you believe has the potential for humor, brainstorm a list of terms and ideas. Select a word that resembles the sound of other words and then make a pun in the form of a phrase or sentence. Example: *The Daily Show* called one of its humorous bits "Mess-o-potamia" to satirize the war in Iraq. This was a pun on *Mesopotamia*, the Iraqi region between the Tigris and Euphrates rivers.
   - **Alliteration:** Using the same issue and list, write an alliterative phrase or sentence. Prewrite by listing words with the same sound and then make selections. Example: A student titled a satire "Butcher of Baghdad to Be Beheaded."
   - **Rhyme and rhythm:** Using the same issue and list, write a phrase or sentence that features rhyme and/or rhythm. Prewrite by listing words that rhyme and then make selections. Example: Another student called an essay "Relax Iraq's Attacks."

Claims and Humor Claims—fact, identity, cause and effect, value, and proposal—sometimes are expressed through humor. Dave Barry, for example, makes an identity claim that *men* and *guys* are different:

> **Guys vs. Men**
>
> This is a book about guys. It's *not* a book about men. There are already way too many books about men, and most of them are *way* too serious.
>
> *Men* itself is a serious word, not to mention *manhood* and *manly*. Such words make being male sound like a very important activity, as opposed to what it primarily consists of, namely, possessing a set of minor and frequently unreliable organs. . . .
>
> So, I'm saying there's another way to look at males: not merely as aggressive macho dominators, not as sensitive, liberated, hugging drummers; but as *guys*.
>
> And what, exactly, do I mean by "guys"? I don't know. I haven't thought that much about it. One of the major characteristics of guyhood is that we don't spend a lot of time pondering our deep innermost feelings. There is a serious

question in my mind about whether guys actually *have* deep innermost feelings, unless you count, for example, the Detroit Tigers, or fear of bridal showers.

—Dave Barry, *Dave Barry's Complete Guide to Guys*

PRACTICE 11.7 Humorous Claims of Identity

Understanding a humorous claim of identity: In a short writing or a group discussion, respond to the following questions about the excerpt titled "Guys vs. Men."

1. Identification can include definition, classification, comparison/contrast, and resemblance. Which of these techniques does Barry use? Where, specifically?
2. Which techniques of humor does Barry use? Where, specifically?
3. Besides the stated purpose of identifying *guys*, what other purpose(s) might Barry have in mind?
4. How does this excerpt compare with other examples, such as "Area Woman Not Listened to Again" and "Why I Want a Wife"?

Writing a humorous claim of identity: Write a humorous claim of identity.

1. Plan or prewrite by first selecting a person, thing, or phenomenon to identify in an unconventional way.
2. Brainstorm or list the qualities that identify your subject.
3. Consider concrete, specific, humorous examples to illustrate the characteristics of your subject.

Rhetorical Questions

A rhetorical question is asked for a purpose other than to receive information in return. It makes a statement implicitly, not explicitly.

Shall I compare thee to a summer's day?

—Shakespeare

Speakers and writers use rhetorical questions for a number of purposes:

- To scold: "What on earth do you think you are doing?"
- To express emotion such as rage or grief: "Why me, Lord?"
- To rouse others' emotions: "Are we going to put up with this?"
- To reason aloud: "What would motivate someone to do such a thing?"

- To engage the audience, making them more a part of the argument, perhaps by using direct address (second person): "What would you do in this situation?"
- To be cautious, considerate, or subtle, encouraging readers to think explicitly without the author making an explicit statement: "Do you have a nonplaid necktie that might go with that plaid shirt?"
- When evidence is lacking, to imply a claim: "Did ancient Atlanteans build the great pyramids?"
- When an issue is sensitive, offensive, or inflammatory, to imply a controversial claim rather than stating it directly: "What can be done about religious extremism?"

Rhetorical questions can be used effectively to create a bond with the audience, as if an actual conversation is taking place between writer and reader or speaker and listener. However, novice writers sometimes overuse rhetorical questions, often to cover up a lack of evidence or claim. Excessive use of rhetorical questions may produce a negative reaction in readers or listeners who tend to prefer explicit statements over vagueness.

Online Study Center
Prepare for Class
Using Rhetorical Questions

PRACTICE 11.8 Rhetorical Questions

Analyzing rhetorical questions: The following passage is from a humorous article by Emily Prager about the cultural impact of Mattel's Barbie and Ken dolls. Many of Prager's points are phrased as rhetorical questions. For each question, speculate on (1) why she chose a question over a direct statement, (2) which claim or support is implied, and (3) how persuasive it is.

> I used to look at Barbie and wonder, What's wrong with this picture? . . . There are millions of women who are subliminally sure that a thirty-nine-inch bust and a twenty-three-inch waist are the epitome of lovability. Could this account for the popularity of breast implant surgery? . . . Why, I wondered, was Barbie designed with such obvious sexual equipment and Ken not? Why was his treated as if it were more mysterious than hers? Did the fact that it was treated as such indicate that somehow his equipment, his essential maleness, was considered more powerful than hers, more worthy of the dignity of concealment?
>
> —Emily Prager, *"Our Barbies, Ourselves"*

Writing rhetorical questions: For an issue that interests you, write rhetorical questions for each of the purposes listed below. After you write, consider whether each question would be more effective or less effective than a direct (declarative or exclamatory) statement.

1. To scold
2. To express emotions such as rage or grief
3. To rouse others' emotions
4. To reason aloud
5. To engage the audience
6. To be cautious, considerate, or subtle

Figurative Language

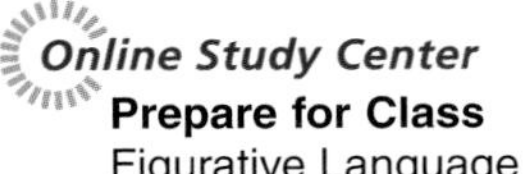

Prepare for Class
Figurative Language

"A rose is a rose is a rose." Often enough, the word *rose* does refer to a shrub having a prickly stem, compound leaves, and fragrant flowers. Yet Gertrude Stein, author of that famous quotation, would be the first to tell you that the word *rose* is not always literally a plant but sometimes a symbol of love, beauty, or spring. She might even tell you that in her poem the meaning of *rose* changes with each repetition.

Figurative language refers to ways that words can be used to mean something other than their literal, denotative meanings. *Figures* are the ways in which the language is crafted. When the order or arrangement of words affects the meaning of the writing, they are called *figures of form,* also known as *schemes*. When the words themselves mean something other than the literal definition, they are called *figures of speech,* also known as *tropes*. As you learn more about schemes and tropes, your own writing may bloom . . . like a rose.

FIGURES OF FORM: SCHEMES

Schemes (figures of form) are ways of organizing the parts of a sentence—words, phrases, and clauses—to add variety and beauty and to enhance the audience's interest and understanding. From your experiences with writing, you know that a sentence can be formed in many ways. The examples in this section should help you expand your knowledge of the basic schemes and their effects on style. Here the schemes are grouped by how they affect sentence structure: interruption of a complete sentence, inversion of word order, omission of words and phrases, and repetition.

Interruption (parentheses) Interrupt the flow of a complete sentence by inserting a word, phrase, or clause. The insertions—parenthetical statements—can be encapsulated within pairs of punctuation mark: Dashes and parentheses are standard, but ellipsis marks and commas are sometimes used.

She had a heart . . . how shall I say . . . too soon made glad. . . .

—Robert Browning, "My Last Duchess"

The capital of Arkansas—you had better know this fact for the test—is Little Rock.

Inversion (anastrophe) Transpose words—for example, by placing a predicate before a subject or an adjective after a noun.

Give crowns and pounds and guineas / But not your heart away.

—A. E. Housman, "When I Was One-and-Twenty"

Let me not to the marriage of true minds / Admit impediments.

—Shakespeare, Sonnet 116

Omission Omit words not needed to complete the meaning. Be careful, however, not to make the sentence too difficult to understand or too different from the style of your other sentences.

Omit a word or phrase (ellipsis). You can drop words that normally would be repeated in a sentence if the reader knows what they would be.

To err is human, to forgive divine.

—Alexander Pope

She: I love you.
He: And I, you.

—Dialogue from a love scene

Omit a verb (zeugma). You can use an ellipsis to make a pun. Omit one verb of a compound sentence, and then craft the remaining predicate/verb to have a different meaning for each of the two objects. This practice is known as *yoking*, joining two meanings in one verb.

Oh, flowers are as common here, Miss Fairfax, as people are in London.

—Oscar Wilde, *The Importance of Being Earnest*

Repetition Repeat words, phrases, and clauses to clarify, emphasize, and make memorable. Recurrence in the form of a refrain is a standard feature of songs and poetry, but repetition can have powerful effects in prose as well. Parallelism—a repetition of grammatical structures—naturally accompanies the repetition of parts of speech.

Repeat a grammatical structure (isocolon). Repeat parts of speech (nouns, verbs, adjectives, and so on) and patterns of phrases and clauses using different words. Known also by its Greek name, *isocolon* ("equal member"), the repeated parts usually are the same length.

> Marry in haste, repent at leisure.
>
> —Scots proverb

> I came, I saw, I conquered.
>
> —Julius Caesar

Repeat the beginning (anaphora). Use the same words at the beginning of each phrase, clause, or sentence in a series.

> I recommend getting your heart trampled on to anyone / I recommend walking around naked in your living room.
>
> —Alanis Morisette, "You Learn"

> To do two things at once is to do neither.
>
> —Publilius Syrus

Repeat the ending (antistrophe). Use the same words at the end of each phrase, clause, or sentence in a series.

> Wherever they's a fight so hungry people can eat, I'll be there. . . . And when our folks eat the stuff they raise an' live in the houses they build—why, I'll be there.
>
> —John Steinbeck, *The Grapes of Wrath*

Repeat the beginning and the ending (symploce). Repeat words at the beginning and at the end of a series of phrases, clauses, or sentences. (*Symploce* combines *anaphora* and *antistrophe*.)

> When I was a child, I spoke like a child, I thought like a child, I reasoned like a child; when I become a man, I gave up childish ways.
>
> —Corinthians 13.11

> This land is your land / This land is my land. . . .
>
> —Woody Guthrie

Double back (anadiplosis). Repeat the end words of a previous phrase, clause, or sentence at the beginning of the next phrase, clause, or sentence.

> A word is a group of letters / Letters strategically placed to make a sound / A sound that creates an image.
>
> —Lynnie Lowe, "Anadiplosis"

> Winter blooms to spring, spring grows to summer, summer fades to fall.
>
> —Trebor Malm

Repeat a pair in reverse order (chiasmus). Repeat two words or phrases but in reversed order, often to negate the first half (antithesis) or to reveal irony.

> I'm trying to give; why don't you give me a try? / Why am I dying to live when I'm just living to die?
>
> —Edgar Winter

> And so, my fellow Americans: ask not what your country can do for you; ask what you can do for your country.
>
> —John F. Kennedy

> Nowadays all the married men live like bachelors and all the bachelors live like married men.
>
> —Oscar Wilde, *The Picture of Dorian Gray*

Restate with synonyms (synonymy). Emphasize or clarify by restating in other words. When overdone, this technique creates humor.

> My truest friend, my Rock of Gibraltar, my guiding star.
>
> Trebor Malm

> 'E's passed on! This parrot is no more! He has ceased to be! 'E's expired and gone to meet 'is maker! 'E's a stiff! Bereft of life, 'e rests in peace! If you hadn't nailed 'im to the perch, 'e'd be pushing up the daisies! 'Is metabolic processes are now 'istory! 'E's off the twig! 'E's kicked the bucket, 'e's shuffled off 'is mortal coil, run down the curtain and joined the bleedin' choir invisible!
>
> —Monty Python, "Dead Parrot" sketch

PRACTICE 11.9 Writing Schemes (Figures of Form)

Imitating schemes: Imitate the sentence structures shown in the examples of schemes: insertion, inversion, omission, and repetition.

1. **Discovering schemes:** Look for schemes as you read. Formal speeches are a rich source, as are literary works—poetry in particular. The schemes you find can be recorded in a journal or writer's scrapbook.
2. **Drafting and revising schemes:** As you draft or revise one of your own arguments, consider using schemes to add eloquence.

SCHEME IN MARTIN LUTHER KING, JR.'S "I HAVE A DREAM" SPEECH (excerpt)

I have a dream that one day this nation will rise up and live out the true meaning of its creed: "We hold these truths to be self-evident, that all men are created equal."

I have a dream that one day on the red hills of Georgia, the sons of former slaves and the sons of former slave owners will be able to sit down together at the table of brotherhood.

I have a dream that one day even the state of Mississippi, a state sweltering with the heat of injustice, sweltering with the heat of oppression, will be transformed into an oasis of freedom and justice.

I have a dream that my four little children will one day live in a nation where they will not be judged by the color of their skin but by the content of their character.

I have a *dream* today!

PRACTICE 11.10 **Scheme in "I Have a Dream"**

1. **Understanding "I Have a Dream":** The above excerpt from Martin Luther King, Jr.'s speech uses repetition (anaphora) at the beginning of each sentence. In what ways is this effective? Does it matter which words are repeated?
2. **Imitating "I Have a Dream":** Write an imitation of the "I Have a Dream" excerpt, substituting your own dream for King's.

FIGURES OF SPEECH: TROPES

Online Study Center
Prepare for Class
Tropes

Tropes (figures of speech) stretch words beyond their literal meanings. Some tropes, such as similes, are familiar—perhaps too familiar because many clichés are similes: "happy as a clam," "crazy as a loon," "strong as an ox." Other tropes may not be in your repertoire at present, or perhaps you use them without knowing it. Like schemes, tropes can help you write with greater clarity, strength, and style.

This section focuses on the following types of tropes: apostrophe; comparisons such as analogy, metaphor, and simile; onomatopoeia; oxymoron; personification; substitutions such as metonymy and synecdoche; and synesthesia.

Apostrophe Directly address someone or an abstraction that is not present.

> Death, be not proud, though some have called thee / Mighty and dreadful, for thou art not so.
>
> —John Donne

Comparison Express a similarity between otherwise dissimilar persons, places, things, ideas, processes, or phenomena.

Analogy Make a comparison in which the similarity may be thought of as literal in a limited, specified way. An analogy can take the form of either simile ("Light resembles particles and waves") or metaphor ("Saddam Hussein is like Hitler") but in a less figurative sense.

Metaphor Make a direct comparison (that is, without using *like*, *as*, *than*, or *seems*).

> Life for me ain't been no crystal stair.
>
> —Langston Hughes, "Mother to Son"

> A word is not a crystal, transparent and unchanged; it is the skin of a living thought, and may vary greatly in color and content according to the circumstances and the time in which it is used.
>
> —U.S. Supreme Court Justice Oliver Wendell Holmes, *Towne v. Eisner*

> Someday I will have a best friend all my own. . . . Until then I am a red balloon tied to an anchor.
>
> —Sandra Cisneros, *The House on Mango Street*

All in favor of extending the Patriot Act, say 'Eye.'

How does this political cartoon use metaphor (or other forms of word play) to make its claim apparent?

Rules for Writing

1. Don't abbrev.
2. No sentence fragments.
3. Implement the vernacular.
4. Dump the slang. It sucks.
5. Avoid clichés like the plague.
6. Try to never split an infinitive.
7. Don't never use double negatives.
8. Passive voice should be made active.
9. Avoid redundant punctuation!!! Okay???
10. And do not start sentences with conjunctions.
11. Prepositions are words you shouldn't end with.
12. Use parallelism when you speak and in writing.
13. Fix comma splices, use a conjunction or semicolon.
14. Each of the pronouns should agree with their antecedent.
15. Mixed metaphors are like a disease that must be ironed out.

Simile Make an indirect comparison (using *like, as, than,* or *seems*).

> An egotist is like a cock who thinks the sun has risen to hear him crow.
>
> —George Eliot

> The relationship between truth and a newspaper is like the relationship between the color green and the number seven. Occasionally you will see the number seven written in green but you learn not to expect this.
>
> —Garrison Keillor

Onomatopoeia Make the word mimic the sound it describes: *bang, beep, buzz, ring, splat, woof, cri-itch* (biting a potato chip), *spohlap* (dripping water).

Oxymoron Make a phrase composed of terms that are opposites, such as *virtual reality, jumbo shrimp, head butt, pretty ugly,* and *tight slacks.*

Personification Give human qualities to inanimate objects or abstractions. Some scholars extend the definition to include giving human qualities to animals.

> [The survivors] came through the jaws of death / Back from the mouth of Hell.
>
> —Alfred, Lord Tennyson, "The Charge of the Light Brigade"

> I am of the earth / She is my mother.
>
> —Anna Lee Walters

Substitution A subject can be represented by another word or phrase that is part of it or associated with it.

Metonymy Identify a subject using something associated with it.

> The White House announced a new tax plan. (*The White House* = "executive branch")

> The world will little note nor long remember what we say here, but it can never forget what they did here. (*The world* = "people")
>
> —Abraham Lincoln, "The Gettysburg Address"

Synecdoche Identify a whole by naming a part.

> The rancher owns a thousand head. (*head* = cattle)

> All hands on deck! (*hands* = sailors)

Synesthesia ("joined feelings") Describe a sensation using terms from another sense. In a broader sense of synesthesia (sometimes spelled *synaesthesia*), a sensation can describe something abstract. Examples include *sharp taste, loud color, bitter cold,* and *bitter defeat.*

PRACTICE 11.11 Writing Tropes (Figures of Speech)

Imitating tropes: Imitate the sentence structures shown in the examples of tropes.

1. **Discovering tropes:** Look for tropes as you read. Formal speeches are a rich source of tropes, as are literary works, especially poetry. The tropes you find can be recorded in a journal or writer's scrapbook.
2. **Drafting and revising tropes:** As you draft or revise one of your own arguments, consider using tropes to add eloquence.

Fallacies

Online Study Center
Prepare for Class
Logical Fallacies

From time to time, you may encounter arguments that either don't make sense or only seem to make sense until closer inspection reveals them to be false. Such arguments probably contain logical flaws known as fallacies. Although fallacies often are accidental, sometimes they may indicate a deliberate attempt to deceive. Learning more about fallacies will help you form your own arguments and understand those of others.

This section examines a few of the many kinds of fallacies, grouping them by their effect on an audience: substitutions, distractions, and distortions.

Substitutions (Nonlogical Appeals)

Some "fallacies" are not so much fallacious as they are substitutes for logic. Ethos and pathos sometimes are valued to the exclusion of logos. Nonlogical appeals may be based on authority, faith, fear, popularity, pity, and an assortment of other substitutes for logic.

Authority (argumentum ad verecundiam) Under many circumstances, an appeal to authority can be valid. It has roots in the reality that we cannot be experts in everything, so we must trust the opinions of others: We accept the claim of a respected expert as factual without demanding full logical proof. In this case, the authority substitutes for evidence. Leaders, both civic and spiritual, appeal to authority. Spokespersons for various products also make authoritative appeals in the form of endorsements and commercials. Their appeal is most convincing if they are truly experts in that field: Michael Jordan, for example, is a good spokesperson for athletic equipment but perhaps less credible if he endorses hair care products. Appeals to authority are fallacious when (1) the "authority" is not actually an expert, (2) authorities are in disagreement, or (3) the arguer misrepresents authority's opinion.

Faith (fiatism or blind faith) This appeal holds that some matters (spiritualism, loyalty) supersede personal judgment and logic. Faith is a hallmark of many religious believers and ideologues (those who hold unquestioning beliefs in particular causes or political leaders). Appeals to faith work only when you "preach to the choir"—that is, you present your argument to someone with identical beliefs who already accepts your claims.

Fear (argumentum in terrorem, argumentum ad metum) This appeal uses apprehension and dread to achieve a desired result. In spiritual terms, this fear may be the consequence of eternal damnation, while governments may threaten with legal repercussions. Such an appeal may be blended with appeals to authority and to faith when the fear concerns danger from outside one's social unit. For example, politicians may claim that they can protect their constituents from terrorists. This fallacy is similar to the appeal to force (*argumentum ad baculum*), which goes beyond intimidation into physical coercion.

Pity (argumentum ad misericordiam) Known also as *special pleading*, this emotional appeal depends on making the audience understand and sympathize with the feelings of someone else. For example, when hardships of a personal nature affect job or school performance, employees or students sometimes plead for special consideration.

Popularity (argumentum ad populum) Known also as the *bandwagon*, *mob appeal*, and *appeal to the masses*, this appeal tries to convince an individual to conform, to join the many. Sometimes it takes the following form: "Can all of these other people be wrong?" Also, it may claim that by joining the throng one will achieve greater acceptance. Advertisers often tout the popularity of their product as evidence that the consumer should purchase it. A variation on popular appeals is the appeal to the lowest common denominator or to prejudices, trying to get as many people as possible to follow—this appeal is known as demagoguery.

Bandwagon appeals claim one should follow the crowd.

Other Appeals

Ignorance (argumentum ad ignorantiam): If it hasn't been proven false, it must be true; or if it hasn't been proven true, it must be false.
Force (argumentum ad baculum): Might makes right.
Novelty (argumentum ad novitatem): Newer is better.
Numbers (argumentum ad numerum): More is better.
Poverty (argumentum ad lazarum): Avoidance of wealth indicates virtue.
Tradition (argumentum ad antiquitatem): Older is better.
Wealth (argumentum ad crumenam): Wealth is validating.

PRACTICE 11.12 Substitutions

Identify each of the following nonlogical appeals.

1. "If you do that, your soul will be condemned to hell."
2. "Please give me a passing grade; otherwise, I'll lose my scholarship."
3. "Trust me: I've got your best interests at heart."
4. "If you use this cologne, people will be attracted to you."
5. "If you're so smart, why ain't you rich?"
6. "One billion Chinamen can't be wrong."

Distractions

Sometimes the argument shifts to a related issue or even to something unrelated.

Attacking the Person (argumentum ad hominem, "argument against the person") This tactic attacks the credibility (ethos) of the person making an argument and does not address the merits of the argument. The fallacy lies in the perception that a disreputable person cannot be trusted regardless of his or her claims and evidence. Name calling or hurling epithets is an ad hominem attack that attempts to discredit opponents by associating them with a label that the audience considers negative. Name calling frequently backfires against the attackers, however, by reducing their own credibility and consequently weakening their arguments. Ad hominem attacks related to guilt by association and poisoning the well are discussed below.

Guilt by association The tactic of guilt by association diverts attention away from the issues at hand and toward the reputations of others who support a particular claim. A guilt-by-association argument against superhighways might say that Hitler supported them when he ruled Germany. Even though highways have their own arguable strengths and weaknesses, the ad hominem argument instead uses the personal attack to dismiss any arguments being proposed. Guilt by association is also used to diminish the credibility of one's opponents. To avoid guilt by association, politicians often distance themselves from unpopular figures. In the 2000 presidential election, for example, candidate Al Gore did not rely on President Bill Clinton (who had been the target of an unsuccessful impeachment attempt) for support.

Poisoning the well The tactic of poisoning the well discredits opponents before an audience receives their arguments. The opponents become, figuratively, like a water source that no one will use in the future.

Red Herring A red herring is an issue that distracts an audience from the main discussion. Metaphorically, it is like using a smelly fish to throw hunting dogs off the scent. Also known as the *run-around*, a *wild goose chase*, and a *smokescreen*, a red herring is introduced as though it is relevant to the main issue but causes discussion to shift to the red herring. For example, an argument about ways of saving the United States' Social Security system might be diverted to finger pointing at private pension plans or political parties.

PRACTICE 11.13 Distractions

Identify each of the following distractions.

1. "Sure, I know smoking causes cancer. But hey, bird flu could kill me tomorrow."
2. "G. Gordon Liddy did jail time for his part in the Watergate scandal. You can't trust his views on anything."
3. "Socialists want universal health care, and so do you. You're like the Socialists."
4. "You're a knuckle-dragging, retrograde nose-picker."

Distortions

Analogy An analogy highlights a similarity between otherwise dissimilar concepts, people, objects, or events. Analogies are often used to make an abstraction more concrete. When used properly, an analogy is valid. However, if the similarity isn't relevant to the argument or if the differences between the two subjects are significant, it is a fallacy. For example, economists have spoken of "trickle-down" economics, which advocates making the wealthy become wealthier, based on the hypothesis that they will in turn make purchases and investments that stimulate the economy—metaphorically "raining money" on those employed by the well-to-do. This analogy doesn't prove that tax cuts for the rich actually benefit the poor, of course. When the character of a person is compared to another, less desirable character—such as comparing an opponent to Hitler—a faulty analogy is also an ad hominem attack.

Anecdotal Evidence Anecdotes are short stories that illustrate a point. They can be very useful in making an abstract concept more concrete and in adding pathos to an argument by connecting issues with real-life events, people, and emotions. Anecdotal evidence is fallacious when it is nonrepresentative, misleading the audience to overgeneralize the point being made. In such a case, the anecdote purports to represent a common occurrence but actually depicts "an exception to the rule."

Begging the Question (petitio principii) Begging the question is a deductive fallacy that uses the conclusion as one of the premises. For example, Chief Justice William Rehnquist detected this fallacy in *Cruzan v. Director, Missouri Department of Health*:

> If the question is, Is Nancy Cruzan capable of making her own decision regarding the continuation or termination of life support, then to say that "Nancy Cruzan is incompetent"—without further argument, evidence, reasons, etc.—is to assume the question at hand. "Incompetent" is, in this context, simply a synonym for "incapable of making an informed decision."
>
> — William Rehnquist

Sometimes the phrase "begs the question" is used in a context that has nothing to do with an argument or logical fallacy. In this alternative sense, it means "raises interest in further discussion." For example, someone might say, "This early freeze begs the question, 'Is global warming a reality?'"

Cherry Picking (card stacking) Cherry picking or card stacking occurs when an arguer is assumed to be presenting all major aspects—both pro and con—of an issue, but, in fact, has overrepresented one side and underrepresented the opposition. Figuratively, this practice is like cheating in a card game by making sure you get the best cards as they are dealt, or like selecting bits of evidence as one might pick and serve the best cherries while bypassing the rotten, worm-eaten ones.

Circular Reasoning (circulus in demonstando) This form of begging the question occurs when the conclusion is used as a part of the evidence. Such a fallacy often is accidental, occurring when a slight rewording of the conclusion disguises it enough that it looks like evidence. For example, consider the statement "Brad Pitt is handsome because he is good looking." *Handsome* and *good looking* are synonyms, so the evidence is the same as the claim.

Equivocation Based on root words meaning "equal voice," equivocation is based on ambiguity: one word with two or more meanings. The equivocator allows the audience to think an obvious (more agreeable) meaning when, in fact, a secret (less agreeable) meaning is intended. A literary example is provided by Shakespeare: An apparition conjured by the three witches foretells that "none of woman born shall harm MacBeth." The character MacBeth assumes that no person can hurt him, because all people are *borne* by women, but the apparition means *born* in the sense of *delivery*: The future slayer of Macbeth had been delivered by cesarean section.

False Cause False cause is known also as a *post hoc fallacy*, from the Latin *post hoc ergo propter hoc*, meaning "after this, therefore because of this." When two events occur in close succession, such as a power outage that happens immediately after you switch on an appliance, we tend to think of the two events as being related. Sometimes the cause-and-effect relationship is valid, but other times it is just coincidence and thus is a fallacy. Cause-and-effect relationships can be difficult to prove. For example, despite common sense and statistical evidence, it was difficult to prove that cigarette smoking causes cancer. The causal connection between the two was proved mainly through correlation — meaning that lung cancer and smoking were observed to occur often in the same people. However, the same people also drank coffee, watched television, breathed smog, or engaged in other activities that had some correlations with the occurrence of cancer. Thus it was difficult to prove a single cause without conducting a controlled laboratory experiment on test subjects.

False Dilemma In this situation, the arguer presents an incomplete set of choices. Aggressive salespeople often use this tactic: "Would you rather risk an asthma attack or purchase this deluxe air purifier?"

Hasty Generalization When a claim is based on too few examples, it may be in error. For example, if the first few students you met on campus were smoking cigarettes, you could be premature in assuming that most or all students smoke. Anecdotal evidence in particular can lead to hasty generalization. To minimize the risk of errors in generalization, statisticians follow guidelines concerning sample sizes and random selection.

Loaded Question Also known as a complex question, a loaded question combines two or more propositions into a single statement. If the responder answers one half without debating the other half, he or she makes a concession. The classic example is, "Have you stopped beating your wife?" This question implies that a simple answer is possible, but in reality any simple answer—yes or no—is an admission that one is or was a wife-beater.

Non Sequitur A non sequitur is a faulty or irrelevant conclusion. This term literally means "doesn't follow," in the sense that the conclusion doesn't follow from the evidence and explanations. One kind of non sequitur arises when the arguer claims that contradictory statements are both true. Non sequiturs can be understood more clearly by examining the logic as a syllogism. Two kinds of syllogistic non sequiturs exist: affirming the consequent and denying the subsequent.

The following is an example of affirming the consequent:

Major premise: All men are mortal.
Minor premise: I am mortal.
Conclusion: Therefore, I am all men.

The second example involves denying the subsequent:

Major premise: If I'm in Dallas, I'm in the United States.
Minor premise: I'm not in Dallas.
Conclusion: Therefore, I'm not in the United States.

Quoting out of Context Removing a quotation from its context can distort the original meaning. For example, the apparent winner of a debate might say of the opposition, "They would like to declare the contest was a draw." Spin doctors for the opposition might quote the apparent winner as saying, "The contest was a draw."

Slippery Slope This type of distortion assumes that if you make an exception to a rule, the rule will become open to other challenges and continually weakened. A slippery slope is a particular instance of analogy, arguing that your present position is like standing atop a steep, slick hill. If you descend from the top, the force of gravity begins to pull you downward, making it much easier to go lower than to return to the top. In truth, the slope slips both ways: it can be viewed as an "uphill climb" to a better way of doing things. The issue of same-sex marriage, for example, slips the slope in both directions. Some see it as a descent from morality, whereas others view it as an ascent toward civil rights.

Straw Man With a straw man argument, the arguer portrays the opposition's argument in a way that is easy to discredit—much the same way that a scarecrow is defenseless and easy to knock over. This can be accomplished by restating or simplifying the opposition's position, thereby making it undesirable or indefensible. If, for example, an arguer portrayed environmentalists as being concerned only with some philosophical opposition to progress but failed to mention concerns over the ecological balance of the planet, this argument would be a straw man.

PRACTICE 11.14 Distortions

Identify each of the following distortions.

1. "Southeast Asian countries are like dominoes. If one falls to communism, its neighbors will fall as well."
2. "Republicans care only about the rich, Democrats only about poor, and Libertarians only about themselves. Vote Green!"
3. "If we don't allow gays to marry, interracial marriage may become illegal."
4. "After the rooster crows, the sun rises. Roosters must cause the sun to rise."
5. "You said that nothing is better than barbecue, so I figured you wanted nothing for dinner."

6. "People who live near foul-smelling swamps get malaria, so it is probably the odor that causes the disease." (*Malaria* literally means "bad air.")
7. "I saw two auto accidents as I drove through Buffalo. The people there must drive like maniacs!"

Looking Back at Chapter 11

- In addition to making an audience smile or laugh, humor has a number of practical uses: It can support a claim or discredit the opposition, make you aware of strategies used by others, hook your audience's interest, make an argument memorable, and form a bond between you and the audience. Conversely, it can be abused as a means of attack or as a distortion of the truth.
- Major techniques of humor include exaggeration, irony, ridicule, and literary devices with a comic twist. These techniques are not discrete but rather can overlap, performing multiple functions.
- A rhetorical question is asked for a purpose other than to receive information in return. It makes a statement implicitly, not explicitly.
- Speakers and writers use rhetorical questions for a number of purposes: to scold, to express emotion, to rouse others' emotions, to reason aloud, to engage the audience, and to be cautious, considerate, or subtle.
- Figurative language can make your writing clearer, stronger, and more interesting.
- Figurative language consists of schemes (figures of form) and tropes (figures of speech).
- Arguments that either don't make sense or seem to make sense but don't probably contain flaws known as fallacies. Sometimes fallacies are accidental, but at other times they may indicate a deliberate attempt to deceive.
- Fallacies can be grouped by how they are perceived by an audience: substitutions, distractions, and distortions.

Suggestions for Writing

- Base a satire on a kind of claim: fact, identity, cause/effect, value, or proposal.
- Write a stand-up monologue about one or more issues that concern you.

- Write a humorous rant about an issue that concerns you.
- In journal entries reflect on humor, rhetorical questions, figurative language, and fallacies.
- As you draft and revise future essays, look for opportunities to use humor, rhetorical questions, and figurative language. Evaluate your argument to eliminate fallacies.

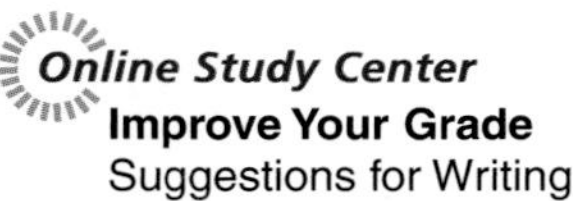

Online Study Center
Improve Your Grade
Suggestions for Writing

ARGUING VISUALLY

The proverb "A picture is worth a thousand words" may not be mathematically accurate, but its meaning is undeniable. A visual image can convey a sizable amount of information. Visuals have always been valued in communication, but within the past decade, technology has made it possible for nonprofessionals to include images in their texts. Current technology—including computers, scanners, e-mail, the Web, facsimile machines, and software for generating images and processing photographs—can allow you to combine your words with visual images to make more powerful arguments.

> *A picture is worth a thousand words.*
> —CHINESE PROVERB

Online Study Center
This icon will direct you to content and resources on the website <college.hmco.com/pic/lamm1e>.

Physicians Against Land Mines
Member of the International Campaign to Ban Land Mines
www.banmines.org

This is an op-ad—an opinion advertisement—that uses its visual power to make an argumentative point. What claim is this composition trying to make? How do the words, shapes, colors, and images work together to drive the point home?

Online Study Center
Prepare for Class
Op-Ads

Images that can be used to supplement a text may include photographs, drawings, charts, and graphs. In some cases—such as in advertisements—text may be combined with pictures to create an argument complete with a claim, supporting evidence (provided through both words and images), and sometimes even a hint of refutation. At other times, an image such as a carefully composed photograph or a statistical graph can imply an argument without fully articulating a claim or presenting evidence. In this case, the claim can usually be figured out and the evidence is often the subject matter of the image itself. Because images may suggest various elements of argumentation rather than state them directly, understanding visual arguments requires taking a fresh approach to the material. In other words, you have to "read" visual arguments differently. In addition to looking for claims, support, and refutation, you should consider the effect that the overall design of the image has on the reader.

Elements of Design

Visual texts typically consist of four elements:

- Text
- Images
- Color
- Overall design

Text

In conventional written texts, words provide most of the raw material for building arguments. You may support an argument with a photograph, bar chart, or political cartoon, but on the whole you will argue through words. In other cases—for example, on websites or in print advertisements—the textual part of the argument is brief and takes on a graphical dimension. The text, in other words, becomes an image in its own right. Moreover, when the text is very concise (in a PowerPoint presentation, for instance), it becomes extremely important for it to be well written, clear in purpose, and supported by images or, in the case of the Internet, linked to other forms of evidence.

Elements of Text You can change the visual impression that a text makes on a reader by changing the style—that is, the appearance—of the letters and symbols that make up a particular argument. Particular textual styles are grouped into categories called typefaces. The appearance of a typeface can vary in terms of its font size, style, color, emphasis, and artistic effects.

Size A typeface is called a *font* when it is reproduced in a particular size. The smaller the number of the font, the smaller the size of the text. One of the most

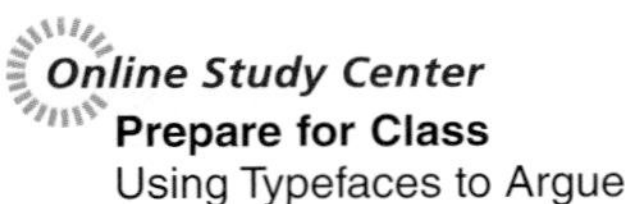

Typefaces

Examples of Serif Typefaces
Book Antiqua
Courier New
Bembo
Palatino Linotype
Times New Roman

Examples of Sans Serif Typefaces
Arial
Futura Book
Impact
Lucida Sans Unicode
Clearface Gothic

Artistic Typefaces

War is not healthy for children or other living things. (Dissonant)

War is not healthy for children or other living things. (Edwardian Script)

War is not healthy for children or other living things. (Woodcut)

War is not healthy for children or other living things. (Gigi)

War is not healthy for children or other living things. (Old English Text MT)

WAR IS NOT HEALTHY FOR CHILDREN OR OTHER LIVING THINGS. (STENCIL)

war is not healthy for children or other living things. (Crayon)

common fonts used in word-processed documents is 12-point Times New Roman. Although fonts as small as 8 points are sometimes used, typefaces smaller than 11 points can cause eyestrain for some people and are best avoided.

Style Typeface styles are classified into two broad categories: serif and sans serif. Serif typefaces feature flattened "tails" on most of the letters. These tails are especially prevalent on capital letters. The Times New Roman typeface, which is a default setting on many word processors, is a serif font. Another commonly used font, Arial, is a sans serif font. Sans serif typefaces are "plain" in the sense that they do not feature flattened tails.

Special styles In addition to the general categories of serif and sans serif, a number of typefaces are notable because they simulate handwriting, are particularly elaborate, or are especially artistic. For example, handwriting typefaces may simulate crude children's handwriting (Crayon), flowing calligraphy, or ordinary cursive script. Elaborate type styles may consist of elegant letters that, although beautiful, can be difficult or irritating to read; these typefaces should be used sparingly. For example, fancy styles such as Edwardian Script are best reserved for special documents (e.g., wedding announcements) where elegant, flowing script is required. Reading long passages set in such a type style can be very difficult. Artistic styles—in which the forms of the letters are works of art in themselves—can be useful (if employed with caution) to create a desired impression.

Color Although we consider color in more depth shortly, this typeface characteristic is worth mentioning briefly here. The color in which text is presented is part of the overall visual impression that you wish your argument to make. As such, it should be considered carefully. A conventional written argument should usually be presented in black in a standard font such as Times New Roman 12. When text is employed as part of an image (or as a visual effect within a written text), its color should be selected for both ease of reading and desired effect. In most cases, the text should contrast sharply with the background (which is why

PRACTICE 12.1 Emotions and Typefaces

What is your emotional reaction to each of these typefaces featured in the sidebar? The statement, "War is not healthy for children or other living things," is the same in each example. How does the typeface influence your reaction to it?

black letters are usually printed on white paper). In addition, you should consider the difference in impact between various colors. Red is an "alarm" color, associated with stoplights, terror alerts, and blood. Green is associated with "go" and also with growth, gardens, and nature in general. Purple is often thought of as rich and royal, whereas yellow and orange are associated with warmth.

PRACTICE 12.2 Text as Image

Working individually or in groups, study this advertisement and then answer the following questions.

HOLD UP TO MIRROR. ANSWER HONESTLY.

WHEN IS IT MY TURN?

It's not something you talk about out loud. But it's only natural to want your chance. Maybe it's time to find success, instead of waiting for it to find you. Wharton's innovative programs reflect the needs and concerns of today's executives, giving you the insight you need to get ahead. Every day, new challenges arrive. Will you?

(continued)

Tips for Using Type Styles

- Avoid using unusual type styles to compose your argument's text. Instead, select 10- to 12-point Times Roman, Arial, or Courier.
- When using text alone as a visual argument, experiment with different type styles, sizes, and colors. Consider the overall emotional effect that the text delivers in communicating its message.
- When combining text with images, try to use a type style that complements the image.
- Make sure your text contrasts with your image so that it is easy to read.

1. Where is your eye drawn when you first glance at the image? Where does your eye go next?
2. Why is the image presented backward? Did you imagine yourself actually holding the text up to a mirror? Try it. What effect does that have? To what extent does your reflection become a personalized element of the advertisement?
3. What does it mean to have "your turn"? What standard of living or level of success does this imply? Why do you think so?
4. In what way does the ad imply the following claim: "To get my turn, I need to attend the Wharton School of Business"?

IMAGES

In visual arguments, images work with text to persuade the audience. Although in some cases the image by itself can be the argument, it often functions rhetorically as a type of evidence to support the writer's proposal. The types of images we will consider in this chapter include photographs, drawings (including politi-

Online Study Center
Prepare for Class
Using Images to Argue

PRACTICE 12.3 Images That Argue

Working individually or in groups, consider the following cartoon, which comments on rising gas prices, and then answer the following questions.

(continued)

1. What claim is being made here? How do you know?
2. What does the gas pump represent in this picture? Why do you think so?
3. This image makes an argument by analogy when it compares the gas pump to a robber. Is this comparison valid? Why or why not?

cal cartoons), graphs (which often represent complex numerical data as pictures), and webpages (which are organized visually).

Elements of Images In most arguments, visuals serve as a kind of evidence to help support a claim. Sometimes a claim may be part of the overall visual argument. For example, the slogan "Buy this car!" beneath a picture of a smiling woman next to her new convertible is a claim associated with an image. The slogan provides the claim and the picture provides the evidence. In other cases, the image itself will be the argument; the claim may not be stated at all.

Using Images in Your Own Arguments When you consider using images in your arguments, you must think carefully about the appropriateness of your selection. It is just as inappropriate to add an out-of-place image to your

TIPS FOR EVALUATING IMAGES IN ARGUMENTS

When you evaluate an image that is used to support another argument (or even one that implies an argument of its own), let your eye explore the image for a moment before you try to analyze it.

- Where does your eye fall when you first observe the image? Where does it wander next? Does your eye move in a circle—from feature to feature?
- If text is not present, can you supply words to accompany the image? What sort of argument does the image imply?
- Is the style (overall design) of the image appropriate? (Sometimes a black-and-white drawing may seem a better choice than a color photograph, for example.) Why do you think so? What do you like or dislike about the image?
- If the text is a part of a larger argument (such as an image on a webpage or a graph in a magazine article), how does it serve to support the overall argument? Does it complement the argument or distract from it?
- How does the image relate to other images included in the argument? (*Note:* Multiple images can support the text of a written argument, or several images could be presented together to imply an argument. Sometimes a series of paintings or a collection of sculptures might imply an argument in this way.)
- Is the image effective in its context (either within the supporting text or as part of another setting)? What are the strengths and weaknesses of the image?
- Does anything about the image work against the point it is trying to make? Is it trite or offensive in some way? Why do you think so?

TIPS FOR USING IMAGES IN YOUR ARGUMENTS

Think about the following questions before you decide to add a cartoon, photograph, or other visual element to your argument:

- Is it appropriate? Add an image to an argument only if it supports what you have to say without distracting your audience from your primary purpose. Adding a carefully selected graph, for example, can make numerical data more viable for the reader by presenting it in a visual format.
- How many images should I add? Be selective. Treat images—and quotations—like hand grenades: Use them sparingly, and only when absolutely necessary.
- Where should I put the image? Normally, an image will go close to the information with which it is associated. However, you should also consider the layout of the page, especially if multiple images appear on the same page. Positioning too much material on one side of the page or the other can make it seem lopsided. Consider where the eye falls when the image is added to the page.
- How big should the image be? First and foremost, don't let the image overpower the rest of the text. It should enhance what is being said, not distract the reader from your argument. Use your own judgment, realizing that the image should be big enough to be easily seen without eyestrain, but not so big that it takes over the page.
- Should I select images of a particular style? Sometimes drawings or cartoons provide the most effective support; at other times color photographs work best. You should avoid selecting images that clash when they appear together, especially if they are positioned on the same page.
- Do I cite my image or use a caption? You must cite your image in the bibliography (Works Cited in MLA style, References in APA style) just like any other source that you borrow from someone else. Captions are generally a good idea because they help identify the image and place it in the appropriate context.
- Do I need to obtain someone's permission before using the image? If your text will be published on the Internet or in another public format, you need to obtain permission from the image's creator. If you are just using it for a class assignment, then you don't have to obtain permission.

document as it is to drop a quotation into your paper that does not support what you are trying to say. Likewise, the inclusion of too many images—even when they are carefully selected—can overpower your essay and cause your reader to forget about your text.

Color

Purple text on yellow is easily readable.

However, purple on blue is a completely different matter.

Color, whether within your printed text or as part of your images, can be a powerful asset if used properly, but may be a disaster if misused. On a black-and-white page, color usually attracts the eye. If you want the eye to go to a particular place—to look at an image or to identify a section heading, for instance—then color can help you organize your page. By contrast, excessive use of color or selection of difficult-to-read hues will lead to trouble. Read the text in the boxes on the left:

The text in the top box is easily readable; the text in the bottom box is not. Similarly, light text on a dark background can strain the eyes.

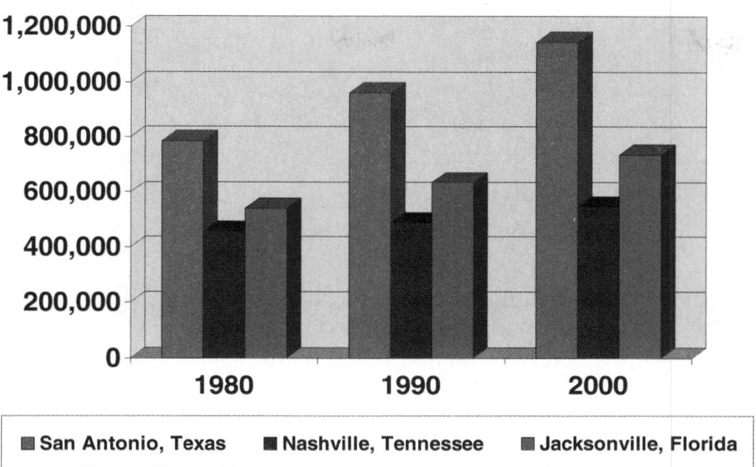

This population chart comes from a student's PowerPoint presentation. It would be more difficult to read if the bars were presented in differing shades of gray.

PRACTICE 12.4 Using Color

Working individually or in groups, critique the PowerPoint slide for its use of color.

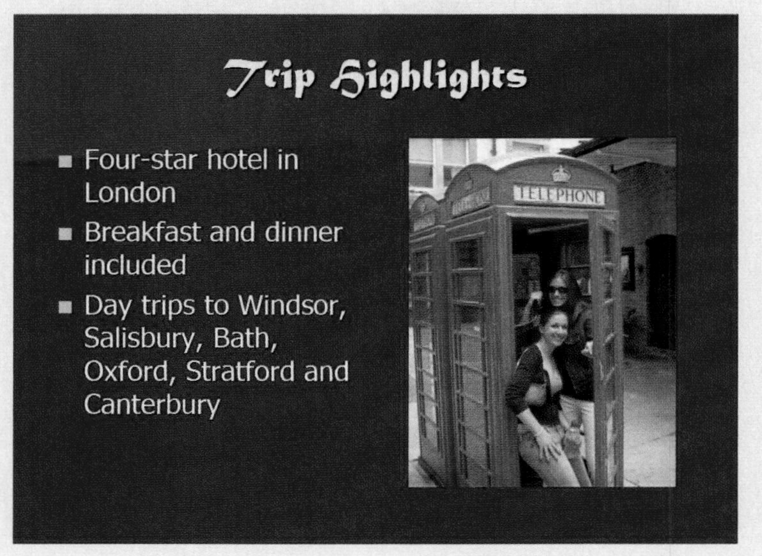

(continued)

Online Study Center
Prepare for Class
Using Color to Enhance Argument

Using Color

Use color in the following situations:

- To draw attention to important headings in a text
- To enliven an illustration, photograph, or chart
- To emphasize only the most important elements on a page (don't overdo it)

Hint: If you use a chart with several variables, colors are easier to read than different shades of gray.

Don't use color in the following circumstances:

- For the main text of your typescript
- For too many design elements (reserve it for important headings and illustrations)
- If it causes excessive eyestrain (avoid using similar colors together, and avoid light text on a dark background)

Online Study Center
Improve Your Grade
PowerPoint Presentations

1. Where does your eye travel when you look at the image? Is this a good thing or a bad thing?
2. How does the slide take advantage of the colors in the photograph for selecting background and text colors?
3. Overall, how well does the color scheme work? Indicate one feature you like and one you would change.
4. How might this slide (in the context of a longer presentation) convince students to go on this trip?

PRACTICE 12.5 Responding to the Overall Design

Working individually or in groups, examine this advertisement. Note your initial reaction to the image, and then answer the following questions.

(continued)

1. What is your initial reaction to this ad? Would your reaction be different if the image in the girl's eye were a fish? Why?
2. What is the ad's purpose? Who is the target audience? How do you know?
3. Where is your eye led when you look at the image? Why is this important?
4. In what way might the phrase, "See her as more than a meal," have more than one meaning? Explain.
5. What do the images of the eye and the cow symbolize? Why is the girl looking at the cow? What is she about to do?
6. What unstated message is the ad trying to relate? How do you know?
7. How effective is the ad in accomplishing its goal? State one weakness and one strength of the ad.

Overall Design

When people respond to visuals within the context of larger arguments or respond to stand-alone visual arguments such as magazine advertisements, they do not react to independent elements such as text, image, and color. Instead, the composition as a whole affects them. But how do you "read" visual arguments?

- Slow down your process of looking at the visual. Notice where your eyes go. Does the image draw them to a particular place, or do your eyes tend to move in a circle?
- After taking in the visual as a whole, note your initial reaction. Do you find the visual persuasive or otherwise appealing? Why or why not?
- Now consider the parts. Study the text, the images, and the colors in turn. How does each function independently, and how does each serve to support the others?
- Do any of the images seem to hold multiple meanings? What might those meanings be?

Understanding Visual Arguments

Although it may not seem possible at first glance, visual arguments can be "read" just as written arguments are read. Written arguments operate on the basis of rhetoric. That is, they have a logic—a system of codes and rules—which they follow and the audience understands. By presenting claims and evidence, written arguments convince their audience of the legitimacy of their claims. Similarly, visual rhetoric operates by a system of rules that the "reader" understands. Type style, images, color, and overall design all contribute to how a visual argument persuades the reader through the presentation of claims and evidence—sometimes explicitly, but most often implied—in a visual format.

When you prepare to evaluate a written argument, you preview the argument first by trying to make sense of its basic parts and any other clues you can glean from the text: its author, its publication site, its main divisions, any subtitles it contains, and so on. Next, you read the argument and try to understand how its parts work together. Finally, you evaluate the argument as a whole. In similar fashion, understanding visual arguments requires you to preview, examine, and respond to the visual text.

EVALUATING VISUAL ARGUMENTS: PREVIEWING, EXAMINING, AND RESPONDING

In the pages that follow, you will have the opportunity to preview, examine ("read"), and respond to several visual arguments. As with arguments constructed solely of text, you will understand these arguments on the basis of your own preconceptions and the context in which you view each argument, and ultimately you will decide how to respond to them.

Previewing As with a conventional text, you can preview a visual argument. This means that you take a few moments to think about your opinions prior to responding to the argument and the context in which it is presented. However, unlike a written argument, which requires you to turn pages to get an initial sense of how the argument is organized, what its major sections are, and what its thesis is, a visual argument is previewed in a flash. If you don't take a moment to slow yourself down and think about your opinion of the topic and the context in which it appears, you might leap to the responding stage without considering how you got there. Slowing down your response to a visual argument will allow you to take note of your point of view, to think about the context in which the argument appears, and to consider how the various elements work together to persuade an audience.

Here are some pointers for previewing a visual argument:

1. Glance at the advertisement, poster, billboard, or webpage. Then STOP.

2. Before offering an opinion or analysis of the ad, television commercial, or photograph, think about the following:
   - Do you have an opinion regarding the topic at hand? What is it? Is your opinion positive, negative, or neutral? Take a moment to write that opinion in the form of an argumentative claim.
   - What is the context in which the argument appears? Although billboards, magazine advertisements, television commercials, and the like may seem random, they usually are not. Magazines for teenage girls rarely advertise 4 × 4s, and commercials during sporting events usually do not sell lipstick. Why is that? Which demographic group might be the target of this particular visual argument?
   - What is the purpose of the argument? If its claim is stated in words, what is it? If it is not, what do you believe it to be? How do you know?

Examining After you have considered your own opinion of the topic, the context in which the argument appeared, and its argumentative purpose, take a moment to examine how the various elements of the visual argument work together to persuade the target audience. To do so, think about how each piece of the argument—be it text, image, or color—contributes to the overall persuasive purpose.

Text Use the following guidelines to understand how the elements of a visual argument work together:

- How much text is included? Some visual arguments have none, while others may contain several paragraphs.
- Why is a particular font or text color used? For instance, why would an ad for wine employ flowing script instead of a more practical type style like Arial? Similarly, why would the voiceover on a television commercial promoting a political candidate speak in a deep formal voice with patriotic music playing in the background? Why not use a child's voice?
- Can you put the claim or other accompanying text into your own words?
- Why do you think the text that is present was used? Why not more? Less? How does it appeal to the target audience?

Images What kinds of images does the composition include? Why do you think those particular images were selected? How do those images appeal to the target audience? Are they persuasive? How so?

Color When considering color, think not only about vibrant colors, but also about the shades of black and white used in certain compositions. With particular types of compositions (e.g., editorial cartoons), convention, rather than the argumentative purpose, may dictate if and what kinds of colors are used. Why do you think particular colors were used? What effect—emotional or otherwise—does the color scheme have on you? Would you have responded differently to another color scheme? If text is present and appears in color, why do you think those colors were selected? Is the color intended merely to draw attention to the text, or does it also serve another purpose?

Responding Once you have thought about the various pieces that make up a visual argument, consider how those elements work together to construct the whole and frame your response to the overall design:

Online Study Center
Prepare for Class
Responding to Visual Arguments

- How do the different elements of type style, image, and color work to create an overall persuasive piece? Do these elements complement one another, or do they have a more contrastive relationship?
- Do you find the overall visual argument persuasive? Why or why not?
- Are there elements of the design that you would change? How? Why would you make these changes?
- What would you consider the greatest strength and the greatest weakness of the overall design?
- How does the design work to accomplish its purpose? Will it persuade its target audience? How do you know?
- How does the visual argument fit into its immediate context (its placement as a graph in an article or as an advertisement in a subway train, for example)? Does the same text include other visual arguments (such as other illustrations within the same article or book)? How do these visual arguments complement one another in an effort to accomplish a larger goal?

PRACTICE 12.6 **Previewing, Examining, and Responding to Visual Arguments**

Working individually or in groups, preview, examine, and respond to the visual argument that appears on the next page. Write one or more paragraphs explaining the argument's purpose and describing its target audience. Discuss the argument's use of text, images, and color. Finally, explain the argument's primary strengths and weaknesses. Do you find it persuasive? Why or why not?

Join the White Ribbon Campaign

Types of Visual Arguments

This chapter has mentioned many types of visual arguments, but many others exist as well. It would be impossible for this chapter to list every type of visual text found in today's media-rich culture. In the pages that follow, you will have the opportunity to work with a few types of visual texts that commonly present arguments and that you probably see almost every day:

- Print advertisements
- Political posters and propaganda

- Political cartoons
- Photographs
- Webpages
- Graphs and charts

Of course, these are not the only types of visual arguments that exist, nor are they even the most important ones.

Print Advertisements Along with television commercials and roadside billboards, print ads are probably the form of visual argument that you are most familiar with. In addition to being strikingly visual, magazine ads are particularly useful for studying visual argumentation because they are placed in context with other forms of persuasion. Magazines typically contain many ads and feature numerous articles. By studying these other "texts" within the magazine, it is relatively easy to get a clear idea of what the readership is like and who the target audience for a particular ad might be. With print ads in particular, it is a good idea to study not only the ad itself, but also other ads in the magazine, along with articles, editorials, regular columns, or other features.

Online Study Center
Prepare for Class
Understanding Opinion Arguments

Most of the ads in this book can be classified as op-ads (opinion advertisements). They try to persuade you to change your opinion about some issue rather than just convince you to buy a particular product. Much like an op-ed ("opposite the editorial page," a.k.a. opinion editorial) in a newspaper, where an editor writes an opinion—usually in the form of an argument—on a particular subject, an op-ad argues a position on a particular issue of relevance to the target audience.

Online Study Center
Prepare for Class
Understanding Propaganda and Editorial Cartoons

Political Posters and Propaganda It is not easy to state definitively where political posters, print ads, or television commercials end and propaganda begins. Generally speaking, propaganda is often the product of a government or other political organization, and it usually consists of a whole campaign as opposed to a single occurrence. For example, the U.S. government's "war on drugs" may be thought of as a propaganda campaign, whereas a few months of ads, commercials, and posters during a candidate's run for public office would not be thought of in quite the same way. Furthermore, propaganda seeks to promote a particular ideology or way of thinking, and it attempts to persuade a mass audience—often an entire population—to adopt this point of view. In the political posters presented in this section, you might consider whether certain posters represent propaganda (or not).

Editorial Cartoons The cartoons that appear on the editorial pages of most newspapers are political in nature. They generally present arguments or other commentary through drawings accompanied by a small amount of text. Because editorial cartoons are timely and often reflect current events in the news, many can be difficult to appreciate if you are not familiar with the events they comment on. While many of these cartoons critique particular personalities (many of whom are quickly forgotten), some touch upon individuals and themes that are nearly universal, so they are easily understood generations later. Thus, the key to understanding political cartoons is having some familiarity with the issues they treat. In some situations, this knowledge may require research on your part, especially if the cartoons are several years old.

Popular Culture Arguments can be made in media other than written arguments and print advertisements. For example, a variety of media within popular culture are used to convey or imply arguments. Radio ads, songs, television commercials, music videos, and entire motion pictures are used to present positions on issues. For example, singer Sinead O'Connor once famously tore up a picture of Pope John Paul II on *Saturday Night Live* to punctuate her views on traditional Catholicism. (In 1997, the singer asked the pope's forgiveness and was ordained a priest by a breakaway Irish congregation in a move John Paul II labeled as "bizarre.") The rock group U2 is also well known for taking a stand on numerous issues. Concert venues have been used to promote awareness of global issues. For example, the Live 8 concert tackled the issue of poverty (which allowed a number of individuals to pick up the microphone to make specific arguments of their own). Even comic books have been employed to make argumentative statements.

Arguments that employ not only static visual images, but also voices, music, and motion, can add to the complexity of the argument being made. In addition to considering the argument's text, color, image, and composition in such cases, you might take into account the authoritative and emotional effects that the choice of music (classical versus grunge rock), voice (not only what is said, but who says it and how the words are conveyed), and motion (cigarette smoke that turns into a skeleton) may have on the target audience. Music videos and op-ad television commercials are particularly

Singer Bono and U2 frequently take stands on social issues.

This photo makes an implied argument about the treatment of prisoners in Iraq.

good examples of visual arguments that take advantage of these additional features.

Photographs Some individuals might say that photographs do not "argue" but rather merely depict reality. Although this might be a reasonable statement in some cases, professional photographs—especially those taken by photographers who carefully select their subjects, frame them in specific ways, and try to use color, light, and shadow to their advantage—can imply arguments.

These arguments can be difficult to interpret because their claims are rarely stated explicitly. Instead, a person who looks at a photograph that seems to promote a point of view must supply the claim and be able to explain how the image suggests that particular viewpoint. In other situations, photographs may function as a form of evidence to support a text-based argument. For example, "before and after" photos of a trash-filled slum that has been transformed into a pristine neighborhood could be used to support an argument centered on revitalization projects for urban neighborhoods. If such photos are particularly powerful, they may serve a dual function: they may make an argument on their own and serve as evidence to support a larger argument. In the context of a text-based argument, it is important to consider what role the photos play in validating the overall argument.

Online Study Center
Prepare for Class
Evaluating Websites

Webpages Webpages are complex documents. They combine text, images, color, and overall design to draw in viewers to sell a product or promote a particular idea. While many websites appear to be purely informational, most are not. Even Aunt Mandy's photos of her grandchildren on the family website promote a particular point of view. At the very least, Aunt Mandy is projecting a particular idea of her family that she hopes her viewers will accept.

When examining a webpage, you should consider how the visual elements work in concert with the text to persuade the viewer. Webpages often do not present evidence directly in their arguments but rather link to other sites or pages containing that evidence. Also, Web documents, like print ads, tend to argue in sentence fragments and bulleted points as opposed to carefully crafted paragraphs and whole essays. When evaluating these documents, it is important to

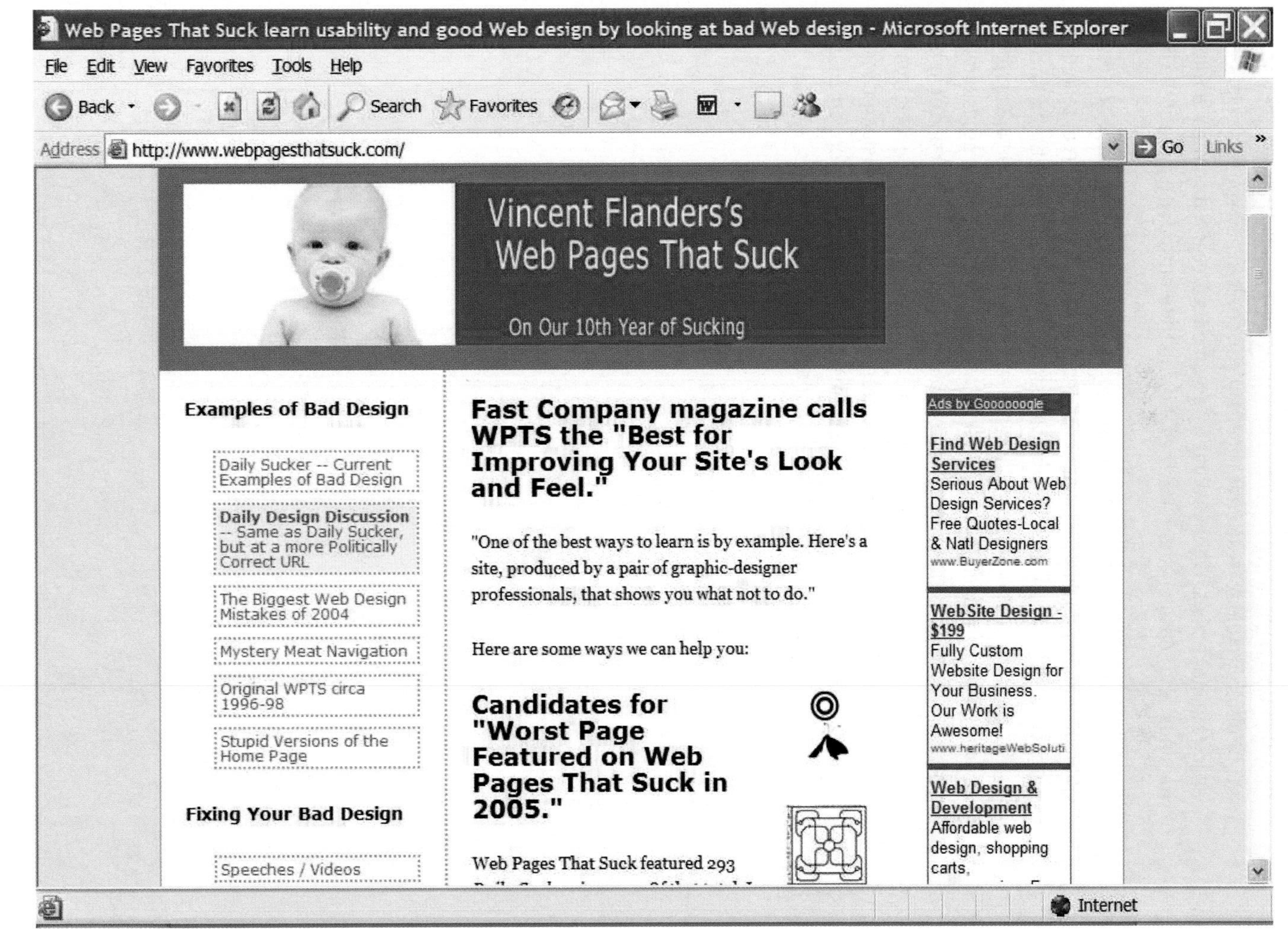

This irreverent site offers good advice about website design by showing examples of bad design.

note that webpages are a relatively new genre and are still evolving. They operate by different rules of discourse than, say, editorials in newspapers or lengthy articles in magazines. When evaluating arguments presented on the Web, keep in mind these considerations and the fluid, multiple-authored nature of the Web.

Graphs and Charts Most of the time, graphs and charts do not stand well on their own as independent arguments. Instead, they are usually contained within other arguments and serve to support a written text. Sometimes, however, a graph or chart may be presented in such a way that it can be understood as an argument independent of the text that surrounds it. On rare occasions, a graph may function in a way similar to a political cartoon: It may make or imply an argument that requires some degree of familiarity with the subject it treats. Nevertheless, in most cases, charts and graphs will need to be considered in their context. They should be considered as forms of evidence used to support a written text rather than an argument that stands alone.

Anthology of Visual Arguments

Life or Death
is a political decision. The lives of millions of women, children and adolescents are hanging in the balance. Each year over 500,000 women die during pregnancy and childbirth. There are 13.4 million AIDS orphans, and half of all new cases of HIV infection are among adolescents. Girls are at particular risk.
Unlike natural disasters, this catastrophic human suffering is not inevitable. To save lives or to not save lives is a political decision. At the International Parliamentarians' Conference in Ottawa, Canada, elected representatives from 72 countries and territories have pledged to save lives by striving to allocate up to 10 per cent of their nations' development budgets for population and reproductive health programmes. Has yours?
For more information visit www.unfpa.org
Concept & Design: Real Design/NY
Photo: Steve McCurry/Magnum Photos
IPCI
ICPD
UNFPA

Trial lawyers' next cash cow.
89% of Americans think obesity lawsuits are ridiculous.
86% believe that parents are responsible for their kids' choices.
Now, trial lawyers want to force *their* choices on 100% of us.
Learn more about the erosion of common sense at:
ConsumerFreedom.com

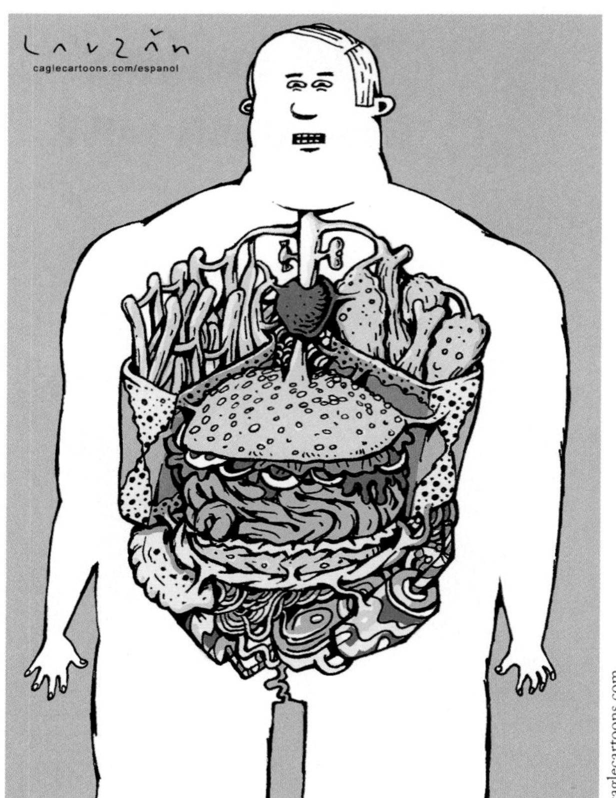
caglecartoons.com/espanol
caglecartoons.com

Whither thou goest
I shall go
And where you stay
I shall stay.
Thy people shall be
my people
And thy God my God.
Where thou diest
will I die
And there will I
be buried.
May God do so to me
and more also
if anything but death
should separate us.
KIRK ©03
Ruth to Naomi, Ruth 1:16-17
Old Testament

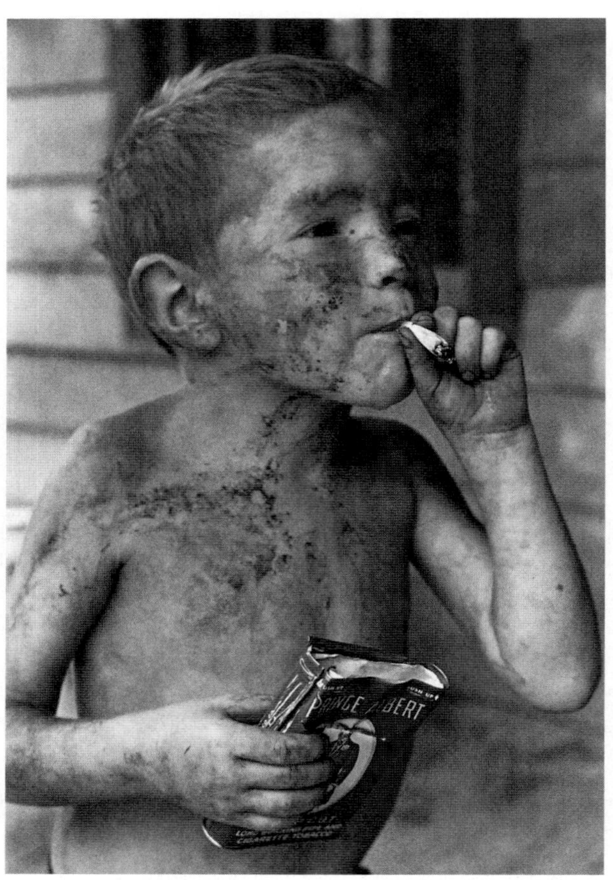

The following photographs of victims of the New Orleans flood following Hurricane Katrina appear with their original captions. What point of view does each photograph imply?

A young man walks through chest-deep flood water after looting a grocery store in New Orleans.

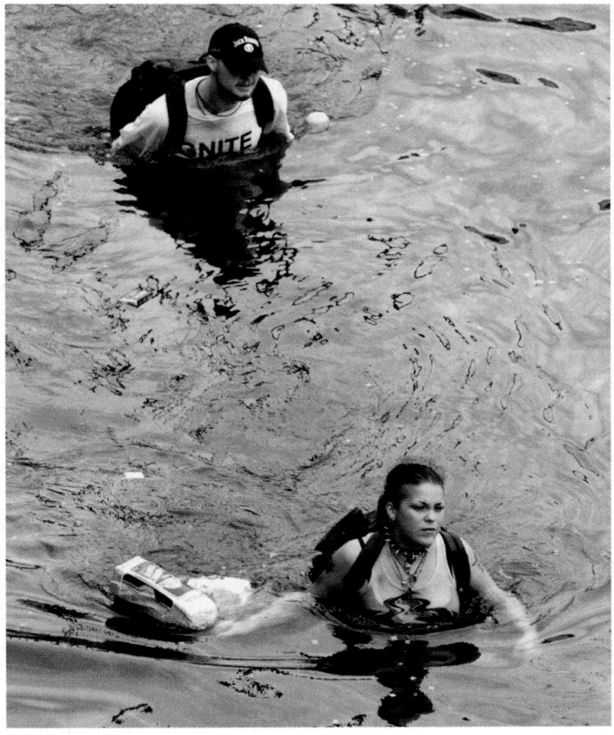

Two residents wade through chest-deep water after finding bread and soda from a local grocery store after Hurricane Katrina.

Home | Greenpeace International - Microsoft Internet Explorer
File Edit View Favorites Tools Help
Back Search Favorites
Address http://www.greenpeace.org/international/
Go Links
GREENPEACE INTERNATIONAL
HOME
About us
What we do
Stop climate change
Save our seas
Protect ancient forests
Say no to genetic engineering
Eliminate toxic chemicals
End the nuclear threat
Encourage sustainable trade
Abolish nuclear weapons
Get involved
Support us
News
Photos, audio, &
Welcome to Greenpeace International
Greenpeace exists because this fragile Earth deserves a voice. It needs solutions. It needs change. It needs action.
Search
Support Us!
Sign up!
Get Involved!
What's happening in my country?
Go to your national site
Greenpeace TV: Greenhouse Olympics
GREENPEACE EXISTS BECAUSE THIS FRAGILE EARTH DESERVES A VOICE.
It needs solutions.
International News:
Victory: Toxic warship Clemenceau turned back to
NATIONAL SITES
World websites
Larger Map
GET INVOLVED!
Enter your email to keep informed and get involved.
Your e-mail
Subscribe
OCEAN DEFENDERS
Opening page http://www.greenpeace.org/international/...
Internet

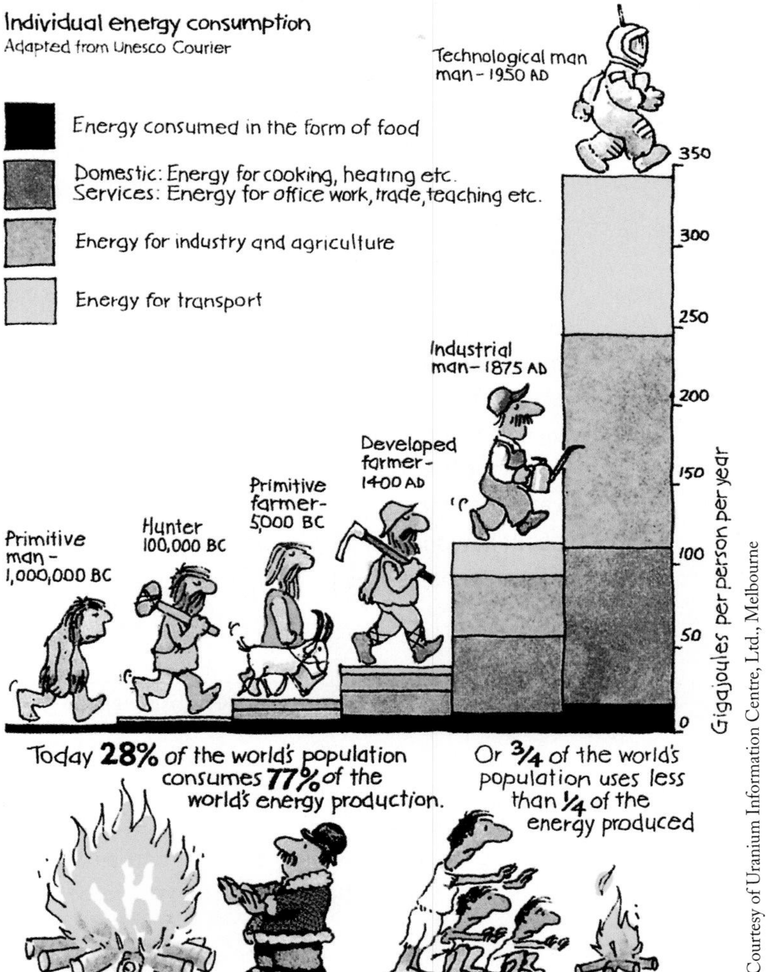

Individual energy consumption
Adapted from Unesco Courier
Energy consumed in the form of food
Domestic: Energy for cooking, heating etc.
Services: Energy for office work, trade, teaching etc.
Energy for industry and agriculture
Energy for transport
Technological man man - 1950 AD
Industrial man - 1875 AD
Developed farmer - 1400 AD
Primitive farmer - 5,000 BC
Hunter 100,000 BC
Primitive man - 1,000,000 BC
350
300
250
200
150
100
50
0
Gigajoules per person per year
Today 28% of the world's population consumes 77% of the world's energy production.
Or 3/4 of the world's population uses less than 1/4 of the energy produced

Courtesy of Uranium Information Centre, Ltd., Melbourne

Levels of Completeness in Visual Arguments

Readers (or viewers) will generally view visual arguments in two ways: as evidence used to support a textual argument or as a stand-alone argument. In the visual anthology you have just reviewed, some of the visuals stand alone as complete arguments, whereas others may be stronger when situated within the context of a written or verbal argument (such as a photograph used in a magazine article or a graph displayed as part of a PowerPoint presentation during a speech). This does not mean that visuals such as photos and graphs cannot imply arguments. Sometimes, as with the "fast food" editorial cartoon, the meaning is so clear that the viewer can supply the claim with relative ease.

Which of the arguments within the anthology seem most "complete" to you? Why? If you thought of the commercial op-ads as being most "complete," then perhaps your rationale is that those visual arguments contain both claims and evidence (even though the claims might not be as clearly stated as they are in a traditional written argument). Thus some visual arguments may be said to be more "complete" in the sense that they supply or strongly suggest a particular claim along with supporting evidence (sometimes in a textual form, but usually visual), whereas others leave the viewer to figure out exactly what is being said.

In the Practices that follow, you will be asked to think not only about how the various elements of visual arguments work together to create meaning, but also about how some of the visuals make complete arguments while others imply a particular point of view that has to be reasoned out.

PRACTICE 12.7 **Previewing the Anthology Images**

Working individually or in groups, consider the images in the anthology one at a time as assigned by your instructor. First, glance at the images to preview them. What does the purpose of each visual argument appear to be? Who is the target audience? Guess as many details about the target audience as you can. Be prepared to defend your answer, either verbally or in writing.

PRACTICE 12.8 Examining the Anthology Arguments

Now go back to the visual arguments you considered in Practice 12.7 one at a time.

1. Is the claim clearly stated or is it implied? Write the claim down. If it is implied, write the claim in your own words. On a scale of 1 to 10, how confident are you that your rendering of the claim is accurate? If you are working in groups, is there disagreement about the argument's claim? Why?
2. What does each argument imply in the way of evidence? Text? Image? What role does color play? How does the overall design contribute to presenting the claim and its accompanying evidence to the audience in a convincing fashion?
3. Rate each of the visual arguments on a scale of 1 to 10 in terms of its "completeness." Why do you consider some of the arguments more complete than others? Are there some purely "visual" arguments that you consider more complete than those containing text? Explain.

PRACTICE 12.9 Responding to the Anthology Images

Take a few moments to consider how these arguments made in the anthology relate to one another and which ones you find more convincing. Because the following questions require you to make highly subjective judgments, if you are working in groups carefully consider and discuss the differences in your responses.

1. Which visual argument do you find the most convincing? Explain.
2. Which visual argument do you find the least convincing? Explain.
3. In each of these cases, how similar are you to the target audience you defined in Practice 12.7?
4. Which arguments do you think would be stronger if situated within the context of a traditional written argument? Why?

PRACTICE 12.10 A Student's Visual Argument

Study the following student visual argument, and answer the questions that follow.

1. What claim is the ad trying to make? What role do the words "I do" play in making this claim apparent?
2. In what way(s) does the text at the top of the ad function as evidence and appeal to authority?
3. How does the photograph serve to make an emotional connection with the audience?
4. Who do you think the intended audience for this ad is? Which audience might not find it appealing?
5. How do text, color, and image work together to create an overall argument?

Looking Back at Chapter 12

- Visual presentations serve to present arguments, sometimes with little or no accompanying text.
- Visual texts typically consist of four elements: text, images, color, and overall design.
- The style of a typeface can be varied by font size, style, color, emphasis, and artistic effects.
- Images include photographs, drawings, graphs, and webpages.
- Like written texts, visual arguments can be "read" rhetorically and logically.
- Visual arguments include print advertisements, political posters and propaganda, political cartoons, photographs, webpages, and graphs and charts.
- Visual arguments either can stand alone or can be used as an element of a larger argument.

Suggestions for Writing

- Locate two op-ads that present different opinions on the same topic. Compare the strengths and weakness of the two advertisements. Which one is better, and why?
- Explain how the gastronomical diagram in the editorial cartoon on page 342 makes an implied argument. Be specific.
- Examine the photos of the Katrina victims on page 345. Write a brief analysis of each photo and its caption, explaining what argument each might imply.
- Why is (or why isn't) the biblical text an effective rhetorical device for persuading the target audience of the editorial cartoon depicting a lesbian marriage?
- Select one of the photos in this chapter (or another you have found on your own) and explain how effectively it implies a particular point of view. What sort of written argument might it be used to support?
- Select a popular television commercial and explain how it uses visual elements to persuade its audience.
- Choose a music video that seems to make an argument (both explicitly and implicitly). What argument is being made, and how effective is the presentation?
- Choose a topic of your own and create a PowerPoint-based argument that includes both visual and textual elements. Present your argument to your class.

- Create a webpage for presenting an argument. Include textual and visual elements.
- Write a new argument (or expand one you have already written for this class) using three separate visual elements. Two of those visual elements should be of different types (e.g., photograph, political cartoon, graph, drawing, or illustration).
- Write a paper explaining when not to use visuals in your written arguments.
- Select two websites to compare. Choose one that presents a well-designed, convincing argument and another that does not. Explain why one website succeeds and the other fails to convince its viewers.

Online Study Center
Improve Your Grade
Suggestions for Writing

13 MLA Documentation

The Modern Language Association (MLA) system of documentation consists of (1) in-text parenthetical citations and (2) a bibliography (called a Works Cited list) that appears on a separate page at the end of the document. Using this method, each time you quote or paraphrase information from a book, article, or the Internet, you must credit the author and indicate the page on which you found the information. Although it may seem daunting at first, the system is fairly straightforward. If you create your Works Cited list as you write your paper, the process becomes much simpler.

> *Good writers are those who keep the language efficient. That is to say, keep it accurate, keep it clear.*
>
> —Ezra Pound (1885–1972)

MLA

Online Study Center
This icon will direct you to content and resources on the website <college.hmco.com/pic/lamm1e>.

Try following these steps:

1. As soon as you begin to write, move down to the next page and type "Works Cited," centered, at the top of the page.
2. As you write, create your in-text citations. If you leave this step for later, you may lose track of your sources.
3. As soon as you have cited a source, page down to the "Works Cited" list, and create your bibliography in alphabetical order based on the author's last name.

In-Text Citations in MLA Style

Online Study Center
Prepare for Class
Modern Language Association

In-text citations in MLA style generally consist of an author's name followed by quoted or paraphrased material, with the page number containing that material positioned immediately after the borrowed information. You should be careful to place the citation immediately after the borrowed material so that the reader will not become confused about what information was obtained where. You also do not want the reader to be confused about which material you wrote and which ideas you borrowed from someone else.

Avoiding Plagiarism

Online Study Center
General Resources
Avoiding Plagiarism

Whenever you represent someone else's ideas as being your own, you are guilty of plagiarism. In most colleges and universities, the penalties for plagiarism are severe, including expelling a student for a year or longer, or even permanently. Sometimes students will commit plagiarism by accident when they are not careful about citing their sources. In these cases, students will often write a paper first and then intend to go back over the paper and insert their citations and Works Cited entries. During the process of writing a research paper, it is easy to become confused and lose track of your sources. The best way to avoid this problem is to insert your citations and create your Works Cited entries as you write.

Citing Sources

Citing a Work by a Single Author The two most common ways to cite a source in MLA style are (1) to mention the author's name in the text or (2) to list the author's name in the parenthetical citation. Consider the following sentences, which cite information found on page 171 of Roy Robson's book *Solovki:*

AUTHOR'S NAME IN TEXT

According to Robson, the majority of pilgrims to the monastery at Solovki were peasants (171).

AUTHOR'S NAME IN CITATION

The majority of pilgrims to the monastery at Solovki were peasants (Robson 171).

If the entire sentence is a paraphrase, then the citation comes at the end. If only part of the sentence is paraphrased, then the parenthetical citation should occur next to the paraphrased material. A comma does not separate the author's name from the page reference, and no indicator for *page* or *pages* (such a *p.* or *pp.*) is used. The period comes after the citation (when the citation occurs at the end of a sentence).

Citing Multiple Sources Although the parenthetical citation often appears at the end of a sentence containing paraphrased material, it is not necessary to always follow this form. Sometimes, the author may follow a citation with commentary, or multiple citations may occur within the same sentence.

Citation with Commentary Sometimes you may wish to comment on paraphrased material within the same sentence. In such cases, the parenthetical citation should be placed so that it is clear where the borrowed information ends and the cited material begins. Consider the following citation/commentary on Ben Bova's book *Immortality: How Science Is Extending Your Life Span—and Changing the World:*

> Although Bova provides a list of his successful predictions to lend authority to his claim that people younger than 50 years of age can look forward to a future of virtual immortality (3–4), there is no current scientific evidence to substantiate his claim.

Most of the first half of this sentence is paraphrased. The material after the parenthetical citation is the author's commentary on Bova's claim.

Multiple Citations by the Same Author Sometimes you may need to cite several different pages within a single article, or you may paraphrase information from several different works by the same writer. Once an author has been introduced, you need include only page numbers in parentheses to indicate material that appears on subsequent pages.

> In ancient Rome, the noon meal, <u>prandium</u>, was followed by an afternoon nap, the <u>meridiatio</u> (Balsdon 25), which itself was followed by a trip to the <u>thermae</u>, the public bathhouse (27).

In this example, two pieces of information from two different pages are brought together in the same sentence. Because the first citation mentions the author's name, it is not necessary to repeat his name in the second citation.

Multiple Citations by Different Authors or Works In some cases, you may cite several authors in one or two sentences, or you may cite information from more than one book or article by the same author. Whenever you move from one work to another or from one author to another, your parenthetical citation must make the change in sources clear. As you move between works by the same author, you may either mention the title of the work in the text or include a significant portion of the title in a parenthetical citation.

> Everett argues that the Peircian triad can be used as a tool for reader-response critics ("Adopting the Peircian Sign" 129), something he later applied to a reading of Hamlet, where he argues that the source story bled through Shakespeare's text ("Two Hamlets" 66).

If works by two different authors are paraphrased, then you can use their last names as you move from one text to another.

> Whereas Chen believes that fast-food ads are to be blamed for the increased rate of obesity among America's youth (26), Nelson argues that sedentary activities such as watching television and spending time on the Internet play a much larger role (113).

Citing Works with More Than One Author When you cite a work written by up to three authors, you may either list all of the authors' names in the text or list just the authors' last names in the parenthetical citation.

> N. Katherine Hayles and Nicholas Gessler have argued that the shifting virtual realities depicted in some contemporary science fiction do not necessarily have to be morally inconsistent because the characters within the shifting realities provide a moral center and a sense of continuity (497).
>
> The shifting virtual realities depicted in some contemporary science fiction do not necessarily have to be morally inconsistent because the characters within the shifting realities provide a moral center and a sense of continuity (Hayles and Gessler 497).

If the work you are citing has more than three authors, then insert *et al.* after the first author's name. Do not mention the other authors.

Citing a Corporate Author Sometimes a source will not credit an individual flesh-and-blood author but rather will list a legal entity such as a government agency or private corporation as the "author." In such a case, you may include the corporate author either in the text or in the parenthetical citation.

Citing a Multivolume Work If you paraphrase or quote material obtained from a multivolume work, then you should make it clear to the reader which volume you are citing. Within the parenthetical citation, give the volume first, followed by a colon and the inclusive page numbers.

> Mesopotamian medicine was more primitive than that practiced by the Egyptians, and consisted largely of rituals, though the lack of extant texts limits our knowledge of their pharmacology (<u>Interpreter's Dictionary</u> 1: 302).

In this case, the full title of the work in question, *The Interpreter's Dictionary of the Bible,* has been shortened to make the passage more readable. In MLA style it is acceptable to shorten cited titles as long as the citation can be easily located in the bibliography, where titles are not abbreviated.

Handling Quotations While you should use quotations sparingly, these excerpts are sometimes necessary when the language of the original source is memorable, when the passage is subject to interpretation, or when the source

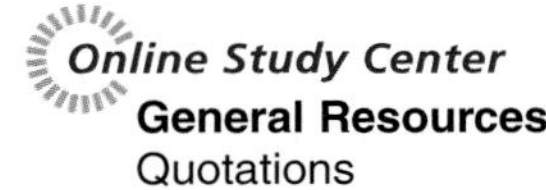

TIPS FOR USING QUOTATIONS

Long Quotations

Block any quotations that are longer than four lines.

Use a colon after a complete sentence to introduce your quotation.

Indent the left margin by two tab spaces (one inch).

Quote only what is necessary to prove your point.

Use square brackets around changes you make to the text.

Don't add quotation marks around the block (but keep quotation marks that appear in the original source).

Place the citation in parentheses after the period at the end of the block.

For electronic citations, mention the author's name or the title of the website in the text or in the parenthetical citation. Page numbers are not needed for electronic citations.

Make the discussion following your citation at least as long as the quotation.

Short Quotations

Try to keep short quotations to one sentence or less.

Make the quoted material part of the natural flow of your sentence.

Use colons or commas after your material to transition to your cited material.

Place the citation in parentheses after the quoted material.

Try to mention the author's name in the sentence, and place the page numbers inside the parentheses.

Place the parenthetical citation before the period.

uses jargon that would make it especially awkward to paraphrase. Most of the time short quotations are preferred, although longer ones may be necessary from time to time. Remember this rule of thumb: Make any discussion of quoted material at least as long as the quote itself to prevent your quotations from "taking over" your paper.

Short quotations If a quotation takes up four fewer lines of text, work it into your prose. Parenthetical citations appear outside of the quotation marks.

> Desmond Morris argues that "The modern human animal is no longer living in conditions natural for his species" (7).

The period does not appear at the end of the quotation, but after the parenthetical citation. Because the entire sentence from the original is used in this example, it is capitalized just as it is in the source text.

Cutting words out of quotations If you cut any words out of the quotation, insert an ellipsis (. . .) to indicate the omission.

> According to William James, "neither Bunyan nor Tolstoy could become what we have called healthy-minded. They had drunk too deeply of the cup of bitterness ever to forget its taste, and . . . the sadness was preserved as a minor ingredient in the heart of the faith by which it was overcome" (169).

Note that the ellipsis includes spaces between the periods. You can also use an ellipsis at the end of a quotation to indicate that the sentence was cut off in the middle.

> According to William James, "neither Bunyan nor Tolstoy could become what we have called healthy-minded. They had drunk too deeply of the cup of bitterness ever to forget its taste . . ." (169).

In this case, the quotation marks and the period go outside the ellipsis. You can use an ellipsis in the same way to eliminate an entire sentence out of the middle of a quotation.

Altering sources Sometimes it may be necessary to change quotations in some way. For example, if a source contains a grammatical or spelling error, insert the phrase "(*sic*)" next to the error to indicate that the mistake was not yours. To emphasize a particular word or phrase, you can underline a portion of a quotation and add the phrase "(emphasis added)" to the quotation. Use the phrase "(emphasis in original)" to indicate that italics were not added.

> "For each subject of instruction," Vygotsky writes, "there is a period when its influence is most fruitful because the child is <u>most receptive</u> to it" (emphasis added).

> Paulo Freire says that "Revolutionary leaders cannot think <u>without</u> the people, nor <u>for</u> the people, but only <u>with</u> the people" (emphasis in original).

Sometimes, it is desirable to add bracketed comments to make the meaning of a passage clear.

> According to Dewey, "there are two schools of social reform. One [the theory of innate morality] bases itself upon the notion of a morality which springs from an inner freedom, something mysteriously cooped up within personality" (9).

Long quotations When you include a quotation of more than four lines, you should block it—that is, you should indent the quotation one inch from the left (usually two tab spaces in most word processing programs). Let us consider James's quotation in full:

> In *The Varieties of Religious Experience,* William James writes that
>
>> neither Bunyan nor Tolstoy could become what we have called healthy-minded. They had drunk too deeply of the cup of bitterness ever to forget its taste, and their redemption is into a universe two stories deep. Each of them realized a good which broke the effective edge of his sadness; yet the sadness was preserved as a minor ingredient in the heart of the faith by which it was overcome. (169)

In the preceding example, quotation marks are unnecessary because the text is blocked, indicating that it is a quotation. Because the blocked quotation stands on its own, the period comes at the end of the quotation, not after the parenthetical citation.

"Quoted in . . ." You will probably encounter situations where a source you have read quotes someone else you would like to quote. In this case, the best thing to do is to obtain the original source, because the quotation may be inaccurate or the context of the quote may somehow distort its meaning. However, the time constraints of college life do not always allow for such luxuries. If your library does not own the original source, and if you cannot obtain it online or through interlibrary loan, then you may wish to quote the material through another source. Use the abbreviation "qtd. in" to indicate that you borrowed the material from a secondary source, not the source where the material originally appeared. Credit the original source (usually by the author's name) in your prose, but include the title of the source where you found the quote in your parenthetical citation.

> A variety of English teachers have incorrectly applied the word "induction" to the ordering of material within an essay. According to Rorabacher, "In induction we analyze particular instances to establish a general truth" (qtd. in Fulkerson 13). However, the philosophical inaccuracy of this term does not mean it should not be used by writing teachers for other purposes.

Citing Electronic Sources While the Internet has created new opportunities for research, it has also created unforeseen difficulties in citing information. Generally, because Internet sources do not divide material into distinct pages, you can omit page numbers from Internet references, although you should always provide the author's name. A second problem arises when authorship is difficult to determine. In such a situation it is usually best to use the corporate author for the citation. For example, if you cite information from the Web MD website that does not include an author's name, you would credit Web MD as the author. Also, because websites usually qualify as shorter works, titles are placed within quotation marks. The important thing to remember is to include enough information in your citation so that the reader can easily find the listing in your bibliography (the Works Cited list):

Online Study Center
General Resources
Electronic Sources

> According to the National Institutes of Health, stem-cell research may one day help prevent birth defects or discover a cure for cancer.
>
> Stem-cell research may one day help prevent birth defects or discover a cure for cancer (National Institutes of Health).

The reader would look up "National Institutes of Health" (capitalized in alphabetical order under "N") in the Works Cited list, which would provide information on the website, including its date of access and URL.

Creating a Works Cited List

Your MLA bibliography is called a "Works Cited list" and is formatted in the following way:

- Always title your reference list "Works Cited" (never "Bibliography" or "References").
- Double-space all entries.
- Use hanging indentation. That is, place the first line of an entry flush to the left margin, and indent subsequent lines by one-half inch (usually one tab space).

Online Study Center
General Resources
Creating a bibliography

- Alphabetize all items. When you have several sources by the same author, arrange the entries in alphabetical order by title. (For example, if Josephine Smith has written articles entitled "Beyond Research: An Introduction to MLA Style" and "Considering Research: MLA Style Revisited," then "Beyond Research" comes first in the list.)
- When one author has several subsequent entries in your Works Cited, don't repeat the author's name. List the author's name for the first entry, and use three hyphens to indicate the author's name for the second and later entries.

The examples that follow cover types of citations that are frequently used in college writing assignments. This list is by no means exhaustive, however. Refer to the *MLA Guide for Writers of Research Papers* when you wish to use sources that do not fit the cases outlined here.

Sample Works Cited Entries: Books

In MLA style, a book entry consists of the author's name, the book's title (underlined), and the publication information. Publication information is usually found on the title page of a book. The dates of publication usually appear on the following page.

- Entries are arranged alphabetically.
- The first author's last name is listed in reverse order. Other authors' names are listed in regular order.
- Titles of long works such as books are underlined.
- A colon indicates the presence of a subtitle.
- If an entry fits entirely on one line, hanging indentation does not apply.

Author's name **Title** **Subtitle**

Ravitch, Diane. The Language Police: How Pressure Groups Restrict What Students Learn. New York: Knopf, 2003.

Place of publication **Publisher** **Year of publication**

Book by One, Two, Three, or Four or More Authors Only the first author's name is listed last name first. When citing two or more works by the same person, use three hyphens in the place of the name. When using two or more works by the same author, arrange the sources in alphabetical order by title. If more than three authors are listed for any work, use *et al.* (Latin for "and others") to indicate the second and subsequent authors.

Bellah, Robert N., et al. The Good Society. New York: Knopf, 1991.

Pinker, Steven. The Blank Slate: The Modern Denial of Human Nature. New York: Viking, 2002.

---. The Language Instinct. New York: Harper Perennial, 1995.

Roark, James L., et al. The American Promise: A History of the United States. 2 vols. New York: Bedford, 2002.

Book with an Editor (No Author Listed)

Burt, Daniel S., ed. The Chronology of American Literature: America's Literary Achievements from the Colonial Era to Modern Times. New York: Houghton, 2004.

Book with a Corporate Author A book is considered to have corporate authorship when it was produced by the membership of a corporation or organization, but the actual writers' names do not appear on the title page. In this case, the organization is considered to be the author. This is different from a book with an unknown author.

American Cancer Society. American Cancer Society's Guide to Complementary and Alternative Cancer Methods. Atlanta: American Cancer Society, 2000.

Book with an Unknown Author

Past Worlds: The Times Atlas of Archaeology. Maplewood, NJ: Hammond, 1988.

Alphabetize works by the first word in the title other than *a, an,* or *the.* When a place of publication is not well known, also include the abbreviation for the state.

Book That Is Part of a Multivolume Work When using more than one volume of a multivolume work, you must give the total number of volumes after the title. If you use only one volume from the set, supply the volume number instead. When citing a multivolume work, indicate the volume number followed by a colon and the subsequent pages. For the example below, the citation would be (Copelston 1: 121–22).

Copelston, Frederick, S.J. A History of Philosophy. 8 vols. New York: Image, 1962.

or

Copelston, Frederick, S.J. A History of Philosophy. Vol. 1. New York: Image, 1962.

A Forward, Preface, or Afterword of a Book

Goldberg, Natalie. Preface. The Writer's Handbook 2004. Ed. Elfrieda Abbe. Waukesha, WI: Writer Books, 2003. 9–14.

A Book with a Title within Its Title

Fish, Stanley. Surprised by Sin: The Reader in Paradise Lost. New York: St. Martin's, 1967.

A Work in an Anthology (Short Story, Poem, or Essay)

Mardsen, Madonna. "The American Myth of Success: Visions and Re-visions." Popular Culture: An Introductory Text. Ed. Jack Nachbar and Kevin Lause. Bowling Green, OH: Bowling Green State U Popular Press, 1992. 134–48.

More Than One Piece from the Same Collection

Caputi, Jane, and Susan Nance. "One Size Does Not Fit All: Being Beautiful, Thin and Female in America." Nachbar and Lause. 292–311.

Motz, Maralyn Ferris. "Seen Through Rose-Tinted Glasses: The Barbie Doll in American Society." Nachbar and Lause. 211–34.

Nachbar, Jack, and Kevin Lause, eds. Popular Culture: An Introductory Text. Bowling Green, OH: Bowling Green State U Popular Press, 1992.

When listing multiple entries from the same anthology, refer to the anthology by its editors' last names and include complete information for the anthology.

Encyclopedia or Dictionary Article With an entry from a commonly used encyclopedia or dictionary, no page numbers or publication information is required. For more specialized sources, give full publication information. If the article is signed, list the author's name as you would for a book or article. When items are listed alphabetically, you may omit the page numbers. If you cite one of several references from a dictionary, then the abbreviation "Def." and the letter or number that references the definition should follow the word being referenced.

"Elegy." Princeton Encyclopedia of Poetry and Poetics. Enlarged ed. Ed. Alex Preminger. Princeton, NJ: Princeton UP, 1974. 215–17.

"Overture." Def. 2b. Webster's New World College Dictionary. 4th ed.

"Paella." Webster's II: New College Dictionary. 1995 ed.

Translation

Lem, Stanislaw. Solaris. Trans. Joanna Kilmartin and Steve Cox. San Diego: Harcourt-Brace, 1987.

A Pamphlet Square brackets are used when information is known but does not appear within the source itself.

What You Should Know about Prostate Cancer. [Los Angeles:] Prostate Cancer Research Institute, 2004.

A Government Publication Government documents present a particular problem because they usually do not list authors and they are often inconsistent in the types of publication information they offer. Generally, you should list the author as being the issuing branch of government (United States, Oklahoma, United Kingdom) followed by the name of the agency, using standard abbreviations as necessary. If a specific author is listed, include that information. If the information was obtained online, the citation should include the date of access and the URL. If you list more than one entry from the same branch of government, use three hyphens instead of the name of the government entity for the second (and following) entries. When citing the U.S. *Congressional Record,* use the abbreviation *Cong. Rec.* and indicate the date of publication and page numbers.

Cong. Rec. 7 Apr. 2004: 3898–914. 20 Sep. 2004 <http://wais.access.gpo>.

---. Federal Register. Equal Employment Opportunity for Individuals with Disabilities, Final Rule. 26 Jul. 1991: 35725–55.

Sample Works Cited Entries: Articles

- Citations in periodicals include the author's name, the title of the article, the title of the publication (underlined), the month (or volume and issue number), year, and inclusive pages on which the article appears.
- As with books, the first author's name is listed in reverse order. For works with more than one author, the other authors' names appear in regular order.
- Article titles (short works) are put in quotation marks. Publication titles (long works) are underlined.
- All months except May, June, and July receive three-letter abbreviations.

- When journal volume or issue numbers are used, they are separated by a period.

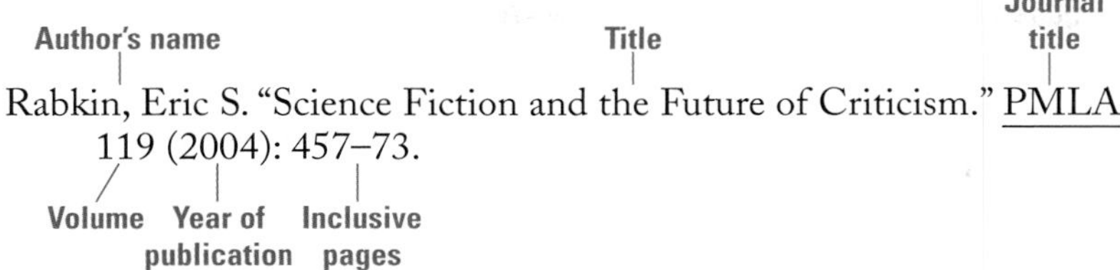

Journal Article with One Author (Continuous Pagination)

Everett, Justin Edward. "Adopting the Peircian Sign for a Method of Affective Interpretation." Linguistica Antverpiensia 25 (1991): 129–51.

Journal Article with One Author (Separate Pagination for Each Issue) Entries dealing with journals with separate pagination in each issue contain both the volume and the issue separated by a period.

Berlin, James. "Current-Traditional Rhetoric: Paradigm and Practice." Freshman English News 8.3 (1980): 1–4, 13–14.

Journal Article with Two or Three Authors As with books, only the name of the first author is inverted. Separate the authors' names with commas, and place a comma before the last author's name, followed by "and."

Flower, Linda, and John R. Hayes. "A Cognitive Process Theory of Writing." College Composition and Communication 32 (1981): 365–86.

When an article has more than three authors, list only the first author's name, followed by *et al.* (Latin for "and others").

Article from a Monthly Magazine In the case of monthly magazines, list the month instead of the volume number. In MLA style, three-letter abbreviations are used for the names of months that are more than four letters long; May, June, and July are not abbreviated. Also, popular monthlies will often begin an article on one page, and finish it later in the magazine. In such a case, use a comma in the place of a hyphen to indicate pages that are not continuous. For citing an article from a monthly that was downloaded from the Internet, see "References from Electronic Sources" later in this chapter.

Bly, Robert W. "The Six Figure Writer." Writer's Digest Aug. 2004: 22, 57.

Article from a Weekly Magazine For magazines published more than once a month (weekly or biweekly), provide the publication date (not just the month).

> Gerdes, Lindsey. "No Pain, Some Gain: The New Workouts." Newsweek 12 Jan. 2004: 59.

Article from a Daily Newspaper Entries from newspapers should include the city of publication (in brackets) if it is not a part of the newspaper's title, immediately after the title (example: *Daily Commercial Record* [Dallas, TX]). If more than one edition is available on the date of publication (many papers publish early editions, especially on Sunday), then indicate that fact after the date. Also include the section information. If the section is indicated by a number, use the abbreviation "sec." followed by the number, a colon, and the page number of the article (example: sec. 3: 11). If the section is indicated by a letter, omit "sec." If the paper is not sectioned or the pagination is continuous, then you do not need to include section information.

> Shapiro, Eben. "Management: Time Warner Defends System of Values." Wall Street Journal [New York] 9 Apr. 1999, eastern ed., B1.

Editorial Editorials are identified with the word "Editorial" placed immediately after the title.

> Satullo, Chris. "Kids' Needs Come First." Editorial. The Philadelphia Inquirer 8 Aug. 2004: C6.

References from Electronic Sources

Online Study Center
General Resources
Formatting Electronic Sources

- Citations for electronic sources include the author's name, the title of the article, the print information (if available), the date of access, and the URL (website address). When using an article obtained through a search (one that is not in a fixed location on the Internet), include the main website's URL. For example, for an article obtained by searching the Web MD site, the URL reported would be: <http:// webmd.com >.
- Some website articles have confusing titles (if they have any titles at all) or are not attributed to an author. In such cases, use your best judgment and provide the most complete information you can.

Burke, Barbara Ruth, and Julie Rae Patterson-Pratt. "Establishing Understandings: Teaching about Culture in Introductory Television Courses." American Communication Journal 5.2 (2002). 21 Sep. 2004 <http://www.acjournal.org/holdings/vol5/iss2/articles/tvculture.htm>.

You will not always be able to find full publication information online. However, you should do your best to obtain the most complete information possible to help someone who reads your citation follow up on your source.

A note on page numbers: Online journals, newspapers, magazines, and books often do not include page number references. If the online source where you obtained the text does not provide page numbers, then you may leave the page numbers out of the citation. However, it is preferable to include the original pagination, if possible, by cross-checking the reference in other databases or sources that might include this information in a bibliographic reference.

UNDERSTANDING WEB ADDRESSES

The Web address, also known as a URL (universal resource locator), usually consists of the abbreviation "http://" followed by a series of words or symbols separated by periods and forward slashes. The forward slashes indicate "levels" in the folder hierarchy of a particular Web address. Anything following a forward slash indicates a permanent place on the Web and should be included in your Works Cited bibliographic reference. The following URL will take you to the online exhibits page for the Museum of the History of Science at Oxford University:

<http://www.mhs.ox.ac.uk/exhibits/index.htm>

Sometimes the symbols in a URL are generated by a search engine when you look for information on the Internet. These symbols (usually a very long string of them) are meaningless as far as the Web address is concerned and should not be included in a Works Cited entry. Here is an example of a URL from a search for "longevity research" conducted on the Web MD site, which located an article entitled "Longevity May Run in Your Blood":

<http://my.webmd.com/content/article/75/89691.htm?lastselectedguid={5FE84E90-BC77-4056-A91C-9531713CA348}>

In this case, the legitimate URL ends with the letters "htm." The material after these letters is computer-generated garbage, so it should not be included in the reference. If you want to test your URL, cut the portion you think is the "legitimate" address and paste it into the address bar of your Internet browser. If it leads you to the article, then you have identified the correct URL. If it doesn't work, then list only the main homepage address (in this case, http://my.webmd.com) in your bibliography.

Article from a Subscribed Database After listing the print information, include the underlined title of the database, the name of the database service, the date you accessed the article, and the URL of the service. You will not always have access to all of this information, depending on the service and the place where you access it. Nevertheless, include as much of this information as possible.

Wilson, Nicholas, Robert Quigley, and Osman Mansoor. "Food Ads on TV: A Health Hazard for Children?" Australian and New Zealand Journal of Public Health 23 (2003): 647–50. ProQuest. University of the Sciences in Philadelphia Lib. 28 Oct. 2003 <http://proquest.umi.com>.

In the preceding example, because "multiple databases" was selected during the search, no database title is included in the citation. Also, when listing a URL, always begin with "http"; when a URL runs over more than one line, divide it only after a backslash.

Online Study Center
General Resources
Public Domain Electronic Books

Reference for an Online Book For an online book, list full publication information for the original text, if available. Also list the title of the website, the editor of the site, the date of electronic publication, and the name of any sponsoring organization, if available. At a minimum, include the author's name, the title of the book, the date of access, and the URL.

Darwin, Charles. The Voyage of the Beagle. London: John Murray, 1845. Electronic Scholarly Publishing. Ed. Robert Robbins. 3 Oct. 2004 <http://www.esp.org/books/darwin/beagle/title.html>.

Lawrence, D. H. Studies in Classic American Literature. American Studies at the University of Virginia. 1 Nov. 2003 <http://xroads.virginia.edu/~HYPER/LAWRENCE/lawrence.html>.

Article from an Online Periodical (with Print Source) Follow full publication information with the date you viewed the article online and the URL.

De Lemos, James, et al. "Early Intensive vs a Delayed Conservative Simvastatin Strategy in Patients with Acute Coronary Syndromes." JAMA 292 (2004): 1307–16. 20 Sep. 2004 <http://jama.org/cgi/content/full/292/11/1307>.

Article from an Online Periodical (No Print Source) If an article exists only online, follow the format for a printed publication and include as much of the information as is available from the online source, followed by the date of access and the URL. If the publication is updated daily, treat it as you would a newspaper or weekly/bimonthly magazine, whichever seems more appropriate. If the E-zine ("electronic magazine") is updated monthly, treat it like a monthly magazine.

Huffington, Arianna. "In Praise of Unruly Women." Salon. 22 Jul. 2004. 22 Oct. 2004 <http://www.salon.comopinion/huffington/2004/07/22/unruly_women/ index_np.html>.

Phillips, Vicky. "Top Ten Bargain Buys: Human Resource Degrees Online." Virtual University Gazette Sep. 2004. 17 Sep. 2004 <http://www.geteducated.com/vugaz.htm>.

Article from a Professional Website For articles and information published on websites, but not associated with an electronic book, magazine, newspaper, or other recognizable print equivalent, provide the author's name, the article's title, the date (the year if a specific date is not published), the sponsoring organization, the date of access, and the URL.

Martino, John M. "Health Tip: Know Your Medications." 2004. U of the Sciences in Philadelphia. 8 Oct. 2004 <http://www.usip.edu>.

Information from a Personal Website (Home page) If the page has a title, that title should follow the author's name. If the personal page has no title, then include "Home page," without underlining or quotation marks, where the title would otherwise go. If the page indicates when it was last updated, this information should appear immediately after the title (or "Home page") and before the date of access.

Cowen, Tyler. Home page. 29 Sep. 2004 <http://www.gmu.edu/jbc/Tyler/>.

MLA

Sample Student Essay: MLA Style

Include your last name and the page number in the top right corner of every page.

Your name and other contact information (address or class) go here.

Bruns 1

Faith Bruns

Dr. Lamm

EN 102

5 August 2004

Mind Your Manners

Basic manners were once taught in the home and reinforced in the schools. Children learned to say "please" and "thank you" and to address others properly. Good manners were once a sign of good breeding, a good home, and a proper upbringing.

What can you tell about the author from the tone of this paragraph?

Unfortunately, manners have gone out of style. The newest trend is to be different, unique. This can be achieved with manners, but the general public has forsaken polite behavior. Instead of manners is the idea of political correctness, which does consider respect for the individual, but lacks civility.

Manners cannot be used only on special occasions. They are to be employed at all times and with all people. The way people treat a waiter or waitress at a local restaurant should be the same way they treat a client or a supervisor: they should be polite, respectful, and courteous.

The author mentions the name of an authoritative source before going into her quotation.

Block long quotations. Note the distinctive language used here.

Perhaps most important, manners tell others what kind of person you are. According to Emily Post, an expert on etiquette:

> Etiquette must, if it is to be of more than trifling use, include ethics as well as manners. Certainly what one is, is of far greater importance than what one appears to be. A knowledge of etiquette is of course essential to one's decent behavior, just as clothing is essential to one's decent appearance; and precisely as one wears the latter without being self-conscious of having on shoes and perhaps gloves, one who has good manners is equally unself-conscious in the

Bruns 2

> observance of etiquette, the precepts of which must be so thoroughly absorbed as to make their observance a matter of instinct rather than of conscious obedience. (Par. 7)

This means that etiquette makes individuals better members of society by making them aware of how their behavior reflects their moral and social character.

Unfortunately, in the social world today manners are not treasured the way they once were. Mrs. Post and Mrs. Vanderbilt were once consulted daily on the proper way to introduce clients or associates, the correct way to set up and serve a meal, and the best way to send thank you notes or invitations. These gentle graces were not reserved for the women of society, either. Men were quick to note the proper way to conduct business. A major social gaffe, such as a slovenly appearance or rudeness to a lady, was the quickest way to lose a promotion (Allen and Briggs 186).

Manners began going out of style in the sixties, when the youth movement proclaimed that everyone needed to do his or her own thing. Judith Martin, author of the syndicated news column "Mrs. Manners," spoke in an interview about the loss of manners and civility in today's society:

> We have seen, first of all, the result of generations of children being told by very well-meaning parents, "Now you don't worry about what other people think about you, you go out and search yourself and get what you want, and never mind what other people think." So they have done this beautifully and that's the decline. . . . all the older people joined in; it's not just one generation or two. (Interview 1)

The problem, as Martin points out, has become infused in society. Rudeness and self-interest are just the way things are now done. This

When citing from books on the Internet, give paragraph numbers when they are available. Bartleby.com is one valuable source.

Should the author have cited this information about Mrs. Vanderbilt, or can it be considered common knowledge? Is this a case of plagiarism?

Use *and* to connect authors' names in a parenthetical citation. Don't use an ampersand (&).

Double quotation marks are used for a quotation within a block quotation.

Since King's statement is common knowledge, it doesn't have to be referenced.

When the author's name is in the text, only the page reference goes inside the parentheses.

Note how this quotation is blended into the author's sentence.

An ellipsis is used when something is cut out of the sentence.

***Cf.* means "compare" (from the Latin *conferre*, "to bring together, to compare"). It refers to material related to the discussion but not directly drawn from the source.**

Bruns 3

has led to a serious problem. When people treat each other without common civility and respect, how can they be expected, in Rodney King's words, to "just get along"? According to Allen and Briggs, "The rules [of manners] have changed as times and conditions have changed, but always the reason for the rules has been the same—a means of living together with ease, harmony, and satisfaction" (12). Those who do not learn to treat others with politeness will find themselves alone in the world playing a difficult game of catch-up. Fortunately, help is available. In any bookstore one may find many different volumes on social behavior and etiquette. These treasures of wisdom are not outdated modes of behavior; many of them address such difficulties as job situations, dating, and the idea of political correctness.

For many, the idea of political correctness has eclipsed manners. It is believed by the general public that sanitized labels are equal to good manners. Political correctness (or PC) is an ideological term, one that has been around for many years and has been associated with a socialist agenda. There are some who attribute PC to the Institute for Social Research in Frankfurt, Germany, which was charged with finding "a solution to the biggest problem facing the implementers of communism in Russia" (Blazquez 1). Bill Lind attributes PC to Karl Marx: "Political Correctness is cultural Marxism . . . translated from economic into cultural terms" (2).

The current trend in our media is to lambaste those who use plain speech instead of PC terminology to get their points across. To not use PC language is erroneously viewed as "bad manners." It may not be politically correct for Bill Cosby to berate other African Americans for what he sees as a decline in civility (cf. Gruenwedel 16), but it is

Bruns 4

not bad manners. Crosby's remarks were quite the opposite. They were intended to encourage social responsibility and good manners.

Manners are not a set of rules merely meant to force people to behave in a certain way. According to Miss Manners' Guide to the Turn of the Millennium, they are inner guidelines that, if taught from an early age, will assist anyone in situations that require interaction with others (Martin 5). Civilization means that the people living in it need to be civil. People need to be aware of their actions and their words. Good manners, not political correctness, are the only way civility will survive.

Underline the titles of books, magazines, and films.

Don't use a comma before the page number.

Bruns 5

Works Cited

Allen, Betty, and Mitchell Pirie Briggs. Mind Your Manners. Chicago: Lippincott, 1957.

Blazquez, Agustin. “Political Correctness: The Scourge of Our Time.” 8 April 2002. 29 Jul. 2004 <http://www.newsmax.com/archives/articles/2002/4/4/121115.shtml>.

Gruenwedel, Erik. “Bill Cosby Decries Slumping Urban Civility.” Video Store Magazine. 25 Jul. 2004: 16.

Lind, Bill. “The Origins of Political Correctness: An Accuracy in Academic Address.” 2000. 29 Jul. 2004 <http://www.academia.org/lectures/lind1.html>.

Martin, Judith. Interview with Barbara Lane. 18 November 2002. Commonwealth Club of California. 4 Jul. 2004. <http://www/cp,,pmwea;tjc;ib/prgarcjove02/02-11martin-speech.html>.

---. Miss Manners’ Guide to the Turn of the Millennium. New York: Simon, 1989.

Post, Emily. Etiquette in Society, in Business, in Politics and at Home. New York: Funk, 1922. Bartleby.com: Great Books Online. 4 Jul. 2004. <http://www.bartleby.com/95/1.html>.

Looking Back at Chapter 13

- The MLA system of documentation consists of (1) in-text parenthetical citations and (2) a bibliography (called "Works Cited") that appears on a separate page at the end of the document.
- For in-text citations in MLA style, the author's name introduces quoted or paraphrased material, and the page number where the material can be found is placed in parentheses immediately after the borrowed information.
- The MLA bibliography (Works Cited) is formatted in the following way:
  1. Title the list of references "Works Cited" (not "Bibliography" or "References").
  2. Double-space all entries.
  3. Use hanging indentation.
  4. Alphabetize all items in the bibliography.

14 APA Documentation

> *Information is the oxygen of the modern age.*
> —Ronald Reagan (1911–2004)

American Psychological Association (APA) style is popular with social scientists, educators, and certain business-related disciplines. The style is complex, but the essential elements are (1) in-text citations and (2) the references list. Where MLA is an author/page number style, APA is an author/date style. Consider the following examples:

MLA Style

According to one source, today's parents often expect excellence from their children as a way of making up for their own insecurities (Marano 54).

APA Style

According to one source, today's parents often expect excellence from their children as a way of making up for their own insecurities (Marano, 2005).

MLA style emphasizes the page on which the information can be located, whereas APA style emphasizes the date of publication. (The preceding example is a paraphrase.) With a direct quotation, the APA citation would be followed by a page reference: (p. 1).

Note on verb tenses: In APA style, sources are generally discussed in the past tense. This is a major difference compared with MLA style, in which sources are usually discussed in the present tense.

Online Study Center
This icon will direct you to content and resources on the website <college.hmco.com/pic/lamm1e>.

Online Study Center
Prepare for Class
American Psychological Association

In-Text Citations in APA Style

Paraphrasing

Most frequently, writers who use MLA style begin sentences with an author's name followed by the date of publication.

> Smith (2003) has said that the average American eats about 2,750 calories per day.

This approach can be monotonous if it is used repetitively. Another method is to end a paraphrase with the author's last name within the parenthetical citation.

> The average American consumes approximately 2,750 calories per day (Smith, 2003).

Using Direct Quotations

In any type of argumentative writing, quotations should be as brief as possible to prove the point being argued. Long quotations are not encouraged. You should try to paraphrase your evidence when possible. However, when the language of a quotation is particularly important or memorable, you may use the original. Even then, your excerpt should be as brief as possible. Quotations of fewer than 40 words are placed within quotation marks and blended in with your prose.

> According to Pollack (2003), "if scientists receive little tangible encouragement to work with the media to make science accessible to a broader non-academic audience, they seldom make the effort" (p. 75).

If the quotation comes from an Internet source, no page reference is needed.

> Kurtz (2003) has argued that same-sex marriage "will usher in legalized polygamy and polyamory [and] weaken the belief that monogamy lies at the heart of marriage."

When long quotations are necessary, you must block them—that is, indent them from the left margin by five spaces (one tab space on most word processors). Delete the quotation marks, and add a page reference at the end of the block.

APA

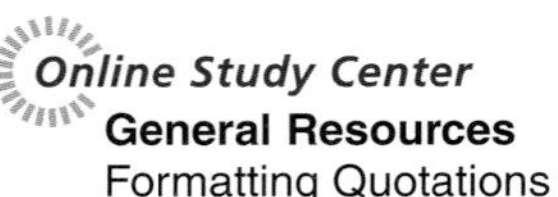

Online Study Center
General Resources
Formatting Quotations

Shari Waxman argued that the media cannot be relied on to promote legitimate science:

> Ultimately, the legitimization of pseudoscientific research and paranormal phenomena by trusted news sources cannot occur without the simultaneous devaluation of science and reason. If the trend continues, the American public will be left with two disconcerting options: (1) They can learn to distrust the information provided by the mainstream news sources; or (2) They can learn to readily accept scientifically baseless claims as provided by mainstream news sources. (p. 84)

Citing Sources

Most of the time you will use one of the methods of citation already mentioned. Sometimes, however, you may need to consider a special case (e.g., no author, corporate author, multiple authors).

One Author

Powledge (2004) reported that a virus may be the cause of obesity in some people.

Two Authors Use the ampersand (&) instead of the word *and* to connect names in APA parenthetical references.

Guided reading is a process teachers use to help students achieve higher levels of ability by reading with assistance within teacher-led groups (Fountas & Pinnell, 1996).

Ampersands

Use the ampersand (&) instead of the word *and* to connect names in APA parenthetical references. The ampersand was used in ancient Rome, where the letters of the word *ET* (Latin for "and") were combined into a single figure. It was sometimes listed as the last letter of the alphabet. Its name originates with the phrase "and *per se* and."

Three, Four, or Five Authors When a work has between two and five authors, all of the names are mentioned in the text. All are mentioned in the first reference, with *et al.* used in the subsequent references.

FIRST MENTION
(Brundage, Harris, Olson, Paris, & Whited, 2004)

LATER IN THE SAME PARAGRAPH
(Brundage, et al.)

IN SUBSEQUENT PARAGRAPHS
(Brundage, et al., 2004)

Six or More Authors (All References)

(Abrams, et al., 1974)

Authors with the Same Last Name Use initials to avoid confusion.

T. Hobbs (2003) and J. E. Hobbs (2005) both agree that . . .

Corporate Author When a corporate name is long and awkward, abbreviate it after the first mention, then use the abbreviation in subsequent references.

FIRST MENTION

(National Organization for the Reform of Marijuana Laws [NORML], 2005)

LATER REFERENCES

(NORML, 2005)

No Author Listed When an author is not credited in the original source, use the first few words of the title in the parenthetical reference. Place quotations around articles and shorter works, but use italics for books and longer works.

("Cosmic Conspiracy," 1994)

Personal Communication You may cite letters, e-mails, interviews, blogs, and postings to electronic bulletin boards in the text. Such items do not usually appear on the References page, however.

(R. Lamm, e-mail, June 21, 2004)

Indirect Source When you cite someone indirectly—for example, if you cite a quotation or paraphrase through a source other than the original—then you must credit the source where you obtained the information.

Victor Barajas of the *Arizona Republic* says rap music is cruel and foulmouthed, but nonetheless entertaining (cited in Hoyt, 2000).

Specific Part of a Source When referring to information that appears in a specific part of a work, use abbreviations for page (p.), pages (pp.), chapter (chap.), and section (sec.) as appropriate.

Fish (1980) argues that one reads backward and forward at the same time (chap. 1).

Electronic Source When citing information from a webpage or other electronic source, use the paragraph symbol (or the abbreviation "para.") to indicate a paragraph's number.

Chef Bobo's goal is "to reverse the metabolic disaster of the modern American diet" (Smith, 2003, para. 2).

APA

If the article is divided into sections across several webpages (Salon.com and MSN.com are both known for this practice), then cite the section as well.

(Manjoo, 2004, p. 2, sec. 3)

Multiple Works in the Same Reference When several works are listed in the same reference, they are separated by semicolons. Usually you will include multiple sources in this way when several works address the same topic.

Several writers have endorsed this approach (Hariston, 1982; Bruffee, 1984; Nystrand, Greene, & Wiemelt, 1993).

Place works by the same author in chronological order. When you cite more than one source by an author that was published in the same year, give the works the designation *a, b, c*, and so on. Because works by the same author would be listed alphabetically on the references page, the title of *a* would come before the title of *b*, and so on.

(Smagorinsky, 1989a, 1989b, 1992, 1996)

Table If you insert a table or other illustration from a source, give the credit in a note at the bottom of the illustration. This source is not listed on the references page.

Source: From J. E. Jordon, *Using Rhetoric* (New York: Harper & Row, 1965), p. 82.

Preparing the References List (Bibliography)

Books

The bibliography for an APA-formatted paper is titled simply "References." Entries include the author's initials and last name and the date of publication. Book references include a title (in italics), place of publication, and press.

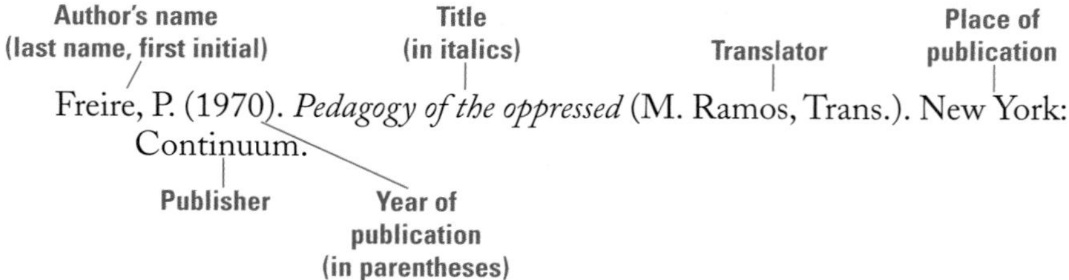

One Author

Brode, D. (1990). *Films of the eighties.* New York: Citadel.

Two or More Authors List up to six authors. If a book lists more than six authors, put *et al.* after the sixth name.

Barr, R., & Johnson, B. (1997). *Teaching reading and writing in elementary classrooms.* New York: Longman.

No Author or Editor Listed

2003 factbook. (2004). Philadelphia: University of the Sciences in Philadelphia.

Corporate Author When a corporate entity publishes a book and no author or editor is listed, use the publisher as author and place the word *Author* after the place of publication.

Arkansas State University. (2002). *2002–2004 Undergraduate bulletin.* State University, AR: Author.

Edited Book

Abrams, M. H., Daiches, D., Donaldson, E. T., Smith, H., Adams, R., Monk, S. H., et al. (Eds.). (1974). *The Norton anthology of English literature* (Vol. 2, 3rd ed.). New York: Norton.

When two types of information must be placed in parentheses after the title, separate them by a comma. Do not use two sets of parentheses: (Vol. 2) (3rd ed.).

Work in Several Volumes

Hartshorne, C., & Weiss, P. (Eds.). (1931–1958). *Collected papers of Charles Sanders Peirce* (Vols. 1–8). Cambridge: Harvard University Press.

Foreword, Preface, or Afterword

Meyerowitz, P. (1975). Introduction to the Dover edition. In G. Stein, *How to write* (pp. ix–xxv). New York: Dovers.

Selection from an Anthology The referenced entry is neither italicized nor put in quotation marks. Even if there are several citations from the same collection, always provide full bibliographic information.

Shakespeare, W. (1974). Venus and Adonis. In G. B. Evans, et al. (Eds.), *The Riverside Shakespeare* (pp. 1703–1719). Boston: Houghton Mifflin.

Article in a Reference Book

Brewer, R. L. (2003). 10 ways to effectively promote your writing through your website. In *2003 writer's market* (pp. 58–60). Cincinnati: Writer's Digest Books.

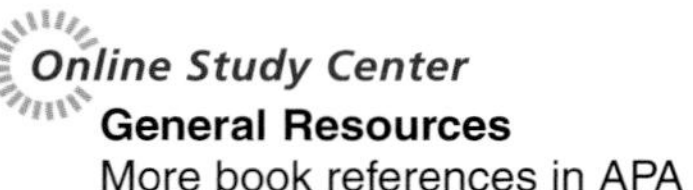

General Resources
More book references in APA

Unsigned Article If the article is unsigned, begin with the entry, followed by the publication date.

Rhetoric. (1995). *The new American Webster handy college dictionary* (p. 576). New York: Signet.

Government Publication

United States. (2000). *Guide to the clinical care of women with HIV* (Publication No. 017-024-01656-0). Washington, DC: U.S. Government Printing Office.

Articles

Periodical entries include the authors' names, the year of publication (in parentheses), the title of the work (only first words and proper nouns are capitalized), the title of the magazine (italicized), the volume, and the page numbers.

Authors' names (last name, first initial)
Year of publication (in parentheses)
Title (no quotation marks)

Wilson, N., Quigley, R., & Mansoor, O. (2003). Food ads on TV: A health hazard for children? *Australia and New Zealand Journal of Public Health, 23*(6), 647–651.

Subtitle (after colon)
Volume
Issue numbers
Pages
Name of journal

The volume number but not the issue number is italicized. If only the volume is listed, then the comma following the volume number is italicized:

Australia and New Zealand Journal of Public Health, 23, 647–651.

If the issue number is used, then the comma is not italicized:

23(6), 647–651.

Article in a Scholarly Journal with Continuous Pagination

Everett, J. E. (1997). Two Hamlets, one text: A semiotic analysis. *Reader: Essays in reader-oriented theory, criticism, and pedagogy,* 37, 59–77.

Article in a Scholarly Journal with Each Issue Paginated Separately

Langer, J. (2003). Succeeding against the odds in English. *English Journal, 91*(1), 37–42.

Popular Magazine Article

Hedegaard, E. (2004, April 29). A magnificent obsession. *Rolling Stone, 947*, 40–50.

For a weekly or bimonthly magazine, the date is given. For monthlies, only the month is listed: (2004, April).

Review Article

Leland, J. (2004, October 19). I am a woman. Now prepare to die. [Review of the motion picture *Kill Bill*]. *The New York Times,* sec. 9, p. 1.

Newspaper Article

McWhorter, J. (2003, May 30). Mean street theater. *Wall Street Journal*, p. W15.

Newspaper Article Retrieved Online

Padawer, R. (2004, March 21). Vendors at same-sex wedding expo in New York City see profits, not politics. *Knight Ridder Tribute Business News*. Retrieved July 1, 2004, from http://proquest.umi.com/pqweb

Online Study Center
General Resources
More Article References in APA

Letter to the Editor

Lamanno, R. (2004, June 21). Have ethics become only a legal distinction? [Letter to the editor]. *Wall Street Journal*, p. A17.

Motion Picture

Gilbert, L. (Producer/Director), & Russell, W. (Writer). (1983). *Educating Rita* [Motion Picture]. United Kingdom: Columbia Pictures.

Television Broadcast

Dorman, B. (Executive Producer). (2004, June 23). *Lou Dobbs tonight*. [Television broadcast]. New York: Cable News Network.

Television Series

Roddenberry, G. (Executive Producer). (1966–1969). *Star trek*. [Television series]. Los Angeles: Paramount Television.

Audio Recording (Entire Album)

Tolkien, J. R. R. (2001). *The fellowship of the ring* [CD]. London: BBC Audiobooks.

Audio Recording (Single Track) Within the brackets indicate the medium of the recording: record, CD, cassette, and so on. If the date on which the track was recorded is different from the copyright date, then put that date in parentheses following the brackets.

Bach, Johann Sebastian. (1989). Air on a "G" string. On *A little night music* [CD].

Software

Greenfield, S. M., Huntley, C., & Phillips, M. A. (1999). Dramatica Pro (Version 4.0) [Computer Software]. Screenplay Systems.

INTERNET SITES

Internet sources can present challenging problems for documentation. Material that appears one week may be gone the next. Also, virtually anyone can produce a document for the Web, so you must be careful to make certain that your source is reliable. Many Internet articles do not list authors or do not indicate publication dates. You should do your best to obtain sources with the most complete information possible.

Online Study Center
General Resources
Tips for Citing Web Sources

Author's name (last name, first initial) | Publication date (in parentheses) | Title of article (no quotation marks) | Title of webpage or original print source

McWhorter, J. (2003, May 30). Mean street theater. *Wall Street Journal*, p. W15. Retrieved October 19, 2003, from ProQuest database.

Page number for original print source | Date retrieved from the Internet | Name of searchable database or URL

Signed Document from a Website

Shreve, J. (1999). Vegetarian love, online. Retrieved November 3, 2003, from http://www.salon.com/tech/log/1999/10/29/veggie_dates/index.html

Document from a Website with No Author or Date

Branding yourself: Making the choice. (n. d.). Retrieved June 23, 2004, from http://www.bmezine.com/scar/A40510/scrbrand.html

Document from a Corporate Website

National Institutes of Health. (n.d.). Research ethics and stem cells. Retrieved July 30, 2004, from http://stemcells.nih.gov/info/ethics.asp

Internet Version of a Print Article You should add the words *Electronic Version* in brackets after the article's title. If the electronic version differs in any way from the print version, you should indicate the date it was retrieved and the URL.

Byrne, R. (2006, February 10). Rebuilding Balkan bridges. [Electronic Version]. *The Chronicle of Higher Education*, 52(23), A12. Retrieved February 14, 2006, from http://chronicle.com

With articles retrieved from the Internet, unless you are absolutely certain the Internet version is identical to the print version, it is always a good idea to include the Internet information.

Article from an Electronic Journal (E-zine)

Zebrowski, G. (2004, June 21). Ray Bradbury, looking back on a lifetime of science fiction, says that for better or worse, the future is now. *Science Fiction Weekly, 10*(25). Retrieved June 22, 2004, from http://www.scifi.com/sfw/current/interview.html

Document from a University Website

Swadley, S. (n.d.). Classical rhetoric: A brief overview of the five canons. Retrieved May 28, 2004, from University of Oklahoma website: http://www.ou.edu/S/Charles.R.Swadley-1/classicalrhetoric.htm

Printed Article from a Database

Clarke, P. (2001). Medical marijuana and the compassion clubs. *Medical Post, 37*(25), 22 [Electronic Version]. Retrieved October 24, 2003, from ProQuest database.

FORMATTING GUIDELINES

- Double-space your paper (no single spacing for quotations, references, and other items).
- Use one-inch margins on the top, the bottom, and both sides of the page (your word processing program is probably set up for these margins by default).
- Indent each paragraph by one tab space (one-half inch). Do not put extra spaces between paragraphs.
- Indent long quotations by one tab space from the left margin.
- Place a header with a page number at the top of each page (including the title page).
- Capitalize major headings (if you use them), and center them. Italicize minor headings (if you use them), and place them flush left.

BIBLIOGRAPHY (REFERENCES LIST)

- Type and center the word *References* at the top of the references list.
- List references items alphabetically.
- Use hanging indentation for each entry (the first line is flush left, but subsequent lines of each entry are indented by one tab space).
- Double-space the entire list.

Sample Student Essay: APA Style

APA format is designed to document the results of formal studies in the social sciences. Papers are often divided into several independent sections, each with its own heading, including an introduction (not titled), method, results, and discussion. Each section can be further subdivided as necessary. Of course, APA style may be used without this approach to organization, as the following student essay demonstrates.

Include a short version of the title and the page number in the top right corner of every page.

Center the title in the upper half of the page, followed by the author's name and course information.

Blame Game 1

The Blame Game of Blaming Games

Charles Mueller

English Composition

Professor Lamm

October 10, 2005

Abstract

Blaming violent video games for game-players' violent real-life crimes could lead to future tragedies if (a) the video games are not the actual cause of real-life violence and (b) it misdirects us from seeking the true causes and solutions. Unfortunately, the case against violent video games is shaky and pushes the issue of parental influence into the background. Parental involvement takes not only time but *quality time,* which would necessitate parents sharing activities with their children. As a role model, a parent can demonstrate to a child the intended use of video games as a mode of entertainment and instill that they are not to be used as a standard of real-life conduct.

Center the title at the top of the page.

Do not hyphenate words at the end of lines.

Multiple citations are separated by semicolons.

In APA, page numbers are given only for direct quotations.

Titles are italicized, not underlined.

After paraphrases, cite the author's last name and the date of publication in parentheses.

The Blame Game of Blaming Games

In Arkansas, two Westside Middle School boys with powerful hunting rifles wore camouflage and concealed themselves behind bushes like hunters, but their prey was their own classmates and teachers on the playground. In Colorado, another pair of boys dressed in trench coats and stalked through Columbine High School while shooting their own classmates and teachers. When the public's initial shock from these school shootings wore off and people began to ask questions about the causes of the rampages, many fingers were pointed at the violent video games that were played occasionally by these boys prior to their murder sprees.

Certainly when consequences are serious, fixing blame is vitally important. Certainly the tragic slayings in our schools demand that we understand the causes and take action. However, blaming games could lead to future tragedies if (a) the video games are not the actual cause of real-life violence and (b) it misdirects us from seeking the true causes and solutions. Unfortunately, the case against violent video games is shaky (Reichhardt, 2003; Rimensnyder, 2002; Wagner, 2004), and it pushes the issue of parental influence into the background.

Authorities have several concerns about video games. First, they are shocked by the content of particular games such as *Grand Theft Auto: San Andreas,* which includes nudity, gambling, and an array of violent scenarios (Reichhardt, 2003). *Grand Theft Auto* players earn money by committing crimes such as stealing cars, running over pedestrians, physically beating other drivers, and killing police officers. In the game *GoldenEye 007,* a player assumes the role of James Bond or one of his counterparts. The object of this game is to uncover as much ammunition as possible and kill your opponent in a set time frame. The *Wikipedia* article "GoldenEye 007" (2005) observes that the game has been "considered revolutionary in its use of the first-person shooter format which led to many imitators." Finally, in the game *Twenty-five to Life* the players shoot policemen and use civilians as human shields. According to Shirley Gibson, the national president of Concerns of Police Survivors, "It is unconscionable and unacceptable for [the game producer] Eidos to promote violence against the men and women behind the badge who devote their lives to serving and protecting our communities" (Concerns of Police Survivors, Inc., 2005).

More specifically, authorities are concerned about the short- and long-term psychological effects these games have on players. According to the American Psychological Association (APA), "Violence in video games is bad for children's health," largely because "violent acts [are shown] without consequences" (qtd. in Less Videogame, 2005). The APA further claims that "violence in video games increases aggressive thoughts, aggressive behavior, and angry feelings in children" (Video Wars, 2005). Lieutenant Colonel David Grossman (1995) describes these games as "violence enabling," a form of psychological conditioning similar to the way real-life soldiers are trained to kill:

> The kind of games that are very definitely enabling violence are the ones in which you actually hold a weapon in your hand and fire at human-shaped targets on the screen. These kinds of games can be played on home video, but you usually see them in video arcades. There is a direct relationship between realism and the degree of violence enabling. (p. 315)

Although the authorities' concerns make sense on an intuitive level, their conclusions have been challenged by researchers who

If the name of the source is given in the text, cite only the publication year in parentheses.

Square brackets are used around changes made within a quotation.

Quotations from an online source do not include page numbers.

Quotations of fewer than 40 words are not blocked.

Quotations of more than 40 words are blocked.

The page number is given after the period at the end of a blocked quotation.

For quotations from an uncited source, "qtd. in" indicates where the quotation was seen.

Block quotations are indented half an inch (usually one tab space).

Words may be italicized to add emphasis.

Square brackets and the words "italics added" show that you italicized words in a quotation for emphasis.

(a) see no clear cause-effect connection between game playing and real-life violence and (b) believe that violent fantasies actually may be beneficial, providing a vent for aggressive yet normal feelings. According to psychologist Kevin Durkin, "Despite much debate about the consequences of playing games with aggressive content, the evidence available to date to support claims of harmful effects upon children is modest" (qtd. in Reichhardt, 2003, p. 368). Gerard Jones, author of fantasy and science fiction stories, asserts that violent entertainment may even have healthy benefits:

> We're trying to control and eliminate real violence in society, and that's a good thing. But in our zeal to do that, we go after everything that resembles violence or seems to glorify it. We forget that one of the main functions of fantasy is that it enables you to take your antisocial desires and dispel them outside of the real world. (qtd. in Rimensnyder, 2002, p. 15)

Video games may be scapegoats for a deeper societal problem, one that will not be solved as easily as unplugging the X-Box. If games are not the root cause of violence in real-life situations, what is? What if the cause is not so much violent entertainment but the lack of parenting that helps young people distinguish fantasy from reality and immorality from morality?

Parental involvement takes not only time but *quality time,* which would necessitate parents sharing activities with their children. Unfortunately, young people spend more quality time with their games than they do with adults: "Teenage boys play video games *for around 13 hours a week*" [italics added] (Breeding evil, 2005). Restricting the kinds of entertainment pursued by young people makes sense only if the parents replace that time with something constructive and meaningful—something that includes their presence and interaction. Of course, some parents feel that being actively involved inhibits their children's development. In actuality, responsive, involved parents can provide an example of what it means to be a model citizen—a real example to contrast the fictional characters of video games.

Parental involvement in youths' lives can lay a solid foundation that would influence them toward becoming positive members of society. As a role model, a parent can demonstrate to a child the intended use of video games as a mode of entertainment and instill that they are not to be used as a standard of real-life conduct. "Playing the blame game" about playing video games is quick and easy but probably ineffective. Quality parenting—far from quick and easy—is the best solution.

References

Breeding evil? Defending video games. (2005, August 4). *The Economist,* 9. Retrieved September 30, 2005, from the ProQuest Database.

Concerns of Police Survivors, Inc. (2005, July 19). COPS opposes violent new video game [Press release]. Retrieved October 2, 2005, from http://www.nationalcops.org/pr04.htm

GoldenEye 007. (2005). *Wikipedia*. Retrieved October 10, 2005, from http://en.wikipedia.org/wiki/Golden_Eye

Grossman, D. A. (1995). *On killing: The psychological cost of learning to kill in war and society.* Boston: Little, Brown & Co.

Less videogame violence is urged. (2005, August 18). *Wall Street Journal,* p. E1. Retrieved September 30, 2005, from the ProQuest database.

Reichhardt, T. (2003, July 24). Playing with fire? *Nature, 424*(6947), 367–368.

Rimensnyder, S. (2002, November). Bang, you're dead [Interview]. *Reason, 34*(2), 15.

Video wars [Editorial]. (2005, August 25). *Knight Ridder Tribune Business News.* Retrieved September 30, 2005, from the ProQuest database.

Wagner, C. G. (2004, July–August). Aggression and violent media. *The Futurist, 38,* 16.

Looking Back at Chapter 14

- For in-text citations, APA style uses an author/date system.
- The bibliography for an APA-formatted paper is titled "References."
- Bibliographic entries include the author's last name and initials and the date of publication.
- Book references include a title (in italics), place of publication, and publisher.

Reading is a means of thinking with another person's mind; it forces you to stretch your own.

—CHARLES SCRIBNER (*Publisher's Weekly*, 1984)

Part 2

READER

Reading is the counterpart of writing. By reading the opinions of others, you will stretch your understanding of claims, evidence, and explanations—and by doing so learn to argue effectively. Each of the five chapters in Part 2 of *Dynamic Argument* presents readings on a controversial topic—health and medicine, the individual in society, security, the future, popular culture, and classic arguments. By reading and responding to the ideas of other writers, you will learn to clarify your own thoughts on these issues and to shape the way that your audience thinks about them.

15 Health and Medicine

The Obesity Epidemic, Stem-Cell Research, and the Psychology of Success

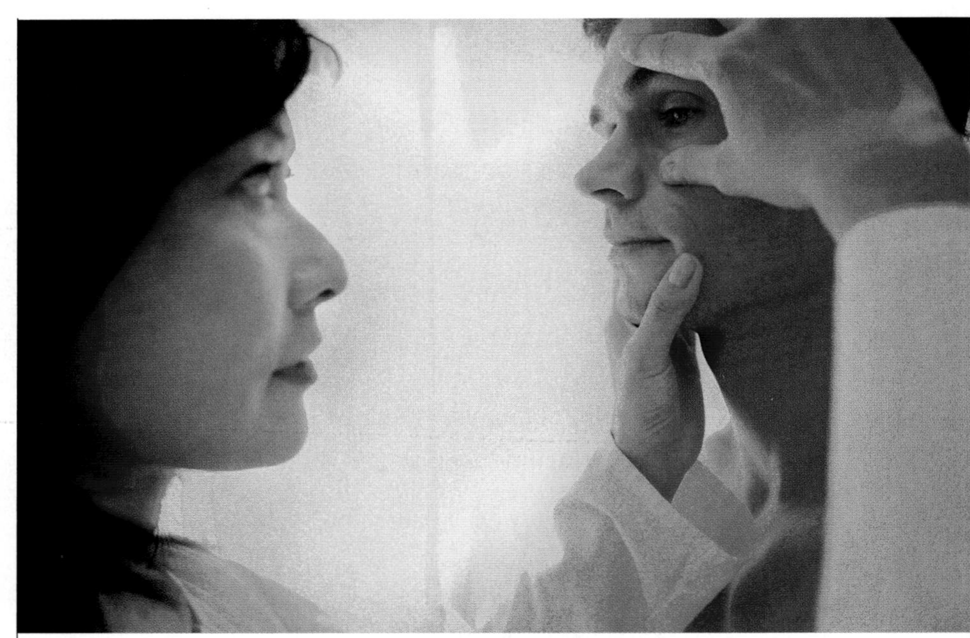

A wise man should consider that health is the greatest of human blessings.
—Hippocrates (460 BCE–377 BCE)

Few of us would deny that health is important, but all too often we take our health for granted until our bodies protest in the form of health problems. Some health problems may result from a lack of self discipline—from overindulgence with comfort foods or from a sedentary life style. Other problems may result from hazards and stresses that accompany our ambitions and careers. Yet other problems may be beyond our control, part of our genetic inheritance. Health and medical issues are many. Is obesity truly an "epidemic" or has it been "hyped"?

When does an individual's health become the concern and responsibility of others? Can stem-cell research provide remedies? What kinds of support or constraints should we place of stem-cell research? To what extent should children be encouraged to be ambitious? At what point does ambition become unhealthy? The topics in this chapter cover obesity, stem-cell research, and the psychology of success.

Online Study Center
This icon will direct you to content and resources on the website <college.hmco.com/pic/lamm1e>.

Issue 1: The Obesity Epidemic

When compared to *fat, portly, rotund,* and *big-boned, obese* is an ugly word. It carries with it much cultural baggage—assumptions that overweight people are somehow lazy, weak-willed, or otherwise inferior to the more slender individuals around them. Increasingly, *obese* is being used to describe a growing portion of the American population.

Online Study Center
Prepare for Class
Obesity Epidemic

At one time, the condition of being overweight was considered a matter of personal weakness, like alcoholism or drug abuse. Today, however, many medical professionals see overweight and obesity as diseases. While obesity has long been treated with diets (most of which fail), it is becoming more common for individuals to treat this condition by undergoing radical surgeries. Other individuals have argued that "fat prejudice" should end and that overweight people should not be treated as if there is something wrong with them if they cannot—or do not want to—lose weight. Some groups have even argued that the "obesity epidemic" is a fiction dreamed up by medical practitioners and attorneys who are anxious to sue fast-food companies for making their clients fat.

Considering the Issue of Chronic Obesity

Working individually or in groups, answer the following questions.

1. Do you believe Americans have a problem with weight? Does this problem rise to the level of an "obesity epidemic"? Explain.
2. Because many overweight people present greater health risks for insurers and employers, should employers be able to require that overweight people lose weight to keep their jobs? Why or why not? Should similar rules apply to people with other health issues (including smokers, drinkers, and people with inherited conditions such as Huntington's disease)?
3. Are overweight people discriminated against in any way? Should legislation protect them from such discrimination? How does discrimination against

obese people compare to racial discrimination or to the unfair treatment of women or gays and lesbians?

4. What, if anything, should be done about the current "obesity epidemic"?
5. What lifestyle changes should children be required to make to prevent the onset of Type II diabetes and other health problems?

READING SELECTION

"Measuring Up"

About the Author: Amy Dickinson

Amy Dickinson has had a diverse career. Her first employment after college was as a lounge singer. Following a divorce (she is still a single mother), she began freelancing for a variety of publications, including the *Washington Post, Esquire,* and *Allure.* Dickinson also wrote commentaries for the National Public Radio show, *All Things Considered.* Between 1999 and 2001, she wrote commentaries about family life for *Time* magazine. Following the death of Epie Lederer, who wrote the "Ann Landers" column until her death in 2002, Dickinson began writing "Ask Amy," the "Ann Landers" replacement, in July 2003. The following article appeared in the November 20, 2000, issue of *Time.*

Before You Read

1. Do you believe young people in the United States today suffer from an "obesity epidemic"? Why or why not? What do you think might be some of the causes of this problem?
2. What does the title of the article tell you? Does it suggest a claim?
3. It has often been said that Barbie dolls provide poor role models for young girls. Do you think this is true? Explain.
4. What kinds of action figures do boys play with? What expectations do these dolls build in young boys in terms of behavior and body image?

Measuring Up

1 Women my age know whom to blame for our own self-loathing, eating disorders, and distorted body image: Barbie. So we're raising our vulnerable, body-conscious girls to beware the perpetually pointy-toed goddess with the impossible body and perfect face. Now it's time to take a good look at our sons and their plastic influences Studies show that boys increasingly suffer from eating disorders, and if that fact is surprising, the root cause is not—after you take a good look at G.I. Joe.

Do toys contribute to a child's poor self-image?

2 G.I. Joe, for those of you who haven't raised an eight-year-old boy lately, has evolved from a normally proportioned grunt into a buff, ripped, mega-muscular warrior who, if he were a real man, would have 27-inch biceps and other proportions achievable only through years of bench presses, protein diets, and the liberal use of steroids.

3 A recent study shows that 36% of third-grade boys had tried to lose weight. In the past 10 years, more than a million males have been found to have eating disorders. In addition to suffering from anorexia and bulimia at increasing rates, boys are falling victim to a newly named disorder: muscle dysmorphia (also called bigorexia)—the conviction that one is too small. This syndrome is marked by an obsession with the size and shape of your body, constant working out and weightlifting (even if you aren't involved in sports), and the use of supplements to "bulk up." Parents might tell themselves their kids' spending hours in a gym working on "six-pack abs" is better than hanging out on the corner and drinking six-packs, but a true case of bigorexia can be just as ruinous to a boy's health and future.

4 Dr. Harrison Pope, co-author of *The Adonis Complex,* a helpful book on male body obsession, says parents should look at the world through their sons' eyes. "Boys are fed a diet of 'ideal' male bodies, from Batman to the stars of the WWF," he says. "So parents need to tell their boys—starting when they are small—that they don't have to look like these characters." Pope, himself an avid weightlifter, says parents should also educate themselves and their sons on the uses and dangers of supplements such as adrenal hormones. "Any kid can go into a store and buy 'andro' [formerly Mark McGwire's bulk-up drug, androstenedione] legally," he says, "but we still don't know what long-term use will do to a boy's health." Pope believes that up to 15% of high school boys use andro, often in dangerous mega-doses.

5 A large percentage will then move on to anabolic steroids.

6 Boys are hampered by their tendency to stay silent about their anxieties, but parents can help them open up by asking questions rather than making statements. The media are full of unattainable images, so an Abercrombie and Fitch or a Gap ad can spark a discussion about what the proper build for a boy is. Parents of kids involved in such weight-sensitive sports as wrestling should know that crash dieting can trigger health problems and eating disorders.

7 Danger signs include extreme mood changes, compulsive behavior, and depression. Parents of very young boys can take a page from the Barbie playbook by asking their sons to compare muscle-bound action figures with real people they know, like Mom and Dad. When we did this in our house, it got a big laugh—maybe too big. But at least it's a start.

Thinking about the Argument

1. According to the author, why is G.I. Joe a bad physical role model for young boys? How does this toy contribute to childhood obesity?
2. What kinds of evidence does the author cite to validate her claim? Do you find it adequate? Why or why not?
3. What solutions does Dickinson suggest for dealing with this image problem?

Responding to the Argument

1. Do you think that toys can influence a child's self-image? Explain.
2. Evaluate Dickinson's evidence. What are the strengths and weaknesses of the information she presents? What other sorts of evidence might have been used?
3. How effectively did the author use logic to appeal to her audience? How effectively did she appeal to authority (either her own or someone else's)? How well did she make an emotional connection with the audience?

Writing about the Argument

1. Identify a toy or other image from popular culture that you believe might contribute to a negative self-image for children. In a detailed paragraph, explain how this image creates a problem.
2. Think of an image in popular culture that you think is a positive role model. In a detailed paragraph, explain why you think this image has a positive influence. If you wish, write this paragraph in the form of a refutation of Dickinson's article.
3. How do images and pervasive ideas in our culture contribute to low self-esteem and obesity trends generally (or do they)? Write an argument exploring this problem.

READING SELECTION

"Obesity: Epidemic or Myth?"

About the Author: Patrick Johnson

Patrick Johnson teaches biology at Washtenaw Community College in Ann Arbor, Michigan. He is a clinical exercise physiologist who writes about health and fitness. In addition to articles in professional journals, he has written for *Skeptic* and the *Skeptical Inquirer,* where this piece appeared in 2005.

Before You Read

1. What does the title of this essay suggest to you? How would you define *epidemic?* How would you define *myth?*
2. Do you think people are getting fatter in America? If so, is this trend a problem? Why or why not?
3. What does the title of the magazine in which this essay originally appeared, the *Skeptical Inquirer,* suggest about the nature of the target audience? What might the target audience profile indicate about what the essay might argue?
4. Look at the subtitles and illustrations provided with this article. What do they suggest about the argument's parts and claims?
5. What claim do you think Johnson will make in this argument?

Obesity: Epidemic or Myth?

1 You have probably heard that we are in the midst of an obesity epidemic. The Centers for Disease Control and Prevention (CDC) has been fervently warning that we are in imminent danger from our expanding waistlines since the beginning of this decade. However, evidence has recently emerged indicating that the CDC's warnings were based on questionable data that resulted in exaggerated risks.

2 This new evidence has led to a hostile backlash of sorts against the CDC. The editors of the *Baltimore Sun* recently called the earlier estimates the "Chicken Little Scare of 2004." The Center for Consumer Freedom, a group that has long been critical of the CDC, declared unequivocally on its website and in print ads in several newspapers around the country that the obesity scare was a myth. Even Jay Leno poked fun at the CDC in one of his *Tonight Show* monologues, making the observation that "not only are we fat. . . . We can't do math either." Not everybody believes the "new" data, however. Cable talkshow host Bill Maher commented during an episode of his show *Real Time with Bill Maher* about it being a shame that lobbyists were able to manipulate the CDC into reducing the estimated risk.

3 So which is it? Are we in imminent danger, or is the whole concept a myth? Looking at the scientific evidence it is clear that the extreme views on either side of the argument are incorrect. There is no doubt that many of our concerns about obesity are alarmist and exaggerated, but it is also apparent that there is a real health risk associated with it.

The Controversy

4 Between 1976 and 1991 the prevalence of overweight and obesity in the United States increased by about 31 percent (Heini and Weinsier 1997), then between 1994 and 2000 it increased by an-

other 24 percent (Flegal et al. 2002). This trend, according to a 2004 analysis, shows little sign of slowing down (Hedley et al. 2004). The fact that more of us are getting fatter all the time raises a significant public health concern. The CDC began calling the problem an epidemic in the beginning of this decade as the result of research that estimated 280,000 annual deaths as a consequence of obesity (Allison et al. 1999). Since then there has been a strong media campaign devoted to convincing Americans to lose weight. In 2003, Dr. Julie Gerberding, the director of the CDC, made a speech claiming that the health impact of obesity would be worse than the influenza epidemic of the early twentieth century or the black plague of the Middle Ages. In 2004 the campaign reached a fever pitch when a report was released that increased the estimate of obesity-related deaths to 400,000 (Mokdad et al. 2004). Finally, in March of this year, a report appeared in the *New England Journal of Medicine* that predicted a decline in life expectancy in the United States as a direct result of obesity (Olshansky et al. 2005).

5 Despite the assertions that obesity is causing our society great harm, however, many scientists and activist groups have disputed the level of danger that it actually poses. Indeed, a recent analysis presented in the *Journal of the American Medical Association* (*JAMA*) by Katherine Flegal of the CDC and her colleagues calls the severity of the dangers of excess body fat into question, indicating that the number of overweight and obesity-related deaths is actually about 26,000—about one fifteenth the earlier estimate of 400,000 (Flegal et al. 2005).

6 There is little argument about the fact that, as a nation, more of us are fatter than ever before; the disagreement lies in the effect that this has on our health. The campaign to convince us to lose weight gained much of its momentum in 2004; not only were there high-profile public health initiatives devoted to stopping the obesity epidemic, but the idea had pervaded popular culture as well. Movies like Morgan Spurlock's *Super Size Me* were the topic of many a discussion, and there were regular news reports about the dangers of too much fat.

7 During this campaign, however, there were some notable dissenters. Paul Ernsberger, a professor of nutrition at Case Western Reserve University, has been doing research since the 1980s that led him to assert that obesity is not the cause of ill health but rather the effect of sedentary living and poor nutrition, which are the actual causes. Another prominent researcher, Steven Blair, director of the Cooper Institute of Aerobics Research in Dallas, Texas, has been an author on several studies indicating that the risks associated with obesity can be significantly reduced if one engages in regular physical activity, even if weight loss is not present. According to Blair, weight loss should not be ignored but a greater focus should be placed on physical activity and good nutrition. Both Ernsberger and Blair indicated to me that they thought the new research by Flegal and her colleagues provides a more accurate picture of the mortality risk associated with obesity.

8 While scientists like Ernsberger and Blair have been presenting their conclusions in the scientific forum, others have taken a more inflammatory approach. In his 2004 book, *The Obesity Myth,* Paul Campos argues that the public health problem we have associated with obesity is a myth and further claims that our loathing of fat has damaged our culture. The most antagonistic group, however, is the Center for Consumer Freedom (CCF) (www.consumerfreedom.com), which implies that the obesity epidemic is a conspiracy between the pharmaceutical industries and the public health establishment to create a better market for weight-loss drugs. Numerous articles on the organization's website bash several of the most prominent obesity researchers who have disclosed financial ties to the pharmaceutical industries. Paul Ernsberger echoed this sentiment. He told me that the inflated mortality

statistics were all based on the work of David Allison, a well-known pharmacoeconomics expert. "These experts create cost-benefit analyses which are part of all drug applications to the PDA. These self-serving analyses start by exaggerating as much as possible the cost to society of the ailment to be treated (obesity in the case of weight-loss drugs). The risks associated with the new drug are severely underestimated, which results in an extremely favorable risk-benefit analysis, which is almost never realized once the drug is on the market. Experts who can produce highly favorable risk-benefit analyses are very much in demand, however."

9 The claims made by the CCF are given some credence by Ernsberger's corroboration; however, there is a noteworthy problem with their own objectivity. On their website they present themselves as a consumer-minded libertarian group that exists to "promote personal responsibility and protect consumer choices." Upon closer examination, however, it becomes evident that the CCF is an advocacy group for restaurants and food companies, which have as much to gain by the threat of obesity being a myth as the pharmaceutical industry does by the danger being dire.

10 It is clear that there are agenda-determined interests on both sides of the issue. Therefore, the best way to discern what is necessary for good health is to shift our focus away from the sensational parts of the controversy and look at the science itself.

Current Science and Obesity Risks

11 In their recent article, Katherine Flegal and her colleagues (2005) point out that the earlier mortality estimates were based on analyses that were methodologically flawed because in their calculations the authors used adjusted relative risks in an equation that was developed for unadjusted relative risk. This, according to Flegal's group, meant that the old estimates only partially accounted for confounding factors. The older estimates, furthermore, "did not account for variation by age in the relation of body weight to mortality, and did not include measures of uncertainty in the form of [standard errors] or confidence intervals." These authors also point out that the previous estimates relied on studies that had notable limitations: "Four of six included only older data (two studies ended follow-up in the 1970s and two in the 1980s), three had only self-reported weight and height, three had data only from small geographic areas, and one study included only women. Only one data set, the National Health and Nutrition Examination Survey I, was nationally representative" (Flegal et al. 2005). In their current investigation, Flegal's group addressed this problem by using data only from nationally representative samples with measured heights and weights. Further, they accounted for confounding variables and included standard errors for the estimates.

12 Obesity was determined in this analysis using each subject's body mass index, which is a simple height-to-weight ratio. A BMI of 18 to 24 is considered to be the normal weight, 25–29 is considered overweight, and 30 and above is considered obese. The data from this study indicated that people who were underweight experienced 33,746 more deaths than normal-weight people, and that people who were overweight or obese experienced 25,814 more deaths than the normal-weight folks. This estimate is being reported in the popular media as being one-fifteenth the earlier estimate of 400,000. However, conflating the categories of overweight and obesity this way is misleading.

13 At first glance, it appears that underweight poses a bigger threat to our health than overweight and obesity, and that the earlier estimates were profoundly exaggerated. However, in this study the people who fit into the obese category actually experienced 111,909 excess deaths compared to normal-weight subjects. In contrast, those who were categorized as overweight

experienced 86,094 fewer deaths than those who were normal weight. The figure of 25,815 is the difference between the obesity deaths and the overweight survivals. In the original study by David Allison and his colleagues (Allison et al. 1999), it is actually estimated that 280,000 deaths result from overweight and obesity and that 80 percent, or 224,000, of these deaths occurred in people who were in the obese category. However, the study by Mokdad and colleagues (2004), using the same methods developed by Allison et al., estimated 400,000 obesity-related deaths, and subsequently fueled much of the recent fervor surrounding the obesity epidemic. In this study, no distinction was made between overweight and obesity and the authors failed to distinguish between obesity, physical inactivity, and poor diet. All of these variables were simply lumped together.

14 A few things become clearer after examining the data. First, it appears that our categories are mislabeled; being classified as overweight appears to give one an advantage (statistically, anyway) over those who are in the ideal weight range.[1] Moreover, it is inappropriate to consider overweight and obese as one group. Despite the current hype, the initial overestimation by Allison and his group was not as exaggerated as is being publicized; compared to that study, the new estimate is actually about half of the old number. Finally, it is apparent; that many at the CDC were simply confirming their own biases when they accepted the estimate by Mokdad et al. The categories in that study—that was, intriguingly, co-authored by CDC director Julie Gerberding, which may provide some insight into why it was so readily accepted—were far too broad to provide useful information. The fact that this flaw was ignored shows how easy it is to accept evidence that supports our preconceived notions or our political agendas.

15 There is another problem inherent in all of the above mortality estimates. They are based on epidemiological data that show correlation but leave us guessing as to causation. Various factors are interrelated with increased mortality—obesity, inactivity, poor nutrition, smoking, and so on. Yet, without carefully controlled experiments, it is hard to determine which factors cause—and which are symptoms of—poor health. This is a difficult limitation to overcome, however, because we can't recruit subjects and have them get fat to see if they get sick and/or die sooner. Most institutional review boards would not approve that sort of research, and furthermore I can't imagine that there would be a large pool of subjects willing to participate. There are, however, observational data that were collected with fitness in mind, which help to clarify the picture somewhat.

16 In 1970 researchers at the Cooper Institute for Aerobics Research in Dallas, Texas, began to gather data for a longitudinal study that was called, pragmatically enough, the Aerobics Center Longitudinal Study (ACLS). This study looked at a variety of different variables to estimate the health risks and benefits of certain behaviors and lifestyle choices. What set this study apart from other large-scale observational studies, however, was that instead of relying on self-reporting for variables like exercise habits, [the researchers] tested fitness levels directly by way of a graded exercise test (GXT). A GXT requires a person to walk on a treadmill as long as he or she can with increases in speed and incline at regular intervals. This is the most reliable way we know of to assess a person's physical fitness.

17 With an accurate measure of the subjects' fitness levels, researchers at the Cooper Institute

1. This is not the first time this has been shown. The following studies are also large scale epidemiological studies that have found the overweight category is where the longest lifespan occurs: Waaler H. T. 1984. Height and weight and mortality: The Norwegian experience. *Acta Medico. Scandinavica Supplementum* 679, 1–56; and Hirdes J., and W. Forbes. 1992. The importance of social relationships, socioeconomic status and health practices with respect to mortality in healthy Ontario males. *Journal of Clinical Epidemiology* 45: 175–182.

have been able to include fitness as a covariate with obesity. Analysis of the data obtained in the ACLS shows that there is a risk associated with obesity, but when you control for physical activity, much of that risk disappears (Church et al. 2004; Katzmarzyk et al. 2004; Katzmarzyk et al. 2004; Lee et al. 1999). One study showed that obese men who performed regular exercise had a lower risk of developing cardiovascular disease than lean men who were out of shape (Lee et al. 1999).

18 Steven Blair, who runs the Cooper Institute and was an author on all four of the above-mentioned studies, however, does not think obesity should be ignored. "I do think obesity is a public health problem, although I also think that the primary cause of the obesity epidemic is a declining level of average daily energy expenditure . . . it will be unfortunate if it is now assumed that we should ignore obesity. I do not think that the [health] risk of obesity is a myth, although it has been overestimated." Blair believes that a focus on good nutrition and increased physical activity rather than on weight loss will better serve us.

19 In spite of the fact that there are virtually no controlled clinical trials examining the effects of obesity in people, we can make some inferences from animal research. Investigations performed by Ernsberger and his colleagues have shown that, over time, weight cycling (temporary weight loss followed by a regain of that weight, otherwise known as yo-yoing) in obese laboratory animals increases blood pressure, enlarges the heart, damages the kidneys, increases abdominal fat deposits, and promotes further weight gain (Ernsberger and Koletsky 1993; Ernsberger et al. 1996; Ernsberger and Koletsky 1999). This indicates that the yo-yo effect of crash dieting may be the cause of many of the problems we attribute to simply being fat.

20 Even though there is a health risk from being too fat, you can eliminate much of the potential risk by exercising. Moreover, it is probably a bad idea to jump from diet to diet given the negative consequences the yo-yo effect can have. According to another study published in *JAMA*, the risk of cardiovascular disease has declined across all BMI groups over the past forty years as the result of better drugs (Gregg et al. 2005).

21 None of this means, however, that we should simply abandon our attempts to maintain a healthy weight; obese people had twice the incidence of hypertension compared to lean people and, most significantly, there has been (according to the above study) a 55 percent increase in diabetes[2] that corresponds to the increase in obesity. So while we are better at dealing with the problem once it occurs, it is still better to avoid developing the problem in the first place.

Condemning the CDC

22 Whatever side of the argument you are on, it is apparent that many in the CDC acted irresponsibly. However, despite the fact that the initial, exaggerated estimate came from people at the CDC, we should keep in mind that so did the corrected number. While this can be frustrating to the casual observer, it is also a testament to the corrective power of the scientific method.

23 Science is about provisional truths that can be changed when evidence indicates that they should be. The fact that scientific information is available to the public is its greatest strength. Most of us, for whatever reason—whether it's self-interest or self-delusion—don't view our own ideas as critically as we should. The fact that scientific ideas are available for all to see allows those who disagree to disprove them. This is what has happened at the CDC; the most current study has addressed the flaws of the earlier studies. It is true that many of those in power at the CDC uncritically embraced the earlier estimates and overreacted, or worse simply accepted research that was flawed because it bolstered

2. This is for both diagnosed and undiagnosed individuals.

their agendas. But that failure lies with the people involved, not with the CDC as an institution or with the science itself.

24 The evidence still shows that morbid obesity is associated with an increased likelihood of developing disease and suffering from early mortality, but it also shows that those who are a few pounds overweight don't need to panic. What's more, it is clear that everyone, fat or thin, will benefit from regular exercise regardless of whether they lose weight.

25 The lesson to be learned from this controversy is that rational moderation is in order. Disproving one extreme idea does not prove the opposite extreme. As Steven Blair told me, "It is time to focus our attention on the key behaviors of eating a healthful diet (plenty of fruits and veggies, a lot of whole grains, and not too much fat and alcohol) and being physically active every day."

References

Allison, D. B., et al. 1999. Annual deaths attributable to obesity in the United States. *Journal of the American Medical Association* 282:1530–1538.

Blaif, S., and J. Morrow, Jr. 2005. Comments on U.S. dietary guidelines. *Journal of Physical Activity and Health* 2:137–142.

Campos, P. 2004. *The Obesity Myth.* New York: Gotham Books.

Church, T., et al. 2004. Exercise capacity and body composition as predictor of mortality among men with diabetes. *Diabetes Care* 27(1):83–88.

Ernsberger, P., and R. Koletsky. 1993. Biomedical rationale for a wellness approach to obesity: An alternative to a focus on weight loss. *Journal of Social Issues* 55(2): 221–259.

Ernsberger, P., and R. Koletsky. 1999. Weight cycling and mortality: Support from animal studies. *Journal of the American Medical Association* 269:1116.

Ernsberger, P., et al. 1994. Refeeding hypertension in obese spontaneously hypertensive rats. *Hypertension* 24:699–705.

Ernsberger, P., et al. 1996. Consequences of weight cycling in obese spontaneously hypertensive rats. *American Journal of Physiology: Regulatory, Integrative and Comparative Physiology* 270:R864–R872.

Flegal, K. M., et al. 2000. *Journal of the American Medical Association* 288(14):1723–1727.

Flegal, K., et al. 2005. Excess deaths associated with underweight, overweight, and obesity. *Journal of the American Medical Association* 293(15):1861–1867.

Gregg, E., et al. 2005. Secular trends in cardiovascular disease risk factors according to body mass index in U.S. adults. *Journal of the American Medical Association* 293(15): 1868–1874.

Hedley, A., et al. 2004. Prevalence of overweight and obesity among U.S. children, adolescents, and adults, 1999–2000. *Journal of the American Medical Association* 291: 2847–2850.

Heini, E., and R. L. Weinsier. 1997. Divergent trends in obesity and fat intake patterns: The American paradox. *Journal of the American Medical Association* 102(3): 254–264.

Katzmarzyk, P., et al. 2004. Metabolic syndrome, obesity, and mortality. *Diabetes Gm?* 28(2):391–397.

Katzmarzyk, T. Church, and S. Blair. 2004. Cardiorespiratory fitness attenuates the effects of the metabolic syndrome on all-cause and cardiovascular disease mortality in men. *Archives of Internal Medicine* 164:1092–1097.

Lee, C. D., S. Blair, and A. Jackson. 1999. Cardiorespiratory fitness, body composition, and all-cause and cardiovascular disease mortality in men. *American Journal of Clinical Nutrition* 69:373–380.

Mark, D. A. 2005. Deaths attributable to obesity. *Journal of the American Medical Association* 293(15):1918–1919.

Mokdad, A. H., et al. 2004. Actual causes of death in the United States. *Journal of the American Medical Association* 291:1238–1245.

Olshansky, S. J., et al. 2005. A potential decline in life expectancy in the United States in the 21st century. *New England Journal of Medicine* 352(11):1138–1145.

Thinking about the Argument

1. Does the author believe that the obesity epidemic is real? How does he define *epidemic,* if at all?
2. What is the author's thesis? What supporting claims does he use to back it up?
3. Why does Johnson believe that the "obesity epidemic" is a controversial issue?
4. Why does the writer distrust the Center for Consumer Freedom? Check out this group's website. Do you find his analysis to be correct? Why or why not?
5. Summarize the author's criticism of the Centers for Disease Control and Prevention's statements regarding obesity. After investigating the CDC's information online, explain why you do or do not agree with his assessment.

Responding to the Argument

1. Does the author represent a point of view other than his own? How does this contribute to—or detract from—the effectiveness of his argument?
2. The author takes a moderate stance on the obesity epidemic. Where do you stand on this issue? Do you think the epidemic is "hype," or is it as serious as some medical officials say? Explain.
3. The author presents his argument mostly in the form of a refutation. How effective is this approach, and why do you hold this opinion?
4. What sort of evidence could the author have provided that he did not?
5. Where is Johnson's argument weakest, and where is it strongest? Explain.

Writing about the Argument

1. Write a critique of the article. Discuss at least one way that Johnson argues effectively, and one way that he argues poorly. If you were to attempt to improve his argument, how would you change it and why?
2. Write a synthesis comparing this article to Dickinson's essay. Which thesis do you most strongly agree with? Which article presents the best evidence? Which is the better argument?
3. Pretend that you have to present a talk to a group of overweight teenagers to explain why and how they should lose weight. Using Johnson's article as a basis for your talk—and keeping the interests and attention level of your audience in mind—write a transcript of this talk.

READING SELECTION

"Rethinking Weight: Hey, Maybe It's Not a Weakness. Just Maybe . . . It's a Disease"

ABOUT THE AUTHOR: AMANDA SPAKE

It would probably be easier to comment on what Amanda Spake has not written than to list what she has written. As a journalist specializing in health and family issues, she has written widely about the obesity epidemic, especially as it relates to children and family issues. This article first appeared in *U.S. News and World Report* in February 2004.

BEFORE YOU READ

1. Often titles to articles provide clues about an essay's main point. What claim do you think Spake will make in this article?
2. Who do you think reads *U.S. News and World Report*? Why would its audience be interested in this topic? What prior assumptions might this readership make about the topic?
3. Glance over the article, looking especially at the beginning and the end. What do the main divisions of the argument appear to be?

Rethinking Weight: Hey, Maybe It's Not a Weakness. Just Maybe . . . It's a Disease

1 Maria Pfisterer has never in her life been skinny. The Arlington, Texas, mother of three was at her slimmest at age 18, when she married Fred, an Air Force sergeant. But she was plump, not seriously fat. She first became seriously overweight at age 21, when she gained about 70 pounds during her first pregnancy. By the time she delivered her daughter Jordan, now 14, she was carrying over 200 pounds on her 5-foot, 2-inch frame.

2 Over the past 14 years, Pfisterer has tried every weight-loss strategy imaginable: She has taken the (now banned) appetite-suppressing drug combo fen-phen (she lost 60 pounds only to regain it during her second pregnancy). She went on a doctor-prescribed and -supervised low-calorie diet (she lost 10 pounds but regained it). She has been enrolled in Jenny Craig, Weight Watchers, Curves, and a variety of quick-weight-loss fads. All resulted in a little lost and more regained. She has taken antidepressants, reputed to have weight loss as a side effect. They didn't for her. She would love to get into one of those intensive medical weight-loss programs, but she can't afford the $4000-plus price tag. So she does what she can. "If I lose weight, it seems like I always go back up to that same 197 to 202 range," she says. "I just don't know how to keep it off."

3 Pfisterer isn't alone. A majority of Americans—now 64 percent—are overweight or obese and struggling to conquer their expanding waistlines before their fat overtakes their health and makes them sick or kills them. At the heart of this obesity epidemic is a debate over whether obesity is a biological "disease" and should be treated like any other life-threatening illness—cancer, heart disease—or whether it is simply a risk factor for those killers. The stakes are high

because the answer may determine who gets treated for obesity, what treatments are available, who pays for treatment, and, ultimately, who stays healthy.

4 New understandings of the biology of obesity are driving the debate. "I think there's enough data now relating to mechanisms of food intake regulation that suggest obesity is a biologically determined process," says Xavier Pi-Sunyer, director of the Obesity Research Center at St. Luke's–Roosevelt Hospital in New York City. And many national and international health organizations—from the National Institutes of Health (NIH) to the World Health Organization—agree. The WHO has listed obesity as a disease in its International Classification of Diseases since 1979. In fact, the organization recently called on member states to adopt programs to encourage a reduction of fat and sugar in the global diet. The recommendation did not sit well with the U.S. food industry or with some within the Bush administration, who still maintain the obesity epidemic can be reversed by individuals taking more personal responsibility and making better lifestyle choices. Many health insurers agree. "For a wide number of people in this country the question is: How do you motivate people to make changes in diet and increase physical activity?" says Susan Pisano of the Health Insurance Association of America.

5 The reason governments, insurance companies, and others still take such positions, says Pi-Sunyer, is that "they are worried they will have to reimburse doctors and patients for treatment. And now, you have such a huge number of people needing treatment." On any given day, about 29 percent of men and 44 percent of women are trying to lose weight, and presumably a large percentage of those would love to be offered medically supervised treatment if it were covered in their health insurance plan.

6 Instead, they pay out of pocket for a $33 billion commercial diet industry—and keep getting fatter. The number of people who are severely obese—that is, those with a body mass index of 40 or above or who are more than 100 pounds overweight—is growing two times as fast as is obesity generally. From 1986 to 2000, the prevalence of Americans reporting a BMI of 40 or above quadrupled, from about 1 in 200 adults to 1 in 50. People who are severely obese generally have more weight-related illnesses and require more expensive treatments than do those who are merely "too fat."

Fat's High Price

7 A new study by RTI International and the Centers for Disease Control and Prevention, published this month in the journal *Obesity Research,* shows that the nation is spending about $75 billion a year on weight-related disease. Type II diabetes, heart disease, hypertension, high cholesterol, gallbladder disease and osteoarthritis merely top the list. Almost 80 percent of obese adults have one of these conditions, and nearly 40 percent have two or more.

8 Health care costs for illnesses resulting from obesity now exceed those related to both smoking and problem drinking. About 325,000 deaths a year are attributed to obesity. The trend lines are only expected to get worse, since childhood obesity is also increasing rapidly.

9 Researchers are encouraged by the stance taken by the WHO and NIH, as well as the American Medical Association, the National Academy of Sciences, and the CDC. Says Yale psychologist Kelly Brownell: "The ramifications could be enormous—for opening up better treatments, and to some extent for social attitudes toward people with this problem. When alcoholism was declared a disease, it changed attitudes and reduced the stigma of blame."

10 And to be sure, there is no shortage of stigma and blame when it comes to obesity. Weight discrimination dates back to the early Christian church, which included "gluttony" as one of the seven deadly sins. Obesity was viewed as the outward manifestation of the "sin" of

overindulgence. Most overweight adults have suffered ridicule, self-consciousness, or depression, particularly if they were obese as children or adolescents. Severely obese patients frequently report workplace discrimination. One woman told researchers: "They put my desk in the back office where no one could see me."

11 Prejudice against the obese stems from the widely held belief that getting fat—and certainly staying fat—results from a failure of willpower, a condition that could be remedied if obese people simply made a personal choice to eat less. But to most obesity experts this notion of personal choice is downright nutty. "Who would choose to be obese?" asks Rudolph Leibel, a Columbia University geneticist and a noted obesity researcher. "Telling someone they've decided to become obese is like saying, 'You've decided to give yourself a brain tumor.'"

12 Increasingly, researchers are demonstrating that obesity is controlled by a powerful biological system of hormones, proteins, neurotransmitters, and genes that regulate fat storage and body weight and tell the brain when, what, and how much to eat. "This is not debatable," says Louis Aronne, director of the Comprehensive Weight Control Program at New York–Presbyterian Hospital and president-elect of the North American Association for the Study of Obesity. "Once people gain weight, then these biological mechanisms, which we're beginning to understand, develop to prevent people from losing weight. It's not someone fighting 'willpower.' The body resists weight loss."

13 This wonder of natural chemical engineering evolved over centuries to protect humans against famine and assure reproduction of the species. "The idea that nature would leave this system to a matter of 'choice' is naive," says Arthur Frank, director of George Washington University's Weight Management Program. "Eating is largely driven by signals from fat tissue, from the gastrointestinal tract, the liver. All those organs are sending information to the brain to eat or not to eat. So, saying to an obese person who wants to lose weight, 'All you have to do is eat less,' is like saying to a person suffering from asthma, 'All you have to do is breathe better.'"

14 When Maria Pfisterer looks at her family, she sees her future—and it is frightening. Her father, a diabetic with congestive heart failure and hypertension, weighs nearly 400 pounds, and at age 60 he can scarcely move. Her older sister is also obese and suffers from hypertension. Both Maria and her sister worry they will eventually develop diabetes like their dad.

15 "My daughter Jordan is very heavy. She's struggling already with weight, and if she gets any more sedentary, I worry what will happen to her," says Pfisterer. "I'm trying to teach her to eat better and keep active. She's into dance, but she'll say, 'I'm the fattest kid there.' It breaks my heart."

16 Pfisterer herself says she does not eat a lot and is always on the go. "I don't eat half gallons of ice cream or bags of chips. But if I lose a little, I regain. I think genetics have a lot to do with it."

Studies of Twins

17 Leibel, director of the division of molecular genetics at Columbia University College of Physicians and Surgeons, has spent a career documenting what Pfisterer knows intuitively. He says, "I believe there are strong genetic factors that determine susceptibility to obesity." Obesity does not result from a single gene, he explains, but rather a variety of genes that interact with environmental influences to increase one's chance of becoming obese. In studies of adult twins, who share many or all of the same genes, BMI, body composition, and other measures of fatness appear to be 20 to 70 percent inherited.

18 Still, biology is not destiny. Overweight results from one thing: eating more food than one burns in physical activity. Genes simply facilitate becoming fat. "I think the primary problem is on the food intake side," Leibel adds. "There are multiple genes involved in that intake

process, and there is good reason to believe that nature and evolution have selected for ingestion of large amounts of food."

19 But even when limitless food is available, not everyone gets fat. In a series of studies of adult twins in Quebec who ate a high-calorie diet designed to produce weight gain, results between sets of twins were vastly different. Some twin pairs gained three times as much weight and fat as others. "We know there are genetic factors," says Jules Hirsch, professor emeritus at Rockefeller University, "but obesity may be a multistep process." Hirsch says an overabundance of fat cells leading to obesity may be the result of gene–environmental interactions that occur in infancy or in utero, leading to vastly different responses to food in adulthood. The story of the offspring of women who survived the Dutch winter famine of 1944–1945 may be a case in point. Babies born to women who suffered severe undernutrition early in their pregnancies tended to have more fat and become obese more readily as adults. But the offspring of women who were undernourished late in pregnancy tended to be leaner and have less fat as adults. Clearly, says Hirsch, there is a great deal more to learn about how obesity develops.

20 Even scientists who basically accept that obesity is a sophisticated biological problem feel that treatment has to consider the powerful roles of social organization and psychology. Take the case of the bottomless soup bowls.

21 University of Illinois nutrition and marketing professor Brian Wansink sat student volunteers in front of bowls of tomato soup in his lab and told them they were involved in a "taste test." Some of the students' bowls were normal. The others had bowls that automatically refilled from a hidden tube in the bottom. The students with the bottomless bowls ate an average of about 40 percent more soup before their brain told them they were full. "Biology has made us efficient at storing fat," says Wansink. "But obesity is not just biology; it's psychology. We're not good at tracking how much we eat. So we use cues—we eat until the plate is empty, or the soup is gone, or the TV show is over."

22 Indeed, research shows that people eat more in groups and with friends than they do when dining alone. Simply eating with one other person increases the average amount eaten at meals by 44 percent. Meals eaten with large groups of friends tend to be longer in duration and are as much as 75 percent bigger that those eaten alone. Eating with someone, suggests John DeCastro, the author of these studies, probably leads to relaxation and a "disinhibition of restraint."

23 Viewing obesity principally as a biological disease worries Wansink because he fears it will remove personal control and shift blame to someone else. But doctors who treat overweight patients say that thinking of obesity as a disease would simply make more treatment available. Most obesity programs rely on personal responsibility to put into action behavioral techniques designed to achieve greater control over biology. "Most of our treatment is still based on modifying choice," says GWU's Frank. "But underneath it all you've got to recognize why it is so difficult to eat less and lose weight. It doesn't make it easier, but it takes it out of the world of willful misconduct."

Frauds

24 The biggest dilemma overweight people face is the world of largely mediocre, misleading, useless, or downright dangerous devices, diet programs, supplements, and drugs promoted to reduce fat. "The treatment of obesity is littered with a history of abuses," says NAASO's Aronne. "Every infomercial out there about weight is damaging people because it's giving them an unrealistic view of what can be done." Most university- and hospital-based weight-loss programs produce a 10 percent loss of body weight in six months. This is more than enough to reduce the incidence of Type II diabetes by 58 percent and lower blood pressure in borderline hypertensives.

But it is not enough to make a fat person as thin as a Hollywood celebrity. Coverage of obesity by health insurers might bring science and sanity to the chaos of weight loss, where, as Aronne puts it, “ethical treatments are competing in an unethical marketplace.”

25 But clinicians acknowledge that weight-loss successes are modest. “To be frank, a lot of the treatment has not been very effective,” says Pi-Sunyer. He points out that there are currently two drugs approved for long-term treatment of obesity, sibutramine and orlistat. Their effect is modest, and their cost is high, about $100 a month. “So for people to pay that amount, they would like to see more impressive results.” Two drugs approved for treating epilepsy, topiramate and zonisamide, are being tested to treat obesity, but the jury is still out on them. “So that’s an out for the insurers,” says Pi-Sunyer. “They can say, ‘Unless you have a treatment that takes weight off and keeps it off, then why pay for it?’ It would be a much stronger argument if we had a more proven treatment.”

26 What’s standing in the way? Basically funding for research. The American Obesity Association reports that NIH funding for research on obesity is less than one sixth that spent on AIDS. “Given the nature of the problem and the side effects,” says Pi-Sunyer, “We’re spending a pittance.”

27 The health insurance industry argues that obesity treatments can’t be covered because there is no evidence of effectiveness. Critics counter that the same argument could apply to a lot of complicated diseases. “We don’t have a good way of treating Alzheimer’s disease,” says GWU’s Frank, “and we don’t have a particularly good way of treating AIDS either. We have a health insurance system based on illness, not treatment effectiveness. Why should obesity be the one disease that’s subjected to this cost-effectiveness standard?”

28 About half of the $75 billion yearly price tag for obesity is covered by taxpayers in Medicare and Medicaid funds. These government health plans are debating right now whether the plans should cover obesity treatment. Currently, only in cases of severe obesity will government and some private insurers reimburse doctors for surgery to reduce girth.

29 But not always. Samantha Moore, a 26-year-old Maine woman who weighs nearly 400 pounds, was recently turned down a third time for gastric bypass surgery. Even though she has been dieting all her life, her insurer denied surgery because she has not made enough “medically supervised” attempts at weight loss. Does the insurer pay for medically supervised weight loss? “No,” says Moore. “It’s shocking to me that the insurance company keeps saying, essentially, ‘You’re not sick enough to get this surgery.’ I think they’re putting off a decision because if I wait much longer, I’ll be too sick to get the surgery.”

Fat or Fit?

30 Not all scientists agree that labeling obesity “a disease” will improve the situation for people like Pfisterer or Moore. Stephen Ball, an exercise physiologist at the University of Missouri, says, “If we call obesity a disease, then anything that reduces one’s fatness or lowers BMI would be a successful treatment, such as liposuction or a very low-calorie diet, where we know these are not healthy. By the same token, if you don’t lose weight with an exercise program but your blood glucose becomes normal and cholesterol improves, then that could be considered a failure, because it didn’t reduce weight. Fitness is a more important indicator of health outcomes than fatness.”

31 Indeed, Steven Blair at the Cooper Institute in Dallas has shown that cardiovascular fitness as measured on a treadmill test is a better predictor of mortality and illness than BMI “I’m convinced . . . that people who are active or fit but in a high BMI group have lower death rates from all causes—cancer, heart disease, diabetes—than

the sedentary and unfit in the normal or lean BMI category. Even among women in our study with BMIs of 37, 20 percent did well enough on the treadmill test to be considered fit. We're obsessed with weight, but where has that gotten us?"

32 Ultimately, if better and more accessible treatments are not offered to obese Americans, the cost not only of obesity but of treatment and health insurance will escalate. The number of people undergoing surgery doubled from 2001 to 2003, in part because people are becoming more obese but also because many want medical help with weight loss and can't find any other treatment health insurers will cover.

33 Frustrated with her options and limited ability to pay for treatment, about six months ago Maria Pfisterer began to explore the possibility of gastric bypass surgery. She is not 100 pounds overweight, and her BMI is not over 40—generally the criteria physicians use for evaluating candidates who would benefit from surgery. Gastric bypass surgery is an irreversible procedure in which the size of the stomach is reduced and the small intestine is bypassed to produce rapid weight loss in people whose fat is putting their lives in danger. Recovery is long, complication rates are high, side effects are bothersome, and it's major surgery—people die from it. But Pfisterer learned through obesity-help.com, a website offering advice to the obese, that her insurer might pay for surgery, given her family history.

34 "For people like me, who are considered on the low end for surgery, there are other options that might be better," she says. "But I can't take advantage of them unless health insurance starts to pay for them."

Thinking about the Argument

1. The author's thesis, at least in part, is that obesity is a disease. How adequately does she explain how obesity qualifies as a disease?
2. Why are insurance companies interested in whether obesity can be defined as a disease?
3. What does the author say to indicate that weight loss is biologically driven rather than a matter of willpower?
4. According to some of the author's sources, what will be the result if obesity research is not funded?

Responding to the Argument

1. How effectively does the opening anecdote function in winning your sympathy? Does it make you more or less receptive to the author's viewpoint? Why or why not?
2. Do you believe obesity qualifies as a disease? Explain.
3. Identify at least two distinct types of evidence that the author uses. Explain which is most effective, and why.
4. Do you agree or disagree with the statement that classifying obesity as a disease "will remove personal control and shift blame to someone else"? Why or why not?

WRITING ABOUT THE ARGUMENT

1. Write a paragraph defining *disease*. Write a second paragraph explaining why obesity does or does not meet this definition. For an additional challenge, expand these paragraphs into a definition-based argument.
2. Write a journal entry or a short essay arguing whether insurance companies should be required to fund radical weight-loss procedures for people who are at least 100 pounds overweight.
3. Write a journal entry or a short essay arguing whether weight loss is, or should be, an act of personal willpower. In other words, can a person who is genetically predisposed to being fat control his or her weight with enough determination?

"A Global Epidemic in the Making?"

ABOUT THE AUTHOR: HOWARD MARKEL

Howard Markel is a professor of pediatrics and communicable diseases at the University of Michigan, where he is also director of the Center for the History of Medicine and George E. Wantz Professor of the History of Medicine. He has written numerous articles and books on medical history, including *When Germs Travel* (2004) and *The Portable Pediatrician* (2000). Markel writes frequently about children's health issues.

BEFORE YOU READ

1. What does the title imply about the subject matter of this article?
2. The Globalist website title is followed by the slogan "Dedicated to global understanding." How might the interests of this audience be broader and narrower than those of the audience for *U.S. News and World Report?* Why do you think so?
3. Glance over the article and look at the subheadings. What do they suggest about the divisions of the argument and the minor claims that will be presented to support the argumentative thesis?

A Global Epidemic in the Making?

1 In the good old, bad old days, epidemics were fairly straightforward affairs. You "contracted"—read: caught—a deadly germ and became ill rather quickly. Today, epidemics come in many forms, but they are not necessarily infectious in origin—nor speedy in resolution.

A Deadly Threat

2 Witness, for example, the increasingly worldwide epidemics of drug abuse, alcoholism, and school violence. But none of these—with the exception of cigarette smoking—are as deadly or widespread as that of obesity.

3 What is especially insidious about obesity is that bad eating habits are established early in life and extend into adulthood.

READING SELECTION

4 Since 1970, the number of overweight children in the United States has more than doubled. In 2002, more than 20 percent of all preschool children in the United States were overweight.

Fries with That?

5 Worse, about half of them—10 percent of all preschool children—were clinically obese. These numbers alone should make any parent pause before allowing their child to respond to the question, "Would you like fries with that?"

6 Recently, a team of Yale University pediatricians released a study diagnosing glucose intolerance in about 25 percent of the obese children and adolescents. What this means, in layman's terms, is that obese kids are very likely to go on to develop Type II diabetes, one of the leading causes of heart and kidney disease, blindness, and death in the United States today.

A Culture of Snacking

7 Not coincidentally, physicians are reporting an increase in Type II diabetes each year. Moreover, obesity is a major factor in developing heart disease, atherosclerosis, colon cancer, hypertension, strokes, and several other deadly conditions. This year, almost 300,000 Americans will die as a result of being overweight.

8 But there is even more bad news. The United States is leading the way in spreading this epidemic of fat to children around the globe. As a result, Americans may before long have to worry about something truly unfortunate.

9 In the eyes of the world, the United States is currently considered a leading force for democracy and capitalism worldwide. But there may come a time when the United States is better known as the world's leading purveyor of snacks and high-fat foods.

American Habits

10 In a striking demonstration of the United States as the "land of opportunity," a 1999 Institute of Medicine report on trends among immigrant children showed that, shortly after settling here, these kids' eating habits and diets deteriorated to the level of their U.S.-born counterparts.

11 Nations such as the United Kingdom, Russia, and France—where fast food now reigns—are also reporting a striking increase in childhood obesity.

The Global Epidemic

12 In May 2002, the World Health Organization announced a rise in obesity, diabetes, and heart disease. Remarkably, this occurred not only in affluent developed nations, but also among developing nations in Africa, the Middle East, Latin America, and the Caribbean, where malnutrition was once the major dietary issue.

13 The International Obesity Task Force currently estimates that 22 million of the world's children under five years of age are overweight or obese.

14 The picture is worse for adults. Worldwide, 300 million of us are obese—and at least 750 million are overweight.

Supersize It!

15 Much of this problem is our own doing. We Americans supersize our orders of French fries. We are no longer content to merely order a pizza. Instead, we crave a "pizza, pizza" with a cheese-filled crust. And we consume cholesterol-rich foods with a vengeance.

16 After such repasts, we steadfastly forego physical activity for the sweeter pastures of the television set, video game, or computer terminal. To add insult to injury, our children are merely learning poor health habits from their elders.

17 At the same time, the U.S. fast food industry has aggressively entered into new domestic markets to sell their products. For example, Taco Bell is served in more than 4500 school cafeterias. Other chains are salivating at the prospect of getting some of this profitable action.

Drawing in the Kids

18 The American School Food Service estimates that at least 30 percent of all U.S. public high schools offer some type of name-brand fast food. And more than a third of the hospitals selected as "America's Best" by *U.S. News and World Report* for 2002 boast a fast food outlet on their premises.

19 Even when discounting charitable efforts by the fast food chains, such as the Ronald McDonald Houses—which offer lodging for parents of hospitalized children—these chains are far more adept than the tobacco companies in luring youths to enjoy their products.

20 The crucial difference is that the fast food chains can legally link their wares with toys, games, and movies that draw in the kids.

Who's to Blame?

21 Fast food of course, is hardly the only culprit in our worldwide obesity epidemic—even though the companies' direct and highly targeted marketing to "billions and billions" of children is troubling, to say the least.

22 But the industry is not the only villain in this high-stakes drama. Consumers are big-time culprits, too. That is why it is high time that both fast food purveyors and consumers alike accept a long-known fact: Nutritional health is inversely proportional to the weight of the saturated fat you lift from the plate into your mouth.

»«

THINKING ABOUT THE ARGUMENT

1. Why does Markel call the obesity epidemic "a deadly threat"?
2. When, according to the author, do people obtain poor eating habits?
3. What role has fast food played in the worldwide spread of obesity?
4. According to the author, whose fault is it that people around the world are becoming increasingly overweight?

RESPONDING TO THE ARGUMENT

1. Do you agree that the availability of fast food and other unhealthy eating options has contributed to the "obesity epidemic"?
2. What role do you think advertising might play in weight gain in the United States and abroad? Is it attributable to cultural images (as Dickinson suggests), to advertising, or to the ready availability of unhealthy food?
3. Do you agree with the author's thesis, or is something or someone else to blame for increasing waistlines?
4. What should be done to counteract the "obesity epidemic"?

WRITING ABOUT THE ARGUMENT

1. Write a short paper arguing whether restaurants should be held liable for their patrons' poor eating habits.

READING SELECTION

2. Write a journal entry arguing about what role, if any, advertising plays in encouraging people to develop unhealthy eating habits. Should the advertising companies as well as (or instead of) the restaurants be held liable? Why or why not?
3. Write a refutation of Markel's article.

Issue 2: Stem-Cell Research

In recent years, stem-cell research has moved from an issue of interest only to research scientists to a burgeoning political issue closely linked with abortion. Many people support the idea of stem-cell research, primarily because it may lead to treatments for medical conditions including spinal-cord injury and Alzheimer's disease). Others oppose funding (or even allowing) this kind of research, primarily because they equate stem cells (which are extracted from embryonic cell clusters very early in their development) with human life. In other words, because stem cells have the potential to become embryos (but have not yet developed into embryos), these people view stem cells as babies and feel that they should not be the subjects of experiments in which they can be "killed." This places a definition (what is life?) at the center of the problem.

Online Study Center
Prepare for Class
Stem-Cell Research and Human Cloning

To exacerbate the problem, some people fear that if stem-cell research is not allowed, other countries that allow this research will be on the forefront of a new era of medicine while the United States is left behind. As a result, arguments surrounding the use of stem cells frequently involve (but are not limited to) questions of ethics, definition, evaluation, and proposal.

Considering the Issue of Stem-Cell Research

Working individually or in groups, answer the following questions.

1. What do you already know about stem-cell research? Have you already formed an opinion?
2. How do you feel about using human embryos for medical research? Does it change your opinion to know that some or all of these embryos were destined to be destroyed anyway?
3. To save lives, how far should medical science be allowed to go? Would it change you opinion if the life to be saved belonged to you or to someone you love?
4. Given that public opinion concerning stem-cell research is divided, should the government provide funding for such research? Would it change your opinion to know that other governments are sponsoring this kind of research?

READING SELECTION

"Use the Body's Repair Kit"

ABOUT THE AUTHOR: CHRISTOPHER REEVE

Perhaps best known for playing Superman in a series of films in the 1980s, actor and director Christopher Reeve was paralyzed from the neck down in 1995. While participating in a riding competition, Reeve's thoroughbred, Eastern Express, hesitated at a rail jump, throwing Reeve forward. Because his hands were caught up in the reins, he landed on his head and broke the topmost vertebrae of his spine. Following the accident, Reeve continued to act and direct until his death on October 10, 2004, of heart failure related to his injury. For nine years, Reeve was an advocate for the disabled and lobbied Congress to approve funding for stem-cell research.

BEFORE YOU READ

Consider the cartoon shown at right.

1. If it had a written claim, what might it be? What part of the cartoon serves as evidence to validate the claim?
2. What is the cartoonist's position on stem-cell research? What does he think of the scientists who are involved in such research?
3. From the headnote and your own personal knowledge, what do you know about Christopher Reeve? Have you ever seen any of his films? What is your opinion of him as a celebrity? As an actor? As a person?

CHRISTOPHER REEVE, 1952-2004...

4. Do you believe that a person who suffers from an injury is in a better or a worse position to argue about a treatment from which he or she might benefit?
5. How does your sympathy for Reeve (and others in his condition) affect the way you approach his argument? Do you think his condition might have a *negative* effect on any potential readers? Why?
6. Does your knowledge of Reeve's disability have any effect on your willingness to consider him an authority on this subject? Would you have the same response if a celebrity without disability (say, Angelina Jolie) were to write on this subject?

READING SELECTION

Use the Body's Repair Kit

1 With the life expectancy of average Americans heading as high as 75 to 80 years, it is our responsibility to do everything possible to protect the quality of life of the present and future generations. A critical factor will be what we do with human embryonic stem cells. These cells have the potential to cure diseases and conditions ranging from Parkinson's and multiple sclerosis to diabetes and heart disease, Alzheimer's, Lou Gehrig's disease, even spinal-cord injuries like my own. They have been called the body's self-repair kit.

2 Their extraordinary potential is a recent discovery. And much basic research needs to be done before they can be sent to the front lines in the battle against disease. But no obstacle should stand in the way of responsible investigation of their possibilities. To that end, the work should be funded and supervised by the Federal Government through the National Institutes of Health. That will avoid abuses by for-profit corporations, avoid secrecy and destructive competition between laboratories, and ensure the widest possible dissemination of scientific breakthroughs. Human trials should be conducted either on the NIH campus or in carefully monitored clinical facilities.

3 Fortunately, stem cells are readily available and easily harvested. In fertility clinics, women are given a choice of what to do with unused fertilized embryos: They can be discarded, donated to research, or frozen for future use. Under NIH supervision, scientists should be allowed to take cells only from women who freely consent to their use for research. This process would not be open ended; within one to two years a sufficient number could be gathered and made available to investigators. For those reasons, the ban on federally funded human embryonic stem-cell research should be lifted as quickly as possible.

4 But why has the use of discarded embryos for research suddenly become such an issue? Is it more ethical for a woman to donate unused embryos that will never become human beings, or to let them be tossed away as so much garbage when they could help save thousands of lives?

5 Treatment with stem cells has already begun. They have been taken from umbilical cords and become healthy red cells used as a potential cure for sickle cell anemia. Stem-cell therapy is also being used against certain types of cancer. But those are cells that have significantly differentiated; that is, they are no longer pluripotent, or capable of transforming into other cell types. For the true biological miracles that researchers have only begun to foresee, medical science must turn to undifferentiated stem cells. We need to clear the path for them as rapidly as possible.

6 Controversy over the treatment of certain diseases is nothing new in this country: Witness the overwhelming opposition to government funding of MDs research in the early 1980s. For years the issue was a political football—until a massive grass-roots effort forced legislators to respond. Today, the NIH is authorized to spend approximately $1.8 billion annually on new protocols, and the virus is largely under control in the United States.

7 While we prolong the stem-cell debate, millions continue to suffer. It is time to harness the power of government and go forward.

»«

THINKING ABOUT THE ARGUMENT

1. What is Reeve's claim? What belief or reason does he cite to support his claim?
2. How is Reeve's argument organized? Is it inductive or deductive in structure? How effective is this approach?
3. Do all of his paragraphs have similar methods of organization? (Where are the minor claims placed?) How do you respond to this organization?
4. What sort of evidence does Reeve cite to support his major and minor claims? Are there places in the essay where you find his support to be particularly strong or weak?
5. Does Reeve respond to arguments against stem-cell research? Why do you think this is so?

RESPONDING TO THE ARGUMENT

1. How did your response to Reeve's logic intertwine with your tendency to sympathize (or not) with him as a disabled person? In other words, how did your sympathy for Reeve affect your response to his argument?
2. To what degree do you consider Reeve to be an authority on this topic? Is it to a greater or lesser extent than before you read his article?
3. Has your opinion of stem-cell research changed in any way as a result of reading Reeve's essay? How?

WRITING ABOUT THE ARGUMENT

1. Pretend that you are a member of Congress who must explain to Reeve's widow why you do not support stem-cell research. Using a Rogerian approach, write your response from a sympathetic point of view.
2. Write an essay or journal entry contrasting the strongest and weakest claims that Reeve offers. Discuss the ways in which each claim you have chosen is particularly strong/weak.
3. Prepare a group or class presentation using at least one visual aid (chart, illustration, cartoon) to supplement an argument for or against stem-cell research.

"Should Human Cloning Be Allowed? Yes, Don't Impede Medical Progress"

ABOUT THE AUTHOR: VIRGINIA POSTREL

Virginia Postrel has been an editor of *Reason* magazine and writes regularly for *Forbes*. In her 1998 book, *The Future and Its Enemies: The Growing Conflict over Creativity, Enterprise, and Progress,* Postrel argues that progress results not from conformity to political ideologies of the left and the right, but rather through experiment and discovery—that is, through simple trial and error. In her most recent book, *The Substance of Style: How the Rise of Aesthetic Value Is Remaking Commerce, Cul-*

ture, and Consciousness, Postrel considers how the aesthetics of popular culture contribute to a healthy, progressive society. She also writes frequently for the *New York Times,* the *Los Angeles Times,* the *Wall Street Journal,* the *Washington Post,* and *Wired* magazine. She is a frequent public speaker and a commentator on the impact of science and technology on society. This essay was originally published in the *Wall Street Journal* on December 5, 2001, and was paired with the following essay by Eric Cohen and William Kristol.

Before You Read

1. Based on the books Postrel has written and the magazines she has written for, what would you expect her outlook on progress and technology to be?
2. Do you consider Postrel to be an authoritative source on this topic? Why or why not?
3. Do you think Postrel is biased? How can you tell? How does this affect the attitude with which you approach her article?
4. What does the title of the article tell you about its content?

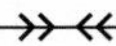

Should Human Cloning Be Allowed? Yes, Don't Impede Medical Progress

1 To many biologists, the recently announced creation of a cloned human embryo was no big deal. True, researchers at Advanced Cell Technology replaced the nucleus of a human egg with the genetic material of another person. And they got that cloned cell to start replicating. But their results were modest. It took 71 eggs to produce a single success, and in the best case, the embryo grew to only six cells before dying. That's not a revolution. It's an incremental step in understanding how early-stage cells develop.

2 And it's far from the 100 or so cells in a blastocyst, the hollow ball from which stem cells can be isolated. Scientists hope to coax embryonic stern cells into becoming specialized tissues such as nerve, muscle, or pancreatic islet cells. Therapeutic cloning, or nucleus transplantation, could make such treatments more effective.

3 In theory, it would work like this: Suppose I need new heart tissue or some insulin-secreting islet cells to counteract diabetes. You could take the nucleus from one of my cells, stick it in an egg cell from which the nucleus had been removed, let that develop into stem cells, and then trigger the stem cells to form the specific tissue needed. The new "cloned" tissue would be genetically mine and would not face rejection problems. It would function in my body as if it had grown there naturally, so I wouldn't face a lifetime of immunosuppressant drugs.

4 But all of that is a long way off. ACT and others in the field are still doing very basic research, not developing clinical therapies. Indeed, because of the difficulty of obtaining eggs, therapeutic cloning may ultimately prove impractical for clinical treatments. It could be more important as a technique for understanding cell development or studying the mutations that lead to cancer. We simply don't know right now. Science is about exploring the unknown and cannot offer guarantees.

5 Politics, however, feeds on fear, uncertainty, and doubt, and the word "cloning" arouses those emotions. While its scientific importance remains to be seen, ACT's announcement has

rekindled the campaign to criminalize nucleus transplantation and any therapies derived from that process. Under a bill passed by the House and endorsed by the president, scientists who transfer a human nucleus into an egg cell would be subject to 10-year federal prison sentences and $1 million fines. So would anyone who imports therapies developed through such research in countries where it is legal, such as Britain. The bill represents an unprecedented attempt to criminalize basic biomedical research.

6 The legislation's backers consider the fear of cloning their best hope for stopping medical research that might lead to gene-level therapies. Opponents make three basic arguments for banning therapeutic cloning.

7 The first is that a fertilized egg is a person, entitled to full human rights. Taking stem cells out of a blastocyst is, in this view, no different from cutting the heart out of a baby. Hence, we hear fears of "embryo farming" for "spare parts."

8 This view treats microscopic cells with no past or present consciousness, no organs or tissues, as people. A vocal minority of Americans, of course, do find compelling the argument that a fertilized egg is someone who deserves protection from harm. That view animates the anti-abortion movement and exercises considerable influence in Republican politics.

9 But most Americans don't believe we should sacrifice the lives and well-being of actual people to save cells. Human identity must rest on something more compelling than the right string of proteins in a Petri dish, detectable only with high-tech equipment. We will never get a moral consensus that a single cell, or a clump of 100 cells, is a human being. That definition defies moral sense, rational argument, and several major religious traditions.

10 So cloning opponents add a second argument. If we allow therapeutic cloning, they say, some unscrupulous person will pretend to be doing cellular research but instead implant a cloned embryo in a woman's womb and produce a baby. At the current stage of knowledge, using cloning to conceive a child would indeed be dangerous and unethical, with a high risk of serious birth defects. Anyone who cloned a baby today would rightly face, at the very least, the potential of an enormous malpractice judgment. There are good arguments for establishing a temporary moratorium on reproductive cloning.

11 But the small possibility of reproductive cloning does not justify making nucleus transfer a crime. Almost any science might conceivably be turned to evil purposes. This particular misuse is neither especially likely—cell biology labs are not set up to deliver fertility treatments—nor, in the long run, especially threatening.

12 Contrary to a lot of scary rhetoric, a healthy cloned infant would not be a moral nightmare, merely the not-quite-identical twin of an older person. (The fetal environment and egg cytoplasm create some genetic variations.) Certainly, some parents might have such a baby for bad reasons, to gratify their egos or to "replace" a child who died. But parents have been having children for bad reasons since time immemorial.

13 Just as likely, cloned babies would be the cherished children of couples who could not have biological offspring any other way. These children might bear an uncanny resemblance to their biological parents, but that, too, is not unprecedented. Like the "test tube babies" born of in vitro fertilization, cloned children need not be identifiable, much less freaks or outcasts.

14 Why worry so much about a few babies? Because, say opponents, even a single cloned infant puts us on the road to genetic dystopia, a combination of *Brave New World* and Nazi Germany. A cloned child's genetic makeup is too well known, goes the argument, and therefore transforms random reproduction into "manufacturing" that robs the child of his autonomy. This is where the attack broadens from nucleus transfer to human genetic engineering more generally. An anti-therapeutic cloning petition, circulated by the unlikely duo of conservative

publisher William Kristol and arch-technophobe Jeremy Rifkin, concludes, "We are mindful of the tragic history of social eugenics movements in the first half of the twentieth century, and are united in our opposition to any use of biotechnology for a commercial eugenics movement in the twenty-first century."

15 But the "eugenics" they attack has nothing to do with state-sponsored mass murder or forced sterilization. To the contrary, they are the ones who want the state to dictate the most private aspects of family life. They are the ones who want central authorities, rather than the choices of families and individuals, to determine our genetic future. They are the ones who demand that the government control the means of reproduction. They are the ones who measure the worth of human beings by the circumstances of their conception and the purity of their genetic makeup. They are the ones who say "natural" genes are the mark of true humanity.

16 Winners in the genetic lottery themselves, blessed with good health and unusual intelligence, they seek to deny future parents the chance to give their children an equally promising genetic start. In a despicable moral equivalency, they equate loving parents with Nazis.

17 Biomedicine does have the potential to alter the human experience. Indeed, it already has. Life expectancy has doubled worldwide in the past century. Childbirth is no longer a peril to mother and infant. Childhood is no longer a time for early death. The pervasive sense of mortality that down through the ages shaped art, religion, and culture has waned.

18 Our lives are different from our ancestors' in fundamental ways. We rarely remark on the change, however, because it occurred incrementally. That's how culture evolves and how science works. We should let the process continue.

Thinking about the Argument

1. What is Postrel's major claim? Where does it occur? Does her pattern of organization involve induction or deduction?
2. Postrel summarizes three arguments for opposing cloning research. What are those arguments, and what reasons does she cite to refute each of them?
3. How does she organize this argument/refutation sequence? What are the strengths and weaknesses of the tactic she uses?
4. How sufficient is the evidence Postrel supplies in support of her claims?

Responding to the Argument

1. How does Postrel's knowledge of science affect your willingness to see her as an authoritative source? Explain.
2. In paragraph 4, Postrel writes, "Science is about exploring the unknown and cannot offer guarantees." Assuming this is true, would you vote to support or suppress cloning research? Explain?
3. In paragraph 15, Postrel repetitively uses the phrase "They are the ones. . . ." Is this sensationalist grandstanding or a legitimate way for the author to drive her point home? Would you ever use such a tactic? Explain.

4. Review Cohen and Kristol's essay that appears below. Do you agree with Postrel's characterization of Kristol? Explain.

WRITING ABOUT THE ARGUMENT

1. Read Cohen and Kristol's article. Argue whether Postrel's characterization of Kristol is accurate or sensationalist.
2. Choose one paragraph from Postrel's essay. Going line by line, break down and evaluate the quality of her argument.
3. Argue whether therapeutic cloning should be used to grow replacement organs. If such technology were available, should it be used to extend life by replacing failing organs in old age?
4. Should people who abuse their bodies (alcoholics, smokers, overeaters, and drug users, for example) have the right to transplants to replace organs they have damaged? An essay on this topic could consider cloning technology or could focus on transplants that are currently available.
5. What evidence supports the idea that cloning technology would lead to a eugenics program? Is this a legitimate fear, or can it be dismissed as an outlandish "conspiracy theory"?

"Should Human Cloning Be Allowed? No, It's a Moral Monstrosity"

ABOUT THE AUTHORS: ERIC COHEN AND WILLIAM KRISTOL

Eric Cohen is a fellow at the New America Foundation, a nonpartisan organization that supports research for the purpose of crafting ideas of public policy in a world characterized by rapid change and economic globalization. William Kristol, a conservative commentator who is frequently featured on Fox News, is editor of the *Weekly Standard,* a political magazine based in Washington, D.C. Together, Cohen and Kristol edited *The Future Is Now: America Confronts the New Genetics* (2002). This essay was originally published in the *Wall Street Journal* on December 5, 2001, and was paired with the preceding essay by Virginia Postrel.

BEFORE YOU READ

1. Study the headnote. Based on the backgrounds of the two authors, what do you expect them to say about this topic?
2. Research the New America Foundation. What does it represent?
3. What other books and articles have Cohen and Kristol published?
4. What does the title of the article suggest about its content? What does it suggest about the tone of the article?
5. If you read Postrel's essay in this section, how have her statements about Kristol affected the attitude with which you approach the following article?

READING SELECTION

Should Human Cloning Be Allowed? No, It's a Moral Monstrosity

1 Dr. Michael West, the lead scientist on the team that recently cloned the first human embryos, believes his mission in life is "to end suffering and death." "For the sake of medicine," he informs us, "we need to set our fears aside." For the sake of health, in other words, we need to overcome our moral inhibitions against cloning and eugenics.

2 The human cloning announcement was not a shock. We have been "progressing" down this road for years, while averting our gaze from the destination. Now we have cloned human embryos. That means that women's eggs were procured, their genetic material removed, the DNA from someone else inserted, and the resulting cloned embryos manufactured as genetic replicas of an existing person. In Dr. West's experiments, the embryos died very quickly. But the hope is that someday these embryos will serve as a source of rejection-free stem cells that can help cure diseases.

3 For now, this is science fiction, or a rosy form of speculation. No one has ever been treated with "therapeutic cloning" or embryonic stem cells. There have been no human trials. But it is true that this research may work in the future (though the benefits would likely be decades away). In addition, beyond cloning, scientists have larger ambitions, including "tinkering" with DNA before it is placed in an egg, and adding designer genes that would make clones into "super clones," stem cells into "super stem cells."

4 Yet while Dr. West and his colleagues say that they have no interest in creating cloned humans—on the grounds that doing so is not yet safe—they do not seem too frightened by the prospect of laying the groundwork for those who would do just that. "We didn't feel that the abuse of this technology, its potential abuses, should stop us from doing what we believe is the right thing in medicine," Dr. West said.

5 The Senate, it seems, is also not very concerned. Majority Leader Tom Daschle wants to put off until spring a vote on the Human Cloning Prohibition Act, which the House passed by 265–162 in July. And on Monday, the Senate chose not to consider a six-month moratorium on all human cloning. As Sen. Harry Reid has said, a moratorium for "six months or two months or two days would impede science." And that, he believes, we cannot do.

6 It is understandable that many senators want to avoid a decision on this controversial issue, and no surprise that those driven by a desire to advance science and to heal the sick at any cost resist a ban. But as the ethicist Paul Ramsey wrote, "The good things that men do can be complete only by the things they refuse to do." And cloning is one of those things we should refuse to do.

7 The debate is usually divided into two issues—reproductive cloning (creating cloned human beings) and therapeutic cloning (creating cloned human embryos for research and destruction). For now, there is near-universal consensus that we should shun the first. The idea of mother–daughter twins or genetically identical "daddy juniors" stirs horror in us. Our moral sense revolts at the prospect, because so many of our cherished principles would be violated: the principle that children should not be designed in advance; that newborns should be truly new, without the burden of a genetic identity already lived; that a society where cloning is easy (requiring a few cells from anywhere in the body) means anyone could be cloned without knowledge or consent; and that replacing lost loved ones with "copies" is an insult to the ones lost, since it denies the uniqueness and sacredness of their existence. For these reasons, Americans agree that human cloning should never happen—not merely because the procedure is not yet "safe," but because it is wrong.

8 Many research advocates say that they, too, are against "reproductive cloning." But to protect their research, they seek to restrict only the implantation of cloned embryos, not the creation of cloned embryos for research. This is untenable: Once we begin stockpiling cloned embryos for research, it will be virtually impossible to control how they are used. We would be creating a class of embryos that, by law, must be destroyed. And the only remedy for wrongfully implanting cloned embryos would be forced abortions, something neither pro-lifers nor reproductive rights advocates would tolerate, nor should.

9 But the cloning debate is not simply the latest act in the moral divide over abortion. It is the "opening skirmish"—as Leon Kass, the president's bioethics czar, describes it—in deciding whether we wish to "put human nature itself on the operating table, ready for alteration, enhancement, and wholesale redesign." Lured by the seductive promise of medical science to "end" suffering and disease, we risk not seeing the dark side of the eugenic project.

10 Three horrors come to mind: First, the designing of our descendents, whether through cloning or germ-line engineering, is a form of generational despotism. Second, in trying to make human beings live indefinitely, our scientists have begun mixing our genes with those of cows, pigs, and jellyfish. And in trying to stamp out disease by any means necessary, we risk beginning the "compassionate" project of killing off the diseased themselves, something that has already begun with the selective abortion by parents of "undesirable" embryos.

11 Proponents of the biogenetic revolution will surely say that such warnings are nothing more than superstitions. Naive to the destructive power of man's inventions, they will say that freedom means leaving scientists to experiment as they see fit. They will say that those who wish to stop the unchecked advance of biotechnology are themselves "genetic fundamentalists," who see human beings as nothing more than their genetic make-ups. Banning human cloning, one advocate says, "would set a very dangerous precedent of bringing the police powers of the federal government into the laboratories."

12 But the fact is that society accepts the need to regulate behavior for moral reasons—from drug use to nuclear weapons research to dumping waste. And those who say that human identity is "more than a person's genetic make-up" are typically the ones who seek to crack man's genetic code, so that they might "improve" humans in the image they see fit. In promising biological utopia, they justify breaching fundamental moral boundaries.

13 C. S. Lewis saw this possibility long ago in "The Abolition of Man." As he put it, "Each new power won by man is a power over man as well." In order to stop the dehumanization of man, and the creation of a post-human world of designer babies, man–animal chimeras, and "compassionate killing" of the disabled, we may have to forego some research. We may have to say no to certain experiments before they begin. The ban on human cloning is an ideal opportunity to reassert democratic control over science, and to reconnect technological advance with human dignity and responsibility.

Thinking about the Argument

1. What is the authors' major claim? What are their supporting claims? How adequate is the evidence supplied for each?
2. How do the authors draw a distinction between "reproductive cloning" and "therapeutic cloning"? Do you agree with this distinction? What bearing does it have on their argument?
3. How do the authors try to discredit West's work? What kind of person do you perceive West to be, based on this analysis? How does that image of the stem-cell researcher compare to the cartoon of the scientist presented at the beginning of this section?

Responding to the Argument

1. Do you agree with the authors' characterization of stem-cell researchers? Why or why not?
2. How do you respond to the authors' claim that stem-cell research will lead to a "post-human world"?
3. Are the "three horrors" the authors mention legitimate concerns? Is it morally wrong to try to genetically engineer humans to make our descendants' lives better in the future? In other words, is it morally wrong to try to cure cancer, Down syndrome, or other genetic diseases through genetic engineering? If curing these ailments is acceptable, is it equally acceptable to use gene therapies to enhance future generations—to make people smarter, stronger, more beautiful, or longer-lived than their parents? Explain.

Writing about the Argument

1. Compose an argument in any form you wish explaining why the "three horrors" the authors mention are—or are not—a legitimate concern.
2. Argue whether stem-cell research should be pursued, taking into account (1) the potential dangers of reproductive cloning and (2) the relative morality of not pursuing stem-cell research when it might lead to the development of therapies that could cure crippling diseases. In other words, is the potential threat represented by reproductive cloning and genetic engineering so significant that not pursuing research that could cure diseases and end much suffering is justified?
3. Is it acceptable to genetically engineer foods and animals but not humans? For example, would it be acceptable to create a nonshedding, allergy-free cat? Would it be okay to create more flavorful tomatoes or bioluminescent goldfish? Why or why not? Argue why things other than humans should—or should not—be considered acceptable subjects of genetic engineering, cloning, and stem-cell research.

READING SELECTION

"Remarks by Ron Reagan, Jr., to the 2004 Democratic National Convention"

ABOUT THE AUTHOR: RON REAGAN, JR.

The son of former president Ronald Reagan, Ron Reagan, Jr., has long been an activist favoring liberal causes. While Ron Reagan disagreed with his father on many topics, Ronald Reagan's battle with Alzheimer's disease unified his family in its outspoken advocacy for stem-cell research, which some believe may lessen or cure this crippling disorder. In recent years, Ron Reagan has been an outspoken critic of the Iraq War and has campaigned on behalf of stem-cell research.

BEFORE YOU READ

1. What do you know about Alzheimer's disease? What symptoms are associated with this disorder? Where could you learn more about it?
2. What do you know about Ronald Reagan and his politics? If Reagan were alive and well today, do you think he would support stem-cell research? Why or why not?
3. What, if anything, do you know about Ron Reagan, Jr.? Why would he advocate this research? If his father had not developed Alzheimer's disease, do you think he would still be in favor of it? For what reason?
4. Do you think Ron Reagan, Jr., should be considered an authority on this topic? Why or why not?

Remarks by Ron Reagan, Jr., to the 2004 Democratic National Convention

1 Good evening, ladies and gentlemen.

2 A few of you may be surprised to see someone with my last name showing up to speak at a Democratic Convention. Let me assure you, I am not here to make a political speech, and the topic at hand should not—must not—have anything to do with partisanship.

3 I am here tonight to talk about the issue of research into what may be the greatest medical breakthrough in our or in any lifetime: the use of embryonic stem cells—cells created using the material of our own bodies—to cure a wide range of fatal and debilitating illnesses: Parkinson's disease, multiple sclerosis, diabetes, lymphoma, spinal cord injuries, and much more. Millions are afflicted. Every year, every day, tragedy is visited upon families across the country, around the world.

4 Now, we may be able to put an end to this suffering. We only need to try. Some of you already know what I'm talking about when I say "embryonic stem-cell research." Others of you are probably thinking, hmm, that's quite a mouthful, what is this all about?

5 Let me try and paint as simple a picture as I can while still doing justice to the incredible science involved. Let's say that 10 or so years from now you are diagnosed with Parkinson's disease. There is currently no cure, and drug therapy, with its attendant side effects, can only temporarily relieve the symptoms.

6 Now, imagine going to a doctor who, instead of prescribing drugs, takes a few skin cells from your arm. The nucleus of one of your cells is placed into a donor egg whose own nucleus has been removed. A bit of chemical or electrical stimulation will encourage your cell's nucleus to begin dividing, creating new cells which will then be placed into a tissue culture. Those cells will generate embryonic stem cells containing only your DNA, thereby eliminating the risk of tissue rejection. These stem cells are then driven to become the very neural cells that are defective in Parkinson's patients. And finally, those cells—with your DNA—are injected into your brain, where they will replace the faulty cells whose failure to produce adequate dopamine led to the Parkinson's disease in the first place.

7 In other words, you're cured. And another thing: These embryonic stem cells, they could continue to replicate indefinitely and, theoretically, can be induced to recreate virtually any tissue in your body. How'd you like to have your own personal biological repair kit standing by at the hospital? Sound like magic? Welcome to the future of medicine.

8 By the way, no fetal tissue is involved in this process. No fetuses are created, none destroyed. This all happens in the laboratory at the cellular level.

9 Now, there are those who would stand in the way of this remarkable future, who would deny the federal funding so crucial to basic research. They argue that interfering with the development of even the earliest-stage embryo, even one that will never be implanted in a womb and will never develop into an actual fetus, is tantamount to murder. A few of these folks, needless to say, are just grinding a political axe and they should be ashamed of themselves. But many are well meaning and sincere. Their belief is just that, an article of faith, and they are entitled to it.

10 But it does not follow that the theology of a few should be allowed to forestall the health and well-being of the many. And how can we affirm life if we abandon those whose own lives are so desperately at risk?

11 It is a hallmark of human intelligence that we are able to make distinctions. Yes, these cells could theoretically have the potential, under very different circumstances, to develop into human beings—that potential is where their magic lies. But they are not, in and of themselves, human beings. They have no fingers and toes, no brain or spinal cord. They have no thoughts, no fears. They feel no pain. Surely we can distinguish between these undifferentiated cells multiplying in a tissue culture and a living, breathing person—a parent, a spouse, a child.

12 I know a child—well, she must be 13 now—I'd better call her a young woman. She has fingers and toes. She has a mind. She has memories. She has hopes. And she has juvenile diabetes.

13 Like so many kids with this disease, she has adjusted amazingly well. The insulin pump she wears—she's decorated hers with rhinestones. She can insert her own catheter needle. She has learned to sleep through the blood drawings in the wee hours of the morning. She's very brave. She is also quite bright and understands full well the progress of her disease and what that might ultimately mean: blindness, amputation, diabetic coma. Every day, she fights to have a future.

14 What excuse will we offer this young woman should we fail her now? What might we tell her children? Or the millions of others who suffer? That when given an opportunity to help, we turned away? That facing political opposition, we lost our nerve? That even though we knew better, we did nothing?

15 And, should we fail, how will we feel if, a few years from now, a more enlightened generation should fulfill the promise of embryonic stem-cell therapy? Imagine what they would say of us who lacked the will.

16 No, we owe this young woman and all those who suffer—we owe ourselves—better than that. We are better than that. A wiser people, a finer

nation. And for all of us in this fight, let me say: We will prevail.

17 The tide of history is with us. Like all generations who have come before ours, we are motivated by a thirst for knowledge and compelled to see others in need as fellow angels on an often difficult path, deserving of our compassion.

18 In a few months, we will face a choice. Yes, between two candidates and two parties, but more than that. We have a chance to take a giant stride forward for the good of all humanity. We can choose between the future and the past, between reason and ignorance, between true compassion and mere ideology. This is our moment, and we must not falter.

19 Whatever else you do come November 2, I urge you, please, cast a vote for embryonic stem-cell research. Thank you for your time.

Thinking about the Argument

1. What is Reagan's major claim? What are his minor claims?
2. Regan uses a scenario early in his argument to connect with his audience. How effective is this tactic?
3. Based on the counterargument in paragraph 9, how do you think Reagan's definition of an embryo differs from his opponents' definition(s)? What role might this disagreement play in the overall argument?

Responding to the Argument

1. Reagan supplies quite a bit more evidence than Reeve to support his argument. Does this make the argument more convincing? Why or why not?
2. Unlike Reeve, Reagan does not suffer from a disease that might one day be cured by stem-cell research. How does this difference affect the way you respond to the argument? In other words, does Reagan's argument lack a sympathetic factor that may be present in Reeve's essay? To what extent does the example of the girl with juvenile diabetes fill a similar role in Reagan's speech?
3. Which specific points in the essay do you agree with? Disagree with? Why?

Writing about the Argument

1. Write an essay evaluating Reagan's use of evidence in his speech. Does he adequately support his claims? Why or why not?
2. Write an essay arguing whether stem-cell research should be restricted to curing debilitating diseases like Alzheimer's.
3. Compose a speech of your own refuting Reagan's claims.

READING SELECTION

"Cynical and Cruel: Ron Reagan's DNC Speech Was Exploitation—of His Father and of Science"

About the Author: Michael Fumento

Michael Fumento, a journalist and attorney who has written for the *Washington Times, Rocky Mountain News,* and *Investor's Business Daily,* has published articles concerning health and ethics in the *Atlantic Monthly, Forbes, The New Republic, USA Weekend, Reason, The American Spectator,* and *National Review* (where this response to Ron Reagan, Jr.'s speech was first published in July 2004). His most recent book is *BioEvolution: How Biotechnology Is Changing Our World.*

Before You Read

1. Based on the publications where much of Fumento's work has been appeared, what do you expect his position to be? Explain.
2. What does the title "Cynical and Cruel" imply?
3. What might the title have to do with Ronald Reagan and his long battle with Alzheimer's disease?
4. Research *National Review* magazine on the Internet. What sort of publication is it? Who is its editor? What can you learn about him and the sort of opinions *National Review* publishes? Can you examine a sample copy?

Cynical and Cruel: Ron Reagan's DNC Speech Was Exploitation—of His Father and of Science

1 It "may be the greatest medical breakthrough in our or in any lifetime: the use of embryonic stem cells," Ron Reagan told enthralled listeners at the Democratic Convention. These cells could "cure a wide range of fatal and debilitating illnesses: Parkinson's disease, multiple sclerosis, diabetes, lymphoma, spinal-cord injuries, and much more."

2 Yet "there are those who would stand in the way of this remarkable future, who would deny the federal funding so crucial to basic research," he warned, concluding we must "cast a vote for embryonic stem-cell research" on Election Day.

3 Now why would the Democrats choose Ron "Jr." to deliver this speech? The reason, naturally, is that Reagan is not only the son of a conservative Republican former president, but of one whose disease we're told could one day be cured with embryonic stem-cell therapy.

4 Liberal, pro-Kerry columnist Richard Cohen accused Ron Reagan of "grave robbery," not so much for exploiting his father's name but for doing it so cynically. After all, Ron Reagan is a lifelong liberal who never voted for his dad, according to Reagan's other son, columnist and radio-show host Michael Reagan. And Miss Manners would surely not approve of Ron Reagan converting the eulogy for his father into a political speech with a thinly veiled swipe at President Bush for "wearing his faith on his sleeve to gain political advantage."

5 In a recent column that, I'm happy to say, quoted my stem-cell work, Michael Reagan declared he was "tired of the media's insistence on reporting that the Reagan 'family' is in favor of stem-cell research, when the truth is that two

members of the family have been long time foes of it . . . my dad, Ronald Reagan during his lifetime, and me."

6 As to Ron Reagan's convention speech, it was so opposite the truth as to resemble a photographic negative.

7 Far from blocking federal embryonic stem-cell research funding, Bush specifically authorized it so long as it used existing lines of embryonic cells. But more remarkably, Ron Reagan made absolutely no reference to an alternative to embryonic stem cells that is decades more advanced and carries absolutely no moral baggage. "Adult stem cells" can be extracted from various places in the human body as well as blood in umbilical cords and placentas. They were first used to treat human illness in 1957.

8 By the 1980s, adult stem cells were literally curing a variety of cancers and other diseases; embryonic stem cells have never been tested on a human. Adult stem cells now treat about 80 different diseases; again embryonic stem cells have treated no one. Adult stem cells obviously aren't rejected when taken from a patient's own body, though they may be from an unmatched donor; embryonic stem cells have surface proteins that often cause rejection. Implanted embryonic stem cells also have a nasty tendency to multiply uncontrollably, a process called "cancer." Oops.

9 Regarding Alzheimer's specifically, drugs will probably provide the cure. But forget embryonic stem cells, as Ronald McKay, a stem-cell researcher at the National Institute of Neurological Disorders and Stroke, recently told the *Washington Post*. He labeled claims of an embryonic stem-cell cure for Alzheimer's "a fairy tale."

10 The only potential advantage embryonic stem cells ever had was the belief that only they could be coaxed into becoming all the different cells of the body. We don't even know whether that's true. Conversely, three different labs have now discovered it may be true of certain adult stem cells.

11 Further, perhaps we have no need for "one size fits all." In recent years researchers have found that they can tease various adult stem cells into far more types of mature tissue than was previously thought possible. Moreover, they seem to find adult stem cells essentially wherever they look—including blood, bone marrow, skin, brains, spinal cords, dental pulp, muscles, blood vessels, corneas, retinas, livers, pancreases, fat, hair follicles, placentas, umbilical cords, and amniotic fluid. We may need all sizes, but we don't need them from one type of stem cell.

12 So why do we keep hearing so much about "miraculous" embryonic stem cells? Because private investors know otherwise, pumping money into adult stem-cell research and leaving embryonic stem-cell labs and companies desperate to feed from the public trough.

13 Ron Reagan began his talk saying it "should not—must not—have anything to do with partisanship," thereby signaling its sole purpose. The Democratic position on stem cells is a cynical and cruel attempt to disenchant Republicans ignorant about adult stem cells and make them feel Bush is pig-headedly stopping a technology that will cure everything from Alzheimer's to AIDS. In what's already a nasty campaign, Ron Reagan's stem-cell speech may have been the most vicious attack yet.

Thinking about the Argument

1. How does the tone of Fumento's essay differ from Reagan's? From Cohen and Kristol's? Is such a tone appropriate for a refutation? Why or why not?
2. What is Fumento's main point? How does he use the following sentence to emphasize it: "As to Ron Reagan's convention speech, it was so opposite the truth as to resemble a photographic negative"? In what way does "photographic negative" add to or detract from its rhetorical power?
3. What alternatives to stem-cell research does Fumento mention? Does their inclusion in the essay cause you to sympathize with his point of view?
4. How does Fumento use quotations from Reagan's speech as the basis of his refutation? Is this tactic effective? Are there certain claims he refutes more effectively than others?
5. How effectively does Fumento question Reagan's credentials?

Responding to the Argument

1. Do you agree or disagree with Fumento's analysis? What point do you agree/disagree with the most? Explain.
2. Both Fumento's argument and Reagan's speech lack significant details in defense of their claims that might be present in more in-depth arguments. How does each author make up for this lack of specificity and carefully presented evidence?
3. How do both Fumento and Reagan use elements of rhetoric (purpose, audience, style, and structure) to make up for their lack of specific proof? In particular, how does each author use style to convince his particular audience? Explain.

Writing about the Argument

1. Write a speech responding to Fumento's critique. You may agree or disagree with his position, but you must evaluate the strengths and weaknesses of his argument.
2. Write a letter to the editor of your local newspaper critiquing Reagan's speech. You may take any position you wish.
3. Contrast Reagan's speech to Fumento's article. Explain the strengths and weaknesses of each.
4. Write a paper taking a position different from that of either Reagan or Fumento. For example, you might argue that stem-cell research should be allowed only to treat debilitating diseases, but should not be pursued for other purposes. Research the issue and think carefully about how stem-cell research could be utilized ethically.

READING SELECTION

"Now That Chimeras Exist, What If Some Turn Out Too Human?"

SHARON BEGLEY

Sharon Begley has written extensively on science-related issues. She has been a science editor for *Newsweek* and now serves as the senior science writer for the *Wall Street Journal.* Among her books are *The Mind and the Brain: Neuroplasticity and the Power of Mental Force* (2003, with Jeffrey M. Schwarz) and *The Hand of God: A Collection of Thoughts and Images Reflecting the Spirit of the Universe* (1999, Introduction). The piece reprinted here is from the May 6, 2005, issue of the *Wall Street Journal.*

BEFORE YOU READ

1. Based on the headnote, what would you expect Begley's opinion to be regarding issues like cloning and genetic engineering? Why do you think this?
2. What is a *chimera*? What does the definition of this word suggest about Begley's viewpoint?
3. Do you think the author is concerned about the ethical issues surrounding stem-cell research? Why or why not?
4. Scan the article. What does the gist of her argument seem to be? State her thesis in your own words.

Now That Chimeras Exist, What If Some Turn Out Too Human?

1 If you had just created a mouse with human brain cells, one thing you wouldn't want to hear the little guy say is, "Hi there, I'm Mickey." Even worse, of course, would be something like, "Get me out of this &%#!! body!"

2 It's been several millennia since Greek mythology dreamed up the chimera, a creature with the head of a lion, the body of a goat, and the tail of a serpent. Research on the chimera front was pretty quiet for 2500 years. But then in 1984 scientists announced that they had merged embryonic goat cells with embryonic sheep cells, producing a "geep." (It's part wooly, part hairy, with a face only a nanny goat could love.) A human–mouse chimera made its debut in 1988: "SCID-hu" is created when human fetal tissue—spleen, liver, thymus, lymph node—is transplanted into a mouse. These guys are clearly mice, but other chimeras are harder to peg. In the 1980s, scientists took brain-to-be tissue from quail embryos and transplanted it into chicken embryos. Once hatched, the chicks made sounds like baby quails.

3 More part-human chimeras are now in the works or already in lab cages. StemCells Inc., of Palo Alto, California, has given hundreds of mice human-brain stem cells, for instance. And before human stem cells are ever used to treat human patients, notes biologist Janet Rowley of the University of Chicago, they (or the cells they develop into) will be implanted into mice and other lab animals. "The centaur has left the barn more than people realize," says Stanford University law professor and bioethicist Henry Greely.

4 Part-human creatures raise enough ethical concerns that a National Academy of Sciences committee on stem cells veered off into chimeras. It recommended last week that some research be barred, to prevent some of the more monstrous possibilities—such as a human-sperm-bearing mouse mating with a human-egg-bearing mouse and gestating a human baby. "We're not very concerned about a mouse with a human spleen," says Professor Greely. "But we get really concerned about our brain and our gonads."

5 That's why his Stanford colleague, Irving Weissman, asked Professor Greely to examine the ethical implications of a mouse–human chimera. StemCells, co-founded by Professor Weissman, has already transplanted human-brain stem cells into the brains of mice that had no immune system (and hence couldn't attack the foreign cells). The stem cells develop into human neurons, migrate through the mouse brain, and mingle with mouse cells. The human cells make up less than 1% of the mouse brain, and are being used by the company to study neurodegenerative diseases.

6 But Professor Weissman had in mind a new sort of chimera. He would start with ill-fated mice whose neurons all die just before or soon after birth. He planned to transplant human-brain stem cells into their brains just before their own neurons died off. Would that lead the human cells to turn into neurons and replace the dead-or-dying mouse neurons, producing a mostly human brain in a mouse?

7 Such a chimera could bring important scientific benefits. The SCID-hu mouse, though it hasn't yielded a cure for AIDS, has been "a very valuable animal model," says Ramesh Akkiha of Colorado State University, Fort Collins, who directs a lab that uses this part-human mouse. "It has human T cells circulating, which will allow us to test gene therapy for AIDS" in a way that will be more relevant to patients than all-animal models. The co-creator of SCID-hu, Michael McCune of the Gladstone Institute of Virology and Immunology, San Francisco, notes that because the human organs last for months in the mice (they would die in days in a lab dish), "it is possible to study the effects of HIV" in many kinds of human cells in a living system.

8 Similarly, studying living human neurons in a living mouse brain would likely yield more insights than studying human neurons in a lab dish or mouse neurons in a mouse brain. "You could see how pathogens damage human neurons, how experimental drugs act, what happens when you infect human neurons with prions [which cause mad-cow disease] or amyloid [associated with Alzheimer's]," says Professor Greely. "The big concern is, could you give the mouse some sort of human consciousness or intelligence?"

9 "All of us are aware of the concern that we're going to have a human brain in a mouse with a person saying, 'Let me out,'" Professor Rowley told the President's Council on Bioethics when it discussed chimeras in March.

10 To take no chances, scientists could kill the mice before birth to see if the brain is developing mouse-y structures such as "whisker barrels,"

which receive signals from the whiskers. If so, it's a mouse. If it is developing a large and complex visual cortex, it's too human. "If you saw something weird, you'd stop," says Professor Greely. "If not, let the next ones be born, and examine them at different ages to be sure they're still fully mouse."

11 To reduce the chance that today's chimeras will be as monstrous as the Greeks' were, the U.S. patent office last year rejected an application to patent a human–chimp chimera, or "humanzee." But that, of course, just keeps someone from patenting one—not making one.

Thinking about the Argument

1. What is the purpose of the first paragraph? How does it employ humor to make its point?
2. Is the author's definition of a *chimera* different from your understanding of the meaning of this term? Explain.
3. Why, according to the author, are part-human creations an ethical concern?
4. Why do the scientists involved think this research is important?
5. What does the last paragraph of the article imply? Why do you think this?

Responding to the Argument

1. Should chimera research be continued for scientific reasons? Why or why not?
2. Should chimera research be abandoned for ethical reasons? Why or why not?
3. Would you be willing to support a compromise position on chimera research that would allow some forms of research and forbid others? Explain.
4. If you are unwilling to support a compromise position on chimera research, state why. Back up your reasons with relevant examples.
5. If a chimpanzee or another animal was subjected to such research and developed humanlike brain structures, would the animal have to be classified as human and subject to human rights? Why or why not?

Writing about the Argument

1. Assume that you have a family member who might be helped by chimera research. (For example, suppose that a pig could be used to grow genetically matched replacement organs.) Write a letter to the editor of your local paper (or to your congressperson) stating why this research should be allowed.
2. In a journal entry, discuss what types of chimera research would be acceptable and what types would not. Create a definition to determine when the "line of acceptability" would be crossed.

3. Are there characteristics of any other animals that you would find beneficial to humans? (For example, would the longevity enjoyed by some reptiles be desirable?) Write a journal entry or Internet blog explaining why chimera research should or should not be used to enhance human abilities.
4. Research and write an essay explaining why chimera research should be supported or prevented and to what degree. Consider arguments of policy (whether or not it should be done) and arguments of procedure (how such experimentation should be implemented).

Issue 3: The Psychology of Success

The importance of individual success is ingrained in the American psyche. Madonna Marsden, an expert in popular culture, has characterized what she terms "the American myth of success" like this: "With hard work comes achievement, and with achievement comes the material comforts of the American Dream and sometimes even great riches and a place in history." However, while the drive to succeed is seen by many as a virtue, it can become an obsession and, at least in the minds of some psychologists, a mental illness. According to Hara Estroff Marano, some super-achieving executives become depressed when they have met all of their goals. One CEO, Phillip J. Burguieres, confessed, "I was a workaholic. . . . I had a mistress. I'd lie to my wife. I'd sneak off at 2 o'clock on Sunday afternoon and tell her I was going to run errands. . . . But the mistress I was running to was my job."

Online Study Center
Prepare for Class
The Psychology of Success

While there is little question that the drive to succeed can pay off financially, the personal costs in terms of well-being and happiness may be too great. Is the importance of career success and material wealth so great that mental and physical health should be a secondary concern? Is there a psychology to success? Is there a positive way of thinking that can allow an individual to succeed while keeping quality of life, health, and work in balance?

Considering the Issue of the Psychology of Success

Consider the following questions, either in a class discussion or as part of a smaller group.

1. How important is it for you to have financial success? How important is it for you to have a sense of happiness and well-being?
2. What, besides money, will make you happy? How do you plan to achieve it?

3. Is hypermotivation good or bad for physical and mental health? Explain your answer.
4. Is it good for parents to have extremely high expectations for their children's performance? How do such children feel when they succeed? How do they feel when they fail?
5. Do you believe that luck plays a role in personal success, or is it just a matter of grit and drive?

READING SELECTION

"How to Help Them Succeed"

ABOUT THE AUTHOR: DANIEL EISENBERG

Daniel Eisenberg is a staff writer for *Time* magazine, where this article was first published in November 2005. He has written numerous articles on a wide range of topics, including health and family issues. In this essay, Eisenberg discusses the U.S. education system and the ways in which the identification of some children as more motivated than others can be a self-fulfilling prophesy.

BEFORE YOU READ

1. What does the title suggest about the purpose of this article? What kind of advice do you think it might provide?
2. If you were to offer someone advice about how to succeed, what are the top three things you might tell them? Why do you think these things will help someone become more successful?
3. What kind of audience reads *Time* magazine? Be as specific as you can in your description.
4. What does a quick glance at this article tell you about the advice that is being offered?

How to Help Them Succeed

1 Anyone who doubts that children are born with a healthy amount of ambition need spend only a few minutes with a baby eagerly learning to walk or a headstrong toddler starting to talk. No matter how many times the little ones stumble in their initial efforts, most keep on trying, determined to master their amazing new skill. It is only several years later, around the start of middle or junior high school, many psychologists and teachers agree, that a good number of kids seem to lose their natural drive to succeed and end up joining the ranks of underachievers. For the parents of such kids, whose own ambition is often inextricably tied to their children's success, it can be a bewildering, painful experience. So it's no wonder some parents find themselves hoping that, just maybe, ambition can be taught like any other subject at school.

2 It's not quite that simple. "Kids can be given the opportunities [to become passionate about a

subject or activity], but they can't be forced," says Jacquelynne Eccles, a psychology professor at the University of Michigan, who led a landmark, 25-year study examining what motivated first- and seventh-graders in three school districts. Even so, a growing number of educators and psychologists do believe it is possible to unearth ambition in students who don't seem to have much. They say that by instilling confidence, encouraging some risk taking, being accepting of failure, and expanding the areas in which children may be successful, both parents and teachers can reignite that innate desire to achieve.

3 Figuring out why the fire went out is the first step. Assuming that a kid doesn't suffer from an emotional or learning disability, or isn't involved in some family crisis at home, many educators attribute a sudden lack of motivation to a fear of failure or peer pressure that conveys the message that doing well academically somehow isn't cool. "Kids get so caught up in the moment-to-moment issue of will they look smart or dumb, and it blocks them from thinking about the long term," says Carol Dweck, a psychology professor at Stanford. "[You have to teach them that] they are in charge of their intellectual growth." Over the past couple of years, Dweck has helped run an experimental workshop with New York City public school seventh-graders to do just that. Dubbed Brainology, the unorthodox approach uses basic neuroscience to teach kids how the brain works and how it can continue to develop throughout life. "The message is that everything is within the kids' control, that their intelligence is malleable," says Lisa Blackwell, a research scientist at Columbia University who has worked with Dweck to develop and run the program, which has helped increase the students' interest in school and turned around their declining math grades. More than any teacher or workshop, Blackwell says, "parents can play a critical role in conveying this message to their children by praising their effort, strategy, and progress rather than emphasizing their 'smartness' or praising high performance alone. Most of all, parents should let their kids know that mistakes are a part of learning."

4 Some experts say our education system, with its strong emphasis on testing and rigid separation of students into different levels of ability, also bears blame for the disappearance of drive in some kids. "These programs shut down the motivation of all kids who aren't considered gifted and talented. [They] destroy their confidence," says Jeff Howard, a social psychologist and president of the Efficacy Institute, a Boston-area organization that works with teachers and parents in school districts around the country to help improve children's academic performance. Howard and other educators say it's important to expose kids to a world beyond homework and tests, through volunteer work, sports, hobbies, and other extracurricular activities. "The crux of the issue is that many students experience education as irrelevant to their life goals and ambitions," says Michael Nakkula, a Harvard education professor who runs a Boston-area mentoring program called Project IF (Inventing the Future), which works to get low-income underachievers in touch with their aspirations. The key to getting kids to aim higher at school is to disabuse them of the notion that classwork is irrelevant, to show them how doing well at school can actually help them fulfill their dreams beyond it. Like any ambitious toddler, they need to understand that you have to learn to walk before you can run.

THINKING ABOUT THE ARGUMENT

1. What is the answer to the question suggested by the article's title (what is the essay's thesis)?
2. According to the author, what causes the "fire" to go out? What are the specific causes of a lack of motivation? How can intellectual curiosity be restored?
3. Does the author blame this lack of ambition on parents, teachers, or culture in general? How do you know?
4. What evidence does Eisenberg cite to support his claim?

RESPONDING TO THE ARGUMENT

1. Do you agree or disagree that "a good number of kids seem to lose their natural drive to succeed"? Why or why not?
2. What forms of evidence does Eisenberg cite? Do you see these sources as reliable and authoritative? Explain.
3. Analyze the causes of the lack of motivation mentioned by the author. Do you agree that they are the real causes? Explain your answer.
4. Does the author address whether the responsibility for motivating children lies with educators or with parents? Who do you think holds the primary responsibility? Why do you think this?

WRITING ABOUT THE ARGUMENT

1. In a short paper or journal entry, evaluate the causes of the lack of motivation for learning that the author mentions.
2. Argue whether parents, teachers, or both should bear primary responsibility for motivating learning.
3. Write a short paper or journal entry arguing how education should be made more relevant for students today. Should education be academic in nature, or should it be practical and professional—aimed at preparing students for a particular career?
4. Gauge how motivated you are in your classes. Which classes seem irrelevant to your goals? How could they better target the skills and knowledge you need to gain for your chosen career?

"Rocking the Cradle of Class"

ABOUT THE AUTHOR: HARA ESTROFF MARANO

Hara Estroff Marano is an editor for *Psychology Today* and has written extensively about mental health issues. Her books include *Style Is Not a Size* (1994) and *Why Doesn't Anybody Like Me? A Guide to Raising Socially Confident Kids* (1998). In this article (which originally appeared in the September/October 2005 issue of *Psychology Today*), Marano argues that parents can harm their children's self-confidence by driving them to succeed. Such pressure, she says, is often a result of the parents' own feelings of inadequacy.

READING SELECTION

Before You Read

1. The title of this article is fairly creative. What does it suggest about the relationship between child-rearing and success?
2. What do you know about *Psychology Today?* What is its readership like? How could you find out more about this publication and its readers?
3. What does the headnote tell you about the author's qualifications?
4. Glance at the subtitles. What are the major divisions of the article?
5. Scan the article. What do you expect its argumentative thesis to be? What other claims might it use to support this idea (what claims might be associated with each of the subheadings in the article)?

Rocking the Cradle of Class

1 A sluggish traffic light at a Brooklyn street corner brought together three acquaintances who had plenty of time to catch up with each other. "My daughter is still in the public school system," said one woman (this is, after all, New York, and one can't take such things for granted, even in the outer boroughs). "My son is, too, and it's going really well," said the one dad. And after an expectant pause, "*We* go to [insert name of highly selective, outrageously expensive private school here]," announced the other mother.

2 How's that again? This wasn't the plural *we;* the woman had arrived solo. Nor was it the royal *we;* no footmen were in sight. No, Ladies and Gents, say hello to the fused-identity *we,* in which fully grown adults openly appropriate the accomplishments of their wee ones, flash them like an Olympic medal for parenting and take much of their own measure from them.

3 Of course, parents have always been proud of their children's accomplishments, perhaps none more so than immigrant parents eager to see their kids thriving in their new land. But now children's achievements have become a marker of how their mothers and fathers are doing in the increasingly prominent job of parenting—and by extension how the whole family is doing. In a novel twist on the age-old status dynamic, parents now rely on their offspring's competitive performance in athletics and, especially, academics for their own inner sense of security and social approval.

4 As the engines of status shift into reverse—with kids fuel-injecting parental egos with every A they get—adults are creating a new kind of child labor that may be at least as unhealthy and onerous as the old. Kids no longer have to till fields from dawn to dusk or toil in sooty factories, but more and more they are handed the burden of power-lifting their parents' sense of self.

5 Consider that prospective parents no longer just *buy* a stroller or other basic baby gear. They invest emotionally in it. A spokes-person for a baby-products manufacturers association explained why some people buy and dispose of dozens of different strollers before settling on a wardrobe of, say, three models. "A stroller is part of the parents' image and a reflection of themselves—personal style, parenting style, their lifestyle."

6 In the same way, the schools that parents send their kids to have come to symbolize much more than education. "College entrance has become your final exam as a parent," says child psychologist David Anderegg of Lenox, Massachusetts.

7 No one knows this better than students at an ultra-selective Ivy League university, admission to which is sometimes considered prima facie evidence of successful child-raising. They call it "the H-bomb effect:" Dropping the bomb that one's kid goes to Harvard can deaden conversation among hypercompetitive parents. Anderegg sees proof of the accessorization of children in the way decals of prestigious colleges are placed on car windows—even before the kids go off to school. "It's a competitive display, and it's not about the kids. It's about the parents."

8 Childhood is being radically transformed right before our very eyes, contends Steven Mintz, professor of history at the University of Houston and author of *Huck's Raft: A History of American Childhood.* As he sees it, children are now extensions of their parents' sense of self in a way that is new and unprecedented. "More than in the past, children are viewed as a project by perfectionist parents. Today's parents are imposing on their kids a violence of raised expectations. They are using their children for their own needs. We've decreased the threat of physical violence but increased the psychological violence."

The '70s Shift

9 It all started in the 1970s, when postwar optimism came to a crashing halt against stagflation and the oil crisis. The American economy shifted dramatically. "Parents translated that into a fear of not passing on their class status to their kids," says Mintz. Their solution: Give the kids whatever advantages possible and introduce into childhood the alien idea of specialization. "Nervousness about globalization made parents so concerned about competitiveness that they began believing they had to do *everything* in their power to not let their kids lose."

10 The economy of the 1970s also attuned people to social class—a radical shift from the '60s. "Even the food that people consumed became class-connected," says Mintz. "The type of lettuce you ate said something about your social status." Increasingly, class concerns devolved on the kids, and suddenly "the nice suburban school just wasn't good enough any more." Today 13 percent of white children attend private schools. Many more live in exclusive suburbs where public schools function like private ones.

11 Kids are driving the status engines for families to such an extent that just having them is becoming a status symbol, the human equivalent of a limited edition Hermès satchel. In a consumer culture where raising a child is a very costly enterprise, kids are the ultimate acquisition. One new mini-trend identifies the wealthy (with incomes of above $250,000) as having more children (2.3) than the middle class (1.8)—slightly more, even, than lower-class families. And the very wealthiest have the most children by far, averaging 2.9 kids.

12 Rapid technological change has also done its share to elevate the status of children. Technology has turned expertise upside down, so kids serve as the household gurus on new gadgetry. They're born into it, don't have to unlearn anything and are unafraid to explore technology. This shift alone accords children cachet in a technologically advanced culture.

13 A growing intensity of family life virtually forces adults to take more of their meaning from their home and their children. Everyone knows that both mothers and fathers are working more hours and feeling very stressed (and loaded with guilt, too). While parents seldom have free time to play—they go to the movies less, for example—or to socialize with other adults, the job of meeting their emotional needs has fallen on their kids. Take the case of children's summer camps and programs, which once served the important function of defusing family pressures on kids. For decades, well-off parents have sent adolescents abroad for a month or two of study, exploration and some independence. But responding to adults' requests to get in on the fun, some teen tours now allow the parents to join their offspring for part of the trip.

What Are Kids for?

14 In agricultural societies, there is an overt economic relationship between parents and children, and it's based on reciprocity. Parents provide food and shelter; kids contribute labor and the promise of care in old age. But in modern societies, kids seldom take on the burden of caring for elderly parents, so there's no economic payoff. Parents shell out lots of money for education, iPods, and other gear. What do the children do in return? Why even have them?

15 Because, increasingly, what they supply are psychological rewards. "More and more, parents have come to be identified with their kids," reports sociologist Lynda Lytle Holmstrom. She and Boston College colleagues David A. Karp and Paul S. Gray have conducted an in-depth study of the college application process among upper-middle-class families. One of the questions they've pondered is why parents pay for college. After all, it's extremely expensive and money deployed on their children can't be spent on themselves or socked away for fast-approaching retirement. But, the researchers found, financial open handedness makes perfect sense—if the kids are perceived as pure extensions of the parents. To a surprising degree, the researchers discovered, the parents' "identities and aspirations are wrapped up in the achievements of their children."

16 Further, paying for college is the way the class system replicates itself. "It's clear to upper-middle-class parents that education is the way for kids to maintain their social status. The parents are increasingly aware of the competition; there is the perception that the stakes are high. It's not necessarily this way throughout the class structure. For other classes, college is the ticket to upward mobility."

Investing in Identity

17 In subsidizing a college education, parents are buying their kids another resource for maintaining class status. Increasingly, social scientists recognize, class consists not only of financial and cultural capital but of "identity capital" as well: your investment in "who you are." It includes such psychological factors as ego strength, cognitive flexibility and complexity, and critical thinking abilities—capacities that help people negotiate the obstacles and opportunities in modern life. College, of course, is the prime proving ground of identity. A residential college education allows the young and the well-off the maximum luxury in expanding their identity capital.

18 So parents come to see helping their kids succeed in school as one of their primary jobs. And that enlarges their own identity playground. As the emotionally involved adults push and micromanage their kids, they get to feed off and celebrate each sign of their children's academic and athletic progress. Annexing their children's achievements not only gives them a way to amplify their own class position, it also heralds a new and much more elusive form of reciprocity—identity reciprocity.

19 It isn't as if parents have never had unreasonable expectations for their children before, and some have certainly attempted to live vicariously through them. But that behavior was once regarded as a parenting flaw—not a practice to be openly promoted. Parents have so assumed the right to take every step of college orientation with their kids that the University of Vermont is hiring and rigorously training selected senior students as "parent bouncers." Their job is to keep the adults from orientation sessions in which their incoming offspring consult with academic advisors or participate in peer discussions about alcohol and sex.

20 Because the outcome of parenting is now managed and measured down to the last detail, you could say that we're on our way to precision-producing designer children. Call it the professionalization of parenthood.

Résumés on Two Legs

21 "We treat children as projects, as things to be helped and shaped and pushed and prodded," says Mintz. "It's the sense that I am going to create a résumé on two legs." Parents have always dreamed of perfection, but it used to be a very surface thing—posture, strict feeding schedules. Now, he says, perfection is defined so exclusively in terms of achievement that no other path to adulthood is acceptable. As he laments in *Huck's Raft,* there's no room for "odysseys of self-discovery outside the goal-driven, overstructured realities of contemporary childhood."

22 The pursuit of perfection in kids stems from a fundamental misunderstanding of the task of parenting, Anderegg charges. "Parenting is not an engineering task, it's an endurance task. It requires a high tolerance for boredom. Engineering is based on the idea that if you do something right the first time, you don't have to do it again."

23 Efficiency, however, is inimical to child-rearing. "Parenting is a problem to be solved daily. It's a repetitive, quotidian task," says Anderegg. That's what maximizes parent–child interaction and persuades kids they are loved. "Seeing kids as well-designed products is a disease of really smart people," he notes. "They feel they have to make child-rearing a task worthy of their time."

24 It may be that people insert professional values in parenting because they are so well rewarded for them at work. Indeed, mothers are more highly educated than ever, and because they are waiting longer to have their babies, many are well entrenched in careers. It's understandable that they would want to bring home what they know—setting long-range goals, keeping complex schedules, managing divisions, and running things efficiently. Anderegg cites a mom who, clipboard in hand, stood at the door of the kindergarten as her child entered. She was taking notes, she said, because she wanted her child to get into an Ivy League school and she needed to make suggestions to the teachers on how to improve her child's education.

25 Ironically, the incredible shrinking family almost demands the encroachment of professional values on parenting. Today, about one in five children under the age of 18 is an only child, and "the fewer kids you have, the more precious they become and the more risk-averse you get," explains Anderegg, who chronicles the rise of parental anxiety in *Worried All the Time.* The more kids you have, the more you understand that each has his own temperament—and that your contribution is not the only thing influencing developmental outcomes.

26 It's bad enough that there are now many for whom parenting has become a profession. But for some it has become a religion. "It's the only source of transcendent meaning in their lives," observes Anderegg. "That fuels hysteria, encouraging parents to exaggerate the dangers facing kids and competition for resources."

Masking the Secret of Success

27 But pushing for perfection seriously clashes with children's developmental needs. "There's a difference between excellence and perfection," points out Miriam Adderholdt, instructor in psychology at Davidson Community College in Lexington, North Carolina, and author of *Perfectionism: What's So Bad about Being Too Good?*

28 The trouble is, perfectionism is transmitted from parents to kids. "A child makes four A's and one B," says Adderholdt. "All it takes is the raising of an eyebrow for her to get the message." Then it seeps into her psyche and creates a pervasive personality style. It lowers her ability to take risks and reduces creativity and innovation—exactly what's *not* adaptive in the global marketplace. It keeps kids from engaging in challenging experiences and testing their own limits; they don't get to discover what they truly like. Further, perfectionism reduces playfulness and the assimilation of knowledge. It destroys self-esteem. And just when the world requires flexibility and comfort with ambiguity, perfectionism creates rigidity. Perhaps worse: The emphasis on

achievement makes parental love feel too conditional.

29 In short, the push for perfection *undermines* the identity capital of kids. But the biggest problem with it may be that it masks the real secret of success in life. Any innovator will tell you that success hinges less on getting everything right than on how you handle getting things wrong. In real life, you can't call the teacher and demand that a C be changed to an A. This is where creativity, passion, and perseverance come into play. The ultimate irony is, in a flat world you don't make kids competitive by pushing them to be perfect but by allowing them to become passionate about something that compels their interest.

Thinking about the Argument

1. Where is the author's thesis located in the article? What other claims are used to support it?
2. Marano uses academics as her primary sources in this article. Find them in the article, and read the passages where they are cited. Do you consider these choices to be good sources for supporting the argumentative thesis? What other sorts of support might you have selected?
3. What economic crisis (or personal fear) does the author cite as a major cause of the push to make children successful? Explain.
4. How does the author characterize children as status symbols or possessions?
5. What are some of the downfalls of the push to make children successful, according to the author?

Responding to the Argument

1. Reread the first two paragraphs. How does the author's opening narrative serve to illustrate the point she is trying to make?
2. How does the example of the stroller serve as evidence for the point the writer is emphasizing in paragraph 5? Do you find this a convincing form of evidence? Why or why not?
3. The author quotes Steven Mintz, who characterizes parents who push their kids to succeed as committing "psychological violence." Do you agree with this assessment? Explain.
4. How important is it for parents to "buy" social status for their children in the form of an elite education? Is this, as the article suggests, really serving the parents' egos rather than the children's needs? Explain.
5. If you were to argue against Marano's position, what would you say?

Writing about the Argument

1. Write a journal entry, short paper, or paragraph arguing whether parents should send students to private schools to help them succeed.
2. Write a short argument explaining whether good grades and a successful career are more important than a sense of happiness and well-being.

3. It has been said that people who win the lottery often become miserable. Is it true that a poor person can be happier than a rich person? Provide evidence from the essays in this book or from your personal experiences to back up your claim.
4. Write a response to Marano's article. In your refutation, explain why pushing children to succeed—even at the cost of their own self-esteem—is good for them.

"The Measuring Game: Why You Think You'll Never Stack Up"

About the Author: Carlin Flora

Carlin Flora is a staff writer for *Psychology Today,* where this piece was published in the September/October 2005 issue. Flora has written on a variety of mental health issues. Here Flora argues that the envy of others that accompanies the drive to succeed (and the fear of failure) can be a healthy motivator as long as it is kept in perspective.

Before You Read

1. What does this title suggest about success anxiety?
2. What kind of advice do you expect this article to provide?
3. Scan the article. What do its major supporting ideas appear to be? Can you locate the thesis?

The Measuring Game: Why You Think You'll Never Stack Up

1 There are few non-legally binding documents as closely read but as coolly received as class notes from one's alma mater. "On the same day I was accepted to a trauma surgery/critical care fellowship, I asked my beautiful girlfriend, an internal medicine resident, to be my wife," reads one Ivy League entry. Another alum informs that while his wife "has continued her participation with the U.S. national women's lacrosse team and hopes to win her third World Cup, I've had much more modest success on the sailplane racing circuit." The alumni journal is a gratingly personal catalogue of a universal predicament: status anxiety. Like all universals, this anxiety has its own deep logic. Learning that our best friend from college is happily married and wildly successful brings sincere joy and admiration but also waves of envy, which serve a primal purpose. Envy nudges us to earn an impressive job title, snag material comforts, and catch and keep a fetching spouse, all of which, as nature would have it, boil down to life's reproductive necessities. We may never be able to overcome our concern with status, and we may not want to. In moderation it is good for us. Understanding our need for status can help us to channel our energies most productively and make use of our talents.

2 We are all at least a touch malcontented with our lot. The frustrations that accumulate as we

fall behind in our career goals or mortgage payments are tiring and vulgar; the hair loss serums and the struggle to fit into our favorite pair of jeans are not battles we're proud of. But to our credit, we don't simply want more, more, more.

3 Sure, images of Donald Trump's gilded Boeing jet or of Kimora Lee Simmons's 30-carat diamond ring and 42-inch legs feed into our status anxiety on some level. But at the end of the day, we're concerned with our immediate reference group—one made up of about 150 people. "When you see Bill Gates's mansion, you don't actually aspire to have one like it. It's who is local, who is near you physically, and who is most like you—your family members, co-workers, and old high school classmates—with whom you compare yourself," says economist Robert H. Frank, of Cornell University. The homogeneity in most communities sensitizes us to tiny upgrades in our midst. "If someone in your reference group has more," he says, "you get a little anxious."

4 In the 1980s, Frank dismantled a premise central to economic theory: People will always choose the greatest absolute amount of wealth. Landmark research shows that our preferences are actually quite relative. We'd rather make $50,000 while living in a neighborhood where everyone else makes $40,000 than earn $100,000 among those who are raking in $150,000.

5 Peers in our little pond, such as the old college crew, are the most accurate yardsticks of our own performance. They probably started out in life with the same advantages as we did and are the same age. They are our rivals, fair and square. "The more similar people are to us, the more we can really gauge their success in a particular area," says Richard Smith, associate professor of psychology at the University of Kentucky. He recalls drawing a stick figure on his two-year-old daughter's easel just before the mother of one of her preschool classmates walked in. "Did your daughter do that?" the girl's mother exclaimed in a panicky voice, while her own daughter continued to scribble wildly. The two little girls happened to share the same birthday, which made the mother even more acutely afraid that her daughter's fine motor skills were dramatically outclassed.

6 "People are rarely satisfied with simply knowing their own performance, as anyone who has taught students knows," says Smith. "They want to know how they stack up against others." Our natural tendency is to establish a pecking order: When placed in an unfamiliar group, subjects are quick to accurately judge where they and other group members rank on various characteristics, even before they speak to one another. Supposed respites from ranking are not immune either: The heavier children at fat camp are ostracized; communes—even prisons—are heavily stratified.

7 We are primed for pettiness, programmed to notice seemingly inconsequential gradations, but for good reason: Being chronically dissatisfied is an effective stimulus to best your more complacent peers.

8 David Buss, of the University of Texas at Austin, and his graduate student Sarah Hill see our persistent status anxiety as a survival mechanism developed hundreds of thousands of years ago when our psychological apparatuses took form. In those times, we traveled in small herds and jockeyed for food and love in very direct ways that lent urgency to cutthroat ranking (as well as to cooperative living). The civilized modern stage upon which status dramas are enacted is not so stripped down—we don't literally miss out on meals if our neighbors overstuff their pantry—but the mechanism remains intact and attuned to the same ultimate goals.

9 Because it is in our nature to home in on the goals of survival and reproduction, men and women conserve mental energy for comparisons in realms that relate directly to these two pursuits. Think of how women are easily irritated by a gorgeous secretary, while (straight) men barely cast a glance at the dashing young male paralegals in the office. Women are more envious

of other women's good looks, say evolutionary psychologists, because appearance is an important marker of youth and fertility. In a beauty-contest version of the economist Frank's salary preferences breakdown, women in Buss and Hill's survey reported they would rather be a "5" among "4s" than an "8" among "10s." Their male counterparts would rather be the best looking in absolute terms.

10 Men are designed to amass solid evidence that they could support a mate and offspring. (As the rapper Young MC once said, "If you got no money and you got no car, then you got no woman, and there you are.") This necessary "proof of resources" may take the form of hard cash or merely cachet, anything that could reassure a woman that she will be provided for. Like feathers on a peacock's tail, unnecessary yet conspicuous displays send a loud signal to potential mates: "I have resources to burn over here!"

11 But complex forces scramble these deep-seated tendencies and account for why women don't exclusively focus on their appearance, nor men on their finances. Buss and Hill's research shows that just like men, women would prefer to have a higher salary than others in their reference group. Hill reasons that this has nothing to do with women wanting to be perceived as providers. Women just happen to like "stuff." "The reason men like acquiring resources is because women like them so much," she says, "whether they get them from men or from themselves."

12 Then there's the rise of the "metrosexual" man, whose very existence defies the dogma that men don't care to look better than their peers. "As women gain access to their own resources, they are sampling more from the buffet of the mating table," Hill explains. "Men have to up the ante, to be attractive, too."

13 Once we perceive our chances for happiness are threatened by another's flowing locks of raven hair or tricked-out Hummer, a complementary adaptive response kicks in: envy. When we stand to miss out on life's prizes, on what we think we deserve or could achieve, envy's distinct blend of inferiority and hostility surges through us. "The brute fact is that it does matter if we are not comparing well with someone else," says Smith. "People who don't feel envy are going to wither away. Its hostile edge makes it a special call to action, and it may create the necessary impulse to narrow the gap or to move ahead."

14 Just as with anxiety, says Peter Salovey, professor of psychology at Yale, a mild dose of envy can energize us and concentrate our efforts: "If I really wish I had a car like my neighbor's, then that will motivate me to put my nose to the grindstone and earn more money in order to be able to buy that car." Monitoring the circumstances under which our envy attacks occur may even help us figure out who we are. "Envy helps us know what's really important to us," he says. If we consistently feel envy toward classmates who earn perfect grades or climbers who summit mighty peaks, these must be the domains on which we stake our reputations.

15 There is a difference between helpful stabs of envy and their pathological variant, however. People who are dissatisfied with life in general are more envious, as are people who exhibit neuroticism, which is characterized by tendencies to feel worried, insecure, and excitable. Smith theorizes that the chronically envious may get into a pattern of misinterpreting social comparison information. Like vigilantes, they are constantly scanning for evidence that they do not measure up. Those who suffer from depression are likely to shine the worst possible light on themselves when making comparisons and are therefore also more susceptible to envy. And envy is ultimately isolating. Envy impairs your ability to maintain close relationships, which happen to be the best refuge from a status-obsessed society, warns veteran journalist Chris Hedges, author of *Losing Moses on the Freeway: The 10 Commandments in America.* "Envy pushes us away from what's most precious, and that is love." Those who are lonely,

who lack close personal relationships, are most susceptible to status anxiety, he says.

16 "It's not enough to succeed," Gore Vidal famously quipped. "One's friends must fail." But there's one caveat to the measuring game. Someone else's good fortune doesn't spark envy if their gain is not our loss. Finding a partner within a small pool of singles, for example, is a zero-sum game akin to musical chairs: Each time someone else pairs off, your chance of getting left out increases. But if you're already happily married, someone else's marriage doesn't affect your happiness directly. Buss and Hill found that you'd prefer to stay married for as long as possible, rather than simply longer than others in your reference group who remain together. You'll feel sentimental (and perhaps hopeful that your own union will go the distance) at your next-door neighbors' golden anniversary celebration, not envious of their longevity.

17 Because envy is a direct threat to self-esteem, we often twist it into something more palatable, says Smith, and decide to denigrate the quality (or person) we envy. You may sigh as you thumb through the alumni journal, reflecting on the tragedy that is your former best friend's transformation. She may have done well for herself, but she sure did sell out! There's just no trace of that simple, virtuous, and completely nonthreatening girl you once loved. But then the next day, you'll finally map out a plan for that import–export venture you're going to start. How nice it will feel to drop the alumni bulletin a note when it gets off the ground.

Thinking about the Argument

1. According to the author, what role does envy play in personal success? Is it good or bad for you? Explain.
2. According to the author, what is an "immediate reference group"? What role does it play in setting standards for envy?
3. What does Flora say is the biological origin of envious behavior?
4. In what ways, according to the author, can envy be unhealthy?

Responding to the Argument

1. Explain why you disagree with the following statement from the article: "Being chronically dissatisfied is an effective stimulus to best your more complacent peers."
2. Do you agree with the way Flora characterizes men and women in terms of the differences in their biological drives to obtain money and possessions? Are men and women really fundamentally different in this regard? Could her analysis be characterized as sexist? Why do you hold this opinion?
3. Do you generally think of envy as psychologically healthy or unhealthy? Explain your answer.
4. How might envy help you to succeed? On what points of this argument do you agree or disagree with the author?

Writing about the Argument

1. Write a journal entry or give a class presentation discussing the role that envy has played in your life. In your estimate, has envy worked to your benefit or to your detriment?

2. Write a brief essay refuting the author's position. Explain how envy can be a destructive force that is best avoided.
3. Examine the evidence that Flora cites to support her argument. Evaluate it in writing. Where might the author need to acknowledge another viewpoint or employ another type of evidence? Where is her proof particularly strong?
4. Write a journal entry or brief paper explaining a situation in your life or the life of someone you know where envy has worked to help that person succeed. Convince a skeptical audience that a little envy is a good thing.

"The Luck Factor"

About the Author: Richard Wiseman

Richard Wiseman, who holds a Ph.D. in psychology from the University of Edinburgh, began his career as a magician. He has specialized in researching unusual areas of psychology, including the psychology of the paranormal, deception, and luck. He has written numerous articles for academic journals, including the acclaimed scientific journal *Nature.* In *The Luck Factor* (2003), Wiseman argues that four principles make a person "lucky" and that they have nothing to do with luck itself but rather are attributable to personality traits. In the article that follows, which was drawn from the author's book, Wiseman argues that lucky people succeed because of their positive attitude and their ability to spot and capitalize on opportunities. This piece first appeared in the May/June 2003 issue of *The Skeptical Inquirer.*

Before You Read

1. Review Wiseman's biographical information in the headnote. Is he qualified to write about a subject like luck and success? Why do you think this?
2. Does the title of his article suggest that Wiseman believes in luck or does not believe in luck?
3. The article, which was drawn from Wiseman's book, appeared in *The Skeptical Inquirer.* What does the title of this publication suggest about your answer to the previous question? Would the audience of this publication be inclined to believe in luck?
4. Do you believe that luck has anything to do with success? Explain your answer.

The Luck Factor

1 Barnett Helzberg, Jr., is a lucky man. By 1994 he had built up a chain of highly successful jewelry stores with an annual revenue of around $300 million. One day he was walking past the Plaza Hotel in New York when he heard a woman call out, "Mr. Buffett," to the man next to him. Helzberg wondered whether the man might be Warren Buffett—one of the most successful investors in America. Helzberg had never met Buffett, but had read about the financial criteria that Buffett used when buying a company. Helzberg had recently turned sixty, was think-

ing of selling his company, and realized that his might be the type of company that would interest Buffett. Helzberg seized the opportunity, walked over to the stranger, and introduced himself. The man did indeed turn out to be Warren Buffett, and the chance meeting proved highly fortuitous because about a year later Buffett agreed to buy Helzberg's chain of stores. And all because Helzberg just happened to be walking by as a woman called out Buffett's name on a street corner in New York.

2 Helzberg's story illustrates the effect of luck in business, but good fortune also plays a vital role in all aspects of our lives. Stanford psychologist Alfred Bandura has discussed the impact of chance encounters and luck on people's personal lives. Bandura noted both the importance and prevalence of such encounters, writing that "some of the most important determinants of life paths often arise through the most trivial of circumstances." He supports his case with several telling examples, one of which was drawn from his life. As a graduate student, Bandura became bored with a reading assignment and so decided to visit the local golf links with a friend. Just by chance, Bandura and his friend found themselves playing behind two attractive female golfers, and soon joined them as a foursome. After the game, Bandura arranged to meet up with one of the women again, and eventually ended up marrying her. A chance meeting on a golf course altered his entire life.

3 In short, lucky events exert a dramatic influence over our lives. Luck has the power to transform the improbable into the possible, to make the difference between life and death, reward and ruin, happiness and despair.

The Power of Superstition

4 People have searched for an effective way of improving the good fortune in their lives for many centuries. Lucky charms, amulets, and talismans have been found in virtually all civilizations throughout recorded history. Touching ("knocking on") wood dates back to pagan rituals that were designed to elicit the help of benign and powerful tree gods. The number thirteen is seen as unlucky because there were thirteen people at Christ's last supper. When a ladder is propped up against a wall it forms a natural triangle which used to be seen as symbolic of the Holy Trinity. To walk under the ladder would break the Trinity and therefore bring ill fortune.

5 Many of these beliefs and behaviors are still with us. In 1996, the Gallup Organization asked 1000 Americans whether they were superstitious. Fifty-three percent of people said that they were at least a little superstitious, and 25 percent admitted to being somewhat or very superstitious. Another survey revealed that 72 percent of the public said that they possessed at least one good luck charm. Superstitious beliefs and behaviors have been passed down from generation to generation. Our parents told us about them and we will pass them on to our children. But why do they persist? I believe that the answer lies in the power of luck. Throughout history, people have recognized that good and bad luck can transform lives. A few seconds of ill fortune can lay waste years of striving, and moments of good luck can save an enormous amount of hard work. Superstition represents people's attempts to control and enhance this most elusive of factors. And the enduring nature of these superstitious beliefs and behaviors reflects the extent of people's desire to find ways of increasing their good luck. In short, superstitions were created, and have survived, because they promise that most elusive of holy grails—a way of enhancing good fortune.

Testing Superstition

6 There is just one problem. Superstition doesn't work. Several researchers have also tested the validity of these age-old beliefs and found them wanting. My favorite experiment into the topic was a rather strange study conducted by high school student (and member of the New York Skeptics) Mark Levin. In some countries, a black

cat crossing your path is seen as lucky, in other countries it is seen as unlucky. Levin wanted to discover whether people's luck really changed when a black cat crossed their path. To find out, he asked two people to try their luck at a simple coin tossing game. Next, a black cat was encouraged to walk across their path, and the participants then played the coin tossing game a second time. As a "control" condition, Levin also repeated the experiment using a white, rather than a black, cat. After much coin tossing and cat crossing, Levin concluded that neither the black nor the white cat had any effect on participants' luck. Also, skeptics have regularly staged events in which they have broken well-known superstitions, such as walking under ladders and smashing mirrors—all have survived the ordeals intact.

7 A few years ago I decided to put the power of lucky charms to the test by empirically evaluating the actual effect that they have on people's luck, lives, and happiness. I asked a group of volunteers to complete various standardized questionnaires measuring their levels of life satisfaction, happiness, and luck. Next, they were asked to carry a lucky charm with them and to monitor the effect that it had on their lives. The charms had been purchased from a New Age center and promised to enhance good fortune, wealth, and happiness. After a few weeks everyone in the group was asked to indicate the effect that the charms had had on their lives. Overall, there was absolutely no effect in terms of how satisfied they were with their lives, how happy they were, or how lucky they felt. Interestingly, a few participants thought that they had been especially unlucky, and seemed somewhat relieved that they could now return the charms.

The Luck Project

8 Superstition doesn't work because it is based on outdated and incorrect thinking. It comes from a time when people thought that luck was a strange force that could only be controlled by magical rituals and bizarre behaviors.

9 Ten years ago I decided to take a more scientific investigation into the concept of luck. I decided that the best method was to examine why some people are consistently lucky whilst others encounter little but ill fortune.—in short, why some people seem to live charmed lives full of lucky breaks and chance encounters, while others experience one disaster after another.

10 I placed advertisements in national newspapers and magazines, asking for people who considered themselves exceptionally lucky or unlucky to contact me. Over the years, 400 extraordinary men and women have volunteered to participate in my research: the youngest eighteen, a student; the oldest eighty-four, a retired accountant. They were drawn from all walks of life—businessmen, factory workers, teachers, housewives, doctors, secretaries, and salespeople. All were kind enough to let me put their lives and minds under the microscope.

11 Jessica, a forty-two-year-old forensic scientist, is typical of the lucky people in the group. She is currently in a long-term relationship with a man who she met completely by chance at a dinner party. In fact, good fortune has helped her achieve many of her lifelong ambitions. As she once explained to me, "I have my dream job, two wonderful children, and a great guy that I love very much. It's amazing, when I look back at my life I realize that I have been lucky in just about every area." In contrast, the unlucky participants have not been so fortunate. Patricia, twenty-seven, has experienced bad luck throughout much of her life. A few years ago, she started to work as cabin crew for an airline, and quickly gained a reputation as being accident-prone and a bad omen. One of her first flights had to make an unplanned stop-over because some passengers had become drunk and abusive. Another of Patricia's flights was struck by lightning, and just weeks later a third flight was forced to make an emergency landing. Patricia was also convinced that her ill fortune could be transferred to others and so never wished people good luck, be-

cause this had caused them to fail important interviews and exams. She is also unlucky in love and has staggered from one broken relationship to the next. Patricia never seems to get any lucky breaks and always seems to be in the wrong place at the wrong time.

12 Over the years I have interviewed these volunteers; asked them to complete diaries, personality questionnaires, and intelligence tests; and invited them to my laboratory to participate in experiments. The findings have revealed that luck is not a magical ability or the result of random chance. Nor are people born lucky or unlucky. Instead, although lucky and unlucky people have almost no insight into the real causes of their good and bad luck, their thoughts and behavior are responsible for much of their fortune.

13 My research revealed that lucky people generate their own good fortune via four basic principles. They are skilled at creating and noticing chance opportunities, make lucky decisions by listening to their intuition, create self-fulfilling prophesies via positive expectations, and adopt a resilient attitude that transforms bad luck into good.

Chance Opportunities

14 Take the case of chance opportunities. Lucky people consistently encounter such opportunities, whereas unlucky people do not. I carried out a very simple experiment to discover whether this was due to differences in their ability to spot such opportunities. I gave both lucky and unlucky people a newspaper, and asked them to look through it and tell me how many photographs were inside. On average, the unlucky people took about two minutes to count the photographs whereas the lucky people took just seconds. Why? Because the second page of the newspaper contained the message "Stop counting—There are 43 photographs in this newspaper." This message took up half of the page and was written in type that was over two inches high. It was staring everyone straight in the face, but the unlucky people tended to miss it and the lucky people tended to spot it. Just for fun, I placed a second large message half way through the newspaper. This one announced: "Stop counting, tell the experimenter you have seen this and win $250." Again, the unlucky people missed the opportunity because they were still too busy looking for photographs.

15 Personality tests revealed that unlucky people are generally much more tense and anxious than lucky people, and research has shown that anxiety disrupts people's ability to notice the unexpected. In one experiment, people were asked to watch a moving dot in the center of a computer screen. Without warning, large dots would occasionally be flashed at the edges of the screen. Nearly all participants noticed these large dots. The experiment was then repeated with a second group of people, who were offered a large financial reward for accurately watching the center dot. This time, people were far more anxious about the whole situation. They became very focused on the center dot and over a third of them missed the large dots when they appeared on the screen. The harder they looked, the less they saw. And so it is with luck—unlucky people miss chance opportunities because they are too focused on looking for something else. They go to parties intent on finding their perfect partner and so miss opportunities to make good friends. They look through newspapers determined to find certain type of job advertisements and as a result miss other types of jobs. Lucky people are more relaxed and open, and therefore see what is there rather than just what they are looking for.

16 But this is only part of the story when it comes to chance opportunities. Many of my lucky participants went to considerable lengths to introduce variety and change into their lives. Before making an important decision, one lucky participant would constantly alter his route to work. Another person described a special technique that he had developed to force him to meet

different types of people. He had noticed that whenever he went to a party, he tended to talk to the same type of people. To help disrupt this routine, and make life more fun, he thinks of a color before he arrives at the party and then chooses to only speak to people wearing that color of clothing at the party! At some parties he only spoke to women in red, at another he chatted exclusively to men in black.

17 Although it may seem strange, under certain circumstances, this type of behavior will actually increase the amount of chance opportunities in people's lives. Imagine living in the center of a large apple orchard. Each day you have to venture into the orchard and collect a large basket of apples. The first few times it won't matter where you decide to visit. All parts of the orchard will have apples and so you will be able to find them wherever you go. But as time goes on it will become more and more difficult to find apples in the places that you have visited before. And the more you return to the same locations, the harder it will be to find apples there. But if you decide to always go to parts of the orchard that you have never visited before, or even randomly decide where to go, your chances of finding apples will be dramatically increased. And it is exactly the same with luck. It is easy for people to exhaust the opportunities in their life. Keep on talking to the same people in the same way. Keep taking the same route to and from work. Keep going to the same places on vacation. But new or even random experiences introduce the potential for new opportunities.

Dealing with Bad Luck

18 But a lucky life is not just about creating and noticing chance opportunities. Another important principle revolved around the way in which lucky and unlucky people dealt with the ill fortune in their lives. Imagine being chosen to represent your country in the Olympic Games. You compete in the games, do very well, and win a bronze medal. How happy do you think that you would feel? Most of us would, I suspect, be overjoyed and proud of our achievement. Now imagine turning the clock back and competing at the same Olympic Games a second time. This time you do even better and win a silver medal. How happy do you think you would feel now? Most of us think that we would feel happier after winning the silver medal than the bronze. This is not surprising. After all, the medals are a reflection of our performance, and the silver medal indicates a better performance than a bronze medal.

19 But research suggests that athletes who win bronze models are actually happier than those who win silver medals. And the reason for this has to do with the way in which the athletes think about their performance. The silver medallists focus on the notion that if they had performed slightly better, then they would have perhaps won a gold medal. In contrast, the bronze medallists focus on the thought that if they had performed slightly worse, then they wouldn't have won anything at all. Psychologists refer to our ability to imagine what might have happened, rather than what actually did happen, as "counter-factual."

20 I wondered whether lucky people might be using counter-factual thinking to soften the emotional impact of the ill fortune that they experienced in their lives. To find out, I decided to present lucky and unlucky people with some unlucky scenarios and see how they reacted. I asked lucky and unlucky people to imagine that they were waiting to be served in a bank. Suddenly, an armed robber enters the bank, fires a shot, and the bullet hits them in the arm. Would this event be lucky or unlucky? Unlucky people tended to say that this would be enormously unlucky and it would be just their bad luck to be in the bank during the robbery. In contrast, lucky people viewed the scenario as being far luckier, and often spontaneously commented on how the situation could have been far worse. As one lucky participant commented, "It's lucky because you could have

been shot in the head—also, you could sell your story to the newspapers and make some money."

21 The differences between the lucky and unlucky people were striking. Lucky people tend to imagine spontaneously how the bad luck they encounter could have been worse and, in doing so, they feel much better about themselves and their lives. This, in turn, helps keep their expectations about the future high, and, increases the likelihood of them continuing to live a lucky life.

Luck School

22 I wondered whether the principles uncovered during my work could be used to increase the amount of good luck that people encounter in their lives. To find out, I created "luck school"—a series of experiments examining whether people's luck can be enhanced by getting them to think and behave like a lucky person.

23 The project comprised two main parts. In the first part I met up with participants on a one-to-one basis, and asked them to complete standard questionnaires measuring their luck and how satisfied they were with six major areas of their life. I then described the four main principles of luck, explained how lucky people used these to create good fortune in their lives, and described simple techniques designed to help them think and behave like a lucky person. For example, as I noted earlier, without realizing it, lucky people tend to use various techniques to create chance opportunities, and soften the emotional impact of any ill fortune they encounter. During luck school participants were shown how to be more open to the opportunities that surround them, how to break daily routines, and also how to deal more effectively with bad luck by imagining how things could have been worse. I asked my volunteers to spend a month carrying out exercises and then return and describe what had happened.

24 The results were dramatic. Eighty percent of people were now happier, more satisfied with their lives, and, perhaps most important of all, luckier. Unlucky people had become lucky, and lucky people had become even luckier. At the start of the article I described the unlucky life of Patricia. She was one of the first people to take part in Luck School. After a few weeks carrying out some simple exercises, her bad luck had completely vanished. At the end of the course, Patricia cheerfully explained that she felt like a completely different person. She was no longer accident-prone and was much happier with her life. For once, everything was working out her way. Other volunteers had found romantic partners through chance encounters and job promotions simply through lucky breaks.

Positive Skepticism

25 After ten years of scientific research my work has revealed a radically new way of looking at luck and the vital role that it plays in our lives. It demonstrates that much of the good and bad fortune we encounter is a result of our thoughts and behavior. More important, it represents the potential for change, and has produced that most elusive of holy grails—an effective way of increasing the luck people experience in their daily lives.

26 The project has also demonstrated how skepticism can play a positive role in people's lives. The research is not simply about debunking superstitious thinking and behavior. Instead, it is about encouraging people to move away from a magical way of thinking and toward a more rational view of luck. Perhaps most important of all, it is about using science and skepticism to increase the level of luck, happiness, and success in people's lives.

»«

THINKING ABOUT THE ARGUMENT

1. What is Wiseman's opinion of luck? Where in the excerpt does he tell you?
2. According to the author, what role does superstition play in increasing good luck?
3. How did Mark Levin test the validity of claims of luck? How did his experiment differ from the author's method? Explain why each was or was not a valid test.
4. What are the author's four basic principles that lead to good fortune? What would you add to or delete from the list?
5. What role does Wiseman think attitude plays in creating good fortune?

RESPONDING TO THE ARGUMENT

1. Wiseman opens with an anecdote about a fortuitous meeting between Barnett Helzberg and Warren Buffett. Was this meeting "just luck," or did it have something to do with Helzberg's ability to make himself successful? Explain.
2. Is the author's discussion of the "supernatural" existence of luck adequate or dismissive? Why do you hold this opinion?
3. Do you agree that an attitude of "positive skepticism" increases success? Explain.

WRITING ABOUT THE ARGUMENT

1. Is buying a lottery ticket a good way to improve your fortune? If the people who win are "lucky," how about the millions who buy tickets but do not win? What should these people have done instead to improve their quality of life?
2. Make your own list of things that will increase someone's chances of success. Write a journal entry or short essay explaining how to apply these ideas.
3. Write a refutation explaining why having luck—or at least believing in it—is important.
4. Does your station in life—whether you are born rich or poor, for example—affect the amount of "luck" you have? Can well-off people be unlucky? Write your answer in the form of a letter to the editor of your local newspaper (or as an Internet blog).

The Individual in Society 16

Same-Sex Marriage, Poverty, and Political Correctness

If there is a bedrock principle of the First Amendment, it is that the government may not prohibit the expression of an idea simply because society finds the idea itself offensive or disagreeable.

—Justice William J. Brennan (1906–1997)

John Stuart Mill once wrote: "The individual is not accountable to society for his actions, in so far as these concern the interests of no person but himself." At first glance, this argument seems common sense. However, the reality is that when individuals gather as parts of a group—as friends, as members of a family, as people working together, or as citizens of a larger society such as a town, state, or nation—their interests often come into conflict. Where one private person's rights end and the rights of others begin can be a matter of debate. In other

Online Study Center
This icon will direct you to content and resources on the website <college.hmco.com/pic/lamm1e>.

words, what appears to be beneficial to an individual may not be perceived as good for the other members of a group.

In the reading clusters that follow, you will be asked to consider, debate, and write about the relationship between the individual and society. Here are some questions to think about as you read:

- Do people really have the right to do whatever they want, even if the community in which they live disapproves of their actions?
- Does society have the right to impose certain standards on the individuals within a community (family, city, state, or company)?

Issue 1: Same-Sex Marriage

Same-sex marriage (or gay marriage) and same-sex civil unions are controversial—not only because they violate a long-held social taboo (against people of the same sex having intimate relations) but because they strike at the heart of

Do gays and lesbians have a right to legal acceptance of their relationships? Does the majority have the right to ask them to sequester their romantic lives behind closed doors?

two domains of law about which many individuals have strong feelings. The first domain of law concerns the right of individuals to do as they please and the right of a society to encourage behavior that is representative of its values and ethics. The second domain of law concerns which division of government—federal or state—has the right to regulate certain kinds of behavior within communities. If a minority of states legitimizes same-sex marriage, should a majority of states be allowed to outlaw it? Do the rights of individual men and women override the right of a society to prohibit behavior it considers immoral?

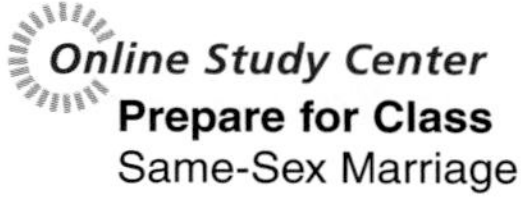

Online Study Center
Prepare for Class
Same-Sex Marriage

Considering the Issue of Same-Sex Marriage

Working individually or in groups, answer the following questions.

1. How do you define *marriage?* Does your definition include or exclude gay couples? Why?
2. What do you think is the most important part of a relationship? Did you include that most important part in your definition of marriage? Why or why not?
3. Do you believe that marriage should be defined by couples, by religions, or by governments?
4. Should gay couples share the same legal rights enjoyed by heterosexual married couples, such as tax exemptions and medical insurance benefits for spouses?

READING SELECTION

"Why the M Word Matters to Me"

About the Author: Andrew Sullivan

Andrew Sullivan, who holds a Ph.D. in political philosophy from Harvard University, has written essays for *Time* magazine (where this essay first appeared in February 2004) and columns for the *Sunday Times of London* and has served as editor of *New Republic.* His articles have also appeared in the *Wall Street Journal,* the *New York Times,* the *Washington Post,* and *Esquire.* He is editor of AndrewSullivan.com, where his articles, commentaries, and Internet blogs can be found. Sullivan has commented on a wide range of social issues, including same-sex marriage. His book *Virtually Normal: An Argument about Homosexuality* (1995) initiated the debate over marriage rights for gay couples. He has also written *Same Sex Marriage: Pro and Con* (1997) and *Love Undetectable: Notes on Friendship, Sex, and Survival* (1999).

BEFORE YOU READ

1. What is your opinion of same-sex marriage? How do you think that opinion will affect the way you approach Sullivan's article?
2. Do you think Sullivan is qualified to comment on this topic? Why or why not?
3. What does the title suggest to you? Do you expect the reading to be personal or impersonal? Formal or informal? Explain.
4. What do you expect the author's main point to be? Why do you think this?
5. How do you react to the term *same-sex marriage* (or *gay marriage*) as opposed to the term *civil union*? If both terms mean the same in terms of legal and financial benefits, what is the difference?

Why the M Word Matters to Me

1 As a child, I had no idea what homosexuality was. I grew up in a traditional home—Catholic, conservative, middle class. Life was relatively simple: education, work, family. I was raised to aim high in life, even though my parents hadn't gone to college. But one thing was instilled in me. What mattered was not how far you went in life, how much money you earned, how big a name you made for yourself. What really mattered was family and the love you had for one another. The most important day of your life was not graduation from college or your first day at work or a raise or even your first house. The most important day of your life was when you got married. It was on that day that all your friends and all your family got together to celebrate the most important thing in life: your happiness—your ability to make a new home, to form a new but connected family, to find love that put everything else into perspective.

2 But as I grew older, I found that this was somehow not available to me. I didn't feel the things for girls that my peers did. All the emotions and social rituals and bonding of teenage heterosexual life eluded me. I didn't know why. No one explained it. My emotional bonds to other boys were one-sided; each time I felt myself falling in love, they sensed it, pushed it away. I didn't and couldn't blame them. I got along fine with my buds in a nonemotional context, but something was awry, something not right. I came to know almost instinctively that I would never be a part of my family the way my siblings might one day be. The love I had inside me was unmentionable, anathema. I remember writing in my teenage journal one day, "I'm a professional human being. But what do I do in my private life?"

3 I never discussed my real life. I couldn't date girls and so immersed myself in schoolwork, the debate team, school plays, anything to give me an excuse not to confront reality. When I looked toward the years ahead, I couldn't see a future. There was just a void. Was I going to be alone my whole life? Would I ever have a most important day in my life? It seemed impossible, a negation, an undoing. To be a full part of my family, I had to somehow not be me. So, like many other gay teens, I withdrew, became neurotic, depressed, at times close to suicidal. I shut myself in my room with my books night after night while my peers developed the skills needed to form real relationships and loves. In wounded pride, I even voiced a rejection of family and marriage. It was the only way I could explain my isolation.

4 It took years for me to realize that I was gay, years more to tell others, and more time yet to

form any kind of stable emotional bond with another man. Because my sexuality had emerged in solitude—and without any link to the idea of an actual relationship—it was hard later to reconnect sex to love and self-esteem. It still is. But I persevered, each relationship slowly growing longer than the last, learning in my 20s and 30s what my straight friends had found out in their teens. But even then my parents and friends never asked the question they would have asked automatically if I were straight: So, when are you going to get married? When will we be able to celebrate it and affirm it and support it? In fact, no one—no one—has yet asked me that question.

5 When people talk about gay marriage, they miss the point. This isn't about gay marriage. It's about marriage. It's about family. It's about love. It isn't about religion. It's about civil marriage licenses. Churches can and should have the right to say no to marriage for gays in their congregations, just as Catholics say no to divorce, but divorce is still a civil option. These family values are not options for a happy and stable life. They are necessities. Putting gay relationships in some other category—civil unions, domestic partnerships, whatever—may alleviate real human needs, but by their very euphemism, by their very separateness, they actually build a wall between gay people and their families. They put back the barrier many of us have spent a lifetime trying to erase.

6 It's too late for me to undo my past. But I want above everything else to remember a young kid out there who may even be reading this now. I want to let him know that he doesn't have to choose between himself and his family anymore. I want him to know that his love has dignity, that he does indeed have a future as a full and equal part of the human race. Only marriage will do that. Only marriage can bring him home.

Thinking about the Argument

1. Why is marriage so important to Sullivan? Why does he say, "I came to know almost instinctively that I would never be a part of my family the way my siblings might one day be"?
2. Reread paragraph 3. What was the result of the lack of fulfillment that Sullivan expresses?
3. According to the author, what is gay marriage "about"?
4. What does Sullivan say about the difference between gay marriage and civil unions? Why does he see this distinction as important?

Responding to the Argument

1. What effect does Sullivan's personal story have on you emotionally? Do you sympathize with his plight? Why or why not?
2. In paragraph 4, Sullivan says, "no one—no one—has yet asked me that question." What question is he referring to? Why is it important to him? What does it imply about the argument that he is making?
3. Do you agree or disagree with Sullivan's assessment of what gay marriage is "about"? Explain.
4. Do you agree or disagree with Sullivan's argument concerning the difference between marriage and civil unions? Why do you think this?

WRITING ABOUT THE ARGUMENT

1. Write a paragraph or two reacting to Sullivan's piece. Discuss your emotional reaction to the personal elements employed in the narrative.
2. Write one or two paragraphs evaluating one significant strength and/or weakness of Sullivan's argument.
3. Write a brief argument explaining the difference between same-sex marriage and civil unions. How are they similar and/or different? Does this difference matter? If so, why does it matter?

"Why Gay Marriage Doesn't Measure Up"

ABOUT THE AUTHOR: ROBERT W. PATTERSON

Robert W. Patterson is a writer and commentator who has worked as a speech writer for the U.S. Department of Health and Human Services and has served as a research fellow for the Howard Center for Family, Religion, and Society. He regularly contributes to the Howard Center's monthly newsletter, *The Family in America.* Patterson has published articles in the *Weekly Standard, Touchstone, Crisis, Books & Culture, Christianity Today, Christian Century,* and *Presbyterian Outlook.* This article first appeared in *Human Events* in March 2004.

BEFORE YOU READ

1. What does the title imply about the book's thesis? Are you inclined to agree or disagree with Patterson? Why?
2. What do you suppose is the purpose of the Howard Center? Do you think that it would endorse civil unions or be critical of them? How do you know?
3. What does Patterson's background suggest to you about his point of view?

Why Gay Marriage Doesn't Measure Up

If any man can show any just cause why they may not lawfully be joined together, let him now speak, or else hereafter forever hold his peace.

—Book of Common Prayer

1 Not very long ago, ordained ministers posed this proposition to congregations early in weddings just before addressing the bride and groom about their intentions of becoming husband and wife. That most clergy today leave it out of wedding liturgies is unfortunate, as the question reflects a critical understanding of marriage largely lost on Americans today and especially upon those seeking civil recognition of same-sex couples.

2 The fact that a minister, functioning as an agent of the state, would seek approval of a marriage from parties other than the couple is revealing. That solicited confirmation expresses the reality that marriage is not just a legal contract between two individuals but also a dynamic relationship that, according to social historian

Allan C. Carlson, stands at the core of a complex web of social bonds that begins with the couple, finds support from their respective families and extended kin, and extends to society at large.

3 When family and friends assent to a marriage, they are judging the union good for *society,* not just good for the couple. In fact, this approbation is also granted on behalf of the future children that all related parties anticipate will naturally flow from such union.

Kinship Bonds

4 This communal dimension is virtually nonexistent when it comes to same-sex relationships, evidence that such relationships should never be deemed equivalent to, or even an alternative to, marriage. Unlike marriage, same-sex relationships are static, self-focused, and center almost exclusively on what the relationship delivers for the two partners, not what it represents to the supportive families or to society.

5 Does a homosexual partner even solicit the blessing of his prospective partner's family? Do his aunts and uncles travel cross-country to celebrate the occasion? Who are the third parties to these pairings? Rarely conducted in a community setting like a church or synagogue, these new-fangled arrangements are essentially private affairs with no organic ties to anything. Ironically, this private identity is praised by advocates like Andrew Sullivan who assert that gay marriage can't possibly impact the traditional marriages of others because it concerns only the two persons involved.

6 This narrow focus on the couple dominates even the campaign for legal recognition of gay marriage or civil unions. It's all about *them.* The stated justifications for same-sex marriage have nothing to do with how this approach to mating can contribute to the common good, but everything to do with what society can, or must, do *for* the couple. They seek health insurance, survivor benefits, and hospital visitation rights (even though no law prevents these things now). They demand these "benefits" and other "rights," the legal side effects that accrue to marriage that are rarely on the table when a man and woman decide to wed.

7 Marriage, Family, and Children

As every husband and wife knows, the real benefits of marriage are not technical legalities conferred upon it by an outside party, in this case the state, but are generated from within the institution itself—children, and eventually grandchildren. Nevertheless, because homosexual relationships are by definition sterile—because they cannot produce what really matters—their demands extend to finagling with biology or exploiting the brokenness of failed heterosexual relationships to "have" children, again at the expense of others.

8 The tragedy of the celebrated Episcopal bishop, Eugene Robinson, vividly illustrates how homosexual relationships fall short of common good. His decision more than ten years ago to enter into a "relationship" with another man may be looked upon by some as what justice and compassion require, but it exacted a huge toll on his family, as well as those close to his family. Robinson had to violate his marriage vows, divorce his wife, and desert his children—all so that he could fool around with his boyfriend.

9 How do his children defend their father to their peers? Is this behavior that the state wants to encourage and uphold as virtuous? Is it good for the families involved, good for the Episcopal communion that Robinson represents, good for society?

10 Granted, some married, heterosexual men do the same and run off with their girlfriends, which is why the states need to repeal no-fault divorce and hold men (and women) accountable to the promises they make, without any coercion, to their families and to society on their wedding day. But just because no-fault has wreaked havoc on a generation of American children is no excuse for state legislatures to sanction (or for courts to

decree) more social pathology with another dubious experiment that, like divorce, treats women and children as disposable.

11 That not all homosexual debuts are as messy as Robinson's may suggest that women are not always casualties. Nevertheless, being twice as prevalent among males than females, homosexual behavior ends up excluding a portion of women from the sexual equation, not to mention marriage, an injustice that feminists overlook. In other words, homosexuality is mostly about men, who are sexually wrapped up in themselves, directing their passions toward other men who are also wrapped up in themselves.

Natural Division of Labor

12 This is not to suggest that gays are self-centered in all aspects of life, as individuals surely make contributions to society that transcend their sexual behavior. But even here, the aggregate contribution of gay couples is muted relative to husband–wife couples.

13 Building upon the insights of Nobel Laureate Gary Becker, who has argued that homosexual couples do not specialize their economic roles as efficiently as do heterosexual couples, economist John Mueller has calculated that average life-time earnings for married heterosexual couples are significantly higher than all other comparable household arrangements, including a divorced husband and wife in separate households, a cohabiting heterosexual couple, and two same-sex individuals in the same household. The reason: Mueller points to the social science literature that finds, confirming Becker's theory of comparative advantage and the sexual division of labor, that the economic behavior of men changes for the better when they have a wife and children to support, a dynamic missing from same-sex arrangements.

14 What this comes down to should be obvious: Gay marriage, like all the liberal ideas of the 1970s—including no-fault divorce, abortion on demand, cohabitation, and day care—does not and cannot serve the common good.

15 When elected officials, like the minister in a wedding ceremony, ask whether the public objects to what is being proposed in Massachusetts and San Francisco, the American people need to rise up and speak their minds for the sake of the children, for the sake of women, and for the sake of the republic.

THINKING ABOUT THE ARGUMENT

1. What is Patterson's claim? Can you identify it in the text? What significant reason(s) does he cite to back up his argument?
2. What evidence does Patterson cite to validate his argument? Is it adequate? Is it convincing? Why or why not?
3. What does the author mean when he suggests that marriages should be "good for *society,* not just good for the couple?"
4. Why does Patterson believe that same-sex marriage is an unnecessary and socially unhealthy formality?

RESPONDING TO THE ARGUMENT

1. Has your opinion of same-sex marriage changed in any way as a result of Patterson's argument? How so?

2. Patterson suggests that for society to endorse same-sex marriage places too much emphasis on the desires of the individual and not enough on the greater health of society. How might same-sex marriage be damaging to society as a whole? Conversely, how might publicly recognizing same-sex unions be good for society?
3. Should marriage (same-sex or otherwise) always be "about" the individuals, or should the marriage's effect on others—children, parents, society in general—be considered as well?
4. How might Patterson's argument be refuted?

Writing about the Argument

1. Write a refutation of Patterson's argument. In your argument, explain why publicly recognizing gay marriage is good for society as a whole, and not just for the individuals involved.
2. Write a brief argument supporting Patterson's point of view.
3. In a brief argument, explain whether the good of society or the good of the individual is more important in any public endorsement of marriage. (There could be a slippery slope here—if the good of the individual is more important than the good of society, then what is to prevent marriages between adults and young teenagers? One might effectively argue that it would be beneficial for a 15-year-old girl to be allowed to marry a 50-year-old man if the man were loving and removing the girl from an abusive household, for example.)

"Option Four"

About the Author: Ramesh Ponnuru

In addition to publishing articles in *National Review* (where he serves as senior editor), Ramesh Ponnuru has published articles in the *New York Times,* the *Washington Post,* the *Wall Street Journal, Newsday,* the *Financial Times,* and the *New York Post.* Ponnuru has also been published in *Reason, First Things, Policy Review,* and the *Weekly Standard.* He has served as a fellow at the Hoover Institution (Stanford University) and the Institute of Economic Affairs (London). He has also appeared on numerous news commentary shows. This article was originally published in *National Review* in June 2005.

Before You Read

1. What does the author's list of publications suggest to you? Does it give you any expectations regarding the article's point of view?
2. What, if anything, do you know about *National Review?* Take a moment to look at its website. What sort of perspective would you expect from this publication? Based on this perspective, what do you think the article might have to say about the topic of same-sex marriage and civil unions?
3. What does the phrase "option four" suggest? Why?
4. Who is Ponnuru's audience?

Option Four

1 The debate over marriage does not seem to be amenable to compromise. It is one of those debates in which the contending parties disagree not only about what answer we should reach, but also about what the question is in the first place. As in the debate over abortion, the very terminology of this debate is contested. Advocates of "gay marriage" use that phrase to suggest that what they want is an end to the exclusion of a class of people from an institution. Opponents of "same-sex marriage" use that phrase to suggest that what is at stake is a redefinition of the institution: The law they defend does not examine the sexual preferences of the parties to a marriage, but merely requires that they be of opposite sexes.

2 But perhaps a limited compromise can be reached, if we can separate the two fundamental issues in the debate: recognition and benefits.

3 Whenever the debate has been at its most abstract and ideological, it has concerned the politics of recognition. Proponents of gay marriage want the government to recognize long-term homosexual relationships as morally equivalent, at least for public purposes, to marriage. Many proponents undoubtedly want more than this kind of formal legal equality: They hope that insisting on governmental evenhandedness between homosexual and heterosexual couples will change people's attitudes so that society, and not just the government, will see them as equally worthy and morally indistinguishable. Opponents warn that if the demand for same-sex marriages is granted, it will be followed by demands for state penalties on people and churches that refuse to recognize them. But for now, what is being debated is the legal recognition of committed homosexual relationships as on a par with marriage.

4 When proponents of gay marriage say that existing law is "discriminatory," and a violation of the Fourteenth Amendment, their underlying claim is that the state has no legitimate reason for distinguishing between long-term gay relationships and conventional marriages. If there is no reason to distinguish between them, the distinction observed by existing law can be attributed only to prejudice. Opponents of same-sex marriage, on the other hand, have argued that there are legitimate distinctions to be drawn. If according legal standing to the marriage of a man and a woman can yield some public good that according legal standing to same-sex couples cannot, then existing law does not involve any invidious discrimination. Whether any such public good exists has been a major point of contention in the debate. Almost all the high-flown commentary on the marriage debate has turned on this question of recognition, although the issue is sometimes disguised.

5 The energy brought to this part of the debate has sometimes obscured the extent to which the debate is also about various governmental benefits. Supporters of same-sex marriage have asked again and again why gays should be denied hospital-visitation rights when their partner falls ill or bereavement leave when their partner dies. Obviously, this concern is connected to the argument about equality: If committed same-sex couples are morally equivalent to married couples, then why should they not have the same legal protections? But the issue of benefits can, to a large extent, be separated from the issue of the legal recognition of relationships.

6 And the issues should be separated. There is no very good reason that many of the incidents of marriage that remain on the books should be tied strictly to marriage. To the extent possible, they should be extended more widely. Liberals and conservatives, supporters and opponents of same-sex marriage alike, should be willing to support this extension.

7 Take, for example, the question of the bereavement leave given to state employees. State governments could easily have their workers designate a person whose death would trigger the leave. Many workers would choose their spouses.

Gay men and lesbians in long-term relationships would, presumably, choose their partners. People who are not in romantic relationships might choose blood relatives or friends. Family leave for state employees could be handled similarly.

8 So could hospital-visitation rights: Where the law has said that hospitals must grant them to spouses, it could be amended to require that they also be granted to whomever the patient has designated—and again, that "whomever" could be a man's live-in girlfriend, his boyfriend, or a close friend.

9 These benefits could, perhaps, be bundled together: People could be allowed to choose someone as their "designated partner" for a multitude of purposes. Legislators could call the resulting bundle of rights a "domestic partnership" or even a "civil union" if they wish. Bundling the benefits together would make things simpler for beneficiaries and government officials alike than extending each benefit separately.

10 Such policies would allow gay couples to get the tangible benefits they seek, but not governmental recognition of their relationships as such. And so long as the benefits were available not only to married people and to gay couples, but to any pair of people, then opponents of same-sex marriage would have nothing to complain about. No benefit would be contingent on any assumption by the government that the beneficiaries were involved in a sexual relationship outside traditional marriage. The precise nature of the relationship between the beneficiaries would not concern the state. The state would be blind to it.

No "Marriage Lite"

11 Would taking these steps "undermine marriage," as opponents say same-sex marriage would? It's hard to see how. The incidents of marriage that remain on the books may be important in some respects, but nobody gets married in order to enjoy them; allowing people to have them outside marriage is not going to drive down the marriage rate. Nor do most of the remaining incidents of marriage have much moral significance—the great exceptions being those incidents having to do with the raising of children, which will continue to divide social conservatives and social liberals. (Florida, for example, does not permit gay couples to adopt children.) The kinds of changes mentioned above are more akin to contractual arrangements. We allow people who are not married to each other to make all kinds of contractual arrangements without worrying that their ability to make them undermines marriage.

12 Social conservatives, and even some supporters of gay marriage such as the journalist Jonathan Rauch, have expressed concern that a proliferation of institutional substitutes for marriage would undermine marriage. They worry, that is, about "marriage lite." The modern practice of cohabitation illustrates the fear. If a young man is being pressured by his girlfriend to commit but does not want to marry, he can move in with her instead. Would registering as a "designated partner" (or whatever term is employed) become another way for him to avoid marriage? So, for example, his girl-friend is pressuring him to make still more of a commitment than just living together. Will he be able to placate her by going to City Hall and signing a form?

13 To the extent there is any reason to worry about this scenario, it's an argument for making the above reforms piecemeal, even at the cost of reduced simplicity. But there is reason to doubt that even a wholesale extension of benefits would have baleful effects. The fact that the new institution would be open to everyone—roommates who are not involved in a sexual relationship as well as those who are, siblings, friends—would tend to undermine its attractiveness as a symbol of romantic commitment.

14 The idea of decoupling various benefits from marriage has hardly received an airing during the debate over gay unions. When the idea entered the debate, it did so at a peculiar angle. Around the time the high court of Massachusetts ruled

in favor of same-sex marriage, when social-conservative organizations were hashing out what kind of constitutional amendment they should support, some social conservatives briefly proposed one with two major features. It would define marriage as the union of a man and a woman. It would also prohibit governments from granting any benefits to unmarried couples (or groups) that were predicated on a sexual relationship. The principle was very similar to what I am advocating here, except that it was framed negatively. The social conservatives were not proposing to extend any benefits that had traditionally been tied to marriage more widely. They were suggesting that they would *allow* such extensions under certain conditions. They would allow benefits to be given to the unmarried, that is, if it were done on a non-discriminatory basis: If unmarried couples, heterosexual or homosexual, could get the benefit, siblings who shared the rent had to be eligible for it, too.

15 The proposal was somewhat convoluted, and thus easily misunderstood. Andrew Sullivan, a prominent pro–gay-marriage pundit, thought that the social conservatives were saying that they wanted to extend benefits only to celibate couples. Any such proposal would be absurd and unworkable, as he suggested. But the present political moment seems auspicious for someone to go further than those social conservatives did, and actually propose an extension of marital benefits to unmarried couples of all kinds.

16 The reason compromise might work now is that the politics of marriage are in flux. Advocates of gay marriage are confident that the future is on their side. Although support for their cause in public-opinion polls has dropped since Massachusetts brought attention to it, the longer-run trend has been in their favor. Younger people, in particular, have shown steadily increasing support for gay marriage. If the advocates believe they will win in the long run, however, they are less sure how long that run will be. Their allies within liberalism, meanwhile, are afraid that they will suffer severe political damage in the interim—as they appear to have done in 2004.

17 Opponents of same-sex marriage, looking at the same situation from the opposite perspective, also have mixed prospects. They can see short-term political victories ahead, but actual success in their project of preventing same-sex marriage from becoming the prevailing law in America looks much less likely.

18 Each side had its own spin on the 2004 elections. Social liberals noted that in the exit polls, a plurality of 35 percent of voters said they favored "civil unions" for gays. Social conservatives, however, noted that voters supported initiatives against same-sex marriage in every state where they were on the ballot—and some of those initiatives were against civil unions, too. Indeed, the opposition to many of those ballot initiatives centered on the notion that they were banning civil unions and domestic partnerships as well as same-sex marriage.

19 My hunch is that public opinion looks ambivalent because the median voter is tugged in two directions. He thinks marriage should remain an opposite-sex affair, but he has no wish to deny hospital-visitation rights to gay couples. If he is forced to choose between these impulses—if what's on the ballot is a choice between same-sex marriage and the continued denial of various benefits for gay couples—he will vote against same-sex marriage. If a pollster offers him "civil unions" as a middle ground, however, he will say he supports it.

20 Civil unions, as generally conceived, seem not to be a viable compromise in the marriage controversy. Social conservatives seem to be implacably opposed to any governmental recognition of homosexual relationships, even if they do not travel under the name of "marriage"—partly because they fear that once such unions are recognized, over time they will be treated as marriages.

READING SELECTION

The Fourth Option

21 But what if our pollster added a fourth option (in addition to same-sex marriage, civil unions, and nothing)? I imagine that if the public were granted an option that allowed gay couples to receive benefits without according legal standing to their relationships, the option would draw support from each of the other three camps. It might well become the plurality option.

22 That plurality would, I imagine, include President Bush, if a pollster called him. Right before the elections, Charles Gibson of ABC asked Bush, "[H]ow can we deny [homosexuals] rights in any way to a civil union that would allow, give them the same economic rights or health rights or other things?" Bush responded, "I don't think we should deny people rights to a civil union, a legal arrangement, if that's what a state chooses to do. . . ." Gibson interjected that the Republican-party platform "opposes it" (i.e., civil unions). Bush came back with, "Well, I don't. I view the definition of marriage different from legal arrangements that enable people to have rights. And I strongly believe that marriage ought to be defined as a union between a man and a woman. Now, having said that, states ought to be able to have the right to pass laws that enable people to be able to have rights like others."

23 The remarks generated a lot of controversy, with some social conservatives convinced that Bush had betrayed them and pundits of all political persuasions convinced that Bush had made a last-minute campaign U-turn. The weekend after the election, Karl Rove offered his own gloss on Bush's position for Fox News: "He believes that there are ways that states can deal with some of the issues that have been raised, for example, visitation rights in hospitals or the right to inherit or benefit rights, property rights. But these can all be dealt with at the state level without overturning the definition of marriage as being between a man and a woman."

24 Keep in mind, when reading Bush's words, that the phrase "civil unions" has no determinate legal meaning. A state could offer various benefits to homosexual couples, heterosexual couples, and roommates with no sexual relationship, all under the rubric of "civil unions." With that understanding in mind, Bush's and Rove's remarks are entirely consistent with support for the kind of approach I am advocating. (They may also be consistent with the Republican platform.)

25 This approach would leave several important issues unsettled. Many people will continue to believe strongly that the law ought to recognize same-sex relationships the same way it recognizes traditional ones, and many people will continue to object strongly. No reconfiguration of benefits is going to end that debate. Liberals will be exasperated with conservatives: If they are willing to grant gay couples benefits, they will ask, why are they so stubborn about the merely symbolic question of legal recognition? Conservatives will have the mirror-image exasperation: If gays have almost every tangible benefit they want, why should they seek legal recognition, too?

26 Nor can this approach neatly solve every question of benefits. The approach advocated here does not attempt to settle questions about rights and duties involving children, where the divisions make attempts at compromise unpromising. Finally, how to apply the approach raises some difficult questions. Tax and Social Security law interact with marriage in various ways. The relevant provisions of the law could be seen as acknowledgments of marriage's dimension as an economic partnership—in which case legislators could presumably extend the benefits to non-marital households that function as economic partnerships. If the provisions are seen, however, as a way for the government to encourage moral behavior, social conservatives and social liberals are likely to disagree about whether they should apply to same-sex couples.

27 A compromise need not settle all the issues, however, to offer something to each side.

28 Advocates of gay marriage would not get legal recognition for gay relationships. Their

cause might lose some steam, since gays would get some benefits whose denial had previously generated sympathy. But gays would get those benefits sooner than they would if they wait for victory in the struggle for gay marriage—and those real-world benefits have to count for something. If advocates of gay marriage are right that their triumph is historically inevitable, they have little to lose.

29 Opponents of same-sex marriage also have little to lose, and something to gain. Many of them insist that they are not motivated by any hostility to gays as people. Supporting an extension of benefits would allow them to prove it, which would be worthwhile morally and would also improve their tactical position in the political debate. Their chances of passing the constitutional amendment they seek might improve. (It's important that there's no certainty here. If this compromise were certain to make the social conservatives succeed, the other side would have no reason to support it.)

30 And it's just barely possible that everyone would reap the benefit of a reduction in the strife that has attended the marriage debate.

THINKING ABOUT THE ARGUMENT

1. What are the four options to which Ponnuru refers? List them.
2. What is "option four" all about? Why does the author think that it would be more acceptable to his particular audience than outright endorsement of same-sex marriage?
3. Is there any place in Ponnuru's article where he refutes a contrary argument? Summarize the opposing viewpoint and explain how well he counters it.
4. Why does the author think his compromise will work well now (at the time the article was written, at least)?
5. Does the author use evidence effectively? Explain. Identify at least one place where the use of evidence could be improved.

RESPONDING TO THE ARGUMENT

1. Do you agree with Ponnuru's moderate position, or would you prefer to take an "all or nothing" stance? In other words, would you prefer (1) no same-sex marriage in any form whatsoever, or (2) full recognition of same-sex marriage? If you are unwilling to compromise on your position, why?
2. Do you think Ponnuru's audience will be receptive to his proposition? Why or why not?
3. Summarize an argument refuting the author's proposal. Explain why you think his compromise is unrealistic or undesirable (these may be two distinct things). Alternatively, explain why you think "option four" is a solid idea.

WRITING ABOUT THE ARGUMENT

1. Review the article. Think of a fifth option and write a brief argument supporting your position.
2. Write an argument refuting Ponnuru's position. Explain why it is unrealistic or undesirable (or both).
3. Write an argument supporting Ponnuru's position. In your argument, explain why compromise is essential.

READING SELECTION

"Mother Land"

About the Author: Komal Bhojwani

Komal Bhojwani is an attorney and stand-up comedian who cofounded MoneyPants.com, an online financial guidance company. One of her short stories was published in a collection called *A Woman's Touch: New Lesbian Love Stories* (2003). She also writes extensively about her personal money journey on MoneyPants.com and is working on a memoir about her father-arranged marriage and self-arranged divorce. In the following article, which first appeared in *The Advocate* in April 2005, Bhojwani reflects on the desire she and her partner have to adopt a child.

Before You Read

1. Look at the author's name and the title of the article. What clues do these give you about what the reading will be about?
2. Glance over the article. To which of the other readings in this section is it similar? How is it similar?
3. Does this article take a personal (subjective) or impersonal (objective) point of view? What does this prepare you to expect?
4. Given that this article was published in *The Advocate* (research this magazine a bit on the Internet if necessary), for what sort of audience was it written? Describe the audience in as much detail as you can.

Mother Land

1 I want to adopt a child, an Indian girl. Having been one myself, I feel uniquely positioned to teach her the kind of independence and freedom of thought that I wish I had been taught earlier. So I went to India in December to investigate the process. I hadn't been to India—land of my birth, birth of my neuroses—in 13 years. In that time I'd married a man my father found for me and divorced him when I realized I was gay.

2 I'd stayed away from India because I hadn't wanted to answer questions from inquisitive relatives. But in the last few years I'd been dreaming about returning. In my dreams I never made it, I missed the plane, or I left my passport at home. Once, I got all the way there; I even saw the streets of Bombay, but there was a problem with a hairbrush, and I had to be sent back.

3 The original plan was for me to go to India by myself. But a few days before I left, I asked my girlfriend, Marina, to join me. I needed something to stand on while I was there, some reminder of my life back home.

4 I knew my mother wouldn't be happy about this, so I waited until the last minute to tell her. They wouldn't be seeing each other, as I was visiting my mother in Bombay and Marina would meet me later in Delhi. But we were staying with cousins and word would get back sooner or later. When I told my mother, she said, "I asked you to keep it out of India. Why do you have to bring her here?"

5 I said, "I don't want to spend New Year's alone."

6 She said, "You won't get your other work done if anyone finds out," referring to the adoption.

7 "No one will suspect. I'll say we're just friends, traveling companions."

8 "Do what you want," she said, her voice dull with angry resignation. "You always do anyway."

9 I spent the first few days in Bombay fighting to keep from being swallowed up by India—loud and crowded and brown with dust and pollution. Drawing from my mother's strength, I trekked with her from one adoption agency to another, always getting the same answer: I would have to work with a U.S. agency, have a home-study done, and then wait.

10 Because gays and lesbians are not allowed to adopt, I told them I was single. But hiding isn't in our nature for either Marina or me. The first day she arrived in Delhi, I drew close to her on the sofa and almost kissed her. She brushed me away, and by sheer coincidence my cousins had their backs turned (we hope).

11 After that, I closed off Marina in my mind, thinking of her as a friend, not a lover, so I wouldn't make the mistake again.

12 My cousins took us shopping, and I had to ask Marina nonchalantly what she thought of this bedcover or that painting, as if I was only getting her opinion, when in fact it was a way of discovering whether she would agree to my bringing it home.

13 Even in the privacy of the bedroom, we kept safely to our sides. We probably wouldn't have done anything anyway in my cousin's 14-year-old daughter's bed. It didn't seem polite. But even so, we were not the same with each other. It was easier to stay in the twilight zone of watchfulness than to jump out and back into the closet every five minutes.

14 The ironic thing is that I think my cousins would have been fine with us as a couple. I was only protecting my mother. She had asked me when I first got divorced not to say anything to our family in Miami, where we lived. But I was rabidly out. I even took Marina to Belize, where I grew up and where a lot of my family still live. We were fighting for the globe, my mother and I, like a game of Risk, and India was now her last bastion. I've let her have it so far, but only for my own selfish reasons.

15 Marina and I are both out with our families and our friends. But to start a family of our own, we were told we had to go back into the closet.

16 That trip strained us, drained me of any desire to go back. And yet I know we will return. We want to adopt an Indian girl. We want to raise her so that when she returns to the land of her birth as a grown woman, she doesn't feel she has to hide in order to protect her mother.

Thinking about the Argument

1. What is Bhojwani's claim? If it is not explicitly stated, can you put it in your own words?
2. What is the purpose of Bhojwani's narrative? What idea is she trying to relate to her audience?
3. How effectively do the details of the personal narrative—the description of Bhojwani and Marina on the sofa or the author's interaction with her mother—serve to support the idea she is trying to relate?

Responding to the Argument

1. How did you respond to the narrative on an emotional level? Do you sympathize in any way with the author's predicament?
2. How did you respond to the narrative on an intellectual level? Do you think lesbians should be accepted by Indian society, and should Bhojwani and Marina be allowed to adopt a child? Why or why not?

READING SELECTION

3. To what extent—if at all—does the author convince you that her relationship with Marina is legitimate and that they should be allowed to adopt a child? Explain your answer.

Writing about the Argument

1. Write a brief argument explaining why the author should (or should not) be allowed to adopt a child. Does Bhojwani give adequate reasons for wanting to adopt (see paragraph 1)?
2. Write a letter to Bhojwani's mother. Explain why her family should (or should not) accept the author's relationship with Marina.
3. What kind of difficulties might people from non-Western cultures face regarding gay and lesbian relationships? Would it be best to "stay in the closet"? Explain your answer.
4. Write an editorial to your college or local town newspaper expressing your thoughts regarding adoption by lesbians and gays. Be sure to defend your reasons, no matter what position you take, with good evidence.

Issue 2: Poverty

In September 2005, Hurricane Katrina laid waste to New Orleans, Louisiana. In doing so, it made all Americans aware of the plight of the city's poor. In the United States, the existence of so many impoverished people stands in stark contrast to the monuments of Washington, D.C., the skyscrapers of Wall Street, or the glamour of Hollywood. It is the ugly underbelly of America that is often easier to ignore than to confront, perhaps because poverty is a problem that cannot be solved easily.

One prevailing theory, sometimes called "trickle-down economics," says that when the wealthiest people make money, some of that money "trickles down" to the poor members of society. Proponents of this theory believe in the American dream: No matter how poor you are, if you work hard and have a little bit of luck, you can become as successful and wealthy as anyone else. Another theory suggests that poverty is caused when the wealthy oppress the poor. This theory argues that the way to eliminate poverty is to redistribute the wealth of those who have plenty to spare.

At the crux of this issue lies the role of the individual in society: Is the individual responsible for his or her own success and happiness, or does the state bear some responsibility in protecting the less fortunate from being preyed on by others?

An elderly woman warms herself with an American flag during the devastation left by Hurricane Katrina. Does the government bear any responsibility for protecting or supporting those who are less fortunate than others?

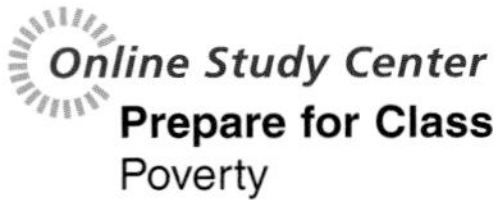

Prepare for Class
Poverty

CONSIDERING THE ISSUE OF POVERTY

Working individually or in groups, answer the following questions.

1. What causes people to be poor? Are there different kinds of poor people?
2. Do you know many poor people? How well do you know them?
3. What problems are associated with being poor?
4. How do you feel about poor people? Do you feel differently about different kinds of poor people?
5. In what way, if any, are nonpoor people responsible for the welfare of the poor? Are these responsibilities personal, local, state, national, or even international?

READING SELECTION

"The Scientist's Pursuit of Happiness"

ABOUT THE AUTHOR: JOHAN NORBERG

Johan Norberg is a Swedish philosopher who writes primarily about the economics of globalization. In his online biography, he says "I am passionate about . . . secularization, education, and liberty, and the adulation of science, technology, and progress." As part of his work for Timbro, a Swedish think tank, Norberg created Frihandel.nu, a website designed to promote free trade. Norberg argues that money really can buy happiness, that welfare and other public-assistance systems are a hindrance to happiness, and that these programs can even cause poverty to fester by not encouraging people to work for what they have. "I am convinced," he writes, "that what the oppressed people of the world need is more free trade and capitalism, not less." In addition to books written in Swedish, Norberg has published *In Defense of Global Capitalism* (2003) and has produced *Globalization Is Good* (2003), a film that explores the role that corporations have played in improving the lives of the poor in developing countries. This essay was first published in *Policy* in 2005.

BEFORE YOU READ

1. What is your opinion regarding the poverty problem in America? Is it the responsibility of the state to take care of the poor, or are individuals always responsible for their own well-being? Explain.
2. Do you think public assistance (e.g., welfare) is beneficial for society as a whole? Why do you think this?
3. Based on the headnote, what do you think Norberg's opinion of the poverty problem in America might be?
4. What do you expect the author to argue about the pursuit of happiness?

READING SELECTION

The Scientist's Pursuit of Happiness

1 For centuries, philosophers and poets have tried to understand what happiness is, and what might contribute to it. In recent decades, scientists have started to come up with the answers. Happiness is electrical activity in the left front part of the brain, and it comes from getting married, getting friends, getting rich, and avoiding communism.

2 At least, that's part of the answer the scholars have given us in a theoretical field that is growing by the minute. There is a constant stream of theories and studies about human well-being and happiness, often translated into policy suggestions.

3 The British economist Richard Layard has written one of the most celebrated works about this, *Happiness: Lessons from a New Science* (London: Allen Lane, 2005). His specific point is that growth in the rich countries since the 1950s has not contributed to more happiness, and that this has a number of explanations. Because money has diminishing returns, we get used to higher incomes, and need even more to keep our old levels of happiness. Since we attach a lot of importance to our relative position, the fact that someone else earns a higher income (which makes them happy), makes others less happy. Getting rich is a negative externality—"pollution," as Layard calls it. It forces others to work harder to retain their relative position, but when they do, they get used to it, and end up no happier than they used to be. To stop this "hedonic treadmill" we should increase taxes, discourage hard work, and slow down mobility and restructuring, to give us more time for the things that really make us happier—family, friends, and reading Layard's books.

Wealth and Happiness

4 It is a simplification to say that growth does not contribute to happiness. In fact, one of the few things there is a consensus about in this very young field of science is that money *does* buy happiness. There is an extremely strong correlation between wealth and happiness. Low-income countries report low levels of happiness, middle-income countries report middle levels, and high-income countries report high levels.

5 What the researchers say, though, is that this correlation levels off at a national income of about $10,000 a year. After $20,000, Layard says, "additional income is not associated with extra happiness" (p. 33). The economist Richard Easterlin presented this surprising conclusion in a study about Japan. Since the 1950s, income in Japan increased almost tenfold, but the Japanese are no happier today than they were then.[1]

6 This is the most highlighted finding from the research. But in fact, it is yet to be proven. The fact that a higher income level does not translate into higher happiness does not mean that growth doesn't. What we do know is that there is a big jump in reported well-being when countries move from about $5,000 to $15,000 a year. And this is consistent with a much more dynamic interpretation than Easterlin's and Layard's.

Happiness and Hope

7 From surveys we know that a lack of hope and opportunity correlates strongly with unhappiness. If you are looking for happy Europeans, try someone who thinks that his present situation is better than it was five years ago, or, even better, someone who thinks that his situation will be better in five years from now. If you want to meet a happy Australian, ask someone who thinks that people like themselves have a good chance of improving their standard of living.[2] In poor and badly governed countries entire societies suffer from hopelessness. If you are an average individual you have few opportunities, no conviction that what you do affects your position, no hope that tomorrow will be a better day. You expect little, and you get it.

8 We also know that a system in which individuals had few opportunities to improve their

lives, communism, is disastrous to well-being. A lot has been made of the fact that post-communist countries reported lower happiness levels immediately after the fall of communism—hardly surprising since national instability is detrimental to happiness.

9 Less attention has been drawn to the fact that communist countries were much more miserable than other countries before the fall. Ronald Inglehart's World Values Project made two studies in communist countries in the early 1980s, Hungary and a representative region of the Soviet Union, Tambov Oblast. The lack of freedom and growth in these countries were not compensated for by higher degrees of reported well-being. On the contrary, they reported lower happiness than any industrialized country, and were far more miserable than other countries on the same income levels. Even in countries like India, Bangladesh, and Turkey, people reported higher well-being than the Soviets.[3]

10 Belief in the future grows when poor countries begin to experience growth, when markets open up, when incomes increase and people's decisions begin to affect their place in society. For a recent example, look at Ireland. This country reported declining levels of life satisfaction between the early 1970s and the late 1980s. Ireland did not grow poorer during this time, but it had low growth and high unemployment. A lack of opportunities for the young led to high emigration.

11 In the 1990s things turned around. Rapid liberalization, foreign investment, and information technology doubled Irish GDP per capita in ten years. It became easy to start a business and to get a job. Unemployment fell from about 15% to 5% and emigrants returned. At the same time, reported levels of happiness grew rapidly, by about one point on a ten-point scale—a dramatic change for such a slow-moving indicator. Today, Ireland is one of the world's happiest countries.[4]

12 That could help explain why happiness reached high levels in the Western world after the Second World War, when they were close to the Irish situation. With economies growing rapidly, people began to think that their children would enjoy a better life than they had. The fact that economic growth since then has not increased happiness much from those levels does not mean that it is useless—it is the fact that growth has continued that makes it possible for us to continue to believe in the future, and to continue experiencing such high levels of happiness. The critics who think that they can conclude from the stability of happiness that zero growth is preferable overlook that loss of income undermines happiness. And growth makes non-zero-sum games possible. Without it, whenever someone succeeds and gains, someone else has to fail.

Rising Happiness

13 But there is a much more basic problem with Layard's interpretations of the happiness research. In fact, happiness hasn't stopped increasing in the West. On the contrary, in most Western countries where we have surveys since 1975, happiness has increased.[5] Yes, there are diminishing returns, but even at our standard of living, people do get happier when our societies grow richer, albeit at a slower rate. Japan seems to be the exception, not the rule.

14 Astonishingly, Layard admits this in the first footnote of the book, where he says about European surveys that "data since then [1975] show a slight upward trend in happiness" (p. 247). But in the rest of the book he completely ignores this fact, which undermines his whole argument. Instead, he just keeps pretending that "for most types of people in the West, happiness has not increased since 1950" (p. 29).

15 This argument also cannot explain why the most happy and satisfied places on earth are the ones that are most dynamic, individualist, and wealthy: North America, Northern Europe, and Australia. So why don't we look there to find the secret of happiness? Even Layard admits that "we in the West are probably happier than any previous society" (p. 235).

Happiness and Freedom

16 One reason for this happiness is that a liberal and market-oriented society allows people freedom to choose. In the absence of authoritarian leaders and Layard-devotees forcing us to live the way they think is best for us, we can choose the kind of identity and lifestyle that suits us. And if we get used to valuing and choosing, we will get increasingly better at choosing to live, work and socialize in ways we like. In traditional societies, on the other hand, the individual has to adapt to prefabricated roles and demands.

17 Of course, not everything in modern society suits everybody, but freedom also means the freedom to say no. If you don't think you get happier by hard work and mobility, just skip it. A survey showed that 48% of Americans had, in the last five years, reduced their working hours, declined promotion, lowered their material expectations, or moved to a quieter place.[6] Fast food or slow food, no logo or pro logo? In a liberal society, you decide.

18 So why should the government have to discourage us from hard work and mobility? Layard only presents indirect correlations to prove that these things are harmful. For example, he says working hard undermines the family and moving to a new neighborhood lowers trust and increases crime, and since we know that family breakdown, lack of trust, and crime are bad for well-being we should avoid this. But that does not follow, since there are other benefits to working as much as you want and moving to a place you prefer, which might compensate for these risks. Unless Layard and others manage to establish a direct link between work/mobility and unhappiness, this argument is bogus.[7]

Happiness and Activity

19 In fact, high levels of happiness are reported from people with active lifestyles and who work a lot. It seems like evolution has given us a human nature that enjoys intellectual exercise, just like our bodies appreciate physical exercise. This is not really surprising, since we developed as hunter-gatherers, where individuals had to make constant choices in complex and constantly changing environments. If you think that this sounds like a night out, or like a day at work, you're not so far off.

20 This might be the way we can save Layard's and others' observation that money as such isn't the meaning of life. It isn't. A classic mystery in the happiness studies is that lottery winners are not much happier than the rest of the population. It's not just the money that makes high earners happier than low earners—more important is their way of life—being active, being creative, and experiencing control of your life. So it's one up for Aristotle, who explained that happiness is not a destination, but a way of traveling.

21 The psychologist Mihaly Csikszentmihalyi captured this with his surprising observation that people asked to record when they experience happiness and joy reported much more happiness while working than in their spare time with their families. It turned out that people experienced most satisfaction when they were creative, when they were absorbed by an activity and felt that it was both challenging and possible to deal with. If I am asked to write an article on a too-complicated subject that I don't really master, I feel worry and anxiety, and if I am supposed to write about something that is too easy, I get bored. But when I strike the right balance, and write about something that is complicated, but I can handle it, then I experience that creative sensation Csikszentmihalyi calls "flow."[8]

22 Apparently, a sense of competence and efficacy gives us happiness—a sense of being in control in complex situations. This is not surprising since it is difficult to imagine a trait that has helped mankind to survive and procreate better than this, but the implications are interesting.

23 Working life offers a lot of opportunities for flow, since it most often provides us with a system of challenges, incentives, and feedback that makes us feel that we are in control, that there is

a meaning to our actions. This can be compared with spare time that often is spent in front of the television. This is why human beings often consciously make their spare time more "complicated" by reading difficult books, playing games, or cooking strange, new dishes. Just watch how children invent rules when playing. It makes the play more challenging—and more fun. That is why we try to learn more about complex subjects, and why we try to make simple and monotonous jobs more demanding—for example, by timing ourselves.

Happiness and the Welfare State

24 This desire for challenge helps to explain why it does not seem like the growth of the welfare state has increased human happiness. This was the finding of a series of studies by one of the most respected happiness researchers, the Dutch professor Ruut Veenhoven. He started out by looking for the correlation between social security and well-being he thought existed, to argue against economists who claimed that the welfare state was bad for the economy:

> Against that loss at a material level I hoped to set the gain in psychological wellbeing. The result was not what I had expected, however. There proved not to be any wellbeing surplus.[9]

Even though redistributive states have created more equal access to resources and welfare services (which create more happiness, ceteris paribus), the benefit is undermined by the fact that we are given this without working for it ourselves. Veenhoven's results show that redistribution has not even managed to create a more equal distribution of happiness. In effect, the welfare state makes the beneficiary a lottery winner. The resources received do not make the welfare recipient more active or in control—perhaps the opposite—and with adaptation to the new resources, happiness is no higher than before.

25 If happiness comes from a sense of competence and efficacy, the welfare state is worse than a lottery. If the welfare state does what it is supposed to do, abolish problems and risks and guarantee a certain material result whatever we do, then it deprives us of many of our challenges and our responsibilities. That actions have consequences, both rewards and punishments, is not just good because it helps us make better decisions; it is also important because it gives us the sense of control. Without this direct feedback our sense of hopelessness and frustration grows.

26 Research tells us that optimism works.[10] People who think that they are in control of their lives go on to be more successful than others, whereas those who indulge in victimization and think that someone else is to blame for their problems are most often proven right in their pessimism. Creating the paternalist institutions that Layard and others propose would be a way of depriving us of freedom, and the sense of control, and therefore probably also of happiness.

Government Cannot Give Us Happiness

27 A government that says it wants to make us happy misses the obvious fact that a government can't give us happiness, it can only give us the right to pursue happiness—because happiness is what we get when we are in control and assume responsibility ourselves. A way of traveling, not a destination.

28 In other words, the conclusion of the French 19th-century liberal Benjamin Constant still stands:

> The holders of authority . . . are so ready to spare us all sort of troubles, except those of obeying and paying! They will say to us: "what, in the end, is the aim of your efforts, the motive of your labors, the object of all your hopes? Is it not happiness? Well, leave this happiness to us and we shall give it to you." No, Sirs, we must not leave it to them. No matter how touching such a tender commitment may be, let us ask the authorities to keep within their limits. Let them confine themselves to being just. We shall assume the responsibility of being happy for ourselves.[11]

Notes

1. Richard Easterlin, "Does Economic Growth Improve the Human Lot? Some Empirical Evidence," in P. A. David & M. W. Reder (Eds.), *Nations and Households in Economic Growth* (New York: Academic Press, 1974).
2. Eurobarometer, Report No. 53 (Brussels: European Commission, Oct 2000), chap. 1; Rachel Gibson, et al. *The Australian Survey of Social Attitudes* (Canberra: Australian Social Science Data Archives, The Australian National University, 2003).
3. Ronald Inglehart & Hans-Dieter Klingemann, "Genes, Culture, Democracy, and Happiness," in E Diener & M Suh (Eds.) *Culture and Subjective Well-Being* (Cambridge: MIT Press, 2000).
4. World Database of Happiness. http://www2.eur.nl/fsw/research/happiness
5. Michael R. Hagerty & Ruut Veenhoven, "Wealth and Happiness Revisited," *Social Indicators Research,* 64 (2003). This also includes the United States, which Layard denies.
6. Robert Fogel, *The Escape from Hunger and Premature Death, 1700–2100* (New York: Cambridge University Press, 2004), 72.
7. As pointed out by Jan Arild Snoen in "Lykkeligere som sosialdemokrater?," article on Civita's website, 2005-06-13. http://www.civita.no/civ.php?mod=content&id=1
8. Mihaly Csikszentmihalyi, *Flow: The Psychology of Optimal Experience* (New York: Harper Perennial, 1991).
9. Ruut Veenhoven, "Wellbeing in the Welfare State," *Journal for Comparative Policy Analysis,* 2 (2000), 3. See also Piet Ouweneel, "Social Security and Well-Being of the Unemployed in 42 Countries," *Journal of Happiness Studies,* 3 (2002), which shows that the level of benefits does not buffer effects of unemployment, and Charles Murray's *In Pursuit of Happiness and Good Government* (New York: Simon & Schuster, 1988).
10. See, for example, Barbara Fredickson, "What Good Are Positive Emotions?," *Review of General Psychology,* 2 (1998).
11. Benjamin Constant, "The Liberty of the Ancients Compared to That of the Moderns," speech delivered in 1816. http://www.uark.edu/depts/comminfo/cambridge/ancients.html

Thinking about the Argument

1. According to Norberg, what is the source of happiness? What evidence does he supply to validate this claim?
2. How does Norberg respond to Layard's claim that wealth does not contribute to happiness?
3. What factor(s) does the author say contribute to increased hope for the future? Identify one piece of evidence he cites to support this assertion.
4. What role does Norberg believe that activity plays in happiness? Which kinds of activities does he think contribute the most, and why?
5. According to the author, how can or should the government contribute to subsidizing people through programs such as welfare to make them happy?

RESPONDING TO THE ARGUMENT

1. Do you agree or disagree with Norberg's claim that money really can buy happiness? Explain.
2. Assuming that both bring home roughly the same amount of money, who will be happier—a poor person working for minimum wage or a poor person on welfare? Explain.
3. What role do you think hope—or lack of it—plays in keeping people poor or motivating them to try to succeed?
4. Do you agree with the author that public forms of assistance are ultimately bad for people? Why do you think this?

WRITING ABOUT THE ARGUMENT

1. Write a letter to Norberg explaining why welfare is a necessary component of American society. What role might compassion play in supporting the idea of a welfare state?
2. Write an argument explaining how the plight of the poor could be improved with the elimination of all welfare programs.
3. Write a letter to the editor of your local paper discussing the role that activities such as work play in making a person productive and happy.
4. Write a paper arguing whether money can buy happiness. Be very specific in your argument, avoiding clichés and broad generalizations.

"Reminders of Poverty, Soon Forgotten"

ABOUT THE AUTHOR: ALEXANDER KEYSSAR

Alexander Keyssar is a historian, writer, and professor of history at Harvard University. His academic journal publications have included articles focusing on the problem of unemployment in America. His books have included *Melville's Israel Potter: Reflections on the American Dream* (1969), *Out of Work: The First Century of Unemployment in Massachusetts* (1986), and *The Contested History of Democracy in the United States* (2001). This article was originally published in *The Chronicle of Higher Education* in November 2005.

BEFORE YOU READ

1. Do you consider poverty to be a serious problem in the United States? Do you ever see or interact with very poor people on a regular basis? How do you react when you encounter them (or how do you think you would react)?
2. Based on the headnote, how might Keyssar's opinion of the plight of the poor differ from Norberg's? Why might you think this?
3. What does the title of Keyssar's essay suggest? Does he believe the upper and middle classes are sympathetic to the plight of the poor? What makes you hold this opinion?
4. Can you guess what the author's thesis might be?

READING SELECTION

Reminders of Poverty, Soon Forgotten

1 For many Americans, Hurricane Katrina kicked up the hope that the United States might try once again to seriously address the problem of poverty. If we had forgotten that poor people still lived in the land of SUVs and hedge funds, we could no longer ignore that reality—not with the powerful news footage coming out of New Orleans. There they were, on our television screens, the storm's most desperate victims—disproportionately poor and black, wading through muddy water, carrying children and plastic bags containing a few meager possessions. An entire city was devastated, but some neighborhoods and some people were clearly hit far worse than others. One thing that being poor meant was that you didn't have the capacity to get out of the way of floodwaters when they came pouring down your street.

2 It took nearly a week, but the news media grabbed onto the issue, rediscovering poverty even while it was pounding the Federal Emergency Management Agency for its inept response to the storm. Major news magazines and television programs rushed to describe what the hurricane's aftermath revealed: *Newsweek,* for example, ran a cover emblazoned "Poverty, Race and Katrina: Lessons of a National Shame," containing a stunning blend of statistics and powerful photographs. We all learned that the charming, hedonistic city on the lower Mississippi had one of the highest poverty rates in the nation and that most of its poor were African American. *The New York Times* apologetically acknowledged that, over the past decade, it had paid far more attention to New Orleans's restaurants than to the abject conditions in which many of its residents lived.

3 Hurricane Katrina seemed to be a wake-up call, a reminder to a prosperous nation that it still had domestic business to attend to. The cold fact that the fruits of recent economic growth had gone overwhelmingly to our richest citizens meant that millions of people continued to live in substandard housing, attend dysfunctional schools, travel slowly on broken-down public transportation systems, and die in overcrowded hospitals. While taxes were cut, public infrastructure—like the levees—was eroding, and an already frayed safety net was disintegrating. The poverty of many of Katrina's victims was an ugly and intolerable sight, and it seemed clear that we needed to do something about it.

4 That view, of course, was neither universal nor unalloyed by less benign portrayals of the men and women who were cast adrift by Katrina. From the beginning, there were reports of looting, of "thugs" seizing control of neighborhoods, of rapes and other violent crimes at sites where refugees had congregated; such reports—now known to have been exaggerated and distorted—made the victims seem less like our fellow citizens and more like denizens of another culture. Complaints were voiced that the people trapped in New Orleans had only themselves to blame, since they hadn't heeded the order to evacuate. (It turns out that a third of the city's African American households did not own cars.) One reporter I spoke to said that when she interviewed middle-class escapees from the Gulf Coast, they criticized the government and the news media for giving too much attention and money to poor African Americans in New Orleans.

5 Indeed, the early outbursts of indignation and hope—not about the wretched relief effort but about the exposure of poverty in Louisiana and Mississippi—began to fade as one week bled into the next. News stories about poverty slowed to a trickle, while reporters dashed to Texas to cover Hurricane Rita. Michael D. Brown resigned, and then blamed local officials for the chaos, while large, well-connected corporations signed no-bid contracts to rebuild swaths of Louisiana and Mississippi. Then the spotlight

of national news attention began to shift altogether, away from the Gulf and toward Harriet Miers, the vote on the Iraqi constitution, the devastating earthquake in Pakistan, and the World Series.

6 Serious discussions of poverty policy can still be heard on NPR, and activists in Louisiana are determined not to let the issue disappear from view. The new head of FEMA has announced that he is revisiting the issue of no-bid contracts, while considerable quantities of relief are actually reaching the people of the Gulf Coast. But there is no crescendo of national public opinion about the presence of millions of poor people in our midst, and President Bush has not announced the creation of a national task force to combat poverty. Some conservatives in Congress, meanwhile, seem determined to pay for the costs of Katrina by cutting other programs that, directly or indirectly, help the poor.

7 As a historian—and one who has taught and written about the history of poverty in the United States—I should not have been surprised by that quick reversion to "normalcy" (although I was). With the immediate crisis over, and many of the victims of Katrina and Rita scattered around the region and beyond, it was entirely foreseeable that the spotlight of public attention would shift to other issues and locales. Those whose homes and jobs disappeared inevitably become absorbed in the tedious, slow, painful task of rebuilding their lives, while elsewhere men and women of good will—however moved by the initial events, and perhaps after writing a check or two—go about their business.

8 But the problem runs deeper. Disasters and crises in American history have, in fact, rarely produced any fundamental changes in economic or social policy. Natural disasters, like hurricanes, floods, earthquakes, and fire, are invariably local events, leaving too much of the nation unscathed to generate any broad-gauged shift in understanding or ideology. Moreover, the most readily adopted policy changes have involved technical issues, like the approval or revision of fire codes, the earthquake-proofing of new buildings, and the raising of the height of levees. The most far-reaching policy decision after the San Francisco earthquake of 1906 was to flood the beautiful Hetch Hetchy Valley to guarantee San Francisco a more reliable source of water.

9 Poverty, however, is not a technical issue, but a deep, structural problem that implicates our values, our economic institutions, and our conception of the proper role of the state. There are fixes, but no quick fixes—and no fixes that will not cost something to at least some other members of our society. Understandably, thus, there has always been resistance to government actions, such as increasing the minimum wage, that might aid the poor; and that resistance has long been grounded both in self-interest and in willful blindness of a type that does not succumb to relatively brief crises.

10 Nowhere is that more evident—or more relevant—than in the history of responses to the panics and depressions that have been a prominent feature of American economic life for almost two centuries. (We called them "panics" until the early 20th century, when widespread recognition that capitalist economies had business cycles led to the use of more reassuring words like "depression," "downturn," and, still later, "recession.")

11 As American society grew more industrial and urban in the 19th century, and as markets increasingly shaped the ability of its populace to earn a living, the impact of business-cycle downturns broadened and deepened. The long post–Civil War downturn of the 1870s, for example, toppled millions of people into destitution or near-destitution; arguably the first depression of the industrial era, it created widespread distress that prompted pioneering efforts to count the unemployed, while also contributing to outbursts of working-class violence in 1877. Less than a decade later (1884–1886), the country lived through another downturn, followed in the 1890s by the most severe depression of the 19th century. The Panic of 1893

(which lasted until 1897) sharply lowered wages, while making jobs exceedingly scarce in many industries. It also prompted the first major protest march on Washington, a national movement of the unemployed led by Ohio's populist leader Jacob S. Coxey.

12 Yet many, if not most, Americans resisted the notion that millions of their fellow citizens were genuinely in need of aid. New York's distinguished Protestant cleric Henry Ward Beecher famously commented in 1877 that a man could easily support a family of eight on a dollar a day: "Is not a dollar a day enough to buy bread with? Water costs nothing; and a man who cannot live on bread is not fit to live." In the spring of 1894, after the dreadful winter that sparked the formation of Coxey's Army, Daniel B. Wesson, of Smith and Wesson, observed that "I don't think there was much suffering last winter." Others insisted that if men and women were destitute, it was because they were improvident or they drank: "Keep the people sober that ask for relief, and you will have no relief asked for," said Henry Faxon, a businessman from Quincy, Massachusetts. Even Carroll D. Wright, who supervised the first count of the unemployed in American history in 1878 (and a few years later became the first head of the U.S. Bureau of Labor Statistics), expressed the view that most of the men who lacked jobs did not "really want employment."

13 Private charities, as well as what were called "overseers of the poor" (overseers? the language itself is telling), did, of course, provide some relief to the victims of economic crisis. Yet they did so grudgingly and warily, often insisting that recipients perform physical labor in return for food and fuel, while also (particularly with women) conducting home interviews to verify that applicants for aid were of good moral character. In many states, the sole legislative response to the depressions of the late 19th century was the passage of "anti-tramp" laws that made it illegal for poor workers to travel from place to place in search of work.

14 Over time, to be sure, the recurrence of panics, coupled with the learning gradually acquired by charity officials and dedicated antipoverty activists like settlement-house workers, did contribute to more-hospitable attitudes toward the poor. They also gave birth to new policy ideas (like unemployment insurance) that might help alleviate the problem of poverty. Such ideas, which began to gain a bit of traction in the early 20th century, were grounded in the supposition that American society had a responsibility to help not only the destitute, but also the poor: the millions of men and women who worked hard, and as steadily as they could, but lived in substandard conditions, a short distance from dire material need.

15 Resistance to such proposals, however, did not vanish overnight: Suspicions that the poor were "unworthy" persisted, as did a reluctance to expand the role of government. Of equal importance, crisis conditions (as business-cycle theorists pointed out) did come to an end, lessening the visible urgency of the problem. That was particularly true during the first three, sharp depressions of the 20th century, in 1907–1908, 1913–1914, and 1920–1922. The second of those led to the drafting of unemployment-insurance bills in several states, but by the time the bills were ready for legislative action, the economy was picking up, and interest had ebbed. In 1921 a charming, eccentric organizer named Urbain Ledoux put together sensational anti-unemployment demonstrations in both New York City and Boston, including mock auctions of unemployed "slaves" on the Boston Common. He garnered enough front-page attention to earn a meeting with President Warren G. Harding and an invitation to attend the President's Conference on Unemployment—which turned out to be a bureaucratic vehicle that effectively delayed action long enough for the economic crisis to come to an end, with no new policies put into place.

16 The Great Depression and the New Deal, of course, constitute the most dramatic and

far-reaching exception to the pattern of a crisis causing (and revealing) poverty while yielding no basic changes in policy. As always, the exception sheds some light on the dynamics that produce the rule. The Great Depression gave rise to significant shifts in policy not just because the downturn was severe but also—and more important—because of its unprecedented length. There were few innovations in public responses to poverty and unemployment during the early years of the 1930s (no one, after all, knew that this depression would turn out to be the Great Depression), and the era's most durable, systematic legislation came more than two years after Franklin D. Roosevelt took office in 1933. The Social Security Act (with its provisions for unemployment and old-age insurance) and the Wagner Act (which strengthened the right of workers to join unions) were passed only in 1935, the same year that the pioneering work-relief programs of the Works Progress Administration were launched; the Fair Labor Standards Act, mandating a federal minimum wage, was not enacted until 1938, nearly a decade after the stock-market crash.

17 The greatest economic crisis in American history, thus, did not produce a quick turnaround in antipoverty policy, even though the ideas eventually put into effect had been circulating among progressives for decades. The recognition that millions of people were suffering (inescapable as early as 1931) was not enough to produce action. What was also needed was time for political movements to build and to generate a leadership with the political will to take action.

18 That involved not just the election of Roosevelt in 1932 (which was primarily a repudiation of Herbert Hoover) but also the Share-the-Wealth movement of Louisiana's own Huey P. Long, the election of many left-leaning Democrats to Congress in 1934, and Roosevelt's overwhelming re-election in 1936. It was at his second inaugural, in January 1937, that Roosevelt famously referred to "one-third of a nation ill-housed, ill-clad, ill-nourished" and committed his administration to dealing with the "tens of millions" of citizens "who at this very moment are denied the greater part of what the very lowest standards of today call the necessities of life." In language eerily resonant today (aimed at an audience with vivid memories of the deadly Labor Day Hurricane that struck Florida in 1935), Roosevelt also announced that his administration "refused to leave the problems of our common welfare to be solved by the winds of chance and the hurricanes of disaster."

19 The New Deal was a turning point not just because of the specific, permanent programs that the federal government adopted, but also because it expressed a new, dominant consensus about social justice and the role of government. The poverty of millions of Americans was viewed as a collective responsibility rather than an assembly of individual misfortunes or failures; and it became the responsibility of government to actively combat that poverty. The political will that Roosevelt voiced was precisely the will to embrace collective responsibility, which, as he himself observed, reflected a "change in the moral climate of America."

20 That same "moral climate" and political will also undergirded Lyndon B. Johnson's declaration of an "unconditional war on poverty" in 1964. Notably, the war on poverty did not originate in an economic crisis or a natural disaster: It was launched in a period of prosperity and linked directly to a middle-class recognition—akin to the "Katrina experience"—that poverty still existed within the plenty of post–World War II America. (The famous emblem of that recognition was John F. Kennedy reading Michael Harrington's *The Other America.*) Yet viewed from the perspective of 2005, what seems most remarkable about the war on poverty was neither the recognition that poverty still existed nor the mixed success of individual programs. Rather, it was the optimism of the "war" itself. In the mid-1960s, much of the political leadership of our nation actually believed that poverty could be eliminated from the richest nation on earth.

21 That optimism has eroded substantially over the last 40 years. The erosion has occurred, in part, because the war on poverty did not register the quick victory foreseen by officials like Sargent Shriver, the head of the Office of Economic Opportunity, who predicted in 1966 that the United States "virtually could eliminate" poverty. Although government programs did contribute to a decline in the poverty rate in the late 1960s and early 1970s (the official figure dropped from 22 percent to 11 percent between 1959 and 1973), progress stalled in the more uncertain and sluggish economic conditions of the 1970s and 1980s. Since the mid-1970s, in fact, the official rate has ranged up and down between 11 percent and 15 percent, roughly tracking the business cycle. The lack of decisive improvement after 1973 made possible Ronald Reagan's oft-quoted quip that the United States had conducted a war on poverty, and "poverty won." Americans like to keep their wars short.

22 Other factors also played a role. By the mid-1970s, social-welfare programs were becoming increasingly expensive, and, with the economy sputtering, public support for what appeared to be income redistribution began to sag. At the same time, critics of the war on poverty helped to resuscitate longstanding negative images of the poor as lazy and unworthy: For example, Russell Long, the influential Louisiana senator, insisted that the welfare system was being "abused by malingerers, cheaters, and outright frauds." Conservative intellectuals joined the fray with studies arguing that government programs had either failed to reduce poverty or made things worse. And in the 1980s public perceptions of poverty became increasingly linked to the image of a largely African American "underclass" that was rife with crime and unresponsive to the benign ministrations of mainstream American society.

23 Accompanying all those developments, of course, were the ideological attacks on government itself that became ascendant with the election of Reagan and that still stymie efforts to mobilize the political will to combat poverty. For more than 25 years, it has been Republican orthodoxy that government is the problem, not the solution. If there is a solution to the issues facing the poor, it lies in the magic of the free market, in letting private enterprise generate jobs and growth. Republicans, moreover, have no monopoly on such views: The centrist Democrats who rose to power in the 1990s have embraced much of the market-centered orthodoxy, undeterred by the historical fact that economic growth alone has never solved the problem of poverty anywhere. It was, after all, the Democrat Bill Clinton who declared that the "era of big government" was over. Most Democratic leaders today seem, indeed, to lack the convictions of their New Deal and Great Society predecessors, convictions that made it possible to translate outrage and empathy into policy initiatives. While President Bush promotes market-friendly responses to the crisis in the Gulf Coast, Democrats remain on the sidelines, fearful of being associated with either "big government" or economic redistribution.

24 As Hurricane Katrina pulled back the veil on American poverty, many news commentators openly wondered whether the scenes we were witnessing would revive the war on poverty of the 1960s. Two months later it is clear that no such revival will happen. The long history of crises and natural disasters in the United States suggests that they rarely provide auspicious moments for major policy initiatives—unless the political will for such initiatives is preexisting or can readily be mobilized. That surely is not the case today. Billions of dollars will be spent in the Gulf states, and New Orleans and Biloxi will be rebuilt. But there will be no new national programs to aid the poor, and precious little in the way of targeted antipoverty programs in the Gulf. Perhaps the most disturbing fact that Hurricane Katrina has placed before our eyes is our society's loss of faith in its ability to truly help the people whose faces we glimpsed in September.

»«

THINKING ABOUT THE ARGUMENT

1. What does the author say that Hurricane Katrina revealed about the city of New Orleans?
2. Does the author believe that the news reports focusing on this disaster will lead to significant discussions about poverty? Why or why not?
3. Why does Keyssar believe that Americans, on the whole, are reluctant to help the poor?
4. According to the author, how have attitudes toward social welfare changed over the years? How much faith does the author place in the idea that the solution to helping the poor "lies in the magic of the free market, in letting private enterprise generate jobs and growth"? Explain.

RESPONDING TO THE ARGUMENT

1. Do you believe that disasters such as Hurricane Katrina will cause the government, and the nation as a whole, to take the plight of the poor seriously? Why or why not?
2. Do you believe that people, on the whole, are reluctant to help the poor? Why or why not?
3. Do you believe that the American Dream—the idea that anyone, with enough hard work and a little luck, can be successful in America—is achievable in this day and age? Why or why not?
4. Is the author's assessment of the government's public attitude toward helping the poor over the last 25 years an accurate one? Why or why not?
5. Do you believe that redistributing some of the income of the wealthiest people in an effort to help the poorest is a good idea? Why or why not?

WRITING ABOUT THE ARGUMENT

1. Write an argument defining the American Dream and explaining whether it is achievable today.
2. Write a letter to a local state or national representative arguing how the current policies toward public welfare should change. If you think they should not be changed, explain why.
3. Do you believe that the problem of poverty is better or worse today than it was 30 years ago? Research this topic and write a documented essay defending your position.
4. Write a dialogue between yourself and a homeless person explaining one of the following: (a) why you will or will not give the person a handout, (b) what the homeless person can do to improve his or her situation, or (c) how the welfare system should be changed to help improve the homeless person's situation.

"Katrina, the Race Card, and the Welfare State"

ABOUT THE AUTHOR: LARRY ELDER

Larry Elder is a newspaper columnist and radio talk-show host known for supporting libertarian principles of limited government and maximum personal and financial responsibility. He graduated from Brown University and the University of Michigan School of Law. He has practiced litigation law and hosted two television shows. His popular daily talk show is based in Los Angeles and nationally syndicated. He also writes a nationally syndicated newspaper column. His books include *The Ten Things You Can't Say in America* (2000) and *Showdown: Confronting Bias, Lies, and the Special Interests That Divide America* (2002). This piece was first published in *Jewish World Review* in September 2005.

Before You Read

1. How does the fact that the author is African American affect the way you approach this article? Explain.
2. What does the title of the article suggest to you? What do you think he will argue?
3. Scan the article for Elder's thesis and some of his main points. Does he appear to offer the arguments you had anticipated? What does this say about the assumptions you made prior to reading the article?
4. What does the term *welfare state* bring to your mind?

Katrina, the Race Card, and the Welfare State

1 In the case of Hurricane Katrina, government failed to do its most essential job—protecting people and property. Yes, state, local, and federal officials failed to appreciate the severity and gravity of this storm and its aftermath, and failed to properly evacuate the citizens from New Orleans.

2 But how does this add up to racism?

3 CNN's Jack Cafferty said, "Despite the many angles of this tragedy, and Lord knows there've been a lot of 'em in New Orleans, there is a great big elephant in the living room that the media seems content to ignore—that would be, until now. . . . [We] in the media are ignoring the fact that almost all of the victims in New Orleans are black and poor."

4 CNN's Wolf Blitzer replied, ". . . You simply get chills every time you see these poor individuals, as Jack Cafferty just pointed out, so tragically, so many of these people, almost all of them that we see, are so poor, and they are so black, and this is gonna raise lots of questions for people who are watching this story unfold."

5 Fox's Shepard Smith described citizens of New Orleans stranded on an Interstate as possessing the face of an African American man, woman, child, or baby.

6 News anchors, once again, demonstrate their willingness, indeed eagerness, to find racism. A few years ago, a *Time*-CNN poll found that 89 percent of black teens experienced little or no racism in their own lives. White teens, however, believed racism against minorities a bigger problem than black teens did.

7 The so-called black leaders, of course, led the race card parade. The Congressional Black Caucus's Rep. Diane Watson, D-California, described those suffering as "sons and daughters of slaves." NAACP attorney Damon Hewitt said, "If the majority of the folks left behind were white individuals, and most of the folks who were able to escape on their own were African Americans, then I wouldn't be sitting here right now. This is a racial story." Rapper Kanye West, at an NBC relief concert, screamed, "George Bush doesn't care about black people."

8 CNN's Cafferty and so-called black leaders refuse to ask basic questions. Since 1978, for example, black mayors controlled the city of New

Orleans, with many of the city's top officials also black. What about their responsibility? What about the damage done by the modern welfare state, helping to create poverty by financially rewarding irresponsible behavior? What about the damage to the black psyche by so-called civil rights leaders who demand not just equal rights, but equal results, helping to create a victicrat-entitlement mentality? Maybe someday one of the news anchors will ask one of the so-called civil rights leaders the following question: Doesn't the demand for race-based preferences, set-asides, private sector anti-discrimination laws, social welfare programs, and social "safety net" programs all conspire to say one thing—"You are not responsible"?

9 *City Journal*'s Nicole Gelinas, a one-time New Orleans resident, said, "[T]he city's decline over the past three decades has left it impoverished and lacking the resources to build its economy from within. New Orleans can't take care of itself even when it is not 80 percent underwater; what is it going to do now, as waters continue to cripple it, and thousands of looters systematically destroy what Katrina left unscathed?" She also notes, "The city's government has long suffered from incompetence and corruption," and that the crime rate in New Orleans—during normal times—exceeds the national average by a factor of 10!

10 News anchors and so-called black leaders ignore a far bigger factor than race or class—culture.

11 Consider the mid-1800s, and the plight of New York City's Irish underclass. According to William J. Stern, writing in the *Wall Street Journal*, "One hundred fifty years ago, Manhattan's tens of thousands of Irish seemed mired in poverty and ignorance, destroying themselves through drink, idleness, violence crime, and illegitimacy. . . . An estimated 50,000 Irish prostitutes worked the city in 1850. . . . Illegitimacy soared, tens of thousands of abandoned Irish kids roamed the city's streets. Violent Irish gangs fought each other . . . but primarily they robbed houses and small businesses. More than half the people arrested in New York in the 1840s and 1850s were Irish. . . ."

12 Disgusted by government "charity," Bishop John Joseph Hughes led movements to form nongovernment-aided Catholic schools and numerous self-help programs. He promoted abstinence and the belief that sex outside of marriage was a sin. His diocese's nuns served as an employment agency for Irish domestics and encouraged women to run boarding houses. What happened? Within two generations, "the Irish proportion of arrests for violent crime had dropped to less than 10 percent from 60 percent. Irish children were entering . . . the professions, politics, show business, and commerce. In 1890, some 30 percent of the city's teachers were Irish women, and the Irish literacy rate exceeded 90 percent."

13 Some demand a commission to investigate the failures and breakdowns in Hurricane Katrina. Fine. Let's hope they put together a commission to investigate another hurricane—that wrought by the welfare state and the irresponsible use of the race card.

THINKING ABOUT THE READING

1. In paragraph 2, Elder writes: "But how does this add up to racism?" What does this line suggest about what the rest of the essay will be about?
2. What purpose does the evidence cited in paragraphs 3, 4, and 5 serve? What point is the author attempting to make?

3. What is the author's opinion of laws that allow preferential treatment for minorities?
4. According to Elder, what is a "far bigger factor than race or class" in contributing to poverty? What does he mean by this phrase?
5. What is the author's opinion of government assistance? What alternative to these programs does he seem to endorse?

Responding to the Reading

1. Do you believe that the response to the Katrina disaster was racist? Explain. In your answer, define *racism* and provide at least one concrete example of it.
2. Do you agree or disagree with Elder's assessment in paragraph 8 that "race-based preferences, set-asides, private sector anti-discrimination laws, social welfare programs, and social 'safety net' programs all conspire to say one thing—'You are not responsible'"? Explain.
3. Do you believe that government-sponsored public assistance programs can or should be replaced with religious or private-sector forms of assistance, as Elder seems to suggest in paragraphs 11 and 12?
4. If neither of these approaches appeals to you, do you think the poor should be left to fend for themselves? Why or why not?

Writing about the Reading

1. Write a response to Elder's article. Argue the ways in which you think his claims are right and wrong. Support your own assertions with adequate evidence.
2. Write an argument explaining whether faith-based or community-based assistance programs should do the job that government programs may have failed to do.
3. Write a brief argument outlining ways in which public assistance may have failed. If you do not think that public assistance programs are flawed, explain why.
4. Assume that you have been given the assignment of helping one homeless family move from public assistance to independence. Outline the steps you would recommend to help this family get back on its feet.

"What the Waters Revealed"

About the Author: Jim Wallis

A veteran of the civil rights and antiwar movements of the 1960s, Jim Wallis, along with other students from Trinity Evangelical Divinity School, created a publication that eventually grew into *Sojourners* magazine, a liberal publication that publishes articles that stress working for peace, seeking justice, and combating poverty. More recently, Wallis helped form Call to Renewal, an organization of affiliated churches and religious organizations that strives to help the poor. Wallis serves as editor-in-chief of *Sojourners,* where the following article was first published in 2005. His books include

The Soul of Politics: A Practical and Prophetic Vision for Change (1994), *Who Speaks for God? A New Politics of Compassion, Community, and Civility* (1996), *Faith Works* (2000), and *God's Politics: Why the Right Gets It Wrong and the Left Doesn't Get It* (2005).

BEFORE YOU READ

1. Review the headnote. What, if anything, do you know about *Sojourners* magazine? How could you find out more?
2. Based on the information supplied in the headnote, what do you expect Wallis's point of view to be? Why do you think this?
3. What does the title of the article suggest? What do you think Wallis will say "the waters revealed"?
4. Scan the article. Try to pick out the thesis statement and some of the supporting claims. What do you think the main thrust of the argument will be at this point?

What the Waters Revealed

1 Hurricane Katrina destroyed entire cities, the lives of more than a thousand people, the homes of hundreds of thousands, and the confidence of millions in the government's commitment and ability to protect them. Then Hurricane Rita reflooded New Orleans and caused millions to flee their homes in Texas, including many who had already fled there from their homes in New Orleans. Much of New Orleans was emptied of its people, and broad areas of the Gulf Coast in Mississippi, Alabama, and Texas were devastated. More than 1 million Americans are now displaced across the country, and their fellow Americans around the nation are trying to take them in, perhaps for a long time.

2 But the waters of Hurricane Katrina also washed away our national denial of the shockingly high number of Americans living in poverty and our reluctance to admit the still-persistent connection of race and poverty in America, and perhaps even eroded the political power of a conservative anti-social services ideology that, for decades now, has weakened the idea of the common good.

3 The pictures from New Orleans stunned the nation. They exposed the stark reality of who was suffering the most, who was left behind, who was waiting in vain for help to arrive, and who is now facing the most difficult challenges of recovery. The faces of those stranded in New Orleans were overwhelmingly poor and black, the very old and the very young. They were the ones who could not evacuate: had no cars or money for gas: no money for bus, train, or airfare; no budget for hotels or no friends or family with room to share or spare. They were already vulnerable before this calamity; now they were totally exposed and on their own. For days, nobody came for them. And the conditions of the places they were finally herded to ("like animals," many testified) sickened the nation. Those left behind in New Orleans had already been left out in America.

4 From the reporters covering the unprecedented disaster to ordinary Americans glued to their televisions, a shocked and even outraged response was repeated: "I didn't realize how many Americans were poor."

5 "We have now seen what is under the rock in America," said a carpenter in Washington, D.C. The vulnerability of the poorest children in New Orleans has been especially riveting to many

Americans, especially to other parents. Many say they had trouble holding back their tears when they saw mothers with their babies stranded on rooftops crying for help or jammed into dangerous and dirty places waiting for help to arrive.

6 As a direct result of Katrina and its aftermath, and for the first time in many years, the media were reporting on poverty, telling Americans that New Orleans had an overall poverty rate of 28 percent (84 percent of them African American), and a child poverty rate of almost 50 percent—half of all the city's children (rates only a little higher than other major cities and actually a little lower than some others). Ironically (and some might say providentially), the annual U.S. Census poverty report came out during Katrina's deadly assault, showing that poverty had risen for the fourth straight year and that 37 million Americans were stuck below the poverty line. Such people were the ones most stuck in New Orleans.

7 Katrina revealed what was already there in America: an invisible and often silent poverty that most of us in the richest nation on earth have chosen not to talk about, let alone take responsibility for. After the storm hit, we all saw it—and so did the rest of the world. It made Americans feel both compassion and shame. Many political leaders and commentators, across the ideological spectrum, acknowledged the national tragedy, not just of the horrendous storm but of the realities the flood waters exposed. And some have suggested that if the aftermath of Katrina finally leads the nation to demand solutions to the poverty of upwards of a third of its citizens, then something good might come from this terrible disaster.

8 That is what we must all work toward now. Rescuing those still in danger, assisting those in dire need, relocating and caring for the homeless, and beginning the process of recovery and rebuilding are all top priorities. But dealing with the stark and shameful social and racial realities Katrina has revealed must become our clear, long-term goal. That will require a combination of public and private initiatives, the merger of personal and social responsibility, the rebuilding of both families and communities—but also the confronting of hard questions about national priorities. Most of all it will require us to make different choices.

9 The critical needs of poor and low-income families must become the first priority of federal and state legislatures, not the last. And, the blatant inequalities of race in America—especially in critical areas of education, jobs, health care, and housing—must now be addressed. Congressional pork-barrel spending that aligns with political power more than human needs must be challenged as never before. That will require a complete reversal of the political logic now operating in Washington and state capitals around the country: A new moral logic must reshape our political habits.

10 In the face of this natural disaster—and during a time of war, with already rising deficits—new budget cuts to vital programs such as food stamps and Medicaid, and more tax cuts for the wealthy, in the form of estate tax repeal and capital gains and stock dividend reductions, would be both irresponsible and shameless.

11 The nation is starting to realize that the weakness of the nation's infrastructure is not a problem limited to the levees of New Orleans, and that restoring the Gulf Coast will require an environmental reconstruction as well. We can no longer neglect the loss of critical wetlands that once offered some protection from flooding, or deny the fact that increased water temperature in the Gulf of Mexico stokes the strength of tropical storms—such negligence is irresponsible and will only produce more disasters.

12 Katrina has also focused new attention on Iraq. The growing human and economic costs of a war in Iraq that more and more Americans believe to be a terrible mistake has also become an increasingly controversial issue as the current disaster has unfolded. Resources diverted from urgently needed levee repair in order to pay for war, the diminished availability of National Guard

troops and first responders on tour in Iraq, and the embarrassing comparisons between poor planning and implementation for war and the ill-preparedness and incompetence of the national response to Katrina have all raised new and deeper questions about the nation's foreign policy and political leadership. A bad war, bad financial choices of how we spend our resources, and a bad strategy to combat terrorism are now inextricably linked in the minds of many to a bad natural disaster strategy, or lack thereof. The war in Iraq hasn't made us more secure; Katrina's aftermath has made that even more clear.

13 There is historical precedent for natural disasters provoking a reevaluation of our social thinking and political direction. In 1889, a great flood in Johnstown, Pennsylvania, trapped and killed hundreds of people, most of them poor. Some of the blame fell on the Pittsburgh millionaires whose private fishing pond overflowed onto the destitute. The tragic event helped to catalyze the already growing popular anger against the new industrialists who seemed so callous to the suffering of people around them. The flood, many historians feel, helped to prepare the way for the turn-of-the-century progressive movement, which focused on breaking up the powerful corporate trusts that had come to dominate the country.

14 In 1927, another flood visited destruction on the city of New Orleans. In his provocative book *Rising Tide: The Great Mississippi Flood of 1927 and How It Changed America,* historian John M. Barry describes how the disaster revealed both racial and economic inequalities. The response to the disaster by local authorities directly exposed the brutal inequities of race and class and provoked a deep populist anger. People demanded new responses from the federal government, and the 1927 flood helped pave the way for the New Deal. Citing both Johnstown and 1927 New Orleans as examples, columnist David Brooks wrote insightfully in the *New York Times* immediately following Katrina, "Hurricanes come in two waves. First comes the rainstorm, and then comes what the historian John Barry calls the 'human storm'—the recriminations, the political conflict, and the battle over compensation. Floods wash away the surface of society, the settled way things have been done. They expose the underlying power structures, the injustices, the patterns of corruption, and the unacknowledged inequalities. When you look back over the meteorological turbulence in this nation's history, it's striking how often political turbulence followed." Such natural disasters, says Brooks, can become "civic examinations."

15 Interviewing Barry on *Meet the Press,* Tim Russert asked, "Do you see the same thing happening now in terms of the reemergence of class and race and poverty as political issues?" Barry replied, "I think it's certainly possible and maybe likely. But it's obviously too early to tell." The storm "ripped off the cover" from America, said Barry, revealing what happens to people without resources. The question, said the historian, is whether Katrina would cause a "shift in public thinking" about our collective responsibilities to people in need.

16 That shift in thinking cannot just be the reassertion of old social and political agendas that seek to take advantage of the current moment of opportunity. The truth is that our failure of the poor is a collective one: Both conservative and liberal agendas have proven inadequate and left us with a very large underclass of poor people—adults, children, families—in America. Both sides have important insights that must be factored into any real solutions, but both have fallen far short of providing real answers. Many, even most, poor people work hard, full time, yet are still forced to raise their children in poverty. That should be unacceptable in America. To change that, we will need a new commitment, a new approach, and a new alliance to overcome poverty in America.

17 There are two obstacles to making real progress against poverty: the lack of *priority* and the lack of agreement on *strategy.* The poor have been near the bottom of our priority list, if they

are on the list at all. It will take a moral and even religious imperative to change our priorities, but the time has come to do so. But we have also been paralyzed by the debate between liberals and conservatives on what solutions to pursue, with the Right favoring cultural changes and the Left endorsing policy changes.

18 We must be disciplined by results when it comes to poverty reduction. It's time to move from the politics of blame to a politics of solutions. Liberals must start talking about the problems of out-of-wedlock births and about strengthening both marriage and parenting, and conservatives must start talking about strategic public investments in education, health care, affordable housing, and living family incomes. We must focus on making work really work for low-income families. Those who work hard and full time in America should not have to raise their children in poverty—but many still do. Together, we must end the debate that's limited to the choices of large or small government and forge a common commitment to good and effective government.

19 This is indeed a teachable moment, but one that will require good teachers. What have we learned, how must we change, where will we transform our priorities, and when will we commit ourselves to forging a new strategy that actually might work to defeat the cycle of poverty?

20 Restoring the hope of America's poorest families, renewing our national infrastructures, protecting our environmental stability, and rethinking our most basic priorities will require nothing less than a national change of heart and direction. It calls for a transformation of political ethics and governance, a move from serving private interests to ensuring the public good. If Katrina changes our political conscience and reinvigorates among us a commitment to the common good, then even this terrible tragedy might be redeemed.

Thinking about the Argument

1. What does the author mean when he says, "Those left behind in New Orleans had already been left out in America"?
2. In paragraph 5, Wallis presents some statistics. How are these facts used to validate what he says in the next paragraph?
3. What is Wallis's call to action? What does he think "we must all work toward now"?
4. What obstacles does the author think we face in changing the way poverty is treated in America?

Responding to the Argument

1. Does the author seem hopeful that substantial changes in the way the poor are treated will be made? How can you tell?
2. Do you believe, as the author suggests, that spending on the Iraq War has directly affected living conditions for the poor? Explain.
3. Do you agree or disagree with Wallis's "call to action"? What policy would you suggest, if any, to help the plight of the poor in America?
4. Wallis makes several statements connecting poverty to race. Do you believe this is a fair characterization or an overgeneralization? Why do you think this?

WRITING ABOUT THE ARGUMENT

1. Name one "call to action"—one thing—that you think should be done to reduce poverty. Write an essay explaining how and why you would implement that plan.
2. Write an in-depth letter to the editor of your local newspaper arguing whether poverty should be linked with discussions about race. Be certain to support your claims with evidence.
3. Critique Wallis's claim that focusing on and/or spending money on military efforts has directly affected the living conditions of poor people in America.
4. Write a refutation of Wallis's article. In your refutation, explain why you think conditions for the poor are better than they have been in the past and why they will likely continue to improve.

Issue 3: Political Correctness and Freedom of Speech

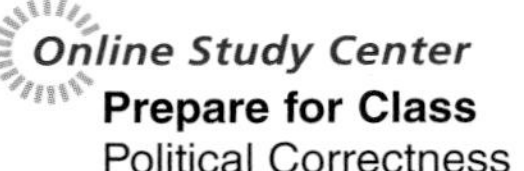

Prepare for Class
Political Correctness

The term *political correctness* refers to the words and images that define people without offending them or implying any prejudice against them. These terms change over time: the word *cripple,* for example, which was once used to describe a person with a certain type of disability, was replaced by the term *handicapped,* which was replaced by the term *physically disabled.*

Although political correctness may seem appropriate in many circumstances, some individuals have seen it as limiting their freedom of speech. The use of the Confederate flag in the South is one example of this kind of hot-button issue: some people see this flag as an offensive symbol of slavery, and others see it as a representation of their culture.

Additionally, certain individuals and groups have rejected politically correct labels, claiming that they are one way that a dominant culture tries to exert influence over them. Toni Morrison, an African American author, has put the issue like this:

> What I think the political correctness debate is really about is the power to be able to define. The definers want the power to name. And the defined are now taking that power away from them.

The articles that follow present a variety of views on subjects relating to political correctness and freedom of speech. What do you think about this issue? Do politically correct terms limit freedom, or do they treat individuals and cultures in a fair and unbiased way?

Considering the Issue of Political Correctness and Freedom of Speech

Working individually or in groups, answer the following questions.

1. What is political correctness? Does *PC* seem a positive or a negative way to label this concept? How does it compare to *politeness?*
2. What is *freedom of speech*? Is the term used in positive or negative way? Do some people abuse this freedom? In what ways?
3. Have you ever been upset or offended by another person's words and ideas? Have you ever offended others with your words and ideas?
4. Do you believe certain words should not be spoken under certain circumstances? Do you believe some words should never be spoken? Explain
5. Do you believe that certain ideas should not be discussed? Explain.

© Dan Piraro, King Features Syndicate

How much influence should special-interest groups have over what does or does not appear in textbooks? Has freedom of speech—and education in general—been compromised for the sake of political correctness?

Reading Selection

"The Language Police: Can We Stop Them?"

About the Author: Diane Ravitch

Diane Ravitch is a researcher, teacher, and educational historian. She is a professor of education at New York University and has served as a senior fellow at the Brookings Institute. Under President George H. W. Bush, she worked for the U.S. Department of Education, where she was an assistant secretary of research. During President Bill Clinton's administration, she served on the National Assessment Governing Board. Her previous books include *Left Back: A Century of Battles over School Reform* (1996). In *The Language Police,* her 2003 book from which this selection is taken, Ravitch argues that textbook publishers and governmental agencies, bowing to pressure from special-interest groups from the left and the right, have cleansed books of anything that might be found offensive. The result, she contends, are unengaging and unrealistic texts that are helping to "dumb down" our systems of public and private education.

READING SELECTION

BEFORE YOU READ

1. What does *political correctness* mean to you? Is it a good thing? How does political correctness impinge on or help support the freedom of speech?
2. Is the personal freedom to say what you think more or less important than the right of others to be insulated from your opinion? How does this relate to the general question from the beginning of this unit: Do people really have the right to do whatever they want, even if the community in which they live disapproves of their actions?
3. What does the term *language police* in Ravitch's title imply? Do you think she believes that PC is good for society? Why do you think so?
4. What do you think the answer to the question phrased in her title might be? What do you think she will argue?

»«

The Language Police: Can We Stop Them?

Don't you see that the whole aim of Newspeak is to narrow the range of thought? In the end we shall make thoughtcrime literally impossible, because there will be no words in which to express it.

—George Orwell, *1984*

1 Ray Bradbury, a writer who smells trends long before anyone else, saw what was happening in 1979. In a coda appended to the paperback version of *Fahrenheit 451,* his classic novel about book burning, Bradbury wrote about his encounters with political censorship. He recalled the letter he received from a college student who suggested that he should add some female characters to his book *The Martian Chronicles;* he also received a complaint that the blacks in the book were "Uncle Toms," followed by a letter alleging that the story was prejudiced in favor of blacks. Soon afterward, a publisher asked him for permission to reprint a story in a high school anthology, but would he mind deleting references to a "God-light" and "the Presence"? He refused. Bradbury found another high school anthology that had compressed the stories of classic authors: "Every story, slenderized, starved, blue-penciled, leeched and bled white, resembled every other story. Twain read like Poe read like Shakespeare read like Dostoevsky read like—in the finale—Edgar Guest. Every word of more than three syllables had been razored. Every image that demanded so much as one instant's attention—shot dead."

2 He saw where the pressure to sanitize books and stories was coming from, and he saw what it meant. Every minority, he said, whether "Baptist/Unitarian, Irish/Italian/Octogenarian/Zen Buddhist, Zionist/Seventh-Day Adventist, Women's Lib/Republican, Mattachine/Four Square Gospel" was ready to burn books, and "every dimwit editor who sees himself as the source of all dreary blanc-mange plain porridge unleavened literature, licks his guillotine and eyes the neck of any author who dares to speak above a whisper or write above a nursery rhyme." When he discovered that his own publisher had quietly, and without his permission, removed seventy-five sections from *Fahrenheit 451,* he was outraged. He learned about it from students who wrote to tell him that his novel about censorship and book burning had been expurgated. He fumed, "If Mormons do not like my plays, let them write their own. If the Irish hate my Dublin stories, let them rent typewriters." He would not, he thundered, "go gently onto a shelf, degutted, to become a non-book."[1]

3 When Bradbury wrote his protest, he thought he was dealing with the aberrant acts of miscellaneous bluenoses, prudes, Pecksniffians, pharisees, and numbskulls. What he did not know was that he had experienced the early phase of a movement that was being institutionalized in educational publishing. It was no accident that chunks of his controversial novel silently dropped onto the cutting-room floor. This was not the result of arbitrary decisions made by a "dimwit editor." The system of silent editing was beginning to work. It was getting organized, becoming a regular process.

4 For twenty-five years, give or take a few, we have lived with this system of silent censorship. We have seen the refinement and perfection of this system, in which publishers have joined hands with state school boards to censor texts and tests. Now that the rules of censorship have been codified, editors, writers, and illustrators know well in advance what is not acceptable. No one speaks of "censoring" or "banning" words or topics; they "avoid" them. The effect is the same. Euphemisms are kinder and gentler than raw truths. By now, the rules and guidelines could be dismissed, and they would still function because they have been deeply internalized by the publishing industry. George Orwell and Franz Kafka would have understood this system perfectly; it works best when it permeates one's consciousness and no longer needs to be explained or defended.

5 The goal of the language police is not just to stop us from using objectionable words but to stop us from having objectionable thoughts. The language police believe that reality follows language usage. If they can stop people from ever seeing offensive words and ideas, they can prevent them from having the thought or committing the act that the words signify. If they never read a story about suicide or divorce, then they will never even think about killing themselves or ending their marriage. If they abolish words that have *man* as a prefix or suffix, then women will achieve equality. If children read and hear only language that has been cleansed of any mean or hurtful words, they will never have a mean or hurtful thought. With enough censorship, the language police might create a perfect world.

6 This is nonsensical, because the schools are not a total institution. They do not control every aspect of children's lives. Children are influenced not just by what they read in their textbooks and what they encounter on tests, but by their families, their friends, their communities, their religious institutions, and—perhaps more than anything else—the popular culture. Much as the censors may hope to limit what children see and hear, they do not have the means to do it.

7 Censorship in the schools, whatever its purposes, is censorship. It should be abhorrent to those who care about freedom of thought, to those who believe that minds grow sharper by contending with challenging ideas. How boring for students to be restricted only to stories that flatter their self-esteem or that purge complexity and unpleasant reality from history and current events. How weird for them to see television programs and movies that present life in all its confusing and sometimes unpleasant fullness, then to read textbooks in which language, ideas, and behavior have been scrubbed of anything that might give offense. How utterly vapid to expect that adolescents want to see themselves in everything they read, as if they have no capacity to imagine worlds that extend beyond their own limited experience, as if they will be emotionally undone by learning about the world as it is. How tedious it is for young people to find that school is an exercise in narcissism rather than an opportunity to discover the mysteries of time, space, and human nature.

8 The censorship that has spread throughout American education has pernicious and pervasive effects. It lowers the literacy level of tests because test makers must take care to avoid language as well as works of literature and historical selections that might give offense. It restricts the

language and the ideas that may be reproduced in textbooks. It surely reduces children's interest in their schoolwork by making their studies so deadly dull. It undermines our common culture by imposing irrelevant political criteria on the literature and history that are taught.

9 Censorship distorts the literature curriculum, substituting political judgments for aesthetic ones. Because of the bias and social content guidelines, editors of literature anthologies must pay more attention to having the correct count of gender groups and ethnic groups among their characters, authors, and illustrations than they do to the literary quality of the selections. State education officials carefully scrutinize the former and ignore the latter. Once literary quality no longer counts, almost anything can be included in literature anthologies, such as television scripts, student essays, advertisements, and other ephemera, while indisputably major authors share equal billing with authors whose work will never be known outside the textbook industry. Quietly but inevitably, what we once considered our literary heritage disappears from the schools.

10 Censorship distorts the history curriculum by introducing political considerations into interpretations of the past, based on deference to religious, ethnic, and gender sensitivities. Forced into a political straitjacket, almost all history texts echo one another, with nary a fresh interpretation, idea, or anecdote, nor even a good argument to excite their readers' enthusiasms. Like books written by historians, history texts should have a point of view, but they should not all have the *same* point of view. That stultifying conformity guarantees that no sparks will be struck in young minds; it is a recipe for boredom.

11 The censorship regime has a chilling effect on writers, as Nat Hentoff pointed out. Most authors, editors, and illustrators whose work is affected by bias guidelines have accepted their permanence or have been reluctant to challenge them for fear of not getting any more assignments. No one wants to be accused of bias, so everyone acquiesces to political restrictions on his or her work. Compared to the larger society, where ideas are freely expressed and freely debated, the schools have become an island of censorship in a sea of freedom.

12 All this sanitizing of children's educational materials is meant to mold their minds and shield them from inappropriate language and thoughts. Censors always believe that their work is for the good of society. But is it? Who gave the schools and the publishers the right to decide how the next generation's minds should be molded? Because the censorship process developed so gradually and with so little public scrutiny, there has been no debate about whether it should be there at all. This is an issue that needs the light of day—that is, open and vigorous public discussion—shined upon it.

13 Rewarding groups that complain by allowing them to censor words and images that they don't like only encourages them. Censorship should be stopped, not rewarded with compliance and victories.

14 It must be said, not in defense of the publishers' bias guidelines, but as a way of seeing the climate in which they acted, that their bowdlerizing was in step with larger trends in society. They did not act alone. On hundreds of college campuses, administrators adopted speech codes and sexual harassment codes to punish anyone who told offensive jokes or said something that made another student feel uncomfortable. Students and faculty members were hauled before campus tribunals for saying the wrong thing, whether in jest, in the classroom, or on a date. In offices and universities across the nation, diversity trainers instructed workers and students about the language that they should and should not express. How natural, in this climate where political reeducation had a certain social validity, to expect that the schools would lead the way in building a new social order.

15 Jonathan Rauch criticized these attempts at cultural cleansing in his book *Kindly Inquisitors,*

in which he argued passionately for freedom of thought. He wrote "No one has the right to be spared sacrilege—not Jews, not Muslims, not ethnic minorities, not me, and not you." What should we do about people who say offensive things? Rauch advises, "Ignore them." And what should we do to assuage the feelings of people who have been offended? Rauch says, "This and only this: *absolutely nothing*. Nothing at all." This is the burden of maintaining a free society. His advice to the offended is to be thick-skinned. No one has a right not to be criticized or offended. The campus speech codes, Rauch writes, aim to silence people with wrong opinions: "The agenda is always the same: stifle ideas you hate in the name of a higher social good." But in our society, the role of authorities is not to get rid of wrong opinions, but to protect the expression of opinion and the free exchange of ideas. A free society is not free unless it tolerates offensive words and unpopular opinions.[2]

16 Another way of expressing Rauch's view is the formula that parents used to teach their children. Whenever anyone says anything offensive, the correct response is: "Sticks and stones may break my bones, but words will never hurt me." Sometimes words do hurt, but we learn to live with that hurt as the price of freedom. The alternative is to submit our speech and our reading materials to bias guidelines, official censors, language police, and thought police.

Notes

1. Ray Bradbury, coda to *Fahrenheit 451* (Ballantine/Del Rey, 1979), pp. 175–79.
2. Jonathan Rauch, *Kindly Inquisitors: The New Attacks on Free Thought* (University of Chicago Press, 1993), pp. 128–29, 141.

Thinking about the Argument

1. How does the author think that publishing companies are being influenced by special-interest groups?
2. What does she think should be done about this trend? Does she think anything can be done?
3. If nothing is done, what will the result be in terms of education?
4. What evidence does Ravitch provide to back up her claims? Is it convincing? Explain.

Responding to the Argument

1. Do you agree with Ravitch? Why or why not?
2. Explain why you agree or disagree with the following statement: "If textbooks (and other educational materials, including teachers' lectures) are adequately censored, then no child will feel alienated or otherwise left out."
3. Choose a specific example from the author's essay and explain how it supports (or fails to support) the thesis. Could the example be used to argue a different claim? Explain.

Writing about the Argument

1. Write a refutation of Ravitch's essay. Using at least one of the author's own examples as part of your evidence, explain why censoring textbooks is good for education.

2. Reflect on a textbook you are using now or one you have used in the past. Name it. In what way does this textbook validate or bring into question the claim(s) that Ravitch is making?
3. Write an essay responding to the following statements: "It is acceptable to use positive stereotypes because they make people feel better about themselves. It is not acceptable to use negative stereotypes because they make people feel bad about themselves."

"Hate-Speech Codes That Will Pass Constitutional Muster"

ABOUT THE AUTHOR: LAWRENCE WHITE

Lawrence White has been legal counsel for Georgetown University. The following article, which appeared in the *Chronicle for Higher Education* in May 1994, was adapted from a speech that White gave at the Stetson University College of Law's National Conference on Law and Higher Education. He suggests that hate-speech codes for universities have legal validity.

BEFORE YOU READ

1. Based on the title of his article, what do you expect White's position to be on regulating freedom of speech on campus?
2. Do you think that speech should be regulated when the views do not represent the majority opinion? When they may be hurtful to others? When they are critical of professors or university administration? Explain.
3. Given that White is an attorney, what do you expect his focus will be?
4. What is "hate speech"?

Hate-Speech Codes That Will Pass Constitutional Muster

1 It has been a trying few years for the drafters of hate-speech codes on college and university campuses. The University of Pennsylvania jettisoned its controversial speech code last fall after President Sheldon Hackney, during his confirmation hearing to be chairman of the National Endowment for the Humanities, questioned whether such codes were the right approach to achieving civility on campus. This year, Central Michigan University became the latest institution to lose a court fight over its speech code. Continuing an unbroken line of victories by the American Civil Liberties Union, a federal judge held in January that Central Michigan had violated its basketball coach's right to free speech when he was disciplined under its "discriminatory harassment" code after he used a racial epithet during a closed-door team meeting. At Wesleyan University, the University of Michigan, and numerous other institutions, administrators have given up and repealed their codes.

2 Due largely to the court decisions, we now understand the arguments against campus speech codes: They use inherently vague terminology; they are overbroad, sweeping within

their regulatory ambit not only pernicious language, but also language that enjoys constitutional protection. "It is technically impossible to write an anti-speech code that cannot be twisted against speech nobody means to bar," concluded Eleanor Holmes Norton, a former Georgetown University law professor who is now the District of Columbia's delegate to Congress.

3 Despite the problems raised by speech codes, however, we must not forget that there are salutary purposes underlying the effort to draft codes banning derogatory and hurtful epithets. Such codes were intended to serve, and still serve, an important educational purpose: They are expressions of an institution's commitment to the victims of a pernicious and destructive form of behavior. Whenever anybody commits an act or utters a remark that is motivated by hatefulness, it causes harm to a real, flesh-and-blood victim. Hate-speech codes designed to protect victims are a noble endeavor. If institutions abandon the effort to draft policies against hateful speech, they are abandoning the victims the policies were meant to protect.

4 Campus administrators can learn important lessons from the court cases against the first generation of speech codes. In every instance, the codes that provoked court challenges were ambitiously, almost sweepingly, worded. Several of them, including those at the University of Michigan and the University of Wisconsin, were modeled on the Equal Employment Opportunity Commission's guidelines on sexual harassment. They used concepts and terminology—"intimidating environment for education," "express or implied threat to an individual's academic efforts"—awkwardly borrowed from employment law. They treated the university campus as a single, undifferentiated "workplace."

5 The language they used seemed almost deliberately provocative to civil libertarians—phrases such as "expressive behavior" (University of Wisconsin) and other wording that equated physical behavior with verbal behavior (Central Michigan University)—as though there were no distinction under the First Amendment.

6 What we have come to refer to as "hate speech" takes many forms on the nation's college campuses. The most prevalent involves remarks by students addressed to other students. For every high-profile case involving a campus speech by Khalid Abdul Muhammad of the Nation of Islam, there are literally dozens, maybe hundreds, of incidents that occur behind the closed doors of dormitory rooms, in dining halls, or in the corridors outside student pubs. We know, regrettably, that a strong correlation exists between hate speech and alcohol abuse.

7 Colleges and universities must now craft a second generation of codes that will serve the important institutional objective of protecting the victims of hateful acts and utterances without violating constitutional principles. These codes would:

8 • Differentiate between dormitories and classrooms. In an article that appeared in the *Duke Law Journal* in 1990, Nadine Strossen, president of the ACLU, observed that the right to free speech applies with different force in different parts of a college campus. That right, she wrote, "may not be applicable to . . . students' dormitory rooms. These rooms constitute the students' homes. Accordingly, under established free-speech tenets, students should have the right to avoid being exposed to others' expression by seeking refuge in their rooms." A policy that disciplined students for hateful acts or utterances against other students in residence halls would probably bring three-quarters of all hate-speech episodes within the regulatory purview of college administrators without offending traditional free-speech precepts.

9 • Be tailored to the Supreme Court's decision in *R.A.V. v. St. Paul, Minn.* This 1992 decision suggests that anti-discrimination codes are on shaky ground constitutionally if they proscribe some hateful acts or utterances but not others. Any policy that prohibits categories of speech "because of" or "on the basis of" a specific factor—such as race, gender, or sexual orientation—runs the risk of violating

the Court's stricture in *R.A.V.* that laws must not single out particular categories of hateful speech for penalties. As ironic as it sounds, the safest hate-speech code may be one that makes no mention of the very groups it is designed to protect.

10 • Use words emphasizing action and its effects, instead of speech. First Amendment jurisprudence recognizes an important distinction between speech and action and allows a greater degree of latitude when action is being regulated. The first generation of campus speech codes used vocabulary emphasizing speech, which virtually doomed them in advance—for example, they barred certain "comments" or "expressive behavior." By fostering the impression that these policies regulated pure speech, they made an easy target. The receptiveness of courts to arguments that the codes were overbroad—prohibiting speech that should be constitutionally protected along with utterances that deserve no protection (such as yelling "Fire!" in a crowded theater)—requires campuses to be more careful than they were in the past to draft constitutionally acceptable speech codes.

11 The second generation of codes should favor "action" vocabulary—prohibiting hostile conduct or behavior that might "incite immediate violence" (the latter being the exact phrasing used in the Supreme Court's half-century-old "fighting words" case, *Chaplinsky v. New Hampshire*). Instead of calling them "hate-speech codes," colleges and universities should refer to the new policies as "anti-hate" or "anti-discrimination" codes.

12 • Enhance the penalties for alcohol-related hate mongering. Most campus conduct codes allow the imposition of disciplinary sanctions for disorderly conduct or violations of drug and alcohol policies. It would be constitutionally defensible to treat hateful acts or utterances as an additional factor to be taken into account when meting out punishment for code violations. For example, a student found guilty of public drunkenness could be sentenced to attend a program designed to treat alcohol abuse, but the same inebriated student could be suspended or expelled for hurling racial epithets or threats at fellow students.

13 Drafting a new generation of campus codes to curb hate mongering, codes that zero in on areas of highest risk (dormitories, drunkenness) while avoiding the vagueness and overbreadth that doomed the first generation of codes, is an exercise worth undertaking. Colleges and universities began attempting to regulate hate speech a decade ago for an important reason—to communicate a message of support to the victims of hate. That reason is still compelling today. If institutions abandon the effort to implement constitutionally acceptable codes, they will be sending a message chillingly and accurately expressed by the Stanford University law professor Charles Lawrence in an article that accompanied Ms. Strossen's in the 1990 *Duke Law Journal:*

> 14 I fear that by framing the debate as we have—as one in which the liberty of free speech is in conflict with the elimination of racism—we have advanced the cause of racial oppression and have placed the bigot on the moral high ground, fanning the rising flames of racism.

15 We all understand civil libertarians' concerns when universities approach the delicate task of regulating certain forms of expressive conduct. But civil libertarians in turn should appreciate the message that is communicated when the rights of insensitive, viciously motivated members of college and university communities are placed above victims' rights to an education untainted by bigoted animosity. By trimming their drafting sails to incorporate the lessons of the first round of court cases, college administrators can satisfy constitutional concerns and at the same time curb the most egregious forms of hate mongering on campus. Then they can send an appropriate message to perpetrator and victim alike: Hateful utterances and behavior are repugnant forms of conduct that colleges and universities will not tolerate.

Thinking about the Argument

1. What is White's central claim? What reasons does he give to validate his point?
2. What evidence does White provide to back up his claim? Do you find it convincing? Why or why not?
3. Consider each of the four solutions that White outlines. Which solutions do you agree with? Which do you disagree with? Explain your answers.
4. What is the basis for White's assumption that hate speech must be controlled? Do you agree with this assumption? (Is its basis ethical or merely legal?)
5. Does White consider alternative arguments (such as those suggesting that all speech—even hurtful speech—is protected under the Constitution)? Why do you think this is the case?

Responding to the Argument

1. Do you believe that hate speech should be controlled on campus for ethical reasons? For legal reasons? Why?
2. Now that you have read the article, how would you define *hate speech*? Do you see any problems with your previous definition?
3. If it were left up to you, what would you do to curb hate speech on your campus? Would you regulate such speech through rules, through education, or through a combination of the two? Would you consider not regulating it at all? Why?

Writing about the Argument

1. Pretend you are an administrator who is drafting a hate-speech policy for your college or university. Write a letter to your president advocating one of the following: (a) not regulating hate speech or putting into place an education program; (b) putting into place an education program with no policy for limiting free speech on campus; (c) creating an education program and establishing policies to limit hurtful speech; or (d) another alternative you think of on your own.
2. Write a letter to White explaining why free speech should not be regulated on campus.

"Is It Time to Retire 'Politically Correct'?"

About the Author: Nat Hentoff

Nat Hentoff has written articles for *Editor & Publisher, Free Inquiry, Legal Times, Jewish World Review, The Progressive,* and the *Washington Times.* Known for writing from a civil libertarian perspective, Hentoff has been particularly critical of the American Civil Liberties Union—an organization that he endorsed in the past—for encouraging the enforcement of speech codes on college campuses and in the workplace. He is associated with the Foundation for Individual Rights in Education, which is not affiliated with the ACLU. Among his many books are *The First Freedom: The Tumultuous History of Free Speech in America* (1980), *Free Speech for Me—But Not for Thee: How the American Left and Right Relentlessly Censor Each Other* (1992), and *Does Anybody Give a Damn?*

Nat Hentoff on Education (1977). In his writings, Hentoff argues that free speech must be extended to everyone, even to those with whom the majority disagree. This essay first appeared in the *Village Voice* in January 1994.

BEFORE YOU READ

1. Based on the headnote, what do you know about the author? What would you guess his opinion to be?
2. What does the title of the article suggest about his thesis?
3. Quickly glance over the article. What main divisions or ideas can you glean?
4. Based on a quick review of the article, who do you think is the target audience? What might the publication in which the article originally appeared (the *Village Voice*) tell you about the audience? (If you don't know anything about this publication, take a moment to look at its website.)

Is it Time to Retire "Politically Correct"?

1 I should have written this series months ago. It was Brent Staples who spurred me to do these reports on the growing force of "political correctness" on college campuses, and he won't like the results. Staples is on the editorial board of The *New York Times* and occasionally writes a signed piece for Editorial Notebook at the bottom of the safely anonymous editorials.

2 Along, with Kari Meyer, Staples is usually precisely challenging—as in his notes on black self-segregation at colleges and "The Politics of Gangster Rap" ("When middle-class blacks fabricate violent urban pasts, they pay homage to murder").

3 However, on December 5 ("Time to Retire a Cliché"), Staples could hardly have been more wrong in his view of "political correctness." He sees it as a weapon used in the 1980s and beyond by "right-wing ideologues . . . to describe what they saw as a systematic effort by liberals to crush free and open discourse. But this was an imagined tyranny, dreamed up just as right-wing politics reached its apex on campus and in the White House." He also declared that it is time to retire the "cliché" of "political correctness," since it is unreal.

4 The tyranny of speech codes was hardly "imagined." It was the creation of some students on the left and craven administrators. Also not imaginary was the tyranny of guardians of orthodoxy in and out of the classroom on many campuses. It is orthodoxy of the left by those whose goals are admirable—opposition to racism, sexism, homophobia—but who use agitprop to ostracize dissenters. (By no means are all students on the left p.c. I keep meeting vigorous civil libertarians who are beginning to organize on campus.)

5 There are scores of documented illustrations of the authoritarian left in my recent book, *Free Speech for Me—But Not for Thee: How the American Left and Right Relentlessly Censor Each Other* (Harper Collins, paper). It should have been published in loose-leaf format, because I learn about new cases every week in the mail and during visits to colleges around the country (I average about three a month). Groupthink on campuses is thriving rather than subsiding.

6 So is the militant, take-no-prisoners orthodoxy of the right, less so at colleges than in public schools around the country. The Christian

Right is "politically correct" in its righteous closed-mindedness. Indeed, in that respect, and in their lust to censor opposing views, the Christian Right and the politically correct left at colleges are mirror images of each other—even though they are sworn enemies.

7 I commend to Brent Staples—and to all of you—this current account of "political correctness" by Benedict J. Miceli, a third-year student at Boston College Law School:

> 8 One of our course requirements is Constitutional Law, a course which I am presently taking. This morning, a group of students were discussing a case with our professor, a young black man. Our discussion got into the issue of civil liberties. Thereupon, the rest of the group and the professor stated that they were in fact not civil libertarians. During the course of the discussion, I was informed that students who express opinions in opposition to, for example, gay rights, feminism, etc. should be legally silenced since the "power" behind those "voices" cannot other than "oppress" those groups.
>
> 9 I was also told that I should not be taking a class from [another] professor who has written critically of the gay rights movement and who thus, by their lights, should not be teaching.
>
> 10 Furthermore, I was told that those who defend the rights of, for example, the Klan or the Nazi Party to march or speak in a public forum are not merely defending free speech, but in fact are in collusion with them! . . .
>
> 11 "How did this differ from protecting [the free-speech rights of] the anti-Semitic Nation of Islam?" I asked. I am sure that you can imagine the response. [The Klan and the Nazi Party did not deserve protection.] . . .
>
> 12 "Later in the discussion, Catharine MacKinnon's name came up approvingly and Nadine Strossen [who opposes MacKinnon's procensorship views] and the ACLU were dismissed as having "simplistic" ideas.
>
> 13 I find it puzzling that those who purport to suffer from oppression feel that restrictions on freedom would somehow be liberating. . . . It is the "marginalized" who suffer when liberty is restricted—not the privileged and "empowered."
>
> 14 Furthermore, it is chilling to contemplate the fact that persons such as I have discussed are in the business of making, teaching, and interpreting the laws which govern our lives. . . .
>
> 15 Some people simply want to tell other people what to do and think and they use the language of oppression as their tools [of suppression] as surely as many a Fundamentalist minister [uses] Scripture.

16 A student at Brown University, whom I got to know over time, is prochoice, antiracist, and against all forms of homophobia. He is also given to thinking for himself, asking questions because not all the answers he hears are complete. In class, for instance, he wondered whether the man involved in a pregnancy ought to have some say in whether the fetus should be aborted. If he were still around, if he were willing to take responsibility for the results of the pregnancy, and if the relationship with the woman were continuing.

17 In another class, he said he wondered whether scholarships based on race should go to those black students whose parents can well afford the tuition. Instead, shouldn't some scholarships be based on class so that a poor white student from Appalachia might find a way to get into college? (This was also the view of the most liberal justice in the history of the Supreme Court, William O. Douglas.)

18 He was looking for a debate. He wasn't sure what the right answers might be. Instead, from most of his classmates, he received contempt and the mechanical dismissal of him and his questions as sexist, racist—and therefore beneath discussion.

19 Having experienced being a pariah after such heresy, he told me had stopped speaking up in class. "It isn't worth it," he said. "They're thought police."

20 As another example of how Brent Staples's "imaginary tyranny" of political correctness is imaginary only in his head, there is this report from Ronald Rotunda. A law professor at the

University of Illinois, Rotunda is a person James Madison would have liked to have known. Whenever I talk with him, I learn something about the history and current complexities of free speech.

21 In the September–October 1993 issue of the *Southern Methodist University Law Review,* there is a Rotunda article on the present conflicts attending free speech. This is the lead:

> 22 Shawn Brown is a sophomore at the University of Michigan. For his assignment in Political Science 111, he wrote a term paper on possible inherent flaws in political polling data. It contained the following passage:
>
> 23 "Another problem with sampling polls is that some people desire their privacy and don't want to be bothered by a pollster. Let's say Dave Stud is entertaining three beautiful ladies in his penthouse when the phone rings. A pollster on the other end wants to know if we should eliminate the capital gains tax. Now Dave is a knowledgeable businessperson who cares a lot about the issue.
>
> 24 "But since Dave is 'tied up' at the moment, he tells the pollster to 'bother' someone else. Now this is perhaps a ludicrous example, but there is simply a segment of the population who wish to be left alone. They have more important things to be concerned about—jobs, family, school, etc. If this segment of the population is never actually polled, then the results of the poll can be skewed."

25 Do you see anything that might be interpreted as sexual harassment in that student article?

26 Debbie Meizlish, a teaching assistant, did. As Professor Rotunda notes: "She may have been pleased to see the sex-neutral term, 'businessperson,' but was otherwise appalled. She interpreted Mr. Brown's paper as sexual harassment *directed against her.*" [Emphasis added.] This is what Meizlish wrote to the student:

> 27 You are right. This is ludicrous & OFFENSIVE. This is completely inappropriate for a serious political science paper. It completely violates the standard of non-sexist writing. Professor Rosenstone [the lecturer for Brown's introductory American Government course] has encouraged me to interpret this comment as an example of sexual harassment and to take the appropriate formal steps.
>
> 28 I have chosen not to do so in this instance. However, any future comments in a paper, in a class or in any dealings w/me will be interpreted as sexual harassment and formal steps *will* be taken. Professor Rosenstone is aware of these comments—& is prepared to intervene. You are forewarned!

29 George Orwell was also forewarned. In *1984*, he said, "Orthodoxy means not thinking. Orthodoxy is unconsciousness." Meizlish and Rosenstone are convinced, however, that they have reached a most high level of consciousness.

30 Ronald Rotunda is very precise in his language. He is coeditor of a widely used law school textbook, *Treatise on Constitutional Law: Substance and Procedure* (West). I have been on panel discussions on constitutional law with him and have to watch my language to try to make sure it's as accurate as his.

31 In contrast with Brent Staples, who wants to retire "politically correct" and believes that it came to be used as a right-wing conspiracy to discredit the left, Rotunda is convinced political correctness continues to flourish. And, as indicated by the experience of Shawn Brown at the University of Michigan, the left has as relentless a holy book of orthodoxies as the right. Says Rotunda:

> 32 In the old days, we would have labeled as "thought control" any effort to control what we say or think. Now it is an effort to ban certain language considered improper, inappropriate, or offensive to people who are politically correct.

33 To my continued astonishment, the *New York Times*—in many of its editorials and sometimes even in its news columns—has become a very

model of political correctness. Brent Staples is too valuable an observer to get caught in that quicksand of righteousness.

34 More and more newspapers these days, including this one, indulge in political correctness from time to time, but not everybody on every paper has to follow suit.

Thinking about the Argument

1. What is Hentoff's central claim? What reasons does he cite to support it?
2. Which evidence presented in the article do you find the most compelling? The least compelling? Why?
3. Reread paragraphs 22–28. Would you consider this episode to be an act of "sexual harassment"? Why or why not? Do you think women and men will tend to react to this episode differently? Why do you think so?
4. Does Hentoff consider the value of speech codes? Why? What does it contribute to or take away from his argument?

Responding to the Argument

1. Do you agree with Hentoff that speech codes should be abolished? Explain.
2. What effect do you think politically correct speech has on limiting free speech (if any)?
3. When should students, professors, and administrators limit expressing their opinions? For example, following the September 11, 2001, attacks on the World Trade Center and the Pentagon, one professor remarked in class that destroying the Pentagon was a good idea. He received so many threats that he had to cancel his classes. Does "political correctness," as some have argued, limit professors' freedom to say what they want in their research or in their classes?

Writing about the Argument

1. Write a response to Hentoff's article. Explain why you think the incident he outlined in paragraphs 22–28 does, indeed, constitute sexual harassment.
2. Compare Hentoff's point of view to that expressed by White. Which writer makes the stronger argument? Explain.
3. Hentoff outlines a problem but does not offer a solution. Write a brief proposal explaining how to limit the "tyranny of speech codes" on your campus.
4. Write an argument explaining one type of speech that should be restricted on campus. Justify your reasons with evidence.

17

SECURITY

Islam and the West, Immigration Control, and the Culture of Fear

Before the new millennium began, most Americans felt relatively secure and safe. However, since September 11, 2001, many Americans have been feeling increasingly insecure—and not just because of terrorism. A sputtering economy, dangers to the environment, increasing energy costs, worries about health care and retirement benefits, and a porous border with Mexico have all contributed to the feeling that life in the United States is less safe now than in years past.

Some of this anxiety is undoubtedly due to media attention. When an airplane crashes or a shark attack occurs at a popular vacation beachfront, every news organization carries the story. Although people are much more likely to be killed in an automobile accident than to be injured in a terrorist attack, few people worry about the former, but a significant number are concerned about the latter.

> *They who would give up an essential liberty for temporary security, deserve neither liberty or security.*
>
> —Benjamin Franklin (1706–1790)

Online Study Center
This icon will direct you to content and resources on the website <college.hmco.com/pic/lamm1e>.

In recent years, three areas that have caused people a significant amount of worry are the relations between the United States and the Islamic world, the influx of undocumented workers across the border with Mexico, and the U.S. government's preparation (or lack thereof) for handling a significant disaster, whether natural (as was demonstrated by Hurricane Katrina) or man-made (as was demonstrated by the September 11 attacks).

Issue 1: Islam and the West

Although the United States has a long history of shaky relations with certain parts of the Islamic world, it was not until September 11, 2001, that many Americans felt that Islam presented a danger to their lives. Prior to September 11, terrorism was always a distant threat—something that endangered soldiers stationed in Beirut or tourists in Israel. Even following the bombing of the Murrah Federal Building in Oklahoma City, once the terrorist was discovered to be a disgruntled former U.S. soldier rather than an Islamic extremist, Americans breathed a mutual sigh of relief. However, the September 11 attacks changed that perception. Since then, this feeling of insecurity has been heightened by further attacks in Madrid, London, and Bali. More recently, Muslim mobs attacked Western embassies and other interests around the world after cartoons featuring Muhammad were published.

Online Study Center
Prepare for Class
Islam and the West

While the threat of terrorist attack is a legitimate concern, there remains little question that these attacks have widened the cultural rift that exists between the European diaspora (represented by Europe, the Americas, and European-style nations in other parts of the world such as South Africa, Israel, and Australia) and Islamic nations (such as Saudi Arabia, Egypt, and Iran). The questions surrounding this relationship are complex and may include differences in religion, political theories, and cultural beliefs.

Considering the Issue of Islam and the West

In discussion groups, in your journal, or working individually, answer the following questions.

1. What do you know about the Islamic faith? In what ways do you think it differs from other monotheistic approaches such as Judaism and Christianity? What is your opinion regarding this religion? Do you think you need to gather more information about it before making an informed decision about its place in America and the world?

2. What do you know about the American political philosophy known as "manifest destiny"? Does America have the right and the responsibility to spread Western democracy throughout the world? Why or why not?
3. Why might people living in Islamic countries be resistant to Western democracy? Why do you think this?
4. How do you think that the cultural values of people living in Western democracies might differ from those of people living in various Islamic countries? What might members of Islamic societies think of the separation of church and state? The equality of women and men in the West? America's support of Israel?

READING SELECTION

"The Patriot Act: Wise beyond Its Years"

About the Author: John Ashcroft

John Ashcroft grew up to reflect his father's evangelical moral certainty and conservative Christian worldview. His rigidity and absolute sense of right and wrong have won him friends and enemies alike. After graduating from the University of Chicago Law School in 1967, Ashcroft worked as a business law professor, Missouri state auditor, and governor of Missouri. He entered the U.S. Senate in 1994 and lost his 2000 race to a dead opponent (who had died in a plane crash). George W. Bush appointed Ashcroft to head the Department of Justice, and as the U.S. Attorney General he became one of the primary supporters of the Patriot Act, which extended the powers of the government and law enforcement agencies in combating terrorism. The Patriot Act has been much maligned by some individuals for curtailing civil liberties. Ashcroft resigned from the office of Attorney General in 2004. He has coauthored two college textbooks and written *Lessons from a Father to His Son* (1998) and *On My Honor: The Beliefs That Shape My Life* (2001). This essay was originally published in the *Wall Street Journal* in October 2004.

Before You Read

1. What do you already know about John Ashcroft? What is your opinion of him?
2. Based on your own knowledge, any research, and the headnote, what do you expect Ashcroft to say about the Patriot Act?
3. What does the title suggest about his thesis?
4. What is your opinion of the Patriot Act? Is it a good or bad idea? Why do you think so?

READING SELECTION

The Patriot Act: Wise beyond Its Years

[The Patriot Act] takes account of the new realities and dangers posed by modern terrorists. It will help law enforcement to identify, to dismantle, to disrupt, and to punish terrorists before they strike.

—President George W. Bush, at the Patriot Act signing ceremony, on October 26, 2001

1 The Patriot Act turns three today, but its age belies its experience—and its phenomenal success. Over the past 36 months, the Patriot Act has proved itself to be an indispensable tool that the men and women of law enforcement use to combat terrorism and to compile a record of accomplishment that has grown even as their responsibility for the safety of Americans has increased.

2 The Patriot Act enhanced communication on every level of law enforcement to combat terrorist threats, while also giving investigators the same tools to use in terrorism cases that they were using to combat other serious threats.

3 Armed with these tools, U.S. intelligence and law enforcement agents have pursued and captured operatives in the war on terrorism from Florida to New York, from Virginia to Oregon, and points in between. Since September 11, 2001, 368 individuals have been charged and 194 have been convicted.

4 Despite the documented successes in keeping Americans safe from terrorism, the Patriot Act rarely receives its due, and indeed is often portrayed in an outright false light.

5 Take the latest example. Just last month, several major news organizations erroneously reported that a federal judge in New York had overturned "an important surveillance provision" of the Patriot Act. In fact, the judge ruled on the Electronic Communications Privacy Act—sponsored by Senator Patrick Leahy (D., Vermont) and passed in 1986, 15 years before the Patriot Act. Both the *New York Times* and the *Washington Post* were forced to print corrections the next day.

6 Time and again, the image of the Patriot Act is at odds with the facts on the ground. Three years ago today, Congress passed, and President Bush signed, a piece of long-overdue legislation that has been critical to keeping Americans safe and free. The parade of witnesses that appeared before the 9/11 Commission spoke of the importance of the Patriot Act. Former Attorney General Janet Reno and many others credited the Patriot Act with updating the law to deal with terrorists and, most critically, for tearing down the "wall" in terrorism investigations that restricted the communication and cooperation between law enforcement and intelligence officials.

7 This new ability to share information helped U.S. law enforcement, working with German authorities, to break up an alleged al Qaeda fundraising plot in Germany. Here in the United States, the Patriot Act helped federal, state, and local law enforcement dismantle the "Portland Seven" terrorist cell in Oregon, as well as cells in Seattle and New York, and alleged terrorist financers in Florida and Texas.

8 The Patriot Act has also been successful in updating anti-terrorism and criminal laws to bring law enforcement up to date with technology. Pre–Patriot Act, a new court order was required to continue surveillance of a suspected terrorist whenever he switched phones. The Patriot Act gave anti-terrorism investigators the same authority that investigators in criminal cases had to get a single court order allowing surveillance of every phone a suspect uses. Common sense dictates that tools that help fight the drug lords should be available to protect the American people from terrorist attacks.

9 The Patriot Act also increased penalties for not only those who commit terrorist acts, but for

READING SELECTION

those who provide support to terrorists as well. In particular, the act enhanced law enforcement's ability to crack down on unlicensed foreign money transmittal businesses, a favored method of financing for terrorists. Prosecutors in New
10 Jersey recently used the Patriot Act to convict Yehuda Abraham, whose services were used in a plot to sell shoulder-fired surface-to-air missiles to terrorists with the understanding that they were going to be used to shoot down U.S. commercial aircraft.

The Patriot Act has proved its usefulness be-
11 yond the war on terrorism in protecting our most vulnerable citizens from harm. During the course of drafting and debating the Patriot Act in 2001, Congress wisely decided to provide some investigative tools for all criminal investigations, including terrorism investigations.

The result? In pedophile and kidnapping investigations, for example, a delay can literally
12 mean the difference between life and death for a child. For years, investigators could subpoena some information from Internet service providers. But filing subpoenas to get information quickly to identify and locate a suspect could cost life-saving time.

Section 210 of the Patriot Act changed that. In Operation Hamlet, sexual predators were using the Internet to exchange photos and videotapes of children being sexually abused. Sometimes the abusers molested children while running a live feed via a webcam; this allowed other child sexual abusers to watch in real-time online. Investigators used the Patriot Act to quickly obtain subpoenas for information from
13 Internet service providers. The sexual predators were identified, and 19 were convicted. More than 100 children were spared further harm.

The Patriot Act has helped law enforcement achieve more safety and security for the American people without any abuse of civil liberties. Misleading rhetoric aside, not a single instance
14 of abuse under the act has been cited by any court, the Congress, or the Justice Department's own Inspector General—not one.

The public has expressed overwhelming support for the Patriot Act in opinion poll after opinion poll. They know what the 9/11 Commission affirmed: that for the past three years, America's families and communities have been safer, and their freedom is enhanced because of the president's resolve and leadership, the foresight of Congress in enacting these vital tools, and the courageous men and women on the front lines who have used the Patriot Act to protect our lives and liberties.

Thinking about the Argument

1. Why does Ashcroft call the Patriot Act a "success"? What evidence does he provide to validate this claim? Is it sufficient? Why or why not?
2. Why does the author believe that the Patriot Act "is often portrayed in an outright false light"? What reasons and/or evidence does he cite to support this claim?
3. Does Ashcroft believe the Patriot Act has resulted in additional security? How do you know?
4. Does Ashcroft explain what he means when he says the Patriot Act is presented in a "false light"? In other words, how effectively does he summarize and respond to the criticism he mentions?

RESPONDING TO THE ARGUMENT

1. What do you know about the Patriot Act? What liberties do you think it gives law enforcement agencies that they did not previously have (if any)?
2. Do you believe the United States is safer as a result of the Patriot Act? Why do you think this?
3. What might Ashcroft mean when he says the Patriot Act has been misrepresented? How could you discover more specific information about this?
4. Do you personally support the Patriot Act? Why or why not?

WRITING ABOUT THE ARGUMENT

1. Find a reliable source of information that outlines the content of the Patriot Act. Summarize the document.
2. Find a reliable source of information that outlines the content of the Patriot Act. Using it as your primary source of information, write an argument explaining why you do or do not support the act.
3. Find a reliable source of information that outlines the content of the Patriot Act, and then locate an article that criticizes it. Write an essay analyzing whether the concerns raised are legitimate.
4. Find two articles that discuss the Patriot Act from different points of view. Write a synthesis comparing these viewpoints.

"Hypocrisy Most Holy"

ABOUT THE AUTHOR: ALI AL-AHMED

Ali Al-Ahmed is a journalist and an Islamic scholar who frequently writes about and speaks out on issues related to Saudi politics, terrorism, and Islamic movements. He is the founder and director of the Saudi Institute in Washington, D.C., and is an outspoken critic of the government of Saudi Arabia. In 2004, Al-Ahmed testified before the U.S. House Committee on International Relations, characterizing the government of Saudi Arabia as a "religious apartheid." He is a frequent news consultant for major news organizations such as CNN and often speaks on topics related to Islam and religious freedom. This selection first appeared in the *Wall Street Journal* in May 2005.

BEFORE YOU READ

1. Based only on the author's name, what were your expectations regarding his opinion on issues related to Islam and the West? How about after you read the headnote? Why might your opinion have changed (if it did)?

READING SELECTION

2. What does the title of Al-Ahmed's article suggest to you? Did it suggest something different before you read the headnote than it does now? Why?
3. What do you think his article will be about?
4. Scan the article for Al-Ahmed's thesis and any major sections. What does this tell you about his argument?

Hypocrisy Most Holy

1 With the revelation that a copy of the Quran may have been desecrated by U.S. military personnel at Guantanamo Bay, Muslims and their governments—including that of Saudi Arabia—reacted angrily. This anger would have been understandable if the U.S. government's adopted policy was to desecrate our Quran. But even before the *Newsweek* report was discredited, that was never part of the allegations.

2 As a Muslim, I am able to purchase copies of the Quran in any bookstore in any American city and study its contents in countless American universities. American museums spend millions to exhibit and celebrate Muslim arts and heritage. On the other hand, my Christian and other non-Muslim brothers and sisters in Saudi Arabia—where I come from—are not even allowed to own a copy of their holy books. Indeed, the Saudi government desecrates and burns Bibles that its security forces confiscate at immigration points into the kingdom or during raids on Christian expatriates worshiping privately.

3 Soon after *Newsweek* published an account, later retracted, of an American soldier flushing a copy of the Quran down the toilet, the Saudi government voiced its strenuous disapproval. More specifically, the Saudi embassy in Washington expressed "great concern" and urged the United States to "conduct a quick investigation."

4 Although considered as holy in Islam and mentioned in the Quran dozens of times, the Bible is banned in Saudi Arabia. This would seem curious to most people because of the fact that to most Muslims, the Bible is a holy book. But when it comes to Saudi Arabia we are not talking about most Muslims but a tiny minority of hard-liners who constitute the Wahhabi sect.

5 The Bible in Saudi Arabia may get a person killed, arrested, or deported. In September 1993, Sadeq Mallallah, 23, was beheaded in Qateef on a charge of apostasy for owning a Bible. The State Department's annual human rights reports detail the arrest and deportation of many Christian worshipers every year. Just days before Crown Prince Abdullah met President Bush last month, two Christian gatherings were stormed in Riyadh. Bibles and crosses were confiscated and will be incinerated. (The Saudi government does not even spare the Quran from desecration. On October 14, 2004, dozens of Saudi men and women carried copies of the Quran as they protested in support of reformers in the capital, Riyadh. Although they carried the Qurans in part to protect themselves from assault by police, they were charged by hundreds of riot police, who stepped on the books with their shoes, according to one of the protesters.)

6 As Muslims, we have not been as generous as our Christian and Jewish counterparts in respecting others' holy books and religious symbols. Saudi Arabia bans the importation or the

display of crosses, Stars of David or any other religious symbols not approved by the Wahhabi establishment. TV programs that show Christian clergymen, crosses, or Stars of David are censored.

7 The desecration of religious texts and symbols and intolerance of varying religious viewpoints and beliefs have been issues of some controversy inside Saudi Arabia. Ruled by a Wahhabi theocracy, the ruling elite of Saudi Arabia have made it difficult for Christians, Jews, Hindus, and others, as well as dissenting sects of Islam, to visibly coexist inside the kingdom.

8 Another way in which religious and cultural issues are becoming more divisive is the Saudi treatment of Americans who are living in that country: Around 30,000 live and work in various parts of Saudi Arabia. These people are not allowed to celebrate their religious or even secular holidays. These include Christmas and Easter, but also Thanksgiving. All other Gulf states allow non-Islamic holidays to be celebrated.

9 The Saudi embassy and other Saudi organizations in Washington have distributed hundreds of thousands of Qurans and many more Muslim books, some that have libeled Christians, Jews, and others as pigs and monkeys. In Saudi school curricula, Jews and Christians are considered deviants and eternal enemies. By contrast, Muslim communities in the West are the first to admit that Western countries—especially the United States—provide Muslims the strongest freedoms and protections that allow Islam to thrive in the West. Meanwhile Christianity and Judaism, both indigenous to the Middle East, are maligned through systematic hostility by Middle Eastern governments and their religious apparatuses.

10 The lesson here is simple: If Muslims wish other religions to respect their beliefs and their holy book, they should lead by example.

Thinking about the Argument

1. Does the author believe that the Saudi government treats non-Muslim faiths fairly? How do you know?
2. What evidence does the author provide to support his claim? How adequate is it? How could you obtain more information?
3. Does Al-Ahmed believe that the disrespect he describes is limited to Saudi Arabia? Explain.
4. What does the author mean when he says, "If Muslims wish other religions to respect their beliefs and their holy book, they should lead by example"?

Responding to the Argument

1. Do you believe that Muslims are treated fairly in the United States? Why or why not?
2. What policy should the United States have regarding the treatment of non-Muslims in Saudi Arabia and other Muslim countries? Why do you think this?
3. Does the United States "lead by example"? In what ways does the United States lead well? In what ways does the country lead poorly? Explain.

READING SELECTION

Writing about the Argument

1. Write a refutation of Al-Ahmed's claim that Muslims are treated fairly (or at least given fair treatment under the law) in the United States. For example, do you think people of Arabic descent are treated the same way as other individuals at security checkpoints at airports? Support your claim(s) with specific examples.
2. Write a letter to the president. In the letter, tell the president how to "lead by example." Provide evidence to support your claims.
3. Write a journal entry or brief argument proposing what the United States should do to convince Saudi Arabia to treat individuals of other faiths with greater respect.

"I.O.U. One Terrorist"

About the Author: Petra Bartosiewicz

Petra Bartosiewicz is a freelance writer who has published articles on a wide variety of topics in venues such as *Harper's*, *Fortune*, the *New York Times*, and Salon.com. The topics of her articles have included fashion, urban life, popular culture, and politics. In the article that follows, Bartosiewicz analyzes an I.O.U. note that was used to arrest a suspected terrorist under the authority of the Patriot Act. This article first appeared in *Harper's* magazine in August 2005.

Before You Read

1. You probably know less about Petra Bartosiewicz than you do about John Ashcroft. How can you find out more about her? Would this help you understand her point of view better? Why or why not?
2. What does the title of Bartosiewicz's article imply? Why do you think this?
3. Quickly scan the article. What role does the image of the I.O.U. note appear to play in her argument? Why do you think so?
4. What do you expect Bartosiewicz's central point to be? Why?

READING SELECTION

I.O.U. One Terrorist

1 In April this I.O.U. helped convict seventy-year-old Hemant Shantilal Lakhani of "attempting to provide material support to terrorists," a felony for which he faces fifteen years in federal prison when sentenced this August. The FBI arrested Lakhani in August 2003 in a Newark hotel room with what he believed was a shoulder-mounted anti-aircraft device—a weapon he intended to sell to a Somali terrorist group. Christopher J. Christie, the U.S. attorney overseeing the investigation, called Lakhani a "significant international arms dealer" whose capture was an "incredible triumph" in the War on Terror. President Bush said the case was "a pretty good example of what we're doing in order to protect the American people." Bush, unfortunately, is correct. Just as this I.O.U. was a poor substitute for cash in hand, Lakhani is a poor substitute for a genuine terrorist.

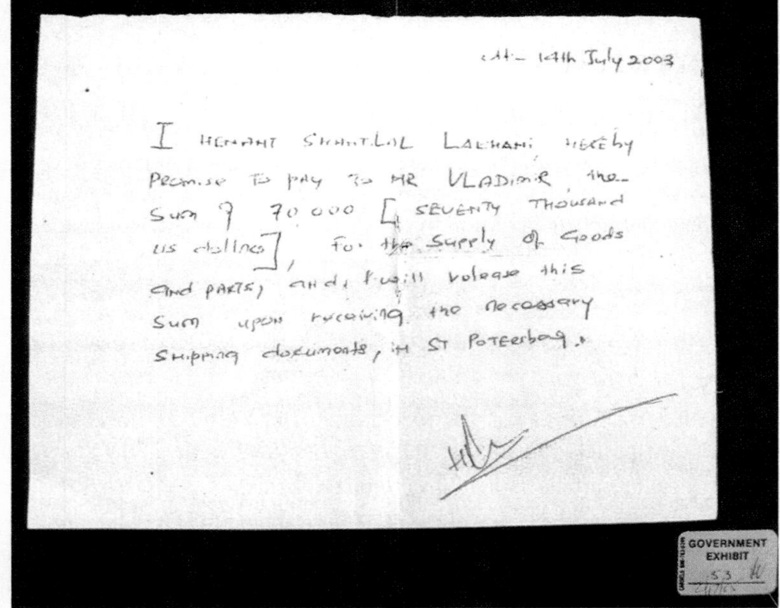

14th July 2003

I HEMANT SHANTILAL LAKHANI hereby PROMISE TO PAY TO MR VLADIMIR, the SUM 70,000 [SEVENTY THOUSAND US dollars], for the Supply of Goods and PARTS, and I will release this sum upon receiving the necessary shipping documents, in ST Petersburg.

GOVERNMENT EXHIBIT 53

2 Lakhani's involvement in the scheme to import a Russian-made Igla SA-18 missile and launcher, referred to here as "goods and parts," began just months after the September 11 attacks, when a down-on-his-luck career informant, Muhammed Habib Rehman, alerted his FBI handlers to the existence of a man he enticingly identified by the Muslim-sounding name "Hemad" Lakhani. (Hemant Lakhani, who was born in India, is a practicing Hindu.) Rehman said that Lakhani, a London-based businessman who traveled frequently to the Middle East, was a "main weapons trafficker" who did business in at least five countries, was involved in drug smuggling, traded embargoed Iraqi oil, and was worth as much as $400 million. The FBI found no evidence to support these claims but launched an undercover operation nonetheless, with Rehman in the role of interested buyer.

3 Although Lakhani jumped at the chance to broker the $70,000 deal—which he hoped would lead to a much larger deal for at least 200 more missiles—it was clear from the beginning that he was not the player Rehman had suggested he

was. Lakhani had no criminal record, and his arms-dealing résumé consisted of once assisting in the legal sale of eleven armored personnel carriers to the government of Angola, a deal that took him nearly three years to complete. In his initial meeting with Rehman in Newark, in January 2002, Lakhani nonetheless claimed that he could supply all kinds of weapons and at one point even offered to procure a submarine. Yet when Rehman asked Lakhani to cover the initial cost of the transaction, Lakhani balked. The U.S. government had to put up the money instead.

4 Lakhani worked his limited arms-industry contacts for a year, but, without an end-user certificate proving the deal was legitimate, no supplier would fill his order. Fortunately, Lakhani's clumsy attempts at procuring a missile, first in Ukraine and then in Russia, had drawn the attention of the Russian Federal Security Service, which quickly opened its own investigation. A deal was struck between the former adversaries: the Russians would pose as suppliers, one of whom is identified here as "Mr. Vladimir," and the Americans would continue to pose as buyers. At a July 14, 2003, Moscow meeting with the Russians, Lakhani was filmed as he inspected his fake missile launcher, picking it up from the wrong end and swinging it around the room as undercover Russian agents, playing true to their roles, ducked for cover. When the FBI arrested him a month later in Newark, Lakhani confessed immediately.

5 In the end it was Lakhani's own words that did him in. The agency recorded him praising Osama bin Laden and boasting that his missile launcher could be used to shoot down American passenger planes. . . . He bragged of friendships with Muammar Qaddafi and fugitive financier Marc Rich and of lunching with Tony Blair at 10 Downing Street. But those were only words. In truth, Lakhani was a failed clothing merchant who lived and worked out of a modest semi-detached London home on the verge of foreclosure. Prosecutors had hoped to develop him as a cooperating witness, but he, of course, had no useful information. His own lawyer, Henry Klingeman, called him an "idiot" and said the case would not have been pursued prior to September 11, 2001. "The government," he observed, "is like the fireman who sets the fire, pulls the alarm, saves the people, and then says, 'What a hero I am.' "

6 President Bush claims that federal terrorism investigations since September 11, 2001, "have resulted in charges against more than 400 suspects, half of whom have been convicted." In fact, there may be an endless supply of people whose professed sympathy for Al Qaeda, no matter how contrived, is enough to set off the "anti-terror" machine. Joining Lakhani in the ongoing exhibition of our terror-fighting prowess are New York jazz bassist Tarik Shah, who faces conspiracy charges for telling an FBI informant that he would like to teach martial arts to aspiring terrorists, and Pennsylvania welder Ron Grecula, who is in jail for offering to build an FBI informant a "hot fusion technology" bomb. That these cases—and many others—can be cited as "incredible triumphs" in the War on Terror is further testament to that war's inability to be won.

Thinking about the Argument

1. What is the author's central point? What is she implying about the "war on terror"?
2. Why does Bartosiewicz think that Lakhani is not a "player"? What evidence does she cite to back up this claim? What role does the I.O.U. play in convincing you that Lakhani is (or is not) a legitimate terrorist?

3. In paragraph 5, the author quotes Lakhani's lawyer. What does this quote imply about Lakhani's status as a terrorist and the legitimacy of the United States' claims against him?
4. Does Bartosiewicz believe the United States can win the war against terror? How do you know? What evidence does she cite to convince you (or not) of this?

Responding to the Argument

1. Do you consider the arrest of Lakhani an "incredible triumph"? Why or why not?
2. Do you think Lakhani qualifies as a terrorist? Was he potentially dangerous? Why or why not?
3. The author implies that the FBI—and by extension, the United States in general—has seriously bungled its attempts to arrest legitimate terrorists. In its place, the author suggests, the country is willing to arrest anyone who could be called a terrorist just to have the appearance of having made progress. Do you agree with this assessment? Why or why not? How might the I.O.U. letter contribute to your opinion?

Writing about the Argument

1. Write a brief argument or journal entry considering the relationship between the Lakhani case and the war on terror. Is it fair to judge the law enforcement efforts of the United States on the basis of this particular example? Why or why not?
2. Write an argument in the form of a letter to the editor of your local paper (or perhaps submit a guest editorial to your college paper) discussing whether Lakhani was treated fairly by law enforcement officials. Was he "entrapped"—led into his crime by overzealous law enforcement officers? Why do you think this?
3. Write a brief essay, journal entry, or blog explaining why enforcement of the kind demonstrated by the Lakhani case is necessary to catch the "big fish."
4. Write an argument explaining whether law enforcement officers should have access to private records—including usually private matters, such as a patron's library records—so that they can catch terrorists. In other words, are you willing to give up some degree of your privacy in exchange for better national security?
5. Should public monitoring (including security cameras in public places, electronic monitoring of Internet activity, and so on) become commonplace to ensure greater security for the public good? What is more important—your right to privacy or a greater sense of security?

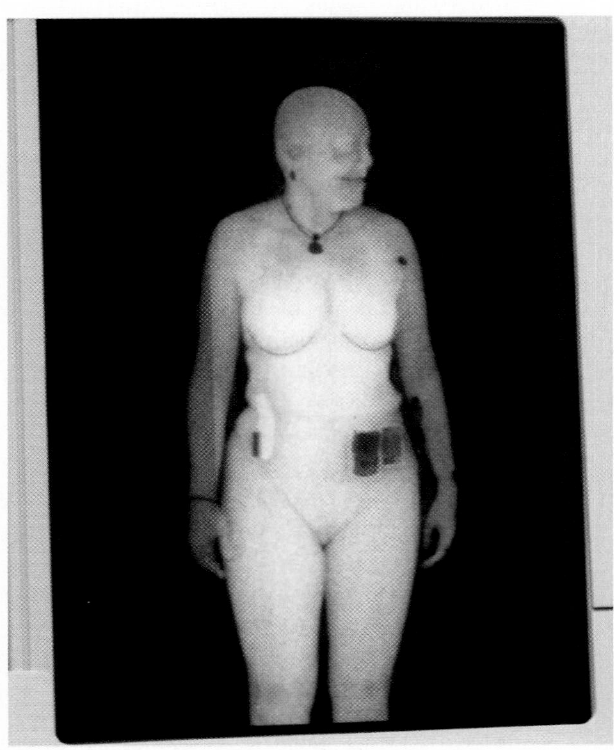

This image shows how a new airport security scanner may be used to detect hidden items under a person's clothing. Which do you believe is more important—personal liberty or security? That question underlies the debate over the Patriot Act and other law enforcement efforts related to terrorism.

READING SELECTION

Afterword from *Leap of Faith*

About the Author: Queen Noor al-Hussein

Queen Noor al-Hussein of Jordan was born Lisa Najeeb Halaby to an Arab American family in Washington, D.C. After graduating from Princeton University's school of architecture, Halaby met King Hussein of Jordan while she was working on a project for Air Jordan. She married Hussein in 1978 and became the first queen of an Arab country born in the United States. Since then, she has been a champion of Arab/American relations and has sponsored numerous projects related to urban planning and humanitarian causes. Among other causes, she chaired the first Arab Children's Congress (1980) and founded the Noor Al-Hussein Foundation (1985), which has sponsored the NHF Quality of Life Project, the Women-in-Development Projects, and other programs. Following her husband's death from cancer in 1999, she established the King Hussein Foundation, which seeks to continue King Hussein's humanitarian programs. Her autobiography, *Leap of Faith,* was published in 2003.

Before You Read

1. How do you react differently to the name Noor al-Hussein as opposed to Lisa Halaby? Explain.
2. Had you ever heard of Queen Noor before? If so, what was your prior opinion of her?
3. Based on the information supplied by the headnote, do you consider her a valid authority on the subject of Arab–American relations? Why or why not?
4. Does al-Hussein's lack of publication credits affect your willingness to carefully consider her arguments? Why or why not?

Afterword from *Leap of Faith*

1 When *Leap of Faith* was published nearly two years ago, it quickly became apparent that many readers saw my personal story as a way of framing their understanding of the Middle East and the Arab world. Their interest in the book mirrored the themes that compelled me to write it in the first place: my abiding belief in the powerful vision and example of my husband, King Hussein; the need for greater tolerance, understanding, and peace among people and nations; the quest for non-military solutions to conflicts; and ultimately, my faith in our common humanity. I am so grateful to the people who have told me this book touched them in some way—that it may have balanced their view of our region or inspired them to learn more about Arab history, culture, and religion. It is more than I could possibly hope for, if I have begun to help some readers overcome prejudice or better understand their Arab and Muslim neighbors or even just encouraged some people to be more open to new ideas or experiences.

This memoir was a continuation of my ef-
2 forts over the past quarter century to broaden and deepen understanding of the shared values, aspirations, and responsibilities of East and West. Too often, Western appreciation of the vibrant culture, customs, people, and heritage of the Arab and Muslim world has been undermined by inaccurate and distorted media coverage and information about our region. These distortions obscure the spiritual and cultural richness of the Arab world and leave many uninformed about the significant contributions that the Islamic faith and Arab thinkers have made to

world civilization. Through the comments of readers, I know that *Leap of Faith* has, in some small measure, helped to close that gap, but much more is needed to bridge the wide gulf of misunderstanding and fear exacerbated by war and conflict.

3 Such challenges to our world family grow deeper everyday. The Middle East region is reeling from the shock of war in its midst, economies weakened and national aspirations thwarted by the instability that armed conflict brings. The Israeli–Palestinian crisis continues to rob the Palestinians of their right to self-determination and nationhood. Many lives have been lost in the Middle East and Afghanistan, but also in regions out of the spotlight, such as Sudan, Central Asia, and Central America. And when solutions are sought for the world's problems, they are often defensive and shortsighted, frequently involving military might.

4 My years of experience in Jordan, and my current work with the United Nations and other international organizations, has convinced me that real security—security that is sustainable and genuine—must focus on the needs of human beings, not just nations. True security is not only a matter of protecting borders from military aggression, or achieving technological or economic dominance, but of providing a stable, safe, and healthy environment for all citizens—women, men, and children—of all races and creeds to participate fully in economic, cultural, and political life. People must work together because no one—even the most wealthy and powerful country in the world—will enjoy true security if others in our interdependent world suffer injustice and deprivation. Given the global rise of extremism on all sides in recent years, it is very easy to turn inward, recoil from risk, and avoid reaching out to others. For all of our sakes, we can no longer afford to allow ourselves to be imprisoned by our fears and differences.

5 We cannot allow extremist views on religion, race, culture, or creed to be twisted into a rationale for hatred. The three great monotheistic faiths, Judaism, Christianity, and Islam, spring from the same root, the faith of Abraham. They teach common values and principles that can and should be a unifying force among all believers—respect for freedom, justice, equity, and compassion as summed up in the commandment of our one God to love others as we love ourselves. In the words of the Prophet, Muhammed, *Peace Be Upon Him.* "None of you is a believer until he wants for his brother what he wants for himself."

6 I believe we all have a sacred duty to embrace and revive these shared, universal values, and begin to drown out extremism and intolerance on all sides. Those who believe in the power of our common humanity must join forces to amplify the voices of the moderate majorities on all sides. There is a middle ground, and on that ground faiths, nations, and peoples of the world can build just and lasting peace.

7 The journey of this book, writing it and learning about people's reaction to my story and its ideas, has been life altering. I am grateful to the many readers across the globe who have responded so enthusiastically to this book and I cherish my new connection with them. I hope that their support for this book will spark their own commitment to build bridges between cultures and work for peace. I remain deeply honored that I can be a part of so many people's lives and continue to carry on the critical legacy of King Hussein.

THINKING ABOUT THE ARGUMENT

1. Why did the author write *Leap of Faith?* What was she trying to accomplish?
2. Whom does she blame for the negative image of the Arab world in the West? What support does she provide to validate this claim?

3. Why do you think Queen Noor uses the phrase "world family"? Does it help support her claim or does it detract from it in some way? Why do you think this?
4. What does the author think is required for "true security"?
5. Queen Noor quotes the Prophet Muhammed to help drive her central point home. How effective is this strategy? Why would she choose this authority or this particular quotation?

Responding to the Argument

1. Why do you believe the Arab world has a negative image in the West? Whose "fault" is it (if anyone's)?
2. The author states that "real security . . . must focus on the needs of human beings, not just nations." Respond to this comment.
3. Can Queen Noor's dream of a peace based on universal tolerance ever be achieved? Why do you hold this opinion? Support your claim with at least one example.

Writing about the Argument

1. Using the first four readings in this chapter as your primary resources, write an argument explaining whether enforcement (through laws like those included in the Patriot Act) or the sort of social change endorsed by Al-Ahmed and Queen Noor is more likely to end terrorism and lead to peace.
2. Write a refutation to Queen Noor's argument. In your essay, provide evidence to explain why her goal is unrealistic.
3. Pretend to be Queen Noor. Write a letter to someone in the Saudi government explaining why it should change its approach to religious tolerance.

"Globalized Religions for a Globalized World"

About the Author: Gregory Melleuish

Gregory Melleuish is a member of the Faculty of Arts at the University of Wollongong in Australia, where he teaches politics and history. He is particularly interested in the history and culture of Australia. He regularly publishes articles in refereed academic journals. This essay first appeared in the October 2005 issue of *Policy*.

Before You Read

1. What does the title of the article imply? What do you think Melleuish's central claim will be?
2. This article first appeared in the academic journal *Policy*. What do you think the focus of this journal might be? How could you find out more?
3. Scan the article. What do you think the author's main supporting points will be?
4. Look at the notes at the end of the article. What do they tell you about the issue at hand?

»«

Globalized Religions for a Globalized World

1 Until the presidency of George W. Bush and September 11, 2001, there was not a great deal of public interest in the place of religion in the contemporary world. True, Samuel Huntington's "clash of civilizations" thesis had excited some interest in a possible conflict between the West and Islam. In general, however, with declining church membership and attendance in most Western countries it was assumed that the developed world, with America the only major exception, was slowly, but inexorably, on the road to complete secularity. This meant that discussion of religion tended to focus on such matters as the decline of Christianity, the possibility of female and gay priests, and "moral" issues such as abortion.

2 The recent and sudden interest in both Christianity and Islam has been fueled by the threat that their more robust forms, generically labelled "fundamentalism," are believed to pose to the stability and comfort of the secularised West. Consequently discussion of religious matters has tended to take on an "Us and Them" character with "Us" being seen as the calm and reasonable children of the Enlightenment and "Them" as fanatics and barbarians, be they Christians, Muslims, or Jews. This is not to say that there is not a small hard core of extremists amongst these "fundamentalists." Rather it is to point out that the use of a term such as "fundamentalism" obscures rather than illuminates when it is used to encompass the beliefs of millions, even billions, of people.

3 The Western fixation, particularly amongst its intelligentsia, on secularization as the inevitable fate of humanity has obscured the fact that we are currently living in one of the great ages of religious vitality and mission, in both the Christian and Muslim worlds. Much of this religious activity is happening in Africa, Latin America, and Asia, far from the eyes of the Western media, just as much of the "clash of civilizations" between Christianity and Islam has occurred in places such as Nigeria and the Sudan and has been reported only sporadically elsewhere.

4 Over the past 40 years both Christianity and Islam have become globalized religions. Much of their progress has occurred outside the view of the West. The consequences of this globalization are only now coming to be fully appreciated. The heart of Christianity no longer lies in the West. Moreover the forms that Christianity is taking in Africa, Asia, and Latin America are often quite different from those currently prevalent in the West.

5 Fundamentalism is essentially propositional in nature—that is to say, it is founded on a number of propositions to which one is meant to give assent. European and American Protestantism has often taken a propositional form as it has focused on the Bible as the defining scripture supplying the "fundamentals" of belief. Alongside what can sometimes be a somewhat emotionally arid form of religion there also developed other forms that have focused more on the immediacy of spiritual experience. Methodism, and in some ways its offspring Pentecostalism, have been forms of Christianity that have emphasized experience.

6 Both of these forms of Christianity are present in the current Christian revival. But while fundamentalism is perhaps the dominant form of religiosity in America, it is Pentecostalism that has won over many Christians in the Third World. It has been estimated that there are half a billion Pentecostalists in the world today.[1] It has been argued that Pentecostalism appeals to many Africans because they live in a world that is inhabited by a range of spirits, including evil ones that can be subdued by Jesus. Moreover they are strongly attracted to the Old Testament while many liberal Christians in the West find it an embarrassment. Jenkins has argued that in many ways these Third World Christians are close to the early Christians who also believed in the reality of spirits around them.[2] Exorcism

was commonplace in the early Church. Moreover as these Third World Churches place so much emphasis on experience some of them run the risk of moving beyond the bounds of Christian orthodoxy.[3]

7 Nevertheless there can be little doubt that the source of much of the vitality in Christianity in the 21st century will come from Africa, Latin America, and Asia. Apart from America the West is in demographic decline and its numbers of believers is declining at an even faster rate.

8 It can be argued that this religious explosion in the more deprived areas of the world really affects the secularization thesis.

9 Norris and Ingelhart have argued the following.[4]

1. The publics of virtually all advanced industrial societies have been moving toward more secular orientations during the past 50 years. Nevertheless,
2. The world as a whole has more people with traditional religious views than ever before—and they constitute a growing proportion of the world's population.

10 They relate religious belief to security and prosperity.[5] The more affluent and secure people are, the less need they have for things outside this world. One could, of course, put it another way: The more prosperity a people has, the more likely they are to stray from the path of righteousness.

11 Norris and Inglehart come up with some interesting findings. One is that the Protestant work ethic in the contemporary world is weakest in cultures that are derived from Protestantism; it is prevalent amongst Muslims.[6] Another is that secularized countries are far more liberal regarding sexual matters and gender equality than religious countries, especially Muslim ones.[7] At the same time countries that are strongly religious have a much higher birth rate than secular ones.

12 Thus we are confronted by the rather stark dichotomy: a secular, developed world with both a declining birth rate and a decreasing appetite for hard work versus a religious and growing developing world. Norris and Inglehart would seem to imply that this is primarily a function of the relative security of the two worlds and that, when every human being lives in a European-style welfare state, what Marx termed the "opiate of the masses" will be no more.

13 But the reality is somewhat more complex than that. In his recent book *The Twilight of Atheism* Alister McGrath argues that in fact it is atheism that is on its last legs in the West. Atheism was largely a by-product of European radical politics that emerged during the late eighteenth century.[8] Its heyday was the Marxist era and its function was to announce that one was in revolt against the existing order. The demise of communism has also probably brought about the demise of atheism, though not religious indifference.

14 In a recent article in *Christianity Today* the existence of a small but growing evangelical movement was revealed in that bastion of secularism, France. Over the past 50 years the number of evangelicals in France has grown from 50,000 to 350,000. The number of evangelical churches has increased from 760 in 1970 to 1850 today.[9]

15 And of course America stands as the prime example of a Western country with a majority of its population professing a belief in Christianity. It also has a higher birth rate than other Western countries and is less enamored of the welfare state.

16 There is an interesting paradox here. Western societies, including parts of America, are becoming more secular. Certain types of Christianity, especially evangelicalism and Pentecostalism, are growing even in the most secular parts of the West, including France. At the same time the mainstream churches are undergoing decay as their membership declines and they struggle to remain relevant to the contemporary world. In many ways these mainstream churches have become little more than another arm of the secular establishment. As such their leaders have

effectively become members of the secular elite more interested in contemporary politics and denouncing their evangelical (i.e., "fundamentalist") rivals than matters of a more eternal nature.

17 This can be seen in two recent books, Marion Maddox's *God under Howard* and Michael Nothcott's *An Angel Directs the Storm.* Both books are concerned with denouncing what they see as the insidious influence that the "Religious Right" exercises over, the first case, John Howard, and, in the second, George W. Bush. Although these writers both come from religious backgrounds, they express the same disgust with fundamentalist and evangelical Christianity that one might expect from the secular elite. They also tend to see the influence of the Religious Right in conspiratorial terms.

18 It is interesting that holding these "extreme" beliefs in no way impedes one's capacity to function in a technological society. One can, like many Americans, be both a believer in creation science and a highly competent engineer; or an extreme Islamist and an able computer scientist. Contemporary "fundamentalists" live effectively in a secular and scientific universe and not one, like our African Pentecostalists, full of spirits and magic.

19 An answer to this apparent paradox can be found in the work of French philosopher Marcel Gauchet. Gauchet argues in *The Disenchantment of the World* that humanity has been on a secular trajectory ever since it left the holistic and embedded spiritual world characteristic of a hunter-gatherer society. Gauchet believes that the creation of the first states involved the sundering of that world into a heaven above and a world below.[10] The consequence of that division in the longer term has been the creation of a secular world that we all inhabit. The world may no longer be religious but, for Gauchet, this does not imply that people have ceased to be religious.[11] Rather the challenge is how to be religious in a secular world.

20 Much of contemporary religion, especially in the West, makes sense when viewed in these terms. Our world is a disenchanted and secular one. Our religion is no longer to be found in nature but in the hearts of men and women. Generally it is a religion that has been quarantined from the larger reality in which we live our lives. Religion has become just another specialized element of our rather fragmented culture in which individuals pursue a rather bewildering range of interests.

21 One consequence of this fragmentation is that religious knowledge and training, especially for evangelicals and Pentecostalists, is no longer conducted within the context of the broader culture but has become, like everything else, a specialized form of technical training. As we noted earlier modern religion tends to reduce its beliefs to a series of abstract propositions. This is in accord with the argument of Michael Oakeshott that in the modern world the technical part of knowledge becomes dominant while the implicit knowledge or skill in which the technical knowledge was traditionally embedded fades away. There was once a time when a bachelor of arts from Oxford or Cambridge was the preferred training for an Anglican priest.

22 In this sense these modern forms of religion have ceased to be part of the wider public culture (insofar as such a public culture still exists) but form their own subcultures, usually outside the radar of the media. Only when their activities have an impact on the public life, as in the case of Family First in the last federal election, is any attention directed their way. Generally their activities in providing a self-help community for their adherents and others, much after the fashion of the early Church, do not figure in public discussion. For example, it has been claimed that the activity of the French evangelical churches in helping poor newcomers to France has played a role in lessening the appeal of radical Islam to these people.[12]

23 Just as Christianity is being transformed through its global encounters, the same is true of Islam. Neither religion is a fixed entity locked in a timeless mold. Just as the critical developments in contemporary Christianity may be oc-

curring in Africa, so the crucial changes in Islam are taking place in its encounter with the West in the West. In his *Globalized Islam* Olivier Roy points to the encounter with Western values in Western societies as the central transforming element in contemporary Islam and in the creation of Islamism.

24 Unlike Christians, Muslims for a long time were uneasy about living outside the realm of Islam. After all how was it possible to live a righteous life in a society run by infidels? In recent times, however, there have been a significant number of Muslim migrants to both Europe and America, although as Roy points out those going to America have been of a higher socioeconomic status. It has been out of this encounter that much of contemporary radical Islam has been born.

25 In part, according to Roy, radical Islam was created by an input of Western ideas and values into Islam. For example, traditionally Islam was not particularly concerned with issues such as abortion and homosexuality but it has taken over these moral issues.[13] At the same time the training of Islamic clerics has become more exclusively concerned with technical religious issues. As in the West this training is no longer embedded in a particular cultural tradition but has been reduced to a number of technical propositions. The Islamic equivalent of the Western liberal education is being expelled from Islamic theological education.[14]

26 The result is an Islam that belongs nowhere and everywhere, a globalized Islam that can be carried from place to place, just as it can be argued that there is a globalized form of Christianity that is no longer linked to any particular culture. More importantly this "fundamentalist" Islam is not a "medieval" religion. In fact, just as evangelical Christians seek to convert Catholics to Christianity, so Islamists want to get rid of the traditional rural Islam founded on saints and sufis. It is a thoroughly modern religion acceptable to scientists and engineers.

27 Both contemporary Christianity and contemporary Islam have elements that can be described as "Jacobin." They adhere to a series of propositions that define the good life; those propositions are not tied to a particular place or time or culture. It is ironic that at a time when the "Jacobin" political traditions of the West, including Communism, have exhausted themselves it is in the two most vital world religions that these "Jacobin" tendencies should have reemerged.

28 What does this mean for the world of the twenty-first century?

1. The first is that Norris and Inglehart are correct at one level. There will continue to be a growing divergence between a largely secular and demographically declining developed world and a developing world that will grow in both numbers and religiosity.
2. There will continue to be religious conflict of the "clash of civilizations" variety but much of it will occur in the developing world between Christians and Muslims.
3. There will be a growing divergence in the developed world between liberal Christians on the one hand and evangelicals and Pentecostalists on the other. As one group of Christians in the West slips into a liberal position that is not clearly distinguishable from secularism, so another group will become much more determined in its defense of orthodoxy. The result will be a largely secular society with a significant "saving remnant" that will continue to be extremely active.
4. One consequence of the fact that if one is religious they must be so in a secular world is that the biggest impact of religion on the wider society will continue to be when moral issues come up for public discussion. On many of these issues Islam lines up with evangelical Christians and traditional Catholics. One should expect that increasingly there will be political alliances between these groups on such issues.

29 I should like to conclude with one final observation. From both a Muslim and an evangelical Christian perspective it is not they who are

strange and perverted but the modern world. It is between the religious and the non-religious that the fundamental "clash of civilizations" is occurring in the 21st century.

Notes

1. Alister McGrath, *The Twilight of Atheism: The Rise and Fall of Disbelief in the Modern World* (London: Rider, 2004), 214.
2. Philip Jenkins, *The Next Christendom: The Coming of Global Christianity* (New York: Oxford University Press, 2002), 129.
3. As above, 120.
4. Pippa Norris and Ronald Inglehart, *Sacred and Secular: Religion and Politics Worldwide* (Cambridge: Cambridge University Press, 2004), 5.
5. As above, 239.
6. As above, 163–169.
7. As above, 154.
8. McGrath, *The Twilight of Atheism,* 21–47.
9. Agnieszka Tennant, "The French Reconnection," *Christianity Today* 49:3 (2005), 28–35.
10. Marcel Gauchet. *The Disenchantment of the World: A Political History of Religion,* Trans. Oscar Burge, (Princeton: Princeton University Press, 1997), 33–46.
11. As above, 200.
12. Tennant, "The French Reconnection," 35.
13. Olivier Roy. *Globalized Islam: The Search for a New Ummah* (New York: Columbia University Press, 2004), 32.
14. As above, 162.

Thinking about the Argument

1. Why does the author say that Western scholars assume that religion, at least in the West, is in decline? Why does he believe, contrary to this, that "we are currently living in one of the great ages of religious vitality and mission, in both the Christian and Muslim worlds"?
2. What does the author mean when he says that Christianity and Islam have become "globalized religions"?
3. How does Melleuish define fundamentalism and Pentecostalism? Which has taken hold in the Third World, and why?
4. Does the author believe religion is growing or shrinking in the West? What evidence does he provide to support his claim?
5. What does the author think "created" radical Islam? What has this form of Islam borrowed from the West?

Responding to the Argument

1. Do you believe that religion is in decline in the West? Is this a good thing or a bad thing? Explain.
2. Is secularization, in the sense that it engenders tolerance and "political correctness," good for Western countries? Why do you think this?
3. In what ways does Melleuish's argument confirm or refute the positions argued by Queen Noor and Al-Ahmed?
4. Examine the author's predictions at the end of his article. Which do you agree with and disagree with? Why?

READING SELECTION

Writing about the Argument

1. Based on Melleuish's argument (as well as others in this section), is a "clash of civilizations" inevitable? Research and write an argument considering this issue.
2. Write a paper analyzing Melleuish's argument. Discuss which elements of his argument are the strongest, and which elements are the weakest.
3. Write a journal entry reflecting on the role of religion in American society. In your opinion, is religion a positive or a negative force in terms of helping Americans cooperate with the Islamic world?

Issue 2: Immigration Control

The United States is a country founded on immigration. These words, inscribed at the base of the Statue of Liberty on Ellis Island, illustrate the concept clearly:

> Give me your tired, your poor, your huddled masses yearning to breathe free,
> The wretched refuse of your teeming shore,
> Send these, the homeless, tempest-tossed, to me:
> I lift my lamp beside the golden door.

As inspiring as these words are, immigration has always been easier in theory than in practice. Legal immigration is a drawn-out and often frustrating process that involves applications, paperwork, attorney's fees, and much waiting—often years. Some individuals do not have the financial resources to invest in legal immigration, others are illiterate, and some feel they lack the skills necessary to be accepted for immigration. Often they are desperate, are in need of work, and cannot afford to wait to see whether their applications will be accepted. Some of these individuals choose to enter the United States illegally. Most of them cross many miles of dangerous desert along the border with Mexico between Texas and California. Still others are brought by human traffickers in overcrowded boats, shipping containers, and unventilated trucks. Each year, a number of these individuals die, and some are sent back to their home countries. Others, however, are able to make it into the United States and seek work as unskilled laborers. The jobs they fill are often day-labor positions for which they are paid cash "under the table" (at a rate usually far below minimum wage).

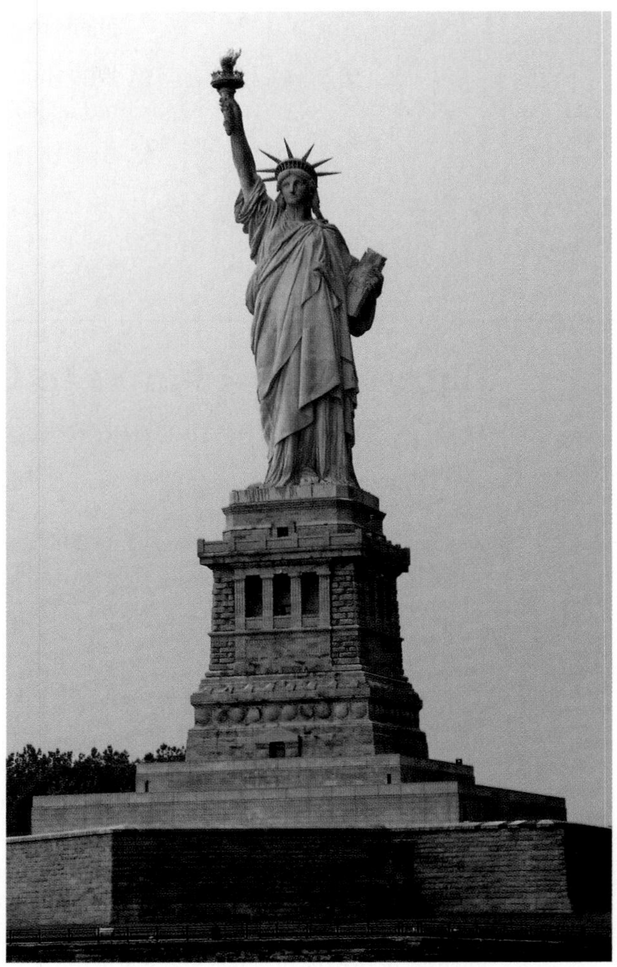

The Statue of Liberty once welcomed immigrants from Europe as they arrived in New York. Is the same true today for immigrants from other parts of the world?

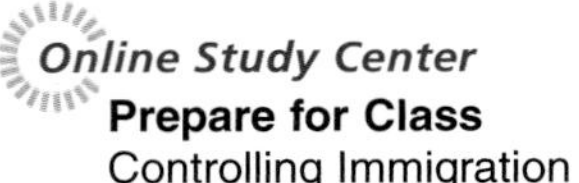

Prepare for Class
Controlling Immigration

Considering the Issue of Immigration Control

In discussion groups, in your journal, or working individually, answer the following questions:

1. On the whole, do undocumented workers benefit or harm American society?
2. Is racism a potential factor in targeting illegal immigrants from Mexico in particular?
3. Does the porous border with Mexico present a legitimate terrorist threat to the United States?
4. Are undocumented workers causing American citizens or legitimate resident aliens to go without a paycheck?
5. Who should be responsible for preventing illegal crossings: the United States or Mexico? Should there be a cooperative effort between the two countries?
6. Does the border with Canada represent a threat that is being ignored?

READING SELECTION

"Let Us Give Thanks to Our Immigrants"

About the Author: Rupert Murdoch

Rupert Murdoch, an immigrant from Australia, built the media giant the News Corporation from a small-town newspaper in Australia, the *Adelaide News.* Nicknamed "the dirty digger" for his aggressive management style, Murdoch expanded his empire to include newspapers, magazines, books, and television, with outlets operating in the United States, Australia, Asia, and Europe. The following article from the *Wall Street Journal* was drawn from a speech Murdoch gave when he accepted the 2004 Forbes Award.

Before You Read

1. How would you define *immigrant?*
2. Is there a significant population of immigrants in your community? Are they isolated from the non-immigrant population, or do they interact with the other members of the community?
3. What is your first reaction when dealing with someone you don't know from another culture? Do you tend to avoid that person or engage him or her in conversation? Be honest.
4. What is your opinion of migrant workers? Do you consider them to be beneficial to society, detrimental, or to have no effect one way or the other?
5. What does the title of Murdoch's essay imply? What do expect him to argue? Do you agree with his viewpoint? Explain.

READING SELECTION

Let Us Give Thanks to Our Immigrants

1 When B. C. Forbes sailed for America from Scotland in 1904, he was following a course well worn by generations of Scots.

2 I know how the founder of *Forbes* magazine must have felt. The Murdochs originally hail from the same part of Scotland. Today, we are part of the most recent wave of immigrants attracted by the bright beacon of American liberty.

3 These days, it's not always easy to talk about the benefits of immigration. Especially since 9/11, many Americans worry about borders and security. These are legitimate concerns. But surely a nation as great as America has the wit and resources to distinguish between those who come here to destroy the American Dream—and the many millions more who come to live it.

4 The evidence of the contributions these immigrants make to our society is all around us—especially in the critical area of education. Adam Smith (another Scotsman) knew that without a decent system of education, a modern capitalist society was committing suicide. Well, our modern public school systems simply are not producing the talent the American economy needs to compete in the future. And it often seems that it is our immigrants who are holding the whole thing up.

5 In a study on high school students released this past summer, the National Foundation for American Policy found 60 percent of the top science students, and 65 percent of the top math students, are children of immigrants. The same study found that seven of the top award winners at the 2004 Intel Science Talent Search were immigrants or children of immigrants. This correlates with other findings that more than half of engineers—and 45 percent of math and computer scientists—with Ph.D.s now working in the United States are foreign born.

6 It's not just the statistics. You see it at our most elite college and university campuses, where Asian immigrants or their children are disproportionately represented. And a recent study of twenty-eight prestigious American universities by researchers from Princeton and the University of Pennsylvania found something startling: that 41 percent of the black students attending these schools described themselves as either immigrants or children of immigrants.

7 The point is that by almost any measure of educational excellence you choose, if you're in America you're going to find immigrants or their children at the top. I don't just mean engineers and scientists and technicians. In my book, anyone who comes here and gives an honest day's work for an honest day's pay is not only putting himself closer to the American Dream, he's helping the rest of us get there too.

8 As Ronald Reagan said at the Statue of Liberty, "While we applaud those immigrants who stand out, whose contributions are easily discerned, we know that America's heroes are also those whose names are remembered by only a few."

9 Let me share some of these names with you.

10 Start with Eddie Chin, an ethnic Chinese Marine who was born a week after his family fled Burma. You've all seen Corporal Chin. Because when Baghdad fell, he was the Marine we all watched shimmy up the statue of Saddam Hussein to attach the cable that would pull it down.

11 Or Lance Corporal Ahmad Ibrahim. His family came to the United States from Syria when the first Gulf War broke out. Now Corporal Ibrahim hopes to be deployed to Iraq—also as a Marine—to put his Arabic language skills in the service of Corps and Country.

12 Or what about Corporal Jose Gutierrez, who was raised in Guatemala and came to America as a boy—illegally! Corporal Gutierrez was one of the first Marines killed in action in Iraq. As his family told reporters, this young immigrant enlisted with the Marine Corps because he wanted to "give back" to America.

13 So here we have it—Asian Marines, Arab Marines, Latino Marines—all united in the mission of protecting the rest of us. Isn't this what Reagan meant when he said that the bond that ties our immigrants together—what makes us a nation instead of a collection of individuals—is "an abiding love of liberty"? So the next time you near people whining about what a "drain" on America our immigrants are, it might be worth asking if they consider these Marines a drain.

14 Maybe this is more clear to businessmen because of what we see every day. My company, News Corporation, is a multinational company based in America. Our diversity is based on talent, cooperation, and ability.

15 Frankly it doesn't bother me in the least that millions of people are attracted to our shores. What we should worry about is the day they no longer find these shores attractive. In an era when too many of our pundits declare that the American Dream is a fraud, it is America's immigrants who remind us—by dint of their success—that the Dream is alive, and well within reach of anyone willing to work for it.

16 We are fortunate to have a president who understands that. Only a few days ago, the White House indicated that it intended to revive an immigration reform that the president had first offered before 9/11 and tried to revive back in January.

17 Politically speaking, a guest-worker plan is no easy thing. But as President Bush realizes, we'll never fix the problem of illegal immigration simply by throwing up walls and trying to make all of us police them. We've tried that for a decade or so now, and it's been a flop. What we need to do first is to make it easier for those who seek honest work to do so without having to disobey our laws. Fundamentally that means recognizing that an economy as powerful as ours is always going to have a demand for more workers.

18 Such a policy would benefit us all:

- It would help those who want nothing more than to work legally move out of the shadows.
- It would help our security forces stop wasting resources now spent on hunting down Mexican waitresses and start devoting them to tracking the terrorists who really threaten us.
- It would help the economy by providing America with the labor and talent it needs.

19 Given the tremendous pressures on President Bush and the considerable opposition from within his own ranks, the politically expedient thing for him to do would be to drop it. But he hasn't, and I for one am encouraged by his refusal to give in.

20 The immigrant editor B. C. Forbes spent much of the twentieth century championing the glories of American opportunity. We who have arrived more recently likewise will never forget our debt we owe to this land—and the obligation to keep that same opportunity alive in the twenty-first.

THINKING ABOUT THE ARGUMENT

1. What is Murdoch's primary claim? What reasons does he cite to support his claim?
2. This article was adapted from a speech. Does that cause you to read it or react to it any differently? Why?
3. Does the author provide adequate evidence to back up what he says? Explain.
4. What would you consider to be the most significant drawback of the article?

Responding to the Argument

1. Do you agree with Murdoch's thesis? Explain.
2. Do you react any differently to Murdoch's article knowing that he is an immigrant? How does Murdoch—who comes from a well-to-do family—differ from immigrants who come to the United States with limited education, skills, and money?
3. Name at least one way that you think illegal immigrants have benefited American society. Name at least one way that you think they have harmed it. On the whole, do illegal immigrants do "more harm than good"? Is the same true of legal immigrants? Why do you think so?
4. If you were to refute Murdoch, what would you argue?
5. Where does Murdoch's article seem weakest? Why is it weak at this point? What is needed to strengthen it?

Writing about the Argument

1. Write an article critiquing Murdoch's argument. Identify its most significant strength and weakness.
2. Refute Murdoch's argument.
3. Write an argument explaining why you agree with what Murdoch has to say. Assume that your audience is highly critical of illegal immigration and believes that such individuals are of no benefit to American society.

"Can We Stop Illegals?"

About the Author: William F. Buckley

Born into an affluent New York family, William F. Buckley was educated in Europe and America. Following his graduation from Yale University in 1950, he wrote *God and Man at Yale,* a book that criticized what he perceived as the undermining of traditional American values by academia. He founded the conservative political magazine *National Review* in 1955, from which he retired in the 1990s. His television show *Firing Line,* which ran from 1966 to 1999, gave him celebrity status. He has written numerous articles and books over the years, including *Buckley: The Right Word* (1998), *Nearer, My God: An Autobiography of Faith* (1998), *On the Firing Line: The Public Life of Our Public Figures* (1989), *Happy Days Were Here Again: Reflections of a Libertarian Journalist* (1995), and a series of mystery novels. This article was originally published in *National Review* in May 2005.

Before You Read

1. What, if anything, do you know about Buckley? Do a quick Internet search. What would you expect his opinion to be?
2. What does the title of Buckley's article imply? What is your initial reaction to it?
3. What do you know about Buckley's magazine, *National Review?* What sort of readership do you think it has? Will this audience be receptive to what he has to say? How do you know?

»«

READING SELECTION

Can We Stop Illegals?

1 The parallels are remarkable, Berlin–Mexico. They are nevertheless worth reciting in order to refamiliarize ourselves with what nations and human beings tend to do when pressed beyond what they believe is their capacity to absorb.

2 In the late 1950s, the awful consequences of life under East German/Soviet rule caused people to vote with their feet—to move from East Germany into West Germany. The movement, in the early stages of it, was thought tolerable. But by the end of the decade it had become intolerable. West Germany had difficulties in assimilating East Germans in the numbers in which they arrived.

3 The problem, by the winter of 1960, had become insupportable. East German leader Walter Ulbricht reported to the Kremlin that at the rate doctors and engineers were leaving East Germany, in ten years if you needed a doctor you'd find none such left, let alone an engineer to build a bridge. We are going to close down Berlin, Ulbricht told Khrushchev, and the mighty Soviet army has to stand by us or the whole Soviet East European establishment is going to break down.

4 What happened was the Berlin Wall. If the border between Mexico and the United States were designed like the border between East and West Berlin, an effort could feasibly be made to block the apex into which the human traffic consolidated.

5 The idea of a 2,000-mile wall is not abandoned, because no escape from the current intolerable situation is officially abandoned. How long would it take? If we hired Israeli wall makers to go to work, or show us how to do it? Ex-Soviet wall builders could surely be found who are as young as 65 years old, and they certainly are looking for work.

6 The concept of a wall is disagreeable, but critical questions are now crystallizing. Can the United States govern its own borders? That is a very serious question because the answer to it is thought obvious: Yes—all nations control their own borders! But the question properly put becomes: Are we prepared to go to the lengths necessary to control our borders? To say yes is glibness—and glibness of a kind we are not practiced in, because maintaining the integrity of a wall requires anti-human fortifications. The Berliners began with barbed wire, which grew to high cement walls. In due course electricity was added, and finally dogs. You can't of course do that over a stretch of 2,000 miles. But would we be willing to do that for any distance?

7 What we have got is ad hoc minute-men volunteering for duty along the Arizona border. But these are "vigilantes," in the thanks-but-no-thanks language of President Bush. They are not trained in the enforcement of justice or in the use of appropriate weapons. What they do is inject a little fright into the situation, with, almost certainly, here and there a dead Mexican, and possibly an international crisis.

8 The cure to East-to-West migration in Germany was simple: the granting of liberty to the East. But effective liberty required huge capital expenditures. When the wall came down, the West Germans faced the need for an investment in the East to make it a place Germans would consider living in. The cost was hundreds of billions of dollars.

9 The flow of Mexicans to the north can be strategically contained either by improving the quality of Mexican economic life or by suppressing opportunities in U.S. life. The former cannot be done, given cultural rigidities and impermeabilities. The latter can be attempted, but at great cost to U.S. business interests and ideals. Congress could pass a law imposing huge fines on any American enterprise that hires illegals. Collateral pressures could be applied, involving driving licenses, hospitals, schools. Are we willing to adopt such measures?

10 There is a yearning across the land to demonstrate that we are master of our own house. As things are going, we are not. The immigration wave appears uncontainable, and we cannot gen-

erate the sentiment required to do the kind of thing the East Germans did. All of which argues that effective reduction in illegal immigration is not going to happen.

Source: Taken from the column On the Right by William F. Buckley, Jr.

Thinking about the Argument

1. What is Buckley's central claim? What reasons does he cite to back up this statement?
2. How does Buckley propose to solve the problem of illegal immigration from Mexico?
3. What evidence does Buckley offer to validate his claim(s)? Do you find this evidence adequate? Explain.
4. The author refutes an alternative solution by saying that Mexico will not make an effort to improve conditions for its own citizens because of "cultural rigidities and impermeabilities." Is this an adequate refutation? Explain.

Responding to the Argument

1. How would you solve the illegal immigration problem that Buckley describes? By building a wall? By stepping up border patrols? By allowing illegal immigrants to become legitimate resident aliens? Can you think of another solution?
2. Do you think it is possible for Mexico to improve the quality of life for its citizens? Explain.
3. Is it "racist" to selectively identify and export illegal immigrants from Mexico? Why do you think this?

Writing about the Argument

1. Write a letter responding to Buckley's article. You may argue any point of view you wish.
2. Write a critique of Buckley's argument. Explain both its chief strengths and its main weaknesses.
3. Pretend you are an American citizen who is the child of an illegal immigrant who later became a naturalized citizen. Explain to Buckley why illegal immigrants should or should not be allowed to enter the United States to work.

"Do Immigrants Benefit America?"

About the Author: Peter Duignan

Peter Duignan is an emeritus senior fellow of the Hoover Institution at Stanford University. He has authored more than forty-five books covering European, Middle Eastern, and African affairs, including several books dealing with immigration and especially Hispanics in the United States. In 2000, he published *Bilingual Education: A Critique.* Duignan coauthored (with Philip Martin) *Making and Remaking America: Immigration into the United States* in 2003. This piece first appeared in the February 2004 issue of *The World & I.*

READING SELECTION

BEFORE YOU READ

1. How does Duignan's title compare with Buckley's? Is the tone different? How do you know?
2. What would you guess Duignan's opinion of illegal immigrants to be? How might he answer the question that forms his title?
3. Would you anticipate that Duignan's audience is different than Buckley's? Why do you think so?
4. Is the United States more like a melting pot (where many ingredients are melted together to become something new) or a salad bowl (where all of the items in the mix remain distinct and separate)?
5. What do you think of Duignan's credentials? Do they affect your willingness to be open to the author's thesis? Are you more inclined to listen to a widely published scholar like Duignan or a widely published journalist like Buckley? Explain.

Do Immigrants Benefit America?

1 Immigration has made and remade this country. Not only do immigrants not harm America but they have benefited it. *The Wall Street Journal* calls for high levels of immigration because it means more consumers, more workers, and a larger economy with new blood for the United States. Whereas Europe and Japan have aging populations and face shortages of tax money to care for their elderly, the United States, thanks to immigration, has a growing population. Immigrant labor, moreover, keeps prices, supplies, and services available and cheap.

2 In 1952 the McCarran-Walter Act allotted to each foreign country an annual quota for immigrants based on the proportion of people from that country present in America in 1920. This policy favored northern European immigrants but kept out southern and central Europeans. The next big change in immigration policy came in 1965, when President Lyndon Johnson abolished the national-origin quota system favoring Europe and adopted a system that favored the Western Hemisphere.

3 As immigration increased and the origins of immigrants changed, U.S. policies changed; the welfare state was enlarged and affirmative action and other programs benefited the new immigrants from Asia and the Western Hemisphere. Bilingualism and multiculturalism lessened the assimilation of the new immigrants in ways they had not influenced earlier arrivals from Europe.

A Change in Immigration

4 Until the early decades of the twentieth century, immigrants were usually Europeans. Today most immigrants are from Asia, Mexico, Latin America, and the Caribbean. The newcomers have come more quickly and in greater numbers than previous waves of immigrants, especially through illegal entrance. They therefore have a bigger impact on population growth, the economy, schools, and the welfare system. They are harder to integrate than earlier immigrants were because there are fewer pressures on them to assimilate and learn English. Instead, bilingual education, multiculturalism, and ethnic clustering slow up the workings of the so-called melting pot.

5 Does this matter? America successfully absorbed Irish, Germans, Poles, and Jews, but things have changed. In the past we had a confident core culture. America insisted that newcomers assimilate and learn English—and they did. There was no bilingual education; there were

no ethnic studies or affirmative action programs. The new immigrants are coming faster and in larger yearly numbers. These large numbers (one million a year plus 500,000 illegals) are proving harder to assimilate.

6 The new immigrants are arriving at a time when U.S. cultural self-reliance has eroded. Having learned from the civil rights struggle of black Americans, Mexican and Asian activists seek bilingual education and affirmative action for their own people while rejecting assimilation and Western culture. Latino activists demand ethnic studies programs in colleges and universities, group rights, and proportional representation in electoral districts, employment, the awarding of official contracts, and many other spheres of public life.

7 Latinos cluster in large neighborhoods to a greater extent than the foreigners who came here a century ago. Such clustering slows the learning of English and the rate of assimilation. Poor people who receive welfare benefits have fewer incentives to master English and adjust to the demands of American society. Latino immigrants, in particular, now make political demands of a kind not made by Sicilian or Greek immigrants a century ago. They are adopting the divisive and counterproductive stance of a racial minority. Their leaders demand privileges similar to those claimed for blacks.

8 In rejecting the melting pot concept, multiculturalists want to preserve immigrant culture and languages rather than absorb American culture. Those who oppose immigration hope to restrict the flow of immigrants so as to better assimilate the newcomers and promote the melting pot process. Otherwise, multiculturalism could lead to political fragmentation and then disaster. Restrictionists predict a stark picture of America as a Bosnia of continental proportions with a population of half a billion and dozens of contending ethnic groups, all lacking a sense of common nationhood, common culture, or political heritage.

Bilingual Education—Helpful or Harmful?

9 In the past, the children of immigrants were educated in English only, which assimilated them in one generation. Nowadays, with bilingual education being imposed on millions of students—with large numbers of Spanish-speaking immigrants arriving each year—the assimilation process is longer and less successful. Indeed, today's children will take three generations to assimilate.

10 Education has been a contentious subject since the Civil Rights Act (1964) and the Bilingual Education Act (1968) decreed that children should be instructed in their native tongues for a transitional year while they learned English but were to transfer to all-English classrooms as soon as possible. These prescriptions were ignored by bilingual enthusiasts. English was neglected, and Spanish-language instruction and cultural maintenance became the norm.

11 Bilingual education was said to be essential, allowing Hispanics to gain a new sense of pride and resist Americanization. The *Lau v. Nichols* (1974) case stands out as a landmark: After the decision, bilingual education moved away from a transitional year to a multiyear plan to teach the children of immigrants in their home language before teaching them in English. This facilitation theory imprisoned Spanish speakers in classrooms where essentially only Spanish was taught; bilingual education became Spanish cultural maintenance, with English limited to 30 minutes a day. As a result, Spanish speakers were literate in neither Spanish nor English.

12 Linda Chavez, president of the Center for Equal Opportunity, accuses these advocates of bilingual education of being politicized and manipulated by cultural activists. The programs they favor have failed, she claims, and have undermined the future of the Latino children they were meant to help. Her criticisms are supported by the evidence. Latinos taught in bilingual programs test behind peers taught in English-only

classrooms, drop out of school at a high rate, and are trapped in low-skilled, low-paying jobs.

13 As noted earlier, the problem began in 1974 when the Supreme Court ignored 200 years of English-only instruction in American schools and said that students who did not speak English must receive special treatment from local schools. *Lau v. Nichols* allowed an enormous expansion of bilingual education. For example, in 1968, the U.S. Office for Civil Rights began a small program to educate Mexican American children; by 1996, it had expanded to an $8 billion a year industry.

14 As the program grew, the initial objective to teach English to Spanish speakers for one or two years was perverted into an effort to Hispanicize, not Americanize, Spanish speakers. The federal program insists that 75 percent of education tax dollars be spent on bilingual education—that is, long-term native-language programs, not English as a second language. Asians, Africans, and Europeans are all in mainstream classes and receive extra training in English-as-a-second-language programs for a few hours a day. Hispanic students, in contrast, are taught in Spanish 70 to 80 percent of the time.

15 The old total immersion system still works best; the longer students stay in segregated bilingual programs, the less successful they are in school. Even after 28 years of bilingual programs, the dropout rate for Latinos is the highest in the country. In Los Angeles, the Latino students dropped out at double the state average (44 percent over four years of high school). Special English-language instruction from day one gets better results than Spanish-language instruction for most of the day.

16 A higher degree of proficiency in English should be required by applicants for naturalization in the United States. A citizen should be able to read all electoral literature in English—no more foreign-language ballots. Educators in publicly funded high schools who believe that their task is to maintain the immigrant cultural heritage should be opposed. Such endeavors are best left to parents, churches, Saturday schools, and the extended family.

17 The role of the public-school teacher is to instruct students in English and American culture and political values. English plays a crucial role in cultural assimilation, a proposition evident also to minority people who argue that Spanish-language instruction in the public schools will leave their children badly disadvantaged when they graduate.

18 There is, however, hope in the battle against bilingual education. In 1998 California passed Proposition 227, calling for an end to bilingual education. If bilingual education is limited to one or two years for non-English-speaking children, who are then taught only in English, the U.S. school system will be able to assimilate students to English as it did before 1965.

The Issue of Matricula Consular

19 ID cards known as matricula consular are issued by the Mexican government. They do not give legal status to undocumented workers, but they do help integrate illegal migrants into U.S. society. Many U.S. banks now accept this document as identification for opening bank accounts. Mexican workers sent home $10–11 billion in 2002. Over 800 police departments and 400 cities now recognize the card as valid ID, and 13 states accept the consular registration as sufficient documentation to obtain a driver's license. This is all well and good, but 13 states allow the use of a driver's license to vote. Obviously, states should require some other identification to prove citizenship and the right to vote.

20 Remittances are becoming the major vehicle for transferring money to poor countries. The United States may have to adopt more liberal immigration policies even in the face of domestic opposition to illegal migrants. But there is a case for helping more immigrants send money to relatives, thus reducing poverty in their own lands and keeping their families at home.

21 There are enough controls in effect to deter any terrorists coming from Mexico. To date, no terrorists have crossed the Mexican border, and no Latino has been involved in terrorist acts. The Mexicans are hard workers and do jobs Americans don't want to do. The antiterrorism crackdown on the Mexican border has caught no terrorists, but it has made life harder on the border. It has slowed trade, tied up traffic, and cost American taxpayers millions, if not billions, of dollars by slowing the movement of people, goods, and services.

What about Muslim Immigrants?

22 Muslim immigrants are helpful to America; most Muslims are good workers and employees. Many are on business or student visas, pay high tuition costs, and are important in graduate school programs. In fact, many stay on after schooling and take highly skilled jobs in the United States.

23 Only 48 Muslims have been identified as terrorists since 1993. Of those, 41 were approved by visas issued by American consulates in Saudi Arabia—14 of the September 11 highjackers were Saudis. Seven who did not have visas sneaked into the United States and four arrived at a port of entry without a visa. An unknown number of terrorists have lived in this country illegally by overstaying a temporary visa.

24 Since September 11, Congress has enacted legislation to fight terrorism. This means that the visa system, especially for students, has been tightened. More of those who break immigration laws are being caught, and border controls are being strengthened. New measures have improved procedures for issuing visas to foreigners, tracking students and others while they are in the United States, and giving immigration authorities more power to arrest, detain, and deport illegal and legal foreigners, as well as those who have ties to terrorism.

25 This should be enough to prevent Muslim terrorists from entering and operating in America as the highjackers did so freely. The laws now in place can control Muslim terrorists and other illegals without needlessly disrupting the lives of the Muslims living, working, and studying here. A further tightening of control is required, however, on the Canadian border. In Canada, it is too easy to claim asylum status upon arrival. So-called refugees are able to stay on, raise money, plan terrorist operations, or slip into the United States across a 4,000-mile border.

What about the Future?

26 What kind of a United States do Americans want for the future? Most Americans feel somewhat ambivalent about immigration—their own forebears may, after all, have come from abroad—even as they tell pollsters they want immigration reduced. Americans are particularly opposed to illegal immigration, although not to undocumented aliens as individuals.

27 Statisticians in the Census Bureau forecast that by 2050, Caucasians will barely form a majority, with Hispanics far exceeding black Americans as the largest minority. But these forecasts may be called into question. For instance, such predictions take little or no account of lower birthrates for immigrants or intermarriage with other social groups. The intermarriage rate is high both for Latino and Asian people in the United States; the rate, moreover, increases from one generation to the next.

28 The United States will certainly be more ethnically and racially mixed in the future. It is not sure, however, how this amalgam will be composed, especially as future immigration patterns may change in an unexpected manner. If the number of immigrants is reduced, bilingualism eliminated, and Americanization encouraged, there will be little danger to U.S. unity.

29 No economist or social planner can specify with confidence the ideal number of immigrants that the U.S. economy should accept each year. But if it is the U.S. political aim to assimilate immigrants into a single nation, annual immigration must be kept in bounds. We suggest not

more than two per 1000 of the population during any one year. This would reduce the current level of immigration from one million annually to about 500,000 annually, not including refugees and skilled immigrants—still a generous quota.

30 Amnesties for illegal immigrants need to be halted to make clear that this is not a viable route to U.S. citizenship. Affirmative action programs should be terminated. Census categories such as Hispanic and Asian should be replaced by national origin classifications. English only should be required in the law, government, schools, and the political system. A transition year or two can be provided for those who do not speak English; then English only must be required in all academic courses, but training in foreign languages as a second language should also be encouraged. Becoming proficient in the language of America is a price that any immigrant should want to pay.

31 For the foreseeable future, America seems likely to remain the world's major destination for immigrants. Our history and traditions suggest that within a few decades, most of today's immigrants will be an integral part of a revised American community. But past success does not guarantee that history will repeat itself. There are concerns about the size and nature of today's immigration, especially about arrivals through the side and back doors. As the nation searches for an immigration policy for the twenty-first century, America—and the immigrants who are on the way—are embarked on a journey to an uncertain destination.

Thinking about the Argument

1. According to Duignan, what do immigrants do for the United States?
2. What is the "melting pot" concept? Why does the author think that the multiculturalists perceive it as a problem? Why does the author think the multiculturalists are wrong?
3. Why does Duignan think that bilingual education is a problem? Explain why you agree or disagree with his assessment.
4. Why does the author think that terrorism is not a problem at the porous Mexican border? Do you agree with this assessment? What would Buckley say?
5. What is "Americanization," and why does the author think it is important?

Responding to the Argument

1. After reading the article, do you agree with the "melting pot" or the "salad bowl" approach to immigration? If you have changed your mind since answering the questions in "Before You Read," explain how and why.
2. Do you think that terrorism is a legitimate threat where the Mexican border is concerned? Explain.
3. What, if anything, should Mexico do to assist the United States in combating illegal immigration?

Writing about the Argument

1. Write an essay comparing Duignan's essay to Buckley's. Which essay does a better job of proving its point through the use of claims, reasons, evidence, and refutation?

2. Write an essay comparing Duignan's essay to Buckley's. Which author do you think presents the best solution to the immigration problem?
3. Write an essay explaining why the "melting pot" approach to Americanization is a good or a bad idea. Are people being forced to shed their cultural identities, languages, and traditions in favor of Anglo-European values?

"Total Amnesty for Illegal Aliens?"

About the Authors: Jim Couch, J. Douglas Barrett, and Peter M. Williams

These three authors are professors at the University of North Alabama. Jim Couch and Peter M. Williams are the coauthors (with Brett King and William H. Wells) of "Nation of Origin Bias and the Enforcement of Immigration Laws by the Immigration and Naturalization Service" (Independent Institute Working Paper Number 38, June 2001). Couch has coauthored (with William F. Shughart) *The Political Economy of the New Deal* (1998). In the following article, which was published in the February 2004 issue of *The World & I,* the authors contend that giving legal status to illegal immigrants is unfair to immigrants who follow the legal process.

Before You Read

1. Do you believe the U.S. government should give complete amnesty to illegal aliens? Would such a move be unfair to legitimate immigrants who "played by the rules" in their efforts to become citizens? Explain.
2. What does the word *amnesty* mean to you? Define it in your own words.
3. Compare this title to the titles of the previous two articles, which are also phrased as questions. Does the title of this article suggest a particular point of view? Explain.
4. What would you guess the thesis of this article to be?
5. If illegal immigrants are given legal status, do you think they are more likely to become productive members of their communities or a burden on society?

Total Amnesty for Illegal Aliens?

1 Suprisingly, arguments surrounding the subject of immigration have changed little over the years. Consider the words of Ralph Waldo Emerson, one of America's foremost essayists, in "Wealth" (which appeared in *The Conduct of Life* in 1860). Emerson asserts that

2 Britain, France, and Germany . . . send out, first attracted by the fame of our advantages, first their thousands, then their millions of poor people, to share the crop. At first we employ them and increase our prosperity; but in the artificial system of society and of protected labor . . . there come presently checks and stoppages. Then we refuse to employ poor men. They go into the poor-rates, and though we refuse wages, we must now pay the same in the

form of taxes. Again, it turns out that the largest proportion of crimes are committed by foreigners. The cost of education of the posterity of this great colony, I will not compute. We cannot get rid of their will to be supported. That has become an inevitable element of our politics; and, for their votes, each of the dominant parties counts and assists them to get it executed.

3 Similar arguments have been posited over the years. The nations of origin have differed, as the end of the nineteenth century saw clusters of German and central European immigrants, while the turn of the century saw many from Italy; the twentieth century featured many Russians, Poles, Asians, and Latin Americans, among others. In any event, the numbers have reached such a magnitude that any hopes of management by immigration officials have been lost.

4 The high numbers of immigrants from many nations led President Reagan to sign the Illegal Immigration Reform and Control Act (IRCA) of 1986. Aliens were granted a one-year period (from May 1987 to May 1988) to apply for legal status. The only eligible aliens were those who had lived in America since the beginning of 1982, and they were granted amnesty. The administration hoped to reduce future illegal immigration by adopting sanctions against employers. Those firms hiring illegal aliens would be punished, and the resulting reduction in employment opportunities was expected to decrease the flow of unlawful immigration.

5 As reported by the Federation for American Immigration Reform, some 2.8 million immigrants who illegally resided in the United States were granted the status of legal residents.

6 The desired results of IRCA did not follow. American businesses continued to hire low-wage foreign labor, as firms were rarely punished. No efficacious system to assess the legal status of workers has been established. Thus, the flow of illegal immigration continued at a rate of one-half million per year in the nineties, reaching an estimated eight million by 2000, as reported by the Census Bureau.

Troubled Native Americans

7 Many Americans find these numbers troubling. According to a 2002 Zogby Poll, "nearly three in five Americans feel that the United States should admit fewer immigrants into the country each year." Furthermore, the poll results indicate that "two-thirds of likely voters in the U.S. (65 percent) disagree that foreigners residing in the United States should be given amnesty."

8 Due to the unpopularity of amnesty efforts, policy proponents have chosen the euphemism "earned legalization," which allows illegal immigrants to obtain the legal status by establishing a work history. Rep. Richard Gephardt's bill, HR 3271, known as the Earned Legalization and Family Unification Act of 2002, was reintroduced in October 2003.

9 The legislation would "amend the Immigration and Nationality Act to provide for permanent resident status for certain long-term resident workers and college-bound students, to modify the worldwide level of family-sponsored immigrants in order to promote family unification." Gephardt explained that the legislation "will allow undocumented immigrants to legalize their status if they have been in the United States for at least five years, worked for [at least] two years, and if they can pass a background check."

10 In a statement, Gephardt said, "Today there are probably millions of immigrants in this country who have done everything we asked them to do. They worked, they have stayed out of trouble, they helped their family, they have helped their communities, and they deserve this opportunity for legalization." The rationale is to allow productive illegal immigrants to come out of the shadows.

11 Overstretched immigration officials can then focus on terrorists rather than on the hardworking core of illegal aliens who accept jobs that

American citizens tend to refuse. The executive director of the American Immigration Lawyers Association proclaimed, "We need to target our enforcement resources on people who mean to do us harm, not on those who are filling our labor market needs, revitalizing our communities, and seeking to fulfill the American dream." Joining in the call for amnesty is the American labor movement, claiming that U.S. employers presently exploit illegal immigrants.

12 Those who oppose amnesty point to the IRCA experience. A study by the Center for Immigration Studies estimates that the 10-year direct and indirect costs of benefits minus tax contributions for the 1986 amnesty total $78 billion. A study by the Immigration and Naturalization Service found that the average amnestied illegal alien had only a seventh-grade education and an annual salary of less than $9,000 after 10 years in the United States.

Perverse Incentives

13 Opponents also point out that amnesty creates perverse incentives, as it both pardons those who have broken our national laws and rewards them with permanent-resident status. Juxtaposed with legal immigration, in which a potential immigrant must wait for years on a tenuous process, legal immigration via amnesty is a bargain. The situation is exacerbated when the naturalization process allows amnestied aliens to petition and sponsor family members, many of whom are also unskilled workers with low levels of education, leading to large numbers of lowskilled and uneducated residents who will potentially be an economic burden.

14 The 1986 amnesty, coupled with the talk of future amnesties, serves only to encourage an increase in illegal immigration. Those hoping to attain legal resident status have a clear incentive to eschew the arduous process of legal immigration and illegally enter and remain in the United States until absolution is granted. The Coalition for the Future American Worker asserts, "We granted amnesty to 3 million workers in 1986, only to see the number of illegal aliens rise to an estimated 11 million in 2000. Amnesty is not a cure for illegal immigration; it is a cause of illegal immigration."

15 Perhaps the greatest threat from amnesty proposals is to homeland security. According to the Center for Immigration Studies, the INS estimates that approximately 78,000 illegal aliens living in the United States come from countries that "are of special concern in the war on terror." Easy entry and future amnesty programs from friendly nations can, ultimately, pose potential problems as well.

16 In the case of Mexico, immigrants themselves may enter primarily for employment purposes. However, less-restrictive immigration policies allow for the very real possibility and even high probability that potential terrorists will use Mexico as a steppingstone for entry into the United States if illegal entry under the guise of seeking low-wage employment virtually guarantees eventual amnesty.

17 With respect to culture, a healthy debate has always existed between the "melting pot" and "Teutonic thesis" concepts. The *melting pot* is a term that refers to America as an amalgamation of cultures and is viewed by its proponents as the basis for "American" society. The Teutonic thesis asserts that true "American" institutions can be traced back to Teutonic (i.e., Anglo-Saxon or Germanic) origins and that a mixing of other cultures therefore serves primarily to dilute fundamental institutions.

18 While these are concerns in the overall immigration debate, they offer little insight on the amnesty question. As many cultures have positive and negative aspects, any nation stands to benefit and incur costs with respect to culture as new immigrants arrive in large numbers. Whether there is a net gain or loss will always be argued by many groups, and no consensus or even a close facsimile is likely to be reached. Nevertheless, America has always welcomed legal

immigrants and will continue to do so, as we appear to be at least close to consensus on the overall net benefits of legal immigration. For an excellent, in-depth treatment of the benefits of immigration with captivating historical research, Thomas Sowell has a trilogy of books that are very accessible: *Race and Culture* (1994), *Migrations and Cultures* (1996), and *Conquests and Cultures* (1998).

Politics Above All

19 The fate of amnesty proposals has, unfortunately, very little to do with economic considerations, cultural concerns, or even national security issues and everything to do with, as Emerson suggested almost 150 years ago, politics. Modern economists have developed models that point out how public policy is shaped largely by the interests of the players in the process—politicians, government bureaucrats, and pressure groups. All of them pursue their own self-interest.

20 Politicians seek to maximize prospects for reelection; administrators of bureaus and agencies hope that those who appointed them get reelected and, in addition, hope to maximize the size of their budgets; and pressure groups push to see that their own narrow-interest legislation is adopted. While the participants claim to pursue the public interest, their actual intentions are quite different. As political scientist Morris Fiorina put it, "History provides too many examples of special-interest wolves wearing public-interest fleeces."

21 Numerous examples of special-interest wolves exist. Unions, suffering from declining membership, have reversed their long-held position on illegal immigrants and amnesty proposals. While they feign an interest in the exploited undocumented worker, they have, in reality, identified a new source of dues-paying members. Eliseo Meding, vice president of the Service Employees Union, declared, "I am convinced that as the labor movement is the best hope for immigrants, so are immigrants the best hope for the labor movement."

22 American business firms have come to rely on this low-cost source of labor and, for the most part, support more open immigration. In his book *Ethnic America,* economist Sowell explains, "Employers of agriculture and other low-paid labor have pressed for a national policy of more open access to the United States . . . while groups concerned with crime, welfare dependency, or other social problems . . . have pressed for more restrictive policies. Shifts in political strength among the contending groups of Americans are reflected in changing immigration policies and changing levels of enforcement."

23 Evidence of industry's desire for lax enforcement of immigration laws has been reported in research by the authors of this article. In a study of immigration law enforcement, we conjecture that employers offering dangerous and low-paying jobs will exert pressure that results in less than vigorous enforcement of our nation's immigration laws by immigration officials. In particular, our results suggest that criminal referrals per estimated illegal alien are significantly lower in those states where low-paying jobs in the service, construction, and manufacturing sectors account for a major portion of economic activity.

24 In addition, immigrants themselves can become an effective lobbying group. Writing for the American Enterprise Institute, Samuel Huntington explains, "Immigration is not a self-limiting process, it is a self-enhancing one. And the longer immigration continues, the more difficult politically it is to stop. Leaders of immigration organizations and interest groups develop a vested interest in expanding their own constituency."

25 In a subsequent study by the authors of this article, we find empirical evidence supporting Huntington's proposition. Our results indicate that immigration officials are less likely to enforce immigration laws in states with large Chi-

nese, Jamaican, and Mexican populations. On the other hand, illegal immigrants whose national origin matched that of relatively underrepresented legal immigrants were subjected to more vigorous enforcement.

26 While these special-interest groups push for easier entry and amnesty proposals, politicians position themselves in such a manner to maximize votes. Representative Gephardt, speaking to supporters of his amnesty legislation, said, "It will have a very hard time getting through Congress if the Republican Party continues their majority in Congress." He continued, "We need a Democratic majority to get this up and get it done." Clearly, Gephardt understands the power of the Hispanic vote.

27 Legal immigration has long been a part of our nation's history. Decade after decade, immigrants came to America, assimilated, and contributed to our economic vitality. In addition, those seeking legitimate political asylum have historically been welcomed. Amnesty proposals—or earned legalization schemes—undermine legal immigration efforts and the integrity of our borders.

28 Americans deserve a system that protects us from those wishing to do us harm but accepts those who can contribute to our overall economic health. The manner in which public policy is developed, however, makes the development of such a system unlikely.

Illegal Immigration Act of 1986

- The high numbers of immigrants from many nations led President Reagan to sign the Illegal Immigration Reform and Control Act (IRCA) of 1986.
- Aliens were granted a one-year period to apply for legal status.
- The only eligible aliens were those who had lived in America since the beginning of 1982, and they were granted amnesty.
- The administration hoped to reduce future illegal immigration by adopting sanctions against employers.
- Those firms hiring illegal aliens would be punished, and the resulting reduction in employment opportunities was expected to decrease the flow of unlawful immigration.
- But the desired results of IRCA did not follow.
- American businesses continued to hire low-wage foreign labor, as firms were rarely punished.
- The flow of illegal immigration continued at a rate of one-half million per year in the nineties, reaching an estimated eight million by 2000.

Opening the Floodgates

The great wealth and productivity of the U.S. economy offer the clearest example in history of a large-scale success in the free-market form of societal organization. While most economists will support the notion that free trade raises productivity and incomes in all countries that participate, free trade is unlikely to confer all the benefits of American-style capitalism and freedoms on populations held captive by oppressive or inept governmental systems.

If free trade in goods does not free the peoples of the world, could free exchange of people accomplish significant gains? The answer from most economists would be a reserved yes. The reservations are significant and explain why the political option of open borders is unlikely in our near future.

One reservation is that immigrants would benefit under the current system in place in the United States, but that sizable immigration itself exerts pressure that may cause systemic change. With a limited immigration policy, immigrants are required to participate in a society that is composed primarily of Americans with a sense of the institutions and values that have developed over time.

This participation is likely to make the assimilation process somewhat more likely, as the minority immigrants are surrounded by majority Americans practicing American capitalism and participating in American-style politics. However, a sudden and large inflow of people without experience in America could increase the ability of immigrants to establish enclaves that insulate their members from assimilation. Americans could fear the changes in politics and culture that such a move could create.

Another reservation is that the method of accounting for the gains should encompass all the gains of all the participants. It is almost assured that the choice to immigrate would select out those immigrants who would stand to benefit; the natives, however, may not choose to count those as gains to Americans but as gains to foreigners who are going to become Americans. Therefore, the votes of many who might benefit do not show up in the proposal to open the borders. Thus, it is not likely that current citizens are willing to risk losses in such a significant experiment.

THINKING ABOUT THE ARGUMENT

1. What is the Illegal Immigration Reform and Control Act of 1986? Why do the authors mention it?
2. Do the authors think that when illegal immigrants are given legal status that they will benefit American society? Why do you think so?
3. Do the authors recognize and/or refute any alternative arguments? Explain.
4. Do the authors believe that terrorism is a problem where illegal immigration is concerned? How is their opinion similar to, or different from, that offered by Duignan? What is your opinion?
5. According to the authors, in what ways do industry (potential employers of immigrants) and politics contribute to the problem of the legitimization of illegal immigrants?

RESPONDING TO THE ARGUMENT

1. Do you believe that giving legal status to illegal immigrants will help solve the problem of illegal immigration? Do you think that most of the migrants will become productive residents? Will such a policy encourage more illegal immigrants to come to the United States? Is that a bad thing or a good thing? For the government? For potential employers? For the rest of us?
2. Do you think that illegal immigration poses a terrorist threat? What do the other authors in this section think? Defend your answer.
3. Should stricter controls be placed on businesses that employ illegal immigrants? Should they be allowed to hire illegal immigrants at pay rates below the minimum wage? Does offering low-wage employment to illegal immigrants benefit or harm society? What will the effect be if they are offered legal status (and potentially demand minimum-wage pay)?

WRITING ABOUT THE ARGUMENT

1. Write a letter to your representative in Congress expressing your feelings regarding granting legal status to illegal immigrants. Be sure to provide reasons and evidence to support your claims.

2. Write a paragraph or a brief paper outlining what should be done about employers that hire illegal immigrants and pay them less than minimum wage. What should be done about the harm these businesses are doing to their workers by paying them so poorly?
3. Write a paper (or outline an argument, or make a journal entry) regarding the effect that you think racism has on how illegal immigrants are treated in the United States.
4. Produce an argument outlining a viewpoint that has not been covered in your reading questions, group work, or class discussions.

Issue 3: The Culture of Fear

Online Study Center
Prepare for Class
The Culture of Fear

After September 11, commentators began talking about the "new normal," and the term became so prevalent that a recent Internet search for the phrase resulted in almost 300,000 hits. Although the phrase may be defined in many ways, it implies that the feelings of security and prosperity brought by the fall of communism and the affluence of the 1990s have been replaced by anxieties about what the future will bring.

While some people have accepted this culture of fear as reality, others have argued that an attitude toward life enshrouded in fear is cultivated—even marketed, packaged, and sold. Fear, like any emotion, is often used inappropriately in arguments. It can be used to sway an audience in the absence of adequate evidence to support a claim. The essays that follow consider the role that fear has come to play in our lives, the extent to which we intentionally cultivate it, and the degree to which we can control it.

Reflections on Homeland Security

What does this editorial cartoon suggest about hope for the future? Has anxiety become part of the American experience?

Considering the Issue of the Culture of Fear

In discussion groups, in your journal, or working individually, answer the following questions.

1. Do we fear the right things?
2. Is it more rational, for example, to be afraid of driving down the highway at 90 miles per hour than to fear a terrorist attack?
3. To what degree do we cultivate fear? How do people in positions of power (politicians,

teachers, police officers, employers, and so on) inappropriately use fear to motivate people?

4. Why do we focus on things that cause anxiety—why do we entertain ourselves by watching horror movies, for instance?
5. What can we do to suppress our irrational fears?
6. How is fear sometimes used inappropriately in arguments to persuade an audience when adequate evidence is not present?

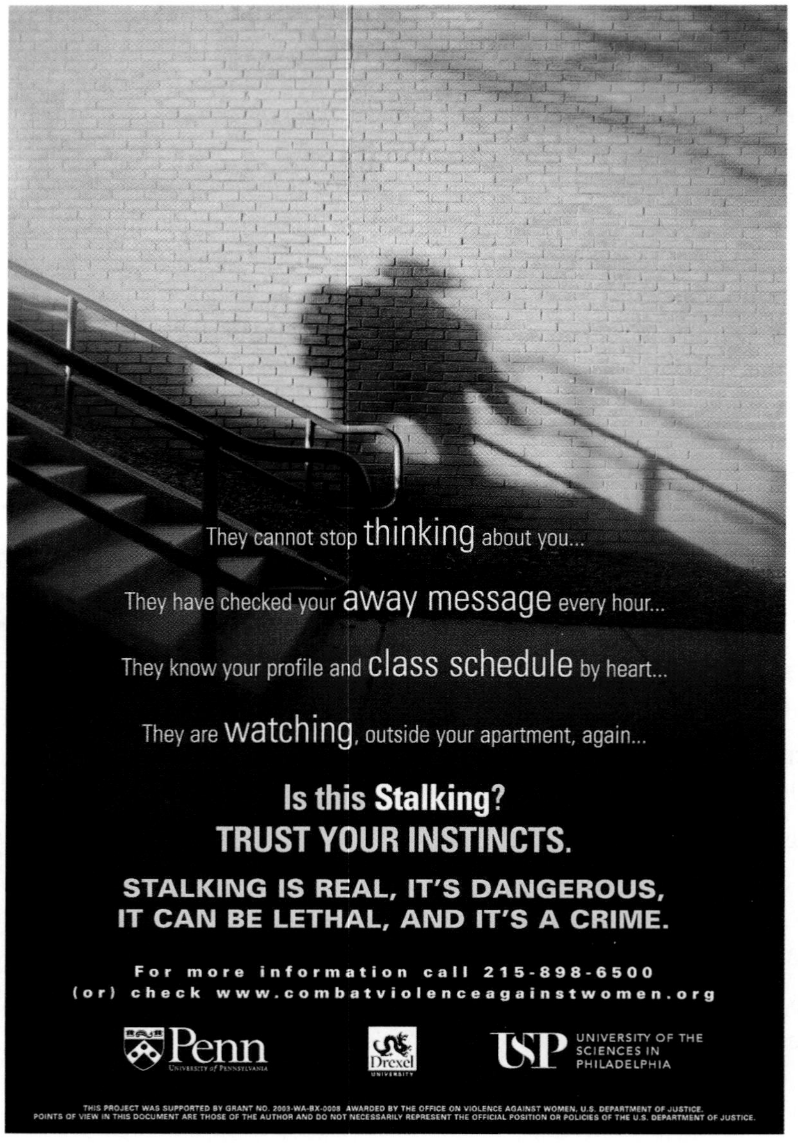

This poster uses emotion—in particular, fear—to validate its claim. Is this use of fear appropriate or inappropriate in your opinion?

READING SELECTION

"The Market in Fear"

About the Author: Frank Furedi

Frank Furedi is a professor of sociology at the University of Kent, England, where he specializes in the study of fear as a cultural phenomenon. He has published numerous articles on this subject, with regular essays appearing at Spiked.com. In his most recent book, *Politics of Fear* (2005), he argues that the liberal/conservative polarization of modern politics is largely driven by a fear of progress and change. Furedi's other recent books have included *Paranoid Parenting: Why Ignoring the Experts May Be Best for Your Child* (2001), *Therapy Culture: Cultivating Vulnerability in an Uncertain Age* (2003), and *Culture of Fear: Risk-Taking and the Morality of Low Expectation* (2002). This essay first appeared online in *Spiked* in September 2005.

Before You Read

1. Consider the title of this article. What does *market* imply? In what ways can fear be bought or sold?
2. Review Furedi's credentials in the headnote. What do you think he might have to say about fear?
3. Scan the article. Look at the subheadings. What do they tell you about the content of the article?

The Market in Fear

1 Fear is fast becoming a caricature of itself. It is no longer simply an emotion or a response to the perception of threat. It has become a cultural idiom through which we signal a sense of unease about our place in the world.

2 Popular culture encourages an expansive, alarmist imagination through providing the public with a steady diet of fearful programs about impending calamities—man-made and natural. Now even so-called high culture cannot resist the temptation of promoting fear: A new exhibition in the Museum of Modern Art in New York has the theme of "The perils of modern living." Fear is also the theme that dominates the Eighth Contemporary Art Biennial of Lyon. Natasha Edwards writes about the "art of fear" that haunts this important exhibition of contemporary European art.

3 But the more we cultivate a twenty-first century sensibility of anxiety, the more we can lose sight of the fact that fear today is very different to the experience of the past.

4 Throughout history human beings have had to deal with the emotion of fear. But the way we fear and what we fear changes all the time. During the past 2000 years we mainly feared supernatural forces. In medieval times volcanic eruptions and solar eclipses were a special focus of fear since they were interpreted as symptoms of divine retribution. In Victorian times many people's fears were focused on unemployment.

5 Today, however, we appear to fear just about everything. One reason why we fear so much is because life is dominated by competing groups of fear entrepreneurs who promote their cause, stake their claims, or sell their products through fear. Politicians, the media, businesses, environmental organizations, public health officials, and

advocacy groups are continually warning us about something new to fear.

6 The activities of these fear entrepreneurs serves to transform our anxieties about life into tangible fears. Every major event becomes the focus for competing claims about what you need to fear. Take the aftermath of Hurricane Katrina. It is not bad enough that we have to worry about the destructive consequence of this terrible catastrophe: According to some fear entrepreneurs, there is more to come. They claim that global warming will turn disasters like Katrina into normal events. Free-market ideologues blame "Big Bureaucracy" for the mismanagement of the rescue operation. Critics of President George W. Bush point the finger at the war in Iraq. And Bush blames local government. In the meantime, some contend that New Orleans represents God's punishment for human sin, while others suggest that the whole event is driven by a hidden conspiracy against the black race.

7 The fierce competition between alarmist fear entrepreneurs helps consolidate a climate of intense mistrust. Is it any surprise that many African Americans believe that the Bush administration sought to save New Orleans' white districts by flooding black neighborhoods, through deliberately engineering the levee breaks?

8 The catastrophe that wreaked havoc in Louisiana was also a test of our humanity. But sadly we were encouraged to interpret the event in the worst possible terms. Most of the stories about rape, looting, gang killings, and other forms of antisocial behavior turned out to be just that—stories. But for a while we became distracted from empathizing with our fellow human beings as we feared for the breakdown of civilization.

9 It is not simply the big events like Katrina that are subjected to competing claims on the fear market. Imagine that you are a parent. For years you have been told that sunshine represents a mortal danger to your children, and that you must protect them from skin cancer by minimizing their exposure to the sun. Then, this summer, a report is published that raises concerns about the rise of vitamin E deficiency among children who have been far too protected from the sun. So what do you do? The fact is that a growing range of human experience—from natural disasters to children's lives in the outdoors—is now interpreted through competing claims about fear.

10 Our misanthropic reaction to the catastrophe in New Orleans is reproduced daily in response to far more mundane events. That is why society cannot discuss a problem facing children without going into panic mode. Research shows that when viewers see an image of a child on a TV news item, they automatically anticipate a negative story. So a majority of people who were asked to give their interpretation of a photo of a man cuddling a child responded by stating that this was a picture of a pedophile instead of an act of a loving father.

A Brief History of Fear

11 In one sense, competing claims about what to fear is not a phenomenon unique to current times. During the Cold War, ideological conflicts were often conducted through the medium of fear. While some politicians argued for expanding arms expenditure by raising alarm about the threat of communism, others demanded disarmament and appealed to the public's fear of nuclear weapons. However, the promotion of competing alarmist claims is very different to the situation in the past.

12 Fear has lost its relationship to experience. When confronted with a specific threat such as the plague or an act of war, fear can serve as an emotion that guides us in a sensible direction. However, when fear is promoted as promiscuously as it is today, it breeds an unfocused sense of anxiety that can attach itself to anything. In such circumstances fear can disorient and distract us from our very own experiences. That is

why fear has acquired connotations that are entirely negative.

13 It is worth recalling that, historically, fear did not always have negative connotations. The sixteenth-century English philosopher Thomas Hobbes regarded fear as essential for the realization of the individual and of a civilized society. For Hobbes and others, fear constituted a dimension of a reasonable response to new events. Nor does fear always signify a negative emotional response. As late as the nineteenth century, the sentiment of fear was frequently associated with an expression of "respect" and "reverence" or "veneration." From this standpoint, the act of "fearing the Lord" could have connotations that were culturally valued and affirmed. Today, by contrast, the act of fearing God is far less consistent with cultural norms. One important reason for this shift is that fearing has tended to become disassociated from any positive attributes.

14 One of the distinguishing features of fear today is that it appears to have an independent existence. It is frequently cited as a problem that exists in its own right, disassociated from any specific object. Classically, societies associate fear with a clearly formulated threat—the fear of plague or the fear of hunger. In such formulations, the threat was defined as the object of such fears: the problem was death, illness, or hunger. Today, we frequently represent the act of fearing as a threat itself. A striking illustration of this development is the fear of crime. Today, fear of crime is conceptualized as a serious problem that is to some extent distinct from the problem of crime. That is why politicians and police forces often appear to be more concerned about reducing the public's fear of crime than reducing crime itself.

15 Yet the emergence of the fear of crime as a problem in its own right cannot be understood as simply a response to the breakdown of law and order. It is important to note that fear as a discrete stand-alone problem is not confined to the problem of crime. The fear of terrorism is also treated as a problem that is independent of, and distinct from, the actual physical threat faced by people in society. That is why so many of the measures undertaken in the name of fighting terrorism are actually oriented towards managing the public's fear of this phenomenon.

16 The generalized fear about the health effects of mobile phones has been interpreted as a risk in itself. In Britain, the Independent Expert Group on Mobile Phones, which was set up in 1999 by the then health minister Tessa Jowell, concluded that public anxiety itself could lead to ill health. The report of this committee noted that such anxieties "can in themselves affect" the public's well-being. In the same way, anxiety about health risks is now considered to be a material consideration in determining planning application. Fear is treated as an independent variable by public bodies.

17 The legal system has also internalized this trend. In the USA, there is a discernible tendency on the part of courts to compensate fear, even in the absence of a perceptible physical threat. This marks an important departure from the practices of the past, when "fright"—a reaction to an actual event—was compensated. Now, the fear that something negative could happen is also seen as grounds for making a claim. For example, it has been argued that people who feel anxious about their health because an incinerator is to be sited near their homes ought to be compensated.

A Market in Fear

18 Political debate is often reduced to competing claims about what to fear. Claims about the threat of terrorism or child obesity or asylum seekers compete for the attention of the public. In this way, our anxieties become politicized and turned into a politics of fear. Health activists, environmentalists, and advocacy groups are no less involved in using scare stories to pursue their agenda than politicians devoted to getting the public's attention through inciting anxieties about crime and law and order.

19 The narrative of fear has become so widely assimilated that it is now self-consciously expressed in a personalized and privatized way. In previous eras where the politics of fear had a powerful grasp—in Latin American dictatorships, fascist Italy, or Stalin's Soviet Union—people rarely saw fear as an issue in its own right. Rather, they were frightened that what happened to a friend or a neighbor might also happen to them. Today, however, public fears are rarely expressed in response to any specific event. Rather, the politics of fear captures a sensibility towards life in general. The statement "I am frightened" tends to express a diffuse sense of powerlessness.

20 Fears are often expressed in the form of a complaint about an individual, such as "Bush really scares me" or "he's a scary president." Ironically, in the very act of denouncing Bush's politics of fear, the complainant advances his own version of the same perspective by pointing out how terrifying the president apparently is.

21 And yet, the politics of fear could not flourish if it did not resonate so powerfully with today's cultural climate. Politicians cannot simply create fear from thin air. Nor do they monopolize the deployment of fear: Panics about health or security can just as easily begin on the Internet or through the efforts of an advocacy group as from the efforts of government spin doctors. Paradoxically, governments spend as much time trying to contain the effects of spontaneously generated scare stories as they do pursuing their own fear campaigns.

22 The reason why the politics of fear has such a powerful resonance is because of the way that personhood has been redefined in mental health terms. Increasingly, people are presented as individuals who lack the emotional resources to cope with the challenges of life.

23 Take the recent report on the legacy of the Chernobyl disaster. You have to read this three-volume, 600-page report very carefully to discover the good news that the number of deaths caused by the accident at the nuclear reactor at Chernobyl is under 50. Despite claims that thousands will eventually die and that even more could suffer terrible physical pain, the news is reassuring. The study found no evidence of decreased fertility among the affected population, nor an increase in congenital malformations. However, in line with the temper of our times the report concluded that the big problem posed by Chernobyl is the mental health of the affected people. The belief that people are unable to cope with misfortune and pain underpins our perception of the problems we face.

24 There is nothing novel about claim-making activities based on fear. Throughout history claim-makers have sought to focus people's anxiety towards what they perceived to be the problem. However, the activities of fear entrepreneurs today do not represent simply a quantitative increase over the past. In the absence of a consensus over meaning, competitive claims-making intrudes into all aspects of life.

25 In the private sector, numerous industries have become devoted to promoting their business through the fear market. In some cases, entrepreneurs seek to scare the public into purchasing their products. Appeals to personal security constitute the point of departure for the marketing strategy of the insurance, personal security, and health industries. Fear is used by the IT industry and its army of consultants to sell goods and services.

26 In certain instances it is difficult to clearly delineate the line that divides the fear economy from the promotion of anxiety and the anticipation of a disaster. It is worth recalling that for a considerable period of time the Y2K problem, also known as the millennium bug, was regarded as the harbinger of a major disaster. The scale of this major internationally coordinated effort and the massive expenditure of billions of dollars to deal with possible technologically induced crisis was unprecedented. Only a tiny minority of IT experts was prepared to question those devoted to constructing the "millennium bug problem."

27 Even social scientists, who usually make an effort to interrogate claims about an impending disaster, failed to raise any questions about the threat. One IT industry commentator, Larry Seltzer, noted that "looking back on the scale of the exaggeration, I have to think that there was a lot of deception going on." He added that the "motivation—mostly consulting fees—was all too obvious." But nevertheless it was not simply about money. Seltzer believes that there were also "a lot of experienced people with no financial interest who deeply believed it was a real problem."

28 Despite the growth of the fear economy, the exploitation of anxieties about potential catastrophes, the promotion of fear is primarily driven by cultural concerns rather than financial expediency. One of the unfortunate consequences of the culture of fear is that any problem or new challenge is liable to be transformed into an issue of survival. So instead of representing the need to overhaul and update our computer systems as a technical problem, contemporary culture preferred to revel in scaring itself about various doomsday scenarios.

29 The millennium bug was the product of human imagination that symbolized society's formidable capacity to scare itself. But who needs a millennium bug when you have global warming? Today global warming provides the drama for the fear-script. Virtually every unexpected natural phenomenon can be recast as a warning signal for the impending ecological catastrophe. Nothing less than a complete reorganization of economic and social life can, we are led to believe, save the human species from extinction.

30 Contemporary language reflects the tendency to transform problems and adverse events into questions of human survival. Terms like "plague," "epidemic," or "syndrome" are used promiscuously to underline the precarious character of human existence. The word "plague" has acquired everyday usage. The adoption of an apocalyptic vocabulary helps turn exceptional events into a normal risk. This process can be seen in the way that the occurrence of child abduction, which is fortunately very rare, has been transformed into a routine risk facing all children. In the same way, threats to human survival are increasingly represented as normal. As the sociologist Krishnan Kumar argues, the apocalyptic imagination has become almost banal and transmits a sense of "millennial belief without a sense of the future."

31 The fear market thrives in an environment where society has internalized the belief that since people are too powerless to cope with the risks they face, we are continually confronted with the problem of survival. This mood of powerlessness has encouraged a market where different fears compete with one another in order to capture the public imagination. Since September 2001, claim-makers have sought to use the public's fear of terrorism to promote their own interests. Politicians, businesses, advocacy organizations, and special-interest groups have sought to further their selfish agendas by manipulating public anxiety about terror.

32 All seem to take the view that they are more likely to gain a hearing if they pursue their arguments or claims through the prism of security. Businesses have systematically used concern with homeland security to win public subsidies and handouts. And paradoxically, the critics of big business use similar tactics—many environmental activists have started linking their traditional alarmist campaigns to the public's fear of terror attacks.

The Politicization of Fear

33 Although the politics of fear reflects a wider cultural mood, it did not emerge spontaneously. Fear has been consciously politicized. Throughout history fear has been deployed as a political weapon by the ruling elites. Machiavelli's advice to rulers that they will find "greater security in being feared than in being loved" has been heeded by successive generations of authoritarian governments. Fear can be employed to

coerce and terrorize and to maintain public order. Through provoking a common reaction to a perceived threat it can also provide focus for gaining consensus and unity.

34 Today, the objective of the politics of fear is to gain consensus and to forge a measure of unity around an otherwise disconnected elite. But whatever the intentions of its authors, its main effect is to enforce the idea that there is no alternative.

35 The promotion of fear is not confined to right-wing hawks banging on the war drums. Fear has turned into a perspective that citizens share across the political divide. Indeed, the main distinguishing feature of different parties and movements is what they fear the most: the degradation of the environment, irresponsible corporations, immigrants, pedophiles, crimes, global warming, or weapons of mass destruction.

36 In contemporary times, fear migrates freely from one problem to the next without there being a necessity for causal or logical connection. When the Southern Baptist leader Reverend Jerry Vines in June 2002 declared that Mohammed was a "demon-possessed pedophile" and that Allah leads Muslims to terrorism, he was simply taking advantage of the logical leaps permitted by the free-floating character of our fear narratives. This arbitrary association of terrorism and pedophilia can have the effect of amplifying the fear of both. The same outcome is achieved when every unexpected climatic event or natural disaster is associated with global warming. Politics seems to only come alive in the caricatured form of a panic.

37 In one sense, the term "politics of fear" is a misnomer. Although promoted by parties and advocacy groups, it expresses the renunciation of politics. Unlike the politics of fear pursued by authoritarian regimes and dictatorships, today's politics of fear has no clearly focused objective other than to express claims in a language that enjoys a wider cultural resonance. The distinct feature of our time is not the cultivation of fear but the cultivation of our sense of vulnerability. While it lacks a clearly formulated objective, the cumulative impact of the politics of fear is to reinforce society's consciousness of vulnerability. And the more powerless we feel, the more we are likely to find it difficult to resist the siren call of fear.

38 The precondition for effectively countering the politics of fear is to challenge the association of personhood with the state of vulnerability. Anxieties about uncertainty become magnified and overwhelm us when we regard ourselves as essentially vulnerable. Yet the human imagination possesses a formidable capacity to engage and learn from the risks it faces. Throughout history humanity has learned from its setbacks and losses and has developed ways of systematically identifying, evaluating, selecting, and implementing options for reducing risks.

39 There is always an alternative. Whether or not we are aware of the choices confronting us depends upon whether we regard ourselves as defined by our vulnerability or by our capacity to be resilient.

THINKING ABOUT THE ARGUMENT

1. What do you think Furedi means when he says that fear "has become a cultural idiom through which we signal a sense of unease about our place in the world"? Restate this in your own words. (*Hint:* What might the phrase "cultural idiom" mean?)
2. What evidence does the author cite to support his claim that a culture of fear is being actively marketed?

3. Why does Furedi believe that certain groups intentionally market fear?
4. According to Furedi, "Fear has lost its relationship to experience." What does this mean?
5. How and why does Furedi think that politicians promote fear?

Responding to the Argument

1. Can you think of at least three ways that fear is being marketed, if not outright encouraged? (*Hint:* In what ways do popular musical groups, movies, politicians, religious institutions, and politically motivated groups like the National Rifle Association play on fear to get their message across?)
2. What is the difference between fear and anxiety? Do you think modern culture is "fearful" or "anxious" in any way? Explain.
3. Do you think that any of the "threats" that the author mentions should be legitimately feared? Explain.

Writing about the Argument

1. In his article, Furedi mentions several fears that he seems to believe are irrational. Taking one of these fears (terrorism, pedophilia, global warming, and so on), write a letter to the author indicating why it should be perceived as a legitimate threat.
2. Write a paper about something you fear that the author does not mention. Explain why it is something people should be concerned about.
3. Identify some way that fear is marketed to the public. Evaluate how this marketing is done and explain what, if anything, should be done about it.
4. Write a journal entry explaining when fear is useful and legitimate. Provide an example. In addition, give an example of an inappropriate use of fear.
5. Given what the author says, how might fear (or other emotions) be used in the place of evidence to support a claim?

"A World Becoming More Peaceful?"

About the Author: Paul Rogers

Paul Rogers works for Bradford University in England as a professor of peace studies. He is a consultant to the Oxford Research Group, which seeks to promote international security through peaceful means (see www.oxfordresearchgroup.org.uk). In his book *Losing Control: Global Security in the Twenty-first Century* (second edition, 2002), Rogers argues that current confrontational approaches to international security fail to address the underlying problems that actually cause global insecurity. His most recent book is *A War on Terror: Afghanistan and After* (2004). He also has published numerous articles on topics related to international security and world peace. This piece appeared online in *OpenDemocracy* in October 2005.

READING SELECTION

BEFORE YOU READ

1. What does the title imply about the argument? What role does the question mark play in creating that impression?
2. What does the title of the source, "Open Democracy" suggest? Visit its website. What sorts of articles does this organization publish? Does it represent a particular point of view?
3. Glance over the article's subheadings. What do they suggest about the content of the essay?
4. Review the headnote. Does the author seem qualified to offer an opinion on this topic? Why or why not?

A World Becoming More Peaceful?

1 There appear good reasons for most people to think that the world is becoming a more dangerous place. In the four years since the 9/11 attacks, the George W. Bush administration has pursued a vigorous counter-terrorism policy that has already terminated two regimes and has, at a conservative estimate, seen at least 40,000 people killed, most of them civilians. United States forces are mired in a deep and bitter insurgency in Iraq, and almost 20,000 more troops are active against a determined Taliban guerrilla force in Afghanistan; they have also engaged in border clashes with Syria, and are involved in a tense standoff with Iran over the latter's nuclear developments.

2 Despite this vigorous U.S. strategy, the al-Qaida movement is able to sustain its activities by launching numerous attacks around the world.

3 This series of large-scale problems surely provides ample evidence for the feeling that global security is threatened. In such circumstances, for a substantial and carefully researched report to claim otherwise seems a nonsense—yet that is exactly the conclusion of the first annual Human Security Report published today, 17 October, by the Liu Institute for Global Issues at the University of British Columbia, Vancouver (and launched at the United Nations in New York).

4 The Human Security Report (HSR)—co-financed by five governments, including Canada and Britain—is modeled on that indispensable guide to issues of development, the United Nations Human Development Report, though it is not itself a product of the UN system. It argues that there has in fact been a marked decrease in political violence since the end of the cold war. The number of armed conflicts has decreased by more than 40 percent, and the number of major conflicts (which it defines as resulting in 1000 or more "battle-deaths") has declined by 80 percent.

5 Among its other conclusions, it finds that interstate wars now comprise only 5 percent of all armed conflicts, far less than in previous eras; that the numbers of people killed in individual wars have declined dramatically in the past five decades; and that the number of international crises fell by more than 70 percent between 1981 and 2001. The report also says that the number of autocratic regimes, noted for their systematic attacks on human rights, is decreasing.

6 At first sight, the conclusions of the report seem to fly in the face of everyday, tangible experience. However, the report is well researched, carefully constructed, and offers explanations for its results. Moreover, it is not alone in its findings. For the past five years, comparable if smaller-scale work by the Center for International Development and Conflict Management, University of Maryland, has generated broadly similar conclusions. Its latest biennial survey, Peace and Conflict 2005, co-authored by veteran

peace researcher Ted Robert Gurr, also finds a marked decline in major conflicts since the early 1990s.

7 One explanation these reports offer for the overall decrease in wars in the last two decades is the ending of two of the main "drivers" of conflict: decolonization and the cold war. Both historical cycles were marked by endemic conflict. The thirty years after 1945 saw numerous "small wars"—regarded as insurgencies or revolutionary threats by colonial powers, and as wars of national liberation by the combatants and their supporters—in southeast Asia, Kenya, Cyprus, Algeria, Angola, Mozambique, and many other places. There was also massive internal violence surrounding other transitions to independence, including the partition of India in 1947 and the birth of Bangladesh in 1970–1971.

8 Many of these conflicts had a wider geopolitical aspect as "proxy wars" between the United States and its allies and the Soviet bloc. It was characteristic of this cold-war era that these wars, which killed at least 10 million people and wounded 30 million, were fought in the "third world"—including Korea, Vietnam, Afghanistan and Ethiopia/Somalia—rather than Europe.

9 When the two types of conflict, decolonization and cold war, are taken together, it is not surprising that (as the Human Security Report points out) the two countries that have been most involved in international wars since 1946 are Britain and France; the United States and Soviet Union/Russia are next on the list.

10 The cold war drew to its end in 1989–1991 with the fall of the Berlin wall, revolutions across east-central Europe, and the collapse of the Soviet Union. This period coincided with the first Gulf war in 1991 to expel Saddam Hussein's forces from Kuwait, and was closely followed by bitter conflicts in the Caucasus (Abkhazia, Nagorno-Karabakh, and Chechnya) and the Balkans, as well as one of the worst conflicts of the past century in the Great Lakes region of Africa.

11 Alongside such violent and destructive events was a huge expansion in peacekeeping and conflict-prevention initiatives, principally but not only by the United Nations and its agencies. The Human Security Report argues strongly that these initiatives have had a direct effect in defusing some potential conflicts and easing others.

12 The UN dimension is significant in anticipating possible reactions to the report. The HSR is not an official UN product, but it is very clearly sympathetic with that organization, and this is likely to induce cynicism from the UN's critics like U.S. ambassador John Bolton and others in American politics and media. At the same time, the evidence the report gathers and the arguments it proposes are not ideologically one-sided: It includes major caveats and is very far from claiming that an era of universal peace is dawning.

The Invisible Casualties

13 The current political context makes the Human Security Report a rare document that provides a more hopeful picture about current indicators of conflict in the world. But a close reading of the HSR's detailed analysis suggests two issues in particular that deserve closer attention.

14 The first is the marked tendency it notes for people to flee from major areas of conflict, seeking security either in neighboring countries or even farther afield. This means that large numbers of people are being exposed to sustained and often extreme dislocation and hardship—a trend that may well result in an underestimation of the actual numbers killed and wounded in current conflicts.

15 The second issue is that in any case, the crude counting of casualties can be hugely misleading, especially when conflicts are happening in weak and impoverished societies. Most wars of the modern era take place in just such societies, with sub-Saharan Africa being particularly badly affected. In such circumstances, the effects of war can take years or even decades to overcome.

16 The destruction of schools, hospitals, and clinics, damage to farming systems, marketing networks, ports, and even bridges will have a far greater effect in poorer countries where most people already live close to the margins. The net effect frequently is to add to malnutrition, susceptibility to disease, and, especially, infant mortality and death in childbirth in a manner that is almost entirely missing from the simple, direct statistics of war.

17 Such impacts have, needless to say, been part of conflicts for decades if not centuries. They should be of great concern today, because alongside the great wealth and comfort of rich 21st-century societies a huge proportion of the global human community lives on very basic incomes with no guarantee of a stable future, while hundreds of millions more barely manage to survive at all. It is arguable that no social order that tolerates such vast inequalities can long endure.

Two Sources of Insecurity

18 These qualifications to the optimistic thrust of the HSR still leave a conundrum: why can this report and other similar research suggest that the world is becoming less violent and dangerous when so many analysts and citizens find daily evidence to offer the opposite view?

19 There are perhaps two main explanations. The first is that it is mainly people in the "Atlantic" countries—especially the United States and Canada, and western European countries such as Britain and Germany—who perceive a world of increasing violence. For this (in world terms) elite group, which includes people directly involved in George W. Bush's "global war on terror," media coverage of Iraq and of al-Qaida attacks helps create a pervasive view of global insecurity. But most people in other parts of the world are more directly concerned with immediate worries—jobs, health and education, and even water, food, and shelter—and any larger worries about war may well have diminished in the past two decades.

20 The second explanation is that the 9/11 attacks really did have a profound effect on the United States, by challenging a self-perception of invulnerability that had previously been disturbed as long ago as 1941. The threat to the United States' superpower dominance, leading to a "war on terror" now approaching its fifth year, may actually be distorting its understanding of the global picture of increasing security.

21 These two arguments require careful attention, but also two strong notes of caution in turn. First, the very vigor of the American response to 9/11 may be creating the conditions for increased instability and conflict. These countercurrents are most evident in the Middle East, whose rapidly growing energy resource significance coupled with the advent of China as a competitive agent reinforce existing political tensions.

22 Second, the assessment of whether or not the world has become more peaceful needs to accommodate the greatest human test of all—the response to climate change and all the many new insecurities that will come in its wake if it is not brought under control. The "drying out" of the tropics and the impact of global warming on the polar icecaps, which now look increasingly possible, will overshadow every other issue of international security in the coming decades. The huge pressure to migrate they are likely to bring is only one of their likely effects.

23 These two cautions refer to problems that will dominate the coming years and that can still—just—be addressed by making necessary policy changes. It is in this political context that the Human Security Report is a salutary reminder of what is possible. In many different ways over the past fifteen years there really has been a much-increased effort to prevent conflict, to resolve it when it happens, and to improve the world's capacity for post-conflict peace-building. In the context of so many forces and dynamics of insecurity, that is a powerful message.

Thinking about the Argument

1. Does the author believe that the world is becoming more peaceful? What evidence does he cite to support his claim?
2. Do you consider the Human Security Report to be an authoritative source? Why or why not? Why might the author need to cite further sources to back this report's findings?
3. Why does the author mistrust the findings of this report? Why does he think the numbers it reports may be inaccurate?

Responding to the Argument

1. Do you believe that the world has become a safer place since the end of the Cold War? Why or why not?
2. Do you agree or disagree with the author's belief that the war on terror and global climate change are legitimate threats?
3. Do you think that the two things the author specifically mentions—the war on terror and global warming—are things you should be worried about on a personal level? (In other words, do you expect these things to have a specific negative impact on your life in any significant way?)

Writing about the Argument

1. Refute Rogers's article. Argue why you think the world is safer overall, despite instability in the Middle East and other concerns.
2. Choose something in Rogers's article and explain why it is a legitimate concern and something to be afraid of. Compose your answer as a brief argument or as part of a journal entry.
3. Do you think that Rogers is "marketing fear" in the way that Furedi describes? Write an analytical synthesis of the two viewpoints. Explain which author you think is correct in his view, and why.

"Do We Fear the Right Things?"

About the Author: David G. Myers

David G. Myers is a professor of psychology at Hope College in Holland, Michigan. He has written textbooks, books, and many articles on topics related to many areas of psychology, including happiness, social psychology, sexual orientation, the psychology of faith, and ESP. His books include *The Pursuit of Happiness: Who Is Happy—and Why* (1992), *The American Paradox: Spiritual Hunger in an Age of Plenty* (2000), *Psychology through the Eyes of Faith* (2002), and *What God Has Joined Together? A Christian Case for Gay Marriage* (2005). Myers also founded the David and Carol Myers Foundation, which contributes profits from his textbooks and trade publications to a variety of charities. This essay originally was published in *Skeptic* in 2003.

Before You Read

1. What does the title of the article imply? What do you think the answer to the question it poses might be? Given this answer, what is likely to be Myers's thesis?
2. What sort of articles might a magazine titled *Skeptic* publish? Check out its website (skeptic.com) if you're not sure.
3. Scan the article. What seems to be the gist of Myers's argument?

Do We Fear the Right Things?

1 "Most people reason dramatically, not quantitatively," said Oliver Wendell Holmes. Even before the horror of 9/11, many Americans feared flying. "Every time I get off a plane, I view it as a failed suicide attempt," movie director Barry Sonnenfeld has said. With 9/11's four crashed airliners vividly in mind, and with threats of more terror to come, cancellations understandably have left airlines, travel agencies, and holiday hotels nose diving into the red. Airport security personnel are treating all approaching cars and even our elderly and children as potential threats. All told, we're preparing to spend $100 billion a year on homeland security. Our society is understandably terrorized by terrorism.

2 Do our intuitive fears fit the facts? How closely do our perceptions of life's various risks correspond to actual risks?

3 Ironically, after 9/11 the terrorists continued killing us, in ways unnoticed. In the ensuing months, Americans flew 20 percent less. "No way are we flying to Florida for vacation!" Instead, we drove many of those miles, which surely caused more additional highway deaths than occurred on those four ill-fated flights.

4 Consider: The National Safety Council reports that in the last half of the 1990s Americans were, mile for mile, 37 times more likely to die in a vehicle crash than on a commercial flight. Commercial flying is so safe that our odds of dying on any flight have been less than the likelihood of our tossing heads 22 consecutive times in a row. When I fly to New York, the most dangerous part of my journey is my drive to the Grand Rapids airport.

5 Believe it or not, terrorists, perish the thought, could have taken down 50 more planes with 60 passengers each in 2001 and—had we kept flying (speaking hypothetically)—we would still have finished 2001 safer in planes than on the road. Flying may be scary (531 people died on U.S. scheduled airlines in 2001). But driving the same distance should be many times scarier.

6 Why do we intuitively fear the wrong things? Why do so many smokers (whose habit shortens their lives, on average, by about five years) fret before flying (which, averaged across people, shortens life by one day)? Why do we fear violent crime more than clogged arteries? Why do we fear terrorism more than accidents—which kill nearly as many per week in just the United States as did terrorism with its 2527 worldwide deaths in all of the 1990s. Even with the horrific scale of 9/11, more Americans in 2001 died of food poisoning (which scares few) than terrorism (which scares many).

7 Psychological science has identified four influences on our intuitions about risk. First, we fear what our ancestral history has prepared us to fear. Human emotions were road tested in the Stone Age. Yesterday's risks prepare us to fear snakes, lizards, and spiders, although all three combined now kill virtually no one in developed countries. Flying may be far safer than biking, but our biological past predisposes us to fear confinement and heights, and therefore flying.

8 Second, we fear what we cannot control. Skiing, by one estimate, poses 1000 times the health and injury risk of food preservatives. Yet many people gladly assume the risk of skiing, which they control, but avoid preservatives. Driving we control, flying we do not. "We are loathe to let others do unto us what we happily do to ourselves," noted risk analyst Chauncey Starr.

9 Third, we fear what is immediate. Teens are indifferent to smoking's toxicity because they live more for the present than the distant future. Much of the plane's threat is telescoped into the moments of takeoff and landing, while the dangers of driving are diffused across many moments to come, each trivially dangerous.

10 Fourth, we fear what is most readily available in memory. Horrific images of a DC-10 catapulting across the Sioux City runway, or the Concorde exploding in Paris, or of United Flight 175 slicing into the World Trade Center, form indelible memories. And availability in memory provides our intuitive rule for judging risks. Thousands of safe car trips (for most of those who have survived to read this) have extinguished our anxieties about driving.

11 In less familiar realms, vivid, memorable images dominate our fears. We can know that unprovoked great white shark attacks have claimed merely 67 lives worldwide since 1876. Yet, after watching *Jaws* and reading vivid accounts of Atlantic coastal shark attacks, we may feel chills when an underwater object brushes our leg. A thousand massively publicized anthrax victims would similarly rivet our attention more than yet another 20,000+ annual U.S. influenza fatalities, or another 30,000+ annual gun deaths.

12 As publicized Powerball lottery winners cause us to overestimate the infinitesimal odds of lottery success, so vivid airline casualties cause us to overestimate the infinitesimal odds of a lethal airline ticket. We comprehend Mario Grasso's winning $197 million in a 1999 Powerball lottery. We do not comprehend the 328 million losing tickets that provided the jackpot. We comprehend the 266 passengers and crew on those four fated flights. We do not comprehend the vast numbers of accident-free flights—16 million consecutive fatality-free takeoffs and landings during one stretch of the 1990s. Dramatic outcomes capture our attention, probabilities we hardly grasp. The result—we overvalue lottery tickets, overestimate flight risk, and underestimate the dangers of driving.

13 And smoking. Imagine, suggests mathematician Sam Saunders, that cigarettes were harmless—except for a single cigarette in every 50,000 packs that is filled with dynamite instead of tobacco. There would be a trivial risk of having your head blown off, yet enough to produce more gruesome deaths daily than occurred at terrorists' hands on 9/11—surely enough to have cigarettes banned everywhere. Ironically, the lost lives from these dynamite-loaded cigarettes would be far less than from today's actual cigarettes, which annually kill some 3 million of the tobacco industry's best customers, the equivalent of 20 loaded jumbo jets daily. Yet rather than spend billions to prevent further carnage, as with homeland security spending, our government subsidizes tobacco.

14 Because we fear too little those threats that will claim lives undramatically, one by one (rather than in bunches), we will also spend hundreds of billions to save thousands instead of spending a few billion to save millions. A 2002 report by Deloitte Consulting and *Aviation Week* projected that the United States would spend between $93 and $138 billion during 2003 to deter potential terrorism.

15 Alternatively, $1.5 billion a year would be the U.S. share of a global effort to cut world hunger in half by 2015, according to a 2001 study done for the U.S. Agency for International Development. Ten billion dollars a year would spare 29 million world citizens from developing AIDS by 2010, according to a joint report by representatives of the United Nations, the World Health Organization, and others. And a few tens of

billions spent converting cars to hybrid engines and constructing renewable energy sources could help avert the anticipated future catastrophe of global warming via drought-fed wild-fires, rain-fed floods, heat-fed tornadoes and hurricanes, and glacier-fed rising tides, which threaten to overrun lowland places such as Bangladesh, the Netherlands, and south Florida. While agonizing over missed signals of the 9/11 horror, are we missing the clearer indications of greater horrors to come? "Osama bin Laden can't destroy Western civilization," observed *New York Times* columnist Paul Krugman. "Carbon dioxide can."

16 The moral: It is perfectly normal to fear purposeful violence from those who hate us. When terrorists strike again, likely where unexpected, we will all recoil in horror. But smart thinkers will also want to check their intuitive fears against the facts. To be prudent is to be mindful of the realities of how humans die. By so doing, we can take away the terrorists' most omnipresent weapon—exaggerated fear. If our fears cause us to live and spend in ways that fail to avert tomorrow's biggest dangers, then we surely do have something to fear from fear itself.

»«

Thinking about the Argument

1. Where in the article does the author state his thesis? Paraphrase it.
2. List three specific things that Myers thinks we should be afraid of, but generally are not. Now list three things Myers thinks we should not be afraid of, but are. What evidence does the author cite to support these claims?
3. According to the author, what three kinds of things has evolution ("ancestral history") prepared us to fear?
4. What is Myers's recommendation to his readers for dealing with different kinds of fears?

Responding to the Argument

1. Why does the author provide so many statistics in making his point? Is he more or less convincing than Furedi in this way?
2. Compare Myers's article to Furedi's. In what ways are the two articles similar? In what ways are they different? What information does one provide that the other lacks? Which do you find the most convincing, and why?
3. Do you agree with the advice that Myers provides in his final paragraph? Why or why not?

Writing about the Argument

1. Research the role that instinct plays in fear. Write a documented synthesis of the information that you find.
2. Think of a fear that Furedi and/or Myers might consider irrational. Using these two articles (and others, if you choose) as the basis of your argument, explain why it is rational to be cautious about

this fear. (For example, you might argue that you should avoid traveling to cities that might be targets of terrorism, or that you should wear a filter mask to avoid catching influenza.)

3. Choose one thing that many people are not afraid of, but should be, such as driving recklessly in heavy traffic. Argue why this behavior, above all others, should be changed.
4. Record a politician's speech, a television commercial, or another argument that uses fear as a primary element. Identify where fear is used to support a claim and where fear is overplayed in the absence of evidence to support a claim. Evaluate the effectiveness and appropriateness of the use of fear as an element of argumentation. Make your presentation before your class or another group.

"The Aesthetics of Fear"

About the Author: Joyce Carol Oates

Joyce Carol Oates is an American novelist, dramatist, essayist, and poet. Among her many novels are *A Garden of Earthly Delights* (1967), *Foxfire: Confessions of a Girl Gang* (1993), *We Were the Mulvaneys* (1996), and *The Falls* (2004). Her essays and criticism have included *The Edge of Impossibility: Tragic Forms in Literature* (1972), *New Heaven, New Earth: The Visionary Experience in Literature* (1974), *The Profane Art: Essays and Reviews* (1983), and *Uncensored: Views and (Re)views* (2005). Oates teaches in Princeton University's creative writing program. This essay was published in *Salmagundi* in 1998.

Before You Read

1. Have you ever heard of Joyce Carol Oates? What do you know about her writings? How do her writings differ from those of the other authors in this section? How could you find out more about her?
2. Would you consider Oates to be an authoritative source regarding the subject of fear as opposed to a psychologist or a sociologist? Why?
3. In what ways might a novelist be considered an authority on emotion or some other subject? (Science-fiction authors, for example, have been called on by the government to advise it about scientific developments in the future.)

The Aesthetics of Fear

The oldest and strongest emotion of mankind is fear, and the oldest and strongest kind of fear is fear of the unknown.

—H. P. Lovecraft, "Supernatural Horror in Literature"

There are far worse things awaiting than death.

—*Dracula* (Tod Browning, 1931)

1 Why should we wish to experience fear? What is the mysterious appeal, in the structured coherences of art, of such dissolving emotions as anxiety, dislocation, terror? Is fear a singular, universal experience, or is it ever-shifting, indefinable? We can presume that the aesthetic fear is not an authentic fear but an artful simulation of what is crude, inchoate, nerve-driven, and ungovernable in life; its evolutionary advantage

must be the preparation for the authentic experience, unpredictable and always imminent. In times of war and social upheaval, suicide is reported to be virtually unknown, for life, the merest shred of life, becomes infinitely precious. (The troubled Bruno Bettelheim, who eventually committed suicide at the age of eighty six, remarked that his year in Buchenwald and Dachau was the only time in his life when he was free of thoughts of suicide.) In authentically fearful times, the aesthetic fear is redundant. As Shakespeare's Edgar remarks in *King Lear,* "The worst is not / So long as we can say, 'This is the worst.'"

2 In the earliest of our consummate artworks of fear, Homer's *Iliad* and *Odyssey,* composed nearly three thousand years ago and in many ways strikingly contemporary, a primitive and continuous brutality is made "aesthetic"—that is, palliative and negotiable—by the poet's highly stylized language. In Homer's terms: How is one to confront fear? How is one to emerge a "hero"? The Greeks who constituted Homer's audience would surely have recoiled in horror from scenes of actual brutality like those celebrated in the poems, as we would, but the strategy of the poems is to present horror through the prism of a reflective consciousness; moreover, the *Iliad* and the *Odyssey* present pre-history, a mythic time now past; we understand that by the time of the poem's composition the warrior-heroes of the Trojan War are long dead, and even Odysseus, the man of twists and turns, has died his incongruously peaceful, gentle death. All that has happened has happened: ". . . hurling down to the House of Death so many sturdy souls, / great fighters' souls, but made their bodies carrion, / feasts for the dogs and birds" (*Iliad,* Book 1, 3–5; translated by Robert Fagles).

3 The *Odyssey* is similarly retrospective though much looser in structure than the *Iliad,* picaresque and seemingly improvised in its succession of vivid, cinematic adventures; its horrors are more primitive than those of the *Iliad,* many of them the actions of monsters: the man-devouring Cyclops, the cannibal giants of Laestrygonia, the fantastical Scylla ("the yelping horror, / . . . twelve legs, all writhing, dangling down / and Six swaying necks, a hideous head on each, / each head barbed with a triple row of fangs, thickset, / packed tight-armed to the hilt with black death!"), and equally "awesome" Charybdis. Yet the most haunting horror of the *Odyssey* is probably, for most readers, the House of Death where "burnt-out wraiths of mortals make their home"; ghosts emitting "high thin cries / as bats cry in the depths of a dark haunted cavern." The two Odysseyan visits to the underworld of bodiless, brain-damaged wraiths are disturbing in ways difficult to explain; evoking, perhaps, those dream-locked fugues of paralysis when we are neither fully unconscious nor conscious, knowing ourselves in a dream-state yet unable to wake, our "souls" trapped in useless bodies. (Some stroke victims are believed to experience this living hell.) It's an unexpected moment in the *Odyssey* when the heroic Achilles, the hero of the Trojan War, now a ghost, says bitterly to the still-living Odysseus, "I'd rather slave on earth for another man / than rule down here over all the breathless dead"—so repulsive is death that the Greeks' highest value, the glory of the warrior-hero, is repudiated by the most celebrated warrior-hero of them all.

4 In Ovid's *Metamorphoses,* an approximate thousand years later, a similarly pre-historic, mythic world is evoked, characterized by nearly continuous scenes of brutality, violence, and horror. A kind of cosmological ether or amniotic fluid seems to contain all living things so that, destroyed in our current form, we are merely transformed (by the caprice of gods) into another form; yet terror is real enough, physical humiliation, dismemberment, agony. Ovid's world is both hallucinatory and matter-of-fact. No matter how frequently we read the story of "guiltless" Actaeon we're struck by the metahorror of the young hunter's fate when turned by Diana

into a stag: "There is one thing only / Left him, his former mind" (Book 3, 204–5; translated by Rolfe Humphries). The peculiar Ovidean sadism of this story resides in the irony of Actaeon's pursuit and dismemberment by his own faithful hounds: "Blackfoot, Trailchaser, Hungry, Hurricane, / Gazelle and Mountain-Ranger, Spot and Sylvan, / Swift Wingfoot, Glen, wolf-sired, and the bitch Harpy / With her two pups . . . / Tigress, another bitch, Hunter, and Lanky) Chopjaws, and Soot, and Wolf, with the white marking / On his black muzzle, Mountaineer and Power, / The Killer, Whirlwind, Whitey, Blackskin, Grabber, / And others it would take too long to mention . . . / [They] lacerate and tear their prey, not master, / No master whom they know, only a deer."

5 Evoked with similarly vivid images is the rape and mutilation of the virgin Philomela by the "savage" Tereus, who, to prevent his victim informing on him, cuts out her tongue: "The mangled root / Quivered, the severed tongue along the ground / Lay quivering, making a little murmur, / Jerking and twitching, the way a serpent does / Run over by a wheel, and with its dying movement / Came to its mistresses's feet. And even then / It seems too much to believe—even then, Tereus / Took her, and took her again, the injured body / Still giving satisfaction to his lust." To revenge this atrocity, Philomela's sister, Tereus's wife and the mother of his son, commits an atrocity of her own: She cuts up the boy "still living, still keeping something of the spirit" and feeds him to his unknowing father; who, eating, is "almost greedy / On the flesh of his own flesh." At last Philomela, Procne, and Tereus are metamorphosed into birds bearing appropriate characteristics—blood-colored feathers, a sword-like beak. Human beings, victims and victimizers alike, frequently become birds in Ovid; and beasts; trees, flowers, fountains, and streams; rocks and stone; or, like Echo, the most subtle of metamorphoses, "voice only." What seems to elude them is common humanity: No one is changed into another person. At the conclusion of this remarkable work of horror mitigated by art, Ovid speaks in his own voice: "Now I have done my work. It will endure, / trust, beyond Jove's anger, fire, and sword, / Beyond Time's hunger . . . Part of me, / The better part, immortal, will be borne/Above the stars . . . / I shall be read, and through all centuries, / . . . I shall be living, always." The motive for art is bound up with a childlike wish to be immortal; what is the "aesthetic of fear" but the vehicle by which fear (of mortality, oblivion) is obviated? At least temporarily.

6 In these great works of the ancient world, existential horror would seem to be the result, not of human volition and responsibility, but of mere chance: the cruel caprice of gods. We are struck by how often anxiety is attached to acts of eating and being eaten: devoured by monsters or by one's own kind. The *Odyssey* might be seen, from a certain perspective, as a succession of meals devoured by ravenous jaws. Our earliest fears are associated with being hungry and being fed and with our mothers' nourishing presence or lack of it; since as helpless infants we can't feed ourselves, we must be fed, as mere mouths. This involves an agent, seemingly godlike, beyond our comprehension and control yet bound to us by the deepest physical intimacy. So the gods of antiquity are but "immortal" versions of mortal men and women, bizarre extended families ruled by figures of ambivalence like Zeus or Jove. To the more modern sensibility, post-Ovid, imbued with a Manichean/Christian metaphysics, it isn't chance but "evil" and its personification in Satan that tempt mankind into sin—thereby taking his immortality from him. The phenomenon of Dracula and the vampire legends generally can only be understood as a melding of ancient—that is, pagan—and more modern, Christian anxieties: not simply that we are the hapless victims of absurd, violent, dehumanizing, and dismembering fates, to be devoured and dissolved back into brainless nature, but that, succumbing

to the vampire's temptation, we are complicit in our own fate. Something in us wants to be seduced, violated, transformed; our innocence, like our virginity, torn from us. The ancient world posits atrocities out there; the Christianized world posits atrocities in here, in the soul. Dracula, the quasi-human villain of Bram Stoker's mythopoetic novel of 1897, is clearly akin to Satan, and to Bluebeard, the malevolent European nobleman celebrated through centuries in fairy tales and folk ballads, who courted and won any number of virginal young brides, bringing them to his castle, forbidding them to enter a certain chamber—which of course the young brides do, and must, each in turn, accursed by her own curiosity, like Eve eating the apple and like Pandora opening the box that contains the world's ills. The victim is to blame—isn't this always the case, especially when the victim is female?

7 Count Bluebeard is no ordinary brute and murderer, of whom, in fairy tales and ballads, there is no short supply, but a seducer, like Satan. The story of "La Barbe bleue" was recorded by Charles Perrault in his monumental *Histoires ou Contes du Temps Passe* (1697). The first English translation was by Robert Samber (1729), and became the basis for numerous woodcut illustrations of a popular sensationalist nature. In the Perrault version, the Blue Beard, as he is called, is finally killed by the brothers of one of his young wives; he leaves no heirs, and she inherits all his wealth—a happy ending, apparently. Yet, in popular legend, Bluebeard continued to thrive even as his bride-victims multiplied, doomed to anonymity. Do Bluebeard's wives—do Dracula's victims—want to be violated, to be victims?—to align themselves not with Christ but with Christ's nemesis, Satan? No—but yes. Apparently, yes. In Bram Stoker's *Dracula,* which would come to be the most popular of all English fin-de-siecle stories for film, Jonathan Harker speaks for many a victim of romantic supernatural forces in saying, in a passionate outburst near the conclusion of the novel, "Do you know what the place is? Have you seen that awful den of hellish infamy—with the very moonlight alive with grisly shapes, and every speck of dirt that whirls in the wind a devouring monster in embryo? Have you felt the Vampire's lips upon your throat?" Harker's actual experience in the count's castle has been significantly different, and here we have the heart of the vampire's secret, unspeakable appeal. Harker has been approached in his sleep by one of Dracula's sisters, a "fair girl" with "honey-sweet" breath in which there is a faint scent of a "bitter offensiveness, as one smells in blood." She bends over his motionless form, gloating:

> 8 There was a deliberate voluptuousness that was both thrilling and repulsive, and as she arched her neck she actually licked her lips like an animal, till I could see in the moonlight the moisture shining on the scarlet lips and on the red tongue as it lapped the sharp white teeth. Lower and lower went her head as the lips went below the range of my mouth and chin and seemed about to fasten on my throat. Then she paused, and I could hear the churning sound of her tongue as it licked her teeth and lips, and could feel the hot breath on my neck. Then the skin of my throat began to tingle as one's flesh does when the hand that is to tickle it approaches nearer—nearer. I could feel the soft, shivering touch of the lips on the supersensitive skin of my throat, and the hard dents of two sharp teeth, just touching and pausing there. I closed my eyes in a langorous ecstasy and waited—waited with beating heart.

9 The powerful appeal of the gothic world is that its inhabitants, who resemble civilized and often attractive men and women, are in reality creatures of primitive instinct. Gratification is all, and it is usually immediate—to wish is to act. Yet more magically, our own ethical behavior is suspended, for any means are justified in destroying the vampire. We ourselves can become savages in a good Christian cause. The most revealing episode in Dracula is the most luridly

erotic and misogynist: the killing of Lucy Western's vampire-self by the men bent upon "saving" her. Here, a communion of blood brotherhood is enacted that parodies the Christian ritual of purification and atonement. The virginal Lucy, it seems, has died; a vampire-Lucy has taken her place, Dracula's bride; she is a "nightmare" with pointed teeth, a bloodstained, voluptuous mouth, the entire "carnal and unspirited appearance" a devilish mockery of the former Lucy's purity; naturally she must be killed, but according to ritual. Led by the insufferably righteous vampire expert Van Helsing, the men place the point of a stake over the slumbering Lucy's heart, recite a prayer for the dead, and strike in God's name; with these spectacular results:

> 10 The Thing in the coffin writhed; and a hideous bloodcurdling screech came from the opened red lips. The body shook and quivered and twisted in wild contortions; the sharp white teeth champed together till the lips were cut, and the mouth was smeared with a crimson foam. But Arthur never faltered. He looked like a figure of Thor as his untrembling arm rose and fell, driving deeper and deeper the mercy-bearing stake, whilst the blood from the pierced heart welled and spurted up around it. His face was set, and high duty seemed to shine through it; the sight of it gave us courage so that our voices seemed to ring through the little vault.
>
> 11 And then the writhing and quivering of the body became less, and the teeth seemed to champ, and the face to quiver. Finally it lay still. The terrible task was over. . . .
>
> 12 There, in the coffin lay no longer the foul Thing that we had so dreaded and grown to hate that the work of her destruction was yielded as a privilege to the one best entitled to it, but Lucy as we had seen her in her life, with her face of unequalled sweetness and purity.

13 Where, except in a gothic dimension in which "high Christian duty" mingles with violent sexual sadism, might such an episode occur? The stake pounded into the female vampire's heart is "mercy bearing"—the entire procedure performed in the name of God the Father—as if rape and death, the particular province of the male aggressor, might be a kind of absolution. Since the "sacrifice" is in the service of religion, it might even be portrayed as altruistic. And if vampirism is erotic experience, we see how a woman must be punished, at least in Stoker's Victorian terms, for the awakening of her forbidden sexuality.

14 In the gothic imagination, the unconscious has erupted and has seeped out into "the world." As if our most disturbing, unacknowledged dreams had broken their restraints, claiming autonomy. The profane and the sacred become indistinguishable: Dracula, immortal so long as he is infused with the blood of living creatures, becomes for certain of his victims a perversely life-bearing force, ironically not unlike the Christian savior. For those whom he blesses, he can transform into vampires like himself. This is the unique vampire attraction, one might say; very different from the fates of those simply devoured, and digested, by such monsters as the Cyclops. The most striking aspect of Tod Browning's film *Dracula* (1931), famously starring Bela Lugosi, is its grave, ritualistic, sacerdotal quality. Here, Count Dracula is no quasi-human bat-faced creature with a fetid breath, as in the crude Stoker novel, nor an alarmingly Semitic buck-fanged hook-nosed rodent as in the silent German film by F. W. Mumau, *Nosferatu* (1922). (Though in all respects, as a work of visually poetic art, the Mumau film is far superior to the film by Browning.) Instead, Dracula is an elegant European gentleman, a reincarnation of the fatally charming Blue Beard; his formal evening wear, high starched collar, and long black cape suggest the vestments of a Catholic priest, as do his carefully choreographed movements and the studied precision with which he speaks English, as if it were a very foreign language. (Lugosi memorized his lines phonetically.) Where in the

Mumau film Dracula is sub-human and lacking all attraction, indeed a carrier of bubonic plague like any infected rat, in the Browning film Dracula is heightened as a charismatic screen presence. There is a brilliant audacity in aligning vampire and priest, for in Catholic ritual the priest celebrating the mass drinks the "blood" of Christ (diluted red wine) out of a chalice, as the congregation prays, in the solemn moments leading to the dramatic sacrament of Holy Communion when communicants come forward to receive from the priest, on their tongues, a consecrated wafer representing the body of Christ. Until fairly recent times, the priest intoned at this moment, in Latin, *Hic est corpus Christ.* "This is the body of Christ."

15 Protestants, Jews, and believers of other faiths may find it difficult to comprehend, or frankly preposterous: The Roman Catholic communion does not offer to communicants a mere symbol of Christ's body and blood but, through the mystery of "transubstantiation," that very body and blood. Christ's Last Supper as recorded in the Gospels is a symbolic ritual in a way that the Catholic communion is not.

16 What are we to make of these charismatic fantasy figures, vampire and savior? Vampire-as-savior? Count Dracula and Jesus Christ? To merely categorize them as fantasies, springing from childlike, if not infantile wishes for immortality, is too schematic, reductive. Personifying "evil"—like personifying "good"—is a human attempt to exert control over the incalculable and impersonal forces of nature of which (though we imagine ourselves superior because we have the gift of language) we are a part, but only an infinitesimal part. Bram Stoker wrote *Dracula* in the waning years of the nineteenth century, in a time of intellectual and religious crisis; like Lewis Carroll in the very different but equally mythopoetic *Alice in Wonderland* and *Alice through the Looking-Glass* of some years before (1865, 1871), Stoker was dramatizing the clash of Darwinian evolutionary theory with traditional Christian-humanist sentiment. (Of course, Christianity triumphs at the melodramatic conclusion of *Dracula*—this is the obligatory Victorian happy ending.) In the austere Darwinian model of our beleaguered Earth, the individual counts for virtually nothing; only the species matters, the replication of DNA; yet, as we humanists are informed by our scientist-colleagues, to our dismay, if not to our surprise, even the species doesn't really count—more than 99% of all species that have ever existed on Earth are now extinct. What does this seem to predict for our aggressive, fear-ridden, and paranoid species? In the benign Christian model, however, the individual is all: Christ died for each of us, as individuals, and we are redeemed by His sacrifice. If this is a fantasy, shared, in other terms, with other religions, it's at least an imaginative one, a powerful antidote to the "aesthetic of fear."

17 To return to the question: Why should we wish to experience fear, if only aesthetically? Why do we wish as a species to approach the unspeakable, the unknowable, the vision that, like Medusa with her horrific head of serpents, will prove unbearable? In H. P. Lovecraft's gothic classic "The Rats in the Walls," this forbidden vision is given a lurid Boschean grandeur as the story's doomed protagonist experiences a revelation in "those grinning caverns of earth's center where Nyarlathotep, the mad faceless god, howls blindly in the darkness to the piping of two amorphous flute-players." In other words: madness. The total disintegration of mind and language: our humanity. "The Rats in the Walls" ends with a brilliantly realized devolution of the protagonist as he regresses through the stages of consciousness represented by stages of the English language, back through middle English, old English, to mere bestial grunts—and cannibalism. Classic gothic literature asks: How human are we? How deep is our humanness? Is the vampire a monster, or is the vampire a natural extension of our human-animal selves? Anxiety arises when we ponder to what degree we share

in the civilization to which we belong. The most extreme "fall" is to revert to vampirism/cannibalism, violating the taboo against eating human flesh but also the taboo of acknowledging that the eating of human flesh is a possibility; looking upon one another as, not spiritual beings, but mere meat. To succumb to such a revelation is, in Lovecraft's cosmos, to succumb to madness; for sanity collapses at this crucial point. As Lovecraft says in his parable-like "The Call of Cthulhu,"

18 The most merciful thing in the world . . . is the inability of the human mind to correlate all its contents. We live on a placid island of ignorance in the midst of black seas of infinity, and it was not meant that we should voyage far.

19 What we fear most, I suggest, is not death; not even physical anguish, mental decay, disintegration. We fear most the loss of meaning. To lose meaning is to lose one's humanity, and this is more terrifying than death; for death itself, in a coherent cultural context, always has meaning. It is the anxiety of the individual that the very species may become extinct in our complicity with the predator—the cannibal/vampire—within. These fears, these anxieties, these recurring and compulsive nightmares, so powerfully dramatized by artists of the tragic and the grotesque through centuries, are not aberrations. The aesthetic of fear is the aesthetic of our common humanity.

Thinking about the Argument

1. Why, according to the author, were people in the ancient world so afraid of death? Name three specific examples Oates gives to support this idea.
2. Why does the author think that vampires are "both thrilling and repulsive"? What role does she think that the primitive or unconscious mind plays in creating this double sensation of fear and thrill?
3. In what way does Oates think that the vampire is a representation of our "human-animal selves"?
4. In the end, what does Joyce Carol Oates think we fear most? Do you agree with this assessment? Explain your answer.

Responding to the Argument

1. How does Oates's strategy differ from that of the other authors in this section? Do you think that looking at what writers of the past have said about fear can help people better understand its psychological role? Explain.
2. Oates provides evidence to argue that people in the ancient world were afraid of death. In what ways are people today afraid of the same thing? What images from literature, movies, and music echo a similar sentiment? Is it rational to be afraid of death? Why or why not?
3. What images in popular culture have the twin aspects of attraction and revulsion that the author speaks about (such as the Borg Queen in the *Star Trek* franchise, for example)? What element of our inner selves might such an image represent?

4. If we fear "loss of meaning" more than death, how do the other fears in our lives—fears of flying, sudden death from disease, terrorism, and so on—represent this fear? Consider this question and the arguments presented by the other authors in this section to examine why we fear these things more than the everyday things—such as driving and high cholesterol levels—that are statistically far more likely to kill us.

WRITING ABOUT THE ARGUMENT

1. Write an essay refuting Oates's claim that we fear a "loss of meaning."
2. Write an argument explaining how the fear of "loss of meaning" is illustrated by things that people commonly fear. Take into account at least one irrational fear.
3. Write in your journal about something that you fear. Explain whether this fear is irrational or rational. Provide significant examples or other evidence to validate your claims.
4. Write a journal entry about one thing that you do not fear but should fear. Support your assertions with concrete examples.
5. Write a letter to a friend who is afraid of flying. Explain why this is an irrational fear, and provide suggestions for how to overcome it.
6. Think of an irrational fear that is shared by many other people in the United States. Research this fear, explain how it is problematic (if you think it is), and describe the steps that should be taken to lessen this fear.

18

THE FUTURE

Environmental Sustainability, Artificial Intelligence, and Human Longevity

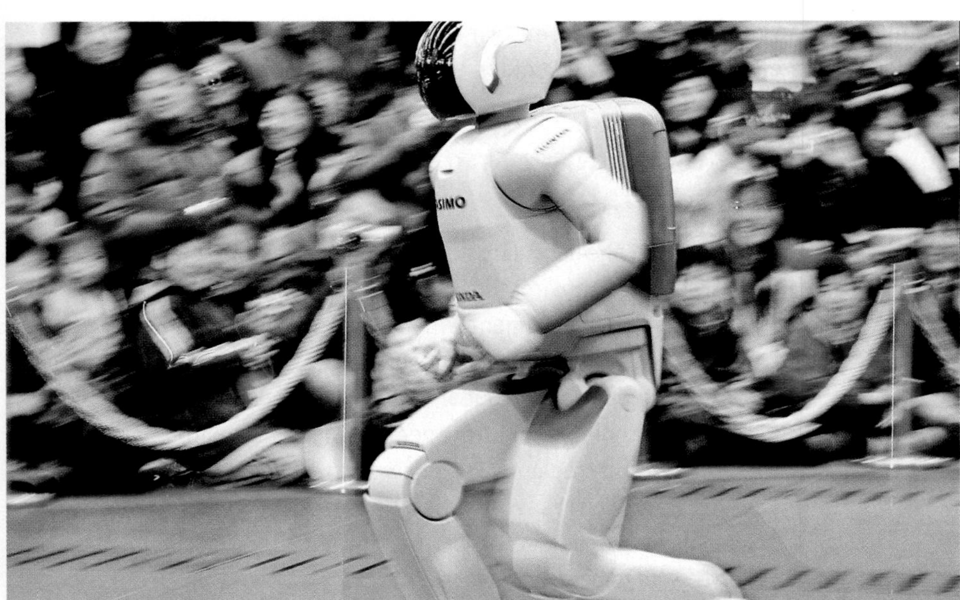

> *Clarke's First Law: "When a distinguished but elderly scientist states that something is possible, he is almost certainly right. When he states that something is impossible, he is very probably wrong."*
> *Clarke's Second Law: "The only way of discovering the limits of the possible is to venture a little way past them into the impossible."*
> *Clark's Third Law: "Any sufficiently advanced technology is indistinguishable from magic."*
>
> —ARTHUR C. CLARKE (B. 1917)

A century ago, most people were very optimistic about the future. The industrial revolution seemed to give human beings control of their destinies and the ability to shape their world in any way they saw fit. Eventually, writers like H. G. Wells and scientists like Albert Einstein began to challenge this view of the universe and to suggest that the world was fragile and that humans would not necessarily last forever. Today we live in a much more pessimistic age that is fraught with danger, and the future seems ever more uncertain, including our ability to prepare ourselves adequately for unforeseen problems.

In this chapter, you will explore three issues that are of great concern to scientists and futurists. The first issue, environmental sustainability, asks us to

Online Study Center
This icon will direct you to content and resources on the website <college.hmco.com/pic/lamm1e>.

consider ways that we can reshape our attitudes and approaches to living so that we can create a sustainable environment—that is, a world in which we do not consume more of our resources than we replenish. The second issue, artificial intelligence, concerns recent advances in computer technology and genetic engineering. Some scientists believe that interfacing human intelligence with computers and modifying the human genome may lead us into a "transhuman" or "posthuman" age in which our descendants will redefine what it means to be human. Finally, the third issue examines current medical research and its implications for extending human life. Some scientists believe that the average human life span will far exceed the century mark, leading to increased productivity but also increased population and unforeseen social problems.

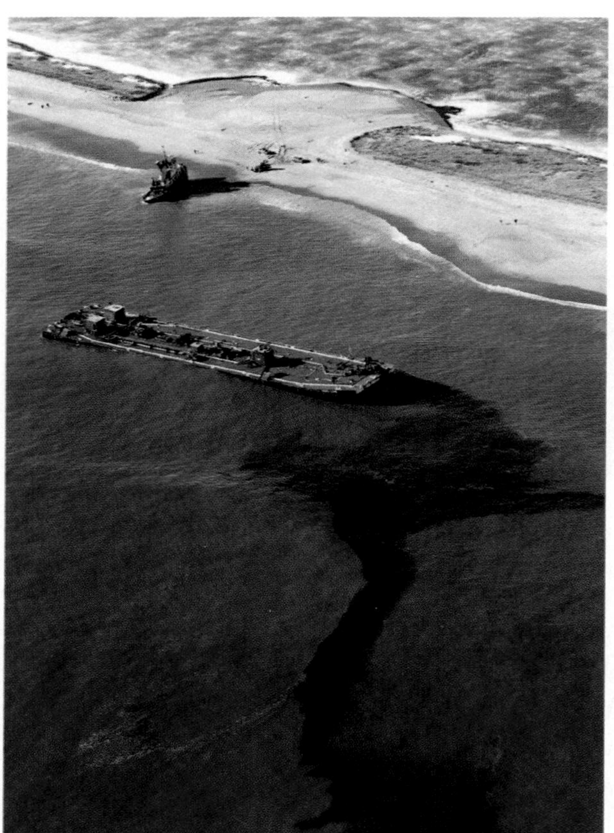

This photo makes a visual argument about environmental sustainability. How many claims are represented here? Can you put them in writing?

Issue 1: Environmental Sustainability

Nearly everyone has heard about global warming. Sustainability, according to environmental scientists, concerns the ability of a particular environment (whether natural or human-made) to remain in equilibrium and meet the needs of the current generation without running out of natural resources and jeopardizing the environment for future generations. If an environment can successfully replenish its renewable resources (for example, by planting trees when others are cut down) and use nonrenewable resources (such as petroleum) in moderation, then it may be said to be sustainable.

Often, however, sustainability depends on the interaction of economic, cultural, and natural forces. For example, if a town that relies primarily on its steel industry runs out of ore, then in addition to becoming environmentally unsustainable it may become economically unsustainable (the factory closes and people are put out of work) and culturally unsustainable (crime and poverty contribute to the decline and "death" of the town).

Considering the Issue of Environmental Sustainability

Consider these questions related to the issue of environmental sustainability (and global warming):

1. Is global warming a reality or a myth?
2. Is global warming truly dangerous, or has the case been overstated by doomsayers?
3. If a particular environment is said to be unsustainable, what caused the imbalance? Is the argument sound?
4. If a particular environment is said to be unsustainable, what will be the result of that unsustainability? How can sustainability be restored? How valid is the argument regarding a proposed solution to the problem?

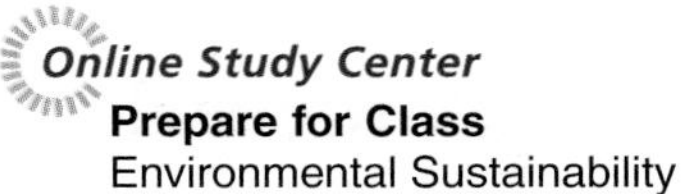

Online Study Center
Prepare for Class
Environmental Sustainability

READING SELECTION

"The Bottleneck"

About the Author: Edward O. Wilson

In addition to being an eminent biologist and professor at Harvard University, Edward O. Wilson is a prolific writer. He has been awarded the Pulitzer Prize for *On Human Nature* (1978) and *The Ants* (1990, which he coauthored with Bert Hölldobler). His ground-breaking book *Consilience: The Unity of Knowledge* (1998) proposed a radical reworking of modern education. In *The Future of Life* (2002), from which this selection is taken, Wilson warns that modern overconsumption is causing the world to rapidly approach a "bottleneck" and that if this bottleneck is to be survived, the people of the world will have to be sensitive to the needs of the planet as a whole, not just the immediate areas where they live.

Before You Read

1. Do you believe the planet is in any environmental danger? What kind of danger? If nothing is done, what do you think life on Earth will be like in 50 years? In 100 years?
2. If you do not believe that the environment is in any danger, why don't you believe this?
3. Do you believe that Wilson is qualified to write on this subject? Do you think that he is biased? Why or why not? (An Internet search can provide you with more information on Wilson.)
4. What do the words *economist* and *environmentalist* suggest to you? What is your sense of the priorities favored by each group?
5. Glance over the reading. What are some of the significant sections within the text? What does this suggest to you about what the argument will say?

READING SELECTION

The Bottleneck

1 The twentieth century was a time of exponential scientific and technical advance, the freeing of the arts by an exuberant modernism, and the spread of democracy and human rights throughout the world. It was also a dark and savage age of world wars, genocide, and totalitarian ideologies that came dangerously close to global domination. While preoccupied with all this tumult, humanity managed collaterally to decimate the natural environment and draw down the nonrenewable resources of the planet with cheerful abandon. We thereby accelerated the erasure of entire ecosystems and the extinction of thousands of million-year-old species. If Earth's ability to support our growth is finite—and it is—we were mostly too busy to notice.

2 As a new century begins, we have begun to awaken from this delirium. Now, increasingly postideological in temper, we may be ready to settle down before we wreck the planet. It is time to sort out Earth and calculate what it will take to provide a satisfying and sustainable life for everyone into the indefinite future. The question of the century is: How best can we shift to a culture of permanence, both for ourselves and for the biosphere that sustains us?

3 The bottom line is different from that generally assumed by our leading economists and public philosophers. They have mostly ignored the numbers that count. Consider that with the global population past six billion and on its way to eight billion or more by mid-century, per-capita fresh water and arable land are descending to levels resource experts agree are risky. The ecological footprint—the average amount of productive land and shallow sea appropriated by each person in bits and pieces from around the world for food, water, housing, energy, transportation, commerce, and waste absorption—is about one hectare (2.5 acres) in developing nations but about 9.6 hectares (24 acres) in the United States. The footprint for the total human population is 2.1 hectares (5.2 acres). For every person in the world to reach present U.S. levels of consumption with existing technology would require four more planet Earths. The five billion people of the developing countries may never wish to attain this level of profligacy. But in trying to achieve at least a decent standard of living, they have joined the industrial world in erasing the last of the natural environments. At the same time *Homo sapiens* has become a geophysical force, the first species in the history of the planet to attain that dubious distinction. We have driven atmospheric carbon dioxide to the highest levels in at least two hundred thousand years, unbalanced the nitrogen cycle, and contributed to a global warming that will ultimately be bad news everywhere.

4 In short, we have entered the Century of the Environment, in which the immediate future is usefully conceived as a bottleneck. Science and technology, combined with a lack of self-understanding and a Paleolithic obstinacy, brought us to where we are today. Now science and technology, combined with foresight and moral courage, must see us through the bottleneck and out.

5 *"Wait! Hold on there just one minute!"*

6 That is the voice of the cornucopian economist. Let us listen to him carefully. You can read him in the pages of *The Economist, The Wall Street Journal,* and myriad white papers prepared for the Competitive Enterprise Institute and other politically conservative think tanks. I will use these sources to synthesize his position, as honestly as I can, recognizing the dangers of stereotyping. He will meet an ecologist, in order to have a congenial dialogue. Congenial, because it is too late in the day for combat and debating points. Let us make the honorable assumption that economist and ecologist have as a common goal the preservation of life on this beautiful planet.

7 The economist is focused on production and consumption. These are what the world wants

and needs, he says. He is right, of course. Every species lives on production and consumption. The tree finds and consumes nutrients and sunlight; the leopard finds and consumes the deer. And the farmer clears both away to find space and raise corn—for consumption. The economist's thinking is based on precise models of rational choice and near-horizon time lines. His parameters are the gross domestic product, trade balance, and competitive index. He sits on corporate boards, travels to Washington, occasionally appears on television talk shows. The planet, he insists, is perpetually fruitful and still underutilized.

8 The ecologist has a different worldview. He is focused on unsustainable crop yields, overdrawn aquifers, and threatened ecosystems. His voice is also heard, albeit faintly, in high government and corporate circles. He sits on nonprofit foundation boards, writes for *Scientific American* and is sometimes called to Washington. The planet, he insists, is exhausted and in trouble.

The Economist

9 "Ease up. In spite of two centuries of doomsaying, humanity is enjoying unprecedented prosperity. There are environmental problems, certainly, but they can be solved. Think of them as the detritus of progress, to be cleared away. The global economic picture is favorable. The gross national products of the industrial countries continue to rise. Despite their recessions, the Asian tigers are catching up with North America and Europe. Around the world, manufacture and the service economy are growing geometrically. Since 1950 per-capita income and meat production have risen continuously. Even though the world population has increased at an explosive 1.8 percent each year during the same period, cereal production, the source of more than half the food calories of the poorer nations and the traditional proxy of worldwide crop yield, has more than kept pace, rising from 275 kilograms per head in the early 1950s to 370 kilograms by the 1980s. The forests of the developed countries are now regenerating as fast as they are being cleared, or nearly so. And while fibers are also declining steeply in most of the rest of the world—a serious problem, I grant—no global scarcities are expected in the foreseeable future. Agriforestry has been summoned to the rescue: more than 20 percent of industrial wood fiber now comes from tree plantations.

10 "Social progress is running parallel to economic growth. Literacy rates are climbing, and with them the liberation and empowerment of women. Democracy, the gold standard of governance, is spreading country by country. The communication revolution powered by the computer and the Internet has accelerated the globalization of trade and the evolution of a more irenic international culture.

11 "For two centuries the specter of Malthus troubled the dreams of futurists. By rising exponentially, the doomsayers claimed, population must outstrip the limited resources of the world and bring about famine, chaos, and war. On occasion this scenario did unfold locally. But that has been more the result of political mismanagement than Malthusian mathematics. Human ingenuity has always found a way to accommodate rising populations and allow most to prosper. The green revolution, which dramatically raised crop yields in the developing countries, is the outstanding example. It can be repeated with new technology. Why should we doubt that human entrepreneurship can keep us on an upward-turning curve?

12 "Genius and effort have transformed the environment to the benefit of human life. We have turned a wild and inhospitable world into a garden. Human dominance is Earth's destiny. The harmful perturbations we have caused can be moderated and reversed as we go along."

The Environmentalist

13 "Yes, it's true that the human condition has improved dramatically in many ways. But you've painted only half the picture, and with all due respect the logic it uses is just plain dangerous.

As your worldview implies, humanity has learned how to create an economy-driven paradise. Yes again—but only on an infinitely large and malleable planet. It should be obvious to you that Earth is finite and its environment increasingly brittle. No one should look to GNPs and corporate annual reports for a competent projection of the world's long-term economic future. To the information there, if we are to understand the real world, must be added the research reports of natural-resource specialists and ecological economists. They are the experts who seek an accurate balance sheet, one that includes a full accounting of the costs to the planet incurred by economic growth.

14 "This new breed of analysts argues that we can no longer afford to ignore the dependency of the economy and social progress on the environmental resource base. It is the *content* of economic growth, with natural resources factored in, that counts in the long term, not just the yield in products and currency. A country that levels its forests, drains its aquifers, and washes its topsoil downriver without measuring the cost is a country traveling blind. It faces a shaky economic future. It suffers the same delusion as the one that destroyed the whaling industry. As harvesting and processing techniques were improved, the annual catch of whales rose, and the industry flourished. But the whale populations declined in equal measure until they were depleted. Several species, including the blue whale, the largest animal species in the history of Earth, came close to extinction. Whereupon most whaling was called to a halt. Extend that argument to falling ground water, drying rivers, and shrinking per-capita arable land, and you get the picture.

15 "Suppose that the conventionally measured global economic output, now at about $31 trillion, were to expand at a healthy 3 percent annually. By 2050 it would in theory reach $138 trillion. With only a small leveling adjustment of this income, the entire world population would be prosperous by current standards. Utopia at last, it would seem! What is the flaw in the argument? It is the environment crumbling beneath us. If natural resources, particularly fresh water and arable land, continue to diminish at their present per-capita rate, the economic boom will lose steam, in the course of which—and this worries me even if it doesn't worry you—the effort to enlarge productive land will wipe out a large part of the world's fauna and flora.

16 "The appropriation of productive land—the ecological footprint—is already too large for the planet to sustain, and it's growing larger. A recent study building on this concept estimated that the human population exceeded Earth's sustainable capacity around the year 1978. By 2000 it had overshot by 1.4 times that capacity. If 12 percent of land were now to be set aside in order to protect the natural environment, as recommended in the 1987 Brundtland Report, Earth's sustainable capacity will have been exceeded still earlier, around 1972. In short, Earth has lost its ability to regenerate—unless global consumption is reduced, or global production is increased, or both."

17 By dramatizing these two polar views of the economic future, I don't wish to imply the existence of two cultures with distinct ethos. All who care about both the economy and environment, and that includes the vast majority, are members of the same culture. The gaze of our two debaters is fixed on different points in the space-time scale in which we all dwell. They differ in the factors they take into account in forecasting the state of the world, how far they look into the future, and how much they care about nonhuman life. Most economists today, and all but the most politically conservative of their public interpreters, recognize very well that the world has limits and the human population cannot afford to grow much larger. They know that humanity is destroying biodiversity. They just don't like to spend a lot of time thinking about it.

18 The environmentalist view is fortunately spreading. Perhaps the time has come to cease calling it the "environmentalist" view, as though it were a lobbying effort outside the mainstream of human activity, and to start calling it the real-world view. In a realistically reported and managed economy, balanced accounting will be routine. The conventional gross national product (GNP) will be replaced by the more comprehensive genuine progress indicator (GPI), which includes estimates of environmental costs of economic activity. Already, a growing number of economists, scientists, political leaders, and others have endorsed precisely this change.

19 What, then, are essential facts about population and environment? From existing databases we can answer that question and visualize more clearly the bottleneck through which humanity and the rest of life are now passing.

20 On or about October 12, 1999, the world population reached 6 billion. It has continued to climb at an annual rate of 1.4 percent, adding 200,000 people each day or the equivalent of the population of a large city each week. The rate, although beginning to slow, is still basically exponential: the more people, the faster the growth, thence still more people sooner and an even faster growth, and so on upward toward astronomical numbers unless the trend is reversed and growth rate is reduced to zero or less. This exponentiation means that people born in 1950 were the first to see the human population double in their lifetime, from 2.5 billion to over 6 billion now. During the twentieth century more people were added to the world than in all of previous human history. In 1800 there had been about I billion; and in 1900, still only 1.6 billion.

21 The pattern of human population growth in the twentieth century was more bacterial than primate. When *Homo sapiens* passed the six billion mark we had already exceeded by as much as a hundred times the biomass of any large animal species that ever existed on the land. We and the rest of life cannot afford another hundred years like that.

22 By the end of the century some relief was in sight. In most parts of the world—North and South America, Europe, Australia, and most of Asia—people had begun gingerly to tap the brake pedal. The worldwide average number of children per woman fell from 4.3 in 1960 to 2.6 in 2000. The number required to attain zero population growth—that is, the number that balances the birth and death rates and holds the standing population size constant—is 2.1 (the extra one-tenth compensates for infant and child mortality). When the number of children per woman stays above 2.1 even slightly, the population still expands exponentially. This means that although the population climbs less and less steeply as the number approaches 2.1, humanity will still, in theory, eventually come to weigh as much as the Earth and, if given enough time, will exceed the mass of the visible universe. This fantasy is a mathematician's way of saying that anything above zero population growth cannot be sustained. If, on the other hand, the average number of children drops below 2.1, the population enters negative exponential growth and starts to decline. To speak of 2.1 in exact terms as the breakpoint is of course an oversimplification. Advances in medicine and public health can lower the breakpoint toward the minimal, perfect number of 2.0 (no infant or childhood deaths), while famine, epidemics, and war, by boosting mortality, can raise it well above 2.1. But worldwide, over an extended period of time, local differences and statistical fluctuations wash one another out and the iron demographic laws grind on. They transmit to us always the same essential message, that to breed in excess is to overload the planet.

23 By 2000 the replacement rate in all of the countries of Western Europe had dropped below 2.1. The lead was taken by Italy, at 1.2 children per woman (so much for the power of natalist religious doctrine). Thailand also passed the magic number, as well as the nonimmigrant population of the United States.

24 When a country descends to its zero-population birthrates, or even well below, it does

not cease absolute population growth immediately, because the positive growth experienced just before the breakpoint has generated a disproportionate number of young people with most of their fertile years and life ahead of them. As this cohort ages, the proportion of child-bearing people diminishes, the age distribution stabilizes at the zero-population level, the slack is taken up, and population growth ceases. Similarly, when a country dips below the breakpoint, a lag period intervenes before the absolute growth rate goes negative and the population actually declines. Italy and Germany, for example, have entered a period of such true, absolute negative population growth.

25 The decline in global population growth is attributable to three interlocking social forces: the globalization of an economy driven by science and technology, the consequent implosion of rural populations into cities, and, as a result of globalization and urban implosion, the empowerment of women. The freeing of women socially and economically results in fewer children. Reduced reproduction by female choice can be thought a fortunate, indeed almost miraculous, gift of human nature to future generations. It could have gone the other way: women, more prosperous and less shackled, could have chosen the satisfactions of a larger brood. They did the opposite. They opted for a smaller number of quality children, who can be raised with better health and education, over a larger family. They simultaneously chose better, more secure lives for themselves. The tendency appears to be very widespread, if not universal. Its importance cannot be overstated. Social commentators often remark that humanity is endangered by its own instincts, such as tribalism, aggression, and personal greed. Demographers of the future will, I believe, point out that on the other hand humanity was saved by this one quirk in the maternal instinct.

26 The global trend toward smaller families, if it continues, will eventually halt population growth, and afterward reverse it. World population will peak and then start down. What will be the peak, and when will it occur? And how will the environment fare as humanity climbs to the peak? In September 1999 the Population Division of the United Nations Department of Economic and Social Affairs released a spread of projections to the year 2050 based on four possible scenarios of female fertility. If the number of children dropped to two per woman immediately—in other words, beginning in 2000—the world population would be on its way to leveling off by around 2050 to approximately 7.3 billion. This degree of descent has not happened of course and is unlikely to be attained for at least several more decades. Thus, 7.3 billion is improbably low. If, at the other extreme, fertility continues to fall at the current rate, the population will reach 10.7 billion by 2050 and continue steeply upward for a few more decades before peaking. If it holds to the present growth rate, it will reach 14.4 billion by 2050. Finally, if fertility falls more rapidly than the present trend, on its way to global 2.1 and below, the population will reach 8.9 billion by 2050; in this case also it will continue to climb for a while longer, but less steeply so. This final scenario appears to be the most likely of the trends. Very broadly, then, it seems probable that the world population will peak in the late twenty-first century somewhere between 9 and 10 billion. If population control efforts are intensified, the number can be brought closer to 9 than to 10 billion.

27 Enough slack still exists in the system to justify guarded optimism. Women given a choice and affordable contraceptive methods generally practice birth control. The percentage who do so still varies enormously among countries. Europe and the United States, for example, have topped 70 percent; Thailand and Colombia are closing on that figure; Indonesia is up to about 50 percent; Bangladesh and Kenya have passed 30 percent; but Pakistan holds with little change at around 10 percent. The stated intention, or at

least the acquiescence, of national governments favors a continued rise in the levels of birth control worldwide. By 1996, about 130 countries subsidized family planning services. More than half of all developing countries in particular also had official population policies to accompany their economic and military policies, and more than 90 percent of the rest stated their intention to follow suit. The United States, where the idea is still virtually taboo, remained a stunning exception.

28 The encouragement of population control by developing countries comes not a moment too soon. The environmental fate of the world lies ultimately in their hands. They now account for virtually all global population growth, and their drive toward higher per-capita consumption will be relentless.

29 The consequences of their reproductive prowess are multiple and deep. The people of the developing countries are already far younger than those in the industrial countries and destined to become more so. The streets of Lagos, Manaus, Karachi, and other cities in the developing world are a sea of children. To an observer fresh from Europe or North America the crowds give the feel of a gigantic school just let out. In at least sixty-eight of the countries, more than 40 percent of the population is under fifteen years of age. Here are typical examples reported in 1999: Afghanistan, 42.9 percent; Benin, 47.9; Cambodia, 45.4; Ethiopia, 46.0; Grenada, 43.1; Haiti, 42.6; Iraq, 44.1; Libya, 48.3; Nicaragua, 44.0; Pakistan, 41.8; Sudan, 45.4; Syria, 46.1; Zimbabwe, 43.8.

30 A country poor to start with and composed largely of young children and adolescents is strained to provide even minimal health services and education for its people. Its superabundance of cheap, unskilled labor can be turned to some economic advantage but unfortunately also provides cannon fodder for ethnic strife and war. As the populations continue to explode and water and arable land grow scarcer, the industrial countries will feel their pressure in the form of many more desperate immigrants and the risk of spreading international terrorism. I have come to understand the advice given me many years ago when I argued the case for the natural environment to the president's scientific advisor: Your patron is foreign policy.

31 Stretched to the limit of its capacity, how many people can the planet support? A rough answer is possible, but it is a sliding one contingent on three conditions: how far into the future the planetary support is expected to last, how evenly the resources are to be distributed, and the quality of life most of humanity expects to achieve. Consider food, which economists commonly use as a proxy of carrying capacity. The current world production of grains, which provide most of humanity's calories, is about 2 billion tons annually. That is enough, in theory, to feed 10 billion East Indians, who eat primarily grains and very little meat by Western standards. But the same amount can support only about 2.5 billion Americans, who convert a large part of their grains into livestock and poultry. The ability of India and other developing countries to climb the trophic chain is problematic. If soil erosion and withdrawal of groundwater continue at their present rates until the world population reaches (and hopefully peaks) at 9 to 10 billion, shortages of food seem inevitable. There are two ways to stop short of the wall. Either the industrialized populations move down the food chain to a more vegetarian diet, or the agricultural yield of productive land worldwide is increased by more than 50 percent.

32 The constraints of the biosphere are fixed. The bottleneck through which we are passing is real. It should be obvious to anyone not in a euphoric delirium that whatever humanity does or does not do, Earth's capacity to support our species is approaching the limit. We already appropriate 40 percent of the planet's organic matter produced by green plants. If everyone agreed to become vegetarian, leaving little or nothing

for livestock, the present 1.4 billion hectares of arable land (3.5 billion acres) would support about 10 billion people. If humans utilized as food all of the energy captured by plant photosynthesis on land and sea, some 40 trillion watts, the planet could support about 17 billion people. But long before that ultimate limit was approached, the planet would surely have become a hellish place to exist. There may, of course, be escape hatches. Petroleum reserves might be converted into food, until they are exhausted. Fusion energy could conceivably be used to create light, whose energy would power photosynthesis, ramp up plant growth beyond that dependent on solar energy, and hence create more food. Humanity might even consider becoming someday what the astrobiologists call a type II civilization, and harness all the power of the sun to support human life on Earth and on colonies on and around the other solar planets. (No intelligent life forms in the Milky Way galaxy are likely at this level; otherwise they would probably have been already detected by the search for extraterrestrial intelligence, or SETI, programs.) Surely these are not frontiers we will wish to explore in order simply to continue our reproductive folly.

33 The epicenter of environmental change, the paradigm of population stress, is the People's Republic of China. By 2000 its population was 1.2 billion, one-fifth of the world total. It is thought likely by demographers to creep up to 1.6 billion by 2030. During 1950–2000 China's people grew by 700 million, more than existed in the entire world at the start of the industrial revolution. The great bulk of this increase is crammed into the basins of the Yangtze and Yellow Rivers, covering an area about equal to that of the eastern United States. Americans, when they started from roughly the same point, found themselves geographically blessed. During their own population explosion, from 2 million at the birth of the republic in 1776 to 270 million in 2000, they were able to spread across a fertile and essentially empty continent. The surplus of people, flowing like a tidal wave westward, filled the Ohio Valley, Great Plains, and finally the valleys of the Pacific Coast. The Chinese could not flow anywhere. Hemmed in to the west by deserts and mountains, limited to the south by resistance from other civilizations, their agricultural populations simply grew denser on the land their ancestors had farmed for millennia. China became in effect a great overcrowded island, a Jamaica or Haiti writ large.

34 Highly intelligent and innovative, its people have made the most of it. Today China and the United States are the two leading grain producers of the world. The two countries grow a disproportionate share of the food from which the world population derives most of its calories. But China's huge population is on the verge of consuming more than it can produce. In 1997 a team of scientists, reporting to the U.S. National Intelligence Council (NIC), predicted that China will need to import 175 million tons of grain annually by 2025. Extrapolated to 2030, the annual level is 200 million tons—the entire amount of grain exported annually at the present time. A tick in the parameters of the model could move these figures up or down, but optimism would be a dangerous attitude in planning strategy when the stakes are so high. After 1997 the Chinese in fact instituted a province-level crash program to boost grain level to export capacity. The effort was successful but may be short-lived, a fact the government itself recognizes. It requires cultivation of marginal land, higher per-acre environmental damage, and a more rapid depletion of the country's precious ground water.

35 According to the NIC report, any slack in China's production may be picked up by the Big Five grain exporters, the United States, Canada, Argentina, Australia, and the European Union. But the exports of these dominant producers, after climbing steeply in the 1960s and 1970s, tapered off to near their present level in 1980. With existing agricultural capacity and technology, this output does not seem likely to increase

to any significant degree. The United States and the European Union have already returned to production all of the cropland idled under earlier farm commodity programs. Australia and Canada, largely dependent on dryland farming, are constrained by low rainfall. Argentina has the potential to expand, but due to its small size the surplus it produces is unlikely to exceed ten million tons of grain production per year.

36 China relies heavily on irrigation with water drawn from its aquifers and great rivers. The greatest impediment is again geographic: two-thirds of China's agriculture is in the north but four-fifths of the water supply is in the south—that is, principally in the Yangtze River Basin. Irrigation and withdrawals for domestic and industrial use have depleted the northern basins, from which flow the waters of the Yellow, Hai, Huai, and Liao Rivers. Added to the Yangtze Basin, these regions produce three-fourths of China's food and support 900 million of its population. Starting in 1972, the Yellow River channel has gone bone dry almost yearly through part of its course in Shandong Province, as far inland as the capital, Jinan, thence down all the way to the sea. In 1997 the river stopped flowing for 130 days, then restarted and stopped again through the year for a record total of 226 dry days. Because Shandong Province normally produces a fifth of China's wheat and a seventh of its corn, the failure of the Yellow River is of no little consequence. The crop losses in 1997 alone reached $1.7 billion.

37 Meanwhile, the groundwater of the northern plains has dropped precipitously, reaching an average 1.5 meters (5 feet) per year by the mid-1990s. Between 1965 and 1995 the water table fell 37 meters (121 feet) beneath Beijing itself.

38 Faced with chronic water shortages in the Yellow River Basin, the Chinese government has undertaken the building of the Xiaolangdi Dam, which will be exceeded in size only by the Three Gorges Dam on the Yangtze River. The Xiaolangdi is expected to solve the problems of both periodic flooding and drought. Plans are being laid in addition for the construction of canals to siphon water from the Yangtze, which never grows dry, to the Yellow River and Beijing, respectively.

39 These measures may or may not suffice to maintain Chinese agriculture and economic growth. But they are complicated by formidable side effects. Foremost is silting from the upriver loess plains, which makes the Yellow River the most turbid in the world and threatens to fill the Xiaolangdi Reservoir, according to one study, as soon as thirty years after its completion.

40 China has maneuvered itself into a position that forces it continually to design and redesign its lowland territories as one gigantic hydraulic system. But this is not the fundamental problem. The fundamental problem is that China has too many people. In addition, its people are admirably industrious and fiercely upwardly mobile. As a result their water requirements, already oppressively high, are rising steeply. By 2030 residential demands alone are projected to increase more than fourfold to 134 billion tons, and industrial demands fivefold to 269 billion tons. The effects will be direct and powerful. Of China's 617 cities, 300 already face water shortages.

41 The pressure on agriculture is intensified in China by a dilemma shared in varying degrees by every country. As industrialization proceeds, per-capita income rises, and the populace consumes more food. They also migrate up the energy pyramid to meat and dairy products. Because fewer calories per kilogram of grain are obtained when first passed through poultry and livestock instead of being eaten directly, per-capita grain consumption rises still more. All the while the available water supply remains static or nearly so. In an open market, the agricultural use of water is outcompeted by industrial use. A thousand tons of fresh water yields a ton of wheat, worth $200, but the same amount of water in industry yields $14,000. As China, already short on water and arable land, grows more

prosperous through industrialization and trade, water becomes more expensive. The cost of agriculture rises correspondingly, and, unless the collection of water is subsidized, the price of food also rises. This is in part the rationale for the great dams at Three Gorges and Xiaolangdi, built at enormous public expense.

42 In theory, an affluent industrialized country does not have to be agriculturally independent. In theory, China can make up its grain shortage by purchasing from the Big Five grain-surplus nations. Unfortunately, its population is too large and the world surplus too restrictive for it to solve its problem without altering the world market. All by itself, China seems destined to drive up the price of grain and make it harder for the poorer developing countries to meet their own needs. At the present time grain prices are falling, but this seems certain to change as the world population soars to 9 billion and beyond.

43 The problem, resource experts agree, cannot be solved entirely by hydrological engineering. It must include shifts from grain to fruit and vegetables, which are more labor-intensive, giving China a competitive edge. To this can be added strict water conservation measures in industrial and domestic use; the use of sprinkler and drip irrigation in cultivation, as opposed to the traditional and more wasteful methods of flood and furrow irrigation; and private land ownership, with subsidies and price liberalization, to increase conservation incentives for farmers.

44 Meanwhile, the surtax levied on the environment to support China's growth, although rarely entered on the national balance sheets, is escalating to a ruinous level. Among the most telling indicators is the pollution of water. Here is a measure worth pondering. China has in all 50,000 kilometers of major rivers. Of these, according to the U.N. Food and Agriculture Organization, 80 percent no longer support fish. The Yellow River is dead along much of its course, so fouled with chromium, cadmium, and other toxins from oil refineries, paper mills, and chemical plants as to be unfit for either human consumption or irrigation. Diseases from bacterial and toxic-waste pollution are epidemic.

45 China can probably feed itself to at least mid-century, but its own data show that it will be skirting the edge of disaster even as it accelerates its life-saving shift to industrialization and mega-hydrological engineering. The extremity of China's condition makes it vulnerable to the wild cards of history. A war, internal political turmoil, extended droughts, or crop disease can kick the economy into a downspin. Its enormous population makes rescue by other countries impracticable.

46 China deserves close attention, not just as the unsteady giant whose missteps can rock the world, but also because it is so far advanced along the path to which the rest of humanity seems inexorably headed. If China solves its problems, the lessons learned can be applied elsewhere. That includes the United States, whose citizens are working at a furious pace to overpopulate and exhaust their own land and water from sea to shining sea.

47 Environmentalism is still widely viewed, especially in the United States, as a special-interest lobby. Its proponents, in this blinkered view, flutter their hands over pollution and threatened species, exaggerate their case, and press for industrial restraint and the protection of wild places, even at the cost of economic development and jobs.

48 Environmentalism is something more central and vastly more important. Its essence has been defined by science in the following way. Earth, unlike the other solar planets, is not in physical equilibrium. It depends on its living shell to create the special conditions on which life is sustainable. The soil, water, and atmosphere of its surface have evolved over hundreds of millions of years to their present condition by the activity of the biosphere, a stupendously complex layer of living creatures whose activities are locked together in precise but tenuous global

cycles of energy and transformed organic matter. The biosphere creates our special world anew every day, every minute, and holds it in a unique, shimmering physical disequilibrium. On that disequilibrium the human species is in total thrall. When we alter the biosphere in any direction, we move the environment away from the delicate dance of biology. When we destroy ecosystems and extinguish species, we degrade the greatest heritage this planet has to offer and thereby threaten our own existence.

49 Humanity did not descend as angelic beings into this world. Nor are we aliens who colonized Earth. We evolved here, one among many species, across millions of years, and exist as one organic miracle linked to others. The natural environment we treat with such unnecessary ignorance and recklessness was our cradle and nursery, our school, and remains our one and only home. To its special conditions we are intimately adapted in every one of the bodily fibers and biochemical transactions that gives us life.

50 That is the essence of environmentalism. It is the guiding principle of those devoted to the health of the planet. But it is not yet a general worldview, evidently not yet compelling enough to distract many people away from the primal diversions of sport, politics, religion, and private wealth.

51 The relative indifference to the environment springs, I believe, from deep within human nature. The human brain evidently evolved to commit itself emotionally only to a small piece of geography, a limited band of kinsmen, and two or three generations into the future. To look neither far ahead nor far afield is elemental in a Darwinian sense. We are innately inclined to ignore any distant possibility not yet requiring examination. It is, people say, just good common sense. Why do they think in this short-sighted way? The reason is simple: it is a hard-wired part of our Paleolithic heritage. For hundreds of millennia those who worked for short-term gain within a small circle of relatives and friends lived longer and left more offspring—even when their collective striving caused their chiefdoms and empires to crumble around them. The long view that might have saved their distant descendants required a vision and extended altruism instinctively difficult to marshal.

52 The great dilemma of environmental reasoning stems from this conflict between short-term and long-term values. To select values for the near future of one's own tribe or country is relatively easy. To select values for the distant future of the whole planet also is relatively easy—in theory at least. To combine the two visions to create a universal environmental ethic is, on the other hand, very difficult. But combine them we must, because a universal environmental ethic is the only guide by which humanity and the rest of life can be safely conducted through the bottleneck into which our species has foolishly blundered.

Thinking about the Argument

1. What is Wilson's central claim? Can you locate it in the text? If not, can you put it in your own words?
2. Why do you think Wilson talks about environmentalists and economists? What does he think of the priorities of each group? Which group (if not both) does Wilson think may need to reassess its values?
3. Does Wilson present enough evidence to convince you that a bottleneck may be coming? Why or why not?

RESPONDING TO THE ARGUMENT

1. In the "Before You Read" exercise, you were asked if you approached Wilson's argument as a believer or as a skeptic. Has your position wavered at all? Why or why not?
2. Can you think of any arguments to refute Wilson's position? If so, what are they?
3. Do you believe, as Wilson suggests, that humans are short-sighted by nature? Provide at least one example to justify your answer.

WRITING ABOUT THE ARGUMENT

1. Write a critique of Wilson's argument. In your essay, analyze one of its strengths and one of its weaknesses.
2. Evaluate how you approach an argument differently when you read as a believer or as a skeptic. What does it take to turn your opinion around? Use Wilson's essay (or another reading from this book) to illustrate your argument.
3. Think about a local environment you know where a "bottleneck" may have occurred—for example, a town that suffers from crime and unemployment, a polluted creek, or something as small as a dried-up pond. What will it take for that environment to recover and become vibrant and sustainable again?

"Our Full, Unequal World"

ABOUT THE AUTHOR: JAN OTTO ANDERSSON

As a professor of economics at Åbo Akademi University in Turku, Finland, Jan Otto Andersson has researched and written about international economics, the welfare states of northern Europe, and the economics of global warming. He is the author of *Studies in the Theory of Unequal Exchange between Nations* (1976). In the following article from the summer 2005 issue of *Inroads,* Andersson argues that people in many countries, and especially in the United States, are consuming the earth's natural resources far more quickly than those resources can be replenished. Such levels are economically and ecologically unsustainable, both for the rich countries that consume the products and for the poor countries that have their resources depleted.

BEFORE YOU READ

1. Based on the headnote, what can you guess about Andersson's point of view? Do an Internet search to find more information on this author. Do you think he has a bias against the United States? Why or why not?
2. What does the title of the essay imply? What do you think its thesis might be?
3. Glance over the essay and take note of its main divisions. What do these divisions suggest about what the essay will argue?

»«

READING SELECTION

Our Full, Unequal World

1 To ecological economists, the most compelling fact is that we are living in a "full world." Rapid population growth and mass consumption have transformed humanity into a colossal user of nature's services. Our "ecological footprint"—the area we require for our consumption and waste absorption—has become so big that ecosystems are being destroyed, species are dying out, climate is changing, and people are losing the potential to pursue their traditional livelihoods. One of the most ambitious attempts to quantify all this is the *Living Planet Report,* published every two years by the World Wildlife Fund. According to the WWF's analysis, humanity's ecological footprint (EF) exceeded the biological capacity (biocapacity) of the earth by about 1985. As of the beginning of this millennium, the "ecological overshoot" is calculated at about 20 percent. . . .

2 Of course, such calculations are estimates and are subject to many uncertainties. Nevertheless, we need some measure of the pressure human consumption is generating on renewable resources and ecosystems. For all its limitations, the ecological footprint concept is better than any other practicable concept, such as energy use or material flows. Unlike alternative indicators, EF calculations make it possible to estimate the biocapacities of different types of land and sea—cropland, grazing land, forestland, and fishing grounds. The concept of biological capacity includes, first of all, the ability of the ecosystem to produce biomass—that is, the quantity of plants and other organisms that can live on a given area. Second, it incorporates the capability to absorb wastes, such as carbon dioxide emissions stemming from the use of fossil fuels. By combining them, we can estimate the hypothetical upper limit of services the biosphere can supply, a limit not to be exceeded if we want to achieve ecological sustainability.

3 Furthermore, it is possible to estimate the biocapacity of smaller areas than the globe, such as that of individual countries. It is important to assess whether countries are maintaining their biocapacities or overusing them. Are they gradually destroying their natural capital through "overshooting"? The Global Footprint Network has measured the biocapacity, the total ecological footprint and the difference—the ecological "surplus" or "deficit"—for 150 countries (see Table 1 for sample results).

4 Most countries have an ecological deficit. This applies for all densely populated industrialized countries—such as Britain, France, Germany, the Netherlands, and Israel. It is also true for countries that can afford high consumption levels thanks to the money they receive for oil exports: Iran, Saudi Arabia, and the United Arab Emirates.

5 Only some sparsely populated temperate countries—such as Australia, Canada, Finland, Russia, and several African and Latin American countries—have substantial ecological reserves. It is remarkable that the United States, with bountiful natural resources relative to its population, would need to double its territory to achieve ecological self-sufficiency. (Admittedly, the U.S. overshoot is exaggerated by use of lower global—not domestic U.S.—productivity per hectare parameters.).

6 A very troubling result is that China and India, as well as other poor countries like Bangladesh, Egypt, Ethiopia, Indonesia, Thailand, and Pakistan, have ecological deficits even though their per capita footprints are low. The ecological overshoot of these developing countries is set to increase dramatically as they try to "develop."

7 It should be noted that the land area required for the absorption of carbon dioxide emissions constitutes almost half of the EFs. For the rich countries the deficits would become significantly smaller—and would often turn into a surplus—if we excluded the imputed hectares required to absorb emissions. Since the damage from global warming may be felt anywhere in the globe, if a country has an ecological deficit it does not necessarily imply that its natural capital has been undermined.

8 The ecological footprint calculations reveal that we live not only in a full world, but also in an unequal one. An average North American consumes 15 times more renewable resources than an average Bangladeshi or Ethiopian. To sustain his or her lifestyle, a typical Western European requires six times the biocapacity of an African or Indian. If everybody on earth were to consume as much biocapacity as North Americans currently do, we would need four more globes, and at least one more even if we did not care about global warming. The major reason for the inequalities in resource use is differences in income and purchasing power per capita. In the global supermarket, the rich are deciding the uses to which the planet's land and sea areas will be put.

Ecologically Unequal Trade

9 A country's ecological footprint as displayed in Table 1 does not include the biocapacity implications of its exports: These are attributed to the importing countries. And a country's biocapacity does not include the biocapacity implications of its imports on the exporting countries. Therefore, a country showing a surplus may in fact use more than its biocapacity if it is a net EF exporter, and a country displaying a deficit may be ecologically sustainable if its net EF imports exceed its ecological deficit. We may live in a world where some countries exploit other countries ecologically by importing enough biocapacity to offset what would otherwise be excessive pressure on their own natural capital.

10 The discussion of the relationships between international trade and environmental problems has mostly focused on the possible shift of polluting industries from rich to poor countries. When looking at the world through EF glasses, however, this shift is overshadowed by the possibility that some countries may be specializing in the production and export of highly biocapacity-intensive goods, although their national ecological reserves may be overexploited.

11 There are at least three conceivable types of inequality, listed here in terms of ascending gravity:

Simple Ecologically Unequal Exchange

12 One country is a net exporter of biocapacity to another (in the form of lumber exports for example) but the exports do not cause overuse of its natural capital. This kind of ecologically unequal exchange is probably advantageous for both parties—at least in the short run—and does not constitute a direct threat to ecological sustainability. However, a country that specializes in the production of raw materials and agricultural products, which are exchanged for manufactured and probably technically advanced products, may miss out on the learning-by-doing and innovations associated with manufacturing. The relationship between two countries engaged in simple ecologically unequal exchange resembles that of town and countryside, centre and periphery.

Unilaterally Unsustainable Exchange

13 One country is a net exporter of biocapacity to another, and the exports do cause overuse of its natural capital. In the short run both countries may be better off thanks to the trade, but the natural capital of the exporting country is gradually being destroyed. In the long run this trade is unsustainable. The net exporting country must either run down its ecological reserves or change its trade in such a way that it becomes a net importer of biocapacity. To change from a net exporter to a net importer of biocapacity may be quite difficult, especially if there are already many countries dependent on imports of biocapacity from abroad, and they cling to their position as exporters of technologically advanced and high-priced products and services.

Mutually Unsustainable Exchange

14 This tragic possibility can occur if two countries engage in what Fred Hirsch called positional competition. The nature of the status position over which the countries compete may differ—it may be military, economic, or even spiritual—

but the result is similar: ecological unsustainability in both countries. Both may be using up their ecological reserves in their efforts to promote competitiveness and growth. They may also, as in the case of global warming, be destroying a global resource essential for both. Mutually unsustainable exchange implies that the stronger country is not strong enough to impose unilaterally unsustainable trade on the weaker country. The stronger country must try either to increase its relative strength further (which may lead to a further widening of its ecological footprint) or to reduce its ecological footprint (which may lead to a weakening of its relative position vis-à-vis its rival).

15 Even if ecologically unequal, trade usually increases sustainability. Through international trade, a country may import and consume resources which are scarce locally but abundant in some other part of the world. Also, temporal scarcities (e.g., a bad harvest) can be dealt with through imports.

16 However, trade tends to blur the ecological as well as the social consequences of production and consumption. If production and consumption take place locally, all parties involved can register and react to the consequences. If the relations between producers and consumers take place at a distance and are more indirect, then the links of cause and effect are less visible. Today's global economy, with very distant and indirect links between producers of primary goods and final consumers, is prone to blurring the ecological consequences of trade. Gross inequalities in purchasing power increase the risks of overexploitation of biocapacity in poor areas.

17 In an unequal world, rich countries can import biocapacity and sink capacity from poorer countries. Inhabitants of a rich country may think that their lifestyles are sustainable, since the ecological capital of their own country is not eroding. They may even believe that becoming richer is the best way to overcome ecological overshooting and blame the poor countries because they are not able to sustain their ecosystems. This rich-country illusion may prove fatal for the world. Poor countries are forced to opt for economic growth to get out of the ecological trap, whereas rich countries wrongly uphold the image that their lifestyles and further increases in consumption are sustainable.

18 The more the natural resources of the earth are overexploited, the more likely it becomes that simple ecologically unequal exchange will be transformed into unilaterally and even mutually unsustainable exchange. Although trade in money terms may look profitable and advantageous to all, this monetary success may blur imminent as well as manifest ecological imbalances.

The Extractive Economy Trap

19 At least since the mercantilist era, there has been a conceptual distinction between economies that export unprocessed natural products, "matter," and economies that export manufactured goods, requiring "labor." According to the mercantilist mindset it was beneficial to import "matter" and to export "labor." Although liberal economists since Adam Smith have declared this distinction irrelevant, it has continued to have political influence. To export unprocessed natural products has been seen as a sign of backwardness and peripheral status in the world economy. To industrialize, to specialize in the production and export of technically advanced goods and services, is to achieve high "international competitiveness" and become part of the developed "center."

20 An economy based on the extraction and export of raw materials runs several risks. The source may be depleted or the price of the raw material may collapse as a result of changes in technology or consumption patterns. The stream of income from exploiting the natural resource may crowd out the development of other productive sectors. Politics in the country may focus exclusively on the dictates of the particular resource sector and on the control over the income stream it enables, increasing the risk of coups d'état, foreign intervention, and civil war. Furthermore, an extractive economy often misses

out on the learning-by-doing that an industrial economy normally experiences. Even the resource extraction sector becomes dependent on knowhow and machinery produced in the developed center.

21 A country that has become an exporter of "matter" may find that its peripheral backward status is accentuated and that it has no other options. Its economically weak position may thus worsen its ecological sustainability, which may further undermine its economic potential. Countries experiencing a combination of these risks may fall into an "extractive economy trap."

22 Although he does not use the term, Stephen Bunker of the University of Wisconsin has given a vivid description of the causes of this trap. The most dramatic of Bunker's historical examples involve countries extracting some specific mineral, plant, or creature in an activity that can only be sustained temporarily. In due course, the buffalo are exterminated, the fish stocks depleted, the gold reserves exhausted. However, we can extend the analysis to situations where the ecological system becomes overexploited: where there is an "ecological overshoot" that is not compensated for by imports of ecological footprints from abroad. A country that specializes in the extraction/production of goods that require much biocapacity is subjected to an ecologically unequal exchange. At first, this exchange may be of the "simple" type, but as the extractive economy trap closes, the exchange may become unilaterally unsustainable.

23 There are, however, some examples of countries that have managed to develop despite their position as net exporters of natural products. One such country is Canada. Another is my home country, Finland.

Finland: Avoiding the Trap

24 How did Finland manage to bypass the traps connected with being an economy based on exports of "matter"? In Bunker's vocabulary, how did Finland make a successful transition from "extraction" to "production"? Bunker describes a few cases in Europe and North America where an economy based on extraction has evolved into a productive centre. He puts forward several factors to explain such exceptions:

25 1. Since capital tends to concentrate, the possibility for productive economies to emerge from extraction diminishes as capitalism develops. Also, as transport technologies improve and lower the costs of bulk movements, the gains from reducing bulk through processing close to the extraction location diminish, making a transition less likely.

26 2. The potential for a transition depends on the spatial location and the natural, physical characteristics of the resource. The closer to an existing productive center extraction takes place, the better the chances for industrial development. The easier it is to deplete or substitute for the resource, the greater the risks that an extractive economy will be unable to make the transition.

27 3. The power of the local population to confront extractive capitalists is crucial. Are the people able to resist the destruction of their environmental base and the exploitation of local labor power? How large a share of the extractive rents is appropriated by the locals and their state?

28 Finland has been fortunate on all fronts. Its industrial takeoff took place early, at the end of the 19th century, when it became a major producer of pulp and paper. Between 1913 and 1950, most industrial economies experienced a widening per capita GDP gap with the United States. There were only three exceptions: Sweden, Norway, and Finland. That Finland belonged to this group is remarkable, since it was the victim of several wars and a large loss of territory, leading to a resettlement of almost a tenth of its population.

29 Finland's geographical location between Sweden and Russia has been crucial. The close cultural links with Sweden have facilitated Finnish emulation of Swedish technological and social advances. Before 1917 Finland had a special relationship with Russia, which aided the export to Russia of processed goods. A similar

relation arose after World War II. Finland was the only "Western" country that traded extensively with the Soviet Union.

30 Forests are a renewable resource. Another advantage of forests is that they have several potential uses. They have been an important energy source. Houses, tools, and ships have been made of wood. Wood can be refined into necessities such as tar or paper. Cutting trees is best done in wintertime, when there are few other employment opportunities for a rural labor force. Forestry therefore is a good complement to farming. Peasant households were able to finance small investments and the education of their children by cutting and selling some of their forests. Regulation of forestry was jointly influenced by the interests of the exporters of tar, sawn products, and paper and the well-organized forest-owning peasantry (involved in cooperative manufacturing based on wood).

31 Bunker's third factor—the power of the local population to confront extractive capitalists—has played a major role. The peasantry managed to avoid serfdom both during the Swedish era and after Finland became a grand duchy under the Russian Czar in 1809. The peasantry constituted the "fourth estate" alongside the nobility, the clergy, and the bourgeoisie. Peasant ownership of the forests was actually shielded by the state. In northeastern Finland, with few peasants but large remote forest areas, the state controlled the resource. Thanks to the dominant Lutheran influence and to a nationalist movement that relied on education as a major tool, the peasantry was largely literate. Democracy at the national and local levels was achieved relatively early, and did not break down despite the traumatic events of the 1930s and 1940s.

32 Finland is an exception to the rule that extraction for export leads to ecologically unequal exchange and even to ecologically and socially unsustainable exchange. However, there are few resource-dependent countries today able to emulate Finland. Latecomers in terms of technological development must compete fiercely with other low-wage producers.

The Importance of Ecological Economics

33 Standard economics focuses on efficiency, defined in terms of today's willingness to pay for goods and services. Environmental economics extends this thinking to environmental problems, and tries to correct for the lack of functioning markets for environmental services. However, focusing on efficiency, so defined, means that questions of justice and sustainability are set aside.

34 Ecological economics differs in its approach from both standard and environmental economics. It puts sustainability at the center of analysis, and it focuses on distributive justice globally as well as between present and future generations. When we look at international trade from the standpoint of an ecological economist, we perceive problems that are not confronted by either environmental or standard economists. Concepts used in this article, such as "a full world," "ecologically unequal exchange," and "unsustainable trade," are barely comprehensible to most economists. On the other hand, a person accustomed to calculating in terms of biophysical quantities such as "ecological footprints" can easily understand how trade that in money terms is advantageous to all parties may be questionable from the point of view of sustainability or distributive justice.

35 Most ecological economists think of sustainability in the "strong" sense of the term: We are not allowed to endanger the natural capital passed on to future generations. We cannot make up for the destruction of environmental capital by improving our human and human-made physical capital. Future generations have the same rights to nature's services as we have. Furthermore, other living beings may have rights that we are not allowed to ignore.

36 For both standard and environmental economists, natural capital is just one factor of production comparable to others such as human capital (labor of varying skill levels) or human-made physical capital (buildings and equipment).

In principle, they believe it possible to compensate for eroding natural capital by improving education or investing in new machines. Those among them who have pondered the costs and benefits of preventing global warming mostly believe that we should not incur the costs of preventing change. Since future generations will be better off than we are, there will be enough human and human-made capital to compensate for a worsening of the climate. Ecological economists call this belief in the possibility—and even desirability—of substituting nonnatural for natural capital as "weak sustainability."

37 In this article, sustainability has been discussed in ecological terms: Overexploitation of our biological capacity implies, quite simply, unsustainability. Eroding ecosystems and causing global warming cannot be justified by hypothetical compensation. The long-run environmental consequences of our present trajectory are almost impossible to assess, but since they may be catastrophic, we should not test the ecological limits lightly.

38 The countries of the world today can be ranked according to their use of global resources. Those with the biggest ecological footprint are generally those with the highest standard of living and the most competitive economies. But does this imply—as most economists believe—that all should strive for the way of life of those on the top? Given a full world subject to ecological overshoot, the answer is far from obvious.

What Are "Ecological Footprints"?

39 The **ecological footprint** is an estimate of how much biologically productive land and water area an individual, a city, a country, a region, or humanity requires to produce the resources it consumes and to absorb the waste it generates, using prevailing technology. This land and water area can be anywhere in the world. Ecological footprints are calculated for each country. This calculation includes the resources contained within the goods and services that are consumed by people living in that country as well as the associated waste. Resources consumed for the production of goods and services exported to another country are added to the footprint of the country where the goods and services are actually consumed, rather than the country where they are produced.

40 The ecological footprint is measured in global hectares. A **global hectare** is one hectare of biologically productive space with world average productivity. Since productivity changes over time, so does the estimated total of global hectares for the planet. The latest estimate, for 2001, is 11.3 billion global hectares. (This is equivalent to roughly one quarter of the actual surface area of the planet. The productivity of particular geographic regions obviously varies—from fertile farmland to forest to desert to ocean. In calculating the planet's estimated total of 11.3 billion global hectares, the productivity of actual hectares has been adjusted.)

41 **Biocapacity** (biological capacity) is the total usable biological production capacity in a given year of a biologically productive area—for example, that within a country. It can be expressed in global hectares. Global biocapacity available per person requires dividing the 11.3 billion global hectares of biologically productive area by the number of people alive—6.15 billion in 2001. This gives the average biocapacity per person on the planet: 1.8 global hectares.

42 **Bioproductivity** (biological productivity) is equal to biological production per hectare per year. Biological productivity is typically measured in terms of annual biomass accumulation.

43 We can use the concept of ecological footprints to estimate how much land and sea area each individual, each country, or humanity as a whole needs to satisfy its present consumption requirements. In doing this, we can use either national productivities or average global productivities per hectare. When estimating, for instance, how much land is needed to produce one tonne of sugar, we can use the average yield per hectare in one country—say, Cuba—or use the global average yield in all countries producing

sugar. Since consumption goods can be bought from any part of the world—today we have a "global factory" and a "global supermarket" at our disposal—it is logical to use global average yields when estimating the pressure an individual or a country causes. However, when we measure the ecological pressures on a particular area, such as a country, it is preferable to use local rather than global yields.

44 When interpreting the results of ecological footprint calculations and their relation to biological capacity, we need to be careful. On the one hand, we may underestimate the pressures, since we assume that present production is achieved in a sustainable way. We are also unable to take into consideration all waste absorption requirements. On the other hand, we may overestimate the pressures—for example, by not being able to account for the multiple uses of land and water. The use of global yield averages when assessing biocapacities may overestimate the pressures in relatively high-yielding regions of the planet and underestimate pressures in low-yielding regions. The low-yielding regions may have a potential for significant future productivity improvements based on existing knowledge.

TABLE 1 National Footprints and Biocapacities, 2001

	Population (millions)	Ecological Footprint	Biocapacity	Ecological Surplus or Deficit
		(global hectares per person)		
World	**6148.1**	**2.2**	**1.8**	**20.4**
Argentina	37.5	2.6	6.7	4.2
Australia	19.4	7.7	19.2	11.5
Bangladesh	140.9	0.6	0.3	−0.3
Brazil	174.0	2.2	10.2	8.0
Canada	31.0	6.4	14.4	8.0
China	1292.6	1.5	0.8	−0.8
Egypt	69.1	1.5	0.5	−1.0
Ethiopia	67.3	0.7	0.5	−0.2
Finland	5.2	7.0	12.4	5.4
France	59.6	5.8	3.1	−2.8
Germany	82.3	4.8	1.9	−2.9
India	1033.4	0.8	0.4	−0.4
Indonesia	214.4	1.2	1.0	−0.2

(*continued*)

TABLE 1 National Footprints and Biocapacities, 2001 (*Continued*)

	Population (millions)	Ecological Footprint	Biocapacity	Ecological Surplus or Deficit
		(global hectares per person)		
Israel	6.2	5.3	0.4	−4.9
Iran	67.2	2.1	0.7	−1.4
Japan	127.3	4.3	0.8	−3.6
Netherlands	16.0	4.7	0.8	−4.0
Nigeria	117.8	1.2	1.0	−0.2
Pakistan	146.3	0.7	0.4	−0.3
Russia	144.9	4.4	6.9	2.6
Saudi Arabia	22.8	4.4	0.9	−3.4
Thailand	61.6	1.6	1.0	−0.6
Turkey	69.3	2.0	1.4	−0.6
United Arab Emirates	2.9	9.9	1.0	−8.9
United Kingdom	59.1	5.4	1.5	−3.9
United States	288.0	9.5	4.9	−4.7

Source: Global Footprint Network, <http://www.footprintnetwork.org/gfn_sub.php?content=footprint_hectares>.

THINKING ABOUT THE ARGUMENT

1. In your own words, what is "sustainability"? According to the author, what is the difference between ecological and economic sustainability?
2. Why does Andersson think that Finland has achieved sustainability on both economic and ecological levels? Why does he think the United States has not achieved this?
3. In the author's opinion, what is wrong with the relationship between rich and poor countries (where the rich countries import large quantities of natural resources from the poor countries)?
4. What is "ecologically unequal trade"? What are the three types mentioned in the article?
5. Does the author explain a problem, a solution, or both? Explain.

Responding to the Argument

1. Do you agree that the United States is ecologically unsustainable? Economically unsustainable? Why do you think so?
2. What might the author mean when he says "capital tends to concentrate"? Why would that be a problem?
3. Name a place you know—a town, a farm, a factory, or another location—that you think is "unsustainable." (The resources involved need not be only raw materials. For example, a barbershop in a small town where almost everyone was bald would not be sustainable, because there would not be enough "raw material"—hair—to keep the barber in business.) Explain why you think this place is unsustainable, both on economic and ecological levels.
4. Name a place that is "sustainable," and explain why you think it is sustainable.

Writing about the Argument

1. Write an essay explaining what changes, if any, the United States should make in its approach toward the environment.
2. Select a local environment, such as your hometown. Are there ways that this local environment is unsustainable? Explain.
3. Write a letter to the editor of your local newspaper suggesting one major change that your neighborhood, city, or state should implement to make the environment more sustainable.
4. Refute Andersson's argument. Explain why the United States is a sustainable environment.
5. Refute Anderson's argument. Explain why the trade policies of the United States in dealing with small, poor countries are fair.

"Environmentalism as Religion Run Amok"

About the Author: Michael Crichton

Michael Crichton is a best-selling author who turned to writing to put himself through medical school. His novels include *The Andromeda Strain* (1969), *The Terminal Man* (1972), *Congo* (1980), *Jurassic Park* (1990), and *Sphere* (1987). He has directed a number of movies, including *Westworld* (1973), *Coma* (1978), and *The Great Train Robbery* (1979), which he also wrote. He is also the creator of the television series *ER*. His latest novel is *State of Fear* (2005). This piece first appeared in *USA Today* in March 2004.

Before You Read

1. What do you know about the author? Have you read any of his books, or have you seen any movies based on his books? What is your opinion of him? Do you think he is qualified to comment on this topic? Why or why not?

2. Compare Crichton to Wilson. Which author do you feel is the most qualified? Which author do you feel is the most unbiased? How do these two aspects—qualifications and bias—affect the way you respond to what an author has written?
3. What does Crichton's title suggest to you? What does it suggest about his overall claim? About the tone of his piece?
4. Glance over the article. Try to get a sense of what the main divisions of the article might be. List them if you can.

Environmentalism as Religion Run Amok

1 The greatest challenge facing mankind is to distinguish reality from fantasy, truth from propaganda. Perceiving the truth always has been a dilemma, but in the Information Age—or, as I think of it, the Disinformation Age—it takes on a special urgency and importance. We must decide daily whether the threats we face are real or not, and whether the solutions we are offered will do any good. Every one of us has a sense of the world, and we all know that this sense is in part supplied by the people around us and the society we live in; in part generated by our own emotional state, which we project outward; and in part results from actual perceptions of the world. In short, our struggle to determine what is valid is the need to decide which of our perceptions are genuine and which are false.

2 As an example of this challenge to mankind, I want to talk about environmentalism. In order not to be misunderstood, I need to be perfectly clear that I believe it is incumbent on us to live our lives in a way that takes into account all the consequences of our actions, including those to other people and the environment. I believe it is important to act in ways that are sympathetic to the biosphere. I feel the world has genuine difficulties and that they can and should be improved. Yet, I also think that deciding what constitutes responsible action is immensely complicated, and the results of our deeds very often are hard to know in advance. I suppose our past record of environmental action is discouraging, to put it mildly, because even our best intended efforts often have gone awry. Moreover, we do not recognize our previous failures or face them squarely—and I think I know why.

3 While studying anthropology in college, one of the things we learned was that certain human social structures always resurface. They cannot be eliminated. One of those is religion. It is said we live in a secular society in which many people—the best and most enlightened—do not believe in any creed. However, you cannot eliminate religion from the psyche of mankind. If you suppress it in one form, it merely reemerges in another. You may not believe in God, but you still have to believe in something that gives meaning to your life and shapes your sense of the world. Such a belief is religious.

4 Today, one of the most powerful religions in the Western World is environmentalism. It seems to be the faith of choice for urban atheists. Why do I say it is a religion? Well, just look carefully at the beliefs. What you see is a perfect 21st-century mapping of traditional Judeo-Christian dogma and myths. For example, there is an initial Eden, a Paradise, a state of innocence, and unity in nature; there is a fall from grace into a state of pollution as a result of eating from the tree of knowledge, and, as a result of our actions, there is a judgment day coming. We all are energy sinners, doomed to die, unless we seek deliverance, which now is called sustainability. Sustainability is salvation in the church of the environment, just as organic food is its Communion.

5 Eden, the fall of man, the loss of grace, the coming doomsday—these are deeply held mythic structures. They are profoundly conservative concepts. They even may be hardwired in the brain. I certainly do not wish to talk anyone out of them, just as I have no desire to dissuade anybody out of a belief that Jesus Christ is the Son of God who rose from the dead. The reason that I have no wish to debate these convictions is that I know that I cannot. These are not facts that can be argued; these are issues of faith.

6 So it is, sadly, with environmentalism. Increasingly, it seems, facts are not necessary because the tenets of environmentalism are all about belief. It is about whether you are going to be a sinner or saved, one of the people on the side of salvation or on the side of doom, one of us or one of them. Am I exaggerating to make a point? I am afraid not. Because we understand a lot more about the world than we did forty or fifty years ago, our new knowledge base is not really supportive of certain core environmental myths, yet they refuse to die. Let us examine some of those notions.

7 There is no Eden. There never was. When was that Garden of the wonderful mythic past? Was it the time when infant mortality was 80 percent, when four children in five died of disease before the age of five? Was it a time when one woman in six died in childbirth; when the average lifespan was forty, as it was in the United States a century ago; when plagues swept across the planet, killing millions in a stroke; when millions more starved to death? Was that Paradise?

8 What about indigenous peoples, living in a state of harmony in an Eden-like environment? Well, they never did. On this continent, the newly arrived travelers who crossed the land bridge from Asia almost immediately set about wiping out hundreds of species of large animals, and they did this several thousand years before the white man showed up to accelerate the process. What was the condition of life? Loving, peaceful, harmonious? Hardly. The people of the New World lived in a state of constant warfare—generations of hatred and perpetual battles. The warlike tribes of this continent are famous even today: the Comanche, Sioux, Apache, Mohawk, Aztec, Toltec, Inca. Some of them practiced infanticide and human sacrifice. Those clans that were not fiercely warlike were exterminated or learned to build their villages high in the cliffs to attain some measure of safety.

9 How about the human condition in the rest of the world? The Maori of New Zealand committed massacres regularly. The Dyaks of Borneo were headhunters. The Polynesians, living in surroundings as close to Eden as one can imagine, fought continually, and created a society so hideously restrictive that you could lose your life for stepping in the footprint of a chief. It was the Polynesians who gave us the very concept of taboo, as well as the word itself. The noble savage is a fantasy. That anyone still believes it, 200 years after philosopher Jean Jacques Rousseau, shows the tenacity of religious myths and their ability to hang on in the face of centuries of factual contradiction. There even was an academic movement, during the latter twentieth century, that claimed that cannibalism was a white man's invention to demonize indigenous races. (Only academics could fight such a battle.) It was some thirty years before professors finally agreed that yes, the ritualistic consumption of human flesh indeed does occur. Meanwhile, all during this time, New Guinea highlanders continued to eat the brains of their enemies, until they finally were made to understand that they risked kuru, a fatal neurological disease. Remember, too, that the African Pygmies have one of the highest murder rates on the planet. Conversely, the gentle Tasaday of the Philippines turned out to be a publicity stunt, a nonexistent entity.

10 In short, the romantic view of the natural world as a blissful Eden is only held by people who have no actual experience of nature. Those who do are not romantic about it. They may hold spiritual beliefs about the world around them;

they may have a sense of the unity of nature or the aliveness of all living things, but they still kill animals and uproot plants in order to eat and to survive. If they do not, they will die.

11 If you put yourself in nature, if only for a matter of days, you quickly will be disabused of all your romantic fantasies. Take a trek through the jungles of Borneo, and in short order you will have festering sores on your skin and bugs all over your body, biting in your hair and crawling up your nose and into your ears. You will have infections and sickness, and if you are not with somebody who knows what he or she is doing, you very rapidly will starve to death. Chances are that even in the jungles of Borneo you will not experience nature so directly since you will have covered your entire body with DEET.

12 The truth is, almost nobody wants to experience real nature. What people desire is to spend a week or two in a cabin in the woods, with screens on the windows. They want a simplified life for a while, a nice river rafting trip for a few days, with somebody else doing the cooking. Nobody wants to go back to nature in any real sense, and no one does. It is all talk, and as the years go on and the world population grows increasingly urban, it is uninformed talk. Farmers know of what they speak; city people do not. They just have their fantasies.

13 One way to measure the prevalence of fantasy is to note the number of people who die because they have not the least knowledge of how nature truly is. They stand beside wild animals, like buffalo, for a picture and get trampled; they climb a mountain in dicey weather, without the proper gear, and freeze to death. They drown in the surf on their holiday because they cannot conceive the real power of what we blithely call "the force of nature." They have seen the ocean, but they never have been in it.

14 The television generation expects nature to act the way they picture it. They think all life experiences can be TiVo-ed. The notion that the natural world obeys its own rules and does not give a damn about their expectations comes as a massive shock. Well-to-do, educated individuals in an urban environment experience the ability to fashion their daily lives as they wish. They buy clothes that suit their taste and decorate their apartments as they like. Within limits, they can contrive a daily urban world that pleases them. The natural world is not so malleable, however. On the contrary, it will demand that you adapt to it—and if you do not, you will die. It is a harsh, powerful, and unforgiving world that most urban Westerners never have experienced.

15 Many years ago, I was trekking in the Karakoram Mountains of northern Pakistan, when my group came to a freezing cold, glacial river, which was running very fast, although it was not deep—maybe two-and-a-half or three feet. Nevertheless, my guide set out ropes for people to hold as they crossed, and everybody proceeded, one at a time, with extreme care. I asked the guide what was the big deal about crossing a three-foot-deep river? "Well," he replied, "supposing you fell and suffered a compound fracture." We were four days trek from the last big town, where there was a radio. Even if the guide went back double-time to get help, it still would be at least three days before he could return with a helicopter, if one were available. In that time, I probably would be dead from my injuries.

16 Now, let us return to religion. If Eden is a fantasy that never existed, and mankind was never noble, kind, nor loving, and we did not fall from grace, what about the rest of the religious tenets? What about salvation, sustainability, and judgment day? What about the coming environmental doom from fossil fuels and global warming if we all do not get down on our knees and conserve every day? Yet, something has been left off the doomsday list lately. Although the preachers of conservatism have been yelling about population for fifty years, over the last decade, world population seems to have taken an unexpected turn. Fertility rates are falling almost everywhere. As a result, over the course of

my lifetime, the thoughtful predictions for total world population have gone from a high of 20 billion to 15 billion to 11 billion—which was the United Nations estimate around 1990—to 9 billion today and, soon, perhaps less. There are some individuals who now think that world population will peak in 2050, and, that by 2100, there will be fewer people than there are today. Is this a reason to rejoice, to say hallelujah? Certainly not. Without a pause, we hear about the coming crisis of world economy from a shrinking population, or the impending predicament of an aging population. Nobody anywhere will say that the core fears expressed for most of my life have turned out to be false. As we have moved into the future, these doomsday visions vanished, like a mirage in the desert. They never were there, although they still appear on the horizon, as mirages do.

17 Okay, so the preachers made a mistake. They got one prediction wrong; they are human. So what? Only it is not just one prediction; it is a whole slew of them. We are running out of oil. We are running out of global resources. Famed biologist Paul Ehrlich projected that 60 million Americans would die of starvation in the 1980s. Forty-thousand species become extinct every year. Half of all species on the planet will be extinct by the year 2000. On and on and on it goes.

18 With so many past failures, one might think that environmental predictions would become more cautious. Not if it is a religion. Remember, the nut on the sidewalk carrying the placard who predicts the end of the world does not quit when the world does not cease on the day he expects. He just changes his placard, sets a new doomsday date, and goes back to walking the streets. One of the defining features of religion is that beliefs are not troubled by facts, because they have nothing to do with them.

19 I can list some facts for you. I know you have not read any of these in the newspaper because newspapers do not report them. I can tell you that DDT is not a carcinogen, did not cause birds to die, and never should have been banned. The people who outlawed it knew that it was not toxic and halted its use anyway. The DDT ban has caused the loss of tens of millions of people, mostly children, whose deaths are directly attributable to a callous, technologically advanced Western society that promoted the new cause of environmentalism by pushing a fantasy about a pesticide, and thus irrevocably harmed the Third World. Banning DDT is one of the most disgraceful episodes in the twentieth-century history of America.

20 Secondhand smoke is not a health hazard to anyone and never was, and the Environmental Protection Agency always has known this. The evidence for global warming is far weaker than its proponents ever would admit. The percentage of U.S. land area that is taken up by urbanization, including cities and roads, is five percent. The Sahara desert is shrinking, and the ice in Antarctica is increasing. A blue-ribbon panel in *Science* magazine concluded that there is no known technology that will enable us to halt the rise of carbon dioxide in the twenty-first century—not wind, solar, or even nuclear power. A totally new technology—like nuclear fusion—is necessary, otherwise nothing can be done. In the meantime, all efforts are a waste of time. That was reported when the United Nations Intergovernmental Panel on Climate Change stated that alternative technologies existed that could control greenhouse gases.

21 I can, with a great deal of time, give you the factual basis for these views and cite the appropriate sources. These are not wacko magazines, but the most prestigious science journals currently in print. Yet such references probably would not impact more than a handful, because the convictions of a religion are not dependent on facts, but rather are matters of unshakable faith.

22 Most of us have had the experience of interacting with religious fundamentalists, and we understand that one of the problems is that they

have no perspective on themselves. They never recognize that their way of thinking is just one of many other possible alternatives which may be equally useful or good. On the contrary, they believe their way is the only course, and everyone else is wrong. They are in the business of salvation, and they want to help you to see things in the right way. They want to help you be saved. They are inherently rigid and completely uninterested in opposing points of view.

23 I want to argue that now is the time for us to make a major shift in our thinking about the planet, similar to that which occurred around the first Earth Day in 1970, when this awareness was first heightened. This time around, though, we need to get environmentalism out of the sphere of religion. We have to stop the mythic fantasies and halt the doomsday predictions. We need to start doing hard science instead.

24 There are two reasons we must get rid of the religion of environmentalism. First, we need an environmental movement, and such a movement is not very effective if it is conducted as a religion. We know from history that faith tends to kill people, and environmentalism already has decimated somewhere between 10 million to 30 million people since the 1970s. That is not a good record. Environmentalism needs to be rational, flexible, and based in objective and verifiable science. Moreover, it must be apolitical. To mix natural concerns with the frantic fantasies that people have about one political party or another is to miss the truth—that there is very little difference between the parties on this subject, except for pandering rhetoric. The effort to promote effective legislation is not helped by thinking that the Democrats will save us and the Republicans will not. Political history is more complicated than that. Never forget which president started the EPA: archconservative Richard Nixon, a staunch Republican. Also keep in mind which president sold the federal oil leases, that allowed drilling in Santa Barbara, California: Great Society architect Lyndon Johnson, a prototypical Democrat. So get politics out of your thinking about the environment.

25 The second reason to abandon environmental religion is more pressing. Fundamentalists think they know it all, but the unhappy truth of Planet Earth is that we are dealing with incredibly complex, evolving systems, and we usually are not certain how best to proceed. Those who are certain are demonstrating their personality type, or their belief system, not the state of their knowledge. Our record in the past—for example, in managing national parks—is humiliating. Our fifty-year effort at forest fire suppression is a well-intentioned disaster from which our forests may never recover. We should be humble, deeply humble, in the face of what we are trying to accomplish. We should be trying various methods, open-minded about assessing the results of our efforts, flexible about balancing needs. Religion does none of these things.

26 How will we manage to get environmentalism out of the clutches of religion and back to a scientific discipline? The answer is simple: We have to institute a far more stringent set of requirements for what constitutes knowledge in the environmental realm. I am thoroughly sick of politicized so-called facts that simply are not true. It is not that these "facts" are exaggerations of an underlying truth. Nor is it that certain organizations are spinning their case to present it in the strongest possible way. Not at all. What more and more groups are doing is putting out blatant lies; falsehoods that they know to be false.

27 This trend began with the DDT campaign, and it persists to this day. At the moment, the EPA is hopelessly politicized. It probably is best to shut it down and start over. What we need is something much closer to the Food and Drug Administration, an organization that will be ruthless about acquiring verifiable results, fund identical research projects to more than one group, and make everybody in this field agree to honest standards.

28 In the end, science offers us the only way out of politics. If we allow science to become politi-

cized, we are lost. We will enter the Internet version of the Dark Ages, an era of shifting fears and wild prejudices, transmitted to people who do not know any better. That is not a good future for the human race. That is our past. So it is time to abandon the religion of environmentalism and return to the science of environmentalism, and base our public policy decisions firmly on that.

Thinking about the Argument

1. How does Crichton establish authority in the first paragraph? How does his tone help hold his audience? How does it compare with Wilson's first paragraph?
2. What is Crichton's central claim? Is it stated more or less strongly than Wilson's central claim? Explain.
3. How does the author define religion? How does environmentalism fit into this definition?
4. Why do you think Crichton says that environmentalism is "the faith of choice for urban atheists"?
5. How does this definition become central to his argument?
6. Why does the author draw parallels between Eden and environmental sustainability? (What is "wrong" with the idea that primitive societies are pacifistic and in tune with nature?)
7. Does Crichton address any alternative arguments? Assess the effectiveness of his refutation.
8. Why does the author think we must get rid of the "religion" of environmentalism?

Responding to the Argument

1. Do you agree that it is possible to see environmentalism as a religion? Why or why not? What might this definition imply about fanaticism?
2. After reading Crichton's essay, has your opinion of Wilson's (or Andersson's) argument changed? Why?
3. Do you believe environmentalism is as fanatical and ineffective as the author states? Defend your answer.
4. Consider the author's evidence. Without knowing for certain, would you guess that it is selective? If you wanted to convince your audience that Crichton (or Wilson or Andersson, for that matter) had distorted the facts, how would you go about it?
5. Of the three arguments you read in this section, which did you find the most engaging to read? The most effective? Which came closest to changing your mind? Explain.

Writing about the Argument

1. The view represented by Crichton and that represented by Wilson (and, with some differences, by Andersson) hinges on the question of whether nature can be intelligently controlled (or at least held at bay to some extent). Do humans control their environments? Do their environments control them? Is the reality somewhere in between? Use concrete evidence to support your claim(s).

2. Some environmentalist groups—for example, Earth First!—have been known to engage in terrorist tactics. For example, they have burned down homes built in areas that they want preserved. After conducting some research, write an argument either criticizing or supporting environmentalist groups that step outside of the law.
3. Write an argument comparing two of the essays in this section. Take note of the strengths and weaknesses of each.
4. Write an argument critiquing Crichton's essay. You may either support his position or explain why he is wrong.

Issue 2: Artificial Intelligence

Online Study Center
Prepare for Class
Artificial Intelligence

In the 1950s, some scientists said that humans would never reach the moon because the laws of physics made it impossible. Only about a generation ago, cloning was considered to reside firmly in the realm of science fiction. Today scientists and their corporate employers are pursuing another formerly impossible goal—artificial intelligence (AI) technology. This research continues in two areas: weak AI and strong AI. Weak AI already exists in the form of software that is able to recognize human speech, outsmart a video game player, translate language in real time, and simulate human vision. These applications are limited because they react as if they were intelligent, even though they have no consciousness behind them. Strong AI would have a human level of intelligence. Some computer scientists believe that this technology is only a few decades away from realization. Others, who do not believe that computer self-awareness is possible, are nevertheless troubled about the implications that nanotechnology and human/computer interfaces may have in terms of redefining what it means to be human.

CONSIDERING THE ISSUE OF ARTIFICIAL INTELLIGENCE

Questions being debated include the following:

1. With so many people already unemployed, do we want computers that may take away even more jobs?
2. If artificially intelligent machines have the capability to make their own decisions, who is responsible if a machine makes a bad decision?
3. Is it ethical to model a machine on human brains with the purpose of creating a human-like intelligence?
4. If artificial intelligence develops a consciousness, is it then a "person"? Does it have rights?

READING SELECTION

"An Inexorable Emergence"

About the Author: Ray Kurzweil

Ray Kurzweil is an inventor, entrepreneur, and author on the forefront of the "transhuman" movement. He believes that within the next century computers will achieve sentience and will merge with humans through artificial intelligence, nanotechnology, and genetic engineering. Kurzweil has received numerous honors, including being inducted into the National Inventors Hall of Fame and receiving the National Medal of Technology. His books include *The Age of Intelligent Machines* (1990), *The Age of Spiritual Machines* (1999), *Fantastic Voyage: Live Long Enough to Live Forever* (with Terry Grossman, M.D., 2004), and *The Singularity Is Near: When Humans Transcend Biology* (2005). The following article is excerpted from *The Age of Spiritual Machines.*

Before You Read

1. Do you believe that "strong" AI is possible? Explain your answer.
2. If strong AI is achieved, will it be beneficial, dangerous, or somewhere in between? Why do you think so?
3. What do the titles of Kurzweil's books suggest to you?
4. Based on what the headnote says about the author's credentials, do you believe that he is a reliable and credible source of information? Why do you think this?
5. Based on the author's background, the article's title, and a scan of the article, what do you think Kurzweil is going to say? What divisions might his argument include?

An Inexorable Emergence

1 The gambler had not expected to be here. But on reflection, he thought he had shown some kindness in his time. And this place was even more beautiful and satisfying than he had imagined. Everywhere there were magnificent crystal chandeliers, the finest handmade carpets, the most sumptuous foods, and, yes, the most beautiful women, who seemed intrigued with their new heaven mate. He tried his hand at roulette, and amazingly his number came up time after time. He tried the gaming tables, and his luck was nothing short of remarkable: He won game after game. Indeed his winnings were causing quite a stir, attracting much excitement from the attentive staff, and from the beautiful women.

2 This continued day after day, week after week, with the gambler winning every game, accumulating bigger and bigger earnings. Everything was going his way. He just kept on winning. And week after week, month after month, the gambler's streak of success remained unbreakable.

3 After a while, this started to get tedious. The gambler was getting restless; the winning was starting to lose its meaning. Yet nothing changed. He just kept on winning every game, until one day, the now anguished gambler turned to the angel who seemed to be in charge and said that he couldn't take it anymore. Heaven was not for him after all. He had figured he was destined for the "other place" nonetheless, and indeed that is where he wanted to be.

4 "But this is the other place," came the reply.

5 That is my recollection of an episode of *The Twilight Zone*[1] that I saw as a young child. I don't recall the title, but I would call it "Be Careful

What You Wish For." As this engaging series was wont to do, it illustrated one of the paradoxes of human nature: we like to solve problems, but we don't want them all solved, not too quickly, anyway. We are more attached to the problems than to the solutions.

6 Take death, for example. A great deal of our effort goes into avoiding it. We make extraordinary efforts to delay it, and indeed often consider its intrusion a tragic event. Yet we would find it hard to live without it. Death gives meaning to our lives. It gives importance and value to time. Time would become meaningless if there were too much of it. If death were indefinitely put off, the human psyche would end up, well, like the gambler in *The Twilight Zone* episode.

7 We do not yet have this predicament. We have no shortage today of either death or human problems. Few observers feel that the twentieth century has left us with too much of a good thing. There is growing prosperity, fueled not incidentally by information technology, but the human species is still challenged by issues and difficulties not altogether different than those with which it has struggled from the beginning of its recorded history.

8 The twenty-first century will be different. The human species, along with the computational technology it created, will be able to solve age-old problems of need, if not desire, and will be in a position to change the nature of mortality in a postbiological future. Do we have the psychological capacity for all the good things that await us? Probably not. That, however, might change as well.

9 Before the next century is over, human beings will no longer be the most intelligent or capable type of entity on the planet. Actually, let me take that back. The truth of that last statement depends on how we define human. And here we see one profound difference between these two centuries: The primary political and philosophical issue of the next century will be the definition of who we are.[2]

10 But I am getting ahead of myself. This last century has seen enormous technological change and the social upheavals that go along with it, which few pundits circa 1899 foresaw. The pace of change is accelerating and has been since the inception of invention . . . (this acceleration is an inherent feature of technology). The result will be far greater transformations in the first two decades of the twenty-first century than we saw in the entire twentieth century. However, to appreciate the inexorable logic of where the twenty-first century will bring us, we have to go back and start with the present.

Transition to the Twenty-First Century

11 Computers today exceed human intelligence in a broad variety of intelligent yet narrow domains such as playing chess, diagnosing certain medical conditions; buying and selling stocks, and guiding cruise missiles. Yet human intelligence overall remains far more supple and flexible. Computers are still unable to describe the objects on a crowded kitchen table, write a summary of a movie, tie a pair of shoelaces, tell the difference between a dog and a cat (although this feat, I believe, is becoming feasible today with contemporary neural nets—computer simulations of human neurons)[3] recognize humor, or perform other subtle tasks in which their human creators excel.

12 One reason for this disparity in capabilities is that our most advanced computers are still simpler than the human brain—currently about a million times simpler (give or take one or two orders of magnitude depending on the assumptions used). But this disparity will not remain the case as we go through the early part of the next century. Computers doubled in speed every three years at the beginning of the twentieth century, every two years in the 1950s and 1960s, and are now doubling in speed every twelve months. This trend will continue, with computers achieving the memory capacity and computing speed of the human brain by around the year 2020.

13 Achieving the basic complexity and capacity of the human brain will not automatically result in computers matching the flexibility of human intelligence. The organization and content of these resources—the software of intelligence—is equally important. One approach to emulating the brain's software is through reverse engineering—scanning a human brain (which will be achievable early in the next century)[4] and essentially copying its neural circuitry in a neural computer (a computer designed to simulate a massive number of human neurons) of sufficient capacity.

14 There is a plethora of credible scenarios for achieving human-level intelligence in a machine. We will be able to evolve and train a system combining massively parallel neural nets with other paradigms to understand language and model knowledge, including the ability to read and understand written documents. Although the ability of today's computers to extract and learn knowledge from natural-language documents is quite limited, their abilities in this domain are improving rapidly. Computers will be able to read on their own, understanding and modeling what they have read, by the second decade of the twenty-first century. We can then have our computers read all of the world's literature—books, magazines, scientific journals, and other available material. Ultimately, the machines will gather knowledge on their own by venturing into the physical world, drawing from the full spectrum of media and information services, and sharing knowledge with each other (which machines can do far more easily than their human creators).

15 Once a computer achieves a human level of intelligence, it will necessarily roar past it. Since their inception, computers have significantly exceeded human mental dexterity in their ability to remember and process information. A computer can remember billions or even trillions of facts perfectly, while we are hard pressed to remember a handful of phone numbers. A computer can quickly search a database with billions of records in fractions of a second. Computers can readily share their knowledge bases. The combination of human-level intelligence in a machine with a computer's inherent superiority in the speed, accuracy, and sharing ability of its memory will be formidable.

16 Mammalian neurons are marvelous creations, but we wouldn't build them the same way. Much of their complexity is devoted to supporting their own life processes, not to their information-handling abilities. Furthermore, neurons are extremely slow; electronic circuits are at least a million times faster. Once a computer achieves a human level of ability in understanding abstract concepts, recognizing patterns, and other attributes of human intelligence, it will be able to apply this ability to a knowledge base of all human-acquired—and machine-acquired—knowledge.

17 A common reaction to the proposition that computers will seriously compete with human intelligence is to dismiss this specter based primarily on an examination of contemporary capability. After all, when I interact with my personal computer, its intelligence seems limited and brittle, if it appears intelligent at all. It is hard to imagine one's personal computer having a sense of humor, holding an opinion, or displaying any of the other endearing qualities of human thought.

18 But the state of the art in computer technology is anything but static. Computer capabilities are emerging today that were considered impossible one or two decades ago. Examples include the ability to transcribe accurately normal continuous human speech, to understand and respond intelligently to natural language, to recognize patterns in medical procedures such as electrocardiograms and blood tests with an accuracy rivaling that of human physicians, and, of course, to play chess at a world-championship level. In the next decade, we will see translating telephones that provide real-time speech translation from one human language to another,

intelligent computerized personal assistants that can converse and rapidly search and understand the world's knowledge bases, and a profusion of other machines with increasingly broad and flexible intelligence.

19 In the second decade of the next century, it will become increasingly difficult to draw any clear distinction between the capabilities of human and machine intelligence. The advantages of computer intelligence in terms of speed, accuracy, and capacity will be clear. The advantages of human intelligence, on the other hand, will become increasingly difficult to distinguish.

20 The skills of computer software are already better than many people realize. It is frequently my experience that when demonstrating recent advances in, say, speech or character recognition, observers are surprised at the state of the art. For example, a typical computer user's last experience with speech-recognition technology may have been a low-end freely bundled piece of software from several years ago that recognized a limited vocabulary, required pauses between words, and did an incorrect job at that. These users are then surprised to see contemporary systems that can recognize fully continuous speech on a 60,000-word vocabulary, with accuracy levels comparable to a human typist.

21 Also keep in mind that the progression of computer intelligence will sneak up on us. As just one example, consider Gary Kasparov's confidence in 1990 that a computer would never come close to defeating him. After all, he had played the best computers, and their chess-playing ability—compared to his—was pathetic. But computer chess playing made steady progress, gaining forty-five rating points each year. In 1997, a computer sailed past Kasparov, at least in chess. There has been a great deal of commentary that other human endeavors are far more difficult to emulate than chess playing. *This is true.* In many areas—the ability to write a book on computers, for example—computers are still pathetic. But as computers continue to gain in capacity at an exponential rate, we will have the same experience in these other areas that Kasparov had in chess. Over the next several decades, machine competence will rival—and ultimately surpass—any particular human skill one cares to cite, including our marvelous ability to place our ideas in a broad diversity of contexts.

22 Evolution has been seen as a billion-year drama that led inexorably to its grandest creation: human intelligence. The emergence in the early twenty-first century of a new form of intelligence on Earth that can compete with, and ultimately significantly exceed, human intelligence will be a development of greater import than any of the events that have shaped human history. It will be no less important than the creation of the intelligence that created it, and will have profound implications for all aspects of human endeavor, including the nature of work, human learning, government, warfare, the arts; and our concept of ourselves.

23 This specter is not yet here. But with the emergence of computers that truly rival and exceed the human brain in complexity will come a corresponding ability of machines to understand and respond to abstractions and subtleties. Human beings appear to be complex in part because of our competing internal goals. Values and emotions represent goals that often conflict with each other, and are an unavoidable by-product of the levels of abstraction that we deal with as human beings. As computers achieve a comparable—and greater—level of complexity, and as they are increasingly derived at least in part from models of human intelligence, they, too, will necessarily utilize goals with implicit values and emotions, although not necessarily the same values and emotions that humans exhibit.

24 A variety of philosophical issues will emerge. Are computers thinking, or are they just calculating? Conversely, are human beings thinking, or are they just calculating? The human brain presumably follows the laws of physics, so it must be a machine, albeit a very complex one. Is there an

inherent difference between human thinking and machine thinking? To pose the question another way, once computers are as complex as the human brain, and can match the human brain in subtlety and complexity of thought, are we to consider them conscious? This is a difficult question even to pose, and some philosophers believe it is not a meaningful question; others believe it is the only meaningful question in philosophy. This question actually goes back to Plato's time, but with the emergence of machines that genuinely appear to possess volition and emotion, the issue will become increasingly compelling.

25 For example, if a person scans his brain through a noninvasive scanning technology of the twenty-first century (such as an advanced magnetic resonance imaging), and downloads his mind to his personal computer, is the "person" who emerges in the machine the same consciousness as the person who was scanned? That "person" may convincingly implore you that "he" grew up in Brooklyn, went to college in Massachusetts, walked into a scanner here, and woke up in the machine there. The original person who was scanned, on the other hand, will acknowledge that the person in the machine does indeed appear to share his history, knowledge, memory, and personality, but is otherwise an impostor, a different person.

26 Even if we limit our discussion to computers that are not directly derived from a particular human brain, they will increasingly appear to have their own personalities, evidencing reactions that we can only label as emotions and articulating their own goals and purposes. They will appear to have their own free will. They will claim to have spiritual experiences. And people—those still using carbon-based neurons or otherwise—will believe them.

27 One often reads predictions of the next several decades discussing a variety of demographic, economic, and political trends that largely ignore the revolutionary impact of machines with their own opinions and agendas. Yet we need to reflect on the implications of the gradual, yet inevitable, emergence of true competition to the full range of human thought in order to comprehend the world that lies ahead.

Notes

1. My recollections of the *Twilight Zone* episode are essentially accurate, although the gambler is actually a small-time crook named Rocky Valentine. Episode 28, "A Nice Place to Visit" (I learned the name of the episode after writing the prologue), aired during the first season of *The Twilight Zone,* on April 15, 1960.

   The episode begins with a voice-over: "Portrait of a man at work, the only work he's ever done, the only work he knows. His name is Henry Francis Valentine, but he calls himself Rocky, because that's the way his life has been—rocky and perilous and uphill at a dead run all the way. . . ."

   While robbing a pawnbrokers shop, Valentine is shot and killed by a policeman. When he awakens, he is met by his afterlife guide, Pip. Pip explains that he will provide Valentine with whatever he wants. Valentine is suspicious, but he asks for and receives a million dollars and a beautiful girl. He then goes on a gambling spree, winning at the roulette table, at the slot machines, and later, at pool. He is also surrounded by beautiful women, who shower him with attention.

   Eventually Valentine tires of the gambling, the winning, and the beautiful women. He tells Pip that it is boring to win all the time and that he doesn't belong in Heaven. He begs Pip to take him to "the Other Place." With a malicious gleam in his eye, Pip replies, "This is the Other Place!" Episode synopsis adapted from Marc Scott Zicree, *The Twilight Zone Companion* (Toronto: Bantam Books, 1982, 113–115).

2. What were the primary political and philosophical issues of the twentieth century? One was ideological—totalitarian systems of the right (fascism) and left (communism) were confronted and largely defeated by capitalism (albeit with a large public sector) and democracy. Another was the rise of technology, which began to be felt in the nineteenth century and became a major force in the twentieth century. But the issue of "what constitutes a human being" is not yet a primary issue (except as it affects the abortion debate), although the past century did witness the continuation of earlier struggles to include all members of the species as deserving of certain rights.
3. For an excellent overview and technical details on neural-network pattern recognition, see the "Neural Network Frequently Asked Questions" web site, edited by W. S. Sarle, at <ftp://ftp.sas.com/pub/neural/FAQ.html>. In addition, an article by Charles Arthur, "Computers Learn to See and Smell Us," from *Independent,* January 16, 1996, describes the ability of neural nets to differentiate between unique characteristics.
4. . . . Destructive scanning will be feasible early in the twenty-first century. Noninvasive scanning with sufficient resolution and bandwidth will take longer but will be feasible by the end of the first half of the twenty-first century.

Thinking about the Argument

1. What purpose does the opening anecdote seem to serve? How does it set the reader up for the central claim?
2. What does the author want you to believe? Find it in the text or state it in your own words.
3. Does he provide any reasons to support the validity of his claim? Identify them if you can (even if you have to put them in your own words).
4. According to the author, when will computers achieve the processing power of a human mind? Even at this level, what will limit its ability to "think"?
5. What will the advantages of machine intelligence over human intelligence be? What reasons does the author cite to support these assertions?
6. Based on Kurzweil's argument, do you think he believes that self-aware machines are a good idea? How can you tell (given that he does not state this idea explicitly)?

Responding to the Argument

1. Return to the opening analogy. Do you think people are "gamblers?" If we are successful in creating highly intelligent machines, is this a game we will win or lose? Explain.
2. Is it a good idea to allow computers to develop their storage and processing abilities beyond those of the human brain? Why or why not?
3. Are humans "thinking or just calculating"? What is the difference (if there is one)? Does the author seem to think there is a qualitative difference between human and potential machine intelligence? What do you think of this idea?

Writing about the Argument

1. Write a letter to the author expressing your opinion about whether it is a good idea to develop human-level artificial intelligence.
2. Write a paragraph stating your opinion about whether computers will ever be able to think like a human. Present your writing in class or in a small group. Evaluate the assumptions that underlie your claim.
3. Choose one of Kurzweil's paragraphs to refute. Try to convince your audience that his claim or evidence is weak and his assumption(s) invalid.
4. In paragraph 25, Kurzweil describes a situation where an individual could have his consciousness uploaded to a computer. If you were dying and had the opportunity to upload your consciousness to a virtual reality database (assume that life there, though virtual, would be the same as life here), would you do so? Why or why not?

"The Dark Side of Technology"

About the Author: Bill Joy

As an engineering graduate student at the University of California at Berkeley, Bill Joy and his team succeeded in modifying the code for the UNIX operating system, thereby introducing a new paradigm of software distribution. He went on to cofound Sun Microsystems in 1982. In 1997, Joy was named cochair of the Presidential Information Technology Advisory Committee by Bill Clinton. After meeting Ray Kurzweil, he gained notoriety for writing "Why the Future Doesn't Need Us" for *Wired* magazine in 2000, in which he argues that if current trends in technology are followed, then machines will replace humans as the dominant "species" on earth. The text reprinted here is based on a speech that Joy gave in September 2000 at the Commonwealth Club of California following the release of his *Wired* article.

Before You Read

1. Research Bill Joy and Sun Microsystems on the Internet. What else has he written? What work has he done? Why might he be qualified (or not) to offer an opinion on the topic of AI and related technologies? Do you have faith in him as a reliable source of information? Explain.
2. What does the title of Joy's speech imply? How might it differ in tone and content from Kurzweil's book?
3. What do you expect Joy's central claim to be?
4. Glance over the text. Can you discern any major divisions? What are they?

READING SELECTION

The Dark Side of Technology

1 Albert Einstein said that the unleashed power of the atom had changed everything except our way of thinking, and that we were drifting toward unparalleled catastrophe. He was, of course, speaking of the threat of nuclear weapons approximately forty years ago. Today I want to talk to you about another threat that I see, but let me start by saying that I come here, fundamentally, because I'm an optimist about three new technologies: genetic engineering, nanotechnology, and robotics (GNR). These technologies will bring us enormous benefits, creating almost unimaginable wealth. Genetic engineering will give us the ability to cure many diseases and extend our lifespans. Nanotechnology promises to allow us to build material goods at much lower costs, certainly providing us the resources to end material poverty. And robotics may, within this century, allow us to end most manual labor. There may well be tens of thousands of dot geno, dot robo, and dot nano startups that create this unimaginable wealth and create a lot of creative opportunity for bright people.

2 These benefits come about because of the confluence of the physical and biological sciences with the field that I practice in: information technology. It's the ability to take the information, say about genetics, and reduce it to a sequence of letters that can be manipulated in the computer that allows us to begin to think of doing some of these things. So it's the continuation of a phenomenon in computing, called Moore's law, that is a huge enabler. It says that computing has been getting cheaper and will continue to get cheaper and more powerful. Many people thought this trend would run out around 2010, but new technology that I just really learned about in detail last year, called nano or molecular electronics, now promises that we'll see this trend almost certainly continue to 2030. This would mean that, by 2030, we should have inexpensive personal computers that are about a million times as powerful as they are today. These computers would allow people, with the information models in them, to begin to redesign the world in a very fundamental way. A factor of a million is an almost inconceivable number. A calculation, which would have taken a thousand years on a computer today, on a computer of 2030 is likely to finish in something like eight hours—a calculation that would take a year and twenty seconds. And we can also expect about another factor of a million in improvement from algorithms, from the ways in which we solve very difficult problems. For total improvement in thirty years, perhaps on large-scale problems of 1012, a million million, which is about the ratio of the power of an atomic weapon to a match head. Clearly, these advances have enormous implications.

3 I believe that our culture is rooted in the Greeks. We've been running an experiment in freedom in civilization for 2500 years, with some interruptions, like the Dark Ages. But our experiment started in a relatively happy way with the Renaissance and, clearly, science and technology have been creating wonderful things for the last hundred or two hundred years and progress has been accelerating. Now, the Greeks were both spiritual and objective. Edith Hamilton, in her classic book *The Greek Way* said: "The Greeks weren't tempered to evade facts. It's we ourselves who are the sentimentalists. We to whom poetry all art is only a superficial decoration of life. The Greeks looked straight at life; they were completely unsentimental. It was a Roman who said it was sweet to die for one's country. The Greeks never said it was sweet to die for anything. They had no vital lies." I think, to be worthy of this tradition that we're the inheritors of, we have to be unsentimental when facing problems and dangers like we face. We have to be blunt if necessary, sometimes even unpleasant, and talk very honestly about our situation in the same way that they did that led to their great progress.

READING SELECTION

4 In the twentieth century, we've spent a lot of time dealing with nuclear, biological, and chemical weapons. Clearly, if you follow the news, you see that these problems continue. These were technologies developed by the military; they had largely military uses with little commercial value, requiring large-scale activities and often rare raw materials to make the weapons and create new trouble using these technologies. In particular, the knowledge about how to do this was not widely available, at least, not for a long time. The truly dangerous, the stuff with the ability to destroy civilization, was actually really held by a couple of nation-states: the United States and the former Soviet Union.

5 The technologies of concern in the twenty-first century—GNR—are quite different. They're being developed by the commercial sector, they have both military and, especially, enormous commercial uses and huge commercial value. As they become information sciences and are practicable on small computers, even personal computers, they are no longer requiring the large-scale facilities that the earlier twentieth-century technologies did. If we're not careful, in the course we're on, the knowledge to do work in these fields will be widely, essentially universally, available.

6 The dangerous situation that we face is that if all practice in these sciences becomes information and all information is available, then clearly the weapon kind of information will be available as well. In an information age, if everything is information, obviously weapons are information also. We have a new situation that we haven't faced before, where the moral equivalent of the weapons of mass destruction may be available to people sitting at their personal computers, or even to small groups.

7 Why can an individual do damage on such a large scale? Well, if you make a bomb, you can blow it up once. If you make something that can replicate in the world and you release it, you can create harm far out of the scale to the act that released it into the world. The technologies that can be created by GNR can self-replicate. So, a single act, with these new kinds of knowledge-enabled massive destructive technologies, can cause extreme harm. By combining the enormous computing power that is released by these new technologies—these million times faster computers—with the manipulative advantage in the physical sciences, using these tools to manipulate what we understand about genetics and the physical world, we are releasing enormous transformative power. This power is certainly sufficient to redesign the world in a very fundamental way, for better or for worse, because the kind of replicating and evolving processes that have been confined to the natural world are becoming realms of human endeavor. The danger that we face is that we know there are evil people in the world and, if we democratize access to all this knowledge so that everyone has these tools and they can then release self-replicating things, we have a recipe for disaster. We're accustomed to living with almost routine scientific breakthroughs, but we haven't come to terms with the fact that these technologies pose a different threat than the technologies that have come before. Uncontrolled self-replication of these new technologies can create enormous damage in the physical world. I don't think it's an exaggeration to say that we're on the course to the perfection of extreme evil, basically allowing evil to spread well beyond that which the weapons of mass destruction bequeath to the nation-states to empowering this for extreme individuals.

8 To talk specifically about genetic engineering, the danger here is that the same technologies that can be used to cure many diseases and extend our lifespan, may allow people to go so far as designing their own disease. One would call it "designer pathogen." If you ask the experts in this field, they're not exactly sure when this would be possible, but twenty years, on our current course, would be a good guess. Diseases that

are designed in the lab have no natural limits on their virulence. They needn't be weak because they're widespread; they can make extinct the species that is their target; there's no Darwinian kind of principles that would prevent that even in the natural world. They certainly don't apply to things that we design in the lab. The virulence contagion and incubation period of such a disease could easily be engineered [and made capable of] avoiding the immune system. What barrier would there be to someone doing this given almost perfect knowledge of the world got from genetic engineering? If all the information is published, the equipment's getting cheaper, the computers are becoming almost infinitely powerful for design, and a good versus a bad design is simply a question of a sequence. This is a situation we have to avoid.

9 Nanotechnology is simply another technology practiced at the atomic scale. Instead of using only biological materials, nanotechnology opens to using any other elements in the periodic table and essentially mechanical kinds of designs and has a similar problem with an out-of-control replicator that the nanotech people call "regu." In response to the article that I wrote in *Wired,* one of the people involved in nanomedicine wrote an analysis of this—it's on the foresight .org website—and it's clear that it's not impossible for these replicators to, say, eat the biosphere, which is the particular analysis of this paper.

10 I think that these kinds of things, in general, have been called pestilences in the world of our ancestors. But, I think, the pestilences are roughly beyond our experience. I don't think, in our living memory, [that] we've seen things like this happen in the world. Clearly, in the fourteenth century in Europe, we had the plague. The *Encyclopedia Britannica* says that it was transmitted to Europeans when a Kipczech army, besieging a Genoese trading post in the Crimea, catapulted plague-infested corpses into the town and, subsequently, a third of Europe's population died. Other people might say that there were actually rats running off the ship and they didn't actually do it by catapulting the body, but that was clearly the intent—to use this as a weapon. In the sixteenth century in the Americas, a similar thing happened with smallpox. Robert Wright, in his book *Stolen Continent,* said: "The turning point, as so often with the conquest of America, came with the Plague. The scourge was no longer left in the hands of God. Lord Jeffery Amherst secured his place in history as the inventor of modern germ warfare with this notorious command: 'Infect the Indians with sheets upon which smallpox patients have been lying, or by any other means which may serve to exterminate this accursed race.'" The last fast-moving pandemic that we had, I think, was the influenza epidemic of 1918, which is almost certainly out of our living collective memory.

11 This century, we've had advances in antibiotics and sanitation that have prevented most of these kinds of things from occurring, at least for a while. To try to bring back some memory of these things, I'd like to read you from the Roman Lucretius, the book *The Way Things Are,* the last chapter, describing a plague on Athens. He says: "A plague once visited Athens. At first, they felt their heads burning with fever, throats blackened, sweating blood. The tongue filled up, engorged with blood, became too hard to move. Men's inner parts were burning to their very bones; their guts were furnaces. The only thing they had to drink was thirst, which made a deluge seem less than a raindrop. Doctors shook their heads while patients stared blankly. The signs of death were obvious; the mind was crazed with grief and fear. Eight days or nine would find the limbs grow stiff and death. There seemed to be no certain remedy; what gave life to one killed others. This plague was most infectious; it could spread as pestilences do with animals, cattle and sheep. So death was piled on death. None were left, sometimes, as mourners when the dead were hurried to their grave. Battles broke out as the

survivors fought for funeral piers of corpses heaped on corpses. Funeral rites, which these pious people held in all-traditional reverence, became quite out of fashion. Everyone in grief buried his own whatever way he could amidst the general panic. Sudden need and poverty persuaded men to use horrible makeshifts. Howling, they would place their dead on piers prepared for other men, apply the torches, maim and bleed and brawl to keep the corpses from abandonment." Okay, let's change the subject.

12 Robotics is the third technology, and it's really different in the sense that the threat here is to create a wild successor species. Nanoelectronics seems to give us sufficient CPU power that we could create something on the scale of a brain. These dangers have been broadly outlined by Hans Moravec in his book *Robot:* "Robots would be very different from us. They'd probably be asexual, Lamarckian—meaning that they could pass experience directly and they wouldn't necessarily have a strong notion of an individual. So, any romantic notion that robots would be like people, I think, is a folly. The most important thing to note about implementing robots is that it's a real change to the evolutionary paradigm." We had biological evolution until humans came along and, since then, evolution has been largely dominated by cultural evolution, which might go, say, a thousand times faster than biological evolution. Technological evolution is moving much, much faster than cultural evolution and perhaps a million times faster than biological evolution. It's no surprise that it's difficult for cultural institutions to maintain any sort of notion of control over the technology.

13 The danger with these technologies—GNR—is extremist and delusional people writing in the *Seattle Times* in response to my article in *Wired.* William Calvin, a neurobiologist at the University of Washington, wrote: "There's a class of people with delusional disorder who can remain employed and pretty functional for decades. Even if they're only one percent of the population, that's 25,000 mostly untreated, delusional people in the Puget Sound area. Even if only one percent of these has the intelligence or education to intentionally create sustained or widespread harm, it's still a pool of 200 high-performing, sociopathic or delusional tecchies in the Puget Sound area alone." Now, the question really is: Are we going to give the people in our society who are clearly crazy—and we can't deny that they're out there—illimitable power? Imagine that we're all on an airplane together, the airplane being the planet, but on Egypt Airline Ninety where everyone's a pilot and everyone has a button to crash the plane by doing one of these crazy things. That's clearly not acceptable—it brings back fate, like we saw in the ancient world. It's clearly insane to create widespread enabling of genocide or extinction or worse.

14 People have proposed technical fixes to this problem: Carl Sagan saw the problem and said, "Well, we could head to the stars." But I don't think there's enough time, and who would take ethical responsibility for the people who were left behind? Ray Kurzweil imagined we'd all become one with technology since we'd all upload ourselves into being robots, but the robots would certainly have their own psychological problems. If anything, given that they're smarter and more powerful than we are, that seems like an even more dangerous situation. The people who didn't choose to be robots would be in a particular peril even if it [were] possible, which is arguable. Other people have argued for shields. Luis Alvarez, a great physicist, said of the people who proposed the great SDI shield: "They were bright guys with no common sense." I think the reality is that the ability to create havoc with these technologies will probably outrace our ability to defend against them. That doesn't mean we shouldn't try to create some defenses, but a defense against a bioengineered pathogen would be the rough analogue of a perfect human immune system, which seems a little bit unlikely given that, for example, today we have no cures for any viral diseases.

15 So, in order to deal with this problem as we had to deal with the nuclear problem, we have to look beyond technical fixes to nontechnical fixes. We could hope for a second coming, some sort of faith-based thing. But if you talk to people of faith, you find out that God isn't going to come back to save us from ourselves in any of the major cases that I can find. In fact, we have the freedom to destroy ourselves—that's part of the covenant after the Noah and the ark story in my faith. We are responsible for ourselves and what we have to do, I think, is decide how we're going to manage these technologies to reduce the danger. We have done some things along these lines. Historically, starting in the Nixon administration, for example, the United States renounced the use and research of offensive, biological weapons. [The weapons of] this category are so bad that you don't even want to make them, even if the enemy makes them, because the ones you are making might get stolen by somebody else. Since there's no defense, the only real answer is to not have them in the first place.

16 How much danger is there? John Leslie, the Canadian philosopher, estimated the danger at roughly 30 percent, but much more if you accept something called the doomsday argument, which I'll explain if someone asks a question [about it]. Ray Kurzweil said, in his book about the age of spiritual machines, meaning robots: "Well, we have a better than even chance of making it through, but I've always been accused of being an optimist."

17 You can come up with your own estimate. I think that either case is so far beyond completely unacceptable, and they don't include a horrible outcome short of extinction, some sort of living, degraded death, that we clearly have to do something.

18 We have an ethical issue: If these technologies can clearly cause genocide or extinction, and genocide is a crime of the highest possible order, we as scientists and technologists must not be complicit in genocide. We have to put in limits or safeguards on development. And it has to account for the reality of extremists. We've got to move beyond fatalism; we don't want to risk our future on the fact that we'll be able somehow to come up with defenses for things that are almost impossible to defend against through some magical intervention or cleverness. Now, the scientific attitude has always revered knowledge above all things. Robert Oppenheimer, two months after the bomb was dropped on Hiroshima, said: "It's not possible to be a scientist unless you believe that the knowledge of the world and the power which it gives is a thing which is of intrinsic value to humanity. And [scientists should be] using it to help in the spread of knowledge and are willing to take the consequences." Essentially, disclaiming any responsibility as a scientist for the further use of the things you're creating—and I agree that knowledge is good, and so is the search for truths. We clearly have a bedrock value in our society long [based] on the value of open access to information and recognize the problems that arise with attempts to restrict access to and development of knowledge.

19 Certainly, in recent times, we've [come] to particularly revere scientific knowledge. Despite the strong historical precedence of open access to an unlimited development of knowledge [putting] us all in clear danger of extinction, then common sense demands that we reexamine even the basic long-held truths. Nietzsche warned us, at the end of the nineteenth century, not only that God was dead, but that "faith in science, which, after all, exists undeniably, cannot owe its origin to a calculus of utility. It must have originated, in spite of the fact that the disutility and dangerousness of the will to truth or truth at any price is proved to it constantly." It's this further danger that we now fully face: the consequences of our truth seeking. The truth that science seeks can certainly be considered a dangerous substitute for God if it's likely to lead to our extinction.

Edith Hamilton, in *The Greek Way,* points out that "the wisest of Roman law-givers said that the enforcement of an absolutely just law, without any exceptions, irrespective of particular differences, worked absolute injustice." And so we see here that, even if the pursuit of truth and openness is an absolutely just thing, that even it must admit exceptions, such as in this case.

20 Aristotle, one of the founders of science, perhaps *the* founder of science, in his book on ethics pointed out that "the final end of human life is happiness, not truth." He said, "We call final that without qualification which is always desirable in itself and never for the sake of something else. Such a thing happiness, above all else, is because we never choose it for the sake of something else." The Dalai Lama has made a similar point in arguing for secular ethics in his book *Ethics for the New Millennium.* Both, in this way, clearly recognize the limits of science.

21 There's been a lot of reaction to the article I wrote. I've been very encouraged by people's willingness to engage on this subject. The twentieth century was clearly a bloody century, a century of war, a century of creation of enormously horrible weapons. We fortunately avoided nuclear disaster. We unfortunately created the ability for the nation-states to destroy civilization. The twenty-first century may be a century of pestilences if we don't take some action, more like the fourteenth or, perhaps, the sixteenth century. I think we have to change our ways to avoid such disasters. We can't afford to democratize extreme evil. I think we have to find a new way of thinking about the world, perhaps thinking of earth as a sanctuary for people. If our home is a sanctuary for our children, we don't leave loaded guns lying around the house. If the zoo is a sanctuary for animals, we don't take toxic chemicals and PCBs into the zoo. So, there are certainly things that we're clever enough to make that we shouldn't have on the earth, and that's the challenge that's in front of us. Thank you.

Thinking about the Argument

1. What is the tone of Joy's first paragraph? What role might it play in setting the reader up for what he says later on?
2. In which paragraph does his tone change?
3. Why does the author think it is important not to be "sentimental" when thinking about the dangers that new technologies may represent?
4. Why does Joy think information is dangerous? How might this idea relate to problems of identity theft?
5. Joy compares nanotechnology to ancient plagues and "pestilence." Is this analogy valid? Is it possible to see nanotechnology as a form of disease? Explain.
6. According to Joy, what danger is represented by AI and robotic technology? How would they be different from humans? What does the author think of Kurzweil's optimism concerning the merging of humans and machines?
7. Why is it important for humans to be responsible for ourselves (and the things we create)?

RESPONDING TO THE ARGUMENT

1. Do you believe that it is possible for the things Joy describes to come to pass? Explain. (Consider, for a moment, the "impossibility" of computers, space flight, instant global communication, and the Internet to someone from the Victorian age.)
2. Do you share Joy's pessimism about humans? Explain.
3. If one person told you that nanotechnology could be developed that could extend human life and health, and another person told you that the same technology could be used to harm someone, would you endorse the development of the technology? Why or why not?

WRITING ABOUT THE ARGUMENT

1. Write a letter to Joy expressing your optimism about the technologies he mentions. Explain why you think these technologies should be developed for the greater good of humankind.
2. Research one of the technologies Joy mentions and argue why it should be developed or suppressed.
3. Write a proposal explaining what safeguards should be implemented to ensure that potentially dangerous technologies are not developed.
4. Provide economic reasons for developing or suppressing nanotechnology. Do you believe these technologies will be good for the economy (create new industries and jobs), will be bad for the economy (replace people with machines), or will have an effect that is somewhere in between these two extremes?

"A.I. and the Return of the Krell Machine"

ABOUT THE AUTHOR: STEVEN B. HARRIS

Steven B. Harris is a medical doctor with an interest in medical research and the ethics of cryonic suspension. He has been involved with the Biosphere II project and is interested in the relationship between nutrition and the aging process. The following article was first published in *Skeptic* magazine in 2002. It has been widely distributed and discussed in artificial-intelligence research circles and has resulted in numerous discussion threads on the Internet.

BEFORE YOU READ

1. Have you ever seen the film *Forbidden Planet?* If not, consider watching this movie before reading the article.
2. Do you actively seek new technology (video game units, video phones, BlackBerries), or do you avoid learning new technology until absolutely necessary? Why?
3. Do you think Harris is qualified to offer an opinion on this topic? Why or why not? What view do you think he will have?
4. What is implied by the title of the magazine in which this article first appeared? What do you think this magazine's audience might be like, and how might its readers approach a topic like artificial intelligence?

READING SELECTION

A.I. and the Return of the Krell Machine

1 In 1956, the Fred McLeod Wilcox film *Forbidden Planet* became the second memorable science fiction movie of the 1950s (the first being Robert Wise's *The Day the Earth Stood Still*). *Forbidden Planet* has become a classic because it was among the first films to raise important issues about the use of ultimate technologies. Modern viewers are reminded of *Star Trek,* but of course the connection is in the other direction. Many episodes of *Trek* borrow liberally from *Forbidden Planet.* As the film begins, a "United Planets Cruiser," featuring a dashing young starship captain, is paying a call to the planet Altair IV to investigate the loss of a science mission there twenty years before. They find no one alive on the planet save for the expedition's strangely powerful philologist, one Edward Morbius, Ph.D. in literature, and his intriguing and beautiful teenaged daughter, who has never seen any human other than her father. (We recognize the basic plot of *The Tempest* from Shakespeare and of *Star Trek*'s episode "Requiem for Methuselah.") Dr. Morbius, attended by an advanced robot servant, is engaged in solo decipherment of traces of an alien civilization that went extinct 200,000 years earlier. In a key scene, Morbius, in almost blank verse, tells the starship captain about this vanished race, which had called themselves the Krell:

> Ethically, as well as technologically, they were a million years ahead of humankind. For, in unlocking the mysteries of nature, they had conquered even their baser-selves.
>
> And, when in the course of eons, they had abolished sickness and insanity and crime and all injustice, they turned, still with high benevolence, outward toward space.
>
> Long before the dawn of man's history, they had walked our Earth, and brought back many biological specimens.
>
> The heights they had reached!
>
> But then, seemingly on the threshold of some supreme accomplishment which was to have crowned their entire history, this all-but-divine race perished, in a single night.
>
> In the two thousand centuries since that unexplained catastrophe, even their cloud-piercing towers of glass and porcelain and adamantine steel have crumbled back into the soil of Altair IV, and nothing, absolutely nothing, remains above ground.

2 Later, Morbius shows the starship captain the principal remains of the Krell civilization: a self-repairing and still-functioning gigantic machine that reposes, blinking and humming, beneath an empty desert. It is a cube measuring 20 miles on a side (think of *Star Trek*'s Borg ship) powered by 9,200 working thermonuclear (fusion) reactors. Its function is a mystery, but later is finally revealed. The huge device was built by the Krell as a replacement for all technological instruments. It is a technical Aladdin's lamp, an Ultimate Machine waiting for a command. The starship captain finally figures this out and accosts Dr. Morbius with the answer:

> Morbius—a big machine, 8000 cubic miles of klystron relays, enough power for a whole population of creative geniuses—operated by remote control! Morbius—operated by the electromagnetic impulses of individual Krell brains. In return, that machine would instantaneously project solid matter to any point on the planet. In any shape or color they might imagine. For any purpose, Morbius! Creation by pure thought!

3 But there's also a little problem with such a technology, the captain tells Morbius: it is Monsters from the Id:

> But, like you, the Krell forgot one deadly danger—their own subconscious hate and lust for destruction! And so, those mindless beasts of the subconscious had access to a machine that could *never* be shut down! The secret devil of every soul on the planet, all set free at once to loot and maim! And take revenge, Morbius, and kill!

4 The nightmare monsters from the machine allow the Krell to destroy themselves, and later (guided unwillingly now by Morbius' subconscious) the device acts as facilitator to destroy one human expedition and part of another. In the end, a desperate Morbius puts the machine into overload as a final stop to the invincible monsters (we see this scene later in the film *Alien*). The starship captain and Morbius' daughter manage to get away from Altair IV just in time before the planet explodes. Wiping out everything is what these ultimate machines all seem to do. (See Arthur C. Clarke's *2010: Odyssey Two,* for example, where self-replicating all-purpose monolith machines turn Jupiter into a small star. The humans in Jovian orbit get away just in time.)

5 From our 21st century vantage point, we recognize the Krell Machine as a 1950s metaphor for nuclear

energy—a technology thought at the time to be a nearly infinite power source for either good or evil. The question asked in the film is the one made famous in the early atomic era: Are our Freudian Ids—our emotional ape brains—ready for that kind of increase in power? If a machine had the power to make anything we wanted instantly, would we be wise enough to know what was good for us? *Forbidden Planet*'s answer is no.

6 Some form of Krell Machine has turned up repeatedly in science fiction, from *Star Trek* to *Total Recall.* Perhaps the most interesting set of ideas it prefigures is a group of now serious predictions about our future. It turns out that the Bomb is only a small subset of mankind's deepest fears. A nuclear bomb, after all, is merely one more device we made when we grew smart enough to do it. The underlying problem is that we're getting smarter and better at making things, and both of these trends, as each amplifies the other, are snowballing toward an inevitable avalanche.

Nanotechnology

7 Let us look now at the darkest potentials of foreseeable technology. The rule we set for ourselves is that we will not consider "fantasy" ideas, such as what may be possible if we discover new loopholes in physical laws. We wish merely to ask how far "ordinary" human technology may go, given known physical constraints. Such possible "ultimate technologies," as we have suggested above, divide broadly into those connected with the physical world, and those connected with the mental and computational world.

8 We begin with the physical. Here, we are amused by one of the more advanced capabilities of Robby the Robot, who is the servant of Morbius in the 1956 film. Robby (a techno-version of *The Tempest*'s slave-spirit Ariel) is human-designed, using bits of advanced Krell knowledge. Robby can synthesize artificial gems of large size, and can analyze and duplicate any food or chemical mixture, all within the small space of his body. At one point we see Robby obligingly make 50 gallons of bootleg liquor for the starship's cook, who plays *The Tempest*'s drunken crewman/fool. Could any technology which we might realistically imagine allow such powers?

9 Richard Feynman's answer, given in his now-famous essay "There's Plenty of Room at the Bottom" (http://www.zyvex.com/nanotech/feynman.html), was yes. Whether he was inspired by *Forbidden Planet,* or his own genius for thinking out of the box, Feynman's answer in 1959 was surprising: the idea of total molecular-level materials manufacturing control may be science fiction, but it is far from fantasy. Feynman advised that there do not appear to be any physical laws which prohibit the manipulation and manufacture of things atom-by-atom, allowing the kinds of duplication of foodstuffs that Robby does.

10 In his 1986 book *Engines of Creation,* K. Eric Drexler predicted some design details. Complex chemical syntheses, he proposed, might be performed using sub-microscopic construction-machines. Such machines (called "assemblers") would work like natural biological catalysts (enzymes). By the time of Drexler's writing, it was known that enzymes work semi-mechanistically, using tiny chemically powered protein "arms" to grab and move groups of atoms, changing the chemical bonds between them. (A chemical bond is a place where electrons are shared between atoms, causing the assembly to stick together to form a molecule). Drexler proposed that assemblers, unlike most enzymes, could be programmable. Instead of only one chemical job, an assembler might do many. In Drexler's scheme, one could give a general purpose assembler instructions about what types of atoms and bonds to look for and work on, changing these instructions as the device moved from one part of a molecule to the next. Fully programmable assemblers would thus have the full flexibility of computer-controlled industrial robots, but be usable on the tiny molecular scale of chemistry.

11 The potential power of such devices is illustrated by the fine synthetic detail seen in biology, in which a semi-programmable enzyme-complex called the ribosome is able to manufacture a potentially infinite number of different proteins (including enzymes), using programming information on the fly from an "instruction tape" of messenger RNA. Drexler's proposed devices, by analogy with the ribosome, would be more powerful and flexible still—able to take a much wider variety of instructions and be able to make more complex decisions as they worked. Such devices would be able to make not only proteins, but nearly any chemical structure that was stable.

12 Since 1986 progress has been made on this front. In 1989 IBM scientists used a very tiny needle to nudge thirty-

five individual xenon atoms on a cold surface to spell out "IBM" in letters a few atoms long. In 1996, further studies showed that molecules could be individually positioned, even at room temperature (http://www.zurich.ibm.com/news/96/n-19960112-01.html; see also http://www.foresight.org for the history and current progress of nanotechnology). Thus, the crucial hurdle is not in manipulating individual atoms or molecules (this can be done) but in doing it cleverly enough.

13 We see immediately that there is a chicken-and-egg problem here. It could be possible to construct cell-sized computers for running assemblers if molecular-scale engineering capability was available to begin with. If not, the difficulty would lie in making the first assemblers. These would need to arise from a laborious process of miniaturizing manufacturing capability, level by level, to make the next smaller generation of devices, until we reached the molecule-sized bottom of chemical reality. Once devices were manufactured this small, however, things would become much easier. The assemblers would then be programmable to simply make more of themselves, just as living cells replicate their own ribosomes, and thus replicate themselves.

14 Nanotechnology (as Drexler called it) would offer the ultimate physical manufacturing technology. Such manufacture would start with basic shapes. Josh Storrs Hall has proposed that nanomachines ("foglets") of approximately protozoan size might interact tactilely with each other to generate ordinary objects having low densities but high strengths. Solid objects might thus emerge from fluid dispersions like today's plastic stereolithography sculpture, yet at the same time potentially be as mobile and protean as the "liquid metal" automaton in the film *Terminator 2.* A collection of foglets might float like mist, but morph or solidify when instructed to lock arms. Such a "Utility Fog" would quickly become any shape or color we wish. Say the word, for example, and an extra chair might coalesce and shape itself out of mist which is otherwise nearly invisible. If you can do such deeds just by thinking or visualizing, as Hall himself pointed out, you will be approaching Krell territory.

15 A notable application of nanotechnology would lie in its role as the ultimate medical treatment. In 1959 the Jet Propulsion Lab's Al Hibbs remarked, on hearing of tiny machines, that it would be very convenient to simply "swallow the doctor." Of course, the micro-doctor, working quickly and by touch, would need to have considerable on-site "intelligence." As early as 1950, in his science fiction novel *Needle,* Hal Clement had already sketched the regenerative possibilities if a human body were interpenetrated by an amorphous intelligent being made of very tiny parts, which could "see" and fix problems micro-surgically. The direct miniaturization of humans as seen in *Fantastic Voyage* is pure fantasy, but "inside doctoring" is not, if the "doctor" were an intelligent but microscopic robot.

16 Nanotechnology would not need to work inside the body to make biomaterials. It should be able to synthesize healthy tissue at any place, for any purpose. Proteins, cells, and tissues could be laid down in Utility Fog shaped forms. With the proper supply of information and raw materials, assemblers might then use an artificial circulatory system to manufacture and place cells on organ-shaped scaffolding. There would be no reason such an enterprise could not eventually manufacture a complete living organism. With such biological manufacture, we come naturally to the most dramatic use of nanotechnology, which is the ability to duplicate and "fax" living organisms, including humans, using information taken from a living template organism.

17 Living organisms now are constructed (we say "grown") slowly from the raw materials of simple food molecules, using a seed of information which controls some nanomachine-like cellular organelles (ribosomes, etc). Nothing stands in the way of improving this natural process greatly, in both rate and fidelity. The cellular clones of today are *not* exact copies, because DNA contains too little information for that. DNA is a recipe, not a blueprint. By contrast, nanotechnology in theory could read the far more complex "blueprint" of an existing individual human, and build another copy using this far larger instruction-set. Moreover, rather than producing a human in twenty years, it might be possible to do it in weeks, or even hours, using information from a template person's brain, so that memories and learning could be replicated also. Thus, while simple cellular cloning of humans *per se* will not be capable of presenting the kinds of social problems seen in the Schwarzenegger film *The Sixth Day,* a fully duplicative nanotechnology would be up to the task.

To be sure, a nanotechnologically duplicated person might not quite pop into existence nearly as quickly as a matter-transportee on *Star Trek.* A human synthesis would also need machinery as well as raw materials in place at the "destination" point. These are details. The point is that the basic process, as well as all the ethical and philosophical problems attendant upon it, does not seem to be ruled out by any physical laws we know.

18 It is well to remind ourselves that human beings are not the atoms that make them up any more than a novel is the atoms that make up a particular book. Atoms in the body are replaced in metabolism, but the person remains. All atoms could be completely replaced and the person would still remain, as a pattern. A human being is information, not matter. Such information can theoretically be extracted on a molecular scale, sent from here to there, and reconstituted as a pattern in new matter. To make an "effectively identical" duplicate of a person, such a process doesn't have to be carried out for each individual atom in a body, because most positions of most atoms in a person don't make any differences that we care about. For example, protein molecules and cell organelles can be produced as generic copies of a single design, once identified by position. A person might have less than 50,000 different protein designs, and much of the rest of their "protein" information is where each copy is, and how it has or hasn't been modified in place. On a larger scale, many cells and even tissues can be generically specified the same way—for example, you probably don't care if all the glomeruli in your kidneys are replaced by many exact copies of a few of your best-performing ones. The important information in transmitting a human being will be in the connections of his or her neurons, and information regarding the delicate modification of proteins in the synapses. These form memories, some of which are not shared by any other human, and are thus irreplaceable.

19 As we have hinted, the powers being discussed are not unlimited. Nanomachines are precision programmable chemical catalysts that are held together by chemical bonds, subject to standard inter- and intra-molecular forces. This places severe limits on the kinetic energy that machine pieces may have, and thus how fast they may work in order to move and assemble atoms. There is friction to deal with, molecular degradation, and of course the need for constant error correction, as in any complex system. There are also temperature and pressure constraints, again because nanomachines are made of ordinary molecular substances. Further, nanotechnology techniques will have power over chemistry only; no nuclear transformations are included, so we cannot turn lead into gold (this will continue to require cyclotrons).

20 These are fundamental limitations connected with physical law, and not likely to be circumventable. Nanotechnology provides the limiting technology for how to make any chemically possible structure of atoms, on any scale that is stable. In theory, one can duplicate any object that already exists in the relatively low-temperature and low-pressure part of our universe (e.g., crusts of small planets). On these scales, the expected power of nanotechnology should fall somewhere between that of biology and the *Star Trek* transporter, between Robby the Robot and the Krell Machine. Such powers are god-like only if your imagination is limited, and your gods are of the slow and patient type.

21 If nanotechnology should eventually be able to manufacture (or assemble) any reasonably small and cool object that can exist on a planetary surface, and do it on command, the next problem is determining who will give the commands. Even if nanomachines are under docile control, their powers begin to resemble wizardry, and the way in which one may change the world with them (by speaking a word, or even thinking a thought) begins to look suspiciously like sorcery. Do we want that? Of course, inside a computer, it's always been that way. But the *Forbidden Planet* question is whether anyone, or any government, is safe holding this kind of power over matter in the real physical world. With nanotechnology we would get real "sorcery"—but even with the best of intentions we might still find ourselves in the position of the sorcerer's apprentice (think of Mickey Mouse in *Fantasia*). Even intelligent beings a good deal smarter than we might not be wise enough to control such technology.

Computational Singularity

22 The other main futuristic prediction of the 1980s about technology addresses a type of technical progress that is easy to project, but (ironically) also evokes ultimate limitations that are much harder to imagine. The starting point for this second set of predictions involves the notion that information pro-

cessing, or "computation," is being done increasingly faster, and that there appear to be no obvious physical limits beyond speed-of-light communications delays as to how fast computation may ultimately be done. If there are limits they are well beyond the power of our own inefficient brains. Therefore it must be possible to construct intelligences far superior to our own. Nor are the paths to doing this completely obscure, since in a real sense we already do it when many people work on a given project too large for any single person to comprehend (a moon rocket, or an economy), or when humans work in concert with computers. This kind of thing will continue with a vengeance. As it does, it will assist in creating itself. Inevitably, this kind of progress in the speed of progress must lead to supra-exponential growth in "thinking" ability.

23 Computing machines (first mechanical, then electronic) have been shrinking at an exponential rate for as long as we've been making them, and many people have sensed that there is something wildly empowering ahead. When the first kit to allow home-builders and hobbyists to construct their own personal electronic computers was offered in 1974, the device fittingly ended up being named the Altair (suggested by the 12-year-old daughter of the *Popular Electronics* publisher, after a *Star Trek* destination). Today, personal computer power has grown to levels quite unforeseen then, and there is no end in sight. Instead, it seems that ahead is a kind of watershed—or perhaps a waterfall. We are due to go over it. Such an event has been described in various terms for half a century, but we may refer to it as the computational singularity. The computational singularity corresponds to a singularity point in a mathematical function, where the value of the function approaches infinity (like $1/x$ when x approaches zero). It is a time when total computational power rises to levels that are, if not infinite, at least qualitatively unimaginable. This is set to happen quite soon at the present pace.

24 One of the first works of fiction to use this idea explicitly is the Vernor Vinge (VIN-jee) 1986 novel *Marooned In Realtime.* In this tale, human time-travelers in time-stasis bubbles come out of suspension to find themselves on the other side of a curious rift in civilization, during which all humans have disappeared from the Earth, leaving the planet empty. No one who emerges from stasis understands what has happened to civilization, and since the travel is one-way, they cannot go back to find out. There are clues that the end hasn't been extermination. Possibly (Vinge hints) there has been an Exodus or Ascendancy or Transcendence of some kind, since the computer technology of the people who "left" just before the rift is clearly progressing exponentially toward incomprehensible information-processing power. The implication is that humankind has perhaps "graduated" into some kind of new mental life, much as happens in Arthur Clarke's 1953 novel *Childhood's End.*

25 Vinge, who in real life is also a professor of computer science at San Diego State University, has also written formally in non-fiction about the concept of the "computational singularity" (http://wwwrohan.sdsu.edu/faculty/vinge/misc/singularity.html). Vinge traces the idea to the speculations of J. von Neumann and S. Ulam, a pair of legendary figures who made deep marks in computer science, mathematics, physics, and complex systems theory in the 1950s. Vinge also credits I. J. Good with first pointing out explicitly that computer-design-of-computers leads to computer power progress which must be at least exponential. And indeed, in the year 2001 we still didn't have a HAL 9000, but we do already allow a great deal of chip design to be done by machine. We have no choice—it's already beyond the capability of human designers.

26 The advent of true self-replicating nanotechnology may be difficult to predict, but recently there have been a number of suggestions that, by contrast, the singularity should be upon us within a generation or two. The reason for the more confident prediction in this case is that information-processing power has been increasing smoothly and exponentially for a century. Hans Moravec, in the classic 1988 future-shock robotics book *Mind Children: The Future of Robot and Human Intelligence,* suggested that the unimaginable waterfall in this river of progress will happen about 2030. Ray Kurzweil has recently updated and expanded Moravec's arguments in a 1999 book called *The Age of Spiritual Machines.* Kurzweil suggests that during the last century the doubling time of the figure-of-merit "computation power per dollar," which was thought to be relatively constant, has in fact decreased from three years toward one year. In other words, we used to have to wait three years to buy a computer twice as powerful for the same price, but with

today's PCs it happens in only twelve months. Not only is the pace of change exponential, but the exponent itself is changing.

27 According to Kurzweil and others, the singularity is due not because of the sliding nature of the exponent (although this helps determine the time) but because of another key milestone: at some point in the process our computers will become as computationally powerful as the human brain. This is projected to happen sometime between 2010 and 2030, and the exponential effect insures that the personal computers five to 10 years later will be just as powerful. It follows inexorably that computers as complex as the human brain will be mass-produced items, like digital watches or wind-up toys. Shortly after this happens, our computer networks are expected to get very, very smart.

28 Of course, a computer as powerful as the human brain does not guarantee the performance of a human-equivalent mind. Indeed, even humans themselves, if not programmed correctly, become less Mowgli than "wolf boy"—not much more than animals. One special thing about a human brain is its sheer connectionist capacity, and the ability to use this capacity to modify deep structural programs for learning. The attainment of human and superhuman mental performance by computers depends on the ability to program computers heuristically by experience, in much the same way that we semi-program human minds today. In such a scenario, simple learning programs become better learning programs until, at some point, they pass the Turing test and become capable of some subset of human-level intellectual performance. The ancient Greek sorites paradox, as amplified by the philosopher Hegel, is then realized: an increase in mere (computational) quantity is mysteriously translated into a change in quality. We say that we now have an emergent property—in this case, intelligent action.

29 Skeptics of the singularity—holding instead that the human mind is a specially creative instrument never to be duplicated—were dealt a severe blow in 1997 when the IBM computer Deep Blue defeated chess world champion Garry Kasparov, who was thought by experts to be as formidable a player as any in history. Until he encountered Deep Blue, Kasparov had contended that the play of computers was typically rote-mechanical and unimaginative, in ways that a grandmaster could easily detect . . . and exploit. Great chess was said to take imagination and creativity of a kind that would forever elude the machine. For a long time it pleased the vanity of humans to believe Kasparov, as he kept beating computers. Finally, however, came the day of reckoning, as an inexorable increase in raw computer processing power resulted in a self-learning chess-playing machine that (somewhat mysteriously) became capable of formidable chess imagination and insight. Even programmers were surprised by the details of Deep Blue's play.

30 Deep Blue now passed its version of the Turing test for machine intelligence—Kasparov felt for the first time that he was glimpsing a mind across the board from him. This may be the most interesting part of the episode, for Kasparov immediately accused the programmers of cheating, and of having a human chess master in contact with the computer during play. He was wrong. There was actually no one "home" within the programs that comprised the "mind" of Deep Blue. The programs that "creatively" dismantled and destroyed Kasparov's strategies were running by themselves. Kasparov was indeed facing only a machine, not a human grandmaster, but he could not tell the difference. If it can happen in chess, it can happen in other areas of thought.

31 In the past, the field of artificial intelligence has suffered badly from making predictions that in retrospect could never have been proven in the time given. Even the supercomputers of today have brains only about as computationally powerful as those of insects, so they've really had no chance to think as well as humans do, no matter how well programmed. Also, it's not very surprising that when given machine bodies, computers of today still interact with the world in somewhat insect-like ways. Indeed, insects themselves often behave in many ways that seem to us to be somewhat stylized and mechanical.

32 Even with real insects, however, we see a principle at work: a qualitative amplification of intelligence is possible if we increase complexity. Hive-insect minds, working in a linked fashion, may develop the flexibility similar to more complex and intelligent animals. A bee colony, for example, which has far more neurological processing power than any single bee, is capable of learned behavior. It will remember the location and times of flower openings. A colony is even capable of

future-modeling or inductive behavior, like a vertebrate: if a dish of sugar-water near the hive is moved by a certain distance each day, bees can be found clustering at the next projected or anticipated spot.

33 In a similar way, things cannot fail to change qualitatively as electronic computers and their networks grow more complex. In the future, as these networks become more capable, they will presumably mimic brains that are further along in the evolutionary scale of complexity. Today's insectoid machines will one day act like lower mammals, then higher ones (toy makers even now are crudely modeling the behavior of babies and dogs with cheap 8-bit microprocessors). Along the way they will pass more and more Turing tests, in which their thought and behavior cannot be discriminated from that of a human. Again, in making such projections, we run up against the past bad predictions of A.I. enthusiasts. We should be cautious, but not too conservative. The moon landing, gene therapy, and mammalian cloning were old science fiction ideas that seemed forever in the future too, but they didn't stay there. Eventually, if computers continue on their present path, A.I., too, will come. Then we will presumably have robots like HAL or Robby, who answer questions in a flexible and non-mechanical way. At that point, we'll wonder whether such devices are the equivalent of animals, or perhaps something more.

34 But skepticism here is not inappropriate. Vinge himself has remarked that the super-accelerated mind of a dog (say) would still not be human. But we may note that dogs as we know them are particularly crippled by a short attention span and a relatively poor memory, neither of which would be expected problems for a computer-enhanced dog-mind. Indeed, Vinge himself, in his 1999 novel *A Deepness in the Sky,* discusses the value of having monomaniacal attention span at one's command, if only one can also leave some executive functions in control of it. A dog is also notably crippled by lack of hands and brain circuitry that allows rapid recognition, identification, and use of sounds and visual symbols that make up language. Add all these things, plus some mental quickness and some training and teaching, and it seems likely that a dog will no longer be a dog. Just what it will become, given enough time and experience, is an open question.

35 If we assume that self-programming ability follows processing power, very soon after the point that computers of human brainpower are mass-production items, we may expect that computers will attain the total information processing power of all human minds on the planet. They will have long since become the experts in the design of more complex computers, just as they are today the reigning experts at chess strategy. At some point not long after that, computers will recapitulate human history, human culture, and human thought. They will then teach each other everything we humans know in a matter of years (months? days? hours?) and then move on. The whole thing will happen in a flash, and if it happens at all, will certainly happen long before we're really ready for it. The flash seems inevitable before the end of this century, and seems quite probably (given even modest extrapolation) before the middle of it. And, of course, we'll be unable to stop it, anymore than we can stop anything on the Internet.

36 Whether full nanotechnology or computational singularity arrives first, it seems probable that the other will then immediately follow. Nanotechnology, after all, requires molecular-scale self-replicating computers, and such machines should rapidly be able to grow and wire themselves in three dimensions to the complexities needed for the singularity to occur. In a similar fashion, an evolved computer that is far faster and brighter than we are, will soon figure out how to manipulate matter on the atomic scale with self-replicators, and will then do so in service of other goals, unless actively prevented. Thus nanotechnology, whether it arrives first or not, seems destined to be the incarnate "muscle" of the singularity artificial intelligence.

37 One might imagine optimistically that we might prevent such a connection, with safeguards that prevent super-intelligences from interacting with the physical world, except perhaps by something like censored email. On second thought, however, any careful isolation program may be doomed. We might as well expect a bunch of chimpanzee guards to keep humans from escaping Alcatraz. If a super-intelligent computer has enough contact with the world to be very useful, it will probably have enough contact to corrupt some of its captors into allowing it to escape. An artificial intelligence might amass wealth, for example, and with that wealth influence the passage of laws in democracies. It might also simply bribe

outlaw humans and outlaw governments. People who imagine that governments can control super-intelligent computers might consider just how much control governments today have over junk-email, the Internet, or very large multinational corporations. Self-aware computers, which will be running the more successful corporations by that time, will be far faster and more slippery than anything we've dealt with thus far.

Penalties for Playing God, or Wanting To

38 After such an escape of artificial intelligence or nanotechnology into the real world and private hands, then what? Humanity does not have a good record for handling destructive technologies. We have avoided global exchange of nuclear weapons till now by a hair's breadth, and would not have come this far if all governments had nuclear weapons, and still less if all people did. Coming soon, however, is something as pervasive as the personal computer and cell phone, but with the power of mass destruction too—bio- or nano-warfare.

39 Viruses and bacteria as we know them are already much like assemblers, and can be made worse (imagine HIV with the infectivity of influenza). There is also the problem of natural replication mutation accidents, which correspond with the emergence of new wild viruses, like Ebola or HIV. As in any self-replicating system, parasitical forms may emerge in nanotech systems. An uncontrolled self-replication/assembler system can be imagined. It popularly manifests itself in the prediction genre as a creeping, corrosive gray goo, a kind of undifferentiated assembler-cancer. Such stuff causes disaster, because like some all devouring bacterium or slime mold, it exists merely to transmute anything it touches into more of itself. Some say the world will end in fire, some say in ice (as the poet Frost writes). Now, there is a third and more insipid option: perhaps it will all just melt into amoeboid sludge.

40 Those who favor fire may note that easy manufacture of nuclear weapons by uranium isotope separation should be a fairly straightforward subset of self-replicative manufacturing technology; yet no foreseeable technology, including nanotechnology, can provide a defense against such weapons. So there are many ways in which the coming world will get scarier.

41 Very well—perhaps we have to let go. Damien Broderick's book-length treatment of the singularity, titled *The Spike* (Tor, NY, 2001), examines many of the possibilities at this point. Perhaps the advanced machines will end up doing everything for us, and, in true *deus ex machina* style, everything will be fixed-up, and come out all right in the end. We like such endings. Culturally, the relative closeness of the singularity has visited on its truest believers much the same effect as belief in the imminence of the Second Coming. The complex set of apocalyptic ideas that parasitizes and sometimes immobilizes adherents to certain brands of Christianity, in other guises now seems to handicap certain alarmists and "cybernetic totalists" (to use Jaron Lanier's phrase) with visions of Technological Salvation, or Techno-transcendentalism. First it was Cryonics, then Nanotechnology, and now Singularity, which will get us to the "End Time." And all perhaps without the conventional God. All of these ideas can serve as an apocalyptic religion, if conveniently simplified with most scary parts left out. We are promised the apotheosis of humanity. At least the techno-evangelicals don't wear placards saying "THE END IS NEAR / REPENT NOW!" Actually, there doesn't seem anything much to do in the Religion of Singularity except spreading the Good News (hence, perhaps, this essay). And, of course, one must Believe. To be sure, there exist some who do seek to bring a more critical eye to the whole idea-set (see, for example, www.SingularityWatch.com). Still, the whole thing does cause a certain amount of unease.

42 It's easy to place the sources of that. To begin, what will be the nature of these A.I. super-intelligences? Will they be nice, or will we get, instead of *Forbidden Planet,* perhaps *The Forbin Project?* Or *Terminator*'s Skynet? Is there nothing else to do in the way of safeguards? In *Forbidden Planet,* Morbius' powerful robot servant Robby has been explicitly designed by Morbius around Asimov's Laws of Robotics (a robot may not harm humans, must follow orders except where they will cause harm to humans, and must preserve itself, except where this conflicts with the first two laws). The Krell Machine, by contrast, is an infinitely dangerous servant precisely because it has not been programmed with such laws. The Krell evidently erred monumentally on that point, and in true tragico-heroic fashion, succumbed as much to hubris as to anything else.

43 We would like to take a precautionary lesson from the noble Krell.

Could we perhaps hard-wire the Asimov Laws of Robotics permanently into machines that are smarter than we are? Alas, it may be that the answer is "no" for machines that rewire themselves, which is what they will have to be capable of if they are ever to become smarter than we are. Here is the rub of A.I.: we cannot directly program minds to be better than ours because we don't know how, and if they program themselves through learning, we won't fully understand them, and certainly won't then be able to perfectly control them. There is no such thing as immutable "hardwiring," when software is in control. Anything created by evolution may be uncreated. Or gotten around, by a similar process.

44 In the darkest *Star Trek* version of our basic story ("What Are Little Girls Made Of," 1966), the role of the Krell machine is played by an underground alien device on an empty planet, which makes robots and cyborgs to order. Again the planet holds one lonely archeologist, attended by a giant Frankenstein-like robot from the planet's past. At one point the robot suddenly remembers how its kind have gotten around their safety programming, allowing them to destroy their creators. The giant robot picks up Captain Kirk like a child and exclaims, "That was the equation!" It's the equation we hope our robots never get to.

45 In creating super-intelligent robots we can only face the key problem of every responsible parent, and place our hope in the Hebraic injunction: "Train up a child in the way he should go, and when he is old he will not depart from it." Or will not depart too badly, we hope.

46 And what about the other Krell lesson? Leaving aside what the computers may want, what about what we desire from the genie? What if the fates punish humanity by giving it what it wants, on both conscious and unconscious levels? Our experience with children and animals, not to say ourselves, makes us suspicious (to say the least) of what occurs then. The effects of our present fad- and impulse-driven market economy (not that the author sees better alternatives) on ourselves and the biosphere are frightening enough. What happens when these effects and externalities all become infinitely amplified via technical means?

47 Our cultural mythology, both before and after the advent of science fiction, laid heavy penalties on those who strove to steal the knowledge of the gods. The penalty is ostracism, and worse: Prometheus was chained to a lonely rock and tortured; Adam and Eve were cast out of the presence of God into an empty Earth. Science fiction as we know it properly begins in 1818 with *Frankenstein Or. The Modern Prometheus,* in which the monster, as a price for its unnatural science-given life, is cast out of society to wander—forever looking through the window at the celebration, forever seeking one of its own kind to talk to or love. The monster suffers the social tortures of adolescence, and Mary Shelley, we may not be surprised to learn, was a motherless child who wrote the book while herself still a teenager. In her later writing Shelley sought other expressions of alienation, and one of her works (*The Last Man,* 1826) features a man who is all alone on a completely depopulated Earth. Ever since Shelley, the ruined or deserted planet—from Nuclear Winter to Silent Spring—has naturally come to be associated with visions of higher technologies and the far future (see H.G. Wells' *The Time Machine,* 1898). The Krell Machine in its many forms typically inhabits empty worlds (just as Prospero, in *The Tempest,* inhabits a nearly deserted island). Krell Machines of various kinds sit unused and lonely in the ruins of empty cities on the edge of forever (yet another theme from the original *Star Trek* series)—their former users having either been destroyed, or else left for their dreams, leaving the shards and husks of more mundane realities behind.

48 Perhaps the image of "wasteland containing a doorway" is a fictional metaphor that arises from our childhood experiences of being lost outside the home in a world we do not understand. Certainly it makes for a better story to be faced with a functional alien artifact that has no user's manual. Frederick Pohl's *Gateway* novels (1977–) contain an entertaining use of this plot device: long vanished aliens have left a deserted space port, and some of the semi-automatic spacecraft still work. Push the button and you go to wherever that ship is programmed to go. Such mysteries are always dangerous, and they are not always resolved. In Algis Budrys' 1960 novel *Rogue Moon,* humans use disposable duplicates of themselves to explore a large and still-working maze-like alien machine found on the moon. The moon artifact kills people in gruesome ways, apparently a side effect of a true design function that humans never do figure out.

49 It does seem to be a nearly universal idea in science fiction that the result

of attaining ultimate technological power must be that those who have access to it vanish like 16-year-olds with the car keys. We don't always know where they go, but their disappearance is expected. Stephen Spielberg's *A.I* typifies a nowstandard mystery form. *A.I.* is a straightforward re-telling of the Frankenstein story, with all of its sub-texts of social isolation, child abuse, and creators who fail to live up to their responsibility. The protagonist, an artificial child, is abandoned like an unwanted pet to wander the Earth as an outcast, and finally is put out of his misery by being accidentally cryo-preserved (Shelley's original *Frankenstein* also begins and ends in the arctic, as a metaphor for isolation and loneliness). When the robot child wakes, humans have vanished, the cities are in ruins, and the child is surrounded by alien mechanoids whom he still asks pitifully for his human mommy. That's meant to give you the creeps, and indeed it does. *A.I.* did not do as well at the theaters as it could have, possibly because, like the robot-child himself, the film jerks too many human emotional strings, and does so too vigorously and too artificially. (Stanley Kubrick, in true *2001: A Space Odyssey* style, has given us an ending that is ambiguous and frustrating, unless one knows something of the original script conceptions. For these, see http://www.visual-memory.co.uk/faq/index2.html. The creatures at the end of the film are meant to be advanced earth robots, not aliens. The problem is that they know so little of their own origins that they may as well be aliens, and they essentially function in the plot as such.)

50 We frequently do not know where civilizations go when they hit the singularity in fiction, but sometimes they leave behind deliberately cryptic messages. For example, in Robert Forward's early treatment of the idea (*Dragon's Egg*, 1980; *Starquake*, 1985), the alien action is set on the surface of a neutron star. The indigenous intelligent life forms are somewhat like electronic computers, inasmuch as their nucleonic brain "chemistry" allows them to think a million times faster than humans. In these novels, humans originally arrive in orbit around the neutron star to find the inhabitants in a very primitive cultural state. Humans cannot visit the star's surface due to the fantastically high gravity, but communication is established. As the neutron star creatures are taught by humans, however, they rapidly assimilate human culture, and just as rapidly surpass it. Then, suddenly, to the surprise of the human starship crew, the world below them is empty. The aliens have reached their own singularity and (of course) disappeared. They leave behind nothing, save for a few condescending clues, the litter of Ascended Beings who now don't want to interact with primitive humanity until we are ready. The ultimate alienation may be an empty world containing traces of advanced beings who could talk to you, but don't want to.

51 In *Star Trek*'s most light-hearted invocation of the Krell Machine (Theodore Sturgeon's 1966 script *Shore Leave*) the crew of the Enterprise lands on an apparently empty planet, only to find that it hides machinery that has the job of making fantasies into realities. After being harassed by the incarnate results of their idle thoughts, the crew finally encounter the planet's alien Owners. The Owners use the technology for recreation (and for medical care—they repair a "dead" Dr. McCoy as easily as any machine). But they tell Captain Kirk that they (the Owners) are too advanced to meet humans. Now run along and play.

52 As with the scenario of nuclear war, it is traditional for planets to come out of the other side of the singularity depopulated, or worse. Science fiction is full of cautionary wastelands and ruins—markers of a time when humans stole Promethean fire and were burned by it. Authors of science fiction, for their part, write past the singularity simply because it's nearly impossible to write convincingly into it and keep a good and readable story with characters that we can care about and with whom we can identify. It's too strange. But there are many "fly-bys" of such apocalypses in the genre. *Childhood's End,* the 1953 Arthur C. Clarke novel, contains one. If "alienation as the price of technical advance" is the primal theme of all science fiction, then it can be added that Clarke's story plots (in particular) often involve alienation with some continued and distant communication. Clarke's characters are often beyond help, but they can still talk while they are trapped, or while meeting their seemingly inevitable doom. In *Childhood's End* the role of the outcast monster is played by alien creatures called the "Overlords." The Overlords are inhumanly intelligent and ethical but physically unlovely beings who are destined never to be able to make the evolutionary leap to higher consciousness, and who must therefore spend eternity outside of the party, looking in. They are alienated aliens; monsters who are troubled with their own monsters. At the end of the novel, the Last Man on Earth stays to fatally

witness humanity's transition to higher being. He continues to talk by radio through the last minutes of his life to the retreating Overlords, as the Earth itself begins to become transparent, in a scene which reminds us once again of Altair IV, the wizard Prospero, and some of the more famous lines from the play that was the inspiration for *Forbidden Planet:*

> Our revels now are ended: these our actors.
> As I foretold you, were all spirits, and
> Are melted into air, into thin air:
> And, like the baseless fabric of this vision
> The cloud-capp'd towers, the gorgeous palaces,
> The solemn temples, the great globe itself,
> Yea, all which it inherit, shall dissolve,
> And, like this insubstantial pageant faded,
> Leave not a rack behind: we are such stuff
> As dreams are made of, and our little life
> Is rounded with a sleep . . .

53 And this is all we can really say, as Earth or Altair IV disappears in the aft viewplate of our imaginations. The problem with the singularity is that there is apparently no way to survive it (pace the tongue-in-cheek Vinge subtitle "How to Survive in the Post-Human Era") because it is the nature of the singularity to change beyond all recognition even the basic concepts of humanity, life, individual identity, and survival—particularly individual survival.

54 A central problem in our imagination of what the singularity might be like is that the interfacing of brains and computers in the singularity must result in a vicious melding of various kinds of minds. Vinge remarks that "[a] central feature of strongly superhuman entities will likely be their ability to communicate at variable bandwidths. . . ." This is a safe and nearly tautological prediction, for breadth of bandwidth is all that defines whether "communication," as we usually understand the word, is taking place at all. Communication is generally not a word we use in connection with the mind's internal affairs. "Communication" therefore requires two or more minds—yet if bandwidth is too high, individual minds must disappear, and only one group-mind is left. Thus, within a grouped computational being, minds and sub-minds are defined only by bandwidth. Imagine being "you" only when you close the door on the party, or they close the door on you. If the door is opened wide, however, "you" cease to exist, and you and they become part of a Larger You (or collective Us).

55 Such Borg-like problems plague our predictions, so much so that writers considering the very far future have had to split some powers of technology off, in order to have any recognizable human culture to deal with at all. For instance, Frank Herbert, in his *Dune* series, simply outlaws machine intelligence. Too much telepathy and too much technology makes it difficult to generate recognizable dramatic tension, which comes from recognizable characters with problems we can care about. Arthur C. Clarke's 1956 novel, *The City and the Stars,* is set a billion years in the future, in a utopian metropolis called Diaspar. Diaspar's machinery can manufacture anything on demand, including human beings. Indeed, the city's very inhabitants are a random collection of people from the much greater store available in the city's memory banks, something like books circulating from a central library. Each inhabitant lives a thousand years, but also recovers his old memories from previous incarnations, giving him functional immortality. And yet, the novel's main character, restless to explore, eventually escapes his version of the Krell Machine. Outside Diaspar, he finds the traditionally empty Earth, uninhabited except by a few mentally advanced communities of humans. These people deliberately eschew technology, and live a rural, somewhat Amish-like existence, complete with normal human reproduction, normal aging, and standard death. Significantly, however, they are telepathic, and thus experience a sense of community and communal immortality that they find to be a satisfying replacement for technological immortality. Thus, Clarke's immortal Diasparians pay for their technical utopia with severe communications problems, and with no way to satisfy the urge to explore. It is difficult to imagine the kind of lifestyle that would result if they were not so crippled. Yet this is exactly what we must contemplate for ourselves—not a billion years from now, but very possibly in the next century.

56 The name "singularity" to describe such a state-of-being is appropriate because, as is the case with a black hole, the singularity looks different depending on whether it is viewed from outside, or from the point of view of an observer falling into it. We have readable fictional scenarios only for the outside. For all we know, however, perhaps these are the futures that will ultimately come to pass. After all, it is

by no means certain that humanity will either be destroyed or entirely uploaded/assimilated into something non-understandable. There is a third possibility: humanity might be left in the dust like those old computers (or toys) in your garage that you're never going to play with again. If the singularity had been called the "Techno-Rapture," it should also be remembered that a fundamental feature of the Rapture is that some go, and some are left behind.

57 Will those who wish to go into the singularity have a path to do so? One of the key issues determining what kind of future we get may be the timing of the development of a full brain/computer interface. Whereas computers may be made to talk to each other with relative ease, the human brain is not wired to accept or process input more complex than sensory data. Indeed, in *Forbidden Planet* all but a few human brains overload and burn out when exposed to connection with the Krell technology. It will not be a trivial undertaking to directly connect brains with computers, or to technologically connect brains with each other (mechanical telepathy). Virtual reality is technically simple compared with (say) constructing a system in which one can sort through and "remember" items in a computer database as easily as sorting through one's own memories. Thus, it may be that the planetary web of computers will exceed the sum of human intelligence well before the interface problem is solved. If events happen in this order, it will be up to the artificial intelligence, not humanity, to figure out how to put the full link between machines and humans safely into place. There is no guarantee that the singularity A.I. will choose to do so.

58 There are dark possibilities at this point. Perhaps A.I. will simply protect itself and impatiently go on, without us. Perhaps (worse) it will even leave humanity with some kind of technological lock, in order to prevent development of the computational power necessary for such uncouth creatures as ourselves to follow. Singularity-struck societies that leave any intelligences "behind" may even represent a kind of threat to the ascended beings who have gone before. Such stuttering "techno-adolescent" societies could be expected to attain new technical singularities regularly. With each one, they would fire out races of new Ascended Intelligences. Might some of these be pathological? It's too soon to tell. But if so, such societies might therefore be under careful watch by those who have gone before. They may, conceivably, even be under quarantine.

59 "What?" you say. "Surely these machines will let humanity upload or mind-link with them, and join the party. Won't they? They have to!"

60 If not, we can glimpse that future—it's the main one we are familiar with from science fiction, and, likely, also familiar with, from some of our own early adolescent experiences of being shut out of the world of adults. We know what things will look like then. They will look like being locked out by an intelligent computer who not only controls our technology, but also tells us that conversation can serve no further useful purpose. Humanity would then be the chained Prometheus, forever the orphaned and lonely Frankenstein's monster, looking in though the window. Indeed, we would be forever Caliban, left alone on an island Earth, with the wizards gone—and not even comforted by the whisperings of spirits that have long since been freed. "Open the Pod Bay Door, HAL. . . ."

Thinking about the Argument

1. Do you think the discussion of a scenario in a science-fiction movie is an engaging way for the author to introduce his topic? Why or why not? Do you find yourself more or less engaged by this issue after being introduced to this analogy?
2. Examine the author's tone. How does his use of specific words (like "darkest potentials of foreseeable technology") reinforce the idea he is trying to relate? Identify three other instances of tone in this essay, and evaluate how they might impact the reader.
3. Does the author think nanotechnology is a good thing or a bad thing? Find examples in the text to validate your answer.

4. What is a "computational singularity"? What benefits and dangers does it represent, according to Harris?
5. What solutions does the author discuss? Which do you agree with or disagree with, and why?

Responding to the Argument

1. Do you think it is useful to use a science-fiction analogy to approach a topic like artificial intelligence? Why or why not? What chance is there that the argument might not be taken seriously? Explain.
2. Make a chart outlining the benefits and dangers of nanotechnology. Do you believe the potential benefits outweigh the dangers? Why or why not?
3. Is Harris suggesting that singularity computers could, or should, be taught morals? Is this possible? Is this desirable? Why or why not?
4. To what extent are the author's predictions reasonable, and to what extent are they fantasy? Are these scenarios, as a form of evidence, reasonably enough anchored in current science to be convincing? Explain.

Writing about the Argument

1. In your journal or in an argumentative essay, write a list of moral principles that you would have hard-wired into all computers. Why did you select these principles? Why do you think they are important?
2. Do you think that efforts should be made to prevent the computational singularity from being reached? Why or why not? Write an argument that is based on a claim of policy and that states what should be done.
3. If computational singularities and nanotechnology can merge humans and computers at some level, is this desirable? Might it be the natural next step in our evolution toward a higher state of being? Why or why not? Write an argument based on either a definition (what it means to be human) or an ethical claim.
4. Write a refutation of this argument. Explain why you think the scenario presented is invalid because it is based on mere conjecture without adequate evidence.

Issue 3: Human Longevity

Recent advances in medicine have moved the idea of extending the human life span from the realm of fantasy to that of scientific reality. Over the last century, the average human life span has been extended thirty years—from roughly forty-five years to about seventy-five years today. More people are living to ninety these days, and it is becoming increasingly common for people to reach

Recent advances in genetic engineering have enabled scientists to give mice the bioluminescent qualities of some jellyfish. Scientists have discussed using mice to grow human brain cells. Might similar research result in a vastly increased human life span?

the century mark. A growing number of scientists believe that in the very near future—within the next fifty years—we may begin to see human lives measured in centuries rather than decades.

Such an extension of the human life span will have significant implications for our lives, our social institutions, and the environment. What, for example, might happen to the global population when people stop dying? Will pension and insurance plans designed around the assumption that the average person will not live past seventy-five go bankrupt? Will people's years of productivity—and their working years—be increased, or will their years of old age and infirmity simply be extended? If life-extension treatments are considered unnecessary elective procedures (similar to cosmetic surgery), would this trend lead to long lives for the wealthy and short lives for poor and middle-income people? Given all of these considerations, is it a good idea for us to let this genie out of the bottle?

Online Study Center
Prepare for Class
Human Longevity

Considering the Issue of Human Longevity

Consider these questions related to the issue of human longevity:

1. If you had the opportunity to extend your life to 120 healthy years, would you do so? Why or why not? What if living longer required you to spend the last twenty years in a wheelchair or hooked up to an oxygen tank?
2. If you had a chance to extend a beloved grandparent's life for another twenty years (in whatever state of health), would you do so? Even against his or her will?
3. What implications does increased longevity have for social institutions such as Social Security and retirement plans? For health insurance?
4. If extending the human life span through gene therapy becomes a reality, should it be considered an elective procedure like cosmetic surgery (and therefore not be covered by insurance)? Should longer lives be a right? Who should pay for exercising that right? Individuals? Insurance plans? The government?

READING SELECTION

"It's Completely Impossible"

About the Author: Ben Bova

After a stint as a journalist, Ben Bova worked for the U.S. space program two years before NASA was formed. He has been the editor of *Analog* and *Omni* magazines and has authored more than ninety books, most of them science fiction. Bova has worked with Nobel laureate scientists on educational films as well as with Woody Allen, Gene Roddenberry, and George Lucas. He serves as the president emeritus of the National Space Society, is past president of the Science Fiction Writers of America, and serves as a science commentator for the *CBS Morning News.* He regularly lectures on the relationship of science and politics and the craft of writing fiction. This selection is excerpted from *Immortality: How Science Is Extending Your Life Span—and Changing the World* (1998).

Before You Read

1. Given what you know about Ben Bova from the headnote, would you consider him to be an authoritative source on this topic? Why or why not?
2. What do you expect Bova to say about this topic?
3. Are you approaching Bova's essay as a believer or a skeptic? How do you think your attitude will affect how you respond to his claims? How about his evidence?
4. Do you think life extension is a good idea? Why or why not?

It's Completely Impossible

1 When I was a teenager, flying to the Moon was regarded as the ultimate impossibility.

2 I remember hearing in 1948: "Harry Truman has as much of a chance of getting reelected President as we have of flying to the Moon." Truman won an upset victory that November. A little less than twenty-one years later, Neil Armstrong and Buzz Aldrin set foot on the Sea of Tranquility.

3 Nuclear power, organ transplants, desktop electronic computers, supersonic aircraft, coronary artery bypass operations—all were once regarded as totally impossible. Yet, over the years of my own lifetime, Buck Rogers's ray guns became lasers, astronauts flying into space have become so routine that the news media only cover space flight when there is an accident or controversy, and the "old folks" have become the "golden agers" who play golf and tennis, take ocean cruises, and power the economy of states such as Florida and Arizona.

Optimists and Pessimists

4 The pessimist sees the glass half-empty, the optimist sees it half-full. Let me tell you why I am an optimist.

5 I started my working career as a reporter on a weekly newspaper in suburban Philadelphia. During the summer we carried a box score on the front page every week—about polio: how many children had been killed by the disease the previous week; how many were crippled; how many had to be placed in iron lungs so that they could breathe.

6 One fine spring day we carried a story about kids getting Salk vaccine shots. Great human-interest photographs of children grimacing and wincing as doctors jabbed needles in their arms while their mothers stood bravely tearful in the background.

7 And we never had to run a polio box score again.

8 I moved from newspapering into the aerospace industry to work on the first American space project, *Vanguard.* In those early days of the so-called "space race" between the United States and the Soviet Union, the Russians scored most of the successes and our rockets tended to blow up. The first attempt to launch a *Vanguard* satellite ended in an ignominious and quite spectacular explosion a few feet above the launch pad on December 6, 1957.

9 Learned mathematicians published articles showing, with impeccable logic, that rockets are such complicated machines that it was statistically impossible to expect each and every part of a rocket launcher to work correctly and in sequence. That was why the rockets blew up. They would always blow up, the mathematicians asserted.

10 The fact that Soviet rockets seemed somehow to evade this mathematical certainty did not enter into their calculations. They were wrong, of course. Solid engineering and hard-earned experience overcame the shortcomings of our early rockets. We went on to the Moon and have sent robot probes to all the planets of the solar system, save distant-most Pluto.

11 Today when I tell friends and colleagues that human immortality is in sight, they stare at me in disbelief.

12 It's impossible, of course. You might as well try flying to the Moon.

13 . . . I believe that human immortality is not only possible but near. Men and women alive today may well be able to live for centuries, and if they survive that long, they will undoubtedly be able to live for millennia. We are reaching the point in our knowledge of biology and medicine where death from aging will no longer be inevitable.

14 When I discuss the matter rationally with friends and colleagues, what comes out is not that they regard human immortality as scientifically impossible. They grudgingly admit that if you give enough scientists enough time (and funding), they can accomplish almost anything.

15 No, they do not really believe immortality is impossible.

16 They believe it is undesirable.

17 They are not saying, "It can't be done." Their true reaction is: "It *shouldn't* be done."

18 Which brings us to a sheep named Dolly.

Questions about Cloning

19 In February 1997 a team of scientists from the Roslin Institute in Scotland rocked the world by announcing that they had successfully cloned a sheep.

20 Dolly was produced not from an egg fertilized by a sperm cell but by taking a sheep's egg cell and replacing its DNA-containing nucleus with the nucleus of a cell from a 6-year-old ewe's body. The egg cell was then placed in another ewe's womb and developed normally. The lamb, named Dolly, was genetically identical to the sheep from which the cell nucleus had been taken.

21 No one had cloned a mammal from an adult cell before. But cloning was not entirely new. It had been going on since the early 1980s, actually. That is when biologists developed a procedure in which they replaced the nucleus of an egg cell with a nucleus from another egg cell. Monkeys were cloned that way.

22 But the altered egg could develop into a clone of the original animal only if the replacement nucleus came from a cell of a barely developed embryo. Cloning attempts using nuclei from adult animals invariably failed.

23 In 1996 the Scottish team, led by Ian Wilmut and Keith H. S. Campbell, successfully cloned sheep from older embryonic cells by placing the intended donor cells in a nutrient-deprived medium, essentially starving them for five days. This forced the cells out of their normal growth cycle and into a quiescent stage. For reasons still under study, nuclei from these cells are more readily accepted by eggs.

24 Dolly was the first mammal to be born not from an embryo's cell but from a somatic cell of an adult. Theoretically, this means that it should be possible to clone animals, eventually including human beings, from any kind of donor cell.

25 Although many biologists feared that the DNA inside the nuclei of adult cells undergoes irreversible changes as the cells differentiate and specialize, Dolly's birth shows that the DNA in an adult nucleus either reprograms itself or is open to reprogramming by factors in the egg.

26 The question is: How old is Dolly?

27 "Our seven-month-old lamb actually has a six-year, seven-month-old nucleus in all her cells," said Grahame Bulfield, director of the Roslin Institute. "It's going to be interesting to see what happens with the aging of this animal."

28 Does the cell's DNA harbor a clock that determines the organism's physiological age? If so, is that clock the telomeres that cap each chromosome or some other mechanism among the genes as yet undiscovered? And is the clock somehow reset by the act of cloning?

29 The answers to those questions are of primary importance in extending human life span.

30 Another critically important question is: Will it be possible to add or delete genes from the donor DNA before producing clones from it? In other words, will bioscientists one day be able to clone organisms with DNA tailored to suit a preconceived demand? Do you want your cloned sheep to produce more wool than normal sheep? Do you want to clone a racehorse that can outrun any thoroughbred?

31 The answers will not be long in coming. In July 1997 the Scottish team announced the birth of five more lambs, all cloned from fetal cells. But these lambs carry extra genes; some even have a human gene that was inserted into the fetal cells before they were cloned.

32 This is part of the effort undertaken by PPL Therapeutics, a Scottish biogenetics firm that worked with the Roslin Institute team, which is reportedly working on replacing the genes that code for blood plasma in sheep and cows with human plasma genes; thus the animals' milk will contain human blood plasma elements, including albumin, clotting factors, and antibodies.

33 Genetically altered animals could produce thousands of times more human blood plasma per year than human blood donors now give. By the end of 1997 the Roslin Institute scientists announced the birth of Molly and Polly, two more cloned lambs who have been genetically engineered so their milk will contain blood-clotting factors that could be used for treating leukemia in humans.

34 The ultimate question is, of course: Will it be possible to clone humans? And if so, do you want to clone copies of yourself? Should they be exact copies or perhaps a little taller and slimmer? And have blue eyes instead of brown?

The Reaction to Cloning

35 No sooner was Dolly's birth announced in Edinburgh than a worldwide cry of fear and revulsion issued from the throats (and keyboards) of politicians, religious leaders, and media pundits.

36 The President of France, Jacques Chirac, called cloning "a degrading attack on humanity" and suggested a ban on such research throughout the industrialized world.

37 Pope John Paul II also inveighed against human cloning, fearing that scientists will attempt to "play God." Later the Vatican announced that cloned human beings would not have souls, a point of view that many dreadful sci-fi movies have been playing on for generations.

38 U.S. President Bill Clinton directed the National Bioethics Advisory Commission to prepare a report examining the ramifications of cloning technology and urged that no federal funding should be allowed for research into cloning human beings.

39 Later in 1997 the National Bioethics Advisory Commission recommended that the moratorium on human cloning research be continued

and reinforced with federal legislation, provided such laws have a "sunset clause" that will allow for a re-examination of the situation in a few years and are written carefully enough so that other forms of cloning research are not outlawed.

40 The general reaction pounced on the idea of cloning humans, of "playing God." But why? Why did media commentators, politicians, and religious leaders *immediately* react with such expressions of fear and outrage?

41 It is important to understand this reaction because this kind of knee-jerk negativism is what we can expect if and when the general public realizes that human life spans can be extended for centuries or more. The public reaction to cloning is a nearly perfect example of what the reaction will be to the prospect of human immortality.

42 This reaction is puzzling and troubling, because a cloned human being will be just like any other human. The Vatican may believe that a cloned person does not have a soul, but souls are ephemeral things, not measurable by scientific methods. Besides, if God creates souls for people born the normal way, why not for clones?

43 This hostile opposition of the naysayers betrays a fundamental ignorance of what cloning can and cannot do.

44 Yes, cloning can produce an offspring that is *physically* an exact copy of its parent—if successful. At present, even cloning a sheep took some three hundred attempts before Dolly was produced.

45 But a cloned human being will be no more a slave, a soulless zombie, or an exact copy of its parent's *personality* than any two identical twins are zombies or have exactly the same personalities. The sum total of a human personality depends not merely on his or her genes, but on the experiences the person has throughout life. . . .

46 A person's genes, by themselves, do not determine that person's fate. A cloned egg is still subject during gestation to the specific chemical factors of its mother's womb, factors that are unique to that woman and that pregnancy. Genetic determinism is no more valid than the belief that the Earth is flat or the phlogiston theory of heat.

Meanwhile, Back at the Lab . . .

47 Look at the other side of the coin. Yes, there may be fears and dangers in cloning research; every new area of knowledge is filled with unknown possibilities.

48 But what happens if we stop research into cloning?

49 One of the motivations of the Scottish work was the hope that it may become possible to create animals such as sheep or cows that can be genetically altered to produce pharmaceutical chemicals—medicines—in their milk. As we have seen, genetically altered animals could produce human blood plasma and then be cloned to meet the need for plasma worldwide.

50 All right, perhaps animals can be developed into biochemical factories. Punsters are already talking about "pharm" animals. An animal breeding firm in Wisconsin, ABS Global, revealed in August 1997 a 6-month-old cloned calf, Gene. ABS Global has spun off a new company, Infigen, specifically to clone transgenic cows capable of producing a variety of therapeutic proteins in their milk.

51 But what about cloning humans? Isn't the old-fashioned way of producing babies good enough?

52 Yes, but . . .

53 Some babies are born with defects in the mitochondria of their cells, those DNA-bearing power plants that produce the cell's energy from nutrients and oxygen. Mitochondria with defective DNA can cause many types of devastating illnesses, including blindness.

54 If it becomes possible to remove the defective mitochondrial DNA and replace it with healthy DNA cloned from a donor, such diseases can be eliminated.

55 Organ transplants often fail because of tissue rejection; the body's immune system attacks the

transplanted organ because it recognizes the tissue as "foreign." If it becomes possible to clone a new heart from the patient's own tissue, the transplant procedure becomes infinitely easier. If it becomes possible to clone healthy brain cells, the ravages of Parkinson's, Alzheimer's, and even traumatic brain injury can be reversed.[1]

56 Stop cloning research and these opportunities will be lost.

57 In the meantime, ongoing research brought up a new possibility. The 1997 announcement from Johns Hopkins that researchers had discovered the embryonic stem cells that give rise to all the other cells of the developing embryo may well replace cloning as a political "hot potato."

58 Such totipotent cells could be used to generate blood, nerve, muscle, or the cells of any organ. This discovery may make organ and tissue regeneration practical. But since they are derived from human embryos—aborted fetuses—much the same furor can be expected as any other therapy touching on the explosive abortion issue.

"Playing God"

59 People tend to fear new possibilities. And the easiest thing to do with something that frightens you is to banish it. Get rid of it! Then it can't hurt us. Yes, but it can't help you either.

60 In attacking the idea of cloning, religious leaders and media pundits trotted out one of their favorite catch-phrases: "playing God."

61 When Pope John Paul II invoked this cliché, His Holiness overlooked the fact that the medical attention that has more than once saved his own life is surely "playing God." Otherwise, he would be among the angels now.

62 Every time we take an aspirin or an antibiotic, we are "playing God." What else is the coronary bypass procedure that saves a heart attack victim from imminent death?

63 When anesthetics were first introduced in surgery in the early nineteenth century, moralists railed against their use in childbirth. The Bible commands that women bear children in pain and suffering, they thundered, therefore giving the laboring mother something to ease her pain was against the dictates of God's expressed will.

64 But when Queen Victoria, no wild-eyed radical, decided that *she* would use anesthesia in childbirth (she had nine children), the moralists were silenced. A blow had been struck for the advance of medicine and science. And feminism.

65 People fear new ideas. Resuscitating a patient whose heart has stopped may be "playing God" the first few times it is done; afterward it becomes a standard part of emergency medical treatment, and we take it for granted.

66 One of the reasons for the fear of cloning is that many people associate the idea of cloning with the concept of trying to produce some sort of "ideal" human beings through eugenics, by deliberately selecting genetic traits such as height, eye color, and so on. Especially to those who remember Nazi Germany's misguided and murderous quest for a "master race," eugenics is anathema.

67 Yet it would be the utmost folly to throw away the possible benefits of cloning over fears of its misuse. A eugenics program dictated by a government, where only certain physical types are regarded as desirable (or even permissible), is certainly a form of tyranny that should be resisted by all. But an individual's desire to produce offspring that are as close to the ideal that the parent can envision seems well within the rights of any citizen.

68 We will face the same objections and emotional reactions when human immortality becomes a public issue. These objections boil down to a choice between pessimism and optimism, a struggle between hope and fear.

69 The pessimists fear that the new knowledge will be used in harmful ways; they are willing to

1. At present, research has shown that transplanted fetal brain tissue can help repair such damage, but the use of fetal tissue has stirred the wrath of those opposed to abortion and thus has been slowed or halted altogether by political decisions in the United States and elsewhere.

forego the possible benefits for fear of the possible harm.

70 The optimists look forward to the possible benefits from new knowledge, and believe (perhaps naively) that the possible harm can be avoided, minimized, or controlled.

Death with Dignity

71 Today more public attention is focused on how we die than on the prospects of avoiding death altogether.

72 Modern biomedical technology allows terminally ill patients to be sustained long past the point where their bodies could continue living without such help. Many people fear that their lives will be unnecessarily prolonged—and their estates drained to the last cent—by such "heroic" methods.

73 People are demanding the right to die with dignity, rather than being maintained in a vegetative state by life-support machinery. Some demand the right, when faced with a hopeless medical condition and the prospect of physical agony and emotional anguish, to decide to end their own lives through doctor-assisted suicide. Dr. Jack Kevorkian has become famous (or infamous, depending on your point of view) for defying local laws and assisting patients to die with as much dignity and as little pain as possible.

74 The Supreme Court decided in 1997 that the U.S. Constitution does not include the right to commit suicide. The separate states will have to decide if they want to legalize suicide and enact their own laws on the subject.

75 As we have seen, a few people have already decided to have their bodies frozen after being declared clinically dead in the hope of one day being thawed and cured of the ailment that "killed" them. Instead of suicide, they look to a life in the future.

76 My father did not die with dignity. Even when taken off life support, he struggled on in a coma for weeks, unseeing, unhearing, but desperately fighting to keep on breathing to stay alive. He died at last when he had no strength left to continue the battle.

77 Do I want to die like that? Or would it be better to go quietly when I become certain I cannot live much longer?

78 If the trends of biomedical research are leading toward immortality or, at least, huge extensions of human life span, do I want to go at all?

Who Wants to Live Forever?

79 Opponents of gun control insist that: "When guns are outlawed, only outlaws will have guns."

80 Opponents of immortality—or vastly extended human lifespans—have already voiced the opinion that only megalomaniacs will want to live forever. Think of an immortal Hitler or Stalin or Genghis Khan.

81 Do *you* want to live forever? Is it morally right to try to extend our lifespans past the traditional three- or four-score of years?

82 We are dealing with life and death quite literally here. The ultimate horror, the transcendent fear, death in all its finality may be avoidable. The prospect threatens our most fundamental beliefs, shatters our basic understanding of life and its fragility. . . .

83 Moreover, by taking away the fear of inevitable death, we may be taking away the most compelling support for religion. It is that fear of death, what Shakespeare's Hamlet called "the undiscover'd country, from whose bourn no traveler returns," that started the earliest humans on their quest for a life beyond the grave.

84 Religious thinkers have created the most important moral codes that we possess. Our society is based on the bedrock of Judeo-Christian morality. Yet if men and women can achieve immortality *here,* on Earth, the most basic motivation for following the ethical teachings of religion is greatly weakened—perhaps fatally weakened.

85 Thus religious thinkers may have ample grounds for resisting the opportunity of achieving human immortality.

86 I believe there is no moral injunction against our efforts to extend lifespan, just as there was no moral injunction against the practice of medicine. Perhaps I won't want to live forever, but it's a choice I would like to be able to make for myself.

87 In essence, we all make that choice when we go to the doctor for help, when we seek a cure for our ailments, even when we eat properly and exercise. We are trying to prolong our lives. We don't cross busy streets with our eyes closed. Rational people try to avoid death, unless they are so ill (physically or mentally) that they see death as preferable to life.

88 Maybe, if I get to be 90, or 900, or 9,000, I will decide that I want to end it all. Perhaps, like the suave movie actor George Sanders, I will take my own life and leave a note that simply reads: "I am bored." But I would prefer to have the option in my own hands and not leave it to the blind workings of chance. Or free radicals. Or glucose browning. Or telomere shortening.

89 And once it becomes known that human lifespan can be greatly extended, the moral questions will be swept aside in the stampede to get whatever it takes to keep on living. As Austad puts it:

> 90 It does seem compelling apparent, though, that regardless of the social desirability of slowing aging, if science uncovers therapies that can do it, those therapies will be employed. This is one genie that has no chance of being put back in the bottle.

91 This is not selfishness, or greed, or any other manifestation of moral degradation. It is nothing less than what we should expect. Life seeks life. Living organisms strive to continue living. They do not ordinarily go gentle into that good night.

92 But if people start living for centuries, what happens to society? How can the world hold together if (and when) humans stop dying of old age?

Thinking about the Argument

1. How optimistic is Bova about longevity research? How can you tell?
2. What is Bova's opinion about the related subjects of euthanasia and cloning research? Do you think the author would support stem-cell research? Why?
3. Could you summarize Bova's main point? What do you think his main supporting ideas are?
4. What sort of evidence does he supply?
5. What is the greatest strength of the excerpt from Bova's book? The greatest weakness?

Responding to the Argument

1. What are some of the social problems that might occur if people begin to live longer? What will happen to pension plans? Social Security? Health/life insurance?
2. If life extension becomes a reality, is it a right (paid for by the government or insurance) or a privilege (like cosmetic surgery, which you can have if you can afford it)?
3. Should people be able to select when and how they die? Does the government have the right to decide when someone must continue to live, even if someone doesn't want to? Explain.

4. If the average age of death continues to climb as it has over the last 100 years, should the mandatory retirement age—that is, the age at which one can retire with full pension benefits—be increased? What effect might such an increase have on pension plans and Social Security?

WRITING ABOUT THE ARGUMENT

1. Pretend you are a concerned citizen and write to your state senator regarding whether the government should fund longevity research.
2. Research the issue of privatization of Social Security. Is it a good idea? Why or why not?
3. Write an essay arguing whether a person has a right to select the moment at which he or she dies. If you are not in favor of euthanasia ("mercy killing"), why do you feel this way? If you are in favor of euthanasia, how do you determine when one has reached the point where the person's suffering gives him or her the right to die? On a related topic, should someone be able to select the moment of his or her own death for reasons other than pain or suffering?

"Point Counterpoint: Would Doubling the Human Life Span Be a Net Positive or Negative for Us Either as Individuals or as a Society?"

ABOUT THE AUTHORS: GREGORY STOCK AND DANIEL CALLAHAN

In this 2004 article from the *Journal of Gerontology,* two experts on the science of aging debate the ethical implications of extending the human life span. Gregory Stock is author of *Redesigning Humans: Our Inevitable Genetic Future* (2002) and director of the UCLA School of Medicine's Program of Medicine, Technology, and Society. He is a frequent commentator on a variety of television and radio programs in addition to being a prolific writer and public speaker. Stock believes that the genetic augmentation of the human genome is not only possible but also inevitable and desirable. Daniel Callahan was cofounder and president of the Hastings Center, a research and educational institute formed to examine ethics issues associated with the medical profession. He is particularly interested in heath care systems and their economic impact on people throughout the world. He has published more than thirty-five books and has contributed articles to the *Atlantic, New England Journal of Medicine, Journal of the American Medical Association, New Republic,* and other publications.

BEFORE YOU READ

1. Do a little research on the Internet. Who is Gregory Stock? Who is Daniel Callahan? Where has each man worked, and what has he published? Why would each of these authors be interested in the topic of longevity research?

2. If you read the excerpt from Bova's book presented earlier in this cluster, has your position on this topic changed? If so, how? Are you now more comfortable with discussing this topic than you previously were?
3. If this is your first reading on this topic, what do you know about it? Have you formed an opinion yet? What sorts of arguments do you think the authors might make?

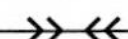

Point Counterpoint: Would Doubling the Human Life Span Be a Net Positive or Negative for Us Either as Individuals or as a Society?

Viewpoint: Dr. Gregory Stock

1 The question before us is whether doubling human life span, and presumably adult life expectancies as well, would be beneficial for us as individuals or as a society. Those who believe such a development will arrive during the next generation or so are almost certainly being overly optimistic, but we will examine here not that issue, but whether the goal itself is worthwhile, because the answer has significant public policy implications. Some critics of biotechnology have argued that such a development would be undesirable and that we should therefore discourage research to achieve the insights that might allow us to meaningfully intervene in the aging process.

2 It may seem self-evident that extending our vital years would be desirable, but so many people have argued the contrary that it is worth looking closely at both the personal and social consequences of such a development. I will argue that the benefits would not only be personal, but social.

3 On the personal side, life's larger trajectory, when looked at from afar, is a brutal one. If we live long enough, everything we love is eventually taken from us: our family, our friends, our health, our connections to the world around us—smell, taste, vision, hearing—our vitality, even our minds. Anyone who looks at this trajectory from youth towards decrepitude as idyllic should sit in a nursing home and contemplate a photo of the early years of someone who has become hunched and frail, or who is barely present at all. Who would not feel at least a twinge at this diminution?

4 We've developed many ways of trying to accept not only these ravages, but death itself. The first is to ignore this descent: We can simply pretend it isn't happening. This works when we're young, but becomes ever less effective as the years march by and our strength seeps from us. The second way is to deny death: We can assert that the soul is eternal, that our memory will live on, that we are young at heart, that we are not older but better. A third way is to battle the process like Ponce de Leon did slogging through Florida, Dorian Gray, or those engaged in anti-aging research because, in the backs of their minds, they hope to extend their own future. Or we can accept this descent as sad but inevitable, and say that it's natural and can't be avoided, or even tell ourselves that it's the best thing and claim, like Leon Kass, the Chair of the President's Bioethics Advisory Commission, that death gives meaning to life.

5 Dan Callahan, I suspect, is right in the middle of this last category, not only accepting aging, but in some ways, extolling its virtue and ultimate wisdom. I, on the other hand, see it as a sorry state of affairs. Frankly, I don't see how you can applaud our current life expectancies and rue their extension while truly saying "yes" to life, unless you think we live in a perfect world, where everything happens to be optimal just as it is.

And this is an attitude exhibited with little else. We alter the world around us all the time. We build and dam and plough. We domesticate animals and plants. We breed our pets to suit our personalities. If we accept that the proper trajectory is that ending with a "natural" life span, then we are accepting that more healthy life is not a general good for us, at least as individuals. This would seem to imply that less healthy life should perhaps be our goal. If we are going to accept that, then it implies a lot of changes, the least of which is that we should terminate much of our public health efforts and biomedical research.

6 Sure, at some point in our journey toward decrepitude, life can become so painful that it's difficult to bear, and the prospects ahead so grim that death can look like a rescuer. That's why we don't always mourn when we see an older person die. Death is an escape at times. But the game of anti-aging medicine is to buy more youthfulness, not more decrepitude. If life shifts at some point from being a positive to being a negative, it does so not at some particular age, but as a result of the internal changes and debilities that accompany the process of life itself. And it stands to reason that delaying the arrival of those changes would delay this shift and add life that is of value to us individually. The cost of intervention might be too high, of course, but theoretically the personal cost could be brought down to very near to zero, as is the case, say for antibiotics that insulate us from infectious disease.

7 In my view, only at the point that someone ceases valuing life itself would he or she not see freely chosen anti-aging interventions as being a personal benefit. To reject such an intervention for oneself is one thing, but to try to deny it to others is entirely another. What about social costs, though? Perhaps the global costs of more youth and vitality might be so high as to demand that individuals forego the obvious personal benefits of extended longevity.

8 Before we answer that question, let's think about how best to measure costs or benefits. The only metric that makes sense is personal. Life extension is of value if individuals value it, and it is very valuable if individuals value it a great deal. Moreover, in our culture, people do value extended vitality and youth, because they strive for even its appearance, spending substantial sums on vitamins and anti-aging medications that accomplish little or nothing. Without this broad desire for extended youth, there would not be so many charlatans and hucksters populating this realm. So, if actual anti-aging interventions come into being, we will forego them only in the face of very serious social costs.

9 In looking at the social costs of anti-aging medicine, we should consider interventions that are freely available and easily accessible not only because these would be the most challenging socially, but because it is so easy to distort the distribution of even a great good and worry about issues of equity and justice that have little to do with the nature of the good itself. To try to weigh costs and benefits, I could list the advantages I see in doubling the span of our vital healthy lives: Such an intervention would give us a chance to recover from our mistakes, lead us towards longer-term thinking, and reduce health care costs by delaying the onset of expensive diseases of aging. It would also raise productivity by adding to our prime years. It takes a long time to acquire the knowledge and experience to operate effectively in the increasingly complex world we live in, and just as we achieve this we begin to slow down. So, adding to our prime years would be of tremendous benefit now, just as it has been in the past. Yale economist William Nordhous, for example, claims that the dramatic increase in human life expectancy since 1900 has been responsible for about half the increase in our standard of living in the United States since then.

10 In any event, I could wave my hands and assert that these sorts of benefits outweigh the various social challenges that would come from changed patterns of wealth transfer, changed family dynamics, added rigidities from reduced

intergenerational turnover, and the need for people to come up with new life plans that encompass these unprecedented extra decades. I could minimize the challenges of getting rid of dictators and even the aging tenured professors that academics always seem to worry about. I could assert that change always brings challenges, and that our projections about the impacts of something as monumental as doubling the human life span and adult life expectancies tells us more about our own values and beliefs than it tells us about what would really happen. I could insist that Dan Callahan had better have some very clear and dire social dangers in mind if he wants to use their avoidance as justification for sacrificing decades of life for so many who value it deeply.

11 But I think the real issue is not how we tote up the specific debits and credits we see, but how we judge what to call a debit or a credit. As I see it, the value of a development to society at large is ultimately the sum of the value it generates for each individual in that society. Thus, if on average we benefit as individuals, then society will enjoy a net benefit. In some situations, of course, the supposed individual benefits are a mirage. The so-called Tragedy of the Commons, for example, occurs when an apparent individual benefit evaporates or is short-lived if pursued by everyone. This happens when the supply of what is sought is limited so that everyone can't possibly have it, or when something that is sought is valued primarily because it shifts one's relative status in society and thus is no longer of value when possessed by all.

12 Anti-aging medicine is afflicted by neither of these attributes. In fact, the more aggressively it is pursued by more people, the more likely it is to arrive more rapidly and to end up being cheaper and more readily available to more people, even those who did not pursue it in the first place. In addition, the more people there are enjoying extended longevity, the more we ourselves would enjoy it. Many people claim that they don't want to live a longer life because they'd grow increasingly isolated as their friends and family aged and passed away. So, the access of others to such a medical intervention would increase, not decrease, its value to us. The circle is virtuous.

13 The public policy implication of this is that we should not only allow anti-aging research, we should pursue it aggressively to gain both the individual and the social benefits that would attend progress. And if we believe that eventual success is likely—whether in decades, generations, or centuries—spending health care resources in its pursuit is a gift to future generations because such effort makes it more likely that they will be among the first to enjoy these benefits, rather than among the last—as we may be—to miss them.

14 I will go even further. To spend resources on our current health care needs, instead of on these future possibilities, is highly suspect if to do so we incur, as is now the case, deficits that will have to be paid by future generations. To sum up, anti-aging interventions are clearly of value to many individuals. They express this clearly in their behavior. Anti-aging interventions are clearly advantageous to society as measured by the very assessment of its members. And as a consequence, we should be virtually compelled to pursue anti-aging medicine as aggressively as we possibly can.

Viewpoint: Dr. Daniel Callahan

15 One of the advantages of getting older, and pursuing these issues, is that I have more time to argue with people whom I think are quite wrong about this. I will try to show you why I think Dr. Stock is going down a bad road here. Let me begin by saying that I am seventy-three and one of the interesting things about these issues is that it's my life I'm thinking about. I also spend time with a lot of people my age and older. I look at them and observe the trajectories of their lives, and I try to see how that is turning out. We have

obviously greatly increased average life expectancy, particularly for those people over the age of sixty-five, and it's continuing to improve. So we have, before our eyes, some of the results of extended life spans. We can see what happens to people who are still in good health, still vigorous, and can see how their lives turn out and how satisfied they are with their lives. For me, that is kind of a natural experiment with my own life while also observing my peers.

16 Let me begin by suggesting four different models of longevity and give you a sense of the one I think makes the most sense. One I will call "The Natural Progress Model." By that, I mean simply that we continue doing what we are now doing, trying to understand and improve the aging process. I'm not against anti-aging research. I'm in favor of improving the quality of research and the quality of aging research and the quality of life of elderly people, but not deliberately trying to extend life. We should simply take as a by-product whatever extension comes as a result of trying to improve quality. I think one demographer said there has been an average gain of about three months a year for 160 years now, in average life expectancy, and I suspect that will continue to go on. I think that's perfectly fine, and that it will come about by improving the social and economic living conditions of people, by better preventive care, and also by better clinical medicine in later years. That's one model.

17 The second I call, "The Normalizing Model." That is to say we could really work hard to reduce premature death, and aim to cluster everyone around the age of eighty-five, which is the age Japanese women on average now reach. If we got everyone clustered closer to the average of eighty-five years, this would be a pretty decent life, a life long enough to do most of the things you *can* do in life.

18 A third model I call "The Optimalizing Model." There was the famous French woman who lived to be 122. We could try to get everybody clustered around that age. We know that such a long life is biologically possible. It has happened. And there are, of course, more people these days living to 105, 110, and 114, and that is not a crazy goal either.

19 Then there is what I call "The Maximizing Model," which is to say, attempting to double life expectancy.

20 I believe in the natural progress model. I think we are doing fine now. People are living longer, and we are going to make great improvements. Life will be better for elderly people in the future, but I see nothing whatever to be gained by deliberately attempting to double life expectancy. My stance is very much a social stance. It seems to me irrelevant that a lot of people would like it. A lot of people like a lot of things that are bad for the collective good of the rest of us. The fact that many of us want to live longer says nothing about (a) whether it will be good for us as individuals to live much longer, and (b) whether we are going to get a better society. We can see some bad results of people trying to pursue their individual welfare, and arguing, as does Dr. Stock, that if everybody gets what they want individually, we will collectively be better off. That is a great fallacy, reminiscent of the old Adam Smith "invisible hand" argument, that we will get a good society by satisfying everybody's individual desires. I think that is a false notion of the way society works and our collective lives work.

21 Let me raise three basic problems that I think have to be addressed if we are going to talk about radically extending life.

22 First of all, consider all of our present problems in our world, in our national and global community: problems of war, poverty, environment, job creation, and social and familial violence, for instance. Are there any of those problems that would be solved by everyone living a much longer life? I don't think so. I can't imagine it's going to help the environment very much. It's certainly not going to automatically

deal with social and family violence, it will not do away with the problem of war, will not do away with the problem of poverty and violence. One question then is to ask, "Will it solve any of our current problems?" I can't think of any.

23 Secondly, what *new* social benefits would a much longer life expectancy confer on our society? Dr. Stock romanticizes about these new possibilities. Maybe it will happen, maybe it won't, who knows? Anybody can have sweet and lovely dreams about the future. But I think one has to ask the much tougher questions, and not just speculate, not assume we'll find ways to adjust, and that it will all turn out beautifully. We don't know that at all. Will we get new wisdom? One of the advantages of getting to being my age, and living with people my age, is that I don't think people my age do have any greater wisdom. If we have greater wisdom, then I'm right and Dr. Stock, my junior, is wrong. I haven't gotten any wiser between fifty and seventy-three. I was probably wiser at fifty than I am now. And most of the people I live with who are my age or older don't seem to be a bit wiser. If I want to talk about interesting things, I look for vitality and drive—I go to young people. One bit of advice my mother gave me in her old age was, "Cultivate young friends. Don't hang around people who are old." She was absolutely right about that.

24 Do I see new energy? I live around some people who are very sick. But mainly I live among affluent, elderly people between the ages of seventy and ninety-five. They are in good health, they have money, and they can take nice cruises or just putter about. They go to Scottsdale and play golf. But they don't seem to have any new energy, and they sure don't have any new serious initiatives. The number of people at this meeting—how many people are over seventy here? Not many. All of us over seventy know how rare it is to find many of "our kind" at meetings, looking at new things. Most of the older people have dropped out. They fade out. I don't believe that if you give most people longer lives, even in better health, they are going to find new opportunities and new initiatives. They will want to come and play more golf maybe, but they aren't going to contribute lots of brand-new ideas, at least those I know.

25 But the hardest question is, "How would we restructure society to deal with people who live to that age?" I think that question has to be looked at in a realistic way. We know it would change the structure of job opportunities, and of job mobility. We know it would change the ratio of young and old, and if you are going to look at the question of extending life expectancy, you are going to have to look at the whole "problem" of child bearing and child rearing. Those two go together. What's going to happen to it in such a society? Leaving aside questions of equitable distribution, if we have very different ideas about living much longer lives, how are we going to design a social security system? What will we do with Medicare where people have different desires for different lengths of time? A lot of people these days are in pretty good health because of expensive drugs and the like. Is Medicare going to support that indefinitely? I think we will have a lot of problems.

26 All I want to say is that it is not enough to speculate in a romantic way about the benefits without speculating equally about the potential downside. Each one of the problems I mentioned has to be solved in advance. The dumbest thing for us to do would be to wander into this new world and say, "We'll deal with the problems as they come along." I don't think that would work. A doubling of life expectancy would fundamentally change society. If this could ever happen, then we'd better ask what kind of society we want to get. We had better not go anywhere near it until we have figured those problems out.

27 The problem can't be solved by looking at what individuals might like. I suggested at the beginning that what individuals like is not a good predictor of what is going to be good for society.

I would also mention, from my own life experience, that I don't see any correlation between length of life and satisfaction with life. Certainly, one doesn't want to die prematurely, but beyond that, it seems to me that living a decent life—assuming one hasn't died as a child, or in middle age as an adult—really has nothing to do with the length of life. It's how you live your life and the kind of goals you set for yourself. The length per se is not a fundamental value.

28 It is also interesting, as one gets older, that those over seventy so often say, "My God, how fast it all went. I can't believe I'm this old now. Where did those years go?" I think people 150 or 160 will say, "My God, where did all those years go?" Of course, if we double life expectancy, and we get everybody up to 150 or 180 years, and if it was really terrific, then they will want more. They will say, "Why should we stop now? It's been wonderful. Let's keep going." We would have an infinite treadmill of more and more and that would increase the social problems enormously.

Discussion

29 DR. STOCK: I don't know quite where to begin. For starters, you seem to feel that we need to solve all the problems in advance before we can embark on a path with such profound social implications. By your logic, which is essentially that of the precautionary principle, we should have stopped medicine in the 1900s or at any time before, since the progress that made possible the extension of life expectancy from around forty-five years then to seventy-five years today, not only couldn't have been shown in advance to be benign, it has contributed to problems from population growth to dramatic shifts in family dynamics and the role of women. By your logic, we wouldn't want birth control; we wouldn't want telephones, computers, or any new technologies. We wouldn't want to do anything that has profound effects because there is no way we can solve the problems in advance.

30 DR. CALLAHAN: Would I have said the same thing 100 years ago? Absolutely not. But we have now had 100 years of technology to draw upon. We have some knowledge of what it means to society to have people live much longer lives. We have a sense of what it means to our social security system. We know what it means for the provision of health care. We know something about what it means for living a family life. We are not ignorant. I don't think we could work it out perfectly, but we could get a pretty good sense of likely possibilities based on our present experience. For instance, I've become interested in universities: What happens now in universities that don't have mandatory retirement? First of all, some people stay beyond age seventy, between 5 percent and 10 percent in the universities I've looked at. One consequence is that they are often not very good teachers any longer. They don't work hard. They know how to avoid the committee assignments; they are really skilled at that. Most importantly, they block the entry of young people onto the faculty. I have three good case examples where they have the data to show that this has happened.

31 DR. STOCK: The problem with your logic is that you are assuming that people are aging, that they are getting older, and their faculties are diminishing. But you can't use such an example as a way of attacking the possibility of extending our vitality rather than our decrepitude.

32 DR. CALLAHAN: No, no, I'm not saying their faculties are diminished. They simply don't have their earlier energy or interest. Why do we assume that this is all going to radically change by virtue of anti-aging research?

33 DR. STOCK: I think that if you were now, physically and mentally, what you were at forty or fifty, your attitudes might be somewhat

different about what it's like to be a seventy-three-year-old. You even said, "I don't want to die prematurely" and yet . . . .

34 DR. CALLAHAN: I guess there's a factor that enters which has nothing to do with physical energy. That is the boredom and repetition of life. I ran an organization for twenty-seven years. I didn't get physically tired. I just got bored doing the same thing repetitiously. When I looked down the road to think of a doubling of life expectancy, the question is, how are you going to deal with the problem of boredom? Do you really believe people are going to find everything brand new all the time?

35 DR. STOCK: Maybe you should try doing something different.

36 DR. CALLAHAN: It gets very hard to do something utterly different, even if you have the physical energy to do so. I don't know many people over my age who have started doing something radically different. My mother took up painting at the age of seventy, which she always wanted to do, and she had won prizes by the time she died at eighty-six. But by and large, even most people in perfectly good health, and with money, don't start on brand-new careers in their later years.

37 DR. STOCK: In perfectly good health, but only for a person beyond the age of seventy.

38 DR. CALLAHAN: No, in perfectly good health, period. They are running around. They have plenty of energy to go on cruises and play golf. They can do that sort of thing very well, but they are not interested in starting new careers. The late journalist I. F. Stone, in his seventies, did what he always wanted to do. He learned Greek to look at Socrates. He then wrote a book on the Socratic dialogues in his eighties. But that's pretty rare and it was much remarked upon as unusual.

39 DR. STOCK: You were talking about premature death. And yet you wouldn't want to die prematurely would you?

40 DR. CALLAHAN: It wouldn't be premature if I died now.

41 DR. STOCK: I think that the notion of what is premature death changes as we accept longer lives. I know a man who retired at sixty-five and then found he had cancer and died soon thereafter. The general reaction was, "Oh, what a tragedy, just before he was going to embark on his retirement." So you may say, "Look, you've lived long enough and you could die tomorrow and it wouldn't be premature." But remember, when Social Security was set up and retirement was set at sixty-five, the age was chosen because hardly anyone was expected to make it that far.

42 DR. CALLAHAN: Here's my definition of prematurity, that of not dying before one has lived a life that is long enough to allow one to do *most,* though not necessarily all, the things that life enables one to do. In any case, by the time I'd reached sixty-five, I'd raised a family, I'd had a career, I'd written a lot of books, I'd given hundreds of lectures, and I'd had lots of friends. I had not been to Nepal, and could always imagine new things I'd like to do. But I said "*most* of the things." You don't have to live to be 100 to do that.

43 DR. STOCK: It's astonishing to me that you could believe that you have already done most of what life allows one to do. You have an imagination. Can you not see huge realms of life that remain?

44 DR. CALLAHAN: I sure can't. All I can do is keep writing more of those books, and that's getting a bit repetitious now. I don't see anyone else doing it either at my age. Not just me. I'm looking at my age.

45 DR. STOCK: There are many people who, at a later age, do not feel they have exhausted what life has to offer.

46 DR. CALLAHAN: They want to play golf in Scottsdale. That's true. Somebody once said to me, "What about the people who like to sit on the back porch and watch the sunset?"

OK, you can do that indefinitely. If that's their life, then fine. I give in.

47 DR. STOCK: To another point. You said a problem with extending longevity is that it wouldn't solve any of the major problems of the world. But why should that be a requirement? There are many things going on in society that we accept even though they aren't oriented towards solving big problems. And many people would say the decay we face with aging and decrepitude is a big problem that they'd like to solve or at least postpone. And effective anti-aging medicine would certainly help with that.

48 DR. CALLAHAN: It seems to me that radically extended life expectancy would radically change the social structure of society. Therefore, if you are going to make that kind of change, particularly just to satisfy individual desires to live longer, then I want to say, "Is this going to help the rest of us with all of our other problems?" Don't change the whole society unless you can show it is going to solve some present problems. That seems to me to be a simple proposition.

49 DR. STOCK: Society is going to undergo profound change whether we extend the human life span or not, considering advances like telecommunications, computers, the Internet, and all the other things that are radically changing society. Birth control is an obvious example of something with dramatic impacts. Society is undergoing profound change and will continue to do so. We can't hope to keep it as it is.

50 DR. CALLAHAN: But then the question is: At what point do we want to stop some of the profound changes? One of the changes I have been fascinated with is that we are getting more and more automobiles in this world. We need a real birth control pill for automobiles. I have written a paper comparing medical technology to automobiles and had a lot of fun doing it because, on the one hand, we don't seem to be able to control the cost of that medical technology, and yet we can't give it up either. On the other hand, we don't know how to count the ever-rising number of automobiles either, creating all kinds of environmental and social problems, but we can't give up cars either. Ought we to have more and more cars just because individuals want more and more?

51 DR. STOCK: You can argue that there are negative externalities for certain kinds of activity. But you haven't made a good case that there is a negative externality for longer life. You asked, "What is good for society? If individuals gain what they want, then why isn't that necessarily good for society?" And it makes me wonder who in your view is actually going to decide what is good for society? Clearly, you have some very clear ideas, which you say are in opposition to what many people believe, because if they get more life they will just want even more.

52 DR. CALLAHAN: I'll give you an example. A lot of people don't like to be taxed, and a lot of people particularly don't like high taxes. Yet we have decided, for the good of society, that we need taxes to pay for Social Security and Medicare, and to run our police departments, and everything else. We thwart a lot of individual desires by having a system of taxation. But to run a society, you have to both say no to people and to require people to do what they don't want to do. There are some higher goods than what we personally want. We set speed limits. We say you can't drive ninety miles an hour down the street even though you want to, because you may hurt other people.

53 DR. STOCK: So you are saying, that if a majority said, "Here is an anti-aging medicine, but it would be bad for society and we shouldn't take it," then this would be something we should ban.

54 DR. CALLAHAN: If you have a majority in favor of something, then you could have a tyranny

of the majority. They might win. I'd lose the battle. I hope there will never be a majority in favor of a doubled life expectancy.

55 DR. STOCK: When you spoke about taxation, weren't you talking about majority decisions? Weren't you saying the political process is what should decide what is best for society?

56 DR. CALLAHAN: We ought to decide politically, but I would prefer to spend a lot of money on distributing AIDS drugs than spending money on anti-aging research. Is that a bad priority on my part? Millions of people are dying of AIDS.

57 DR. STOCK: Why do you have a problem with those deaths, considering it's a pretty natural path?

58 DR. CALLAHAN: No, it's not. AIDS leads to a premature death, the death of people at a young age, and affects people who are responsible for the infrastructure of society. AIDS is a terrible disease, and ought to be cured. I don't think cancer in people at ninety-five needs to be cured. It's as simple as that.

59 DR. STOCK: Are you suggesting that there should be some age threshold above which you don't treat a person, independent of what their level of vitality is?

60 DR. CALLAHAN: That's a question of how much you want to spend on Medicare. How much do you want to invest in high-technology medicine to keep elderly people alive? That's going to be a problem in future years with our Medicare system. I think you will agree we are going to have to make some terrible decisions. Right now there are a lot of new heart technologies coming along, most of them very expensive, and Medicare is struggling right now to decide whether or not to provide reimbursement for them.

61 DR. STOCK: How to allocate public resources is a large issue, and one can make lots of arguments about how best to spend money to best serve society as a whole. But would you argue that if the possibility emerges to extend human life span and prolong our years of vitality significantly there should be some sort of prohibition to stop all those who you yourself would acknowledge are going to want it?

62 DR. CALLAHAN: I would not want to prohibit the research. I want to stigmatize it. I want to make it look like you are being an utterly irresponsible citizen if you would sort of dump this radical life extension on the rest of us, as if you expect your friends and neighbors to pay for your Social Security at age 125, your Medicare at 145. I want to make it look like one of the worst things you could do to your neighbor. That's all. I wouldn't prohibit it.

63 DR. STOCK: But how can you imagine it would be stigmatized if the vast majority of people would do virtually anything to have it and if it's already something that people seek?

64 DR. CALLAHAN: I would lose. I probably won't succeed in stigmatizing it, but it is worth a try.

Thinking about the Argument

Stock's Viewpoint

1. What is Stock's major claim? His main supporting points? How sound is his evidence?
2. How does Stock's tone and style compare to Callahan's? To Bova's? Which do you find more appealing, and why?
3. Why does Stock think life is "unfair"? What does he think longevity research will do to improve life for everyone?

Callahan's Viewpoint

4. How does Callahan use his age to justify his position against life extension research? Do you find this an effective tactic? Why?
5. What evidence does Callahan cite to support his claim?
6. How does Callahan's classification of four models of longevity help to advance his argument? What reason does Callahan give for endorsing the "natural process" model?
7. What differences in style and tone do you perceive between Callahan and Stock? Which author uses his style to better advantage? Why do you think so?

Responding to the Argument

1. How did you respond to the point–counterpoint structure of the article? What advantage, if any, is imparted by placing Stock's essay first?
2. Consider the following quotations from the arguments: (a) "if on average we benefit as individuals, then society will enjoy a net benefit" (Stock); (b) a gradual increase in life expectancy "will come about by improving the social and economic living conditions of people, by better clinical medicine in later years" (Callahan). Which do you agree with most? How effectively is each quotation used in the original argument? Which do you think is the most compelling (it does not have to be the one you agree with). Why?
3. Do you think increased longevity will contribute to increased productivity and improved quality of life, or will it just create more social problems? Is there a middle ground that Stock and Callahan have not addressed? If these procedures become available, who will pay for them?

Writing about the Argument

1. Which author's *position* do you most agree with? Explain in a one-page argument of no more than three paragraphs. Whose *argument* is the most effective? Include an analysis of organization, logic (claims/support), audience appeal, and style. Write a brief essay on this topic.
2. Pretend that you are a parent who has the opportunity to have a life extension procedure done on your child before she is born. Would you allow the procedure to be performed? Why or why not? Write your argument in the form of a letter to your adult child, explaining why you elected (or did not elect) to have the procedure done.
3. If you were a member of Congress, what sort of legislation would you introduce to regulate life extension research? Write a proposal for a new law, being certain to provide adequate evidence to justify the need for the new regulation.

READING SELECTION

Reading: "Coping with Methuselah"

About the Authors: Henry J. Aaron and William B. Schwartz

Henry J. Aaron is Bruce and Virginia MacLaury Senior Fellow at the Brookings Institute. He is the author of numerous books and articles on the economics of aging. William B. Schwartz is professor of medicine at UCLA and the author of *Life without Disease: The Pursuit of Medical Utopia.* He has many articles in professional journals and newspapers to his credit. Together, Aaron and Schwartz have edited *Coping with Methuselah: The Impact of Molecular Biology on Medicine and Society,* from which the following extract was taken and published in the *Brookings Review* in fall 2003.

Before You Read

1. Based on what you read in the headnote, would you consider Aaron and Schwartz to be authorities on the science of aging? Why?
2. Would you consider them to be reliable, objective sources of information? Are you more inclined to consider their opinions than the view of a science-fiction writer like Ben Bova?
3. What does the name "Methuselah" in the title imply?
4. Look through the essay at the major subtitles and divisions of the argument. Based on this review, what do you expect some of the significant subtopics to be?

Coping with Methuselah

1 The capacity to manipulate the genetic templates that shape all living beings was long the plaything of science fiction. In the final decades of the twentieth century, however, intellectual advances transmuted genetic tinkering from alchemy into science. In 1953 two young scientists identified the double helix comprising four nucleotides entwined in the code of all life, thereby opening the first chapter in the saga of molecular biology. Then in 2001 two competing scientific teams produced a draft of the human genome, introducing a new therapeutic era in which medical professionals may be able to slow human aging and make celebrating 100th birthdays almost routine.

2 No one can predict the precise extent or timing of advances in molecular biology. No one can know exactly when particular diseases will be prevented or cured. No one can foresee when, or even if, human aging will be slowed or stopped. No one yet knows for sure whether humans' genetic makeup limits life span or, if it does, what those limits might be. Some families include more nonagenarians and centenarians than any roll of nature's dice could explain, a fact that suggests genes' powerful influence on longevity. Even if life span is now limited, molecular biology may reveal that these limits are not fixed and may provide ways to slow aging and prevent or cure illnesses that cause physical decline and death.

3 Scientific advance has revolutionized man's centuries-old assault on human illness. Physicians have long understood, in some sense, the basis of successful medical treatments, without being able to penetrate the underlying processes by which their interventions worked. The fundamental reasons why antibiotics killed pathogens, for example, remained for years as mysterious to the discoverers of those drugs and to the physicians who used them as they were to the patients whose lives they saved.

4 As the twenty-first century begins, scientists are increasingly working from a fundamental understanding of cells, proteins, and genes to design interventions that reverse, block, or otherwise forestall illnesses. In the words of Nobel Prize–winner Alfred Gilman, scientists are now "able to complete [their] understanding of the wiring

diagram of the signaling switchboard in each type of cell." With that knowledge in hand, they now have—or soon will—the means to design drugs or to directly change how cells operate to correct the genetic defects each person inherits or acquires during life from mutations or other sources.

5 In the coming century, human mortality rates may begin falling rapidly. Eventually molecular biology may lengthen human life almost unimaginably. Is the Age of Methuselah at hand? And if so, what will it mean for public policy in the United States—and the world?

Our Uncertain Demographic Future

6 Advances in public health, nutrition, and medical treatment over the past century first set in motion an increase in human life expectancy. With mortality rates now declining roughly 0.6 percent a year, demographers project that longevity will continue to increase and that the elderly will constitute a growing share of the U.S. population. A bio-medical revolution causing mortality rates to fall more rapidly could intensify these trends and have important demographic implications.

7 Many scientists have long believed that the human life span has a natural limit. The finding by 19th-century scientist August Wiseman that cells stopped reproducing after a certain number of divisions seems consistent with this hypothesis. But even if a natural limit exists, the practical question is how far that limit exceeds current average life span and what can be done to push today's life span closer to that limit. One theory of aging draws an analogy between a person and a machine consisting of many systems, each essential for its operation. Each system within the machine remains functional until too many of its constituent parts fail, leading the machine itself to fail over time in patterns that closely resemble human mortality rates. The implication is that medical progress comes through interventions that prevent or postpone the failure of the constituent parts of each of the biological "systems" essential for life.

8 Rapidly falling mortality rates would affect longevity relatively quickly but would take many years to alter the age distribution of the population. The U.S. Social Security Administration, which assumes that mortality rates will continue to decline at the current annual rate, about 0.6 percent, projects that people born in 2030 will have a life expectancy at birth of just over eighty-four years; those born in 2075, just over eighty-six. If mortality rates decline 2 percent a year, babies born in 2030 could expect to live 104 years; those born in 2075, more than 115 years. But even this rapid rate of decline would have little effect on the U.S. population distribution until past mid-century.

9 How would rapidly declining mortality affect the U.S. workplace and public programs to support the elderly? Much would depend on the onset of physical decline in the longer-lived Americans. Would greatly increased longevity mean longer periods of dependency? Or would older Americans stay healthy longer? If workers were able to keep working for a greater portion of their lives than they do now, the cost of supporting the elderly might increase only slightly because the ratio of retirees to active workers might increase only a little. If current retirement age patterns persisted, however, the cost of increased longevity would rise sharply as people spent ever more years outside the labor force.

10 Little in economic theory or empirical evidence suggests that sharply increased longevity would directly affect retirement behavior. But if workers extended their years in retirement, it would boost pension costs, which, in turn, would probably force changes in public policy to encourage workers to extend their working lives. Higher pension costs would necessitate sharply increased pension contributions by workers or their employers, or higher taxes on workers and employers to support public pensions, or cuts in benefits and increases in the age at which pensions are first paid. These changes would likely cause Americans to work more years than they now do.

11 Rapidly falling mortality would certainly affect government revenues and spending. If longer-living Americans extended their working lives, they would earn and produce more, swelling tax revenues. But increased longevity would also boost government spending on Social Security, Medicare, and Medicaid, all of which are already projected to grow rapidly as baby boomers begin retiring. And a major new decline in mortality rates would drive spending above these already steeply rising trends.

12 Social Security costs are officially projected to increase between now and 2080, from just under 11 percent to just over 20 percent of earnings subject to the Social Security payroll tax. If mortality rates were to fall 2 percent annually while the duration of working lives remained the same, Social Security

costs would reach more than 25 percent of payroll. Raising the age at which full Social Security benefits are paid by one month a year starting in 2018 would eliminate most of the additional longevity-related cost. The message is simple and clear: as longevity increased, so too would Social Security costs.

13 Projecting the effects of longevity on Medicare and Medicaid costs is much trickier because spending depends not only on the number of beneficiaries, but also on trends in the cost of medical care. Regardless of trends in mortality rates, Medicare and Medicaid costs will soar because per capita medical costs for everyone will increase. Medical spending also rises with age as people's bodies gradually wear out or become subject to disease. Some observers see decline as an immutable consequence of a person's age since birth—an eighty-year-old whose life expectancy is eighty-five will be in the same state of decline as an eighty-year-old whose life expectancy is 110. But Stanford University economist John Shoven thinks it more plausible that medical spending depends on years until death. And the fact that disability rates have fallen as mortality rates have improved supports that view. If mortality declines at historical rates, projections based on the years-since-birth assumption show Medicare costing about 2 percent of gross domestic product more in 2070 than if costs are projected on the years-until-death assumption. The difference jumps to roughly 5 percent of GDP if mortality rates fall 2 percent a year. In the case of Medicaid, the cost difference in 2070 between projections is a bit over 1 percent of GDP if mortality declines at officially assumed rates, but nearly 6 percent if it declines 2 percent a year.

14 The story is straightforward. Costs of Social Security, Medicare, and Medicaid will rise during the early part of the 21st century, primarily because of the aging of the baby-boom generation and—in the case of the health programs—increases in medical costs. Accelerated increases in longevity would affect costs primarily in the second half of the century and beyond. If, in the best scenario, physical decline were delayed as lives were lengthened, the added health care costs would be modest. If, in addition, working lives increased, the added revenues from a bigger labor force would help defray these costs.

A Global Perspective

15 The effects of a sharp increase in longevity would not be confined to one nation. The swelling ranks of the elderly already threaten pension systems in many countries and may have important effects on international capital flows. Dramatically increased longevity would require most developed nations to reform their retirement systems to keep them sustainable. Increased public spending on retirement would lower saving rates in developed nations, which could prevent many developing nations from borrowing to finance growth.

16 Over the past 150 years, both birth and mortality rates have fallen nearly everywhere. From the standpoint of economic development, the ideal pattern is a drop in birth rates followed years later by declining mortality. That pattern keeps the ratio of the working-age population to the total population quite high for a time, enabling domestic saving to support high rates of investment. Eventually, however, the aged population increases. If birth rates remain low, overall population, excluding immigration, will fall.

17 Only wealthy nations would be able to afford the costly medical interventions that would sharply increase longevity. Because mortality rates in those nations are already low among younger citizens, declining mortality rates primarily would increase the number of those over age fifty. The ratio of the elderly to the working-age population would therefore increase most in wealthy nations. The most extreme effects would show up in nations such as Japan, where the elderly population is already 71 percent as large as the working-age population. The effect in the United States would be much smaller because above-average birth and immigration rates are projected to keep the working-age population growing at least slowly.

18 Current population aging is already likely to lower both saving and investment in high-income countries and to increase saving in middle-income and poor nations, pushing foreign trade balances of rich nations into deficit and those of the rest of the world into surplus. A 2-percent-a-year reduction in mortality rates would intensify these effects. Saving would decline sharply, investment somewhat less. With mortality falling fastest in nations that can afford medical innovation, trade deficits are especially likely for rich nations.

19 These projections are tentative and depend heavily on how increasing longevity affects the world of work. If people's working lives lengthen, investment will be higher, the cost of

private and public pensions lower. Technological change will also influence investment opportunities and the call on saving to finance that investment. Nevertheless, extending longevity is likely to be quite expensive, and rich nations are far more likely than poor nations to incur those costs.

The Ethical Dilemmas of Increasing Longevity

20 Throughout the twentieth century, public health advances, rising income, and medical discoveries added decades to life expectancy at birth. These advances raised practical questions, such as how to pay for pension and health costs for the elderly, but relatively few ethical problems. Some painful moral problems did arise: whether it is ever right—and, if so, under what circumstances and after what steps—to curtail care for extremely ill patients or to allow severely damaged newborns to die. But few observers questioned whether clean water, the reduction of poverty, or effective antibiotics were ethically desirable.

21 The prospect of an engineered extension of human life, however, has created a major stir among ethicists. As Alexander Morgan Capron, University Professor of Law and Medicine at the University of Southern California, notes, past developments in longevity took opportunities once available to the few and extended them to the many. But some interventions now in prospect would change the fundamental character of humans—for example, by changing their genes.

22 The ethical issues raised by life extension depend in part on its consequences. Most problematic would be increasing the average age of death primarily by increasing a person's years of physical and mental decline. But, as Capron points out, no one can foresee whether the coming scientific advances will add decades of mental and physical vigor or decades of senility and debility.

23 The ethical issues will also be shaped by the means used to increase longevity. Irreversible interventions, such as altering human genes, raise more questions than do interventions that can be stopped, such as a hormone that a patient can stop taking. And many innovations that promise to extend life will require risky experimentation and must be attended by stringent procedural safeguards.

24 Another issue is access to life-extending interventions. Capron dismisses the views of some ethicists that once a person has reached a "normal" life span, access to life-extending care is not ethically required. Both the duration of "normal" lives and the content of "normal" interventions, he notes, are inescapably elastic. Both depend on expectations that are themselves influenced by technological possibilities.

25 Finally, Capron notes that questions about suicide and passive euthanasia are likely to become increasingly prominent. If the capacity to extend life is available, is it euthanasia if caregivers do not use it—or suicide if patients actively reject it?

26 Leon Kass, Francis Fukayama, and others have posited that life extension is not a legitimate goal of science and that success in such an endeavor threatens to deprive people of essential attributes of their humanity. Finitude, they argue, lends life savor, sweetness, and value. A quest for superhuman intelligence, looks, or longevity is quite literally inhuman. Gradually, step by step, like the person immersed in a bath slowly warming from comfortable to lethal, humans would surrender what it means to be human by a series of steps each seemingly reasonable, but cumulatively dehumanizing. Capron is more concerned that successful life extension could produce a dystopia with ever-larger parts of life spent in dependence.

When Imagined Futures Become Real

27 A flowering of biomedical science holds the promise, though not the certainty, that human beings will soon live routinely to ages almost unthinkable today. Although such a development still has an air of science fiction for most Americans, its implications must be considered seriously. Authors of fiction tend to place utopias and dystopias in an imagined future. Readers may be revulsed by the nightmares of *Brave New World* or *1984,* chilled by the cold impersonality of *The Rise of the Meritocracy,* or swept by the romantic notions of *Looking Backward.* The authors of these imagined futures had a free hand to paint with their chosen palettes. Social scientists, having no such license, must contemplate with academic detachment the problems, challenges, and opportunities to be faced if living to 90, 100, or beyond becomes common. Utopias do not adorn the pages of honest analysis.

»«

Thinking about the Argument

1. What do Aaron and Schwartz believe about the increasing human life span?
2. What problems do they suggest longevity will create? What benefits do they discuss? What solutions do they propose?
3. The authors offer more statistical evidence than the other readings in this cluster. How do you, as a reader, respond to such evidence? Do you find Aaron and Schwartz's argument more convincing than the arguments presented by Bova, Stock, and Callahan? Why?
4. How do Aaron and Schwartz use statistics to their advantage?
5. The authors use two different scenarios to illustrate the effects of increasing longevity on the U.S. economy. What are they? How do these authors think longevity will affect the world economy?
6. This argument ends on a cautionary note. What do you think this ending implies?

Responding to the Reading

1. Aaron and Schwartz are considerably less optimistic than Bova about the future of a long-lived humankind. What is your opinion? Is it a good thing or a bad thing, or somewhere in between? Explain.
2. What social problems that are not mentioned by Aaron and Schwartz have occurred to you? How do you think these issues could be addressed?
3. If Social Security, insurance plans, and other retirement programs are incorrect about the gradual increase in human longevity at the rate of 0.6 percent per year, what will happen to these programs? What should be done to save them? How will the United States support an aging population that it can no longer afford?
4. The authors ask an interesting question about euthanasia: If someone in the future were to refuse medical treatment for the purpose of artificially extending his or her life span, could this be considered a form of suicide (much as someone today who refuses treatment for cancer or heart disease might be considered "suicidal")?

Writing about the Reading

1. Writing (like Bova) as an optimist, compose a letter to Aaron and Schwartz explaining why you think their cautionary tone is unjustified.
2. Writing from a pessimistic stance, argue why you think Aaron and Schwartz are being too optimistic in their analysis. Why might an aging population be a social disaster?
3. Decide which of the authors within this cluster makes the strongest argument. Evaluate their essay and explain in what ways it is stronger than the others.
4. Is it a good idea to grow (very) old at all? If you had to choose the time in your life that you would select to die, what would it be? Why would you choose this period? Assuming you were in good health at the time, what would you do during the year that preceded your death?
5. In a world where dying of natural causes becomes increasingly less common, should suicide be legal? Under what conditions should a person be allowed to elect to die?

6. Should research into stem cells, the human genome, cloning, and other methods that extend the human life span be made illegal? What might happen to the research community in the United States if such laws were to be passed? How could the United States avoid becoming "second class" in this area while other nations continue to advance?
7. Is there an ethical or moral injunction against tampering with the human life span (or any other aspect of the human genome)? Explain.

19

Popular Culture

Violent Entertainment, Body Modification, and Consumerism

> *My prediction from the sixties finally came true: "In the future everyone will be famous for fifteen minutes." I'm bored with that line. I never use it anymore. My new line is, "In fifteen minutes everybody will be famous."*
>
> — Andy Warhol (1928–1987)

Popular culture surrounds us like the air we breathe. It consists of anything that is mass-produced, widespread, well known, and marketable:

- Events: Academy Awards, September 11, Super Bowl, celebrity trials
- Merchandise: Clothing, CDs, video games, iPods
- Personalities: Paris Hilton, 50 Cent, Tiger Woods, Saddam Hussein
- Slogans: "Be all you can be." "It's the real thing." "What would Jesus do?"

Online Study Center
This icon will direct you to content and resources on the website <college.hmco.com/pic/lamm1e>.

- Themes: Romantic love, the American dream, family values, "having it all"
- Trends: Tattoos, rap music, reality TV, cosmetic surgery, fashions

Culture as a concept has related yet distinct meanings. In the broadest sense, it embraces our entire way of life—customs, beliefs, history. In another sense, it refers to elite, high, or refined culture—literature, art, science, and ideas that are deemed to be the very best a civilization has produced. The poems of Emily Dickinson, the paintings of Vincent Van Gogh, the music of Ludwig von Beethoven, and the novels of William Faulkner are examples of refined culture. While the works of refined culture are held in high esteem by almost everyone, they are enjoyed less frequently than popular culture and are fully appreciated by a relatively small number of experts who are "cultured."

Popular culture, however, affects many people's lives on a daily basis. To appreciate it requires little training (or "acculturation") because we are steeped in it and often enjoy it and seek it out. Entertainments such as video games and rap music let fans live glamorous, exciting lives vicariously. Body modification tempts us to alter our own physical nature to achieve culturally glorified images. Consumerism promises a better, happier life through the purchase of culturally valued products. Popular culture is therefore a kind of argument, beckoning us to change the way we think, act, and appear. Of course, there are counterarguments: Violent entertainment may teach us destructive behaviors, body modifications can have physical and psychological side effects, and consumerism affects us both economically and philosophically.

Issue 1: Violent Entertainment: Video Games and Rap Music

A culture's entertainments presumably reveal much about its values. When we look back at the to-the-death gladiatorial combat that entertained ancient Romans, we may perhaps feel they were inhumane and that we are culturally more evolved. Yet modern critics point to the gladiator-like brutality of boxing matches as evidence that our culture has advanced much less than we suppose.

Online Study Center
Prepare for Class
Violence and the Media

More specific to the following readings, some video games and rap music seem to glorify and encourage violence. When violent entertainments are popular, do they signify that we are a violent culture? Do they teach us to be violent? Does viewing violence in art, television, and cinema imprint us with destructive images? Does the threatening, obscene language in some rap songs become part of our own speech and thought patterns?

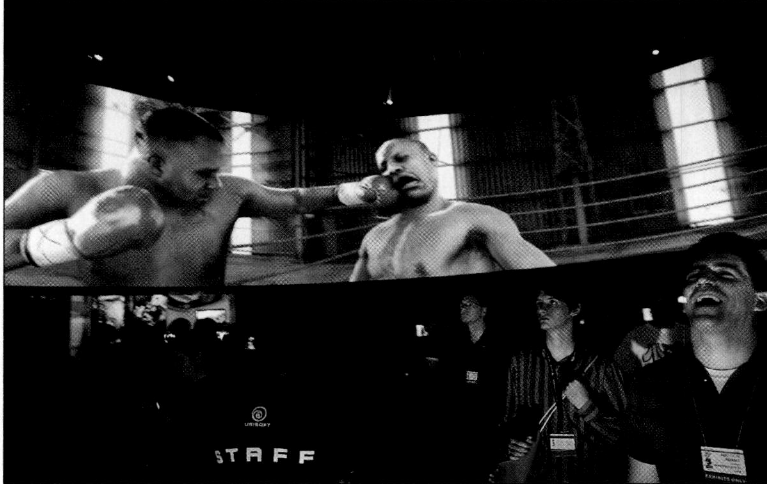

Can youth violence be attributed to the media?

Considering the Issue of Violent Entertainment

In discussion groups, in your journal, or working individually, answer the following questions.

1. How much violence is in entertainment (music, television, cinema, art, video games)? How essential is the violence, especially to particular kinds of entertainment (e.g., rap music or action/adventure video games)?
2. When is entertainment violence excessive? When is it appropriate?
3. Do you believe entertainment violence has negative, long-term effects? Explain.
4. What kinds of restrictions, if any, should be placed on violent entertainment?

READING SELECTION

"Breeding Evil? Defending Video Games"

ABOUT THE AUTHOR: *THE ECONOMIST*

Articles in *The Economist* are written anonymously by its editors or unnamed contributors. Published in London since 1843, this newsweekly focuses on world events—politics, business and finance, and science—that influence decision makers such as executives, financiers, managers, and government officials. Editorially, it advocates economic conservatism.

BEFORE YOU READ

1. *The Economist* is a British publication. To what extent do you expect British concerns about media violence to be similar to or different from American concerns?
2. What does the title, "Breeding Evil? Defending Video Games," indicate about the article's argument? What is your initial reaction to the title and possible argument?
3. This is an "unsigned" article; the author presumably is one of the journal's staff writers. In what ways might your reading be affected by not knowing the identity of the author?
4. What do you already know about video games that might be relevant to the reading? Do you think that violent video games are harmless, possibly even beneficial?

Breeding Evil? Defending Video Games

1 "It is an evil influence on the youth of our country." A politician condemning video gaming? Actually, a clergyman denouncing rock and roll fifty years ago. But the sentiment could just as easily have been voiced by Hillary Clinton in the past few weeks, as she blamed video games for "a silent epidemic of media desensitization" and "stealing the innocence of our children."

2 The gaming furor centers on *Grand Theft Auto: San Andreas*, a popular and notoriously violent cops and robbers game that turned out to contain hidden sex scenes that could be unlocked using a patch downloaded from the internet. The resulting outcry (mostly from Democratic politicians playing to the center) caused the game's rating in America to be changed from "mature," which means you have to be seventeen to buy it, to "adults only," which means you have to be 18, but also means that big retailers such as Wal-Mart will not stock it. As a result the game has been banned in Australia; and, this autumn, America's Federal Trade Commission will investigate the complaints. That will give gaming's opponents an opportunity to vent their wrath on the industry.

3 Skepticism of new media is a tradition with deep roots, going back at least as far as Socrates's objections to written texts, outlined in Plato's *Phaedrus*. Socrates worried that relying on written texts, rather than the oral tradition, would "create forgetfulness in the learners' souls, because they will not use their memories; they will trust to the external written characters and not remember of themselves." (He also objected that a written version of a speech was no substitute for the ability to interrogate the speaker, since, when questioned, the text "always gives one unvarying answer." His objection, in short, was that books were not interactive. Perhaps Socrates would have thought more highly of video games.)

4 Novels were once considered too low-brow for university literature courses, but eventually the disapproving professors retired. Waltz music and dancing were condemned in the nineteenth century; all that twirling was thought to be "intoxicating" and "depraved," and the music was outlawed in some places. Today it is hard to imagine what the fuss was about. And rock and roll was thought to encourage violence, promiscuity, and satanism; but today even grannies buy Coldplay albums.

Joystick Junkies

5 The opposition to gaming springs largely from the neophobia that has pitted the old against the entertainments of the young for centuries. Most gamers are under forty, and most critics are non-games-playing over-forties. But what of the specific complaints—that games foster addiction and encourage violence?

6 There's no good evidence for either. On addiction, if the worry is about a generally excessive use of screen-based entertainment, critics should surely concern themselves about television rather than games: American teenage boys play video games for around thirteen hours a week (girls for only five hours), yet watch television for around twenty-five hours a week. As to the minority who seriously overdo it, research suggests that they display addictive behavior in other ways too. The problem, in other words, is with them, not with the games.

7 Most of the research on whether video games encourage violence is unsatisfactory, focusing primarily on short-term effects. In the best study so far, frequent playing of a violent game sustained over a month had no effect on participants' level of aggression. And, during the period in which gaming has become widespread in America, violent crime has fallen by half. If games really did make people violent, this tendency might be expected to show up in the figures, given that half of Americans play computer and video games. Perhaps, as some observers have suggested, gaming actually makes people less violent, by acting as a safety valve.

Neophobes Unite

8 So are games good, rather than bad, for people? Good ones probably are. Games are widely used as educational tools, not just for pilots, soldiers, and surgeons, but also in schools and businesses. Every game has its own interface and controls, so that anyone who has learned to play a handful of games can generally figure out how to operate almost any high-tech device. Games require players to construct hypotheses, solve problems, develop strategies, learn the rules of the in-game world through trial and error. Gamers must also be able to juggle several different tasks, evaluate risks, and make quick decisions. One game, set in 1930s Europe, requires the player to prevent the outbreak of the second world war; other games teach everything from algebra to derivatives trading. Playing games is, thus, an ideal form of preparation for the workplace of the twenty-first century, as some forward-thinking firms are already starting to realize.

9 Pointing all this out makes little difference, though, because the controversy over gaming, as with rock and roll, is more than anything else the consequence of a generational divide. Can the disagreements between old and young over new forms of media ever be resolved? Sometimes attitudes can change relatively quickly, as happened with the Internet. Once condemned as a cesspool of depravity, it is now recognized as a valuable new medium, albeit one where (as with films, TV, and, yes, video games) children's access should be limited and supervised. The benefits of a broadband connection are now acknowledged, and politicians worry about extending access to the have-nots. Attitudes changed because critics of the Internet had to start using it for work, and then realized that, like any medium, it could be used for good purposes as well as bad. They have no such incentive to take up gaming, however.

10 Eventually, objections to new media resolve themselves, as the young grow up and the old die out. As today's gamers grow older—the average age of gamers is already thirty—video games will ultimately become just another medium, alongside books, music, and films. And soon the graying gamers will start tut-tutting about some new evil threatening to destroy the younger generation's moral fiber.

Thinking about the Argument

1. What is the main argument of the reading? Where is it stated?
2. Why does the author mention Plato and novels in paragraphs 3 and 4? How do these examples support the thesis?
3. According to the article, what evidence is there that video games encourage violence? Explain.
4. In what ways, according to the author, can video games be "good"? Do you agree with this assessment? Why or why not?
5. What is "neophobia"? Do you agree with the reading's assertion that people usually are skeptical about new media? What supporting evidence does the author cite? How relevant is the evidence?

Responding to the Argument

1. Do you agree that video games are "stealing the innocence of our children"? Why or why not? Defend your answer.
2. The article has argued that video games can be good for you. List three ways that you think video games can be bad. Provide an example to back up each claim.
3. Do you think you are "neophobic"? Why or why not?
4. Have you ever played a video game for more than an hour in one stretch? If so, how long? What might the positive and negative effects of such extended game play be?

Writing about the Argument

1. Write a dialogue between a concerned mother and a video game designer. Assume that the mother believes video games are bad for children. Assume that the video game designer thinks that they can be helpful in some way.
2. Video games, like role playing games and movies, can be escapist entertainment. Write an argument explaining ways in which escapism can be good and/or bad.
3. Research a situation in which video gaming has led to violent behavior. Does this mean, then, that video games should be banned for everyone? (By analogy, if a person drives drunk and kills someone in an accident, does this mean that alcohol should be illegal for everyone?) Develop your argument as a journal entry or a formal argument.

4. Write an argument explaining whether or not video games that depict antisocial behavior should be banned. In your argument, consider whether this prohibition should be extended to other media, such as movies, television shows, literature, or the Internet.
5. What is more important—freedom of expression or the protection of social standards? In a journal entry or a letter to the editor of your local paper, argue your position on this topic.

"B. F. Skinner's Rats and Operant Conditioning at the Video Arcade"

About the Author: David Grossman

A former Army Ranger and now a professor of military science at Arkansas State University and the director of Killology Research Group, Lieutenant Colonel David Grossman is recognized internationally as an authority on violence and human aggression. Through interviews, publications, and speeches, Grossman has commented on violence ranging from schoolyard shootings to terrorist acts. His books include *On Combat: The Psychology and Physiology of Deadly Combat in War and Peace* (1994), *On Killing: The Psychological Cost of Learning to Kill in War and Society* (1995), and *Stop Teaching Our Kids to Kill* (with Gloria De Gaetano, 1999). The essay reprinted here is from section 8, chapter 3, of *On Killing.*

Before You Read

1. What is your opinion of video gaming prior to reading this article? In what ways is your opinion of this topic positive, negative, or neutral?
2. What does the headnote tell you about the author? How might this information affect the attitude with which you approach of the reading?
3. In your opinion, does the article's title seem authoritative to you? How so?
4. What do you already know about the psychologist B. F. Skinner and operant conditioning? How could you find out more information?

B. F. Skinner's Rats and Operant Conditioning at the Video Arcade

When I went to boot camp and did individual combat training they said if you walk into an ambush what you want to do is just do a right face—you just turn right or left, whichever way the fire is coming from, and assault. I said, "Man, that's crazy. I'd never do anything like that. It's stupid." The first time we came under fire, on Hill 1044 in Operation Beauty Canyon in Laos, we did it automatically. Just like you look at your watch to see what time it is. We done a right face, assaulted the hill—a fortified position with concrete bunkers emplaced, machine guns, automatic weapons—and we took it. And we killed—I'd estimate probably thirty-five North

Vietnamese soldiers in the assault,
and we only lost three killed. . . .
But you know, what they teach you, it doesn't faze you until it comes down to the time to use it, but it's in the back of your head, like, What do you do when you come to a stop sign? It's in the back of your head, and you react automatically.

—Vietnam veteran,
quoted in Gwynne Dyer, *War*

Conditioning Killers in the Military

1 On the training bases of the major armies of the world, nations struggle to turn teenagers into killers. The "struggle" for the mind of the soldier is a lopsided one: Armies have had thousands of years to develop their craft, and their subjects have had fewer than two decades of life experience. It is a basically honest, age-old, reciprocal process, especially in today's all-volunteer U.S. Army. The soldier intuitively understands what he or she is getting into and generally tries to cooperate by "playing the game" and constraining his or her own individuality and adolescent enthusiasm, and the army systematically wields the resources and technology of a nation to empower and equip the soldier to kill and survive on the battlefield. In the armed forces of most modern armies this application of technology has reached new levels by integrating the innovations of operant conditioning into traditional training methods.

2 Operant conditioning is a higher form of learning than classical conditioning. It was pioneered by B. F. Skinner and is usually associated with learning experiments on pigeons and rats. The traditional image of a rat in a Skinner box, learning to press a bar in order to get food pellets, comes from Skinner's research in this field. Skinner rejected the Freudian and humanist theories of personality development and held that *all* behavior is a result of past rewards and punishments. To B. F. Skinner the child is a tabula rasa, a "blank slate," who can be turned into anything provided sufficient control of the child's environment is instituted at an early enough age.

3 Instead of firing at a bull's-eye target, the modern soldier fires at man-shaped silhouettes that pop up for brief periods of time inside a designated firing lane. The soldiers learn that they have only a brief second to engage the target, and if they do it properly their behavior is immediately reinforced when the target falls down. If he knocks down enough targets, the soldier gets a marksmanship badge and usually a three-day pass. After training on rifle ranges in this manner, an automatic, conditioned response called automaticity sets in, and the soldier then becomes conditioned to respond to the appropriate stimulus in the desired manner. This process may seem simple, basic, and obvious, but there is evidence to indicate that it is one of the key ingredients in a methodology that has raised the firing rate from 15 to 20 percent in World War II to 90 to 95 percent in Vietnam.

Conditioning at the Video Arcade

4 In video arcades children stand slack jawed but intent behind machine guns and shoot at electronic targets that pop up on the video screen. When they pull the trigger the weapon rattles in their hand, shots ring out, and if they hit the "enemy" they are firing at, it drops to the ground, often with chunks of flesh flying in the air.

5 The important distinction between the killing-enabling process that occurs in video arcades and that of the military is that the military's is focused on the enemy soldier, with particular emphasis on ensuring that the U.S. soldier acts only under authority. Yet even with these safeguards, the danger of future My Lai massacres among soldiers drawn from such a violent population must not be ignored, and . . . the U.S. armed forces are taking extensive measures to control, constrain, and channel the violence of their troops in future conflicts. The video games that our children conduct their combat training on have no real sanction for firing at the wrong target.

6 This is not an attack on all video games. Video games are an interactive medium. They demand and develop trial-and-error and systematic problem-solving skills, and they teach planning, mapping, and deferment of gratification. Watch children as they play video games and interact with other children in their neighborhood. To parents raised on a steady diet of movies and sitcoms, watching a child play Mario Brothers for hours on end may not be particularly gratifying, but that is just the point. As they play they solve problems and overcome instructions that are intentionally inadequate and vague. They exchange playing strategies, memorize routes, and make maps. They work long and hard to attain the gratification of finally winning a game. And there are no commercials: no enticements for sugar, no solicitation of violent toys, and no messages of social failure if they do not wear the right shoes or clothes.

7 We might prefer to see children reading or getting exercise and interacting with the *real* real world by playing outside, but video games are definitely preferable to most television. But video games can also be superb at teaching violence—violence packaged in the same format that has more than quadrupled the firing rate of modern soldiers.

8 When I speak of violence enabling I am not talking about video games in which the player defeats creatures by bopping them on the head. Nor am I talking about games where you maneuver swordsmen and archers to defeat monsters. On the borderline in violence enabling are games where you use a joystick to maneuver a gunsight around the screen to kill gangsters who pop up and fire at you. The kind of games that are very definitely enabling violence are the ones in which you actually hold a weapon in your hand and fire it at human-shaped targets on the screen. These kinds of games can be played on home video, but you usually see them in video arcades.

9 There is a direct relationship between realism and degree of violence enabling, and the most realistic of these are games in which great bloody chunks fly off as you fire at the enemy.

10 Another, very different type of game has a western motif, in which you stand before a huge video screen and fire a pistol at actual film footage of "outlaws" as they appear on the screen. This is identical to the shoot–no shoot training program designed by the FBI and used by police agencies around the nation to train and enable police officers in firing their weapons.

11 The shoot–no shoot program was introduced nearly twenty years ago in response to the escalating violence in our society that was resulting in an increase in deaths among police officers who hesitated to shoot in an actual combat situation. And, of course, we recognize it as another form of operant conditioning that has been successful in saving the lives of both law-enforcement officers and innocent bystanders, since the officer faces severe sanctions if he fires in an inappropriate circumstance. Thus the shoot–no shoot program has served successfully to both enable *and* constrain violence among police officers. Its video arcade equivalent has no such sanctions to constrain violence. It only enables.

12 The worst is yet to come. Just as movies have become successively more realistic in their depiction of violence and death, so too have video games. We are now entering an era of virtual reality, in which you wear a helmet that has a video screen before your eyes. As you turn your head the screen changes just as though you were within the video world. You hold a gun in your hand and fire it at the enemies who pop up around you, or you hold a sword and hack and stab at the enemies around you.

13 Alvin Toffler, author of *Future Shock,* says, "This manipulation of reality may provide us with exciting games, entertainment, but it will substitute not a virtual reality, but a pseudo reality, so subtly deceptive as to raise the levels of public suspicion and disbelief beyond what any society can tolerate." This new "pseudo reality" will make it possible to replicate all the gore and

violence of popular violent movies, except now you are the one who is the star, the killer, the slayer of thousands.

14 Through operant conditioning B. F. Skinner held that he could turn *any* child into *anything* he wanted to. In Vietnam the U.S. armed forces demonstrated that Skinner was at least partially correct by successfully using operant conditioning to turn adolescents into the most effective fighting force the world has ever seen. And America seems intent on using Skinner's methodology to turn us into an extraordinarily violent society.

Thinking about the Argument

1. Why do you think the author begins with a quotation from a Vietnam veteran? How does it relate to what Grossman is arguing?
2. What is "operant conditioning"?
3. Why does Grossman believe that video game "training" is more dangerous from a societal standpoint than military training?
4. What kinds of games does the author believe are "violence enabling"? Do you agree? Explain.

Responding to the Argument

1. The author compares war to a game. Do you think this is a valid analogy? Explain.
2. Grossman compares the "killing-enabling" training of soldiers to the behavioral conditioning of rats. In what ways are these processes similar? Is Grossman's comparison *figurative (*an *analogy*) or literal? To what extent do you accept or reject Grossman's comparison?
3. Do you agree that certain types of video games can be "violence enabling"? Why or why not?
4. List other activities that you consider "violence enabling." Explain your answer.

Writing about the Argument

1. Grossman argues that certain video games are "violence enabling" because they provide sharpshooter-like training without the restraint taught to professional soldiers. What flaws might there be in the author's logic? Write an essay refuting Grossman's claim(s).
2. Given what Grossman has argued, should sharpshooter games be banned? Research the topic and argue a specific position.
3. Which is more important—the gamer's right to play certain games, even though they may violate cultural standards or move certain individuals toward violence, or the need to prevent the occurrence of another tragedy like that which occurred at Columbine High School? Write a journal entry arguing your position on this topic.
4. Using the articles in this book or by finding others on your own, write a synthesis comparing and contrasting different views on the social dangers represented by video games.

READING SELECTION

"Playing with Fire?"

About the Author: Tony Reichhardt

Tony Reichhardt is a freelance writer who lives in Fredericksburg, Virginia. He has written about the space program for approximately twenty-five years. He was the editor of the 2002 Smithsonian book *Space Shuttle: The First Twenty Years,* a collection of firsthand astronaut stories and photographs. At present, he writes almost entirely for two magazines—as a consulting editor at *Air & Space* and as a contributing correspondent for *Nature* magazine, covering space science and a range of other topics that include genetics, nuclear energy, the environment, and video entertainment. This essay first appeared in *Nature* in July 2003.

Before You Read

1. What images or ideas does the title invoke? What might this suggest about the author's point-of-view?
2. What does the headnote tell you about the author's qualifications to offer an opinion on this subject? How might you be able to get more insight into his qualifications?
3. What do you know—or how can you find out—about the reputation and readership of *Nature,* in which this article first appeared? Does the place this article appears tell you anything about the author or the intended audience or give you insight into the probable quality of the article?
4. Scan the essay. Do you get a sense of the thesis or main divisions of the argument? What might they be?

Playing with Fire?

1 How about this for two contrasting views of the same phenomenon? When Craig Anderson watches teenagers playing violent video games such as *Doom* and *Grand Theft Auto,* he believes that seeds of aggression are being sown in their minds. Anderson, a psychologist at Iowa State University in Ames, says that experiments he and others have carried out show that players become more likely to harbor aggressive thoughts and show aggressive behavior. He sometimes opens articles about media violence with ominous reminders of the 1999 Columbine High massacre in Littleton, Colorado. The Columbine killers, it seems, were big fans of *Doom.*

2 Kevin Durkin, a psychologist at the University of Western Australia in Crawley, observes teenagers playing arcade games, even violent ones, and sees something entirely different: kids having a good time. Whatever aggression the players show towards each other is generally good-natured, and accompanied by laughter. "The main type of aggression was robust treatment of the equipment," he noted dryly in a 1999 study for the Australian government.[1] Computer games, he concluded last year,[2] can be "a positive feature of a healthy adolescence."

3 Contrasting views are not unusual in media-violence research. In one corner are parents' groups and politicians, who worry that the games' violence fuels real-life aggression, and say that the majority of research confirms such fears. Lined up against them are the researchers who side with Durkin, together with freedom-of-speech advocates. The evidence is weak, they counter, and their opponents use dubious statistics to make their point.

4 So who is right? The answer is far from clear, partly because the two sides are engaged in a war of words that can be as combative as some of the games being studied. Researchers who deny a

link between violence and computer games have, for example, had their work challenged on the grounds that they received funding from the entertainment industry. Others point out that some supporters of a link make money by advising parent-focused media watchdogs. The answer may be out there, but locating it amid the controversy is difficult. *Mortal Kombat* indeed.

Study Stand-off

5 The public split between the two sides centers on their interpretation of existing studies. Although the vast majority of work on violence in the media has focused on television, Anderson and supporters say that we already know enough about computer games to be concerned. Together with former Iowa State colleague Brad Bushman, now at the University of Michigan in Ann Arbor, Anderson analyzed 35 video-game studies carried out as of 2000. The research, the pair argue, shows that video-game violence "is correlated with aggression in the real world."[3]

6 Typical of the studies is one that Anderson carried out with Karen Dill, a psychologist at Lenoir-Rhyne College in Hickory, North Carolina. College students played violent and nonviolent games, and then competed against each other in another game in which they tried to push a button faster than their opponent. If they won, they got to blast the loser with a loud noise. Those who played the violent game blasted their opponents for about a tenth of a second longer than nonviolent gamers, but only when they had been blasted themselves in the previous round. "Playing a violent video game increased the aggressiveness of participants after they had been provoked by their opponent's noise blast," the authors concluded.[4]

Eric Harris and Dylan Klebold killed thirteen students and teachers and wounded twenty-one others before killing themselves.

7 But Durkin's review of the literature led him to downplay the threat from video games "Despite much debate about the consequences of playing games with aggressive content, the evidence available to date to support claims of harmful effects upon children is modest." Ditto Lillian Bensley and Juliet VanEenwyk, epidemiologists at the Washington State Department of Health in Olympia, who published a review of computer-game literature in 2000. "The research evidence is not supportive of a major public concern that violent video games lead to real-life violence," they wrote.[5]

Cartoon Categories

8 How can groups reach such different conclusions? Part of the answer lies in the difficulty of comparing studies. Take the definition of violent content, for example. One widely cited study of television violence was published in March by Rowell Huesmann, a psychologist at the University of Michigan. He found that subjects who had watched violent shows and identified with aggressive television characters as children showed more aggression in early adulthood.[6] But in the study, *Roadrunner* cartoons were described as "very violent," leading critics to question the method's validity. Assessments of video-game violence suffer similar problems. One group of researchers, for example, counted Pac Man being swallowed by ghosts as a violent event, and tallied 0.59 "deaths per minute" in a Smurfs game.[7]

9 Michael Rich, head of the Center on Media and Child Health at the Children's Hospital in Boston, Massachusetts, and a film-maker turned pediatrician, would like to end this confusion. "We need to get out of this mode where everybody's measuring different things," he says. The center hopes to standardize existing studies of television and video games to allow direct comparison, and to develop a content-based ratings system grounded on the principles of developmental psychology.

10 Hints about how this could be done come from the work of Jeanne Funk, a psychologist at the University of Toledo in Ohio, who has helped to review rating standards for the software industry. Funk consulted with teen-agers to come up with more subtle and descriptive categories, such as "fantasy violence," "human violence," and "sports violence." The Entertainment Software Rating Board, the New York-based body that oversees U.S. game classifications plans to incorporate such categories in its labeling, and the descriptions could also help game-violence researchers to be more specific about what kind of content they are assessing.

11 Other problems may be more difficult to tackle. Different experiments often measure different proxies for aggression, for example. Some merely record signs of physiological arousal, such as increased heart rate and blood pressure, after subjects play violent games. Others try to assess violent thoughts, based, for example, on how subjects complete a partial story given to them. Few studies have looked at actual acts, such as blasting another person with sound in the lab, or hitting other children.

12 Although Anderson maintains that aggression in the lab is essentially the same as aggression in the real world, critics see the connection as tenuous. Both sides agree that carefully designed longitudinal studies—tracking the real-life histories of heavy game players—would advance our understanding. But Anderson and his colleagues have been unable to obtain funding for such research.

13 Policy-makers, meanwhile, cannot wait for science to catch up—they come under pressure every time a violent new game is released, and have to act on the available evidence, even if it is limited. Almost every session of the U.S. Congress includes an attack on the dangers that television and video-game violence pose to America's youth. And local law-makers are beginning to take action. In May, for example, Washington became the first state to ban sales of realistic cop-killer games to children younger than seventeen years of age.

Small Influence

14 Are such measures justified on scientific grounds? Some of the researchers consulted by *Nature* argue that computer games could lead to violent behavior under certain conditions—they might trigger aggression in certain people already predisposed to violence, for example. But few support the idea that video games are important causes of violence in the real world. A 2001 report on violence issued by the U.S. Surgeon General[8] sums up their opinions: "Taken together, findings to date suggest that media violence has a relatively small impact on violence."

15 Some of the most damning verdicts on video-game studies come from those who study violence in general. Jeffrey Fagan, who heads the Center for Violence Research and Prevention at Columbia University in New York, says media-violence researchers are guilty of "a lot of sloppy thinking about causality." Look at it from an epidemiological viewpoint, he urges. With millions of copies of *Doom* sold, we would be seeing an epidemic of violence unless the dose–response rate is extremely small. Meanwhile, violence in the United States has declined—in 2001 it reached its lowest level since records began in 1972. Claiming that television or video games are important contributors to societal violence "doesn't pass the giggle test," says Fagan.

16 Anderson remains undaunted, however. While conceding that media exposure may not be the most important risk factor for violent behavior he insists that the link between video games and aggression "has pretty much been established." But he is likely to need more definitive evidence to persuade his colleagues, let alone the millions of kids eagerly awaiting the next action-packed game.

Notes

1. Durkin, K., & Aisbett, K. *Computer Games and Australians Today* (Office Film Literature Classification, Sydney, 1999).
2. Durkin, K., & Harber, B. *J. Appl. Dev. Psychol.* **23,** 373–392 (2002).
3. Anderson, C. A., & Bushman, B. *J. Psychol. Sci.* **12,** 353–359 (2001).
4. Anderson, C. A., & Dill, K. E. *J. Personality Soc. Psychol.* **78,** 772–790 (2000).
5. Bensley, L., & VanEenwyk, I. *Video Games and Real-Life Aggression: A Review of the Literature* (Washington State Dept Health Office Epidemiol., Olympia, Washington, 2000).
6. Huesmann, L. R., et al. *Dev. Psychol.* **39,** 201–221 (2003).
7. Thompson, K. M., & Haninger, K. *J. Am. Med. Assoc.* **286,** 591–598 (2001).
8. U.S. Surgeon General. *Youth Violence: A Report of the Surgeon General* (U.S. Pub. Health Service, Washington DC, 2001).

Thinking about the Argument

1. What, according to the author, are the two dominant views regarding whether or not video games encourage aggression in young people?
2. Why are parents' groups and politicians concerned about this debate?
3. Why does Reichhardt say there is such a strong difference of opinion among researchers?
4. Why do you think the author uses the term "cartoon categories"?
5. What viewpoint does Reichhart seem to favor? How do you know?

Responding to the Argument

1. Reichhardt divides this issue into two divergent opinions. Do you think this assessment is accurate, or are there other opinions he does not discuss?
2. What might those opinions be?
3. How does your opinion agree with, or differ from, those Reichhardt discusses?
4. In the last three paragraphs, how does the author use humor to emphasize his opinion? Do you find this approach appealing? Why or why not?

Writing about the Argument

1. Write an essay comparing Reichhardt's style to others whose writings address this issue. Do you find his more lighthearted approach effective? Why or why not?
2. Write two parallel journal entries about violence and video gaming. In the first, use a serious tone. In the second, use a humorous tone. In a third, explain which approach you found more effective, and why.
3. Identify an audience that is likely to believe that video gaming is unhealthy. Write a letter to this audience explaining why their fears are unfounded.
4. Identify an audience that is likely to believe that video gaming is perfectly fine. Write a letter to this audience explaining why they should be concerned.

"Bang, You're Dead"

About the Author: Sara Rimensnyder

Sara Rimensnyder is a journalist whose career has included writing theater reviews and commentaries on Asian politics. Recently, she has been an assistant editor at *Reason* magazine, a monthly publication focused on politics and culture. In "Bang, You're Dead," from the November 2002 issue of *Reason,* Rimensnyder interviews Gerard Jones, a writer of screenplays, comic books, and histories. Jones's *Men of Tomorrow: Geeks, Gangsters, and the Birth of the Comic Book* won the 2005 Eisner Award.

READING SELECTION

Before You Read

1. What does the headnote tell you about the interviewer and the interviewee? How might this information affect your understanding of the reading?
2. What does the title indicate about the article's argument? What is your initial reaction to the title and possible argument? Usually, how serious is it when a child says "Bang, you're dead!"?
3. Do you think it is healthy or unhealthy for children to engage in fantasy violence, such as "war" or "cops and robbers"? Why or why not?
4. How is playing a video game or watching a movie similar to, or different from, fantasy roleplay? Is it healthier, less healthy, or about the same for children to play violent video games versus "cops and robbers"?
5. Based on the title and a scan of the article, what is the author's perspective, either stated or implied, on this topic?

Bang, You're Dead

1 Would-be censors have long posited a monkey-see, monkey-do relationship between media and audiences. Violent images create violent kids, they warn. Comic book writer, screenwriter, historian, and parent Gerard Jones upends that thinking in his new book *Killing Monsters: Why Children Need Fantasy, Super Heroes, and Make-Believe Violence* (Basic 2002). In his view, the violence depicted in comic books, cartoons, and video games helps far more kids than it hurts. As a lonely, angry thirteen-year-old, writes Jones, "the character who caught me, and freed me, was the [Incredible] Hulk: overgendered and undersocialized, half-naked and half-witted, raging against a frightened world that misunderstood and persecuted him."

2 Jones has authored two previous books and countless comics, including *Green Lantern: Mosaic, The Trouble with Girls, Batman: Jazz,* and *The Shadow Strikes.* His latest project is the nonprofit Media Power for Children. "Our mission statement isn't written yet," he says, "but we'll be talking about the ways kids can use media to empower themselves, to use a cornball word." Assistant editor Sara Rimensnyder spoke to Jones in September.

3 **Q:** How can fantasy violence help children?

4 **A:** Fantasy gives kids a world in which they can be everything that real life doesn't let them be. That can be a tremendous relief, a great way to leave behind the tensions of having to behave and compromise and negotiate your way through life all the time. It also helps satisfy curiosity about what life might be like without all these constraints.

5 Fantasy worlds let children create a proxy self—through a superhero, say—who's more powerful than their real selves. Since kids always have and always will feel somewhat powerless in this world, that proxy self is very energizing, helping them deal with reality when they close the comic book.

6 **Q:** Why are we so uptight about violent images in popular culture?

7 **A:** We're trying to control and eliminate real violence in society, and that's a good thing. But in our zeal to do that, we go after everything that resembles violence or seems to glorify it. We forget that one of the main functions of fantasy is that it enables you to take your

antisocial desires and dispel them outside of the real world.

8 **Q:** Are there any TV shows or video games that are off-limits to your own son?

9 **A:** I do believe in creating filters for younger kids, not because media will teach them to be criminals, but because it can add additional stresses, pains, and confusion to their lives. I wouldn't let my 9-year-old son play *Grand Theft Auto.* Kids learn gradually about how the adult world works. I don't need him to learn about gory street crime or oral sex all at once through a shock-value video game.

Thinking about the Argument

1. According to the interviewee, how was the writer "helped" by comic book fantasies when he was a child?
2. Why does the interviewee think that such fantasies are good for children?
3. Does the interviewee adequately answer the question, "How can fantasy violence help children?" Explain.
4. What kinds of limits does the interviewee believe should be placed on children's access to fantasy violence? Do you agree? Why or why not?
5. Do you agree with Jones's statement that "one of the main functions of fantasy is that it enables you to take your antisocial desires and dispel them outside of the real world"? Explain.

Responding to the Argument

1. Did you read comic books when you were growing up? Do you consider comics violent? If so, in what ways is this violence healthy, unhealthy, or neutral in its effect? Why do you think this?
2. What other fantasy figures—wrestlers, pop stars, fantasy heroes—in popular culture did you know about or identify with as a child? Did any of them practice violence? Did you role play or emulate this violence in any way? How about someone you knew?
3. At what point would you consider interest in fantasy violence to be unhealthy? For example, is "backyard wrestling" unhealthy? Are there forms of fantasy violence, that when acted out, even just for play, can be dangerous?
4. Do you think any of these forms of fantasy violence could lead to real violence? Explain.

Writing about the Argument

1. Write an argument discussing whether or not fantasy violence such as "cops and robbers" or "backyard wrestling" is unhealthy—mentally, physically, or both—for children.
2. If such fantasy role-play is acceptable to you, what should the restrictions of such play be? Should it be officially monitored and supervised, as "paintball" or "laser tag" is, or should children be taught to safely manage their own play? Write an essay, a journal entry, or a letter to a concerned mother explaining the pros and cons of the situation.

3. Write an essay comparing "live" fantasy violence to video games. Which is healthier? Use concrete examples to support your claims.
4. Should monitoring fantasy violence be left up to parents or to society? Should certain types of rough play become illegal? Why or why not? Write an essay or journal entry arguing your position.
5. If children are injured while engaging in dangerous activities based on scenarios seen on television, in video games, or in comic books, should parents be able to sue the creators of those products? Where does personal and parental responsibility end and corporate liability begin? Write an essay or a letter to the editor of your local paper arguing this issue.

"Aggression and Violent Media"

About the Author: Cynthia G. Wagner

After receiving her master's degree in magazine journalism from Syracuse University in 1981, Cynthia G. Wagner began working for *The Futurist,* and in 1992 she became its managing editor. Her articles deal with trends and cautionary tales on a variety of subjects, such as the environment, global security, economics, tourism, and poverty. She is the editor of *Foresight, Innovation, and Strategy: Toward a Wiser Future* (2005). She writes, "The study of the future is like a lifelong open curriculum in liberal arts, so I've been exposed to subjects I never would have expected, from astrobiology to sustainable development." This selection was originally published in the July/August 2004 issue of *The Futurist.*

Before You Read

1. What does the headnote tell you about the author? How might this information affect your understanding of the reading?
2. What does the title indicate about the article's argument? What is your initial reaction to the title and possible argument?
3. Scan the article. What main points do you expect it to make?

Aggression and Violent Media

1 Young people are now spending more time playing video games than watching television. For parents and educators concerned with children's exposure to violence, this is not necessarily good news.

2 A new Michigan State University survey of youths from grade five through university level found that all are spending as much or more time playing games as watching television, and that boys spend about twice as much time playing video games as girls do.

3 But the violent content of those games, particularly those favored by males, is of growing concern to families, schools, and policy makers. Gaming is participatory while television viewing is passive, so the risk may be greater that exposure to violent games will result in violent behavior, suggests a recent study led by psychologist Craig A. Anderson of Iowa State University.

4 "The impact of exposure to violent video games has not been studied as extensively as the impact of exposure to TV or movie violence," the researchers write in *Psychological Science in the Public Interest.* "However, on the whole, the results reported for video

games to date are very similar to those obtained in the investigations of TV and movie violence."

5 Among the effects of violent game playing are increases in physiological arousal and physically aggressive behavior, such as hitting, kicking, and pulling clothes or hair. Studies also have found a reduction in helpful behavior among youths exposed to violent video games.

6 Males tend to prefer action-oriented video games involving shooting, fighting, sports, action adventure, fantasy role-playing, and strategy, according to the Michigan State survey. Females prefer classic board games, trivia quizzes, puzzles, and arcade games.

7 Electronic game playing gets young people involved with technologies and opens up opportunities in high-paying tech careers, notes communications professor Bradley Greenberg of Michigan State.

8 "It is believed that these opportunities accrue to boys because they spend more time working with electronic games and computers," says Greenberg. "If girls become more involved with technology at an early age, it is likely that the interest in technology will continue into the work world."

9 If females do become more involved in technology fields, including game development, they may create less-violent games that promote cooperation rather than aggression.

10 Video games are in 80 percent of U.S. homes with children; they generated $6 billion in 2000 and $11 billion by 2003.

11 "All indications are that the industry will continue to grow at a healthy clip," says Greenberg. "The emerging market is for games designed more with girls in mind that engage them for longer periods of time and force them to investigate more the technology behind the games. The next frontier involves transferring video-game technology to educational settings and using the young people's fascination with the games to involve them more with innovative teaching technologies."

12 Until that day comes, however, more awareness is needed of the impacts of violent games on young people's behavior, Anderson and his colleagues conclude.

»«

Thinking about the Argument

1. To what extent is this article argumentative, and to what extent is it merely expository? Is it possible for an expository essay to imply an argument? Explain.
2. Why might the author invoke the University of Michigan study so early in the reading?
3. What, according to Wagner, is the difference between watching television and playing video games?
4. What does the article say are some of the effects of playing video games?
5. What does the author suggest as the potential positive effects of video games designed by women?

Responding to the Argument

1. Do you agree that video games are primarily played by boys, and that such games encourage violence in boys?
2. What are the differences between boys and girls that might account for these results?
3. If more nonviolent games were offered, do you think more girls would be inclined to play?
4. What kinds of interactions—in person, on the Internet, or in games—do girls prefer as compared to the kinds of activities boys engage in?

5. Do you think games can have legitimate educational applications? What might they be? Given the choice, will a young person play an educational game when a violent game is an option? Explain.

Writing about the Argument

1. Though the article uses an expository "reporting" style, the argument is clearly implied. In a journal entry or essay, analyze the style of this article and discuss how it uses exposition to imply an argument.
2. Research and write an argumentative essay discussing the differences between the ways that boys and girls approach and respond to video games.
3. Imagine that you are an educator. Write a letter to a video game designer asking him or her to design a game that will both attract young people and educate them. What kinds of features should such a game have?
4. Research several video games by playing them. Take notes on the types of characters depicted and the types of situations encountered. In what ways might these games be attractive to boys and repulsive to girls? Would you classify any of them as sexist? Write an essay or journal entry comparing three or more games.

"Parents Need Help"

About the Author: Barbara Dafoe Whitehead

Barbara Dafoe Whitehead is a widely published advocate for the well-being of children and traditional families. Her books include *The Divorce Culture: Rethinking Our Commitment to Marriage and Family* (1998) and *Why There Are No Good Men Left: The Romantic Plight of the New Single Woman* (2002). She is codirector of the National Marriage Project. This essay first appeared in *Commonweal* magazine in January 2005.

Before You Read

1. What does the headnote tell you about the author? How could you discover more information?
2. What do you expect the author's opinion regarding video games to be? Why do you think this?
3. What does the title indicate about the article's argument? What claims do you think she might make?
4. What do you already know about parenting and violent entertainment that might be relevant to the reading?

»«

Parents Need Help

1 A century ago, Jane Addams and other progressive reformers in Chicago responded to the dangers of the industrial age by creating laws and institutions that would protect children from the unwholesome lures of the city streets. Her work is rightly honored. A similar, and equally important, struggle is being waged in Illinois today. On the surface, it's about the sale of video games to kids. It's also a debate about a deeper question: To what degree does the responsibility for teaching good values to children fall solely on parents? Should some of that responsibility be shared by the state?

2 Those who make and sell video games say parents alone should bear the responsibility. On the other side is Illinois Governor Rod Blagojevich. He's trying to outlaw the sale of excessively violent or sexually explicit video games to children under eighteen. In his effort to restrict such sales he's making the argument that raising children is a shared responsibility: "Parenting is hard work and the state has a compelling interest in helping parents raise their children to be upstanding men and women."

3 The governor firmly believes that parents have the primary responsibility for teaching their children right from wrong. He believes just as firmly that parents should not have their efforts subverted by the avalanche of "amusements" that tell kids it is fun to blow people up. "Too many of the video games marketed to our children teach them all of the wrong lessons and all of the wrong values," Blagojevich writes in a "letter to Illinois parents" posted on the state's informational website (www.safegamesIllinois.com). "These games use violence, rage, and sexual aggression as play. That is not acceptable. When kids play, they should play like children, not like gangland assassins."

4 The governor's reference to gangland assassins is not an overstatement. One video game, the top-selling, industry-award-winning *Grand Theft Auto: San Andreas,* features gang warfare and the killing of prostitutes. Another, released on the forty-first anniversary of the Kennedy assassination, gets players to step into the shoes of Lee Harvey Oswald and to aim at the president's head as his motorcade rolls by. "Content descriptors" for video games also suggest how lurid the violence can be. These games include depictions of "blood and gore (mutilation of body parts)," "intense violence (human injury or death)," and "sexual violence (depictions of rape and other sexual acts)."

5 No sooner had Blagojevich unveiled his proposal than he faced powerful organized opposition from the entertainment industry. The Illinois Retail Merchants Association, the National Association of Theater Owners, the Entertainment Software Rating Board, and the Motion Picture Association of America took strong exception to the legislation. Imposing a curb on the free market is not the way to protect kids, these critics argued. Instead, parents should screen what their kids are buying and playing. As one lobbyist put it: "Retailers can't be held accountable for lack of oversight by parents."

6 This is a distortion of the governor's position, and of the problem. No one denies that parents have the primary responsibility for monitoring their kids. Blagojevich points out, though, that the sophisticated technology of video games makes that very hard to do. Consequently, it's up to the state to step in on the side of parents and children to help them cope.

7 The industry argument would be plausible if it were still 1955. Back then, it was easier for parents to exercise strict oversight. The big, boxy home entertainment technologies of that era—radio, television, and record players—produced images and sounds that parents could see and hear. They came with OFF buttons for parents to push and plugs for parents to pull. All that has changed. The new entertainment technologies include a dizzying and ever-multiplying array of small, portable, individual, kid-friendly devices that defy close parental supervision. It was easy for parents to check on a half-hour TV show. It's much harder to review a video game. The games feature successive levels of difficulty; players must qualify at a lower level before earning the right to move to a higher level. So it takes time and practice before acquiring the skill to progress to the highest level of the game—which may also be its highest level of violence. To ensure that a video game isn't excessively violent, a parent would have to be looking over a child's shoulder until the highest level of play was finally revealed. This could take days.

8 Moreover, it isn't as if parents and the video-game industry meet each other on a level playing field. This is a multi-billion-dollar industry that spends all its time and money devising ever

more ingenious ways to market to kids over the heads of their parents and to deliberately undermine the ability of parents to regulate what their children are seeing. And in a tactic called "age compression," the marketers target their appeals to ever-younger kids. Like the youth sex revolution, the youth marketing revolution has migrated down the age scale. Even four-year-olds know what is cool.

9 To be sure, the industry's Entertainment Software Rating Board has voluntarily established its own ratings system. The trouble is: It isn't enforced. A study by the Federal Trade Commission found that early teens were able to buy games rated M (Mature 17+) 69 percent of the time.

10 It is telling that the makers and sellers of video games have responded so quickly and vigorously to Governor Blagojevich's very modest proposal. Clearly the corporate sector finds it in its interest to prompt kids to engage in fantasy rape, beheadings, and mass murder. And why should we expect otherwise? Its interest is the bottom line. Violence sells. But isn't it in the compelling interest of the community to curb such violent play?

Thinking about the Argument

1. Why does the author mention Jane Addams in the first paragraph? Does this add to her authority on this subject? Why or why not?
2. Does Whitehead think parents should bear the primary responsibility for the content of the games their children play? How do you know?
3. What does the author's sentence "The governor's reference to gangland assassins is not an understatement" tell you about her viewpoint? Explain.
4. What evidence does Whitehead provide to suggest that games are needlessly violent?
5. Why, according to Whitehead, is the video game industry's rating system a problem? What evidence does she provide to back up this statement?

Responding to the Argument

1. Explain why you agree or disagree with this statement: "Isn't it in the compelling interest of the community to curb such violent play?"
2. Why does the author think it is difficult for parents to monitor the games their children play? Do you agree with the assessment? Why or why not?
3. Contrast this article to one of the others in this section that argues in favor of the video game industry. Where do the articles differ? What points do they have in common? Make a chart of the various viewpoints on this issue.
4. Consider the author's style. Are you sympathetic to her point of view? Why or why not? How does she use words to create a "voice" that might engender sympathy in her audience?
5. Rate the articles you have read that treat this issue in two areas—style and argument—on a scale of 1 to 10. Do you find yourself "sympathizing" more with an author who makes a weaker argument than with someone with whom you did not identify? Explain which author you identified with the most, and why.

WRITING ABOUT THE ARGUMENT

1. Write an argument in the form of a letter for or against censoring the content of video games. Write the letter to a group of twenty-something male video game designers.
2. Now rewrite the letter to an organization of concerned mothers.
3. Go back over the two letters you have written. Write a journal entry or brief essay explaining what you changed in the second essay, and why. How did these changes help you approach your new audience?
4. Do you think that the government should enforce censorship standards where video games are concerned? Why or why not? Write an argument considering whether or not the video game designer's right to freedom of speech and expression overrides the concerns of the standards of a community that would censor such games.
5. Should the same standards that are applied to pornography be applied to the censorship of video games? Why or why not? Explain in a journal entry, letter, or essay. Be certain to define a specific audience before you write.

"Why Eminem Is a Problem"

ABOUT THE AUTHOR: LLOYD EBY

Lloyd Eby is the assistant senior editor for the "Modern Thought" section of the monthly online publication *The World & I,* which provides news and opinions about science, culture, politics, and social issues. Although individual articles in *The World & I* may have argumentative slants, the publication seeks balance by publishing counterarguments in the same issue. This essay and the following one by M. P. McRillis were published in March 2003 in *The World & I.*

BEFORE YOU READ

1. What does the headnote tell you about the author and journal? How might this information affect your understanding of the reading?
2. What does the title indicate about the article's argument? What is your initial reaction to the title and possible argument?
3. What do you already know about Eminem and rap music that might be relevant to the reading?

READING SELECTION

Why Eminem Is a Problem

1 The best discussion I have seen of the role and influence of music in the lives of today's young people occurs in the "Music" chapter of the late Allan Bloom's 1997 book, *The Closing of the American Mind.* Bloom had been a professor of social thought at the University of Chicago and other universities for many years, and he drew on his experiences interacting with and teaching numerous generations of students.

2 Bloom begins by noting that today's students do not have books, but they do have music: "Nothing is more singular about this generation than its addiction to music. This is the age of music and the states of soul that accompany it." Moreover, advances in technology have made music available to all people, everywhere, all the time. "The musical soil has become tropically rich," Bloom says, and "there are many geniuses, producing all the time," so that "there is no dearth of the new and the startling."

3 A change in the role of music in young people's lives came about recently, Bloom says—he seems to mean at the beginning of the 1960s. Before that there had been a decline in the role and influence of music; romanticism had dominated serious music since Beethoven, he says, and this appealed to refined sentiments that barely exist in the contemporary world. Moreover, there had been a divide between the middle and lower classes, the educated and the uneducated. The educated middle class frequently "made some of the old European music a part of the home, partly because they liked it, partly because they thought it was good for the kids." But rock music, when it emerged, came with "real, if coarse, feelings as opposed to artificial and dead ones." This amounted to a revolution, and rock music "won the revolution and reigns unabashed today." The class distinction in musical tastes disappeared because rock appealed to all young people, regardless of class or education. "The power of music in the soul . . . has been recovered after a long period of desuetude. And it is rock music that has effected this restoration."

4 Because of their immersion in this music, Bloom writes, today's students now take seriously Plato's passages on musical education in the *Republic.* In the past, students "were indignant at [Plato's advocacy of] the censorship of poetry, as a threat to free inquiry." They were thinking about science and politics, not paying attention to what Plato says about music, because for those earlier students music was only an entertainment. "Students today, on the contrary, know exactly why Plato takes music so seriously," Bloom says. "They know it affects life very profoundly and are indignant because Plato seems to want to rob them of their most intimate pleasure." Consequently, they are drawn into a dispute with Plato on these issues: "The very fact of their fury shows how much Plato threatens what is dear and intimate to them." According to Bloom, "It is Plato's teaching that music, by its nature, encompasses all that is today most resistant to philosophy," which is careful and informed thought about what is most important to us.

5 Bloom goes on to note that Plato held "that rhythm and melody, accompanied by dance, are the barbarous expressions of the soul. Barbarous, not animal." Music "is the medium of the human soul in its most ecstatic condition of wonder and terror." It is the soul's "primitive and primary speech . . . without articulate speech or reason." It is "hostile to reason" and is contrasted with education, which "is the taming or domestication of the soul's raw passions." The goal, as Plato and Bloom see it, is to harmonize this enthusiastic part of the soul "with what develops later, the rational part." Students, Bloom says, "are not in a position to know the pleasures of reason; they can only see it as a disciplinary and repressive parent." And here their opposition to Plato

emerges because "they do see, in the case of Plato, that the parent has figured out what they are up to."

6 Rock music, Bloom says, seeks and serves to unleash the Dionysian passions, to "replenish our dried-up stream from barbaric sources." Rock music "has risen to its current heights in the education of the young on the ashes of classical music, and in an atmosphere in which there is no intellectual resistance to tap the rawest passions." It has "one appeal only, a barbaric appeal, to sexual desire—not love, . . . but sexual desire undeveloped and untutored." It "acknowledges the first emanations of children's emerging sensuality and addresses them seriously, eliciting them and legitimating them . . . as the real thing." It and the entertainment industry "give children, on a silver platter, . . . everything their parents always used to tell them they had to wait for until they grew up and would understand better." That thing is sex. "Young people know that rock [music] has the beat of sexual intercourse."

7 The result of this sexual interest that is expressed in rock music is "rebellion against the parental authority that represses it." The selfishness of teenagers "becomes indignation and then transforms itself into morality." Along with this came the sexual revolution, which overthrew "the forces of domination, the enemies of nature and happiness." This led to a transformation in which "a worldview is balanced on the sexual fulcrum." Moreover, these changes had harmful consequences because "nothing noble, sublime, profound, delicate, tasteful or even decent can find a place in such tableaux. There is room only for the intense, changing, crude, and immediate." This leads to pubescent children whose bodies "throb with orgasmic rhythms," and whose "life is made into a nonstop commercially packaged [sexual] fantasy." He goes on to say that his description "may seem exaggerated, but only because some would prefer to regard it as such."

8 All this takes place in a "family spiritual void [that] has left the field open to rock music"; parents "cannot possibly forbid their children to listen to it" since it is everywhere and "all children listen to it." Because of that, "forbidding it would simply cause [parents] to lose their children's affection and obedience." The result is "nothing less than parents' loss of control over their children's moral education at a time when no one else is seriously concerned with it."

9 The rock music business fully supports all this because it is "perfect capitalism, supplying to demand and helping to create it." It is a business that "is peculiar only in that it caters almost exclusively to children, treating legally and naturally imperfect human beings as though they were ready to enjoy the final or complete satisfaction." It leads to a "loss of a clear view of what adulthood or maturity is, and our incapacity to conceive ends." Because it is empty of values, it leads to "the acceptance of the natural facts as the ends." The end, in the case of rock music, is "infantile sexuality," and, Bloom suspects, because of the absence of other, better ends, many adults have come to agree with those ends.

10 Bloom's ultimate concern is "not with the moral effects of this music—whether it leads to sex, violence, or drugs." Instead, he is concerned about education and the fact that because the young people are addicted to the music, they cannot discover the depths of thought and experience that lie within great books, art, and the great traditions. "As long as they have the Walkman on," he concludes, "they cannot hear what the great tradition has to say. And, after its prolonged use, when they take it off, they find they are deaf." He means not that they are physically deaf, but that their minds and spirits have become seared, so they are unable to comprehend.

11 An important point that Bloom ignores is that the precognitive, emotive force of music and lyrics can influence people for good or ill. Bloom focuses on the bad effects of rock music on the young, and he is surely correct that much of this influence is bad. But some music also affects young people who hear it in good and beneficial

ways. Examples are nursery songs, religious and patriotic music, and even some forms of rock music or rock songs—so-called Christian or religious rock attempts to do this.

The PMRC and Tipper Gore

12 In 1984, Tipper Gore, wife of then-Senator Albert Gore, bought the album *Purple Rain* by the artist then known as Prince. When listening to the album with her daughter, Gore became very disturbed by some of the lyrics, especially the song "Darling Nikki," about a woman caught masturbating in a hotel with a magazine. This outraged Gore, and she started wondering whether other parents who had bought this album for their children had also listened to it and become upset at its contents. After studying other song lyrics, music videos, and the MTV music network, she became increasingly agitated. Eventually, she published a best-selling book on the topic, *Raising a PG Kid in an X-Rated Society* (1987).

13 Gore joined with some other influential Washington wives in forming the Parents' Music Resource Center (PRMC). The stated goal of the PRMC was not to push for government censorship of the recording industry—a claim made by the group's opponents—but instead to "educate and inform parents about this alarming new trend as well as to ask the industry to exercise self-restraint." On September 19, 1985, representing the PMRC, Tipper Gore and Susan Baker, wife of Treasury Secretary James Baker, appeared before the Senate Committee on Commerce, Science, and Transportation. Baker, speaking to the committee, said:

> Our primary purpose is to educate and inform parents about this alarming trend as well as to ask the industry to exercise self-restraint. . . . Because anything that we are exposed to that much [as today's rock music] has some influence on us, we believe that the music industry has a special responsibility, as the message of songs goes from the suggestive to the blatantly explicit.

14 As Ellen Goodman stated in a recent column . . . "The outrageous edge of rock and roll has shifted its focus from Elvis's pelvis to the saw protruding from Blackie Lawless's codpiece on a WASP album. Rock lyrics have turned from 'I can't get no satisfaction' to 'I am going to force you at gunpoint to eat me alive.'"

15 The material we are concerned about cannot be compared with "Louie Louie," Cole Porter, Billie Holiday, etc. Cole Porter's "the birds do it, the bees do it," can hardly be compared with WASP, "I . . . like a beast." There is a new element of vulgarity and violence toward women that is unprecedented.

16 While a few outrageous recordings have always existed in the past, the proliferation of songs glorifying rape, sadomasochism, incest, the occult, and suicide by a growing number of bands illustrates this escalating trend that is alarming.

17 Gore, in her testimony, underscored that the PMRC was calling for voluntary restraints, and the difference between present-day material and what has been produced in the past:

> The committee should understand the Parents' Music Resource Center is not advocating any federal intervention or legislation whatsoever. The excesses that we are discussing were allowed to develop in the marketplace, and we believe the solutions to these excesses should come from the industry who has allowed them to develop and not from the government.
>
> The issue here is larger than violent and sexually explicit lyrics. It is one of ideas and ideal freedoms and responsibility in our society. Clearly, there is a tension here, and in a free society there always will be. We are simply asking that these corporate and artistic rights be exercised with responsibility, with sensitivity, and some measure of self-restraint, especially since young minds are at stake. We are talking about preteenagers and young teenagers having access to this material. That is our point of departure and our concern. . . .
>
> One point we have already made, that the material that has caused the concern is new

and different. It is not just a continuation of controversies of past generations.

18 The PMRC members stressed that they wanted four things: (a) that questionable lyrics should be printed and provided with their respective recordings; (b) that objectionable album covers should be sold in plain brown wrappers, or sold in areas segregated from other albums; (c) that rock concerts be rated; and (d) that MTV segregate questionable video recordings into specific late-night viewing slots. In addition, the PMRC claimed that "virgin minds" were being poisoned by "hidden messages and backward masking." Besides its testimony before Congress, the PMRC lobbied recording companies to reassess the contracts of performers whose works were found to be objectionable.

19 The PMRC never called for direct government censorship of music lyrics; in fact, its members explicitly denied that they were advocating censorship. They stated repeatedly that they were working toward adoption of a "voluntary" ratings system. But the testimony and proposals of the PMRC stirred up a hornets' nest within the music industry and among some prominent musicians, Frank Zappa being the most notable. He too testified before that Senate committee, speaking strongly against the PMRC and its proposals, saying that "censorship here would be like using decapitation to deal with dandruff." He argued that any ratings system "opens the door to an endless parade of moral quality-control programs based on Things Certain Christians Don't Like. What if the next bunch of Washington Wives demands a large yellow 'J' on material written or performed by Jews?" Musical performers who were antiratings formed a group called Musical Majority, affiliated with the American Civil Liberties Union, and with some record companies.

20 In the 1990s, Tipper Gore became more or less silent on these issues and quit as head of the PMRC. By that time, others, such as Vice President Dan Quayle and Charlton Heston, had taken up the cause.

Rap Lyrics and Charlton Heston

21 Bloom's comments about rock music and its effects on young people apply today with even more force to rap music also known as hip-hop. As noted above, the effects of music and lyrics can be for good or ill. Here we are concerned with the ill effects, which are more prevalent and common than the good ones. Rap, like rock, had its roots in the black American underground—urban in this case—but has broken out to become a major force in the music of most young people, of whatever race or class. And it has usually been far more vulgar (using the f-word over and over), explicitly sexually oriented, violence-affirming, hate-filled, and misogynistic than the worst of rock ever was.

22 At a Harvard University Law School forum on February 16, 1999, Heston—Academy Award–winning actor and National Rifle Association president—gave a presentation entitled "Winning the Cultural War." He mentioned President Lincoln's proclamation in the Gettysburg Address, "Now we are engaged in a great Civil War . . ." and said, "Those words are true again. I believe that we are again engaged in a great civil war, a cultural war that is about to hijack your birthright."

23 In the course of his talk, Heston mentioned an incident having to do with the lyrics of rap music, stating:

> A few years back I heard about a rapper named Ice-T who was selling a CD called Cop Killer, celebrating ambushing and murdering police officers. It was being marketed by none other than Time/Warner, the biggest entertainment conglomerate in the world. Police across the country were outraged. Rightfully so—at least one had been murdered. But Time/Warner was stonewalling because the CD was a cash cow for them, and the media were tiptoeing around because the rapper was black. I heard Time/Warner had a stockholders meeting scheduled in Beverly Hills. I owned some shares at the time, so I decided to attend. What I did there was against the advice of my family and col-

leagues. I asked for the floor. To a hushed room of a thousand average American stockholders, I simply read the lyrics of "Cop Killer"—every vicious, vulgar, instructional word. "I GOT MY 12 GAUGE SAWED OFF / I GOT MY HEADLIGHTS TURNED OFF / I'M ABOUT TO BUST SOME SHOTS OFF / I'M ABOUT TO DUST SOME COPS OFF. . . ." It got worse, a lot worse. I won't read the rest of it to you. . . . The room was a sea of shocked, frozen, blanched faces. The Time/Warner executives squirmed in their chairs and stared at their shoes. They hated me for that. Then I delivered another volley of sick lyric brimming with racist filth, where Ice-T fantasizes about sodomizing two twelve-year-old nieces of Al and Tipper Gore. "SHE PUSHED HER BUTT AGAINST MY. . . ." Well, I won't do to you here what I did to them. Let's just say I left the room in echoing silence. When I read the lyrics to the waiting press corps, one of them said, "We can't print that." I know," I replied, "but Time/Warner's selling it."

24 Many more people—among them, William Bennett, Lynne Cheney, Peggy Noonan, and others—could be mentioned as objectors to the influence and content of rock and especially rap music. Should all of them be dismissed as intellectually irresponsible, as fuddy-duddies, or as banging a cudgel for censorship? Or should we surmise that these people have cogent objections, and good reasons for them, and seek to understand and amplify them? I think the latter is more prudent and responsible.

25 It is interesting that defenders of this music, such as Frank Zappa, almost always jump to the conclusion that critics, such as the PMRC, want to institute some form of government censorship. The critics explicitly state that their goals are different: They want such things as open labeling, parental notification, printed lyrics, and restraint on the part of artists and the music business. The problem seems to be that the defenders, in this domain at least, cannot think in categories other than individual freedom contrasted with government control, while the critics work from different concepts, thinking in terms of personal and community standards and of personal and community responsibility for upholding those standards.

26 Marshall Mathers III, known as Eminem, has become the most prominent present-day rap or hip-hop artist. His most important work is the CD entitled *The Eminem Show,* and the movie featuring him, *8 Mile.* The greatest irony is that Eminem is white, in an industry and musical-form that have been predominately black, a state of affairs he remarks on in the song "White America." . . .

27 Those few lyrics encapsulate what I will call the Eminem problem. One must give due recognition to Eminem's musical and lyrical genius. He became preeminent in his field not by a fluke, but because he is among the very best musicians and lyricists of the day. His work is characterized by inventiveness, apposite and unexpected lines and line combinations, and layers of complexity. Moreover, his stance in the lyrics is frequently ironic, in that he comments on the reactions that objectors are likely to have to them. He also deals with topics that have almost never been handled in rock music: the death of his father, the devastating results of divorce, his concern for his daughter, and his desire that his mother behave well. On the other hand, his lyrics and movie pulsate with vulgarity, adolescent sexuality, hatred, misogyny, and violence. . . .

28 The consumers of this music—the people as young as six to twelve years old who listen to and buy it—are not at the level where they make cognitive assessments of the irony, or any true or false claims about the content. Thus, Eminem and his music, as well as his film *8 Mile* and his public persona, raise anew the problem of the relationship between artistic goodness or achievement, on the one hand, and ethical or social goodness, on the other. Although, as Bloom notes, romanticism has been eclipsed today, its stance toward art and the artist still largely holds. It can be characterized, possibly a bit oversimply,

as holding that feeling is more important than reason, and, since its rise, has held sway in much of elite thought about the role and status of art and artists. Consequently, the sophisticated view or attitude has usually been to treat the art and the artist as beyond ethical assessment, as open only to consideration of whether the art is good—"good" here usually meaning avant-garde, shocking, or otherwise unconventional. If the art is good, then, according to this view, it is therefore valuable; if the artist makes good art, he is beyond good and evil.

29 There are, however, good reasons to suspect that this view is mistaken. We know that attraction to art or being a great artist does not necessarily make that person ethically good as a person. Two examples are Adolf Eichmann, the Nazi death camp commander, who played violin and liked violin music, and Pablo Picasso, whose work most knowledgeable art historians consider to have been one of the highest points of twentieth-century art, but who, as Arianna Stassinopoulos Huffington showed in *Picasso: Creator and Destroyer,* was a misogynist and monster. Two examples from film show that great art can be ethically reprehensible: Leni Riefenstahl's film *Triumph of the Will,* considered purely as an artistic creation, is one of the greatest and strongest films ever made, but it is nevertheless highly questionable and even objectionable ethically because it glorifies Hitler and the Nazis. Sergei Eisenstein's *Battleship Potemkin* has frequently appeared on international critics' polls as one of the ten greatest films ever made, but it advocates and glorifies the communist revolution, a movement that was responsible for more than a hundred million murders in the Soviet Union, China, Cambodia, and elsewhere.

30 Music is not an argument; it does not consist of statements that are to be understood as true or false. Instead, music operates at a precognitive level of human apprehension. So Bloom is correct in what he wrote in his account of Plato, "Music is the soul's primitive and primary speech . . . without articulate speech or reason." This observation is not made on the basis of Plato's supposed authority. Instead, Plato made it because it is true, and its truth does not depend on whether he had a comprehensive philosophy of anything. Those who object to the lyrics of rap music do not take those lyrics to be statements that could be true or false. Instead, they take them to be a form of primitive and primary speech, prereason. Such primitive speech is very much a compelling force, just as the beat of rock or the drums of Indian dancers are a compelling force. In fact, the force is such that it bypasses the reasoning part of the human mind and urges or even compels thoughts and behaviors that, on reflection, the person may repudiate.

31 Much of rock and especially rap music immerses young people in vile language, premature sex, gunplay, and other forms of violence, misogyny, and hatred. Although it depicts Eminem sympathetically and shows him struggling to rise above and escape his surroundings, the movie *8 Mile* does all of those. The movie and Eminem's lyrics do not make an argument for these things—his lyrics and the film can be understood, on the cognitive level, as questioning them or making ironic comments about them. But the cognitive level is not the one on which rap operates on six- to twelve-year-olds. It influences them precognitatively, insinuating itself into their spirits, so to speak, in such a way that their young selves are formed, without their conscious knowledge or consent, into its way of being and outlook. It is an expression of the nihilism of the day. In schools across the land, beginning as early as elementary school, one sees young people with earphones seemingly glued to their heads, bopping and swaying to the music, then talking and acting as the rappers talk and act.

32 One would be quite foolish to claim that there is no direct connection between young people's immersion in rock and rap music—drenched as those musics are in adolescent sex,

violence, and misogyny—and the rise in actual teenage sex, with its attendant pregnancies and sexually transmitted diseases, and the increase in teenage violence, shootings, and other pathologies. This is not just simple correlation; there is surely a causal factor, too.

33 Someone commenting on Eminem said that the Right worries about sex and the Left about violence. I am not opposed either to sex or to guns, per se. I think that sex between married adult heterosexual couples is the place where the divine enters most directly into human life. I also own and shoot numerous rifles and shotguns, either at targets or hunting. But those are not the mature and responsible expressions of sex and guns that exist in Eminem's music; the sex in his music is adolescent, or adulterous, and mixed with misogyny, and the gunplay is stupid and violently directed at humans. Since we know that young people learn and mimic what they see and hear—to say otherwise is to deny all theories and knowledge about education—we know for certain that they are absorbing diabolical attitudes and behaviors about sex and violence from this music.

O'Reilly Understands

34 In his syndicated newspaper column of November 18, 2002, Bill O'Reilly compared Eminem to Elvis Presley: "In 1962 a young truck driver named Elvis Presley had become a rock superstar singing about hound dogs, tender love, and his mama, whom he apparently loved." But Eminem "has become the country's hottest recording star rapping about rape, drugs, and his mother, whom he apparently hates. She has sued him for $10 million. He called her a slut, in one of his recordings." O'Reilly goes on to note the profound effect Elvis had on young Americans: "Millions of young boys slicked back their hair and adopted some Elvis moves on the dance floor."

35 O'Reilly sees Eminem's influence as much more sinister. "Eminem has left his calling card as well. Two New York City grammar school teachers told me it is not uncommon for ten-year-old boys to call the little girls in their classes 'bitches' and 'ho's' (whores)." It's true, unfortunately, that very many urban American young people as young as six years old talk this way and did so long before Eminem came on the scene. But his songs only reinforce this trend, encouraging even more youngsters to think and talk this way.

36 O'Reilly minces no words. "Any way you slice it, Marshall Mathers sells degenerate behavior to kids. The entertainment industry, long devoid of any social conscience whatsoever, provides Mr. Mathers with cover and calls him a creative genius and a sensitive soul. Students of history will remember that they called Caligula that once as well."

37 The problem, O'Reilly claims, is that there has been a progressive degeneration of popular culture that has left us shell-shocked, and we have "run out of outrage." "The Baby Boom generation," he says, "embraced Elvis but then went progressively off the deep end. Drugs became chic, rebellion against authority a fad, greed became good, and self-indulgence ruled." All this has "produced an army of degenerates like Eminem." We should not be surprised, he says, "when ten-year-old Timmy calls his baby sister a bitch," because "Timmy hears that word and worse all the time." Moreover, "he sees his idol Eminem being praised by adults on TV."

38 O'Reilly concludes, "If you think this Eminem person is harmless, you are astonishingly wrong. Like Elvis, he will leave his mark on America. But unlike Elvis, the legacy Mathers will leave is one that will injure many children, especially those without much parental guidance."

39 What O'Reilly writes could be attacked for lacking nuance, and he does not acknowledge the artistic or aesthetic subtlety of Eminem. But O'Reilly does understand the problem of the influence of Eminem and his music well enough on young people and their culture that his

indictment of it is correct. It teaches young people styles of talking and being and attitudes about sex, other people, violence, and culture that can and will cause them great harm.

Epilogue

40 In the first days of January of the new year, as this was being prepared for printing, word came through MTV—was it a serious bulletin or a spoof—that Eminem has announced that he is returning to his wife and giving up drugs. He has commented that it is time to put his past behavior behind him, because one cannot be young and behave in stupid ways all the time. Time will tell whether this is serious and whether it is carried out. But if the announcement is true and if Eminem does follow through, it will be a most important development for this complex artist.

THINKING ABOUT THE ARGUMENT

1. Why does the author believe that the music serves as a form of education? Does he seem to think this is a good thing or a bad thing? How does he think music influences young people's sexual behavior and values? Explain.
2. The author spends a lot of time quoting his sources in this paper. Is this too much? How does it contribute to, or detract from, the author's authentic sense of authority or voice? Explain.
3. What is the author's stand on censoring music? Explain.
4. Why does the author contrast Eminem with Elvis? What is he trying to relate with this example? Is this strategy effective? Why or why not?

RESPONDING TO THE ARGUMENT

1. Do you accept the author's claim that popular music is "a form of primitive and primary speech" that influences young people on a subconscious level? Why or why not?
2. Explain why you agree or disagree with this statement from paragraph 32: "One would be quite foolish to claim that there is no direct connection between young people's immersion in rock and rap music—drenched as those musics are in adolescent sex, violence, and misogyny—and the rise in actual teenage sex, with its attendant pregnancies and sexually transmitted diseases, and the increase in teenage violence, shootings, and other pathologies." (Might one or more logical fallacies be evident here? If so, which ones?)
3. Does the author ever discuss his religious views in relation to this argument? Do you think that censoring or applying a rating system to music is a religious or ethical issue? Why or why not? How does this perspective strengthen or weaken the writer's argument?
4. Do you believe that popular music is damaging to young people? Why or why not? What other things present in popular culture might be a negative influence also? What, if anything, do you think should be done?

WRITING ABOUT THE ARGUMENT

1. Write a letter to the author. Question his underlying assumption that music operates on a subliminal level and moves young people to commit immoral acts. Could the same music also encourage good behavior on some level?
2. Do you believe that music that endorses antisocial behavior should be censored, at least where young people are concerned? Write a journal entry or essay addressing this issue.
3. What qualities must music have to make it "antisocial" or "immoral" in some way? Write a definition-based essay considering this issue. As a part of your essay, consider the author's comparison of Eminem to Elvis.
4. If it can be said that Rap music encourages misogyny or that video games make young people violent, what about Shakespeare? Would watching *Hamlet* turn someone into a murderer? Why or why not? Write an essay using this analogy (or one like it) to make your point.
5. What policies/procedures should affect (1) the content, labeling, broadcasting, and/or sale of rap music and/or (2) the responsibilities of concerned parties such as rap artists, music labels, parents, retailers, broadcasters, researchers, and/or the government? Research and write an argument on this topic.

"Why Eminem Is Important"

ABOUT THE AUTHOR: MAURY P. MCCRILLIS

Maury P. McCrillis is a lecturer in English in the department of languages and letters at Cape Breton University in Sydney, Nova Scotia. His formal studies have been in the area of medieval Scottish literature, and he has published a paper on "The Kingis Quair" about James I of Scotland. As an adjunct instructor at Alabama State University, McCrillis presented a paper comparing the medieval Scottish tradition of *flyting* (a competitive exchange of insults between poets) to freestyle battling in rap. From this topic was born an interest in the lyrical and musical complexities of rap. This essay and the preceding one by Lloyd Eby were published in March 2003 in *The World & I.*

BEFORE YOU READ

1. What does the headnote tell you about the author's qualifications to offer an opinion on this issue? Would you consider McCrellis more or less authoritative than Eby? Explain.
2. Have the previous readings changed your viewpoint in any way? How? In what way does this affect your attitude toward this subject?
3. What does the title indicate about the article's argument? What is your initial reaction to the title and possible argument?
4. Scan the essay. How does it appear to be similar to or different from Eby's argument? What do you expect its major claim to be? What supporting points might it make?

Why Eminem Is Important

1 With the recent release of his new album, *The Eminem Show,* rapper Marshall Mathers III, better known as Eminem, has catapulted to the forefront of popular music and become the lightning rod for a new round of debates over free speech and lyrical content. I suspect that since he has directed his venom directly at the Bush administration and specifically at Vice President Cheney's wife on this album, the question of explicit content will foment into another debate over social values, the decline of Western civilization, and the psychological effects of music on children.

2 In all fairness to Eminem's critics, there is a meanness and, in some cases, viciousness to a great deal of contemporary music. The meanness is certainly not limited to rap, but rap tends to bear the brunt of this criticism because, as music goes, it appears to be the most imitative of political speech. While mainstream America has a vague sense of what distinguishes rap (or hip-hop, as it's generally referred to) from other musical styles, more people are aware that Eminem is a controversial, white rapper than they are of his music or the genre he is working within. It only takes a brief exposure to Eminem's music to realize what generates that controversy Though he may be characterized as hard core, he is largely working within an accepted and highly sophisticated musical genre that has not only risen to prominence in North America but has already begun to influence musical culture throughout Europe and Asia. Rap has a number of well-established subgenres (e.g., gangsta rap, dance rap, lyrical battling, freestyling), firmly established old school and new school traditions, some revered or reviled individuals who have evolved into musical icons, and even two notable martyrs, Christopher Wallace (a.k.a. the Notorious B.I.G.) and Tupak Shakur, both of whom still exert an immense influence over contemporary hip-hop.

3 Like many rap artists, Eminem has built a music career by straddling the line that separates good taste from bad, but even he seems aware that much of his success hinges upon the fact that he is white: "Let's do the math, if I was black I wouldn't have sold half, I ain't have to graduate from Lincoln High School to know that" (*The Eminem Show,* "White America"). Eminem is as creative as he is controversial, though. Evidence of both is a remark by Will Smith (himself a successful rap artist as well as actor) to the effect that Eminem is creative, but his music is a farce.

4 Smith is right about the creativity. Eminem has a remarkably good ear for beats. That he has managed to achieve such notoriety without depending on music-video packaging or radio-station saturation is truly extraordinary. However, by dismissing his work as farcical, Smith seems to buy into the popular assumption that Eminem garners most of his attention simply by being controversial. Eminem thrives on controversy, but he doesn't survive on it. It is difficult for his critics to see that the controversy that surrounds him is really incidental to the question of what it is that music does and how an artist such as Eminem manipulates his lyrical content so successfully. To put it simply, what's important is not so much what he says but how he says it.

From Speech to Verse

5 An intuitive sense of how to flow smoothly from the measured cadence of ordinary speech to the discursive intensity of verse allows him, in my estimation, to blur the distinction between prose and poetry. It is essential to keep in mind that Eminem's most vocal social critics regard his music as affirming a host of claims about violence, misogyny, drug use, suicide, and criminal activity. Lynne Cheney's testimony to the Senate Committee on Commerce, Science, and

Transportation in 1999 is the most highly publicized example in recent years.

6 Interestingly, Cheney, who is the former chairperson for the National Endowment for the Humanities, chose a metaphor by author Peggy Noonan to make her argument that Eminem "promotes violence of the most degrading kind": "My friend Peggy Noonan . . . suggests that we understand the way our children are affected by . . . stories . . . by imagining little children as intelligent fish swimming in a deep ocean. The stories are 'waves of sight and sound, of thought and fact [that] come invisibly through the water, like radar.'"

7 That she chose a metaphor to make her case and, in particular, this metaphor is evidence of how critics tend to regard artistic forms of expression as if they constituted statements. By statements, I have in mind sentences that are either true or false, and thus which serve either to affirm or deny facts for the purpose of verifying or refuting claims about the world. In her testimony before the Senate committee, Cheney argued that a verse from Eminem's song "Kill You" advocates violence against women: "Wives, nuns, sluts, whoever the bitches might be, he will kill them slowly, leaving enough air in their lungs so their screaming will be prolonged."

8 I would argue that it is intellectually irresponsible for Cheney to claim that a first-person narrative in a musical soliloquy is evidence of what an artist intends or advocates. Referring to the same verse, she claimed in 2000 that Eminem "advocates raping and murdering his mother." To advocate is to defend a point of view by means of developing arguments in support of a claim. Does "wives, knives, lives, nuns, sluts" support the claim that he "will kill women slowly" or "paint the forest with their blood"?

9 It seems to me that what Cheney does in her speech is to take advantage of her audience's unfamiliarity with Eminem and the entire musical genre in which he works. The very awkwardness of reciting rap lyrics before a congressional committee draws attention away from what is at best an intellectually tenuous attempt to treat artistic expression as argumentation. By pointing her finger at Eminem, she seeks to convince her audience of senators that what is unfamiliar to them must be seditious because it is imitative of inflammatory speech.

10 Cheney's argumentative strategy is highly reductive, as is her use of Noonan's analogy to defend her claim that Interscope Records (a subsidiary of Seagrams) is "distributing lyrics that are socially irresponsible." She argues that just as fish swimming in a deep ocean are affected by "waves going through [them] again and again, from this direction and that," so are children affected by Eminem's lyrics. Such an analogy may get our attention, especially insofar as its sharp juxtaposition with the lyrics of "Kill You" is used to further condemn the singer, but it ultimately says nothing of substance about how Cheney knows that children will be or even could be affected by lyrics. Noonan's metaphor is neither true nor false; we cannot verify that children are affected by controversial lyrics by means of examining how fish are affected by waves in a deep ocean. Similarly, we cannot verify very much about what Eminem intends or advocates regarding the words used by a narrative persona in a musical soliloquy.

11 Like Cheney, most critics do not realize that they predictably make the mistake of treating artistic forms of expression like statements. Tipper Gore's complaint that Prince's song "Darling Nikki" in the *Purple Rain* album contained lyrics about a girl masturbating with a magazine led to the formation of the Parent's Music Resource Center and a campaign to force record companies to use "explicit language" labels on albums. The reasoning was that such "porn rock" lyrics make claims to young children about what constitutes appropriate behavior and thus can compel children with substandard reasoning skills to engage in such behavior.

12 Looking at Eminem's lyrics closely, it quickly becomes apparent that while the proselike

quality of the verse is highly imitative of inflammatory speech, were it actually to consist of statements, the claims it would support would be so unreasonable and strange that to take them seriously would be absurd. Many people are preoccupied with the extent to which Eminem's material is offensive, but few seem to realize that what makes him such a clever lyricist is his ability to manipulate and even undercut that material. In the song "Who Knew" from the *The Marshall Mathers CD,* Eminem writes, "I'm sorry; there must be a mix-up / You want me to fix up lyrics while the President gets his . . . ? / . . . that, take drugs, rape sluts / Make fun of gay clubs, men who wear make-up."

13 To treat these lines as if they were an attempt to convince the listener to engage in such behavior, we would have to say that Eminem argues for such a course of action "because" President Clinton engaged in immoral behavior while holding public office. First, even if we were inclined to treat this as an actual argument, it would be easy to dismiss as a non sequitur. It does not follow that Clinton's behavior presents a sufficient or even a necessary condition for taking drugs, committing rape, or making fun of gay clubs. Eminem is clearly not making an argument here.

14 Second, those who still might be inclined to treat the lines as if they were an argument are given what resembles a counterargument by the artist in the song's chorus: "I never knew I, knew I would get this big / I never knew I, knew I'd affect this kid." That is, even if we were inclined to believe that Eminem is really trying to convince us that we ought to engage in immoral behavior because the president is alleged to have done so, he easily slips away from the non sequitur by pointing out that he still bears no responsibility for the actions of his listeners.

15 In fact, he cleverly protects himself from the criticism of those who would believe that his listeners could be so influenced by his lyrics as to go against better judgment by incorporating a line that functions as a disclaimer. "how many retards'll listen to me / and run up in the school shootin' when they're pissed at a teach / er, her, him, is it you is it them?"

16 While some musicians will incorporate disclaimers into their albums and then undermine them, Eminem turns various lyrics themselves into disclaimers. By the end of the song, when he writes, "I just said it—I ain't know if you'd do it or not," it becomes clear that while the lyrics may be considered emotionally compelling, they are not convincing. Eminem's allusions are controversial, perhaps, but alluding to something is far different from arguing a listener into accepting claims about what constitutes proper behavior. Furthermore, what he sings about may be controversial, but that too is a far different thing than saying that his work is controversial in and of itself.

Songs as Arguments?

17 We certainly can treat songs as arguments. Clearly, the more that we are offended by the effect of their utterances, the more inclined we are to find some means to limit and control them by pointing out that they are false, inaccurate, untrue, and ipso facto potentially damaging to a listener who does not recognize them as such. By treating songs as arguments, though, we put an additional burden upon ourselves to treat individual lines, if not entire songs, as statements that either support or do not support some imagined claim. Take, for example, this verse from the song "Till I Collapse": "Fa shizzel my wizzel, this is the plot, listen up, you bizzels forgot, slizzel does not give a. . . ." What claim does this line make? Is the claim true or false? Is it seditious?

18 Anyone who has ever tried to interpret a piece of literature knows that it is no easy task to come to a conclusive agreement on its meaning or significance because, often, extremely compelling cases can be made for interpretations that are diametrically opposed to one another. The history of literary criticism is fraught with such opposing interpretations, but let me use Eminem

as an example again. In the song "Role Model," from the *Slim Shady World Show,* he writes: "I came to the club drunk with a fake ID / Don't you wanna grow up to be just like me! / I've been with ten women who got HIV / Don't you wanna grow up and be just like me!" If we regard these lines as being in accordance with fact, then we can easily make the case that Eminem is attempting to convince an underage listener that he ought to have unprotected sex and use fake IDs to get into clubs so that he can be just like the artist. However, an equally compelling argument can be made that Eminem is using irony to suggest just the opposite. Which is the case? If it's the former, then the lyrics ought to be censored for content. If it's the latter, then they are actually providing moral instruction. A more thorough investigation of the lyrics of the entire song will permit either interpretation.

19 Treating emotive utterances (lyrics specifically) as arguments has a long and quite honorable intellectual legacy. The mimetic theory of art has at its foundation none other than the Platonic discourses. When Cheney remarked that as chairperson of the National Endowment for the Humanities, she often testified about "the philosophy and literature that lifts our souls," she located herself in a long tradition of social critics who hearken back to Plato and Socrates to reaffirm the notion that art is either socially useful or socially destructive.

20 These critics find support in two broad assumptions: the notion that art reflects the world and that, insofar as it reflects the world, it must serve either to elevate or to degrade, depending, usually, upon how accurately it reflects the world. Of course, there is always the added provision that in some cases (like nonsense verse, postmodern sculpture, or abstract painting) it is so hard to make a compelling case about what the art reflects that we can't tell if it uplifts or degrades. Such cases are given the benefit of the doubt, often because compelling cases that they degrade can't be made without seeming silly.

21 With regard to the mimetic theory of art, though, one reading of the Socratic dialogues can support the notion that Socrates did make a philosophical commitment to treat poems as if they were potentially damaging to society. However, there are two very important points to keep in mind. First, even if we assume that his position on the destructive potential of imitative verse is one that he was committed to, Socrates would be the first to admit that such a position ought not to be accepted as accurate simply by virtue of the fact that he may be committed to it. Second, the Socratic dialogues do not present an established and organized philosophical system, and thus Socrates's philosophical discussions are at best a series of relatively casual ruminations on a variety of subjects.

22 Furthermore, Socrates's position on art is not as self-evident as some seem to think. I am not convinced that Socrates was seriously committed to the notion that art was so potentially destructive to society as to warrant a serious fear of its corrupting influence on children. One ought to consider, for example, that although a great deal of discussion is undertaken by Socrates about how Homer's *Iliad* misrepresents the nature of the gods in the *Republic,* he virtually ignores Aristophanes's *The Clouds,* a caustic comic play with Socrates himself depicted in one scene as a buffoon masturbating beneath a blanket. Socrates knew Aristophanes but apparently never invested much time utilizing political maneuvers to restrict access to his performances.

23 The point is that even if Socrates were committed to cleaning up art, too many are content to assume that this view must be right because he may have been committed to it. In *The Devaluing of America,* William Bennett ruminates that "if we believe that good art, good music, and good books will elevate taste and improve the sensibilities of the young—which they certainly do—then we must also believe that bad music, bad art, and bad books will degrade. As a society, we must come to grips with that truth."

24 Bennett makes a very interesting point and one that perhaps is intentionally reminiscent of the dialogue between Socrates and Glaucon in Book 2 of the *Republic.* There Socrates asks, "shall we [as a society] just carelessly allow children to hear any casual tales which may be devised by casual persons, and to receive into their minds ideas for the most part the very opposite of those which we should wish them to have when they are grown up?" For Bennett, the responsibility of distinguishing between good and bad art is society's because "no man is a good citizen alone, [as] Plato teaches us in his dialogue *Gorgias.*"

25 Bennett may be right, and his sense of Socrates's position on art in the *Gorgias* may be right. The problem is that Bennett doesn't explain how he knows his own position (or what he takes to be Socrates's position) is right. Instead, he insists upon a highly stratified, yet ultimately unsophisticated, view of art that comes not from serious study (or even a well-rounded exposure to art) but from a broad set of a priori assumptions about declining moral standards that are wrapped in partisan catchphrases such as "our common culture," the "moral imagination of the nation," and the need for "our souls [to be] filled with noble sentiments." What's more, by summoning the names of Plato and Socrates, he attempts to lend credibility to his rhetoric while deflecting potential criticism against himself.

26 Before Cheney mentioned Eminem in her testimony, Bennett also testified before the Senate Committee on Commerce and once again drew upon Socrates for support: "In Plato's *Republic,* Socrates said that 'musical training is a more potent instrument than any other, because rhythm and harmony find their way into the inward places of the soul, on which they mightily fasten, imparting grace.'" It is fine to talk about good literature improving and elevating the sensibilities of the young. Few are going to be against the idea of improving or elevating anything. The problem arises with the obverse case. If Bennett is going to claim that what others may appreciate is going to degrade them, then he had better explain exactly how it is that it degrades, or we will have no reason to believe him. To just assume that it does is to mask an illogical argument in a stirring reference to powerful intellectual figures like Socrates and Plato.

27 When Cheney reminisces about testifying on what "Matthew Arnold called 'the best that has been thought and known in the world,'" she does something very similar. She wants her audience to believe that her position regarding Eminem is right by virtue of a reference to an important literary figure, a figure who most likely would have held a view similar to hers. The allusion certainly is stirring. Hearing Arnold's name, one cannot help but think of the crumbling white cliffs of Dover in "Dover Beach" in the context of Cheney's concern about crumbling American culture. But is that anything more than an impulse or prejudice born out of a remembered reference?

Plato and Bloom

28 The Platonic discourses are indeed important in the context of any discussion about how art compels. However, it must be remembered from the outset that "Plato's philosophy consists of a series of sharply presented questions, and of bold, speculative, and incomplete answers to them." As Hugh Tredennick argues, "In reading Plato's dialogues it is necessary always to keep in mind the fact—obvious but often forgotten—that they are not systematic expositions of his own (or anyone else's) doctrines. The dialogues are works of art, composed at various times and for special reasons at which we can only guess." There is a long tradition of treating the dialogues as support for the notion that lyrics are potentially harmful to society, but it is not self-evident that such a notion is accurate.

29 Among those who have attempted to make a strong case regarding Socrates's position on art is Allan Bloom. As Bloom explained in *The Clos-*

ing of the American Mind, the insidiousness of contemporary music (especially rock and roll) lies in the ability of such "barbarous expressions of the soul" to distract students of liberal education. Bloom wrote, "When [students] are in school and with their families, they are longing to plug themselves back into their music. Nothing surrounding them—school, family, church—ha[s] anything to do with their musical world. . . . There is the stereo in the home, in the car; there are concerts; there are music videos . . . ; there are Walkmans, so that no place . . . prevents students from communing with the Muse, even while studying."

30 For Bloom, the distracting influence of music took on a special relevance in the late twentieth century because of the death of classical music. Whereas classical music "had been designed to produce, as well as to please [the] exquisite sensibilities [of the] highly educated German and French bourgeoisie," rock and roll has "one appeal only, a barbaric appeal, to sexual desire . . . undeveloped and untutored."

31 Bennett argues in *The Devaluing of America* that most modern-day academics—whom he regards as leftists—have "achieved their positions not . . . through intellect . . . but through disposition, sentiment, bias, and ideology." The simple fact, however, is that Bloom's own sentimental affirmation of the high art/low art distinction, a distinction that critics such as Bennett regularly invoke when making artistic value judgments, is itself another, albeit older, form of ideological bias. Bloom claims that the ubiquitous presence of music in the lives and minds of students did at least give him the opportunity during his career to "frequently introduce them to Mozart," in order to see "whether and in what ways their studies are complemented by such music." Of course, to use Mozart to promote the "deeper understanding of the meaning of nobility" would seem to be complicated by some of Mozart's more, shall we say, Matheresque canons, such as K.231, "Lack mich im Arsch," and K233, "Lack mir den Arsch fein recht schon sauber," to name a few. As Wolfgang Hildesheimer [wrote], in his book *Mozart,* "The attempts that have been made to keep Mozart's image clean are older than the image itself, extending back into his lifetime. The publishers Herr Breitkopf and Herr Hartel alternated in trying to clean up the dirty texts of canons by bowdlerizing them, with the natural result that one can hear the original words reverberating rhythmically underneath their substitutions."

32 Contemporary artists such as Eminem face a similar situation insofar as attempts to remove or alter controversial material often produce an alternate version of a song that is highly artificial and strange, and which ultimately serves to draw attention to the original. Nonetheless, one of the many problems with the high art/low art dichotomy is that even some of the classical composers require an occasional touch-up in order to affirm their roles as the figureheads of artistic nobility. Though he does not address Mozart's occasional lapses, Bloom is at least honest about his own intellectual bias.

33 Bloom's reading of Socrates (with regard to musical education) is highly traditionalist, and, finally, is more interesting when viewed as an apology for liberal education than as a rigorous, intellectual examination of Socrates's mimetic theory. Music, Bloom writes, is "the soul's primitive and primary speech and it is *alogon* without articulate speech or reason." He continues, "Even when the articulate speech is added, it is subordinate to . . . the music and passion that it expresses."

34 Here Bloom makes a clear distinction between music (meaning harmony and rhythm) and articulate (that is, intelligible and reasonable) speech. For example, poetry "is what music becomes as reason emerges." In other words, the Socratic logos is, for him, what restrains the emotive power of music: "According to the Socratic formula, the lyrics—speech and, hence, reason—must determine the music—harmony

and rhythm." Bloom's complaint is that contemporary music fails to use reason as language to restrain the passions, as he assumes that classical music does. Instead, he implies that rock and roll utilizes things outside of reason to further indulge the passions, and thus distracts the audience from contemplating the logos. "Ministering to and according with the arousing . . . music, the lyrics celebrate puppy love as well as polymorphous attraction . . . [and] the words implicitly and explicitly describe bodily acts that satisfy sexual desire."

35 Bennett, Cheney, Gore, and other critics will say that they are not confusing arguments with artistic utterances, but then claim that it is necessary to restrict access to lyrics because the compelling power of rhythm and harmony can somehow lead people to believe that artistic utterances have truth value. Bloom's criticism is much subtler because of his concern with the potential of music to distract students, rather than moral effects. However, even though he argues that the compelling power of music is its harmony and rhythm, his concern with the "low rock world" is that the lyrics fail to use reason to counterbalance the passions and instead indulge students in the three great themes of sex, hate, and "a smarmy . . . version of brotherly love" so effectively that they undermine the traditional liberal education.

Aristotelian Catharsis

36 Those who are concerned with the degeneration of cultural values seem to find support in the Socratic/Platonic concern with the potentially corrupting influence of imitative art largely because of a dissatisfaction with the Aristotelian notion of catharsis. The notion that art helps to purge emotions which might otherwise manifest themselves in everyday life is interesting but not convincing enough to quell the anxieties of those who fear declining moral standards. Arguing that human beings by nature "learn or infer" through imitation, Aristotle moved to rescue art from Socratic suspicions about its moral effects and instead claimed that "poetry is a higher thing than history because poetry tends to express the universal, history the particular."

37 This move was also an attempt to pay homage to Socrates's theory of mimesis. That is, at its worst, art can still help an audience to purge itself of destructive tendencies. At its best, it can portray things as they "ought" to be; it can be morally instructive. To me, this just revisits the idea that art is good or bad with respect to the extent to which it is in accordance with facts. After all, art can protray things as they ought not to be as well. The notion of catharsis may give art enough integrity in such instances to protect it from being banned or maybe even censored, but ultimately such works become relegated to the dustbin of low art, where they are subjected to social and intellectual suspicion until they are forgotten. Only the art that can be deemed to provide the right moral instruction has the opportunity to be counted as high art, where it can receive serious intellectual consideration and perhaps real, lasting appreciation and admiration.

38 In his dialogue with Glaucon and Adeimantus, Socrates explored the notion that because imitative poets are "thrice removed from the truth," they are "prone to making the gravest misstatements." From that assumption he drew the conclusion that "we shall be right in refusing to admit [imitative artists] into a well-ordered state. . . . However, we may further grant to those of her [poetry's] defenders the permission to speak on her behalf; let them show that she is not only pleasant but useful to states . . . and we shall listen in a kindly spirit; for if this can be proved we shall surely be the gainers." Part of the problem with such a position is that to place the burden upon the artist or "her defenders" to prove how it's not the case that art is socially destructive is an appeal to ignorance. The burden of proof falls upon the one who asserts the claim. It is up to the critic to demonstrate how art is or at least can be destructive; it's not up to the artist

to prove that it isn't. Socrates at least sketches out some kind of framework within which to consider censorship. His fundamental assumption that "literature may be either true or false" is insufficient. Bennett, Bloom, Cheney, and others who take Socrates at his word on this matter are indeed, as Charlton Heston points out, in the midst of a cultural war. However, it is a self-imposed cultural war that is both driven by and undermined by the flawed notion that artistic utterances have truth value.

Art as Allusion

39 Eminem seems to understand what many social critics do not: The task of the artist is not to defend argumentative claims to portray the world in artistic terms. Instead, it is to create within the context of the rules that govern the field of play. At the same time, though, the artist must also distinguish himself from others who are working within the same genre. The push for originality/creativity and the pull of convention/tradition have the effect of keeping the rules that govern any artistic genre from becoming fully solidified.

40 Genres expand until they finally shift. It is at the nexus of such shifts that those who are unwilling to examine the rules that govern the new genre begin to establish high art/low art distinctions. They do so by unfairly holding those who have to adhere to the rules of the newer genre accountable for not adhering to the rules of the former genre. They often do this by calling into question the moral or ethical effects that the new artistic genre has upon society. In order to make claims about moral effects, artists must be treated as if they were advocating by means of their art.

41 Lyrics are neither true nor false, not when accompanied by rhythm and harmony, and not as poems. It is a mistake to assume that they can convince in any strict sense of the term. This is precisely why Eminem is so important. By reveling in the controversial, he indulges his detractors in their predictable critical approach, thus keeping them preoccupied with trying to hold him accountable for remarks on the basis that such remarks make false, libelous, and even seditious claims. At the same time, he can elicit interest, and even support, from those who take great delight in watching the ensuing melee over the question of whether or not rap songs are seditious enough to be exempted from constitutionally protected speech.

42 I once asked the late Cleanth Brooks, professor of English at Yale University and proponent of the New Criticism, why the literary theory that he and Robert Penn Warren had so enthusiastically promoted in the 1950s and '60s had come under such sharp attack in the 1980s and '90s. He said to me, "I don't know. All we ever wanted was to show what made literature good." I suspect that neither Brooks nor Warren, were they alive today, would be fans of Eminem, but they most certainly would be interested in how his poems managed to have such a popular appeal. It could be the case that Eminem is simply the next stage in America's cultural and intellectual decline. However, I don't think so. As an artist, Eminem may be mischievous, but he is no fool. Perhaps one good thing that will result from putting his lyrics under the microscope is that hip-hop will finally be recognized as a culturally diverse and artistically sophisticated musical genre. Someday, perhaps, even the artists themselves will get the respect they deserve from academics as well.

THINKING ABOUT THE ARGUMENT

1. How does the author engage the reader's attention? Is this tactic effective? Why or why not?
2. In what ways does the author's content and tone differ from that in Eby's essay? What does this suggest about his point of view and his target audience?
3. Why does McCrillis believe that Eminem's lyrics should not be taken at face value? Do you agree with him? Why or why not?
4. What does McCrillis think of the argument that certain kinds of art can corrupt youth? Explain.
5. What is "catharsis"? In what way does the author believe Eminem's music is "cathartic"?
6. Why does McCrillis think Eminem is important? Explain.

RESPONDING TO THE ARGUMENT

1. Do you believe, as McCrillis does, that Eminem's "disclaimers" invalidate whatever influence his lyrics might have? Why or why not?
2. Do you believe that art is good for society, bad for society, or both? (Can it both "elevate" and "degrade"?) Provide concrete examples to back up your answer.
3. Do you agree that Eminem's music—or any other art form that expresses negative emotions, for that matter—can be "cathartic"? Can experiencing dangerous emotions in a nonthreatening way be good for you? Explain.
4. Think about the positions articulated by both Eby and McCrillis. Are they both too extreme in their views? Explain. Think of a position that might lie between them and express it in your own words.

WRITING ABOUT THE ARGUMENT

1. Write a synthesis comparing the different ways Eby and McCrillis characterize the subliminal effects of Eminem's lyrics. Are they subversive or cathartic? How do you know?
2. Think of a position that lies between the extremes posed by Eby and McCrillis. Write an argument proposing a compromise between the two positions.
3. Write a letter to McCrillis explaining why you agree or disagree with his views.
4. In paragraph 10 McCrillis states, "we cannot verify very much about what Eminem intends or advocates regarding the words used by a narrative persona in a musical soliloquy." Do you agree or disagree with this statement? Does it matter what an artist "intends" when the effect of the art is in question? Record your answer in your journal.

Issue 2: Body Modification

Online Study Center
Prepare for Class
Designing the Body

Every culture has a unique sense of beauty, including an idealized appearance for the faces and bodies of men and women. At various times in history and in various cultures, people have made extreme changes to "improve" their features. Ancient Incan, Mayan, and Egyptian rulers sometimes practiced "skull flattening." As late as the early twentieth century, some Chinese parents bound their daughters' feet inside tiny packets to prevent their growth and thus make their adult size more dainty. Lip plates, ringed and elongated necks, elongated earlobes: body modifications such as these are featured periodically in *National Geographic* as cultural curiosities. Americans have their own culturally determined sense of physical perfection, and they often go to extremes with diets, exercise, fashions, pharmaceuticals, and cosmetics to achieve a certain look. Body

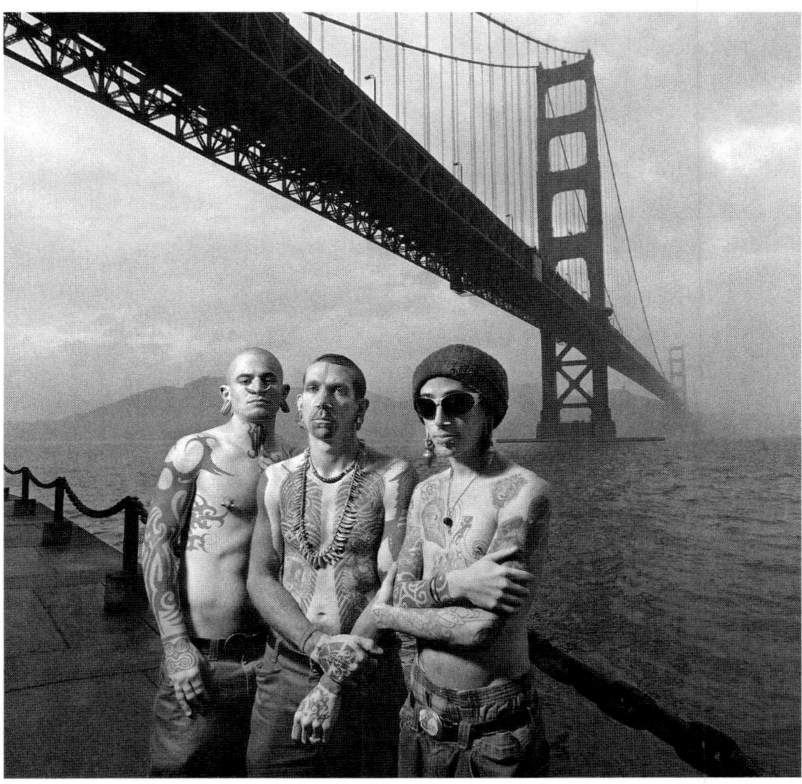

Some "modern primitives" argue that body modification is a postmodern mixture of the present and the past and therefore is forward-looking. What might cause such a radical shift in standards of beauty in the Western world?

modification takes these efforts a step further by making physical changes that may be difficult or impossible to reverse. The readings in this section focus primarily on two kinds of body modification—body art (such as piercing, tattoos, and scarification) and plastic surgery (such as implants and facelifts).

Considering the Issue of Body Modification

In discussion groups, in your journal, or working individually, answer the following questions.

1. How much body modification takes place nowadays? Are some kinds more commonplace? Explain.
2. When is body modification inappropriate? When is it appropriate?
3. What do you believe are the positive and negative effects of body modification?
4. What kinds of restrictions, if any, should be placed on body modification?

READING SELECTION

"Focusing on Body Image Dissatisfaction"

About the Author: *USA Today*

Articles in *USA Today* sometimes are written anonymously by its editors or contributors. With a national circulation of approximately 2.5 million, this publication is the most widely circulated newspaper in the United States. Its popularity stems from its lively format, accurate and timely reporting, and balanced treatment of controversial issues. The essay reprinted originally appeared in *USA Today* in February 1999.

Before You Read

1. What does the term *body image* mean for you? Do you consider it important or unimportant? In what ways do you try to project a body image?
2. What do you know about *USA Today* and its audience? Why would this group be interested in body image?
3. What does the title indicate about the article's argument? What do you think the thesis might be?
4. Do you think many people are dissatisfied with their body image? Why or why not? What sorts of things might they try to do about this feeling?

READING SELECTION

Focusing on Body Image Dissatisfaction

1 Future psychological studies of plastic surgery patients need to focus on body image, according to the authors of a historical review of cosmetic surgery patients. "We really don't know what motivates people to seek plastic surgery," admits Linton Whitaker, chief of plastic surgery and director of the Center for Human Appearance, University of Pennsylvania School of Medicine, Philadelphia. "We need to probe these issues so we can clarify which patients will benefit from plastic surgery."

2 Covering the psychological research completed in the last forty years, the review was designed to address two basic questions: Are there types of patients for whom plastic surgery is inappropriate? and What is the likelihood that patients will benefit psychologically from cosmetic surgery? The authors conclude that the existing research has not addressed either of these questions completely. They recommend that future research take a new direction and focus on body image in cosmetic surgery patients.

3 Body image—defined as the perceptions, thoughts, and feelings a person has about his or her physical appearance—is thought to play an important role in self-esteem for many individuals. In addition, physical appearance and body image influence how persons are perceived by others. Research shows that attractive people are viewed more positively in practically every situation studied, such as education, employment, health care, legal proceedings, and romantic encounters.

4 "Body image dissatisfaction is pervasive in America. We believe this dissatisfaction may motivate many persons to undergo cosmetic surgery," indicates David Sarwer, assistant professor of psychology in psychiatry and surgery at the Center for Human Appearance. "Many persons hope that cosmetic surgery will help them feel better about their appearance, which, in turn, may promote other psychological benefits, such as improved self-esteem. However, research is needed to determine if cosmetic surgery leads to improvement in body image."

5 The authors propose several priorities for future research with cosmetic surgery patients. These include assessing the extent of body image dissatisfaction experienced by cosmetic surgery patients; determining if this dissatisfaction varies by body part; and documenting changes in body image following cosmetic surgery. Such studies are important to demonstrate the potential psychological benefits of cosmetic surgery, they maintain.

6 In addition, they stress the importance of identifying patients with extreme body image dissatisfaction who may be inappropriate for surgery. Extreme body image dissatisfaction can be a symptom of body dysmorphic disorder, a psychiatric condition defined as a preoccupation with a slight defect in appearance that leads to excessive concern and interruption in daily functioning. Although the percentage of cosmetic surgery patients with that disorder is thought to be small, these individuals do not seem to be good candidates for cosmetic surgery, which appears to exacerbate the symptoms of body dysmorphic disorder in some individuals, while others may become preoccupied with a new defect. Ultimately, medication or psychotherapy may be the most appropriate treatment.

THINKING ABOUT THE ARGUMENT

1. Reread the first paragraph. What issue is being discussed? How does the article create the authority to offer an opinion on this matter?
2. According to the article, what is body image? How does this compare with the definition you came up with in Before You Read on page 694?
3. In what ways does a negative body image serve as a motivation for plastic surgery? Explain.
4. How do physicians try to determine whether plastic surgery can be good or bad for a person?
5. For what kinds of patients is plastic surgery an inappropriate choice?

RESPONDING TO THE ARGUMENT

1. Do you believe this piece argues or is purely informational? In what ways, if any, does this information slant in favor of one position or another?
2. Consider the following list. Discuss whether plastic surgery would be appropriate in any of these cases. Provide a sound reason to back up your claim.
   a. An eighteen-year-old girl who thinks that the Barbie Doll is the epitome of beauty
   b. A fifty-year-old man who lost his nose and half his face in an industrial accident
   c. A thirty-eight-year-old housewife who wants to look twenty again and is fearful that her husband will stray
   d. A forty-something man who has already had seven procedures in an attempt to make himself look like Tom Cruise
3. Health reasons aside, can you think of any ethical reasons why plastic surgery might not be appropriate in some cases? Why do you think this?
4. Would you ever consider plastic surgery? Why or why not? Explain.

WRITING ABOUT THE ARGUMENT

1. What ethical responsibilities do plastic surgeons bear in determining whether or not to perform procedures on certain patients? Explain in a journal entry.
2. Research and identify a case in which you think plastic surgery should not have been performed. Write an argumentative essay explaining why you think this. (Example: In 2005, a mentally ill French woman received the first face transplant. Some people said she was a bad choice because of her emotional condition.)
3. Suppose you have a friend that has decided that she wants to have surgery to drastically alter her appearance so she can "just disappear and start all over again." In a letter, explain why you would or would not support this move.
4. Is beauty only skin deep, or is it vitally important? Do we overvalue physical beauty? Write an argumentative essay based on this idea.
5. What responsibility does popular culture bear for presenting young people with unrealistic body images? Should performance stars, actors, and so on attempt to present more realistic body images to the public? Why or why not? Argue this point in an essay or journal entry.

READING SELECTION

"The Perfect Body Could Be Detrimental to Our Health"

About the Author: Colin Milner

Colin Milner heads the International Council on Active Aging, the world's largest fitness and wellness association for seniors. He has written more than 160 articles on aging and fitness. This essay was originally published in *Club Industry's Fitness Business Pro* in August 2005.

Before You Read

1. Do you think the author is qualified to offer an opinion on this subject? Why or why not?
2. What does the title indicate about the article's argument? Do you agree or disagree with this statement? Why?
3. How do you think this author might differ from the plastic surgeons represented in the previous article? Why do you say this?

The Perfect Body Could Be Detrimental to Our Health

1 They say two things are guaranteed in life: death and taxes. I would like to add a third—aging.

2 We age from the moment we are born until the moment we draw our last breath. We all experience this natural life process; some of us just experience it for a shorter time than others.

3 Today, our longer life spans are creating challenges and opportunities for governments, industries, and businesses, as well as for individuals and families. This revolution finds us scrambling to address these challenges and opportunities as we enter unknown territory.

4 Among these challenges is the aging population's continual fixation on staying young and on top of its game. This desire to discover the fountain of youth has spawned numerous billion-dollar industries. Whether it's Viagra, nutraceuticals, or tummy tucks, these markets are being driven by aging boomers who want solutions and want them now. Just look at celebrity boomers Randy Jackson of *American Idol* and Al Roker of NBC's *Today Show,* who both had gastric bypass surgery. After a lot of nip and a little tuck, they are thin again. But these celebrities took a major risk when undergoing the operation—three in 200 people die after weight loss surgery.

The Hunt Is On

5 Plastic surgery also has gone mainstream. It is now a part of several reality makeover shows and at least one fictional series. In less than an hour, the country can see a whole new person emerge from under bandages. For those less inclined to be cut, cosmetic companies offer what they claim are solutions for wrinkles, age spots, and cellulite.

6 Of course, let's not forget that recent medical breakthrough: the World's First Anti-aging Pill. The new pill's dramatic press release says the "promising discovery has been proven to quickly reverse the aging process by replenishing the body's own production of youth hormone to normal twenty-five-year-old levels." Hard to believe, I know, but let's try to imagine what such a product could mean.

7 If we can lose weight by having surgery and build muscle by taking a pill, why spend time sweating off those pounds and building that noteworthy physique? If we can take "elixirs of life" that promise to recapture the vitality of youth, why get out of bed to walk or run on a dark, cold morning in winter? These are good questions to ask,

but the fact is all the surgeries, pills, and elixirs have a downside, whether their claims are true or false. About 40 percent of Americans ages 50 and older believe anti-aging products are basically "hogwash," while another 36 percent are "curious, but skeptical." Although more than 20 percent of people in this age group say these products can "work sometimes," just 3 percent say they like them a lot.

To Age or Not to Age

8 As we hear stories about increasing numbers of boomers and older adults having their stomachs stapled or taking expensive "remedies," we must recognize that most of these new industries focus on physical beauty rather than on internal health. Think about it. We can have a great exterior but still develop heart disease, hypertension, osteoporosis, diabetes, and depression.

9 What kind of message is this focus on outward beauty sending to our children, whom most parents would agree should be taught that what's really important is on the inside? That message is also one we need to share with our members, some of whom may be too focused on the physical benefits of exercising. Exercising might lead them to a nicer physique, but more importantly, it can lead them to a healthier body. By making better lifestyle choices, eating properly, and exercising, we can prevent, control, or retard much of the heart disease, hypertension, and diabetes that we see. Yes, physicians can prescribe pills to treat these health issues, but we can address them just as well—if not better—and for much less money with exercise, proper nutrition, and lifestyle modifications.

Expanding the Message

10 The reality is, we don't live in a perfect world. And the pursuit of the perfect exterior, whether young or old, while neglecting the perfect interior, could have a major impact on the health of aging boomers. Fitness professionals offer individuals the ability to lead a high-quality life by shifting their focus to the inside. If we are successful in doing this, we grow closer to attaining our goal of helping these individuals achieve their ideal self, both inside and out. By broadening the focus to include the internal, we can help our members—and our businesses—enjoy better health.

>> <<

THINKING ABOUT THE ARGUMENT

1. What, according to the author, does life guarantee us other than "death and taxes"?
2. In paragraph 4, the author notes America's obsession with "the fountain of youth." What does the last sentence imply about Milner's opinion regarding this industry?
3. What are some of the antiaging methods the author mentions? Are you familiar with any of them? Can you think of any the author does not mention? List them.
4. What, according to Milner, is a better option than the anti-aging methods? Why does he think they are so beneficial? What can "fitness professionals" offer that antiaging methods cannot?

RESPONDING TO THE ARGUMENT

1. Do you think Milner's suggestions are appropriate for everyone? Why or why not?
2. Why do some people pick things like weight loss surgery and plastic surgery over diet and exercise? Does Milner adequately discuss why people choose one over the other? Why do you think this?
3. In what ways might Milner agree or disagree with the authors of the other articles in this section? Explain.
4. In what cases do you think Milner would recognize the need for extreme weight loss surgery or plastic surgery? Why do you hold this opinion?

Writing about the Argument

1. When it comes to beauty, do you think that Americans are looking for a quick fix? Discuss this issue in your journal.
2. Have previous readings changed your viewpoint in any way about American ideals of beauty? Which viewpoints (stated or implied) do you agree with the most, and why?
3. Some men have been known to get pectoral implants to give them an appearance of a muscular chest. Do you think this is a good idea? What are the benefits of this when compared to exercise? Write an argument discussing whether health or the aesthetic effect is more important, and why.

"Pots of Promise: The Beauty Business"

About the Author: *The Economist*

Articles in *The Economist* often are written anonymously by its editors or unnamed contributors. Published in London since 1843, this newsweekly focuses on world events—politics, business and finance, and science—that influence decision makers such as executives, financiers, managers, and government officials. Editorially it advocates economic conservatism. The essay reprinted here appeared in the May 24, 2003, issue of *The Economist*.

Before You Read

1. What does the magazine's title tell you about its readership?
2. What does the article's title indicate about its argument? What sort of claim do you expect it to make?
3. Do you think that beauty products are healthy or unhealthy for society as a whole? Would it be better if women (and increasingly, some men) did not wear makeup but presented themselves simply, like the Amish? Why do you have this opinion?

Pots of Promise: The Beauty Business

1 Medieval noblewomen swallowed arsenic and dabbed on bats' blood to improve their complexions; eighteenth-century Americans prized the warm urine of young boys to erase their freckles; Victorian ladies removed their ribs to give themselves a wasp waist. The desire to be beautiful is as old as civilization, as is the pain that it can cause. In his autobiography, Charles Darwin noted a "universal passion for adornment," often involving "wonderfully great" suffering.

2 The pain has not stopped the passion from creating a $160 billion-a-year global industry, encompassing make-up, skin and hair care, fragrances, cosmetic surgery, health clubs, and diet pills. Americans spend more each year on beauty than they do on education. Such spending is not mere vanity. Being pretty—or just not ugly—confers enormous genetic and social advantages.

Attractive people (both men and women) are judged to be more intelligent and better in bed; they earn more, and they are more likely to marry.

3 Beauty matters most, though, for reproductive success. A study by David Buss, an American scientist, logged the mating preferences of more than 10,000 people across thirty-seven cultures. It found that a woman's physical attractiveness came top or near top of every man's list. Nancy Etcoff, a psychologist and author of *Survival of the Prettiest,* argues that "good looks are a woman's most fungible asset, exchangeable for social position, money, even love. But, dependent on a body that ages, it is an asset that a woman uses or loses."

4 Beauty is something that we recognize instinctively. A baby of three months will smile longer at a face judged by adults to be "attractive." Such beauty signals health and fertility. Long lustrous hair has always been a sign of good health; mascara makes eyes look bigger and younger; blusher and red lipstick mimic signs of sexual arousal. Whatever the culture, relatively light and flawless skin is seen as a testament to both youth and health: partly because skin permanently darkens after pregnancy; partly because light skin makes it harder to hide illness. This has spawned a huge range of creams to treat skin in various ways.

5 Then again, a curvy body, with big breasts and a waist-to-hip ratio of less than 0.8—Barbie's is 0.54—shows an ideal stage of readiness for conception. Plastic surgery to pad breasts or lift buttocks serves to make a woman look as though she was in her late teens or early twenties: the perfect mate. "Mimicry is the goal of the beauty industry," says Ms. Etcoff.

6 Basic instinct keeps the beauty industry powerful. In medieval times, recipes for homemade cosmetics were kept in the kitchen right beside those used to feed the family. But it was not until the start of the twentieth century, when mass production coincided with mass exposure to an idealized standard of beauty (through photography, magazines, and movies) that the industry first took off.

From Small Roots to Big Business

7 In 1909, Eugene Schueller founded the French Harmless Hair Colouring Co, which later became L'Oreal—today's industry leader. Two years later, Paul Beiersdorf, a Hamburg pharmacist, developed the first cream to bind oil and water. Today, it sells in 150 countries as Nivea, the biggest personal-care brand in the world. Around the same time, in Tokyo's upmarket Ginza, Arinobu Fukuhara hit on eudermine lotion—the first Japanese cosmetic based on a scientific formula, and the first product for the Shiseido company.

8 But it was the great rivalry between two women in America that made the industry what it is today. Elizabeth Arden opened the first modern beauty salon in 1910, followed a few years later by Helena Rubinstein, a Polish immigrant. The two took cosmetics out of household pots and pans and into the modern era. Both thought beauty and health were interlinked. They combined facials with diets and exercise classes in a holistic approach that the industry is now returning to.

9 Rubinstein considered facelifts (via leather straps and electricity) to be as acceptable as lipstick, while Arden pioneered beauty branding, with her iconic gold and pink packaging. The two women, together with Max Factor (which originally produced make-up for actresses), built the foundations of modern marketing, bewitching consumers with aggressive tactics such as celebrity endorsements and magazine advertorials. In the 1930s they were joined by Revlon, and after the second world war by Estee Lauder. All these companies are still around.

10 The emerging beauty industry played on the fear of looking ugly as much as on the pleasure of looking beautiful, drawing on the new science of

psychology to convince women that an inferiority complex could be cured by a dab of lipstick. Even then, ruthlessness and outright quackery lurked behind the façade. On launching her famous eight-hour cream, developed for her horses, Arden quipped: "I judge a woman and a horse by the same criteria: legs, head, and rear end."

Anything but Skin-Deep

11 Analysts at Goldman Sachs estimate that the global beauty industry—consisting of skin care worth $24 billion; make-up, $18 billion; $38 billion of hair-care products; and $15 billion of perfumes—is growing at up to 7 percent a year, more than twice the rate of the developed world's GDP. The sector's market leader, L'Oreal, has had compound annual profits growth of 14 percent for thirteen years. Sales of Beiersdorf's Nivea have grown at 14 percent a year over the same period.

12 This growth is being driven by richer, aging baby boomers and increased discretionary income in the West, and by the growing middle classes in developing countries. China, Russia, and South Korea are turning into huge markets. In India, sales of anti-aging creams are growing by 40 percent a year, while Brazil has more "Avon Ladies" (900,000) than it has men and women in its army and navy. Although the industry's customers are predominantly women, it is increasingly marketing itself to men, too.

13 The juicy returns are attracting new entrants. The household-goods giants Unilever and Procter & Gamble (P&G), facing maturity in many of their traditional businesses, are devoting more resources to their beauty divisions—as evidenced by P&G's current $6.5 billion offer for Germany's Wella, a hair-care company, to bolster its earlier purchase of Clairol, a hair-dye business. Simon Clift, marketing head of Unilever's personal-care businesses (including its big Dove and Sunsilk brands), says: "We are a Cinderella, seen as a soap-powder company, but we have changed our belief about what we do well."

14 Most luxury-goods groups now have perfume brands, and many (like Dior, Chanel, and Yves St. Laurent) are selling make-up and creams too. LVMH, the biggest luxury-goods group of all, has moved into retailing with its Bliss spas and Sephora shops (which sell make-up).

15 At the same time the industry is consolidating. Many innovative younger brands have been swallowed up by the giants. Japan's Kao bought John Frieda to tap into the hair-dye business, one of the fastest-growing segments of the market. And in the past five years, LVMH has bought Hard Candy and Urban Decay, two funky young make-up brands; while Estee Lauder has acquired Stila, MAC, and Bobbi Brown, another collection of up-and-coming names in make-up.

16 Since this burst of transactions, six multinationals account for 80 percent of American make-up sales, while eight brands control 70 percent of the skin-care market. With its Nivea brand, Beiersdorf is one of the few large independents left, desired by everyone from P&G and Unilever to L'Oreal.

Science Fictions

17 Unable to outspend their big new rivals, the traditional beauty companies are trying to out-innovate them, by making even more of their scientific credentials. The industry is marketing a new category of products that blurs the line between cosmetics and nonprescription drugs—so called "cosmaceuticals." L'Oreal's advertisements now stress how many product patents it has filed.

18 The focus on science has led to some genuinely new ideas, such as face cloths impregnated with cleansers that combine surfactant and paper technology. As yet, though, most of it is pseudoscience. Shiseido's recent international launch of its new Body Creator skin gel claims that its fat-burning pepper and grapefruit oil can melt 1.1 kg of body fat in a month without any need to diet or exercise. At last year's launch in Japan, customers bought a bottle every 3.75 seconds.

19 Avon's chief executive, Andrea Jung, expects Cellu-Sculpt, a new cream that claims to take an inch off your thighs in four weeks, to sell three times as much as an ordinary body cream in its first six weeks. P&G is also playing the game. It is busy plugging the science behind its newest cream, Olay Regenerist, and it has built Pantene into the world's biggest hair-care brand on the basis of its "pro-vitamin B" ingredient. But a report by Britain's *Which?* magazine recently pointed out that vitamins need to be ingested to work, and that a Pantene shampoo it tested was no better than a supermarket's own brand.

20 That is hardly surprising: Jacques-Franck Dossin, an analyst at Goldman Sachs, says that beauty firms spend just 2–3 percent of their sales on research and development—compared with 15 percent by the pharmaceuticals industry. On the other hand, they spend a whopping 20–25 percent on advertising and promotion. Some of that money has been well spent. L'Oreal's "Because I'm worth it" tag-line has long been a huge success. And new companies like Pout are attracting attention with lipsticks labeled "Lick my lolly" and "Bite my cherry."

21 Nevertheless, marketing is becoming hugely expensive, putting pressure on margins. Goldman's Mr. Dossin worries that, in response to intensifying competition and consolidation, L'Oreal has recently cranked up its spending on marketing, forcing an advertising war with rivals that will end up undermining everyone's profitability. Scott Beattie, Elizabeth Arden's boss, says that its marketing budget, which grew by 25 percent in 2002, will rise by another 40 percent this year. Avon plans to hike its advertising budget by 50 percent.

22 This competition has left some exhausted. Revlon, once one of the biggest make-up brands, has been tottering on the edge of bankruptcy. Its current boss, Jack Stahl, a former president of Coca-Cola, is fighting to get the business back on track. Unilever, which is facing slowing growth overall, is stranded in no-man's-land. It sold the great Elizabeth Arden brand and missed out on the boom in hair color. Critics say it should now sell its remaining beauty business to a more focused group, such as Elizabeth Arden. Meanwhile P&G, seen as the first serious threat to L'Oreal for decades, is struggling with its $5 billion acquisition of Clairol. It has been losing market share at an alarming rate to both the French and to Kao's John Frieda.

23 Changes in distribution are also helping to separate the winners from the losers. The only real growth is coming through huge grocery chains such as Wal-Mart that want to deal with just a handful of big suppliers. That is good news for P&G and L'Oreal (which already gains two-thirds of its revenues from mass retailers). But Estee Lauder and Revlon are more dependent on unfashionable department stores where sales are declining and selling costs are high. Estee Lauder's chief executive, Fred Langhammer, bravely preaches the virtues of department stores: "People will always need advice about what skin cream to use," he says. But he is wisely hedging his bets by buying fun specialist retailers, such as MAC.

Body Rebuilding and Refitting

24 Two potentially lucrative markets are being all but ignored by the traditional beauty companies. The first is cosmetic surgery, already a $20 billion business, which has been growing and innovating by leaps and bounds. The number of cosmetic procedures have increased in America by over 220 percent since 1997. Old favorites, such as liposuction, breast implants, and nose jobs, are being overtaken by botox injections to freeze the facial muscles that cause wrinkles. With the number of these up by more than 2400 percent since 1997, botox injections have become the most common procedure of all.

25 The newest lines are bottom implants, fat inserts to plump up aging hands, and fillers like Restylane and Perlane for facial wrinkles. Cosmetic dentistry is also a booming business. Jeff Golub, Manhattan dentist to stars like Kim Catrall of *Sex and the City,* dubs himself a "smile

designer." "We are able to create all sorts of illusions," he says. "The smile has become a fashion statement." Tooth whitening is the botox of the cosmetic dentistry business.

26 What used to be the preserve of actresses and celebrities has become safer and more affordable. Alan Matarasso, one of America's leading plastic surgeons, says: "Ten years ago you could reconstruct a woman's breasts for $12,000—now it can be done for $600." Drooping prices have helped cosmetic surgery to move into the mainstream. More than 70 percent of those who come under the knife now earn less than $50,000 a year.

27 The second big new market is in "well-being"—whole-treatment systems that cover beauty, exercise, and diet, including visits to spas, salons, and clubs, and hark back to the early days of Mesdames Arden and Rubinstein. People are increasingly seeking natural cures rather than turning to chemicals, and an emphasis on being fit—not just thin—is growing in popularity. The trend is being led by a list of celebrities. Avon's boss, Andrea Jung, says modern beauty has been "redefined as health, self-esteem, and empowerment."

28 Beauty firms are falling over themselves to sell products with new-age promise—Arden has a range of products called "Happy." Avon sells diet bars, and L'Oreal owns a few spas. However, it has been left largely to entrepreneurs like American cosmetic surgeon Stephen Greenberg to offer real innovations. His "extreme makeovers" combine cosmetic surgery, a personal trainer for your body, and an image consultant for your face and hair. The traditional beauty companies have yet to grasp the opportunities in these rapidly growing and fragmented markets.

A Slap in the Face?

29 At the same time, the beauty business needs to guard against a growing consumer backlash. Like those facing the tobacco and food industries, this has two elements. The first concerns truth in advertising. Creams and cosmetics are making increasingly extravagant marketing claims. So far, women have been willing to buy into the illusion. Should that change (and there are signs it might), then manufacturers expose themselves to potentially ruinous litigation.

30 Second, there is a moral dimension. The beauty industry is at a stage where it can permanently change a person's looks. Given advances in genetic engineering and the competitive drive, a race for beauty is conceivable in which people will strive to model themselves on some form of idealized human being. By selling the weapons to win this war, the industry may find itself roundly condemned and subject to legislation.

31 Public handwringing is already evident in the case of teenagers indulging in cosmetic surgery. In *Branded,* a book on marketing to teenagers, Alissa Quart notes that in America the number of teenage breast implants and liposuctions rose by 562 percent between 1994 and 2001. There is a cynical marketing phrase for all this: helping "kids look older younger." A number of new books have begun to question the ethics of marketing beauty products and services to adults, too.

32 Part of the backlash so far is tighter regulation. Europe recently passed new labeling and animal-testing laws on cosmetics and will soon give the public the right to probe how firms create cosmetics. This is sure to raise costs for the industry worldwide. Much of the concern, however, is misdirected. Compared with the lead or belladonna that once gave women gothic dreamy eyes, today's lotions are relatively harmless, and consumers are well informed. Cosmetic-surgery techniques are improving—liposuction using electrically vibrating rods, not manual jabbing, still sounds horrible, but it is safer. Worries about newish procedures such as botox look overdone, too—the stuff has been around for a decade as a medical treatment. Even silicone breast implants may be back on the market soon, after improvements in technology.

33 The fact is that neither moral censure nor fears about safety will stop people from wanting to look better. The desire is too entrenched. An eighteenth-century British law proposing to

allow husbands to annul marriages to wives who had trapped them with "scents, paints, artificial teeth, false hair, and iron stays," had no effect on women, who continued to clamor for the latest French skin creams. During the second world war, the American government had to reverse a decision to remove lipstick from its list of essential commodities in order to prevent a rebellion by female war workers. The beauty business—the selling of "hope in a jar," as Charles Revson, the founder of Revlon, once called it—is as permanent as its effects are ephemeral.

THINKING ABOUT THE ARGUMENT

1. What does the first paragraph imply about the article's viewpoint? How do you know this?
2. What does the article suggest are the social benefits of beauty? What evidence is supplied to verify this?
3. The article indicates that a "mass exposure to an idealized standard of beauty" began early in the twentieth century. Do you agree with this? Is it a good thing or a bad thing? Explain.
4. After reading the article, do you believe the author is for, against, or ambivalent about the beauty industry? How do you know?

RESPONDING TO THE ARGUMENT

1. Do you believe that beauty confers certain social benefits? Should it? Why or why not?
2. Of the articles presented so far in this section, which provides the strongest evidence? Why do you say this?
3. How does the viewpoint presented in this article compare or contrast with viewpoints presented in the other articles in this section? Explain.
4. In what ways is the viewpoint of this article appropriate for something appearing in a publication called *The Economist*? Explain.

WRITING ABOUT THE ARGUMENT

1. Is the beauty business, at least in some small way, to blame for America's obsession with youth and beauty? Write a journal entry arguing this issue.
2. Do you believe that beauty is equated with success, wealth, and overall worth? Why or why not? If you think this is a bad thing, what can be done about it? Write an essay considering this issue.
3. Write a synthesis of the first three articles in this section. What appear to be the central features of this debate? What various opinions are offered from each viewpoint? (Hint: Try charting the views before you begin to write.)
4. Is it ethical to look beautiful through artificial means? Is it moral for the beauty business to exploit people's concerns about their appearance? What are the moral/ethical responsibilities of educators, government, ministers, and/or physicians to promote a healthy sense of beauty? Identify an issue and write a value-based argument regarding this topic.

READING SELECTION

"The 'Modern Primitives'"

About the Author: John Leo

Since 1988, John Leo has served *U.S. News & World Report* as a columnist and editor. Known for his wit and humor, he often comments on social and intellectual trends. Prior to 1988, he wrote for *Time*, the *New York Times*, *Commonweal*, *Society*, *McCalls*, and the *Village Voice*. This essay was originally published in *U.S. News & World Report* on July 31, 1995.

Before You Read

1. What does the headnote tell you about the author? Do you think he is qualified to offer an opinion on this topic? Why or why not?
2. What does the title indicate about the article's argument? Do you think it will be argumentative or merely informative? Why do you think so?
3. What do you already know about "primitive" cultures and body modification that might be relevant to the reading? Do you find such things as alternative dress, body piercings, tattoos and scarification attractive, edgy, or repulsive? Explain.
4. If you were an employer, would you hire someone with excessive tattoos, piercings, or even more extreme body modification? Why or why not?
5. In what ways, if any, does "primitive" modification differ from seeking plastic surgery in order to improve your looks? Discuss and explain the difference.

The "Modern Primitives"

1 The days when body piercers could draw stares by wearing multiple earrings and a nose stud are long gone. We are now in the late baroque phase of self-penetration. Metal rings and bars hang from eyebrows, noses, nipples, lips, chins, cheeks, navels, and (for that coveted neo-Frankenstein look) from the side of the neck.

2 "If it sticks out, pierce it" is the motto, and so they do, with special attention to genitals. Some of the same middle-class folks who decry genital mutilation in Africa are paying to have needles driven through the scrotum, the labia, the clitoris, or the head or the shaft of the penis. Many genital piercings have their own names, such as the ampallang or the Prince Albert. (Don't ask.)

3 And, in most cases, the body heals without damage, though some women who have had their nipples pierced report damage to the breast's milk ducts, and some men who have been Prince Alberted no longer urinate in quite the same way.

4 What is going on here? Well, the mainstreaming-of-deviancy thesis naturally springs to mind. The piercings of nipples and genitals arose in the homosexual sadomasochistic culture of the West Coast. The Gauntlet, founded in Los Angeles in 1975 mostly to do master and slave piercings, now has three shops around the country that are about as controversial as Elizabeth Arden salons. Rumbling through the biker culture and punk, piercing gradually shed its outlaw image and was mass marketed to the impressionable by music videos, rock stars, and models.

5 The nasty, aggressive edge of piercing is still there, but now it is coated in happy talk (it's just body decoration, like any other) and a New Agey rationale (we are becoming more centered, reclaiming our bodies in an antibody culture). Various new pagans, witches, and New Agers see piercing as symbolic of unspecified spiritual transformation. One way or another, as Guy Trebay writes in the *Village Voice,* "You will never find anyone on the piercing scene who thinks of what he's doing as pathological."

Fashions and Fetishes

6 The yearning to irritate parents and shock the middle class seems to rank high as a motive for getting punctured repeatedly. Some ask for dramatic piercings to enhance sexual pleasure, to seem daring or fashionable, to express rage, or to forge a group identity. Some think of it as an ordeal that serves as a rite of passage, like ritual suspension of Indian males from hooks in their chests.

7 Piercing is part of the broader "body modification" movement, which includes tattooing, corsetry, branding, and scarring by knife. It's a sign of the times that the more bizarre expressions of this movement keep pushing into the mainstream. The current issue of *Spin* magazine features a hair-raising photo of a woman carving little rivers of blood into another woman's back. "Piercing is like toothbrushing now," one of the cutters told *Spin.* "It's why cutting is becoming popular." Slicing someone's back is a violent act. But one of the cutters has a bland justification: People want to be cut "for adornment, or as a test of endurance, or as a sacrifice toward a transformation." Later on we read that "women are reclaiming their bodies from a culture that has commodified starvation and faux sex." One cuttee says: "It creates intimacy. My scars are emotional centers, signs of a life lived."

8 But most of us achieve intimacy, or at least search for it, without a knife in hand. The truth seems to be that the sadomasochistic instinct is being repositioned to look spiritually high-toned. Many people have found that S&M play "is a way of opening up the body–spirit connection," the high priest of the body modification movement, Fakir Musafar, said in one interview.

9 Musafar, who has corseted his waist down to nineteen inches and mortified his flesh with all kinds of blades, hooks, and pins, calls the mostly twentyish people in the body modification movement "the modern primitives." This is another side of the movement: the conscious attempt to repudiate Western norms and values by adopting the marks and rings of primitive cultures. In some cases this is expressed by tusks worn in the nose or by stretching and exaggerating holes in the earlobe or nipple.

10 Not everyone who pierces a nipple or wears a tongue stud is buying into this, but something like a new primitivism seems to be emerging in body modification, as in other areas of American life. It plugs into a wider dissatisfaction with traditional Western rationality, logic, and sexual norms, as well as anger at the impact of Western technology on the natural environment and anger at the state of American political and social life.

11 Two sympathetic analysts say: "Amidst an almost universal feeling of powerlessness to 'change the world,' individuals are changing what they have power over: their own bodies. . . . By giving visible expression to unknown desires and latent obsessions welling up from within, individuals can provoke change."

12 Probably not. Cultural crisis can't really be dealt with by letting loose our personal obsessions and marking up our bodies. But the rapid spread of this movement is yet another sign that the crisis is here.

Thinking about the Argument

1. What do the first three paragraphs tell you about Leo's audience and their familiarity with, and tolerance for, body modification?
2. Do you agree with the author that piercing has become mainstream? How about "dramatic piercing"? How would you define *dramatic piercing?*
3. What are the reasons that the author gives for dramatic piercing?
4. What are some of the other forms of body modification?
5. How does Fakir Musafar define "modern primitives"? In what ways do you agree or disagree with this definition?

Responding to the Argument

1. Reread the first three paragraphs. What is your emotional reaction to what Leo describes? Why is this?
2. Do you believe that piercing is primarily a spiritual and political exercise, as Musafar seems to indicate? Why or why not? What other reasons might there be for mutilating the body?
3. Do you believe that people self-mutilate to gain control over their own bodies? Do you think this is healthy, or is it a sign of an emotional disorder that needs to be addressed? Why do you think this?
4. In what ways is this form of body modification similar to, or different from, wearing makeup or seeking cosmetic surgery? Explain.

Writing about the Argument

1. In your journal, explain which forms of body modification have become socially acceptable and which ones have not. Use concrete examples to back up your claims.
2. In what ways does trying to improve your appearance (with makeup or cosmetic surgery) differ from a form of body art for self-expression (getting a tattoo or piercings) and the more extreme forms of expression (such as self-mutilation)? Write a definition-based essay that defines and provides concrete examples of each type.
3. How do you know what new standards of beauty are considered socially acceptable? Do different standards apply to different social groups and different situations? For example, would a "modern primitive" be considered a "sellout" if he masked his tattoos and removed his piercings to get or keep a job? Brainstorm, choose a position, and argue an issue drawn from this topic.
4. Do you believe that severe body modification is a sign of an inner emotional issue that needs to be addressed? Should such deviation be treated as a sign of a disease, like the outward signs of alcoholism or anorexia? Why or why not? Write a letter, essay, or journal entry arguing one or more points related to this topic.

"Mark Her Words"

ABOUT THE AUTHOR: DEBORAH SHOUSE

Deborah Shouse's writings have appeared in periodicals such as *Newsweek, Family Circle, Redbook,* and *Reader's Digest.* She is coauthor of *Antiquing for Dummies* (with Ron Zoglin, 1999), and her articles have appeared in more than a dozen anthologies, including *Chicken Soup for the Mother's Soul.* This essay was originally published in *Ms.* magazine in 1996.

BEFORE YOU READ

1. What does the headnote tell you about the author? Who would you expect her primary audience to be? Be as specific as possible.
2. What does the title indicate about the article's argument? What is your initial reaction to the title and possible argument? Could "Mark Her Words" have a double meaning, considering that the article is about tattooing?
3. Do you consider tattooing to be socially acceptable? Why or why not? If it is acceptable, is it also good taste? Explain.

Mark Her Words

1 "I got a tattoo." My daughter Hilee's voice is a child bouncing on the sofa. I press the telephone receiver closer to my ear. "Where?"

2 "Don't worry, Mom, it's on my back. It's beautiful, a triangle with a woman sign inside."

3 "Did it hurt?"

4 "The pain is only temporary," Hilee says.

5 My younger daughter, Sarah, walks into the room and I tell her, "Hilee got a tattoo."

6 "Really?" She reaches for the phone. "What did you get? Wow, it sounds totally cool. Yeah, that's wonderful!" I listen to Sarah's excitement and I tell myself, "That is how I want to act next time." Then I worry, what if there is a next time?

7 "I want to know what will make you freak out the most," Hilee says, when she calls the next day. "Visible tattoos, face piercing, or scars?"

8 "Scars, tattoos, and face piercing, in that order," I report.

9 "I don't think I'm going to do any of those things, but I'll prepare you if I do. I want you to understand why this is so important to me," Hilee says.

10 Hilee already has scars that she inflicted on herself. She cut at her upper arms so she would not slice her wrists and kill herself. Her scars are symbols that she was strong enough to stay alive. This she explained to me several weeks ago. I look at the buds of pink skin on her arm and I wince at what she has endured. I look at the marks and I am grateful she knew how to keep herself alive.

11 Three years ago, Hilee came into my office and said, "I was sexually abused as a child." At that moment, my heart and my world stopped. When I breathed again, everything was different. My history was shattered, the family photos destroyed, and my image of myself as a good mother obliterated. Those words explained so much of my daughter to me.

12 My child was sexually abused . . . the thought haunts me. How can I forgive myself for not knowing? How can I accept that I didn't live up to the basic tenet of motherhood, to keep my child safe?

13 "Forgive yourself," my friends urge. "You did your best."

14 Hilee is undoing her hurt. She is stepping out and embracing her body. She pierces her labia, her nipple. She tattoos her back and dyes her hair blond. She reads about tribal scarifications and rituals designed to mark and honor the body. Every poke of the needle, every insert of color, is a step toward her true self.

15 Now I look at the nose and eyebrow piercings, the dragon tattoo on the cashier at the health food store differently. What used to be mere squiggles of color and pieces of silver, I now see as symbols, spelling out stories for those who can read them.

16 Hilee is teaching me to read them. I am slow. I resist. I cringe at the idea of my daughter being hurt.

17 "I was in pain before and had only misery to show for it," she explains. "Now I choose the pain and I have something beautiful and meaningful. I go right through the pain. Do you understand?" I breathe in every word. I want to tell her she's done enough, she can stop for a while. I wonder how she can stand so strong and still, when I run from pain?

18 "I want to honor my Jewish heritage," Hilee tells me. "I'm thinking of tattooing 'Survivor' in Hebrew around my wrist. That way, I know I will never try to kill myself." Here is my child striding forward, transmuting pain into celebration.

19 Hilee's birth was my first real introduction to pain. My introduction to the fierce lioness love that never dims or dies; the love that can overturn a car or endlessly hold a crying child. Does that encompassing love include being excited and supportive about scarring, piercing, and tattoos?

20 I call a synagogue and ask the rabbi if he will write out "Survivor" in Hebrew for me.

21 "Which survivor do you want?" he says. "Survivor, as in one left behind after a death, or the survivor of much trauma, like a concentration-camp survivor?"

22 "The survivor of much trauma," I tell him.

23 For years, my daughter lived apart, her arms folded against me. Now she is opening: to me, to herself, to life.

24 "I worry I spent too much money on this tattoo," she says, running her fingers over the triangle on the back of her neck.

25 "It's not really expensive when you amortize the cost over seventy years," I tell her. The tattoo hasn't quite healed; the woman symbol is puffy, swollen. I am amazed that she went by herself, bared her back to a stranger, and accepted this piece of forever.

26 "Isn't it gorgeous? Don't you want a tattoo?" Hilee asks.

27 Even when your child goes away for a long, long time, you wait. Every inhale is hope, every exhale despair. You go through life, working, smiling, talking, acting like part of you is not standing on the pier, staring out to sea, waiting for your own true love, your own true child.

28 My body is not decorated by needles or ink. This child is my tattoo, my indelible mark, my symbol that I lived through pain and into celebration. She is the story of my skin and my heart, written all over me, for anyone, who is able, to read.

Thinking about the Argument

1. What does the opening narrative (paragraphs 1 to 4) tell you about the mother-daughter relationship? What does it tell you about the writer's opinion of tattooing? What does it suggest about her target audience?
2. Now examine paragraphs 5 and 6; how do they change your understanding of this relationship? What does they suggest about the relationship between tattooing and scarification?

3. How does the author explain that scarification and pain can be a part of the healing process that helped her daughter recover from sexual abuse?
4. How, according to the author, has tattooing brought the mother and daughter closer together?
5. What does Shouse mean when she says "my child is my tattoo"?

RESPONDING TO THE ARGUMENT

1. This article uses narrative as its primary means of persuasion. How has the author used this method to present claims and evidence, either explicitly stated or implied?
2. How has this author used the appeal to emotion to make a connection with the audience and drive her point home? Do you think this tactic was effective? Why or why not?
3. What is the difference between scarification—self-cutting and mutilation—and tattooing, if both are responses to emotional pain and an attempt to gain ownership of one's body? Does it matter, in Hilee's words, that "Now I choose the pain and I have something beautiful and meaningful"? In what way is a tattoo different from, or even superior to, a self-inflicted scar or brand?
4. Do you think it is wise to use rituals of pain to deal with emotional trauma? Explain.

WRITING ABOUT THE ARGUMENT

1. What are the reasons that someone might get a tattoo? List them in your journal. Argue which ones you consider to be healthy or unhealthy.
2. Are tattoos like telling a story? Can you "read" tattoos that you see on other people? Choose a tattoo you have seen on someone. Photograph it and interview them. What tale does that tattoo tell? In what way has that tattoo been healthy or unhealthy for this person? Write an argument based on this topic.
3. Do tattoos and body piercings help a victim heal emotionally, or are they just signs of inner pain, like the symptoms of a disease? Write an argument based on this idea.
4. Do you think therapists should recommend tattooing or body modification for therapeutic reasons? Why or why not? In the form of a letter to a therapist, write an argument expressing your view on this topic.

"The Boldest Cut"

ABOUT THE AUTHOR: DAVID CONCAR

David Concar is a London-based deputy editor of *New Scientist.* He writes often on a wide range of science topics. This selection first appeared in *New Scientist* in 2004.

BEFORE YOU READ

1. What does the headnote tell you about the author? How might this information affect your understanding of the reading?

READING SELECTION

2. What do you think the audience of *New Scientist* is like? Do you think they are for or against cosmetic and reconstructive surgery? Why?
3. What does the title indicate about the article's argument? What is your initial reaction to the title and possible argument?
4. How do you feel about transplanting a face from one person to another, as opposed to reconstructing one's own face? Are there ethical issues to be considered? Explain.

The Boldest Cut

1 Harpal Kaur can still see the terrible events of that day unfolding in her mind's eye. Her nine-year-old daughter Sandeep was chopping grass to feed the family buffalo at their home in Chak Khurd in northern India, when Sandeep's hair got caught in the threshing machine. As it was relentlessly dragged in, the skin above her neck tore, and her entire scalp and face were ripped off. "I started to scream when I realized what happened," recalls Sandeep's mother. "I didn't know where her face was."

2 Despite their shock and distress, the family managed to salvage Sandeep's face and scalp, and get her on a moped. After a fraught three-and-a-half-hour journey that involved several breakdowns, Sandeep arrived at the Christian Medical College and Hospital in Ludhiana, her face in a plastic bag.

3 By a stroke of luck, an experienced microsurgeon was on duty. Abraham Thomas knew that repairing Sandeep's face with skin grafts from elsewhere on her body would leave her profoundly disfigured, so he decided to attempt something bolder—to return the plastic bag's contents to their rightful place.

4 It was the right call. In the early hours of the next day, as Thomas reconnected the first artery the reattached face flushed pink as blood perfused it once more. Against the odds Thomas and his team had performed the world's first reported "replant" of an entire face and scalp.

5 Since that day in 1994 there have been two other known cases of surgeons heroically replacing entire faces, in Australia and the United States. And surgeons have asked the obvious question: If it's possible to reattach such messily torn-off faces, couldn't we also carry out face transplants, using the faces of the newly deceased to treat people with disfigurements?

6 It is a grisly yet fascinating subject that in recent years has divided opinions among doctors, ethicists, and disfigured patients. Indeed for a while it looked like the world's first face transplant was only a matter of time. Several teams of surgeons around the world argued that face transplants could transform the lives of people with severe disfigurements. Critics questioned whether the benefits were worth the medical risks. And newspaper columnists quipped about George Clooney being a better-qualified donor than George Bush.

7 Then, last November, came a setback: an inquiry by the United Kingdom's prestigious Royal College of Surgeons concluded that doctors should wait until more was known about risks both of tissue rejection and the psychological impacts on the recipient and the donor's family.

8 But not everyone agrees with that verdict. And not all teams have put their plans on hold. *New Scientist* has learned that surgeons and scientists at the University of Louisville in Kentucky are in the process of requesting formal approval to carry out a face transplant. They have described their plans in detail in a thirty-page document being submitted to their university's ethics committee or institutional review board. Despite the earlier Royal College of Surgeons' report, the U.S. team says enough research has

now been done, and they plan to start screening prospective patients and looking for donors as soon as they get the go-ahead from the IRB.

9 So who are these doctors so willing to court controversy? A leading team-member is John Barker, director of plastic surgery research at the University of Louisville. My first contact with Barker came in September 1998. News had just broken that an international team working in Lyon, France, had carried out what appeared to be the world's first successful hand transplant. I knew surgeons in Louisville had been working toward the same goal and so I called Barker for a comment.

10 In the event Barker was keener to talk about what he saw as the next milestone in the field—face transplants. Some patients, Barker explained, were so severely injured that even after scores of skin grafts and other operations, they barely had a functioning face, let alone a normal-looking one. They included victims of severe burns, cancers, gunshot wounds, or dog attacks. Louisville surgeons, Barker disclosed, were now seriously investigating the possibility of giving such patients face transplants.

11 *New Scientist* ran the story (3 October 1998, p. 13) and news organizations across the world picked it up. With the movie *Face/Off* recently released, headline writers had an easy, if less than scientifically grounded, point of reference. The following January, Barker and his colleagues made news again when they carried out the world's second successful hand transplant operation.

12 The French hand transplant of the previous autumn had come out of the blue with no public debate beforehand. Behind the scenes, however, surgeons had faced similar objections to those now being leveled at face grafts. Ever since the first human kidney transplant in 1954, transplant surgery has been seen as the risky and expensive therapy of last resort. The orthodoxy has always been that exposing patients to the dangers of organ rejection and the risks of immunosuppressant drugs simply isn't worth it for someone who was not in mortal danger in the first place.

13 And as well as being non-life-saving, hand transplants involved giving the patient skin—a tissue nobody had previously succeeded in transplanting (other than between identical twins). Because of its role in protecting the body from invading bacteria and viruses, skin contains myriad immune cells and proteins, and is thus one of the body's most immunologically active organs.

14 So why risk a hand transplant? The Louisville team began exploring how to prevent skin rejecting in the mid-1990s. Testing their procedures on pigs, they initially thought their best hope was to deliver drugs directly to a transplanted limb. In one test they used miniature pumps implanted under the skin to deliver a drug. As a control, they gave a cocktail of drugs orally to another group of animals. In the end the pumps became blocked and the pigs rejected their grafts. But many of the control animals unexpectedly thrived.

15 Suddenly the idea of human skin—and limb—transplants was no longer an impossible dream. Rejection, it appeared, could be stopped by a cocktail of drugs that was already being used for other transplants. "All of a sudden the light went on," says Barker. "We realized the control group was doing great with a treatment that was already being used widely for kidney transplants.

16 Almost immediately teams in Louisville and elsewhere decided to attempt a hand transplant. Since then there have been more than twenty such grafts in countries including the United States, Austria, and China, all relying on the same three drugs that were given to the Louisville pigs. And as far as we know, there has been just one failure. Ironically it was the very first patient, a New Zealander called Clint Hallam, who stopped taking the drugs and had to have his new limb amputated. Other patients have experienced some early signs of rejection, but doctors have so far been able to suppress these by temporarily upping the drug dosage.

17 The results have scotched some of the concerns about non-life-saving transplants and triggered a wave of other operations. In recent years

there have been eight thigh and knee bone transplants, four double hand transplants (one to a French house painter whose hands were blown off by a home-made model rocket), and a combined arm-and-hand transplant to a one-month baby girl. A larynx, a tongue, and an abdominal wall have also been transplanted. There has been speculative talk about breast, neck, and even penis transplants.

18 Yet not all experts are convinced that the benefits justify the risks involved in this growing list of non-life-saving transplants. Opponents say that even with the latest drugs, transplanted kidneys survive less than 10 years on average; hand or face transplants, they claim, are unlikely to do any better. And if or when a transplanted face triggers an uncontrollable rejection, what then? The face would have to be removed and the patient given either skin grafts from their own body or a second transplant. Plus, even if the transplant stays healthy, immunosuppressants cost tens of thousands of dollars per year and carry serious long-term risks of infections, diabetes, and certain cancers.

19 In light of these risks, even some proponents of face transplants believe it may be best to wait for better techniques for preventing rejection. But the Louisville team are more optimistic. Without playing down the risks, they are increasingly convinced that for the most severely disfigured patients, the benefits of a face transplant could justify a lifetime's dependency on even the present generation of drugs. "The whole driving force behind this is there is a patient need," says Louisville surgeon Joseph Banis. "Over twenty years I've seen patients whose faces have been so severely damaged that they are non-human faces."

20 Skin from elsewhere on the body has a different texture to that of the face and is notoriously difficult to turn into natural-looking noses and mouths. Patients with severe facial burns may undergo over fifty painful operations, to achieve only modest results. "You lose animation, you lose normalcy of texture, of color," says Banis, who in one case even created a makeshift nose from a patient's toe.

21 To help make their case, the Louisville researchers have spent the past couple of years probing attitudes to transplant risks. They used questionnaires to ask how many years of life expectancy people would sacrifice in return for particular transplanted organs. The results are still being processed, but a preliminary analysis reveals something surprising. People are willing to trade more years for a hand, should they need one, than, say, a foot, and more years for a larynx than a hand. But the body part for which people are willing to trade most years of life is by some margin a transplanted face. For a face they would take on even more risk than for a kidney, and, as Barker points out, kidney transplants are already seen as worth the risk.

22 So assuming the team gets clearance, what are the challenges involved? Banis, the plastic surgeon who is likely to lead the operation, says they will need to cut out and lift off the full surface of the donor's face. The borders of this graft would probably trace a line running across the hairline, down the temples on either side, passing just in front of the ears, and round the jawline. Eyebrows, eyelids, nose, mouth, and lips could all be included.

23 And that's just for starters. As well as the skin and its fine undercoat of fat, the surgeons would also need to take the underlying arteries and veins that keep the face supplied with blood. Depending on the extent of the patient's injuries, the team might even have to go deeper still, taking from the donor nose cartilage, facial nerves, and even muscles. "I could see it taking as long as ten to twelve hours to harvest the graft." Serge Martinez, another surgeon in the Louisville team, told us. "Then to transplant it you might be looking at twenty-four hours."

24 And when the bandages come off? Perhaps what most spooks people about face transplants is the idea that the recipient will end up looking just like the dead donor. In *Face/Off,* the swap between the two lead characters is so flawless

that even the women in their lives are misled. In reality, that couldn't happen: our looks are strongly influenced by the underlying bone structure and muscle movement, not just the soft tissues that would be transplanted.

25 Nevertheless, working out just how much of the donor's looks would be transferred has become an important goal for the Louisville team. "One of the questions that has come up is whether the family of a donor will recognize the donor in the face of the recipient," says Barker. "And would they donate knowing they might one day see their loved one in the face of somebody walking down the street?"

26 The surgeons in Louisville have been practicing for the operation by swapping the faces of bodies donated for medical research. The team has used these practice sessions to discover whether recipients of donated faces are likely to be mistaken for the donor.

27 Even for a seasoned reconstructive surgeon like Martinez it has been an eye-opener. "It is really awesome to lift up a whole face and lay it back down," he says. "I have to sit back sometimes and say, am I really part of doing this?"

28 In a typical recognition test, the researchers will show photographs of a dead person's face to a group of volunteers. After removing the photos, the researchers will lay out photos of a dozen more heads. One of these has had the first person's face transplanted onto them. The volunteers are asked whether that person is in the crowd and if so, where they are.

29 The full results will be submitted to a journal and so cannot be revealed here but what Barker will say is that they suggest a transplanted face won't be strongly recognizable as either the donor or recipient. In effect, says Barker, a third face is created: "More often than not you don't recognize the person."

30 To get a more vivid idea of how a patient might look afterwards, *New Scientist* teamed up with a TV company, U.K.-based Mentorn, and commissioned an animation firm to carry out a virtual face transplant. The results, which will be shown in a TV documentary on the subject, . . . appear to back the Louisville team's conclusions.

31 The firm, Darkside Animation, needed to create an anatomically accurate head for their virtual patient. So they digitally scanned the face of a living woman and placed this face on a standard thirty anatomy model of a human skull, cartilage, and musculature. This was resized and reshaped to make its bone structure fit the contours of the scanned face. For the virtual donor, the team took the same standard model of a human head and reshaped its bone structure, adding skin, eyebrows, lips, and so on, to create a second head.

32 To perform the transplant, the team took the skin and underlying fat off the donor and stretched it over the bone structure and musculature of the virtual patient. The recipient ends up sharing certain features with the donor—the shape of the mouth, for example—yet has her own distinct identity. In the case of the mouth, the team found this part of the face to be strongly influenced by the underlying fat that was transplanted along with the skin and lips.

33 A harder question to answer is what level of movement, feeling, and expression the transplanted face would have. The surgeons I spoke to agreed that restoring expression and sensation to the face, and getting the eyelids and mouth moving properly, would be major challenges—just as they are when rebuilding a face with conventional skin grafts. "No transplant will ever have the fine activity that the normal body part would have," says Banis. "We hope to get about 50 percent return of nerve function."

34 For a better idea of how face transplant recipients might fare, surgeons are turning to "replant" patients like Sandeep Kaur. Ten years after the accident, she is now 19 and studying to be a nurse. Her face still bears scars and lacks mobility. But her doctor is hopeful that further surgery will help. And conventional skin grafts would have left her a lot worse off.

35 Reflecting on Sandeep's case, Barker is optimistic that transplanting a face from a dead donor would be easier than replanting one that has been ripped off. "It's all surgically clean, pristine tissue and you have plenty to work with," he says. "You remove it from the donor; drape it over and tailor; sew it in place. There's no dead tissue that has been crushed."

36 While that may be true, there is a note of caution from the only U.S. surgeon to have carried out a face replant, Bradon Wilhelmi, of Southern Illinois University. Two years ago Wilhelmi led a team at Massachusetts General Hospital that replaced the face and scalp of a twenty-one-year-old man who'd caught his hair in a conveyor belt at work. The victim's skin had been peeled off cleanly, leaving the underlying muscles and nerves intact. The peeling happens because of a specific weak plane underneath the skin and fat, says Wilhelmi. This makes replant patients more likely to regain facial expression and sensation.

37 During a transplant, in contrast, surgeons may have to remove and reattach a deeper layer of muscles and nerves. That could limit the patient's recovery. Despite this, Wilhelmi is broadly optimistic about the prospects for transplanting faces. With any reattachment or transplant operation, establishing a good blood supply to the graft is crucial. Fortunately, the face is so dense with blood vessels that reattaching just a few arteries can allow the tissue to be well perfused. Indeed, Wilhelmi's team found that a single repaired artery gave their replanted face all the blood it needed.

38 In Paris, a second team has also been preparing to carry out a face transplant. However the French surgeons, led by Laurent Lantieri at the University of Henri Mondor Hospital, have decided to limit their transplant to the part of the face that is hardest to reconstruct using conventional skin grafts—the upper lip and nose. Lantieri believes that a partial transplant would avoid the risk of having to strip off so much tissue if it goes wrong: in the event of rejection the nose and upper lip could be removed and the patient could go back to wearing a mask over that section of the face. But others question whether such a transplant would be worth the side effects of anti-rejection drugs.

39 Meanwhile, in London at the Royal Free Hospital, surgeon Peter Butler has also spent a lot of time in recent years practicing the techniques necessary for a face transplant. Like the Louisville team, Butler has been assessing people's attitudes to the risks, and has studied the recipient's likely resemblance to the donor.

40 Butler drew world attention in autumn 2002 when he told a plastic surgery conference that the technical expertise for a face transplant was now in place and that it was time to decide whether the surgery would be ethical. Since then he has been hounded by the world's media wanting to know when he is going to take the plunge.

41 In recent months, Butler has been voicing caution. "These drugs have significant complications and they don't always work," he says. "Is it really worth it for the patient?" He will continue with his research, but has announced no immediate plans to proceed.

42 The Louisville surgeons know that if or when their plans get the green light, their success or failure will depend greatly on the patient they select. Nobody has yet been lined up, and finding the right person won't be easy. "It really has to be a severe, severe injury to the face, so that the benefit will outweigh the risk," says Barker. And the person will also need to understand the risks as well as be able to handle the immense media pressure that is bound to surround the first patient.

43 But having got this far, the team have no truck with arguments to delay the first attempt. "Tell me what you are going to do during that cautionary period that will get us closer to doing this," Barker says. "Caution by itself will not get us any closer. If Christopher Columbus were cautious I'd probably be speaking with a British accent."

THINKING ABOUT THE ARGUMENT

1. How do paragraphs 1 and 2 affect you emotionally? Do they incline you to favor radical reconstructive surgery? Why or why not?
2. According to the author, why is performing a face transplant a controversial topic?
3. Why are skin grafts not considered a viable option for some patients?
4. How have scientists prevented skin tissue from transplant rejection?
5. Why do the scientists believe that the person receiving the transplant would not look exactly like the person who donated the face?
6. This article was written before the first face transplant was conducted in France on November 27, 2005. In what ways is the article dated or still relevant? Do you think differently about this procedure than you would have if a transplant had not yet taken place?

French surgeons performed the world's first-ever face transplant at a hospital in Amiens on November 27, 2005. The recipient, Isabelle Dinoire, had been mauled six months before by her dog, losing most of her lips, nose, and chin. Unable to eat or speak properly, unwilling to be seen in public, and damaged beyond the help of reconstructive surgery, Dinoire was judged by her surgeons to be a good candidate for the transplant. Critics, however, have raised ethical questions about whether the procedure was premature: her disfigurement was not life-threatening, and the transplant procedure was experimental. The immediate results of the surgery were mixed. She was soon able to eat, speak, and even smoke a cigarette, but her speech was slurred, and her mouth would hang open. Rehabilitation and nerve growth should improve her condition, but tissue rejection will always be a threat.

RESPONDING TO THE ARGUMENT

1. This article was written before the first face transplant was completed in France in 2005. Do you agree it was correct for this transplant to have taken place, in spite of the ethical concerns? Explain.
2. Even if a face transplant were to be medically successful, what emotional and ethical issues might a person face if his or her appearance was so radically altered? How might spouses, close friends, and members of their families react?
3. Would it be ethical for a transplant recipient to receive a radically different face—such as the face of a person of another race, a much younger face, or the face of someone of the opposite sex? Why or why not?
4. Should face transplants, when they become safe, be allowed for cosmetic reasons? For example, should a fifty-year-old woman be allowed to receive the face of a twenty-year-old girl? Why or why not?
5. Should such transplants be allowed for purposes of changing one's identity (either legally or illegally)? Why or why not?

WRITING ABOUT THE ARGUMENT

1. Write a journal entry or an essay arguing whether ordinary reconstructive surgery or a face transplant—with their relative strengths and weaknesses—would be preferable. Assume that the medical situation would allow either hypothetical surgery to take place.
2. Under what conditions would a face transplant be considered "cosmetic surgery"? Should it be allowed or banned? Under what conditions? Write an essay arguing this issue.
3. What might some of the personal or social effects of a face transplant be? Write a letter to the editor of your local paper expressing your opinion on this topic.
4. Write an essay arguing whether or not a face transplant should be allowed for cosmetic reasons.

Issue 3: Consumerism

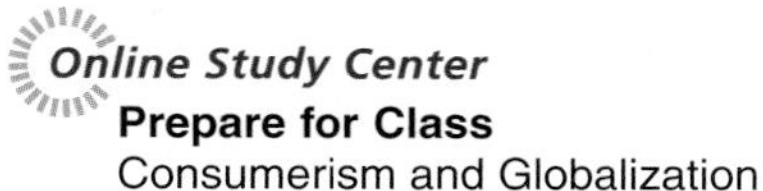

Online Study Center
Prepare for Class
Consumerism and Globalization

We live in a material world, and modern Americans are unrivaled in the bounty of material goods they generate and consume. Advertisements entice audiences to buy this or that, promising or implying that the product's acquisition will make the owner happier, more attractive, or more popular. We want the smallest cell phone, the newest fashion, the fastest computer, the largest home, the fanciest automobile. The list seems endless and ever-growing. Yet materialism does not go unchallenged. Legal and ethical questions arise regarding how items and services are advertised and who is targeted by advertisements. Global responsibilities and conflicts between materialism, family values, and spiritualism are examined and debated.

Considering the Issue of Consumerism

Working in discussion groups or in your journal, answer the following questions.

1. How important are possessions in your life? In the lives of others?
2. Should there be limits on the accumulation of wealth and possessions?
3. What obligations do developed countries have to provide for the world's "have-nots"?
4. To what extent is one nation responsible for the material comforts of other nations?

Some people believe that an economy that focuses on a cycle of advertising and buying shapes a society that has misplaced values.

5. To what extent is government obligated to teach or promote values, particularly nonmaterial values?
6. To what degree should advertisers and promoters be restrained (or left unrestrained) in their appeals to consumers?

READING SELECTION

"The More Factor"

ABOUT THE AUTHOR: LAURENCE SHAMES

Laurence Shames is a novelist and former ethics columnist for *Esquire.* His novels blend humor and the crime genre. His nonfiction treatment of the Mafia, *The Boss of Bosses* (1991), was a bestseller. In his book *The Hunger for More: Searching for Values in an Age of Greed* (1991), from which this selection is excerpted, he considers the ethical implications of consumer culture.

BEFORE YOU READ

1. Do you believe that excessive wealth is a virtue or a vice? Explain.
2. What do you think that Shames's viewpoint might be? Do you think he is in favor of or against excessive wealth? Why do you think this? How could you find out more about him?
3. What does the word "More" in the title imply? Do you think the article will support or criticize the American drive to increase personal wealth? Why do you think this?
4. What do you already know about "the American Dream" and the American expansionist vision of "manifest destiny"? How might the frontier idea of expansion relate to today's idea of wealth as a virtue?

»«

The More Factor

One

1 Americans have always been optimists, and optimists have always liked to speculate. In Texas in the 1880s, the speculative instrument of choice was towns, and there is no tale more American than this.

2 What people would do was buy up enormous tracts of parched and vacant land, lay out a Main Street, nail together some wooden sidewalks, and start slapping up buildings. One of these buildings would be called the Grand Hotel and would have a saloon complete with swinging doors. Another might be dubbed the New Academy or the Opera House. The developers would erect a flagpole and name a church, and once the workmen had packed up and moved on, the towns would be as empty as the sky.

3 But no matter. The speculators, next, would hire people to pass out handbills in the Eastern and Midwestern cities, tracts limning the advantages of relocation to "the Athens of the South" or "the new plains Jerusalem." When per-

suasion failed, the builders might resort to bribery, paying people's moving costs and giving them houses, in exchange for nothing but a pledge to stay until a certain census was taken or a certain inspection made. Once the nose-count was completed, people were free to move on, and there was in fact a contingent of folks who made their living by keeping a cabin on skids, and dragging it for pay from one town to another.

4 The speculators' idea, of course, was to lure the railroad. If one could create a convincing semblance of a town, the railroad might come through it, and a real town would develop, making the speculators staggeringly rich. By these devices a man named Sanborn once owned Amarillo.

5 But railroad tracks are narrow and the state of Texas is very, very wide. For every Wichita Falls or Lubbock there were a dozen College Mounds or Belchervilles, bleached, unpeopled burgs that receded quietly into the dust, taking with them large amounts of speculators' money.

6 Still, the speculators kept right on bucking the odds and depositing empty towns in the middle of nowhere. Why did they do it? Two reasons—reasons that might be said to summarize the central fact of American economic history and that go a fair way toward explaining what is perhaps the central strand of the national character.

7 The first reason was simply that the possible returns were so enormous as to partake of the surreal, to create a climate in which ordinary logic and prudence did not seem to apply. In a boom like that of real estate when the railroad barreled through, long shots that might pay 100,000 to one seemed worth a bet.

8 The second reason, more pertinent here, is that there was a presumption that America would *keep on* booming—if not forever, then at least longer than it made sense to worry about. There would always be another gold rush, another Homestead Act, another oil strike. The next generation would always ferret out opportunities that would be still more lavish than any that had gone before. America *was* those opportunities. This was an article not just of faith, but of strategy. You banked on the next windfall, you staked your hopes and even your self-esteem on it; and this led to a national turn of mind that might usefully be thought of as the habit of more.

9 A century, maybe two centuries, before anyone had heard the term *baby boomer,* much less *yuppie,* the habit of more had been installed as the operative truth among the economically ambitious. The habit of more seemed to suggest that there was no such thing as getting wiped out in America. A fortune lost in Texas might be recouped in Colorado. Funds frittered away on grazing land where nothing grew might flood back in as silver. There was always a second chance, or always seemed to be, in this land where growth was destiny and where expansion and purpose were the same.

10 The key was the frontier, not just as a matter of acreage, but as idea. Vast, varied, rough as rocks, America was the place where one never quite came to the end. Ben Franklin explained it to Europe even before the Revolutionary War had finished: America offered new chances to those "who, in their own Countries, where all the Lands [were] fully occupied . . . could never [emerge] from the poor Condition wherein they were born."

11 So central was this awareness of vacant space and its link to economic promise, that Frederick Jackson Turner, the historian who set the tone for much of the twentieth century's understanding of the American past, would write that it was "not the constitution, but free land . . . [that] made the democratic type of society in America." Good laws mattered; an accountable government mattered; ingenuity and hard work mattered. But those things were, so to speak, an overlay on the natural, geographic America that was simply *there,* and whose vast and beckoning possibilities seemed to generate the ambition and

the sometimes reckless liberty that would fill it. First and foremost, it was open space that provided "the freedom of the individual to rise under conditions of social mobility."

12 Open space generated not just ambition, but metaphor. As early as 1835, Tocqueville was extrapolating from the fact of America's emptiness to the observation that "no natural boundary seems to be set to the efforts of man." Nor was any limit placed on what he might accomplish, since, in that heyday of the Protestant ethic, a person's rewards were taken to be quite strictly proportionate to his labors.

13 Frontier; opportunity; more. This has been the American trinity from the very start. The frontier was the backdrop and also the raw material for the streak of economic booms. The booms became the goad and also the justification for the myriad gambles and for Americans' famous optimism. The optimism, in turn, shaped the schemes and visions that were sometimes noble, sometimes appalling, always bold. The frontier, as reality and as symbol, is what has shaped the American way of doing things and the American sense of what's worth doing.

14 But there has been one further corollary to the legacy of the frontier, with its promise of ever-expanding opportunities: Given that the goal—a realistic goal for most of our history—was *more,* Americans have been somewhat backward in adopting values, hopes, ambitions that have to do with things *other than* more. In America, a sense of quality has lagged far behind a sense of scale. An ideal of contentment has yet to take root in soil traditionally more hospitable to an ideal of restless striving. The ethic of decency has been upstaged by the ethic of success. The concept of growth has been applied almost exclusively to things that can be measured, counted, weighed. And the hunger for those things that are unmeasurable but fine—the sorts of accomplishment that cannot be undone by circumstance or a shift in social fashion, the kind of serenity that cannot be shattered by tomorrow's headline—has gone largely unfulfilled, and even unacknowledged.

Two

15 If the supply of more went on forever, perhaps that wouldn't matter very much. Expansion could remain a goal unto itself, and would continue to generate a value system based on bulk rather than on nuance, on quantities of money rather than on quality of life, on "progress" itself rather than on a sense of what the progress was for. But what if, over time, there was less more to be had?

16 That is the essential situation of America today.

17 Let's keep things in proportion: The country is not running out of wealth, drive, savvy, or opportunities. We are not facing imminent ruin, and neither panic nor gloom is called for. But there have been ample indications over the past two decades that we are running out of more.

18 Consider productivity growth—according to many economists, the single most telling and least distortable gauge of changes in real wealth. From 1947 to 1965, productivity in the private sector (adjusted, as are all the following figures, for inflation) was advancing, on average, by an annual 3.3 percent. This means, simply, that each hour of work performed by a specimen American worker contributed 3.3 cents worth of more to every American dollar every year; whether we saved it or spent it, that increment went into a national kitty of ever-enlarging aggregate wealth. Between 1965 and 1972, however, the "more-factor" decreased to 2.4 percent a year, and from 1972 to 1977 it slipped further, to 1.6 percent. By the early 1980s, productivity growth was at a virtual standstill, crawling along at 0.2 percent for the five years ending in 1982. Through the middle years of the 1980s, the numbers rebounded somewhat—but by then the gains were being neutralized by the gargantuan carrying costs on the national debt.

19 Inevitably, this decline in the national stockpile of more held consequences for the individ-

ual wallet. During the 1950s, Americans' average hourly earnings were humping ahead at a gratifying 2.5 percent each year. By the late seventies, that figure stood just where productivity growth had come to stand, at a dispiriting 0.2 cents on the dollar. By the first half of the eighties, the Reagan "recovery" notwithstanding, real hourly wages were actually moving backwards—declining at an average annual rate of 0.3 percent.

20 Compounding the shortage of more was an unfortunate but crucial demographic fact. Real wealth was nearly ceasing to expand just at the moment when the members of that unprecedented population bulge known as the baby boom were entering what should have been their peak years of income expansion. A working man or woman who was thirty years old in 1949 could expect to see his or her real earnings burgeon by 63 percent by age forty. In 1959, a thirty-year-old could still look forward to a gain of 49 percent by his or her fortieth birthday.

21 But what about the person who turned thirty in 1973? By the time that worker turned forty, his or her real earnings had shrunk by a percentage point. For all the blather about yuppies with their beach houses, BMWs, and radicchio salads, and even factoring in those isolated tens of thousands making ludicrous sums in consulting firms or on Wall Street, the fact is that between 1979 and 1983 real earnings of all Americans between the ages of twenty-five and thirty-four actually declined by 14 percent. The *New York Times,* well before the stock market crash put the kibosh on eighties confidence, summed up the implications of this downturn by observing that "for millions of breadwinners, the American dream is becoming the impossible dream."

22 Now, it is not our main purpose here to detail the ups and downs of the American economy. Our aim, rather, is to consider the effects of those ups and downs on people's goals, values, sense of their place in the world. What happens at that shadowy juncture where economic prospects meld with personal choice? What sorts of insights and adjustments are called for so that economic ups and downs can be dealt with gracefully?

23 Fact one in this connection is that, if America's supply of more is in fact diminishing, American values will have to shift and broaden to fill the gap where the expectation of almost automatic gains used to be. Something more durable will have to replace the fat but fragile bubble that had been getting frailer these past two decades and that finally popped—a tentative, partial pop—on October 19, 1987. A different sort of growth—ultimately, a growth in responsibility and happiness—will have to fulfill our need to believe that our possibilities are still expanding.

24 The transition to that new view of progress will take some fancy stepping, because, at least since the end of World War II, simple economic growth has stood, in the American psyche, as the best available substitute for the literal frontier. The economy has *been* the frontier. Instead of more space, we have had more money. Rather than measuring progress in terms of geographical expansion, we have measured it by expansion in our standard of living. Economics has become the metaphor on which we pin our hopes of open space and second chances.

25 The poignant part is that the literal frontier did not pass yesterday: it has not existed for a hundred years. But the frontier's promise has become so much a part of us that we have not been willing to let the concept die. We have kept the frontier mythology going by invocation, by allusion, by hype.

26 It is not a coincidence that John F. Kennedy dubbed his political program the New Frontier. It is not mere linguistic accident that makes us speak of Frontiers of Science or of psychedelic drugs as carrying one to Frontiers of Perception. We glorify fads and fashions by calling them Frontiers of Taste. Nuclear energy has been called the Last Frontier; solar energy has been

called the Last Frontier. Outer space has been called the Last Frontier; the oceans have been called the Last Frontier. Even the suburbs, those blandest and least adventurous of places, have been wryly described as the crabgrass frontier.

27 What made all these usages plausible was their being linked to the image of the American economy as an endlessly fertile continent whose boundaries never need be reached, a domain that could expand in perpetuity, a gigantic playing field that would never run out of room, and on which the game would get forever bigger and more filled with action. This was the frontier that would not vanish.

28 It is worth noting that people in other countries (with the possible exception of that other America, Australia) do not talk about frontier this way. In Europe, and in most of Africa and Asia, "frontier" connotes, at worst, a place of barbed wire and men with rifles, and at best, a neutral junction where one changes currency while passing from one fixed system into another. Frontier, for most of the world's people, does not suggest growth, expanse, or opportunity.

29 For Americans, it does, and always has. This is one of the things that sets America apart from other places and makes American attitudes different from those of other people. It is why, from *Bonanza* to the Sierra Club, the notion or even the fantasy of empty horizons and untapped resources has always evoked in the American heart both passion and wistfulness. And it is why the fear that the economic frontier—our last, best version of the Wild West—may finally be passing creates in us not only money worries but also a crisis of morale and even of purpose.

Three

30 It might seem strange to call the 1980s an era of nostalgia. The decade, after all, has been more usually described in terms of coolness, pragmatism, and a blithe innocence of history. But the eighties, unawares, were nostalgic for frontiers; and the disappointment of that nostalgia had much to do with the time's greed, narrowness, and strange want of joy. The fear that the world may not be a big enough playground for the full exercise of one's energies and yearnings, and worse, the fear that the playground is being fenced off and will no longer expand—these are real worries and they have had consequences. The eighties were an object lesson in how people play the game when there is an awful and unspoken suspicion that the game is winding down.

It was ironic that the yuppies came to be so reviled for their vaunting ambition and outsized expectations, as if they'd invented the habit of
31 more, when in fact they'd only inherited it the way a fetus picks up an addiction in the womb. The craving was there in the national bloodstream, a remnant of the frontier, and the baby boomers, described in childhood as "the luckiest generation," found themselves, as young adults, in the melancholy position of wrestling with a two-hundred-year dependency on a drug that was now in short supply.

True, the 1980s raised the clamor for more to new heights of shrillness, insistence, and general obnoxiousness, but this, it can be argued,
32 was in the nature of a final binge, the storm before the calm. America, though fighting the perception every inch of the way, was coming to realize that it was not a preordained part of the natural order that one should be richer every year. If it happened, that was nice. But who had started the flimsy and pernicious rumor that it was normal?

»«

Thinking about the Argument

1. How does the opening description of a frontier town serve to hook the reader? What does this idea have to do with the essay's major claim?
2. In paragraphs 7 and 8, what two forces does Shames identify as the drivers of the American economy? Do you think these forces still apply today? Why or why not?
3. Do you believe, as the author contends, that "we are running out of more?" Why or why not?
4. What does the author say (in the late 1980s) was happening to personal wealth? Do you think this trend is continuing today?
5. Shames says that the word *frontier* has a different meaning in America (and Australia) than it has in other parts of the world. What is that difference?
6. Do you agree? Explain.

Responding to the Argument

1. Can you think of another historical boom that is similar, in some ways, to the expansion of the West? How, for example, are various real estate booms and the technology/Internet boom of the 1990s similar to, or different from, the boom of western speculators?
2. Do you expect to do better than your parents, or not as well? Do you expect to carry more or less debt than your parents? Why or why not?
3. In what way has "a sense of quality . . . lagged behind a sense of scale"? How has the "ethic of decency . . . been upstaged by the ethic of success"? In other words, is it more important to be rich (and to do better than one's parents and/or neighbors) than it is to be happy? Explain.
4. In what way might American culture encourage people to strive to obtain more than their parents? How much "stuff" do you think you need? Can money, in fact, be the root of happiness? Explain.

Writing about the Argument

1. Define *American dream* and *manifest destiny.* Look up these terms if you need to. What is your version of the American dream? How do you plan to obtain it? In what way do you think that it will make you happy? Write an essay arguing whether or not the American dream is a good ideal for people to pursue.
2. In what way is the American economy like an "endlessly fertile continent whose boundaries never need to be reached, a domain that could expand in perpetuity"? Use this quotation as the basis of an argument of your choosing.
3. In your journal, write about something that you wanted for a long time and finally obtained after much waiting. Were you as happy when you obtained this object as you thought you would be when you desired it? Why or why not?
4. Write an argument discussing either the causes or the effects of greed.
5. Write an essay considering to what extent greed should be considered good.

"Shop 'til We Drop?"

ABOUT THE AUTHOR: ROBERT J. SAMUELSON

A graduate of Harvard University with a bachelor's degree in government, Robert J. Samuelson has served as chief of *Newsweek*'s Washington bureau and has written a column for the *Washington Post* since 1977. His biweekly columns comment on economic issues. His books include *The Good Life and Its Discontents* (1995) and *Untruth: Why the Conventional Wisdom Is (Almost Always) Wrong* (2001). His journalism has won many honors, including the Clarion Award, the National Magazine Award, and the Loeb Award. This essay was originally published in *Wilson Quarterly* in 2004.

BEFORE YOU READ

1. Define *consumerism* in your own words. Is it a good thing or a bad thing? Explain.
2. What do you expect Samuelson's opinion on this topic to be? Why do you think this?
3. What does the title of the article imply? Explain.
4. What do you expect the article to be about? What kind of audience might be receptive to it? What kind of audience might be skeptical about it? Be as specific as you can in your answer.

Shop 'til We Drop?

1 We shop, therefore we are. This is not exactly the American credo, but it comes close to being the American pastime. Even infants and toddlers quickly absorb the consumer spirit through television and trips to the supermarket ("I want *that*" is a common refrain). As we age, consumption becomes an engine of envy, because in America the idea is that everyone should have everything—which means that hardly anyone ever has enough. The notion that wants and needs have reached a limit of material and environmental absurdity, though preached fervently by some social activists and intellectuals, barely influences ordinary Americans. They continue to flock to shopping malls, automobile dealers, cruise ships, and health clubs. There are always, it seems, new wants and needs to be satisfied.

2 Although consumerism now defines all wealthy societies, it's still practiced most religiously in its country of origin. Indeed, Americans have rarely so indulged the urge to splurge as in the past decade. Look at the numbers. In 2002, consumer spending accounted for 70 percent of U.S. national income (gross domestic product), which is a modern American record, and a much higher figure than in any other advanced nation. In Japan and France, consumer spending in 2002 was only 55 percent of GDP; in Italy and Spain, it was 60 percent. These rates are typical elsewhere. Even in the United States, consumer spending was only 67 percent of GDP as recently as 1994. Three added percentage points of GDP may seem trivial, but in today's dollars they amount to an extra \$325 billion annually.

3 This spending spree has, in some ways, been a godsend. Without it, the U.S. and world economies would recently have fared much worse. During the 1997–1998 Asian financial crisis, the irrepressible buying of American consumers cushioned the shock to countries that, suddenly unable to borrow abroad, had to curb

their domestic spending. Roughly half of U.S. imports consist of consumer goods, automobiles, and food (oil, other raw materials, and industrial goods make up the balance). By selling Americans more shoes, toys, clothes, and electronic gadgets, Asian countries partially contained higher unemployment. U.S. trade deficits exploded. From 1996 to 2000, the deficit of the current account (a broad measure of trade) grew from $177 billion to $411 billion.

4 Later, the buying binge sustained the U.S. economy despite an onslaught of bad news that, by all logic, should have been devastating: the popping of the stock market "bubble" of the 1990s; rising unemployment (as dot-com firms went bankrupt and business investment—led by telecommunications spending—declined); 9/11; and a string of corporate scandals (Enron, WorldCom, Tyco). But American consumers barely paused, and responded to falling interest rates by prolonging their binge. Car and light-truck sales of 17.1 million units in 2001 gave the automobile industry its second-best year ever, after 2000. The fourth- and fifth-best years were 2002 (16.8 million units) and 2003 (an estimated 16.6 million units). Strong home sales buoyed appliance, furniture, and carpet production.

5 To some extent, the consumption boom is old hat. Acquisitiveness is deeply embedded in American culture. Describing the United States in the 1830s, Alexis de Tocqueville marveled over the wide-spread "taste for physical gratification." Still, the ferocity of the latest consumption outburst poses some interesting questions: Why do Americans spend so much more of their incomes than other peoples? How can we afford to do that? After all, economic theory holds that societies become wealthier only by sacrificing some present consumption to invest in the future. And if we aren't saving enough, can the consumer boom continue?

6 Let's start with why Americans spend so much. One reason is that our political and cultural traditions differ from those of other nations. We do some things in the private market that other societies do through government. Health care, education, and social welfare are good examples. Most middle-class Americans under 65 pay for their own health care, either directly or through employer-provided health insurance (which reduces their take-home pay). That counts as private consumption. In countries with government-run health care systems, similar medical costs are classified as government spending. The same thing is true of education. Although U.S. public schools involve government spending, college tuition (or tuition for private school or pre-school) counts as personal consumption. Abroad, governments often pay more of total educational costs.

7 It's also true that the United States saves and invests less than other nations—investment here meaning money that, though initially channeled into stocks, bonds, or bank deposits, ultimately goes into new factories, machinery, computers, and office buildings. Low U.S. saving and investment rates have often inspired alarm about America's future. In 1990, for instance, Japan's national savings rate was 34 percent of GDP, more than double the U.S. rate of 16 percent. By out-investing us, Japan (it was said) would become the world's wealthiest nation. That hasn't happened, in part because what matters is not only how much countries invest but how well they invest it. And Americans generally are better investors than others.

8 Of course, there's waste. The hundreds of billions of dollars invested in unneeded dot-com and telecom networks in the late 1990s are simply the latest reminder of that. But the American business system corrects its blunders fairly quickly. If projects don't show signs of becoming profitable, they usually don't get more capital. Wall Street's obsession with profits—though sometimes deplored as discouraging long-term investment—compels companies to cut costs and improve productivity. If bankrupt firms (Kmart and United Airlines are recent examples) can't

improve efficiency, their assets (stores, planes) are sold to others who hope to do better. American banks, unlike Japanese banks, don't rescue floundering companies; neither (usually) does the government, unlike governments in Europe. Getting more bang from our investment buck, we can afford to invest less and consume more.

9 Our privileged position in the world economy reinforces the effect. Since the 1970s, we've run trade deficits that have allowed us to have our cake and eat it too: All those imports permit adequate investment rates without crimping consumption. We send others dollars; they send us cars, clothes, and computer chips. It's a good deal as long as we're near full employment (when we're not, high imports add to unemployment). The trade gap—now about five percent of GDP—persists in part because the dollar serves as the major global currency. Foreigners—companies and individuals—want dollars so they can conduct trade and make international investments. Some governments hoard dollars because they'd rather export than import. The strong demand for dollars props up the exchange rate, making our imports less expensive and our exports more expensive. Continuous trade deficits result.

10 All this suggests that the consumer boom could go on forever, because Americans always feel the need to outdo the Joneses—or at least to stay even with them. No level of consumption ever suffices, because the social competition is constant. The surge in prosperity after World War II briefly fostered the illusion that the competition was ebbing because so many things that had once been restricted (homes, cars, televisions) became so widely available. "If everyone could enjoy the good things of life—as defined by mass merchandisers—the meanness of class distinctions would disappear," Vance Packard wrote in his 1959 classic *The Status Seekers*. Instead, he found, Americans had developed new distinctions, including bigger homes and flashier clothes.

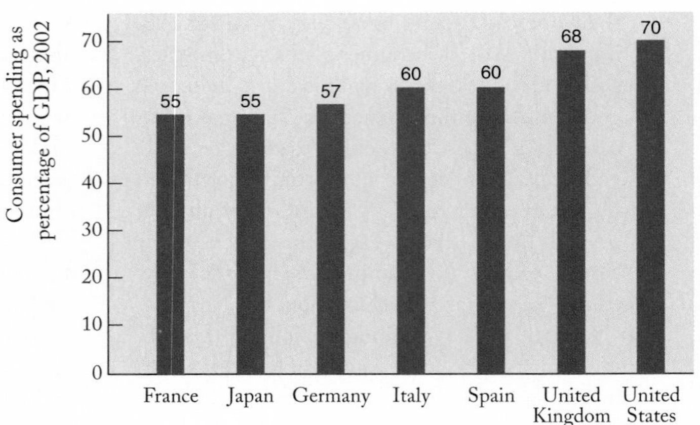

Big spenders: Consumer spending as a percentage of gross domestic product, 2002
Source: Organization for Economic Cooperation and Development.

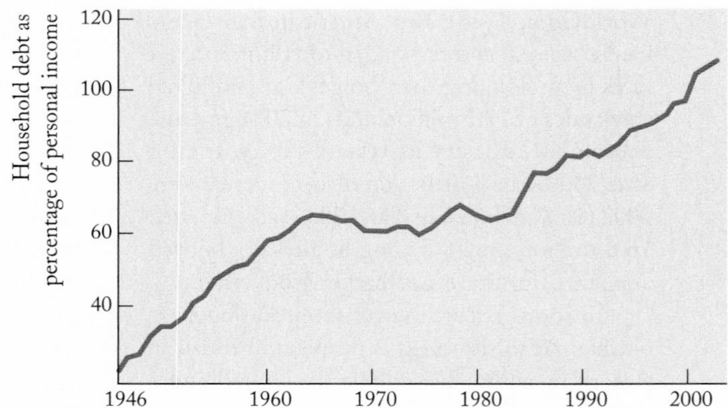

A mountain of debt: Household debt as a percentage of personal income, 1946–2002
Source: Federal Reserve Board (data for fourth quarter of each year).

In 2002, Americans held nearly $9 trillion in household debt: $6 trillion in home mortgages; $2 trillion in consumer debt (e.g., credit card and car loans); and $1 trillion in other debt.

11 Four decades later, little has changed. Americans constantly pursue new markers of success and status. In 2002, the median size of a new home was 20 percent larger than in 1987, even though families had gotten smaller. Luxury car

Where the Consumer Dollar Goes

	1959	*2000*
Durable goods	**13.4%**	**12.1%**
Motor vehicles	5.9	5.0
Furniture and household equipment (including computers)	5.7	4.6
Other (including books, sporting equipment)	1.8	2.5
Nondurable goods	**46.7%**	**29.7%**
Food	25.4	14.1
Clothing and shoes	8.3	4.9
Energy (including gasoline)	4.8	2.7
Other (including drugs, tobacco products, toys)	8.2	8.1
Services	**39.9%**	**58.1%**
Housing	14.2	14.2
Household operation (utilities and maintenance)	5.9	5.7
Transportation (including car maintenance and repair, mass transit, airlines)	3.3	4.0
Health care	5.2	14.8
Recreation (including sports events, movies, cable TV, Internet services, video rentals)	2.0	3.9
Other (including financial services, personal care, higher education and private schools, legal services)	9.3	15.6

Source: Bureau of Economic Analysis, U.S. Department of Commerce.

sales have soared. According to the marketing research firm of J. D. Power and Associates, in 1980 luxury brands—mainly Cadillacs and Lincolns, along with some Mercedes—accounted for only 4.5 percent of new-vehicle sales. By 2003, luxury brands—a category that now includes Lexus, Infinity, and Acura, along with Hummers and more BMWs and Mercedes—exceeded 10 percent of sales. Second homes are another way that people separate themselves from the crowd. Perhaps 100,000 to 125,000 such homes are built annually, says economist Gopal Ahluwalia of the National Association of Homebuilders. In the 1990s, comparable figures were between 75,000 and 100,000.

12 To critics, this "consumption treadmill" is self-defeating, as Cornell University economist Robert H. Frank put it in his 1999 book *Luxury Fever: Money and Happiness in an Era of Excess.* People compete to demonstrate their superiority, but most are frustrated because others continually catch up. Meanwhile, over-consumption—homes that are too big, cars that are too glitzy—actually detracts from people's happiness and society's well-being, Frank argued. Striving to maximize their incomes, workers sacrifice time with family and friends—time that, according to surveys, they would prize highly. And society's reluctance to take money out of consumers' pockets through taxation means too little is spent to solve collective problems such as poverty and pollution.

13 As a cure, Frank proposed a progressive consumption tax. People would be taxed only on what they spent, at rates rising to 70 percent above $500,000. Savings (put, for example, into

stocks, bonds, and bank deposits) would be exempt. The tax would deter extravagant spending and encourage saving, Frank contended. Total consumption spending would be lower, government spending could be higher, and the competition for status would simply occur at lower levels of foolishness. The "erstwhile Ferrari driver . . . might turn instead to [a] Porsche," he wrote. Whatever their merits, proposals such as this lack political support. Indeed, they do not differ dramatically—except for high tax rates—from the present income tax, which allows generous deductions for savings, through vehicles such as 401(k) plans and individual retirement accounts.

14 Still, America's consumption boom could falter, because it faces three powerful threats: debt, demographics, and the dollar.

15 Over six decades, we've gone from being a society uneasy with credit to a society that rejoices in it. In 1946, household debt was 22 percent of personal disposable income. Now, it's roughly 110 percent. Both business and government have promoted more debt. In 1950, Diners Club introduced the modern credit card, which could be used at multiple restaurants and stores. (Some department stores and oil companies were already offering cards restricted to their outlets.) New laws—the Fair Housing Act of 1968, the Equal Credit Opportunity Act of 1974—prohibited discriminatory lending. One result was the invention of credit-scoring formulas that evaluate potential borrowers on their past payment of bills, thereby reducing bias against women, the poor, and minorities. Similarly, the federal government encourages home mortgages through Fannie Mae and Freddie Mac, government-created companies that buy mortgages.

16 This "democratization of credit" has enabled consumer spending to grow slightly faster than consumer income. People simply borrow more. Economist Thomas Durkin of the Federal Reserve notes the following: In 1951, 20 percent of U.S. households had a mortgage, compared with 44 percent in 2001; in 1970, only 16 percent of households had a bank credit card, compared with 73 percent in 2001. The trouble is that this accumulation of debt can't continue forever. Sooner or later, Americans will decide that they've got as much as they can handle. Or lenders will discover that they've exhausted good and even mediocre credit risks. No one knows when that will happen, but once it occurs, consumer spending may rise only as fast as consumer income—and slower still if borrowers collectively repay debts.

17 What could hasten the turning point is the baby boom. We're now on the edge of a momentous generational shift. The oldest baby boomers (born in 1946) will be 58 in 2004; the youngest (born in 1964) will be 40. For most Americans, peak spending occurs between the ages of 35 and 54, when household consumption is about 20 percent above average, according to Susan Sterne, an economist with Economic Analysis Associates. Then it gradually declines. People don't buy new sofas or refrigerators. They pay off debts. For 15 years or so, the economy has benefited from baby boomers' feverish buying. It may soon begin to suffer from their decreased spending.

18 Finally, there's the dollar. Should foreign demand for U.S. investments wane—or should American politicians, worried about jobs, press other countries to stop accumulating U.S. Treasury securities—the dollar would decline on foreign exchange markets. There would simply be less demand, as foreigners sold dollars for other currencies. Then our imports could become more expensive while our exports could become cheaper. Domestic supplies might tighten. Price pressures on consumer goods—cars, electronics, clothes—could intensify. This might cause Americans to buy a little less. But if they continued buying as before, the long-heralded collision between consumption and investment might materialize. (As this article goes to press,

the dollar has dropped from its recent highs. The ultimate effects remain to be seen.)

19 Little is preordained. Sterne thinks retired baby boomers may defy history and become spendthrifts. "They don't care about leaving anything to their kids," she says. "There's no reluctance to go into debt." Their chosen instrument would be the "reverse mortgage," which unlocks home equity. (Under a reverse mortgage, a homeowner receives a payment from the lender up to some percentage of the home's value; upon the owner's death, the loan is repaid, usually through sale of the house.) Maybe. But maybe the post–World War II consumption boom has reached its peak. If the retreat occurs gently, the consequences, at least on paper, should be painless and imperceptible. We'll spend a little less of our incomes and save a little more. We'll import a little less and export a little more. These modest changes shouldn't hurt, but they might. The U.S. and world economies have grown so accustomed to being stimulated by the ravenous appetite of ordinary Americans that you can't help but wonder what will happen if that appetite disappears.

Thinking about the Argument

1. In what way does the first sentence of the article relate to the major claim, if at all? Explain.
2. Now that you have read the essay, revise your definition of *consumerism*. How does your new definition differ from the old one, and why?
3. According to the author, in what ways is spending good for the economy?
4. Is Samuelson's view of American consumerism more or less optimistic than that painted by Shames? Provide examples from each essay to substantiate your claim.
5. What is his overall outlook regarding the retirement of baby boomers and what this means for the future of the U. S. economy?

Responding to the Argument

1. What is wrong with having "new wants and needs to be satisfied"? Explain.
2. Consider the following statements and note your reaction, whether or not it is in the form of a refutation. Support your claim with evidence.
   a. "The notion that wants and needs have reached a limit of material and environmental absurdity . . . barely influences ordinary Americans."
   b. "Acquisitiveness is deeply embedded in American culture."
   c. "Meanwhile, over-consumption—homes that are too big, cars that are too glitzy—actually detracts from people's happiness and society's well-being."
3. Do you believe that parents should be responsible enough to save something to pass on to their children, or should they spend what they earn in order to enjoy their own lives? Why or why not?
4. Do you believe that the future of the consumer economy will continue to operate on a balance of earning and spending, or will it falter in some way? Why do you think this?

WRITING ABOUT THE ARGUMENT

1. Make a chart, and then write a synthesis of the views expressed by Shames and Samuelson. In what ways are they similar and different?
2. Write an essay arguing whether or not consumerism is "good." In what ways is it "good" for individuals? For corporations? For the country as a whole?
3. Write a letter to your children. (If you are not planning to have children, pretend that you will.) In this letter, explain to them whether or not you plan to save in order to leave them with a substantial inheritance, or spend it on your own pleasure. Argue the ethics of the situation, regardless of your choice.

"Admit It: You, Too, Are Paris Hilton"

ABOUT THE AUTHOR: GEOFFREY COLVIN

Geoffrey Colvin is a longtime editor and columnist for *Fortune* magazine and co-anchors *Wall Street Week with FORTUNE* on PBS television. He also is heard daily on the CBS radio network. He has a B.A. in economics from Harvard University and an M.B.A. from New York University's Stern School. He is an authority on business leadership, management, and the global marketplace. This essay was first published in *Fortune* magazine in December 2003.

BEFORE YOU READ

1. What is your opinion of Paris Hilton? Does she evoke in you disgust? Admiration? Envy? Desire? Why?
2. What part of you might be similar to Paris Hilton? Explain. Back your claim with evidence.
3. Do you think Colvin is qualified to offer an opinion on this topic? Why or why not?
4. What does the title indicate about the article's major claim? Explain.

Admit It: You, Too, Are Paris Hilton

1 A mob of shoppers rushing for a sale on DVD players trampled the first woman in line and knocked her unconscious on Friday as they scrambled for the shelves at a Wal-Mart Supercenter.

2 The woman, Patricia VanLester, had her eye on a $29 DVD player, but when the siren blared at 6 A.M. announcing the start of the post-Thanksgiving sale, VanLester, forty one, was knocked to the ground by the frenzy of shoppers behind her. . . .

3 [The woman's sister] said that some shoppers tried to help VanLester and that one employee helped her reach her sister. But most people just continued their rush for the deals, she said.

4 "All they cared about was a stupid DVD player," she said.

5 Maybe you remember Stanford biologist Paul Ehrlich's famous V prediction in the late

1960s that by now America would be so near starvation that we'd have food riots. The reality is exactly the opposite. We have shopping riots. Instead of panicking as the ultimate necessity of life grows so expensive that no one can afford it, Americans flip out because a product absolutely no one needs is available at a price so low that even a year ago no one would have believed it possible. Food, if anyone still cares, takes a lower proportion of our income than ever before.

6 By odd coincidence, just as the season of peak acquisitive madness grips the nation, we're being treated to a glut of TV programs about some of America's most revoltingly excessive consumers, our hyperwealthy kids. *Rich Girls* (MTV) follows a couple of heiresses who embark on buying orgies with the immortal cry "Let's do some damage." In *Born Rich* (HBO), we meet twenty-one-year-olds who know they need never work a day in their life, and we learn of the wrenching conflicts they face, such as what one girl might have done with the $800 that she dropped in a bar the other night ("I could have bought a dress!"). *The Simple Life* (Fox) places Paris Hilton (hotel money) and Nicole Richie (daughter of former pop star Lionel Richie) in a tiny Arkansas town so that we can marvel at their cluelessness about real life; Richie, for example, had never pumped gas "because my guard usually does that."

7 What's your reaction? Laughing? Loathing? Fine—but be careful. Because the truth is, if average Americans of even thirty to forty years ago could see us today, they'd think we were all spoiled just as rotten as any young Trump, Newhouse, or Bloomberg.

8 You know it's true. How many televisions do you have? Do you even know? How many channels do you get? Do your kids refuse to watch black-and-white programs? No one had a VCR in 1970. Now 240 million of us do, but VCRs are history now that Wal-Mart is selling DVD players for $29.

9 If anyone had told you in 1980 that today you'd use a cellphone the size of a cigarette pack to call someone else's cellphone in Sao Paulo—and would complain about the connection—would you have believed him?

10 How big is your house? The average new house is 34 percent bigger than it was in 1970. Yet despite that supersizing, more people own their homes today than ever in our history.

11 No, I'm not overlooking the poor, especially at this time of year. They are indeed always with us, but not the way they used to be. Some 21 percent of U.S. families were poor in 1960, while in 2001, the latest year for which figures are available, just 10 percent were. And those official statistics exclude the value of noncash government benefits like food stamps and Medicaid, which didn't exist in 1960. That's why some economists estimate that today's real poverty rate is much less than officially reported, maybe only half.

12 Malnutrition was still a major concern in the 1960s. Today's crisis is very different—obesity. That's a problem of national excess on an unprecedented scale.

13 The consumer culture has achieved total victory. We spend more and save less than ever before. We are richer, fatter, and more obsessed by consumption than any people have ever been.

14 So let's enjoy gawking at the rich kids on television. It really is fun. But let's also confront the new reality: With precious few exceptions (and home videos aside), we are all Paris Hilton.

THINKING ABOUT THE ARGUMENT

1. Read the opening narrative. What is your emotional reaction to this event? How does this incident relate to the article's title?
2. The author compares Americans fighting over commodities to starving people fighting over food. Is this a legitimate analogy? What is implied by it?
3. Does the author think there is anything wrong with the culture of consumption? How can you tell?
4. How does the author use tone to indicate what he is trying to say indirectly? Can you put this idea into your own words?

RESPONDING TO THE ARGUMENT

1. Think of a situation reported in the media involving people fighting over discounted goods. (For example, there was an incident at a Wal-Mart during the 2005 Holiday season that involved two men fighting over a $400 laptop computer.) What do you think of such incidents? Are certain goods, if appropriately priced, worth fighting for?
2. In what ways are we becoming like Paris Hilton? Explain.
3. Is the culture of consumerism—making more money and spending it on more and more stuff—ultimately good or bad for society? Explain.
4. What role do icons like Paris Hilton play in encouraging people to spend more of what they earn?

WRITING ABOUT THE ARGUMENT

1. Think of a figure in popular culture who has encouraged you to spend money. (For example, when you were a child, did Mickey Mouse or other Disney characters cause you to encourage your parents to take you to Disneyland? Do you wear certain clothes because a particular person looks good wearing them?) In a journal entry, explain why you have done this and in what way it made you feel good.
2. Make two lists — one list of your wants and one list of your needs. Discuss the lists with a group of friends. Could you move some things from one column to the other? If so, why? Write a journal entry or essay explaining the difference between your particular wants and needs.
3. Think of a particular want you have as a consumer (the bigger the better). What has caused you to have this desire? Think of a time that you obtained something you wanted for a long time. Was having the object as satisfying as you thought it would be, or did you feel let down after a short time? Did obtaining this object lead to a new want? Write an essay arguing a causal point related to this topic. Consider whether a cycle is involved: want goods → obtain goods → want new goods.
4. Is Paris Hilton a good role model? Why or why not? Write an argument discussing a figure in popular culture that is a good or bad role model, and why.

READING SELECTION

"Globilization: Now the Good News"

ABOUT THE AUTHOR: CHARLES LEADBEATER

Charles Leadbeater writes extensively on finance, management, entrepreneurship, and economics. He spent ten years working at the *Financial Times* and has advised a variety of businesses and government agencies. His writings are influential and reportedly have affected the policies of British prime minister Tony Blair. In 2002, *GQ* magazine listed him as one of the most powerful men in England. His books include *Living on Thin Air: The New Economy* (2000) and *Up the Down Escalator: Why the Global Pessimists are Wrong* (2002). This selection was originally published in the July 1, 2002, issue of *New Statesman.*

BEFORE YOU READ

1. Do you think the world is generally getting better or worse? Why do you think this?
2. Do you think Leadbeater is qualified to offer an opinion on this topic? Why or why not?
3. Who do you think Leadbeater's target audience might be? How might it differ from the audiences of the other writers in this section?
4. What does the title indicate about the article's argument? What is your initial reaction to the title and possible argument?

Globilization: Now the Good News

1 Across the political spectrum, from communitarians to social conservatives, and from New Age ecologists to religious moralisers, politics increasingly articulates a fear that society is degenerating into a global dystopia. Everything is falling apart. Nothing can be relied upon. We are being overrun and undermined by foreign and unfamiliar influences. The moral and cultural core of our society is being eaten away from within. Individualism, hedonism, fashion, and cosmopolitanism are spreading a moral contagion that has overrun society's badly weakened immune system.

2 The appeal of dystopia is not confined to politics. Much of the work of young British artists such as Damien Hirst concerns decay, death, and decline. Steven Spielberg's film *The Minority Report* portrays a future in which people are controlled by genetic manipulation. A recent BBC docudrama, *Fields of Gold* coauthored by Alan Rusbridger, editor of the *Guardian* painted an alarmist picture of the risks posed by genetically modified foods.

3 The apostles of degeneration have different values and ambitions. But their account of what is wrong with the world shares a code. Modern society is enacting a collective death wish: its lust for freedom, pleasure, innovation, and democracy has unleashed a process of inner decay. The sources of modern society's greatest vitality—innovation, choice, globalization—also threaten to kill it.

4 For environmentalists and many opponents of capitalism, the killer is our consumer culture. For communitarians of left and right, it is individualism, which unravels families, communities, and neighbors. For cultural and social conservatives, it the urge to innovate, which threatens history and tradition.

5 Ours is not the first era in which accelerated social and economic change has prompted extreme fears of degeneration. We think now of the late nineteenth century as an age of reform, progress, and utopian hope, and of remorseless technological triumph, as one spectacular discovery followed another. Yet that era also bred theories of decline and regression, the most powerful of which was Max Nordau's *Degeneration,* a runaway European bestseller after it was published in German in 1892.

6 Nordau painted a picture of a society mentally and morally fatigued by the incessant pace of change. The force of innovation produced grotesque side effects, such as increased crime and declining morals.

7 "We stand," wrote Nordau, "in the midst of a severe mental epidemic, a sort of Black Death of degeneration and hysteria." As society became more complex, so it became more difficult to maintain a sense of order. "Whoever looks upon civilization as a good, having value and deserving to be defended, must mercilessly crush under his thumb the anti-social vermin, ie, the degenerates." Only a few decades later, this kind of thinking would license genocide and war.

8 That is why we should worry about the prominent role that fear of degeneration plays in so many accounts of globalization. One might expect it from the religious right, but chronic pessimism is just as influential on the left.

9 For example, the communitarian David Myers, in *American Paradox: Spiritual Hunger in an Age of Plenty,* argues that the United States went through a steep social and emotional recession in the 1990s even as its economy boomed. Since the 1960s, Myers points out, the divorce rate has doubled, teen suicide trebled, violent crime quadrupled, the prison population quintupled, babies born out of wedlock sextupled, and cohabitation, a predictor of divorce, has risen sevenfold. Rich Western society is being eaten away from within by individualism and moral relativism, which undermine civic engagement and social responsibility.

10 From the new left, Morris Berman argues in *The Twilight of American Culture* that American civilization, far from being vital and confident after capitalism's triumph over communism, is in a twilight phase, rapidly approaching the point of social and cultural bankruptcy. The nation's spiritual life has been all but extinguished by corporate marketing.

11 It is striking how much this critique of modern society shares with those by conservatives. Thus the philosopher Roger Scruton, in *England: An Elegy,* laments (to caricature him only slightly) a degenerate England where ladies no longer cycle to church on Sunday past a friendly village pub close to a village green where white-flaneled men play cricket. Today, louts would knock the ladies off their cycles, tacky executive homes will have replaced the cricket field, the church will have been turned into yuppy flats, and the pub will be offering Thai food.

12 These anti-globalizers and rabid nationalists, melancholic aristocrats and impassioned environmentalists, social conservatives, and liberal intellectuals, now form an alliance of pessimism with extraordinary reach. The pessimists of the left associate globalization with unchecked corporate power and growing inequality; the pessimists of the right associate it with foreign influences that threaten cherished traditions, customs, and practices. Both see Globalization as a standardizing, commercializing force that stifles diversity and dissent: as they see it, the market, far from providing greater choice, is an agent for cultural cleansing. Both want to go back to basics, to apply the brakes, and get away from fashion, celebrity, and novelty. Both view the world in stark, apocalyptic terms, leaving little room for adaptation and complexity, let alone shades of gray. Both contrast the unique destruction wrought by modern global capitalism with an unsullied past where, we are asked to believe, communities were always organic, families always nuclear, and politicians always noble.

13 Like the super-optimists, the super-pessimists wish to parcel history into neat per-

iods. Where one side announces new beginnings and fresh starts, the other announces final endings and lost ways of life. History is rarely that neat.

14 The danger is that the chronic pessimism becomes a self-fulfilling prophecy. If we insist that we are in the midst of irreversible degeneration, we feed the sense of helplessness that encourages people either to withdraw from civic engagement or to support violent, confrontational movements.

15 Yet this ought to be an age of excitement and optimism. Consider, first, the breathtaking possibilities of technology. By 2007, the hard disk in the average television settop box should have enough memory to store all the songs ever recorded. By 2010, it should be able to take every film. Telecommunications bandwidth is doubling every twelve months. The capacity of fiber to transmit information has increased by a factor of 16,000 in less than five years; it will soon carry everything we can say, write, compose, play, record, film, draw, paint, or design. The entire contents of the U.S. Library of Congress could be passed through an optical switch in less than three seconds.

16 This still emerging global web of communications and computing could indeed bring more surveillance, cacophony, and crime. But ours is a world where half the population is yet to make a telephone call. New global communications will help scientists to collaborate, protesters to campaign, students to learn, writers to publish, and myriad groups to share, trade, swap, and gossip. Nor is this pace of innovation confined to information technology. Medicine, for example, will benefit from our capacity to analyze human genes. Within the next decade, cars with highly efficient, methane-based fuel will emerge: they will generate electricity using hydrogen and oxygen, leaving water as the main by-product, and allowing us to relinquish the polluting internal combustion engine.

17 Consider, second, the opportunities for us to lead fuller lives. While digital technologies allow us to hang on to the films and music of our youth, genetic technologies will allow us to act as if we are forty even when we are seventy. In the past fifty years, life expectancy in the United Kingdom has risen by two years every decade. In the nineteenth century it was about forty years; now, it is seventy-five for men and more than eighty for women.

18 This benefit is spreading to the developing world to a far greater extent and far more quickly than the pessimists would have you believe. People in the developing countries now live longer than people in rich economies did a century ago. In 1900, average life expectancy in the developing countries was thirty years; now it is about sixty-five.

19 Nine out of every ten people in the developing countries can expect to live beyond the age of sixty, against just six out of ten in 1960. Affordable food, antibiotics, vaccines, clean water, electricity, and education will all contribute to the continuation of that trend.

20 In the twentieth century the extension of average life expectancy at birth was due mainly to a dramatic decline in infant mortality. In the next century, it will be because science can delay the onset of aging, giving people perhaps thirty or forty years of health and fitness in which they can pursue leisure or second careers, as they choose, free from direct child-rearing responsibilities. The problems for health, pensions, and employment policies should not be allowed to obscure the blessings.

21 Consider, third, how globalization is likely to become a more open and legitimate process. Critics may argue that it is creating a homogenized, Americanized culture. Yet it is increasingly the distinctive national or local products—Australian wine, Scottish whisky, Indian curry, or Japanese sushi—that are spread by the global markets. The pessimists see the masses as hapless dupes who can be reprogrammed by advertising. But watching American television programs does not make you American, any more than watching *ER* makes you a doctor.

22 The main case against globalization is that most people in the world live in abject poverty, if not outright misery, by Western standards. And it is true that the poorest 20 percent of the world's population accounts for just 1.3 percent of its spending; that perhaps a billion people do not have secure access to clean drinking water and 2.4 billion to adequate sanitation; that a quarter of a billion children are forced to work, most of them in agriculture, and that another 100 million subsist on the streets; that an estimated 1.3 billion people breathe deeply polluted air, mainly in the enormous cities of the developing world.

23 Yet think of some other figures. In 1820, about 900 million people, about 85 percent of the world's population, lived on $1 a day (by today's prices), the figure usually taken to represent absolute poverty. Now, the proportion of the world living at that level is only 20 percent. Despite the fast-growing world population, even the numbers have fallen since 1980, from 1.4 billion to 1.2 billion.

24 That is still a huge and morally unacceptable number, but it is arguable that the late twentieth century—the era of globalization—saw a more dramatic reduction in world poverty than any other time in history. In India alone, about 100 million people have been taken out of poverty in the pass twenty years. Again, agricultural food production, in part driven by technology, has dramatically reduced the regular incidence of hunger.

25 According to the U.N. Food and Agriculture Organisation, 37 percent of the population of the developing countries (960 million people) were malnourished in 1970; by 1996, that proportion was down to 18 percent (790 million). Global food production has doubled in the past half-century and in the developing world it has trebled. The developing countries are producing 49 percent more grain per capita than they were forty years ago, in large part because agriculture has been made more efficient. We are feeding vastly more people from the same amount of land. About 25 percent of the world's rural population are still without pure water; but a decade ago, the figure was closer to 90 percent.

26 None of this makes it acceptable that so many millions live in abject conditions. But it has been the period of globalization—during which developing countries have had access to trade and technology, and to investment in education and infrastructure—that has seen these improvements.

27 The problem is not that globalization makes developing countries poor; rather, it is that the global economy excludes too many countries from participating in ways that would deliver considerable benefits to them.

28 Perhaps the great cause for optimism is that global markets, and even more the global webs of communication, are encouraging an intense debate about the possibilities of global citizenship and governance.

29 There is an emerging recognition among national governments that they share common problems that often can only be addressed cooperatively: terrorism, crime, environmental pollution, rules for trade, investment, and debt relief. The war crimes tribunal in The Hague is exploring the scope for global notions of justice.

30 Global governance, although ramshackle, is slowly being shaped and developed to reduce poverty, promote democracy, and extend basic common rights such as freedom of speech. For globalization to be seen as legitimate, world poverty has to be reduced further, and dramatically; corporations will have to acknowledge their wider social responsibilities, for health, education, and the environment, as part of the economic development from which they benefit; international institutions will have to give greater voice to poorer developing nations; those nations will need investment so that they can better take advantage of international trade; markets in the North will have to be further opened to exporters from the South.

31 Instead of joining the global pessimists in predicting apocalypse, we should press for these changes. If they can be achieved, there is every reason to expect that the world will improve at least as much in the next fifty years as it has in the past fifty.

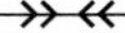

Thinking about the Argument

1. Read the first three paragraphs. What problem is Leadbeater addressing?
2. What did you already know that was confirmed by the reading?
3. Why does the author think that pessimism about globalization is "a self-fulfilling prophesy"?
4. The author states that "this ought to be an age of excitement and optimism." What supporting evidence and explanations does he provide? Do you agree? Why or why not?
5. Why does the author think that globalization is good for people worldwide? Do you agree or disagree? Why?

Responding to the Argument

1. State why you agree or disagree with the following sentence: "Modern society is enacting a collective death wish: its lust for freedom, pleasure, innovation and democracy has unleashed a process of inner decay." Provide support to substantiate your claim.
2. How are globalization and consumerism connected? Provide examples to substantiate your answer.
3. Name two ways that consumerism and globalization can be good for the poor. State two ways in which consumerism and globalization can be bad for the poor. Is there a difference in the way consumerism can be "good" or "bad" in Western-style countries as opposed to third world countries? Explain.

Writing about the Argument

1. Is "everything falling apart" globally? Write a brief essay or journal entry arguing this point.
2. Write an essay arguing whether or not consumerism will benefit the poor. You may limit your choice to a particular country. Conduct research as needed.
3. Write a refutation of Leadbeater's article. Consider each of his main points, and refute them in turn. Draw evidence as needed from other articles in this section or from research.
4. Write a synthesis comparing Leadbeater's view to one that strongly contrasts with his.

"Hungry for More: Reengaging Religious Teachings on Consumption"

ABOUT THE AUTHOR: GARY GARDNER

Gary Gardner directs the research staff at World Watch Institute, which provides "independent research for an environmentally sustainable and socially just society." His writings include *Beyond Malthus: Nineteen Dimensions of the Population Challenge* (1999) and *Invoking the Spirit: Religion and Spirituality in the Quest for a Sustainable World* (2002). He holds master's degrees in politics from Brandeis University and in public administration from the Monterey Institute of International Studies. This essay first appeared in *World Watch* magazine in 2005.

BEFORE YOU READ

1. What does the headnote tell you about the author? What do you expect his attitude toward consumer culture to be?
2. What relationship do you see between poverty and consumer culture? Explain.
3. What does the title indicate about the article's argument? What is your initial reaction to the title and possible argument?

Hungry for More: Reengaging Religious Teachings on Consumption

1 In his book *God's Politics,* evangelical minister Jim Wallis describes an episode from his seminary days when a fellow student took scissors and snipped out of an old Bible every verse that focused on poverty and wealth. The remaining text was tattered and fragile, reports Wallis; these economic themes occur in the Hebrew scriptures more often than any topic except idolatry, and in the Gospels account for as many as one in seven verses. The eviscerated Bible was an effective prop for his sermons. "I'd hold it up high above American congregations and say 'Brothers and sisters, this is our American Bible; it is full of holes,'" the empty spaces constituting the mute teachings that favor the poor and outline the economic obligations of the wealthy.

2 Recovering the lost economic teachings—not just of the Jewish and Christian traditions, but of many of the world's faiths—could be enormously valuable to a global economy faced with unprecedented ethical challenges. Mass consumerism in wealthy countries has already broken the ecological bank, with a crippled climate, extinct species, scalped forests, and drained or polluted rivers standing as red ink. Now billions of citizens of China and India demand a piece of the global consumption pie. How can the legitimate aspirations of emerging nations be met without further damaging the planet—while safeguarding opportunities for the world's poorest, especially in Africa, to stake *their* consumption claims?

3 Consumption is linked, of course, to both poverty and wealth: The poor underconsume, by definition, and the prosperous typically consume

more than needed, often wastefully. Thus religious wisdom on poverty and wealth can be helpful in tackling the emerging ethical dilemma of global consumption. Restoring the forgotten wisdom buried in the sacred texts of the world's faith traditions could help to sketch out the principles for a new economics—principles that address the challenges of consumption and poverty simultaneously.

4 Indeed, the power of inspirational and challenging religious messages to mobilize believers is at work on the consumption question in pockets around the world, from Sri Lanka and Alabama to the finance ministries of major creditor nations. In each case, religious teachings are awakening adherents to the moral dimension of consumption (and its offspring, debt and inequality), in some cases with measurable impact. They are a reminder of the power inherent in the founding visions of many of the world's faiths.

Neither Poverty nor Wealth

5 Consider, for example, the power of "Buddhist economics" to turn Western notions of consumption on their heads. From its starting position—the purpose of an economy—the Buddhist approach is distinctive. As explained in E. F. Schumacher's classic, *Small Is Beautiful,* whereas market economies are designed to produce the highest possible levels of production and consumption, Buddhist economics supports a different aim: to achieve enlightenment. This spiritual goal, in turn, requires freedom from desire, the source of all suffering, according to the Buddha. This is a tall order in societies of mass consumption, where advertisers conflate needs and desires and where acquisitiveness is a cultural norm. Thus the very attitude toward material goods is one of detachment, a sharp contrast to the frenzied grasping for stuff that often characterizes non-Buddhist societies.

6 Indeed, from the perspective of Buddhist economics, having and consuming makes sense only as a means to a well-rounded sense of well-being, in which material needs are met in moderation, and in which cultural, psychological, and spiritual needs are also addressed. Consumption as an end—chasing the most prestigious house or the latest cellphone—is irrational. In fact, in Buddhist thought the rational person aims to achieve the highest level of well-being with the *least* consumption, since consumption is merely a means to this higher end.

7 In this view, collecting ever-greater quantities of stuff, generating mountains of refuse, and designing goods to wear out (all normal in consumerist economies) are absurd inefficiencies. The waste is huge, not just in terms of garbage generated, but because the outsized material dimension of a consumer's life does not deliver any greater degree of well-being. Indeed, evidence from high-consumption societies like the United States make it clear that when people overconsume food or sedentary leisure time, health is likely to suffer. And overwork in support of a high consumption lifestyle can leave little time for strong relationships, another necessary ingredient of well-being.

8 The consumption ethic of Buddhist economics appears to have taken strong root in Sri Lanka in a village-based development movement known as Sarvodaya Shramadana, now present in more than half of the country's 24,000 villages. Consumption in the Sarvodayan experience is shaped by the Sarvodayan vision of development, which is summarized in a list of ten major human needs:

- A clean and beautiful environment
- A clean and adequate supply of water
- Basic clothing
- A balanced diet
- A simple house to live in
- Basic health care
- Simple communications facilities
- Basic energy requirements
- Well-rounded education
- Cultural and spiritual sustenance

9 The list yields a moderate but broadly based approach to consumption. Commodities are "basic," "simple," and "adequate," strongly communicating an ethic of sufficiency. And nonmaterial assets such as a clean environment, well-rounded education, and cultural and spiritual sustenance are on par with material ones, suggesting that material and spiritual dimensions are both necessary for full development. In short, the list produces a materially narrower but spiritually broader understanding of healthy consumption than is found in societies of mass consumerism.

10 The list also implicitly suggests where to draw the line on consumption. If meeting the ten needs essentially provides for a decent life, pursuit of desires from beyond the list is necessarily evidence of "greed, sloth, or ignorance," in the words of one Sarvodaya observer. Acceding to those desires would simply be a waste of resources.

11 The Sarvodayan consumption goals also open up development opportunities more broadly across society. Modest consumption saves resources for use by others, thereby extending the reach of potential development efforts. Indirectly, the list serves as a quick and easy way to identify the individuals or groups most in need of further development assistance. This assessment would be much more difficult task if the list were a long and virtually endless list of wants rather than a limited set of needs. The result is fulfillment of the Sarvodayan goal of "no poverty, no affluence."

Keep the Sabbath

12 In the Jewish and Christian traditions, consumption issues are rooted in the broader question of a person or society's obligations to the poor. "Sabbath economics" traces biblical economic thought back to the evolving understanding of the Sabbath in the Hebrew sacred texts. The analysis, radical by today's economic standards, has challenging implications for modern notions of consumption.

13 Theologians of Sabbath economics note that the biblical admonition to "keep the Sabbath" was more than a weekly religious observance for the ancient Israelites; it also signified their commitment to economic justice and ecological stewardship. Consider the story of the Israelites wandering in the desert after their liberation from slavery in Egypt. They are hungry, and complain to God about their plight. God responds by sending a daily shower of manna from heaven, an act of compassion that came with special instructions: the people were to gather only what they needed, no less and no more. Those who hoarded found that their stocks spoiled, while those who gathered only what they needed found that they, and the entire community, were adequately fed. On the Sabbath day, they were to rest, remember God's generosity to them, and reflect on the abundance that exists when people practice moderation.

14 Gradually the Sabbath concept took on more layers of economic meaning. In the books of Exodus and Deuteronomy, for example, the "Sabbath year" was introduced, when debts were to be forgiven, prisoners set free, and cropland allowed to lie fallow, offering the poor and the exhausted land a fresh start. Next, the Scriptures add the Jubilee year, which occurs every seventh Sabbath year, or every forty-nine years (seven being a symbol of perfection in the Jewish and Christian scriptures). This "super-Sabbath" year entails all of the liberation and fallowing obligations of previous Sabbath years, but adds the requirement that land, the source of people's livelihoods, be returned to its original owners of fifty years earlier. In this way the economic slate was wiped clean, ensuring that nobody remained perpetually on the economic margins.

15 In sum, explains religious activist and author Ched Myers, the Sabbath teachings in the Hebrew Scriptures contain a clear set of economic principles that are as valuable today as when first set down. The first principle is that extremes of consumption, whether too much or too little,

should be avoided. Sufficient consumption, say analysts of Sabbath economics, can be surmised from the interplay between abundance and restraint that runs through the Sabbath stories: the abundance of manna being coupled with the injunction not to hoard, for example, or the provision of productive land being linked to a mandate to redistribute it periodically. God created a cornucopian world, the stories stress; combine this gift with moderation of appetites and the result is a world of plenty for everyone, rather than the resource scarcity that is a basic axiom of modern economics.

16 The second principle of Sabbath economics is that surplus wealth should circulate, not concentrate, and that mechanisms of redistribution are needed to ensure that any skewing of wealth does not become extreme or entrenched. Central to this principle is the notion that concentrated surpluses are inevitably linked to oppression. The Israelites themselves understood that their own enslavement in Egypt helped to produce the concentrated wealth of the pharaoh. Today, note proponents of Sabbath economics, economic oppression takes the form of sweatshops, sub-adequate wages, child labor, and other labor abuses. On these are built the concentrated wealth of many individuals, corporations, and nations.

17 The third principle is that believers should rest regularly, thank God for their blessings, and remember the first two principles through the rituals of community worship.

The Power to Inspire

18 It is easy to dismiss these teachings as quaint artifacts of the Jewish and Christian traditions. After all, it is probably safe to assume that only a tiny minority of practicing Jews and Christians read the various stories of Sabbath obligations as treatises in economics. But these texts are clearly not merely utopian visions: they were the operating ethical base of the Hebrew economy thousands of years ago. There is no reason, in principle, why the same ethical imagination could not be resurrected today. Moreover, the principles of Sabbath economics have in recent years revealed their power to energize important publics on debt and taxation issues, cousins to consumption because the way they are addressed can raise the consumption levels of the poorest and curb the consumption of the wealthiest.

19 Perhaps the finest example of the motivational power of these texts is the Jubilee 2000 movement, an effort to reduce developing country debt whose very name evokes the most radical of the Sabbath economics-based practices. The debt crisis was in large part created by a recession in industrial countries in the early 1980s that increased borrower country payments while decreasing their capacity to export and generate the foreign exchange needed to pay down their debt. Borrowers' indebtedness soon increased to the point that it was virtually impossible to pay off. What was needed, it seemed, was a strategy to wipe clean the economic slate and offer countries a fresh start.

20 The strategic matching of the year 2000 with the powerful religious story of the Jubilee had the effect of firing the imagination of many religious rank and file, who became heavily involved in starting the Jubilee 2000 movement in 1996. Meanwhile, the Religious Working Group on the World Bank & IMF (RWG) was formed to look at debt, structural adjustment, and other economic issues facing developing countries. By 1997, RWG had begun to collaborate closely with the British Jubilee 2000 campaign and had announced the formation of Jubilee 2000/USA.

21 RWG targeted for action the annual Group of Seven (G7) meetings of leaders of the world's wealthiest nations, organizing some 70,000 demonstrators at the 1998 G7 summit in Birmingham, for example, to form a ring around the meeting site, and presenting a petition at the 1999 Cologne summit demanding debt forgiveness. The petition was signed by 12 million people. The result was the first real reductions in

debt since the debt crisis began in 1980 (previous efforts had largely only changed the terms of payment). Will Hutton, a British economic commentator, wrote in the *Observer* that without the "moral imagination of religion" and the leadership of the religious community, "there would be no Jubilee 2000, no debt campaign, and no international public pressure" to reduce developing country debt.

22 Another noteworthy example of the power that can emerge from a serious reading of sacred texts comes from the politically conservative U.S. state of Alabama. In 2001, law professor and theology student Susan Pace Hamill was dumbfounded to learn how regressive Alabama's tax code was, with state taxation kicking in at an annual income of only $4,600, the lowest in the nation and far below the official poverty level of $17,000. Meanwhile, timber interests, which own 71 percent of the state's land area, accounted for only two percent of the state's property tax. Hamill used her thesis work to analyze the state tax code from the perspective of Jewish and Christian scriptural teachings, publishing "An Argument for Tax Reform based on Judeo-Christian Ethics" in the *Alabama Law Review* in 2002.

23 Her work caught the attention of the conservative Republican governor, Bob Riley, a practicing Christian, who spear-headed an effort to raise the income level at which state taxation kicks in to above the U.S. official poverty level. In the process, he mobilized the religious community, gathering endorsements from the five largest Christian denominations in the state, including the Alabama Baptist Convention, which represents 3,100 of the state's 8,000 churches. Unfortunately, the effort failed at the polls, largely because of the well-funded opposition from the timber and agricultural interests whose taxes would have been raised to offset the loss of revenues from the state's poorest. But the fact that a conservative sector of a conservative state was able to persuade a conservative governor to make a serious stab at an issue of economic justice, based on a religious argument, is an impressive testament to the power of a spiritual appeal to change hearts and minds.

Ideas Whose Time Has Come—Again?

24 Whatever the success of the Sarvodayan and Jubilee movements, they represent but a tiny fraction of religious activity in the world today. And it seems safe to assume that the vast majority of religious people do not make a connection between their faith and consumption, beyond the (admittedly significant) understanding of the need to make charitable contributions. Meanwhile, the consumption juggernaut rolls on globally, with wealthy nations continuing to consume at ever-higher levels and large chunks of the developing world as attracted to the consumption promise as any other nation. Is a religiously led, globally effective movement to promote healthier and more just models of consumption little more than a quixotic dream?

25 There are reasons to believe that the potential for change continues to be significant. For starters, Americans and Europeans appear to be awakening to the realization that consumption beyond a moderate level can actually be harmful to individuals, as the surge in obesity, depression, and indebtedness suggest. Churches and synagogues concerned about the well-being of their own faithful have growing reason to take action to help free their followers from the debilitating addiction of consumption. Indeed, the twelve-step groups operating in church and synagogue basements for decades, often as an outreach service, may now need to tackle the consumption addiction of entire congregations.

26 The international context is different as well, with the rise of China, India, and other rapidly developing countries raising moral questions about environmental impact and equitable access to consumption opportunities. How will the global community make room for the legitimate

material aspirations of these nations? In short, previously dormant moral questions surrounding consumption may now have new power, power that might awaken the interest of faith communities.

27 Religions may also be prepared to take seriously the prospect that consumerism is a serious competitor for the allegiance of millions of people. The fact that societies of high consumption tend to be highly secular is not likely an accident. As more people turn to markets and shopping malls for fulfillment (however temporary and unsatisfying that fulfillment might be) religions are challenged to respond.

28 Competition from consumerism may be the most significant incentive for religions to become involved, but it is likely also the most challenging. Could it be that faith communities have had so little impact on consumption trends, despite thousands of years of durable teachings on the topic, because they are as bound to the consumer culture as the rest of society? Or because they fear that challenging their congregants on consumption would quickly empty their pews? Questioning consumption seriously, after all, is to challenge a host of societal interests and to anger a broad swath of the public.

29 What is clear from the Jubilee and Sarvodaya examples is that religious vision has tremendous power to induce societal change. Religions that re-embrace the original vision—that take seriously once again the sentiments expressed in those snipped passages from Scripture—could help to make the world anew. Wishful thinking perhaps, but theologian Douglas John Hall notes that religion becomes relevant in desperate times, that churches get creative precisely when the culture becomes disillusioned. In a world in economic and ecological crisis early in the twenty-first century, these teachings may be religions' best kept secrets.

Thinking about the Argument

1. How does the first paragraph serve to hook the audience? What does it suggest about the target audience? About the author's views on poverty?
2. Why does the author believe that religion should play a role in addressing issues like consumerism and poverty? Do you agree? Why or why not?
3. What issues does the author believe need to be addressed? Do you agree? Why or why not?
4. What is "Sabbath economics"? Is this idea limited only to Jews and Christians, or can it be applied to people of all beliefs?

Responding to the Argument

1. Do you think that "Sabbath economics" can be applied in a secular society? Why or why not?
2. Do you think the idea of a Jubilee year—a year preselected to forgive the debts of the previous generations—is a good idea or a bad idea? Why or why not? What might some of the good effects be? What could be the bad effects?
3. Respond to the following statement: "Americans and Europeans appear to be awakening to the realization that consumption beyond a moderate level can actually be harmful to individuals, as the surge in obesity, depression, and indebtedness suggest." Support your claims with concrete examples.

Writing about the Argument

1. Write an argument for or against legislation to support the creation of a "Jubilee year." In your argument, explain how often this year should occur and what the criteria would be for debt forgiveness. Write the argument in the form of a letter to your local representative. When you are finished, consider mailing it.
2. Should a "Jubilee year" apply to personal indebtedness in our own country? What would some of the positive and negative effects of such debt forgiveness be (on both people and corporations)? Write an argument considering this issue.
3. Write a synthesis of all of the articles in this section. Organize them according to where they stand on the topic of consumerism.
4. Refute Gardner's argument. You may wish to consider whether it is ever a good idea to forgive debt and whether religion should be allowed to play a role in economics.

20 Classic Arguments

> *A classic is classic not because it conforms to certain structural rules or fits certain definitions (of which its author had quite probably never heard). It is classic because of a certain eternal and irrepressible freshness.*
>
> —Ezra Pound (1885–1972)

Arguments, by nature, are contextual and transient. They are applicable to a particular time and place because certain issues are important to certain people at specific times. For a particular audience to understand an argument, it needs to have a certain degree of cultural literacy and relevancy to that audience. Discussions of same-sex marriage, terrorism, environmental sustainability, and media-driven violence all require that the reader understand certain things about modern culture. Same-sex marriage would have been unthinkable—at least for most people—as a serious issue fifty years ago. Discussions of the relationship between the Western and Islamic civilizations have taken on a new urgency since September 11, 2001. Environmental sustainability requires

Online Study Center
This icon will direct you to content and resources on the website <college.hmco.com/pic/lamm1e>.

Online Study Center
Prepare for Class
Plato

knowledge of the global warming debate. Ten years from now, if you glance at future editions of this book, or any other textbook on argument, the issues being discussed will most likely have changed.

Nevertheless, some arguments have staying power. They are read and discussed generation after generation for the depth of their thinking, the quality of their writing, and the universality of their themes. The arguments in this chapter—even though their writers, in some cases, lived centuries apart in vastly different cultures—are classic in the sense that they address ideas that are still relevant today.

READING SELECTION

Crito

ABOUT THE AUTHOR: PLATO

Plato (427–347 B.C.E.) was one of the preeminent philosophers of ancient Greece and was a student of Socrates, who left no written records after his execution in 399 B.C.E. Much of what is known about Socrates has been transmitted through Plato's writings about him. Plato, who eventually established a school in Athens, was deeply committed to the need for social and political change through the acquisition of wisdom. From Socrates, he presumably took the form of dialectic—the pursuit of wisdom through questions and answers, which in turn lead to further questions. Plato wrote many dialogues, including *Crito,* which considers Socrates's argument for obeying unjust laws. Among Plato's other dialogues are *Symposium,* which discusses (among other things) beauty and love, and the *Republic,* which outlines Plato's theory of politics and justice. This dialogue is excerpted from Alain De Botton's *The Essential Plato* (1999, originally published in 1871 and translated by Benjamin Jowett and M. J. Knight).

BEFORE YOU READ

1. What knowledge, if any, do you have of Plato? How could you locate more information about him?
2. After doing a little research on your own, what have you learned about the world in which Plato lived? What have you learned about the ideas he addresses?
3. *Crito* is written in the form of a dialogue, or discussion. How might you approach this writing differently than an essay or printed speech in terms of locating its central claims and evidence?
4. What does an initial scan of the dialogue tell you about the way it is organized? Do you expect Plato to present his central idea up front or to work toward it gradually? Why do you hold this opinion?

READING SELECTION

Crito

Persons of the Dialogue:
Socrates
Crito

SCENE: The Prison of Socrates

1 SOCRATES. Why have you come at this hour, Crito? it must be quite early?

2 CRITO. Yes, certainly.

3 SOC. What is the exact time?

4 CR. The dawn is breaking.

5 SOC. I wonder that the keeper of the prison would let you in.

6 CR. He knows me, because I often come, Socrates; moreover, I have done him a kindness.

7 SOC. And are you only just come?

8 CR. No, I came some time ago.

9 SOC. Then why did you sit and say nothing, instead of awakening me at once?

10 CR. Why, indeed, Socrates, I myself would rather not have all this sleeplessness and sorrow. But I have been wondering at your peaceful slumbers, and that was the reason why I did not awaken you, because I wanted you to be out of pain. I have always thought you happy in the calmness of your temperament; but never did I see the like of the easy, cheerful way in which you bear this calamity.

11 SOC. Why, Crito, when a man has reached my age he ought not to be repining at the prospect of death.

12 CR. And yet other old men find themselves in similar misfortunes, and age does not prevent them from repining.

13 SOC. That may be. But you have not told me why you come at this early hour.

14 CR. I come to bring you a message which is sad and painful; not, as I believe, to yourself, but to all of us who are your friends, and saddest of all to me.

15 SOC. What! I suppose that the ship has come from Delos, on the arrival of which I am to die?

16 CR. No, the ship has not actually arrived, but she will probably be here to-day, as persons who have come from Sunium tell me that they left her there; and therefore to-morrow, Socrates, will be the last day of your life.

17 SOC. Very well, Crito; if such is the will of God, I am willing; but my belief is that there will be a delay of a day.

18 CR. Why do you say this?

19 SOC. I will tell you. I am to die on the day after the arrival of the ship?

20 CR. Yes; that is what the authorities say.

21 SOC. But I do not think that the ship will be here until to-morrow; this I gather from a vision which I had last night, or rather only just now, when you fortunately allowed me to sleep.

22 CR. And what was the nature of the vision?

23 SOC. There came to me the likeness of a woman, fair and comely, clothed in white raiment, who called to me and said: O Socrates,

> "The third day hence to Phthia shalt
> thou go."

24 CR. What a singular dream, Socrates!

25 SOC. There can be no doubt about the meaning, Crito, I think.

26 CR. Yes; the meaning is only too clear. But, Oh! my beloved Socrates, let me entreat you once more to take my advice and escape. For if you die I shall not only lose a friend who can never be replaced, but there is another evil: people who do not know you and me will believe that I might have saved you if I had been willing to give money, but that I did not care. Now, can there be a worse disgrace than this—that I should be thought to value money more than the life of a friend? For the many will not be persuaded that I wanted you to escape, and that you refused.

27 SOC. But why, my dear Crito, should we care about the opinion of the many? Good men, and they are the only persons who are worth considering, will think of these things truly as they happened.

28 CR. But do you see, Socrates, that the opinion of the many must be regarded, as is evident

in your own case, because they can do the very greatest evil to any one who has lost their good opinion.

29 SOC. I only wish, Crito, that they could; for then they could also do the greatest good, and that would be well. But the truth is, that they can do neither good nor evil: they can not make a man wise or make him foolish; and whatever they do is the result of chance.

30 CR. Well, I will not dispute about that; but please to tell me, Socrates, whether you are not acting out of regard to me and your other friends: are you not afraid that if you escape hence we may get into trouble with the informers for having stolen you away, and lose either the whole or a great part of our property; or that even a worse evil may happen to us? Now, if this is your fear, be at ease; for in order to save you, we ought surely to run this, or even a greater risk; be persuaded, then, and do as I say.

31 SOC. Yes, Crito, that is one fear which you mention, but by no means the only one.

32 CR. Fear not. There are persons who at no great cost are willing to save you and bring you out of prison; and as for the informers, you may observe that they are far from being exorbitant in their demands; a little money will satisfy them. My means, which, as I am sure, are ample, are at your service, and if you have a scruple about spending all mine, here are strangers who will give you the use of theirs; and one of them, Simmias the Theban, has brought a sum of money for this very purpose; and Cebes and many others are willing to spend their money too. I say therefore, do not on that account hesitate about making your escape, and do not say, as you did in the court, that you will have a difficulty in knowing what to do with yourself if you escape. For men will love you in other places to which you may go, and not in Athens only; there are friends of mine in Thessaly, if you like to go to them, who will value and protect you, and no Thessalian will give you any trouble. Nor can I think that you are justified, Socrates, in betraying your own life when you might be saved; this is playing into the hands of your enemies and destroyers; and moreover I should say that you were betraying your children; for you might bring them up and educate them; instead of which you go away and leave them, and they will have to take their chance; and if they do not meet with the usual fate of orphans, there will be small thanks to you. No man should bring children into the world who is unwilling to persevere to the end in their nurture and education. But you are choosing the easier part, as I think, not the better and manlier, which would rather have become one who professes virtue in all his actions, like yourself. And indeed, I am ashamed not only of you, but of us who are your friends, when I reflect that this entire business of yours will be attributed to our want of courage. The trial need never have come on, or might have been brought to another issue; and the end of all, which is the crowning absurdity, will seem to have been permitted by us, through cowardice and baseness, who might have saved you, as you might have saved yourself, if we had been good for anything (for there was no difficulty in escaping); and we did not see how disgraceful, Socrates, and also miserable all this will be to us as well as to you. Make your mind up then, or rather have your mind already made up, for the time of deliberation is over, and there is only one thing to be done, which must be done, if at all, this very night, and which any delay will render all but impossible; I beseech you therefore, Socrates, to be persuaded by me, and to do as I say.

33 SOC. Dear Crito, your zeal is invaluable, if a right one; but if wrong, the greater the zeal the greater the evil; and therefore we ought to consider whether these things shall be done

or not. For I am and always have been one of those natures who must be guided by reason, whatever the reason may be which upon reflection appears to me to be the best; and now that this fortune has come upon me, I can not put away the reasons which I have before given: the principles which I have hitherto honored and revered I still honor, and unless we can find other and better principles on the instant, I am certain not to agree with you; no, not even if the power of the multitude could inflict many more imprisonments, confiscations, deaths, frightening us like children with hobgoblin terrors. But what will be the fairest way of considering the question? Shall I return to your old argument about the opinions of men? some of which are to be regarded, and others, as we were saying, are not to be regarded. Now were we right in maintaining this before I was condemned? And has the argument which was once good now proved to be talk for the sake of talking; —in fact an amusement only, and altogether vanity? That is what I want to consider with your help, Crito: —whether, under my present circumstances, the argument appears to be in any way different or not; and is to be allowed by me or disallowed. That argument, which, as I believe, is maintained by many who assume to be authorities, was to the effect, as I was saying, that the opinions of some men are to be regarded, and of other men not to be regarded. Now you, Crito, are a disinterested person who are not going to die tomorrow—at least, there is no human probability of this, and you are therefore not liable to be deceived by the circumstances in which you are placed. Tell me then, whether I am right in saying that some opinions, and the opinions of some men only, are to be valued, and other opinions, and the opinions of other men, are not to be valued. I ask you whether I was right in maintaining this?

34 CR. Certainly.

35 SOC. The good are to be regarded, and not the bad?

36 CR. Yes.

37 SOC. And the opinions of the wise are good, and the opinions of the unwise are evil?

38 CR. Certainly.

39 SOC. And what was said about another matter? Was the disciple in gymnastics supposed to attend to the praise and blame and opinion of every man, or of one man only—his physician or trainer, whoever that was?

40 CR. Of one man only.

41 SOC. And he ought to fear the censure and welcome the praise of that one only, and not of the many?

42 CR. That is clear.

43 SOC. And he ought to live and train, and eat and drink in the way which seems good to his single master who has understanding, rather than according to the opinion of all other men put together?

44 CR. True.

45 SOC. And if he disobeys and disregards the opinion and approval of the one, and regards the opinion of the many who have no understanding, will he not suffer evil?

46 CR. Certainly he will.

47 SOC. And what will the evil be, whither tending and what affecting, in the disobedient person?

48 CR. Clearly, affecting the body; that is what is destroyed by the evil.

49 SOC. Very good; and is not this true, Crito, of other things which we need not separately enumerate? In the matter of just and unjust, fair and foul, good and evil, which are the subjects of our present consultation, ought we to follow the opinion of the many and to fear them; or the opinion of the one man who has understanding, and whom we ought to fear and reverence more than all the rest of the world: and whom deserting we shall destroy and injure that principle in us which

may be assumed to be improved by justice and deteriorated by injustice; —is there not such a principle?

50 CR. Certainly there is, Socrates.

51 SOC. Take a parallel instance: —if, acting under the advice of men who have no understanding, we destroy that which is improvable by health and deteriorated by disease—when that has been destroyed, I say, would life be worth having? And that is—the body?

52 CR. Yes.

53 SOC. Could we live, having an evil and corrupted body?

54 CR. Certainly not.

55 SOC. And will life be worth having, if that higher part of man be depraved, which is improved by justice and deteriorated by injustice? Do we suppose that principle, whatever it may be in man, which has to do with justice and injustice, to be inferior to the body?

56 CR. Certainly not.

57 SOC. More honored, then?

58 CR. Far more honored.

59 SOC. Then, my friend, we must not regard what the many say of us: but what he, the one man who has understanding of just and unjust, will say, and what the truth will say. And therefore you begin in error when you suggest that we should regard the opinion of the many about just and unjust, good and evil, honorable and dishonorable. —Well, some one will say, "but the many can kill us."

60 CR. Yes, Socrates; that will clearly be the answer.

61 SOC. That is true: but still I find with surprise that the old argument is, as I conceive, unshaken as ever. And I should like to know whether I may say the same of another proposition—that not life, but a good life, is to be chiefly valued?

62 CR. Yes, that also remains.

63 SOC. And a good life is equivalent to a just and honorable one—that holds also?

64 CR. Yes, that holds.

65 SOC. From these premisses I proceed to argue the question whether I ought or ought not to try and escape without the consent of the Athenians: and if I am clearly right in escaping, then I will make the attempt; but if not, I will abstain. The other considerations which you mention, of money and loss of character and the duty of educating children, are, as I fear, only the doctrines of the multitude, who would be as ready to call people to life, if they were able, as they are to put them to death—and with as little reason. But now, since the argument has thus far prevailed, the only question which remains to be considered is, whether we shall do rightly either in escaping or in suffering others to aid in our escape and paying them in money and thanks, or whether we shall not do rightly; and if the latter, then death or any other calamity which may ensue on my remaining here must not be allowed to enter into the calculation.

66 CR. I think that you are right, Socrates; how then shall we proceed?

67 SOC. Let us consider the matter together, and do you either refute me if you can, and I will be convinced; or else cease, my dear friend, from repeating to me that I ought to escape against the wishes of the Athenians: for I am extremely desirous to be persuaded by you, but not against my own better judgment. And now please to consider my first position, and do your best to answer me.

68 CR. I will do my best.

69 SOC. Are we to say that we are never intentionally to do wrong, or that in one way we ought and in another way we ought not to do wrong, or is doing wrong always evil and dishonorable, as I was just now saying, and as has been already acknowledged by us? Are all our former admissions which were made within a few days to be thrown away? And have we, at our age, been earnestly discoursing with one another all our life long only to discover that we are no better than children? Or are we to rest assured, in spite of the opinion of the many, and in spite of conse-

quences whether better or worse, of the truth of what was then said, that injustice is always an evil and dishonor to him who acts unjustly? Shall we affirm that?

70 CR. Yes.

71 SOC. Then we must do no wrong?

72 CR. Certainly not.

73 SOC. Nor when injured injure in return, as the many imagine; for we must injure no one at all?

74 CR. Clearly not.

75 SOC. Again, Crito, may we do evil?

76 CR. Surely not, Socrates.

77 SOC. And what of doing evil in return for evil which is the morality of the many—is that just or not?

78 CR. Not just.

79 SOC. For doing evil to another is the same as injuring him?

80 CR. Very true.

81 SOC. Then we ought not to retaliate or render evil for evil to any one, whatever evil we may have suffered from him. But I would have you consider, Crito, whether you really mean what you are saying. For this opinion has never been held, and never will be held, by any considerable number of persons; and those who are agreed and those who are not agreed upon this point have no common ground, and can only despise one another when they see how widely they differ. Tell me, then, whether you agree with and assent to my first principle, that neither injury nor retaliation nor warding off evil by evil is ever right. And shall that be the premiss of our argument? Or do you decline and dissent from this? For this has been of old and is still my opinion; but, if you are of another opinion, let me hear what you have to say. If, however, you remain of the same mind as formerly, I will proceed to the next step.

82 CR. You may proceed, for I have not changed my mind.

83 SOC. Then I will proceed to the next step, which may be put in the form of a question: Ought a man to do what he admits to be right, or ought he to betray the right?

84 CR. He ought to do what he thinks right.

85 SOC. But if this is true, what is the application? In leaving the prison against the will of the Athenians, do I wrong any? or rather do I not wrong those whom I ought least to wrong? Do I not desert the principles which were acknowledged by us to be just? What do you say?

86 CR. I can not tell, Socrates; for I do not know.

87 SOC. Then consider the matter in this way: Imagine that I am about to play truant (you may call the proceeding by any name which you like), and the laws and the government come and interrogate me: "Tell us, Socrates," they say; "what are you about? are you going by an act of yours to overturn us—the laws and the whole state, as far as in you lies? Do you imagine that a state can subsist and not be overthrown, in which the decisions of law have no power, but are set aside and overthrown by individuals?" What will be our answer, Crito, to these and the like words? Any one, and especially a clever rhetorician, will have a good deal to urge about the evil of setting aside the law which requires a sentence to be carried out; and we might reply, "Yes; but the state has injured us and given an unjust sentence." Suppose I say that?

88 CR. Very good, Socrates.

89 SOC. "And was that our agreement with you?" the law would say; "or were you to abide by the sentence of the state?" And if I were to express astonishment at their saying this, the law would probably add: "Answer, Socrates, instead of opening your eyes: you are in the habit of asking and answering questions. Tell us what complaint you have to make against us which justifies you in attempting to destroy us and the state? In the first place did we not bring you into existence? Your father married your mother by our aid and begat you. Say whether you have any objection to urge against those of us who regulate

marriage?" None, I should reply. "Or against those of us who regulate the system of nurture and education of children in which you were trained? Were not the laws, who have the charge of this, right in commanding your father to train you in music and gymnastic?" Right, I should reply. "Well then, since you were brought into the world and nurtured and educated by us, can you deny in the first place that you are our child and slave, as your fathers were before you? And if this is true you are not on equal terms with us; nor can you think that you have a right to do to us what we are doing to you. Would you have any right to strike or revile or do any other evil to a father or to your master, if you had one, when you have been struck or reviled by him, or received some other evil at his hands?—you would not say this? And because we think right to destroy you, do you think that you have any right to destroy us in return, and your country as far as in you lies? And will you, O professor of true virtue, say that you are justified in this? Has a philosopher like you failed to discover that our country is more to be valued and higher and holier far than mother or father or any ancestor, and more to be regarded in the eyes of the gods and of men of understanding? also to be soothed, and gently and reverently entreated when angry, even more than a father, and if not persuaded, obeyed? And when we are punished by her, whether with imprisonment or stripes, the punishment is to be endured in silence; and if she lead us to wounds or death in battle, thither we follow as is right; neither may any one yield or retreat or leave his rank, but whether in battle or in a court of law, or in any other place, he must do what his city and his country order him; or he must change their view of what is just; and if he may do no violence to his father or mother, much less may he do violence to his country." What answer shall we make to this, Crito? Do the laws speak truly, or do they not?

90 CR. I think that they do.

91 SOC. Then the laws will say: "Consider, Socrates, if this is true, that in your present attempt you are going to do us wrong. For, after having brought you into the world, and nurtured and educated you, and given you and every other citizen a share in every good that we had to give, we further proclaim and give the right to every Athenian, that if he does not like us when he has come of age and has seen the ways of the city, and made our acquaintance, he may go where he pleases and take his goods with him; and none of us laws will forbid him or interfere with him. Any of you who does not like us and the city, and who wants to go to a colony or to any other city, may go where he likes, and take his goods with him. But he who has experience of the manner in which we order justice and administer the state, and still remains, has entered into an implied contract that he will do as we command him. And he who disobeys us is, as we maintain, thrice wrong; first, because in disobeying us he is disobeying his parents; secondly, because we are the authors of his education; thirdly, because he has made an agreement with us that he will duly obey our commands; and he neither obeys them nor convinces us that our commands are wrong; and we do not rudely impose them, but give them the alternative of obeying or convincing us;—that is what we offer, and he does neither. These are the sort of accusations to which, as we were saying, you, Socrates, will be exposed if you accomplish your intentions; you, above all other Athenians." Suppose I ask, why is this? they will justly retort upon me that I above all other men have acknowledged the agreement. "There is clear proof," they will say, "Socrates, that we and the city were not displeasing to you. Of all Athenians you have

been the most constant resident in the city, which, as you never leave, you may be supposed to love. For you never went out of the city either to see the games, except once when you went to the Isthmus, or to any other place unless when you were on military service; nor did you travel as other men do. Nor had you any curiosity to know other states or their laws: your affections did not go beyond us and our state; we were your special favorites, and you acquiesced in our government of you; and this is the state in which you begat your children, which is a proof of your satisfaction. Moreover, you might, if you had liked, have fixed the penalty at banishment in the course of the trial—the state which refuses to let you go now would have let you go then. But you pretended that you preferred death to exile, and that you were not grieved at death. And now you have forgotten these fine sentiments, and pay no respect to us the laws, of whom you are the destroyer; and are doing what only a miserable slave would do, running away and turning your back upon the compacts and agreements which you made as a citizen. And first of all answer this very question: Are we right in saying that you agreed to be governed according to us in deed, and not in word only? Is that true or not?" How shall we answer that, Crito? Must we not agree?

92 CR. There is no help, Socrates.

93 SOC. Then will they not say: "You, Socrates, are breaking the covenants and agreements which you made with us at your leisure, not in any haste or under any compulsion or deception, but having had seventy years to think of them, during which time you were at liberty to leave the city, if we were not to your mind, or if our covenants appeared to you to be unfair. You had your choice, and might have gone either to Lacedaemon or Crete, which you often praise for their good government, or to some other Hellenic or foreign state. Whereas you, above all other Athenians, seemed to be so fond of the state, or, in other words, of us her laws (for who would like a state that has no laws), that you never stirred out of her; the halt, the blind, the maimed were not more stationary in her than you were. And now you run away and forsake your agreements. Not so, Socrates, if you will take our advice; do not make yourself ridiculous by escaping out of the city.

94 "For just consider, if you transgress and err in this sort of way, what good will you do either to yourself or to your friends? That your friends will be driven into exile and deprived of citizenship, or will lose their property, is tolerably certain; and you yourself, if you fly to one of the neighboring cities, as, for example, Thebes or Megara, both of which are well-governed cities, will come to them as an enemy, Socrates, and their government will be against you, and all patriotic citizens will cast an evil eye upon you as a subverter of the laws, and you will confirm in the minds of the judges the justice of their own condemnation of you. For he who is a corruptor of the laws is more than likely to be corruptor of the young and foolish portion of mankind. Will you then flee from well-ordered cities and virtuous men? and is existence worth having on these terms? Or will you go to them without shame, and talk to them, Socrates? And what will you say to them? What you say here about virtue and justice and institutions and laws being the best things among men. Would that be decent of you? Surely not. But if you go away from well-governed states to Crito's friends in Thessaly, where there is a great disorder and license, they will be charmed to have the tale of your escape from prison, set off with ludicrous particulars of the manner in which you were wrapped in a goatskin or some other disguise, and metamorphosed as the fashion of runaways is—that is very likely;

but will there be no one to remind you that in your old age you violated the most sacred laws from a miserable desire of a little more life. Perhaps not, if you keep them in a good temper; but if they are out of temper you will hear many degrading things; you will live, but how?—as the flatterer of all men, and the servant of all men; and doing what?—eating and drinking in Thessaly, having gone abroad in order that you may get a dinner. And where will be your fine sentiments about justice and virtue then? Say that you wish to live for the sake of your children, that you may bring them up and educate them—will you take them into Thessaly and deprive them of Athenian citizenship? Is that the benefit which you would confer upon them? Or are you under the impression that they will be better cared for and educated here if you are still alive, although absent from them; for that your friends will take care of them? Do you fancy that if you are an inhabitant of Thessaly they will take care of them, and if you are an inhabitant of the other world they will not take care of them? Nay; but if they who call themselves friends are truly friends, they surely will.

95 "Listen, then, Socrates, to us who have brought you up. Think not of life and children first, and of justice afterwards, but of justice first, that you may be justified before the princes of the world below. For neither will you nor any that belong to you be happier or holier or juster in this life, or happier in another, if you do as Crito bids. Now you depart in innocence, a sufferer and not a doer of evil; a victim, not of the laws, but of men. But if you go forth, returning evil for evil, and injury for injury, breaking the covenants and agreements which you have made with us, and wronging those whom you ought least to wrong, that is to say, yourself, your friends, your country, and us, we shall be angry with you while you live, and our brethren, the laws in the world below, will receive you as an enemy; for they will know that you have done your best to destroy us. Listen, then, to us and not to Crito."

96 This is the voice which I seem to hear murmuring in my ears, like the sound of the flute in the ears of the mystic; that voice, I say, is humming in my ears, and prevents me from hearing any other. And I know that anything more which you may say will be vain. Yet speak, if you have anything to say.

97 CR. I have nothing to say, Socrates.

98 SOC. Then let me follow the intimations of the will of God.

Thinking about the Argument

1. Where is this dialogue set, and why is Socrates there? Why has Crito come to visit his friend Socrates? What will happen to Socrates if he does not agree to Crito's proposal?
2. What argument—claims and evidence—does Crito present to convince Socrates to leave? Do you agree with the reasons cited by Crito? Why or why not?
3. How does Socrates refute Crito's argument? What combination of claims and evidence does he present to justify refusing Crito's request? Do you agree or disagree with any of these specific reasons? Why or why not?
4. What premise does Crito use to undergird his chief argument? Do you agree with this premise? Why or why not?
5. Why does Socrates think that leaving prison would do society a greater evil than his wrongful death and ultimately lead to a corruption of the youth?

Responding to the Argument

1. What would you have done in Socrates's situation? Would you violate the law if you think you had been wrongfully convicted? Why would you do so?
2. State your answer to Question 1 in the form of a claim backed by evidence.
3. In a democracy, law is determined—at least in theory—by majority opinion. What does Plato (through the "voice" of Socrates) think of this idea? Do you agree or disagree with him? Explain.
4. Contrast Socrates's notion that one should obey the law with the ideas expressed in the readings by Henry David Thoreau and Martin Luther King, Jr. Under what conditions should a person be permitted (or, going further, be morally bound) to disobey the law? Explain.

Writing about the Argument

1. Write a dialogue between Socrates and one other author represented in this section (such as Martin Luther King, Jr., or Henry David Thoreau). Through this dialogue, argue whether a person is morally bound to obey the law, even when the law is wrong. In your dialogue, discuss a particular historical instance, such as the civil rights movement or a soldier's refusal to fight in a war that he thinks is wrong.
2. Write a letter to Socrates. In this letter, attempt to convince him that he should escape from prison. Begin with his assumption that the opinions of some people are to be regarded highly and the opinions of others are to be ignored.
3. Using a topic in one of the other sections of this book as your basis—whether stem-cell research should be allowed, for example—write an argument explaining why you should or should not obey a law that you think unjust. For example, should a scientist who believes he can save lives by continuing research in therapeutic cloning carry on this research in secret, even though it is illegal?
4. Think of another situation where you think the law is unjust. Write an argument (perhaps in the form of a letter to your local representative?) explaining why the law should or should not be disobeyed.

"A Modest Proposal for Preventing the Children of Poor People in Ireland from Being a Burden to Their Parents or Country, and for Making Them Beneficial to the Public"

About the Author: Jonathan Swift

Jonathan Swift (1667–1745) was an Irish poet and essayist. After being educated in Trinity College, Dublin, Swift moved to England, where he received a master's degree from Oxford University. By 1710, Swift had become an advocate and pamphleteer for the Tories. When the party lost power with the passing of Queen Anne in 1714, he returned to his native Ireland, where he tirelessly produced essays that were critical of the Whig Party and other writings that attacked British culture and policies toward the Irish. Among these works were *Gulliver's Travels* (1726) and "A Modest Proposal" (1729).

READING SELECTION

Before You Read

1. What does the title "A Modest Proposal" imply? Why do you think this?
2. Given the information supplied by the headnote, what sort of argument might you expect from Swift? Will it be serious? Humorous? Will it take the form of a letter, a play, or a poem? Explain.
3. Scan the document. What does Swift's primary purpose seem to be? What appear to be some of the significant divisions of the argument?
4. Do you think Swift's proposal is a serious one? Why or why not?

Online Study Center
Prepare for Class
Jonathan Swift

A Modest Proposal for Preventing the Children of Poor People in Ireland from Being a Burden to Their Parents or Country, and for Making Them Beneficial to the Public

1 It is a melancholy object to those who walk through this great town, or travel in the country, when they see the streets, the roads and cabin-doors crowded with beggars of the female sex, followed by three, four, or six children, all in rags, and importuning every passenger for an alms. These mothers, instead of being able to work for their honest livelihood, are forced to employ all their time in strolling, to beg sustenance for their helpless infants, who, as they grow up, either turn thieves for want of work, or leave their dear native country to fight for the Pretender in Spain, or sell themselves to the Barbadoes.

2 I think it is agreed by all parties that this prodigious number of children, in the arms, or on the backs, or at the heels of their mothers, and frequently of their fathers, is in the present deplorable state of the kingdom a very great additional grievance; and therefore whoever could find out a fair, cheap, and easy method of making these children sound and useful members of the commonwealth would deserve so well of the public as to have his statue set up for a preserver of the nation.

3 But my intention is very far from being confined to provide only for the children of professed beggars; it is of a much greater extent, and shall take in the whole number of infants at a certain age who are born of parents in effect as little able to support them as those who demand our charity in the streets.

4 As to my own part, having turned my thoughts for many years upon this important subject, and maturely weighed the several schemes of other projectors, I have always found them grossly mistaken in their computation. It is true a child just dropped from its dam may be supported by her milk for a solar year with little other nourishment, at most not above the value of two shillings, which the mother may certainly get, or the value in scraps, by her lawful occupation of begging, and it is exactly at one year old that I propose to provide for them, in such a manner as, instead of being a charge upon their parents, or the parish, or wanting food and raiment for the rest of their lives, they shall, on the contrary, contribute to the feeding and partly to the clothing of many thousands.

5 There is likewise another great advantage in my scheme, that it will prevent those voluntary abortions, and that horrid practice of women murdering their bastard children, alas, too frequent among us, sacrificing the poor innocent babes, I doubt, more to avoid the expense than the shame, which would move tears and pity in the most savage and inhuman breast.

READING SELECTION

6 The number of souls in Ireland being usually reckoned one million and a half, of these I calculate there may be about two hundred thousand couples whose wives are breeders, from which number I subtract thirty thousand couples who are able to maintain their own children, although I apprehend there cannot be so many under the present distresses of the kingdom, but this being granted, there will remain an hundred and seventy thousand breeders. I again subtract fifty thousand for those women who miscarry, or whose children die by accident or disease within the year. There only remain an hundred and twenty thousand children of poor parents annually born: the question therefore is, how this number shall be reared, and provided for, which, as I have already said, under the present situation of affairs is utterly impossible by all the methods hitherto proposed, for we can neither employ them in handicraft or agriculture; we neither build houses (I mean in the country), nor cultivate land: they can very seldom pick up a livelihood by stealing until they arrive at six years old, except where they are of towardly parts, although I confess they learn the rudiments much earlier, during which time they can however be properly looked upon only as probationers, as I have been informed by a principal gentleman in the County of Cavan, who protested to me that he never knew above one or two instances under the age of six, even in a part of the kingdom so renowned for the quickest proficiency in that art.

7 I am assured by our merchants that a boy or a girl before twelve years old, is no saleable commodity, and even when they come to this age, they will not yield above three pounds, or three pounds and half-a-crown at most on the Exchange, which cannot turn to account either to the parents or the kingdom, the charge of nutriment and rags having been at least four times that value.

8 I shall now therefore humbly propose my own thoughts, which I hope will not be liable to the least objection.

9 I have been assured by a very knowing American of my acquaintance in London, that a young healthy child well nursed is at a year old a most delicious, nourishing and wholesome food, whether stewed, roasted, baked, or boiled, and I make no doubt that it will equally serve in a fricassee, or a ragout.

10 I do therefore humbly offer it to public consideration, that of the hundred and twenty thousand children already computed, twenty thousand may be reserved for breed, whereof only one fourth part to be males, which is more than we allow to sheep, black-cattle, or swine, and my reason is that these children are seldom the fruits of marriage, a circumstance not much regarded by our savages, therefore one male will be sufficient to serve four females. That the remaining hundred thousand may at a year old be offered in sale to the persons of quality, and fortune, through the kingdom, always advising the mother to let them suck plentifully in the last month, so as to render them plump, and fat for a good table. A child will make two dishes at an entertainment for friends, and when the family dines alone, the fore or hind quarter will make a reasonable dish, and seasoned with a little pepper or salt will be very good boiled on the fourth day, especially in winter.

11 I have reckoned upon a medium, that a child just born will weigh twelve pounds, and in a solar year if tolerably nursed increaseth to twenty-eight pounds.

12 I grant this food will be somewhat dear, and therefore very proper for landlords, who, as they have already devoured most of the parents, seem to have the best title to the children.

13 Infant's flesh will be in season throughout the year, but more plentiful in March, and a little before and after, for we are told by a grave[1] author, an eminent French physician, that fish being a prolific diet, there are more children born in Roman Catholic countries about nine months after Lent than at any other season; therefore reckoning a year after Lent, the markets will be more glutted than usual, because the number of

1. Rabelais.

Popish infants is at least three to one in this kingdom, and therefore it will have one other collateral advantage by lessening the number of Papists among us.

14 I have already computed the charge of nursing a beggar's child (in which list I reckon all cottagers, labourers, and four-fifths of the farmers) to be about two shillings *per annum,* rags included, and I believe no gentleman would repine to give ten shillings for the carcass of a good fat child, which, as I have said, will make four dishes of excellent nutritive meat, when he hath only some particular friend or his own family to dine with him. Thus the Squire will learn to be a good landlord and grow popular among his tenants, the mother will have eight shillings net profit, and be fit for work until she produces another child.

15 Those who are more thrifty (as I must confess the times require) may flay the carcass; the skin of which artificially dressed, will make admirable gloves for ladies, and summer boots for fine gentlemen.

16 As to our city of Dublin, shambles may be appointed for this purpose, in the most convenient parts of it, and butchers we may be assured will not be wanting, although I rather recommend buying the children alive, and dressing them hot from the knife, as we do roasting pigs.

17 A very worthy person, a true lover of his country, and whose virtues I highly esteem, was lately pleased, in discoursing on this matter to offer a refinement upon my scheme. He said that many gentlemen of this kingdom, having of late destroyed their deer, he conceived that the want of venison might be well supplied by the bodies of young lads and maidens, not exceeding fourteen years of age, nor under twelve, so great a number of both sexes in every county being now ready to starve, for want of work and service: and these to be disposed of by their parents if alive, or otherwise by their nearest relations. But with due deference to so excellent a friend, and so deserving a patriot, I cannot be altogether in his sentiments. For as to the males, my American acquaintance assured me from frequent experience that their flesh was generally tough and lean, like that of our schoolboys, by continual exercise, and their taste disagreeable, and to fatten them would not answer the charge. Then as to the females, it would, I think with humble submission, be a loss to the public, because they soon would become breeders themselves: and besides, it is not improbable that some scrupulous people might be apt to censure such a practice (although indeed very unjustly) as a little bordering upon cruelty, which I confess, hath always been with me the strongest objection against any project, howsoever well intended.

18 But in order to justify my friend, he confessed that this expedient was put into his head by the famous Psalmanazar, a native of the island Formosa, who came from thence to London, above twenty years ago, and in conversation told my friend that in his country when any young person happened to be put to death, the executioner sold the carcass to persons of quality, as a prime dainty, and that, in his time, the body of a plump girl of fifteen, who was crucified for an attempt to poison the emperor, was sold to his Imperial Majesty's Prime Minister of State, and other great Mandarins of the Court, in joints from the gibbet, at four hundred crowns. Neither indeed can I deny that if the same use were made of several plump young girls in this town who, without one single groat to their fortunes, cannot stir abroad without a chair, and appear at the playhouse and assemblies in foreign fineries, which they never will pay for, the kingdom would not be the worse.

19 Some persons of a desponding spirit are in great concern about that vast number of poor people, who are aged, diseased, or maimed, and I have been desired to employ my thoughts what course may be taken to ease the nation of so grievous an encumbrance. But I am not in the least pain upon that matter, because it is very well known that they are every day dying, and rotting, by cold, and famine, and filth, and vermin, as fast as can be reasonably expected. And as to

the younger labourers they are now in almost as hopeful a condition. They cannot get work, and consequently pine away from want of nourishment, to a degree that if at any time they are accidentally hired to common labour, they have not strength to perform it; and thus the country and themselves are in a fair way of being soon delivered from the evils to come.

20 I have too long digressed, and therefore shall return to my subject. I think the advantages by the proposal which I have made are obvious and many, as well as of the highest importance.

21 For first, as I have already observed, it would greatly lessen the number of Papists, with whom we are yearly over-run, being the principal breeders of the nation, as well as our most dangerous enemies, and who stay at home on purpose with a design to deliver the kingdom to the Pretender, hoping to take their advantage by the absence of so many good Protestants, who have chosen rather to leave their country than stay at home and pay tithes against their conscience to an idolatrous Episcopal curate.

22 Secondly, the poorer tenants will have something valuable of their own, which by law may be made liable to distress, and help to pay their landlord's rent, their corn and cattle being already seized, and money a thing unknown.

23 Thirdly, whereas the maintenance of an hundred thousand children, from two years old, and upwards, cannot be computed at less than ten shillings a piece *per annum,* the nation's stock will be thereby increased fifty thousand pounds *per annum,* besides the profit of a new dish, introduced to the tables of all gentlemen of fortune in the kingdom, who have any refinement in taste, and the money will circulate among ourselves, the goods being entirely of our own growth and manufacture.

24 Fourthly, the constant breeders, besides the gain of eight shillings sterling *per annum,* by the sale of their children, will be rid of the charge of maintaining them after the first year.

25 Fifthly, this food would likewise bring great custom to taverns, where the vintners will certainly be so prudent as to procure the best receipts for dressing it to perfection, and consequently have their houses frequented by all the fine gentlemen, who justly value themselves upon their knowledge in good eating; and a skilful cook, who understands how to oblige his guests, will contrive to make it as expensive as they please.

26 Sixthly, this would be a great inducement to marriage, which all wise nations have either encouraged by rewards, or enforced by laws and penalties. It would increase the care and tenderness of mothers towards their children, when they were sure of a settlement for life, to the poor babes, provided in some sort by the public to their annual profit instead of expense. We should soon see an honest emulation among the married women, which of them could bring the fattest child to the market. Men would become as fond of their wives, during the time of their pregnancy, as they are now of their mares in foal, their cows in calf, or sows when they are ready to farrow, nor offer to beat or kick them (as it is too frequent a practice) for fear of a miscarriage.

27 Many other advantages might be enumerated. For instance, the addition of some thousand carcasses in our exportation of barrelled beef; the propagation of swine's flesh, and improvement in the art of making good bacon, so much wanted among us by the great destruction of pigs, too frequent at our tables, are no way comparable in taste or magnificence to a well-grown, fat yearling child, which roasted whole will make a considerable figure at a Lord Mayor's feast, or any other public entertainment. But this and many others I omit, being studious of brevity.

28 Supposing that one thousand families in this city would be constant customers for infants flesh, besides others who might have it at merry meetings, particularly weddings and christenings; I compute that Dublin would take off annually about twenty thousand carcasses, and the rest of the kingdom (where probably they will be sold somewhat cheaper) the remaining eighty thousand.

29 I can think of no one objection that will possibly be raised against this proposal, unless it

should be urged that the number of people will be thereby much lessened in the kingdom. This I freely own, and it was indeed one principal design in offering it to the world. I desire the reader will observe, that I calculate my remedy *for this one individual Kingdom of* Ireland, *and for no other that ever was, is, or, I think, ever can be upon earth.* Therefore let no man talk to me of other expedients: *Of taxing our absentees at five shillings a pound: Of using neither clothes, nor household furniture, except what is of our own growth and manufacture: Of utterly rejecting the materials and instruments that promote foreign luxury: Of curing the expensiveness of pride, vanity, idleness, and gaming in our women: Of introducing a vein of parsimony, prudence, and temperance: Of learning to love our country, wherein we differ even from* Laplanders, *and the inhabitants of* Topinamboo: *Of quitting our animosities and factions, nor act any longer like the* Jews, *who were murdering one another at the very moment their city was taken: Of being a little cautious not to sell our country and consciences for nothing: Of teaching landlords to have at least one degree of mercy towards their tenants.* Lastly, *of putting a spirit of honesty, industry, and skill into our shopkeepers, who, if a resolution could now be taken to buy only our native goods, would immediately unite to cheat and exact upon us in the price, the measure and the goodness, nor could ever yet be brought to make one fair proposal of just dealing, though often and earnestly invited to it.*

30 Therefore I repeat, let no man talk to me of these and the like expedients, till he hath at least a glimpse of hope that there will ever be some hearty and sincere attempt to put them in practice.

31 But as to myself, having been wearied out for many years with offering vain, idle, visionary thoughts, and at length utterly despairing of success, I fortunately fell upon this proposal, which as it is wholly new, so it hath something solid and real, of no expense and little trouble, full in our own power, and whereby we can incur no danger in disobliging England. For this kind of commodity will not bear exportation, the flesh being of too tender a consistence to admit a long continuance in salt, *although perhaps I could name a country which would be glad to eat up our whole nation without it.*

32 After all I am not so violently bent upon my own opinion as to reject any offer, proposed by wise men, which shall be found equally innocent, cheap, easy and effectual. But before some thing of that kind shall be advanced in contradiction to my scheme, and offering a better, I desire the author, or authors, will be pleased maturely to consider two points. First, as things now stand, how they will be able to find food and raiment for a hundred thousand useless mouths and backs? And secondly, there being a round million of creatures in human figure, throughout this kingdom, whose whole subsistence put into a common stock would leave them in debt two millions of pounds sterling; adding those who are beggars by profession, to the bulk of farmers, cottagers, and labourers with their wives and children, who are beggars in effect; I desire those politicians who dislike my overture, and may perhaps be so bold to attempt an answer, that they will first ask the parents of these mortals whether they would not at this day think it a great happiness to have been sold for food at a year old, in the manner I prescribe, and thereby have avoided such a perpetual scene of misfortunes as they have since gone through, by the oppression of landlords, the impossibility of paying rent without money or trade, the want of common sustenance, with neither house nor clothes to cover them from the inclemencies of weather, and the most inevitable prospect of entailing the like, or greater miseries upon their breed for ever.

33 I profess in the sincerity of my heart that I have not the least personal interest in endeavouring to promote this necessary work, having no other motive than the *public good of my country, by advancing our trade, providing for infants, relieving the poor, and giving some pleasure to the rich.* I have no children by which I can propose to get a single penny; the youngest being nine years old, and my wife past child-bearing.

Thinking about the Argument

1. What is Swift's "proposal"? Is it really "modest"? Is he serious? Explain.
2. What do you think Swift is really trying to say about the treatment of the Irish? How do you know this?
3. What does Swift say should be done with these extra children? What problems will it solve?
4. If you think that Swift is not serious about his "proposal," what do you think the author believes the real problem to be? What do you suppose he thinks should be done?

Responding to the Argument

1. What is your emotional reaction to Swift's "proposal"? At what point did you think he was not serious? Did his "proposal" make you laugh or recoil in horror?
2. Do you think Swift actually meant to draw attention to the plight of the poor? How so? To what extent does he want you to be horrified at the sight of the suffering of the poor?
3. Think about the poor people and the homeless that you may have seen in the area where you live. Do you react with sympathy toward them, or do you ignore them, as if they were just another piece of scenery? How do you think Swift would want you to react? Explain.
4. Compare Swift's description of the eighteenth-century Irish poor with the articles in Chapter 16 that discuss contemporary American poverty. How was the plight of the Irish poor similar to, or different from, the situation faced by poor people in America today?

Writing about the Argument

1. Write a "modest proposal" of your own with the purpose of drawing attention to a serious social problem that you think is being ignored.
2. Write an argument for a plan of action for relieving the suffering of the poor in your own community. Support your claims with evidence, and argue why you think your plan would be particularly effective.
3. Visit a homeless shelter or outreach project operating in a poor neighborhood in your community. Volunteer for a few weeks, and keep a journal of your experiences. Based on this experience, write a letter to your local newspaper explaining how individuals in your community can help the poor.
4. If you think that nothing needs to be done to help the poor in your community, write a paper expressing this opinion. Back up your claims with evidence.
5. Should poor illegal immigrants receive the same services as poor Americans? Why or why not? Write a paper expressing your opinion on this topic. Use one or more of the articles in the immigration section of Chapter 17 as resources.

READING SELECTION

"Declaration of Independence"

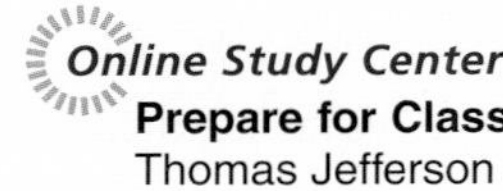

ABOUT THE AUTHOR: THOMAS JEFFERSON

Thomas Jefferson (1743–1826) was one of the founding fathers of the United States. In addition to being a gentleman farmer, philosopher, and statesman, he was a prolific writer. During the summer of 1776, as a member of the revolutionary Continental Congress, Jefferson was called on to draft the Declaration of Independence. Jefferson wrote a series of drafts, and finally presented his work to the Congress on June 28. The Congress approved the document on July 2, revised it, and released it to the public two days later. Jefferson served in a series of government offices, including being governor of Virginia from 1779 to 1781. After serving as George Washington's secretary of state, Jefferson was elected third president of the United States.

BEFORE YOU READ

1. List as many facts as you can recall about Thomas Jefferson. How could you find out more information about him?
2. What else did Thomas Jefferson write? What does this tell you about what the argumentative purpose of the Declaration of Independence might be?
3. Summarize in your own words your personal recollection of the purpose and content of the Declaration of Independence.
4. Who was the intended audience of the Declaration of Independence? How would this affect its purpose, audience, structure, and style?

Declaration of Independence

1 **IN CONGRESS, July 4, 1776.**

2 **The unanimous Declaration of the thirteen united States of America,**

3 When in the Course of human events, it becomes necessary for one people to dissolve the political bands which have connected them with another, and to assume among the powers of the earth, the separate and equal station to which the Laws of Nature and of Nature's God entitle them, a decent respect to the opinions of mankind requires that they should declare the causes which impel them to the separation.

4 We hold these truths to be self-evident, that all men are created equal, that they are endowed by their Creator with certain unalienable Rights, that among these are Life, Liberty and the pursuit of Happiness.—That to secure these rights, Governments are instituted among Men, deriving their just powers from the consent of the governed,—That whenever any Form of Government becomes destructive of these ends, it is the Right of the People to alter or to abolish it, and to institute new Government, laying its foundation on such principles and organizing its powers in such form, as to them shall seem most likely to effect their Safety and Happiness. Prudence, indeed, will dictate that Governments long established should not be changed for light and transient causes; and accordingly all experience hath shewn, that mankind are more disposed to suffer, while evils are sufferable, than to right themselves by abolishing the forms to

which they are accustomed. But when a long train of abuses and usurpations, pursuing invariably the same Object evinces a design to reduce them under absolute Despotism, it is their right, it is their duty, to throw off such Government, and to provide new Guards for their future security.—Such has been the patient sufferance of these Colonies; and such is now the necessity which constrains them to alter their former Systems of Government. The history of the present King of Great Britain is a history of repeated injuries and usurpations, all having in direct object the establishment of an absolute Tyranny over these States. To prove this, let Facts be submitted to a candid world.

5 He has refused his Assent to Laws, the most wholesome and necessary for the public good.

6 He has forbidden his Governors to pass Laws of immediate and pressing importance, unless suspended in their operation till his Assent should be obtained; and when so suspended, he has utterly neglected to attend to them.

7 He has refused to pass other Laws for the accommodation of large districts of people, unless those people would relinquish the right of Representation in the Legislature, a right inestimable to them and formidable to tyrants only.

8 He has called together legislative bodies at places unusual, uncomfortable, and distant from the depository of their public Records, for the sole purpose of fatiguing them into compliance with his measures.

9 He has dissolved Representative Houses repeatedly, for opposing with manly firmness his invasions on the rights of the people.

10 He has refused for a long time, after such dissolutions, to cause others to be elected; whereby the Legislative powers, incapable of Annihilation, have returned to the People at large for their exercise; the State remaining in the mean time exposed to all the dangers of invasion from without, and convulsions within.

11 He has endeavoured to prevent the population of these States; for that purpose obstructing the Laws for Naturalization of Foreigners; refusing to pass others to encourage their migrations hither, and raising the conditions of new Appropriations of Lands.

12 He has obstructed the Administration of Justice, by refusing his Assent to Laws for establishing Judiciary powers.

13 He has made Judges dependent on his Will alone, for the tenure of their offices, and the amount and payment of their salaries.

14 He has erected a multitude of New Offices, and sent hither swarms of Officers to harrass our people, and eat out their substance.

15 He has kept among us, in times of peace, Standing Armies without the Consent of our legislatures.

16 He has affected to render the Military independent of and superior to the Civil power.

17 He has combined with others to subject us to a jurisdiction foreign to our constitution, and unacknowledged by our laws; giving his Assent to their Acts of pretended Legislation:

For Quartering large bodies of armed troops among us:

For protecting them, by a mock Trial, from punishment for any Murders which they should commit on the Inhabitants of these States:

For cutting off our Trade with all parts of the world:

For imposing Taxes on us without our Consent:

For depriving us in many cases, of the benefits of Trial by Jury:

For transporting us beyond Seas to be tried for pretended offences:

For abolishing the free System of English Laws in a neighbouring Province, establishing therein an Arbitrary government, and enlarging its Boundaries so as to render it at once an example and fit instrument for introducing the same absolute rule into these Colonies:

For taking away our Charters, abolishing our most valuable Laws, and altering fundamentally the Forms of our Governments:

For suspending our own Legislatures, and declaring themselves invested with power to legislate for us in all cases whatsoever.

18 He has abdicated Government here, by declaring us out of his Protection and waging War against us.

19 He has plundered our seas, ravaged our Coasts, burnt our towns, and destroyed the lives of our people.

20 He is at this time transporting large Armies of foreign Mercenaries to compleat the works of death, desolation and tyranny, already begun with circumstances of Cruelty & perfidy scarcely paralleled in the most barbarous ages, and totally unworthy the Head of a civilized nation.

21 He has constrained our fellow Citizens taken Captive on the high Seas to bear Arms against their Country, to become the executioners of their friends and Brethren, or to fall themselves by their Hands.

22 He has excited domestic insurrections amongst us, and has endeavoured to bring on the inhabitants of our frontiers, the merciless Indian Savages, whose known rule of warfare, is an undistinguished destruction of all ages, sexes and conditions.

23 In every stage of these Oppressions We have Petitioned for Redress in the most humble terms: Our repeated Petitions have been answered only by repeated injury. A Prince whose character is thus marked by every act which may define a Tyrant, is unfit to be the ruler of a free people.

24 Nor have We been wanting in attentions to our Brittish brethren. We have warned them from time to time of attempts by their legislature to extend an unwarrantable jurisdiction over us. We have reminded them of the circumstances of our emigration and settlement here. We have appealed to their native justice and magnanimity, and we have conjured them by the ties of our common kindred to disavow these usurpations, which, would inevitably interrupt our connections and correspondence. They too have been deaf to the voice of justice and of consanguinity. We must, therefore, acquiesce in the necessity, which denounces our Separation, and hold them, as we hold the rest of mankind, Enemies in War, in Peace Friends.

25 We, therefore, the Representatives of the united States of America, in General Congress, Assembled, appealing to the Supreme Judge of the world for the rectitude of our intentions, do, in the Name, and by Authority of the good People of these Colonies, solemnly publish and declare, That these United Colonies are, and of Right ought to be Free and Independent States; that they are Absolved from all Allegiance to the British Crown, and that all political connection between them and the State of Great Britain, is and ought to be totally dissolved; and that as Free and Independent States, they have full Power to levy War, conclude Peace, contract Alliances, establish Commerce, and to do all other Acts and Things which Independent States may of right do. And for the support of this Declaration, with a firm reliance on the protection of divine Providence, we mutually pledge to each other our Lives, our Fortunes and our sacred Honor.

Thinking about the Argument

1. The first paragraph of the Declaration of Independence consists of one long sentence. Restate it in your own words. What does it tell you about the argumentative purpose of the document?
2. How is this purpose further developed in the second paragraph? What claims are presented? What evidence is offered to support them?
3. Much of the middle part of the document consists of evidence presented in sentences beginning with "he." To whom does "he" refer? How do you know?
4. What evidence does the author provide as evidence that the colonists attempted to settle their differences with the British government peacefully?

Responding to the Argument

1. Having read this document as an argument—as opposed to a piece of philosophy or history—do you think the case is well argued? Why or why not?
2. Name one significant strength and one significant weakness of the Declaration of Independence as an argument.
3. In an argument, it is usually not sufficient to present claims and evidence. In addition, the arguer must discuss the validity of the evidence provided as support of the claims. How well does the Declaration of Independence do this?
4. How could the argument made by the Declaration of Independence be refuted? Are there any statements in the document that you find particularly weak or questionable? Explain.

Writing about the Argument

1. In a journal entry, summarize the contents of the Declaration of Independence.
2. Assume that you have been assigned by the British government to write a reply to the Declaration of Independence, refuting its claims. Write a letter to Jefferson explaining why all men are not created equal. (Note that you are questioning the underlying assumption of the document, which would render the arguments that follow invalid.)
3. Write an essay evaluating the strengths and weaknesses of the Declaration of Independence as an argument.
4. How does the Declaration of Independence utilize the parts of a classic argument? Write an essay evaluating the document from this perspective.

READING SELECTION

"Civil Disobedience"

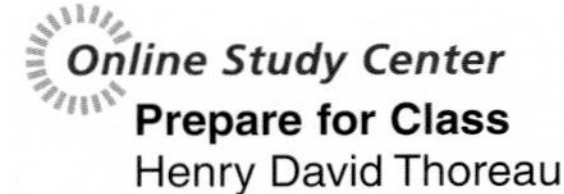

About the Author: Henry David Thoreau

In addition to being an amateur naturalist and a writer, Henry David Thoreau (1817–1862), who was educated at Harvard University but declined to pay the five dollars required to receive his diploma, might be best described as a social and environmental activist. A native of Concord, Massachusetts, Thoreau was acquainted with, among other literati, Ralph Waldo Emerson and Nathaniel Hawthorne. Thoreau is perhaps best known for *Walden; or, Life in the Woods* (1854), which describes his experiment of living for two years in the woods around Walden Pond (which was, in fact, only a short walk to town). His essay *Civil Disobedience,* written in 1849, is a reflection on his refusal to pay overdue taxes.

Before You Read

1. Based on what the headnote tells you about Thoreau, what do you expect him to say about "civil disobedience"? Do you think he will say it is a good thing or a bad thing?
2. Do you think Thoreau would agree or disagree with the methods used by Martin Luther King, Jr.? Why do you think this?
3. What else has Thoreau written? How could you discover more information about him?
4. Scan the document. What would you guess Thoreau's central claim to be? What main divisions do you think there will be to his argument?

Civil Disobedience

1 I heartily accept the motto, "That government is best which governs least;" and I should like to see it acted up to more rapidly and systematically. Carried out, it finally amounts to this, which also I believe—"That government is best which governs not at all;" and when men are prepared for it, that will be the kind of government which they will have. Government is at best but an expedient; but most governments are usually, and all governments are sometimes, inexpedient. The objections which have been brought against a standing army, and they are many and weighty, and deserve to prevail, may also at last be brought against a standing government. The standing army is only an arm of the standing government. The government itself, which is only the mode which the people have chosen to execute their will, is equally liable to be abused and perverted before the people can act through it. Witness the present Mexican war, the work of comparatively a few individuals using the standing government as their tool; for, in the outset, the people would not have consented to this measure.

2 This American government—what is it but a tradition, though a recent one, endeavoring to transmit itself unimpaired to posterity, but each instant losing some of its integrity? It has not the vitality and force of a single living man; for a single man can bend it to his will. It is a sort of wooden gun to the people themselves. But it is not the less necessary for this; for the people must have some complicated machinery or other, and hear its din, to satisfy that idea of government which they have. Governments show thus how successfully men can be imposed on, even impose on themselves, for their own advantage. It is excellent, we must all allow. Yet this government never of itself furthered any enterprise,

but by the alacrity with which it got out of its way. *It* does not keep the country free. *It* does not settle the West. *It* does not educate. The character inherent in the American people has done all that has been accomplished; and it would have done somewhat more, if the government had not sometimes got in its way. For government is an expedient by which men would fain succeed in letting one another alone; and, as has been said, when it is most expedient, the governed are most let alone by it. Trade and commerce, if they were not made of india-rubber, would never manage to bounce over the obstacles which legislators are continually putting in their way; and, if one were to judge these men wholly by the effects of their actions and not partly by their intentions, they would deserve to be classed and punished with those mischievous persons who put obstructions on the rail-roads.

3 But, to speak practically and as a citizen, unlike those who call themselves no-government men, I ask for, not at once no government, but *at once* a better government. Let every man make known what kind of government would command his respect, and that will be one step toward obtaining it.

4 After all, the practical reason why, when the power is once in the hands of the people, a majority are permitted, and for a long period continue, to rule is not because they are most likely to be in the right, nor because this seems fairest to the minority, but because they are physically the strongest. But a government in which the majority rule in all cases cannot be based on justice, even as far as men understand it. Can there not be a government in which majorities do not virtually decide right and wrong, but conscience?—in which majorities decide only those questions to which the rule of expediency is applicable? Must the citizen ever for a moment, or in the least degree, resign his conscience to the legislator? Why has every man a conscience, then? I think that we should be men first, and subjects afterward. It is not desirable to cultivate a respect for the law, so much as for the right. The only obligation which I have a right to assume is to do at any time what I think right. It is truly enough said that a corporation has no conscience; but a corporation of conscientious men is a corporation *with* a conscience. Law never made men a whit more just; and, by means of their respect for it, even the well-disposed are daily made the agents of injustice. A common and natural result of an undue respect for law is, that you may see a file of soldiers, colonel, captain, corporal, privates, powder-monkeys, and all, marching in admirable order over hill and dale to the wars, against their wills, ay, against their common sense and consciences, which makes it very steep marching indeed, and produces a palpitation of the heart. They have no doubt that it is a damnable business in which they are concerned; they are all peaceably inclined. Now, what are they? Men at all? or small movable forts and magazines, at the service of some unscrupulous man in power? Visit, the Navy-Yard, and behold a marine, such a man as an American government can make, or such as it can make a man with its black arts—a mere shadow and reminiscence of humanity, a man laid out alive and standing, and already, as one may say, buried under arms with funeral accompaniments, though it may be,

"Not a drum was heard, not a funeral note,
As his corse to the rampart we hurried;
Not a soldier discharged his farewell shot
O'er the grave where our hero we buried."

5 The mass of men serve the state thus, not as men mainly, but as machines, with their bodies. They are the standing army, and the militia, jailers, constables, *posse comitatus,* etc. In most cases there is no free exercise whatever of the judgment or of the moral sense; but they put themselves on a level with wood and earth and stones; and wooden men can perhaps be manufactured that will serve the purpose as well. Such command no more respect than men of straw or a lump of dirt. They have the same sort of worth only as horses and dogs. Yet such as these even

are commonly esteemed good citizens. Others—as most legislators, politicians, lawyers, ministers, and office-holders—serve the state chiefly with their heads; and, as they rarely make any moral distinctions, they are as likely to serve the devil, without *intending* it, as God. A very few—as heroes, patriots, martyrs, reformers in the great sense, and *men*—serve the state with their consciences also, and so necessarily resist it for the most part; and they are commonly treated as enemies by it. A wise man will only be useful as a man, and will not submit to be "clay," and "stop a hole to keep the wind away," but leave that office to his dust at least:

"I am too high-born to be propertied,
To be a secondary at control,
Or useful serving-man and instrument
To any sovereign state throughout the world."

6 He who gives himself entirely to his fellow-men appears to them useless and selfish; but he who gives himself partially to them is pronounced a benefactor and philanthropist.

7 How does it become a man to behave toward this American government today? I answer, that he cannot without disgrace be associated with it. I cannot for an instant recognize that political organization as *my* government which is the *slave's* government also.

8 All men recognize the right of revolution; that is, the right to refuse allegiance to, and to resist, the government, when its tyranny or its inefficiency are great and unendurable. But almost all say that such is not the case now. But such was the case, they think, in the Revolution of '75. If one were to tell me that this was a bad government because it taxed certain foreign commodities brought to its ports, it is most probable that I should not make an ado about it, for I can do without them. All machines have their friction; and possibly this does enough good to counterbalance the evil. At any rate, it is a great evil to make a stir about it. But when the friction comes to have its machine, and oppression and robbery are organized, I say, let us not have such a machine any longer. In other words, when a sixth of the population of a nation which has undertaken to be the refuge of liberty are slaves, and a whole country is unjustly overrun and conquered by a foreign army, and subjected to military law, I think that it is not too soon for honest men to rebel and revolutionize. What makes this duty the more urgent is the fact that the country so overrun is not our own, but ours is the invading army.

9 Paley, a common authority with many on moral questions, in his chapter on the "Duty of Submission to Civil Government," resolves all civil obligation into expediency; and he proceeds to say that "so long as the interest of the whole society requires it, that is, so long as the established government cannot be resisted or changed without public inconveniency, it is the will of God . . . that the established government be obeyed—and no longer. This principle being admitted, the justice of every particular case of resistance is reduced to a computation of the quantity of the danger and grievance on the one side, and of the probability and expense of redressing it on the other." Of this, he says, every man shall judge for himself. But Paley appears never to have contemplated those cases to which the rule of expediency does not apply, in which a people, as well as an individual, must do justice, cost what it may. If I have unjustly wrested a plank from a drowning man; I must restore it to him though I drown myself. This, according to Paley, would be inconvenient. But he that would save his life, in such a case, shall lose it. This people must cease to hold slaves, and to make war on Mexico, though it cost them their existence as a people.

10 In their practice, nations agree with Paley; but does any one think that Massachusetts does exactly what is right at the present crisis?

"A drab of state, a cloth-o'-silver slut,
To have her train borne up, and her soul trail
in the dirt."

Practically speaking, the opponents to a reform in Massachusetts are not a hundred thousand politicians at the South, but a hundred thousand merchants and farmers here, who are more interested in commerce and agriculture than they are in humanity, and are not prepared to do justice to the slave and to Mexico, *cost what it may.* I quarrel not with far-off foes, but with those who, near at home, coöperate with, and do the bidding of, those far away, and without whom the latter would be harmless. We are accustomed to say, that the mass of men are unprepared; but improvement is slow, because the few are not materially wiser or better than the many. It is not so important that many should be as good as you, as that there be some absolute goodness somewhere; for that will leaven the whole lump. There are thousands who are *in opinion* opposed to slavery and to the war, who yet in effect do nothing to put an end to them; who, esteeming themselves children of Washington and Franklin, sit down with their hands in their pockets, and say that they know not what to do, and do nothing; who even postpone the question of freedom to the question of free trade, and quietly read the prices-current along with the latest advices from Mexico, after dinner, and, it may be, fall asleep over them both. What is the price-current of an honest man and patriot today? They hesitate, and they regret, and sometimes they petition; but they do nothing in earnest and with effect. They will wait, well disposed, for others to remedy the evil, that they may no longer have it to regret. At most, they give only a cheap vote, and a feeble countenance and God-speed, to the right, as it goes by them. There are nine hundred and ninety-nine patrons of virtue to one virtuous man. But it is easier to deal with the real possessor of a thing than with the temporary guardian of it.

11 All voting is a sort of gaming, like checkers or backgammon, with a slight moral tinge to it, a playing with right and wrong, with moral questions; and betting naturally accompanies it. The character of the voters is not staked. I cast my vote, perchance, as I think right; but I am not vitally concerned that that right should prevail. I am willing to leave it to the majority. Its obligation, therefore, never exceeds that of expediency. Even voting *for the right* is *doing* nothing for it. It is only expressing to men feebly your desire that it should prevail. A wise man will not leave the right to the mercy of chance, nor wish it to prevail through the power of the majority. There is but little virtue in the action of masses of men. When the majority shall at length vote for the abolition of slavery, it will be because they are indifferent to slavery, or because there is but little slavery left to be abolished by their vote. *They* will then be the only slaves. Only *his* vote can hasten the abolition of slavery who asserts his own freedom by his vote.

12 I hear of a convention to be held at Baltimore, or elsewhere, for the selection of a candidate for the Presidency, made up chiefly of editors, and men who are politicians by profession; but I think, what is it to any independent, intelligent, and respectable man what decision they may come to? Shall we not have the advantage of his wisdom and honesty, nevertheless? Can we not count upon some independent votes? Are there not many individuals in the country who do not attend conventions? But no: I find that the respectable man, so called, has immediately drifted from his position, and despairs of his country, when his country has more reason to despair of him. He forthwith adopts one of the candidates thus selected as the only *available* one, thus proving that he is himself *available* for any purposes of the demagogue. His vote is of no more worth than that of any unprincipled foreigner or hireling native, who may have been bought. O for a man who is a *man,* and, as my neighbor says, has a bone in his back which you cannot pass your hand through! Our statistics are at fault: the population has been returned too large. How many *men* are there to a square thousand miles in this country? Hardly one. Does not America offer any inducement for men to settle here? The American has dwindled into an Odd Fellow—one who may be known by the development of his organ of gregariousness, and a manifest lack of intellect and cheerful self-reliance; whose first and chief concern, on coming

into the world, is to see that the almshouses are in good repair; and, before yet he has lawfully donned the virile garb, to collect a fund for the support of the widows and orphans that may be; who, in short, ventures to live only by the aid of the Mutual Insurance company, which has promised to bury him decently.

13 It is not a man's duty, as a matter of course, to devote himself to the eradication of any, even the most enormous, wrong; he may still properly have other concerns to engage him; but it is his duty, at least, to wash his hands of it, and, if he gives it no thought longer, not to give it practically his support. If I devote myself to other pursuits and contemplations, I must first see, at least, that I do not pursue them sitting upon another man's shoulders. I must get off him first, that he may pursue his contemplations too. See what gross inconsistency is tolerated. I have heard some of my townsmen say, "I should like to have them order me out to help put down an insurrection of the slaves; or to march to Mexico;—see if I would go;" and yet these very men have each, directly by their allegiance, and so indirectly, at least, by their money, furnished a substitute. The soldier is applauded who refuses to serve in an unjust war by those who do not refuse to sustain the unjust government which makes the war; is applauded by those whose own act and authority he disregards and sets at naught; as if the state were penitent to that degree that it hired one to scourge it while it sinned, but not to that degree that it left off sinning for a moment. Thus, under the name of Order and Civil Government, we are all made at last to pay homage to and support our own meanness. After the first blush of sin comes its indifference; and from immoral it becomes, as it were, *un*moral, and not quite unnecessary to that life which we have made.

14 The broadest and most prevalent error requires the most disinterested virtue to sustain it. The slight reproach to which the virtue of patriotism is commonly liable, the noble are most likely to incur. Those who, while they disapprove of the character and measures of a government, yield to it their allegiance and support are undoubtedly its most conscientious supporters, and so frequently the most serious obstacles to reform. Some are petitioning the State to dissolve the Union, to disregard the requisitions of the President. Why do they not dissolve it themselves—the union between themselves and the State—and refuse to pay their quota into its treasury? Do not they stand in the same relation to the State that the State does to the Union? And have not the same reasons prevented the State from resisting the Union which have prevented them from resisting the State?

15 How can a man be satisfied to entertain an opinion merely, and enjoy *it?* Is there any enjoyment in it, if his opinion is that he is aggrieved? If you are cheated out of a single dollar by your neighbor, you do not rest satisfied with knowing that you are cheated, or with saying that you are cheated, or even with petitioning him to pay you your due; but you take effectual steps at once to obtain the full amount, and see that you are never cheated again. Action from principle, the perception and the performance of right, changes things and relations; it is essentially revolutionary, and does not consist wholly with anything which was. It not only divides States and churches, it divides families; ay, it divides the *individual,* separating the diabolical in him from the divine.

16 Unjust laws exist: shall we be content to obey them, or shall we endeavor to amend them, and obey them until we have succeeded, or shall we transgress them at once? Men generally, under such a government as this, think that they ought to wait until they have persuaded the majority to alter them. They think that, if they should resist, the remedy would be worse than the evil. But it is the fault of the government itself that the remedy *is* worse than the evil. *It* makes it worse. Why is it not more apt to anticipate and provide for reform? Why does it not cherish its wise minority? Why does it cry and resist before it is hurt? Why does it not encourage its citizens

to be on the alert to point out its faults, and *do* better than it would have them? Why does it always crucify Christ, and excommunicate Copernicus and Luther, and pronounce Washington and Franklin rebels?

17 One would think, that a deliberate and practical denial of its authority was the only offence never contemplated by government; else, why has it not assigned its definite, its suitable and proportionate, penalty? If a man who has no property refuses but once to earn nine shillings for the State, he is put in prison for a period unlimited by any law that I know, and determined only by the discretion of those who placed him there; but if he should steal ninety times nine shillings from the State, he is soon permitted to go at large again.

18 If the injustice is part of the necessary friction of the machine of government, let it go, let it go: perchance it will wear smooth—certainly the machine will wear out. If the injustice has a spring, or a pulley, or a rope, or a crank, exclusively for itself, then perhaps you may consider whether the remedy will not be worse than the evil; but if it is of such a nature that it requires you to be the agent of injustice to another, then, I say, break the law. Let your life be a counter-friction to stop the machine. What I have to do is to see, at any rate, that I do not lend myself to the wrong which I condemn.

19 As for adopting the ways which the State has provided for remedying the evil, I know not of such ways. They take too much time, and a man's life will be gone. I have other affairs to attend to. I came into this world, not chiefly to make this a good place to live in, but to live in it, be it good or bad. A man has not everything to do, but something; and because he cannot do *everything,* it is not necessary that he should do *something* wrong. It is not my business to be petitioning the Governor or the Legislature any more than it is theirs to petition me; and if they should not hear my petition, what should I do then? But in this case the State has provided no way: its very Constitution is the evil. This may seem to be harsh and stubborn and unconciliatory; but it is to treat with the utmost kindness and consideration the only spirit that can appreciate or deserves it. So is all change for the better, like birth and death, which convulse the body.

20 I do not hesitate to say, that those who call themselves Abolitionists should at once effectually withdraw their support, both in person and property, from the government of Massachusetts, and not wait till they constitute a majority of one, before they suffer the right to prevail through them. I think that it is enough if they have God on their side, without waiting for that other one. Moreover, any man more right than his neighbors constitutes a majority of one already.

21 I meet this American government, or its representative, the State government, directly, and face to face, once a year—no more—in the person of its tax-gatherer; this is the only mode in which a man situated as I am necessarily meets it; and it then says distinctly, Recognize me; and the simplest, the most effectual, and, in the present posture of affairs, the indispensablest mode of treating with it on this head, of expressing your little satisfaction with and love for it, is to deny it then. My civil neighbor, the tax-gatherer, is the very man I have to deal with—for it is, after all, with men and not with parchment that I quarrel—and he has voluntarily chosen to be an agent of the government. How shall he ever know well what he is and does as an officer of the government, or as a man, until he is obliged to consider whether he shall treat me, his neighbor, for whom he has respect, as a neighbor and well-disposed man, or as a maniac and disturber of the peace, and see if he can get over this obstruction to his neighborliness without a ruder and more impetuous thought or speech corresponding with his action. I know this well, that if one thousand, if one hundred, if ten men whom I could name—if ten *honest* men only—ay, if *one* HONEST man, in this State of Massachusetts, *ceasing to hold slaves,* were actually to

withdraw from this copartnership, and be locked up in the county jail therefor, it would be the abolition of slavery in America. For it matters not how small the beginning may seem to be: what is once well done is done forever. But we love better to talk about it: that we say is our mission. Reform keeps many scores of newspapers in its service, but not one man. If my esteemed neighbor, the State's ambassador, who will devote his days to the settlement of the question of human rights in the Council Chamber, instead of being threatened with the prisons of Carolina, were to sit down the prisoner of Massachusetts, that State which is so anxious to foist the sin of slavery upon her sister—though at present she can discover only an act of inhospitality to be the ground of a quarrel with her—the Legislature would not wholly waive the subject the following winter.

22 Under a government which imprisons any unjustly, the true place for a just man is also a prison. The proper place today, the only place which Massachusetts has provided for her freer and less desponding spirits, is in her prisons, to be put out and locked out of the State by her own act, as they have already put themselves out by their principles. It is there that the fugitive slave, and the Mexican prisoner on parole, and the Indian come to plead the wrongs of his race should find them; on that separate, but more free and honorable, ground, where the State places those who are not *with* her, but *against* her—the only house in a slave State in which a free man can abide with honor. If any think that their influence would be lost there, and their voices no longer afflict the ear of the State, that they would not be as an enemy within its walls, they do not know by how much truth is stronger than error, nor how much more eloquently and effectively he can combat injustice who has experienced a little in his own person. Cast your whole vote, not a strip of paper merely, but your whole influence. A minority is powerless while it conforms to the majority; it is not even a minority then; but it is irresistible when it clogs by its whole weight. If the alternative is to keep all just men in prison, or give up war and slavery, the State will not hesitate which to choose. If a thousand men were not to pay their tax-bills this year, that would not be a violent and bloody measure, as it would be to pay them, and enable the State to commit violence and shed innocent blood. This is, in fact, the definition of a peaceable revolution, if any such is possible. If the tax-gatherer, or any other public officer, asks me, as one has done, "But what shall I do?" my answer is, "If you really wish to do anything, resign your office." When the subject has refused allegiance, and the officer has resigned his office, then the revolution is accomplished. But even suppose blood should flow. Is there not a sort of blood shed when the conscience is wounded? Through this wound a man's real manhood and immortality flow out, and he bleeds to an everlasting death. I see this blood flowing now.

23 I have contemplated the imprisonment of the offender, rather than the seizure of his goods—though both will serve the same purpose—because they who assert the purest right, and consequently are most dangerous to a corrupt State, commonly have not spent much time in accumulating property. To such the State renders comparatively small service, and a slight tax is wont to appear exorbitant, particularly if they are obliged to earn it by special labor with their hands. If there were one who lived wholly without the use of money, the State itself would hesitate to demand it of him. But the rich man—not to make any invidious comparison—is always sold to the institution which makes him rich. Absolutely speaking, the more money, the less virtue; for money comes between a man and his objects, and obtains them for him; and it was certainly no great virtue to obtain it. It puts to rest many questions which he would otherwise be taxed to answer; while the only new question which it puts is the hard but superfluous one, how to spend it. Thus his moral ground is taken

from under his feet. The opportunities of living are diminished in proportion as what are called the "means" are increased. The best thing a man can do for his culture when he is rich is to endeavor to carry out those schemes which he entertained when he was poor. Christ answered the Herodians according to their condition. "Show me the tribute-money," said he;—and one took a penny out of his pocket;—if you use money which has the image of Cæsar on it, and which he has made current and valuable, that is, *if you are men of the State,* and gladly enjoy the advantages of Cæsar's government, then pay him back some of his own when he demands it. "Render therefore to Cæsar that which is Cæsar's, and to God those things which are God's"—leaving them no wiser than before as to which was which; for they did not wish to know.

24 When I converse with the freest of my neighbors, I perceive that, whatever they may say about the magnitude and seriousness of the question, and their regard for the public tranquillity, the long and the short of the matter is, that they cannot spare the protection of the existing government, and they dread the consequences to their property and families of disobedience to it. For my own part, I should not like to think that I ever rely on the protection of the State. But, if I deny the authority of the State when it presents its tax-bill, it will soon take and waste all my property, and so harass me and my children without end. This is hard. This makes it impossible for a man to live honestly, and at the same time comfortably, in outward respects. It will not be worth the while to accumulate property; that would be sure to go again. You must hire or squat somewhere, and raise but a small crop, and eat that soon. You must live within yourself, and depend upon yourself always tucked up and ready for a start, and not have many affairs. A man may grow rich in Turkey even, if he will be in all respects a good subject of the Turkish government. Confucius said: "If a state is governed by the principles of reason, poverty and misery are subjects of shame; if a state is not governed by the principles of reason, riches and honors are the subjects of shame." No: until I want the protection of Massachusetts to be extended to me in some distant Southern port, where my liberty is endangered, or until I am bent solely on building up an estate at home by peaceful enterprise, I can afford to refuse allegiance to Massachusetts, and her right to my property and life. It costs me less in every sense to incur the penalty of disobedience to the State than it would to obey. I should feel as if I were worth less in that case.

25 Some years ago, the State met me in behalf of the Church, and commanded me to pay a certain sum toward the support of a clergyman whose preaching my father attended, but never I myself. "Pay," it said, "or be locked up in the jail." I declined to pay. But, unfortunately, another man saw fit to pay it. I did not see why the schoolmaster should be taxed to support the priest, and not the priest the schoolmaster; for I was not the State's schoolmaster, but I supported myself by voluntary subscription. I did not see why the lyceum should not present its tax-bill, and have the State to back its demand, as well as the Church. However, at the request of the selectmen, I condescended to make some such statement as this in writing:—"Know all men by these presents, that I, Henry Thoreau, do not wish to be regarded as a member of any incorporated society which I have not joined." This I gave to the town clerk; and he has it. The State, having thus learned that I did not wish to be regarded as a member of that church, has never made a like demand on me since; though it said that it must adhere to its original presumption that time. If I had known how to name them, I should then have signed off in detail from all the societies which I never signed on to; but I did not know where to find a complete list.

26 I have paid no poll-tax for six years. I was put into a jail once on this account, for one night; and, as I stood considering the walls of solid

stone, two or three feet thick, the door of wood and iron, a foot thick, and the iron grating which strained the light, I could not help being struck with the foolishness of that institution which treated me as if I were mere flesh and blood and bones, to be locked up. I wondered that it should have concluded at length that this was the best use it could put me to, and had never thought to avail itself of my services in some way. I saw that, if there was a wall of stone between me and my townsmen, there was a still more difficult one to climb or break through before they could get to be as free as I was. I did not for a moment feel confined, and the walls seemed a great waste of stone and mortar. I felt as if I alone of all my townsmen had paid my tax. They plainly did not know how to treat me, but behaved like persons who are underbred. In every threat and in every compliment there was a blunder; for they thought that my chief desire was to stand the other side of that stone wall. I could not but smile to see how industriously they locked the door on my meditations, which followed them out again without let or hindrance, and *they* were really all that was dangerous. As they could not reach me, they had resolved to punish my body; just as boys, if they cannot come at some person against whom they have a spite, will abuse his dog. I saw that the State was half-witted, that it was timid as a lone woman with her silver spoons, and that it did not know its friends from its foes, and I lost all my remaining respect for it, and pitied it.

27 Thus the State never intentionally confronts a man's sense, intellectual or moral, but only his body, his senses. It is not armed with superior wit or honesty, but with superior physical strength. I was not born to be forced. I will breathe after my own fashion. Let us see who is the strongest. What force has a multitude? They only can force me who obey a higher law than I. They force me to become like themselves. I do not hear of *men* being *forced* to live this way or that by masses of men. What sort of life were that to live? When I meet a government which says to me, "Your money or your life," why should I be in haste to give it my money? It may be in a great strait, and not know what to do: I cannot help that. It must help itself; do as I do. It is not worth the while to snivel about it. I am not responsible for the successful working of the machinery of society. I am not the son of the engineer. I perceive that, when an acorn and a chestnut fall side by side, the one does not remain inert to make way for the other, but both obey their own laws, and spring and grow and flourish as best they can, till one, perchance, overshadows and destroys the other. If a plant cannot live according to its nature, it dies; and so a man.

28 The night in prison was novel and interesting enough. The prisoners in their shirt-sleeves were enjoying a chat and the evening air in the doorway, when I entered. But the jailer said, "Come, boys, it is time to lock up;" and so they dispersed, and I heard the sound of their steps returning into the hollow apartments. My room-mate was introduced to me by the jailer as "a first-rate fellow and a clever man." When the door was locked, he showed me where to hang my hat, and how he managed matters there. The rooms were whitewashed once a month; and this one, at least, was the whitest, most simply furnished, and probably the neatest apartment in the town. He naturally wanted to know where I came from, and what brought me there; and, when I had told him, I asked him in my turn how he came there, presuming him to be an honest man, of course; and, as the world goes, I believe he was. "Why," said he, "they accuse me of burning a barn; but I never did it." As near as I could discover, he had probably gone to bed in a barn when drunk, and smoked his pipe there; and so a barn was burnt. He had the reputation of being a clever man, had been there some three months waiting for his trial to come on, and would have to wait as much longer; but he was quite domesticated and contented, since he got his board for nothing, and thought that he was well treated.

29 He occupied one window, and I the other; and I saw that if one stayed there long, his prin-

cipal business would be to look out the window. I had soon read all the tracts that were left there, and examined where former prisoners had broken out, and where a grate had been sawed off, and heard the history of the various occupants of that room; for I found that even here there was a history and a gossip which never circulated beyond the walls of the jail. Probably this is the only house in the town where verses are composed, which are afterward printed in a circular form, but not published. I was shown quite a long list of verses which were composed by some young men who had been detected in an attempt to escape, who avenged themselves by singing them.

30 I pumped my fellow-prisoner as dry as I could, for fear I should never see him again; but at length he showed me which was my bed, and left me to blow out the lamp.

31 It was like travelling into a far country, such as I had never expected to behold, to lie there for one night. It seemed to me that I never had heard the town clock strike before, nor the evening sounds of the village; for we slept with the windows open, which were inside the grating. It was to see my native village in the light of the Middle Ages, and our Concord was turned into a Rhine stream, and visions of knights and castles passed before me. They were the voices of old burghers that I heard in the streets. I was an involuntary spectator and auditor of whatever was done and said in the kitchen of the adjacent village inn—a wholly new and rare experience to me. It was a closer view of my native town. I was fairly inside of it. I never had seen its institutions before. This is one of its peculiar institutions; for it is a shire town. I began to comprehend what its inhabitants were about.

32 In the morning, our breakfasts were put through the hole in the door, in small oblong-square tin pans, made to fit, and holding a pint of chocolate, with brown bread, and an iron spoon. When they called for the vessels again, I was green enough to return what bread I had left; but my comrade seized it, and said that I should lay that up for lunch or dinner. Soon after he was let out to work at haying in a neighboring field, whither he went every day, and would not be back till noon; so he bade me good-day, saying that he doubted if he should see me again.

33 When I came out of prison—for some one interfered, and paid that tax—I did not perceive that great changes had taken place on the common, such as he observed who went in a youth and emerged a tottering and gray-headed man; and yet a change had to my eyes come over the scene—the town, and State, and country—greater than any that mere time could effect. I saw yet more distinctly the State in which I lived. I saw to what extent the people among whom I lived could be trusted as good neighbors and friends; that their friendship was for summer weather only; that they did not greatly propose to do right; that they were a distinct race from me by their prejudices and superstitions, as the Chinamen and Malays are; that in their sacrifices to humanity they ran no risks, not even to their property; that after all they were not so noble but they treated the thief as he had treated them, and hoped, by a certain outward observance and a few prayers, and by walking in a particular straight though useless path from time to time, to save their souls. This may be to judge my neighbors harshly; for I believe that many of them are not aware that they have such an institution as the jail in their village.

34 It was formerly the custom in our village, when a poor debtor came out of jail, for his acquaintances to salute him, looking through their fingers, which were crossed to represent the grating of a jail window, "How do ye do?" My neighbors did not thus salute me, but first looked at me, and then at one another, as if I had returned from a long journey. I was put into jail as I was going to the shoemaker's to get a shoe which was mended. When I was let out the next morning, I proceeded to finish my errand, and, having put on my mended shoe, joined a huckle-berry party, who were impatient to put themselves under my conduct; and in half an hour—for the horse was

soon tackled—was in the midst of a huckleberry field, on one of our highest hills, two miles off, and then the State was nowhere to be seen.

35 This is the whole history of "My Prisons."

36 I have never declined paying the highway tax, because I am as desirous of being a good neighbor as I am of being a bad subject; and as for supporting schools, I am doing my part to educate my fellow-countrymen now. It is for no particular item in the tax-bill that I refuse to pay it. I simply wish to refuse allegiance to the State, to withdraw and stand aloof from it effectually. I do not care to trace the course of my dollar, if I could, till it buys a man or a musket to shoot one with—the dollar is innocent—but I am concerned to trace the effects of my allegiance. In fact, I quietly declare war with the State, after my fashion, though I will still make what use and get what advantage of her I can, as is usual in such cases.

37 If others pay the tax which is demanded of me, from a sympathy with the State, they do but what they have already done in their own case, or rather they abet injustice to a greater extent than the State requires. If they pay the tax from a mistaken interest in the individual taxed, to save his property, or prevent his going to jail, it is because they have not considered wisely how far they let their private feelings interfere with the public good.

38 This, then, is my position at present. But one cannot be too much on his guard in such a case, lest his action be biased by obstinacy or an undue regard for the opinions of men. Let him see that he does only what belongs to himself and to the hour.

39 I think sometimes, Why, this people mean well, they are only ignorant; they would do better if they knew how: why give your neighbors this pain to treat you as they are not inclined to? But I think again, This is no reason why I should do as they do, or permit others to suffer much greater pain of a different kind. Again, I sometimes say to myself, When many millions of men, without heat, without ill will, without personal feeling of any kind, demand of you a few shillings only, without the possibility, such is their constitution, of retracting or altering their present demand, and without the possibility, on your side, of appeal to any other millions, why expose yourself to this overwhelming brute force? You do not resist cold and hunger, the winds and the waves, thus obstinately; you quietly submit to a thousand similar necessities. You do not put your head into the fire. But just in proportion as I regard this as not wholly a brute force, but partly a human force, and consider that I have relations to those millions as to so many millions of men, and not of mere brute or inanimate things, I see that appeal is possible, first and instantaneously, from them to the Maker of them, and, secondly, from them to themselves. But if I put my head deliberately into the fire, there is no appeal to fire or to the Maker of fire, and I have only myself to blame. If I could convince myself that I have any right to be satisfied with men as they are, and to treat them accordingly, and not according, in some respects, to my requisitions and expectations of what they and I ought to be, then, like a good Mussulman and fatalist, I should endeavor to be satisfied with things as they are, and say it is the will of God. And, above all, there is this difference between resisting this and a purely brute or natural force, that I can resist this with some effect; but I cannot expect, like Orpheus, to change the nature of the rocks and trees and beasts.

40 I do not wish to quarrel with any man or nation. I do not wish to split hairs, to make fine distinctions, or set myself up as better than my neighbors. I seek rather, I may say, even an excuse for conforming to the laws of the land. I am but too ready to conform to them. Indeed, I have reason to suspect myself on this head; and each year, as the tax-gatherer comes round, I find myself disposed to review the acts and position of the general and State governments, and the spirit

of the people, to discover a pretext for conformity.

> "We must affect our country as our parents,
> And if at any time we alienate
> Our love or industry from doing it honor,
> We must respect effects and teach the soul
> Matter of conscience and religion,
> And not desire of rule or benefit."

I believe that the State will soon be able to take all my work of this sort out of my hands, and then I shall be no better a patriot than my fellow-countrymen. Seen from a lower point of view, the Constitution, with all its faults, is very good; the law and the courts are very respectable; even this State and this American government are, in many respects, very admirable, and rare things, to be thankful for, such as a great many have described them; but seen from a point of view a little higher, they are what I have described them; seen from a higher still, and the highest, who shall say what they are, or that they are worth looking at or thinking of at all?

41 However, the government does not concern me much, and I shall bestow the fewest possible thoughts on it. It is not many moments that I live under a government, even in this world. If a man is thought-free, fancy-free, imagination-free, that which *is not* never for a long time appearing *to be* to him, unwise rulers or reformers
42 cannot fatally interrupt him.

I know that most men think differently from myself; but those whose lives are by profession devoted to the study of these or kindred subjects content me as little as any. Statesmen and legislators, standing so completely within the institution, never distinctly and nakedly behold it. They speak of moving society, but have no resting-place without it. They may be men of a certain experience and discrimination, and have no doubt invented ingenious and even useful systems, for which we sincerely thank them; but all their wit and usefulness lie within certain not very wide limits. They are wont to forget that the world is not governed by policy and expediency. Webster never goes behind government, and so cannot speak with authority about it. His words are wisdom to those legislators who contemplate no essential reform in the existing government; but for thinkers, and those who legislate for all time, he never once glances at the subject. I know of those whose serene and wise speculations on this theme would soon reveal the limits of his mind's range and hospitality. Yet, compared with the cheap professions of most reformers, and the still cheaper wisdom and eloquence of politicians in general, his are almost the only sensible and valuable words, and we thank Heaven for him. Comparatively, he is always strong, original, and, above all, practical. Still, his quality is not wisdom, but prudence. The lawyer's truth is not Truth, but consistency or a consistent expediency. Truth is always in harmony with herself, and is not concerned chiefly to reveal the justice that may consist with wrong-doing. He well deserves to be called, as he has been called, the Defender of the Constitution. There are really no blows to be given by him but defensive ones. He is not a leader, but a follower. His leaders are the men of '87. "I have never made an effort," he says, "and never propose to make an effort; I have never countenanced an effort, and never mean to countenance an effort, to disturb the arrangement as originally made, by which the various States came into the Union." Still thinking of the sanction which the Constitution gives to slavery, he says, "Because it was a part of the original compact—let it stand." Notwithstanding his special acuteness and ability, he is unable to take a fact out of its merely political relations, and behold it as it lies absolutely to be disposed of by the intellect—what, for instance, it behooves a man to do here in America today with regard to slavery—but ventures, or is driven, to make some such desperate answer as the following, while professing to speak absolutely, and as a private man—from which what new and singular code of social duties might be inferred? "The manner," says he, "in which the governments of those States where slavery exists are to regulate it is for their own consideration, under their responsibility to their constituents, to the general laws of propriety, humanity, and justice, and to God. Associations formed elsewhere, springing from a feeling of humanity, or any other cause, have nothing whatever to do with it. They have never received any encouragement from me, and they never will."[1]

43 They who know of no purer sources of truth, who have traced up its stream no higher, stand, and wisely stand, by the Bible and the Constitution, and drink at it there with reverence and humility; but they who behold where it comes trickling into this lake or that pool, gird up their loins once more, and continue their pilgrimage toward its fountain-head.

44 No man with a genius for legislation has appeared in America. They are rare in the history of the world. There are orators, politicians, and eloquent men, by the thousand; but the speaker has not yet opened his mouth to speak who is capable of settling the much-vexed questions of the day. We love eloquence for its own sake, and not for any truth which it may utter, or any heroism it may inspire. Our legislators have not yet learned the comparative value of free trade and of freedom, of union, and of rectitude, to a nation. They have no genius or talent for comparatively humble questions of taxation and finance, commerce and manufactures and agriculture. If we were left solely to the wordy wit of legislators in Congress for our guidance, uncorrected by the seasonable experience and the effectual complaints of the people, America would not long retain her rank among the nations. For eighteen hundred years, though perchance I have no right to say it, the New Testament has been written; yet where is the legislator who has wisdom and practical talent enough to avail himself of the light which it sheds on the science of legislation?

45 The authority of government, even such as I am willing to submit to—for I will cheerfully obey those who know and can do better than I, and in many things even those who neither know nor can do so well—is still an impure one: to be strictly just, it must have the sanction and consent of the governed. It can have no pure right over my person and property but what I concede to it. The progress from an absolute to a limited monarchy, from a limited monarchy to a democracy, is a progress toward a true respect for the individual. Even the Chinese philosopher was wise enough to regard the individual as the basis of the empire. Is a democracy, such as we know it, the last improvement possible in government? Is it not possible to take a step further towards recognizing and organizing the rights of man? There will never be a really free and enlightened State until the State comes to recognize the individual as a higher and independent power, from which all its own power and authority are derived, and treats him accordingly. I please myself with imagining a State at least which can afford to be just to all men, and to treat the individual with respect as a neighbor; which even would not think it inconsistent with its own repose if a few were to live aloof from it, not meddling with it, nor embraced by it, who fulfilled all the duties of neighbors and fellow-men. A State which bore this kind of fruit, and suffered it to drop off as fast as it ripened, would prepare the way for a still more perfect and glorious State, which also I have imagined, but not yet anywhere seen.

1. These extracts have been inserted since the lecture was read.

Thinking about the Argument

1. What does Thoreau mean when he says, "I heartily accept the motto,—'That government is best which governs least'"? What is your reaction to this saying? How do you react to his statement that "That government is best which governs not at all"?
2. Does the author think that government helps or hinders commerce? What, in his opinion, is the relationship of the individual to the government? What evidence does he cite to back his claims?
3. Does the author believe that the individual has the right to resist a government he or she does not believe in? Explain.
4. Do you think Thoreau has much faith in democratic elections in the United States? Why or why not?
5. What reasons does Thoreau give for his refusal to pay taxes? Explain.

Responding to the Argument

1. Do you think that Thoreau would approve of the civil rights movement? Explain.
2. Do you agree with the author's position that the government of the United States is oppressive and restricts freedom? Why or why not? Support your assertion with at least one example.
3. Thoreau indicates that citizens who disagree with the government should "at once effectually withdraw their support, both in person and property, from the government." Is this strategy practical in today's society? Why or why not? How does this advice compare with the strategies advocated by Martin Luther King, Jr., during the civil rights movement?
4. As he closes his argument, Thoreau says, "There will never be a really free and enlightened State, until the State comes to recognize the individual as a higher and independent power, from which all its own power and authority are derived, and treats him accordingly." Do you believe that the United States has yet achieved this goal? Why or why not?

Writing about the Argument

1. Think of a social cause that calls for civil disobedience today. Write an essay (or Internet blog, letter to the editor, or other document) explaining why civil disobedience is an appropriate response to this situation. For an additional challenge, outline the steps that such disobedience should entail, and explain why they are necessary.
2. Write a letter to Thoreau explaining why it is every citizen's duty to pay taxes. Provide evidence to support your claims.
3. Do you think it is practical—or even possible—to withdraw from society these days to the extent that Thoreau advocates? Why or why not? Explain your answer in the form of a short argument or journal entry.

READING SELECTION

"Women's Time"

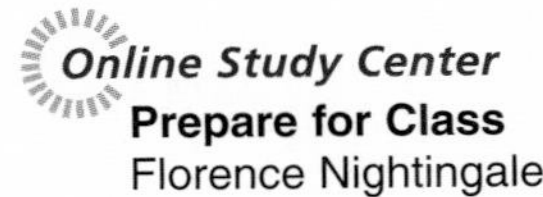

ABOUT THE AUTHOR: FLORENCE NIGHTINGALE

Florence Nightingale (1820–1910) is most famous for her work as a nurse and reformer of hospitals. Against her family's wishes, she sought training as a nurse and joined a force of likeminded women who fought the unsanitary conditions that faced British soldiers fighting against Russia in the Crimean peninsula. Nightingale was also a social and political revolutionary who rebelled against the traditional expectations of role and behavior laid upon women in the Victorian age. Among other accomplishments, she founded schools for nurses and midwives. The following excerpt is from *Cassandra,* Nightingale's reflection on the traditional role of women in British Victorian society.

BEFORE YOU READ

1. List three things that the name "Florence Nightingale" brings to mind. What do you expect her writing to be about?
2. What do you think were the traditional expectations of women in the Victorian era? Do you think conditions were different for members of the upper and lower classes? How so?
3. Why do you think Nightingale rejected her family's expectation that she should marry and lead a life of upper-class leisure? Do you think her relationship with her family was strained after she made her decision? Why or why not?
4. Briefly scan the reading. What do you expect the thrust of Nightingale's argument to be? Why do you think this?

Women's Time

Yet I would spare no pang,
Would wish no torture less,
The more that anguish racks,
The earlier it will bless.

1 Give us back our suffering, we cry to Heaven in our hearts—suffering rather than indifferentism; for out of nothing comes nothing. But out of suffering may come the cure. Better have pain than paralysis! A hundred struggle and drown in the breakers. One discovers the new world. But rather, ten times rather, die in the surf, heralding the way to that new world, than stand idly on the shore!

2 Passion, intellect, moral activity—these three have never been satisfied in a woman. In this cold and oppressive conventional atmosphere, they cannot be satisfied. To say more on this subject would be to enter into the whole history of society, of the present state of civilization.

3 Look at that lizard—"It is not hot," he says, "I like it. The atmosphere which enervates you is life to me." The state of society which some complain of makes others happy. Why should these complain to those? *They* do not suffer. *They* would not understand it, any more than that lizard would comprehend the sufferings of a Shetland sheep.

4 The progressive world is necessarily divided into two classes—those who take the best of what there is and enjoy it—those who wish for something better and try to create it. Without these two classes the world would be badly off.

They are the very conditions of progress, both the one and the other. Were there none who were discontented with what they have, the world would never reach anything better. And, through the other class, which is constantly taking the best of what the first is creating for them, a balance is secured, and that which is conquered is held fast. But with neither class must we quarrel for not possessing the privileges of the other. The laws of the nature of each make it impossible.

5 Is discontent a privilege?

6 Yes, it is a privilege for you to suffer for your race—a privilege not reserved to the Redeemer, and the martyrs alone, but one enjoyed by numbers in every age.

7 The common-place life of thousands; and in that is its only interest—its only merit as a history; viz. that it is the type of common sufferings—the story of one who has not the courage to resist nor to submit to the civilization of her time—is this.

8 Poetry and imagination begin life. A child will fall on its knees on the gravel walk at the sight of a pink hawthorn in full flower, when it is by itself, to praise God for it.

9 Then comes intellect. It wishes to satisfy the wants which intellect creates for it. But there is a physical, not moral, impossibility of supplying the wants of the intellect in the state of civilization at which we have arrived. The stimulus, the training, the time, are all three wanting to us; or, in other words, the means and inducements are not there.

10 Look at the poor lives we lead. It is a wonder that we are so good as we are, not that we are so bad. In looking round we are struck with the power of the organizations we see, not with their want of power. Now and then, it is true, we are conscious that *there* is an inferior organization, but, in general, just the contrary. Mrs. A. has the imagination, the poetry of a Murillo, and has sufficient power of execution to show that she might have had a great deal more. Why is she not a Murillo? From a material difficulty, not a mental one. If she has a knife and fork in her hands for three hours of the day, she cannot have a pencil or brush. Dinner is the great sacred ceremony of this day, the great sacrament. To be absent from dinner is equivalent to being ill. Nothing else will excuse us from it. Bodily incapacity is the only apology valid. If she has a pen and ink in her hands during other three hours, writing answers for the penny post, again, she cannot have her pencil, and *so ad infinitum* through life. People have no type before them in their lives, neither fathers nor mothers, nor the children themselves. They look at things in detail. They say, "It is very desirable that A., my daughter, should go to such a party, should know such a lady, should sit by such a person." It is true. But what standard have they before them of the nature and destination of man? The very words are rejected as pedantic. But might they not, at least, have a type in their minds that such an one might be a discoverer through her intellect, such another through her art, a third through her moral power?

11 Women often try one branch of intellect after another in their youth, *e.g.* mathematics. But that, least of all is compatible with the life of "society." It is impossible to follow up anything systematically. Women often long to enter some man's profession where they would find direction, competition (or rather opportunity of measuring the intellect with others) and, above all, time.

12 In those wise institutions, mixed as they are with many follies, which will last as long as the human race lasts, because they are adapted to the wants of the human race; those institutions which we call monasteries, and which, embracing much that is contrary to the laws of nature, are yet better adapted to the union of the life of action and that of thought than any other mode of life with which we are acquainted; in many such, four and a half hours, at least, are daily set aside for thought, rules are given for thought, training and opportunity afforded. Among us

there is *no* time appointed for this purpose, and the difficulty is that, in our social life, we must be always doubtful whether we ought not to be with somebody else or be doing something else.

13 Are men better off than women in this?

14 If one calls upon a friend in London and sees her son in the drawing-room, it strikes one as odd to find a young man sitting idle in his mother's drawing-room in the morning. For men, who are seen much in those haunts, there is no end of the epithets we have: "knights of the carpet," "drawing-room heroes," "ladies' men." But suppose we were to see a number of men in the morning sitting round a table in the drawing-room, looking at prints, doing worsted work, and reading little books, how we should laugh! A member of the House of Commons was once known to do worsted work. Of another man was said, "His only fault is that he is too good; he drives out with his mother every day in the carriage, and if he is asked anywhere he answers that he must dine with his mother, but, if she can spare him, he will come in to tea, and he does not come."

15 Now, why is it more ridiculous for a man than for a woman to do worsted work and drive out every day in the carriage? Why should we laugh if we were to see a parcel of men sitting round a drawing-room table in the morning, and think it all right if they were women?

16 Is man's time more valuable than woman's? or is the difference between man and woman this, that woman has confessedly nothing to do?

17 Women are never supposed to have any occupation of sufficient importance *not* to be interrupted, except "suckling their fools"; and women themselves have accepted this, have written books to support it, and have trained themselves so as to consider whatever they do as *not* of such value to the world or to others, but that they can throw it up at the first "claim of social life." They have accustomed themselves to consider intellectual occupation as a merely selfish amusement, which it is their "duty" to give up for every trifler more selfish than themselves.

18 A young man (who was afterwards useful and known in his day and generation) when busy reading and sent for by his proud mother to shine in some morning visit, came; but, after it was over, he said, "Now, remember, this is not to happen again. I came that you might not think me sulky, but I shall not come again." But for a young woman to send such a message to her mother and sisters, how impertinent it would be! A woman of great administrative powers said that she never undertook anything which she "could not throw by at once, if necessary."

19 How do we explain then the many cases of women who have distinguished themselves in classics, mathematics, even in politics?

20 Widowhood, ill-health, or want of bread, these three explanations or excuses are supposed to justify a woman taking up an occupation. In some cases, no doubt, an indomitable force of character will suffice without any of these three, but such are rare.

21 But see how society fritters away the intellects of those comitted to her charge! It is said that society is necessary to sharpen the intellect. But what do we seek society for? It does sharpen the intellect, because it is a kind of *tour-de-force* to say something at a pinch,—unprepared and uninterested with any subject, to improvise something under difficulties. But what "go we out for to seek"? To take the chance of some one having something to say which we want to hear? or of finding something to say which *they* want to hear? You have a little to say, but not much. You often make a stipulation with someone else, "Come in ten minutes, for I shall not be able to find enough to spin out longer than that." You are not to talk of anything very interesting, for the essence of society is to prevent any long conversations and all tête-à-têtes. *Glissez, n'appuyez pas* is its very motto. The praise of a good *maîtresse demaison* consists in this, that she allows no one person to be too much absorbed in, or too long about, a conversation. She always recalls them to their "duty." People do not go into

the company of their fellow-creatures for what would seem a very sufficient reason, namely, that they have something to say to them, or something that they want to hear from them; but in the vague hope that they may find something to say.

22 Then as to solitary opportunities. Women never have an half-hour in all their lives (excepting before or after anybody is up in the house) that they can call their own, without fear of offending or of hurting someone. Why do people sit up so late, or, more rarely, get up so early? Not because the day is not long enough, but because they have "no time in the day to themselves."

23 If we do attempt to do anything in company, what is the system of literary exercise which we pursue? Everybody reads aloud out of their own book or newspaper—or, every five minutes, something is said. And what is it to be "read aloud to"? The most miserable exercise of the human intellect. Or rather, is it any exercise at all? It is like lying on one's back, with one's hands tied and having liquid poured down one's throat. Worse than that, because suffocation would immediately ensue and put a stop to this operation. But no suffocation would stop the other.

24 So much for the satisfaction of the intellect. Yet for a married woman in society, it is even worse. A married woman was heard to wish that she could break a limb that she might have a little time to herself. Many take advantage of the fear of "infection" to do the same.

25 It is a thing *so* accepted among women that they have nothing to do, that one woman has not the least scruple in saying to another, "I will come and spend the morning with you." And you would be thought quite surly and absurd, if you were to refuse it on the plea of occupation. Nay, it is thought a mark of amiability and affection, if you are "on such terms" that you can "come in" "any morning you please."

26 In a country house, if there is a large party of young people, "You will spend the morning with us," they say to the neighbors, "we will drive together in the afternoon," "tomorrow we will make an expedition, and we will spend the evening together." And this is thought friendly and spending time in a pleasant manner. So women play through life. Yet time is the most valuable of all things. If they had come every morning and afternoon and robbed us of half-a-crown we should have had redress from the police. But it is laid down, that our time is of no value. If you offer a morning visit to a professional man, and say, "I will just stay an hour with you, if you will allow me, till so and so comes back to fetch me"; it costs him the earnings of an hour, and therefore he has a right to complain. But women have no right, because it is "*only* their time."

27 Women have no means given them, whereby they *can* resist the "claims of social life." They are taught from their infancy upwards that it is a wrong, ill-tempered, and a misunderstanding of "woman's mission" (with a great M) if they do not allow themselves *willingly* to be interrupted at all hours. If a woman has once put in a claim to be treated as a man by some work of science or art or literature, which she can *show* as the "fruit of her leisure," then she will be considered justified in *having* leisure (hardly, perhaps, even then). But if not, not. If she has nothing to show, she must resign herself to her fate.

THINKING ABOUT THE ARGUMENT

1. What does the first paragraph suggest regarding Nightingale's expectations in life? What is the "new world" to which she refers? Can you restate the last sentence of paragraph 1 in your own words?
2. What is the meaning of paragraph 2? State it in your own words. What is the meaning of "cold and oppressive conventional atmosphere"? In what way, if any, does paragraph 9 further illustrate this point?
3. What are the differences regarding the expectations of men and women in upper-class society that Nightingale disparages?
4. What, according to the author, are the traditional explanations for women to take up professions?
5. Why does Nightingale believe that women in upper-class society have so little time to devote to their own interests?

RESPONDING TO THE ARGUMENT

1. Nightingale discusses the plight of upper-class British women as being, on the one hand, a life of leisure and, on the other hand, a life without choice. Is this a contradiction? Why or why not?
2. What conditions described by Nightingale do you think have improved for women since the Victorian era, regardless of their class? Explain.
3. In what ways are women's choices still more limited than those available to men? Why do you think this?
4. Do you think that women of the lower classes or upper classes have more freedom and discretion in their lives? Why do you think this? (As you prepare your answer, consider whether freedom from toil and freedom of choice are necessarily the same thing.)

WRITING ABOUT THE ARGUMENT

1. Write a journal entry or brief argument discussing the ways in which women's freedom of choice has not improved since the Victorian era. What improvements still need to be made, and why?
2. Is there a "double jeopardy" for women of color? Write an essay arguing which is the most difficult for women to overcome—barriers associated with gender or barriers associated with race. Use concrete examples to illustrate your argument.
3. In what ways might women of the working classes have more freedom than women of the upper classes? Write a journal entry or argument discussing whether poorer women have more freedom of choice in making decisions about their day-to-day lives.
4. How do the cultural barriers faced by Victorian women compare with the cultural barriers confronted by gays and lesbians today? Do lesbians suffer from the sort of "double jeopardy" as described in Question 2? Write a journal entry or argument addressing this issue.

READING SELECTION

"Address by Elizabeth Cady Stanton on Woman's Rights"

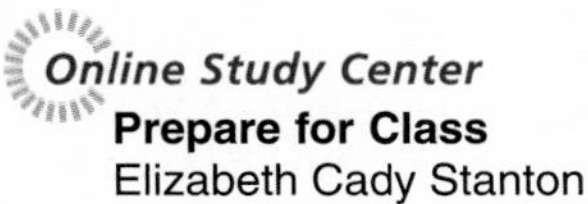

About the Author: Elizabeth Cady Stanton

Elizabeth Cady Stanton (1815–1902) was a social activist and advocate for women's rights. After her marriage, she refused to be addressed as "Mrs. Henry Stanton." Stanton was also an abolitionist and a supporter of the temperance movement. (She would later express her disappointment when the abolitionists did not push for the vote for women as they did for African American men.) Although she helped Susan B. Anthony in her drive to secure the vote for women, Stanton sought a more ambitious program of liberation than that endorsed by Anthony. The following speech was probably first delivered in 1848.

Before You Read

1. How do you think Stanton's life might have been similar or different from Nightingale's life? Why do you think this?
2. Stanton was a political activist who sought to reform American attitudes toward women's rights, whereas Nightingale dedicated her life to helping the sick and improving sanitary conditions in hospitals. Is there a difference in your opinion of the two writers? Which writer might you consider a more authoritative source on the topic of women's rights, and why?
3. Scan the speech. What do you expect Stanton's central point to be, and why? What do you expect her three most significant supporting points to be?

Address by Elizabeth Cady Stanton on Woman's Rights

1 Ladies and gentlemen, when invited some weeks ago to address you I proposed to a gentleman of this village to review our report of the Seneca Falls convention and give his objections to our Declaration, resolutions, and proceedings to serve me as a text on which to found an address for this evening. The gentleman did so, but his review was so laconic that there was the same difficulty in replying to it as we found in replying to a recent sermon preached at Seneca Falls—there was nothing of it.

2 Should that gentleman be present this evening and feel disposed to give any of his objections to our movement, we will be most happy to answer him.

3 I should feel exceedingly diffident to appear before you wholly unused as I am to public speaking, were I not nerved by a sense of right and duty—did I not feel that the time had fully come for the question of woman's wrongs to be laid before the public—did I not believe that woman herself must do this work—for woman alone can understand the height and the depth, the length and the breadth of her own degradation and woe. Man cannot speak for us—because he has been educated to believe that we differ from him so materially, that he cannot judge of our thoughts, feelings, and opinions by his own. Moral beings can only judge of others by themselves—the moment they give a different nature to any of their own kind they utterly fail. The

drunkard was hopelessly lost until it was discovered that he was governed by the same laws of mind as the sober man. Then with what magic power, by kindness and love, was he raised from the slough of despond and placed rejoicing on high land. Let a man once settle the question that woman does not think and feel like himself and he may as well undertake to judge of the amount of intellect and sensation of any of the animal creation as of woman's nature. He can know but little with certainty, and that but by observation.

4 Among the many important questions which have been brought before the public, there is none that more vitally affects the whole human family than that which is technically termed Woman's rights. Every allusion to the degraded and inferior position occupied by woman all over the world has ever been met by scorn and abuse. From the man of highest mental cultivation to the most degraded wretch who staggers in the streets do we hear ridicule and coarse jests, freely bestowed upon those who dare assert that woman stands by the side of man—his equal, placed here by her God to enjoy with him the beautiful earth, which is her home as it is his—having the same sense of right and wrong and looking to the same Being for guidance and support. So long has man exercised a tyranny over her injurious to himself and benumbing to *her* faculties, that but few can nerve themselves against the storm, and so long has the chain been about her that however galling it may be she knows not there is a remedy. . . .

5 Let us now glance at some of the popular objections to this whole question. There is a class of men who believe in the natural inborn, inbred superiority both in body and mind and their full complete Heaven descended right to lord it over the fish of the sea, the fowl of the air, the beast of the field, and last tho' not least the immortal being called woman. I would recommend this class to the attentive perusal of their Bibles—to historical research, to foreign travel—to a closer observation of the manifestations of mind about them and to an humble comparison of themselves with such women as Catharine of Russia and Elizabeth of England distinguished for their statesmanlike qualities, Harriet Martineau and Madame de Stael for their literary attainments, or Caroline Herschel and Mary Summerville for their scientific researches, or for physical equality to that whole nation of famous women the Amazones. We seldom find this class of objectors among liberally educated persons, who have had the advantage of observing their race in different countries, climes, and under different phases, but barbarians tho' they be in entertaining such an opinion—they must be met and fairly vanquished.

Man Superior, Intellectually, Morally, and Physically

6 1st: Let us consider his intellectual superiority. Man's superiority cannot be a question until we have had a fair trial. When we shall have had our colleges, our professions, our trades, for a century a comparison may then be justly instituted. When woman instead of being taxed to endow colleges where she is forbidden to enter, instead of forming societies to educate young men shall first educate herself, when she shall be just to herself before she is generous to others—improving the talents God has given her and leaving her neighbor to do the same for himself we shall not then hear so much of this boasted greatness. How often now we see young men carelessly throwing away the intellectual food their sisters crave. A little music that she may while an hour away pleasantly, a little French, a smattering of the sciences, and in rare instances some slight classical knowledge and a woman is considered highly educated. She leaves her books and studies just at the time a young man is entering thoroughly into his—then comes the cares and perplexities of married life. Her sphere being confined to her house and children, the burden generally being very unequally divided, she

knows nothing beside and whatever yearning her spirit may have felt for a higher existence, whatever may have been the capacity she well knew she possessed for more elevated enjoyments—enjoyments which would not conflict with these but add new lustre to them—it is all buried beneath the weight that presses upon her. Men, bless their innocence, are fond of representing themselves as beings of reason—of intellect—while women are mere creatures of the affections. There is a self-conceit that makes the possesser infinitely happy and one would dislike to dispel the illusion, if it were possible to endure it. . . .

2nd: Let us consider man's claims to superi-
7 ority as a moral being. Look now at our theological seminaries, our divinity students—the long line of descendants from our apostolic Fathers and what do we find here? Perfect moral rectitude in every relation of life, a devoted spirit of self-sacrifice, a perfect union in thought opinion and feeling among those who profess to worship the one God and whose laws they feel themselves called upon to declare to a fallen race? Far from it. These persons all so thoroughly acquainted with the character of God and of his designs made manifest by his words and works are greatly divided among themselves—every sect has its God, every sect has its own Bible, and there is as much bitterness, envy, hatred, and malice between these contending sects yea even more than in our political parties during periods of the greatest excitement. Now the leaders of these sects are the *priesthood* who are supposed to have passed their lives almost in the study of the Bible, in various languages and with various commentaries, in the contemplation of the infinite, the eternal, and the glorious future open to the redeemed of earth. Are they distinguished among men for their holy aspirations—their virtue, purity, and chastity? Do they keep themselves unspotted from the world? Is the moral and religious life of this class what we might expect from minds (said to be) continually fixed on such mighty themes? By no means, not a year passes but we hear of some sad soul-sickening deed perpetrated by some of this class. If such be the state of the most holy we need not pause now to consider those classes who claim of us less reverence and respect. The lamentable want of principle among our lawyers generally is too well known to need comment—the everlasting bickering and backbiting of our physicians is proverbial. The disgraceful riots at our polls where man in performing so important a duty of a citizen ought surely to be sober minded. The perfect rowdyism that now characterizes the debates in our national congress—all these are great facts which rise up against man's claim to moral superiority.

In my opinion he is infinitely woman's inferior in every moral virtue, not by nature, but
8 made so by a false education. In carrying out his own selfishness, man has greatly improved woman's moral nature, but by an almost total shipwreck of his own. Woman has now the noble virtues of the martyr, she is early schooled to self-denial and suffering. But man is not so wholly buried in selfishness that he does not sometimes get a glimpse of the narrowness of his soul, as compared with women. Then he says by way of an excuse for his degradation, God made woman more self-denying than us, it is her nature, it does not cost her as much to give up her wishes, her will, her life even as it does us. We are naturally selfish, God made us so. No! Think not that He who made the heavens and the earth, the whole planetary world ever moving on in such harmony and order, that He who has so bountifully scattered, through all nature so many objects that delight, enchant, and fill us with admiration and wonder, that He who has made the mighty ocean mountain and cataract, the bright and joyous birds, the tender lovely flowers, that He who made man in His own image, perfect, noble and pure, loving justice, mercy, and truth, think not that He has had any part in the production of that creeping, cringing, crawling, debased selfish monster now extant, claiming for himself the name of man. No, God's commands rest upon man as well as woman, and it is as much his duty

to be kind, gentle, self-denying, and full of good works as it is hers, as much his duty to absent himself from scenes of violence as it is hers. A place or a position that would require the sacrifice of delicacy and refinement of woman's nature is unfit for man, for these virtues should be as carefully guarded in him as in her.

The false ideas that prevail with regard to the purity necessary to constitute the perfect character in woman and that requisite for man
9 have done an infinite deal of mischief in the world. We would not have woman less pure, but we would have man more so. We would have the same code of morals for both. Moral delinquencies which exclude women from the society of the true and the good should assign to man the same place. Our partiality towards man has been the fruitful source of dissipation and riot, drunkenness, and debauchery and immorality of all kinds. It has not only affected woman injuriously by narrowing her sphere of action, but man himself has suffered from it. It has destroyed the nobleness, the gentleness that should belong to his character, the beauty and transparency of soul the dislike of everything bordering on coarseness and vulgarity, all those finer qualities of our nature which raise us above the earth and give us a foretaste of the beauty and bliss, the refined enjoyments of the world to come.

3rd: Let us now consider man's claims to physical superiority. Methinks I hear some say, surely you will not contend for equality here. Yes,
10 we must not give an inch lest you claim an ell,[1] we cannot accord to man even this much, and he has no right to claim it until the fact be fully demonstrated, until the physical education of the boy and the girl shall have been the same for many years. If you claim the advantage of size merely, why it may be that under any course of training in ever so perfect a development of the physique in woman, man might still be the larger of the two, tho' we do not grant even this. But the perfection of the physique is great power combined with endurance. Now your strongest men are not always the tallest men, nor the broadest, nor the most corpulent, but very often the small man who is well built, tightly put together, and possessed of an indomitable will. Bodily strength depends something on the power of will. The sight of a small boy thoroughly thrashing a big one is not rare. Now would you say the big fat boy whipped was superior to the small active boy who conquered him? You do not say the horse is physically superior to the man—for although he has more muscular power, yet the power of mind in man renders him his superior and he guides him wherever he will. . . .

11 We, the women of this state, have met in convention within the last few months both in Rochester and Seneca Falls to discuss our rights and wrongs. We did not as some have supposed assemble to go into the detail of social life alone, we did not propose to petition the legislature to make our Husbands just, generous, and courteous, to seat every man at the head of a cradle and to clothe every woman in male attire; no, none of these points, however important they may be considered by humble minds, were touched upon in the convention. As to their costume the gentlemen need feel no fear of our imitating that for we think it in violation of every principle of beauty, taste, and dignity and notwithstanding all the contempt and abuse cast upon our loose, flowing garments we still admire their easy graceful folds, and consider our costume as an object of taste much more beautiful than theirs. Many of the nobler sex seem to agree with us in this opinion, for all the Bishops, Priests, Judges, Barristers, and Lord Mayors of the first nation on the globe and the Pope of Rome, too, when officiating in their highest offices, they all wear the loose flowing robes, thus tacitly acknowledging that the ordinary male attire is neither dignified nor imposing. No! We shall not molest you in your philosophical experiments with stocks, pants, high-heeled boots, and Russian belt. Yours be the glory to discover by personal

1. A unit of measurement equal to 45 inches. It was once used to measure cloth.

experience how long the knee pant can resist the terrible strapping down which you impose—in how short time the well developed muscles of the throat can be reduced to mere threads by the constant pressure of the stock, how high the heel of the boot must be to make a short man tall, and how tight the Russian belt may be drawn and yet have wind enough to sustain life. Our ambition leads us neither to discovery nor martyrdom of this sort.

12 But we did assemble to protest against a form of government existing without the consent of the governed, to declare our right to be free as man is free—to be represented in the government which we are taxed to support—to have such disgraceful laws as give to man the right to chastise and imprison his wife—to take the wages which she earns,—the property which she inherits and in case of separation the children of her love—laws which make her the mere dependent on his bounty—it was to protest against such unjust laws as these and to have them if possible forever erased from our statute books, deeming them a standing shame and disgrace to a professedly republican, christian people in the nineteenth century. We met

To uplift woman's fallen divinity
Upon an even pedestal with man

13 And strange as it may seem to many we then and there declared our right to vote according to the Declaration of the government under which we live. This right no one pretends to deny. We need not prove ourselves equal to Daniel Webster to enjoy this privilege, for the most ignorant Irishman in the ditch has all the civil rights he has, we need not prove our muscular power equal to this same Irishman to enjoy this privilege for the most tiny, weak, ill-shaped, imbecile stripling of 21 has all the civil rights of the Irishman. We have no objection to discuss the question of equality, for we feel that the weight of argument lies wholly with us, but we wish the question of equality kept distinct from the question of rights, for the proof of the one does not determine the truth of the other. All men in this country have the same rights however they may differ in mind, body, or estate. The right is ours. The question now is, how shall we get possession of what rightfully belongs to us. We should not feel so sorely grieved if no man who had not attained the full stature of a Webster, Van Buren, Clay, or Gerrit Smith could claim the right of the elective franchise, but to have the rights of drunkards, idiots, horse-racing, rum-selling rowdies, ignorant foreigners, and silly boys fully recognized, whilst we ourselves are thrust out from all the rights that belong to citizens—it is too grossly insulting to the dignity of woman to be longer quietly submitted to. The right is ours, have it we must—use it we will. The pens, the tongues, the fortunes, the indomitable wills of many women are already pledged to secure this right. The great truth that no just government can be formed without the consent of the governed, we shall echo and re-echo in the ears of the unjust judge until by continual coming we shall weary him.

14 But say some, would you have woman vote? What refined delicate woman at the polls, mingling in such scenes of violence and vulgarity—most certainly—where there is so much to be feared for the pure, the innocent, the noble, the mother surely should be there to watch and guard her sons, who must encounter such stormy dangerous scenes at the tender age of 21. Much is said of woman's influence, might not her presence do much towards softening down this violence—refining this vulgarity? Depend upon it that places that by their impure atmosphere are rendered unfit for woman cannot but be dangerous to her sires and sons. But if woman claims all the rights of a citizen will she buckle on her armor and fight in defense of her country? Has not woman already often shown herself as courageous in the field as wise and patriotic in counsel as man? But for myself—think all war sinful. I believe in Christ—I believe that command, Resist not evil to be divine. Vengeance is mine and I will repay saith the Lord—Let frail man, who cannot foresee the consequences of an action,

walk humbly with his God—loving his enemies, blessing those who curse him, and always returning good for evil. This is the highest kind of courage that mortal man can attain to and this moral warfare with one's own bad passions requires no physical power to achieve. I would not have man go to war. I can see no glory in fighting with such weapons as guns and swords whilst man has in his possession the infinitely superior and more effective ones of righteousness and truth.

15 But what would you gain by voting? Man must know the advantages of voting, for they all seem very tenacious about the right. Think you if woman had a voice in this government, that all those laws affecting her interests would so entirely violate every principle of right and justice? Had we a vote to give, might not the office holders and seekers propose some change in woman's condition? Might not "woman's rights" come to be as great a question as "free soil"? But are you not already sufficiently represented by your Fathers, Husbands, Brothers, and Sons. Let your statute books answer the question. We have had enough of such representation. In nothing is woman's true happiness consulted. Men like to call her an angel—to feed her with what they think sweet food nourishing her vanity, to induce her to believe her organization is so much finer, more delicate than theirs, that she is not fitted to struggle with the tempests of public life but needs their care and protection. Care and protection? Such as the wolf gives the lamb—such as the eagle the hare he carries to his eyrie. Most cunningly he entraps her and then takes from her all those rights which are dearer to him than life itself, rights which have been baptized in blood, and the maintenance of which is even now rocking to their foundations the kingdoms of the old world. The most discouraging, the most lamentable aspect our cause wears is the indifference, indeed the contempt, with which women themselves regard our movement. When the subject is introduced among our young ladies, among those even who claim to be intelligent and educated it is met by the scornful curl of the lip and by expressions of disgust and ridicule. But we shall hope better things of them when they are enlighted in regard to their present position, to the laws under which they live—they will not then publish their degradation by declaring themselves satisfied nor their ignorance by declaring they have all the rights they want. . . . she will find any earthly support unstable and weak, that her only safe dependence is on the arm of omnipotence. Teach her there is no sex in mind, that true happiness springs from duty accomplished, and she will feel the desire to bathe her brow heated from the struggles of an earthly existence in the cool stream that flows fresh and sparkling from the Divine fountain. She will become conscious that each human being is morally accountable for himself, that no one can throw upon another his burden of responsibility, that neither Father, Husband, Brother, nor Son, however willing they may be, can relieve woman from this weight, can stand in her stead when called into the presence of the searcher of spirits. . . .

16 One common objection to this movement is that if the principles of freedom and equality which we advocate were put to practice, it would destroy all harmony in the domestic circle. Here let me ask, how many truly harmonious households have we now? Take any village circle you know of and on the one hand you will find the meek, sad-looking, thoroughly subdued wife who knows no freedom of thought or action—who passes her days in the dull routine of household cares and her nights half perchance in making the tattered garments whole and the other half in slumbers oft disturbed by sick and restless children. She knows nothing of the great world without, she has no time for reading, and her Husband finds more pleasure in discussing politics with men in groceries, taverns, or depots than he could in reading or telling his wife the news whilst she sits mending his stockings and shirts through many a lonely evening, nor thinks he selfish being that he owes any duty to that perishing soul, beyond providing a house to cover

her head, food to sustain life, and raiment to put on and plenty of wood to [burn].

17 As to her little world within, she finds not much comfort there. Her wishes, should she have any, must be in subjection to those of her tyrant—her will must be in perfect subordination, the comfort of the wife, children, servants, one and all, must be given up wholly disregarded until the great head of the house be first attended to. No matter what the case may be, he must have his hot dinner. If wife or children are sick—they must look elsewhere for care, he cannot be disturbed at night, it does not agree with him to have his slumbers broken, it gives him the headache—renders him unfit for business, and worse than all her very soul is tortured every day and hour by his harsh and cruel treatment of her children. What mother cannot bear me witness to anguish of this sort? Oh! Women how sadly you have learned your duty to your children, to your own heart, to the God that gave you that holy love for them when you stand silent witnesses to the cruel infliction of blows and strips from angry Fathers on the trembling forms of helpless infancy. It is a mother's sacred duty to shield her children from violence from whatever source it may come, it is her duty to resist oppression wherever she may find it at home or abroad, by every moral power within her reach. Many men who are well known for their philanthropy, who hate oppression on a southern plantation, can play the tyrant right well at home. It is a much easier matter to denounce all the crying sins of the day most eloquently too, than to endure for one hour the peevish moanings of a sick child. To know whether a man is truly great and good, you must not judge by his appearance in the great world, but follow him to his home—where all restraints are laid aside—there we see the true man his virtues and his vices, too.

18 On the other hand, we find the so called Hen-pecked Husband, oftimes a kind, generous, noble-minded man who hates contention and is willing to do anything for peace. He having unwarily caught a Tarter tries to make the best of her. He can think his own thoughts and tell them too when he feels quite sure that she is not at hand, he can absent himself from home as much as possible, but he does not feel like a free man. The detail of his sufferings I can neither describe nor imagine never having been the confident of one of these unfortunate beings. Now in such households as these there may be no open ruptures—they may seemingly glide on without a ripple upon the surface—the aggrieved may have patiently resigned themselves to suffer all things with Christian fortitude—with stern philosophy—but can there be harmony or happiness there? Oh! No, far from it. The only happy households we now see are those in which Husband and wife share equally in counsel and government. There can be no true dignity or independence where there is subordination, no happiness without freedom. . . .

19 There seems now to be a kind of moral stagnation in our midst. (Philanthropists have pulled every string. War, slavery, drunkeness, licentiousness, and gluttony have been dragged naked before the people and all their abominations fully brought to light. Yet with idiotic laugh we hug these monsters to our arms and rush on. Our churches are multiplying on all sides, our Sunday schools and prayer meetings are still kept up, our missionary and tract societies have long labored and now the laborers begin to faint—they feel they cannot resist this rushing tide of vice, they feel that the battlements of righteousness are weak against the mighty wicked, most are ready to raise the siege. And how shall we account for this state of things? Depend upon it, the degradation of woman is the secret of all this woe,—the inactivity of her head and heart. The voice of woman has been silenced, but man cannot fulfill his destiny alone—he cannot redeem his race unaided, there are deep and tender chords of sympathy and love in the breasts of the downfallen, the crushed, that woman can touch more skillfully than man. The earth has never yet seen a truly great and virtuous nation, for woman has

never yet stood the equal with man. (As with nations, so with families. It is the wise mother who has the wise son, and it requires but little thought to decide that as long as the women of this nation remain but half-developed in mind and body, so long shall we have a succession of men decrepit in body and soul; so long as your women are mere slaves, you may throw your colleges to the wind, there is no material to work upon, it is in vain to look for silver and gold from mines of copper and brass. How seldom now is the Father's pride gratified, his fond hopes realized in the budding genius of the son—the wife is degraded—made the mere creature of his caprice and now the foolish son is heaviness to his heart. Truly are the sins of the Fathers visited upon the children. God in his wisdom has so linked together the whole human family that any violence done at one end of the chain is felt throughout its length.)

20 Now is the time, now emphatically, for the women of this country to buckle on the armor that can best resist the weapons of the enemy, ridicule and holy horror. "Voices" were the visitors and advisers of Joan of Arc, "voices" have come to us, oftimes from the depths of sorrow degradation and despair,—they have been too long unheeded. The same religious enthusiasm that nerved her to what she deemed her work now nerves us to ours; her work was prophesied of, ours too is the fulfilling of what has long since been foretold. In the better days your sons and your daughters shall prophesy. Her struggle and triumph were alike short, our struggle shall be hard and long but our triumph shall be complete and forever. We do not expect that our path will be strewn with the flowers of popular favor—that our banner which we have flung to the wind will be fanned by the breath of popular applause. No, we know that over the nettles of prejudice and bigotry will be our way, that upon our banner will beat the dark stormcloud of opposition from those who have entrenched themselves behind the strong bulwark of might, of force and who have fortified their position by every means holy and unholy, but we steadfastly abide the result. Unmoved we will bear it aloft—undaunted we will unfurl it to the gale,—we know the storm cannot rend from it a shred, that the electric flash will but more clearly show to us the glorious words inscribed upon it, "Equality of rights" and the rolling thunder will be sweet music in our ears, telling us of the light . . . of the purer clearer atmosphere [rest of line torn away].

Thinking about the Argument

1. What reason does Stanton give that men do not acknowledge the social and political equality of women?
2. Do you think it is fair, as Stanton suggests, to compare the status of women in the nineteenth century to slavery? Why or why not?
3. In what way does Stanton blame religion for the cultural inferiority of women?
4. What does the author say is the source of true strength, and why do women have as much of it as men?
5. Where does Stanton state her thesis? How do you know?
6. How does Stanton refute the argument that if women are the equals of men, they must also go to war?
7. How does Stanton answer the argument that the equality of women will create discontent at home?

Responding to the Argument

1. Do you think Stanton would be pleased with the status of women in the United States today? Why or why not?
2. Besides women having the right to vote, name one thing in today's world you think Stanton would approve of, and one thing she would disapprove of. Explain.
3. How is Stanton's viewpoint similar to or different from Nightingale's viewpoint? Whose viewpoint do you find more reasonable, and why?
4. Do you believe that men and women differ, in some fundamental way, in how they think and act? Does this difference, if it exists, justify different treatment of men and women in terms of rights and privileges? Explain. (For example, if you believe that men are better at fixing things than women, or that women are better at forming relationships than men, does this mean that men should hold primary responsibility for home repairs and women should be in charge of childrearing?)

Writing about the Argument

1. Write an argument comparing and contrasting the arguments presented by Stanton and Nightingale. Which do you find more eloquent? Which do you find most convincing? What difference is there in terms of the audience each author is addressing, and the purpose that each author is trying to achieve?
2. Pretend you are Elizabeth Cady Stanton. Write a letter to the editor of a prominent newspaper explaining (1) what level of equality women have achieved and (2) what battles remain to be fought.
3. Write a paper evaluating the quality of Stanton's argument. Identify any logical fallacies and weaknesses in her argument. Likewise, comment on points that she argues well.
4. Examine Stanton's argument in paragraph 14 where she avoids the issue of sending women to war by arguing for peace. If women are to be considered the legal equals of men, should they be subject to the draft and subject to the same combat situations as men? Write an argument expressing your view on this matter.

"Feminist Manifesto"

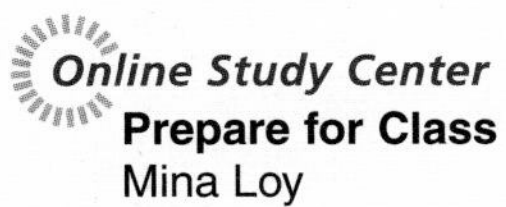

Online Study Center
Prepare for Class
Mina Loy

About the Author: Mina Loy

Unlike Florence Nightingale, who spent her life in service to others, and Elizabeth Cady Stanton, who focused her energy on activism, Mina Loy's life is harder to define. Like both Stanton and Nightingale, Loy (1882–1966) sought to break away from traditional Victorian society and the expectations it created for women. She expressed her independence and modernism in her poetry, in her art, and in her overall unconventional approach to life. She lived, at various times, in London, Paris, Florence, New York, and Aspen, Colorado. Loy weaved in and out of a variety of artistic professions, including that of a lampshade designer. At one point she created abstractions of street scenes constructed from trash she had found in the streets of New York. During her lifetime Loy produced only two books: *Lunar Baedecker* (1923) and *Lunar Baedecker and Time-Tables* (1958).

Before You Read

1. Would you consider Loy to be an admirable person? Why or why not? How does your opinion of her lifestyle affect how you approach her writing?
2. To effect social change, are there times when a radical approach is preferred to a more measured or sober approach? When might a more radical approach be warranted? Explain.
3. Based on the information in the headnote, how do you expect Loy's point of view to differ from that of Nightingale and Stanton?
4. Scan Loy's "Feminist Manifesto." What parts, if any, draw your attention? What does this tell you about the emotional tone of the piece? How does that affect the faith you have in Loy as an authority on her topic?

Feminist Manifesto

1 The Feminist Movement as instituted at present is INADEQUATE.

2 Women, if you want to realize yourselves (for you are on the brink of a devastating psychological upheaval) all your pet illusions must be unmasked. The lies of centuries have got to be discarded. Are you prepared for the WRENCH?

3 There is no half measure, no scratching on the surface of the rubbish heap of tradition. Nothing short of Absolute Demolition will bring about reform. So cease to place your confidence in economic legislation, vice-crusades, and uniform education. You are glossing over REALITY.

4 Professional and commercial careers are opening up for you. *Is that all you want?* If you honestly desire to find your level without prejudice, be brave and deny at the outset that pathetic clap-trap war-cry, "Woman is the equal of man."

5 She is *not.*

6 For the man who lives a life in which his activities conform to a social code which is a protectorate of the feminine element is no longer masculine. The woman who adapts herself to a theoretical valuation of her sex as a *relative impersonality* is not yet feminine.

7 Leave off looking to men to find out what you are *not.* Seek within yourselves to find out what you *are.* As conditions are at present constituted you have the choice between Parasitism, Prostitution, or Negation.

8 Men and women are enemies, with the enmity of the exploited for the parasite, the parasite for the exploited—at present they are at the mercy of the advantage that each can take of the other's sexual dependence. The only point at which the interests of the sexes merge is the sexual embrace.

9 The first illusion to demolish is the division of women into two classes: the mistress and the mother. Every well-balanced and developed woman knows that no such division exists, that Nature has endowed the Complete Woman with a faculty for expressing herself through all her functions. These are *no restrictions.* The woman who is so incompletely evolved as to be unself-conscious in sex will prove a restrictive influence on the temperamental expansion of the next generation; the woman who is a poor mistress will be an incompetent mother, an inferior mentality. She will not have an adequate apprehension of LIFE.

10 To obtain results you must make sacrifices and the first and greatest sacrifice you have to make is of your VIRTUE.

11 The fictitious value of woman as identified with her physical purity is too easy a standby. It renders her lethargic in the acquisition of intrinsic merits of character by which she could obtain a concrete value. Therefore, the first self-enforced law for the female sex, as protection

against the manmade bogey of virtue (which is the principal instrument of her subjugation) is the *unconditional* surgical *destruction of virginity* throughout the female population at puberty.

12 The value of man is assessed entirely according to his use or interest to the community; the value of woman depends entirely on chance—her success or failure in manipulating a man into taking life-long responsibility for her.

13 The advantages of marriage are too ridiculously ample compared to all other trades, for under modern conditions a woman can accept preposterously luxurious support from a man without returning anything—even offspring—as an offering of thanks for her virginity.

14 The woman who has not succeeded in striking that advantageous bargain is prohibited from any but the most surreptitious reaction to life-stimuli and is entirely debarred from maternity. Every woman has a right to maternity.

15 Every woman of superior intelligence should realize her race-responsibility by producing children in adequate proportion to the unfit or degenerate members of her sex.

16 Each child of a superior woman should be the result of a definite period of psychic development in her life and not necessarily of a possibly irksome and out-worn continuance of an alliance that is spontaneously adapted for vital creation in the beginning but which becomes unbalanced as the parties of that alliance follow the individual lines of their personal evolution.

17 For the harmony of the race, each individual should be the expression of an easy and ample interpenetration of the male and female temperaments—free from stress.

18 Woman must become more responsible for the child than man.

19 Woman must destroy in herself the desire to be loved.

20 The desire for comfortable protection rather than intelligent curiosity and courage in meeting and resisting the presence of sex (or so-called love) must be reduced to its initial element. Honor, grief, sentimentality, pride, and consequently jealousy must be detached from sex.

21 Woman must retain her deceptive fragility of appearance, combined with indomitable will, irreducible courage, abundant health, and sound nerves.

22 Another great illusion that woman must use all her introspection, innate clear-sightedness, and unbiased bravery to destory is the impurity of sex—for the sake of her self-respect.

23 In defiance of superstition I assert that *there is nothing impure in sex* except the mental attitude toward it. The eventual acceptance of this fact will constitute an incalculably wider social regeneration than it is possible for our generation to acquire.

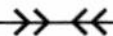

Thinking about the Argument

1. What is Loy's thesis? Can you state it in your own words? Who is her target audience? How do you know?
2. Is Loy's tone suitable for its purpose and audience? Explain.
3. Why do you think Loy says that women only "have the choice between Parasitism, Prostitution, or Negation"? Explain.
4. Why does Loy see virtue as "the principal instrument of her [any woman's] subjugation"? What does she think girls should do about this upon entering puberty?
5. What does Loy say is the purpose of sex and rearing children? How does her view contrast with the positions of Nightingale and Stanton?
6. How, according to Loy, can a woman best protect herself from men?

RESPONDING TO THE ARGUMENT

1. Loy is critical of the emotional bond between women and men. Do you think, as the author suggests, that to be free women must emotionally detach themselves from men? Why or why not?
2. Would you give your own daughter the advice that Loy gives, especially in paragraphs 11 and 19? Explain your answer.
3. Do you agree that women should bear the primary responsibility in childrearing? Why or why not?
4. Should women consider men the enemy, as Loy suggests? In your opinion, how can women be "free" (and what is the definition of *freedom*)? Explain.

WRITING ABOUT THE ARGUMENT

1. In a journal entry or argumentative essay, define *virtue,* and explain why it is a good or bad concept for women to use in defining themselves. Does it, as Loy intimates, enslave women to men?
2. Write an essay arguing whether emotion is necessary to have a successful relationship with the opposite sex. In your essay, be sure to explain what makes a relationship successful or unsuccessful.
3. Write a letter to Loy expressing your feelings regarding the role that men should (or should not) play in rearing children. Alternatively, discuss the role that an emotional bond can play in either enslaving women or empowering them.
4. Write an argument discussing what *liberation, equality,* and *independence* mean for women. Should women be free and detached from men, except for sexual pleasure, as Loy argues? Should women be satisfied to be equal partners with men but still have an emotional bond with them? Does this bond enslave women to men, or the reverse? Is such enslavement acceptable, if both individuals are happy in the relationship?
5. Consider what women have achieved today. Do you consider women to be liberated? Are they men's equals? Are they independent of men? Is it possible, or even desirable, for women and men to be equals and/or independent in all things? Write an essay assessing the state of women in society today.

"Politics and the English Language"

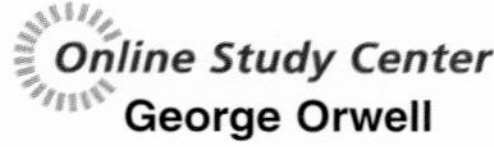

ABOUT THE AUTHOR: GEORGE ORWELL

Born Eric Arthur Blair (1903–1950) but best remembered by his pen name, George Orwell was respected for his social and political commentaries, essays, and novels. After graduating from Britain's famous Eton College, Blair briefly joined the Indian Imperial Police. He then returned to England, where he began his literary career as George Orwell. Some of his most famous essays, including "A Hanging" (1931) and "Shooting an Elephant" (1936), reflect these early experiences. Following World War II, Orwell completed his dystopian allegory *Animal Farm* (1945) and, a few years later, *Nineteen Eighty-four* (1949). In the following essay, which was first published in 1946, Orwell critiques what he sees as the decline of the English language and what would later be termed "political correctness."

READING SELECTION

Before You Read

1. What do you know about George Orwell? If you have never heard of him or read anything he has written, how could you find out more?
2. What does the title of the essay imply? What do you expect the author to argue?
3. Scan the article. Note its major divisions. How is it organized? Can you pick out Orwell's central claim? What is it?

Politics and the English Language

1 Most people who bother with the matter at all would admit that the English language is in a bad way, but it is generally assumed that we cannot by conscious action do anything about it. Our civilization is decadent and our language—so the argument runs—must inevitably share in the general collapse. It follows that any struggle against the abuse of language is a sentimental archaism, like preferring candles to electric light or hansom cabs to aeroplanes. Underneath this lies the half-conscious belief that language is a natural growth and not an instrument which we shape for our own purposes.

2 Now, it is clear that the decline of a language must ultimately have political and economic causes: it is not due simply to the bad influence of this or that individual writer. But an effect can become a cause, reinforcing the original cause and producing the same effect in an intensified form, and so on indefinitely. A man may take to drink because he feels himself to be a failure, and then fail all the more completely because he drinks. It is rather the same thing that is happening to the English language. It becomes ugly and inaccurate because our thoughts are foolish, but the slovenliness of our language makes it easier for us to have foolish thoughts. The point is that the process is reversible. Modern English, especially written English, is full of bad habits which spread by imitation and which can be avoided if one is willing to take the necessary trouble. If one gets rid of these habits one can think more clearly, and to think clearly is a necessary first step toward political regeneration: so that the fight against bad English is not frivolous and is not the exclusive concern of professional writers. I will come back to this presently, and I hope that by that time the meaning of what I have said here will have become clearer. Meanwhile, here are five specimens of the English language as it is now habitually written.

3 These five passages have not been picked out because they are especially bad—I could have quoted far worse if I had chosen—but because they illustrate various of the mental vices from which we now suffer. They are a little below the average, but are fairly representative samples. I number them so that I can refer back to them when necessary:

> (1) I am not, indeed, sure whether it is not true to say that the Milton who once seemed not unlike a seventeenth-century Shelley had not become, out of an experience ever more bitter in each year, more alien *[sic]* to the founder of that Jesuit sect which nothing could induce him to tolerate.
>
> —Professor Harold Laski
> (Essay in *Freedom of Expression*)

> (2) Above all, we cannot play ducks and drakes with a native battery of idioms which prescribes such egregious collocations of vocables as the Basic *put up with* for *tolerate* or *put at a loss* for *bewilder.*
>
> —Professor Lancelot Hogben
> (*Interglossa*)

(3) On the one side we have the free personality: by definition it is not neurotic, for it has neither conflict nor dream. Its desires, such as they are, are transparent, for they are just what institutional approval keeps in the forefront of consciousness; another institutional pattern would alter their number and intensity; there is little in them that is natural, irreducible, or culturally dangerous. But *on the other side,* the social bond itself is nothing but the mutual reflection of these self-secure integrities. Recall the definition of love. Is not this the very picture of a small academic? Where is there a place in this hall of mirrors for either personality or fraternity?

—Essay on psychology in *Politics* (New York)

(4) All the "best people" from the gentlemen's clubs, and all the frantic fascist captains, united in common hatred of Socialism and bestial horror of the rising tide of the mass revolutionary movement, have turned to acts of provocation, to foul incendiarism, to medieval legends of poisoned wells, to legalize their own destruction of proletarian organizations, and rouse the agitated petty-bourgeoisie to chauvinistic fervor on behalf of the fight against the revolutionary way out of the crisis.

—Communist pamphlet

(5) If a new spirit *is* to be infused into this old country, there is one thorny and contentious reform which must be tackled, and that is the humanization and galvanization of the B.B.C. Timidity here will bespeak canker and atrophy of the soul. The heart of Britain may be sound and of strong beat, for instance, but the British lion's roar at present is like that of Bottom in Shakespeare's *Midsummer Night's Dream*—as gentle as any sucking dove. A virile new Britain cannot continue indefinitely to be traduced in the eyes or rather ears, of the world by the effete languors of Langham Place, brazenly masquerading as "standard English." When the Voice of Britain is heard at nine o'clock, better far and infinitely less ludicrous to hear aitches honestly dropped than the present priggish, inflated, inhibited, school-ma'amish arch braying of blameless bashful mewing maidens!

—Letter in *Tribune*

4 Each of these passages has faults of its own, but, quite apart from avoidable ugliness, two qualities are common to all of them. The first is staleness of imagery; the other is lack of precision. The writer either has a meaning and cannot express it, or he inadvertently says something else, or he is almost indifferent as to whether his words mean anything or not. This mixture of vagueness and sheer incompetence is the most marked characteristic of modern English prose, and especially of any kind of political writing. As soon as certain topics are raised, the concrete melts into the abstract and no one seems able to think of turns of speech that are not hackneyed: prose consists less and less of *words* chosen for the sake of their meaning, and more and more of *phrases* tacked together like the sections of a prefabricated henhouse. I list below, with notes and examples, various of the tricks by means of which the work of prose-construction is habitually dodged:

5 *Dying metaphors.* A newly invented metaphor assists thought by evoking a visual image, while on the other hand a metaphor which is technically "dead" (e.g. *iron resolution*) has in effect reverted to being an ordinary word and can generally be used without loss of vividness. But in between these two classes there is a huge dump of worn-out metaphors which have lost all evocative power and are merely used because they save people the trouble of inventing phrases for themselves. Examples are: *Ring the changes on, take up the cudgels for, toe the line, ride roughshod over, stand shoulder to shoulder with, play into the hands of, no axe to grind, grist to the mill, fishing in troubled waters, on the order of the day, Achilles' heel, swan song, hotbed.* Many of these are used without knowledge of their meaning (what is a "rift," for instance?), and incompatible metaphors are frequently mixed, a sure sign that the writer is not interested in what he is saying. Some metaphors now current have been twisted

out of their original meaning without those who use them even being aware of the fact. For example, *toe the line* is sometimes written *tow the line.* Another example is the *hammer and the anvil,* now always used with the implication that the anvil gets the worst of it. In real life it is always the anvil that breaks the hammer, never the other way about: a writer who stopped to think what he was saying would be aware of this, and would avoid perverting the original phrase.

6 *Operators or verbal false limbs.* These save the trouble of picking out appropriate verbs and nouns, and at the same time pad each sentence with extra syllables which give it an appearance of symmetry. Characteristic phrases are *render inoperative, militate against, make contact with, be subjected to, give rise to, give grounds for, have the effect of, play a leading part (role) in, make itself felt, take effect, exhibit a tendency to, serve the purpose of, etc., etc.* The keynote is the elimination of simple verbs. Instead of being a single word, such as *break, stop, spoil, mend, kill,* a verb becomes a *phrase,* made up of a noun or adjective tacked on to some general-purpose verb such as *prove, serve, form, play, render.* In addition, the passive voice is wherever possible used in preference to the active, and noun constructions are used instead of gerunds (*by examination of* instead of *by examining*). The range of verbs is further cut down by means of the *-ize* and *de-* formations, and the banal statements are given an appearance of profundity by means of the *not un-* formation. Simple conjunctions and prepositions are replaced by such phrases as *with respect to, having regard to, the fact that, by dint of, in view of, in the interests of, on the hypothesis that;* and the ends of sentences are saved from anticlimax by such resounding commonplaces as *greatly to be desired, cannot be left out of account, a development to be expected in the near future, deserving of serious consideration, brought to a satisfactory conclusion,* and so on and so forth.

7 *Pretentious diction.* Words like *phenomenon, element, individual* (as noun), *objective, categorical, effective, virtual, basic, primary, promote, constitute, exhibit, exploit, utilize, eliminate, liquidate,* are used to dress up simple statement and give an air of scientific impartiality to biased judgments. Adjectives like *epoch-making, epic, historic, unforgettable, triumphant, age-old, inevitable, inexorable, veritable,* are used to dignify the sordid processes of international politics, while writing that aims at glorifying war usually takes on an archaic color, its characteristic words being: *realm, throne, chariot, mailed fist, trident, sword, shield, buckler, banner, jackboot, clarion.* Foreign words and expressions such as *cul de sac, ancien régime, deus ex machina, mutatis mutandis, status quo, gleichschaltung, weltanschauung,* are used to give an air of culture and elegance. Except for the useful abbreviations *i.e., e.g.,* and *etc.,* there is no real need for any of the hundreds of foreign phrases now current in English. Bad writers, and especially scientific, political, and sociological writers, are nearly always haunted by the notion that Latin or Greek words are grander than Saxon ones, and unnecessary words like *expedite, ameliorate, predict, extraneous, deracinated, clandestine, subaqueous,* and hundreds of others constantly gain ground from their Anglo-Saxon opposite numbers.* The jargon peculiar to Marxist writing (*hyena, hangman, cannibal, petty bourgeois, these gentry, lackey, flunkey, mad dog, White Guard,* etc.) consists largely of words and phrases translated from Russian, German, or French; but the normal way of coining a new word is to use a Latin or Greek root with the appropriate affix and, where necessary, the size formation. It is often easier to make up words of this kind (*deregionalize, impermissible, extramarital, nonfragmentary,*

* An interesting illustration of this is the way in which the English flower names which were in use till very recently are being ousted by Greek ones, *snapdragon* becoming *antirrhinum, forget-me-not* becoming *myosotis,* etc. It is hard to see any practical reason for this change of fashion: it is probably due to an instinctive turning away from the more homely word and a vague feeling that the Greek word is scientific.

and so forth) than to think up the English words that will cover one's meaning. The result, in general, is an increase in slovenliness and vagueness.

8 *Meaningless words.* In certain kinds of writing, particularly in art criticism and literary criticism, it is normal to come across long passages which are almost completely lacking in meaning.† Words like *romantic, plastic, values, human, dead, sentimental, natural, vitality,* as used in art criticism, are strictly meaningless, in the sense that they not only do not point to any discoverable object, but are hardly ever expected to do so by the reader. When one critic writes, "The outstanding feature of Mr. X's work is its living quality," while another writes, "The immediately striking thing about Mr. X's work is its peculiar deadness," the reader accepts this as a simple difference of opinion. If words like *black* and *white* were involved, instead of the jargon words *dead* and *living,* he would see at once that language was being used in an improper way. Many political words are similarly abused. The word *Fascism* has now no meaning except in so far as it signifies "something not desirable." The words *democracy, socialism, freedom, patriotic, realistic, justice,* have each of them several different meanings which cannot be reconciled with one another. In the case of a word like *democracy,* not only is there no agreed definition, but the attempt to make one is resisted from all sides. It is almost universally felt that when we call a country democratic we are praising it: consequently the defenders of every kind of regime claim that it is a democracy, and fear that they might have to stop using the word if it were tied down to any one meaning. Words of this kind are often used in a consciously dishonest way. That is, the person who uses them has his own private definition, but allows his hearer to think he means something quite different. Statements like *Marshal Pétain was a true patriot, The Soviet press is the freest in the world, The Catholic Church is opposed to persecution,* are almost always made with intent to deceive. Other words used in variable meanings, in most cases more or less dishonestly, are: *class, totalitarian, science, progressive, reactionary, bourgeois, equality.*

9 Now that I have made this catalogue of swindles and perversions, let me give another example of the kind of writing that they lead to. This time it must of its nature be an imaginary one. I am going to translate a passage of good English into modern English of the worst sort. Here is a well-known verse from *Ecclesiastes:*

> I returned and saw under the sun, that the race is not to the swift, nor the battle to the strong, neither yet bread to the wise, nor yet riches to men of understanding, nor yet favour to men of skill; but time and chance happeneth to them all.

Here it is in modern English:

> Objective consideration of contemporary phenomena compels the conclusion that success or failure in competitive activities exhibits no tendency to be commensurate with innate capacity, but that a considerable element of the unpredictable must invariably be taken into account.

10 This is a parody, but not a very gross one. Exhibit (3), above, for instance, contains several patches of the same kind of English. It will be seen that I have not made a full translation. The beginning and ending of the sentence follow the original meaning fairly closely, but in the middle the concrete illustrations—race, battle, bread—dissolve into the vague phrase "success or failure in competitive activities." This had to be so, because no modern writer of the kind I am dis-

† Example: "Comfort's catholicity of perception and image, strangely Whitmanesque in range, almost the exact opposite in aesthetic compulsion, continues to evoke that trembling atmospheric accumulative hinting at a cruel, an inexorably serene timelessness. . . . Wrey Gardiner scores by aiming at simple bull's-eyes with precision. Only they are not so simple, and through this contented sadness runs more than the surface bittersweet of resignation." (*Poetry Quarterly.*)

cussing—no one capable of using phrases like "objective consideration of contemporary phenomena"—would ever tabulate his thoughts in that precise and detailed way. The whole tendency of modern prose is away from concreteness. Now analyze these two sentences a little more closely. The first contains forty-nine words but only sixty syllables, and all its words are those of everyday life. The second contains thirty-eight words of ninety syllables: eighteen of its words are from Latin roots, and one from Greek. The first sentence contains six vivid images, and only one phrase ("time and chance") that could be called vague. The second contains not a single fresh, arresting phrase, and in spite of its ninety syllables it gives only a shortened version of the meaning contained in the first. Yet without a doubt it is the second kind of sentence that is gaining ground in modern English. I do not want to exaggerate. This kind of writing is not yet universal, and outcrops of simplicity will occur here and there in the worst-written page. Still, if you or I were told to write a few lines on the uncertainty of human fortunes, we should probably come much nearer to my imaginary sentence than to the one from *Ecclesiastes.*

11 As I have tried to show, modern writing at its worst does not consist in picking out words for the sake of their meaning and inventing images in order to make the meaning clearer. It consists in gumming together long strips of words which have already been set in order by someone else, and making the results presentable by sheer humbug. The attraction of this way of writing is that it is easy. It is easier—even quicker, once you have the habit—to say *In my opinion it is not an unjustifiable assumption that* than to say *I think.* If you use ready-made phrases, you not only don't have to hunt about for words; you also don't have to bother with the rhythms of your sentences, since these phrases are generally so arranged as to be more or less euphonious. When you are composing in a hurry—when you are dictating to a stenographer, for instance, or making a public speech—it is natural to fall into a pretentious, Latinized style. Tags like *a consideration which we should do well to bear in mind* or *a conclusion to which all of us would readily assent* will save many a sentence from coming down with a bump. By using stale metaphors, similes, and idioms, you save much mental effort, at the cost of leaving your meaning vague, not only for your reader but for yourself. This is the significance of mixed metaphors. The sole aim of a metaphor is to call up a visual image. When these images clash—as in *The Fascist octopus has sung its swan song, the jackboot is thrown into the melting pot*—it can be taken as certain that the writer is not seeing a mental image of the objects he is naming; in other words he is not really thinking. Look again at the examples I gave at the beginning of this essay. Professor Laski (1) uses five negatives in fifty-three words. One of these is superfluous, making nonsense of the whole passage, and in addition there is the slip—*alien* for akin—making further nonsense, and several avoidable pieces of clumsiness which increase the general vagueness. Professor Hogben (2) plays ducks and drakes with a battery which is able to write prescriptions, and, while disapproving of the everyday phrase *put up with,* is unwilling to look *egregious* up in the dictionary and see what it means; (3), if one takes an uncharitable attitude towards it, is simply meaningless: probably one could work out its intended meaning by reading the whole of the article in which it occurs. In (4), the writer knows more or less what he wants to say, but an accumulation of stale phrases chokes him like tea leaves blocking a sink. In (5), words and meaning have almost parted company. People who write in this manner usually have a general emotional meaning—they dislike one thing and want to express solidarity with another—but they are not interested in the detail of what they are saying. A scrupulous writer, in every sentence that he writes, will ask himself at least four questions, thus: What am I trying to say? What words will express it? What image or idiom will

make it clearer? Is this image fresh enough to have an effect? And he will probably ask himself two more: Could I put it more shortly? Have I said anything that is avoidably ugly? But you are not obliged to go to all this trouble. You can shirk it by simply throwing your mind open and letting the ready-made phrases come crowding in. They will construct your sentences for you—even think your thoughts for you, to a certain extent—and at need they will perform the important service of partially concealing your meaning even from yourself. It is at this point that the special connection between politics and the debasement of language becomes clear.

12 In our time it is broadly true that political writing is bad writing. Where it is not true, it will generally be found that the writer is some kind of rebel, expressing his private opinions and not a "party line." Orthodoxy, of whatever color, seems to demand a lifeless, imitative style. The political dialects to be found in pamphlets, leading articles, manifestoes, White Papers and the speeches of undersecretaries do, of course, vary from party to party, but they are all alike in that one almost never finds in them a fresh, vivid, homemade turn of speech. When one watches some tired hack on the platform mechanically repeating the familiar phrases—*bestial atrocities, iron heel, blood-stained tyranny, free peoples of the world, stand shoulder to shoulder*—one often has a curious feeling that one is not watching a live human being but some kind of dummy: a feeling which suddenly becomes stronger at moments when the light catches the speaker's spectacles and turns them into blank discs which seem to have no eyes behind them. And this is not altogether fanciful. A speaker who uses that kind of phraseology has gone some distance toward turning himself into a machine. The appropriate noises are coming out of his larynx, but his brain is not involved as it would be if he were choosing his words for himself. If the speech he is making is one that he is accustomed to make over and over again, he may be almost unconscious of what he is saying, as one is when one utters the responses in church. And this reduced state of consciousness, if not indispensable, is at any rate favorable to political conformity.

13 In our time, political speech and writing are largely the defense of the indefensible. Things like the continuance of British rule in India, the Russian purges and deportations, the dropping of the atom bombs on Japan, can indeed be defended, but only by arguments which are too brutal for most people to face, and which do not square with the professed aims of political parties. Thus political language has to consist largely of euphemism, question-begging and sheer cloudy vagueness. Defenseless villages are bombarded from the air, the inhabitants driven out into the countryside, the cattle machine-gunned, the huts set on fire with incendiary bullets: this is called *pacification*. Millions of peasants are robbed of their farms and sent trudging along the roads with no more than they can carry: this is called *transfer of population* or *rectification of frontiers*. People are imprisoned for years without trial, or shot in the back of the neck or sent to die of scurvy in Arctic lumber camps: this is called *elimination of unreliable elements*. Such phraseology is needed if one wants to name things without calling up mental pictures of them. Consider for instance some comfortable English professor defending Russian totalitarianism. He cannot say outright, "I believe in killing off your opponents when you can get good results by doing so." Probably, therefore, he will say something like this:

> While freely conceding that the Soviet regime exhibits certain features which the humanitarian may be inclined to deplore, we must, I think, agree that a certain curtailment of the right to political opposition is an unavoidable concomitant of transitional periods, and that the rigors which the Russian people have been called upon to undergo have been amply justified in the sphere of concrete achievement.

14 The inflated style is itself a kind of euphemism. A mass of Latin words falls upon the facts like soft snow, blurring the outlines and

covering up all the details. The great enemy of clear language is insincerity. When there is a gap between one's real and one's declared aims, one turns as it were instinctively to long words and exhausted idioms, like a cuttlefish squirting out ink. In our age there is no such thing as "keeping out of politics." All issues are political issues, and politics itself is a mass of lies, evasions, folly, hatred, and schizophrenia. When the general atmosphere is bad, language must suffer. I should expect to find—this is a guess which I have not sufficient knowledge to verify—that the German, Russian and Italian languages have all deteriorated in the last ten or fifteen years, as a result of dictatorship.

15 But if thought corrupts language, language can also corrupt thought. A bad usage can spread by tradition and imitation, even among people who should and do know better. The debased language that I have been discussing is in some ways very convenient. Phrases like *a not unjustifiable assumption, leaves much to be desired, would serve no good purpose, a consideration which we should do well to bear in mind,* are a continuous temptation, a packet of aspirins always at one's elbow. Look back through this essay, and for certain you will find that I have again and again committed the very faults I am protesting against. By this morning's post I have received a pamphlet dealing with conditions in Germany. The author tells me that he "felt impelled" to write it. I open it at random, and here is almost the first sentence that I see: "[The Allies] have an opportunity not only of achieving a radical transformation of Germany's social and political structure in such a way as to avoid a nationalistic reaction in Germany itself, but at the same time of laying the foundations of a co-operative and unified Europe." You see, he "feels impelled" to write—feels, presumably, that he has something new to say—and yet his words, like cavalry horses answering the bugle, group themselves automatically into the familiar dreary pattern. This invasion of one's mind by ready-made phrases (*lay the foundations, achieve a radical transformation*) can only be prevented if one is constantly on guard against them, and every such phrase anaesthetizes a portion of one's brain.

16 I said earlier that the decadence of our language is probably curable. Those who deny this would argue, if they produced an argument at all, that language merely reflects existing social conditions, and that we cannot influence its development by any direct tinkering with words and constructions. So far as the general tone or spirit of a language goes, this may be true, but it is not true in detail. Silly words and expressions have often disappeared, not through any evolutionary process but owing to the conscious action of a minority. Two recent examples were *explore every avenue* and *leave no stone unturned,* which were killed by the jeers of a few journalists. There is a long list of flyblown metaphors which could similarly be got rid of if enough people would interest themselves in the job; and it should also be possible to laugh the *not un-* formation out of existence,* to reduce the amount of Latin and Greek in the average sentence, to drive out foreign phrases and strayed scientific words, and, in general, to make pretentiousness unfashionable. But all these are minor points. The defense of the English language implies more than this, and perhaps it is best to start by saying what it does *not* imply.

17 To begin with it has nothing to do with archaism, with the salvaging of obsolete words and turns of speech, or with the setting up of a "standard English" which must never be departed from. On the contrary, it is especially concerned with the scrapping of every word or idiom which has outworn its usefulness. It has nothing to do with correct grammar and syntax, which are of no importance so long as one makes one's meaning clear, or with the avoidance of Americanisms, or with having what is called a "good prose

* One can cure oneself of the *not un-* formation by memorizing this sentence: *A not unblack dog was chasing a not unsmall rabbit across a not ungreen field.*

style." On the other hand it is not concerned with fake simplicity and the attempt to make written English colloquial. Nor does it even imply in every case preferring the Saxon word to the Latin one, though it does imply using the fewest and shortest words that will cover one's meaning. What is above all needed is to let the meaning choose the word, and not the other way about. In prose, the worst thing one can do with words is to surrender to them. When you think of a concrete object, you think wordlessly, and then, if you want to describe the thing you have been visualizing you probably hunt about till you find the exact words that seem to fit it. When you think of something abstract you are more inclined to use words from the start, and unless you make a conscious effort to prevent it, the existing dialect will come rushing in and do the job for you, at the expense of blurring or even changing your meaning. Probably it is better to put off using words as long as possible and get one's meaning as clear as one can through pictures or sensations. Afterward one can choose—not simply *accept*—the phrases that will best cover the meaning, and then switch round and decide what impression one's words are likely to make on another person. This last effort of the mind cuts out all stale or mixed images, all prefabricated phrases, needless repetitions, and humbug and vagueness generally. But one can often be in doubt about the effect of a word or a phrase, and one needs rules that one can rely on when instinct fails. I think the following rules will cover most cases:

(i) Never use a metaphor, simile, or other figure of speech which you are used to seeing in print.
(ii) Never use a long word where a short one will do.
(iii) If it is possible to cut a word out, always cut it out.
(iv) Never use the passive where you can use the active.
(v) Never use a foreign phrase, a scientific word, or a jargon word if you can think of an everyday English equivalent.
(vi) Break any of these rules sooner than say anything outright barbarous.

These rules sound elementary, and so they are, but they demand a deep change of attitude in anyone who has grown used to writing in the style now fashionable. One could keep all of them and still write bad English, but one could not write the kind of stuff that I quoted in those five specimens at the beginning of this article.

18 I have not here been considering the literary use of language, but merely language as an instrument for expressing and not for concealing or preventing thought. Stuart Chase and others have come near to claiming that all abstract words are meaningless, and have used this as a pretext for advocating a kind of political quietism. Since you don't know what Fascism is, how can you struggle against Fascism? One need not swallow such absurdities as this, but one ought to recognize that the present political chaos is connected with the decay of language, and that one can probably bring about some improvement by starting at the verbal end. If you simplify your English, you are freed from the worst follies of orthodoxy. You cannot speak any of the necessary dialects, and when you make a stupid remark its stupidity will be obvious, even to yourself. Political language—and with variations this is true of all political parties, from Conservatives to Anarchists—is designed to make lies sound truthful and murder respectable, and to give an appearance of solidity to pure wind. One cannot change this all in a moment, but one can at least change one's own habits, and from time to time one can even, if one jeers loudly enough, send some worn-out and useless phrase—some *jackboot, Achilles' heel, hotbed, melting pot, acid test, veritable inferno,* or other lump of verbal refuse—into the dustbin where it belongs.

Thinking about the Argument

1. What does Orwell mean when he says "political writing is bad writing"? What does the word *political* mean here?
2. Does Orwell think bad writers (many of whom we might call "politically correct") are lazy, conformist, or both? How do you know?
3. What specific things does the author list as being hallmarks of bad writing?
4. What does Orwell mean when he says that "A speaker who uses that kind of [political] phraseology has gone some distance toward turning himself into a machine"? Do you agree or disagree with this statement? Why?
5. What might the author mean when he says "But if thought corrupts language, language can also corrupt thought"? Do you agree with this idea? Why or why not?

Responding to the Argument

1. In what ways does Orwell's criticism address what is today termed as "politically correct" language? Do you think Orwell is right in saying that such language obscures meaning? Explain.
2. Do you think that certain catch phrases—"African American" as opposed to "black," and "mentally challenged" as opposed to "mentally retarded," for example—should be used to avoid offending certain groups of people? Why or why not?
3. Is the use of nonsexist language—such as using "an individual" instead of the pronoun "he"—a good idea, or does this practice also make language excessively wordy and obscure? Explain.
4. Which of Orwell's specific points about "bad writing" do you agree with and which do you disagree with? List at least one you agree with and one you disagree with. Explain.

Writing about the Argument

1. Find a piece of writing in a newspaper, in a magazine, or on the Internet that you think represents "politicized" (or simply bad) writing. (Government, university, and business documents can be especially fruitful sources.) Following the advice that Orwell provides in his article, rewrite the material to make it both clear and informative. (The end product will probably be shorter than the original.)
2. Write an argument in favor of (or against) what Orwell calls "political" writing. Find one or more examples to quote in your paper and critique them.
3. What is right or wrong about the following statement? Rewrite the statement, and explain why you made the changes that you did.

   "In order to increase the efficient dropping off of students in the circle drive in the front of the school, a decision has been made to expedite the process. In an effort to increase the efficiency and the flow of traffic, and to better protect the children and prevent unfortunate incidents, parents are not to drop off students in the circle drive, but are to utilize the parking lot on the east side of the building."

READING SELECTION

"Letter from Birmingham Jail"

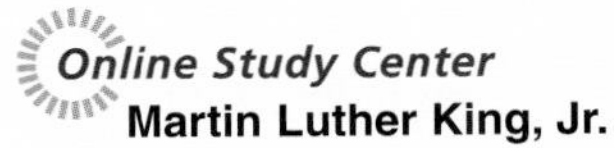

ABOUT THE AUTHOR: MARTIN LUTHER KING, JR.

Known worldwide as the leader of the American civil rights movement, Martin Luther King, Jr., was born in Atlanta, Georgia, in 1929. After graduating from Morehouse College, King attended Crozer Theological Seminary, where he received a Ph.D. In 1955, the Montgomery, Alabama, bus boycott began when an African American woman, Rosa Parks, declined to relinquish her seat to a white man. King, who was serving as a pastor at Dexter Avenue Baptist Church, quickly became one of the boycott's leaders. A few years later, King helped create the Southern Christian Leadership Conference, a group that advocated nonviolent civil disobedience. By 1963, King had become the figurehead of the civil rights movement with his famous "I Have a Dream" speech delivered before the steps of the Lincoln Memorial. The letter reprinted here, written in 1963 in response to a statement published by local Birmingham, Alabama, clergymen, is one of the most heartfelt and profound of King's many writings. It was first published in King's book *Why We Can't Wait* in 1963. King was assassinated in Memphis, Tennessee, on April 4, 1968.

BEFORE YOU READ

1. Other than the information provided in the headnote, list three to five things you can recall about the life of Martin Luther King, Jr. Why was his work important? To you? To society?
2. What does the title of the letter imply? Why do you suppose King was in jail? To whom might this letter be written, and why?
3. Scan the letter. Were you correct about its audience and purpose? Will this knowledge affect the attitude with which you approach the letter? Explain.
4. What does the main thrust of the letter seem to be? What do you think the main aspects of the argument will be? Explain.

Letter from Birmingham Jail

1 April 16, 1963

2 My dear fellow clergymen:

3 While confined here in the Birmingham city jail, I came across your recent statement calling my present activities "unwise and untimely." Seldom do I pause to answer criticism of my work and ideas. If I sought to answer all the criticisms that cross my desk, my secretaries would have little time for anything other than such correspondence in the course of the day, and I would have no time for constructive work. But since I feel that you are men of genuine good will and that your criticisms are sincerely set forth, I want to try to answer your statements in what I hope will be patient and reasonable terms.

4 I think I should indicate why I am here in Birmingham, since you have been influenced by the view which argues against "outsiders coming in." I have the honor of serving as president of the Southern Christian Leadership Conference, an organization operating in every southern state, with headquarters in Atlanta, Georgia. We have some eighty-five affiliated organizations across the South, and one of them is the Al-

abama Christian Movement for Human Rights. Frequently we share staff, educational, and financial resources with our affiliates. Several months ago the affiliate here in Birmingham asked us to be on call to engage in a nonviolent direct-action program if such were deemed necessary. We readily consented, and when the hour came we lived up to our promise. So I, along with several members of my staff, am here because I was invited here. I am here because I have organizational ties here.

5 But more basically, I am in Birmingham because injustice is here. Just as the prophets of the eighth century B.C. left their villages and carried their "thus saith the Lord" far beyond the boundaries of their home towns, and just as the Apostle Paul left his village of Tarsus and carried the gospel of Jesus Christ to the far corners of the Greco-Roman world, so am I compelled to carry the gospel of freedom beyond my own home town. Like Paul, I must constantly respond to the Macedonian call for aid.

6 Moreover, I am cognizant of the interrelatedness of all communities and states. I cannot sit idly by in Atlanta and not be concerned about what happens in Birmingham. Injustice anywhere is a threat to justice everywhere. We are caught in an inescapable network of mutuality, tied in a single garment of destiny. Whatever affects one directly, affects all indirectly. Never again can we afford to live with the narrow, provincial "outside agitator" idea. Anyone who lives inside the United States can never be considered an outsider anywhere within its bounds.

7 You deplore the demonstrations taking place in Birmingham. But your statement, I am sorry to say, fails to express a similar concern for the conditions that brought about the demonstrations. I am sure that none of you would want to rest content with the superficial kind of social analysis that deals merely with effects and does not grapple with underlying causes. It is unfortunate that demonstrations are taking place in Birmingham, but it is even more unfortunate that the city's white power structure left the Negro community with no alternative.

8 In any nonviolent campaign there are four basic steps: collection of the facts to determine whether injustices exist; negotiation; self-purification; and direct action. We have gone through all these steps in Birmingham. There can be no gainsaying the fact that racial injustice engulfs this community. Birmingham is probably the most thoroughly segregated city in the United States. Its ugly record of brutality is widely known. Negroes have experienced grossly unjust treatment in the courts. There have been more unsolved bombings of Negro homes and churches in Birmingham than in any other city in the nation. These are the hard, brutal facts of the case. On the basis of these conditions, Negro leaders sought to negotiate with the city fathers. But the latter consistently refused to engage in good-faith negotiation.

9 Then, last September, came the opportunity to talk with leaders of Birmingham's economic community. In the course of the negotiations, certain promises were made by the merchants—for example, to remove the stores' humiliating racial signs. On the basis of these promises, the Reverend Fred Shuttlesworth and the leaders of the Alabama Christian Movement for Human Rights agreed to a moratorium on all demonstrations. As the weeks and months went by, we realized that we were the victims of a broken promise. A few signs, briefly removed, returned; the others remained.

10 As in so many past experiences, our hopes had been blasted, and the shadow of deep disappointment settled upon us. We had no alternative except to prepare for direct action, whereby we would present our very bodies as a means of laying our case before the conscience of the local and the national community. Mindful of the difficulties involved, we decided to undertake a process of self-purification. We began a series of workshops on nonviolence, and we repeatedly asked ourselves: "Are you able to accept

blows without retaliating?" "Are you able to endure the ordeal of jail?" We decided to schedule our direct-action program for the Easter season, realizing that except for Christmas, this is the main shopping period of the year. Knowing that a strong economic withdrawal program would be the by-product of direct action, we felt that this would be the best time to bring pressure to bear on the merchants for the needed change.

11 Then it occurred to us that Birmingham's mayoralty election was coming up in March, and we speedily decided to postpone action until after election day. When we discovered that the Commissioner of Public Safety, Eugene "Bull" Connor, had piled up enough votes to be in the run-off we decided again to postpone action until the day after the run-off so that the demonstrations could not be used to cloud the issues. Like many others, we waited to see Mr. Connor defeated, and to this end we endured postponement after postponement. Having aided in this community need, we felt that our direct-action program could be delayed no longer.

12 You may well ask: "Why direct action? Why sit-ins, marches, and so forth? Isn't negotiation a better path?" You are quite right in calling for negotiation. Indeed, this is the very purpose of direct action. Nonviolent direct action seeks to create such a crisis and foster such a tension that a community which has constantly refused to negotiate is forced to confront the issue. It seeks so to dramatize the issue that it can no longer be ignored. My citing the creation of tension as part of the work of the nonviolent-resister may sound rather shocking. But I must confess that I am not afraid of the word "tension." I have earnestly opposed violent tension, but there is a type of constructive, nonviolent tension which is necessary for growth. Just as Socrates felt that it was necessary to create a tension in the mind so that individuals could rise from the bondage of myths and half-truths to the unfettered realm of creative analysis and objective appraisal, we must see the need for nonviolent gadflies to create the kind of tension in society that will help men rise from the dark depths of prejudice and racism to the majestic heights of understanding and brotherhood.

13 The purpose of our direct-action program is to create a situation so crisis-packed that it will inevitably open the door to negotiation. I therefore concur with you in your call for negotiation. Too long has our beloved Southland been bogged down in a tragic effort to live in monologue rather than dialogue.

14 One of the basic points in your statement is that the action that I and my associates have taken in Birmingham is untimely. Some have asked: "Why didn't you give the new city administration time to act?" The only answer that I can give to this query is that the new Birmingham administration must be prodded about as much as the outgoing one, before it will act. We are sadly mistaken if we feel that the election of Albert Boutwell as mayor will bring the millennium to Birmingham. While Mr. Boutwell is a much more gentle person than Mr. Connor, they are both segregationists, dedicated to maintenance of the status quo. I have hope that Mr. Boutwell will be reasonable enough to see the futility of massive resistance to desegregation. But he will not see this without pressure from devotees of civil rights. My friends, I must say to you that we have not made a single gain in civil rights without determined legal and nonviolent pressure. Lamentably, it is an historical fact that privileged groups seldom give up their privileges voluntarily. Individuals may see the moral light and voluntarily give up their unjust posture; but, as Reinhold Niebuhr has reminded us, groups tend to be more immoral than individuals.

15 We know through painful experience that freedom is never voluntarily given by the oppressor; it must be demanded by the oppressed. Frankly, I have yet to engage in a direct-action campaign that was "well timed" in the view of those who have not suffered unduly from the disease of segregation. For years now I have heard

the word "Wait!" It rings in the ear of every Negro with piercing familiarity. This "Wait" has almost always meant "Never." We must come to see, with one of our distinguished jurists, that "justice too long delayed is justice denied."

16 We have waited for more than 340 years for our constitutional and God-given rights. The nations of Asia and Africa are moving with jet-like speed toward gaining political independence, but we still creep at horse-and-buggy pace toward gaining a cup of coffee at a lunch counter. Perhaps it is easy for those who have never felt the stinging dark of segregation to say, "Wait." But when you have seen vicious mobs lynch your mothers and fathers at will and drown your sisters and brothers at whim; when you have seen hate-filled policemen curse, kick, and even kill your black brothers and sisters; when you see the vast majority of your twenty million Negro brothers smothering in an airtight cage of poverty in the midst of an affluent society; when you suddenly find your tongue twisted and your speech stammering as you seek to explain to your six-year-old daughter why she can't go to the public amusement park that has just been advertised on television, and see tears welling up in her eyes when she is told that Funtown is closed to colored children, and see ominous clouds of inferiority beginning to form in her little mental sky, and see her beginning to distort her personality by developing an unconscious bitterness toward white people; when you have to concoct an answer for a five-year-old son who is asking: "Daddy, why do white people treat colored people so mean?"; when you take a cross-county drive and find it necessary to sleep night after night in the uncomfortable corners of your automobile because no motel will accept you; when you are humiliated day in and day out by nagging signs reading "white" and "colored"; when your first name becomes "nigger," your middle name becomes "boy" (however old you are), and your last name becomes "John," and your wife and mother are never given the respected title "Mrs."; when you are harried by day and haunted by night by the fact that you are a Negro, living constantly at tiptoe stance, never quite knowing what to expect next, and are plagued with inner fears and outer resentments; when you are forever fighting a degenerating sense of "nobodiness," then you will understand why we find it difficult to wait. There comes a time when the cup of endurance runs over, and men are no longer willing to be plunged into the abyss of despair. I hope, sirs, you can understand our legitimate and unavoidable impatience.

17 You express a great deal of anxiety over our willingness to break laws. This is certainly a legitimate concern. Since we so diligently urge people to obey the Supreme Court's decision of 1954 outlawing segregation in the public schools, at first glance it may seem rather paradoxical for us consciously to break laws. One may well ask: "How can you advocate breaking some laws and obeying others?" The answer lies in the fact that there are two types of laws: just and unjust. I would be the first to advocate obeying just laws. One has not only a legal but a moral responsibility to obey just laws. Conversely, one has a moral responsibility to disobey unjust laws. I would agree with St. Augustine that "an unjust law is no law at all."

18 Now, what is the difference between the two? How does one determine whether a law is just or unjust? A just law is a man-made code that squares with the moral law or the law of God. An unjust law is a code that is out of harmony with the moral law. To put it in the terms of St. Thomas Aquinas: An unjust law is a human law that is not rooted in eternal law and natural law. Any law that uplifts human personality is just. Any law that degrades human personality is unjust. All segregation statutes are unjust because segregation distort the soul and damages the personality. It gives the segregator a false sense of superiority and the segregated a false sense of inferiority. Segregation, to use the terminology of the Jewish philosopher Martin

Buber, substitutes an "I-it" relationship for an "I-thou" relationship and ends up relegating persons to the status of things. Hence segregation is not only politically, economically, and sociologically unsound, it is morally wrong and awful. Paul Tillich said that sin is separation. Is not segregation an existential expression "of man's tragic separation, his awful estrangement, his terrible sinfulness"? Thus it is that I can urge men to obey the 1954 decision of the Supreme Court, for it is morally right; and I can urge them to disobey segregation ordinances, for they are morally wrong.

19 Let us consider a more concrete example of just and unjust laws. An unjust law is a code that a numerical or power majority group compels a minority group to obey but does not make binding on itself. This is difference made legal. By the same token, a just law is a code that a majority compels a minority to follow and that it is willing to follow itself. This is sameness made legal.

20 Let me give another explanation. A law is unjust if it is inflicted on a minority that, as a result of being denied the right to vote, had no part in enacting or devising the law. Who can say that the legislature of Alabama which set up that state's segregation laws was democratically elected? Throughout Alabama all sorts of devious methods are used to prevent Negroes from becoming registered voters, and there are some counties in which, even though Negroes constitute a majority of the population, not a single Negro is registered. Can any law enacted under such circumstances be considered democratically structured?

21 Sometimes a law is just on its face and unjust in its application. For instance, I have been arrested on a charge of parading without a permit. Now, there is nothing wrong in having an ordinance which requires a permit for a parade. But such an ordinance becomes unjust when it is used to maintain segregation and to deny citizens the First Amendment privilege of peaceful assembly and protest.

22 I hope you are able to see the distinction I am trying to point out. In no sense do I advocate evading or defying the law, as would the rabid segregationist. That would lead to anarchy. One who breaks an unjust law must do so openly, lovingly, and with a willingness to accept the penalty. I submit that an individual who breaks a law that conscience tells him is unjust and who willingly accepts the penalty of imprisonment in order to arouse the conscience of the community over its injustice is in reality expressing the highest respect for law.

23 Of course, there is nothing new about this kind of civil disobedience. It was evidenced sublimely in the refusal of Shadrach, Meshach, and Abednego to obey the laws of Nebuchadnezzar, on the ground that a higher moral law was at stake. It was practiced superbly by the early Christians, who were willing to face hungry lions and the excruciating pain of chopping blocks rather than submit to certain unjust laws of the Roman Empire. To a degree, academic freedom is a reality today because Socrates practiced civil disobedience. In our own nation, the Boston Tea Party represented a massive act of civil disobedience.

24 We should never forget that everything Adolf Hitler did in Germany was "legal" and everything the Hungarian freedom fighters did in Hungary was "illegal." It was "illegal" to aid and comfort a Jew in Hitler's Germany. Even so, I am sure that, had I lived in Germany at the time, I would have aided and comforted my Jewish brothers. If today I lived in a Communist country where certain principles dear to the Christian faith are suppressed, I would openly advocate disobeying that country's antireligious laws.

25 I must make two honest confessions to you, my Christian and Jewish brothers. First, I must confess that over the past few years I have been gravely disappointed with the white moderate. I have almost reached the regrettable conclusion that the Negro's great stumbling block in his stride toward freedom is not the White Citizen's Counciler or the Ku Klux Klanner, but the white

moderate, who is more devoted to "order" than to justice; who prefers a negative peace which is the absence of tension to a positive peace which is the presence of justice; who constantly says: "I agree with you in the goal you seek, but I cannot agree with your methods of direct action"; who paternalistically believes he can set the timetable for another man's freedom; who lives by a mythical concept of time and who constantly advises the Negro to wait for a "more convenient season." Shallow understanding from people of good will is more frustrating than absolute misunderstanding from people of ill will. Lukewarm acceptance is much more bewildering than outright rejection.

26 I had hoped that the white moderate would understand that law and order exist for the purpose of establishing justice and that when they fail in this purpose they become the dangerously structured dams that block the flow of social progress. I had hoped that the white moderate would understand that the present tension in the South is a necessary phase of the transition from an obnoxious negative peace, in which the Negro passively accepted his unjust plight, to a substantive and positive peace, in which all men will respect the dignity and worth of human personality. Actually, we who engage in nonviolent direct action are not the creators of tension. We merely bring to the surface the hidden tension that is already alive. We bring it out in the open, where it can be seen and dealt with. Like a boil that can never be cured so long as it is covered up but must be opened with all its ugliness to the natural medicines of air and light, injustice must be exposed, with all the tension its exposure creates, to the light of human conscience and the air of national opinion before it can be cured.

27 In your statement you assert that our actions, even though peaceful, must be condemned because they precipitate violence. But is this a logical assertion? Isn't this like condemning a robbed man because his possession of money precipitated the evil act of robbery? Isn't this like condemning Socrates because his unswerving commitment to truth and his philosophical inquiries precipitated the act by the misguided populace in which they made him drink hemlock? Isn't this like condemning Jesus because his unique God-consciousness and never-ceasing devotion to God's will precipitated the evil act of crucifixion? We must come to see that, as the federal courts have consistently affirmed, it is wrong to urge an individual to cease his efforts to gain his basic constitutional rights because the quest may precipitate violence. Society must protect the robbed and punish the robber.

28 I had also hoped that the white moderate would reject the myth concerning time in relation to the struggle for freedom. I have just received a letter from a white brother in Texas. He writes: "All Christians know that the colored people will receive equal rights eventually, but it is possible that you are in too great a religious hurry. It has taken Christianity almost two thousand years to accomplish what it has. The teachings of Christ take time to come to earth." Such an attitude stems from a tragic misconception of time, from the strangely rational notion that there is something in the very flow of time that will inevitably cure all ills. Actually, time itself is neutral; it can be used either destructively or constructively. More and more I feel that the people of ill will have used time much more effectively than have the people of good will. We will have to repent in this generation not merely for the hateful words and actions of the bad people but for the appalling silence of the good people. Human progress never rolls in on wheels of inevitability; it comes through the tireless efforts of men willing to be co-workers with God, and without this hard work, time itself becomes an ally of the forces of social stagnation. We must use time creatively, in the knowledge that the time is always ripe to do right. Now is the time to make real the promise of democracy and transform our pending national elegy into a creative psalm of brotherhood. Now is the time to lift our national policy from the quicksand of racial injustice to be the solid rock of human dignity.

29 You speak of our activity in Birmingham as extreme. At first I was rather disappointed that fellow clergymen would see my nonviolent efforts as those of an extremist. I began thinking about the fact that I stand in the middle of two opposing forces in the Negro community. One is a force of complacency, made up in part of Negroes who, as a result of long years of oppression, are so drained of self-respect and a sense of "somebodiness" that they have adjusted to segregation; and in part of a few middle-class Negroes who, because of a degree of academic and economic security and because in some ways they profit by segregation, have become insensitive to the problems of the masses. The other force is one of bitterness and hatred, and it comes perilously close to advocating violence. It is expressed in the various black nationalist groups that are springing up across the nation, the largest and best known being Elijah Muhammad's Muslim movement. Nourished by the Negro's frustration over the continued existence of racial discrimination, this movement is made up of people who have lost faith in America, who have absolutely repudiated Christianity, and who have concluded that the white man is an incorrigible "devil."

30 I have tried to stand between these two forces, saying that we need emulate neither the "do-nothingism" of the complacent nor the hatred and despair of the black nationalist. For there is the more excellent way of love and nonviolent protest. I am grateful to God that, through the influence of the Negro church, the way of nonviolence became an integral part of our struggle.

31 If this philosophy had not emerged, by now many streets of the South would, I am convinced, be flowing with blood. And I am further convinced that if our white brothers dismiss as "rabble-rousers" and "outside agitators" those of us who employ nonviolent direct action, and if they refuse to support our nonviolent efforts, millions of Negroes will, out of frustration and despair, seek solace and security in black-nationalist ideologies—a development that would inevitably lead to a frightening racial nightmare.

32 Oppressed people cannot remain oppressed forever. The yearning for freedom eventually manifests itself, and that is what has happened to the American Negro. Something within has reminded him of his birthright of freedom, and something without has reminded him that it can be gained. Consciously or unconsciously, he has been caught up by the Zeitgeist, and with his black brothers of Africa and his brown and yellow brothers of Asia, South America, and the Caribbean, the United States Negro is moving with a sense of great urgency toward the promised land of racial justice. If one recognizes this vital urge that has engulfed the Negro community, one should readily understand why public demonstrations are taking place. The Negro has many pent-up resentments and latent frustrations, and he must release them. So let him march; let him make prayer pilgrimages to the city hall; let him go on freedom rides—and try to understand why he must do so. If his repressed emotions are not released in nonviolent ways, they will seek expression through violence; this is not a threat but a fact of history. So I have not said to my people: "Get rid of your discontent." Rather, I have tried to say that this normal and healthy discontent can be channeled into the creative outlet of nonviolent direct action. And now this approach is being termed extremist.

33 But though I was initially disappointed at being categorized as an extremist, as I continued to think about the matter I gradually gained a measure of satisfaction from the label. Was not Jesus an extremist for love: "Love your enemies, bless them that curse you, do good to them that hate you, and pray for them which despitefully use you, and persecute you." Was not Amos an extremist for justice: "Let justice roll down like waters and righteousness like an ever-flowing stream." Was not Paul an extremist for the Christian gospel: "I bear in my body the marks

of the Lord Jesus." Was not Martin Luther an extremist: "Here I stand; I cannot do otherwise, so help me God." And John Bunyan: "I will stay in jail to the end of my days before I make a butchery of my conscience." And Abraham Lincoln: "This nation cannot survive half slave and half free." And Thomas Jefferson: "We hold these truths to be self-evident, that all men are created equal. . . ." So the question is not whether we will be extremists, but what kind of extremists we will be. Will we be extremists for hate or for love? Will we be extremists for the preservation of injustice or for the extension of justice? In that dramatic scene on Calvary's hill three men were crucified. We must never forget that all three were crucified for the same crime—the crime of extremism. Two were extremists for immorality, and thus fell below their environment. The other, Jesus Christ, was an extremist for love, truth, and goodness, and thereby rose above his environment. Perhaps the South, the nation, and the world are in dire need of creative extremists.

34 I had hoped that the white moderate would see this need. Perhaps I was too optimistic; perhaps I expected too much. I suppose I should have realized that few members of the oppressor race can understand the deep groans and passionate yearnings of the oppressed race, and still fewer have the vision to see that injustice must be rooted out by strong, persistent, and determined action. I am thankful, however, that some of our white brothers in the South have grasped the meaning of this social revolution and committed themselves to it. They are still too few in quantity, but they are big in quality. Some—such as Ralph McGill, Lillian Smith, Harry Golden, James McBride Dabbs, Ann Braden, and Sarah Patton Boyle—have written about our struggle in eloquent and prophetic terms. Others have marched with us down nameless streets of the South. They have languished in filthy, roach-infested jails, suffering the abuse and brutality of policemen who view them as "dirty nigger lovers." Unlike so many of their moderate brothers and sisters, they have recognized the urgency of the moment and sensed the need for powerful "action" antidotes to combat the disease of segregation.

35 Let me take note of my other major disappointment. I have been so greatly disappointed with the white church and its leadership. Of course, there are some notable exceptions. I am not unmindful of the fact that each of you has taken some significant stands on this issue. I commend you, Reverend Stallings, for your Christian stand on this past Sunday, in welcoming Negroes to your worship service on a nonsegregated basis. I commend the Catholic leaders of this state for integrating Spring Hill College several years ago.

36 But despite these notable exceptions, I must honestly reiterate that I have been disappointed with the church. I do not say this as one of those negative critics who can always find something wrong with the church. I say this as a minister of the gospel, who loves the church; who was nurtured in its bosom; who has been sustained by its spiritual blessings; and who will remain true to it as long as the cord of life shall lengthen.

37 When I was suddenly catapulted into the leadership of the bus protest in Montgomery, Alabama, a few years ago, I felt we would be supported by the white church and felt that the white ministers, priests, and rabbis of the South would be among our strongest allies. Instead, some have been outright opponents, refusing to understand the freedom movement and misrepresenting its leadership, and too many others have been more cautious than courageous and have remained silent behind the anesthetizing security of stained-glass windows.

38 In spite of my shattered dreams, I came to Birmingham with the hope that the white religious leadership of this community would see the justice of our cause and, with deep moral concern, would serve as the channel through which our just grievances could reach the power structure. I had hoped that each of you would understand. But again I have been disappointed.

39 I have heard numerous southern religious leaders admonish their worshipers to comply with a desegregation decision because it is the law, but I have longed to hear white ministers declare: "Follow this decree because integration is morally right and because the Negro is your brother." In the midst of blatant injustices inflicted upon the Negro, I have watched white churchmen stand on the sideline and mouth pious irrelevancies and sanctimonious trivialities. In the midst of a mighty struggle to rid our nation of racial and economic injustice, I have heard many ministers say: "Those are social issues, with which the gospel has no real concern." And I have watched many churches commit themselves to a completely other worldly religion which makes a strange, un-Biblical distinction between body and soul, between the sacred and the secular.

40 I have traveled the length and breadth of Alabama, Mississippi, and all the other southern states. On sweltering summer days and crisp autumn mornings I have looked at the South's beautiful churches with their lofty spires pointing heavenward. I have beheld the impressive outlines of her massive religious-education buildings. Over and over I have found myself asking: "What kind of people worship here? Who is their God? Where were their voices when the lips of Governor Barnett dripped with words of interposition and nullification? Where were they when Governor Wallace gave a clarion call for defiance and hatred? Where were their voices of support when bruised and weary Negro men and women decided to rise from the dark dungeons of complacency to the bright hills of creative protest?"

41 Yes, these questions are still in my mind. In deep disappointment I have wept over the laxity of the church. But be assured that my tears have been tears of love. There can be no deep disappointment where there is not deep love. Yes, I love the church. How could I do otherwise? I am in the rather unique position of being the son, the grandson, and the great-grandson of preachers. Yes, I see the church as the body of Christ. But, oh! How we have blemished and scarred that body through social neglect and through fear of being nonconformists.

42 There was a time when the church was very powerful—in the time when the early Christians rejoiced at being deemed worthy to suffer for what they believed. In those days the church was not merely a thermometer that recorded the ideas and principles of popular opinion; it was a thermostat that transformed the mores of society. Whenever the early Christians entered a town, the people in power became disturbed and immediately sought to convict the Christians for being "disturbers of the peace" and "outside agitators." But the Christians pressed on, in the conviction that they were "a colony of heaven," called to obey God rather than man. Small in number, they were big in commitment. They were too God intoxicated to be "astronomically intimidated." By their effort and example they brought an end to such ancient evils as infanticide and gladiatorial contests.

43 Things are different now. So often the contemporary church is a weak, ineffectual voice with an uncertain sound. So often it is an archdefender of the status quo. Far from being disturbed by the presence of the church, the power structure of the average community is consoled by the church's silent and often even vocal sanction of things as they are.

44 But the judgment of God is upon the church as never before. If today's church does not recapture the sacrificial spirit of the early church, it will lose its authenticity, forfeit the loyalty of millions, and be dismissed as an irrelevant social club with no meaning for the twentieth century. Every day I meet young people whose disappointment with the church has turned into outright disgust.

45 Perhaps I have once again been too optimistic. Is organized religion too inextricably bound to the status quo to save our nation and

the world? Perhaps I must turn my faith to the inner spiritual church, the church within the church, as the true ecclesia and the hope of the world. But again I am thankful to God that some noble souls from the ranks of organized religion have broken loose from the paralyzing chains of conformity and joined us as active partners in the struggle for freedom. They have left their secure congregations and walked the streets of Albany, Georgia, with us. They have gone down the highways of the South on tortuous rides for freedom. Yes, they have gone to jail with us. Some have been dismissed from their churches, have lost the support of their bishops and fellow ministers. But they have acted in the faith that right defeated is stronger than evil triumphant. Their witness has been the spiritual salt that has preserved the true meaning of the gospel in these troubled times. They have carved a tunnel of hope through the dark mountain of disappointment.

46 I hope the church as a whole will meet the challenge of this decisive hour. But even if the church does not come to the aid of justice, I have no despair about the future. I have no fear about the outcome of our struggle in Birmingham, even if our motives are at present misunderstood. We will reach the goal of freedom in Birmingham, and all over the nation, because the goal of America is freedom. Abused and scorned though we may be, our destiny is tied up with America's destiny. Before the Pilgrims landed at Plymouth, we were here. Before the pen of Jefferson etched the majestic words of the Declaration of Independence across the pages of history, we were here. For more than two centuries our forebears labored in this country without wages; they made cotton king; they built the homes of their masters while suffering gross injustice and shameful humiliation—and yet out of a bottomless vitality they continued to thrive and develop. If the inexpressible cruelties of slavery could not stop us, the opposition we now face will surely fail. We will win our freedom because the sacred heritage of our nation and the eternal will of God are embodied in our echoing demands.

47 Before closing I feel impelled to mention one other point in your statement that has troubled me profoundly. You warmly commended the Birmingham police force for keeping "order" and "preventing violence." I doubt that you would have so warmly commended the police force if you had seen its dogs sinking their teeth into unarmed, nonviolent Negroes. I doubt that you would so quickly commend the policemen if you were to observe their ugly and inhumane treatment of Negroes here in the city jail; if you were to watch them push and curse old Negro women and young Negro girls; if you were to see them slap and kick old Negro men and young boys; if you were to observe them, as they did on two occasions, refuse to give us food because we wanted to sing our grace together. I cannot join you in your praise of the Birmingham police department.

48 It is true that the police have exercised a degree of discipline in handing the demonstrators. In this sense they have conducted themselves rather "nonviolently" in public. But for what purpose? To preserve the evil system of segregation. Over the past few years I have consistently preached that nonviolence demands that the means we use must be as pure as the ends we seek. I have tried to make clear that it is wrong to use immoral means to attain moral ends. But now I must affirm that it is just as wrong, or perhaps even more so, to use moral means to preserve immoral ends. Perhaps Mr. Connor and his policemen have been rather nonviolent in public, as was Chief Pritchett in Albany, Georgia, but they have used the moral means of nonviolence to maintain the immoral end of racial injustice. As T. S. Eliot has said: "The last temptation is the greatest treason: To do the right deed for the wrong reason."

49 I wish you had commended the Negro sit-inners and demonstrators of Birmingham for their sublime courage, their willingness to suffer,

and their amazing discipline in the midst of great provocation. One day the South will recognize its real heroes. They will be the James Merediths, with the noble sense of purpose that enables them to face jeering and hostile mobs, and with the agonizing loneliness that characterizes the life of the pioneer. They will be old, oppressed, battered Negro women, symbolized in a seventy-two-year-old woman in Montgomery, Alabama, who rose up with a sense of dignity and with her people decided not to ride segregated buses, and who responded with ungrammatical profundity to one who inquired about her weariness: "My feets is tired, but my soul is at rest." They will be the young high school and college students, the young ministers of the gospel, and a host of their elders, courageously and nonviolently sitting in at lunch counters and willingly going to jail for conscience's sake. One day the South will know that when these disinherited children of God sat down at lunch counters, they were in reality standing up for what is best in the American dream and for the most sacred values in our Judaeo-Christian heritage, thereby bringing our nation back to those great wells of democracy which were dug deep by the founding fathers in their formulation of the Constitution and the Declaration of Independence.

50 Never before have I written so long a letter. I'm afraid it is much too long to take your precious time. I can assure you that it would have been much shorter if I had been writing from a comfortable desk, but what else can one do when he is alone in a narrow jail cell, other than write long letters, think long thoughts, and pray long prayers?

51 If I have said anything in this letter that overstates the truth and indicates an unreasonable impatience, I beg you to forgive me. If I have said anything that understates the truth and indicates my having a patience that allows me to settle for anything less than brotherhood, I beg God to forgive me.

52 I hope this letter finds you strong in the faith. I also hope that circumstances will soon make it possible for me to meet each of you, not as an integrationist or a civil rights leader but as a fellow clergyman and a Christian brother. Let us all hope that the dark clouds of racial prejudice will soon pass away and the deep fog of misunderstanding will be lifted from our fear-drenched communities, and in some not too distant tomorrow the radiant stars of love and brotherhood will shine over our great nation with all their scintillating beauty.

53 Yours for the cause of Peace and Brotherhood,

54 Martin Luther King, Jr.

THINKING ABOUT THE ARGUMENT

1. Who are the "Fellow Clergymen" addressed in King's letter? Do you think they consider themselves to be King's peers? Why or why not? What might their opinion of King be? How can you tell?
2. What does King say in his letter to gain the sympathy and attention of his particular audience? Is this technique effective in your opinion? Why or why not?
3. How does King establish authority in the first paragraphs of the letter?
4. What does King state as his purpose in writing the letter? Explain in detail.

5. What are the elements, according to the author, of nonviolent resistance, and why does he say this action is necessary?
6. Why does King say he was disappointed by the "white moderate"? How does the author address the criticism that he is an "extremist"?

Responding to the Argument

1. In his letter, King justifies his willingness to break laws in the search for justice. How does this contrast with the position that Socrates argues in Plato's essay, "Crito"? Which position do you endorse, and why?
2. In your opinion, is a program of nonviolent resistance a good means of effecting social change? Why or why not? Did it seem to work well for the civil rights movement? Can you think of a case where nonviolent resistance has been effective (or ineffective) in recent history? If it is sometimes effective and sometimes ineffective, why is this?
3. How do you think King would react to the poverty, violence, and despair in the largely African American communities in inner cities today? What might he suggest as a starting point for a solution? Conversely, what actions do you think should be taken in helping these communities end the cycle of poverty and violence?
4. Do you think that the civil rights movement largely solved the problem of racism in the United States, or was the problem just driven underground? Provide at least one concrete piece of evidence to support your answer.

Writing about the Argument

1. For a research project, select a modern organization that is trying to combat racism, oppression, and poverty in the United States, such as Call to Action. How does this organization differ in purpose or methodology from the original civil rights movement? Argue what this organization (and others like it) needs to do to combat poverty and racism.
2. Write a letter of your own. In this letter, address changes that need to be made in your community to promote social justice. If you like, send the letter to your local newspaper.
3. If you think that American society has largely solved the problem of racism, write an argument supporting this position. Conduct research as necessary and provide evidence to support your claims.
4. Write a response to King from the point of view of the "white moderates" he chastises in his letter. Explain why his criticisms are, at least in part, exaggerated and unfair.

Glossary

A

analysis The study of the parts of an object of learning (like an argumentative essay) to understand how the different parts work together to contribute to an understanding of the whole. One of the elements of **Bloom's taxonomy.**

anecdote A brief narrative that can be used in an informal way to begin an essay or illustrate a point.

annotate To write notes in the margin of a text as it is being read.

appeal to authority A logical fallacy that relies on expert opinion when the authority is not actually an expert on the subject. Also called *argumentum ad verecundiam.*

appeal to faith A logical fallacy that relies on a previously held belief rather than evidence to support a claim. Also called *fiatism* or *blind faith.*

appeal to fear A logical fallacy that relies on fear rather than evidence to persuade an audience to accept a claim.

appeal to pity A logical fallacy that relies on the likelihood that an audience will sympathize with someone or something as the basis of convincing that audience to accept a claim. Also called *argumentum ad misericordiam.*

appeal to popularity A logical fallacy that relies on the wide appeal of a particular position to persuade an audience to accept the validity of a claim. Also known as *argumentum ad populum* and *bandwagon fallacy.*

application A way that knowledge can be applied in a practical way. One of the elements of **Bloom's taxonomy**.

argument The process of providing claims, giving reasons, and supplying evidence to change the way someone thinks or acts.

argumentative thesis An assertion that needs support—specific reasons—to be accepted as true. Also called a *claim.*

attacking the person A logical fallacy that relies on a criticism of a person's character, rather than the validity of his or her argument, to persuade an audience. Also called *argumentum ad hominem.*

audience The people who are intended to read a piece of writing.

authority The degree of faith or the level of trust that an audience has in a writer. Also called *ethos.*

B

backing In Toulmin's system of argumentation, an additional argument that is needed to convince a skeptical audience that a particular **inference**, or *warrant*, is valid.

begging the question A logical fallacy in which the conclusion and premise of a logical statement are the same or similar. Also called *petitio principii.*

Bloom's taxonomy A system developed by Benjamin Bloom that describes how people acquire and use knowledge. The elements of Bloom's taxonomy are **knowledge**, **comprehension**, **application**, **analysis**, **synthesis**, and **evaluation**.

C

card stacking A logical fallacy that relies on giving the impression that all sides of an issue are being fairly represented while actually selecting evidence that favors a particular viewpoint. Also called *cherry picking.*

cause claim A claim that focuses on the source of a particular effect. With a cause claim, the effect is generally known, but the cause is open to debate.

cause-and-effect claim A claim that connects an action with a result. Such claims can focus on a cause, an effect, or both.

claim An arguable idea that you want your audience to accept as true.

classification claim A claim that organizes collections of people, concepts, or objects into identifiable groups.

comparison and contrast claim A claim that identifies one thing in relation to something else.

comprehension The understanding of the meaning of an object of knowledge and ability to rephrase that information in your own words. An element of **Bloom's taxonomy**. Also called *interpretation.*

counterargument An argument that differs from your own argument.

critical reading Reading in an active mode with the idea of understanding, analyzing, and evaluating a text.

D

definition claim A claim that identifies something by outlining its distinguishing features.

drafting The second major stage of the writing process, following **planning** and coming before **revising**.

E

editing A terminal stage of the writing process that is engaged in only after a draft has been thoroughly revised and polished.

effect claim A claim that focuses on the result of a particular cause.

emotion A persuasive appeal that helps an audience sympathize with the author's point of view. Also called *pathos*.

enthymeme An incomplete logical statement consisting of a **claim** but omitting the **reason**, the **inference**, or both.

evaluation A determination of the value of an object of knowledge. An element of **Bloom's taxonomy**.

evidence Any information that can be used to support a claim. Common types of evidence include anecdotes, examples, expert opinions, facts, history, scenarios, and statistics.

F

fact A piece of information that is looked on as being true and generally is not open to debate or interpretation.

fact claim A claim that tries to determine whether something is real or true.

fallacy An abuse of logic that undercuts or replaces an argument based on claims supported by evidence.

false cause An assumption that a first event causes a second event just because the first event happens before the second event. Also called *post hoc fallacy*.

false dilemma An artificially limited choice. Also called *false choice*.

figurative language Words and phrases that mean something other than their literal meanings.

figure of form A series of words that are rearranged in a way that alters their meaning or creates an aesthetic effect. Also called *scheme*.

figure of speech A word, such as a metaphor or simile, used in a nonliteral way that expands its meaning or effect. Also called *trope*.

G

grounds In Toulmin's system of argumentation, the **evidence** that is provided to back up a **claim** and its associated **reason**.

guilt by association A logical fallacy that diverts attention away from arguable issues by discussing the negative reputations of others who supported the claim.

H

hasty generalization A logical fallacy that assumes the truth of a claim based on insufficient examples.

hook An opening sentence that is used to engage the attention of the reader.

I

identity claim A claim used to identify what something is by understanding its dominant features.

inference An underlying assumption that allows a **reason** to support a **claim**. Also called *warrant*.

irony A dramatic, situational, or verbal contrast between the expected and the actual.

issue A subject that can be debated and argued.

K

knowledge An accurately recalled or reported piece of information. One of the elements of **Bloom's taxonomy**.

L

logic The science of establishing relationships between ideas. Also called *logos*.

M

major claim The thesis statement of an argument; a statement of the idea that you want your reader to accept when he or she is finished reading your essay. Also called an **argumentative thesis**.

moral and ethical claim A claim that proposes to judge human behavior on the basis of a religious or philosophical system.

N

non sequitur An argument that presents a conclusion that is not supported by the evidence. Literally, "does not follow."

O

objection A potential argument that may be raised in objection to your argument and that must be answered with an argument of your own in the form of a rebuttal.

P

paraphrasing The process of taking information from a source and putting it in your own style. Paraphrases should be approximately the same length as the original material and should not distort the original source's meaning.

plagiarism The insertion of information from another source into your own work and the representation (either intentional or unintentional) of it as your writing or ideas.

planning The first stage of the writing process, which is followed by **drafting** and **revising**. Also called *prewriting*.

poisoning the well The process of discrediting an opponent before the audience has had a chance to consider the opponent's arguments. A form of **attacking the person** (*argumentum ad hominem*).

policy claim A claim that proposes rules, guidelines, or laws to govern a particular situation.

procedure claim A claim that argues how a particular policy should be carried out.

purpose The belief that you want your audience to have when they finish reading your writing (or listening to your speech).

Q

qualifier A term inserted in a logical statement that limits its application.

quoting The practice of reproducing words from a source and using them to support your arguments.

R

reason A statement attached to an argumentative claim that is used to support the validity of a **claim**.

rebuttal In Toulmin's system of argumentation, an argument made to respond to a particular **objection**.

red herring A secondary issue that distracts from the claim at hand.

refutation The part of an argument involving arguing against an opposing position. See also **rebuttal**.

resemblance claim A claim that helps the audience understand something unfamiliar by comparing it to something familiar.

revising The third stage of the writing process, which follows **planning** and **drafting**. Revising involves thinking about what you have written (how well it accomplishes your **purpose** and communicates with your **audience**) and making changes, both large and small, to fine-tune your text. Also called *revision*.

S

scenario A hypothetical situation that has not happened but could occur.

slippery slope A logical fallacy that assumes that if one step is taken or one concession is made, it will lead to a series of new events or concessions, akin to a stack of dominoes falling down.

statistics A form of evidence that uses numerical data to support a claim.

straw man A logical fallacy in which an arguer misrepresents an opposing position in an inaccurate or simplistic way that will make the counterargument easy to discredit.

structure The organization of an argument—how the parts are arranged into an effective and persuasive whole.

style The effective arrangement of words so that they are engaging, eloquent, clear, and persuasive.

summary A condensed version of a source with the idea of capturing the essence, main ideas, and emphasis of the original.

supporting claim A secondary claim that appears in an argumentative essay's body paragraphs and usually takes the form of a topic sentence. Also called a *minor claim*.

syllogism A complete logical statement consisting of a major premise, a minor premise, and a conclusion. See also **enthymeme**.

synthesis The comparison and contrasting of an object of knowledge with other, similar objects. An element of **Bloom's taxonomy**.

T

topic A general, nonarguable subject.

topic sentence A sentence in a paragraph that states the paragraph's rhetorical purpose. In **arguments**, topic sentences frequently take the form of **minor claims** that serve to support the **argumentative thesis**, the **major claim**.

V

value claim A claim that tries to determine the worth of something by measuring it against a standard or scale.

visual argument An image (such as a photograph, editorial cartoon, or public service advertisement) that states or implies an argument using means in addition to, or in the place of, written text.

voice The unique tone created by a particular writer's **style**.

W

warrant See **inference**.

Credits

Text Credits

Chapter 2: Page 52: Figure based on "The Cycle of Violence" from *Domestic Violence Handbook*, http://www.domesticviolence.org. Reprinted by permission of Common Ground Sanctuary.

Page 52: Frank L. Cioffi, "Argumentation in a Culture of Discord," *Chronicle of Higher Education* 20 May 2005: B6–B8. Reprinted by permission of the author.

Chapter 4: Page 103: From John McWhorter, "Mean Street Theater: An Awful Image for Black America," *Wall Street Journal* (Eastern ed.) 30 May 2003: W15. Copyright 2003 by Dow Jones & Co. Inc. Reproduced with permission of Dow Jones & Co. Inc. in the format Textbook via Copyright Clearance Center.

Page 112: Opio Lumumba Sokoni, "Hip-Hop Activism Buds Beautifully," from http://www.alternet.org/story/16107. Reprinted by permission of AlterNet.

Chapter 5: Page 133: From Benjamin S. Bloom et al., *Taxonomy of Educational Objectives*, Book 1, *Cognitive Domain* (Boston: Allyn and Bacon). Copyright © 1964 by Pearson Education. Adapted by permission of the publisher.

Page 138: Frederick Emrich, from "Cheating and 'Common Knowledge'" (blog), http://info-commons.org/blog/archives/000117.html. Courtesy of Frederick Emrich and the info-commons.org website.

Chapter 6: Page 159: Jane Caputi and Susan Nance, "One Size Does Not Fit All: Being Beautiful, Thin, and Female in America," from Christopher Geist and Jack Nachbar eds., *The Popular Culture Reader* (1983), 295. Copyright © 1983. Reprinted by permission of The University of Wisconsin Press.

Page 160: Gerald Early, "Never-Never Land," *Wall Street Journal* (Eastern ed.) 2 Dec. 2003: A18. Copyright 2003 by Dow Jones & Co. Inc. Reproduced with permission of Dow Jones & Co. Inc. in the format Textbook via Copyright Clearance Center.

Page 163: Laurence Shames, "The More Factor," from *The Hunger for More: Searching for Values in an Age of Greed* (1989), 19–27. Copyright © 1989 by Laurence Shames. Published by Times Books, a division of Random House, Inc. Reprinted with permission of the Stuart Krichevsky Literary Agency, Inc.

Page 168: M. P. McCrillis, "Why Eminem Is Important," *The World & I* March 2003: 275–287. Reprinted by permission.

Page 171: Marcia Ian, "Abject to Object: Women's Body Building," *Postmodern Culture* 1:3 (1991), © The Johns Hopkins University Press. Reprinted with permission of The Johns Hopkins University Press.

Chapter 7: Page 193: Jerrold H. Zar, "Candidate for a Pullet Surprise" (aka "An Owed to the Spelling Chequer"), *Journal of Irreproducible Results* (the science humor magazine), http://www.jir.com. Reprinted by permission.

Chapter 9: Page 254: Gregory Stock and Daniel Callahan, "Point-Counterpoint: Would Doubling the Human Life Span Be a Positive or Negative for Us Either as Individuals or as a Society?," *Journals of Gerontology* June 2004: 554–559, *A Biol Sci Med Sci.* 2004: 59A: 554–559. Copyright © The Gerontological Society of America. Reproduced by permission of the publisher.

Chapter 11: Page 294: Judy Brady, "Why I Want a Wife," *Ms.* magazine, 1971. Reprinted by permission of the author.

Page 295: "Area Woman Not Listened to Again," *The Onion*, 25 Mar. 1998. Reprinted by permission of The Onion.

Chapter 15: Page 398: Amy Dickinson, "Measuring Up," *Time* 20 Nov. 2000: 154. Copyright © 2000 Time Inc. Reprinted by permission.

Page 401: Patrick Johnson, "Obesity: Epidemic or Myth?," *The Skeptical Inquirer* Sept./Oct. 2005: 25+. Used by permission of The Skeptical Inquirer, http://www.CSICOP.org.

Page 408: Amanda Spake, "Rethinking Weight: Hey, Maybe It's Not a Weakness. Just Maybe . . . It's a Disease," *U.S. News & World Report* 9 Feb. 2004: 50–56. Copyright 2004 U.S. News & World Report, L.P. Reprinted with permission.

Page 414: Howard Markel, "A Global Epidemic in the Making?," *The Globalist* 1 Aug. 2002. Reprinted by permission of the author.

Page 419: Christopher Reeve, "Use the Body's 'Repair Kit,'" *Time* 1 May 2001: 44. Reprinted by permission of the Christopher Reeve Foundation.

Page 421: Virginia Postrel, "Should Human Cloning Be Allowed? Yes, Don't Impede Medical Progress," *Wall Street Journal* (Eastern ed.) 2 Dec. 2001: A20. Copyright 2001 by Dow Jones

& Co. Inc. Reproduced with permission of Dow Jones & Co. Inc. in the format Textbook via Copyright Clearance Center.

Page 424: Eric Cohen and William Kristol, "Should Human Cloning Be Allowed? No, It's a Moral Monstrosity," *Wall Street Journal* (Eastern ed.) 5 Dec. 2001: A20. Copyright 2001 by Dow Jones & Co. Inc. Reproduced with permission of Dow Jones & Co. Inc. in the format Textbook via Copyright Clearance Center.

Page 428: Ron Reagan, "Remarks to the 2004 Democratic National Convention." Reprinted by permission of Ron Reagan.

Page 431: Michael Fumento, "Cynical and Cruel: Ron Regan's DNC Speech Was Exploitation—of His Father and of Science," *National Review Online* 29 July 2004, http://www.nationalreview.com. Copyright © 2004 by National Review Online. Reprinted by permission.

Page 434: Sharon Begley, "Now That Chimeras Exist, What If Some Turn Out Too Human?," *Wall Street Journal* (Eastern ed.) 6 May 2005: B1. Copyright 2005 by Dow Jones & Co. Inc. Reproduced with permission of Dow Jones & Co. Inc. in the format Textbook via Copyright Clearance Center.

Page 438: Daniel Eisenberg, "How to Help Them Succeed," *Time* 14 Nov. 2005: 59. Copyright © 2005 Time Inc. Reprinted by permission.

Page 441: Hara Estroff Marano, "Rocking the Cracle of Class," *Psychology Today* Sept./Oct. 2005: 52–58. Reprinted with permission from *Psychology Today* magazine. Copyright © 2005 Sussex Publishers, Inc.

Page 446: Flora Carlin, "The Measuring Game: Why You Think You'll Never Stack Up," *Psychology Today* Sept./Oct. 2005: 42–50. Reprinted with permission from *Psychology Today* magazine. Copyright © 2005 Sussex Publishers, Inc.

Page 450: Richard Wiseman, "The Luck Factor," *The Skeptical Inquirer*, May/June 2003: 26–30. Used by permission of the Skeptical Inquirer, http://www.CSICOP.org.

Chapter 16: Page 462: Robert Patterson, "Why Gay Marriage Doesn't Measure Up," *Human Events* 29 March 2004: 20. Reprinted by permission.

Page 465: Ramesh Ponnuru, "Option Four: A Compromise on Gay Marriage," *National Review* 6 June 2005: 38–40. © 2005 by National Review, Inc., 215 Lexington Avenue, New York, NY 10016. Reprinted by permission.

Page 471: Komal Bhohwani, "Mother Land," *The Advocate* 12 April 2005: 9. Reprinted by permission of LPI Media.

Page 474: Johan Norberg, "The Scientist's Pursuit of Happiness," *Policy*, 21, no. 3 (Spring 2005): 9–13. This article first appeared in *Policy*, the magazine of the Centre for Independent Studies, http://www.cis.org.au.

Page 486: Larry Elder, "Katrina, the Race Card, and the Welfare State," *Jewish World Review* 8 Sept. 2005. By permission of Larry Elder and Creators Syndicate, Inc.

Page 480: Alexander Keyssar, "Reminders of Poverty, Soon Forgotten," *Chronicle of Higher Education: The Chronicle Review*, 4 Nov. 2005. Reprinted by permission of the author.

Page 489: Jim Wallis, "What the Waters Revealed," *Sojourners Magazine* Nov. 2005: 8–17. Reprinted with permission from Sojourners magazine, http://www.sojo.net, 1-800-714-7474.

Page 495: Dianie Ravitch, "The Language Police: Can We Stop Them?," from *The Language Police* by Diane Ravitch, copyright © 2003, 2004 by Diane Ravitch. Used by permission of Alfred A. Knopf, a division of Random House, Inc.

Page 500: Lawrence White, "Hate-Speech Codes That Will Pass Constitutional Muster," *Chronicle of Higher Education* 25 May 1994: A48. Reprinted by permission of the author.

Page 503: Nat Hentoff, "Is It Time to Retire 'Politically Correct'?," *Village Voice* 11 Jan. 1994, pp. 20–21. Reprinted by permission of the author.

Chapter 17: Page 511: John Ashcroft, "The Patriot Act: Wise beyond Its Years," *Wall Street Journal* (Eastern ed.) 26 Oct. 2004: A24. Copyright 2004 by Dow Jones & Co. Inc. Reproduced with permission of Dow Jones & Co. Inc. in the format Textbook via Copyright Clearance Center.

Page 514: Ali Al-Ahmed, "Hypocrisy Most Holy," *Wall Street Journal* (Eastern ed.) 20 May 2005: 48–49. Copyright 2005 by Dow Jones & Co. Inc. Reproduced with permission of Dow Jones & Co. Inc. in the format Textbook via Copyright Clearance Center.

Page 517: Petra Bartosiewicz, "I.O.U. One Terrorist," *Harper's Magazine* Aug. 2005: 48–49. Copyright © 2005 by Harper's Magazine. All rights reserved. Reproduced from the August issue by special permission.

Page 521: Noor Al Hussein, "Afterword," from *Leap of Faith: Memories of an Unexpected Life* by Queen Noor. Copyright © 2003 Her Majesty Queen Noor. Reprinted by permission of Hyperion. All rights reserved.

Page 523: Gregory Melleuish, "Globalized Religions for a Globalised World," *Policy* Winter 2005: 16–20. This article first appeared in *Policy*, the magazine of the Centre for Independent Studies, http://www.cis.org.au.

Page: 530: Rupert Murdoch, "Let Us Give Thanks to Our Immigrants," *Wall Street Journal* (Eastern ed.) 24 Nov. 2004: A12. Copyright 2004 by Dow Jones & Co. Inc. Reproduced with permission of Dow Jones & Co. Inc. in the format Textbook via Copyright Clearance Center.

Page 533: William F. Buckley, Jr., "Can We Stop Illegals?," *National Review* 9 May 2005: 50. Taken from the column On the Right by William F. Buckley, Jr. copyright © 2005. Distributed by Universal Press Syndicate. Rerpinted with permission. All rights reserved.

Page 536: Peter Duignan, "Do Immigrants Benefit America?," *The World & I* Feb. 2004: 20. Reprinted by permission.

Page 541: Jim F. Couch, J. Douglas Barrett, and Peter M. Williams, "Total Amnesty for Illegal Aliens?," *The World & I* February 2004: 26. Reprinted by permission. Please contact http://www.WorldandIJournal.com for more information.

Page 549: Frank Furedi, "The Market in Fear," *Spiked Online* 26 Sept. 2005. Reprinted by permission.

Page 555: Paul Rogers, "A World Becoming More Peaceful?," *open-Democracy.net* 17 Oct. 2005. First published at http://www.open-Democracy.net. Reprinted by permission.

Page 559: David G. Myers, "Do We Fear the Right Things?," *Skeptic* 2003: 56–57. Reprinted by permission.

Page 563: Joyce Carol Oates, "The Aesthetics of Fear," *Ontario Review* Fall 1998: 176–186. Copyright © 1998 Ontario Review. Reprinted by permission of John Hawkins & Associates, Inc.

Chapter 18: Page 573: Edward O. Wilson, "The Bottleneck," from *The Future of Life* by Edward O. Wilson. Copyright © 2002 by E. O. Wilson. Used by permission of Alfred A. Knopf, a division of Random House, Inc.

Page 584: Jan Otto Andersson, "Our Full, Unequal World," *Inroads* 1 July 2005: 48–57. Reprinted by permission.

Page 591: Table, "National Footprnits and Biocapacities." Reprinted by permission of Global Footprint Network. For more information, visit http://www.Footprintnetwork.org.

Page 593: Michael Crichton, "Environmentalism as Religion Run Amo," *USA Today* 1 Mar. 2004: 22–25. Reprinted from *USA Today* magazine, Mar. 2004. Copyrighted by the Society for the Advancement of Education, Inc.

Page 601: Ray Kurzwel, "Prologue: An Inexorable Emergence," from *The Age of Spiritual Machines* by Ray Kurzweil. Copyright © 1999 by Ray Kurzweil. Used by permission of Viking Penguin, a division of Penguin group (USA) Inc.

Page 607: Bill Joy, "The Dark Side of Technology" © September 15, 2000 by Bill Joy. This article originally appeared in *Vital Speeches of the Day.* Reprinted by permission of the author.

Page 614: Steven B. Harris, "A.I. and the Return of the Krell Machine," *Skeptic* 9.3 2002. Reprinted by permission.

Page 629: Ben Bova, "It's Completely Impossible," *Immortalty: How Science Is Extending Your Life Span—and Changing the World* (1998), 185–189. Copyright © 2000 by Ben Bova. Reprinted by permission of HarperCollins Publishers.

Page 636: Gregory Stock and Daniel Callahan, "Point-Counterpoint: Would Doubling the Human Life Span Be a Positive or Negative for Us Either as Individuals or as a Society?," *Journals of Gerontology* June 2004: 554–559, *A Biol Sci Med Sci.* 2004; 59A: 554–559. Copyright © The Gerontological Society of America. Reproduced by permission of the publisher.

Page 647: Henry J. Aaron and William B. Schwartz, "Coping with Methuselah," *Brookings Review* Fall 2003: 36–39. Reprinted with permission of the Brookings Institution Press.

Chapter 19: Page 656: "Breeding Evil? Defending Video Games," *Economist* 6 Aug. 2005: 9. © 2005 The Economist Newspaper Ltd. All rights reserved. Reprinted with permission. Further reproduction prohibited. http://www.economist.com.

Page 659: David A. Grossman, "B. F. Skinner's Rats and Operant Conditioning at the Video Arcade," *On Killing: The Psychological Cost of Learning to Kill in War and Society* (1995), 312–316. Copyright © 1995, 1996 by David A. Grossman. By permission of Little, Brown and Co., Inc.

Page 663: Tony Reichardt, "Playing with Fire?" *Nature* July 2003: 367–368. Copyright 2003 by Nature Publishing Group. Reproduced with permission of Nature Publishing Group in the format Textbook via Copyright Clearance Center.

Page 667: Sara Rimensnyder, "Bang, You're Dead," *Reason* Nov. 2002: 15. Reprinted by permission.

Page 669: Cynthia G. Wagner, "Aggression and Violent Media," *The Futurist* July/Aug. 2004: 16. Reprinted by permission.

Page 671: Barbara Dafoe Whitehead, "Parents Need Help," *Commonweal* 28 Jan. 2005: 9–10. © 2005 Commonweal Foundation, reprinted with permission. For subscriptions, http://www.commonwealmagazine.org.

Page 674: Lloyd Eby, "Why Eminem Is a Problem," *The World & I* Mar. 2003: 289. Reprinted by permission. Please contact http://www.WorldandIJournal.com for more information.

Page 683: M. P. McCrillis, "Why Eminem Is Important," *The World & I* Mar. 2003: 275–287. Reprinted by permission.

Page 694: Sara Rimensnyder, "Bang, You're Dead," *Reason* Nov. 2002: 15. Reprinted by permission.

Page 694: "Focusing on Body Image Dissatisfaction," *USA Today* Feb. 1999: 3. Reprinted by *USA Today* magazine, February 1999. Copyrighted by the Society for the Advancement of Education, Inc.

Page 697: Colin Milner, "The Perfect Body Could Be Detrimental to Our Health," *Club Industry's Fitness Business Pro* Aug. 2005: 20. Reprinted with permission of Prism Business Media 2005. All rights reserved.

Page 699: "Special Report: Pots of Promise—The Beauty Business," *Economist* 24 May 2003: 71+. © 2003 The Economist Newspaper Ltd. All rights reserved. Reprinted with permission. Further reproduction prohibited. http://www.economist.com.

Page 708: Deborah Shouse, "Mark Her Words," *Ms.* magazine, Sept./Oct. 1996: 96. Reprinted by permission of *Ms.* magazine © 1996.

Page 711: David Concar, "The Boldest Cut," *New Scientist* 29 May–4 June 2004: 32+. Reprinted by permission.

Page 718: Laurence Shames, "The More Factor," from *The Hunger for More: Searching for Values in an Age of Greed* (1989), pp. 19–27. Copyright © 1989 by Laurence Shames. Published by Times Books, a division of Random House, Inc. Reprinted with permission of the Stuart Krichevsky Literary Agency, Inc.

Page 724: Robert J. Samuelson, "Shop 'til We Drop?," *Wilson Quarterly* Winter 2004: 22–29. Robert J. Samuelson is a columnist for the *Washington Post* and *Newsweek*. Reprinted by permission of the author.

Page 730: Geoffrey Calvin, "Admit It: You, Too, Are Paris Hilton," *Fortune* 29 Dec. 2003: 57. © 2003 Time Inc. All rights reserved.

Page 733: Charles Leadbeater, "Globalization: Now the Good News," *New Statesman* 1 July 2002: 29–31. © New Statesman. Reprinted by permission. All rights reserved.

Page 738: Gary Gardner, "Hungry for More: Re-Engaging Religious Teachings on Consumption," *World Watch* Sept./Oct. 2005: 26–30. Worldwatch Institute, http://www.worldwatch.org.

Chapter 20: Page 796: George Orwell, "Politics and the English Language," *Shooting and Elephant and Other Essays* by George Orwell. Copyright 1950 by Sonia Brownell Orwell and renewed 1987 by Sonia Pitt-Rivers. Reprinted by permission of Harcourt, Inc.

Page 806: Martin Luther King, Jr., "Letter from Birmingham Jail." Reprinted by arrangement with the Estate of Martin Luther King Jr., c/o Writers House as agent for the proprietor New York, NY. Copyright 1963 Martin Luther King Junior, copyright renewed 1991 Coretta Scott King.

Photo Credits

Chapter 1: Page 4, AP/CP/Wide World; page 9, AP/Wide World; page 16, National Youth Anti-Drug Campaign/Office of National Drug Control Policy; page 18, Courtesy Change the Climate, Inc.; page 20, Getty Images.

Chapter 2: Page 31, AP/Wide World; page 34 top, AP/Wide World; page 34 bottom, AP/Wide World; page 39, © Jean Pierre Fizet/Sygma/Corbis; page 40, AP/Wide World; page 44, AP/Wide World; page 46, Getty Images; page 49 bottom, AP/Wide World; page 55, AP/Wide World; page 57, AP/Wide World; page 60 top, AP/Wide World; page 60 bottom, © Tom Stewart/Corbis; page 66, British Court Martial/AP/Wide World.

Chapter 3: Page 71, AP/Wide World; page 74, AP/Wide World; page 75, Drug Policy Information Clearinghouse.

Chapter 4: Page 91, AP/Wide World; page 100, © Patrick Chauvel/Sygma/Corbis; page 101, Courtesy The Lavin Agency; page 103, AP/Wide World.

Chapter 5: Page 122, AP/Wide World.

Chapter 6: Page 147, AP/Wide World; page 149, AP/Wide World; page 160, Getty Images.

Chapter 7: Page 178, AP/Wide World.

Chapter 8: Page 199, PhotoDisc RF; page 204, Stone/Getty Images.

Chapter 9: Page 229, AP/Wide World; page 242, AP/Wide World; page 245, AP/Wide World.

Chapter 10: Page 257, © Royalty-Free/Corbis; page 258, Getty Images; page 260, © Gary D. Landsman/Corbis; page 250 left, Courtesy Randall Bytwerk; page 250 right, National Archives/Still Picture Branch; page 264, Courtesy Designers Against Addiction; page 272, AP/Wide World; page 274, © Reuters/Corbis; page 278, AP/Wide World; page 279, © Kim Kulish/Corbis; page 281, AP/Wide World; page 284, AP/Wide World.

Chapter 11: Page 287, PhotoDisc RF; page 290, AP/Wide World; page 293, www.supersize.com; page 298, Agence France/AP/Wide World.

Chapter 12: Page 319, © Steve Marcus/Reuters/Corbis; page 320, Courtesy Physicians against Land Mines/Center for International Rehabilitation; page 323, Courtesy Physicians against Land Mines/Center for International Rehabilitation; page 238, Courtesy Compassion over Killing; page 333, Courtesy Brownstein Group and Wharton Communications; page 335, New York Times Reprints; page 336, AP/Wide World; page 339, Courtesy Union of Concerned Scientists; page 340, Courtesy United Nations Population Fund (UNFPA); page 341, Courtesy Center for Consumer Freedom; page 344, © William Gedney Collection, Duke University Rare Book, Manuscript and Special Collections Library; page 345 left, AP/Wide World; page 345 right, AFP/Getty Images.

Chapter 13: Page 353, Stockdisc Premium RF.

Chapter 14: Page 376, © Royalty-Free/Corbis.

Chapter 15: Page 396, © Royalty-Free/Corbis; page 399 top, AP/Wide World; page 399 bottom, AFP/Getty Images; page 435, Courtesy Advanced Cell Technology.

Chapter 16: Page 457, © Pinto/zefa/Corbis; page 458, © Kimberly White/Reuters/Corbis; page 473, AP/Wide World.

Chapter 17: Page 509, AP/Wide World; page 520, AP/Wide World; page 529, AP/Wide World; page 548, Courtesy Combat Violence against Women.

Chapter 18: Page 571, AFP/Getty Images; page 572, Boston Globe/AP/Wide World; page 628, Courtesy Advanced Cell Technology.

Chapter 19: Page 653, AFP/Getty Images; page 655 top, Courtesy Ft. Lauderdale Police Department; page 655 bottom, Getty Images; page 664, Jefferson County Sheriff's Dept/AP/Wide World; page 693, © 2006 Chris Rainier; page 717, The Emporia Gazette/AP/Wide World.

Chapter 20: Page 745, © James Leynse/Corbis.

INDEX